To our families and friends,
who have loved and supported us,
and to our students, who have taught us,
we dedicate this book.

Preface

Welcome to the study of psychology. We, the authors, are students as well as teachers of psychology and hope to share with you the fascination we have found in the study of human and animal behavior. After years of teaching the introductory psychology course and paying close attention to the comments of our students, we have developed strong ideas about what a textbook should (and can) accomplish. Students have asked: "Why do texts have to be so cluttered and confusing?" "Am I responsible for all the material in the boxes, margins, and at the beginning and end of the chapters?" We asked ourselves: "Why do texts seem to be either condescendingly easy or overly difficult and encyclopedic?" "Can a text be both comprehensive and comprehensible, scientific yet practical, classic in foundation yet contemporary in application?"

1. Learning as an Activity

These are but a few of the questions that initiated our interest in writing this text. But our primary goal is to write a text that promotes learning as an *activity* of the student. Hence the title, *Psychology in Action.* Most texts encourage the reader to be passive. Research, however, shows that learning is greatly facilitated when the learner is an active participant. We have made every effort to engage the reader to participate with us in studying psychology.

Indeed, the study of psychology should not be just a one-way activity wherein the student receives a body of knowledge. Our title, *Psychology in Action,* also signifies actively applying psychological principles and research findings to aspects of life around us.

2. Critical Thinking Activities

"Critical Thinking" is a term that is currently receiving considerable attention from textbook authors. We have noticed that texts advocating critical thinking limit its implementation to exhorting students to think critically without giving them any specific suggestions or activities that will lead to critical thought. For example, if a student's ability to empathize is limited, what activities can be performed to improve this important component of critical thinking? Frequently, the student is put into a passive role as the recipient of vague exhortations to be empathetic.

Using the most recent research on critical thinking, we have developed highly focused exercises in each chapter to help students practice critical thinking skills. Each exercise is labeled "Critical Thinking: Psychology in Action." For example, in Chapter 5, the reader learns how to distinguish fact from opinion using the topic of drug use and abuse. Chapter 12 offers practice in recognizing illegitimate appeals to emotion. Additional specific exercises and activities that promote critical thinking are provided in the student study guide and the instructor's manual, which are available from the publisher.

An explanation of the 21 basic elements that are necessary for critical thinking are introduced and explained in the Prologue.

3. The Scientific Method in Action

The scientific method is an excellent example of critical thinking in action. One of our primary goals in writing this text is to enhance the reader's appreciation of psychology as an empirical study of human experience and to demonstrate the advantages of the scientific method over speculation and "common sense."

Throughout the text, the reader is exposed to the successes and failures of the empirical method of discovery. By actively encouraging readers to evaluate research findings and to imagine themselves as participants in classic experiments, we have attempted to present the scientific method as an exciting voyage of discovery and an opportunity to practice critical thinking. Readers will discover how the tool of empiricism will help them think more clearly about popular media claims, EST, subliminal advertising, "brainwashing," and the dangers of electroshock therapy.

4. SQ3R Learning Activities

To overcome the passive-learner syndrome, we have structured the entire text to employ the SQ3R (Survey, Question, Read, Recite, Review) technique. Each chapter follows this format beginning with an outline that provides a *survey* of the major topics. To encourage questioning, we have included overview *questions* at the end of each chapter's introductory vignette and have included questions our students have asked us as part of the ongoing discussion of the text.

Reading is facilitated by the clear and concise explanations. In addition, we have eliminated boxed essays. Many students feel that these boxed essays break up the continuity of the text. Placing specific studies or applications in special areas also conveys the impression that these topics are less important than the rest of the material. If something is worth discussing, we integrated it into our presentation.

To encourage *recitation* and *review,* we offer "Review Questions" after each major section. Again, these "Review Questions" provide an opportunity for active participation and provide the correct answers printed upside down for immediate feedback. Finally, each chapter concludes with a "Review of Major Concepts."

Some educators recommend *writing* as an additional "R" (SQ4R). The reader is encouraged to write brief summary notes while reading the chapter material. The student study guide that accompanies this text was specifically designed to encourage this fourth "R." Both the SQ3R and SQ4R methods are explained in greater detail in the study guide.

5. Glossaries

In addition to the SQ3R techniques, we have incorporated other learning aids that are known to increase comprehension and retention. New and important terms are identified with boldface type and are immediately defined in the text and in the margin of that page. In addition, there is a complete cumulative glossary at the end of the text. These aids alert readers to important terms and concepts while providing a useful review tool and increasing overall comprehension.

Note to the Student

We hope you will enjoy reading our second edition of *Psychology in Action.* As the name implies, we believe that psychology is, and should remain, a vital science that is practical, fascinating, and fun to learn. You will be the best judge of how well we have reached our goals. Please send us your comments, complaints, and questions while you are reading the text. We value your opinion and would appreciate your feedback.

Address correspondence to:
Karen Huffman, Mark Vernoy,
Judy Vernoy, or Barbara Williams
Palomar College
San Marcos, CA 92069

Note to the Instructor

We want to make your teaching time as exciting and rewarding as possible. We thought that the best way to do this was to create a student-centered, readable text that covers the material so clearly that students can achieve a high level of comprehension. Instead of using valuable class time to clarify the text, you will be free to present your own special topics, invite guest speakers to class, and allocate time for small and large group discussions. In other words, you can use class time for other learning activities.

Supplements
Psychology in Action is accompanied by a host of carefully crafted ancillary materials that will facilitate active learning.

Studying Psychology in Action is a student study guide that provides learning objectives, key terms, and multiple-choice practice tests for each chapter. "Critical Thinking: Psychology in Action" sections provide more focused exercises for practicing skills essential to critical thinking. Selected application sections show the student how text material can be used to lose weight, remember names, and so on. In addition, the guide includes detailed information on the SQ3R method and helpful information concerning study habits, test taking, and general college success.

Teaching Psychology in Action, a guide for the instructor, provides chapter overviews, film lists, learning objectives, key terms, lecture lead-ins, lecture extenders, and suggested classroom activities and demonstrations. "Critical Thinking: Psychology in Action" sections provide exercises and discussion formats to help your students practice skills that lead to critical thinking. The "lecture organizer" section is integrated with the chapter outline and page referenced to the text to make it easy for the instructor to illustrate or expand on major topics in each chapter.

The ***Testing Psychology in Action*** includes at least 100 multiple-choice items for each chapter. These test items are separated into two sections. One contains factual and the other contains application items. The test bank is available in both printed and easy-to-use computer formats. The computerized test banks are available for both Macintosh and IBM PC compatible computers.

Two sets of ***Transparencies*** are available. One set is made up of more than 95 illustrations from the text. The other set is comprised of 100 transparencies that provide extra scope with illustrations on topics that aren't covered in the text. This set is accompanied by a 100-page instructor's guide.

The ***Discovering Psychology*** videotapes aired on Public Television are available to instructors who order at least 100 copies of *Psychology in Action*. A complete instructor's manual shows how these tapes can be used in the classroom to enhance material in the text.

Wiley Computer Tutor Study Software. Available for IBM PC compatible computers, this software game is the fun way to study. The game can be played by one to five players. The game quizzes the players on the content of the text, keeps score, and identifies the winner. All incorrect answers are explained.

The ***PSYCHAID*** simulation software is available for IBM PC compatible computers. This easy-to-use, interactive software leads the student through a number of exercises, demonstrations, and activities that reinforce concepts in the text. For example, the sensation unit asks students to discriminate between the varying pitches of paired tones to illustrate the concept of thresholds.

We hope that these supplements will help both beginning and experienced instructors enrich their classroom presentations and create the lively environment that is Psychology in Action.

ACKNOWLEDGMENTS

From the beginning, our writing of this text has been a group effort, involving the input and support of our families, friends, and colleagues. To each person we offer our sincere thanks. A special note of appreciation goes to Jay Alperson, Bill Barnard, Haydn Davis, Ann Haney, Herb Harari, Terry Humphrey, Bob Miller, and Kate Townsend-Merino.

To the reviewers and adopters who gave their time and constructive criticism, we offer our sincere appreciation. We are deeply indebted to the following individuals and trust that they will recognize their contributions throughout this text.

Worthon Allen Utah State University	Thomas Linton Coppin State College
Daniel Bellack Lexington Community College	Tom Marsh Pitt Community College
Terry Blumenthal Wake Forest University	Nancy Meck University of Kansas Medical Center
Mark Covey University of Idaho	Michael Miller College of St. Scholastica
Thomas Eckle Modesto Junior College	John Near Elgin Community College
Eric Fiazi Los Angeles City College	Steve Neighbors Santa Barbara City College
Sandra Fiske Onondague Community College	Sarah O'Dowd Community College of Rhode Island
Pamela Flynn Community College of Philadelphia	Richard S. Perrotto Queensborough Community College
William F. Ford Bucks City Community College	Christopher Potter Harrisburg Community College
Paul Fuller Muskegon Community College	Derrick Proctor Andrews University
Fredrick Gault Western Michigan University	Antonio Puente University of North Carolina-Wilmington
Judith Gentry Columbus State Community College	Leonard S. Romney Rockland Community College
Joseph Giacobbe Adirondack Community College	Tirzah Schutzengel Bergen Community College
Sylvia Haith Forsyth Technical College	Lawrence Scott Bunker Hill Community College
Frederick Halper Essex County Community College	Art Skibbe Appalachian State University
George Hampton University of Houston-Downtown	Ronald Testa Plymouth State College
Sidney Hochman Nassau Community College	John L. Vogel Baldwin Wallace College
Kathryn Jennings College of the Redwoods	Paul Wellman Texas A & M University
Seth Kalichman University of South Carolina	Charles Wiechert San Antonio College
Paul Kaplan Suffolk Community College	Jeff Wolper Delaware Technical and Community College
Bruno Kappes University of Alaska	Brian T. Yates American University

Special thanks also go to the staff at John Wiley and Sons. This project benefited from the wisdom and insight of many individuals: Stella Kupferberg, Elizabeth Austin, Gilda Stahl, Carol Einhorn, and others. In particular, we thank Deborah Moore, the psychology editor, who masterminded this second edition and whose charm and enthusiasm served to "refuel" us whenever our spirits flagged. Our developmental editor, Jackie Estrada, has been an essential contributor to both editions. Her hard work, commitment to quality, and barrage of wonderful suggestions have greatly improved the book.

Finally, we would like to express our continuing appreciation to our students. They taught us what students want to know and inspired us to write the book. Two students deserve special recognition for their research assistance: Greg Nelson and Richard Hosey. Our warm appreciation is also extended to Kandis Hosey for her tireless efforts, thoughtful feedback, and unique sense of what should and should not go into an introduction to psychology text.

Contents in Brief

Critical Thinking Exercises

Contents

Critical Thinking   Psychology in Action
CONDUCTING SOCRATIC DISCUSSIONS: Thinking
About Sensation

Critical Thinking   Psychology in Action
RECOGNIZING FAULTY REASONING: Problems with
the Belief in ESP

Critical Thinking   Psychology in Action
DISTINGUISHING FACT FROM OPINION:
Understanding Claims About Drug Use and Abuse

Critical Thinking Psychology in Action
TRANSFERRING IDEAS TO NEW CONCEPTS:
Operant Conditioning and the College Classroom

chapter seven
Memory 196

Critical Thinking Psychology in Action
PRACTICING REFLECTIVE THINKING: Exploring
Your Early Childhood Memories

chapter eight
Thinking and Intelligence 228

Critical Thinking Psychology in Action
MAKING SOUND DECISIONS: Recognizing the Role
of Personal Values in Conflict Resolution

chapter nine
Early Development 260

Critical Thinking Psychology in Action
DEVELOPMENT INSIGHT INTO EGOCENTRICITY:
Adult Versus Childhood Egocentrism

Critical Thinking   Psychology in Action

DEVELOPING THE ABILITY TO EMPATHIZE:
Abortion, Adoption, or Keeping the Child

Critical Thinking   Psychology in Action

DEVELOPING ONE'S PERSPECTIVE: Clarifying Your
Sexual Values

Critical Thinking   Psychology in Action

RECOGNIZING ILLEGITIMATE APPEALS TO
EMOTION: Ads and Everyday Attempts to Persuade

chapter seventeen
Social Interaction 546

Critical Thinking   Psychology in Action

DEVELOPING SELF-UNDERSTANDING: Social Perception and Attitude Formation

chapter eighteen
Living in Society 576

Critical Thinking   Psychology in Action

FOSTERING INDEPENDENT THINKING: Would You Have Followed Jim Jones?

appendix
Statistics and Psychology A-1

CRITICAL THINKING — Psychology in Action

> *A great many people think they are thinking
> when they are merely rearranging their prejudices.*
>
> WILLIAM JAMES

> *Think critically? That's what others don't do, isn't it?*
>
> KIRK MONFORT

Although the ability to think critically has always been important, it is now imperative. For the first time in history, the human race has the capacity to destroy itself. The choices we make regarding nuclear weapons, preservation of the natural environment, and the world's rapidly expanding population will affect future generations and all people who currently inhabit this planet.

On a more personal level, people today are facing choices about such life and death matters as surrogate motherhood, sustaining coma patients on respirators, and fetal tissue transplants. Even when relaxing with a snack in front of the television set, viewers are bombarded with misleading statements by advertisers and politicians and by emotional appeals on subjects ranging from racism and homelessness to the latest carcinogen.

There is no shortage of information available on many of these issues. Today's college student has easy access to mountains of information. When assigned a research project, students can go beyond traditional local library resources by using a personal computer and modem to search thousands of daily newspapers, research journal articles, and encyclopedia services.

The problem for modern college students is not a lack of data but knowing what to do with the "information explosion." Information must be interpreted, evaluated, digested, synthesized, and applied in a logical, rational manner. In short, the student must be a critical thinker.

What is "critical thinking"?

Critical thinking has many meanings, and some books have dedicated entire chapters to its definition. The word *critical* comes from the Greek word "kritikos," which means to question, make sense of, to be able to analyze. *Thinking* is the cognitive activity involved in making sense of the world around us. *Critical thinking* is "thinking about our thinking so that we can clarify and improve it" (Chaffee, 1988, p. 29).

To understand critical thinking better, study the following list of processes that comprise it. As authors of this text, we have incorporated many of these elements into every facet of this book. Each of the critical thinking exercises is devoted to step-by-step training in one aspect of the process. *Psychology in Action* invites active use of this list as a way to improve critical thinking.

While all of us employ some form of these intellectual behaviors, the list can be used to identify areas that need strengthening through practice. They may also suggest additional opportunities for critical thinking in aspects of life where strong emotional reactions to the issues have previously hampered the application of the critical thinking process.

THE CRITICAL THINKING PROCESS

Affective Components — the emotional foundation that either enables or limits critical thinking.

- *Valuing truth above self-interest.* You must hold yourself and those you agree with to the same intellectual standards to which you hold your opponents.

- *Accepting change.* Critical thinkers remain open to the need for adjustment and adaptation throughout the life cycle. Because critical thinkers fully trust the processes of reasoned inquiry, they are willing to use these skills to examine even their most deeply held values and beliefs, and to modify these beliefs when evidence and experience contradict them.

- *Empathizing.* Noncritical thinkers view everything and everyone else in relationship to the self. They fail to understand or appreciate another's thoughts, feelings, or behaviors, as critical thinkers do.

- *Welcoming divergent views.* Since critical thinkers value examining issues from every angle, they know that it is especially important to explore and understand positions with which they disagree.

- *Tolerating ambiguity.* Although formal education often trains students to look for a single "right" answer, critical thinkers recognize that many issues are complex, intricate, and subtle, and that complex issues may not have a "right" answer. They recognize and value qualifiers such as "probably," "highly likely," and "not very likely."

- *Recognizing personal biases.* Using your highest intellectual skills to detect personal biases and self-deceptive reasoning, you can then design reasonable procedures for self-correction.

Cognitive Components — the thought processes actually involved in critical thinking.

- *Thinking independently.* Critical thinking is autonomous, independent thinking. You do not passively accept the beliefs of others and are not easily manipulated.

- *Defining problems accurately.* A critical thinker identifies the issues in clear and concrete terms, to prevent confusion and lay the foundation for gathering relevant information.

- *Analyzing data for value and content.* By carefully evaluating the nature of evidence and the credibility of the source, you will recognize illegitimate appeals to emotion, unsupported assumptions, and faulty logic. This will enable you to discount sources of information that lack a record of honesty, contradict themselves on key questions, or have a vested interest in selling a product or idea.

- *Employing a variety of thinking processes in problem solving.* Among these are the ability to use each of the following skills: *inductive logic*—reasoning that moves from the specific to the general; *deductive logic*—reasoning that moves from the general to the specific; *dialogical thinking*—thinking that involves an extended verbal exchange between differing points of view or frames of reference; and *dialectical thinking*—thinking conducted in order to test the strengths and weaknesses of opposing points of view.

- *Synthesizing.* Critical thinkers recognize that comprehension and understanding result from combining various elements into meaningful patterns.
- *Resisting overgeneralization.* Overgeneralization is the temptation to apply a fact or experience to situations that are only superficially similar to the original context.
- *Employing metacognition.* Metacognition, also known as reflective or recursive thinking, involves a review and analysis of your own mental processes — thinking about your own thinking.

Behavioral Components — the actions necessary for critical thinking.

- *Delaying judgment until adequate data is available.* A critical thinker does not make "snap judgments."
- *Employing precise terms.* Such terms help you to identify the issues in clear and concrete terms that can be objectively defined and empirically tested.
- *Gathering data.* Collecting up-to-date, relevant information on all sides of an issue is done before making decisions.
- *Distinguishing fact from opinion.* Facts are statements that can be proven true. Opinions are statements that express how a person feels about an issue or what someone thinks is true.
- *Encouraging critical dialogue.* Critical thinkers are active questioners who challenge existing facts and opinions and welcome questions in return. Socratic questioning is an important type of critical dialogue where the questioner deeply probes the meaning, justification, or logical strength of a claim, position, or line of reasoning.
- *Listening actively.* Critical thinkers fully engage their thinking skills when listening to another.
- *Modifying judgments in light of new information.* Your previous judgments can be abandoned or modified if later evidence or experience contradicts them.
- *Applying knowledge to new situations.* When critical thinkers master a new skill or discover an insight, they are able to transfer this information to new contexts. Noncritical thinkers can often provide correct answers, repeat definitions, and carry out formulae, yet remain unable to transfer their knowledge to new situations because of a basic lack of understanding.

Psychology in Action

chapter one

Introducing Psychology

OUTLINE

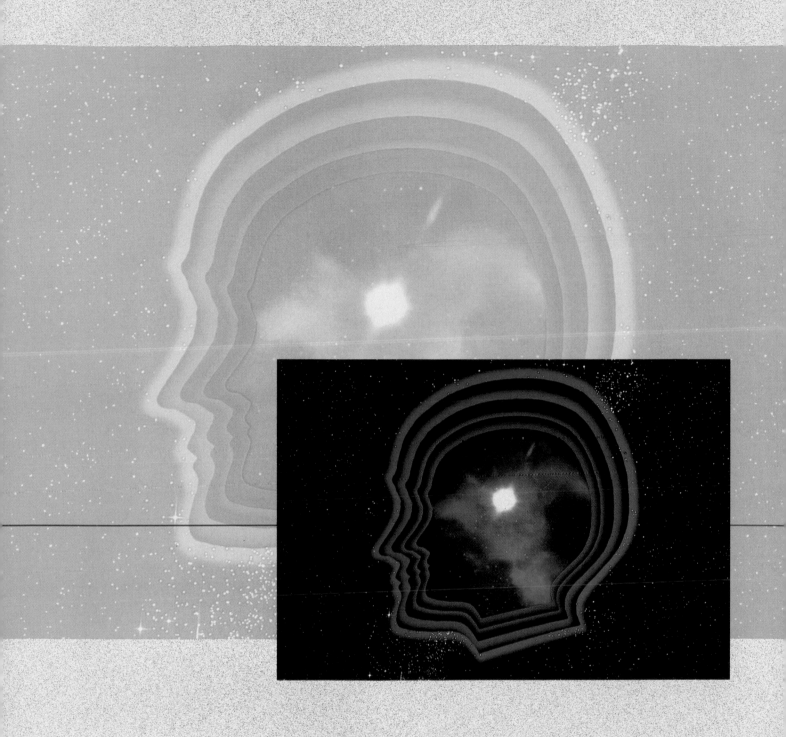

PRETEND for the moment that you are one of the people responding to this ad. As you arrive at the Yale University laboratory, you are introduced to the experimenter and to another **subject** (another participant in the experiment). The experimenter explains that he is studying the effects of punishment on learning and memory, and that one of you will play the role of a learner and the other will play the role of a teacher. You draw lots, and on your paper is written "teacher." The experimenter leads you into a room where he straps the other subject—the "learner"—into an "electric chair" apparatus that looks escape-proof. The experimenter then applies some electrode paste to the learner's wrist "to avoid blisters and burns" and attaches an electrode that is connected to a shock generator.

You are then shown into an adjacent room and asked to sit in front of the shock generator, which is wired through the wall to the chair of the "learner." As you can see in Figure 1.1, the shock machine consists of 30 switches that represent succeedingly higher levels of shock in 15-volt increments. In addition, labels appear below each group of levers, ranging from "slight shock," to "danger: severe shock," all the way to "XXX." The experimenter explains that it is your job to teach the learner a list of word pairs and to punish any errors by administering a shock. With each wrong answer, you are to give a shock one level higher on the shock generator—for example, at the first wrong response, you give a shock

of 15 volts, at the second wrong response, 30 volts, and so on.

As the experiment begins, the learner seems to be having problems with the task because the responses are often wrong. Thus, you find that before long you are inflicting shocks that must be extremely painful. Indeed, after you administer 150 volts, the learner begins to protest and demands, "Get me out of here . . . I refuse to go on."

You hesitate and wonder what you should do. The experimenter urges you to continue and insists that, even if the learner makes no response, you must keep increasing the shock levels. But the other person is obviously in pain. What should you do? Should you keep giving the shocks or should you stop?

Actual subjects participated in a series of such experiments and suffered real conflict when confronted with this problem. The following dialogue took place between the experimenter and a subject in one of these experiments (Milgram, 1974, pp. 73–74):

Subject: I can't stand it. I'm not going to kill that man in there. You hear him hollering?

Experimenter: As I told you before, the shocks may be painful, but [there is no permanent tissue damage].

Learner (screaming): Let me out of here, you have no right to keep me here. Let me out of here, let me out, my heart's bothering me, let me out! *(Subject shakes head, pats the table nervously.)*

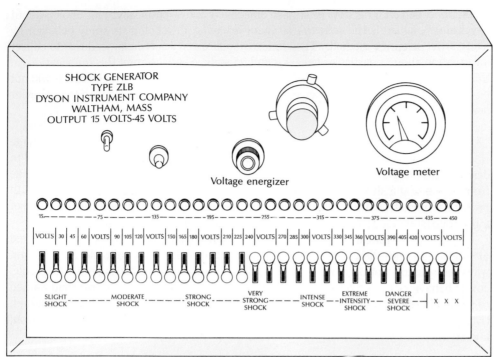

Figure 1.1 The shock generator used by the "teacher" in Stanley Milgram's experiment.

Subject: You see, he's hollering. Hear that? Gee, I don't know.

Experimenter: The experiment requires . . .

Subject (Interrupting): I know it does, sir, but I mean—huh! He don't know what he's getting in for. He's up to 195 volts! *(Experiment continues, through 210 volts, 225 volts, 240 volts, 255 volts, 270 volts, at which point the teacher, with evident relief, runs out of word-pair questions.)*

Experimenter: You'll have to go back to the beginning of that page and go through them again until he's learned them all correctly.

Subject: Aw, no I'm not going to kill that man. You mean I've got to keep going up with the scale? No sir. He's hollering in there. I'm not going to give him 450 volts.

SUBJECT: A participant in a research study.

What do you think happened? Did the man continue? It may surprise you that this particular subject continued to give shocks in spite of the learner's strong protests and even continued to the highest level when the learner refused to give any more answers. As you may have guessed, the purpose of this experiment was not really to study the effects of punishment on learning. The psychologist who designed the experiment, Stanley Milgram, was investigating the question of obedience to authority. In fact, no shocks were administered at all—the "learner" was an accomplice of the experimenter and simply pretended to be shocked.

How obedient do you think you would have been? Milgram conducted a survey to determine how people expected they would perform in such an experiment. No one predicted that they would go past the 300-volt level, and fewer than 25 percent predicted that they would go beyond 150 volts. Even Milgram was surprised and dismayed when a full 65 percent of the subjects in this experiment actually administered the maximum shock intensity.

Milgram's experiment demonstrates that we cannot always rely on common sense to accurately predict behavior, whether it be our own or others'. Rather, to ensure reliable

PSYCHOLOGY: *The scientific study of behavior.*

predictions, behavior needs to be studied objectively and scientifically. This book is about **psychology,** which is the *scientific* study of behavior. Psychologists study behavior by using strict scientific methods. They follow standardized scientific procedures to collect information about a particular behavior and to analyze and interpret this information. In this way, psychologists can be reasonably assured that the results of their studies will not be contaminated by their own personal attitudes or by factors unrelated to the behavior being studied.

Question: Isn't "behavior" a rather narrow area of study?   In everyday language **behavior** may refer primarily to the way people act, but in psychology it is used to

BEHAVIOR: *Anything a person or animal does, feels, thinks, or experiences.*

describe anything a person or animal does, feels, thinks, or experiences. Behaviors range from depressing a shock lever to running a marathon, from solving a complicated math problem to forgetting the name of a long-time friend, from suffering the delightful thrill of a roller-coaster ride to experiencing the utter relaxation of meditation.

OVERT: *Observable, not concealed.*
COVERT: *Hidden or unobservable.*

Some behaviors are **overt** — easily seen or identified. Others are **covert** — covered or hidden, and not directly observable. Psychologists have been quite clever in finding ways to measure not only overt but also covert behaviors. To measure unobservable, covert behaviors, researchers use a variety of creative techniques. If Milgram had wanted to study his subjects' anxiety levels, for example, he could have used electrocardiograph (EKG) and other machines to measure their heart rate, blood pressure, muscle tension, and so on.

UNDERSTANDING PSYCHOLOGY

The definition of psychology as the study of behavior is surprising to many students. Most people think of psychology and psychologists as they are portrayed by popular books, magazines, movies, and television programs. When asked to define psychology at the beginning of the course, students often give such responses as "The study of people," "How the mind operates," "What makes people break down or go crazy," "How to raise children," "The meaning of dreams and personality tests," and so on. Although psychology does include these topics, it is also concerned with such questions as: How do people learn? How is intelligence measured? What motivates some people to starve themselves to the point of death while others eat themselves into obesity? Should anger be controlled and suppressed or should its expression be encouraged? How does stress affect both our physical and our psychological functioning? Why do we like some people and not others? What makes some people so influential and powerful, while others seem to be mindless followers and socially ineffective? In this book we will address these difficult questions and many others as well.

The goals of psychology: Describe, explain, predict, and change

One of the first steps in understanding the complex world of psychology is to look at its four basic goals: to describe, explain, predict, and change behavior. In some studies, psychologists attempt merely to *describe* particular behaviors by making careful scientific observations. In other studies, psychologists also try to *explain* behaviors by conducting experiments to determine their causes. Whatever the approach, psychologists often use research information to *predict* when the behavior being studied will occur in the future. When indicated, they can also apply research findings to *change* inappropriate behavior or circumstances.

Milgram's study achieved all these goals. He was able to *describe* how his subjects behaved when an authority figure told them to do something that was opposed to their sense of right and wrong. He was able to *explain* why subjects acted in this way by systematically varying certain experimental conditions. For example, by varying such factors as whether or not the teacher and the learner were in the same room, Milgram found that remoteness from the "victim" (the learner) is a contributing cause of obedience.

By applying Milgram's results to the real world, it is possible to *predict* the behavior of people in similar situations. For example, officers in the armed forces might use Milgram's findings to predict that pilots would be more likely to obey orders to fire a missile at a distant obscure city than to kill someone with their bare hands.

Findings from Milgram's and similar research are being used today to *change* behavior. For example, parents and educators are teaching children to question authority in critical or dangerous situations rather than to automatically obey. In an effort to prevent sexual molestation, many schools are presenting special programs to young children. Puppet shows, role playing, class discussion, and other techniques are being used to teach children to say "no" when adults touch them inappropriately or do something they feel is uncomfortable. On a personal note, you might find ways to apply Milgram's results in changing your own behavior when someone insists that you do something questionable. For instance, you might seek a second opinion when your doctor says you need surgery.

Often, researchers such as Milgram study some aspect of behavior with no thought of how their results can be applied to the real world. This is known as **basic research,** and these studies are usually conducted in universities or in research laboratories and may or may not have immediate real-world applications. On the other hand, **applied research** is conducted to solve specific problems, such as finding ways to help scuba divers adapt to underwater visual distortions (Vernoy and Luria, 1977). Applied researchers are often employed by the government or industry to perform research in a particular area.

BASIC RESEARCH: *Research conducted to study theoretical questions without trying to solve a specific problem.*
APPLIED RESEARCH: *Research that utilizes the principles and discoveries of psychology for practical purposes, to solve real-world problems.*

Question: Don't psychologists do other things besides research? Of course. Psychologists perform a wide variety of roles (Figure 1.2). One of the most obvious is that of a mental health service provider such as a clinical psychologist, a psychiatrist, or a marriage and family counselor. These professionals work with mentally or emotionally disturbed people by engaging in therapy or counseling. They are employed in hospitals, mental health clinics, or their own private practice facilities.

Other types of specialists in psychology include:

Educational psychologists, who study the process of education — how people, particularly children, learn and what teaching techniques work best;

Industrial/organizational psychologists, who are employed by industry to help factories, offices, and companies run more smoothly and efficiently;

Developmental psychologists, who study physical and mental development from conception to death;

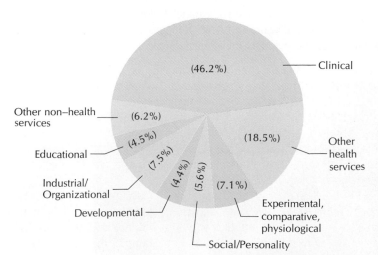

Figure 1.2 The percentage of American Psychological Association members employed in each of the major areas of psychology.

Social psychologists, who are interested in the behavior of people in social (group) situations;

Comparative psychologists, who are interested in gaining insights into human behavior by studying the behavior of animals;

Physiological psychologists, who study the relationship of the physiology of the brain and nervous system to behavior;

Experimental psychologists, who design and conduct experiments to study specific behaviors in such areas as perception, sensation, learning, memory, and cognition.

Psychology in your life: Separating fact from fiction

Psychology is a compelling field of study because it deals with topics that you can apply to your everyday life. For example, by reading about how people learn and remember, you might develop better study habits and create a better learning environment for yourself. By reading about interpersonal relationships, you might learn effective ways to maintain long-term friendships. By reading about motivation, you might be able to modify undesirable behaviors, such as overeating or smoking.

The study of psychology will also give you a greater awareness of the distinction between scientifically verified explanations of behavior and explanations that have been developed through mere subjective observation. Many "scientific" claims publicized in the popular press, for example, are in fact bogus — they do not follow from scientifically collected data.

Similarly, there is no scientific basis for the many **pseudopsychologies,** or "false psychologies," that are popular attempts to explain behavior or personality differences using nonscientific methods. Pseudopsychologies include palmistry (reading people's character from the markings on the palms of their hands), psychometry (the ability to determine facts about an object by handling it), psychokinesis (the movement of objects by purely mental means), and astrology (the study of how the positions of the stars and planets influence people's personalities and affairs). Although these pseudopsychologies are entertaining (horoscopes are fun to read and are great conversation starters), there has never been any documented proof that they are legitimate means of explaining complex human behavior.

In fact, horoscopes may at times be harmful. When Ronald Reagan was president of the United States, his wife Nancy would not allow him to make certain public appearances solely on the basis of information from her astrologer. Many astrologers and other pseudopsychologists have been proven to be frauds by a magician named James Randi. In his book *Flim-Flam!* (1982), he has described how time and time again, under carefully controlled, standardized conditions, he has exposed their phony claims.

Psychology Today magazine poked fun at pseudopsychologies when in September 1983 it announced its first "Invent-a-Scam" contest. Readers were asked to invent a pseudopsychology similar to those previously mentioned. Some of the winners included

PSEUDOPSYCHOLOGIES: *"False psychologies"; popular systems that pretend to discover psychological information through nonscientific or deliberately fraudulent methods.*

Have you ever wondered what makes one person more popular than another? Interpersonal attraction is a major research topic for social psychologists.

Psychology can help you identify nonscientific claims such as these.

Interior Seating Therapy, which deals with psychological disorders associated with furniture, such as "anorexia newsofa"; Autozodiac, in which clients are asked to send in the make, model, year, and serial number of their car in return for an astrological chart containing such information as descriptions of the car's individual temperament and days on which it is safe to take trips; and Fetal Terpsicology, in which babies are taught to tap dance before birth. Although these "scams" were created to have fun, they help illustrate the absurdity of the various pseudosciences and help point out the fact that we should be aware of the difference between false psychology and objective, scientific studies of behavior.

Review Questions

1 Psychology is the _____ study of behavior.

2 _____ behaviors are observable and _____ behaviors are hidden.

3 The goals of psychology are to _____, _____, _____, and _____ behavior.

4 The main criticism of _____ is that they attempt to explain behavior using nonscientific methods and cannot be proven true when objective, standardized techniques are used.

5 _____ research is conducted to solve a specific problem.

Answers: 1 scientific; *2* overt, covert; *3* describe, explain, predict, control; *4* pseudopsychologies; *5* applied

PSYCHOLOGICAL RESEARCH

As we have mentioned, psychology involves studying behavior *scientifically.* This means that psychologists, like scientists in biology, chemistry, or any other scientific field, need to conduct investigations in which they methodically collect their data. They then piece it together bit by bit until they come to an objective conclusion. So that other people — lay people as well as other scientists — can understand, interpret, and repeat their research, psychologists must follow standardized scientific procedures, or methods, in conducting their studies. These procedures are collectively known as **research methodology.** A distinct methodology is used in each of the two basic approaches to the study of psychology, experimental and nonexperimental research. In this section, we will discuss the distinguishing features and examine the methodology used in each approach.

RESEARCH METHODOLOGY: *Standardized scientific procedures for conducting investigations.*

Experimental research: The study of cause and effect

Any research study begins with an idea or question that inspires inquiry. Stanley Milgram, for example, wanted to know what causes people to obey authority figures who ask them to do something totally opposed to their moral values. The only way he could answer this question was to conduct an **experiment.**

EXPERIMENT: *A carefully controlled scientific procedure conducted to determine whether certain variables manipulated by the experimenter have an effect on other variables.*

Question: Why was an experiment the only way to answer it? Only through an experiment can researchers isolate a single factor and examine the effect of that factor alone on a particular behavior (Cozby, 1985). For example, when you are studying for an upcoming test, you probably try a lot of methods—studying in a quiet room, rereading highlighted sections, repeating key terms with their definitions over and over to yourself, and so on—to help you remember the material. It is impossible to determine which study methods are truly effective because you probably use several at the same time. The only way you could discover which one is most effective would be to isolate each method in an experiment. (Numerous experiments have been conducted concerning memory and study techniques. If you're interested in how to develop better study habits, refer to the Study Guide and to Chapter 7, which discuss the findings from such research.)

An experiment has several critical components. In this section, we will discuss a few of the major ones: the hypothesis, independent variables, dependent variables, and experimental controls. A more in-depth discussion of experiments and the analysis of experimental results is provided in the appendix at the end of the book.

The hypothesis After Milgram formulated his question, reviewed related research, and considered possible ways to study obedience to authority, he generated a hypothesis to explain why obedience occurs. A **hypothesis** is an "educated guess" or a possible explanation for a behavior being studied that is expressed as a prediction or a statement of cause and effect.

HYPOTHESIS: *A question or a possible explanation for a behavior being studied that can be answered or affirmed by an experiment or a series of observations.*

People generate informal hypotheses all the time. For example, we sometimes hear such statements as "Children today are illiterate because they watch too much TV" or "Cloudy days make people feel depressed." These are informal explanations for behaviors

Reprinted courtesy Omni Magazine © 1990.

"I know how to get out, but I wouldn't give them the satisfaction."

that are based only on observations or personal experiences. A *scientific* hypothesis is based on facts and theories that have been gathered and investigated by previous researchers, as well as on personal experience and observations. It is posed in a way that indicates how the results can be measured. A hypothesis may or may not be correct; it is merely a *possible* explanation for a behavior and is subject to verification through scientific study.

 Question: What was Milgram's hypothesis?   Milgram had one basic hypothesis:

People do obey authorities. When directed to do so by an authority figure, people will perform tasks that are totally opposed to common ethical behavior.

However, he also developed and tested variations of this hypothesis, such as:

Group effects. Subjects will display a different level of obedience when they are members of a group, as opposed to when they are acting as individuals.

Subjects' perceived personal responsibility. When subjects feel less responsible, they will administer greater levels of shock.

Results of experiments conducted to test these hypotheses revealed that the first hypothesis — people *do* obey authority — was supported throughout the many variations of Milgram's basic experiment. Brief summaries of these variations as well as their results are shown in Figure 1.3. As you may be able to tell from the figure, Milgram found that the modeling, or imitation, of defiance and the increased sense of responsibility are the two most important factors in obedience. You might keep these findings in mind when you are questioning whether your "one voice of dissent" can make a difference in the world.

Independent and dependent variables   After generating a hypothesis, an experimenter decides on an appropriate research design to test that hypothesis. A basic part of the design is to make a decision about what factors will be directly manipulated by the experimenter and what factors will be examined for possible changes. These factors are

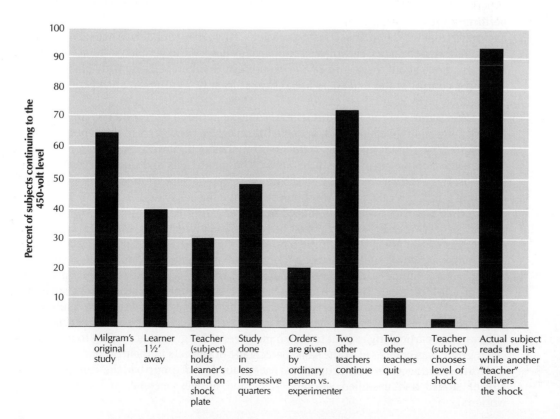

Figure 1.3 Degrees of obedience according to various hypotheses and conditions of Milgram's experiment.

known as **variables** and are just that—factors that can vary, that can assume more than one value. Variables include such factors as weight, time, distance between people, scores on a test, number of responses, and so on. The two major types of variables used in an experiment are independent and dependent variables.

An **independent variable** is a factor that is selected and manipulated by the experimenter and is totally independent of anything the subject does. Initially, Milgram obtained a basic measurement of obedience to authority by recording responses of subjects who had been directed by the experimenter to shock a learner in a separate room. He then manipulated various factors—the proximity of the learner to the subject, whether or not the experimenter was present, the gender of the subject and several others—to determine their effect on the obedient behavior. These manipulated factors were Milgram's independent variables.

In contrast to the independent variable, which is selected and manipulated by the experimenter, the **dependent variable** is a measurable behavior exhibited by the subject. It is a result of, or is dependent on, the independent variable. In Milgram's experiments, the dependent variable was always the same—the highest level of shock administered by any one subject.

Experimental controls Experimental design requires that there be at least two groups of subjects so that the performance of one group can be compared with that of another. Ideally, the only way these groups differ is in the amounts or levels of the independent variable. For example, Helene Intraub (1979) conducted an experiment to determine whether rehearsal (repeating something over and over) improves memory for faces. Her independent variable was the amount of rehearsal time between presentations of the faces. Results of the experiment indicated that subjects in the groups that were allotted greater amounts of rehearsal time were able to recognize more faces than those given lesser amounts. Since the only difference between the groups was rehearsal time, it can be concluded that increased rehearsal time *causes* better recognition for faces.

Often, one group of subjects will be assigned to a zero or **control condition** in which they are not exposed to any amount or level of the independent variable. If, in her memory experiment, Intraub had wanted to have a control group, she might have asked subjects to perform a totally unrelated task between presentations of the faces, such as counting backward from 998 by sevens as fast as possible. Thus, they would have had no opportunity to rehearse the faces. Having a control group allows the experimenter to make wider generalizations about the results of the experiment than can be made with experiments lacking a control group, but there are always at least two groups in an experiment for comparison purposes.

Oftentimes, in drug-related research, subjects in the control condition are given a pill or an injection that appears identical to the one given to subjects in the **experimental condition.** The pills or injections in the control condition, however, contain only inert substances such as sugar or distilled water. These fake pills and injections are called **placebos.** It is necessary to use placebos because researchers have found that the mere act of taking a pill or receiving an injection can change the behavior of a subject. Thus, to ensure that a particular effect is indeed due to the drug being tested and not to the "placebo effect," control subjects must be treated exactly as the experimental subjects, even if this means going through the motions of giving them drugs or medications.

When assigning subjects to the groups, the experimenter may choose to randomly assign them and hope that subjects with similar characteristics do not all wind up in the same group. However, if there are factors that may have a bearing on the results, such as intellectual level in a memory experiment, the experimenter may decide to *match* subjects as closely as possible. This can be done via a pretest, a survey, or some other means. Milgram was particularly careful to match members of his groups according to age level (each group was composed of the same percentage of subjects in their twenties, thirties, and forties) and according to occupational background (each group had the same percentage of skilled and unskilled workers, sales and business people, and professional workers).

In every experiment, the researcher takes care to assure that all extraneous variables (those that are not being directly manipulated or measured) are held *constant*. That is, factors that should have no bearing on the experimental results, such as the on-again, off-again noise of the air conditioner, need to be kept constant (the same) for all subjects so that they do not affect subjects' responses.

Milgram's experiment was particularly well controlled. For example, the instructions were the same for all conditions and the learner gave identical responses for the level of shock being administered. At 285 volts, he merely let out an agonized scream; at 300 volts, he let out an agonized scream, then said, "I absolutely refuse to answer any more. Get me out of here. You can't hold me here. Get me out. Get me out of here." At 315 volts, he let out an intensely agonized scream, then said, "*I told you I refuse to answer.* I'm no longer part of this experiment." Some variables, of course, are irrelevant to the research and can be ignored; there was no need for Milgram to control for subjects' eye color or handedness, for example. If the appropriate variables have been controlled, any change found in the dependent variable should be attributable *only* to the independent variable and the researcher should be reasonably able to assume that the independent variable is the *cause* of the change in behavior.

Besides extraneous variables, there are other details that must be controlled. Experimenters, like everyone, have their own personal beliefs and expectancies. In the process of data collection they may inadvertently give subtle cues or treat subjects differently in accordance with these expectations. For example, an experimenter may breathe a sigh of relief when a subject gives a response supporting the hypothesis. This tendency of experimenters to influence the results in the expected direction is called **experimenter bias.**

EXPERIMENTER BIAS: *The tendency of experimenters to influence the results of a research study in the expected direction.*

There are several devices that experimenters use to prevent experimenter bias. One technique is to run a **double-blind experiment,** in which both the experimenter and the subjects are unaware of which subjects are part of the control group and which are part of the experimental group. For instance, in a double-blind experiment testing a new drug, both the experimenter administering the drug and the subjects taking the drug are blind as to who is receiving a placebo and who is receiving the drug itself. Other techniques to prevent experimenter bias include using recording methods that are as objective as possible and enlisting neutral people other than the experimenter to interact with the subjects and collect the data. Milgram employed both these techniques: he used an automatic recording device to record subjects' responses, and he hired a high school teacher to play the role of experimenter.

DOUBLE-BLIND EXPERIMENT: *An experiment in which neither the subject nor the experimenter knows which treatment is being given to the subject or to which group the subject has been assigned.*

Another type of bias is called sample bias. A **sample** is a group of experimental subjects selected to represent a larger group, or **population. Sample bias** is the tendency for the sample to be not truly representative, or typical, of the population being studied. If, for example, a therapist wished to study normal behavior but used emotionally disturbed people as the sole sample, the behavior of the sample would not represent the behavior of average people. The purpose of conducting experiments is often to apply, or *generalize,* the results to a wide population. Thus, it is of considerable importance that the sample represent this general population. It is also important that the sample be of sufficient size — the larger the sample, the more likely it is that it will represent a cross section of the entire population.

SAMPLE: *A selected group of subjects that is representative of a larger population.*
POPULATION: *The total of all possible cases from which a sample is selected.*
SAMPLE BIAS: *The tendency for the sample of subjects in a research study to be atypical of a larger population.*

Question: Isn't a lot of research conducted with college students or with animals? How can you generalize these results to people in the real world? This can present a problem. Milgram realized that Yale undergraduates represented only a small percentage of the general population, since they were highly intelligent, they were in their late teens or early twenties, and many had had some recent experience with psychological studies. Thus, Milgram recruited subjects ages 20 to 50, with a wide variety of occupational backgrounds, from the community around Yale and paid them to participate in the experiment.

Not all researchers have funds to pay their subjects, however. Thus, a large percentage of psychological research is conducted with animals and college students. Most often,

Using naturalistic observation, Jane Goodall has been a major contributor to our knowledge of animal behavior.

these subjects are sufficiently similar to the general population in behaviors under investigation that the study results can validly be generalized to the population at large. For example, David Hubel (1984), who has conducted extensive research on brain physiology, has stated: "The principles of [nerve] function are remarkably similar in animals as far apart as the snail and man. . . . Even the major structures of the brain are so similar in, say, the cat and man that for most problems it seems to make little difference which brain one studies" (p. 4).

Review Questions

1. Experiments are used to determine _____ relationships.
2. A _____ is a tentative explanation for behavior.
3. _____ are factors capable of change or variation.
4. A response of subjects in an experiment is the _____ variable.
5. Subjects in a _____ condition are exposed to a zero level of the independent variable.
6. Experimenter _____ is the tendency of experimenters to influence results in the expected direction.

Answers: 1 cause-and-effect; 2 hypothesis; 3 variables; 4 dependent; 5 control; 6 bias

Nonexperimental research techniques: Studying the correlates of behavior

Sometimes it is not feasible for ethical or practical reasons to study behavior experimentally, so a number of nonexperimental techniques have been devised. These techniques include naturalistic observation, surveys, and individual case studies. Although none of these methods can be used to determine the causes of behavior, they can be quite valuable in determining relationships between variables and in providing information vital to making predictions of future behavior.

NATURALISTIC OBSERVATION: The systematic recording of behavior in the subject's natural state or habitat.

Naturalistic observation When using **naturalistic observation**, researchers systematically record the behavior of subjects in their natural state or habitat. This habitat may be the jungle, in a study of chimpanzees, or a classroom, in a study of third graders (Josephson, 1987). Cheney and Foss (1984) used naturalistic observation in a study involving social problems encountered by mentally impaired workers. They recorded observations of mentally retarded people in their work setting. These observations revealed 355 distinct social problems encountered by mentally retarded workers. Most of them involved interpersonal problems with supervisors or coworkers or disruptive and distractive behavior patterns on the part of the mentally retarded workers. Analysis of the nature of such problems can yield valuable information in the assessment and training of mentally retarded people.

Ideally, a researcher using naturalistic observation tries to prevent subjects from detecting that they are being observed because their behavior becomes unnatural when they know they are being watched. For example, have you ever been driving down the street, singing along with a song on the radio, only to stop in the middle of a phrase as you realized that the person in the next car was watching? The same type of thing normally happens when subjects of scientific studies realize they are being observed.

The chief advantage of using naturalistic observation is that researchers are able to obtain data about a truly natural behavior rather than a behavior that is a reaction to a contrived experimental situation. If the Cheney–Foss study had taken place in a lab, the workers would probably have acted quite differently from how they behaved in their actual workplace. On the other hand, naturalistic observation can be difficult and time-consuming, controls are lacking, it is difficult to generalize the results of the research, and scientific objectivity may be lost if the experimenters somehow interact with their subjects.

Surveys   **Surveys,** tests, questionnaires, and interviews (we will refer to them all as "surveys") are similar techniques that sample a wide variety of behaviors and attitudes. They range from personality inventories that probe into the character makeup of individual people to public opinion surveys such as the well-known Gallup and Harris polls. A lesser-known survey is one conducted by Jon D. Miller (1986). He designed a telephone survey to assess how well people living in the United States understand the technological advances made during the past century. As can be seen in Table 1.1, Miller found that many people do not understand or do not apply available technology to everyday life. For example, 41 percent of the people sampled believe that rocket launchings have caused changes in our weather.

SURVEYS: *Nonexperimental research techniques that sample behaviors and attitudes of a population.*

Surveys enable researchers to obtain a description of the characteristics of a relatively small sample of, perhaps, a few thousand people, and then generalize that information to a larger population. Miller, for example, sampled 1,992 people and generalized his findings to the entire U.S. population. For surveys to be truly effective research tools, it is critical that the wording of questions be as unambiguous and unbiased as possible. Considerable attention must also be given to details such as ensuring that the sample is truly representative of the population. Miller took great pains to ensure a representative sample. His survey involved 150 distinct nationwide sampling units and he used a random-digit dialing procedure to avoid any sampling bias.

Survey techniques, of course, cannot be used to explain causes of behavior, but they can be used to predict behavior. Miller could not pinpoint the inadequacy of school science programs as being the *cause* of technological illiteracy. He could, however, *predict* the level of such illiteracy in the United States. Moreover, Miller's research supports his

TABLE 1.1
Public Acceptance of Selected Technological Ideas

	Agree	Not Sure	Disagree
It is not wise to plan ahead because many things turn out to be a matter of good or bad luck anyway.	20%	2%	78%
Some numbers are especially lucky for some people.	40	4	56
Smoking causes serious health problems.	95	1	3
There are good ways of treating sickness that medical science does not recognize.	75	8	18
Rocket launchings and other space activities have caused changes in our weather.	41	12	47
It is likely that some of the unidentified flying objects that have been reported are really space vehicles from other civilizations.	43	11	46

$N = 1992.$

Drawing by David Sipress.

"Just pretend we're not here, Ms. Robinson..."

recommendation that primary and secondary education be directed more toward establishing a firm scientific background.

Case studies   Suppose a researcher wanted to investigate the problem of "photophobia," or fear of light. Most people are not afraid of light, so it would be next to impossible to gather enough subjects to conduct an experiment or to use surveys or naturalistic observation. In the case of such rare disorders, researchers usually find a single person who has the problem and study him or her intensively. Such an in-depth study of a single research subject is called an individual **case study.**

CASE STUDY: *An in-depth study of a single research subject.*

In a case study, many aspects of a single subject's life are studied in depth in an attempt to explain the person's behavior and to evaluate any treatment techniques that are used. Consider, for example, the case of H. M., a man who underwent brain surgery to alleviate severe epilepsy (Milner, 1959). The surgery was successful in that it lessened the severity of the epilepsy, but it had an unexpected side effect. H. M. could not form *new* memories. He could remember things from the past before the surgery but could not remember things that happened after the surgery. (This case is described in more detail in Chapter 7.) Because of Milner's study, surgeons faced with similar cases have avoided destroying the brain areas that seem to be involved in the formation of new memories.

Correlation versus experimental methods   Now that we have studied both experimental and nonexperimental research techniques, it is important to understand the advantages and disadvantages of each. As we discovered in the previous section, carefully controlled experiments are very powerful tools for discovering the *causes* of behavior. In his research on H. M., however, Milner used the case study because it was the only appropriate technique. In many instances, the only appropriate research technique is a nonexperimental one, especially when studying human behavior. In fact, it would be impossible to study some variables in any other way. For example, it would be unethical to administer a drug to one group of pregnant women and none to another group to see whether the drug causes birth defects. The only way to study such topics as suicide, mental illness, alcoholism, divorce, and drug abuse would be to observe them as they occur naturally (Cozby, 1977).

CORRELATIONS: *Relationships between variables.*

Although nonexperimental techniques do not allow researchers to determine the causes of behavior, they enable researchers to determine **correlations,** or relationships, between variables being studied. When any two variables are correlated, a change in one variable is accompanied by a concurrent change in the other. For example, there is a well-known correlation between heredity and schizophrenia (a type of mental disorder characterized by disorganized thinking and disturbed emotions — see Chapter 15). Stud-

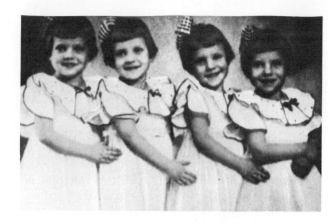

Correlation studies have shown that schizophrenia tends to run in families. Each of the Genain quadruplets was diagnosed a schizophrenic.

ies have been done comparing the development of schizophrenia in identical twins with its development in fraternal twins. Identical twins inherit identical genes from the parents, whereas fraternal twins are no more alike than brothers and sisters born at different times. If one identical twin develops schizophrenia, the other twin has a 41–63 percent chance of also becoming schizophrenic; but when one fraternal twin is schizophrenic, the other twin has only a 12–21 percent chance (Bernheim and Lewine, 1979; Gottesman and Shields, 1982).

Question: Does this prove that schizophrenia is inherited?   Absolutely not. Investigators may *guess* at the reasons for correlations between variables, but nonexperimental techniques provide no means for *proving* them. In the case of schizophrenia, some researchers believe that psychological factors such as stress and childhood trauma are the most important factors (Stabenau and Pollin, 1969), but only further *experimental* research will enable us to prove the cause or causes of schizophrenia.

A study conducted in Taiwan demonstrates how absurd it is to assume that when two factors are correlated, one must cause the other. Li (1975) wanted to determine which factors correlate with the use of birth control methods. Of the variables tested, it was found that the variable most strongly related to the use of contraceptives was the number of electric appliances (toasters, can openers, popcorn poppers, and so on) in the home. Does this mean, then, that Planned Parenthood should pass out toasters to cut down on teenage pregnancy? Of course not. Just because electrical appliances and the use of birth control methods are correlated, it does not follow that the electrical appliances *cause* people to use birth control. We cannot state this strongly enough: *Correlation does not imply causation.*

This is not to say that nonexperimental studies are useless. The descriptions and correlations obtained from nonexperimental studies can lead to predictions of behavior, and these predictions can be of considerable value. For example, the Taiwan study may lead researchers to seek a variable that relates to both the number of appliances and contraceptive use, such as socioeconomic level. If a strong correlation exists between these three variables, we might be able to predict that the higher the socioeconomic level, the greater the contraceptive use. By knowing this, family planning agencies can target people of lower socioeconomic levels when designing and distributing birth control information.

Evaluating the research: Are the findings significant?

Question: How do researchers know whether the information they have collected really measures the behavior they are studying?   There are criteria to be followed to ensure that research results will be accurate, legitimate measures of the hypothesis. These criteria vary according to the type of study being conducted, but they include controlling for experimenter or researcher bias, controlling extraneous influences, ensur-

STATISTICS: *Data collected in a research study and the procedures used to analyze data.*

STATISTICALLY SIGNIFICANT: *A relationship believed not to be caused by chance.*

REPLICATE: *To conduct a research study again, following the same procedure.*

ing that the sample size is substantial, and ensuring that the sample is representative of the population to which the results will apply. However, even though the proper procedures and controls have been used, the results need to be analyzed statistically. **Statistics** consist not only of the data (the numbers) that are recorded when some behavior is measured but also analyses of these data according to specific rules and mathematical formulas. Statistical analysis is used to determine whether any relationships or differences among the variables are significant. A **statistically significant** relationship or difference is one that the experimenter has good reason to believe is true or real and not due merely to chance or coincidence. Statistics and the concept of significance are examined in detail in the appendix at the end of the book.

Another way to determine whether research results are legitimate is to **replicate** the research project by conducting the same study again following the same procedure. Milgram's study has been replicated countless times, with similar results, both by Milgram himself and by other researchers (Kilham and Mann, 1974; Shanab and Yahya, 1977). Replication is often done as a means of substantiating research. As more and more replications confirm the results of the original research, it becomes more evident that the research findings are valid and can legitimately be applied to real-world situations. Replication is also conducted for other reasons. When examining research reports, psychologists might question some aspect of the research. For example, they may dispute results that are not consistent with other research findings or with common expectation. Or they may detect an error in methodology, in procedure, or in some other aspect of the study. As a result, they decide to replicate the study. The findings of such replications may either support or refute the original research. If replications do not support the research, it is necessary to study the problem further.

Review Questions

1 With the research technique of _____ _____, behavior is studied in its natural state or habitat.

2 Surveys measure a relatively small sample in order to generalize the information to a larger _____.

3 An individual _____ _____ measures a single subject in depth.

4 _____ are relationships between two variables that are used to predict behaviors.

5 _____ include both data and their interpretation.

6 _____ is repeating a research study to determine whether the same results can be obtained.

Answers: 1 naturalistic observation; *2* population; *3* case study; *4* correlations; *5* statistics; *6* replication

ETHICS IN PSYCHOLOGY

The American Psychological Association (APA), the professional organization of psychologists, recognizes the importance of maintaining high ethical standards in research, therapy, and all other areas of professional psychology. The preamble to their publication *Ethical Principles of Psychologists* (1981) admonishes psychologists to maintain their competence, to retain objectivity in applying their skills, and to preserve the dignity and best interests of their clients, colleagues, students, research participants, and society.

APPLYING ABSTRACT TERMINOLOGY
Becoming a Better Consumer of Scientific Research

The news media, advertisers, politicians, teachers, close friends, and other individuals frequently use research findings in their attempts to change your attitudes and behavior. How can you tell whether such information is accurate and worthwhile?

Using terms and concepts from the previous discussion on psychological research techniques, the following exercise will improve your ability to critically evaluate sources of information. Read each "research" report and decide what is the *primary* problem or research limitation. In the space provided, make one of the following marks:

CC = The report is misleading because correlational data are used to suggest causation.

CG = The report is inconclusive since there was no control group.

EB = The results of the research were unfairly influenced by experimenter bias.

SB = The results of the research are questionable because of sample bias.

_____ *1* A clinical psychologist strongly believes that touching is an important adjunct to successful therapy. For two months he touches half his patients (Group A) and refrains from touching the other half (Group B). He then reports a noticeable improvement in Group A.

_____ *2* A newspaper reports that violent crime corresponds to phases of the moon. The reporter concludes that the gravitational pull of the moon controls human behavior.

_____ *3* A researcher interested in women's attitudes toward premarital sex sends out a lengthy survey to subscribers of *Playboy* and *Cosmopolitan* magazines.

_____ *4* An experimenter is interested in studying the effects of alcohol on driving ability. Prior to testing on the experimental driving course, Group A consumes 2 ounces of alcohol, Group B consumes 4 ounces of alcohol, and Group C consumes 6 ounces of alcohol. The researcher reports that alcohol consumption adversely affects driving ability.

_____ *5* After reading a scientific journal that reports higher divorce levels among couples who lived together before marriage, a college student decides to move out of the apartment she shares with her boyfriend.

_____ *6* A theater owner reports increased beverage sales following the brief flashing of subliminal messages (such as "Drink Coca-Cola") during the film showing.

ANSWERS: 1 EB; 2 CC; 3 SB; 4 CG; 5 CC; 6 CG

Research ethics: Respecting the rights of subjects

Think back to Milgram's experiment for a moment. In that study subjects were led to believe that they were administering shocks to an unfortunate "learner." The learner was actually a **confederate,** or accomplice, of the experimenter, who only pretended to be in pain. The role was played by a 47-year-old accountant who delivered a believable performance as the desperate, protesting learner. Can you imagine how Milgram's subjects must have felt when they discovered they had been tricked and that the turmoil they had gone through had been purposely created?

CONFEDERATE: *An accomplice of the experimenter who pretends to be another subject.*

Because of this deception, Milgram's experiment has been criticized on ethical grounds. Critics point out that subjects may have suffered from feelings of guilt and remorse after the experiment, as well as intense inner conflict and stress during the experiment (Baumrind, 1964, 1985). Milgram (1974) argues that he took great care to assure both the short- and long-term psychological well-being of his subjects. In postexperimental sessions, Milgram informed subjects about the true nature of the experiment, discussed the research with them, and took pains to reassure them that whatever behavior they exhibited—obedient or defiant—was normal and in keeping with that of other subjects. He also sent a five-page summary of the research results to each subject.

Studies such as Milgram's raise a number of questions regarding ethics in psychological research. These questions are addressed in a specialized publication of the APA, *Ethical Principles in the Conduct of Research with Human Participants* (1982). One of the chief principles set forth in the document is that an investigator should obtain the subject's "informed consent" before initiation of an experiment. The researcher should fully inform the subject as to the nature of the study and establish a reciprocal agreement with the subject clarifying the responsibilities of each. Milgram, of course, did not obtain such "informed consent." He deceived subjects by telling them that they were involved in a study of learning and memory.

Question: But if Milgram had told his subjects he was studying obedience, wouldn't they have behaved differently?   Yes, that's probably true. That's the reason why deception research is conducted. If subjects knew the true purpose behind some studies, they would almost certainly not respond normally. Therefore, APA acknowledges the need for some deception research. However, researchers conducting this research are expected to follow strict guidelines, which include debriefing subjects at the end of the experiment. When **debriefing** subjects, researchers explain the reasons for conducting the research and clear up any misconceptions or concerns on the part of the subject. It is expected that subjects will be debriefed at the end of all experiments. Milgram did indeed debrief his subjects and send them research results.

DEBRIEFING: *Explaining the research process to subjects who participated.*

Question: Milgram's learner may not have been really shocked, but I've heard of animals being given electric shocks in psychological experiments. That doesn't sound ethical to me. Why is it done?   There has been some research in which electric shock or some other type of unpleasant or aversive treatment has been administered to animals. In recent years, this type of research has been brought to the public's attention by animal rights groups opposed to such research and to improper care of laboratory animals. Such research is extremely rare, however, and psychologists argue that it is conducted only when there is no alternative way to study the behavior and when applications of the research justify the nature of the experiment. Only about 7 to 8 percent of all psychological research is done on animals, and 90 percent of that is done with rats and mice (APA, 1984). In most research institutions where animal research is conducted, animal care committees have been established to ensure proper treatment of research animals, to review projects, and to set guidelines that are in accordance with the APA standards for the care and treatment of research animals.

Most studies involving animals consist of naturalistic observation or learning experiments using rewards rather than punishments (Mesirow, 1984; Gallup and Suarez, 1985). Animals are used instead of humans because "time requirements [as in studies of aging], risk, or other conditions make it impossible to use humans" (APA, 1984). Animal research has benefited humans in many ways. Research on learning in rats and pigeons has led to the development of programmed learning materials. Research projects involv-

Considerable media attention has been paid to animal rights groups who continue to protest the use of animals in psychological and medical research.

ing the teaching of sign language to chimps and gorillas have led to a better understanding of the structure of human language. Research involving the effects of drugs on unborn animals has demonstrated the risks of maternal alcohol and other drug use for human babies. Animal research has also led to benefits for animals. For example, more natural environments have been created for zoo animals, successful breeding techniques have been developed for endangered species, and effective training techniques have been devised for pets and wild animals in captivity.

Clinical practice ethics: Respecting the rights of clients

Successful **psychotherapy** requires that clients reveal their innermost thoughts and feelings during the course of treatment. Thus, clients need to develop a sense of trust in their therapists. This places a burden of responsibility on therapists to maintain the highest of ethical standards in upholding this trust.

PSYCHOTHERAPY: *Application of psychological principles and techniques to the treatment of mental disorders or to the problems of everyday adjustment.*

Therapists are expected to conduct themselves in a moral and professional manner. They should remain objective while becoming sufficiently involved with the clients' problems to know how to help the client deal with them. They should encourage the client to become involved not only in deciding the type of treatment to be given but also in the treatment process itself.

A therapist is expected to make adequate measures of clients' progress and to report that progress to them. All personal information and therapy records must be kept confidential, with records being available only to authorized persons of whom the client is aware. Such confidentiality can become an ethical issue when a client reveals a fact that will affect and possibly injure other people. For example, if you were a therapist, what would you do if a client revealed plans to commit murder — would you alert the police or uphold your client's trust? It is a difficult decision, but therapists have the responsibility not only of ensuring clients' interests but ensuring the interests of others as well; thus, they are expected to report such cases. Similarly, they are required by law to disregard their pledge of confidentiality when confronted with disclosures of child and spouse abuse by reporting such cases to appropriate authorities.

Question: I've heard psychologists hand out advice to callers on radio and TV talk shows. Is this ethical? Many psychologists condemn such talk-show psychology because of the impossibility of accurately assessing people's problems in such a short period of time. They also disapprove of the practice on the grounds that listeners may apply to themselves advice bestowed on another, which may lead to problems since no two people or situations are alike. However, others argue that the nature of the on-air interview is supportive and rather general in nature, and talk-show psychologists maintain that when indicated, they refer the caller for direct counseling with a qualified therapist. They maintain that radio psychologists can benefit thousands of listeners by acquainting them with psychologists and with psychological principles and techniques that they might apply to their own personal problems (Schwebel, 1982).

SCHOOLS OF PSYCHOLOGY

During the early 1800s research into biology, physiology, chemistry, and physics got under way, and such research led to an interest in the behavior of both animals and humans. Physiologists conducted investigations into the structure and function of the nervous system, while physicists determined relationships between physical stimuli and the sensations they evoke. However, it was not until the first psychological laboratory was founded in 1879 that psychology as a science officially began. Since then, psychologists have studied behavior from a variety of different approaches, and they have grouped together under various schools with distinct approaches and beliefs regarding the study of behavior (see Table 1.2).

in the behaviorist approach. This criticism has been summarized by one of the best-known humanists, Carl Rogers (1964):

> In this world of inner meanings, humanistic psychology can investigate all the issues which are meaningless for the behaviorist — purposes, goals, values, choice, perceptions of self, perceptions of others, the personal constructs with which we build our world, the responsibilities we accept or reject, the whole phenomenal world of the individual with its connective tissue of meaning. Not one aspect of this world is open to the strict behaviorist. Yet that these elements have significance for man's behavior seems certainly true. (p. 119)

HUMANISTIC PSYCHOLOGY: *A school of psychology that emphasizes the importance of the inner, subjective self and stresses the positive side of human nature.*

From Rogers' statement, it is evident that **humanistic psychology** emphasizes the importance of the inner, subjective self, of consciousness and feelings. Humanists stress the fact that human nature is naturally positive, creative, and growth-seeking unless thwarted by experience. In humanistic therapy, people are viewed in a positive light, as "clients" rather than "patients," and are encouraged to express their feelings and find their own solutions to problems while engaged in a supportive relationship with their therapist.

In contrast to the behaviorist view of behavior as mere responses to stimuli, humanists emphasize the capacity for people to exercise free will in making their own choices and their own decisions in the way they behave. As a result, each person is seen as a unique individual. All people, according to humanist Abraham Maslow, have both the need and the ability to fulfill their unique and optimum potential.

Cognitive psychology: The return to thought processes

COGNITIVE PSYCHOLOGY: *A school of psychology that focuses on reasoning and the mental processing of information.*

Cognitive psychology focuses on the mental processing of information. It is concerned with the acquisition, storage, retrieval, and use of knowledge, whether that knowledge be about the intricacies of the atom or about how to change a flat tire. Cognitive psychologists study how we gather, encode, and store information from our environment using such mental processes as perception, memory, imagery, concept formation, problem solving, reasoning, decision making, and language. If you were listening to a friend describe her whitewater rafting trip, a cognitive psychologist would be interested in how you decipher the meaning of her words, how you form mental images of the turbulent water, how you incorporate your impressions of her experience into your previous concepts of rafting, and so on.

INFORMATION PROCESSING APPROACH: *An approach to studying mental processes that views people and computers in similar terms, as processors of information that has been gathered from the environment, then encoded for memory storage and retrieval.*

The major perspective used by cognitive psychologists to study these topics is known as the **information processing approach,** which was derived from the computer sciences. According to this approach, we gather information from the environment, then process it in a series of stages. A certain type of processing is performed at one level before the information is passed on to another level for a different kind of processing. The information processing approach is based on the idea that humans are like computers in that both take in information, process it, and produce a response. In fact, cognitive psychologists often express models of human thought processes with techniques used in the computer sciences, such as flowcharts (diagrams with arrows leading from one box to successive others) and mathematical formulas. For example, cognitive psychologists studying memory have devised a model (which can be seen in Figure 7.1) that illustrates the sequence of stages in the acquisition of memory.

Psychobiology: The brain and behavior

PSYCHOBIOLOGY: *The study of the biology of behavior.*

During the last couple of decades, significant advances have been made in our understanding of the structure and function of the brain and nervous system. This new knowledge has given rise to an increasingly important school of psychology known as physiological psychology, or **psychobiology.** Psychobiologists explain behavior as a result of complex chemical and biological events within the brain. Recent research has been productive in exploring the role of biological factors in sensation, perception, learning, memory, language, sexual behavior, and schizophrenia.

The roots of psychobiology can easily be traced to the beginnings of experimental physiology and Johannes Müller, whose most important contribution was his *doctrine of specific nerve energies.* This doctrine stated that all nerves carry the same basic message, an electrical impulse. Other significant nineteenth-century physiologists and anatomists who made contributions to this area include Paul Broca, a French surgeon who studied patients with brain injuries; Luigi Galvani, who was the first to use electrical stimulation to study the workings of the brain; Hermann von Helmholtz, who among other things was the first to attempt to measure the speed of the nerve impulse; and Charles Darwin, whose theory of evolution inspired research into comparative physiology. Unlike their predecessors, today's psychobiologists have access to modern technological equipment to help them study the functioning of individual nerve cells, the roles of various parts of the brain, the effects of various drugs on brain functions, and so on. Chapter 2 is devoted to modern research into the biological basis of behavior. As you will discover, the biology of behavior is a theme that is woven into the discussion of many types of behavior throughout this text.

Psychology today: An eclectic view

Rather than speak of "schools of psychology," most modern psychologists talk about the five basic "perspectives" that influence the topics psychologists study, how they conduct their research, and what information they consider important. These are the *psychoanalytic, behavioristic,* and *humanistic,* as well as the increasingly important *cognitive* and *biological* perspectives. As you study this text or read of general information about psychology, you will find numerous references to each of these perspectives.

In discussing the various schools or perspectives within psychology, we have necessarily examined them separately and made distinctions between their philosophies and practices. Today most psychologists recognize the value of each orientation, but at the same time concede that no one view has all the answers. They take an *eclectic* approach in adopting principles from several orientations and recognizing that the variety of complex behaviors we humans exhibit requires complex ways of dealing with them.

Question: Is any one school of thought more "right" than the others? Most students begin by agreeing with one major school, then another, and another, as they learn more about each one. Ultimately, most come to realize the value of different orientations for distinct situations as they look for ways to apply psychological concepts to their everyday lives. For example, they can see the value of behaviorism in training their dog not to jump up on people, or the value of humanism in building responsibility for their own lives.

One final note as you begin your study of psychology: You will learn a great deal about psychological functioning, but take care that you don't overestimate your expertise. Once friends and acquaintances know that you're taking a course in psychology, they may ask you to interpret their dreams, help them to discipline their children, or even offer your opinion on whether they should break up their relationships. As David L. Cole, the recipient of the APA Distinguished Teaching in Psychology award, has stated, "Undergraduate psychology can, and I believe should, seek to liberate the student from ignorance, but also the arrogance of believing we know more about ourselves and others than we really do" (1982). It is also important to remember that the ideas, philosophies, and even experimental findings of the science of psychology are continually being revised. But like those from any other science, psychological findings and ideas, developed through careful research and study, can make important contributions to our lives. As Albert Einstein once said, "One thing I have learned in a long life: that all our science, measured against reality, is primitive and childlike — and yet, it is the most precious thing we have."

Review Questions

1 Subjects are _____ at the end of an experiment so they will understand the purposes of the research study.

2 The _____ school of psychology originated the method of introspection to examine thoughts and feelings.

3 Freud's approach to studying unconscious conflicts of the mind is called _____.

4 A _____ is an organized whole or pattern of perception.

5 The _____ approach considers more than one approach or perspective in studying behavior.

6 The _____ approach emphasizes the importance of inner meanings and feelings.

7 _____ attempts to explain behavior as complex chemical and biological events within the brain.

Answers: 1 debriefed; *2* structuralist; *3* psychoanalysis; *4* gestalt; *5* eclectic; *6* humanistic; *7* psychobiology

---

REVIEW OF MAJOR CONCEPTS

UNDERSTANDING PSYCHOLOGY

1 Psychology is the scientific study of behavior. Psychologists use scientific research methods to investigate overt, or observable, behaviors and covert behaviors such as thoughts and feelings.

2 The goals of psychology are to describe, explain, predict, and change behavior.

3 Psychologists perform research and can specialize in several areas, including clinical, counseling, educational, school, physiological, developmental, social, or industrial and organizational psychology.

4 Basic research involves the study of theoretical issues; applied research involves solving specific problems.

5 Psychological findings can be applied to improve our personal lives. The study of psychology leads to an appreciation for scientific methods of research, as opposed to pseudoscientific methods.

PSYCHOLOGICAL METHODOLOGY

6 Research methodology includes experimental techniques designed to investigate cause-and-effect relationships and nonexperimental techniques that provide descriptions of behavior.

7 An experiment begins with a hypothesis or possible explanation for behavior. Independent variables are the factors the experimenter manipulates and dependent variables are measurable behaviors of the subjects. Experimental control includes assigning subjects to groups and holding extraneous variables constant.

8 Nonexperimental research techniques are used to obtain descriptions of behavior. Naturalistic observation is used to study behavior in its natural habitat. Surveys use interviews or questionnaires to obtain information on a sample of subjects. Individual case studies are in-depth studies of single subjects.

9 Experiments enable us to determine causes for behaviors, whereas correlational relationships enable us to predict behaviors.

10 Psychologists use statistics to judge whether research findings are statistically significant or due to chance.

ETHICS IN PSYCHOLOGY

11 Psychologists are expected to maintain high ethical standards in their relations with human and animal research subjects and in therapeutic relationships with clients. The APA has established and published specific guidelines detailing these ethical standards in order to guarantee the rights and welfare of experimental participants as well as clients undergoing therapy.

SCHOOLS OF PSYCHOLOGY

12 Psychologists have grouped together to form various schools of psychology with distinct approaches to the study of behavior. Structuralists attempted to identify elements of consciousness through the technique of introspection to determine how these elements form the structure of the mind. Functionalists studied the functions of mental pro-

cesses in adapting the individual to the environment and broadened the scope of psychology, while extending its influence to such fields as education and industry.

13 Freud's psychoanalytic theory examined conflicts that were presumed to be caused by unconscious conflicts. The Gestalt school studied organizing principles of perceptual processes and encouraged the eclectic approach.

14 Behaviorism emphasizes observable behaviors and the ways they are learned. Humanistic psychology focuses on inner meanings and assumes our nature is positive and growth-seeking. Cognitive psychology examines reasoning and mental processes.

15 Psychobiology attempts to explain behavior as complex chemical and biological events within the brain.

SUGGESTED READINGS

AMERICAN PSYCHOLOGICAL ASSOCIATION (1980). *Careers in psychology.* Washington, DC: APA. This booklet is available free to students from the American Psychological Association, 1200 17th Street NW, Washington, DC 20036.

AMERICAN PSYCHOLOGICAL ASSOCIATION (1982). *Ethical principles in the conduct of research with human participants.* Washington, DC: APA. This book lists and discusses the ethical principles involved in research with humans.

COZBY, P. C. (1985). *Methods in behavioral research.* Palo Alto, CA: Mayfield. An introduction to the use of research methods in psychology.

MILGRAM, S. (1974). *Obedience to authority.* New York: Harper & Row. This book describes the original experiments conducted by Milgram on obedience to authority.

SCHULTZ, D. (1981). *A history of modern psychology.* New York: Academic Press. An introduction to the short history of psychology.

STANOVICH, K. E. (1986). *How to think straight about psychology.* Glenview, IL: Scott, Foresman. An interesting book on how to evaluate psychological and pseudopsychological research.

chapter two

The Brain and Nervous System

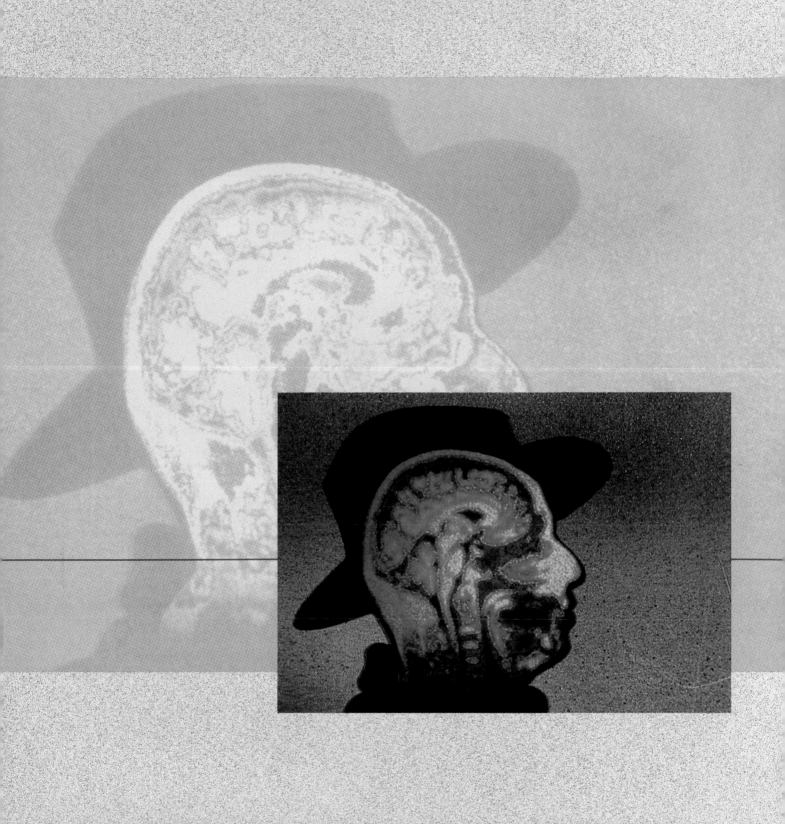

RED	BLUE	RED	RED	BLUE
GREEN	BLUE	GREEN	YELLOW	YELLOW
RED	YELLOW	GREEN	YELLOW	GREEN
BLUE	RED	YELLOW	BLUE	YELLOW
YELLOW	GREEN	BLUE	GREEN	BLUE
GREEN	RED	GREEN	RED	RED
YELLOW	BLUE	RED	YELLOW	RED
RED	YELLOW	YELLOW	GREEN	BLUE
BLUE	GREEN	RED	BLUE	YELLOW
GREEN	RED	GREEN	YELLOW	BLUE
YELLOW	RED	RED	YELLOW	RED
GREEN	RED	YELLOW	BLUE	GREEN
GREEN	BLUE	YELLOW	GREEN	RED
BLUE	BLUE	BLUE	RED	GREEN
BLUE	YELLOW	GREEN	BLUE	RED
YELLOW	GREEN	BLUE	BLUE	GREEN

TAKE a look at the list of words printed above. Try to read the entire list out loud as fast as you can, beginning with the left-hand column and reading down each column. That was easy, wasn't it? Now try again, but this time say aloud *not* the words themselves but the colors of the ink in which the words are printed.

Could you do it without making a mistake? Did you stutter and stammer, hesitate, get all confused? It took you a lot longer to say the colors, didn't it? This is a version of the "Stroop effect" that has fascinated psychologists since 1935 when J. R. Stroop first studied it in a learning experiment. How do you think the Stroop effect works? Why do you think it is so easy to read the words and so hard to say the colors of ink?

Whenever one of your five senses detects a stimulus — a stop sign, the voice of a friend, chocolate ice cream — the resulting sensation is changed into neural (nerve) signals that are sent to your brain. So when you read a word or identify a color on the Stroop list, your eyes sense the word or color and transcribe the sensation into neural signals, which are sent via nerves to your brain. After processing the information, your brain "decides" what you should say and sends a message to your mouth and vocal cords to produce it.

When you are directed to say the colors rather than the words in the list, confusion results somewhere within the maze of interconnected brain cells. Why? One very plausible explanation is that your brain has become so accustomed to reading words that reading any word, no matter what its color, is automatic. However, when you try to name a color different from the word it forms, your deeply ingrained reading habit interferes, resulting in confusion in your brain.

When you think about it, it is astounding that confusion in the brain does not occur more often than it does. Our brain is an extraordinarily complex structure composed of billions of cells working in concert with one another to enable us to move, perceive, feel, and think. As if the brain itself is not complex enough, a system of thousands of nerves is scattered throughout the body carrying messages to and from the brain, enabling us to do anything from jump hurdles to memorize poems. The brain is ultimately responsible for all our actions and is the part of the body that makes each of us unique — even identical twins, who have developed from the same fertilized egg, do not have identical brains.

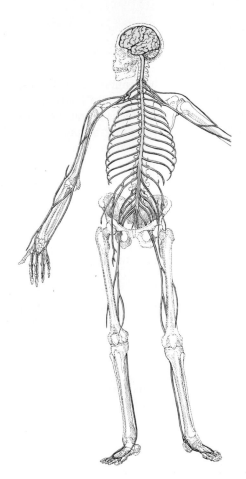

Figure 2.1 The central nervous system is found within the skull and spinal column, whereas the peripheral nervous system connects the nervous system to muscles and internal organs.

Unique as they are, all brains are made up of similar parts. Psychobiologists study these brain parts and the rest of the nervous system to see how they affect our behavior. For example, they know what area of your brain was responsible for your feelings of frustration when you were stumbling over the ink colors in the Stroop test. Moreover, they know along which neural pathways the color messages traveled from your eyes to your brain, and how the messages were passed from one nerve cell to another. In this chapter we will discuss the major findings of these psychobiologists, as well as the techniques they have developed to conduct their investigations. In our discussion, we will examine the two major divisions of the nervous system: the **central nervous system (CNS),** which consists of the brain and the spinal cord, and the **peripheral nervous system (PNS),** which consists of the remaining nerves outside the CNS (see Figure 2.1). Before studying the nervous system, however, we will take a look at its basic unit, the neuron.

THE NEURON

The brain and the rest of the nervous system essentially consist of neurons. **Neurons** are cells that are responsible for transmitting information throughout the body, as well as within the brain. All behavior, everything you do, think, or feel, is a result of neuronal activity. Your every movement, every thought, and every heartbeat ultimately depends on what happens at the level of the neuron. Each neuron is a tiny information-processing system with thousands of connections through which it receives and sends signals to other neurons. Although nobody knows for sure, it has been estimated that the brain alone contains on the order of 100 billion neurons (Hubel, 1984). Translated into more comprehensible terms, this means that if placed end to end, the body's neurons would reach to the moon and back.

CENTRAL NERVOUS SYSTEM (CNS): *The part of the nervous system that consists of the brain and the spinal cord.*
PERIPHERAL NERVOUS SYSTEM (PNS): *The part of the nervous system outside the central nervous system that consists of the nerves going to and from the brain and spinal cord.*
NEURON: *Individual nerve cells responsible for transmitting information throughout the body.*

Structure of a neuron: Three basic parts

Just as no two people are alike, no two neurons are exactly alike, although most share three basic features: dendrites, a soma (cell body), and an axon (see Figure 2.2). Information from other cells normally enters the neuron through the numerous dendrites, passes through the soma, and is transmitted to other cells via the axon. **Dendrites** are branching structures that receive information from other neurons. Each neuron may have hundreds or thousands of dendrites. The cell body, or **soma**, serves several functions: It integrates the electrical information coming from the dendrites; it absorbs needed nutrients; and because it contains the nucleus, it produces the majority of protein molecules needed for normal functioning of the cell. The **axon** is a long tubelike structure specialized for transmitting neural information. It is highly sensitive to changes in the electrical charge of its membrane. If the electrical change is sufficient, an **action potential** (an electrochemical impulse) is initiated at the junction between the soma and the axon. This action potential travels down the length of the axon to its end, where it branches into small structures called **axon terminal buttons**. These terminal buttons form junctions with other neurons and with muscles.

Question: Is a nerve the same thing as a neuron? No. A neuron is a single cell. A **nerve** is a bundle of axons that have a similar function (see Figure 2.3). This distinction is similar to the difference between a single telephone wire and a telephone cable containing thousands of wires. A noteworthy example is the optic nerve, which has over a million axons transmitting visual information from the eye to the brain. When you were looking at the Stroop list, several thousand individual neurons were activated. Their messages were transmitted to your brain along thousands of axons bundled together

DENDRITES: *Branching neuron structures that receive neural impulses from other neurons and convey impulses toward the cell bodies.*

SOMA: *The cell body of the neuron; it integrates incoming information from the dendrites, absorbs nutrients, and produces the majority of the protein molecules needed by the neuron.*

AXON: *A long tubelike structure attached to the neuron cell body that conveys impulses away from the cell body toward other neurons.*

ACTION POTENTIAL: *An electrochemical impulse that travels down an axon from the soma to the axon terminal buttons.*

AXON TERMINAL BUTTONS: *Small structures at the ends of axons that release neurotransmitter chemicals.*

NERVE: *A bundle of axons that have a similar function.*

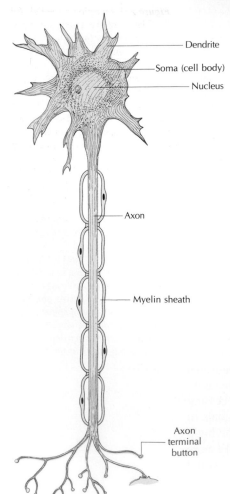

— Dendrite
— Soma (cell body)
— Nucleus
— Axon
— Myelin sheath
Axon terminal button

Figure 2.2 The structure of a typical neuron.

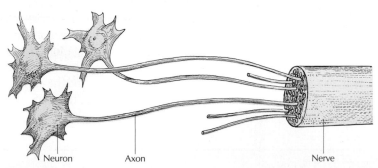

Neuron   Axon   Nerve

Figure 2.3 A nerve is a bundle of axons.

within the two optic nerves, one leading from each eye. Thus, the loss of a single neuron would be insignificant compared to the loss of an entire nerve.

Resting potential and action potential: To transmit or not to transmit, that is the question

Question: What happens when neurons are activated? Neurons are activated through a rather complicated electrochemical process that produces an action potential. Because of its complexity, we will greatly simplify our description of the process. During our discussion, it would be of great help to you if you would refer to Figures 2.4 and 2.5.

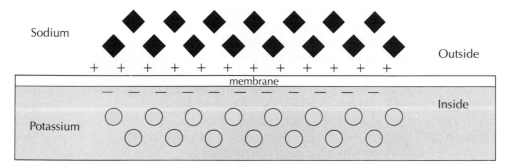

Figure 2.4 Resting potential. The sodium ions are represented by diamonds; the potassium ions are represented by circles. Although the sodium and potassium ions are both positively charged, the inside of the membrane has a net negative charge because of the large number of negatively charged protein ions (not shown) inside the cell.

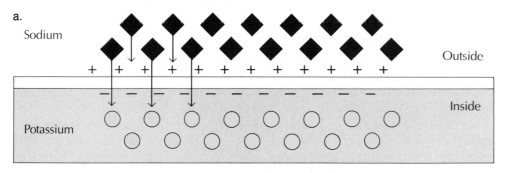

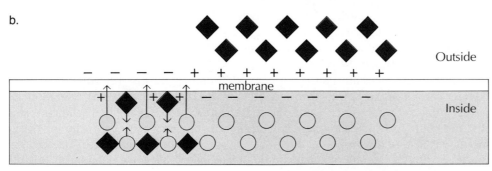

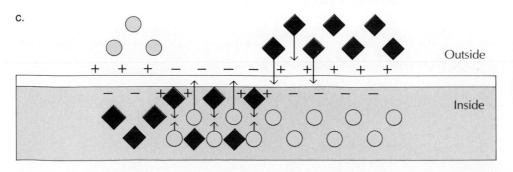

Figure 2.5 An action potential. *(a)* Stimulation of the axon causes the membrane barrier to break down and sodium to enter the cell. *(b)* As the sodium enters the cell, the charge inside the membrane goes from negative to positive. *(c)* Potassium exits the cell, restoring the inside of the membrane to a negative charge. Meanwhile, sodium enters the next segment of the membrane as sodium pores open.

IONS: *Molecules that carry positive or negative electrical charges.*

RESTING POTENTIAL: *The resting state of the axon membrane, which consists of a high concentration of sodium molecules outside the axon and a high concentration of potassium and protein molecules inside the axon.*

SODIUM–POTASSIUM PUMP: *An ongoing process whereby sodium ions are continually moved out and potassium ions are continually moved into the axon to restore and preserve the resting potential.*

MYELIN: *Fatty insulation that serves to greatly increase the speed at which an action potential moves down an axon.*

Many complex cognitive or motor tasks, such as reading or riding a bicycle, require continued development of the brain and nervous system.

Picture the axon as a tube of membranous tissue filled with chemicals. This tube is floating within a liquid sea of still more chemicals. The chemicals are **ions,** molecules that carry a particular electrical charge, either positive or negative. When nerve impulses are not being passed along the neural membrane, the chemical ions and their electrical charges outside and inside the membrane are balanced in such a way that the neuron is in a state of rest. This is known as the **resting potential.** During the resting potential, sodium ions, which carry a positive electrical charge, lie predominantly outside the axon membrane. Inside the membrane are positively charged potassium ions and negatively charged protein ions. Overall, the outside of the membrane is more positively charged than the inside (see Figure 2.4).

An action potential is initiated when enough stimulation is received at the dendrites or soma to change the electrical properties of the soma and the axon membrane. When this happens, pores in the axon membrane open and sodium ions rush in, temporarily giving the inside of the cell a positive charge. Almost immediately, potassium ions leave the cell, restoring the negative internal charge. These events at one spot on the neuron membrane trigger pores to open in the next section of the membrane, allowing sodium to move in and potassium to move out (see Figure 2.5). In short, a chain reaction occurs, with the impulse traveling down the axon, one section at a time, until it reaches the terminal buttons at the end. Arrival of an action potential at the terminal buttons causes them to squirt a tiny amount of chemical into the space between their neuron and another neuron (or muscle). If the other neuron receives sufficient chemical stimulation, an action potential will be initiated along its axon membrane and the process will be repeated.

Question: How does the axon return to its resting state?   The resting potential is reestablished in the axon by means of the **sodium–potassium pump.** This is a process that continually moves sodium ions out and potassium ions into the axon to maintain the electrochemical balance essential to the resting potential.

Question: The movement of the nerve impulse sounds like a really slow process. Is there any way it could be speeded up?   True, the nerve impulse does move slowly, much more slowly than electricity through a wire. Because it does so by a purely physical process, electricity can move through a wire as fast as the speed of light, approximately 300 million meters per second. A nerve impulse, on the other hand, can travel along a bare axon at only about 20 meters per second. Some axons, however, are enveloped in a fatty insulation called **myelin** that greatly increases the speed of an action potential. The myelin blankets the axon, with the exception of periodic nodes, points at which the myelin is very thin or absent (see Figure 2.2). The action potential jumps from node to node rather than traveling along the full membrane. Whereas an action potential might move at less than 20 meters per second in a bare axon, it can move at over 120 meters per second in a myelinated axon (Kalat, 1984).

In humans, myelinization is not completed until about age 12. This means that children cannot be expected to learn and react as fast as nor in the same way as an adult. It is impossible to teach most two-year-olds to read and write, for example. Their brains are just not ready to handle information at the speed and complexity necessary for these tasks. Certain diseases such as multiple sclerosis destroy the myelin sheath. This results in the slowing of the rate of conduction of action potentials and a subsequent loss of coordination within the nervous system.

Review Questions

1 The nervous system is broken into two major parts: the _____ nervous system, which includes the brain and spinal cord, and the _____ nervous system, which includes all the nerves entering or exiting the brain or spinal cord.

2 _____ , or nerve cells, are responsible for transmitting information throughout the brain and the body.

3 The major parts of the neuron are _____, _____, and _____.

4 An electrochemical impulse that travels down an axon is called an _____ _____.

5 Small structures at the end of axons that form synapses with other cells and release neurotransmitters are called _____ _____ _____.

6 A _____ is a bundle of axons that have a similar function.

7 The electrical potential that exists when an axon is not conducting an action potential is called a _____ potential.

8 When an action potential is first initiated, _____ ions rush into the axon and _____ ions move out.

9 The resting potential is restored and maintained in the axon by means of the _____ _____.

10 The fatty insulation that covers the axon and increases the speed of the action potential is called _____.

Answers: 1 central, peripheral; *2* neurons; *3* dendrites, soma, axon; *4* action potential; *5* axon terminal buttons; *6* nerve; *7* resting; *8* sodium, potassium; *9* sodium – potassium pump; *10* myelin

CHEMICAL MESSENGERS

Before reading about the action potential, you may not have realized the extent to which your body depends on electrical and chemical processes. But if you stop a moment to think about it, you are in fact a conglomeration of chemicals. You think, you move, you feel because of information conveyed throughout your body by chemicals. This information can be conveyed by the nervous system, via chemicals working within and between neurons, or by the **endocrine system,** via chemicals distributed by the bloodstream.

ENDOCRINE SYSTEM: *A system of glands that, by releasing bodily chemicals into the bloodstream, is responsible for distributing chemical information throughout the body to effect behavioral change or to maintain normal bodily functions.*

Nervous system messengers: Neurotransmitters

Information from our senses or from our brain or spinal cord travels throughout our body from neuron to neuron. For example, when you looked at the first word on the Stroop list, neurons at the back of your eye were stimulated. They in turn stimulated other neurons in the optic nerve, which stimulated other neurons in your brain, which stimulated still other brain neurons, and so on. This successive neural stimulation, this relaying of information from one neuron to another, begins at the juncture between the neurons. This juncture is known as the **synapse.** Figure 2.6 shows the basic components of a synapse. When the action potential reaches the end of the axon terminal, it causes a minute amount of **neurotransmitter** to be released into the synaptic gap. Neurotransmitters are special chemicals that cross the synapse and stimulate another cell.

When neurotransmitter is released into the synaptic gap, it binds to receptor sites on the membrane of the receiving cell. These receptor sites are highly sensitive to neurotransmitters. As a result of this binding, there is a slight electrical change in the membrane. If enough receptors are bound, the electrical change will be enough to initiate an action potential in the cell.

Action potentials are not always fired, however, even when enough receptor sites are bound, because some neurotransmitters inhibit action potentials from being fired. Basically, there are two types of transmitters: excitatory and inhibitory. Excitatory neurotransmitters cause the receiving cell to be more likely to initiate an action potential; inhibitory neurotransmitters cause it to be less likely to initiate one. Excitatory transmitters, which are affected by such common drugs as alcohol or caffeine, include acetylcho-

SYNAPSE: *The junction between two neurons where neurotransmitter passes from the axon of one neuron to the dendrite or soma of another.*
NEUROTRANSMITTERS: *Special chemicals released from axon terminal buttons that cross the synapse and bind to receptor sites on the membrane of another neuron.*

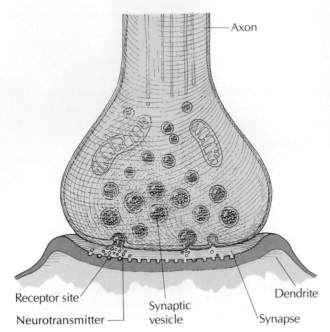

— Axon

Receptor site

Neurotransmitter —

Synaptic
vesicle

Dendrite

Synapse

Figure 2.6 A schematic view of a synapse. Neurotransmitter chemicals are stored in small vesicles (fluid-filled pouches) found in the axon terminal button. When the action potential reaches the axon terminal button, these vesicles release the stored neurotransmitter into the synapse.

line, norepinephrine, serotonin, and dopamine. A major inhibitory transmitter is endorphin, which is produced within the body and has been found to block neural signals in the pain pathways.

Question: Does the strength of the action potential depend on how much neurotransmitter reaches the neuron?　　No. All action potentials that occur in any neuron are of the same intensity. The neuron either fires an action potential or it doesn't. This is known as the **all-or-nothing principle.** In a way, the conduction of an action potential in a neuron is similar to the firing of a bullet out of a gun. An action potential is fired by the binding of neurotransmitters; a gun is fired by pulling a trigger. In a gun, the only factor in ejecting the bullet is a minimum amount of pressure on the trigger. Whether the pressure is exactly the minimum required or 20 times the minimum, the bullet comes out of the barrel with the same force. In a neuron, if the necessary amount of excitatory neurotransmitter is received at the receptor sites, an action potential will be generated in the axon. If the neuron receives 20 times the minimum amount of neurotransmitter, it will still initiate an action potential of the same intensity as all other action potentials.

ALL-OR-NOTHING PRINCIPLE: *The principle whereby an axon either fires an action potential or does not — there are no gradations; if one is fired, it is of the same intensity as any other.*

Distributed by King Features Syndicate, Inc.

How the brain works.

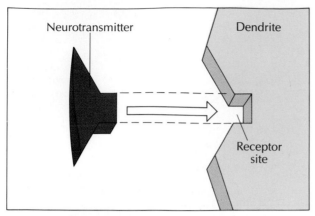 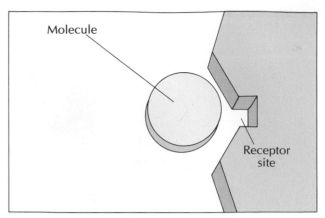

Figure 2.7 (a) Receptor sites recognize neurotransmitters because of their three-dimensional shape. (b) Molecules without the correct shape will not fit the receptors.

Although the strength of action potentials does not vary, the *rate* at which they are fired can differ. Indeed, information is encoded in the nervous system by the rate of firing of individual neurons. Generally, a high level of stimulation will cause a neuron to fire many action potentials in succession, whereas a low level of stimulation will produce only intermittent firing. Sensory, motor, and informational systems in the brain must then interpret and respond to these changes in the firing rate.

Question: How exactly do neurotransmitters act to cause action potentials? Neurotransmitters bind to receptor sites in much the same way as a key fits into a lock. Just as different keys have distinct three-dimensional shapes, various chemical molecules, including neurotransmitters, have distinguishing three-dimensional characteristics. If the neurotransmitter has the proper three-dimensional shape, it will bind to the receptor site (see Figure 2.7 *a*) and thereby influence the firing of the receiving cell (Bloom, 1983; S. H. Snyder, 1984). Molecules that do not have the correct three-dimensional shape will not fit into the receptor site and will therefore fail to affect the cell (see Figure 2.7 *b*).

The synapse is really where most of the action takes place in the nervous system. Anything that causes neurotransmitters to be released or blocked at the synapse will also affect perceptions or moods. For example, most **psychoactive drugs** (drugs that affect the nervous system in some way, like alcohol or caffeine) have their effect at the synapse by either decreasing or enhancing the amount of neurotransmitter released.

PSYCHOACTIVE DRUGS: *Drugs that affect the nervous system and cause a change in perception or mood.*

Because of their role in nervous system functioning, changes in the levels of certain neurotransmitters can alter people's moods or perceptions. The "runner's high" is an example of how a person's pain perception can be reduced. As muscles become extremely fatigued during a long run, they begin to activate pain pathways. To counter this pain and enable the runner to keep going, the brain releases endorphins (inhibitory transmitters) that bind to receptor sites and slow the pain signals. These receptor sites are the same as those to which the opiate drugs morphine and heroin bind. Under certain circumstances, when enough endorphin is released, a natural euphoria such as the runner's high can be produced. This state is remarkably similar to one produced by heroin and morphine.

Question: Exactly how do psychoactive drugs act at the synapse? Some drugs, such as amphetamine, cocaine, and caffeine, act by increasing the amount of neurotransmitter in the synapse or by directly activating receptor sites on the dendrites. They can do this because they have a three-dimensional shape similar to that of the neurotransmitter. These drugs thus have a stimulating effect on the nervous system. Other drugs, such as barbiturates and alcohol, work by suppressing the release of neurotransmitter or by competing with the transmitter for the receptor sites on the dendrite. To use our lock-and-key analogy, these drugs fit into the lock but do not turn the tumblers. If the

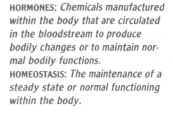

Neurotransmitter

Drug

Receptor site

Figure 2.8 Drugs can block transmission by filling a receptor site and thus not activating that site.

false "key" is taking up space in the lock, the lock will not open, and the real key will be prevented from getting into the lock (see Figure 2.8). These drugs thus depress nervous system functioning. Psychoactive drugs are discussed in further detail in Chapter 5.

Endocrine system messengers: Hormones

HORMONES: *Chemicals manufactured within the body that are circulated in the bloodstream to produce bodily changes or to maintain normal bodily functions.*

HOMEOSTASIS: *The maintenance of a steady state or normal functioning within the body.*

The nervous system and the endocrine system work hand in hand in effecting changes in our behavior as well as in maintaining our body's "status quo." The endocrine system consists of several glands that manufacture bodily chemicals, called **hormones.** Upon receiving signals from the brain, the glands release these hormones into the bloodstream, which circulates them throughout the body. The primary function of many endocrine glands, including the pituitary, the thyroid, the adrenals, and the pancreas (see Figure 2.9), is to maintain **homeostasis,** the normal functioning of bodily processes. They

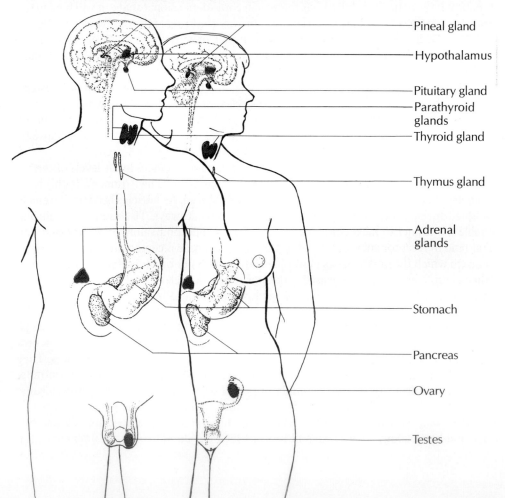

- Pineal gland
- Hypothalamus
- Pituitary gland
- Parathyroid glands
- Thyroid gland
- Thymus gland
- Adrenal glands
- Stomach
- Pancreas
- Ovary
- Testes

Figure 2.9 The major glands of the endocrine system.

accomplish this by maintaining the tissue and blood levels of certain chemicals within a specific range. For example, sugar is a chemical that must remain within a certain concentration for the body to function normally. If too much sugar enters the bloodstream, the pancreas (an endocrine gland) will secrete the hormone insulin to lower the blood sugar level to a more normal, safer level.

Another major function of the endocrine glands, particularly the ovaries and the testes, is to secrete hormones that regulate reproductive functions and to turn on the genes responsible for the development of such sexual characteristics as breast development and facial hair. The major endocrine glands, the hormones they secrete, their target tissues, and their functions are listed in Table 2.1.

The major link between the endocrine system and the nervous system is the **hypothalamus,** a tiny brain structure that lies next to the pituitary gland. The pituitary is usually considered the master endocrine gland because it releases hormones that tend to activate the other endocrine glands. However, the hypothalamus is the area of the brain that controls the pituitary, through direct neural connections and through the release of its own hormones into the blood supply of the pituitary. Thus, the real "master endocrine gland" is the hypothalamus. Specific endocrine functions will be described in future chapters that discuss such topics as sexuality (Chapter 11), eating and feeding behavior (Chapter 12), and health psychology (Chapter 13).

HYPOTHALAMUS: *A subcortical group of neuron cell bodies lying below the thalamus that ultimately controls the endocrine system and is responsible for the regulation of drives such as hunger, thirst, sex, and aggression.*

TABLE 2.1
The Endocrine System

Tissue	Hormone	Function
Anterior pituitary	Follicle-stimulating hormone	Ovulation, spermatogenesis
	Luteinizing hormone	Ovarian/spermatic maturation
	Thyrotropin	Thyroxin secretion
	Adrenocorticotropin	Corticosteroid secretion
	Growth hormone	Somatomedin secretion
		Protein synthesis
	Prolactin	Growth and milk secretion
Posterior pituitary	Vasopressin	Water retention
		Increase in blood pressure
	Oxytocin	Uterine contraction, milk production
Ovaries	Estrogens	Female secondary sex characteristics; female sex drive; ovulation
	Progesterone	Maintenance of pregnancy
Testes	Androgens	Male secondary sex characteristics; male sex drive; sperm production
Thyroid	Thyroxin	Increase in metabolic rate
Parathyroid	Calcitonin	Calcium retention
Adrenal cortex	Corticosteroids	Use of energy resources
		Inhibition of antibody formation and inflammation
	Aldosterone	Sodium retention
	Androgens	Male sex characteristics
	Estrogens	Female sex characteristics
Adrenal medulla	Epinephrine	Activation of sympathetic responses
	Norepinephrine	
Pancreas	Insulin	Decrease in blood sugar; increase in glucose storage after conversion to fat
	Glucagon	Increase in blood sugar; conversion of stored fat to glucose

We have examined the workings of the individual neuron in passing neural information throughout the body. We have also noted the role of glands in sending hormonal information through the bloodstream. In the next section, we shall see how the neurons and the glands work together to form a coordinated system responsible for our most basic bodily movements and functions.

Review Questions

1 Neurotransmitters are bodily chemicals that are released at the _____.

2 There are two basic types of neurotransmitters: _____ transmitters, which cause the receiving cell to be more likely to initiate an action potential, and _____ transmitters, which cause it to be less likely to initiate an action potential.

3 The endocrine system consists of several glands that secrete _____ into the bloodstream to maintain appropriate levels of certain chemicals within the body.

4 The primary function of many endocrine glands is to maintain _____, or the normal functioning of the body.

Answers: 1 synapse; *2* excitatory, inhibitory; *3* hormones; *4* homeostasis

---

SOMATIC NERVOUS SYSTEM: *A subdivision of the peripheral nervous system that consists of nerves carrying afferent sensory information and efferent motor information to and from the central nervous system, the sense organs, the skeletal muscles, and the skin.*
AFFERENT: *Incoming sensory information.*

THE PERIPHERAL NERVOUS SYSTEM

The peripheral nervous system (PNS) includes all nerves going to and from the brain and spinal cord. The PNS has two major subdivisions—the somatic nervous system and the autonomic nervous system. They work jointly with the central nervous system and the endocrine system in carrying out their functions. The somatic nervous system sends and receives sensory messages and controls motor movements, whereas the autonomic nervous system regulates more automatic bodily functions, such as heart rate and breathing (see Figure 2.10).

The somatic nervous system: A network for sensory and motor messages

The **somatic nervous system** consists of all nerves carrying incoming sensory information and outgoing motor information. Incoming **(afferent)** information comes toward the spinal cord or the brain from the sense organs or from muscles. It includes the

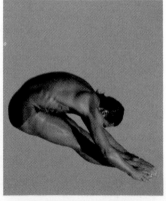

When a diver such as Greg Louganis executes a complicated series of twists and turns, the information necessary for the control of his body moves through both the afferent and efferent nerves of the somatic nervous system.

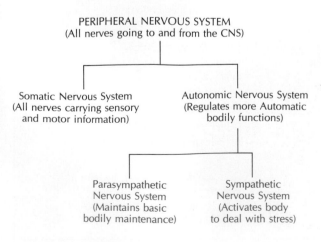

PERIPHERAL NERVOUS SYSTEM
(All nerves going to and from the CNS)

Somatic Nervous System
(All nerves carrying sensory and motor information)

Autonomic Nervous System
(Regulates more Automatic bodily functions)

Parasympathetic Nervous System
(Maintains basic bodily maintenance)

Sympathetic Nervous System
(Activates body to deal with stress)

Figure 2.10 Subdivisions of the peripheral nervous system.

awareness of external stimulation and the position of the skeletal muscles and limbs. Outgoing **(efferent)** information travels from the brain or spinal cord in the form of neural impulses with instructions for skeletal muscles to contract or relax. When you were saying the colors of the words in our chapter preview, afferent information traveled from your eyes to your brain and efferent information traveled from your brain to your mouth, vocal cords, and other speech-producing organs.

EFFERENT: *Outgoing motor information.*

Depending on the origin and complexity of the stimulation, the somatic nervous system may deal with neural information in one of three ways. First, information originating in the face and head enters and exits the brain through one of 12 cranial nerves. Second, in the case of a simple reflex, neural information is processed solely in the spinal cord. (A reflex is an involuntary reaction to a stimulus that is performed without involving the brain.) Finally, in more complex behavior requiring input from the brain, afferent information enters the spinal cord and is sent to the brain, where it is analyzed. Then efferent messages are sent down the spinal cord and out to target muscles.

The somatic nervous system responds to external stimuli and regulates voluntary actions. However, the peripheral nervous system is also responsible for several involuntary tasks, such as control of heart rate, digestion, and breathing. These involuntary actions and many others are carried out by the second half of the PNS, the autonomic nervous system.

The autonomic nervous system: Preparing for fight or flight

The primary function of the **autonomic nervous system (ANS)** is to maintain homeostasis, the maintenance of body balances necessary for survival. It does this by regulating the endocrine glands, the heart muscle, and the smooth muscles of the blood vessels and internal organs. The autonomic nervous system is divided into two branches, the parasympathetic and the sympathetic. These tend to work in opposition to each other in regulating the functioning of such target organs as the heart, the intestines, and the lungs (see Figure 2.11).

AUTONOMIC NERVOUS SYSTEM (ANS): *A subdivision of the peripheral nervous system that maintains normal functioning of glands, heart muscles, and the smooth muscles of the blood vessels and internal organs.*

The **parasympathetic nervous system** is normally dominant when the person is in a relaxed, nonstressful physical and mental state. The main function of the parasympathetic system is to slow heart rate, lower blood pressure, and increase digestive and eliminative processes. In short, it performs basic housekeeping and bodily maintenance. As Chapter 13 points out, there is a definite advantage to one's health when the parasympathetic system remains dominant over the sympathetic system.

PARASYMPATHETIC NERVOUS SYSTEM: *The part of the autonomic nervous system that is normally dominant when a person is in a relaxed, nonstressful physical and mental state.*
SYMPATHETIC NERVOUS SYSTEM: *The part of the autonomic nervous system that dominates when a person is under mental or physical stress.*

When a person is under some type of stress, some type of mental or physical strain, the **sympathetic nervous system** takes over. The sympathetic nervous system stops digestive and eliminative processes, increases respiration, increases heart rate, increases

Both of these animals are in sympathetic dominance, with the fight-or-flight response activated.

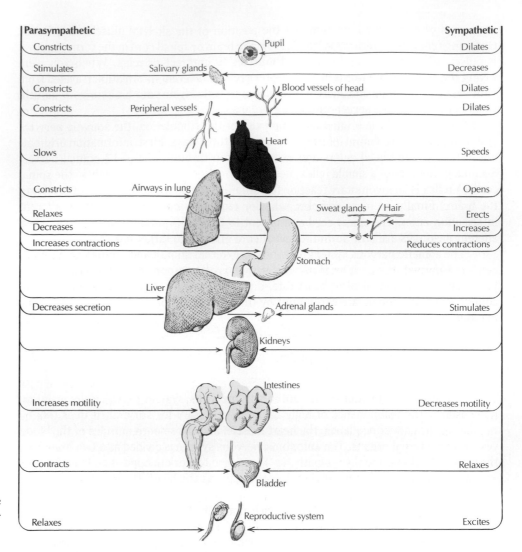

Figure 2.11 The functions of the parasympathetic and the sympathetic branches of the ANS.

blood pressure, and causes several hormones to be released into the bloodstream. The net result of this sympathetic activation is to get more oxygenated blood to the skeletal muscles, thus making a person better able to deal with the source of stress. Because the sympathetic system is most active during times of stress, it sometimes is referred to as the *fight–flight system*—it prepares the body to fight or flee from whatever is causing the stress.

Review Questions

1 The two major parts of the peripheral nervous system are the _____ nervous system and the _____ nervous system.

2 Afferent nerves carry information _____ the brain or spinal cord; efferent nerves carry information _____ the brain or spinal cord.

3 The part of the autonomic nervous system that is dominant during normal nonstressful times is the _____ nervous system.

4 The part of the autonomic nervous system that is dominant during mental or physical stress is the _____ nervous system.

Answers: 1 somatic, autonomic; *2* to, from; *3* parasympathetic; *4* sympathetic

THE CENTRAL NERVOUS SYSTEM

The central nervous system (CNS) consists of the **brain** and the **spinal cord.** The brain is the control center for all voluntary behavior (such as brushing your teeth) and a good part of involuntary behavior (such as feeling embarrassed). The spinal cord contains the structures responsible for reflex actions and the nerve fibers that are the links between the brain and other parts of the body.

The spinal cord: The link between the brain and the body

Beginning at the base of the brain and continuing down the back, the *spinal cord* is surrounded and protected by the vertebrae, the bones of the spinal column. The spinal cord is involved in all the voluntary and reflex responses of the body below the neck. Serving as a communications link between the brain and the body, it relays incoming sensory information to the brain and sends messages from the brain to muscles.

The spinal cord has two major components: gray matter and white matter (see Figure 2.12). The gray matter, found near the center of the spinal cord, contains mostly cell bodies. It is within the gray matter that information is processed in the spinal cord itself. The white matter, found in the outer layers of the spinal cord, contains mostly myelinated axons. It is within the white matter that axons transmit information to and from the brain.

Imagine you are a child who has just glimpsed your first icicle. Delighted, you rush over to where it dangles and break it off. After a few licks, you become aware of how cold your hand is growing. The cold receptors in your skin are being stimulated and are firing nerve impulses. This incoming *afferent* information from the receptors in your hand travels through neurons to your spinal cord, where it enters the gray matter in the center of the cord. It then travels via axons in the white matter to your brain. Although researchers do not yet fully comprehend how, the brain analyzes this sensory information and may decide to initiate a voluntary movement in response, such as dropping the icicle or insulating your hand with a mitten. This message is sent down axons in the white matter to the cell bodies of the appropriate motor nerves in the gray matter. The *efferent* motor information travels to the muscles, which contract and enable you to let go of the icicle or grab a mitten.

BRAIN: *An extremely complex mass of nerve tissue organized into structures that control all voluntary and much involuntary behavior.*

SPINAL CORD: *The part of the nervous system found within the spinal column that is involved in reflexes and the relay of neural information to and from the brain.*

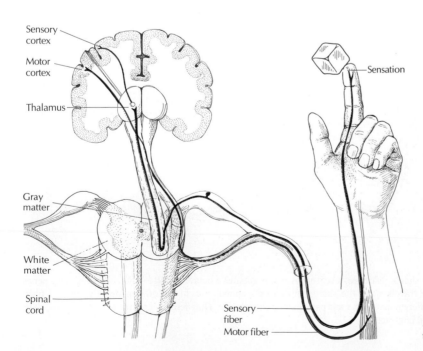

Sensory cortex

Motor cortex

Thalamus

Gray matter

White matter

Spinal cord

Sensation

Sensory fiber

Motor fiber

Figure 2.12 The spinal cord and the pathway of messages through it.

When a person suffers damage to the spinal cord, muscles served by sections of the spinal cord below the damaged area will not function normally and the person may be paralyzed.

> *Question:* Then people with damage to their spinal cord can't move at all?
> That's not totally true. They can move all parts of their body that are served by nerves above the injured area, and other areas of the spinal cord may still be able to provide reflex movement. **Reflexes** are important because they enable us to respond immediately to possibly dangerous or painful stimuli without involving the brain. Suppose you grabbed a hot pan and the pain signal had to travel from your hand to your brain and back to your hand. It might take several seconds, and meanwhile the tissue in your hand could be severely damaged. But by bypassing the brain and following a simple *reflex arc* through the spinal cord, the pain message would speed directly to an arm muscle. You would withdraw your hand almost instantly, avoiding serious injury. Please take the time to examine the simple reflex arc, which is detailed in Figure 2.13.

With a damaged spinal cord, information may not be able to travel to and from the brain, but many reflexes may still remain intact. For instance, you might not be able to voluntarily move your legs, but you may still exhibit a knee jerk reflex when tapped just below the kneecap.

Even though it is impossible for the brain to control muscles through a damaged spinal cord, recent research has made it possible for some patients who have lost the use of their legs to walk again. The photograph on this page shows a very determined woman, Jennifer Smith, who participated in the Honolulu Marathon in December 1985. Jennifer's spinal cord had been severed by a sniper's bullet in 1980, rendering her unable to control the muscles in her legs. With the help of a computerized electronic muscle-stimulation system developed by the National Center for Rehabilitation Engineering at Wright State University in Dayton, Ohio, she was able to perform this miraculous achievement.

REFLEXES: *Movements that are initiated by an external stimulus and do not require input from the brain.*

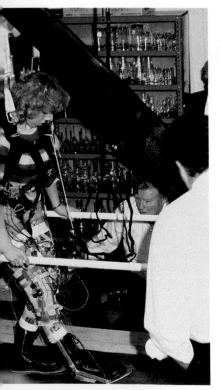

Researchers at Wright State University help a paraplegic walk by using a computer to directly stimulate the muscles in her legs. This is necessary because a spinal cord injury makes it impossible for the motor cortex to send nerve impulses which would control the muscles in her legs.

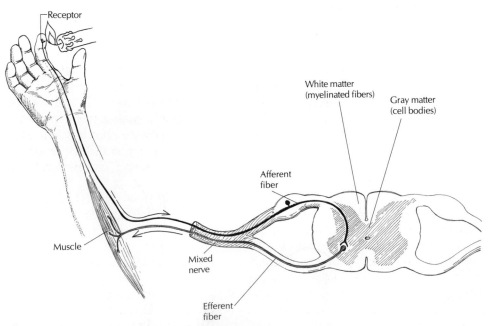

Figure 2.13 In a simple reflex arc, a sensory receptor initiates a neural impulse in an afferent sensory nerve fiber. The impulse travels along the afferent fiber to the spinal cord. In the gray matter, the afferent fiber synapses with an efferent motor fiber and passes along the impulse. The efferent signal travels to the appropriate muscle, which then contracts.

The New Breed

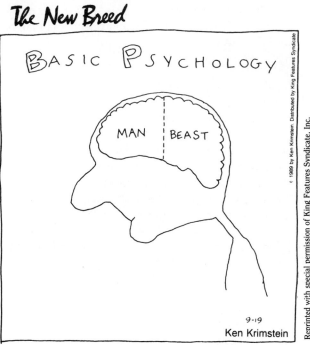

BASIC PSYCHOLOGY

MAN | BEAST

9-19
Ken Krimstein

© 1989 by Ken Krimstein. Distributed by King Features Syndicate

Reprinted with special permission of King Features Syndicate, Inc.

The brain: The body's control center

The brain is an extremely complex bundle of billions of neurons that are organized in such a way that they control what we think, feel, and do. Brain size and complexity vary significantly from species to species. Lower species of animals such as fish and primitive reptiles have brains that are generally smaller and less complex than those of higher species such as cats and dogs. The most complex brains belong to whales, dolphins, and higher primates such as chimps, gorillas, and humans.

In this chapter, we will restrict our discussion to the physiology — the structure and functions — of the various parts of the human brain. The major divisions of the human brain are the cerebral cortex, subcortical areas, cerebellum, and brain stem.

The cerebral cortex The bumpy convoluted area making up the outside surface of the brain is the **cerebral cortex**. The cortex can be divided into two halves, the right and left hemispheres, that resemble the halves of a walnut. An interesting and significant fact is that each hemisphere processes information about the opposite side of the body. When you arrive home from a late date, you probably fumble around in your pocket or purse for the key to your door. If you touch the key with your left hand, the sensation travels to your spinal cord and crosses over to your right hemisphere. On the other hand, if you insert the key into the lock with your right hand, motor information travels from your left hemisphere to enable your right hand to move.

Each of the two cerebral hemispheres is further divided into four areas, or lobes, according to their general functions and structure. These areas, shown in Figure 2.14, are known as the frontal, parietal, occipital, and temporal lobes. As we describe the functions of each lobe, it would be helpful for you to refer to this figure.

The **frontal lobes** are responsible for many of the functions that distinguish humans from most other animals. Self-awareness, initiative, and the ability to plan ahead, among other qualities that are traditionally considered uniquely human, are regulated by the frontal lobes. For example, what are you going to be doing twenty minutes from now, two hours from now, tomorrow, next week, next year? These are questions that, as far as we currently know, only humans can answer, and we use the frontal lobes to do so. By far the largest of the cortical lobes, the frontal lobes are located at the top front portion of the brain.

CEREBRAL CORTEX: *The bumpy, convoluted area on the outside surface of the brain that contains primary sensory centers, motor control centers, and areas responsible for higher mental processes.*

FRONTAL LOBES: *The cortical lobes located at the front of the brain whose functions include motor and speech control, the ability to plan ahead, initiative, and self-awareness.*

Figure 2.14 The four lobes of the cerebral cortex.

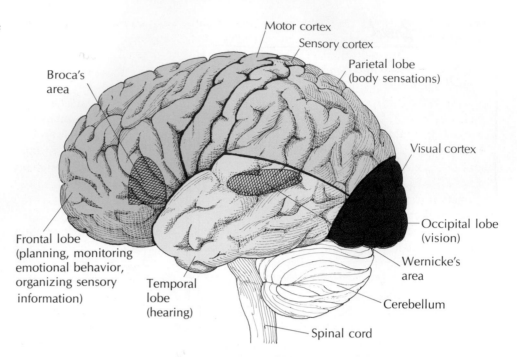

Motor cortex

Sensory cortex

Parietal lobe (body sensations)

Broca's area

Visual cortex

Occipital lobe (vision)

Wernicke's area

Cerebellum

Frontal lobe (planning, monitoring emotional behavior, organizing sensory information)

Temporal lobe (hearing)

Spinal cord

MOTOR CONTROL AREA: *The area located at the back of the frontal lobes of the cortex that is responsible for instigating voluntary movements.*

BROCA'S AREA: *A brain area found in the left frontal lobe that controls the muscles used to produce speech.*

ASSOCIATION AREAS: *The areas in the cerebral cortex that are involved in such mental operations as thinking, memory, learning, and problem solving.*

At the very back of the frontal lobes lies the **motor control area.** All neural signals that instigate voluntary movement originate here. For instance, when you reach out to choose a candy bar from a vending machine, it is the motor control area of the frontal lobes that guides your hand in pulling the proper lever. A specialized area in the *left* frontal lobe, on the surface of the brain near the bottom of the motor control area, is **Broca's area,** which controls the muscles used to produce speech. When you read aloud the words on the Stroop list, it was your Broca's area that sent the signals to your lips, tongue, jaws, and vocal cords to produce the words.

The remainder of the frontal lobes consists of association cortex. **Association areas** in the cortex are those areas that have no specific motor or sensory function but are thought to involve such mental operations as perception, emotion, memory, language, and thinking (Luria, 1973, 1980). These areas, which make up a large portion of the cortex, are used when we solve a complicated math problem, plan a weekend camping trip, or create a modern sculpture. It seems that association areas organize sensory information received from other brain areas and integrate this information in performing such functions.

Although researchers do not fully comprehend the mechanisms involved — indeed, research into the exceedingly complex functions of the brain is just beginning (Hubel, 1984) — we can deduce from what is known that association areas must play an important role in the Stroop effect. Color and word information from the list is converted to neural signals that are processed in the visual area of the brain. This neural information is then sent to association areas, where it is organized, integrated with other information, analyzed, and in the case of the Stroop effect, confused. It appears that these areas then send signals to other parts of the brain, such as signals for speech production to Broca's area.

Recent research has found that the frontal lobes are especially important for planning or changing a course of action. When the solution to a problem involves planning, damage to the frontal lobes can severely limit a person's abilities (Damasio, 1979; Pines, 1983). Research has also indicated that the frontal cortex appears to be the brain area that monitors emotional behavior, and damage to this area can severely affect the emotionality of an individual (Nauta, 1972). These findings are substantiated by the famous case of Phineas Gage. Gage was a construction supervisor who in 1848 had a large rod blown through his frontal lobes during an explosion. He seemed to recover fairly rapidly from the physical damage, but psychologically he was never again quite himself. He had difficulty in making decisions and was unable to perform his duties as supervisor. His personality was also affected in that he became undependable, indecisive, vulgar, and profane — a different person from the original Phineas Gage. From this case and from other research, it appears that much of our individual personality and much of what makes us uniquely human is regulated by our frontal lobes.

Located at the top of the brain just behind the frontal lobes are the **parietal lobes,** which are the seat of body sensations and much of our memory about the environment. It is at the front of the parietal lobes just behind the motor control area that the **projection areas** for body sensations are found (see Figure 2.15). These are areas where information about such bodily sensations as touch, pain, and heat is projected from nerves throughout the body. For example, when you step on a tack, you don't feel the pain until the sensory information from the pain and pressure receptors in the skin of your foot reaches the sensory projection areas.

As in the frontal lobes, the remainder of the parietal lobes is made up of association areas, which are involved chiefly with integrating information from the environment and reconciling tactile (touch) information with visual and auditory (hearing) information. In these association areas, therefore, lie such abilities as using memory to orient oneself in space and identifying objects within that space. For instance, if something touches your shoulder, identifying whether that touch is a friend's tap or an acorn dropping from a tree will require information not only from the sensory areas of the parietal lobes but also from the visual and auditory areas of the brain. If you see a friendly face and hear a familiar voice, the touch on the shoulder is probably from a friend rather than a message from nature.

Located at the very back of the brain, the **occipital lobes** are dedicated entirely to vision and visual perception. When you were reading the Stroop list, visual information was processed here in the occipital lobes before being sent to the association areas and possibly other parts of the brain.

Question: Is that why I see stars when I'm hit on the back of the head — because the visual area of the brain is located there? Absolutely. When you are hit on the back of the head, the blow activates the nerve cells in the occipital lobes of the cerebral cortex. Since this type of stimulation is not systematic and does not come from the normal sensory channels, you just see flashes of light, or "stars."

David Hubel and Torsten Wiesel (1962, 1968) extensively researched this brain area. They placed electrodes (small electrical wires) in the occipital lobes of cats and recorded how individual neurons in this lobe responded when the cats were presented with a simple stimulus, such as a picture of a horizontal bar. Their research demonstrated that the occipital cortex is organized in columns of neurons lying perpendicular to the surface of the cortex. All the neurons in the same column tend to respond only to similar visual stimuli. This type of organization seems to hold true for the rest of the cortex as well.

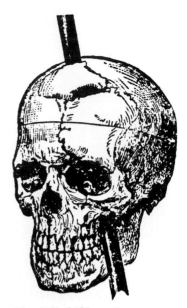

The skull of Phineas Gage showing the path of the tamping iron through his brain.

PARIETAL LOBES: *The lobes of the cerebral cortex located at the top of the brain that contain the major projection areas for body sensation.*
PROJECTION AREAS: *Any area in the brain that receives incoming sensory information.*
OCCIPITAL LOBES: *The cortical lobes located at the back of the brain that are dedicated entirely to vision and visual perception.*

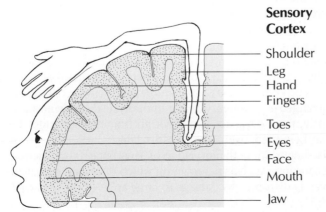

Sensory Cortex

Shoulder
Leg
Hand
Fingers

Toes
Eyes
Face
Mouth

Jaw

Figure 2.15 In this drawing, the area of cortex responsible for processing sensory information from various parts of the body corresponds to the body part adjacent to the cortex.

The size of the body parts of this homunculus indicates the amount of cortex dedicated to processing sensory information from that part of the body.

TEMPORAL LOBES: *The cortical lobes whose functions include auditory perception, language, memory, and some emotional control.*

WERNICKE'S AREA: *An area of the cerebral cortex responsible for the thinking and interpreting aspect of language production.*

DYSLEXIA: *An inability or difficulty in reading.*

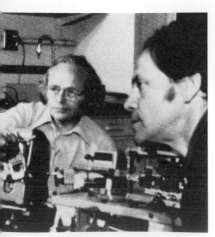

David Hubel and Torsten Wiesel conducting research in their laboratory.

The last of the four major cortical lobes, the **temporal lobes,** are found on the sides of the brain. Their major functions are auditory perception (hearing), language, memory, and some emotional control. The auditory perception areas are located at the top front of the temporal lobe. On reaching this area of the cortex, incoming sensory information from the ears is processed and then sent to the parietal lobes, where it is combined with visual and other body sensation information.

Wernicke's area is found at the top of the left temporal lobe, near its junction with the parietal lobe. This language area is responsible for the thinking and interpreting aspect of language production. Damage to this area of the brain can cause severe difficulties in communication. For example, people with damage to Wernicke's area may not be able to read, write, speak, or interpret any kind of language at all.

Question: Do people with dyslexia have a problem with this area of the brain?
People with **dyslexia** have normal intelligence and their ability to speak and understand spoken language is normal, but they have trouble reading. Often, they do not see letters in words or inadvertently reverse letters. For example, dyslexics might read the word "read" and see it as the word "red," or they might read "rat" and process it as "tar." Obviously this can present quite a problem.

Although there are several theories, no one is quite sure what causes dyslexia; it may in fact have several different causes (Bloom, Lazerson, and Hofstadter, 1985). Dyslexics may have visual problems that do not allow them to see the words correctly. There may be problems with areas of the cortex that integrate visual and auditory information. This results in difficulties in matching letter combinations with the sounds those combinations make. Finally, to answer the question, yes, there is evidence that some dyslexics may have abnormalities in Wernicke's area (Galaburda and Kemper, 1979). In the normal brain, the cells are arranged in columns, whereas in the dyslexic brain no such organization is evident. Currently, most dyslexics can, through training, be taught to process information in ways that help them overcome their disability.

The temporal lobes are also important in the formation of new concepts and memories. The ability to form simple concepts, such as determining which of several stimuli is different from the others, is severely disrupted by damage to large areas of the temporal lobes (Mishkin and Pribram, 1954).

The temporal lobes also seem to be involved, along with several other brain structures, in emotional behavior. Research with cats and monkeys has shown that damage to areas of the brain attached to the temporal lobes known as the *amygdala* and the *hippocampus* can severely disrupt emotionality. Kluver and Bucy (1939) removed both temporal lobes of monkeys, including the amygdala and the hippocampus. As might be expected, the monkeys were quite different after the surgery. Their emotional behavior was noticeably flat. For example, they showed no fear of snakes after the surgery, whereas they had previously been terrified of snakes; and they tried to put everything into their mouths that they could get their hands on. Similar results have been reported in humans whose temporal lobes have been damaged by illness (Marlowe, Mancall, and Thomas, 1975). The temporal lobes, as well as the other cortical lobes, have many interconnections with other areas of the brain, including the subcortical areas.

Subcortical brain areas What makes us feel like hitting people when we're mad at them? How does your body maintain a temperature of 98.6 degrees? What part of your brain is responsible for your sexual drives? Tucked into the center of the brain and surrounded by the cerebral cortex are the areas of the brain that hold the answers to these questions. Called subcortical brain areas, they include the corpus callosum, the thalamus, the hypothalamus, and a group of structures collectively known as the limbic system. Most of these structures can be viewed if the brain is sliced lengthwise down the middle (see Figure 2.16).

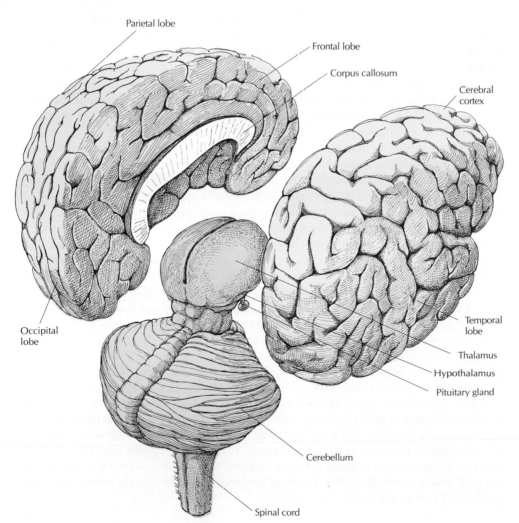

Parietal lobe

Frontal lobe

Corpus callosum

Cerebral cortex

Occipital lobe

Temporal lobe

Thalamus

Hypothalamus

Pituitary gland

Cerebellum

Spinal cord

Figure 2.16 The subcortex and the cerebellum.

CORPUS CALLOSUM: *A connecting bridge of nerve fibers between the left and right hemispheres of the cerebral cortex.*

THALAMUS: *A subcortical area located below the corpus callosum that serves as the major relay area for incoming sensory information.*

The **corpus callosum** serves as a bridge between the two cerebral hemispheres and makes it possible for the hemispheres to communicate with each other. Severing the corpus callosum creates two separate brains that can function independently of each other, as we will see later in the chapter when we discuss split-brain research techniques.

The **thalamus** is located below the corpus callosum. It looks like two football-shaped areas, one on each side of the brain, connected by a thinner group of nerve fibers (see Figure 2.16). Serving as the major sensory relay center for the brain, the thalamus receives input from nearly all the sensory systems, then projects this information to the appropriate cortical areas. Visual information from the words in the Stroop list, for example, first goes to the thalamus before it is projected to the occipital lobe for further processing. The thalamus also relays information from the primary sensory areas of the cerebral cortex to other areas of the cortex.

The thalamus may also play a role in learning and memory. Damage to the thalamus is known to cause memory problems as evidenced by the case of "H.M." H.M.'s thalamus was damaged when a fencing foil went up through his nose and entered his brain. The damage to his thalamus caused him to have severe difficulties in making new memories. For instance, he was unable to learn new shopping lists or remember new faces (Bloom, Lazerson, and Hofstadter, 1985).

The hypothalamus is a group of neuron cell bodies lying below the thalamus. Its general function is homeostasis, which it accomplishes through regulating the endocrine system. The hypothalamus also serves as the major brain center for temperature regulation and the control of such drives as hunger, thirst, sex, and aggression. It accomplishes these regulatory functions directly, by generating some behaviors itself, and indirectly, by controlling parts of the autonomic nervous system. Research has shown that when the hypothalamus is damaged or disconnected, mammals and birds no longer exhibit behaviors such as sweating or shivering to maintain normal body temperatures. Even when outside temperatures remain constant, their internal body temperatures can fluctuate over a wide range (Satinoff, 1974; Satinoff, Liran, and Clapman, 1982). Research has also shown that animals exhibit increased or decreased eating and drinking patterns depending on what area of the hypothalamus is affected. More detailed discussion of the functions of the hypothalamus can be found in Chapters 11 and 12.

Even if the entire brain above the hypothalamus were disconnected or otherwise rendered nonfunctional, animals would still exhibit survival behaviors, although they would be particularly primitive and often without direction. Their mechanisms prompting them to breathe, to eat and quench their thirst, to shiver when cold and pant when hot, to exhibit sexual behaviors, and to sleep and awaken would remain functional. They would still be able to move in a smooth, coordinated fashion. They would also be capable of some emotional reactions and aggressive behaviors, such as fear and attack behaviors, although these would be generalized behaviors — not directed toward any particular stimulus (Bard, 1934).

LIMBIC SYSTEM: *An interconnected system of mainly subcortical brain structures involved with many types of emotional behavior, particularly aggression. The brain structures making up the limbic system include the hypothalamus, the fornix, the hippocampus, the amygdala, the septum, parts of the thalamus, and parts of the frontal and temporal lobes of the cerebral cortex.*

The hypothalamus is also a part of a group of subcortical and cortical structures known collectively as the **limbic system,** an interconnected system of structures involved with many types of emotional behavior, particularly aggression. The brain structures making up this system include the hypothalamus, the fornix, the hippocampus, the amygdala, the septum, parts of the thalamus, and parts of the frontal and temporal cortical lobes. The areas of the limbic system most involved with aggression are the amygdala and the septum. Research on cats and rats has shown that stimulation of the amygdala can increase aggressive behavior (Egger and Flynn, 1967). The septum, on the other hand, seems to have a moderating effect on aggression. Animals that have had their septum removed tend to attack anything that comes near them. The hypothalamus can also have some effect on aggressive behavior. Through its regulation of the pituitary gland, it can cause the release of the male hormone testosterone — a hormone related to aggressiveness in several species. The more testosterone available in the bloodstream, the more likely the animal will be aggressive.

Cerebellum   The **cerebellum** is located at the base of the brain behind the brain stem (see Figure 2.16). In evolutionary terms, it is a very old structure. (Generally, the lower brain structures are older and more primitive than the higher structures.) The cerebellum is responsible for the maintenance of smooth movement and for coordinated motor activity. Although the motor control area of the frontal lobe is involved in the initiation of voluntary movements, it is the cerebellum that makes these movements smooth, coordinated, and on target. For example, as we type words into our word processors, it is the cerebellum that is responsible for the coordinated movement necessary to hit the correct keys in succession.

CEREBELLUM: *The brain area responsible for the maintenance of smooth movement and for coordinated motor activity.*

The cerebellum also controls the automatic adjustments of posture that allow us to stay upright when we walk and that keep us from falling out of our chairs when we are listening to a lecture or reading a book. To know what postural adjustments to make, the cerebellum receives input from all areas of the brain, including the cortex, the subcortex, and the brain stem.

Brain stem   You are sleeping. Your eyes dart back and forth as you begin your last dream of the night. Your heart rate, blood pressure, and respiration increase as the dream gets more exciting. Then your dream is shattered by the obnoxious buzzing of your alarm clock. All your behaviors and responses in this situation have been either controlled or influenced by areas located in the brain stem. The **brain stem** lies below the subcortical brain areas and in front of the cerebellum. Three major brain stem areas are of interest to us: the pons, the medulla, and the reticular formation.

BRAIN STEM: *An area of the brain below the subcortex and in front of the cerebellum that includes the pons, the medulla, and the reticular formation.*

The **pons** is located in the upper portion of the brain stem below the subcortex. It is in front of the cerebellum and above the medulla. The pons contains several types of fibers. Some connect the two halves of the cerebellum, whereas others carry visual and auditory information either to the brain or to the cerebellum. Still other fibers are associated with respiration, movement, facial expression, and sleep. One of the most interesting functions of the pons is regulation of sleep, including initiation of the rapid eye movements associated with dream sleep (see Chapter 5).

PONS: *A brain structure located at the top of the brain stem that is involved with functions such as respiration, movement, and sleep.*

The **medulla** is found below the pons at the bottom of the brain stem and the top of the spinal cord. Its functions are similar to those of the pons. Because it is essentially an extension of the spinal cord, the medulla has many nerve fibers passing through it carrying information to and from the brain. The medulla also contains many nerve fibers that control automatic bodily functions such as respiration. Damage to the medulla can lead to failure of bodily functions and death.

MEDULLA: *A structure in the brain stem responsible for automatic body functions, such as respiration.*

The **reticular formation**, also known as the *reticular activating system (RAS)*, is, like the limbic system, a diffuse set of cells in the medulla, pons, hypothalamus, and thalamus. The reticular formation serves as a filter for incoming sensory information. After receiving input from most of the sensory systems, the reticular formation filters it and rejects unimportant or nonvital sensory input. Have you ever been to a party where you tried to hold a conversation with a friend over the din of several other conversations? Your reticular formation was helping you make sense of what your friend was saying by allowing the sensory information from your friend to pass to other parts of the brain, while screening or blocking information from other conversations. Because the reticular formation serves as a sensory filter, it is also important for attention and arousal. For example, if someone across the room at the party says your name, the reticular formation will let that information through to your cortex, and you might try to zero in on that voice and hear what is being said about you.

RETICULAR FORMATION: *A diffuse set of cells in the medulla, pons, hypothalamus, and thalamus that serves as a filter for incoming sensory information.*

This has been a brief discussion of the major brain structures and their functions. Keep in mind that in this discussion, we have isolated each structure in detailing its functions. In a fully operational brain, each brain part has many interconnections with other parts — cortical areas with other cortical areas, cortical areas with subcortical areas, and so on. As you may have noticed when we pointed out the part played by various brain structures in the Stroop effect, several brain areas, both cortical and subcortical, contribute to it.

How do we know the role of each brain structure in certain types of behavior? By what means have researchers been able to pinpoint the precise brain site responsible for, say, aggressive attacks? In the next section, we will examine the variety of research methods that have been used to study the brain.

Review Questions

1 The dorsal root and the ventral root are pathways into and out of the _____ _____.

2 The bumpy, convoluted area making up the outside surface of the brain is the _____ _____.

3 The lobes of the brain that contain the area for motor control and Broca's speech area are the _____ lobes.

4 The major projection area at the front of the parietal lobes is involved with _____ information.

5 Visual information is processed primarily in the _____ lobes.

6 Areas for hearing and Wernicke's area are found in the _____ lobes.

7 The connecting bridge between the two cerebral hemispheres that makes it possible for the hemispheres to communicate with each other is the _____ _____.

8 The _____ is a subcortical brain structure that is the major sensory relay center for the brain.

9 The major function of the hypothalamus is _____.

10 The interconnected system of subcortical and cortical structures involved with many types of emotional behavior is the _____ system.

11 The brain structure located at the base of the cerebral cortex that is responsible for the maintenance of smooth movement and coordinated motor activity is the _____.

12 The major brain stem structures are the _____, _____, and _____ _____.

Answers: 1 spinal cord; *2* cerebral cortex; *3* frontal; *4* sensory; *5* occipital; *6* temporal; *7* corpus callosum; *8* thalamus; *9* homeostasis; *10* limbic; *11* cerebellum; *12* pons, medulla, reticular formation

It is possible to learn a great deal about the structure of the human brain by generating computerized views of actual human brains.

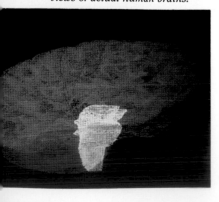

STUDYING THE BRAIN

Information about the brain presented in this chapter has been gleaned from research that has made use of a variety of techniques. They include anatomical techniques, lesion techniques, electrical recording, electrical stimulation, split-brain techniques, computerized axial tomography (CAT), positron emission tomography (PET), and magnetic imaging (MI).

Anatomical techniques: From cadavers to computers

Most of the early data on nervous system structure and function came from the study of human anatomy. The dissection of human cadavers in the early 1800s allowed the basic mapping of the peripheral nervous system and of certain brain structures. One

CLARIFYING TERMS AND CONCEPTS
Understanding Brain Anatomy and Function

One of the most important elements of critical thinking is clarity of thought. A clear thinker understands that the simple ability to define a term is not evidence of true understanding. One must be able to extend basic definitions to higher, more complex applications. The clear, critical thinker allows his or her curiosity to roam to the "outer limits." They ask questions such as "What does this mean?" "What would happen if . . . ?" "What if this were different?" They explore core terms and concepts from several different angles. This type of "free-wheeling" exploration not only improves comprehension of the original terms but also encourages the development of general critical thinking skills.

The following exercise will help to clarify your understanding of brain terminology and function. While so doing, it provides a model for the types of questions one asks that lead to critical thinking.

Situation #1

A neurosurgeon is about to perform brain surgery. The surgeon touches (stimulates with an electrode) a tiny portion of the patient's brain, and the patient's right finger moves. After noting the reaction, the surgeon stimulates a portion of the brain a short distance away and the patient's right thumb moves.

Questions to Answer

1 What strip (or section) of the brain has been stimulated? _____ What lobe is this in? _____

2 What hemisphere of the brain is being stimulated? _____

3 During this stimulation, would the patient experience feelings of pain? Why or why not? _____

4 Given that some parts of the brain seem to be specialized for certain functions (e.g., receiving sensory information and controlling motor output), what would happen if the brain was disconnected from the rest of the body? Does brain functioning require feedback from the receptors in the body? If your brain could be kept alive outside your body, what could it do? Would you be able to think without sensory input or motor output?

Situation #2

The scene: An emergency room in a hospital. Two interns are talking about a car crash victim who has just been wheeled in.

First Intern: "Good Grief! The whole cerebral cortex is severely damaged; we'll have to remove the entire area."

Second Intern: "We can't do that. If we remove all that tissue the patient will die in a matter of minutes."

First Intern: "Where did you get your medical training —watching "General Hospital"? The patient won't die if we remove his whole cerebral cortex."

Second Intern: "I resent your tone and insinuation. I went to one of the finest medical schools, and I'm telling you the patient *will* die if we remove his whole cerebral cortex."

Questions to Answer

1 If the whole cerebral cortex *is* removed, *will* the patient die? Explain your answer.

2 If the patient *is* kept alive without a cerebral cortex, what kinds of behaviors or responses would be possible? What changes would you expect in personality, memories, and emotions?

3 What kinds of behaviors could be expected with only the subcortex, medulla, and spinal cord intact? What if only the medulla and spinal cord were functioning? With only the spinal cord intact?

4 If a patient could be kept alive without a cerebral cortex, would life be worth living? What parts of your brain could be removed before you would want to stop living?

early physiologist was Paul Broca (1861), who located an area of the brain (now known as Broca's area) that, when damaged, causes a partial or complete loss of the ability to use language. Broca was able to identify this brain area by dissecting brains of deceased patients who had had language disabilities.

More recently, investigators have used sophisticated microscopes and advanced computer methods to study the fine detail of brains removed from the body. A good example of the use of computers in research on brain structure is shown on p. 54. This computer-generated view of the human brain was produced by Robert Livingston at the University of California, San Diego. Livingston and his group produced this image by feeding a computer hundreds of images previously recorded on slides containing slices of a human brain. By using a sophisticated computer graphics system, Livingston was able to add color to certain parts of the brain and even make motion pictures of different areas of the brain.

Just as it is impossible for us to determine the function of many machines just by looking at them, researchers cannot effectively determine brain function merely by examining dead brain tissue. Researchers have, however, developed a number of sophisticated techniques to allow them to examine and better understand the function of the living brain.

Lesion techniques: Studying the brain through systematic deactivation

LESION TECHNIQUE: *Any brain research technique that systematically destroys brain tissue to observe the effect of the destruction on behavior.*

The first techniques used to examine living brains were invasive; that is, they caused some kind of damage to the brain of an animal and then studied the results of that damage. (Fortunately, more modern techniques do not need to resort to such destruction.) Any technique that systematically destroys brain tissue to observe the effect of the destruction on behavior is a **lesion technique.** In the earliest experimental research using this approach, both large and small amounts of brain tissue were destroyed in order to better understand the function of the brain.

Although lesion techniques have helped researchers determine specific functions for some portions of the brain, these techniques have two severe drawbacks: (1) the researcher is doing permanent damage to the brain of a living, thinking animal; and (2) once part of the brain of an animal is destroyed, the researcher is no longer observing the brain of a normal animal. Research techniques that do not have these drawbacks include electrical recording techniques and electrical stimulation of the brain.

Electrical recording: Measuring electrical changes in the brain

ELECTRODES: *Small devices (normally wires) used to conduct electricity to or from brain tissue.*

Because the action potential that travels down an axon generates a small electrical current, it is possible to measure the electrical activity of a single neuron, a group of neurons, or an intact nerve. Such measurement requires a recording electrode, an amplifer, and an output (or recording) device (see Figure 2.17). **Electrodes** are small devices that conduct electricity. Of many shapes and sizes, most electrodes used in recording neural activity are similar to thin wires. Amplifiers are necessary to intensify the tiny electrical currents into signals that can be recorded on an output device. This recording device can be electronic, such as an oscilloscope, or mechanical, such as a paper chart recorder.

Question: Do you have to put the electrodes inside the brain of a person or an animal to record brain activity?   No. It is possible to record large changes in brain activity with electrodes that are attached to a person's skin or scalp. This brain activity is

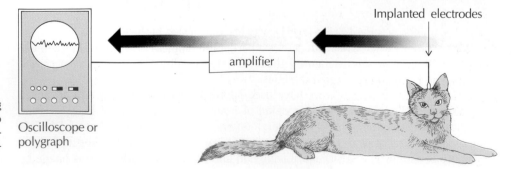

Figure 2.17 An electrical recording system. Such a system is used to monitor changes in individual neurons or groups of neurons in particular brain areas.

Oscilloscope or polygraph

Implanted electrodes

amplifier

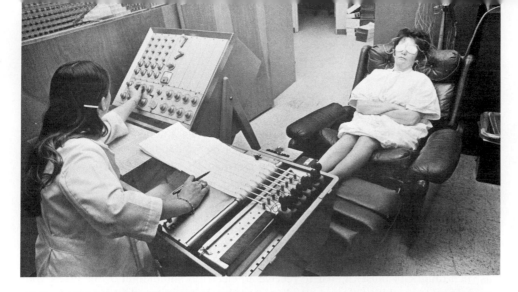

Electrical activity of the brain can be recorded using the electroencephalograph (EEG). The electrodes are taped to the person's scalp.

measured by an **electroencephalograph (EEG)** machine, which can be used to monitor a person's general state of consciousness. This type of recording is widely used with humans because it requires no surgery. EEG recording is used in the study of sleep and dreaming, as we will see in Chapter 5.

ELECTROENCEPHALOGRAPH (EEG): *A machine that monitors large changes in brain activity with electrodes that are attached to a person's scalp.*

Electrical stimulation: Eliciting brain activity

A researcher can activate certain areas of the brain by using electrodes to deliver small electrical currents to those areas. These electrical currents will then cause the person or animal to move a muscle, experience a feeling, remember something, or perhaps see or hear something. This type of research is usually done with humans, since animals can give us only a limited amount of information. For example, if a rat is stimulated in the visual area, it cannot say, "Oh, wow, what a beautiful blue color!" Thus, most of the functional mapping of the brain using electrical stimulation has involved human subjects who are undergoing brain surgery for some reason. In such cases, the brain surgeons have needed to determine the functions of the brain areas to be lesioned or removed. In the process they have mapped areas dealing with specific functions.

Wilder Penfield in particular has been able to electrically stimulate the brains of many of his patients during the course of surgery. Since the brain itself does not feel pain, it is possible for humans to be aware and alert during brain surgery. When Penfield

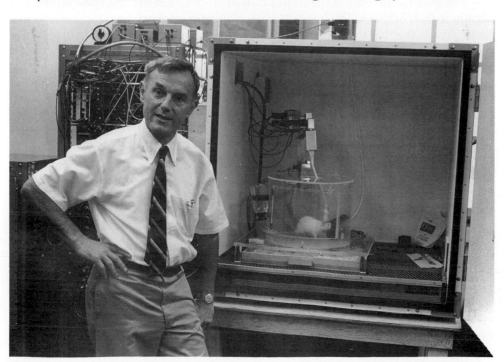

James Olds with an experimental rat that has been implanted with an electrode.

57

stimulated particular brain areas, his subjects reported feeling various sensations, seeing visual images, hearing musical passages, experiencing memories from the past, and so on. For example, one patient told him that she felt she was in her kitchen listening to the voice of her little boy playing outside in the yard. Another reported that he was watching a small town baseball game and saw a young boy crawl under the fence and join the other spectators (1975, pp. 21–22).

One researcher who did manage to overcome the difficulties in using animals in brain stimulation research was James Olds. In the early 1950s, Olds designed an experiment that allowed him to determine whether a rat liked or disliked a particular brain stimulation (Olds and Milner, 1954). Within the rat's brain, he implanted a permanent electrode that was hooked up to a stimulator connected to a bar in the rat's cage. The rat was then taught to press the bar to receive an electrical stimulation of the brain. Olds found that rats would rapidly press the bar when the electrode was placed in specific brain areas. The areas that caused the most vigorous bar pressing were called **reward centers.** Of course, it is not clear exactly what the rats felt or why they pressed the bar. Whatever the reason, the brain stimulation was apparently very rewarding. In some cases, hungry rats preferred the electrical stimulation to food.

REWARD CENTERS: *Areas in the brain that, when stimulated, invoke a highly satisfying feeling.*

Split-brain research: Two brains rather than one

Some fascinating aspects of brain functioning have been uncovered from split-brain research. This type of research had its beginnings in 1961, when Joseph Bogen, a neurosurgeon, severed the corpus callosum of a patient with severe epilepsy, a chronic disease of the nervous system in which patients suffer from seizures and sometimes unconsciousness. He undertook this dramatic procedure because previous research had led him to believe that his patient's seizures could be greatly reduced or completely eliminated by doing so. As noted earlier, the corpus callosum normally connects the two cerebral hemispheres. After this type of surgery has been performed, the two halves of the brain are no longer able to communicate with each other. Each tends to operate independently. Although fewer than 100 split-brain operations have been done since 1961, the resulting research has had a profound impact on our understanding of how the two halves of the brain function.

Despite the severing of the corpus callosum, split-brain patients show no outward change in their behavior. They can talk, walk, play catch, and perform complicated mental tasks. Nor do they behave as if they have a "split personality." However, careful testing of these subjects has revealed subtle differences in their functioning. Because split-brain patients cannot transfer information from one half of the brain to the other, tasks that require this sharing of information may be difficult or impossible for them to perform.

The following example illustrates this difficulty. Two split-brain people are blindfolded. Subject L picks up a key with his left hand. Because information from the left side of the body crosses over and is received in the right brain, the information about the key travels to L's right hemisphere (see Figure 2.18). Subject R picks up a key with her right hand; this information is received and processed in the left hemisphere. Thus, for each subject, information about the key travels from one side of the body to the opposite brain hemisphere but cannot be shared with the other hemisphere because of the severed corpus callosum.

When the subjects are asked to say what is in their hands, subject L, cannot verbally say, "a key," whereas subject R can. However, if the blindfolds are removed and the subjects are asked to point out the object they were holding from among other objects, both subjects are able to do so. The right brain (which receives information from the left hand) knows what the key is but cannot verbally identify it. The left brain also knows what the key is and *can* verbally identify it. The reason for this discrepancy is that language areas are in the left hemisphere; thus, the left brain can talk but the right brain is mute.

As a result of research on split-brain patients (Gazzaniga, 1970; Sperry, 1968;

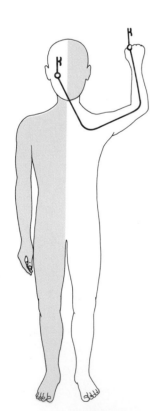

Figure 2.18 Information from the left side of the body crosses over to the right brain.

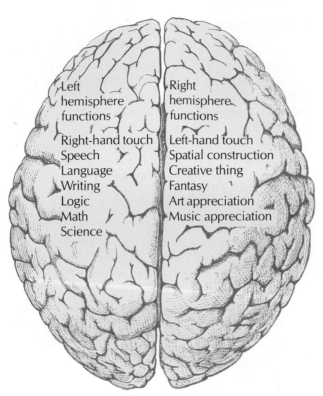

Left
hemisphere
functions

Right-hand touch
Speech
Language
Writing
Logic
Math
Science

Right
hemisphere
functions

Left-hand touch
Spatial construction
Creative thing
Fantasy
Art appreciation
Music appreciation

Figure 2.19 Functions of the left and right hemispheres.

Zaidel, 1975), a clear pattern of the differences between the two brain hemispheres has emerged (summarized in Figure 2.19). The left hemisphere appears to be specialized for language functions — for speaking, reading, writing, and understanding language — and for analytical functions, such as mathematics. The right hemisphere appears to be specialized for nonverbal abilities. These include musical abilities and perceptual and "spatio-manipulative" skills, such as maneuvering through space, drawing or building geometric designs, working puzzles, and painting pictures (Springer and Deutsch, 1981).

Question: Is this left- and right-brain specialization reversed in left-handed people? Not necessarily. Most people who use their left hands to write, hammer a nail, and throw a ball still have their language areas on the left side of the brain. Springer and Deutsch (1981) describe a study in which 95 percent of right-handers were found to have speech localized on the left side of their brain and 70 percent of left-handers showed the same pattern. This research suggests that even though the right side of the brain is the dominant hemisphere for movement in left-handers, other types of skills are often localized in the same brain areas as for right-handers.

Although it is true that left-handers are generally penalized for living in a right-handed world, there may be some benefits to being left-handed. Statistics show that left-handed people tend to recover better from strokes that damage the language areas in their brain (Seamon and Gazzaniga, 1973). This may be because the nonspeech hemisphere in left-handers is better able to take over speech functions if the primary speech areas are damaged.

Research into hemispheric specialization has provided possible answers to many psychological puzzles that have arisen over the years. For example, a possible explanation for the confusion experienced in the Stroop effect is that the words and the colors are processed in separate hemispheres, the words in the left hemisphere and the colors in the right. For people to name the color, the right brain must first identify it and send this information to the left brain, which takes time. Meanwhile, the left hemisphere might mistakenly process and speak the printed word.

Drawing by John Chase.

CAT (COMPUTERIZED AXIAL TOMOGRA-PHY) SCAN: *X-ray pictures of internal organs and different parts of the brain that are clearer and more accurate than normal X rays.*

PET (POSITRON EMISSION TOMOGRAPHY) SCAN: *A type of brain scan in which radioactive glucose is injected into the bloodstream in order to see brain activity in an intact, living brain.*

CAT, PET, and MI: Techniques that scan the brain

Brain research techniques are dependent on the cleverness of the researcher and on technology. Recent technological advances have provided several techniques in which brain researchers can study intact, functioning brains by taking pictures of them. These techniques include CAT scans, PET scans, and magnetic imaging.

CAT stands for **computerized axial tomography.** The CAT scan uses X rays to take pictures of internal organs and different parts of the brain. CAT scans are much more useful than regular X rays because they pinpoint exact locations of tumors or other problem areas quite clearly, whereas normal X rays are not nearly as clear and accurate. Although CAT scans can reveal structural problems with the brain, they cannot provide information about the function of any particular brain area.

PET scans, on the other hand, can yield information that is helpful in determining brain function. **PET** stands for **positron emission tomography.** In a PET scan, a chemical such as glucose is made radioactive and injected into the bloodstream of the subject. This radioactive glucose emits positively charged particles called "positrons." The positrons react with other particles to generate gamma rays, which are detected by the PET scanner (Li and Shen, 1985). The more gamma rays detected in a certain area of the brain, the more glucose is being used in that area. Glucose consumption is directly related to brain activity; therefore, the more glucose that is being used by a particular area of the brain, the more neural activity is occurring in that brain area (Phelps and Mazziotta, 1985). PET scans, then, can clearly show which areas of the brain are active and which are not (see the photograph on this page). This can be particularly helpful when studying mental disorders and problems associated with strokes (Andreasen, 1988).

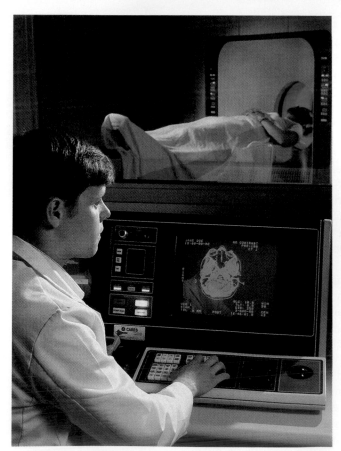

Computerized axial tomography (CAT) uses X rays to provide images to the brain.

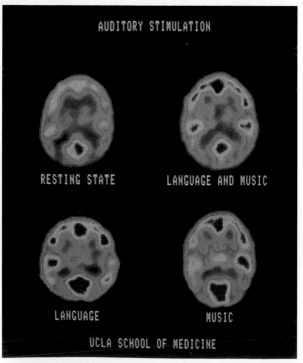

A PET scan can be used to indicate the function of different brain areas. You can see in these four scans that the left hemisphere shows more activity when we process music, and both hemispheres are active when we process both language and music.

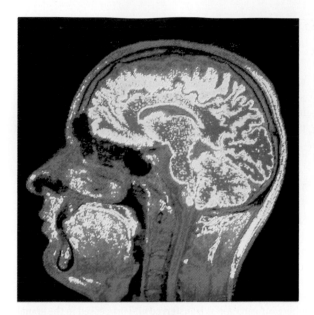

Magnetic imaging enables researchers to see clearly the internal structures of the brain. At the top of this image lies the cerebral cortex, which is colored green, yellow, and red. Immediately to the left of the cerebellum, also in yellow and red, is the brain stem. The throat and nasal airways and the cerebrospinal fluid surrounding the brain and spinal cord are shown in black.

A more recent technique that shows the structure of a living brain much more clearly even than CAT scans is **magnetic imaging,** or **MI.** It uses radio waves instead of X rays to enable researchers to see structures within the brain (see the photograph on this page). MI can reveal the distribution of specific types of atoms within any brain area (Pykett, 1982) by utilizing the magnetic properties of the nuclei of different atoms to make clear pictures of the structure of the brain. Structures within the brain show up much more clearly than when CAT scans are used to examine the same areas.

As we have seen in this chapter, behavior is a complex process that has its roots in the nervous and endocrine systems. Even though it is currently not possible to understand all behavior merely by examining the biology of the body, the brain and the nervous system are slowly revealing their secrets to an army of dedicated psychologists, physiologists, and physicians. The more we learn about the brain and the nervous system, the more we will be able to understand how and why people and animals behave the way they do.

MI (MAGNETIC IMAGING): *A research technique utilizing radio waves instead of X rays to allow researchers to see structures within the brain.*

Review Questions

1 Dissection of human cadavers and the studying of the brains of patients who have died are examples of _____ research techniques.

2 _____ research techniques involve damaging neural tissue in order to observe behavioral changes.

3 Small wires inserted into the brain to record electrical activity of different brain structures are called _____.

4 The discovery of reward centers in the brain was the result of research that used electrical _____ of the brain.

5 Severing the corpus callosum of a patient results in a person with a _____ brain.

6 Most people (both right- and left-handed) have their language abilities localized in the _____ side of their brain.

7 The three major techniques used for scanning the brain are _____, _____, and _____.

Answers: 1 anatomical; *2* lesion; *3* electrodes; *4* stimulation; *5* split; *6* left; *7* CAT, PET, MI

REVIEW OF MAJOR CONCEPTS

THE NEURON

1 Neurons are cells that are responsible for transmitting information throughout the body. The main parts of the neuron are the dendrites, which receive information from other neurons; the soma, or cell body; and the axon, which transmits neural information. At the end of the axon are small structures called axon terminal buttons that form synapses with other nerve cells and that secrete neurotransmitters.

2 Nerves are bundles of axons from neurons having similar functions.

3 The axon is a tubelike structure that may be covered with an insulating substance called myelin. The axon is specialized for transmitting neural impulses, or action potentials. During times when no action potential is moving down the axon, the axon is at rest. The resting potential gives way to the action potential when a stimulus causes chemical ions to move across the axon membrane. All action potentials in a given neuron are of the same intensity.

CHEMICAL MESSENGERS

4 Information is transferred from one neuron to another at the synapse via chemical called neurotransmitters. Neurotransmitters are released by axon terminal buttons when an action potential reaches the buttons. Most psychoactive drugs have their effect on the nervous system by affecting the amount of neurotransmitter that crosses the synapse.

5 Closely associated with the autonomic nervous system is the endocrine system, which is a system of several glands that release hormones into the bloodstream to regulate the level of critical chemicals within the body. The major link between the endocrine and nervous systems is the hypothalamus.

THE PERIPHERAL NERVOUS SYSTEM

6 The peripheral nervous system includes all nerves going to and from the brain and spinal cord. Its two major subdivisions are the somatic nervous system and the autonomic nervous system.

7 The somatic nervous system includes all nerves carrying afferent (incoming) sensory information and efferent (outgoing) motor information to and from the sense organs and skeletal muscles.

8 The autonomic nervous system includes those nerves outside the brain and spinal cord that function to maintain normal functioning of glands, heart muscles, and the smooth muscles of the blood vessels and internal organs. The autonomic nervous system is divided into two branches, the parasympathetic and the sympathetic, which tend to work in opposition to one another.

9 The parasympathetic nervous system is normally dominant when a person is relaxed and not under any physical or mental stress. Its main function is to slow heart rate, lower blood pressure, and increase digestion and elimination.

10 The sympathetic nervous system is normally dominant when a person is under physical or mental stress. It functions to increase heart rate and blood pressure and slow digestive processes, mobilizing the body for fight or flight.

THE CENTRAL NERVOUS SYSTEM

11 The central nervous system is composed of the brain and the spinal cord.

12 The spinal cord is the communications link between the brain and the rest of the body below the neck and is involved in all voluntary and reflex responses of the body below the neck. Its major components are the gray matter and the white matter. Gray matter contains cell bodies and synapses where information is transferred and processed in the spinal cord. The white matter is made up wholly of axons carrying information to and from the brain.

13 The major divisions of the brain are the cerebral cortex, the subcortical areas, the cerebellum, and the brain stem.

14 The cerebral cortex, the bumpy, convoluted area making up the outside surface of brain, is divided into four lobes: frontal, parietal, occipital, and temporal. The frontal lobes control movement and speech and are involved with self-awareness and the ability to plan ahead. The parietal lobes function as the receiving area for sensory information from the limbs and skin. The occipital lobe is almost entirely involved with visual sensation and visual information processing. The major functions of the temporal lobes include hearing and language.

15 The subcortex lies in the middle of the brain under the cerebral cortex and includes many different areas, the most important being the corpus callosum, the thalamus, the hypothalamus, and the limbic system. The corpus callosum is a connecting bridge of axons between the two cerebral hemispheres. The thalamus is the major incoming sensory relay area of the brain. The hypothalamus regulates functioning of the endocrine system and is the major brain center for the regulation of temperature, thirst, hunger, sex, and aggression.
The limbic system is an interconnected system of brain structures involved with many types of emotional behavior.

16 The cerebellum is located at the base of the brain behind the brain stem and is responsible for the maintenance of smooth movement and for coordinated motor activity.

17 The brain stem lies below the subcortex and in front of the cerebellum. Its major areas are the pons, the medulla, and the reticular formation. The major functions of the pons involve respiration, movement, facial expression, and sleep. The main function of the medulla is control of respiration. The reticular formation is a diffuse set of neurons that are associated with attention and arousal.

STUDYING THE BRAIN

18 Anatomical research techniques involve the study of the brain's structure through direct observation, such as examining the brains of cadavers or studying slices of brain tissue by using a microscope.

19 Lesion techniques involve destroying part of an animal's brain and studying resultant changes in the animal's behavior.

20 Electrical recording techniques involve insertion of electrodes into the brain or on its surface to study the brain's electrical activity.

21 Electrical stimulation techniques involve passing small electrical currents through parts of the brain to activate neurons in a particular brain area. One finding from this research has been the discovery of reward centers in the brain.

22 In split-brain research, patients who have had their corpus callosum severed are studied to determine the differences in functional abilities between the left and right brain hemispheres.

23 Split-brain research has led to findings suggesting that the left hemisphere appears to be specialized for language and analytical functions, whereas the right hemisphere appears to be specialized for nonverbal abilities, including musical abilities and perceptual and spatiomanipulative skills.

24 CAT, PET, and MI scans are used to study the structure and function of intact, living brains without having to place electrodes in the brain or destroy normal brain tissue.

SUGGESTED READINGS

BLOOM, F. E., LAZERSON, A., & HOFSTADTER, L. (1988). *Brain, mind, and behavior.* New York: Freeman.

CARLSON, N. R. (1986). *Physiology of behavior.* Boston: Allyn & Bacon. An introduction to physiological psychology.

Editors of *Scientific American* (1980). *The brain.* San Francisco: Freeman. A readable collection of articles on the brain from the journal *Scientific American.*

HUNT, M. (1982). *The universe within: A new science explores the human mind.* New York: Simon & Schuster. A fascinating book about the brain and brain research.

SPRINGER, S. P., & DEUTSCH, G. (1981). *Left brain, right brain.* San Francisco: Freeman. A book about the research on split-brain surgery and the difference between the left and right hemispheres of the cerebral cortex.

chapter three
Sensation

Helen Keller (1880–1968).

I have just touched my dog. He was rolling on the grass, with pleasure in every muscle and limb. I wanted to catch a picture of him in my fingers, and I touched him as lightly as I would cobwebs. . . . He pressed close to me, as if he were fain to crowd himself into my hand. He loved it with his tail, with his paw, with his tongue. If he could speak, I believe he would say with me that paradise is attained by touch. (pp. 3–4)

Thus Helen Keller began her book *The World I Live In*. Her world was totally different from that of most people: She couldn't see it or hear it because she was blind and deaf, but she learned to know it through her sense of touch. Although deprived of two senses, she was as capable and as appreciative of life — if not more so — as any person with all five senses. This was because she made the most of those senses she did have. Excerpts from her book describe how she used these senses:

> Through the sense of touch I know the faces of friends, the illimitable variety of straight and curved lines, all surfaces, the exuberance of the soil, the delicate shapes of flowers, the noble forms of trees, and the range of mighty winds. Besides objects, surfaces, and atmospherical changes, I perceive countless vibrations. . . . Footsteps, I discover, vary tactually according to the age, the sex, and the manners of the walker. . . . When a carpenter works in the house or in the barn near by, I know by the slanting, up-and-down, toothed vibration, and the ringing concussion of blow upon blow, that he is sawing or hammering. . . .

> In the evening quiet there are fewer vibrations than in the daytime, and then I rely more largely upon smell. . . . Sometimes, when there is no wind, the odors are so grouped that I know the character of the country and can place a hayfield, a country store, a garden, a barn, a grove of pines, a farmhouse with the windows open. . . . I know by smell the kind of house we enter. I have recognized an old-fashioned country house because it has several layers of odors, left by a succession of families, of plants, perfumes, and draperies. (pp. 43–44, 46, 68–69)

Helen Keller wasn't born deaf and blind. When she was 19 months old, she suffered a fever that left her without sight or hearing and thus virtually isolated from the world. As a young child, Helen learned to function by substituting her other senses for those she lacked. She discovered her father's facial features not through sight, but by feeling them; she knew when the door slammed not through hearing it, but by feeling the resulting vibrations; she found out where she had wandered not by looking around, but by smelling the fragrances in that part of the yard.

Although Helen did manage to maneuver through her silent world, she remained isolated from any communication with others. This isolation was a constant source of frustration and anger, leading her to violent temper tantrums. In fact, she noted that "after awhile the need of some means of communication became so urgent that these outbursts occurred daily, sometimes hourly" (1902, p. 32).

Helen's parents recognized the need to find help for their daughter, and after diligently searching they found Anne Sullivan, a young woman who was able to break through Helen's barrier of isolation by taking advantage of her sense of touch. From the moment she arrived, Anne began finger-spelling names of objects by placing her hand in Helen's and forming letters used in sign language. Although Helen learned to finger-spell many words, she didn't understand that these finger movements could signify names for things. Then one day, Anne took Helen to the pump-house and, as Anne (1902) wrote:

> I made Helen hold her mug under the spout while I pumped. As the cold water gushed forth, filling the mug, I spelled "w-a-t-e-r" in Helen's free hand. The word coming so close upon the sensation of cold water rushing over her hand seemed to startle her. She dropped the mug and stood as one transfixed. A new light came into her face. (p. 257)

From that moment on, Helen had an unquenchable desire to learn the names of everything and everybody, to learn to interact and communicate with everyone possible. That one moment, brought on by the sensation of cold water on her hand, became the impetus for a lifetime of learning about, understanding, and appreciating the world through her remaining senses. In 1904, Helen Keller graduated cum laude from Radcliffe, one of the most respected women's colleges in the world, and following her graduation went on to become a well-known author and lecturer, inspiring hope and encouragement to the handicapped throughout the world.

The story of Helen Keller has been told and retold as an example of how people can overcome sensory deficiencies by using their other senses to the optimum. In this chapter, we will discuss each sense in detail and examine the sensory mechanisms by which each operates. We will describe, for instance, how environmental stimuli—light from a flashlight, the odor of a skunk, heat from a campfire—are received by sensory receptors, converted into a language the brain can understand, then transmitted to the brain. This process of receiving, converting, and transmitting information from the outside world ("outside" the brain, not necessarily outside the body) is called **sensation**. Our study of sensation will be concerned not only with what are commonly known as the five senses—vision, hearing, taste, smell, and touch—but also with those senses that provide the brain with data from inside the body. These internal senses include the vestibular sense (the sense of balance) and kinesthesis (the sense of bodily position and movement).

SENSATION: *The process of receiving, translating, and transmitting information to the brain from the external and internal environments.*

EXPERIENCING SENSATIONS

To experience sensations, we must have both a means of detecting stimuli and a means of converting them into a language the brain can understand. By their nature, our sensory organs accomplish both goals. They are effective in detecting light, sound, tastes, odors, heat, and other stimuli, which they then convert into signals that can be sent to the brain.

Sensory processing: Transduction, reduction, and coding

Our sense organs contain cells called **receptors** that receive and process sensory information from the environment. For each sense, these specialized cells respond to a distinct stimulus, such as sound waves and odor molecules. Through a process called **transduction,** the receptors convert the stimulus into neural impulses, which are sent to the brain. In hearing, for example, tiny receptor cells in the inner ear transduce mechanical vibrations (induced by sound waves) into electrochemical signals. These signals are carried via neurons to the brain. Each type of sensory receptor is designed to detect a wide variety of stimuli and a wide range of stimulation. However, also built into our sensory systems are structures that purposefully reduce the amount of stimuli we receive.

RECEPTORS: *Body cells specialized to detect and respond to stimulus energy.*

TRANSDUCTION: *The process by which energy stimulating a receptor is converted into neural impulses.*

Question: Why would we want to reduce the amount of sensory information we receive? Can you imagine what would happen if some natural filtering of stimuli did not occur? You would constantly hear blood rushing through your veins or continually feel your clothes brushing against your skin. Obviously, some level of filtering is needed so that the brain is not constantly overwhelmed with unnecessary information. It needs to be free to respond to those stimuli that have meaning for survival. Each of our senses is therefore custom-designed to respond to only a select range of potential sensory information. All species have evolved selective receptors that suppress or amplify information in order to survive. For example, hawks have an acute sense of vision but a poor sense of smell. Similarly, although we humans cannot sense many stimuli (such as ultraviolet or infrared light), some stimuli we can detect are truly astounding. We can see a candle burning 30 miles away on a dark, clear night, hear the tick of a watch at 20 feet under quiet conditions, and smell one drop of perfume in a six-room apartment (Galanter, 1962).

In the process of sensory reduction, our sensory system not only filters incoming sensations but also analyzes their relative importance before sending a neural impulse to the cortex of the brain. This analysis is performed by nerve cells in the **reticular activating system (RAS)** within the brain stem (see Chapter 2). The RAS determines whether or not incoming sensory information is important. If important, it passes the information on to the cerebral cortex. Because of this screening process, parents of a newborn baby, for example, will learn to sleep through passing sirens and blaring stereos yet will awaken to the slightest whimper of their baby.

Question: How does the brain differentiate between various incoming sensations, such as sounds and smells? It does so through the process of **coding,** in which the experiencing of specific sensations depends on the number and type of sensory cells that are activated, on the precise nerve that is stimulated, and ultimately on the part of the brain that the nerve stimulates. In other words, sounds and smells are interpreted as distinct sensations not because of the environmental stimuli that activate them but because their respective neural impulses travel by different routes and arrive at different parts of the brain. Figure 3.1 illustrates the parts of the brain involved in sensory reception.

If you need help in your comprehension of coding, try this experiment: Close your eyes, and with your fingertips press *gently* on your eyelids for about 30 seconds. The visual sensations you experience (circles; streams of light) reflect the fact that the receptor cells at the backs of your eyes are prepared to code any kind of stimulation, including pressure, into visual patterns. So even though you aren't looking at an object in your environment, you still "see" something because your visual receptors have been stimulated.

Sensory thresholds: Testing the limits and changes

Suppose that you were the parent of a schoolage daughter who, like Helen Keller, has just suffered from an intense illness accompanied by a high fever. During her period of recovery, you notice that she does not seem to hear as well as before her illness, so you immediately take her to a hearing specialist. The specialist administers a series of tests based on principles of **psychophysics,** which is the study of the relationships between physical stimuli and the sensations they evoke.

In a test for hearing loss, the specialist uses a tone generator that produces sounds of differing pitches and intensities. Your daughter listens to the sounds over earphones and is asked to indicate the earliest point at which she can hear a tone. She thereby indicates her **absolute threshold,** or the smallest magnitude of sound that she can detect. To test your daughter's **difference threshold,** the examiner presents a small change in volume and asks the child to respond when she notices a difference. By noting your daughter's thresholds and comparing them to those of people with normal hearing, the

---

RETICULAR ACTIVATING SYSTEM (RAS): *A network of neurons in the brain stem that filters and selects sensory input to the cerebral hemispheres.*

CODING: *The process that converts a particular sensory input into a specific sensation.*

PSYCHOPHYSICS: *The study of the relationships between physical stimulation and the sensations evoked by such stimulation.*
ABSOLUTE THRESHOLD: *The smallest magnitude of a certain stimulus energy that can be detected.*
DIFFERENCE THRESHOLD: *The smallest magnitude of difference in stimulus energy that a person can detect.*

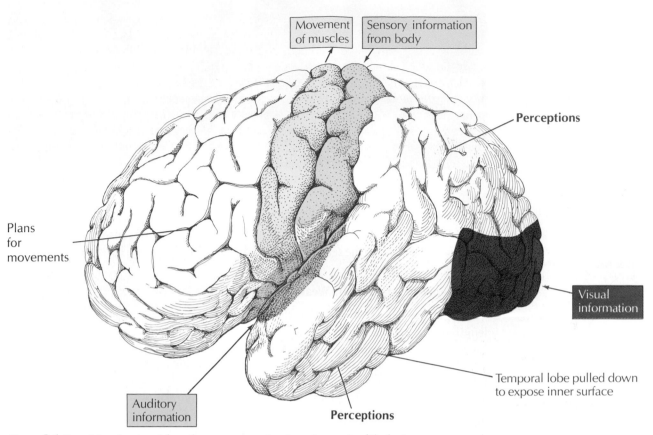

Figure 3.1 Neural impulses travel from the sensory receptors to various parts of the brain.

specialist is able to determine whether she has a hearing loss and, if so, the extent of the loss.

Sensory thresholds exist not only for hearing but also for vision, taste, smell, and the skin senses. In fact, much of the research done in all areas of sensation originally began by studying various thresholds.

Question: Do people's thresholds vary?   People with sensory impairments obviously have thresholds that differ from the norm. But even among individuals with no sensory difficulties there is a considerable range in sensitivities, and the sensitivity of

Hearing tests measure a person's absolute threshold for sound.

People exposed to noise quickly adapt to it.

each individual can also vary from moment to moment, depending on his or her physiological state. Lack of food and the use of certain drugs, for example, can cause a change in thresholds. Also, if your senses have gone through any type of **sensory deprivation** (a condition where use of the senses is restricted), your thresholds will be lower than normal.

Sensory adaptation: Weakening the response

An interesting thing happens when a constant stimulus is presented to a person for a length of time: the sensory structures involved begin to adapt to that stimulus, a process known as **sensory adaptation.** For example, if you are presented with a constant tone for a long time, your hearing receptors will decrease their firing rates and you will perceive the tone as less loud. All sensory systems display adaptation, but some senses adapt quickly, such as smell and touch, whereas others adapt very slowly, such as the sense of pain. When you walk into a kitchen, the aroma from freshly baked cookies can be delightfully overwhelming, but the baker, who has been in the kitchen for some time, hardly notices the smell. By deemphasizing repetitive information, the process of sensory adaptation allows us to operate efficiently in a wide range of stimulus intensities and makes us more alert to novel stimuli.

In some instances, adaptation can also distort sensation. To fully appreciate this, try the following experiment: Place one hand in icy water and the other in very warm water. After you have adapted to the two temperatures, place both hands into a pail of lukewarm water. If you are like most people, you will find that the water feels hot to the hand that had been in ice water but feels cold to the hand that had been in warm water. This phenomenon applies not only to touch, but to all our senses. For example, a friend's voice sounds much louder when we have adapted to silence than when we have adapted to the blaring music of a rock band. Thus, our sensory experiences are relative, depending on our level of adaptation.

Each of the sensory principles we've discussed thus far — reduction, transduction, coding, thresholds, and adaptation — applies to all the senses. Yet each sense is uniquely different, as we shall see in the remainder of the chapter.

Review Questions

1 The process of receiving, translating, and transmitting information from the "outside" to the brain is called _____.

2 _____ involves the conversion of environmental information into a language the brain can understand.

3 The part of the brain that analyzes the importance of incoming sensory information is the _____ _____ _____.

4 If a researcher were testing to determine the dimmest light a subject could perceive, the researcher would be measuring the _____ _____.

5 If you douse yourself with perfume or after-shave and after a few minutes you can't smell it, this would be an example of _____ _____.

Answers: 1 sensation; *2* transduction; *3* reticular activating system; *4* absolute threshold; *5* sensory adaptation.

VISION

While on a lengthy train trip, Helen Keller's aunt improvised a doll for six-year-old Helen out of a few towels. It had no nose, no mouth, no ears, no eyes—nothing to indicate a face. But the one thing that disturbed Helen most of all was the lack of eyes—in fact it agitated her so much that she was not content until she found some beads and had her aunt attach them as makeshift eyes.

Even the untutored Helen Keller, ignorant as she was of the myriad sensations our eyes bring us, seemed to know the importance of having eyes. But few of us realize the fantastic capabilities of our visual systems. Have you ever taken the time to consider these capabilities? At a football game, you can watch a distant action on the field and in the next instant consult a program as near as your lap. You can see a whole range of brightness, from pure white to jet black, and all the colors of the rainbow unless, of course, you're color-blind.

To fully appreciate the marvels of sight, we first need to examine the properties of light, since without it we wouldn't be able to see. We will then examine the structure and function of the eye, and finally the way in which visual input is processed.

Light: Electromagnetic energy

Light is a form of electromagnetic energy. Electromagnetic energy is made up of tiny particles called photons that move in waves similar to the movement of waves in the ocean. There are many different types of electromagnetic waves, from the short X rays to the long radio waves, that form the **electromagnetic spectrum** (see Figure 3.2). Most of these wavelengths are invisible to the human eye; only a small part of the spectrum, known as visible light, can be detected by our visual receptors. This visible light can be emitted by a source such as the sun or a light bulb, or it can be reflected from an object. Most often, it is by reflected light that we see our world.

ELECTROMAGNETIC SPECTRUM: *The band of radiant energy generated by the sun; visible light is only a small part of this spectrum.*

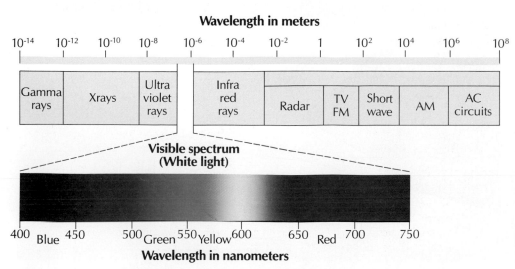

Figure 3.2 The electromagnetic spectrum. Most of the spectrum is invisible to the human eye, with visible light making up only a small part. Gamma radiation and X radiation have short wavelengths, visible light has medium wavelengths, and TV and radio waves have long wavelengths.

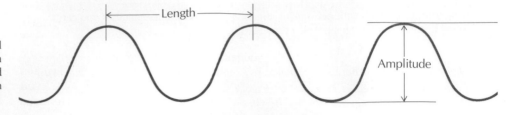

Figure 3.3 The two major physical properties of light waves: wavelength (the distance from peak to peak) and amplitude (the distance from trough to peak).

WAVELENGTH: *The length of a sound or light wave, measured from the crest of one wave to the crest of the next.*
HUE: *The visual dimension seen as a particular color; determined by the length of a light wave.*
AMPLITUDE: *The height of a light or sound wave; pertaining to light, it refers to brightness.*

Light waves vary in length and amplitude, each with a distinct effect on vision (see Figure 3.3). The **wavelength** — the distance between the crest of one wave and the crest of the next — determines its **hue,** or color. When white light strikes a prism or water droplets, it is separated into the individual colors found in the visible spectrum (see Figure 3.4). The **amplitude,** or height, of a light wave determines its brightness — the higher the wave, the brighter the light.

The eye: The anatomy of vision

The eye is uniquely designed to capture light and focus it on the receptors. These in turn convert light energy into neural signals to be interpreted by the brain. Many important structures in the eye contribute to the vision process. To explain how light is converted into neural signals that the brain can understand, we will trace a path of light through these structures. As we do, please take the time to refer to Figure 3.5, which summarizes this process.

CORNEA: *The transparent bulge at the front of the eye where light enters.*
SCLERA: *The white opaque outer wall of the eye.*
AQUEOUS HUMOR: *The clear fluid that fills the front chamber of the eye.*

Structures of the eye   Light waves enter the eye through a tough transparent shield called the **cornea.** Its bulging shape allows it to bend the entering light rays in order to fix an image on the receptors in the back of the eye. The cornea is attached to the **sclera,** the white, opaque outer wall of the eye. Within the cornea is a clear fluid known as the **aqueous humor,** which nourishes the cornea. At times, you may have noticed "spots" floating before your eyes. Actually, these spots are impurities floating in the aqueous humor. Since this fluid is recycled about once every four hours, the "floaties" are sometimes brought in and then carried away in the recycling process.

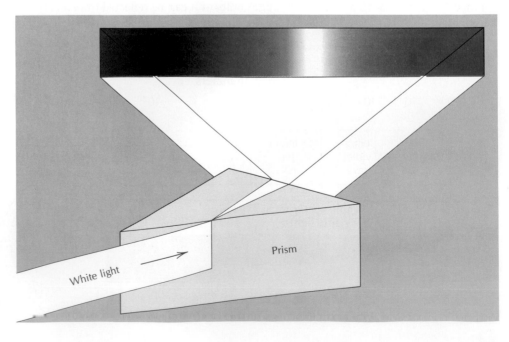

Figure 3.4 The visible color spectrum.

Light passes from the cornea through the **pupil,** an opening that can be enlarged or reduced to regulate the amount of light entering the eye. The muscles that control the size of the pupil are known as the **iris,** which is the colored part of the eye.

After passing through the pupil, light travels through the **lens,** a transparent elastic structure that focuses light on the back of the eye by changing its shape — by bulging and thinning. This focusing process is known as **accommodation** (see Figure 3.6). When you look at a faraway object, your lens accommodates by growing thinner, in order to focus the far object onto the back of the eye. When your glance shifts back to a near object, such as the book you're reading, your lens accommodates by bulging. The muscles responsible for changing the shape of the lens during the accommodation process are the **ciliary muscles,** which attach the lens to the sclera. Muscles attached to the outer surface of the sclera are responsible for movement of the eye itself. From the lens, light passes through the **vitreous humor,** a semiliquid gel that nourishes the eye and is responsible for the eye's spherical shape.

Ultimately, incoming light waves fall on the **retina.** This is an area at the back of the eye that contains light receptors, blood vessels, and a network of neurons that transmit

PUPIL: *An opening surrounded by the iris through which light passes into the eye.*
IRIS: *The colored part of the eye consisting of muscles that control the size of the pupil.*
LENS: *The transparent elastic structure in the eye that focuses light on the retina by changing shape.*
ACCOMMODATION: *The bulging and flattening of the lens in order to focus an image on the retina.*
CILIARY MUSCLES: *Muscles attached to the lens that stretch and relax it in order to focus images on the retina.*
VITREOUS HUMOR: *A semiliquid gel that nourishes the inside of the eye and is responsible for maintaining the eye's shape.*
RETINA: *An area at the back of the eye containing the rods and cones.*

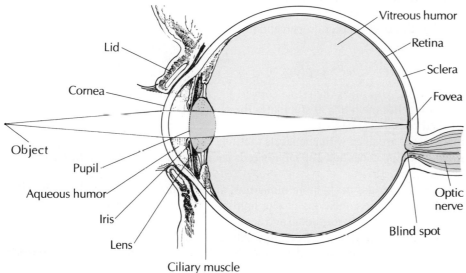

Figure 3.5 Anatomy of the eye. Follow the path of light from the point where it enters the eye to the point where neural impulses leave the eye through the optic nerve.

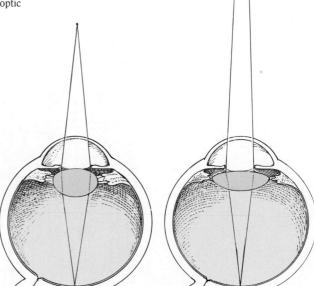

Figure 3.6 Accommodation. The lens bulges to focus on a near object. The lens is stretched and thinned by muscles to focus on a distant object.

Figure 3.7 To experience your blind spot, hold the book about one foot in front of you, close your right eye, and stare at the ✕ with your left eye. Very slowly, move the book closer to you. You should see the worm disappear and the apple become whole.

FOVEA: *The point on the retina containing only cones, where light from the center of the visual field is focused; the point responsible for our clearest vision.*

BLIND SPOT: *A part of the retina containing no receptors; the area where the optic nerve exits the eye.*

OPTIC NERVE: *The cranial nerve that carries visual information from the retina to the brain.*

PHOTORECEPTORS: *Receptors for vision, the rods and cones.*

RODS: *Receptors in the retina that are most sensitive in dim light; they do not respond to color.*

neural information to the brain. In the center of the retina is the **fovea,** a tiny pit in which are concentrated specialized receptor cells. The fovea is responsible for our sharpest vision. In contrast to the fovea, there is an area called the **blind spot** that has no visual receptors at all because it is the point where blood vessels and nerve pathways enter and exit the eyeball. We are not normally aware of the existence of this blind spot because we "fill in" the missing information with data from other parts of the retina. Figure 3.7 describes how you can experience the "disappearance" of objects that fall on your blind spot. After the retinal receptors have converted incoming light waves to neural signals, they are sent via the **optic nerve** to the brain for interpretation (a process that will be discussed in the next chapter on perception).

The retina and its visual receptors

Question: How does the retina convert light waves into neural signals?   When light reaches the retina, it stimulates the **photoreceptors.** These are light-sensitive cells, called rods and cones, that are named for their distinctive shapes (see Figure 3.8). Photoreceptors are filled with chemicals that react to the characteristics of light. There are about 7 million cones and 120 million rods packed tightly together at the back of the retina (Kaufman, 1974).

The **rods,** besides being more numerous, are also more sensitive to light than the cones and are used in conditions of dim lighting. This greater sensitivity, however, is achieved at the expense of fine detail and acuity in space and time — the job of the cones. You've probably noticed how increasingly difficult it becomes to play tennis, softball, or basketball as the afternoon sun fades into early twilight. At such times, your vision relies more and more on the rods. When rods are being used, there is a measurable delay in the

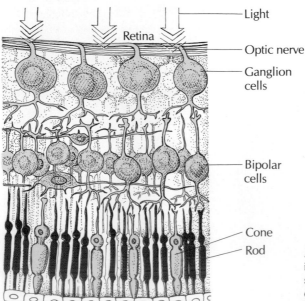

Figure 3.8 The physiology of the retina. The retina of the eye is a complicated structure with many different types of cells, the most important of which are the rods and cones.

message going from the eye to the brain and a consequent decline in the precise localization of moving objects. This is not to say that rods do not detect movement — they are very sensitive to motion — but only that the fine detail and timing of the movement are impeded. You can demonstrate this for yourself by extending your arms out at shoulder height and staring straight ahead while wiggling your fingers. Without moving your head, you can readily detect the movement of your fingers but can see little detail and no color. This is because the outer parts of your eyes — the periphery of the retina — contain only rods and no cones.

Cones become more numerous toward the center of the retina. In fact, they are concentrated in the fovea, where only cones are found. Any image that you want to examine carefully should be focused on the fovea. When you are reading and you detect something moving in your peripheral vision, you immediately turn your head to focus the moving object on your fovea. You do so because it is the cones that enable you to see the object in fine detail. Cones function better in bright light and diminish in function as the light dims.

CONES: Receptors in the retina that respond to color and fine detail.

Question: When the brightness level suddenly changes, how do the rods "take over" from the cones, and vice versa?   You've probably noticed when walking into a dark movie theater on a sunny afternoon that you are momentarily blinded during rapid changes from cones to rods. Under conditions of bright light, the pigment inside the rods is bleached and therefore the rods become temporarily nonfunctional. But as you enter a darkened theater, light is reduced and the rods start reacting immediately. They continue to adjust for longer than half an hour, until your maximum light sensitivity is reached. This process is known as **dark adaptation** (Hecht, Haig, and Wald, 1935). The visual adjustment that takes place when you go out of the theater back into the sunlight — **light adaptation** — takes about seven minutes and is the work of the cones. This adaptation process is particularly important to remember when driving your car from a brightly lit garage into a dark night.

DARK ADAPTATION: Visual adjustment that increases the sensitivity of the rods and cones and allows us to see better in dim light.
LIGHT ADAPTATION: The visual adjustment of the rods and cones that reduces sensitivity to bright light.

Cones not only enable us to see things in fine detail, they also enable us to see in color. All cones are sensitive to many wavelengths, but each is maximally sensitive to one color — red, green, or blue (Boynton, 1988). We will discuss color vision in the section on color perception in Chapter 4.

Question: I've heard that the eye is like a camera. Is this really true?   Yes and no. Like a camera, the eye admits light through a small hole that adjusts its size to various intensities and passes the light through to a lens that focuses an image on a photosensitive surface. However, unlike the camera lens, which moves forward or backward in the focusing process, the human lens focuses by bulging and thinning. Furthermore, the eye does not produce an actual "image" on the retina but rather sends information to the brain in the form of electrical impulses. In this regard, the eye is more analogous to a video camera than to a still camera.

The eye also differs from a camera in that a camera must be held steady when shooting, whereas the eye works quite well during bodily movement. In fact, the eyeball itself is in constant motion. This motion is necessary to prevent fatigue of the receptor cells in the retina. When nerve cells are continually stimulated, their receptivity tends to "fade" (an adaptation process). Thus, if the muscles of the eye weren't continually in motion and weren't shifting the image to neighboring cells when we looked at something for more than a few seconds, the image would disappear. You can check this for yourself by placing a finger at the corner of each eye and gently, being very careful, pressing on your eyeball for a few seconds to hold the eye still. Your visual field will soon fade to black.

Problems with vision: Eyes that are too long, too short, or too old

Our visual system, when all its structures are intact and working properly, enables us to see forms and shapes, colors, brightness levels, moving objects — everything necessary to function in our world. However, numerous things can affect vision. For example,

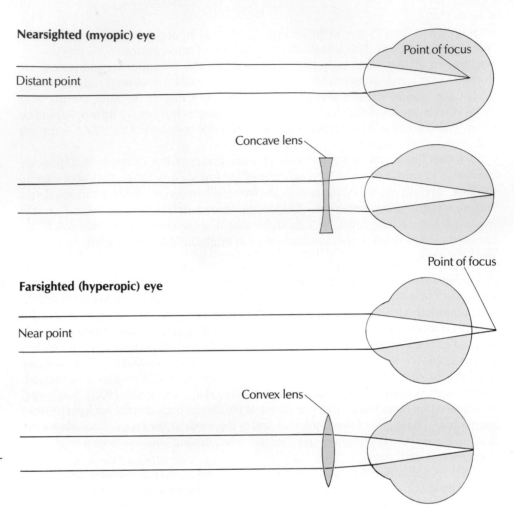

Nearsighted (myopic) eye

Distant point

Point of focus

Concave lens

Point of focus

Farsighted (hyperopic) eye

Near point

Convex lens

Figure 3.9 Corrections for near-sighted and farsighted vision.

many people are born with or develop eyes that are too long or too short, yet their lenses function as if they had normal-sized eyes. Thus, light is focused either in front of or in back of the retina. These people have trouble seeing either near or far objects, depending on whether they are myopic (having an eye that is longer than normal) or hyperopic (having an eye that is shorter than normal).

Myopia is commonly called "nearsightedness." People who are myopic have trouble focusing on distant objects, although they can see normally when they view the same objects from a near position. The opposite of myopia is **hyperopia,** or "farsightedness." Hyperopic people have trouble focusing on near objects because their eyes are too short, but they can see things clearly in the distance. Both myopia and hyperopia can be corrected through the use of eyeglasses or contact lenses that refocus the path of incoming light so that it falls in the right place on the retina (see Figure 3.9).

MYOPIA: *Nearsightedness; the eye is longer than normal and the image falls in front of the ideal position on the retina.*

HYPEROPIA: *Farsightedness; the eye is shorter than normal and the image falls behind its ideal position on the retina.*

Question: Don't all people get farsighted when they get old?   It is true that as we grow older, we tend to have trouble viewing close objects while we still see faraway objects relatively well. But the cause of this farsightedness is different from hyperopia. Our lenses grow stiffer as we age, and therefore do not bulge as easily as they once did. Consequently, older people have trouble focusing on near objects and need to hold things such as books farther and farther away to see them clearly. Eventually, the time comes when their arms are not long enough and they must wear reading glasses if they want to look at something close.

Other problems with vision may arise from disorders of the retina or the optic nerve. Eye problems involving the retina normally develop as a result of disease or trauma (some type of violent blow or action). Sometimes a portion of the retina is damaged from trauma,

As people age, the lenses in their eyes do not bulge as easily as they did when they were younger, so they need to wear glasses to see normally.

resulting in a partial loss of vision in the form of a blind spot. Many times the brain will ignore the blind spot if it is not too large, and the person will almost never notice the small absence of vision. Another problem often related to trauma is a **detached retina.** A sudden severe jolt to the head can cause the retina to detach from the back of the eye, causing total or partial blindness in the affected eye. Treatment involves surgically reattaching the retina to the back of the eye by "spot welding" it many times with a laser. World champion boxer Sugar Ray Leonard had his career jeopardized by a detached retina.

DETACHED RETINA *A disconnection of the retina from the back of the eye, which causes total or partial blindness of that eye.*

Damage to the optic nerve or to the visual cortex of the brain can cause many different problems, from partial loss of sight to total blindness. Although we will never know the cause of Helen Keller's blindness, it is relatively certain that it was due to some type of brain damage from her high fever. Just as in the days of her youth, there is currently no effective treatment for nerve cell damage, so visual problems resulting from damage to these areas are permanent.

There are several artificial visual systems that may help those who are totally blind in distinguishing basic forms and outlines. One of these enables the blind to "see" with their sense of touch through televised images projected onto their skin (Collins, 1970). A television camera translates images into electrical signals, and the individual learns to interpret the patterns of vibrations created by the signals as representations of objects. By using this system, blind students have been able to find and retrieve objects around a room, to read meters, and even to use an oscilloscope (Hechinger, 1981).

Review Questions

1 Light waves vary in two major ways: _____ and _____.

2 Light waves entering the eye pass through the outer transparent _____ and the opening called the _____ and are focused by the elastic _____ on the _____ at the back of the eye.

3 The lens of the eye focuses by _____ and _____. The focusing process is known as _____.

4 The two kinds of photoreceptors found on the retina are the _____ and _____.

5 An increased sensitivity to light after being in the dark for several minutes is called _____ _____.

6 A person whose eyeball is longer than normal is _____. A person whose eyeball is too short is _____.

Answers: 1 wavelength (hue), amplitude (brightness); *2* cornea, pupil, lens, retina; *3* thinning, bulging, accommodation; *4* rods, cones; *5* dark adaptation; *6* nearsighted (myopic), farsighted (hyperopic)

HEARING

AUDITION: *The sense of hearing.*

In this section, we will examine **audition,** the sense of hearing, which we use nearly as much as our sense of vision. Our auditory sense is as remarkable as our visual sense when we consider all that our ears can do. For instance, while listening to music, we can distinguish among many different instruments by discerning subtle differences in tonal qualities. Our hearing receptors can accommodate wide differences in volume, from the delicate sound of a mouse nibbling at a sunflower seed to the sharp bark of Rover sitting at our feet. Our hearing is so sensitive that we can quickly recognize friends' voices over the telephone, and from their voices even detect their moods.

Obviously, Helen Keller couldn't hear distinct sounds like these. But she recalled the time during her childhood when she went upstairs to dress herself in "company clothes" because she had sensed the door shutting and sensed that company had just arrived. How could she know the door had shut without being able to hear it? What is it about sound that allows hearing people to discriminate between a flute and a violin and enables a deaf person to tell that a door has been closed?

Sound: Mechanical energy

SOUND WAVES: *The mechanical movement of air molecules produced by a vibrating object.*

Sound is actually the mechanical movement of air molecules in a particular wave pattern. The waves produced by this movement of molecules are known as **sound waves.** They result from rapid changes in air pressure caused by vibrating objects, such as vocal cords or guitar strings. It was differences in the patterns of vibration that enabled Helen Keller to sense "sounds."

The vibrations from people's voices or musical instruments are like the ripples in a pond created by a bobbing cork on a fishing line. As vocal cords vibrate back and forth, they make ripples in the air around them. The sound waves then travel through the air, just as the ripples from a cork travel across the surface of a pond.

FREQUENCY: *The number of sound pressure waves per second; perceived as the pitch of a sound.*
PITCH: *The highness or lowness of tones or sounds, depending on their frequency.*

Like light waves, sound waves vary in two basic ways, frequency and amplitude, each with a distinct sensory effect (see Figure 3.10). **Frequency** refers to the number of sound pressure waves per second. Sounds of different frequencies are perceived as being high or low. This is known as **pitch.** For instance, the faster a particular vocal cord vibrates (the more waves per second), the higher the pitch of a person's voice. Frequency is measured in *hertz,* which is the number of sound wave cycles per second. Just as the eye responds only to light waves within a particular range, the ear responds only to frequencies from about 16 hertz (cycles per second) to 20,000 hertz. Dogs can detect sounds up to 30,000 hertz, and bats and dolphins up to 100,000 hertz. Humans are most sensitive to sounds that fall in the range of speech, about 500 to 3,000 hertz.

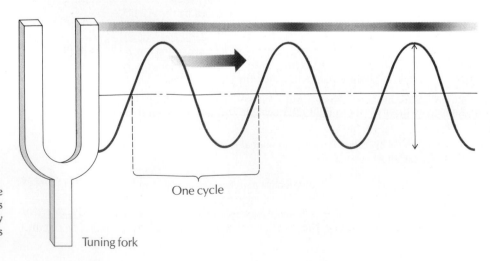

One cycle

Tuning fork

Figure 3.10 Sound is caused by the vibration of objects, which produces sound waves of varying frequency and amplitude. The number of cycles per second determines frequency.

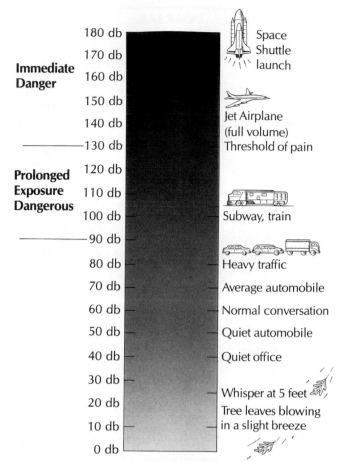

Figure 3.11 Decibel levels and examples of situations that generate sounds of varying intensity. One decibel is the faintest sound a normal person can hear. Normal conversation takes place at about 60 decibels. Constant noise above about 90 decibels can cause permanent nerve damage to the ear.

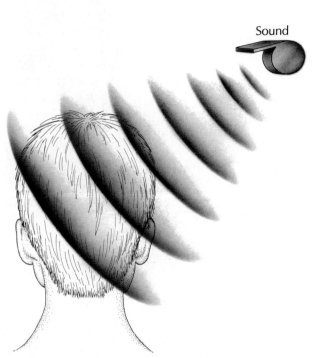

Figure 3.12 When a sound is generated to a person's right, the sound waves reach the right ear before they reach the left ear. This difference in arrival time can be used to localize the sound.

Amplitude refers to the amount of pressure (height) of sound waves. The amplitude of the wave determines loudness, which is measured in units known as decibels. Figure 3.11 gives decibel ratings for various sounds.

AMPLITUDE: *The height of a light or sound wave; pertaining to sound, it refers to loudness.*

Question: How do we know what direction a sound is coming from?   Locating sounds in space is aided by the slight time difference necessary for sounds to reach the two ears. When a bell rings somewhere to the right of us, the sound will reach the right ear slightly before it reaches the left (see Figure 3.12). Also, the sound reaching the right ear will be slightly louder than the sound reaching the left ear. We often have difficulty in locating a sound that is directly in front of or directly behind us, since the sound enters both ears at the same time. Sometimes a turn of the head will allow enough of a time or loudness differential to determine whether the sound is in front of or behind us.

The ear: The anatomy of hearing

The ear is composed of three major sections: the outer ear, the middle ear, and the inner ear. The outer ear is responsible for gathering and focusing sound waves. The middle ear serves to amplify and concentrate sounds. The inner ear contains the receptor cells that ultimately transduce the mechanical energy created by sounds into neural

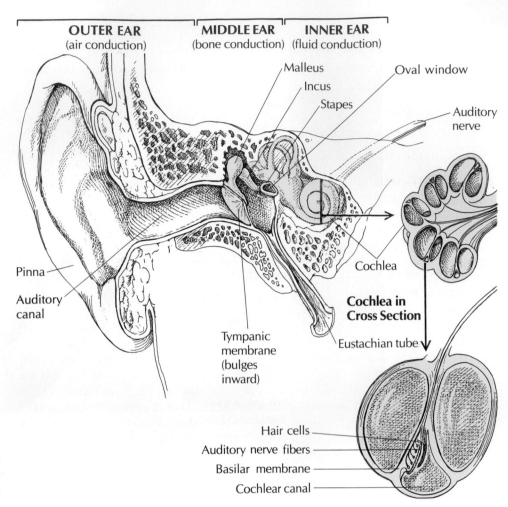

OUTER EAR
(air conduction)

MIDDLE EAR
(bone conduction)

INNER EAR
(fluid conduction)

Malleus

Incus

Stapes

Oval window

Auditory
nerve

Pinna

Auditory
canal

Cochlea

Tympanic
membrane
(bulges
inward)

**Cochlea in
Cross Section**

Eustachian tube

Hair cells

Auditory nerve fibers

Basilar membrane

Cochlear canal

Figure 3.13 Anatomy of the ear.
Sound waves enter the outer ear, are
amplified and concentrated in the
middle ear, and are transduced in the
inner ear.

PINNA: *The fleshy part of the outer
ear that we think of as "the ear."*
AUDITORY CANAL: *A tubelike structure
into which sound is channeled by
the pinna.*
EARDRUM (TYMPANIC MEMBRANE): *A
membrane located between the
auditory canal and the middle ear
that vibrates in response to sound
waves.*
OSSICLES: *Three small bones of the
middle ear: the malleus, the incus,
and the stapes.*
MALLEUS: *The first of the ossicles,
attached to the eardrum and the
incus.*
INCUS: *The middle ossicle, attached
to the malleus and the stapes.*
STAPES: *The last of the ossicles, attached to the incus and to the oval
window.*
OVAL WINDOW: *The membrane of the
cochlea that is moved by the
motions of the stapes.*
COCHLEA: *The inner ear structure
that contains the receptors for
hearing.*
HAIR CELLS: *Auditory receptors in the
cochlea.*

impulses. As we trace the path of sound waves through the ear, it will help to refer to
Figure 3.13.

Sound waves are gathered and funneled into the outer ear by the **pinna,** the
external, visible part of the ear that we automatically envision when we think of an "ear."
The pinna channels the sound waves into the **auditory canal,** a tubelike structure that
serves as a resonator to amplify the sound. At the end of the auditory canal is a thin, tautly
stretched membrane known as the **eardrum,** or tympanic membrane. As sound waves hit
the eardrum, it vibrates. The eardrum is so sensitive and elastic that it matches any
incoming sound waves in exact frequency and amplitude.

The eardrum separates the outer ear from the middle ear. When the eardrum
vibrates, it causes the three tiniest bones in the body, known as the **ossicles,** to vibrate in a
rocking motion in synchrony with the sound waves. During this rocking process, the
sound is further amplified and concentrated. The ossicles are named for objects they
resemble. They include the **malleus** (or hammer), which is connected to the eardrum; the
incus (or anvil), which is connected to the malleus; and the **stapes** (or stirrup), which is
connected to the incus. When the eardrum vibrates, it sets the malleus to rocking, which
sets the incus to rocking, which sets the stapes to rocking. As it rocks, the stapes presses
on a membrane known as the **oval window,** which is much like the eardrum, and causes it
to vibrate.

The oval window separates the middle ear from the inner ear. The movement of the
oval window creates waves in the fluid that fills the **cochlea.** This is a snail-shaped
structure that is sometimes referred to as the "retina of the ear" because it contains the
receptors for hearing. The hearing receptors are known as **hair cells** and they do in fact

resemble hairs. As the waves travel through the cochlear fluid, they displace the **basilar membrane,** to which the hair cells are attached. This displacement causes the hair cells to bend from side to side. It is at this point that the mechanical energy of the wave is transduced into electrochemical impulses that are carried via the **auditory nerve** to the brain.

BASILAR MEMBRANE: *The membrane in the cochlea that contains the hearing receptors.*
AUDITORY NERVE: *The cranial nerve that carries auditory information from the hair cells to the brain.*

Question: How do we hear differences in pitch or loudness? We hear various pitches and loudness levels by a combination of mechanisms, depending on the frequency of the sound. First, let's discuss how we hear various pitches of sounds. It seems that we hear high-pitched sounds according to the place along the basilar membrane that is most stimulated. When we hear a particular sound, it causes the eardrum, the ossicles, and the oval window to vibrate, which in turn produces a "traveling wave" through the fluid in the cochlea. This wave produces some bending of hair cells all along the basilar membrane, but there is a single point where the hair cells are maximally bent for each distinct pitch. This is known as the *place theory* and explains how we hear higher-pitched sounds (Kalat, 1984). The explanation of how we hear lower-pitched sounds is offered by the *frequency theory.* This theory proposes that we hear a particular low sound because it causes hair cells along the basilar membrane to bend and fire action potentials at the same rate as the frequency of that low sound (Kalat, 1984). For example, a sound with a frequency of 90 hertz would produce 90 action potentials per second in the auditory nerve.

How we detect loudness levels also differs according to the frequency of the sounds. When a sound has a high pitch, we hear it as louder because the neurons fire at a faster rate. Louder sounds produce more intense vibrations, which result in a greater bending of the hair cells, a greater release of transmitter, and consequently a higher firing rate of action potentials. However, there must be an alternate explanation for the perception of the loudness of low sounds, because as just described, rate of firing explains how we hear the pitch of a low sound. Most researchers think that the loudness of lower-pitched sounds is detected by the number of axons that are firing at any one time (Carlson, 1988).

Hearing problems: When things go wrong

Hearing problems vary according to their cause and location. For example, people suffering from a problem in the eardrum or the middle ear (a conductive hearing loss) might ask you to "speak louder." People suffering from an inner ear problem (nerve deafness) might ask you to "speak more clearly." And people suffering from damage to the auditory areas of the brain either cannot hear at all or cannot interpret the sounds that are sent to the cerebral cortex.

In conduction deafness, sound waves are unable to reach the mechanism of the inner ear. The most common cause of this condition is a middle ear infection, in which a building of fluid in the middle ear prevents the eardrum and the ossicles from vibrating. If ear infections in young children are left untreated, the hearing loss during this critical time of cognitive and language development could lead to severe speech impairments, problems in cognitive development, and impeded social development. Another cause of conduction deafness is a bony growth that develops in the region where the stapes connects to the oval window, thus preventing the stapes from rocking freely. This condition is normally corrected with a hearing aid (although hearing with hearing aids is distorted and is not the same as normal hearing). It can also be treated through a surgical technique that frees the stapes.

Hearing losses due to inner ear problems are much more serious than those due to conduction problems, since they stem from damage to the nerve cells in the cochlea. These nerve cells cannot regenerate, so any damage done to them is irreversible. Nerve deafness is normally a result of disease, birth defects, frequent exposure to loud sounds, or the simple process of aging. (Many older people can no longer hear higher-pitched sounds, so you might remember that instead of shouting when talking to older people who have hearing difficulties, first try lowering the pitch of your voice.)

Exposure to loud noise can cause nerve deafness. These crew members are wearing helmets that protect them from the extreme noise levels present on the flight deck of an aircraft carrier.

Question: Is it true that loud music can damage your hearing?   Yes. One of the most common causes of nerve deafness is a condition known as stimulation deafness, in which continuous exposure to loud sounds damages the hair cells. If a noise is loud — 150 decibels or more, such as blaring music or jet airplane engine — even a brief exposure can cause permanent deafness. Daily exposure to approximately 85 decibels (such as heavy traffic or motorcycles) may lead to permanent hearing loss.

Because nerve deafness is caused by irreversible damage to the nerve or receptor cells, the best treatment is undoubtedly prevention. That means avoiding areas with exceptionally loud noises (rock concerts, jackhammers, stereo headphones at full blast), wearing earphones when such areas cannot be avoided, and paying attention to bodily warnings. These warnings might include a change in your normal hearing threshold or tinnitus, a whistling or ringing sensation in the ears.

An artificial ear has been developed that may restore the hearing of about 70 percent of the 500,000 people in the United States with nerve deafness who cannot benefit from traditional hearing aids. This "bionic" ear attempts to electronically duplicate the function of the cochlea. A tiny microphone worn around the pinna picks up sounds and transmits them to a microprocessor worn on a belt. The microprocessor then transduces the information into electrical impulses that are sent to a small number of tiny electrodes that are surgically implanted in the cochlea. With this device, some patients have regained to some extent understanding of the spoken word, although in groups they can understand only one voice at a time.

Review Questions

1 _____ _____ result from rapid changes in air pressure caused by vibrating objects.
2 A 20,000-hertz tone will have a _____ pitch, whereas a 100-hertz tone will have a _____ pitch.
3 Loudness is related to the _____ of a sound wave.
4 The external visible part of the ear, or the _____, channels sound waves into the _____ _____, which ends at the _____.
5 The eardrum vibrates against the three _____, which in turn set in motion the _____.
6 The receptors for sound are the _____ _____, which are located in the _____

7 We hear _____ -pitched sounds according to the place on the basilar membrane that is most stimulated; we hear _____ -pitched sounds according to the rate of action potentials fired.

8 A form of nerve deafness caused by continuous exposure to loud sounds is called _____ _____ .

Answers: 1 sound waves; *2* high, low; *3* amplitude; *4* pinna, auditory canal, eardrum (tympanic membrane); *5* ossicles, oval window; *6* hair cells, cochlea; *7* high, low; *8* stimulation deafness

SMELL AND TASTE

Smell and taste are sometimes referred to as the chemical senses because they both involve chemoreceptors. These are receptors that are sensitive to certain chemical molecules rather than to electromagnetic or mechanical energy. Chemical stimulation of these receptors initiates transduction and the transmission of nerve impulses to the brain.

Smell and taste receptors are located near each other and often interact so closely that we have difficulty in separating the sensations. You can test this for yourself by closing your eyes and biting into an onion, an apple, and a potato while holding your nose closed. You will find that it is much more difficult to distinguish the three tastes without the aid of your smell receptors. In fact, smell plays a major role in the sense of taste. Have you ever noticed how food seems bland when your nose is blocked by a cold and you are unable to smell your food? The interaction between taste and smell is also affected by the temperature of food. Pizza and pancakes are much tastier when hot than cold. The steam from the hot foods enhances their taste because it can stimulate the smell receptors.

Chemical senses play an important role in the survival of many animals — in mating, detecting enemies, and locating food. Some people, like Helen Keller, have come to rely on these senses more than the average person. Helen told of times when she would row a boat and would "steer by the scent of watergrasses and lilies, and of bushes that grow on the shore" (Keller, 1908, p. 100). However, for most people, smell and taste seem to be more a matter of aesthetics than survival. Thus, these senses have received much less research attention than vision and hearing, although researchers have uncovered some interesting information.

Olfaction: The sense of smell

The sense of smell, or **olfaction,** results from stimulation of receptor cells in the nose (see Figure 3.14). These receptors are embedded at the top of the nasal cavity in a mucus-coated membrane called the **olfactory epithelium.** The olfactory epithelium is accessible from the mouth, via the oral–nasal connection at the top of the throat, which accounts for the strong contribution of smell to taste. The olfactory receptors are actually modified neurons, with a branched set of dendrites extending out of the epithelium. When air molecules in the nasal cavity come in contact with the dendrites, they initiate a neural impulse. The impulse travels along the neuron's axon directly to the olfactory bulb just below the frontal lobes. In the olfactory bulb, most of the olfactory information is processed before being sent to other parts of the brain. Pevsner, Reed, Feinstein, and Snyder (1988) have recently identified an odorant-binding protein in the nasal epithelium of several animals. This protein attaches to odorant molecules and then transports them to olfactory receptors. Since the major function of the protein is to concentrate odorant molecules, its presence can explain why we can smell some odors at extremely low concentrations.

As noted earlier, smell receptors adapt quickly. Odors that initially seem overpowering soon seem to wear off. Furthermore, some people adapt to smells more quickly than

OLFACTION: *The sense of smell.*
OLFACTORY EPITHELIUM: *The mucus-coated membrane lining the top of the nasal cavity and containing the receptors for smell.*

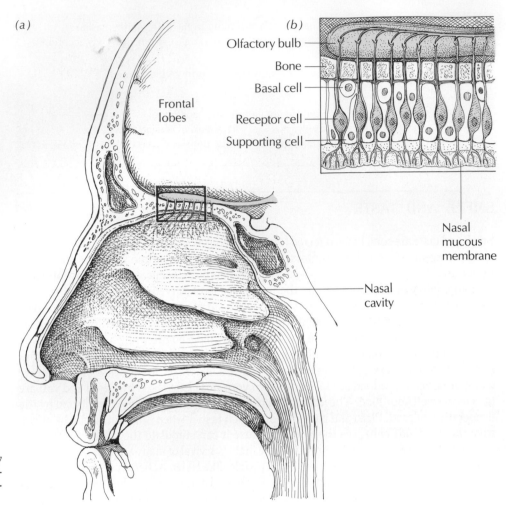

(a)

Frontal lobes

(b)

Olfactory bulb

Bone

Basal cell

Receptor cell

Supporting cell

Nasal mucous membrane

Nasal cavity

Figure 3.14 *(a)* The nasal cavity showing location of olfactory receptors. *(b)* Detail of the olfactory receptor system.

others. (It's too bad that many of us didn't know this when we were first learning to use after-shave lotion and cologne.) Smell acuity is generally keen — we can detect up to tens of thousands of different odors — but it also seems to vary among individuals. Some of us are totally "blind" to certain odors (such as musk and sweat), and some older people suffer a complete loss of smell (Cohen, 1981). The exact reasons for these variations are still unclear, but current research is looking at the roles of heredity, hormones, and learning.

Question: How do we distinguish different odors?   Although researchers have proposed a number of explanations, there are two basic theories. One suggests that all the complex odors are made up of between 6 and 32 primary qualities, such as camphor (mothball), floral, peppermint, ether (dry-cleaning fluid), musk, pungent (spices), putrid (rotten eggs), fishy, malty, and sweaty (Amoore, Johnston, and Rubin, 1964; Amoore, 1977). As Figure 3.15 shows, the complex molecules responsible for each of these odors are different in shape and size. According to this **lock-and-key theory**, each odor will fit into only one type of receptor cell, like a key into a lock. Some molecules, such as carbon monoxide, have a shape that will not fit into any receptor and are therefore odorless.

The other major theory proposes that, as opposed to specific receptors responding only to distinct odors, all receptors contribute to the detection of all odors. Any one receptor may respond more to some odors than to others, but most receptors respond in varying degrees to a wide range of odors (Tanabe, Iino, and Takagi, 1975). According to this theory, we perceive any particular odor because it excites a certain *pattern* of activity within all the olfactory receptors.

LOCK-AND-KEY THEORY: *The idea that each odor molecule will fit into only one type of smell receptor cell according to shape.*

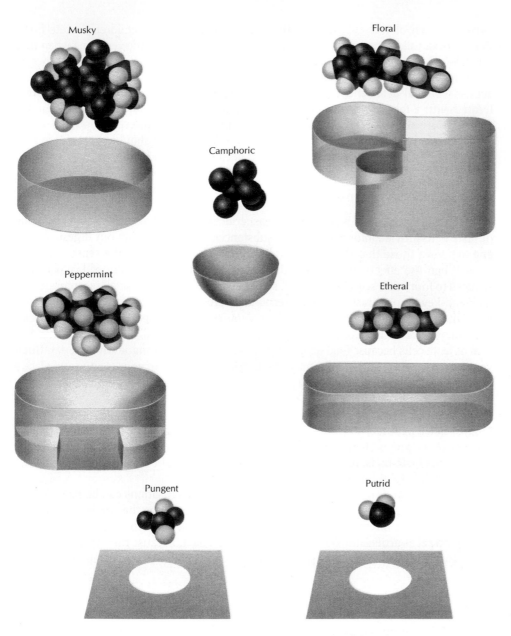

Figure 3.15 Examples of different types of odor molecules and the shapes of the receptor sites they activate.

Question: Does smell really have an effect on sexual attraction? Since ancient times, human beings have been interested in finding ways to increase their sexual attractiveness. One popular means has been the use of perfumes, after-shave lotions, and other odorous substances to try to enhance attraction. Is there any scientific basis to such practices? One line of research has focused on **pheromones** — chemical odors we give off that are thought to affect the behavior of others (e.g., it is thought that we may give off sexual pheromones that increase our attractiveness).

Pheromones have been found in a number of animals species. Michael and Keverne (1970) found, for example, that female monkeys secrete chemicals called copulins that are sexually attractive to males. Similarly, Morris and Udry (1978) found that when human females were instructed to rub perfume containing copulins on their chests, a definite increase occurred in the sexual behavior of both their partners and themselves. Researchers looking for male copulins have found that ovulating women are much better than men or children at detecting the musky fragrance of a synthetic substance called exaltolide, which chemically resembles a substance found in human urine. Males secrete

PHEROMONES: *Bodily chemicals that affect others' behavior.*
GUSTATION: *The sense of taste.*

twice as much of this substance in their urine as women, and children secrete none. Perhaps exaltolide is a male pheromone that attracts females at the very time when they are most likely to conceive (Hassett, 1978). At the other extreme, Gustavson, Dawson, and Bonett (1987) have suggested that women may secrete a "spacing" pheromone that acts as a sexual deterrent. These researchers report that men are likely to avoid areas treated with a female pheromone called androstenol. It is possible that androstenol is secreted during times when a woman's fertility rates are at their lowest. Although perfume companies have eagerly responded to pheromone research, we should be careful to note that these studies are very controversial and need further validation.

Gustation: The sense of taste

Taste, or **gustation,** is perhaps the least critical of all our senses. The major function of taste is to provide information about substances that are entering our digestive tract and to screen those that may be harmful. This function is aided by the sense of smell.

When the effects of smell are eliminated, the enormous variety of tastes can be reduced to four basic sensations: sweet, sour, salty, and bitter. Like smell receptors (in the lock-and-key theory), taste receptors respond differentially to the varying shapes of food and liquid molecules. But unlike smell receptors, taste receptors for the four basic sensations have specific locations (see Figure 3.16). We generally don't notice this division of taste cells because food usually reaches all parts of the tongue while we eat. But if you want to avoid tasting a pill, throw a salty pill on the back of your tongue and place a bitter pill on the exact center. If you want to savor a sweet treat, you should roll it around on the tip of your tongue.

Note in Figure 3.16 that the major taste buds are clustered together under little bumps, called **papillae,** that you can see on the surface of your tongue. When liquids enter the mouth or food is chewed and dissolved, the fluid runs over the papillae and into the pores to the taste buds. (Can you now understand why we should chew our food slowly and completely to get maximum taste satisfaction?)

Some research has found that the four basic taste sensations can be mimicked by artificial substitutes. Aspartame, for example, is a derivative from the artichoke plant that appears to mimic the molecular shape of sweet substances. Both Nutrasweet and saccharin can act as artificial sweeteners in many diet products because they have a molecular shape that is similar enough to sugar that they can stimulate sweet receptors.

PAPILLAE: *Small bumps on the surface of the tongue that contain the taste receptors.*

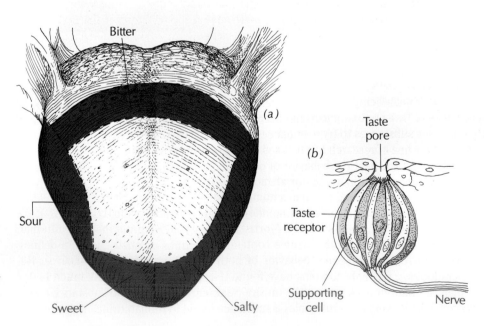

Figure 3.16 (a) Taste regions of the tongue. (b) Detail of a taste receptor.

Question: Why are children so "picky" regarding the foods they like?   In young people, taste buds die and are replaced about every seven days; as we age, the buds are replaced more slowly, so taste declines as we grow older. Thus, children, who have abundant taste buds, often dislike foods with strong or unusual tastes (such as liver and spinach), but as they grow older and lose taste buds, they may come to like these foods.

Pickiness is also related to learning. Many food and taste preferences are results of childhood experiences and cultural influences. For example, Japanese children eat raw fish and Chinese children eat chicken feet as part of their normal diet, whereas American children declare these foods as being "yucky." Likewise, many smells we perceive as offensive or alluring are learned and often are culturally defined, as evidenced by the extreme measures Americans take to disguise their body odors.

Review Questions

1 The chemical senses are _____ and _____ .

2 The sense of smell is called _____ .

3 According to the _____ theory, we are able to smell a particular odor because the shape and size of its molecule enable it to fit into a certain type of receptor cell.

4 Bodily chemicals that may affect the behavior of others are called _____ .

5 The four basic taste sensations are _____ , _____ , _____ , and _____ .

6 Taste buds are found under the _____ , which can be seen on the surface of the tongue.

Answers: 1 smell, taste;   *2* olfaction;   *3* lock-and-key;   *4* pheromones;   *5* salty, sweet, sour, bitter;   *6* papillae

THE BODY SENSES

Pretend for a moment that you are an Olympic skier, and you're anxiously awaiting the starting signal that will begin your once-in-a-lifetime race for the gold medal in the giant slalom. What senses will you need if you are to manage the subtle and ever-changing balance adjustments required for Olympic-style skiing? How will you make your skis carve the cleanest, shortest, fastest line from start to finish? What will enable your arms, legs, and trunk to work in perfect harmony so that you can record the shortest time and win the gold? The senses that will allow you to do all this, and much more, are the **body senses.**

The body senses tell the brain how the body is oriented, where and how the body is moving, the things it touches or is touched by, and so on. These senses include the vestibular sense, the kinesthetic sense, and the skin senses.

BODY SENSES: *The senses that include the skin senses of pressure, warmth and cold, and pain; the vestibular sense of balance; and the kinesthetic sense of body position and movement.*

The skin senses: More than just touch

The **skin senses** are perhaps the most vital of all our senses. Skin not only protects the internal organs but also provides the brain with basic survival information. With their nerve endings in the various layers of skin, our skin senses tell us when a pot is dangerously hot, when the weather is freezing cold, when we have been hurt. Helen Keller realized the value of her skin senses early in life. Indeed, it was through feeling the cool gush of water over her hand that Helen was able to understand the "mystery of language" by associating objects with finger-spelled words.

SKIN SENSES: *The sensory system for detecting pressure, temperature, and pain.*

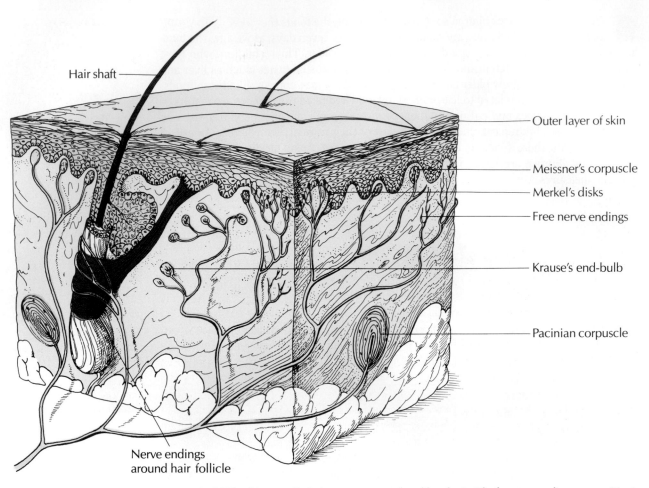

Hair shaft

Outer layer of skin

Meissner's corpuscle

Merkel's disks

Free nerve endings

Krause's end-bulb

Pacinian corpuscle

Nerve endings
around hair follicle

Figure 3.17 The skin senses include pressure, warmth, cold, and pain. The free nerve endings are sensitive to pressure and pain. The Pacinian corpuscles, Meissner's corpuscles, and Merkel's disks, as well as some free nerve endings, are sensitive to touch and pressure. Temperature may be sensed via myelinated axons located in the upper layers of the skin.

Researchers have "mapped" the skin by applying probes to skin areas all over the body. Using this method, they have determined that there are four basic types of skin sensations: pressure, warmth, cold, and pain. Receptors for these sensations lie at various depths in the skin and connect to neurons that transmit the sensory information to the appropriate parts of the brain (see Figure 3.17). At present, the relationship between the types of receptors and the different sensations is not clear. It used to be thought that each receptor responded to only one type of stimulation, but recent research has shown that some receptors respond to more than one. For example, pressure receptors will also respond to certain sound waves (Green, 1977), and itching, tickling, and vibrating sensations seem to be produced by light stimulation of both pressure and pain receptors. Nevertheless, each of the four skin senses has been studied separately, and research has revealed some interesting facts about them.

Pressure   Pressure receptors are not evenly distributed. For example, the fingertips, lips, tip of the tongue, inner forearm, and genitals all contain densely packed receptors and are extremely sensitive to pressure or touch, whereas portions of the back are relatively insensitive. Like Helen Keller, many blind people use their fingertip sensitivity to "see" the world. They can recognize people and objects through their sense of touch and can read books by using the Braille alphabet.

Question: Are women more sensitive to touch than men?   Newborn boys and girls seem equally sensitive to touch—both are quieted when soothed with a blanket or soft fabric (Richmond-Abbott, 1983). But both parents tend to touch, as well as talk to, their girl babies more than their boy babies, and by adulthood women do test out as being more sensitive to touch stimuli than men (Tavris and Offir, 1984).

Question: Is touch really necessary to the bonding between parent and child?   In recent years, the popular press has given a great deal of attention to research on the importance of touch in the early bonding process between parent and child (Minde, 1986; Montagu, 1971). This research has suggested that skin contact in the first few hours of life can increase the amount of time mothers spend with their babies, their success in nursing, the babies' intellectual development, and so on. More recent studies have refuted this bonding research. They conclude that a strong bond between parent and child develops not because of skin contact immediately after birth but by continual contact between parent and child throughout infancy and subsequent childhood (Lamb, 1982; Reed and Leiderman, 1983). These later findings can do much to alleviate the guilt and concern that might have been experienced by parents who adopted, by mothers who had cesarean deliveries, and by parents who gave birth before the bonding research was done. As we noted in Chapter 1, psychological research often has wide-ranging influences on public opinion, and this is a good example of why we all need to be more alert to both supportive and refutational findings.

Continued contact between parent and child throughout infancy is important for the bonding process.

Warmth and cold   The average square centimeter of skin contains about six cold spots where only cold can be sensed, and one or two warm spots where only warmth can be felt. Researchers have found no "hot" receptors, but by using a device called a "heat grill" (see Figure 3.18), they have found that the sensation of "hot" is created by stimulation of both warm and cold receptors at the same time.

As noted earlier in this chapter, skin adapts quite readily to temperature changes, so that the same bucket of water can be perceived as warm or cold depending on skin temperature. Thus, we can tell when something is hotter or colder than our skin, but not how hot or cold it is on an absolute scale. When conducting studies involving temperature receptors, researchers must therefore establish the subject's normal temperature in the skin area under study. This baseline temperature is referred to as *physiological zero*. They then record sensory reactions to changes from this baseline.

Pain   Many kinds of stimuli can initiate pain—scratches, cuts, burns, abscessed teeth, even hungry stomachs. We feel pain as a result of the overstimulation of sensory receptors (when we burn our mouth on piping hot pizza) and as a result of the stimulation of specific pain receptors (when we prick our finger with a needle). Although classified as a skin sense, the sense of pain is not restricted only to the skin. Pain that is perceived as "dull and achy" can be felt in the internal organs as well as in the deeper layers of the skin. On the other hand, pain experienced as either "sharp" or "bright" is felt in the superficial layers of the skin.

The common function for all types of pain is to serve as a warning device for real or potential damage to bodily tissues. During a long-lasting headache, we would like to trade away our ability to sense pain, but this would be a dangerous move. People with diseases or injuries that reduce or eliminate pain perception are in constant danger. These individuals often suffer extensive burns and deep cuts without even noticing them—one women even chewed off the tip of her tongue without feeling a thing (Cohen et al., 1955; McMurray, 1950).

At the other end of the pain continuum are those who suffer from chronic pain as a result of cancer, arthritis, or other causes. Chronic pain is the most common reason both for going to the doctor and for taking medication, yet it has received relatively little attention in research and in the training of doctors.

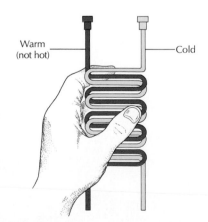

Warm (not hot)   Cold

Figure 3.18 An example of a heat grill. When you grasp it, you get the sensation of intense heat.

Question: Why don't we adapt to pain? The sensation of pain is transmitted along both rapid and slow neural pathways in the spinal cord. Thus, we tend to experience "first and second pain" (Sternbach, 1978). The initial pain from burning one's hand on a hot stove is a clear, localized feeling that is carried over rapid pathways to the brain. This warning pain fades quickly. The pain that doesn't fade is the second, follow-up pain that is more diffused and long-lasting and is carried by the slower neural pathways. The fact that we don't adapt to pain is generally quite functional — it serves as a reminder to do something about the tissue that has been hurt, such as putting some ice on that burned hand.

Question: If we don't adapt to pain, how do athletes keep playing despite painful injuries, and soldiers keep fighting after they've been wounded? In certain situations, the body releases natural pain killers called **endorphins.** Endorphins are chemicals that act in the same way as morphine to relieve pain by inhibiting pain perception. An extremely painful injury, along with the motivation of winning an athletic contest or the sense of danger during battle, can cause the release of these endorphins and the closing of the pain pathways.

There are many theories explaining pain transmission and perception, but no one theory is adequate in explaining every type of pain. One of the most accepted and useful theories (useful as it applies to pain relief) is the **gate-control theory,** developed by Ronald Melzack and Patrick Wall (1965) (see Figure 3.19). As mentioned earlier, there are both large, fast nerve fibers and smaller, slower fibers that transmit sensory information from receptors to the brain via the spinal cord. The large fibers are responsible for sensations of touch, pressure, and dull pain; the smaller fibers are responsible solely for pain sensations. According to the gate-control theory, if a person receives some type of painful stimulation (e.g., a bee sting), the small fibers will carry the pain information to the spinal cord and open a pain "gate" that allows this information to be sent on to the brain. If the person receives some type of alternate stimulation (such as pressing on or rubbing the bee sting), information from the larger, faster nerve fibers will arrive sooner than pain information from the small, slow fibers. This will close the gate, thereby reducing the amount of pain information that is sent to the brain (Warga, 1987).

Recent research has suggested that the gate may be controlled by chemical means. It seems that a neurotransmitter called substance P works as a chemical opener for the pain gate and that endorphins close it. Although the gate-control theory has generated a good deal of debate (Nathan, 1976), it quite effectively explains why several pain control techniques are successful. These techniques include back rubs and massages, applica-

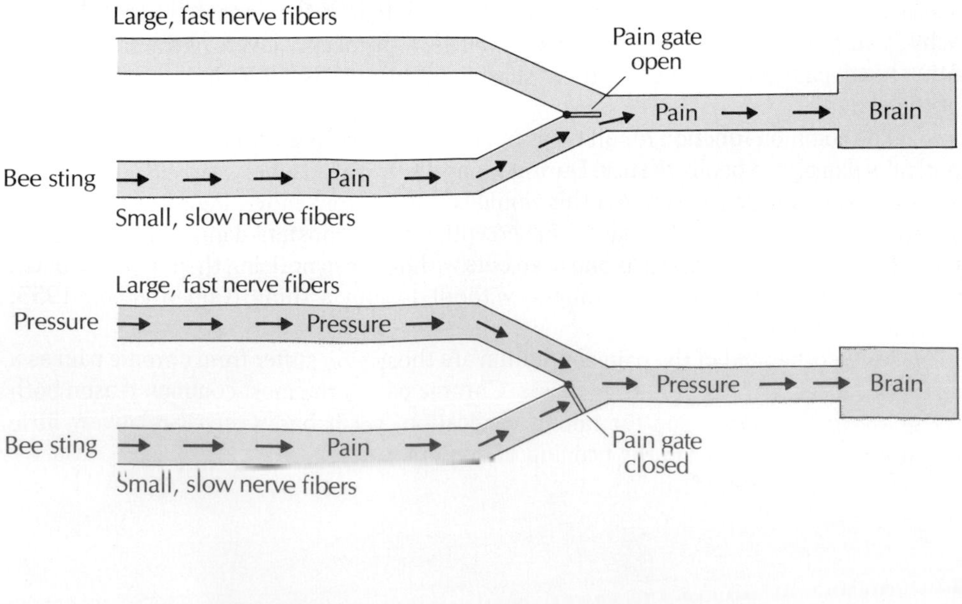

ENDORPHINS: *Morphinelike chemicals occurring naturally in the brain that can lessen pain responses.*

GATE-CONTROL THEORY OF PAIN: *The idea that pain sensations are processed and altered by mechanisms within the spinal cord.*

Figure 3.19 The gate-control theory of pain.

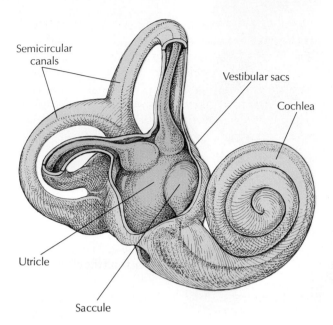

Semicircular
canals

Vestibular sacs

Cochlea

Utricle

Saccule

Figure 3.20 Vestibular apparatus.
The receptor cells for body position
are located in the semicircular canals.

tions of heat, acupuncture, and the use of electrical nerve-stimulating devices. According
to the gate-control theory, these procedures stimulate the touch and pressure fibers,
thereby causing the gate to close on pain information.

The vestibular sense: The sense of balance

The **vestibular sense** is the sense of body orientation and position with respect to
gravity and three-dimensional space (in other words, the sense of balance). Even the most
routine activities — riding a bike, walking, or even sitting up — would be impossible
without this sense. The vestibular apparatus is located in the inner ear and is composed of
two smaller sensory organs: the vestibular sacs, consisting of the saccule and the utricle,
and the semicircular canals (see Figure 3.20).

The **semicircular canals** are three arching structures located above and attached to
the entrance to the cochlea. They provide the brain with balance information, particularly
information about the rotation of the head. Because space has three dimensions — length,
breadth, and height — the semicircular canals are arranged in three planes to detect
movement in each dimension. As the head moves, hair cells are bent by liquid moving in
the canals. At the end of the semicircular canals are the **vestibular sacs,** which contain
hair cells sensitive to the specific angle of the head — straight up and down or tilted.
Information from the semicircular canals and the vestibular sacs is converted to neural
impulses that are then carried to the appropriate section of the brain.

VESTIBULAR SENSE: *The sense of how
the body is oriented in relation to
the pull of gravity; the sense of
gravity.*

SEMICIRCULAR CANALS: *Three arching
structures in the inner ear that
contain the hair receptors that provide balance information from head
movements.*

VESTIBULAR SACS: *Inner ear structures
containing hair receptors that
respond to the specific angle of the
head, to provide balance information.*

*The vestibular sense and the
kinesthetic sense work in harmony
to enable us to move and
maintain our balance. This skier is
using her vestibular and kinesthetic senses to their limits.*

Random, unpredictable movement can cause motion sickness.

Question: What causes motion sickness?   Information from the vestibular sense is used by the eye muscles to maintain visual fixation and sometimes by the body to change body orientation. When this sense is overloaded or is confused by boat, airplane, or automobile motion, the result is often dizziness and nausea. Research has found that random versus expected movements are more likely to produce motion sickness (Geeze and Pierson, 1986). Thus, automobile drivers are better prepared than passengers for upcoming movement and are less likely to feel sick. Motion sickness seems to vary with age: Infants are generally immune, children from 2 to 12 have the highest susceptibility, and the incidence declines in adulthood.

Motion sickness has been a particular problem for space travelers (Kohl, 1987). Conditions such as a gravity-free environment, rapid changes in altitude, and loss of visual reference with respect to the ground and horizon all contribute to the motion sickness often experienced by astronauts. Research by NASA, the Air Force, and the Navy has produced several methods for helping to prevent motion sickness. In addition to using drugs, such as Dramamine, that reduce sensitivity within the semicircular canals and antinausea patches that are worn behind the ear, it is beneficial to close your eyes and imagine that you are fixing your gaze on a stable object. Relaxation techniques such as lying down, slowly and rhythmically tensing and untensing muscles, and open-mouth deep breathing also seem to help (Fromer, 1983).

The kinesthetic sense: The sense of movement

KINESTHESIS: *The sensory system that provides information on body posture and orientation.*

Kinesthesis (from the Greek word for "motion") is the sense responsible for providing the brain with information about bodily posture and orientation, as well as bodily movement. Unlike the receptors for sight, hearing, smell, taste, and balance, which are clumped together in one organ or area, the kinesthetic receptors are diffused throughout the muscles, joints, and tendons of the body. As we sit, walk, bend, and ski, our kinesthetic

92

receptors respond by sending messages to the brain. They tell us which muscles are being contracted and which relaxed, how our body weight is being distributed, where our arms and legs are in relation to the rest of our body, and so on. Without these sensations, we would literally have to watch every step.

Despite its importance, we generally take our kinesthetic sense for granted. Helen Keller certainly did. She praised her senses of smell, taste, and touch in compensating for her lack of vision and hearing, but she never mentioned the value of her kinesthetic sense. However, she relied on kinesthesis heavily when climbing trees (which she did frequently), paddling a rowboat (she could feel by the resistance of the water if she was holding the oars correctly), writing or typing a letter or a lesson, or making any kind of movement.

Sighted and hearing people likewise rely on kinesthesis constantly. Yet they seldom acknowledge it, since this sense is rarely disturbed in their everyday lives. In one study, an experimenter intentionally disturbed subjects' wrist tendon receptors by producing certain vibrations. Subjects reported sensations of having multiple forearms and impossible positions of their arms (Craske, 1977). But we don't have to go through experimental procedures to appreciate our kinesthetic sense. All we have to do is observe children learning new skills and remember when we were just learning to ride a bike, jump rope, or catch a football. During the learning process, we consciously move certain body parts and certain muscles, but gradually we learn to operate on "automatic pilot." Thus, just as wine tasters need training in knowing what smells and tastes to notice, our kinesthetic sense needs training in recognizing how various postures and movements should feel.

SENSORY DEPRIVATION

Although Helen Keller was deprived of two critical senses, she compensated for her deficiencies with her other senses and thus lived a successful, satisfying life. What would it be like, however, to be deprived of all our senses? In 1954, Bexton, Heron, and Scott conducted a classic study of such sensory deprivation. They offered $20 a day (a good wage at that time) to students at McGill University to do nothing more than rest on a comfortable bed, shielded from any stress or distractions. Sensations from outside their bodies were diminished as much as possible. The subjects wore translucent plastic visors that prevented recognition of any type of visual patterns. They heard the continuous hum of an air conditioner to muffle any incoming sounds, and they lay on a U-shaped foam pillow and wore cotton gloves and cardboard cuffs to prevent any sensation of touch.

After just a few hours, students began to feel bored and irritable, and most of them began to experience "blank periods" when they couldn't focus their attention on anything. Continued lack of sensory stimulation led several subjects to embark on drugless "trips" in which they experienced visual, tactile, and auditory hallucinations. The visual hallucinations chiefly took the form of simple geometrical patterns or dots of light. However, one subject saw little yellow men wearing black caps parading past with open mouths; another saw distorted eyeglasses marching down a street; and another, squirrels hurrying by, carrying sacks over their shoulders.

Many subjects quit during the first day, with few remaining after two days, despite the financial incentive to continue. Thus, it seems that our bodies need some sort of sensory stimulation to function normally and that deprivation of stimulation for long periods of time can lead to adverse effects.

Intentional deprivation: The benefits of boredom

Considering the hallucinations, extreme boredom, and occasional panic experienced by the students in the original studies of sensory deprivation, it is surprising that researchers have found beneficial uses for it. In the early 1960s, a psychiatrist named John C. Lilly set out to study deprivation effects by donning a diving helmet and immersing himself in a dark, soundproof tank of highly saline, buoyant water. During his immersion,

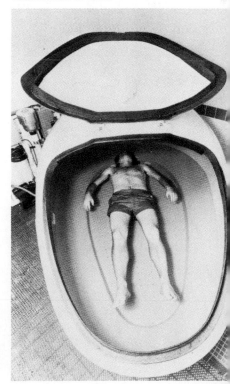

When "tanking," people float in a dark, water-filled chamber. They claim this produces a blissful, relaxed state of mind.

Critical Thinking — PSYCHOLOGY IN ACTION

CONDUCTING SOCRATIC DISCUSSIONS
Thinking About Sensation

Perhaps the single most important ingredient of critical thinking is that of critical questioning. The ability to delve beneath the superficial or to rise above mere appearances by considering the logical consequences and possible boundaries is at the heart of critical thinking. Socrates, an ancient Greek philosopher, modeled this type of thinking in his question-and-answer method of teaching. During a Socratic discussion the questioner uses probing questions to learn what another thinks, to help the respondent develop his or her ideas, and to mutually explore the implications, consequences, and values of core ideas. In turn, the respondent is comfortable being questioned. He or she welcomes good questions and doesn't become offended, defensive, or intimidated.

In this exercise, we offer several questions related to content within Chapter 3 that will help you practice the method of Socratic discussions. Select a good friend or classmate to simulate the roles of "questioner" and "respondent." One of you should play Socrates and question the other for half the questions, and then you should reverse roles for the remaining questions. We are providing sample questions that "Socrates" might ask, and the respondent's answers should be followed up with questions such as: "Why?" "How do you know?" "What is your reason for saying that?" "For example?" "Can I summarize your point as . . . ?" Remember to relax and enjoy your role as both the questioner and respondent. Critical, Socratic questioners do not attempt to make another look stupid. This should be a fun "mind game" that stretches your intellectual capacity and develops your critical thinking skills. (A healthy by-product of this exercise is that it will also help you to master the chapter material.)

Sample Socratic Questions

1 Is there a sound if no one is there to hear it? Or, does a hamburger have a taste if no one is there to taste it?

2 What would the world be like if the absolute thresholds for sensation were changed? If we could see X rays and ultraviolet light or infrared rays and radar? If we were like bats and dolphins and could hear sounds up to 100,000 hertz?

3 What would happen if each sensory receptor (e.g., eyes, ears, skin) was receptive to every type of incoming stimuli? If your eyes were also sensitive to sound waves and odor molecules, could the brain distinguish and integrate this information?

4 William James, a famous early psychologist, suggested that, "If a master surgeon were to cross the auditory and optic nerves, then we would hear lightning and see thunder." How would you explain this statement?

5 How would you explain the fact that blind people tend to be better adjusted psychologically and less subject to emotional difficulties than deaf people?

6 If you had to choose between losing vision, hearing, or touch, which sense would you choose to lose? Why? What effect would it have on your life?

Lilly reportedly experienced "out of body" sensations, mind trips to other dimensions, and a general sense of being born again (Lilly, 1972). Other proponents of "tanking" claim that it produces a blissful, relaxed state of mind and vivid, enjoyable hallucinations.

Question: Why did Bexton, Heron, and Scott's subjects experience such an unpleasant state if people who engage in tanking find it so enjoyable? One of the major reasons for this difference may be the power of suggestion. In Bexton, Heron, and Scott's studies, participants were unwittingly led to expect negative experiences, since they were given medical release forms to sign and "panic buttons" to push if they became too stressed. The negative results may have been furthered by the researchers' assumptions that deprivation was harmful. However, the results may also be due to a time factor. Whereas the McGill students experienced derivation for a long period of time, people in isolation tanks stay for only a few hours.

Despite the discrepancies in the effects of sensory deprivation, it has proven beneficial when applied to certain clinical situations involving problem behaviors. In recent years, many psychologists have used a sensory deprivation approach called *restricted environmental stimulation therapy* (REST) as a treatment for clients with phobias or motivational problems in overeating, smoking, or drinking (Suedfeld, 1975; Suedfeld and Baker-Brown, 1986). One of the most interesting applications of the REST technique is with autistic children. Autism is one of the most severe childhood psychological disorders.

It is generally characterized by self-imposed isolation, major language difficulties, intellectual impairment, insistence on sameness in the environment, and violent, self-destructive temper tantrums. The autistic child seems to withdraw into a private world and appears to have no need for affection or interaction with others. There is considerable debate over the cause and treatment of autism (see Chapter 15), but use of REST is based on the idea that autism may be the result of sensory overload. Autistic children may be unable to selectively reduce the normal bombardment of sensory stimuli. Acting on this assumption, many therapists have had some success in treating the violent temper tantrums and other maladaptive behaviors of autistic children with two or three days of sensory isolation (Suedfeld, 1977).

Another approach to treating autism has involved an input-control device called a phonic ear, which consists of a set of earphones connected to an FM radio and a wireless microphone that broadcasts to the radio (Smith et al., 1981). This device allows autistic children to select and control their own audio input. They simply adjust the volume and point the microphone toward any sound they wish to hear. The phonic ear has been enthusiastically received by autistic children, as well as by their parents and teachers. In some children, inappropriate behavior is dramatically reduced, while spontaneous speech is greatly increased. These benefits arise, it seems, merely because the child can now control the previous sensory overload. Thus, it appears that limited sensory deprivation can be beneficial for some people.

Sensory substitution: Natural and artificial compensation

Another interesting finding from deprivation research is that when sensory stimulation is blocked for only one sense, the body compensates by increasing the sensitivity in other senses. In a study by Bross, Harper, and Sicz (1980), the visual sensitivity of experimental subjects made artificially deaf first dropped and then rebounded to above starting levels. Researchers have also been successful in developing sensory substitution systems utilizing devices that substitute vibrations on the skin for other sensory impairments (Lechet, 1986).

Similar substitutions can be noted in the case of Helen Keller. Helen learned to "see" and "hear" with her sense of touch, and she often recognized visitors by their smell or by vibrations from their walk. Despite the heightened sensitivity of her functioning senses, however, Helen professed a lifelong yearning to experience a normal sensory world. She gave this advice to those whose senses are "normal":

> I who am blind can give one hint to those who see: use your eyes as if tomorrow you would be stricken blind. And the same method can be applied to the other senses. Hear the music of voices, the song of a bird, the mighty strains of an orchestra as if you would be stricken deaf tomorrow. Touch each object as if tomorrow your tactile sense would fail. Smell the perfume of flowers, taste with relish each morsel as if tomorrow you could never smell and taste again. Make the most of every sense, glory in all the facets of pleasure and beauty which the world reveals to you through the several means of contact which nature provides.
>
> *(1962, p. 23)*

Review Questions

1 The body senses include the _____ senses, the _____ sense, and the _____ sense.

2 There are four basic types of skin receptors: _____, _____, _____, and _____.

3 The _____ theory of pain suggests that pain-related information is let through to the brain when small, slow fibers are stimulated and is prevented from getting through when large, fast fibers are stimulated.

4 Endorphins are chemicals that _____ the pain gate, whereas substance P _____ the pain gate.

5 The _____ _____ in the inner ear provide the brain with information about the body's balance.

6 The sense responsible for providing the brain with information about bodily posture and orientation and bodily movement is _____.

7 Bexton, Heron, and Scott demonstrated that _____ _____ can lead to such adverse effects as hallucinations and an inability to focus attention.

Answers: 1 skin, vestibular, kinesthetic; *2* pressure, warmth, cold, pain; *3* gate-control; *4* close, opens; *5* semicircular canals; *6* kinesthesis; *7* sensory deprivation

---

REVIEW OF MAJOR CONCEPTS

EXPERIENCING SENSATION

1 Sensory processing includes reduction, transduction, and coding. The reticular activating system is responsible for much of the sensory reduction that takes place. Transduction, or the conversion of physical stimuli into neural impulses, occurs at the receptors in our sense organs. Each sensory modality is specialized to code its stimuli into unique sets of neural impulses that will eventually reach the brain and be perceived as light, touch, and so on.

2 Psychophysics is the study of the relationships between physical stimuli and the sensations they evoke, including the study of thresholds. The absolute threshold is the smallest magnitude of a stimulus we can detect. The difference threshold is the smallest change in a stimulus we can detect.

3 The process of sensory adaptation allows us to operate efficiently in a wide range of stimulus intensities by decreasing our sensitivity to constant, unchanging stimuli.

VISION

4 Light is a form of energy that is part of the electromagnetic spectrum. The wavelength of a light determines its hue, or color; the amplitude, or the height of a light wave, determines its intensity.

5 The function of the eye is to capture light and focus it on the visual receptors that convert light energy to neural impulses.

6 The major parts of the eye include the cornea, the clear bulge at the front of the eye where light enters; the sclera, the white outer covering of the eye; the pupil, the hole through which light passes into the eye; the iris, the colored set of muscles that surround the pupil; the lens, the elastic structure that bulges and stretches to focus an image on the retina; and the retina, the back part of the eye that contains the visual receptor cells.

7 The visual receptors, called photoreceptors, are the rods and cones. The rods are very sensitive to light and enable us to see at night. The cones are specialized for bright light conditions and enable us to see close and fine detail.

8 The major visual problems include myopia and hyperopia. Myopia occurs when the lens focuses the image in front of the retina, resulting in nearsightedness. Hyperopia occurs when the lens focuses the image in back of the retina, resulting in farsightedness.

HEARING

9 The sense of hearing is known as audition.

10 Sound waves result from rapid changes in air pressure caused by vibrating objects. The frequency of these sound waves is sensed as the pitch of the sound and is measured in cycles per second, whereas the amplitude of the waves is perceived as loudness and is measured in decibels.

11 The structures of the ear include the pinna, the external visible part of the ear; the eardrum, or tympanic membrane, that vibrates when hit by sound waves; the ossicles — the malleus, incus, and stapes — that transmit the sound vibrations through the middle ear; the oval window, the membrane separating the middle ear from the inner ear; and the cochlea, the structure that forms the inner ear. The major structures of the cochlea are the basilar membrane and the auditory receptor cells (hair cells).

SMELL AND TASTE

12 The sense of smell (olfaction) and the sense of taste (gustation) are called the chemical senses and are closely interrelated.

13 The receptors for olfaction are in the olfactory epithelium located at the top of the nasal cavity. According to the lock-and-key theory, we can smell diverse odors because each

three-dimensional odor molecule fits only into one type of receptor.

14 The receptors for taste are located on the tongue and throat. Taste receptors are sensitive to the four major tastes: salty, sweet, sour, and bitter.

THE BODY SENSES

15 The body senses include the skin senses, the vestibular sense, and the kinesthetic sense.

16 The skin senses, which include touch, temperature, pain, and pressure, not only protect the internal organs but also provide basic survival information.

17 The vestibular sense is the sense of body orientation and position with respect to gravity and three-dimensional space. The vestibular apparatus is located in the inner ear and is composed of two smaller sensory organs: the semicircular canals and the vestibular sacs.

18 The kinesthetic sense provides the brain with information about bodily posture and orientation, as well as bodily movement. The kinesthetic receptors are spread throughout the body in muscles, joints, and tendons.

SENSORY DEPRIVATION

19 Sensory deprivation is the restricting of incoming sensory information to the brain. This phenomenon has been studied by isolating people from external sensory stimulation.

20 Sensory substitution occurs when one sensory modality takes over for an impaired sensory modality.

SUGGESTED READINGS

GOLDSTEIN, E. B. (1984). *Sensation and perception* (2nd ed.). Belmont, CA: Wadsworth. An introduction to the study of sensation and perception.

GREGORY, R. L. (1977). *Eye and brain: The psychology of seeing* (3rd ed.). New York: World University Library. A wonderful book on the wonders of seeing.

chapter four
Perception

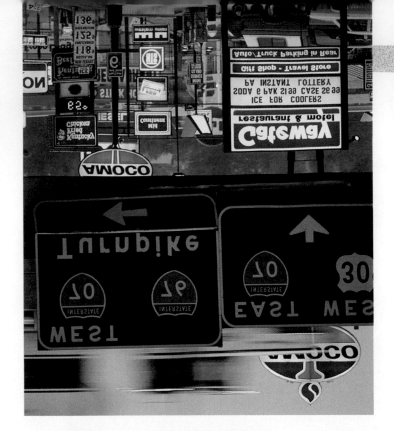

IF you were to put on some glasses that so inverted your world that it looked like the picture above, how do you think you would react? Do you think you could still walk? write a paper? ride a bike? take a shower? You would probably have a lot of trouble at first, but do you think you'd get used to it? Would you "adapt"?

Psychologist George Stratton (1896) purposefully wore a special lens over one eye and a patch over the other for eight days to answer just such questions. Whenever he removed the lens he covered both eyes. For the first few days, Stratton had a great deal of difficulty navigating in his environment and dealing with everyday problems and tasks. His arms and legs generally seemed to be in the wrong places and the world had an unreal feeling about it. But by the third day he noted:

Walking through the narrow spaces between pieces of furniture required much less care than hitherto. I could watch my hands as they wrote, without hesitating or becoming embarrassed thereby.

By the fifth day Stratton's adjustment to this strange perceptual environment was almost complete, and he could walk around his house with ease. When he removed the lens on the eighth day of his experience, he was surprised to find that his view of the world was somewhat perplexing, even though his vision had theoretically been restored to "normal." Stratton wrote:

. . . the scene had a strange familiarity. The visual arrangement was immediately recognized as the old one of pre-experimental days; yet the reversal of everything from the order to which I had grown accustomed during the last week gave the scene a surprising bewildering air which lasted for several hours. It was hardly the feeling, though, that things were upside down.

Stratton's experiment is considered a classic today because he demonstrated for the first time the crucial role of learning in perception. You can gain a sense of what Stratton experienced from the inverted photograph, which shows what you would see if your visual field were inverted, and from trying to read the following passage:

This is how a written text would have appeared to George Stratton when he was wearing his spectacles. Although it may be hard for you, you can probably read this appear. If you had been taught to read words upside down and backwards, this would appear normal.

With some difficulty, or by turning the book upside down and holding it up to a mirror, you can decipher the picture and decode the inverted passage. But can you interpret the following?

ジョージ・ストラットン氏が眼鏡を掛けていた時
文書が氏にはこんな風に見えたでしょう。たとえ
難しくても、おそらく読むことができます。もし文字を
さかさまや逆から読むように習えば、たぶんこれは、
普通と思われるでしょう。

Your success in understanding this passage depends on your experience with, or prior learning of, Japanese characters. If you could read Japanese, you would know that this passage says the same thing as the inverted English paragraph above. Without learning and experience, raw sensory data such as these Japanese characters are just meaningless jumbles of lines that cannot be *perceived* by the brain.

Question: What is the difference between sensation and perception? Sensation and perception are intimately related and difficult to separate, but there is a distinct difference. Figure 4.1 may help you to understand this difference. **Sensation** generally refers to the process of detecting and transducing raw sensory information, whereas **perception** refers to the process of selecting, organizing, and interpreting sensory data into a usable mental representation of the world. To better understand how perception differs from sensation, look at Figure 4.2. Do you see a downward curving spiral? Now try putting your finger on the outermost circle and tracing the "spiral" downward with your fingertips. If you do this carefully, you will discover that in fact there is no spiral, only concentric circles, one inside the other. Your senses have not lied — they have accurately reported the available information. The problem is in your perception of the sensory information. What you have just encountered is the first of many *illusions* that will be presented in this chapter.

Question: What is an illusion? An **illusion** is a false impression of the environment. Our perceptions are normally in agreement with our actual sensations. Occasionally, however, sensations and perceptions do not match and an illusion results. Illusions can be produced by actual physical distortion of stimuli, as is the case with a desert mirage caused by refracted light, or by distortions in the perceptual process, as in

SENSATION: *The process of detecting and transducing raw sensory information.*

PERCEPTION: *The process of selecting, organizing, and interpreting sensory data into usable mental representations of the world.*

ILLUSION: *A false impression of the environment.*

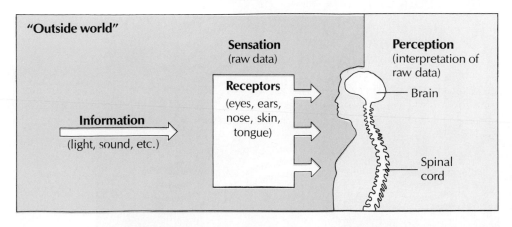

Figure 4.1 A drawing illustrating the difference between sensation and perception. Sensation is the entering of raw data from the senses into the brain. Perception involves the interpretation of that raw sensory data.

Figure 4.2 Is this a spiral or a series of concentric circles?

Highway guidelines appear much shorter to the driver than they actually are.

the spiral illusion (Figure 4.2) and an M. C. Escher print. Illusions offer psychologists an indirect method for studying the normal modes of perception. By studying how and where the perceptual system breaks down, researchers can obtain valuable information on perceptual processes.

Psychologists have also studied illusions that are found in everyday situations. For instance, we commonly misperceive the length of the dashed guidelines that separate the lanes on streets and highways as shorter than they actually are. Most people estimate that the lines are 2 to 5 feet long; in reality, they are longer than 10 feet, and some are as long as 18 feet (Harte, 1975). Information gained from this type of research can be applied to improving conditions in everyday life. In this case, the findings can be used to determine the best placement of safety features along our highways, such as the optimum height of lettering painted on roadways.

Most illusions you will encounter in this chapter will involve the visual sense. But you should remember that illusions do occur in all the senses. For an example of a touch illusion, try this: With the tip of your *retracted* ball-point pen, trace a letter or numeral on the palm of your hand as it faces you. Then turn your palm away from you and ask a friend

The art of M. C. Escher uses illusions to trick the brain and produce "impossible images."

to do the same tracing. If you are like many subjects, the second tracing will seem backward (Kaufman, 1980).

Whichever senses are involved, perception consists of three basic processes: (1) selection, in which we select which stimuli to focus on while disregarding the rest; (2) organization, in which we assemble selected sensations into usual patterns or shapes; and (3) interpretation, in which we attempt to explain the selected and organized sensations and to make reasonable judgments from them.

These three processes can be seen in the example of a major league baseball player, like Tony Gwynn or Don Mattingly, coming up to bat. The first thing he does is to *select* the sensory input: He directs his attention to the players on the field rather than the people in the stands and listens to the directions from his coach rather than to the cheers, boos, or other comments from the fans. As he takes his stance, he *organizes* his sensory input. He notes positions of the players on both teams and gaps in the opposing team's defense. As he gets ready to swing, he *interprets* the information he has selected and organized to judge where he should hit the ball and how hard he should swing.

In the rest of the chapter we will examine each of these stages in perception (selection, organization, and interpretation) and present a number of facts and theories to help explain how perception works and why people often differ in their view of the world.

SELECTION

The first step in perception is *selection,* in which we select the stimuli to which we will pay attention. Imagine that you are at a three-ring circus, with dancing bears and clowns in ring one, a troupe of high-wire trapeze artists in ring two, and a lion-taming act in ring three. With such an array of stimuli, how can you keep from being overwhelmed? In almost any situation there is an excess of sensory information, but the brain manages to sort out the important messages and discards the rest. This process is known as **selective attention.** While watching the circus, for example, you generally direct your attention to only one of the three rings at a time and ignore the others.

An interesting feature of selective attention is that while you are attending to a stimulus with one of your senses, you are particularly insensitive to other incoming stimuli acting on the same sense organ. For example, although you can listen to the friends sitting next to you while you're watching the clowns in ring one, you cannot watch both the clowns in ring one and the trapeze artist in ring two. It seems that the mental processes involved in perception work fairly well when two different kinds of sensory information are involved. However, processing is impaired when messages come through on the same sensory channel.

Question: Why does the brain decide to pay attention to some sensory stimuli but not to others? There are three major factors involved in this selection decision: physiological factors, stimulus factors, and psychological factors.

Physiological factors: Biological influences on selection

One of the major physiological factors in selection is the presence of specialized cells in the brain called **feature detectors** (or feature analyzers) that respond only to certain sensory information. In 1959 researchers discovered there are specialized nerve cells, which they called "bug detectors," in the optic nerve of the frog that responded only to moving bugs (Lettvin et al., 1959). In the early 1960s, David Hubel and Torsten Wiesel, in studies of the visual system of cats, found feature detectors that respond to specific lines and angles in the visual field (Hubel, 1963; Hubel and Wiesel, 1965). In addition to these specialized cells that select for visual movement and patterns, cells have also been found in the auditory area of animal brains that respond to different and changing pitches of sound (Whitfield and Evans, 1965).

Tony Gwynn is selecting, organizing, and interpreting information about the baseball that is approaching him at faster than 90 miles per hour.

SELECTIVE ATTENTION: *The process whereby the brain manages to sort out and attend only to the important messages from the senses.*

FEATURE DETECTORS: *Specialized cells in the brain that respond only to certain sensory information.*

Although the basic mechanisms for perceptual selection are built into the brain, a certain amount of interaction with the environment is apparently necessary for these cells to develop normally. In one well-known study it was found that early visual deprivation can lead to permanent degeneration of the retina in chimpanzees (Riesen, 1950). Another study demonstrated that kittens raised in a cylinder with walls consisting of vertical or horizontal stripes develop severe behavioral and neurological impairments (Blakemore and Cooper, 1970). When "horizontal cats" — those cats raised with only horizontal lines in their environment — were removed from the cylinder and allowed to roam, they could easily jump onto horizontal surfaces but had great difficulty in negotiating objects with vertical lines, such as chair legs. The reverse was true for the "vertical cats": They could easily avoid table and chair legs but never attempted to jump onto horizontal structures. Examination of the visual cortex of these cats revealed that, because of their restricted environment, they had failed to develop their potential feature detectors for either vertical or horizontal lines and angles. Unlike these cats, however, George Stratton was able to adjust to his new environment because, during development, his brain had been organized along principles that applied to both his normal and his distorted environments.

Visual deprivation research has several practical applications. For one thing, it gives scientific backing to the idea, long advocated by both pediatricians and psychologists, that infants need a certain amount of sensory stimulation even in the earliest days of life. Furthermore, such research suggests that certain childhood visual defects, such as squinting or astigmatism, must be corrected early in life. If they are not dealt with until later, they may not be correctable, since the perceptual "wiring" within the brain will be at fault, not the sensory processes in the eye.

HABITUATION: *The tendency of the brain to ignore environmental factors that remain constant.*

An additional physiological factor important in selecting sensory data is **habituation,** the tendency to ignore environmental factors that remain constant. The brain seems "prewired" to pay more attention to *changes* in the environment than to stimuli that remain constant. Have you ever noticed that when you first get a new car, you hear every squeak or rattle it makes? After driving it for a short time, however, you become so accustomed to its sounds that you pay attention only to unusual or changing noises. This happens because you have *habituated* to the original sounds of the car.

Question: Is habituation the same as sensory adaptation?   No. As you may remember from Chapter 3, sensory receptors respond to a constant stimulus by slowing down their firing rates. This process is called *adaptation.* When this same type of adaptive process occurs at the level of the brain — when the brain "decides" not to pay attention to the constant stimulus — it is called *habituation.* To illustrate the difference between these two processes, picture yourself walking into a room full of people smoking. The smell of smoke is overwhelming at first but your smell receptors will *adapt* to the smell after you have been in the room for awhile. Conversely, you will not adapt to the smoke burning your eyes and hindering your breathing; but if you become engrossed in some hot topic of conversation, your brain will ignore the discomfort caused by the smoke — you will habituate to it.

In October 1985, the American Cancer Society, the American Lung Association, and the American Heart Association joined forces in launching a large-scale media advertising program. Aware of the effects of habituation, they began changing their message every three months. One message emphasizes the harmful effects of carbon monoxide in cigarette smoke. Another warns that people who smoke are at risk for serious disease. Still another cautions that smoking during pregnancy may be detrimental to the fetus. As people become habituated to one warning, it is replaced with a new one that will attract attention.

Stimulus factors: Environmental influences on selection

When given a wide variety of stimuli to choose from, we will automatically select stimuli that are intense, novel, moving, contrasting, or repetitious. Parents and teachers often use these attention-getting principles, but advertisers have developed them to a fine art. Have you ever noticed how commercials seem so much louder and brighter than the preceding program? Or how talking tigers, space creatures, and dancing cats are used to sell products because of their novelty effects? Repetition, of course, has been so overused as an advertising technique that it often makes us feel like throwing things at our TV sets.

Question: Doesn't this type of obnoxious advertising make us less likely to buy these products?   Advertisers are well aware of the potential for irritating their audience, but they have found that the single most important factor in sales is getting people's attention. For sheer volume of sales, the question of whether you *like* a product or company isn't nearly as important as whether you *notice* the product.

Psychological factors: Intrapsychic influences on selection

In addition to physiological and stimulus factors, certain psychological characteristics are important in explaining why you attend to some stimuli and not to others. Motivation and personal needs are two of these factors. What you choose to see or hear or perceive is determined largely by your current level of satisfaction or deprivation. For example, when you are hungry, you are much more likely to notice television commercials for doughnuts, hamburgers, or pizza than those for cars or detergent. In a similar way, you'll find that when you're lonely, your perceptions will be so affected that it will seem that everyone is part of a happy couple except you.

In addition to the strong influence of needs and motivations on perceptual selection, personality and interests play a role. At a typical college football game, for example, an ex-quarterback may be paying close attention to plays being called on the field, while his wife, a musician, may be listening to the band, and a broadcasting major sitting next to them may be focusing on the announcer's vocal qualities.

Question: Isn't it possible to perceive something without paying attention to it, such as perceiving hidden advertising messages and backward messages on records?   There has been quite a lot of research conducted on the effectiveness of **subliminal** messages in advertising (messages that are below the threshold of our conscious awareness) and backward messages on records. Even though research has not shown any support for this phenomenon, many people believe that subliminal advertising does somehow gain our attention and "make" us do things without our being aware of it (Zanot et al., 1983). One researcher who believes this is Lloyd Silverman (1980; Silverman and Lachmann, 1985), who has proposed that subliminal messages can be perceived by the unconscious mind, where they can affect personality and behavior.

Whether or not the unconscious mind can really perceive these messages, it is clear from the research that they have little or no influence on consumer behavior. In 1956 managers of a New Jersey theater allegedly inserted the messages "Drink Coca-Cola" and "Hungry? Eat popcorn" on the screen every five seconds. They flashed the messages so fast that people were unable to "see" them, but the managers claimed that their sales of Coke and popcorn increased. This claim was never supported by any data, and subsequent research has been unable to document any significant change in buying behavior (Moore, 1982).

Some people have also been concerned that messages recorded backward on popular records are being used to encourage immoral or aberrant behavior in unsuspecting listeners. This backward recording, known as "backmasking," has been extensively investigated by John Vokey and Don Read (1985) across a wide variety of different tasks. They have been unable to find any evidence that backmasking affects behavior in any way. The fact that people sometimes claim to hear messages when a record is played backward

Don't Smoke Yourself To Death.

GIVE SMOKING A KICK IN THE BUTT.

With every puff, your health could be going up in smoke. If you'd like to kick the habit but you need help, call your local American Cancer Society office. It could be the first step to quitting for life.

Examples of antismoking ads produced by the American Cancer Society. These ads change every three months to combat habituation.

SUBLIMINAL: *Pertaining to any stimulus presented below the threshold of conscious awareness.*

is understandable, since most of us can also see animals and other shapes in clouds. However, Vokey and Read's research shows that even if there are messages, they have *no* effect on behavior when played backward, because of the simple fact that they are impossible to understand at either a conscious or unconscious level.

Review Questions

1 The process of selecting, organizing, and interpreting raw sensory data is called _____.

2 A(n) _____ is a false impression of the environment caused by the physical distortion of a stimulus or by an error in the perceptual process.

3 The three basic processes of perception are: _____, _____, and _____.

4 The process that allows us to sort out the important sensory information from the unimportant is _____ _____.

5 Specialized cells in the brain called _____ _____ respond only to certain types of sensory information.

6 _____ occurs when we stop noticing things in our environment that never change.

Answers: 1 perception; *2* illusion; *3* selection, organization, interpretation; *4* selective attention; *5* feature detectors; *6* habituation

ORGANIZATION

Once we have completed our selection of incoming information, we must organize this information into patterns or principles that will help us to understand the world. Raw sensory data are like the parts of a watch — they must be assembled in a meaningful way before they are useful. The *organization* of sensory data can be divided into five areas: form perception, perceptual constancies, depth perception, color perception, and motion perception.

Form perception: Organizing stimuli into patterns or shapes

GESTALT: *A German word meaning "whole" or "pattern".*

Gestalt psychologists were among the first to study how sensory impressions are organized by the brain. The German word **gestalt** means "whole" or "pattern." Accordingly, Gestaltists emphasized the importance of organization and patterning in enabling us to perceive the *whole* stimulus rather than perceiving its discrete parts as separate entities. The Gestaltists proposed a set of laws of organization that specify how people perceive form. These basic laws are summarized in Figure 4.3. Although these examples are all visual, each law applies to other modes of perception as well.

FIGURE AND GROUND: *A Gestalt law of perceptual organization stating that our perceptions consist of two aspects: the figure, which stands out and has a definite contour or shape, and the ground, which is more indistinct.*

The most fundamental Gestalt principle or law of organization is that we tend to distinguish between **figure and ground.** For example, while reading this material your eyes are receiving sensations of black lines and white paper, but your brain is organizing these sensations into letters and words that are perceived against a backdrop of white pages. The letters constitute the figure and the pages, the ground. The discrepancy between figure and ground is sometimes so vague that we have difficulty in perceiving which is which, as can be seen in the photograph on p. 125 at the end of this chapter. This

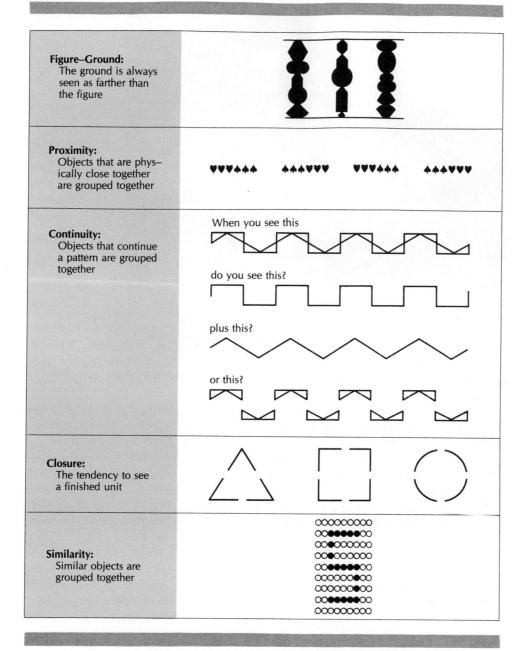

Examples 4.3 Examples of some basic Gestalt principles.

is known as a **reversible figure**. It is also possible to "see" a figure and background where none actually exist. The figure–ground principle is the basis for explaining why people wear makeup. Makeup highlights the figures of the face, making the eyebrows, eyes, cheeks, and lips stand out against the background of the skin. This principle also illustrates why camouflage works. The similarity between the color and/or shape of the figure and its background makes the contour of the figure nearly indistinguishable — hence the difficulty in distinguishing such figures as tigers from their natural surroundings. Since camouflage often depends on color blending, many "color-blind" soldiers were employed during World War II to detect camouflaged enemy targets (color blindness will be discussed later in this chapter).

According to the principle of **proximity**, elements that are physically close together will be grouped together and perceived as a single unit. Most young children in the United

REVERSIBLE FIGURE: *An ambiguous figure that has more than one possible figure and ground organization.*

PROXIMITY: *The Gestalt principle proposing that elements that are physically close together will be grouped together and perceived as a single unit.*

This M. C. Escher print illustrates the Gestalt principle of figure and ground. You can see each form either as figure or as ground.

States initially learn their alphabet through singing it to the tune of "Twinkle, Twinkle, Little Star." The principle of proximity can be used to explain why these children often conclude that L, M, N, O, and P are one letter, since in the song those letters are sung as a phrase and sound like the name of one letter, LMNOP.

According to the principle of **continuity**, patterns or objects that continue in one direction, even if interrupted by another pattern, are perceived as being grouped together. Thus, the contour of distant hills will be perceived as being continuous even though interrupted by intervening trees and buildings. Sounds heard on the radio will be perceived as part of the same song even if horns honking and blaring street noises interrupt them occasionally. The similar principle of **closure** proposes that we have a tendency to perceive a finished or whole unit even if there are gaps in it. Therefore, when the outside noises blot out some of the words of the song on the radio, you can generally fill in missing words via the principle of closure.

Many other principles of organization cannot be shown here because they involve sensations other than vision. An example is the law of **contiguity**, which states that when two events happen at a time and place near to each other, one is perceived as causing the other. Suppose a three-year-old playing in her father's used-car office observes that every time her dog barks, a customer walks in. She could very well conclude that the barking dog *causes* the customer to come into the office.

Gestalt principles also apply to perceptions involving other people. For example, blacks, women, senior citizens, and Mexican Americans are often thought of and treated as members of a group rather than as individuals — the **similarity** principle at work. In the same way, the figure–ground principle can be used to explain why a white person will stand out in an all-black group. And the proximity principle suggests that we tend to make judgments about others on the basis of the company they keep. Thus, the rules for organizing stimuli can also help us to understand areas of human behavior other than the physical modes of perception (see Chapters 17 and 18).

Perceptual constancies: Stabilizing a changing world

Although we are particularly alert to changes in our sensory input, we also manage to perceive a great deal of consistency in the environment, thanks to the principle of perceptual **constancy**. Although the visual sensory input of George Stratton was drastically altered by his inverting lens, his world was not completely foreign to him since, through prior experience, he had learned certain consistencies that transferred to his

CONTINUITY: *The Gestalt principle proposing that patterns or objects that continue in one direction, even if interrupted by another pattern, tend to be perceived as being grouped together.*
CLOSURE: *The Gestalt principle proposing that people have a tendency to perceive a finished unit even if there are gaps in it.*

CONTIGUITY: *The Gestalt principle stating that when two events happen at a time and place near to each other, one is perceived as causing the other.*

SIMILARITY: *The Gestalt principle proposing that things that appear similar or act in a similar fashion are perceived as being the same.*

CONSTANCY: *The tendency for the environment to be perceived as remaining the same even with changes in sensory input.*

newly distorted world. Without perceptual constancies, our world would seem totally chaotic. Things would seem to grow as we got closer to them, to change shape as our viewing angle changed, and to change color as light levels changed.

Size constancy   Most perceptual constancies are based on prior experience and learning. For example, preschoolers express wonder at the fact that the car parked down the street is only "this high" (as they show about two inches between their fingers), while the car they are standing next to is taller than they are. Their size judgment is mistaken because they haven't yet had the experiences necessary for learning **size constancy.** According to this principle, the perceived size of an object remains the same even though the size of its retinal image changes. Research shows that adults consistently outperform young children in tasks involving size constancy. But when children reach about age six or seven they have had enough experience with relative sizes that their size judgments remain constant with varying distances and their size constancy skills match those of adults (Teghtsoonian and Beckwith, 1976).

SIZE CONSTANCY: *The process in which the perceived size of an object remains the same, even though the size of the retinal image changes.*

A famous example of an adult who had never acquired size constancy was provided by anthropologist Colin Turnbull (1961). While he was studying pygmies living in the dense rain forest of the Congo River Valley in Africa, Turnbull once took a native named Kenge for a jeep ride to the African plains. Kenge had lived his entire life in an area so dense with foliage that he had never seen distances further than about 100 yards. Now he was suddenly able to see for almost 70 miles. Lacking perceptual experience with such wide open spaces, Kenge had great difficulty judging sizes. When he first saw a herd of water buffalo in the distance, he thought they were insects. When Turnbull insisted they were buffalo that were very far away, Kenge seemed insulted and asked, "Do you think that I am ignorant?" To Kenge's surprise, as they drove toward the "insects" the creatures seemed to grow into buffalo. He concluded that witchcraft was being used to fool him, and after Turnbull showed him a lake so large that its opposite shore couldn't be seen, he asked to be taken back to his rain forest.

Shape constancy   Other constancies also develop through individual experience. When you look at a chair directly from the front or the back, it has a rectangular shape. When you look at it directly from the side, it has an "h" shape. Yet you still perceive the chair as having a single shape because your brain remembers past experiences with objects that only *seemed* to change shape as you moved but actually remained constant. This is known as **shape constancy.** Without shape and size constancy, a romantic kiss would become a nightmare as your partner's nose and eyes grew larger and more prominent as he or she approached you.

SHAPE CONSTANCY: *The process in which the perceived shape of an object remains the same, even though the retinal image of that object changes.*

A perceptual psychologist named Adelbert Ames demonstrated the power of shape and size constancies by creating what is now known as the *Ames room* (see the photograph on p. 110). After examining this photograph, your first impression might be that the person on the left is a midget and the person on the right is a giant. In actuality, both people are of normal size. This illusion is based on the unusual construction of the room. As can be seen in the diagram in Figure 4.4, linear perspective is used to trick the observer into perceiving the room as square when it is actually shaped like a trapezoid. This illusion is so strong that when a person walks from the left corner to the right, the observer perceives the person to be "growing," even though that is not possible.

Question: If we know the truth of this illusion, why does it still work?   Our brain has had a lifetime of interaction with normally constructed rooms, and our desire to perceive the room according to our experience is so powerful that we overrule common "truth." This is not a breakdown in perception but rather a result of trying to apply the standard perceptual processes of shape and size constancy to an unusual situation. You *can* learn not to see such illusions, but this normally takes lots of practice and experience in the distorted environment. Although Stratton was not having to overcome illusions of constancy, he did have to adjust to a distorted environment, which he accomplished only after wearing the lens for several days. Similarly, divers wearing masks underwater

The Ames room illusion. The boy on the right is seen as much taller than the woman on the left, when actually she is taller.

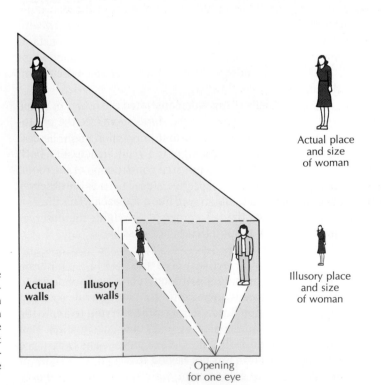

Actual place and size of woman

Illusory place and size of woman

Actual place and size of boy

Actual walls   **Illusory walls**

Opening for one eye

Figure 4.4 An explanation for the Ames room illusion. This drawing illustrates why the boy in the bottom photo above appears to be taller than the woman. We assume that both the boy and the woman are equidistant from the front wall. In actuality, however, the woman is standing quite some distance away.

experience severe distortions of their normal visual fields, yet they can learn to adapt to these distortions, given enough practice (Vernoy and Luria, 1977).

Color and brightness constancy   A third form of constancy that adds stability to our world is **color** and **brightness constancy.** This enables us to perceive things as retaining the same color or brightness level even though the amount of light may vary. For example, if you place a piece of gray paper in bright sunlight and a piece of white paper in shade, you will still perceive the white as lighter and the gray as darker. This is true regardless of the amount of reflected light actually coming from their surfaces. As is the case with shape and size constancy, color constancy is the result of learning and experience and occurs primarily with familiar objects. If an object is unfamiliar, its color will be determined by the *actual* wavelength of reflected light — it will not be affected by prior experience with the object.

COLOR CONSTANCY: *The tendency for the color of objects to be perceived as remaining the same even when illumination varies.*

BRIGHTNESS CONSTANCY: *The phenomenon in which objects tend to maintain their appropriate brightness, even when illumination varies.*

Review Questions

1 The distinction between _____ and _____ is the most fundamental Gestalt principle of organization.

2 The Gestalt principle of _____ asserts that elements that are physically close together will be perceived as a single unit.

3 The Gestalt law of _____ states that when two events happen at a time and place near each other, one is perceived as causing the other.

4 Without _____ _____ , the world would seem totally chaotic.

5 The principle of _____ _____ is at work when, as your brother walks away from you, you don't perceive him to be shrinking.

6 _____ _____ allows us to see a white blouse as equally bright in sunlight and in shade.

Answers: 1 figure, ground;   *2* proximity;   *3* contiguity;   *4* perceptual constancy;   *5* size constancy;   *6* brightness constancy.

Depth peception: Seeing the world as three dimensional

Evidence for the role of experience and learning in the organization of perceptions is particularly clear in the case of **depth perception,** or the ability to see the world in three dimensions. Take the example of a patient known as S.B., blind since the age of 10 months, whose sight was restored at the age of 52. Following the operation that removed cataracts from both eyes, S.B. had great difficulty learning to use his newly acquired vision for judging distance and depth. On one occasion, he was found trying to crawl out of the window of his hospital room. He thought he would be able to lower himself by his hands to the ground below, even though the window was on the fourth floor.

DEPTH PERCEPTION: *The ability to see the world in three dimensions.*

Question: Didn't S.B. have some inborn depth and distance perception?   The answer is not clear. The question of innate depth perception has been the subject of general debate for many years, with the *nativists* arguing that depth perception is inborn and the *empiricists* insisting that it is learned. As is often the case, most psychologists have concluded that there is truth in both viewpoints.

Evidence for the innate position comes from a set of interesting experiments with an apparatus called the *visual cliff,* which can be seen in the photograph on p. 112. The apparatus consists of a table top with a slightly raised platform across the middle. On one side of the platform the table top is clear glass, with a black-and-red-checked pattern running down the side of the table and onto the floor several feet below the glass,

The visual cliff. Once children can crawl, they will refuse to cross the "deep" side even to get to their parent.

simulating a steep cliff. The other side of the table top has the checked pattern directly on it. When an infant is placed on the platform and is coaxed by his or her mother to crawl to one side of the table, the infant will readily move to the "shallow"' side but will hesitate or refuse to move to the "deep" side (Gibson and Walk, 1960). This reaction is given as evidence of innate depth perception—the infant's hesitation is attributed to fear of the apparent cliff.

The empiricists argue, however, that by the time infants are crawling and old enough to be tested, they may have *learned* to perceive depth. Nevertheless, similar research with baby chickens, goats, and lambs—animals that walk almost immediately after birth—supports the hypothesis that some depth perception is inborn, since these animals hesitate in stepping onto the steep side. The question is further complicated by still more research. In two separate studies, infants as young as two months of age have been lowered face-down on both the deep and shallow sides of the visual cliff. In a study done by Campos, et al. (1978), the infants showed a change in heart rate only when lowered on the deep side, whereas a study done by Campos, et al. (1982) generated conflicting results.

Although the nativist versus empiricist debate remains unsettled, there is general agreement that in our three-dimensional world, the ability to perceive depth and distance is essential. But how do we perceive a three-dimensional world with a two-dimensional receptor system? Although the rods and cones do not respond to depth and distance, we have at least two other mechanisms that provide depth cues. One mechanism is the interaction of both eyes to produce *binocular* depth cues; the other involves *monocular* depth cues, which work with each eye separately.

Binocular cues   One of the most important cues to depth and distance perception comes from **retinal disparity**. Because of the separation of the two eyes, each retina receives a slightly different view of the world. You can demonstrate this for yourself by pointing at some distant object across the room with your arm extended straight in front of you. Holding your pointing finger steady, close your left eye and then your right. You will

RETINAL DISPARITY: *A binocular cue to distance in which the separation of the eyes causes different images to fall on each retina.*

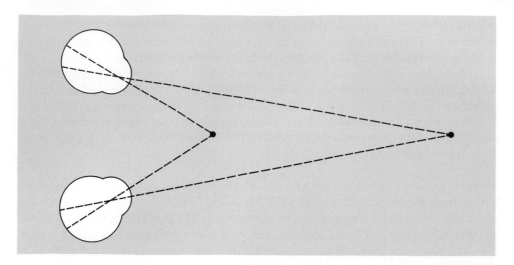

Figure 4.5 Through the process of retinal disparity, objects at different distances will project their images on different parts of the retina. Far objects project on the retinal area near the nose, whereas near objects project farther out, closer to the ears.

notice that your finger will seem to jump around in relation to the rest of the room as you change eyes, because of retinal disparity (Kaufman, 1974).

The brain fuses the different images received by the two eyes into one overall visual image, and a powerful and accurate sensation of depth occurs (see Figure 4.5). Such **stereoscopic vision** offers a distinct physical advantage over animals that have only monocular cues for depth. Animals such as horses, deer, and fish have two eyes, but the eyes are set on each side of their heads, enabling them to have nearly a 360° field of view. This broad view gives them a better chance of detecting predators. Their predators, on the other hand, have eyes set in the front of their heads, like ours, and can use their ability to judge depth for distinguishing their prey from surrounding camouflage.

As we move closer and closer to an object, another binocular cue helps us judge depth and distance. The closer the object, the more our eyes are turned inward, toward our noses (see Figure 4.6). You can try this for yourself: Hold your index finger at arm's

STEREOSCOPIC VISION: *Three-dimensional vision that is due to overlapping views of the eyes.*

(a)

(b)

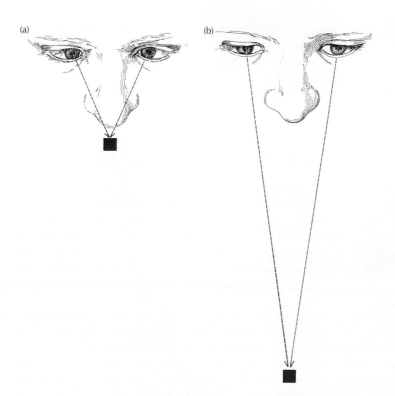

Figure 4.6 Convergence. Your eyes turn in to view close objects *(a)* and turn out to view distant objects *(b)*.

length in front of you and watch it as you bring it closer and closer until it is right in front of your nose. The amount of muscular strain in your eyeball created by this **convergence**, or turning inward, is used as a cue by your brain to interpret distance.

A recent study of how convergence operates might help you improve your performance in athletic endeavors. Allen Souchek (1986) found that depth perception is better when looking directly at an object, rather than out of the corner of your eye. Thus, if you turn your body or your head so that you look straight at your tennis opponent or at a pitcher, you will be more accurate in judging the distance of the ball and thereby more likely to swing at the right time.

Monocular cues　Retinal disparity and convergence are inadequate in judging distances farther than the length of a football field. According to R. L. Gregory (1969), ''we are effectively one-eyed for distances greater than perhaps 100 meters'' (p. 67). Luckily, we can take advantage of several additional cues for distance and depth that do not require two eyes. Known as *monocular cues,* they are available separately to each eye. Many of them can be used to depict our three-dimensional world on a two-dimensional page and are used extensively by artists to create an illusion of depth on a flat canvas. These cues, illustrated in Figure 4.7, include:

Figure 4.7 Monocular depth cues. *(a)* Perspective. *(b)* Interposition. *(c)* Relative size. *(d)* Texture gradient.

(a) Perspective

(b) Interposition

(c) Relative size

(d) Texture gradient

1. *Linear perspective.* As two parallel lines recede away from us, they appear to come together at the horizon. Any time you have a long, unobscured view of a street, a tall building, railroad tracks, or anything that is delineated by two parallel lines, you experience this cue — see Figure 4.7a. An interesting illusion based on this principle is the Ponzo illusion shown in Figure 4.8.

2. *Aerial perspective.* Objects that are far away look "fuzzy" and blurred in comparison to near objects because of intervening particles of dust, haze, or smoke in the atmosphere. This becomes noticeable when there is an absence of haze or smog: On a really clear day, we are often startled at the seeming nearness of skyscrapers, silos, or mountains that normally appear far away.

3. *Texture gradients.* Close objects appear to have a rough or detailed texture; as distance increases, the texture appears to become finer and finer — see Figure 4.7d. You may have noticed this effect when driving on a gravel road: The road in the distance looks much smoother than the road directly in front of you.

4. *Interposition.* An object that partially obscures another is perceived as being closer — see Figure 4.7b.

5. *Relative size.* Objects that are far away look smaller than close objects of the same size — see Figure 4.7c. This principle is exploited by the Ames room illusion.

6. *Light and shadow.* Brighter objects are perceived as closer, whereas darker, dimmer objects are perceived as farther away. The variations in light produced by irregular surfaces also give cues for depth and distance as well as for shapes of objects (Ramachandran, 1988).

Two additional monocular cues — ones that cannot be used by artists — are accommodation of the lens of the eye and motion parallax. As you may remember from the previous chapter, **accommodation** refers to changes in the shape of the lens of the eye in response to the distance of the object being focused. For near objects the lens bulges, for far objects it flattens. Information from the muscles that move the lens is sent to the brain, which interprets the signal and perceives the distance of the object. **Motion parallax** (also known as relative motion) refers to the fact that when an observer is moving, objects at various distances move at different speeds across the retinal field. Close objects appear to whiz by, farther objects appear to move past slowly, and very distant objects appear to remain stationary. This effect can easily be seen when traveling by car or train, as telephone poles and fences next to the road or track seem to move by very rapidly, houses and trees in the midground seem to move by relatively slowly, and the mountains in the distance seem not to move at all.

One of the most interesting everyday experiences that result from inappropriate use of these monocular cues is the distortion in perception known as the *moon illusion*

LINEAR PERSPECTIVE: *The principle that as parallel lines recede, they appear to come together at the horizon.*

AERIAL PERSPECTIVE: *A monocular depth cue based on the fact that more distant objects appear less distinct than closer objects because of dust or haze in the air.*

TEXTURE GRADIENTS: *Monocular cue to distance based on the fact that texture changes from coarse to fine as the distance of an object increases.*

INTERPOSITION: *A monocular depth cue in which the object that partially obscures another object is seen as closer.*

RELATIVE SIZE: *A monocular cue to distance in which smaller objects appear more distant than larger objects.*

LIGHT AND SHADOW: *A monocular depth cue in which brighter objects are perceived as closer, whereas darker, dimmer objects are perceived as farther away.*

ACCOMMODATION: *A change in the shape of the lens to focus on near or far objects.*

MOTION PARALLAX: *A monocular depth cue that occurs when a moving observer perceives that objects at various distances move at different speeds across the retinal field.*

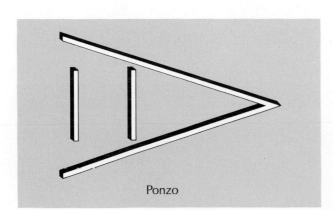

Ponzo

Figure 4.8 The Ponzo illusion. The vertical line at the right is seen as being farther away and therefore longer than the vertical line at the left. This is due to the linear perspective created by the converging lines.

The moon illusion. The moon appears larger on the horizon because of the many cues to distance.

(Baird, 1982; Baird and Wagner, 1982). Perhaps you've noticed that a full moon can look truly gigantic when seen on the horizon but tiny by comparison when at its zenith, straight overhead. Nevertheless, the moon's physical distance from the earth and the size of its image remain constant.

Question: Why, then, does the moon look larger on the horizon?   When we look at the moon on the horizon, we use the monocular depth cue interposition in judging that intervening objects, such as houses, trees, and hills, are rather close, as compared to the moon, which we perceive as very far away. Because the moon seems so far away, our brain assumes that it must be quite large. The zenith moon has no accompanying depth cues, so we do not perceive it as being as far away and thus, we do not judge it to be as large. You can demonstrate this difference for yourself by looking at a horizon moon through a rolled-up paper tube — the moon will "shrink" when observed without its accompanying depth cues.

Distance and depth cues can also be used to explain certain visual illusions known as impossible figures (see Figure 4.9). In these instances, we initially perceive the figures as real objects, but as we examine them, we realize that they can't really exist. Can you explain these impossible figures in terms of the cues we've just explored?

Color perception: Discriminating among hues

We humans are able to discriminate among literally hundreds of different hues. Such color perception seems to be inborn: Studies of infants old enough to focus and move their eyes have shown that they are able to see color nearly as well as adults (Teller, Peeples, and Sekel, 1978; Werner and Wooten, 1979). So, practically from the moment of

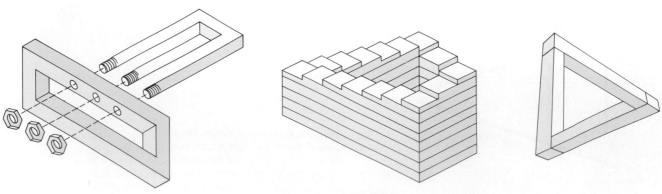

Figure 4.9 Some examples of impossible figures.

116

birth, we are able to see a world rich in greens and oranges, blues and red, yellows and purples.

As mentioned in Chapter 3, color is produced by different wavelengths of light, ranging from the short wavelengths of purple and blue to the long wavelengths of orange and red. The actual way in which we perceive color has been a matter of scientific debate for over a hundred years. Traditionally, there have been two theories of color vision, the trichromatic (three-color) theory and the opponent-process theory. The **trichromatic theory** was first proposed by Thomas Young in the early nineteenth century and was later refined by Hermann von Helmholtz and others. It states that there are three "color systems," as they called them — one system that is maximally sensitive to blue, another maximally sensitive to green, and another maximally sensitive to red (Young, 1802). The proponents of this theory demonstrated that mixing lights of these three colors could yield the full spectrum of colors we perceive. A major flaw associated with this theory, however, was that it did not account for color blindness or color weakness, the inability to see certain colors.

The **opponent-process theory,** proposed by Ewald Hering in the nineteenth century, also claims that there are three color systems but that each is sensitive to two opposing colors — blue and yellow, red and green, black and white — in an "on–off" fashion. In other words, each color receptor responds to either blue *or* yellow, red *or* green, with the black and white system responding to differences in brightness levels. This theory makes a lot of sense, since when different colored lights are combined, people are unable to see reddish greens and bluish yellows; in fact, when red and green lights or blue and yellow lights are mixed in equal amounts, we see white.

This theory accounts for the phenomenon of **color aftereffects,** images that are perceived after staring at a particular colored pattern for a period of time. To experience this effect, look at Figure 4.10. After staring at it for several minutes, look at a plain sheet of white paper. You will perceive color aftereffects — red in place of green, blue in place of yellow, and so on. The opponent-process theory also adequately explains color vision defects, since most people who have a color weakness are unable to see *either* red and green *or* blue and yellow. Have you ever tested yourself to see if you're color blind? Try it. Figure 4.11 consists of a color vision test.

Question: It sounds like the opponent-process theory is the correct one. Is this right? Actually, both theories are correct. In 1964, George Wald demonstrated that there are indeed three different types of cones in the retina, each with its own type of photopigment. One type of pigment is sensitive to blue light, one is sensitive to green light, and the third is sensitive to red light (see Figure 4.12). At nearly the same time that Wald was doing his research on cones, R. L. DeValois (1965) was doing electrophysio-

TRICHROMATIC THEORY: *The theory of color vision first proposed by Thomas Young stating that there are three color systems — red, green, and blue.*

OPPONENT-PROCESS THEORY: *The theory of color vision first proposed by Ewald Hering that claims that there are three color systems — blue–yellow, red–green, and black–white.*

COLOR AFTEREFFECTS: *Color images that are seen after staring at a particular colored pattern for a long time.*

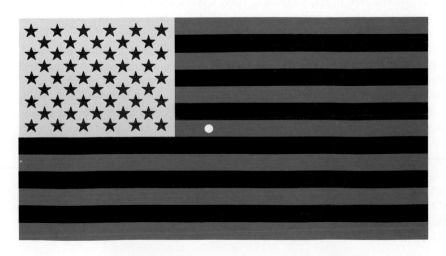

Figure 4.10 Color aftereffect. Stare at the center of this color-distorted American flag for a minute or more. Then look at a white sheet of paper to see a color aftereffect of a "genuine" American flag.

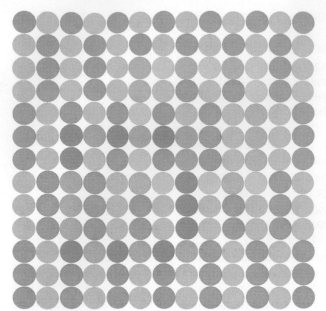

Figure 4.11 Color vision test. People with normal color vision see two squares, with the green square being clearer. People with red–green color weakness see only the green square; people with blue–yellow color weakness see only the blue square.

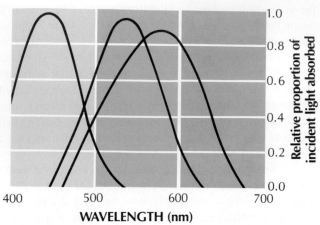

Figure 4.12 The three types of cones in the human retina absorb different wavelengths of light.

logical recording of cells in the optic nerve and optic pathways to the brain. DeValois discovered cells that responded to color in an *opponent* fashion in the thalamus. Thus, it appears that the two theories have been correct all along. Color is processed in a trichromatic fashion at the level of the retina (in the cones) and in an opponent fashion at the level of the optic nerve and the thalamus (in the brain).

Question: You mentioned that we see white light when blue and yellow lights are mixed—why is this? Shouldn't we see green? When blue and yellow paint pigments are mixed together, they do indeed produce the color green. However, mixing lights is different from mixing pigments. The reason we perceive the red from a red stop light is that a long wavelength of light (red light) is projected into our eyes. On the other hand, the reason we perceive the red from a stop sign is that the pigments in the red paint absorb all colors except red, which is reflected into our eyes. So we see colored light by an *additive* process because our visual system adds the colors together. We see colored pigments by a *subtractive* process because some colors are reflected and others are subtracted, or absorbed, by the object.

Question: What causes color blindness? People who are totally *color-blind,* known as **monochromats** (meaning "one color"), have just rods and no cones, and can therefore see things only in black and white and shades of gray. What they see is similar to what we see when we are watching a black-and-white television show. Monochromats are rare; much more common are people with a *color weakness.* Known as **dichromats** (meaning "two colors"), these people are missing one type of cone pigment and thus are either unable to distinguish red and green or, less commonly, blue and yellow (Nathans et al., 1986; Nathans et al., 1986). Because people with a color weakness are unable to distinguish between certain colors by using wavelength (hue) information, they must rely on brightness information. For example, a red–green dichromat cannot distinguish a green traffic light from a red one on the basis of color, and so must distinguish between the brighter (green) and the darker (red) light or read the signal by the position of the lights.

MONOCHROMAT: *A person who is truly color-blind because he or she has only rods and no cones.*

DICHROMAT: *A person having the type of color weakness in which only two types of cones are present, rather than the normal three.*

Color blindness and color weakness can create a number of problems in everyday life. People who are unable to discriminate between red and green are restricted to certain ranks and duties within the armed forces. They would be unable to tell at night whether another airplane or ship was approaching or receding. (This is determined by noting the colors of lights on the wings or the sides of the ship — green lights denote the right side, whereas red lights denote the left.) You can probably imagine some of the inconveniences faced by a red–green dichromat in trying to choose clothing that matches or in picking out red apples from green ones at the supermarket.

Research on color blindness has been useful, but research on other types of color perception has also had practical applications. For example, what color do you think of when the word "fire engine" is mentioned? Most people respond with "red." However, many new fire engines are now being painted light green, yellow, or white because research has found that these colors are seen equally well at night and during the day. Another study found that it is easier to see and estimate the distance of lights when one light is red and the other blue, as opposed to both lights being the same color (Berkhout, 1979). This research supports the current practice of placing one red and one blue light on top of emergency vehicles. There is an additional safety reason for the placement of these lights: Red shows up better in low light, blue better in brighter conditions. Other studies have been done involving the color of the print on computer video screens: It has been found that, contrary to the white-on-black that many people expect, amber or green on a black background is more readable. These and many other perceptual studies have been applied to practical situations to make our lives safer and more comfortable.

Motion perception: Seeing movement, both real and apparent

Another important factor in perceptual organization and everyday survival is the perception of movement. Each day we avert disaster by responding to movement in our environment — we move out of the way of oncoming trucks, we avoid collisions with hurrying shoppers in the mall, and so on. Occasionally, our perceptual processes are fooled by objects that look as if they're moving when they really aren't. It therefore seems necessary to differentiate between real and apparent motion.

Real motion   The perception of real movement is the result of an actual change in the object's position in space. There are basically two ways that we perceive real motion: (1) an image moves across the retina, and (2) the eye moves in the head, to follow the path of the moving object (see Figure 4.13).

Much real movement perception has been explained by the work of Hubel and Wiesel (1968). Their research has shown that, just as there are line and angle detectors in the visual cortex, there are also motion detectors that respond specifically to the movement of an object across the retina. Another explanation for movement perception stems from the fact that when the eyes move to follow an object, the brain sends signals to the

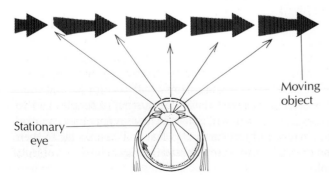

Stationary eye

Moving object

Figure 4.13 Real motion is perceived when objects move across the field of vision and the retina is stimulated in various locations.

eye muscles to keep the image on the fovea, or the center of the retina. This tracking motion thereby provides additional cues for motion perception (Kasamatsu, 1976).

An important practical application of the study of movement and depth perception comes from research into collisions between cars and trains. Have you ever wondered why so many people are killed in such accidents when virtually every railroad crossing has a warning device to signal approaching trains? You might think that the people don't hear the train whistle or see the flashing lights. However, through analysis of several such accidents, it has been found that, although most drivers probably did see the approaching trains and were well aware of the warning signals, they chose to ignore them. Leibowitz (1985) suggests that aspects of motion perception could explain these accidents. Large objects are perceived as moving more slowly than small objects and objects seem to move more slowly when tracked, as opposed to keeping the head and eyes still. Thus, the drivers apparently perceived the trains as moving slower than they really were. These proved to be fatal misperceptions.

Apparent motion   It is also possible to perceive movement in the absence of any real motion. If you are seated in a darkened room and look at two adjacent lights being turned on, one after the other, it will seem that a single light is jumping back and forth. This is known as **stroboscopic motion,** or the "phi phenomenon." This illusion makes it possible to construct "moving arrows" on electric signs and to put "motion" into motion pictures. What you see on the movie screen is actually a series of still images illuminated in rapid succession. Old black-and-white movies and home movies sometimes seem jerky because only 16 still pictures are projected per second, whereas modern movie films flash 24 pictures per second. Even at this speed, some flicker would occur except for the fact that sound movie projectors have a three-bladed shutter that rotates in front of the light source. This shutter causes each frame of film to be projected three times, for an effective projection rate of 72 pictures a second.

Another form of apparent movement is the **autokinetic effect** — perceived motion of a single stationary light or object. You can experience this illusion by looking at a small dim light at the far end of a completely dark room (the glowing end of a cigarette is a good target). If you stare at the light for a few seconds, it will appear to wander around erratically. This apparent movement occurs because there are no cues to tell you that the light is really stationary, and the slight constant movement of the eye (mentioned in Chapter 3) makes the light appear to move. Another explanation for the autokinetic effect is that the eye muscles fatigue from their effort to obey the commands of the brain to maintain their fixation on the spot of light (Gregory, 1977).

In the past, this illusion created a safety problem for night-flying pilots who were trying to judge the position of beacon lights or of tail and wing lights on other airplanes. You may have noticed that lights on airplanes and beacons now flash on and off, which helps to reduce the autokinetic illusion. This illusion could also explain some of the thousands of reported sightings each year of unidentified flying objects (UFOs). A common element in the description of UFOs is their "erratic" movements and strange abilities to "hover." Can you see how a simple steadily beaming light on a dark night and the autokinetic illusion could lead to a UFO "sighting"?

STROBOSCOPIC MOTION: *The illusion of motion in which alternating lights are seen as one moving light.*

AUTOKINETIC EFFECT: *The perceived motion of a single stationary light in the dark.*

TELEPATHY: *The ability to read other people's minds.*

CLAIRVOYANCE: *The ability to perceive objects or events that are inaccessible to the normal senses.*

PRECOGNITION: *The ability to predict the future.*

PSYCHOKINESIS: *The ability to move or affect objects without touching them.*

EXTRASENSORY PERCEPTION (ESP): *Perceptual, or "psychic," abilities that go beyond the "known" senses, including telepathy, clairvoyance, precognition, and telekinesis.*

Question: It may be possible to explain UFOs in terms of misperception, but what about ESP — can perception research explain that?   A number of people claim to have perceptual abilities that go beyond the "known" senses. They say that they can read other people's minds (**telepathy**), perceive objects or events that are inaccessible to their normal senses (**clairvoyance**), predict the future (**precognition**), or move or affect objects without touching them (**psychokinesis**). Such "psychic abilities," or **extrasensory per-**

ception (ESP), have captured the public imagination, and popular tabloids are filled with the accounts of psychics claiming to be able to find lost children or predict assassinations.

Many psychologists believe that people who claim to have ESP are frauds who use magic and perceptual illusions to mislead general audiences, as well as scientific observers. James ("The Amazing") Randi, a famous magician and self-proclaimed "professional charlatan," has offered $10,000 to anyone who can perform even *one* example of psychic abilities under previously agreed upon standards of control. After over 600 would-be psychic inquires and more than 20 years, Randi still has his money (Morris, 1980; Randi, 1980).

Randi believes that the positive results of some ESP studies are due to scientist's inability to detect trickery. In 1983, Randi planted two of his most accomplished magician friends as "psychics" in the McDonnell Laboratory for Psychic Research at Washington University in St. Louis. Although these magicians had agreed in advance to answer honestly if they were ever accused of trickery, the confrontation never occurred. As a matter of fact, the administrator of the laboratory proclaimed that, of all the subjects tested, they were the most reliable examples of people having true psychic abilities. With their skills in sleight-of-hand spoon bending, "mind reading," and "psychic photography," the two conjurers lulled the researchers into a euphoria of scientific success, until Randi called a press conference to expose these "natural psychics" (Cornell, 1984). Randi has repeatedly suggested that all ESP research should include an experienced stage magician who can detect trickery that scientists easily miss.

Question: Has any legitimate scientific research been conducted to determine whether ESP really exists?   Scientific investigations of ESP began in the early 1900s when Joseph B. Rhine conducted experiments to test psychic abilities in his subjects. Many of his experiments, as well as those done by subsequent ESP researchers, involved *Zener cards*, a deck of 25 cards that bear five different symbols — a plus sign, a square, a star, a circle, and wavy lines. When experimenters want to study telepathy, for instance, they ask a "sender" to concentrate on a card; then they ask the "receiver" to try to "read the mind" of the sender. With luck alone, the receiver will guess the symbols on about five cards correctly. A subject who consistently scores above "chance" is credited with having ESP.

Although reports from Rhine's Laboratory have been impressive, critics find much to condemn in terms of scientific methodology, particularly in the area of experimental control. In many early experiments, for example, the Zener cards were so cheaply printed that a faint outline of the symbol could be seen from the back. Also, since experimenters knew which cards were correct, they could unknowingly give subjects cues through subtle facial gestures. Later experiments that used necessary controls, such as double-blind procedures, reported contradictory results (Hansel, 1980).

Another criticism of studies indicating the existence of ESP is their lack of stability and replicability. Findings in ESP are notoriously "fragile" (Gardner, 1977). Not only do different researchers find conflicting evidence, but the same subject will show psychic abilities in some laboratories but not others. Rhine himself has stated that he has never found a subject whose ESP powers did not disappear over time (Rhine, 1972).

Question: If scientific evidence is so strongly against ESP, why do so many people still believe in it?   When people hear about or personally experience unusual incidents that cannot be easily explained, they grab hold of any explanation that sounds feasible. Because ESP is by nature subjective and *extra*ordinary, people tend to accept it as an explanation for personal, out-of-the-ordinary experiences. Moreover, as was mentioned earlier in the chapter, people's motivations and interests can influence their perceptions. They tend to pay extra attention to things they want to see or hear. Often both subjects and researchers exhibit this strong motivation to believe in ESP. People generally have difficulty in evaluating and processing complex scientific information. In the case of psychic abilities it is hard to distinguish chance and coincidental events from the multitude of experiences in daily life. But the most important underlying reason for why people believe in ESP is that they *want* to. A quick glance at children's fairy tales, comic books, and popular movies finds an abundance of superhuman characters and violations of the laws of physics. It seems that release from natural law is one of the most common and satisfying human fantasies (Moss and Butler, 1978). When it comes to ESP, people eagerly engage in a process known as "the willing suspension of disbelief." We seem to have a hard time accepting our finiteness, and a belief in psychic phenomena offers an increased feeling of power and control.

In addition to personal motivation, there are several social reasons why people believe in ESP. For example, Singer and Benassi (1981) point out that the public generally tends to believe what they see in print or on TV. Yet most newspapers and TV programs that report stories about ESP seldom demand scientific proof. This media belief is particularly strong when the source is perceived as "scientific" or as a "documentary," but Singer and Benassi found that many college students listed *Reader's Digest,* the *National Enquirer,* and movies such as *Star Wars* as examples of "scientific sources." Finally, our fast-paced technological world reinforces a belief in ESP. Our scientific progress leads many people to believe that virtually anything is possible, and possible is often translated as "probable."

Review Questions

1 Binocular cues to distance require _____ eye(s), whereas monocular cues to distance require _____ eye(s).

2 The two main binocular cues to distance are _____ _____ and _____ .

3 List the eight monocular cues to distance:

_____   _____

_____   _____

_____   _____

_____   _____

4 The color theory that states that there are three color systems—red, green, and blue—is known as the _____ theory.

5 The color theory that claims that there are red–green, blue–yellow, and black–white color systems is the _____ theory.

6 The illusion that allows us to perceive movement in motion pictures is called _____ motion.

Answers: 1 two, one; *2* retinal disparity, convergence; *3* linear perspective, aerial perspective, texture gradient, interposition, light and shadow, relative size, accommodation, motion parallax; *4* trichromatic; *5* opponent-process; *6* stroboscopic

INTERPRETATION

After selectively sorting through incoming sensory information and organizing it into patterns, the brain uses this information to explain and make judgments about the external world. This final stage of perception, *interpretation,* is influenced by several factors, including early life experiences, perceptual expectations, cultural factors, and a number of others.

Critical Thinking

RECOGNIZING FAULTY REASONING
Problems with the Belief in ESP

The subject of ESP often generates great interest and emotional responses in people, and individuals who feel strongly about an issue sometimes fail to recognize the faulty reasoning that forms the foundation of their beliefs. Belief in ESP is particularly susceptible to this type of illogical, noncritical thinking.

In this exercise, you have a chance to examine common reports of ESP and to practice identifying possible examples of faulty reasoning. Begin by studying the following list of "common problems with ESP."

(a) Fallacy of Positive Instances Noting and remembering events that confirm personal expectations and beliefs (the "hits") and ignoring nonsupportive evidence (the "misses").

(b) Innumeracy Failing to recognize chance occurrences for what they are due to a lack of training in statistics and probabilities. Unusual events are misperceived as statistically impossible and extraordinary explanations, such as ESP, are seen as the logical alternative.

(c) Willingness to Suspend Disbelief Refusing to engage one's normal critical thinking skills because of a personal need for power and control. Although few people would attribute a foreign country's acquisition of top-secret information to ESP, some of these same individuals would willingly believe that a psychic could help them find their lost child.

(d) The "Vividness" Problem Human information processing and memory storage and retrieval are often based on the initial "vividness" of the information. Sincere personal testimonials, theatrical demonstrations, and detailed anecdotes easily capture our attention and tend to be remembered better than rational, scientific descriptions of events.

Now read the following ESP reports and decide which "problem with ESP" is MOST appropriate. More than one problem may be applicable, but try to limit your choice. Enter only one letter beside each report, and then compare your answers with those of your classmates or friends. This comparison of results will help to sharpen your critical thinking skills.

_____ John hadn't thought of Paula, his old high school sweetheart, for years. Yet one morning he woke up thinking about her. He was wondering what she looked like and whether she was married now, when suddenly the phone rang. For some strange reason, he felt sure the call was from Paula. He was right. John now cites this call as evidence for his personal experience with extrasensory perception.

_____ A psychic visits a class in introductory psychology. He predicts that, out of this class of twenty-three students, two individuals will have birthdays on the same day. When a tally of birthdays is taken, his prediction is supported and many students leave class believing that ESP has been supported.

_____ A National League baseball player dreams of hitting a bases-loaded triple. Two months later, during the final game of the World Series, he gets this exact triple and wins the game. He informs the media of his earlier dream and the possibility of ESP.

_____ A mother is sitting alone in her office at work and suddenly sees a vivid image of her home on fire. She immediately calls home and awakens the sitter who excitedly reports smoke coming under the door. The sitter successfully extinguishes the fire, and the mother later attributes her visual images to ESP.

Early life experiences: The effects of environmental interaction

As we discovered in the section on selection, early life experiences can have a dramatic effect on the biological development of perceptual systems. Early experiences also influence the process of interpretation. Held and Hein (1963) conducted a famous experiment that dramatically demonstrated the influence of early learning on perceptual development. These researchers raised 20 kittens in total darkness except for one hour a day when they were allowed to see. During that one hour, one group of kittens was placed in body harnesses that allowed them to walk in a circular path around a patterned "kitty carousel." Another group of kittens was suspended passively above the floor of the carousel in a gondola that could be pulled by the movement of the active kittens (see the photograph on p. 124). When all kittens were later released, the active kittens displayed normal visual perception (avoiding the deep side of a visual cliff, blinking when faced with

In the "kitty carousel," both kittens get the same visual stimulation, but only the free-moving kitten develops normal depth perception.

an approaching object, and so on), but the passive kittens displayed none of these behaviors. After several days of being allowed to move about freely, the kittens who rode passively in the gondola did finally catch up to their active partners.

The importance of being able to actively explore and experiment with the environment can also be seen in the experiences of George Stratton. On the first day of his experiment, he was unable to manage the simple act of pouring and drinking a glass of milk, but by the third day he was able to sit down and enjoy a full meal.

Question: Why does it seem so easy for "blind" characters in movies to adjust after having their sight restored?   Although previously blind characters seem to immediately adjust and live "happily ever after" in the movies, such adjustment is often lengthy and traumatic in real life. This can be seen in the example of the cataract patient known as S.B. (the fellow who tried to crawl out a fourth-floor window). The following is an account of the difficulty S.B. had in trying to get used to his newly acquired sense of sight:

> We saw in dramatic form the difficulty that S.B. had in trusting and coming to use his vision whenever he had to cross the road. Before the operation, he was undaunted by traffic. He would cross alone, holding his arm or his stick stubbornly before him, when the traffic would subside as the waters before Christ. But after the operation, it took two of us on either side to force him across a road: he was terrified as never before in his life.
>
> *Gregory (1966), p. 197*

S.B.'s adjustment to vision was not only difficult and terrifying but also depressing. Although he was initially excited about his newfound sight, as the days passed he became progressively more despondent. After a while, he seemed to revert to life without vision and in the evening would sit alone in darkness, not bothering to turn on the lights. His depression and disappointment gradually deepened, and three years after his surgery he died. Although most cases of visual restoration do not end in such a tragic way, depression *is* a common reaction.

Perceptual expectancy: The effects of prior experience

When George Stratton tried to maneuver about his house after initially donning his inverting lens, he undoubtedly had some difficulty. To function during the initial period of wearing the lens, Stratton most likely relied on his expectations of the way objects in his environment *ought* to look, based on his prior experiences with them. Similarly, in our normal, everyday world, our expectations often bias our perceptions. If batter Tony Gwynn is thrown three fast balls in a row, he will expect another fast ball and will not be prepared to hit a curve ball. In fact, he may even misperceive the next pitch and actually

124

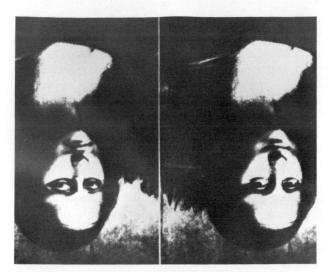

Does this picture bother you? You expect that the picture has been printed upside down and will be O.K. when it is righted. Now turn the book so that the picture is rightside up and you'll see that your expectations are mistaken.

When you first look at this photograph, you will see either the silhouette of two people or a vase, depending on your perceptual expectations.

see it as a fast ball when indeed it is a curve. The incoming sensory information will be correct, but the perception of that information may be influenced by his *perceptual expectations.*

You can test your reliance on perceptual expectations with the photograph above. Do you notice anything unusual in this photo? All the facial features seem to be in the correct positions for an upside-down face. But when you turn the face right side up, you'll be surprised (and probably a little disgusted) to find that your expectations are wrong. The strong influence of perceptual expectancies can especially be noted when viewing ambiguous figures. If someone had been discussing the Royal Family and then showed you the picture at the right, you would probably see the faces first, rather than the vase.

Cultural factors: Social influences on interpretation

Many psychologists believe that cultural factors are the most important influences on the way we perceive the world. For example, children and adults raised in industrialized cultures generally have better acuity for horizontal and vertical lines than they do for lines oriented at an angle. One explanation for this differential acuity is the **carpentered environment hypothesis,** which suggests that the perceptions of industrialized people are influenced by having grown up in a world of objects such as buildings and roads that have numerous horizontal and vertical lines and right angles. When this hypothesis was tested on a group of Canadian Cree Indians who live in a noncarpentered environment (a rural area without the strong domination of rectangular influences), it was found that the Cree's visual acuity was about the same for lines of all orientation (Annis and Frost, 1973).

This carpentered world concept is also used to explain why industrialized people are more susceptible to visual illusions such as the Müller–Lyer illusion shown in Figure 4.14 than are people from nonindustrialized countries. Western civilization is filled with houses and buildings constructed with straight lines, corners, and right angles. These structures provide us with a perceptual background that leads us to use the angles in the Müller–Lyer illusion to infer distance. It was found that people from noncarpentered worlds make no such inference (Segall, Campbell, and Herskovits, 1966).

Other influences on interpretation: Personal motivations and frames of reference

Among other factors that influence our interpretations of what we perceive are our personal interests and needs that influence our perceptions and the frames of reference surrounding what is being perceived. As we discovered in the process of selection, our

CARPENTERED ENVIRONMENT HYPOTHESIS: *The idea that the perceptions of industrialized people are influenced by having grown up in a world of constructed objects that have numerous horizontal and vertical lines and right angles.*

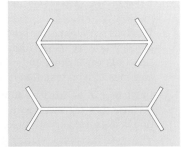

Figure 4.14 The Müller–Lyer illusion. Which line is longer? Both are actually the same length, but people from industrialized countries normally see the bottom line as longer than the top. This is because they are used to making size and distance judgments from perspective cues created by right angles and horizontal and vertical lines of buildings and streets.

individual needs and interests can color what we selectively attend to; they can also affect how we judge or interpret the information selected. For example, Stephan, Berscheid, and Walster (1971) found that sexually aroused men judged photographs of women as more attractive than did nonaroused males, and this reaction was particularly strong when the men believed they would actually have a date with the women. Thus, when men's sexual needs were stimulated and their interests were piqued because of an impending date, the men perceived the photographs more favorably.

Our perceptions of people, objects, or situations are also affected by their frames of reference or the context surrounding them. Whereas a man might judge a woman's photograph as attractive when seen by itself, he might judge it as unattractive when seen next to that of Miss America.

In this chapter we have seen that a number of internal and external factors affect all three stages of perception—selection, organization, and interpretation. In upcoming chapters, we will continue our study of perception by examining how incoming sensory information is processed and retrieved in the different types of memory (Chapter 7), how perception develops in infants (Chapter 9), and how we perceive ourselves and others (Chapter 17).

Review Questions

1 Held and Hein's "kitty carousel" experiment showed that _____ _____ is especially important in learning how to perceive the world.

2 _____ _____ occurs when expectancies influence what we perceive.

3 The carpentered environment hypothesis is an example of the way in which _____ factors influence perception.

4 The _____ illusion demonstrates the influence of an industrialized environment on perception.

Answers: 1 early experience;   *2* perceptual expectancy;   *3* cultural;   *4* Müller–Lyer

REVIEW OF MAJOR CONCEPTS

1 Whereas sensation is the process of detecting and transducing raw sensory information, perception is the process of selecting, organizing, and interpreting this data into a usable mental representation of the world.

2 Illusions can be used to study the process of perception because they represent a situation where sensory information is organized or interpreted improperly.

3 The three basic processes of perception are selection, organization, and interpretation.

SELECTION

4 The selection process allows us to choose which of the billions of separate sensory messages will eventually be processed.

5 Selective attention allows us to direct our attention to the most important or critical aspect of the environment at any one time.

6 Feature detectors distinguish between different sensory inputs. Early deprivation may lead to problems with feature detectors.

7 The selection process is very sensitive to changes in the environment. Those stimuli that remain the same can cause either sensory adaptation, in which the receptors slow down their firing rates, or perceptual habituation, in which the brain ignores the constant stimuli.

ORGANIZATION

8 The process of organization was studied very intensely by the Gestalt psychologists, who set forth some laws of organization explaining how people perceive form. Their most fundamental principle is the distinction between figure and ground. Other principles include proximity, continuity, closure, contiguity, similarity, and contrast.

9 Through the perceptual constancies—size constancy, shape constancy, and brightness constancy—we are able to perceive consistencies in our environment, even though the actual sensory information we receive may be constantly changing. These constancies are based on our prior experiences and learning.

10 There are two major types of cues to size and distance: binocular cues, which require two eyes, and monocular cues, which are available to one or two eyes. The binocular cues include retinal disparity and convergence. Monocular cues include linear perspective, aerial perspective, texture gradients, interposition, light and shadow, relative size, accommodation, and motion parallax.

11 The perception of color is explained by a combination of the two traditional color theories, the trichromatic theory and the opponent-process theory. The trichromatic theory proposes that there are three kinds of color systems maximally sensitive to blue, green, and red. The opponent-process theory proposes that there are three color systems but that each is sensitive to two opposing colors — blue and yellow, red and green, and black and white — and that they operate in an on–off fashion. It appears that the trichromatic system operates at the level of the retina, whereas the opponent-process system occurs at the level of the brain.

12 Some people cannot perceive color normally. Monochromats have only rods and no cones and see things only in black and white and shades of gray. Dichromats are missing only one type of cone system and cannot distinguish between red and green or blue and yellow.

13 We are able to perceive both real motion and apparent motion. The perception of real motion is due to the movement of an object across the retina or the movement of the eye to follow a moving object. The perception of apparent motion can be due to stroboscopic motion, in which two stimuli are presented in close succession, or the autokinetic effect, the apparent movement of a single light in a dark room.

14 Extrasensory perception (ESP) is the ability to perceive things through senses that go beyond the "known" senses. Although ESP research has led to impressive results, critics condemn its scientific validity because it lacks experimental control and replicability.

INTERPRETATION

15 Interpretation, the final stage of perception, can be influenced by early life experiences, perceptual expectancy, cultural factors, needs and interests, and frames of reference.

SUGGESTED READINGS

GOLDSTEIN, E. B. (1984). *Sensation and perception* (2nd ed.). Belmont, CA: Wadsworth. An introduction to the study of sensation and perception.

GREGORY, R. L. (1977). *Eye and brain: The psychology of seeing* (3rd ed.). New York: World University Library. A wonderful book on the wonders of seeing.

HANSEL, C. E. M. (1980). *ESP and parapsychology.* Buffalo, NY: Prometheus. This book takes a critical look at research into ESP and parapsychology.

RANDI, J. (1982). *Flim-flam.* Buffalo, NY: Prometheus. The "Amazing Randi" takes on all kinds of pseudoscientists and con artists in demonstrating how the claims and accomplishments of famous psychics are based on mere magicians' tricks.

chapter five
States of Consciousness

HALF an hour after swallowing the drug, I became aware of a slow dance of golden lights. A little later there were sumptuous red surfaces swelling and expanding from bright nodes of energy that vibrated with a continuously changing, patterned life. I saw the books . . . all of them glowed with living light and in some the glory was more manifest than in others. The legs . . . of that chair . . . how miraculous their tubularity, how supernatural their polished smoothness! I spent several minutes — or was it several centuries? — not merely gazing at those bamboo legs, but actually being them — or rather being myself in them: or, to be still more accurate . . . being my Not-self in the Not-self which was the chair.

*Aldous Huxley, 1954,
The Doors of Perception, p. 45*

Now that you have read Aldous Huxley's account of his personal experience with a chemically induced state of consciousness, compare that description with the experiences of Peter Tripp, a New York disc jockey who stayed awake in a 200-hour "wake-a-thon" to benefit charity.

After little more than two days [without sleep] as he changed shoes in the hotel, he pointed out [to a psychiatrist] a very interesting sight. There were cobwebs in his shoes — to the eyes at least. . . . Specks on the table began to look like bugs. . . . He was beginning to have trouble remembering things. By 110 hours there were signs of delirium. . . . A doctor walked into the recording booth in a tweed suit that Tripp saw as a suit of furry worms. On the morning of the final day [of the 200-hour period] a famous neurologist arrived to examine him . . . [Tripp] came to the morbid conclusion that this man was an undertaker, there for the purpose of burying him [and] leapt for the door with several doctors in pursuit.

Luce and Segal (1966), p. 91

CONSCIOUSNESS: *The external stimuli and internal events that we are aware of at any given moment, as opposed to mind, which is the sum of past consciousness.*

To a reader in a "normal" state of consciousness, these passages may seem rather bizarre and confusing — what is a "Not-self in a Not-self," and why would a tweed suit look like "furry worms"? But to many who purposely seek to alter their consciousness, these descriptions may seem quite familiar and attractive.

Question: What exactly is meant by the term "consciousness"? **Consciousness** is the general state of being aware and responsive to stimuli and events in both the external and internal environments. William James observed in 1890 that "normal" waking consciousness is seldom fixed on any one event for any length of time. Instead, it seems to consist of a continuous flow of awareness, a *stream of consciousness,* that shifts from event to event, from stimuli to stimuli, from past to present to future, and from external to internal worlds. You can easily recognize this shift from external to internal worlds by watching your own stream of consciousness during a typical classroom lecture. If you're not actively concentrating on the lecture, you're likely to "tune out" and focus on internal events. When the tuning out becomes detailed to the point of active daydreaming, you have entered the dimension of altered or alternate states of consciousness. In recent years, the term "altered" has been used to refer to changed states of consciousness that must be deliberately evoked through drugs, hypnosis, meditation, and so on, whereas changes that occur spontaneously, such as sleeping and dreaming, are generally called "alternate states." Since this distinction may be unnecessarily confusing and because the term *altered* has been criticized for implying a single "desirable" state of consciousness, we will use *alternate* to refer to all states that differ from "normal" consciousness.

Question: How are alternate states of consciousness distinguished from normal consciousness? **Alternate states of consciousness (ASCs)** differ from normal, waking states of consciousness primarily in the dimensions of *awareness* and *control.* When a person is in a drug-induced ASC, for example, his or her awareness of the world is often lessened or distorted, as in Aldous Huxley's seeing his books as glowing with a "living light." The dimension of control (or actually lack of control) can be seen in an experience we've probably all had — being in a dream where we desperately needed to run but couldn't control our legs to make them move.

Although ASCs are hard to identify precisely, they generally contain one or more of the following characteristics (Ludwig, 1966; Nideffer, 1976; A. Smith, 1982; Tart, 1975):

1. Distortions of perceptual processes, sense of time, and body image (such as Huxley's loss of time while staring at the "supernatural smoothness" of the chair legs).
2. Emotional intensity ranging from quiet, profound peace or depression to rapturous joy or extreme anger and paranoia (such as the paranoia in Peter Tripp's belief that the examining doctor was an undertaker coming for his body).
3. Disruptions in normal thinking and memory (as when people drink too much and can't remember what happened the next morning).
4. Inability to communicate the experience, particularly in the language understood by the normal type of consciousness.
5. Feelings of unity and fusion, with a loss of boundaries between self and others and loss of physical constraints such as time and space (as evidenced by Huxley's feelings of being a "Not-self in the Not-self which was the chair.")

While reading this list, you may have recognized some of these same qualities in descriptions of people who experience alternate states from high fevers and intense religious experiences. These qualities are also found during biofeedback and the "runner's high" (see Chapter 2) and during sensory deprivation (see Chapter 3).

In this chapter we will begin our exploration of various states of consciousness with a general overview of the nature of consciousness. We will then examine the changes in consciousness that occur during sleep and dreaming, with use of psychoactive drugs, under hypnosis, and with meditation.

ALTERNATE STATES OF CONSCIOUSNESS (ASCs): *Any state of consciousness other than normal waking consciousness.*

THE NATURE OF CONSCIOUSNESS

Our understanding of the nature of consciousness is a result of both scientific and popular explorations.

INTROSPECTION: *A research method popular during the late nineteenth century in which trained subjects reported their current conscious experience.*

Scientific approach: Psychology's study of consciousness

In the late nineteenth century, when psychology first established itself as a scientific discipline separate from philosophy, the structuralists defined psychology as "the study of human consciousness." Early research consisted of having subjects examine and report their awareness through the method of **introspection**. Sigmund Freud also felt that consciousness was an important focus of psychology and in particular emphasized the role of *unconscious* feelings and drives in motivating people's behavior.

As the field of psychology grew, however, many psychologists became disenchanted with the method of introspection and with Freud's disproportionate emphasis on the unconscious. In particular, the behaviorists, led by John Watson, believed that consciousness was not the proper focus of psychology. In fact, he declared that "the time seems to have come when psychology must discard all references to consciousness; when it need no longer delude itself into thinking that it is making mental states the object of observation" (1913, p. 164). This behavioristic approach dominated the field of psychology during the first half of the twentieth century, and the goal of establishing a science of consciousness was nearly abandoned.

In recent times, psychology has experienced a quiet return to the study of consciousness. This revived interest is due in part to advances in scientific technology that provide objective means of measuring states of consciousness (such as through brain wave monitoring). The development of the humanistic branch of psychology and the work of cognitive psychologists have also helped to refuel scientific interest in consciousness.

Popular approach: The public's study of consciousness

While psychologists' interest in consciousness may have waxed and waned over the years, the interest of the general public has almost always been intense — especially in the alternate states. In a survey of 488 societies in all parts of the world, 90 percent were found to practice institutionally recognized methods of changing consciousness (Bourguignon, 1973), which included drug ingestion, ritualistic fasting, dancing, and chanting among others. The fact that very young children are commonly observed engaging in practices designed to alter their consciousness has led some researchers to suggest there is a basic inborn human need to experience nonordinary reality (Duncan and Gold, 1982). According to Harvard researcher and physician Andrew Weil (1972): "Three and four-year-olds commonly whirl themselves into vertiginous stupors, hyperventilate, and have other children squeeze them around the chest until they faint. They also choke each other to produce loss of consciousness" (p. 19).

Similar attempts to alter consciousness can be found throughout the entire life span. Adolescents and young adults, for example, will sometimes wait in long lines to ride "death-defying" roller coasters, or will purposely choose front row seats in ear-blasting rock concerts. This is also a time when many individuals take their first drink of alcohol or smoke their first marijuana cigarette. For many, drug use (and abuse) continues throughout middle and late adulthood.

Each of these examples involves deliberate, artificial means for obtaining an alternate state of consciousness. Our next section deals with ASCs that result from unplanned, "natural" sources.

Meditation, religious chants, and childhood "experiments" with swings are common methods of changing consciousness.

DAILY VARIATIONS IN CONSCIOUSNESS

Whether you recognize it or not, your consciousness goes through regular variations every day. These variations include changes in biological rhythms, daydreaming, and sleep and dreaming.

Biological rhythms: Can time cause an alternate state?

Have you ever wondered whether bio-rhythm charts can really predict your "critical" accident-prone days? Whether premenstrual tension can cause some women to become so aggressive or depressed that they will do something they would never do under a normal waking state of consciousness? Whether jet lag is a contributing factor in airline disasters? If so, the relatively new science of **chronobiology,** or the study of biological rhythms, will be of great interest to you. Over the past three decades, researchers in this area have found that in virtually every function of life, time is of the essence. Month by month, day by day, and hour by hour, biological rhythms have been found to affect thoughts, emotions, and behaviors.

CHRONOBIOLOGY: *The study of biological rhythms.*

Many biological rhythms occur on a *circadian,* or daily, cycle. **Circadian rhythms** govern the amount of sleep we need each day and influence more than 40 aspects of bodily activity, including body temperature, pulse rate, blood pressure, blood sugar level, and cell growth. These daily rhythms help explain why most people's sleep/waking cycle is relatively regular and why we often feel irritable, hungry, listless, or energetic at different times of the day. These daily rhythms can also vary from person to person. For example, "morning people" tend to reach their peak body temperature and corresponding alertness and efficiency at mid-morning, whereas "night people" have higher temperatures and better functioning in the evening (Luce, 1971).

CIRCADIAN RHYTHMS: *Biological changes that occur on a 24-hour cycle.*

Other cycles occur over much longer periods. The female menstrual cycle, for example, is about 28 days. During the cycle, hormones are secreted in varying amounts to control egg release from the ovaries and changes in the lining of the uterus.

Question: Does the monthly menstrual cycle really affect women's moods and performance?   Approximately 70 percent of menstruating women report at least one emotional, physical, or behavioral change in the week or so prior to the onset of menstruation (Hopson and Rosenfeld, 1984). For most women these changes are usually mild or moderate. For a few (approximately 3 to 10 percent), however, the changes are numerous and of such a severe nature that their lives are seriously disrupted. The type and severity of premenstrual changes vary from woman to woman. The most common physical symptoms are headaches, backaches, breast swelling and tenderness, water retention, and sleep disorders. Emotional changes include tension, irritability, anger, depression, and low self-esteem. Some women also report impaired motor function such as decreased coordination and clumsiness.

Medical authorities are still debating the actual definition of **premenstrual syndrome (PMS).** Is it really a collection of symptoms — a syndrome — or a separate, identifiable disorder? There is also considerable controversy over its cause and treatment (Abplanalp, 1983; Gordon and Snyder, 1989; Rolker-Dolinsky, 1987). For some women who experience severe reactions, multidimensional therapy emphasizing diet, exercise, vitamin and hormone supplements (Achtigal, 1986; Demarest, 1985), and/or specific psychological techniques (Weiss et al., 1985) has proven helpful in reducing symptoms.

PREMENSTRUAL SYNDROME (PMS): *A loose cluster of symptoms that supposedly occurs in some women just prior to menstruation.*

Although the research concerning monthly biological changes for women remains inconclusive, there is consistent evidence that interference with our daily (circadian) rhythms has several deleterious effects. Studies of employees whose work schedules are not in synchrony with their circadian rhythms (such as shift workers) are much less productive and more accident-prone on the job than those who *are* in synchrony (Chollar, 1989; Coleman, 1986). It is interesting to note that the Union Carbide chemical accident in Bhopal, India, and the nuclear power plant disaster in Chernobyl both occurred during the night shift (Coleman, 1986; Hilts, 1986). Although this may well be a simple coincidence, it could also reflect the fact that the circadian cycle of these workers was oriented toward sleep at a time when full attention and critical thinking were required.

College life, with its late night study sessions, early morning classes, and weekend parties, also causes disruption in the typical circadian rhythm. Have you ever experienced bouts of extreme sleepiness during the day, difficulty sleeping at night, and a strong need to sleep in on the weekend? This could be the result of problems with your body's

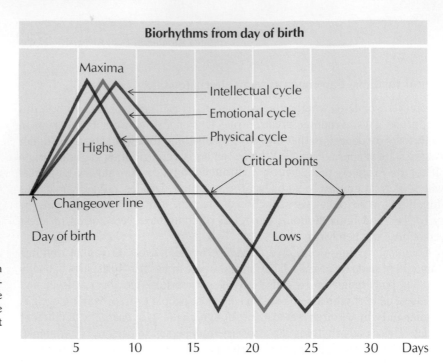

Biorhythms from day of birth

Maxima

Intellectual cycle
Emotional cycle
Physical cycle

Highs

Critical points

Changeover line

Day of birth

Lows

5   10   15   20   25   30   Days

Figure 5.1 A typical chart used in biorhythm theory. If this hypothetical person was born on the first of the month, then their physical cycle would peak around the 6th and be at the lowest around the 16th.

circadian rhythm. Your overall college productivity could be improved by minimizing these disruptions and also by adjusting your class schedule and study time to match your personal times of highest energy and alertness. To find your best times, start by keeping a daily record of your sleeping patterns and mood and energy levels throughout the day. After two weeks, analyze your records for patterns of peak and low times and then make your adjustments.

Question: Is this the same kind of record as those prepared by biorhythm experts who predict "critical" days? **Biorhythm theory** proposes that at the moment of birth we all start off at specific spots on three biological cycles (physical, emotional, and intellectual) and that these cycles continue throughout our lifetime (see Figure 5.1). When a cycle turns from positive to negative, it is considered a "critical" day, and when all three cycles line up on the same critical day, we're considered to be at high risk for disaster. Unlike circadian cycles, the existence of these cycles has received little or no scientific support (see Palmer, 1983). Nevertheless, this "theory" enjoys considerable financial support from the public.

Question: Do body rhythms have something to do with jet lag? The sleepy, uncomfortable feeling that often accompanies long airline flights, commonly known as *jet lag,* is generally due to a disruption in the body's circadian rhythm. Jet lag has been found to be correlated with decreased alertness, decreased mental agility, and overall reduced efficiency (Hilts, 1984). In response to such findings, many airlines now allow pilots additional adjustment time on international flights. If you want to avoid jet lag in your own life, you may want to follow the "anti-jet-lag" diet and behavior suggestions developed by Dr. Charles Ehret (Perry, 1982):

1. Eat lightly the day before a long flight, and stick to a low-calorie, low-carbohydrate diet such as eggs, fish, salad, and fruit.
2. When you board the plane, set your watch to correspond to the time zone of your planned destination and then eat and sleep according to this new timetable.
3. On the plane and at your destination, avoid alcohol and stick to a high-protein breakfast and lunch and a high-carbohydrate dinner.
4. At your destination, go to bed early and according to the new time zone.

Daydreaming: A special type of alternate state

Daydreaming, that personal form of reverie or inwardly focused thought, is thought to be one of the most commonly experienced ASCs. Scientists have found that during a typical 24-hour period we spend as much as one-third of our waking hours

DAYDREAMING: *An alternate state of consciousness characterized by internal reverie or inwardly focused thought.*

Figure 5.2 The favorite topics of daydreams, as reported by 2,000 men and women responding to a Roper poll. (*Source: USA TODAY,* October 18, 1984. Reprinted with permission.)

Although an alert, "normal" state of consciousness is recommended during class time, daydreaming also occurs.

daydreaming (Foulkes and Fleisher, 1975; Webb and Cartwright, 1978). As you can see in Figure 5.2, the content of these daydreams is varied.

Question: Why do we daydream?   Most people daydream during quiet, private moments when outside events are boring or automatized, such as while waiting at bus stops or washing dishes. It appears that while our brain responds to unchanging or repetitive stimuli by simply tuning them out (perceptual habituation), our consciousness responds to an unchanging external world by turning inward and creating more interesting thoughts and images. Daydreaming while sitting in a lecture or driving a car may be counterproductive and potentially dangerous, but under other circumstances it can be helpful. Daydreams not only help us to cope with boring tasks and difficult situations but also seem to allow mental relaxation, improve intellectual functioning, and release creative abilities (Klinger, 1987; Starker, 1982).

Since daydream content sometimes reflects frustrated desires and wishes (Giambra, 1974), some researchers have suggested that daydreaming may serve as a healthy outlet for these desires and ultimately increase self-control (Klinger, 1987; Lynn and Rhue, 1985). Keeping track of the content of your daydreams may increase your awareness of consistent sources of frustration that you may want to modify.

Review Questions

1 The general state of being aware and responsive to stimuli and events in both the external and internal environments is _____.

2 Alternate states of consciousness differ from normal, waking states of consciousness primarily in the dimensions of _____ and _____.

3 Distortions of perceptual processes, distortions of emotional intensity, disruptions in normal thinking, the inability to communicate the experience, and feelings of unity and fusion are all characteristics of _____ _____ _____.

4 Biological rhythms that occur on a daily basis are called _____ rhythms.

5 _____ _____ is a loose cluster of symptoms—such as depression, pain, irritability, and anxiety—that occur in some women just prior to menstruation.

6 Most people spend up to _____ of their waking hours daydreaming.

Answers: 1 consciousness;   *2* awareness, control;   *3* alternate states of consciousness;   *4* circadian;   *5* premenstrual syndrome;   *6* one-third

Sleep: The most common alternate state

Sleep has always been a welcome but mysterious and sometimes elusive guest in our lives. The ancient Greeks attributed its properties and control to the god Morpheus. How do you explain this profound alteration in consciousness? Many people equate sleep with unconsciousness or liken it to "turning the motor off." But if awareness is turned off during sleep, how are some people able to set a "mental alarm clock" and awaken themselves at prearranged times? Why is it that mothers will sleep soundly despite the noises of an urban environment yet quickly awaken to the sound of their baby's cry?

Although people spend more than one-third of their lives sleeping, little research was done in this area until the mid-1930s. A breakthrough in sleep study came with the development of the **electroencephalograph (EEG),** which records brain waves through small disklike electrodes placed on the surface of the scalp. With the help of the EEG, it was discovered that brain waves change in an orderly fashion throughout the sleep period and that eye movements during sleep are related to dreaming (Aserinsky and Kleitman, 1953). Results of EEG and related sleep studies have allowed researchers to describe the mental and physical changes of a typical night's sleep.

The function of sleep

Question: Why do we need to sleep?   One of the earliest explanations, the **adaptive theory,** suggests that sleep evolved because it allows animals to conserve their energy during the time of day when they are not foraging for food or seeking mates and keeps them still at times when predators are active (Allison and Cicchetti, 1976; Hobson, 1989). **Repair theory** suggests that sleep serves an important restorative function, allowing us to recuperate not only from physical fatigue but also from emotional or intellectual demands (Webb, 1983).

Some researchers have studied the reasons for sleep by looking at the role of specific parts of the brain. For example, research on the reticular activating system (RAS) in cats has shown that during sleep this area seems to be "dampened down," which serves to reduce the arousal level in the higher centers of the brain. When an animal is sleeping, stimulation of the RAS will cause it to wake up (Schneider and Tarshis, 1980). In a similar way, humans will quickly awaken when their RAS receives important or emergency

ELECTROENCEPHALOGRAPH (EEG): *An instrument that measures the voltage that the brain produces (brain waves). Recordings of these voltages on sheets of paper are known as electroencephalograms.*

ADAPTIVE THEORY: *A theory suggesting that sleep evolved as a means for conserving energy and for protecting individuals from predators.*
REPAIR THEORY: *A theory suggesting that sleep serves a restorative function, allowing organisms to recuperate from physical, emotional, and intellectual demands.*

Using electrodes connected to EEG's, scientists can monitor brain-wave changes in this sleeping subject.

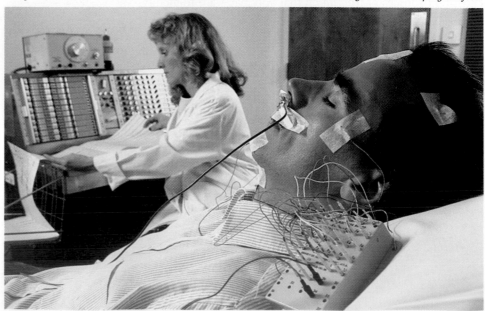

The Reticular Activating System (RAS) would awaken these sleeping animals in an emergency situation.

messages (the smell of smoke or the cries of their children). But since the RAS is dampened during sleep, most sensory information is ignored or incorporated into a dream. For example, sleepers who are sprinkled with water may sometimes dream that it has begun to rain, and those who wish to disregard their alarm clock may dream of a fire station alarm or similar sound.

The second major brain area that has been studied in relation to the production of sleep is the brain stem. Within the brain stem, researchers have located a "sleep center" with two separate areas that seem to be separately responsible for REM and NREM states of sleep. When either area is removed, the animal does not have the type of sleep for which the area is responsible.

Types of sleep

Question: What are REM and NREM types of sleep? During a typical night's sleep, each of us tends to experience two basic types of sleep: **rapid eye movement (REM) sleep** and **non-rapid eye movement (NREM) sleep.** During REM periods, the eyes dart about under the lids, in patterns very much like those of waking eye movements. In contrast, little or no eye movement occurs during NREM sleep. The two sleep states also differ in brain wave patterns and in heart and respiration rates (Aserinsky and Kleitman, 1953).

REM sleep is particularly fascinating to researchers because it is so clearly identifiable and because it signals that dreaming is taking place. You may have watched your sleeping pets making darting eye movements and occasional body twitches and wondered whether they were dreaming and what they were dreaming about. It is generally impossible to answer these questions with dogs or cats. However, human subjects can be wired to an EEG (to measure their brain waves) while they're sleeping in a laboratory and then wakened during REM states to find out what they're dreaming about. Research of this type led to the discovery of the correlation between REM sleep and dreaming. We now know that when attached to such electronic equipment, people who claim never to dream do report dreaming if they are awakened during REM sleep. Researchers have also found that when subjects are selectively deprived of REM sleep (by waking them each time they enter the state), they will later show a *rebound* effect — that is, they will try to "catch up" on REM sleep on subsequent occasions by spending more time than the usual amount in

RAPID EYE MOVEMENT (REM) SLEEP: *A stage of sleep marked by rapid eye movements, high-frequency brain waves, and dreaming.*
NON-RAPID EYE MOVEMENT (NREM) SLEEP: *Sleep stages 1 through 4, which are marked by an absence of rapid eye movements, relatively little dreaming, and variations in EEG activity.*

this state. Although the loss of REM sleep is generally harmful, some depressed individuals have been helped by a systematic program of REM deprivation (Borbely, 1986). By preventing or reducing the total amount of REM sleep, brain neurotransmitters are also altered and the individual experiences an improved mood.

REM sleep is also intriguing because it entails some important and apparently impossible contradictions, leading it to be called *paradoxical sleep.* For one thing, the brain in REM sleep is aroused and "awake" according to the measured brain waves, yet the person remains nonresponsive and asleep. In addition, signals from the brain suppress voluntary muscular activity during REM sleep, thereby effectively "paralyzing" the sleeper. At the same time, however, the involuntary system shows bursts of activity, including erratic blood pressure, changes in pupil size, rapid eye movements, muscle twitches, and erection of the penis and vaginal swelling. Early researchers believed that sexual dreams were the cause of the sexual arousal that occurs during the REM state, but in sleep laboratories it was later discovered that sexual arousal tends to come first, and the plot of the dream sometimes then changes to create a sexual theme.

Stages of sleep

Question: How many REM periods are there in a typical night's sleep?   In eight hours of sleep, there are typically four or five REM periods (see Figure 5.3). To understand the relation of REM to NREM sleep more fully, let's follow an "average" sleeper through a typical night of sleep. During the initial phase of sleep, the sleeper begins to relax and feel drowsy, the eyes close, the muscles relax, the breathing becomes slow and regular, and brain waves slowly move from **beta waves,** associated with normal wakefulness, to **alpha waves,** which indicate drowsy relaxation (see Figure 5.4). This period is sometimes referred to as a special type of ASC called the **hypnogogic state.** During this state many people report visual images (such as flashing lights and colors), auditory sensations (music or chimes), and kinesthetic experiences (bodily sensations such as feelings of falling).

As can also be seen in Figure 5.4, this hypnogogic state is followed by four stages of NREM sleep. As the sleeper moves through these stages, he or she becomes progressively less responsive and harder to awaken. Each of these stages is also characterized by a reduction in brain wave speed (there are fewer cycles per second) and an increase in voltage (on the graph, this can be seen by the higher "peaks" and lower "valleys").

After spending some time in the light sleep of *Stage 1,* the sleeper enters *Stage 2* and bursts of brain waves, known as *sleep spindles,* appear on the EEG. The stages of sleep that follow (*Stages 3 and 4*) are marked by **delta waves.** The delta wave, or slow wave, sleep is the deepest stage; as people age, their sleep becomes slighter and less of their sleep time is spent in Stages 3 and 4.

BETA WAVES: *Brain waves associated with normal wakefulness.*
ALPHA WAVES: *Brain waves that indicate drowsy relaxation.*
HYPNOGOGIC STATE: *A state of consciousness at the beginning of sleep in which many people experience visual, auditory, and kinesthetic sensations.*

DELTA WAVES: *Brain waves associated with the deepest level of sleep (Stages 3 and 4).*

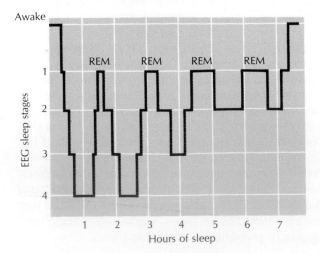

Figure 5.3 During a normal night's sleep, the sleeper moves in and out of various stages of sleep. Starting off alert, the sleeper gradually shifts from drowsiness into Stage 1, then Stages 2, 3, and 4. Note how the sleep cycle then reverses. During Stage 2, the sleeper stays a short time in REM and then the cycle starts downward again. As the night continues, the sleeper repeats this cycle four to five times. Note that progressively less time is spent in Stage 4, while more time is spent in REM.

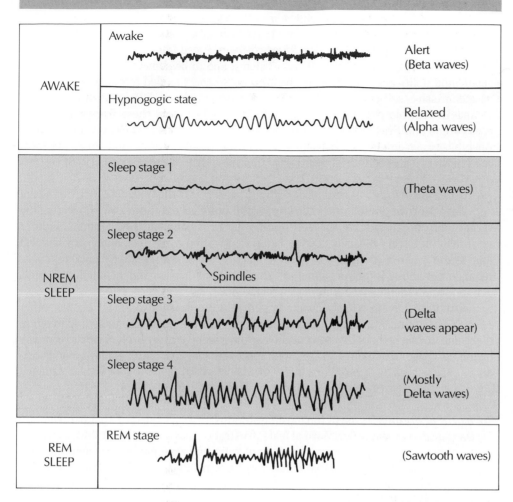

AWAKE	Awake	Alert (Beta waves)
	Hypnogogic state	Relaxed (Alpha waves)
NREM SLEEP	Sleep stage 1	(Theta waves)
	Sleep stage 2 — Spindles	
	Sleep stage 3	(Delta waves appear)
	Sleep stage 4	(Mostly Delta waves)
REM SLEEP	REM stage	(Sawtooth waves)

Figure 5.4 As an individual moves from being awake to deeply asleep, the brain produces remarkable differences in brain waves that can be measured by an electroencephalograph.

After spending some time in Stage 4, the sleep cycle shifts into reverse. From Stage 4, the sleeper goes back through Stages 3 and 2. During Stage 2, the sleeper enters REM sleep for the first time (refer back to Figure 5.3). After 8 to 15 minutes of REM sleep, the brain waves slow again and the cycle starts over. Each cycle generally lasts between 60 and 90 minutes, and most people experience four or five cycles in an average 7 to 8-hour night of sleep. As the night continues, the proportion of time spent in REM and NREM states changes, with REM sleep time lengthening and Stages 3 and 4 often being omitted. Thus, if you are accustomed to 8 hours of sleep and you sleep less than that, you will be losing out on a larger proportion of REM sleep.

Adults of all ages spend about 20 percent of their sleep time in REM and 80 percent in NREM, whereas the ratio is about 40 : 60 for infants (Long, 1987). Some researchers use this difference to suggest that REM sleep may be associated with the integration of new information. Since infants must learn more in a day than the average adult, they are believed to need longer periods in REM sleep (Dewan, 1970). The fact that REM sleep undergoes a dramatic increase when adult subjects wear inverting lenses, such as those discussed in Chapter 4, also supports this integration of information function (Herman and Roffwirg, 1983). REM sleep also increases with life stresses, such as marital conflict, death in the family, and financial worries (Hartmann, 1973), situations that call for additional information and adjustment.

Question: How many hours of sleep do I really need?   Most people average 7.6 hours of sleep a night, although some individuals seem to get by on less than 15 to 30 minutes of sleep a night (Meddis et al., 1973; Moore-Ede et al., 1982). In a study of men over the age of 20, it was found that *short sleepers* tended to be energetic, efficient, and ambitious, to complain rarely, to deny problems, and to be somewhat conforming both socially and politically. On the other hand, *long sleepers* tended to be more depressed, anxious, passive, self-critical, and inhibited (Hartmann et al., 1972). Other studies, using 17- and 18-year-old first-year college students, failed to show these personality differences (Webb and Friel, 1971). There does seem to be agreement, however, on the relationship between amount of sleep and physical health. Both "short" and "long" sleepers are at higher risk of serious stress-related illnesses (Kripke and Simons, 1976).

Question: How long could I go without sleep before doing damage?   Studies of sleep deprivation, such as Peter Tripp's 200-hour sleep-a-thon, have shown that the average person can tolerate up to 60 hours or so of complete sleeplessness without measurable ill effects (Borbely, 1986). But if deprivation continues, many subjects will begin to show increased irritability, delayed reaction times, and impaired mental functioning, and after about 100 hours some will show signs of distress and mental disturbance, such as Tripp's visual and auditory hallucinations.

Although having to stay awake is generally unpleasant for most people, other research has found little or no negative side effects from even prolonged deprivation (Webb and Cartwright, 1978). Seventeen-year-old Randy Gardner broke Tripp's record by staying awake for 264 hours and showed none of the bizarre hallucinations and disturbances experienced by Tripp. When interviewed on his final day as to how he had managed it, Gardner commented, "It's just mind over matter" (Dement, 1974, p. 12).

The world of dreams   One of the most mysterious aspects of sleep is that of dreaming. The average dream may reflect normal fears, frustrations, and personal desires, as well as events that violate laws of physics, principles of logic, and personal codes of morality. One survey of dream content found that dreams about being chased or about falling were the most common, followed by dreams of returning to a childhood home, flying, appearing naked or scantily clad in a public place, and being unprepared for an exam (Stark, 1984b). Thirty-nine percent of dreamers in this survey also claimed to be able to control the course of their dreams.

Question: Why do we dream?   A number of theories attempt to explain the purpose of dreams (Hunt, 1989). One of the oldest and most influential explanations is Freud's **psychoanalytic theory**, which suggests that dreams are disguised symbols of repressed desires. In one of his first books, *The Interpretation of Dreams* (1900), Freud argued that dreams are "the royal road to the unconscious," because dreaming is one of the few times when forbidden and personally unacceptable desires rise to the surface of consciousness. Using this reasoning, it is easy to see why we often dream of food when we're hungry or of having sex with someone other than our spouse, but how would forbidden desires explain the following dream, reported by a patient of analyst Louis Breger (1967)?

> I was walking down this street and I saw this booth and it said "help fat people" or something like this, and it was full of ugly fat people. [The sign said] "Pay here and we will give you the means" or something like this. So I went up and paid a lot of money and, ah, went away. I didn't refuse it. That was the end of the dream. (p. 20)

Since the dreamer was a slim and attractive young woman who had never had trouble with her weight, the dream seems difficult to understand on the basis of frustrated desires. However, when asked to explain her associations to the dream, the woman mentioned that she had secretly had an abortion the previous year and regretted the loss of the child. In response to this, Breger interpreted the "ugly" aspects of the fat people as a symbol for the guilt she experienced over her pregnancy and abortion.

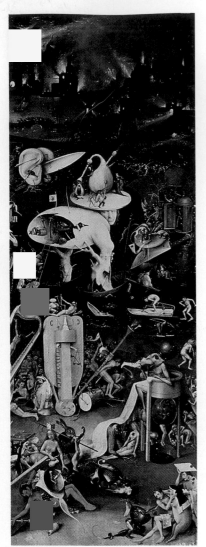

This painting by Hieronymos Bosch is a portrayal of the state of dreaming and it exemplifies how dreams sometimes violate the laws of physics and normal perception.

PSYCHOANALYTIC THEORY: *Freud's theory of personality that emphasizes the influence of the unconscious mind.*

According to Freud and other psychoanalysts, dreams sometimes offer us direct insight into the unconscious but more often the dream content is so threatening and anxiety producing that it must be couched in symbols. In this particular dream, the description of the "fat and ugly" people may be a symbol or disguise for the dreamer's underlying, hidden feelings associated with the pregnancy and abortion. Freud referred to such symbols as the **manifest content** of dreams, and the underlying, true meaning as the **latent content.**

In contrast to the Freudian model of dreaming is the **activation – synthesis hypothesis** advanced by J. Alan Hobson and Robert W. McCarley (1977) of Harvard Medical School. In their view, dreams have no real significance. On the basis of their research conducted on the brain activity of cats during REM sleep, these investigators proposed that dreaming is a simple and unimportant by-product of random stimulation of brain cells. According to this theory, certain cells in the sleep center of the brain stem are activated during REM sleep. The brain struggles to "synthesize" or make sense out of this random stimulation by searching through stored memories and manufacturing dreams.

One of the most popular recent dream theories is the **mental housecleaning hypothesis,** which suggests that we need to dream to get rid of useless, bizarre, or redundant information (Crick and Mitchinson, 1983). This housecleaning model, along with Freud's theory, has been synthesized by Evans (1984) into a theory that sees dreaming as analogous to a computer's process of program inspection. According to this theory, the brain, like a large computer system, must regularly shut down to update, rewrite, or test the complex programs it runs every day. Like a computer, the brain shuts down by going to sleep, whereas the computer goes "off-line." While the computer-brain is "down," it occasionally comes "on-line" by accident (dreaming), and the sleeper gets a glimpse of the program that is being run. As in the Freudian model, the programs that are being run during "down time" are those that have not been successfully resolved during the day, and as in the housecleaning model, the brain does work primarily to rid itself of "old programs."

Regardless of the exact reasons for dreaming, modern day psychotherapists still find dream analysis useful in uncovering core issues in therapy, and others have found their own positive ways to interpret and use their dreams to improve their everyday life. A leading dream researcher, Calvin Hall (1966), suggests that a dream can be seen as a "letter to oneself" and that by studying and analyzing a series of dreams one can often gain important personal insight. Similarly, Carl Jung (1933) believed that dreams help us to recognize ignored or suppressed aspects of our personality. And research by Rosalind Cartwright (1978) suggests that after dreaming subjects are better equipped to recognize the full dimension of their problems and to find realistic solutions.

Question: Can people sometimes tell that they're dreaming while the dream is going on? *Lucid dreaming,* in which the dreamer recognizes the dream as a dream, has been reported for many years and has recently been documented in studies where sleepers are trained to signal when they were dreaming by voluntarily moving their eyes and clenching their fists (Hunt, 1989; Laberge et al., 1981). Since this type of training also allows "on the scene" reporting versus after-the-fact recall, scientists are especially interested in this reporting technique. In this particular study they found that lucid dreamers were able to not only evaluate their dreams as they were occurring but on occasion to even influence the outcome.

Controlling your dreams might be particularly useful when they're bad. In fact, the problem of nightmares and other sleep disorders has gained considerable research attention in recent years.

Sleep disorders For most of us sleep is a strange opponent — we fight and welcome it at the same time. But for approximately 50 million Americans, sleep is a different kind of enemy. These people have the problem of sleeping too little (insomnia), sleeping too much (hypersomnia), or having troubled sleep (nightmares and night terrors).

MANIFEST CONTENT: *The surface content of a dream, containing dream symbols that distort and disguise the true meaning of the dream, according to Freudian dream theory.*
LATENT CONTENT: *The true, unconscious meaning of a dream, according to Freudian dream theory.*
ACTIVATION – SYNTHESIS HYPOTHESIS: *The idea that dreams have no real significance, but in fact are simply unimportant by-products of random stimulation of brain cells.*
MENTAL HOUSECLEANING HYPOTHESIS: *A theory suggesting that the function of dreaming is to rid the brain of useless, bizarre, or redundant information.*

INSOMNIA: *A sleep disorder in which a person has repeated difficulty in falling asleep, or staying asleep, or awakens too early.*

Insomnia is said to occur when a person has repeated difficulty falling asleep (taking longer than 20 minutes), staying asleep, or waking up too early. Although many people often think they have insomnia because they wrongly assume that everyone *must* sleep eight hours a night or because they think they aren't sleeping when they really are, a large percentage of the population (between 10 to 25 percent) does suffer from this disorder. Insomnia is often associated with alcohol and other drug abuse, with emotional disturbances (such as anxiety and depression), and with a variety of physiological conditions. Unfortunately, the most popular treatment for insomnia is drugs — either over-the-counter pills such as Sominex and Sleep-eze or prescription drugs such as tranquilizers and barbiturates. The problem with nonprescription pills is that they generally don't work (Kales and Kales, 1973). Prescription pills, on the other hand, create a type of artificial sleep — they put you to sleep but they decrease Stage 4 and REM sleep, thereby seriously disrupting the quality of sleep. People who regularly use sleeping pills also run the risk of psychological and physical drug dependence (Roth and Zorick, 1983). (We will discuss these terms in the next section, on chemical alterations of consciousness.)

Question: What is recommended instead of drugs? If you're having difficulty falling asleep at night, try concentrating on simple relaxation. Instead of monitoring the clock and nervously waiting to "fall asleep," close your eyes and try to systematically relax each part of your body. If this fails, you may want to try some of the more specific techniques listed in Table 5.1.

SLEEP APNEA: *A temporary cessation of breathing during sleep; one of the causes of snoring and a suspected cause of sudden infant death syndrome.*

A type of sleep disorder that is generally more serious and difficult to treat is **sleep apnea,** a temporary cessation of breathing. It is one of the causes of snoring and is a suspected factor in the *sudden infant death syndrome* (*SIDS,* or "crib death") (Guilleminault, 1979; Harper, 1983). Sleep apnea seems to result from blocked upper air passages or from the brain ceasing to send signals to the diaphragm, thus causing breathing to stop. Obstruction of the breathing passages is sometimes treated with reducing diets for obese patients. For others, surgery may be the answer. If you have friends who snore loudly, they may be suffering from sleep apnea and should be encouraged to seek medical attention, since the condition may eventually lead to heart damage. Babies with a suspected risk of SIDS can be helped by a special monitor that is mounted above the crib and sounds an alarm when the breathing weakens (Naeye, 1980). Since many adult sufferers are often unaware that sleep apnea is the cause of their sleep disturbances, they often seek help from doctors who may prescribe drugs to help them sleep more soundly. Such medications, as well as alcohol and other depressant drugs, are potentially dangerous since they also suppress the normal reflexes that would otherwise awaken the sleeper when breathing stops (Coleman, 1986).

NARCOLEPSY: *A disease marked by sudden and irresistible onsets of sleep during normal waking hours.*

A serious type of sleep disorder that is somewhat the opposite of insomnia is **narcolepsy** — excessive daytime sleepiness characterized by sudden and irresistible demands for sleep. During an attack, the narcoleptic's muscles unexpectedly go limp and he or she drops directly into the REM state of sleep. These attacks are obviously dramatic and incapacitating. Can you imagine what it would be like to be driving along the highway or walking across the campus and suddenly have an attack that would drop you immediately into REM sleep? Although stimulant drugs may help to reduce the frequency of attacks, the causes and cure of narcolepsy are still unknown. The fact that researchers at Stanford University's Sleep Disorders Center have selectively bred a group of narcoleptic dogs suggests a genetic basis for the disorder and a promising avenue for future research (Dement, 1983).

NIGHTMARES: *Anxiety-arousing dreams that generally occur near the end of the sleep cycle and during REM sleep.*
NIGHT TERRORS: *Abrupt awakenings from NREM sleep accompanied by intense physiological arousal and feelings of panic.*

Much more common among sleep disorders are **nightmares,** or bad dreams that occur toward the end of the sleep cycle during REM sleep. Less common but more frightening are **night terrors,** which occur early in the cycle during Stage 4 of NREM sleep. Night terrors are more upsetting than nightmares because the dreamer often awakens suddenly, in a state of panic, but with no clear recollection of the dream. Night terrors are most prevalent among preschool-age children but can also occur in adults, particularly during times of stress (Hartmann, 1983). Nightmares also seem to decrease

TABLE 5.1
Methods for Enhancing Sleep

Send yourself to slumberland

You can help yourself to a good night's sleep by preparing during the day and at bedtime. These suggestions come from the Better Sleep Council, a nonprofit educational organization in Burtonsville, Md.

During the day:

Exercise. Daily physical activity works away tension. But don't exercise vigorously late, or you'll get fired up instead.

Keep regular hours. An erratic schedule can disrupt biological rhythms. Get up at the same time each day.

Avoid stimulants. Coffee, tea, soft drinks, chocolate, and some medications contain caffeine. Nicotine may be an even more potent sleep disrupter.

Avoid late meals. Heavy or spicy meals at bedtime keep you awake. Have light snacks.

Eschew heavy drinking. Overindulgence can shatter your normal sleep pattern.

Stop worrying. Focus on your problems at a set time earlier in the day. If you worry in bed, tell yourself you'll resolve the problems tomorrow.

Use presleep rituals. Follow the same routine every evening: listen to music, write in a diary, meditate.

In bed:

Use progressive muscle relaxation. Alternately tense and relax various muscle groups.

Apply yoga. These gentle exercises help you relax.

Light a candle in your mind. Focus on the flame to get rid of distracting thoughts.

Try sandman's snacks. Eggs, tunafish, chicken, turkey, and soy beans contain L-tryptophan, an amino acid called nature's sleeping pill.

Have a nightcap. Warm milk and herbal teas can promote sleep. If your drink is alcohol, have only one.

Use fantasies. Imagine yourself in a tranquil setting. Feel yourself relax.

Use deep breathing. Take deep breaths, telling yourself you're falling asleep.

Try a splashdown. A warm bath can induce drowsiness because it sends blood away from the brain to the skin surface.

Use mind games. Imagine you're writing 6-foot-high numbers. Start at 100 and count backwards.

Count sheep. It works by relaxing both sides of the brain.

Source: USA Today, October 18, 1984. Reprinted with permission.

Cockroach nightmares

with age, are more likely to occur toward morning, and, contrary to popular opinion, are probably not the result of eating spicy foods (Hartmann, 1985).

Sleepwalking and *sleeptalking* also tend to accompany night terrors and generally occur during NREM sleep (which explains the movement). Nightmares, night terrors, sleepwalking, and sleep-talking all seem to be found more often in young children and in adults during times of stress. Thus, patience and soothing reassurance at the time of the sleep disruption are all that are generally recommended for treatment.

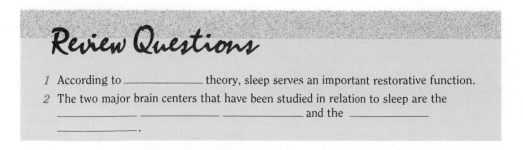

Review Questions

1 According to _____ theory, sleep serves an important restorative function.
2 The two major brain centers that have been studied in relation to sleep are the
_____ _____ _____ and the _____
_____.

3 Dreaming occurs primarily during _____ sleep, which has also been called _____ sleep.

4 As a person begins to relax before going to sleep, the brain waves of that person move from _____ waves associated with normal wakefulness to _____ waves that indicate drowsy relaxation.

5 The deepest stage of sleep is _____ or slow-wave sleep.

6 As the night continues, the amount of REM sleep _____ .

7 Freud believed that dreams were the road to the _____ mind.

8 According to Freud, dreams have two different types of content: the _____ content, which distorts the true meaning of the dream, and the _____ content, which represents the true meaning of the dream.

9 In contrast to the Freudian model of dreaming, the _____ _____ states that dreams have no real significance.

10 The major sleep disorders include _____, in which a person has difficulty falling asleep, _____ _____, in which a person has difficulty sleeping and breathing at the same time, and _____, in which the person has sleep attacks or excessive daytime sleepiness.

Answers: 1 repair; *2* reticular activating system, brain stem; *3* REM, paradoxical; *4* beta, alpha; *5* delta or Stage 4; *6* lengthens; *7* unconscious; *8* manifest, latent; *9* activation–synthesis hypothesis; *10* insomnia, sleep apnea, narcolepsy

CHEMICALLY ALTERED STATES OF CONSCIOUSNESS

PSYCHOACTIVE DRUGS: *Drugs that alter consciousness, perception, or mood.*

Since the beginning of civilization, **psychoactive drugs** (chemicals that change consciousness, perception, or mood) have been used, and abused, by people of all cultures (Julien, 1988). As an adult in contemporary times, you may use drugs like caffeine (in coffee, tea, chocolate, or cola) and nicotine (in cigarettes) to pick you up. On the other hand, you may use drugs like alcohol (in beer, wine, and cocktails) to relax you and lessen your inhibitions. How this use differs from abuse and how these chemical alterations in consciousness affect you both psychologically and physically are important topics in psychology.

Understanding drugs: Major physical and psychological effects

The line between use and abuse of mind-altering drugs is obviously ill defined, but the term *drug abuse* is generally used to refer to drug taking that causes emotional or physical harm to the individual or others, that is compulsive, or that follows a high-frequency, intense pattern.

Question: Is drug abuse the same as addiction? The term *addiction* was initially used to describe heavy and compulsive drug use, but in recent times it has been enlarged to include almost any type of compulsive activity. Psychologist Stanton Peele (1984a), for example, suggests that people may become "addicted" to television watching, work, or physical exercise programs like jogging, weight-lifting, or aerobics. One of the supposedly strongest addictions is that of romantic love (see Chapter 11).

PSYCHOLOGICAL DEPENDENCE: *A desire or craving to achieve the effects produced by a drug.*
PHYSICAL DEPENDENCE: *A condition in which bodily processes have been so modified by repeated use of a drug that continued use is required to prevent withdrawal symptoms.*

Because of the problems associated with such an all-encompassing definition, most drug researchers no longer use the term at all. Instead they use **psychological dependence** to refer to the mental desire or craving to achieve the effects produced by a drug and **physical dependence** to refer to the modifications of bodily processes such that continued drug use is required for normal daily functioning. The state of physical dependence is shown most clearly when the drug is withheld, as the user undergoes a series of painful physical reactions known as **withdrawal symptoms.**

Although psychological dependence is sometimes considered to be less dangerous than physical dependence, the effects on the drug user's life can be just as damaging (Orford, 1985). The desire or craving in psychological dependence can be so strong that the user ingests the drug regularly and maintains a constant drug-induced state. In addition, the psychological aspects of drug taking are often so powerful that an "addict" will return to his or her habit even after all signs of physical dependence are removed. Psychological and physical dependence may or may not occur together, as can be seen in Table 5.2.

WITHDRAWAL SYMPTOMS: *Unpleasant, painful, or agonizing physical reactions resulting from discontinued use of a drug.*

TABLE 5.2
Effects of the Major Psychoactive Drugs

Category	Desired Effects	Undesirable Effects	Physical Dependence	Psychological Dependence	Tolerance
Depressants					
Morphine, heroin, codeine	Euphoria, "rush" of pleasure, pain relief, prevention of withdrawal discomfort	Nausea, vomiting, constipation, painful withdrawal, shallow respiration, convulsions, coma, death	Yes	Yes	Yes
Alcohol, barbiturates, tranquilizers	Tension reduction, euphoria, disinhibition, drowsiness	Anxiety, nausea, disorientation, impaired reflexes and motor functioning, loss of consciousness, shallow respiration, convulsions, coma, death	Yes	Yes	Yes
Stimulants					
Cocaine, amphetamines, dexedrine	Exhilaration, euphoria, high physical and mental energy, perceptions of power, sociability, loss of appetite	Irritability, anxiety, paranoia, hallucinations, psychosis, convulsions, death	Yes[a]	Yes	Yes
Caffeine	Increased alertness	Insomnia, restlessness, increased pulse rate, sleep disruption, mild delirium, ringing in the ears, tachycardia	Yes[b]	Yes	Some
Nicotine	Relaxation, increased alertness, sociability	Irritability, raised blood pressure, stomach pains, vomiting, dizziness, cancer, heart disease, emphysema, death	Yes	Yes	Some
Hallucinogens					
LSD (lysergic acid diethylamide)	Delusions, hallucinations, distorted perceptions and sensations	Longer and more extreme delusions, hallucinations, and perceptual distortions ("bad trips"), psychosis, death	No	No	Yes
Marijuana	Relaxation, mild euphoria, increased appetite	Perceptual and sensory distortions, hallucinations, fatigue, lack of motivation, paranoia, possible psychosis	No	Yes[b]	Yes

Sources: Griffith (1983); Groves and Rebec (1988); Julien (1988); Leavitt (1984).

[a] Data are inconclusive concerning cocaine.
[b] Contradictory results.

The term *addiction* is also commonly confused with the physiological process of **tolerance,** in which larger and more frequent doses of a drug are required to produce the desired effect. After repeated use of a drug, many of the body's physiological processes adjust to higher and higher levels of the drug. Amounts far above what might be a lethal dose for nonusers can be ingested with virtually no effect, pleasurable or adverse. Tolerance is also what leads many users to escalate their drug use and to experiment with other drugs in an attempt to recreate the originally pleasurable altered state.

Question: Isn't there a lot of individual variation in the effects of various drugs? How a drug will affect a particular individual depends on several factors. These factors include the form in which the drug is taken (powder, liquid, vapor, pill, and so on) and the route by which it enters the body (through the lungs, the digestive tract, a vein, and so on) (Van Dyke and Byck, 1982). For example, tobacco can be smoked, snorted, or chewed, but each method has different effects. Obviously, the form of a drug will determine its route — it would be rather difficult to inhale a beer or to inject marijuana leaves.

Drug effects also depend on physical and psychological characteristics of the individual — "some people experience nothing even at high doses, while many others describe overwhelming sensations" (Snyder, 1980, p. 99). Physical characteristics that influence drug effects include individual metabolic variations, disease conditions, and variations in body weight and structure. The effects of alcohol, for example, can vary dramatically on the simple basis of body weight (see Figure 5.5). As a general rule of thumb, the greater a person's body weight, especially if the body has more muscle than fat, the more alcohol the person can drink without feeling the effects (Leavitt, 1982).

Among the most important psychological determinants of a drug's effects are the *set,* or internal state of the drug taker (including his or her beliefs and expectations), and the *setting,* or physical and interpersonal environment surrounding the individual at the time the drug is being taken (Duncan and Gold, 1982). According to Andrew Weil (1980), "drugs do not work unless set and setting encourage us to interpret their direct physical effects in ways that allow us to be high" (p. 41).

The various factors that influence drug experiences — including potentials for dependence, the form and route of the drug, and the person's set and setting — should be kept in mind as you read the rest of this section on psychoactive drugs. For convenience, psychologists commonly divide these drugs into three broad categories: *depressants,* *stimulants,* and *hallucinogens.* As we consider each category, we will discuss those drugs most widely used by college students. Our attention will focus on how these drugs affect states of consciousness. (How drugs affect the brain and nervous system was

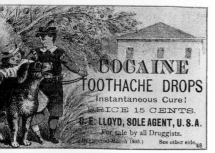

Before the Food and Drug Administration began to regulate the sale of drugs, substances like heroin, opium, and cocaine were easily available in over-the-counter nonprescription drugs.

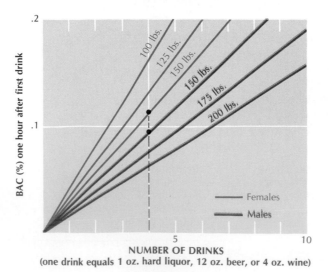

Figure 5.5 How weight and sex affect individual response to alcohol. Note that a 150-pound female, with four drinks in an hour, would have a blood alcohol concentration (BAC) of about 0.12 percent (legally drunk), whereas the same weight male drinking similarly would be just below the legal limit with a BAC of 0.095 percent. This is due to the female's normal larger fat-to-muscle ratio. These reactions assume all other factors are equal — stomach contents, speed of consumption, etc.

discussed in Chapter 2, how they affect prenatal development will be discussed in Chapter 9, and the types of therapy for substance abuse disorders will be discussed in Chapter 16.)

Depressants: Drugs that suppress the central nervous system

Depressants are drugs that act on the central nervous system to suppress or slow down bodily processes and reduce overall responsiveness. On the basis of differing effects, depressants are sometimes classified into opiates, barbiturates, and alcohol.

Opiates, which include morphine, heroin, and related substances, numb the senses and thus are used medically to relieve pain. They are appealing to those seeking an alternate state of consciousness because of their ability to produce feelings of relaxation and euphoria. The euphoria generally results from relief of pain, tension, anxiety, and feelings of inferiority. Users generally report a happy glow of contentment and a rosy perception of reality. The reaction to heroin sometimes includes a "rush," or ecstatic thrill of pleasure that reportedly resembles sexual experiences—an "abdominal orgasm."

If the opiate drugs are removed or withheld, the user experiences a very painful withdrawal. As we noted in Chapter 2, the brain produces chemicals closely resembling opiates (endorphins) and it contains special receptor sites for them. Regular opiate use overloads the endorphin receptor sites, and the brain soon stops producing these substances. When the drugs are no longer taken, neither opiates nor endorphins are available for regulating pain and discomfort. Thus, the user experiences excruciating pains of withdrawal (Platt, 1986).

Barbiturates, contained in sleeping pills and tranquilizers, constitute a second important type of depressant. The most widespread clinical uses are for short-term treatment of insomnia and to relieve anxiety. Tranquilizers, such as Valium, Librium, and Quaalude, initially produce feelings of relaxation and euphoria, but with extended use they also generate feelings of confusion, memory lapses, and reduced ability to concentrate. Because tolerance and dependence (both physical and psychological) are rapidly acquired with both sleeping pills and tranquilizers, there is a strong potential for abuse.

Alcohol is the most widely used (and abused) drug in our society. It is also a powerful central nervous system depressant.

Question: How can alcohol be a depressant? Doesn't it lift people's spirits? This classification is confusing to many people since alcohol has the popular reputation for being a "party drug." Because the initial effects of alcohol serve to relieve anxiety, many people have noticed that a drink or two does seem to relax them and to put them in a party mood. In addition to these initial effects, increasing doses of alcohol also disinhibit or reduce normal constraints on behavior and provide an overall sense of euphoria. Based on these effects it is easy to see why alcohol has so often been seen as a stimulant rather than as a depressant. The depressant qualities are more easily understood when we look at the effects of increasing drug dosage or blood alcohol level (as shown in Figure 5.6).

Question: Can you explain why with similar doses some people become silly or the life of the party, whereas others become angry and abusive? The disinhibitory effects of alcohol and the label of "drunkenness" are sometimes used as an excuse for inappropriate or antisocial behaviors—"He was drunk and didn't know what he was doing." Research has also explained these individual differences as a reflection of varying expectancies (*set*) concerning the effects of alcohol (Bauman et al., 1985; Massey and Goldman, 1988). This set can then lead to a *self-fulfilling prophecy* in which the drinker acts in ways that are consistent with his or her expected behavior. The environment or *setting* in which people drink alcohol may also affect behavior. Suppose you've just broken up an important love relationship and then see your previous partner with someone else at a party. If you have a few drinks, the alcohol may encourage a variety of

DEPRESSANTS: *Psychoactive drugs that act on the central nervous system to suppress or slow down bodily processes and reduce overall responsiveness.*

Alcohol maintains its popular reputation as a "party drug" because it relaxes and disinhibits the user.

BLOOD ALCOHOL CONTENT (%)	EFFECT
.05	Relaxed state; judgment not as sharp
.08	Everyday stress lessened
.10*	Movements and speech become clumsy
.20	Very drunk; loud and difficult to understand; emotions unstable
.40	Difficult to wake up; incapable of voluntary action
.50	Coma and/or death

* Most states use .10 as the lowest indicator of driving while intoxicated. A few states use .08, while some go as high as .12.

Figure 5.6 Alcohol's effects on the body and behavior. Responses to a given blood alcohol concentration (BAC) vary from one person to the next and even in the same person under different situations.

reactions — feelings of sadness and self-recrimination, flirting with others, or even jealous violence toward the "interloper."

Research on the puzzling effects of alcohol on behavior has important implications for some of our most serious social problems. Did you know, for example, that alcohol is a factor in nearly half of all murders, suicides, and accidental deaths in the United States (Lord et al., 1987)? Or did you know that drinking drivers presently account for about one-half of all highway fatalities (Leavitt, 1982)? Medical authorities also list alcohol as the third leading cause of birth defects (Julien, 1985). When we add in the fact that about 7 percent of all adults in the United States are considered *problem drinkers* — people who get drunk at least once a month — we can see that alcohol abuse is indeed an important social issue.

Question: Why haven't the repeated warnings about drinking reduced these statistics?   For many in our society, alcohol is not considered a "drug." Although the American Medical Association has long considered alcohol to be the most dangerous and physically damaging of all psychoactive drugs, drinking still enjoys wide social acceptance. Most people would undoubtedly be shocked and outraged by someone publicly "shooting up" a dose of heroin, yet they calmly accept alcohol consumption at major sporting events, parties, business lunches, and dinner get-togethers. In addition, many parents express relief when they discover that their teenagers are "only drinking," yet recent surveys find this group to be one of the largest of alcohol abusers (Foderaro, 1989; Leary, 1988). And teens, like most problem drinkers, will often deny that they have a problem. According to the American Psychiatric Association (1985), you have an alcohol dependency if you experience three or more of the following:

1. You are frequently preoccupied with alcohol.
2. You often drink more than you intend.
3. You need more and more alcohol to get drunk.
4. You suffer withdrawal symptoms.
5. Despite repeated attempts, you fail to cut down on drinking.
6. You are frequently drunk or impaired when expected to fulfill social or occupational obligations.
7. You are willing to give up important social, occupational, or recreational opportunities to drink.
8. You drink despite a significant social, occupational, or legal problem, or a physical disorder worsened by alcohol.

Question: Why do authorities warn us about mixing alcohol and barbiturates? The combination of alcohol and barbiturates can be particularly dangerous because of the **synergistic effect,** which means that the two drugs interact in such a way that the combined effects are much stronger than a simple summation of their individual doses. The combination of alcohol and barbiturates can easily become fatal because it causes the diaphragm muscles to relax to such a degree that the person literally suffocates. Actress Judy Garland is among celebrities known to have died from barbiturate and alcohol mixture.

SYNERGISTIC EFFECT: *The interaction of two or more drugs such that the combined effects are much stronger than a simple summation of their individual doses.*

Due to the synergistic effect, combining coffee and cigarettes results in a stronger effect than taking similar quantities of either drug alone.

Review Questions

1 Drugs that change conscious awareness or perception are called _____ drugs.

2 A desire or craving to achieve the effects produced by a drug is termed _____ .

3 People have developed a physical dependence on a drug when their bodily processes have been affected so severely that without repeated use of the drug they will experience _____ symptoms.

4 The need for larger and larger doses of a drug to achieve the same effects is called _____

5 Among the most important psychological determinants of a drug's effects are the _____ and the _____ .

6 _____ are drugs that act on the central nervous system to suppress or slow down bodily processes and reduce overall responsiveness.

7 Drugs such as heroin, valium, and alcohol are classified as _____ .

8 That alcohol is a severe social problem can be seen from the fact that about _____ of all fatal automobile accidents are associated with drinking drivers.

9 When two drugs interact in such a way that the combined effects are much stronger than a simple summation of their individual doses, they are said to have a _____ effect.

Answers: 1 psychoactive; *2* psychological dependence; *3* withdrawal; *4* tolerance; *5* set, setting; *6* depressants; *7* depressants; *8* one-half; *9* synergistic

Stimulants: Drugs that activate the central nervous system

Whereas depressants are "downers," stimulants are "uppers." **Stimulant** drugs act on the brain and nervous system, increasing its overall activity and general responsiveness. Nicotine, caffeine, amphetamines, and cocaine are by far the most common uppers used and abused in our society.

In low initial doses, the stronger stimulants (amphetamines and cocaine) promote feelings of high physical and mental energy and perceptions of power and invulnerability. This alternate state is highly reinforcing, leading the person to make repeated attempts at recapturing the high and avoiding the inevitable comedown. The inevitable low that accompanies stimulant abuse is seldom acknowledged by the general public. Instead of recognizing that the high is a result of actual depletion of their own bodily energy stores, many people seem to falsely attribute the extra energy to some sort of magic quality of the drug. Just as credit card purchases sometimes seem like an easy source of extra money, stimulants also seem to offer an easy source of extra energy. But after continued use of

STIMULANTS: *Drugs that act on the brain and nervous system, increasing their overall activity and general responsiveness.*

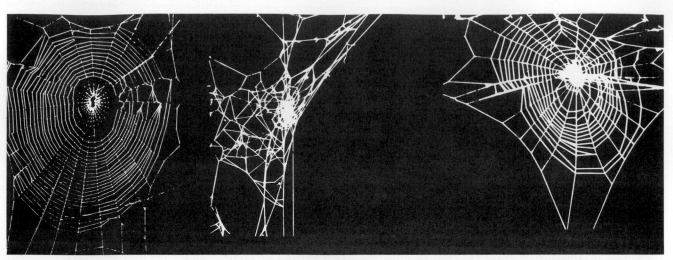

Notice the symmetry and precision of the normal web of the female spider (left), and contrast it with the irregularity when the spider was interrupted (center photo) or exposed to cocaine (right).

stimulants and higher doses, the "bills" come in: irritability, anxiety, paranoia, and auditory or visual hallucinations. [In relation to this, it's interesting to note that Peter Tripp was using a substantial dose of amphetamines during his wake-a-thon, which may account for the hallucinations he reported, instead of the supposed lack of sleep (Luce and Segal, 1966).]

Stimulant use often leads to psychological dependence, increased tolerance, and ultimately abuse. There are cases in which stimulants have legitimate medical value, as in the treatment of narcolepsy. However, these drugs tend to be widely abused, especially by many medical professionals (such as doctors and dentists) and by airline pilots, professional athletes, truck drivers, and railroad personnel.

Question: What do these particular groups have in common that would explain this abuse? The last two groups (truck drivers and railroad personnel) seem to use stimulants to counteract long hours and the boring or repetitive nature of their work. Although doctors, pilots, and athletes sometimes share these same problems, they often cite occupational pressures and stresses as the major reason for their use of stimulants. Athletes, for example, must endure an incredible amount of physical and psychological abuse, and stimulants help them to cope—at least in the beginning. Because of the increase in physical and mental energy experienced with initial doses, athletes generally believe that their performance is improved, setting the stage for continued drug use that sometimes slips into abuse. Whether or not the drug really does improve the athlete's performance, the fact that he or she *believes* that it does is all important.

Question: Why are there so many warnings about cocaine abuse in particular? Although cocaine was once considered to be a relatively harmless "recreational drug," its potential for physical damage and severe psychological dependence has generally been underestimated (Fackelmann, 1989a; Long, 1989). Sigmund Freud is often cited as a supporter of cocaine use, but few people know that in his later writings Freud also warned that overuse of the drug could lead to severe depression and psychosis. The tragic death of the college basketball star Len Bias also brought widespread attention to the fact that even small, initial doses can sometimes be fatal (Leo, 1986).

Question: How can cocaine cause death? It can interfere with the electrical system of the heart causing ventricular fibrillation and resultant heart failure. It can also produce heart attacks by temporarily constricting blood supplies (Barnes, 1988).

Although there is still controversy over whether cocaine produces physical dependence, animals who are allowed unlimited access will self-administer the drug in long

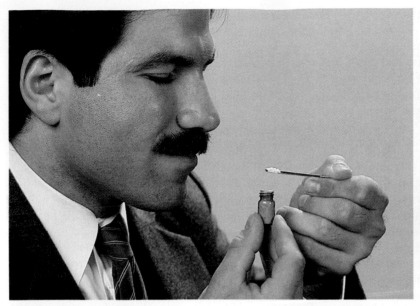

Although many people associate cocaine use with teenage gangs and prostitutes, cocaine is most widely consumed among white, upper- and middle-class adults.

Singer Andy Gibb, died at the age of 30 as a result of cocaine abuse.

binges, and a significant number will self-administer a lethal dose (Koob and Bloom, 1988). Cocaine seems to have similar ill effects on human users. Some individuals may remain "social sniffers" who restrict their use to occasional recreational purposes, yet many individuals become "cokeaholics" who lose control over their consumption and will jeopardize everything for the drug (Stone et al., 1985). The potential dangers for cocaine abuse used to be somewhat limited by its relatively high cost. In recent years, however, increased production and supply have lowered the cost and the development of cheaper forms of the drug (such as "crack") has made it widely available to all groups.

Question: Why is cocaine so popular?   One of the primary reasons for its popularity is that it reportedly induces strong feelings of power, security, and individual dynamism—emotions that are highly valued in our culture (Stone et al., 1985). In addition to these initial effects, repeated use of cocaine seems to create an inability to feel pleasure without the drug. Drug researchers Frank Gawin and Herbert Kleber (1984) have found that cocaine abusers "can't get off on the real world." They take the drug initially to obtain the feelings of unusual power and dynamism but then find they can no longer obtain satisfaction from everyday life.

Question: Isn't this the way all drug addictions work?   Although each psychoactive drug alters the user's "normal" state of consciousness, which may affect their enjoyment of everyday life, cocaine seems to be one of the most rewarding of all known chemicals. As mentioned earlier, rats apparently find cocaine so irresistible that they will self-administer to the point of death, and Wise (1984) suggests that this may be due to cocaine's unique effect on the reward or pleasure centers of the brain (see Chapter 2). It is also known that cocaine and amphetamines have a strong effect on feelings of energy and power largely because they increase the amount of available neurotransmitters in the synapse (the depressants decrease the amount or block the transmission). The initial high is due to the prolonging of the neurotransmitters' effects, and the inevitable crash afterward is due to the depletion of these neurotransmitters. In response to this, Gawin and Kleber have helped some cocaine abusers kick their habit by administering certain drugs that mimic the effect of cocaine but are not habit forming and do not cause the same overall depletion of neurotransmitters.

APHRODISIACS: *Substances that supposedly increase sexual desire.*

One additional reason for the current popularity of cocaine is its reputation as a "love drug." Throughout history, people have gone to great lengths in search of **aphrodisiacs,** or substances that increase sexual desire. But cocaine, like alcohol, probably maintains its sexual reputation because it lowers inhibitions and because of the self-fulfilling nature of expectations. If people believe cocaine or any other substance will improve their sexual performance and enjoyment, they will act in such a way that they will make this belief come true.

Hallucinogens: Drugs that alter perception

HALLUCINOGENS: *Drugs that produce visual, auditory, or other sensory hallucinations.*

One of the most popular ways to alter consciousness is through the use of **hallucinogens,** drugs that produce visual, auditory, or other sensory hallucinations. According to some reports, colors are brighter and more luminous, patterns often seem to pulsate and rotate, and senses may seem to fuse — colors are "heard" or sounds "tasted." Perhaps as a result of these changes in normal sensory or perceptual experiences, hallucinogens are highly valued by some artists as a way of increasing creativity (Leavitt, 1982). Some cultures have also used these drugs for religious purposes as a way to experience "other realities" or to communicate with the supernatural. In Western societies, most people use hallucinogens for their reported "mind-expanding" potentials, but there have also been reports of terror-filled "bad trips" and dangerous *flashbacks,* where the effects of the drug spontaneously reoccur long after the initial ingestion.

Hallucinogens are also commonly referred to as *psychedelic* (from the Greek for "mind manifesting"). Drugs in this category include mescaline (derived from the peyote cactus, its effects on Aldous Huxley are described in the opening example), psilocybin (from mushrooms), phencyclidine (chemically derived), and LSD (derived from ergot, a rye mold). Marijuana ("pot," "grass," or hashish) is sometimes classified as a hallucinogen since in sufficient dosages it can produce mental effects similar to the stronger hallucinogens. We will focus on LSD and marijuana in our discussion because they are the most widely used of these drugs.

According to psychologist Ronald Siegel, white lights that appear to explode from the center to the periphery or spiral tunnels that seem to pulsate and rotate are often reported during drug-induced hallucinations.

LSD Lysergic acid diethylamide (LSD), an odorless, tasteless, and colorless substance, is one of the most potent drugs known. As little as 10 micrograms of LSD can produce a measurable effect in one individual, while an amount the size of a five-grain aspirin is enough to produce effects in 3000 people. In 1943 Albert Hofman, the Swiss chemist who first synthesized LSD in a laboratory, accidentally licked some of the drug off his finger and later recorded in his journal:

> Last Friday, April 16, 1943, I was forced to stop my work in the laboratory in the middle of the afternoon and to go home, as I was seized by a peculiar restlessness associated with a feeling of mild dizziness. Having reached home, I lay down and sank in a kind of drunkenness which was not unpleasant and which was characterized by extreme activity of imagination. As I lay in a dazed condition with my eyes closed (I experienced daylight as disagreeably bright) there surged upon me an uninterrupted stream of fantastic images of extraordinary plasticity and vividness and accompanied by an intense, kaleidoscope-like play of colors. This condition gradually passed off after about two hours.
>
> *Hofman (1968), pp. 184–185*

Perhaps because the LSD experience is so powerful, few people actually "drop acid" on a regular basis, which may account for the fact that it has a relatively low reported abuse rate ("Psychedelic drugs," 1990).

Question: Is it true that LSD was used for experimental purposes by the army? LSD has been used experimentally in the treatment of schizophrenia and alcoholism, and it has been tried by the military as a possible drug for "brainwashing" and inducing prisoners to talk. Any potential therapeutic or military value has been clouded, however, by the negative associations created by early controversial proponents such as

The potential harm of marijuana use is still a matter of uncertainty and debate for both scientists and the general public.

Timothy Leary and by the well-publicized case of the U.S. Army's experiment in which LSD was given to subjects without warning them of its effects. The ability of LSD to so strongly affect consciousness makes it a particularly dangerous drug if ingested without warning. Suicide and serious psychological reactions are possible if the user is not aware of the potential of the drug and fails to interpret the LSD trip in the "appropriate" manner.

Marijuana   Marijuana is a hard drug to classify. It has some of the properties of depressants, as well as those of stimulants and hallucinogens. Regardless of its classification, it is one of the most popular of all illegal consciousness-altering drugs today. In low doses it induces a sense of relaxation and mild euphoria sometimes characterized by detachment or uncontrollable giggles. With higher doses subjects often report disruptions in time perception and sensory experiences and, with very high doses, visual or auditory hallucinations.

With the exception of alcohol during the time of Prohibition, there has never been a drug more hotly debated than marijuana — or more heavily researched (Weil and Rosen, 1983). For every study that lists no ill effects with moderate usage, there exists a conflicting study that lists dangers. These dangers include throat and respiratory disorders, impaired lung functioning and immune response, declines in testosterone levels, reduced sperm count, impairment of short-term memory, disruption of the menstrual cycle and ovulation, and brain atrophy (Bower, 1988b; Fackelmann, 1989a; Scott, 1988; Wallace and Fisher, 1983). It has also been suggested that using marijuana may make people infected with the AIDS virus more likely to develop the disease (Ost, 1987).

Arguments over the short-term and long-term dangers associated with marijuana use will undoubtedly continue for many years. However, some research has found marijuana to be therapeutic in the treatment of glaucoma, in alleviating the nausea and vomiting associated with chemotherapy, in increasing appetite, and in treating asthma, seizures, and anxiety (Leavitt, 1982; Leo, 1988).

Question: My friends tell me that marijuana improves their driving abilities. Is this true?   The human limits of attention and memory are the prime sources of failures in human–machine control situations (Moskowitz, 1973), and marijuana and similar drugs clearly affect these abilities. Like alcohol, marijuana and the other psychedelic drugs also affect motor coordination in addition to their alteration in sensory and perceptual abilities. Research with aircraft pilots in computer-simulated flight tasks has shown that a "social dose" of marijuana will hamper performance for as long as 24 hours (Bower, 1985b).

We have just completed our whirlwind trip through the drugs used to induce alternate states of consciousness. Before we go on, we'd like to offer a brief warning. We've tried to be as factual as possible in our presentation of this material, but the information is obviously limited and will quickly become dated. With all drug consumption, both prescription and "recreational," the consumer must assume the responsibility for maintaining a complete and up-to-date drug education. This warning is particularly important for illicit "street drugs." Since there are no truth-in-packaging laws to protect buyers from unscrupulous practices, sellers often substitute unknown, cheaper, and potentially even more dangerous substances for the ones they claim to be selling. The cocaine-related deaths of sports stars like Don Rogers can be traced to very potent or adulterated forms of the drug (Gold, Gallanter, and Stimmel, 1987). When you add in the danger of transmission of deadly infectious diseases such as AIDS and hepatitis, which can be passed through the sharing of nonsterile needles, and the problem of the high variability in potency from one supply of drugs to another, you can see that drug use has several dangers outside the ones associated with the particular drug itself.

In addition to these "old" problems that have been with us for many years, we also face some new dilemmas. New and untried drugs like clove cigarettes, and the so-called **designer drugs** created by "street chemists," pose unknown threats. **Polydrug use**, in which several drugs are used at the same time, increases the problem. In early studies of polydrug use, scientists found that heavy alcohol abusers are also more likely to smoke and that the combination seems to increase the chances for cancers of the mouth, larynx, and throat (University of California, Berkeley Wellness Letter, 1986). A new synthetic drug that has caused particular concern is crystal methamphetamine (a form of amphetamine). This drug, the cheapest form is known as "ice," produces insomnia, anxiety, depression, and serious psychotic symptoms that are sometimes indistinguishable from paranoid schizophrenia (Largent, 1989). Given that almost all drugs, including those usually derived from plants, can be synthesized in a laboratory, many drug enforcement experts are warning the public that efforts to control drugs may be doomed to failure (Browne, 1989).

Given the basic human desire to experiment with other states of consciousness, we would like to offset the serious concerns associated with drugs by encouraging more positive routes to alternate states. The fact is that many benefits associated with drugs, such as relaxation and improved mood, can be achieved through such nondrug methods as hypnosis and meditation.

DESIGNER DRUGS: *Drugs produced by slightly altering the molecular structure of psychoactive drugs, thereby creating a new drug that has similar effects.*

POLYDRUG USE: *The combining of several drugs, which results in unknown and potentially serious side effects.*

Review Questions

1 A desire or craving to achieve the effects produced by a drug is known as _____ _____ ; whereas_____ _____ refers to a condition in which repeated use of the drug is necessary to prevent withdrawal symptoms.

2 Drugs that act on the brain and nervous system to increase its overall activity are called _____ .

3 The strongest illegal stimulants most commonly abused are _____ and _____ .

4 Drugs that cause visual, auditory, or other sensory hallucinations are called _____ .

5 The use of _____ leads to a powerful experience characterized mostly by visual hallucinations.

6 _____ has been found to be effective in the treatment of glaucoma and in alleviating the nausea and vomiting associated with chemotherapy.

7 When street chemists take a known drug and slightly alter its molecular structure, they have created a _____ _____ .

Answers: 1 psychological dependence, physical dependence; *2* stimulants; *3* amphetamines, cocaine; *4* hallucinogens; *5* LSD; *6* marijuana; *7* designer drug

DISTINGUISHING FACT FROM OPINION
Understanding Claims about Drug Use and Abuse

The topic of drugs often generates heated debate between people of differing perspectives. When discussing controversial issues, it is helpful to make a distinction between statements of *fact* and statements of *opinion*. (A fact is a statement that can be proven true. An opinion is a statement that expresses how a person feels about an issue or what someone thinks is true.) Although it is also important to later determine whether the facts *are* true or false, in this exercise simply mark "O" for opinion and "F" for fact.

_____ *1* Marijuana is now one of America's principal cash crops.

_____ *2* Friends don't let friends drive drunk.

_____ *3* People who use drugs aren't hurting anyone but themselves.

_____ *4* Legalizing drugs such as cocaine, marijuana, and heroin would make them as big a problem as alcohol and tobacco.

_____ *5* The number of cocaine addicts is small compared with the number of alcoholics.

_____ *6* The American Medical Association considers alcohol to be the most dangerous of all psychoactive drugs.

_____ *7* Once legalized, drugs would become cheaper and more accessible to people who previously had not tried them.

_____ *8* Random drug tests are justified for personnel involved with public safety (e.g., air traffic controllers, police officers, etc.).

_____ *9* Eventually all employers will require urinalysis for prospective employees.

_____ *10* One-quarter of all Fortune 500 companies now administer urinalysis tests to applicants or current employees.

_____ *11* If parents use drugs, their children are more likely to use drugs.

_____ *12* You're not living life if you're high on drugs.

_____ *13* Mothers who deliver cocaine-addicted babies are guilty of child abuse.

_____ *14* Alcohol abuse by pregnant mothers is one of the most important factors in mental retardation.

ANSWERS: Rather than offering specific answers to these questions, we suggest that you discuss your answers with your classmates and friends. Listening to the reasons others give for their answers often provides valuable insights in distinguishing between fact and opinion. (Adapted from Bach, 1988.)

ADDITIONAL ROUTES TO ALTERNATE STATES

As we have discovered thus far in this chapter, alternate states of consciousness may be reached through everyday means such as sleep and dreaming or through the chemical channel of drugs. In this section we will explore two additional routes for changing consciousness: hypnosis and meditation.

Hypnosis: A true alternate state?

Many students are initially surprised to find that hypnosis has become a respectable topic for a college textbook. Because of its "shady" past and its association with quackery and magic, hypnosis has often been dismissed rather than considered a possibly legitimate psychological phenomenon and medical technique.

Question: What exactly is hypnosis? **Hypnosis** is believed to be an alternate state of consciousness characterized by one or more of the following: (1) heightened suggestibility (increased willingness to respond to proposed changes in perceptions — "this onion is an apple"); (2) narrowing and focusing of attention (the subject is able to "tune out" competing sensory stimuli); (3) an effortless use of imagination and hallucina-

HYPNOSIS: *An alternate state of heightened suggestibility characterized by relaxation and intense focus.*

For many years stage hypnotists have used suspension tricks of this type to convince audiences of their special powers, but any well-motivated, nonhypnotized person can duplicate this "plank effect" (left photo). One of the most widely-used professional tests of hypnosis involves measurements of arm rigidity, hand lowering, and eye closure (right photo).

tions (in the case of visual hallucinations, subjects may see things that aren't there or not see things that are); (4) a passive and receptive attitude; and (5) decreased responsiveness to pain (Hilgard, 1986; Groot et al., 1988; Wilkes, 1986).

The characteristic of increased suggestibility is often used as support of the argument that hypnosis is *not* a separate and distinct state of consciousness. Theodore X. Barber (1969), for example, suggests that hypnosis is simply the result of experimental demand characteristics (the subject attempts to please the experimenter and tries not to "ruin the show") and of role playing (the subject plays the role he or she believes a "hypnotized" person is expected to play). Studies by Kirsch (1985) and Council et al. (1986) have agreed that the subject's expectancy of how easily he or she can be hypnotized or of what hypnosis is like may be the most important variable in so-called hypnotic behavior. It has also been difficult to demonstrate physiological differences between hypnotized and unhypnotized subjects in terms of eye movements, brain wave patterns, and other physiological measures like respiration and heart rate.

One of the most convincing theories supporting the idea that hypnosis *is* a unique and separate state of consciousness is that of **dissociation.** In dissociation one part of your mind is conscious of certain experiences (and can report on them) and another part is not (Kelly and Kelly, 1985). Have you ever arrived at your destination and realized that you didn't remember a single detail of the drive? The fact that you managed to make all the right turns, stopped at stop signs, and maneuvered through traffic is evidence of your own experience with dissociation or "highway hypnosis." In a similar fashion, people can be hypnotized and one part of their mind will be unaware of strong sensations of pain while another part seems to be watching and monitoring. This "hidden observer" is easily seen in research where subjects are hypnotized not to feel pain while their hands are in ice water for 45 seconds, a situation that normally produces intense pain (Hilgard, 1978). However, when these same subjects are asked to report the pain through "the eyes" of the hidden observer, they will press a key that indicates a higher level of pain. As shown in Figure 5.7, one part of the mind is apparently aware of the pain while the other is fully hypnotized and unaware.

Dissociation theory is an intriguing explanation of hypnosis, but it is not universally accepted (Coe, 1987; Spanos and Chaves, 1988). Some critics have argued that the "hidden observer" in dissociation is also engaging in a subtle form of role playing. While psychologists continue to debate whether hypnosis *is* or is *not* a separate form of consciousness, magicians and entertainers continue to amuse large audiences by asking volunteers to impersonate the opposite sex, to "cluck like a chicken," and so on.

DISSOCIATION: *A splitting or separating of consciousness. Under hypnosis, one part of consciousness seems to be aware and observing hypnotic suggestions, while a separate type of consciousness is responding to the suggestion.*

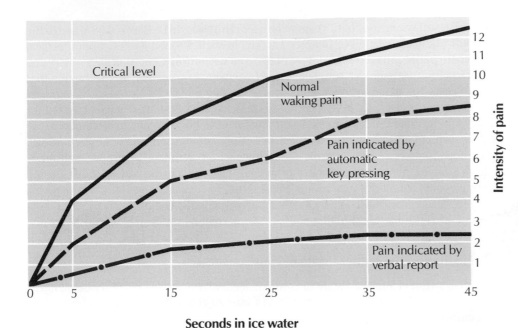

Critical level

Normal
waking pain

Pain indicated by
automatic
key pressing

Pain indicated by
verbal report

Intensity of pain

Seconds in ice water

Figure 5.7 Compared to unhypnotized subjects, hypnotized ones will verbally report little pain while their hands are submerged in ice water. When asked to report the pain through the "eyes" of the hidden observer, however, the subjects will press a key indicating a higher level of pain. [*Source:* Hilgard, E.R. (1977). *Divided consciousness: Multiple controls in human thought and action.* New York: Wiley. Copyright © 1977. Reprinted with permission of John Wiley & Sons Inc.]

Question: Can I be hypnotized even if I don't want to be? Research on hypnosis has cleared up a number of popular misconceptions about the phenomenon. One popular misunderstanding is the idea that people can be hypnotized against their will. Because hypnosis requires the subject to make a conscious decision to willingly relinquish control of his or her consciousness to another person, it is virtually impossible to hypnotize an unwilling subject. As a matter of fact, about 8 to 9 percent of the population *cannot* be hypnotized even when they are willing and trying very hard to cooperate. The best potential subjects are those who are able to focus attention, are open to new experience, and are capable of imaginative involvement or fantasy (Hilgard, 1979; Lynn and Rhue, 1988).

A related misconception is that hypnosis can make a person do dangerous or immoral actions against his or her will. Generally speaking, people will not go against their basic value system. In the face of morally conflicting suggestions from the hypnotist, the subject will simply come out of the hypnosis. It is also a misconception that under hypnosis people can perform acts of superhuman strength. When unhypnotized subjects are simply asked to try their hardest on tests of physical strength, they can generally do anything that a hypnotized subject can do (Barber, 1976).

A controversial question about hypnosis concerns its role in memory. In spite of widely publicized success stories about witnesses or victims who under hypnosis were able to remember crucial facts that led to the arrest and conviction of dangerous criminals, many judges and state bar associations have banned the use of hypnosis and the testimony of hypnotized subjects from the courtroom (Spiegel, 1985; Stark, 1984a). Researchers such as Elizabeth Loftus (1980, 1983) have shown that memories are imperfect. Unlike videotape recordings, memories are inaccurate records, and they become further distorted by the process of recollection (see Chapter 7). Researchers *have* found that under hypnosis some parts of recall memory are improved (because the subject is able to relax and focus intently on a particular topic), but the number of errors also increases (because the subject has more difficulty in separating fact and fantasy and is more willing to guess) (Dywan and Bowers, 1983; Dywan, 1984).

Question: Can hypnotized people really undergo major surgery without anesthesia? Before the discovery of anesthetics like ether and chloroform, hypnosis was widely used with surgical patients. In more recent times, hypnosis has occasionally been successful when anesthetics cannot be used (Hilgard and Le Baron, 1984) and in the treatment of chronic pain (see Chapter 13). Hypnosis has found its best use in medical areas where patients have a high degree of fear and misinformation, such as dentistry and obstetrics. Because pain is strongly affected by tension and anxiety, any technique that helps to relax the patient is medically useful.

Hypnosis is also used in psychotherapy to help patients relax, remember, or reduce anxiety and has had limited success in the treatment of phobias, and in attempts to lose weight, stop cigarette smoking, and improve study habits (Long, 1986; Miller, 1982). Many individuals have used a form of self-hypnosis to regulate their pain, and many athletes use self-hypnosis techniques of mental imagery and focused attention during sporting events. Long-distance runner Steve Ortiz, for example, mentally relives all his best races before a big meet, and by the time the race actually begins he says, "I'm almost in a state of self-hypnosis. I'm just floating along" (cited in Kiester, 1984, p. 23).

Meditation: A "higher" state of consciousness?

MEDITATION: *A relaxed state of consciousness that is characterized either by detachment from the external world or by directed focus on the external world.*

Meditation is a relaxed state of consciousness characterized by either detachment from the external world through a process of intense concentration and contemplation (*concentrative meditation*) or directed focus on the external world such that the meditator experiences a heightened awareness of environmental stimuli (*opening-up meditation*).

Meditation has only recently gained acceptance and popularity in America, primarily for its relaxation and anxiety reduction value. It has, however, been a worldwide practice for centuries, primarily as a means for spiritual development. Among the most interesting claims of meditation is that it offers a "higher" and more enlightened form of consciousness, superior to that of all other levels, and that it allows meditators to have remarkable control over bodily processes.

Question: What can be achieved with meditation?   In the beginning stages of meditation, subjects generally report a mellow type of relaxation, followed by a mild euphoria. With long practice, some advanced meditators may report experiences of profound rapture and joy or of strong hallucinations (Smith, 1982). A particularly vivid description of these experiences is provided by Gopi Khrishna (1971).:

> Suddenly, with a roar like that of a waterfall, I felt a stream of liquid light entering my brain through the spinal cord. The illumination grew brighter and brighter, the roaring louder. I experienced a rocking sensation and then felt myself slipping out of my body, entirely enveloped in a halo of light. I felt the point of consciousness that was myself growing wider, surrounded by waves of light. (pp. 12–13)

With sophisticated electronic equipment, Western scientists have verified that meditation can produce dramatic changes in basic physiological processes such as brain waves, heart rate, oxygen consumption, and sweat gland activity (Benson, 1988; Pagano and Warrenberg, 1983). For the one out of four Americans who suffer from high blood pressure, it may be useful to know that meditation has proven successful in reducing stress and in lowering blood pressure (Benson, 1987, 1988; Raskin, Bali, and Peeke, 1980). Blood pressure, visual acuity, and auditory threshold are often used to calculate an individual's "biological age," and on all three measures long-term meditators have been found to be significantly "younger" than a chronologically matched age group (Wallace et al., 1982).

Although some research has shown that just sitting quietly and resting can produce similar physiological and psychological benefits (Holmes, 1984b), concentrative meditation seems to be particularly effective for those individuals who find it difficult to shut off disturbing or exciting thoughts when they need to relax. You can experience many of the benefits of meditation by practicing the relaxation technique developed by Herbert Benson (1977):

1. Pick a focus word or short phrase that is firmly rooted in your personal value system (such as "love," "peace," "one," "shalom," "Hail, Mary, full of grace").

2. Sit quietly in a comfortable position, close your eyes, and relax your muscles.

3. Focusing on your breathing, you should breathe through your nose, and as you breathe out say your focus word or phrase silently to yourself. Continue for 10 to 20 minutes. You may open your eyes to check the time, but do not use an alarm. When you have finished, sit quietly for several minutes, at first with closed eyes and later with opened eyes.

4. Maintain a passive attitude throughout the exercise — permit relaxation to occur at its own pace. When distracting thoughts occur, ignore them and gently return to your repetition.

5. Practice the technique once or twice daily, but not within two hours after a meal — the digestive processes seem to interfere with a successful relaxation response.

At this point you may be feeling more attracted to the alternate states of consciousness than to the so-called normal waking consciousness and wonder why so little attention has been focused on such an important aspect of psychology. If so, you are not alone. In its treatment of consciousness, traditional Western psychology has been criticized on several grounds: for being too bound by "left-brained," linear thinking models (Ornstein, 1973; Weil, 1985); for focusing on the lower *levels* of consciousness such as the unconscious rather than on higher levels that may provide a path to greater intellectual and spiritual enlightment (Rama et al., 1976); and for relying on a scientific model that cannot be used to study alternate states of consciousness.

Review Questions

1 _____ is an alternate state of heightened suggestibility characterized by relaxation and intense focus.

2 In _____, one part of the "mind" is conscious of certain experiences and another part is not conscious.

3 It is virtually _____ to hypnotize an unwilling subject.

4 A relaxed state of consciousness that is characterized by detachment from the external world or a heightened awareness of the world is known as _____.

5 Unlike hypnosis, _____ produces verifiable changes in basic physiological processes.

Answers: 1 hypnosis; *2* dissociation; *3* impossible; *4* meditation; *5* meditation

REVIEW OF MAJOR CONCEPTS

THE NATURE OF CONSCIOUSNESS

1 Consciousness is the general state of being aware and responsive to stimuli and events in both the external and internal environments. Alternate states of consciousness differ from normal waking consciousness in the dimensions of awareness and control.

2 The scientific study of consciousness has waxed and waned in psychology. Whereas the structuralists and psychoanalytic theorists emphasized consciousness, the behaviorists discarded it. Today interest in the topic has been revived. The general public in particular has been interested in ASCs.

DAILY VARIATIONS IN CONSCIOUSNESS

3 The study of biological rhythms (chronobiology) has focused on the effects of normal internal biological processes on states of awareness. These biological factors can influence behavior on a regular cycle. Biological rhythms that occur on a daily cycle, such as sleep, are called circadian rhythms. Disruption of circadian rhythm is the cause of jet lag.

4 The menstrual cycle in women is an example of a biological rhythm lasting on the average about 28 days. Premenstrual syndrome (PMS) is a loose cluster of symptoms that supposedly occur in some women just prior to menstruation.

5 One of the most commonly experienced alternate states of consciousness is daydreaming. Daydreaming is a personal form of reverie or inwardly focused thought. Most people daydream frequently during private quiet moments.

6 Sleep and dreaming are states of consciousness that occupy nearly one-third of our lives. The exact function of sleep is not known, but it is thought to be necessary for its restorative value, both physically and psychologically. Sleep seems to be controlled in two areas of the brain, the reticular activating system and the brain stem.

7 REM, or rapid eye movement, sleep is a period of sleep where the eyes dart rapidly about under the eyelids. During REM sleep, the brain pattern of the sleeper is similar to the waking state and the person often is dreaming.

8 NREM, or nonrapid eye movement, sleep occurs when the person is sleeping without the rapid eye movements and is usually not dreaming. There are four NREM sleep stages that the sleeper moves in and out of during a normal night's sleep.

9 During a normal night's sleep, the sleeper will experience four to five entire sleep cycles, which include both REM and NREM sleep. Most people average 7.6 hours of sleep per night, although some sleep much less (short sleepers) or much longer (longer sleepers).

10 According to Freudian theory, dreams can be used as a window into the unconscious mind. But according to the activation–synthesis hypothesis, dreams have no real significance. Some dream researchers suggest that individuals can use dream analysis to gain insights into themselves.

11 There are several different types of dreams: lucid dreams, in which the person knows that they are dreaming; nightmares, which are bad dreams experienced during REM; and night terrors, which are terrifying dreams usually experienced in Stage 4 of NREM sleep.

12 Sleep problems can include insomnia, sleep apnea, and narcolepsy. Insomnia is experienced by people who have repeated difficulty in falling asleep. Sleep apnea is a condition in which a person temporarily stops breathing during sleep, causing loud snoring or poor quality sleep. Narcolepsy is excessive daytime sleepiness characterized by sudden sleep attacks.

CHEMICALLY ALTERED STATES OF CONSCIOUSNESS

13 Psychoactive drugs are those drugs that change conscious awareness or perception. The major categories of psychoactive drugs are depressants, stimulants, and hallucinogens.

14 Psychoactive drug use can lead to psychological dependence or physical dependence or both. Psychological dependence is a desire or craving to achieve the effects produced by a drug. Physical dependence is a change in bodily processes due to continued drug use that results in withdrawal symptoms when the drug is withheld. Tolerance to a drug is a physiological process that results in the need for larger and more frequent doses of a drug to produce the desired effect. The effects of a particular drug depend on many factors, including the setting and the person's psychological set.

15 Depressant drugs slow down bodily processes by depressing central nervous system functioning. There are three major classes of depressants: opiates, barbiturates, and alcohol. Opiates such as morphine and heroin numb the senses. Barbiturates such as sleeping pills and tranquilizers are used to induce sleep or to relieve anxiety. Alcohol is the most widely used and abused drug.

16 Stimulant drugs such as cocaine and amphetamine act on the central nervous system to increase activity and mood. Although these drugs supposedly do not create a physical dependence, the potential for physical damage and psychological dependence is high.

17 Hallucinogens are psychoactive drugs such as LSD and marijuana that produce visual, auditory, or sensory hallucinations.

ADDITIONAL ROUTES TO ALTERNATE STATES

18 Hypnosis is an alternate state of heightened suggestibility characterized by relaxation and intense focus. Hypnosis has been used to reduce pain and to increase concentration. Some researchers argue that hypnosis is not a separate state of consciousness, whereas others argue that it is a distinct dissociative state.

19 Meditation is a relaxed state of consciousness characterized by either detachment from the external world or a directed focus in which the meditator experiences a heightened awareness of the external world. Meditation can produce dramatic changes in physiological processes.

SUGGESTED READINGS

BORBELY, A. (1986). *Secrets of sleep.* New York: Basic Books. A good overview of sleep, dreams, and sleep disorders.

DAVIS, W. (1986). *The serpent and the rainbow.* New York: Simon & Schuster. A fascinating account of the plants and animals used to produce the paralytic and hallucinogenic experiences found in voodoo practices and zombiism.

DEMENT, W. C. (1976). *Some must watch while some must sleep.* New York: Norton. Intended for nonprofessional readers, this paperback offers a survey of major sleep disorders, as well as normal sleeping and dreaming.

JULIEN, R. (1988). *A primer of drug action* (5th ed.). San Francisco: Freeman. An excellent resource for the background, mechanisms of action, and effects of a wide variety of psychoactive drugs.

KELLY, S. F., & KELLY, R. J. (1985). *Hypnosis: Understanding how it can work for you.* Reading, MA: Addison–Wesley. An interesting and helpful text that describes the use of hypnosis in overcoming common problems (such as anxiety, smoking, and overeating) and how it is used and misused in detective work and the courtroom.

WALLACE, B., & FISHER, L. E. (1983). *Consciousness and behavior.* Boston: Allyn & Bacon. A far-ranging discussion of the general topic of consciousness.

chapter six
Learning

WHEN you visit the gorillas, orangutans, and chimpanzees at the zoo, do you ever have the feeling that they are scrutinizing you just as much as you are them? Do their behaviors strike you as being amazingly humanlike? Have you ever felt like crossing over the wall or moat separating you and trying to see if you can somehow communicate with them? Francine (Penny) Patterson did cross barriers to do just this. Thanks to the San Francisco Zoo, she acquired a gorilla, Koko, whom she taught to communicate through American Sign Language. After less than a month of watching people use sign language and only two days of formal training, Koko signed her first word. As Patterson describes the experience:

> [Koko] consistently responded with close approximations of the *food* sign when I offered her tidbits of fruit. Most frequently she put her index finger to her mouth, but she also made the sign correctly — putting all the fingers of one hand, held palm down, to her mouth. As it dawned on me that for the first time she was consistent and deliberate in her signing, I wanted to jump for joy. Finally she seemed to have made the connection between the gesture and the delivery of food, to have discovered that she could direct my behavior with her own.
>
> *Patterson and Linden, 1981, p. 28*

Thus, Koko learned to associate a specific gesture with the object it represented. How did she learn this? How could an ape learn to use hand symbols to communicate her needs to others when neither she nor her predecessors had done this in the past? Below, Patterson explains the procedure she used to teach Koko the *food* sign.

> I praised Koko profusely and seized every chance to get her to sign *food*, showering her with treats in the process. Whenever she reached for some food, I would prompt her by signing *food*, and almost every time she responded. I made sure that she realized she was supposed to ask for things by name by pushing her hand away and signing *no* when she did not make the sign. On several occasions Koko signed *food* without any prompting on my part. After her nap I gave Koko another twenty or so opportunities to sign *food*, and she responded incorrectly only toward the end of the afternoon, by which time the stuffed gorilla had no interest in food whatsoever.
>
> *Patterson and Linden, 1981, p. 28*

At first, Penny Patterson rewarded Koko with pieces of fruit if the gorilla made any sign that even resembled the correct one. Gradually, Patterson rewarded only those gestures that were formed correctly until in the end, if Koko failed to produce an exact duplicate of the *food* sign, she was punished by not being given any food for the faulty sign. Thus, through a system of rewards and punishments Koko learned sign language. This system has proven to be quite successful. Today Koko knows over 600 different signs and is continuing to acquire new ones.

164

There is no doubt that Koko has learned to communicate with humans at a very basic level. That is not to imply that the language abilities of gorillas are comparable to those of humans: They very decidedly are *not*. Human language is exceedingly complex and involves much more than simple associations of signs or sounds with objects (see Chapter 8). The acquisition of human language is likewise exceedingly complex and should not be confused with the more simplistic training methods used in teaching Koko sign language.

Nevertheless, people and animals do learn many behaviors through systems of rewards and punishments that are similar to those employed by Penny Patterson. Rewards and punishments are effective in teaching seals to honk horns in order to get tidbits of fish, students to study intensively in order to get A's on final exams, and drivers not to speed in order to avoid getting tickets. We also learn — and unlearn — through a variety of other methods besides rewards and punishments. In this chapter, we will examine these methods of learning and will discuss what psychologists have discovered about how we learn. We will also investigate how we can apply their research findings to our lives.

LEARNING AND INNATE BEHAVIORS

All animal behaviors are not learned. Although the extent depends on the species, at least some behavior is **innate,** or inborn, either in the form of reflexes or in the form of instincts. It appears that animals of any particular species are "preprogrammed" to engage in certain innate behaviors at a predetermined point in their maturation. Often, an innate behavior emerges when some type of environmental stimulus triggers the behaviors. We have all experienced reflexive reactions. When a gnat suddenly flies too close to our eyes, we automatically blink. When we touch a hot pan, we reflexively pull our hand away. When infants feel a light touch on the cheek, they turn their heads toward the touch, with their mouths searching for that milk-giving nipple. Reflexes allow animals to deal with specific stimuli that are critical to their survival with rigid, automatic responses.

Although humans do exhibit reflexive behaviors, it is generally agreed that we do not engage in instinctive behaviors. Whereas a reflex consists of a single response, an instinct comprises a complex sequence of responses, such as the elaborate mating rituals of some species of birds or the instinctive paddling responses of dogs thrown into deep

INNATE: *Referring to any inborn behavior that emerges during a predetermined period of an organism's life as a result of maturation only and not as a result of practice.*

These tigers have learned to perform in response to the commands of their trainer.

water. For many years, it was thought that instincts were totally genetically determined and were completely independent of environmental influence. Recent research has shown, however, that many behaviors, such as singing in birds, arise from a combination of genetic factors and environmental influences (Gordon, 1989; Marler & Mundinger, 1971).

In stark contrast to innate behavior is learned behavior. We engage in learned behavior as a result of environmental influence, as opposed to some type of genetic programming. We learn through actively doing things, we learn through associating one item with another, we learn through observing others, and the behaviors we learn result from interactions with people, events, or objects in our environment.

Learning is defined as a relatively permanent change in behavior or behavioral potential as a result of practice or experience. Let's take a moment to examine this definition bit by bit. Because learning is a *change* in behavior or *behavioral potential,* it might consist of changes in immediate behavior (e.g., changing your breaststroke immediately after your swim instructor suggests an improvement). Or it might consist of behavioral changes that occur much later but are the result of experience (changing your breaststroke after watching the moves of a champion swimmer on TV). It could even consist of changes that could potentially be initiated but never are because the opportunity never arises (by watching that champion swimmer, you know how to improve your stroke but never again go swimming).

Note in this definition that learning is *relatively* permanent. This means that any learned behavior is not necessarily permanent and can possibly be unlearned. Also, learning is a *result of practice or experience.* This reflects the fact that learning can result from actively performing a behavior or merely from passively experiencing (watching or hearing) someone or something else.

Question: It sounds like we learn things in different ways. Is this true?   Most psychologists and educators agree that we learn our myriad behaviors through a variety of methods. However, there are some learning theorists who staunchly proclaim one type of learning as the method by which we learn everything we know. In our overview of learning principles, we will isolate the major types of learning and discuss them separately, but you should keep in mind that most of our complex human behaviors are not learned solely by one learning method.

In the opening preview to this chapter, we read how Koko learned the appropriate gesture for food by receiving a bite to eat after associating the *food* sign with actual food. One theory of learning views learning solely in this way: as an association between some external stimulus (food, a bell, a snake) and a response (salivation, an eyeblink, a change in blood pressure). This learning of an association between a stimulus and a response is called **conditioning.** One type of conditioning, called **classical conditioning,** involves learning reflexive, involuntary responses to stimuli that don't normally cause such responses. Another type of conditioning, called **operant conditioning,** the one by which Koko learned the *food* sign, involves learning voluntary responses to stimuli through the consequences of previous responses.

Another theory of learning is more concerned with the thinking processes involved in learning. Known as **cognitive learning theory,** it proposes that learning involves more than observable responses to stimuli. Proponents of this theory believe that there is an inner, subjective element in learning that sometimes cannot be directly observed or measured. Consequently, they study the thought processes underlying the observable behaviors of their subjects.

Observational learning theory combines elements of conditioning and cognitive learning theories. It explains how we can learn certain behaviors through watching models perform them. Depending on our esteem for the model or the consequences of the behavior we observe, we learn to mimic or not to mimic the model's behavior.

Now that we have briefly introduced the three major approaches to the study of learning, let us look at each one in greater detail. Remember as you read that few psychologists adhere strictly to any one theory as the explanation for all of learning.

LEARNING: *A relatively permanent change in behavior or behavioral potential as a result of practice or experience.*

CONDITIONING: *The type of learning involving stimulus–response connections, in which the response is conditional on the stimulus.*

CLASSICAL CONDITIONING: *Learning a response to a neutral stimulus when that neutral stimulus is paired with a stimulus that causes a reflex response.*

OPERANT CONDITIONING: *Learning that occurs when a response to an environmental cue is reinforced.*

COGNITIVE LEARNING THEORY: *The idea that learning involves more than an observable response, that often the learning that occurs involves thought processes that may not be directly observed or objectively measured.*

OBSERVATIONAL LEARNING THEORY: *The idea that we learn certain behaviors merely by watching someone else perform them.*

CONDITIONING

As we mentioned previously, *conditioning* is a type of learning that occurs when an association is made between a stimulus and a behavioral response. The two major types of conditioning are classical conditioning and operant conditioning.

Classical conditioning: Learning through passive pairing

Have you ever noticed that sometimes, when you are hungry and see a large slice of chocolate cake or a juicy steak, your mouth starts to water? It seems natural that your mouth should water if you put food into it, but why should your mouth water simply when you see food or sometimes merely think of food? This is one of the questions Ivan Pavlov was contemplating over 80 years ago. Pavlov was a Russian physiologist who conducted pioneering work on the digestive system and digestive processes, work for which he was eventually awarded the first Russian Nobel Prize for physiology and medicine.

One of Pavlov's experiments involved salivary responses in dogs. In studying how the salivary glands respond to different types of food, Pavlov attached to a dog's salivary gland a glass funnel that directed the saliva into a container where it could be measured. In this way, he was able to determine that dry food required more saliva than moist food and that nonfood objects required varying amounts of saliva, depending on how hard it was to spit them out. During this research, Pavlov noticed that many of his dogs would begin to salivate as soon as they entered the experimental room or saw the people who normally fed them. Although this "unscheduled" salivation originally irritated him because it interfered with his original research design, Pavlov eventually decided that he would conduct a systematic investigation into the reason behind it.

Pavlov designed an experiment (see Figure 6.1) in which he could measure and record the amount of saliva produced when a **neutral stimulus** was paired with the presentation of food. He used a bell as the neutral stimulus, since a bell was something that wouldn't normally elicit salivation when presented by itself. He paired the bell with meat powder, which when presented to the dogs *would* naturally produce a salivation reflex. Pavlov's experimental procedure went as follows:

Drawing by John Chase.

NEUTRAL STIMULUS: *An external stimulus that does not ordinarily cause a reflex response or an emotional response.*

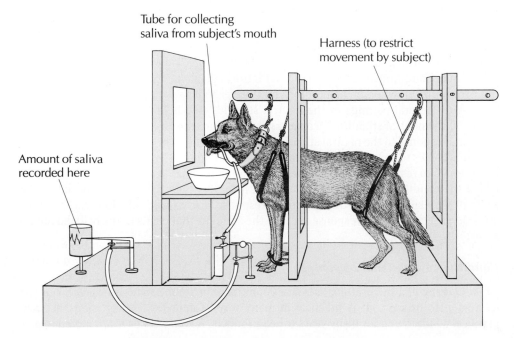

Figure 6.1 A drawing of the apparatus used by Pavlov.

THE FAR SIDE   By GARY LARSON

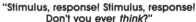

"Stimulus, response! Stimulus, response!
Don't you ever *think?*"

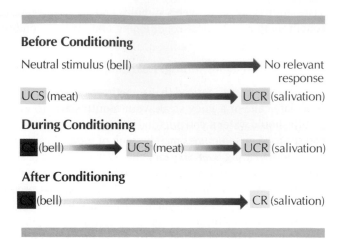

Before Conditioning

Neutral stimulus (bell) ⟶ No relevant response

UCS (meat) ⟶ UCR (salivation)

During Conditioning

(bell) ⟶ UCS (meat) ⟶ UCR (salivation)

After Conditioning

(bell) ⟶ CR (salivation)

Figure 6.2 A summary of classical conditioning.

1. The bell was rung (neutral stimulus).
2. Meat powder was given to the dog (a stimulus that elicits a reflex).
3. The dog salivated (reflex response).

After several trials of pairing the bell with the meat powder, Pavlov found that the mere ringing of the bell would elicit salivation. In this way, the dog had been *conditioned* — it had *learned* — to salivate to the bell in the same way that the other dogs had unintentionally been conditioned to salivate to the sight of the experimental room.

This stimulus–response type of learning acquired by Pavlov's dogs is known as *classical conditioning.* It involves learning reflexive, involuntary responses to stimuli that do not usually cause such responses. In classical conditioning, a subject is initially presented with a neutral stimulus such as a bell. This neutral stimulus is anything that does not ordinarily elicit a particular reflexive or emotional response from the subject. For example, dogs do not naturally salivate to a bell; Pavlov's dogs had to be conditioned, or taught, to do so. Immediately after being introduced, the neutral stimulus is paired with a stimulus that *does* elicit a reflex or emotional response. This reflex-producing stimulus is known as the **unconditioned stimulus (UCS).** It is called "unconditioned" because it involves no learning. It always causes a specific *unlearned* reflex-type response, which is called an **unconditioned response (UCR).** Figure 6.2 summarizes the classical conditioning procedure. It would be helpful for you to refer to it as we continue our discussion.

After several pairings of the neutral stimulus (the bell) with the UCS (the meat powder), the neutral stimulus becomes associated with the UCS, and the subject makes the same response to the neutral stimulus as it does to the UCS. At this point, the neutral stimulus comes to be known as the **conditioned stimulus (CS),** since the subject has been conditioned to respond to it, and the response the subject has been conditioned to make is called the **conditioned response (CR).** The CR (in this case, salivation) is normally the same or very similar to the unconditioned response (also salivation). However, it is now considered a conditioned response because the stimulus that elicits it (the bell) did not do so prior to learning.

UNCONDITIONED STIMULUS (UCS): *Any stimulus that causes a reflex or emotional response without the necessity of learning or conditioning.*
UNCONDITIONED RESPONSE (UCR): *The reflex response evoked by a stimulus without the necessity of learning.*
CONDITIONED STIMULUS (CS): *A previously neutral stimulus that, through conditioning, now causes a classically conditioned response.*
CONDITIONED RESPONSE (CR): *A learned response to a previously neutral stimulus that has been associated with the stimulus through repeated pairings.*

Conditioned emotional responses

Question: How useful is classical conditioning? No one wants to teach his or her dog to drool.   It is practical in many ways. Commercial advertising has used classical conditioning for many years to sell products. Advertisers have attempted to pair

168

their products with male or female models who just happen to be celebrities or just happen to have gorgeous bodies. These models automatically trigger favorable responses in the people reading or viewing the ads. After repeated viewings, advertisers hope that the products alone will elicit those same favorable responses in the prospective consumers.

Conversely, many of the most troublesome behaviors that humans and animals exhibit result from unintentional classical conditioning. For example, many of our deepest fears may be classically conditioned. John B. Watson (Watson and Rayner, 1920) demonstrated the classical conditioning of fears with an 11-month-old infant named Albert. Using the fact that infants are generally very trusting and afraid of only a few things, like loud noises or falling from high places, Watson gave little Albert a small white rat to play with. After a few minutes, Watson deliberately produced a loud noise that scared Albert and made him cry. He continued to pair the loud noise with the rat and, unfortunately for Albert, was immensely successful in classically conditioning the child to fear white rats.

Watson's research design is shown in Figure 6.3. First, Albert was presented with the white rat, the neutral stimulus. The neutral stimulus was then paired with the noise, the unconditioned stimulus (UCS), which elicited the crying, the unconditioned response (UCR). Later, after many pairings of the rat with the noise, the presence of the rat alone became the conditioned stimulus (CS), and crying at the mere sight of the rat was the conditioned response (CR).

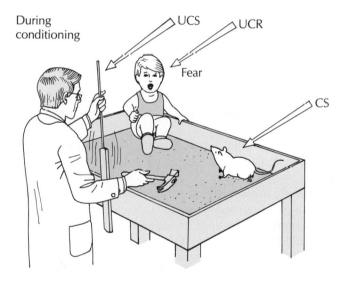

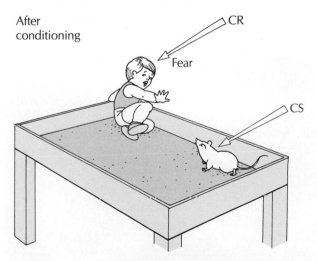

Figure 6.3 Little Albert learned to fear rats through classical conditioning.

Little Albert's fear of white rats is an example of a **conditioned emotional response (CER).** Many **phobias,** or severe and irrational fears of certain objects or situations, can be thought of as CERs. Every time a phobic person is near or even thinks about the object causing the phobia, that person becomes extremely fearful and anxious. A student in one of our classes had a phobia about rats and mice. When she was younger, she had been bitten by a large rat and had been terrified of rats ever since. By the time she reached college, her phobia had become so severe that she refused to read her psychology textbook because it contained references to rats, and whenever rats were brought up in classroom discussions, she would leave the room. If you're interested in how this fear could have been "deconditioned," a more in-depth discussion of phobias, the problems they can cause, and methods of treatment will be found in Chapters 15 and 16.

Although not as severe as phobias, many of our everyday emotional responses have been classically conditioned. For example, Michael, a son of one of the authors, did not touch flowers growing in the yard for a long time because as a young boy he had picked a flower containing a bee and was stung. For Michael, the flower was the CS, the bee's sting was the UCS, the resulting pain and fear were the UCR, and the fear of touching the flower was the CR.

Higher order conditioning You have undoubtedly been conditioned to undergo unique emotional responses to certain words. For example, what do you *feel* as you read the following words?

honky	black	Nixon	Hannukah
Democrat	final exams	mother	Communist
father	Republican	Hitler	Santa Claus
vacations	Lincoln	sexist	atomic bomb

Did you feel angry or "tight" when you read some words and happy or "warm" with others? Your reactions, whether positive or negative, are a result of your own personal history of classical conditioning.

The type of conditioning in the preceding example is known as **higher order conditioning** (as opposed to the conditioning Pavlov used with his dogs). Whereas in Pavlovian conditioning the neutral stimulus is paired with an unconditioned stimulus, in higher order conditioning a neutral stimulus is paired with a *conditioned* stimulus, another stimulus that already produces a learned response. If Pavlov had wanted to experiment with higher order conditioning in his dogs, he could have trained a dog to salivate to the *word* "bell." He could have done this by first conditioning the dog to salivate to the ringing of the bell and then pairing the word "bell" to the ringing of the bell. Eventually, the dog would salivate only to the word itself.

In a classic study of conditioned emotional responses, Arthur and Carolyn Staats (1958) conditioned subjects to experience emotional responses to the names "Tom" and

Advertisers have attempted to pair their products with models who automatically trigger favorable responses in people seeing the ads.

"Bill." They paired a neutral word (such as the name "Tom") with a conditioned stimulus (such as the word "bad") that their subjects had already been conditioned to associate with negative stimuli. The pairing produced a new learned emotional response (a negative, unhappy feeling) to the neutral word. This distinction between Pavlovian and higher order conditioning can be very important. In the rest of this section, see if you can identify which kind of conditioning is involved in the examples we cite.

Question: Can any other responses besides salivation and emotions be classically conditioned? Yes. For a response to be classically conditioned, it must be elicited by some kind of unconditioned stimulus. Thus, most classically conditioned responses involve either reflexive or autonomic responses (those produced by the autonomic nervous system) and are therefore either physical or emotional responses. One interesting example of a conditioned physical response is a *taste aversion*. Most people dislike some foods to some degree, but some people dislike a particular food so strongly that they get physically ill when they smell or even think about it. Many of these aversions to food are classically conditioned. For example, some people have acquired "beer aversions" from college drinking contests in which they drank until they got violently ill; from that time on, they have not been able to tolerate the taste or smell of beer.

Researchers have applied their knowledge of taste aversions toward solving an economic problem of western ranchers: the killing of sheep by coyotes. One "solution" to this problem would be to kill all the coyotes. Of course, this would be irresponsible and would cause serious ecological problems, since the coyotes also eat rabbits, ground squirrels, and other rodents that compete with sheep for the limited grass and edible plants in their particular region. A better solution would be to use classical conditioning to teach the coyotes not to eat sheep. Gustavson and Garcia (1974) were able to condition coyotes to develop a taste aversion to sheep by lacing freshly killed sheep with a chemical that causes coyotes to get sick when they eat the tainted meat. Their scheme worked so well that the mere sight and smell of sheep caused coyotes not only to avoid eating sheep but to run away from them when they were near.

Coyotes find sheep a readily available source of food, but those coyotes who have developed a conditioned taste aversion to sheep will avoid them and seek other food.

Review Questions

1 A behavior that is inborn, emerges at a predetermined point of maturation, and is often triggered by some type of environmental stimulus is _____.

2 Any behavior that is relatively permanent and is *solely* a result of environmental influence is _____.

3 In classical conditioning, a(n) _____ _____ is paired with a(n) _____ _____.

4 After conditioning, the _____ _____ elicits the _____ _____.

5 The conditioning of little Albert is an example of a _____ _____ _____.

6 Pairing a neutral stimulus with an existing conditioned stimulus is called _____ _____.

7 Feelings of revulsion at the sight or smell of certain foods because of bad experiences with those foods are characteristics of _____ _____.

Answers: 1 innate; *2* learned; *3* neutral stimulus, unconditioned stimulus; *4* conditioned stimulus, conditioned response; *5* conditioned emotional response; *6* higher order conditioning; *7* taste aversion

Figure 6.4 The graph on the left illustrates the "acquisition phase" of classical conditioning, during which Pavlov counted the number of drops of saliva produced in response to the conditioned stimulus. He plotted the number of drops on the vertical axis and the number of trials on the horizontal axis. After 16 acquisition trials, extinction trials began. Extinction results are shown in the graph on the right. Note in this graph the sharp "peaks" in response rate that are characteristic of spontaneous recovery. (After Pavlov, 1927.)

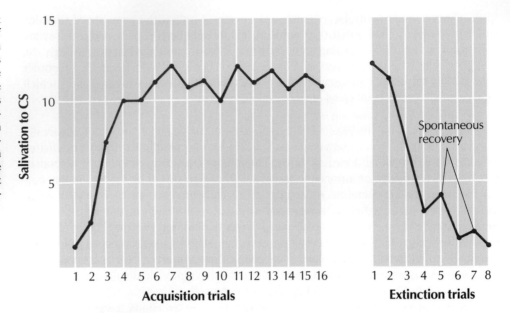

Extinction and spontaneous recovery

Question: As a child, I once ate 18 hot dogs at a picnic, got sick, and had difficulty eating hot dogs for several years. Why can I eat them now?   Classical conditioning, like all learning, is "relatively" permanent. However, most things that are learned through classical conditioning can be unlearned. The process of unlearning a behavior or a response is called **extinction.** Extinction occurs when the unconditioned stimulus (the stimulus causing the unlearned, or reflex, behavior) is repeatedly withheld whenever the conditioned stimulus is presented. The previous association between the CS and the UCS is thereby broken. Pavlov (1927) demonstrated extinction in his dogs. After conditioning a dog to salivate to a tone by using meat powder as the unconditioned stimulus, he then withheld the meat powder. The salivary response to the tone decreased over several trials until it was finally extinguished (see Figure 6.4).

EXTINCTION: *The gradual unlearning of a behavior or a response that occurs when a CS is repeatedly presented without the UCS with which it had been previously associated.*

In the case of eating 18 hot dogs, the taste of the hot dogs was the CS, the overfull stomach was the UCS, and the resulting nausea and vomiting was the UCR. After the eating spree, either the sight of a hot dog or the attempt to eat one became the CS that elicited the CR, the sick feeling. For a conditioned response to be maintained, it is necessary to occasionally reintroduce the unconditioned stimulus; if it is never again presented, the strength of the conditioned response will weaken over time and will eventually cease altogether. Thus, if you don't get violently ill when you subsequently take a bite of a hot dog, you don't have another occurrence of that unconditioned stimulus producing an undesired response; therefore, extinction occurs and hot dogs are again a neutral stimulus.

Question: Isn't extinction just a fancy name for forgetting?   No, there is an important difference between extinction and forgetting. Extinction occurs only when the conditioned stimulus is presented alone, without the UCS, leading to a gradual weakening of the conditioned response over several trials. **Forgetting,** on the other hand, occurs most often when neither the conditioned stimulus nor the unconditioned stimulus is presented for a long period of time. Perhaps an example would help clarify the difference. Suppose that the first time you rode a horse it tripped and fell, the second time it tried to bite you, and the third time the horse threw you off. Given these experiences, you can bet you wouldn't be wild about riding horses — you might even have a conditioned emotional response of fear for horses. One solution to this problem would be to avoid

FORGETTING: *The unlearning of a behavior due to continued withholding of the CS as well as the UCS.*

horseback riding, whereby several years later, you might have *forgotten* the experience altogether. Another solution, which would be faster and would allow you to still enjoy horseback riding with your friends, would be to continue riding the horse, with the probability that the horse would get used to you and mishaps would stop occurring each time you rode. Your fear of horses would then have *extinguished* over time. (Do you now understand the difference? In the forgetting example, what are the CS and the UCS that are withheld? In the extinction example, what is the UCS that is withheld?)

Extinction of a classically conditioned response is often accompanied by a process called **spontaneous recovery,** in which a conditioned response that had been extinguished spontaneously reappears. If you go horseback riding without any mishaps, your fear of the horse at the end of the ride will probably have decreased considerably — extinction will have begun. On your next ride, however, some of the fear you lost the week before will have returned — it will have recovered. You will not fear the horse as much as you did at the beginning of the previous ride, but you will fear it more than you did at the end of the previous ride (see Figure 6.4). This cycle will continue through many trials, with your fear response spontaneously recovering, at lesser and lesser intensities, between trials.

Spontaneous recovery occurs when a significant amount of time has elapsed after an extinction trial. For this reason, it is not a simple matter to extinguish a classically conditioned response. To be effective, the extinction process must extend over several days or even weeks, depending on the response to be extinguished. Even when a response is completely extinguished, it can be relearned in fewer trials than it was originally learned.

SPONTANEOUS RECOVERY: The reappearance of a previously extinguished response.

Generalization and discrimination

Question: Would I be afraid of all horses if I had a particularly bad experience with one horse? Yes, you probably would. Remember Watson's experiment with Little Albert, in which he conditioned the infant to fear the white rat by using a loud noise as a UCS? After the conditioning experience, Albert feared not only rats but also furry white rabbits, cotton wool, and even a Santa Claus mask, with its white beard. This process, in which stimuli similar to the conditioned stimulus elicit the conditioned response, is called **generalization.** The more similar a stimulus is to the original stimulus, the greater the response. Thus, furry white rabbits frightened Albert more than Santa Claus masks because the rabbits were more similar to the white rat (Watson and Rayner, 1920).

GENERALIZATION: A tendency to respond in the same way to stimuli in the environment that have similar characteristics.

Question: Would Little Albert still be afraid of Santa Claus as he grew older? Probably not, since through the process of **discrimination** he would probably have learned that there is a difference between rats and people. Normally, generalization occurs initially in classical conditioning. However, as conditioning continues we begin to discriminate between stimuli when only one specific stimulus is paired with the UCS. A friend of the authors has lived for several years in Brawley, California, which is situated on a large earthquake fault. Being terrified of earthquakes, she at first panicked whenever she heard any low, rumbling noise, whether it signaled an earthquake, faraway thunder, or distant aircraft. However, after living through a severe earthquake and several serious aftershocks that were all preceded by a distinctive rumbling sound, she can now differentiate the sound of a quake from all others. Now our friend no longer panics when the rumble she hears is due to thunder or a jet plane.

DISCRIMINATION: The process whereby a subject learns to differentiate one stimulus from others that are similar because that stimulus is the only CS that is paired with the UCS.

Discrimination learning takes place when the target stimulus is the *only* CS that is paired with the UCS. In Pavlov's experiment, each time a specific tone was sounded the dog was presented with the meat powder. Whenever a similar but different tone was sounded, no UCS was presented. Eventually, the dog learned to discriminate between tones and salivated only to the target tone. Discrimination can also be seen in the coyote study, where coyotes learned to associate sheep with sickness but did not stop eating other sources of food.

Review Questions

1 Extinction occurs when only the _____ _____ is withheld.

2 The difference between extinction and forgetting is that in forgetting neither the _____ _____ nor the _____ _____ is presented.

3 Spontaneous recovery occurs when a previously extinguished response _____.

4 _____ occurs when stimuli similar to the conditioned stimulus evoke the conditioned response.

5 The opposite of generalization is _____.

Answers: 1 unconditioned stimulus; *2* conditioned stimulus, unconditioned stimulus; *3* returns (reappears); *4* generalization; *5* discrimination

Operant conditioning: Learning from consequences

Through classical conditioning, we learn to associate a neutral stimulus with a stimulus that naturally produces an involuntary, reflexive response. Operant conditioning also involves learning through association, except that in operant conditioning, we associate a *voluntary* response with a particular *cue* in our environment. We make an intentional response to something — an object, a sound, a situation — and learn that our response produces an environmental change. We learn to repeat the response or not to repeat it depending on whether or not the change is favorable. For example, suppose you were playing a video game for the first time. When you pushed the white button, a little man jumped up and hit his head on a brick, resulting in 20 points. In all likelihood, you would try to make the same response the next time he walked under a brick. If making the man bump the brick resulted in losing 20 points, you would learn *not* to make that response.

It is through operant conditioning that we learn to type, children learn to say "Thank you," and students learn good study habits. It was through operant conditioning that Koko learned sign language. As described in the chapter preview, Koko voluntarily made a distinctive gesture for the word "food" and learned to repeat it because she was given a piece of fruit for doing so. In fact, operant conditioning is involved any time we learn a new motor skill or a new social behavior (Gordon, 1989). By *operating* in the environment and observing the effects of our behavior, we learn which behaviors will lead to desired outcomes.

Note that two important factors distinguish operant from classical conditioning: (1) in operant conditioning, the stimulus that leads to a voluntary response is really just a cue — it does not *evoke* the response in the same way an unconditioned stimulus evokes an unconditioned response; (2) an operant response is *voluntary,* not the reflex type of response in classical conditioning.

FEEDBACK: *Knowledge of the results of a particular response.*

A critical element in operant conditioning is **feedback,** in which learners are made aware of the results of their behavior. When an animal or a person makes a response, the feedback that occurs after that response determines whether it will be repeated. During her training sessions, Koko received immediate feedback from Patterson by receiving praise and food when she made appropriate responses and by receiving a "no" sign and not being rewarded when she made inappropriate responses.

The first psychologist to study operant conditioning was Edward Thorndike. His most famous experiment involved placing a cat inside a "puzzle box" (see Figure 6.5). Once inside the box, the only way the cat could escape was to pull on a rope or step on a pedal, whereupon the door would open and the cat could exit and eat the food just outside. As you might imagine, the cat would spend some time wandering around inside the box

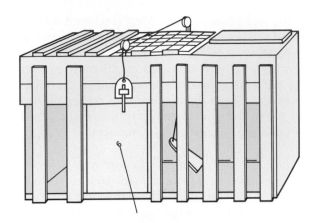

Figure 6.5 This is typical of the boxes used by Thorndike in his trial-and-error experiments with cats. When a cat stepped on a pedal inside the box, the door bolt was released and a weight attached to the door pulled the door open so that the cat could escape. (From Thorndike, 1898.)

This white rat has been placed in a typical Skinner box, which will be used to condition it to press a bar for a food reward.

but eventually, by trial-and-error, would perform the necessary response to open the door. The amount of time the cat took to escape usually decreased with each trial until it would step on the pedal or pull the rope immediately upon being placed in the box. Thorndike concluded that the probability of a response being repeated is related to the effect that response has on the animal or the environment. This he called the *law of effect* (Thorndike, 1931).

Reinforcement and punishment   The effects that Thorndike referred to are now called reinforcement and punishment. **Reinforcement** is any operation or procedure that results in an increase in a response; conversely, **punishment** is any procedure that results in a decrease in a response. The distinction between reinforcement and punishment is critical to your understanding of this section and can significantly affect your relationships with others. For example, have you ever tried to punish someone and found that the person's behavior only got *worse?* As we will soon see, this could happen because you're actually *reinforcing* the person's undesirable behavior, rather than punishing it, or it could mean that the person is angry or resentful about being punished and the increase in undesirable behavior is a retaliatory act.

B. F. Skinner was the first to conduct systematic research on the effects of reinforcement. Although most of Skinner's original research was done with animals (rats and pigeons), the relationships he demonstrated between responses and reinforcement can easily be applied to human beings. A typical Skinner experiment would require an animal, such as a rat, and an apparatus he designed, which has come to be called a *Skinner box.* In one of his classic experiments, Skinner trained a rat to push a lever in order to receive a food reinforcer. The Skinner box automatically gave the rat a pellet of food each time it pushed the lever. At the same time, the number of responses made by the rat was recorded. Skinner used this basic experimental design to demonstrate a number of operant conditioning principles.

Skinner found that food was an effective reinforcer for responses in rats, but many other factors can also serve as reinforcers, including water, sex, money, attention, and material possessions. Reinforcers such as food, water, and sex are called **primary reinforcers** because they normally lead to the satisfaction of an *unlearned* biological need. Reinforcers such as money, praise, and material possessions that have no *intrinsic* value are called **secondary reinforcers**; the only power they have to reinforce behavior results from their *learned* value. A baby, for example, would find milk much more reinforcing than a hundred dollar bill. Needless to say, by the time this baby has grown to adolescence, he or she will have learned to prefer the money. In our adult culture, money is by far the most widely used secondary reinforcer because of its learned association with desirable commodities. During her training sessions with Koko, Patterson used a combination of primary (food) and secondary (praise) reinforcers to teach the gorilla sign language. She probably selected "food" as her first sign because Koko could thereby associate this sign with the primary reinforcer.

REINFORCEMENT: *Any action or event that increases the probability that a response will be repeated.*
PUNISHMENT: *Any action or event that decreases the likelihood of a response being repeated.*

PRIMARY REINFORCERS: *Stimuli that increase the probability of a response and whose value does not need to be learned, such as food, water, and sex.*
SECONDARY REINFORCERS: *Stimuli that increase the probability of a response and whose reinforcing properties are learned, such as money and material possessions.*

A behavior can be reinforced by the application or withholding of relevant stimuli. For instance, suppose you talk to a friend and she smiles at you. You are likely to talk to her again because she has, through her smiling, applied a reinforcer for your talking. On the other hand, suppose you are learning to drive a stick-shift car. Because of your inexperience, it is continually bouncing and jerking. Suddenly, you coordinate the pedals in such a way that the annoying jerkings cease. Their absence reinforces the coordinated motions you just made. In the first case, the smile is **positive reinforcement.** In the second case, the cessation of the jerking and bouncing is **negative reinforcement.**

POSITIVE REINFORCEMENT: *Reinforcement in which a stimulus is given or added that is desirable to the subject.*
NEGATIVE REINFORCEMENT: *Reinforcement in which a painful or annoying stimulus is taken away.*

Question: Time out! I thought negative reinforcement was punishment. Right? Wrong! Negative reinforcement is probably one of the most misunderstood terms in psychology. Negative reinforcement is *not* punishment. In thinking about the term, you must not dwell on the word "negative"; think more of the word "reinforcement." A reinforcer is anything that will cause a behavior to increase or a response to be repeated. When you think of the two different kinds of reinforcers, positive and negative, think of them in mathematical terms (+ and −), not in terms of good and bad. *Positive reinforcement* occurs when something desirable is given or *added.* If your boss compliments you on a job well done, you are receiving positive reinforcement, with the praise being a secondary reinforcer. If a mild foot shock ceases whenever a rat pushes a lever, the rat will probably continue to push it. The elimination of the shock provides negative reinforcement.

In these examples, the behavior or the response being demonstrated is *more* likely to be repeated after the reinforcement. You will try to continue producing good work and the rat will continue to push the lever. Of course, when you use either positive or negative reinforcement to increase individual response in others, be aware that their behavior may affect you as well. If you as a boss begin to praise your employees and production increases, the increase will serve as positive reinforcement and you will probably continue praising your workers.

This process helps explain why so many bad situations often seem to escalate — two parties get locked into a vicious cycle where one is being negatively reinforced, the other is being positively reinforced, and both of their behaviors *increase!* Take the simple example of a little girl in a supermarket screaming for a lollipop. Her parents are embarrassed and frustrated, so they give in, the crying stops, and the parents are negatively reinforced. But what do you think is happening for the little girl? She is being positively reinforced for screaming. Do you see what the parents and their daughter learned in this exchange? Can you see how the girl might scream louder and more readily the next time, thereby causing her parents to give in sooner? The lesson to be learned here is that if you find yourself in a situation where things are rapidly escalating, try to step back and analyze what's going on: What are the reinforcers? How can I remove them? How can I change them? Try to *use* your psychology.

Question: I can see that negative reinforcement is not punishment. So what *is* punishment? Punishment occurs when some procedure or some type of event leads to a decrease in a response. There are two kinds of punishment, positive and negative (Gordon, 1989). As with reinforcement, remember to think in the mathematical terms of adding and taking away, rather than good and bad. **Positive punishment** is the application of an *aversive* (painful, disgusting, or otherwise undesirable) stimulus to decrease a response to a particular cue. If your dog digs a hole every time it sees a gopher mound and you swat it with a newspaper to decrease the digging, you are applying (literally!) positive punishment.

POSITIVE PUNISHMENT: *Punishment in which an aversive or undesirable stimulus is applied or added to decrease a response.*

Opposed to positive punishment is **negative punishment,** which is the removal of a desired stimulus to decrease a response. If your puppy has an accident while being house-trained, you could use negative punishment by taking away its privilege of being in the house by putting it outside.

NEGATIVE PUNISHMENT: *Punishment in which a desired stimulus is removed or taken away to decrease a response.*

Punishment can help decrease unwanted behaviors, but it also has serious side

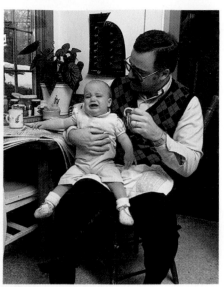

This killer whale is receiving positive reinforcement in the form of a fish. If the baby stops crying, her father will be negatively reinforced for picking her up which is the behavior he engaged in just before the crying ceased.

effects and should therefore be avoided if possible. A major side effect of punishment is its tendency to lead to frustration in the person or animal being punished, which can lead to anger and eventually aggression. Although research has found a clear and direct connection between punishment and aggression in animals (Baenninger, 1974; Cairns, 1972; Hyman, 1981), the relationship is more complicated with humans. For example, most of us have learned from previous experience that retaliatory aggression toward a punisher (who is usually bigger and more powerful) is usually followed by more punishment. We therefore tend to control our impulse toward open aggression and instead resort to more subtle techniques, such as procrastination, pouting, stubbornness, or intentional inefficiency. Such behavior is commonly known as **passive aggressiveness** (Coleman, Butcher, and Carson, 1984).

As well as leading to subversive behaviors on the part of the recipient, punishment may also lead to an escalation of aggression on the part of the punisher. Because the punishment generally produces a decrease in undesired behavior, at least for the moment, the punisher is in effect rewarded for applying punishment. Thus, a vicious cycle can be set up in which both people are actually being reinforced for inappropriate behavior — the punisher for punishing and the recipient for being submissive and subversive. Can you see how this cycle may partially explain the escalation of violence seen in spouse and child abuse cases, and the reluctance of the recipients to leave the situation?

Some researchers have pointed out that in places like China, Taiwan, and Tahiti, where physical punishment is far less common than it is in the United States, there is also far less child abuse. They suggest that by making physical punishment acceptable as a normal disciplinary method, Americans may be inadvertently encouraging its abuse (Parke and Collmer, 1975).

Another side effect of punishment is avoidance behavior. People and animals do not like to be punished, so they try to avoid the punisher if they can. Suppose you come home from school and find that your dog just dug another hole in the yard. He has been repeatedly punished for this in the past, and runs and hides with his tail between his legs as soon as he sees you, to avoid your anger. This also happens with people. If every time you came home your parents or your spouse started yelling at you, you would find another place to go. You would come to perceive home as a place for punishment. This aspect of punishment is one reason children sometimes lie to their parents: They want to avoid punishment, so they fabricate any kind of explanation to help them avoid being yelled at, spanked, and so on.

PASSIVE AGGRESSIVENESS: *A subtle form of aggression characterized by pouting, procrastination, stubbornness, or intentional inefficiency.*

LEARNED HELPLESSNESS: *A state in which people or animals give up and quietly submit to punishment that they have previously been unable to escape.*

Learned helplessness   It seems that people and animals *must* have a way to escape from punishment. If they don't, they often find themselves in a state of **learned helplessness.** Overmeier and Seligman (1967) investigated this condition of helplessness by conducting experiments in which they used dogs as subjects. The first step was to expose each dog in the experimental condition to a series of inescapable shocks; dogs in the control condition were not thus shocked. The next step was to place each dog in a *shuttle box*—a box with two compartments separated by a low barrier—and electrify the floor of only one of the compartments. When the control dogs were shocked in the shuttle box, they ran around frantically, trying to escape, and eventually jumped the barrier into the nonelectrified compartment. However, when the experimental dogs received the shocks in the shuttle box, they ran around for only a few seconds, then lay down in a corner and whined without making any attempt to escape.

One thing is clear from such research. Constant and unavoidable punishment will eventually cause people and animals to give up attempts of escape, and they will quietly submit to the punishment. This learned helplessness has been offered as an explanation for many behaviors. Huesmann (1978) claims that it is the source for such psychological problems as withdrawal, apathy, and severe depression. Gentile and Monaco (1986) have studied its role in low mathematical achievement. Feinberg, Miller, and Weiss (1983) have found a strong correlation between learned helplessness and depression in college-age subjects.

Greer and Wethered (1984) claim that the "burnout" experienced by many teachers of exceptional children (children who have severe mental or physical handicaps) is due to learned helplessness. *Burnout* is a state of physical and emotional exhaustion associated with a job or situation. The lack of control over the children's handicaps and the lack of reinforcement inherent in teaching children who make such slow progress lead to learned helplessness and, consequently, to burnout. Greer and Wethered suggest that, to fight burnout, teachers (1) set realistic and attainable goals; (2) recognize the control they do have; and (3) develop a realistic understanding of the cause for their failures. They also suggest that, because burnout results at least partially from a lack of positive reinforcement, there should be an increase in positive reinforcers—for example, monetary rewards or frequent praise from supervisors.

As you have seen, punishment leads to such negative behaviors as aggression, avoidance, lying, and learned helplessness. What is ironic is that punishment does not really eliminate a response; it only temporarily suppresses it. Usually, the individual who is being punished merely stops or decreases the undesirable behavior as long as the punisher is directly in sight. You have no doubt noticed, for example, the large number of people who drive well above the posted speed limit and slow down only when they see the distinctive markings of a police car.

Review Questions

1. Anything that increases the probability that a particular response will be repeated is a _____ .

2. _____ decreases the probability that a response will be repeated.

3. Food and water are _____ reinforcers, whereas money is a _____ reinforcer.

4. Positive reinforcement occurs when something is _____ that the person or animal _____ .

5. Negative reinforcement occurs when something is _____ _____ that the person or animal _____ .

6. When you remove something good in order to decrease a response, you have used _____ punishment.

7 When you spank your dog for wetting on your carpet, you have used _____ punishment.

8 Techniques such as stubbornness and intentional inefficiency are called _____ _____.

9 The behavior of a person or animal passively enduring punishment while making no attempt to escape is called _____ _____.

Answers: 1 reinforcer or reinforcement; *2* punishment; *3* primary, secondary; *4* given (added), likes; *5* taken away (subtracted), dislikes; *6* negative; *7* positive; *8* passive aggressiveness; *9* learned helplessness

Extinction and spontaneous recovery   *Extinction,* the elimination of a response, occurs in operant conditioning as well as in classical conditioning. To extinguish a classically conditioned response, the unconditioned stimulus is withheld whenever the conditioned stimulus is presented. To extinguish an operantly conditioned response, the reinforcement is withheld whenever the learned behavior is performed. In the usual operant conditioning experiment, a rat is conditioned to press a bar for a pellet of food (bar pressing is the response and food is the positive reinforcement). To eliminate this bar-pressing behavior, the experimenter simply turns off the food dispenser. Since the bar-pressing response is no longer being reinforced, the response rate decreases until it ultimately ceases altogether (see Figure 6.6).

Question: After extinction, does spontaneous recovery occur as it does in classical conditioning?   Yes. If the rat that has undergone several successful extinction trials is taken out of the box for a few hours, it will show spontaneous recovery by pressing the bar on its return to the experimental box (see Figure 6.7). Similarly, if you had always kept your underwear in the top drawer of your dresser and them moved them to the bottom drawer, it may take several days for your "top drawer" habit to be extinguished. So you can see that for a response to be completely extinguished, the extinction process must be continued in several sessions extending over several days. The actual amount of time required to extinguish an operantly conditioned response is directly related to the schedule of reinforcement.

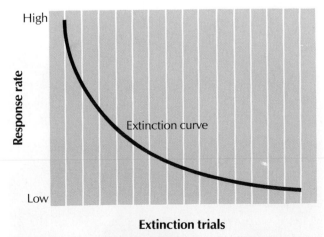

Figure 6.6 The graph from a typical experiment demonstrating extinction would look something like this.

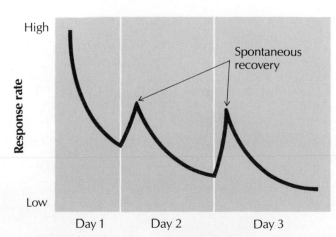

Figure 6.7 A hypothetical graph depicting spontaneous recovery of a response that is no longer being reinforced.

Schedules of reinforcement   The term **schedule of reinforcement** refers to a program designating at what rate or at what intervals responses are reinforced. Although there are many different schedules of reinforcement, they can all be grouped into two types: continuous reinforcement and partial reinforcement. In **continuous reinforcement,** every response is reinforced. For example, every time a rat pushes a lever, it gets a pellet of food, and every time you make the correct response in a video game, you are rewarded with more points. In **partial reinforcement,** only *some,* but not all, responses are reinforced. For example, a cat may wait beside a mouse hole for hours to catch a delectable snack. When a mouse finally does appear, the cat may not be quick enough and the mouse may escape. But once in a while, a mouse will see the cat too late and the cat will be reinforced.

Question: Which schedule enables us to learn faster, continuous or partial reinforcement?   Continuous reinforcement leads to more rapid learning. Imagine you are learning to play a video game in which you need to guide your starship with a joystick and press the firing button at the appropriate moment so that you can blast alien ships and win points. If you are rewarded for every hit (continuous reinforcement), you will learn how to play faster than if you are rewarded for every third or fourth hit (partial reinforcement).

Although a continuous schedule of reinforcement does lead to faster initial learning, it is an inefficient system for long-term maintenance of behaviors. You simply cannot reward someone constantly for every appropriate response. Can you imagine parents of teenagers having to reward their children every day for getting up, dressing, making their beds, brushing their teeth, and so on? It is therefore important to move to a partial schedule of reinforcement once a task is well learned. Under partial schedules behavior is more resistant to extinction. To use the example of the slot machine, have you ever noticed how intense and serious people become as they're gambling, and how they will stand for hours pulling a lever in hopes of winning the elusive jackpot? (Sounds a bit like Skinner's rats, doesn't it?) This high response rate and the compulsion to keep on gambling in spite of significant losses are evidence of the maintenance power and the strong resistance to extinction that are characteristic of a partial schedule of reinforcement.

Partial schedules of reinforcement may be based on the number of responses between reinforcements *(ratio schedules)* or on the interval of time between reinforced responses *(interval schedules).* In addition, either type of schedule may be fixed or

Video games provide continuous reinforcement, while slot machines provide partial reinforcement.

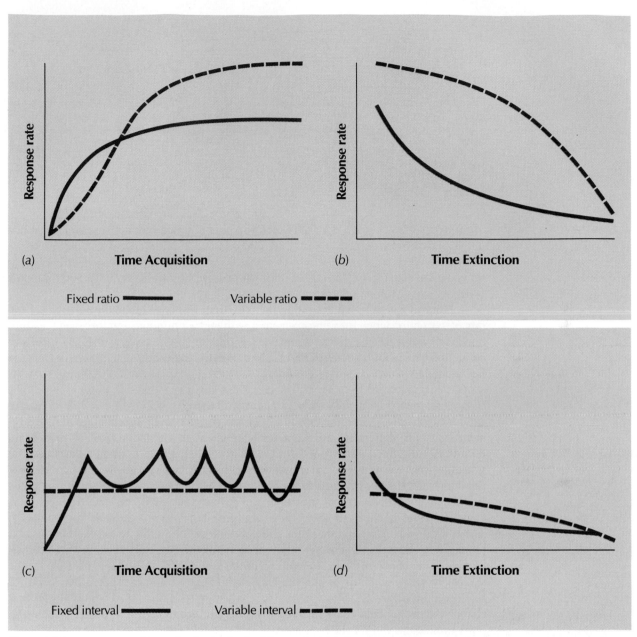

Figure 6.8 Response rates and rates of extinction for the different schedules of reinforcement. (*a*) and (*c*) show the response rates during learning; (*b*) and (*d*) show the response rates during extinction.

variable. There are thus four main partial schedules of reinforcement: fixed ratio, variable ratio, fixed interval, and variable interval. The type of schedule selected by the experimenter depends on the type of behavior being studied and on the speed of extinction desired by the experimenter. Figure 6.8 compares the response rates and extinction patterns for the four types of reinforcement schedules. Please refer to this figure as we continue our discussion of the schedules.

Suppose you want to teach your dog to sit. Initially you reinforce your dog for each occurrence of the behavior. Each time the dog sits, you give it a cookie. To save on your cookie bill, you eventually reinforce the animal only every other time it sits, or every third time, or every fifth time. This is known as a **fixed ratio** reinforcement schedule: the animal must make a *fixed* number of responses before it receives the reinforcement. A fixed ratio

FIXED RATIO: *A partial schedule of reinforcement in which a subject must make a certain number of responses before being reinforced.*

*"It's most interesting. By pushing this lever twenty
times you can get him to walk across here with a banana."*

schedule can lead to a high response rate, especially if the ratio is very high, such as five or more responses to one reinforcement.

Reinforcement schedules influence more than response rates; they also affect the rate of extinction when the reinforcement is withheld. Continuous reinforcement leads to rapid extinction when the reinforcement is withheld. Higher fixed ratios lead to slower extinction rates, but the subject eventually comes to realize that no more reinforcers are forthcoming.

Question: Is it possible to set up a reinforcement schedule that will never lead to extinction?   Never is a long time. But it is possible to set up schedules of reinforcement that will make a behavior extremely resistant to extinction. Rather than being reinforced for a fixed number of responses, the subject is reinforced on a **variable ratio** schedule, in which reinforcers may be given for the first response, then the third response, then the twenty-third. *On the average,* the subject will be reinforced on a specific schedule (such as every fifth time), but the number of required responses on each trial will vary.

Most slot machines are designed to reinforce gamblers on a variable ratio schedule. They might win on the first try or the thirteenth try — they never know whether the next try might be the jackpot. Whereas in a fixed ratio schedule the subject learns that a certain number of responses will lead to reinforcement, in a variable ratio it is impossible for the subject to know when he or she will receive the next reinforcer. That is why behavior reinforced on a variable ratio schedule is so resistant to extinction. There is always that chance that as soon as you walk away from the slot machine, the very next person who pulls the handle will hit the big jackpot.

Partial reinforcement may also be given on a **fixed interval** schedule, in which the subject is reinforced for the first response *after* a fixed interval of time has elapsed. What are your study habits like when you know that you will have a psych quiz every Friday and you really care about your grade? Do you study at a moderate level at the beginning of the week and harder on Wednesday and Thursday so that you'll be reinforced with an "A" on Friday's quiz? If you do, you are like most animals (including humans) who, when put on a fixed interval schedule, tend to respond at a slow or moderate rate during most of the time interval and begin to respond more rapidly toward the end of the interval.

It is relatively easy to extinguish a response that has been conditioned using a fixed interval schedule, since it is possible for a person or animal to predict approximately when a reinforcement will be given. If no reinforcement is forthcoming, there is no point in continuing the behavior.

On **variable interval** schedules, subjects are reinforced the first time they perform the target behavior after a variable, unpredictable interval of time. Imagine, for example, that you are a hungry rat who is undergoing a learning session in which you are placed in a cage with a lever jutting out of one wall. After exploring the cage, you hit the lever a

VARIABLE RATIO: *A schedule of reinforcement in which the subject is reinforced, on the average, for making a specific number of responses, but the number of required responses on each trial is varied.*

FIXED INTERVAL: *A schedule of reinforcement in which a subject is reinforced for the first response after a definite period of time has elapsed.*

VARIABLE INTERVAL: *A schedule of reinforcement in which the subject is reinforced for the first response after a specified period of time has elapsed. This period of time varies from one reinforcement to the next.*

couple of times and then receive a bit of food. Having been reinforced for the behavior, you hit the lever several more times, with no result. You wait, then again hit the lever several times before you are again reinforced. After eating your food, you hit the lever and immediately receive more food. In this case, you have been rewarded after intervals of varying lengths.

Contrary to the response rates using fixed interval schedules, most animals trained on a variable interval schedule learn that the most efficient way to earn their reinforcers is to respond at a slow steady rate. This is so because the determining factor is not the actual number of responses but the length of time that has elapsed. Thus, if in your psych class you know that you will have occasional quizzes but you never know when they will be sprung on you, you are more likely to study at a constant rate and try to keep up with your reading assignments.

In this discussion of reinforcement schedules, continuous and partial reinforcement have been dealt with separately. Normally, however, learning occurs through a combination of the two. Initially, in learning a particular response we are continuously reinforced for that behavior; then, after the initial learning has taken place, we are only partially reinforced, enough so that the behavior will be continued. For example, when Patterson was teaching Koko her first sign, she noted that by the end of the session, in which she had used a continuous reinforcement schedule, Koko was "stuffed" and had no more interest in the food reinforcers. Such satiation also occurs when training people and other animals. A partial reinforcement schedule eliminates the problem of trying to train a subject who has lost interest in the reinforcer. Thus, it seems that most behavior is ultimately reinforced on a partial schedule, especially after it has been well established.

Superstitious behavior   In 1948, B. F. Skinner conducted an experiment in which he altered the feeding mechanism on the cages for eight of his pigeons so that it would drop food pellets into the cages once every 15 seconds. No matter what the birds did, they were reinforced in intervals of 15 seconds. Of the eight pigeons, six acquired very noticeable types of behavior that they repeated over and over, even though the behaviors were not necessary to receive the food. For example, one pigeon kept turning in counterclockwise circles, and another kept making jerking movements with its head.

Why did the pigeons engage in such repetitive and unnecessary behavior? It's easy to understand. Recall that a reinforcer increases the probability that a response just performed will be repeated. Although Skinner was not using the food to reinforce any particular behavior, the pigeons came to associate the food with whatever behavior they were engaged in when the food was originally dropped into the cage. Thus, if the bird was circling counterclockwise when the food was dropped into the cage, it would repeat that motion in order to receive more food: It had formed a meaningless connection between the food and the behavior. This type of behavior is called **superstitious behavior** — behavior that is continually repeated because it is thought to be the cause of "something good," even though in reality it has no connection with the reinforcer.

It is surprising how many people exhibit superstitious behavior. In a poll of junior high, senior high, college, and university athletes, 40 percent of those interviewed confessed to having superstitions (Buhrmann and Zaugg, 1981). Indeed, many professional and Olympic-level athletes carry lucky charms or engage in ritualistic behavior before every competition. Phil Esposito, a hockey player with the Boston Bruins and the New York Rangers for 18 years, performed the same superstitious actions before each game: He would always wear the same black turtleneck and drive through the same tollbooth on his way to each game. Upon arrival in the locker room, he would put on all his clothes in the same order and lay out his equipment in exactly the same arrangement as he had in every other game. All this because once when he had engaged in such behavior years before, he had been the team's high scorer.

Sports psychologists tend to agree that superstitions *can* get out of control and interfere with the athlete's faith in his or her own abilities. If this happens, they step in and use such methods as relaxation training to help the athletes rely on their own resources

SUPERSTITIOUS BEHAVIOR *Behavior that is continually repeated because it is thought to cause desired effects, though in reality the behavior and the effects are totally unrelated.*

Fifty-seven years, and I haven't stepped on a crack yet!

Drawing by W. Miller; © 1982 The New Yorker Magazine, Inc.

instead of on the ritual or object they believe is the source of their "luck." But many sports psychologists and coaches support a reasonable amount of reliance on superstition, since it serves as a source of confidence and assurance, leading to better concentration on the game.

Review Questions

1 For extinction to occur in operant conditioning, you must withhold the _____.

2 If you reinforce every third response, you are using a _____ _____ reinforcement schedule.

3 The _____ _____ reinforcement schedule leads to the slowest extinction.

4 A person or an animal who is reinforced on a _____ _____ schedule responds with bursts of responses around the end of the time period.

5 The best way to generate a slow, steady response rate is to use a _____ _____ reinforcement schedule.

6 _____ behavior occurs when reinforcers are not connected to the behavior.

Answers: 1 reinforcement; *2* fixed ratio; *3* variable ratio; *4* fixed interval; *5* variable interval; *6* superstitious

Shaping

Question: Could I use operant conditioning to teach my dog Charlie to bring me my newspaper? You would probably not use the operant conditioning principles presented thus far. They would require you to follow Charlie around until he happened to pick up your paper so that you could finally reinforce him. This could take a long, long time. To train Charlie in a relatively short time, you could use the process of **shaping,**

SHAPING: *Teaching a desired response by reinforcing a series of successive steps leading to this final response.*

which is the process of rewarding successive approximations to the desired behavior. When shaping the behavior of animals or people, you initially reward the slightest look or movement toward the target object or response (you give Charlie a dog biscuit when he looks in the direction of the paper). Then you reinforce the subject when he or she makes a more distinct movement toward the desired response (Charlie walks toward the paper), and so on until—it may take a while—the response you wanted to shape has been performed (Charlie picks up the paper and gives it to you).

Penny Patterson used shaping during one of her initial training sessions. When Koko approximated the food sign by placing only her index finger on her mouth, she was rewarded with tidbits of fruit. She was then rewarded for closer and closer approximations to the appropriate sign, until she finally made the correct sign, placing all the fingers of one hand on the mouth. After that, only the correct sign was reinforced.

Sometimes behavior is not purposely shaped. Instead, it is shaped by circumstances and the environment. One of the authors has a pony that often roams around the yard, grazing on the grass. Lately, however, she has not been eating the grass; she has been eating apples off the apple tree. Picking apples is not an innate horse behavior; the pony's behavior was shaped. During her wanderings, the pony would sometimes graze under the apple tree, occasionally finding apples on the ground, which, since horses love apples, served as excellent reinforcers for grazing in this area. After eating all the apples from the ground, the pony noticed the apples on the lower branches of the tree, ate those, and then learned that there were apples on the entire tree and that she could eat as many as she could reach. In this way, the pony's ability to pick apples off the apple tree was shaped by her environment.

Through the process of shaping, animals and people can learn to perform many complex behaviors, as can be seen in circuses and animal shows (lions jumping through hoops and seals playing horns). Shaping is essentially a method of indicating to a person or animal those responses that lead to a desired behavior, which in turn is ultimately "controlled" by a particular cue or stimulus in the environment. When a certain stimulus is present, a shaped response sequence is likely to occur. For example, when the pony sees the apple tree (the stimulus), she responds by looking for apples on the ground and on the tree. Her shaped behavior (apple picking) is under the control of the stimulus (the apple tree) with which it is associated.

Generalization and discrimination

Question: Shaping sounds a lot like the discrimination training involved in classical conditioning. Is it?   Yes, both generalization and discrimination occur in operant conditioning as well as in classical conditioning. A rat that is learning to push a lever to receive a pellet of food may at first push the lever with its paw, its nose, or any other part of its anatomy. This generalized behavior may be reduced to discriminative behavior only if a specific response is reinforced, such as pushing the bar with its paw.

The principles of generalization and discrimination can also be seen in the case of three-year-old Michael. His family was eating dinner at a local restaurant when a small man (a dwarf) walked in. Michael said in a voice loud enough for everyone in the restaurant to hear, "Look, Daddy, a hobbit." Michael had just seen the movie *The Hobbit* and had been reinforced for correctly identifying the hobbits in the film. To the embarrassment of his parents, he had *generalized* the term to people as well as to cartoon characters. *Generalization* is, basically, a tendency to respond in the same way to cues in the environment that have similar characteristics. *Discrimination,* on the other hand, is the ability to distinguish relevant cues from irrelevant ones.

Discrimination occurs only when responses to specific stimuli are reinforced, so that responses to irrelevant stimuli are extinguished. You can imagine Michael's disappointment when he was told that the man in the restaurant was not a hobbit but a dwarf. This was the beginning of discrimination training, in that the boy was not reinforced for generalizing the term "hobbit" to all short people but *was* reinforced for using the correct word, "dwarf."

A REVIEW OF CONDITIONING

	Classical Conditioning	Operant Conditioning
OTHER NAMES	Respondent conditioning	Instrumental condition
	Pavlovian conditioning	Skinnerian conditioning Law of Effect (Thorndike)
PIONEERS	Ivan Pavlov John B. Watson	Edward Thorndike B. F. Skinner

EXAMPLES	Sound of bell (CS) begins to
	    produce salivation
		Baby cries and parent picks
		    baby up

MAJOR TERMS	Unconditioned stimulus (UCS)
	Conditioned stimulus (CS)
	Unconditioned response (UCR)
	Conditioned response (CR)
	Conditioned emotional response
	    (CER)
		Reinforcers
		    (primary and secondary)
		Reinforcement
		    (positive and negative)
		Punishment
		    (positive and negative)
		Shaping
		Reinforcement Schedules
		    (continuous and partial)

SHARED TERMS	Extinction Spontaneous recovery Generalization Discrimination	Extinction Spontaneous recovery Generalization Discrimination
MAJOR DIFFERENCES		
BEHAVIOR ORDER	Involuntary (subject is passive) CS must come *before* the UCS	Voluntary (subject is active) Reinforcement comes *after* the behavior

Figure 6.9 *A review of conditioning.*

B. F. Skinner (1979) conducted a series of interesting experiments during World War II involving the discriminative abilities of pigeons. In these experiments, Skinner taught pigeons to discriminate enemy ships from other variables in the surrounding environment. The object was to place the pigeons inside missiles and have them, through a previously trained pecking behavior, "guide" the missile into enemy ships. "Project Pigeon" was never approved by the U.S. Defense Department, so no pigeons were asked to give their lives for their country. The U.S. Coast Guard has, however, successfully used pigeons to help in search and rescue operations at sea by training the birds to respond only to the color orange, which is the color of life jackets.

There are many other intriguing ways in which operant conditioning principles have been applied to everyday life, but before we describe them we'd like to pause here to encourage you to review Figure 6.9, which summarizes the major differences and similarities between classical and operant conditioning.

Reinforcement and punishment: How to use them effectively

Now that you have learned some basic principles governing operant conditioning, how can you effectively apply reinforcement in your own life? Here are some important rules to keep in mind:

1. *Feedback.* In using both reinforcement and punishment, be sure to provide immediate and clear feedback to the person or animal whose behavior you wish to change.

When using punishment, it is particularly important to make clear the desired response, since punishment is merely an indication that the response is undesirable. In other words, give the subject an alternative response to the punished one.

2. *Timing.* Reinforcers and punishers should be presented as close in time to the response as possible. The old policy of "waiting till Father gets home" is obviously inappropriate for many reasons, the chief one being that the delayed punishment is no longer associated with the inappropriate response. The same is true for reinforcement. If you're trying to lose weight, don't say you'll buy yourself a new wardrobe when you lose 30 pounds; reward yourself with a small treat (like a new blouse or shirt) after every few pounds.

3. *Consistency.* With both reinforcement and punishment, be consistent in your responses. Take our example of the parents who gave in to their child's screaming for a lollipop. Many such parents create a tremendous problem for themselves because they are firm one time, refusing to give in or even punishing the temper tantrum, but the next time are so embarrassed or hassled that they go ahead and buy the lollipop. It would be much easier and more effective to use extinction (by ignoring the tantrum) all the time, since punishment requires such a high level of surveillance and consistency that few parents can effectively use it. (Can you see how, if you don't punish every instance of the undesired behavior, children can get into a partial schedule of reinforcement?)

4. *Order of presentation.* To use reinforcement or punishment effectively, be sure that it comes *after* the behavior, never before. Can you imagine how angry you would be if your instructor assumed that all students cheat on tests when given the chance and thus punished you ahead of time with restrictive rules during a testing situation? Undoubtedly you've managed to obtain a few unearned rewards by plying your parents with empty promises of washing the car or mowing the grass on Saturday if they would just let you use the car on Friday night. When you're teaching your own students or raising your own children, remember to use your psychology and only punish them *after* they've cheated or reward them *after* they've washed the car.

The best rule to follow in the use of operant conditioning is to use a combination of each of the major techniques: *Reinforce* appropriate behavior, *extinguish* inappropriate behavior, and save *punishment* for the most extreme cases (such as a two-year-old's running into the street). Remember that you have grown up in a culture that often considers reinforcement to be "bribery" and slightly unethical and that ironically stresses the need for more punishment. We encourage you to explore the technique of reinforcement—you'll find it very rewarding!

Conditioning in action: Using learning principles in everyday life

Biofeedback   During the mid-1960s, Neal Miller and Leo DiCara (1967), among others, found that operant conditioning could be used to train rats to control their heart rates. The heart rate is regulated by the autonomic nervous system (see Chapter 2). Until this time, it had been thought that autonomic system function was totally automatic and not subject to conscious control, but Miller and DiCara demonstrated that autonomic functions *can* be regulated. Through implanting an electrode in the pleasure center of a rat's brain, they were able to train the rat to increase its heart rate by stimulating the pleasure center every time the heartbeat increased. Very slowly, the rat began to increase its heart rate by itself. In the same way, Miller and DiCara were able to train rats to *lower* their heart rates.

Shortly after it had been shown that rats could learn to control their autonomic functions, several other researchers showed that humans could control not only their heart rates but also their blood pressure, their skin temperature, and even the electrical activity of their brains. The ability to do so is achieved through a procedure known as biofeedback.

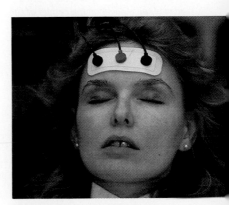

This woman is attending a pain clinic that is using biofeedback in an attempt to control her chronic pain.

BIOFEEDBACK: *A procedure in which people's biological functions are monitored and the results made known to them so that they can learn to control these functions.*

During the process of **biofeedback,** which means "biological feedback," information about some biological function, such as heart rate, is fed back to the individual in the form of a signal of some type. Sit quietly for a moment and try to determine your heart rate without feeling your pulse. Is it high or low? Is it different from a few minutes ago? You can't tell, can you? Therefore, it is impossible for you to learn to control your heart rate consciously. But if we were to hook you up to a device that could display your heart rate to you, you would have access to the information (feedback) that you need to learn to control it.

Biofeedback is actually a type of secondary reinforcement, since it reinforces a desired physiological change that has beneficial results (the primary reinforcement). Several researchers have successfully used biofeedback techniques to treat problems such as epilepsy, by changing brain wave patterns (Psatta, 1983); hypertension, by lowering blood pressure (Erbeck et al., 1983; McGrady et al., 1983); and migraine headache, by redirecting blood flow (Labbe and Williamson, 1983).

The relief from migraine headache is a good example of the current use of biofeedback. Migraine headaches are caused, in part, by an increase in blood flow to the head. If this blood flow can be slightly decreased, some relief can be obtained. Biofeedback can be used to help people direct blood to other parts of the body, thereby reducing the flow of blood to the head. The usual technique is to use temperature biofeedback to teach afflicted people how to increase the temperature of their hands. The increased temperature of the hands results from blood vessels in the hands dilating to allow more blood to flow to this area instead of to the brain. Biofeedback wires are attached to subjects' hands and they think of various things (warm sun shining down) to try to heat their hands. When they think the right thoughts and their hands are warm, the machine sounds a signal, which serves as a reinforcer for their behavior. At the same time, the headache pain begins to subside; this serves as a negative reinforcement.

When it was first discovered that biofeedback could be applied to humans, there was much enthusiasm and optimism for its ability to relieve a multitude of disorders, from high blood pressure to asthma. This enthusiasm has waned over the years because biofeedback techniques are difficult to learn. Even when they have been learned in a clinical setting, they are difficult to practice on returning to everyday life. However, biofeedback is still being used with considerable success in conjunction with other techniques, especially in pain control and stress management programs.

PROGRAMMED INSTRUCTION: *Personalized learning that makes use of operant conditioning techniques, whereby students read a section of text, then test themselves on the material. They continue on to the next section or review the previous one, depending on the results of the test.*

Programmed instruction **Programmed instruction,** or personalized instruction, is another example of the practical use of operant conditioning techniques (see Figure 6.10). In programmed instruction, you are encouraged to learn at your own pace. Typically, you read a chapter or section of a textbook and are then tested on the section. If you pass the test, you are "rewarded" by being allowed to continue to the next section. If you fail the test, you are "punished" by being told not to advance to the following section until you have reread and mastered the previous section. In this way, you can proceed at a pace that is right for you, not at a pace that is dictated by a professor. Programmed instruction can be presented in the form of a workbook, a computer program, a record, a videotape, or any combination. The main idea behind programmed learning is to allow students to learn at their own pace by rewarding appropriate study habits and punishing poor habits.

Review Questions

1 Reinforcing successive approximations to the desired behavior is called _____.

2 _____ is a tendency to respond to cues in the environment that are similar, whereas _____ is the ability to distinguish relevant cues from irrelevant cues.

3 _____ involves giving a person or animal information about heart rate, blood pressure, or other biological functions in order to bring these bodily functions under conscious control.

4 The technique of presenting material to be learned at the learner's own pace and with frequent tests to provide feedback on the learner's progress is a form of _____ _____ .

5 For reinforcement or punishment to be effective, it must be administered _____ _____ the target behavior.

Answers: 1 shaping; *2* generalization, discrimination; *3* biofeedback; *4* programmed instruction; *5* immediately after

Critical Thinking — PSYCHOLOGY IN ACTION

TRANSFERRING IDEAS TO NEW CONTEXTS
Operant Conditioning and the College Classroom

One of the major problems with "learning about learning" is that many students find it difficult to integrate the new terminology and concepts into their daily lives. They are so involved with the memorization of labels that they fail to appreciate the extensive power of simple learning principles. Critical thinking requires the learner to rise above rote memorization and to integrate basic information with practical applications. When an idea or concept is transferred from one situation to another, the idea becomes richer and the learner's insight grows.

This exercise is designed to improve your basic understanding of operant conditioning while also developing your ability to apply learning terms to an important part of your life—the college classroom.

Situation # 1
A professor is disturbed by the large number of students arriving late to class. She wants to reduce this behavior.

Questions to Answer:

1 Would you recommend that the professor punish students for being late or reinforce students for being on time? Why?

2 If the professor decides to use punishment, what type of positive punishment could she employ? Negative punishment?

3 What type of positive reinforcement and negative reinforcement could be used if she decides to reinforce being on time?

4 Once the goal of reduced tardiness is met, what type of reinforcement schedule would be best to avoid either extinction of the behavior of coming on time or eventual ineffectiveness of the reinforcement?

Situation # 2
You are in your second year of graduate school in psychology, and you have been assigned the coveted position of Teaching Assistant (TA) for a large lecture course in Introductory Psychology. Your supervising professor, a strong advocate for learning theory, suggests that your evaluation as a TA will depend on your ability to incorporate learning principles in your classroom.

Questions to Answer

1 How will you design the operation of your classroom and testing format to implement the basic principles of positive reinforcement, negative reinforcement, extinction, and shaping?

2 Under what conditions would you be willing to use punishment?

3 What use would you make of programmed instruction?

4 Given that at least some student behaviors can be controlled through conditioning techniques, what is to prevent you from taking advantage of your students? Should there be some built-in controls on the controllers? What would happen if specialists in learning theory had full control of the academic world? Would you want such individuals in powerful political positions? Why or why not?

COGNITIVE LEARNING

So far, we have examined learning processes that involve associations between a stimulus and an observable behavior. We have described how associations are formed between bells and salivation, between white rats and fear, between Koko's making a sign for food and her receiving a piece of fruit. Although behaviorists like B. F. Skinner argue that all learning can be explained in stimulus – response terms, many psychologists feel that there is more to learning than tangible, observable factors. *Cognitive psychologists* maintain that much, if not all, of learning involves internal mental processes that cannot be seen, and they are interested in studying these thinking, or *cognitive,* processes. According to cognitive psychologists, we begin learning at the instant we pay attention to some stimulus, such as a winged creature alighting on the branch outside our window. We mentally compare it to similar creatures we already know and discover how it "fits" into our existing cognitive structure. In this way, we form a concept about the new animal and store it in memory according to how that concept fits with our preexisting ones.

Cognitive psychologists think of the learner as an information processing system. They are interested in how we acquire information about our world and process that information to store it in our memories. They study our perceptual processes of attention, selection, and organization. They examine our abilities to form mental images, to conceptualize, to reason, to solve problems. They probe into how we remember information we've acquired through examining the various stages and types of memory. Because these topics of study are discussed elsewhere in this book, particularly in the perception, memory, thinking, and development chapters, we will focus on the background of cognitive learning in this chapter.

1 It is important when using punishment to make clear to the subject what response is appropriate and acceptable. True or false? Go to Question 5.

2 False. Both reinforcement and punishment are most effective when presented as soon after the response as possible. If incorrect, read the section on *Timing.* Next, go to Question 6.

3 It is agreed that sometimes reinforcement and punishment are best used *before* the behavior has been exhibited. True or false? Go to Question 7.

4 Waiting a couple of hours to reinforce good behavior is just as effective as immediate reinforcement. True or false? Go to Question 2.

5 True. Punishment is most effective when accompanied by feedback indicating what behavior *is* appropriate. If incorrect, reread the section on *Feedback,* then go on to Question 4.

6 It is best to be consistent when disciplining children. We should try to avoid being firm and unyielding sometimes and being lax and indulgent at other times. True or false? Go to Question 8.

7 False. For reinforcement and punishment to be truly effective, they should always be given *after* the behavior. If incorrect, read the section on *Order of Presentation.*

8 True. Whether using punishment or reinforcement, it is important to be consistent when disciplining. If incorrect, read the section on *Consistency* again. Now go to Question 3.

Figure 6.10 Programmed questions. If you haven't already done so, read the section in the text entitled "Reinforcement and Punishment: How to Use Them Effectively." Then see how well you do on these programmed learning questions.

Cognitive learning as a learning theory is relatively new — in fact, it did not gain full recognition until the 1960s. That is not to say that there was no research investigating thinking processes before this time. There were several researchers who studied these processes and "set the stage" for the cognitive psychologists of today. The most influential of these early researchers were Wolfgang Köhler and Edward C. Tolman.

The study of insight: Köhler's work with chimpanzees

Because such internal events as thinking and reasoning are not directly observable, it is difficult to design experiments in which such processes can be directly observed and measured. This, along with the fact that most experiments had been conducted with animals that have less developed thinking abilities than humans, is a major reason why conditioning theories remained dominant for so long. However, Wolfgang Köhler was quite successful in the earlier part of this century in designing experiments to study the cognitive element in learning.

Köhler believed that there is more to learning than isolated stimulus–response relationships — that learning to solve a complex problem, for instance, involves more than a series of responses to stimuli made in a trial-and-error fashion. He investigated this idea by conducting several experiments designed to study the role of insight in learning. **Insight** is a sudden flash of understanding that occurs when one is trying to solve a problem.

In his experiments, Köhler posed several different types of problems to chimpanzees. In one conducted in 1917, he placed a banana outside the reach of a caged chimpanzee. To reach the banana, the chimp would have to use a stick placed near the cage to extend its reach. The chimp did not solve this problem in the random trial-and-error fashion of Thorndike's cats or Skinner's rats and pigeons, but rather sat and seemed to "think about the situation for awhile." Then, in a flash of insight (as Köhler termed it), the chimp picked up the stick and retrieved the banana (Köhler, 1925).

Another of Köhler's chimps, an intelligent fellow named Sultan, was put in a similar situation. But this time there were two sticks available to him and the banana was placed even farther away, too far to reach with a single stick. Sultan played with the sticks and seemed to think about the problem for a period of weeks. One day, he got up and inserted one bamboo stick into the hollow end of another, producing a stick that was twice as long. With this longer stick he was able to retrieve the distant banana. Köhler designated this type of learning as *insight learning,* because there was obviously some mental event that we can only describe as "insight" that went on between the presentation of the banana and its retrieval with the stick.

Latent learning: Tolman's "hidden learning"

Most learning theorists, certainly the behaviorists, hold that for learning to occur, a response must be reinforced. Perhaps this is true for certain types of learning, but consider for a moment: Aren't you filled with "useless" knowledge that you have yet to demonstrate, simply because the right situation hasn't arisen? Children often ride their bikes around their neighborhoods for no particular purpose. In so doing, they learn names of streets, locations of mailboxes, which houses have RVs in their driveways, which streets end in cul-de-sacs, and so on. In effect, they form a map of the neighborhood in their minds, with no thought of ever having to retrieve the information for a reward.

Edward Tolman was a researcher who felt that a significant amount of learning consists of such **latent learning.** Such learning occurs in the absence of any reward and remains hidden until some future time when it can be retrieved. If you were one of those aimlessly wandering bike riders, you probably learned a lot about your neighborhood, but this learning remained latent unless you needed to mail a letter or give directions to a newcomer to the neighborhood. (The information about the locations of the RVs, on the other hand, would probably never need to be retrieved.) Your learning was clearly cognitive in nature — you did not learn the locations of the mailboxes and RVs in exchange for any type of reward.

One of Köhler's chimps solving a problem using "insight."

INSIGHT: *A sudden flash of understanding that occurs when one is trying to solve a problem.*

LATENT LEARNING: *Learning that occurs in the absence of a reward and remains hidden until some future time when it can be retrieved.*

Question: It's easy to see that we humans can learn without being immediately reinforced, but is that true of other animals as well? Tolman found that latent learning does indeed occur in other animals. He designed an experiment in which there were two groups of rats. One group explored a maze in an aimless fashion and received no reinforcement for doing so, while the rats in another group were reinforced with food when they reached the far end of the maze. The rats were allowed to explore their mazes for 10 days. On the eleventh day, food reinforcers were placed at the far end of the maze for both the control and the experimental groups. The previously unrewarded rats, after only one or two reinforced trials, reached the food as quickly as the rewarded rats (Tolman and Honzik, 1930). From this research, Tolman proposed that people and animals learn to navigate in their environment by creating **cognitive maps** of the area. In the case of his experimental rats, information in their cognitive maps remained latent until they discovered the food at the end of the maze. So it seems that rats, as well as people, learn information that remains latent until there is sufficient reason to retrieve it.

COGNITIVE MAP: *A mental image of a maze or an area that a person or animal has navigated.*

OBSERVATIONAL LEARNING

Can you remember when you got into the driver's seat of a car for your first driving lesson? On your first time at the wheel, did you *randomly* push buttons, pull levers, and turn the steering wheel? Of course not. You had watched others drive cars countless times before. During the months immediately preceding your first chance at the wheel, you probably paid especially close attention to the intricacies of driving. You had learned driving procedures through observation. Many things we do, from driving a car to brushing our teeth, have been learned by watching someone else, by reading a "how-to" book, or by being given direct instruction. This type of learning is called *observational learning.* Although early animal research with this type of learning met with little success (Thorndike, 1898, 1901), research in this area gained recognition in the 1960s when Albert Bandura conducted a series of research studies on social learning in children.

Bandura's research illustrated how children learn through observation. In one of his experiments he asked children to view a videotape of a model performing aggressive acts on a number of toys in a playroom (Bandura and Walters, 1963). Later, the children were given the opportunity to play in the same room with the same toys. The children who had seen the videotape were much more aggressive with the toys than children who had not seen it. They had learned how to act in a particular situation by observing another person in that situation. Bandura called this "social learning," which is essentially the same as observational learning. His **social learning theory** proposes that people learn various behaviors by observing others who serve as *models.*

According to Bandura, there are four processes involved in learning through observation: (1) we must attend to the model (of course, if we aren't paying attention, we won't know what behavior is being exhibited); (2) we must call on our cognitive abilities to organize and remember the modeled behavior; (3) we must be able to put into practice what was observed (for instance, we wouldn't be able to imitate someone riding a bike if we were paralyzed); and (4) we must decide whether we want to repeat the modeled behavior, based on whether the model was reinforced or punished and/or based on our esteem for the model. We can see these processes at work when we apply them to the subjects in Bandura's experiment who learned to imitate the aggressive behavior they had observed in models. The children were paying attention to the aggressive behavior of the models. Their cognitive processes were organizing and remembering what they had seen, as confirmed by their subsequent actions. The children were able to physically perform the modeled behaviors. And many of the children made the decision to imitate the observed behaviors (Josephson, 1987).

Through **modeling** procedures, we learn to imitate all kinds of behavior. Patterson and her associates served as models for Koko as she was learning to acquire new signs. Student teachers learn teaching and discipline techniques by observing their master

Children often learn by observing adults. In this photograph, a child is learning by watching his father demonstrate the proper way to cast.

SOCIAL LEARNING THEORY: *A theory developed by Bandura proposing that people learn various behaviors by observing others who serve as models.*

MODELING: *Learning by imitating the behaviors of others.*

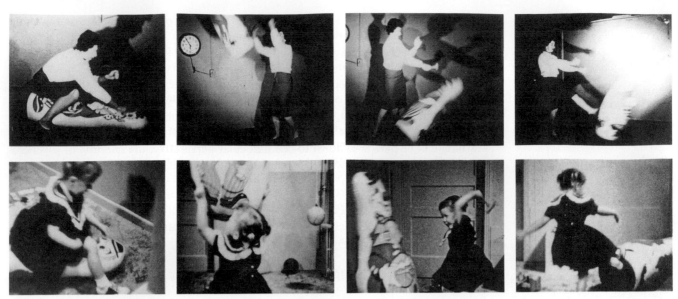

The top series of photographs shows the woman model hitting the "Bobo" doll. The bottom series of photographs shows a girl imitating the model.

teachers. Children, as Bandura's study showed, can learn aggression from watching aggressive models. Thus, if you as a parent were to spank your daughter for hitting her brother, you might temporarily suppress your daughter's hitting behavior, but you would also be serving as an aggressive model yourself. If you were to handle the same situation in a calm, courteous manner, you would be modeling a behavior more consistent with how you would like your daughter to behave.

It has been found that we can be classically conditioned through observational learning. Patricia Barnett and David Benedetti (1960) have called this **vicarious conditioning.** In one of their experiments they asked subjects to observe a model who was being classically conditioned to react to a buzzer. The model heard a buzzer and a few seconds later received a shock. Each time the shock was administered, the model would quickly remove his or her hand from the shock plate. When the observers were subsequently tested, they also reflexively removed their hands from the shock plate in response to the buzzer, even though they had never actually been shocked. Vicarious conditioning has also been demonstrated with operant conditioning (Bandura, 1971).

VICARIOUS CONDITIONING: *Learning by watching a model or reading about a task.*

An interesting warning is in order concerning the power of modeling (Chance, 1979). If you are out with a friend or your child and observe some other person acting in a way that is against your standards or morals, be sure that you let the person you're with know how you feel about that act. If you don't, he or she may think that you approve of the behavior. Parents are especially concerned about their children imitating good role models, so they must be doubly sure that they make their opinions known. For example, if you take your child to see a movie in which the stars exhibit excessive violence and you say nothing — or worse yet, you cheer on the violence — your child will learn that you consider violence to be an acceptable behavior. Make sure that you let your children know by your words and actions, not by your silence, which people you consider to be good models.

In this chapter we have discussed a number of learning principles. Effective application of these principles can benefit all of us in our everyday learning situations. Classical conditioning techniques are commonly applied to situations in which our emotions and reflexes are involved (e.g., extinguishing a fear of heights). Operant conditioning techniques are applied to "training" situations involving rewards and punishments (e.g., giving candies as positive reinforcers when toilet training a toddler). Cognitive learning techniques are applied to situations involving thinking, problem solving, and memory processes (e.g., learning and remembering information in a textbook). Finally, observational learning techniques are applied when learning how to perform a new behavior through observation and modeling (e.g., learning how to tune up a car).

Keep in mind, however, that since human behavior is so very complex, most human learning is *not* a result of one specific learning method. Most behaviors such as human language are learned through a combination of conditioning, cognitive, and observational learning methods. Thus, although some learning theory purists really believe that all learning can be narrowed down to one particular perspective, the majority of psychologists agree that our knowledge is gained through a combination of learning methods.

Review Questions

1 The _____ aspects of learning, such as thinking, reasoning, and memory processes, are unobservable processes that go on within the individual.

2 Köhler's chimp Sultan showed _____ when he solved the two-stick problem to get a banana.

3 Sometimes we learn information that is not connected to any apparent reinforcement. This type of learning is called _____ learning.

4 Learning by watching others is called _____ learning.

5 When you show another person how to perform a task, you are _____ that behavior.

Answers: 1 cognitive; *2* insight; *3* latent; *4* observational; *5* modeling

REVIEW OF MAJOR CONCEPTS

LEARNING AND INNATE BEHAVIORS

1 Learning is a relatively permanent change in behavior or behavioral potential as a result of practice or experience. A learned behavior is opposed to an innate, or instinctual, behavior, which is affected by maturation only and not by practice. Both learned behaviors and innate behaviors are exhibited in humans, as well as in animals.

2 Conditioning emphasizes the relationship between a stimulus and a response. These theories include both classical and operant conditioning.

3 Cognitive learning emphasizes thinking processes as they are related to learning.

4 Observational learning explains how people and animals learn by watching a model perform a task.

CONDITIONING

5 Classical conditioning is the type of learning investigated by Ivan Pavlov in which an originally neutral stimulus is paired with another stimulus that causes a reflex response. After several pairings, the neutral stimulus will cause the response to occur.

6 The terminology used in classical conditioning consists of the following:

a The neutral stimulus does not normally cause any particular reflex or emotional response. In classical conditioning, it is paired with a stimulus that does cause such a response.

b The stimulus that causes a reflex or emotional response is called the unconditioned stimulus (UCS).

c The reflex or emotional response is called the unconditioned response (UCR).

d When the neutral stimulus begins to cause the response, it is then called the conditioned stimulus (CS).

e When the response is caused by the conditioned stimulus, it is called the conditioned response (CR).

7 In higher order conditioning, the neutral stimulus is paired with a conditioned stimulus, one to which the subject has already been conditioned, rather than being paired with an unconditioned stimulus as in primary conditioning.

8 In classical conditioning, extinction occurs when the unconditioned stimulus is repeatedly withheld and the previous association between the CS and the UCS is broken. Spontaneous recovery occurs when a conditioned response that had been extinguished spontaneously reappears.

9 Generalization occurs when stimuli similar to the original CS elicit the CR. Discrimination occurs when only the CS elicits the CR.

10 Operant conditioning is the type of learning originally investigated by B. F. Skinner in which people or animals learn by the consequences of their responses.

11 In operant conditioning, when a response is made it is either reinforced or punished. Reinforcement is anything that is likely to cause an increase in the response. Punishment is anything that is likely to cause a decrease in the response.

12 Positive reinforcement occurs when something desirable is given or added so that subjects will increase their response rates. Negative reinforcement occurs when something bad or aversive is removed to increase the response rate.

13 Positive punishment occurs when something bad or aversive is given to decrease the response rate. Negative punishment occurs when something good is removed to decrease the response rate.

14 In operant conditioning, extinction occurs when the reinforcement is withheld until the subject stops responding to the stimulus, and spontaneous recovery occurs just as it does after the classical conditioning extinction process. The amount of time required for extinction is directly related to the schedule of reinforcement being used.

15 In operant conditioning, there are several schedules of reinforcement. Continuous schedules of reinforcement consist of subjects being reinforced for each response. Partial schedules of reinforcement consist of subjects being reinforced for some, but not all, responses.

16 Superstitious behaviors occur when people or animals make responses they think are connected to rewards when in reality their responses have nothing to do with the rewards.

17 Suggestions for the effective use of both reinforcement and punishment include the following:
 a Provide clear and immediate feedback when the person or animal makes the desired response.

 b Apply reinforcers or punishers as soon as possible after the response is made.
 c Be consistent in applying both reinforcers and punishers.
 d Be sure to reinforce or punish after the behavior has been exhibited.

18 Shaping is the process of teaching a person or animal a complex task by reinforcing successive approximations to a desired response.

19 Biofeedback is the "feeding back" to subjects of biological information such as heart rate or blood pressure to help them use the information to learn to control normally automatic functions of the body.

20 Programmed instruction is an application of operant conditioning techniques whereby people learn at their own pace.

COGNITIVE LEARNING

21 Cognitive psychologists are interested in investigating the mental or cognitive processes that lead to responses.

22 Wolfgang Köhler, in working with chimpanzees, demonstrated that learning could occur with a sudden flash of insight.

23 Latent learning is learning that occurs in the absence of reinforcements and remains latent until it is needed.

OBSERVATIONAL LEARNING

24 Observational learning is the process of learning how to do something by watching a behavior occur or reading about one, rather than learning through doing.

25 Social learning theory was proposed by Albert Bandura to explain how people learn by observing others who serve as models.

SUGGESTED READINGS

BANDURA, A. (1977). *Social learning theory.* Englewood Cliffs, NJ: Prentice–Hall. A brief overview of social learning theory.

CHANCE, P. (1979). *Learning and behavior.* Belmont, CA: Wadsworth. An introduction to the study of learning.

GORDON, W. C. (1989). *Learning and memory.* Pacific Grove, CA: Brooks/Cole. A readable introduction to both learning and memory, detailing the basics of both.

SKINNER, B. F. (1979). *The shaping of a behaviorist.* New York: Knopf. The autobiography of America's most influential behaviorist.

chapter seven
Memory

IN August 1979, Father Pagano, a polite and gentle Roman Catholic priest, was on trial for a long string of armed robberies. He was accused of being the "Gentleman Bandit," a thief who had impressed his victims with his mild-mannered behavior. At the time of the trial, conviction seemed certain, since seven witnesses had positively identified Father Pagano as the guilty person. It seemed impossible to believe that so many people could all be mistaken in identifying the same man as the one who had robbed them. The overwhelming certainty of the crime victims was particularly surprising in light of Father Pagano's status as a priest—a champion of the poor—who had maintained his innocence from the time of his arrest. Was he a modern-day Robin Hood who stole from the rich to help the downtrodden?

Father Pagano's trial was finally terminated when the real robber, Ronald Clouser, confessed. Clouser said he had committed the robberies because his marriage was disintegrating and he was deeply in debt. Being a decent man, he did not want an innocent man to be punished for his crimes. This story could have gone down as a simple case of mistaken identity except for the fact that the two men were so unalike. At the time of the trial, Clouser was 39 and Father Pagano was 53 and balding (Loftus, 1980).

Above Photo: Do these two men look alike to you? Father Pagano is on the left and the real "Gentleman Bandit" is on the right.

How could seven people have made such a mistake? Perhaps, through pure coincidence, all seven were born with bad memories. But is anyone really born with a good or bad memory? You would probably give anything for a memory like the winning contestants on TV's *Jeopardy* or those history buffs who can remember countless dates and facts. Are these people born with their abilities, or do they develop techniques that enable them to efficiently store and retrieve facts and figures?

Most early psychologists felt that some people have good memories whereas others have poor ones, and that not much could be done to change one's memory abilities. On the basis of these assumptions, they focused on devising tests to measure and diagnose individual differences in memory. More recently, psychologists have realized that memory is not a "given" but rather an ever-changing ability strongly influenced by internal and situational factors. Such factors could indeed account for such memory errors as Father Pagano's mistaken identity.

A THREE-STAGE MEMORY MODEL

Researchers have identified at least three distinct stages of memory: sensory memory, short-term memory, and long-term memory. **Sensory memory** is the initial storage of information within the senses, such as a visual or an auditory image. **Short-term memory (STM)** is the working memory where information is briefly stored and processed. **Long-term memory (LTM)** contains information and experiences that have been stored for future use.

The flow of information from one type of memory to another is diagrammed in Figure 7.1. From the figure, you can see that sensory memory is mainly an input into STM. Information can then move from STM into LTM. Since STM is the "working memory," information that is stored in LTM can also be moved back into STM. Note that forgetting can occur at any of the three stages in the model.

Sensory memory: The first stage of the process

Hold your hand about 12 inches in front of you and look at it steadily for awhile. Now, close your eyes, and notice how long a clear image of your hand lasts. A clear visual image of an object will last in sensory memory about a half second after a stimulus is no longer received by the receptors (Sperling, 1960). Any stimulus that is registered in sensory memory is available to be selected for attention and for processing into a more permanent type of memory. All the objects in your visual field and all sounds loud enough for you to hear are available for processing at this first stage. Thus, sensory memory is assumed to be unlimited in capacity.

The information in sensory memory is temporary. As you just noticed, visual images last about ¼ to ½ second, whereas sounds last a bit longer, up to four seconds (Neisser, 1967). Although these times seem very brief, four seconds of availability of auditory information is generally enough to reanalyze what we have heard and figure out what a person said before the sounds disappear completely. If you have ever said, "What?" to someone and then responded before the person had time to repeat the statement, you were able to refocus on the sound in auditory sensory memory and figure out what was said. When you refocus on a sound or visual image, it is entered into STM, the working space

SENSORY MEMORY: *The type of memory that occurs within the senses while incoming messages are being transmitted to the brain.*
SHORT-TERM MEMORY (STM): *Memory containing things a person is presently thinking about and having a capacity limited to about seven items and a duration of about 30 seconds.*
LONG-TERM MEMORY (LTM): *A relatively permanent memory in which information is stored for use at a later time.*

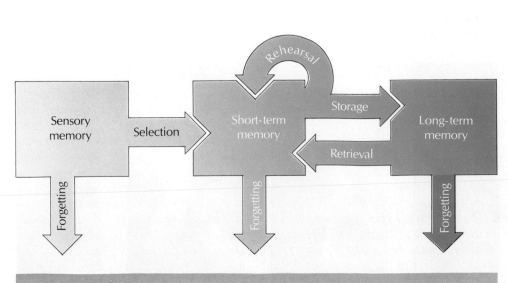

Figure 7.1 The three-stage memory model.

for current attention where the sounds or sights can be interpreted. Only the information selected for passage into STM receives further processing and has a chance of being stored permanently.

Short-term memory: Selecting and concentrating

Look up from this book for a moment and notice what occupies your visual attention. What do you see around you? Now try to identify the sounds and sensations you are currently experiencing and the thoughts that are occurring at this moment. What you have just identified is the contents of your short-term memory (STM).

Short-term memory, otherwise known as "working memory," is actually the working area for the contents of our minds, much like the surface of a desk is the working area for material objects. We keep an item on our desktop long enough to work on it, then either dispose of it or store it for later retrieval. So it is with short-term memory. Depending on what we select for attention, the contents of STM can be dismissed, can be changed rapidly (Baddelely, 1981), or can be retained for awhile. We hold information in STM long enough to evaluate it, organize it, and combine it with both new information and old information retrieved from storage (Norman, 1982). In a sense then, short-term memory can be thought of as a limited working memory that is used in two ways: to select and process ongoing information and to store memories for a short duration (Johnson and Hasher, 1987).

Selection

Question: How do we decide what to allow into short-term memory? **As you may** remember from Chapter 4, we either pay attention to stimuli or do not pay attention via a process called *selective attention.* During the sensory memory stage, we select what should be sent on to STM either *automatically* or *deliberately.* If we don't deliberately direct our attention to certain stimuli, the nervous system will automatically make some choices for us. Because the novelty of stimuli was often an important consideration for survival during evolutionary development, any new stimuli entering sensory memory were given top priority for selection. Paying attention to new or unusual signals helped early humans avoid becoming meals for predators. That's why movements in the visual field or a new noise outside the room are likely to be selected for STM. In addition to novel stimuli, any input related to satisfying basic needs such as hunger or thirst will be automatically selected. This is also a survival mechanism, but it can be quite unpleasant if you are on a diet and find yourself constantly noticing food stimuli.

The nice part about selecting contents for short-term memory is that it *can* be a deliberate process. It is possible to use the information stored in long-term memory to

When you look up a telephone number, you can rehearse it to keep it in short-term memory; however, you might not remember it after you dial.

guide your attention at any particular time. For instance, if you are determined to do well in a course, you can direct your attention to the instructor's voice and make yourself think about what is happening in class rather than filling your short-term memory with distractions or daydreams.

Whenever your attention is diverted to something happening around you, it is possible to stop selecting that input and concentrate on whatever is more important to you. Such choices depend on the goals and information stored in long-term memory. These can take priority over novel or drive-related stimuli like a person walking by or the smell of spaghetti.

Once something has been selected for attention in short-term memory, its ability to be processed further is affected by two important characteristics of STM: its limited duration and its limited capacity. Both of these qualities can seriously affect our ability to remember things.

Duration of short-term memory   Researchers have found that a sound or visual image will last for a maximum of 30 seconds in STM unless it is reentered (Craik and Lockhart, 1972). There are two ways a stimulus can be reentered to gain more time for processing in STM. Look back to the memory model in Figure 7.1. Note that there are two arrows indicating how STM contents can be reentered. The first method involves sensory memory: If the sensation (sound, smell, and so on) is still present, it is still available for selection into STM. The other method is maintenance rehearsal, indicated by the looping arrow in the figure. When you use **maintenance rehearsal,** you maintain information in STM by repeating or reviewing it mentally. Maintenance rehearsal is commonly used to keep a phone number in STM long enough to dial it. When you look up a number, you can repeat it to yourself to keep it in STM. If something interrupts you for as long as 30 seconds, you have to look up the number again to reenter it through sensory memory.

In laboratory research, rehearsal can be prevented by the use of an interference task. An **interference task** gives subjects something to do that takes their complete attention so that no other information can be reentered into STM. One frequently used interference task is to have the subjects count backward by 3's, starting with a number like 574, as soon as they have read a list of words to memorize (Peterson and Peterson, 1959). For most subjects, this type of interference task is difficult enough to prevent rehearsal of the words they are attempting to memorize. Within 18 seconds, the words are forgotten (see Figure 7.2).

When we are able to use maintenance rehearsal, information is reentered into STM so that further processing can occur. Rehearsal is an important technique for coping with the limited duration of memory in this second stage, since information often needs to be revised and rearranged before it can be stored. The one drawback to maintenance rehearsal is that when information is continually reentered into STM, the amount of new information that can enter is curtailed because of STM's limited capacity.

MAINTENANCE REHEARSAL: *The process of repeating the contents of short-term memory over and over to maintain it in STM.*

INTERFERENCE TASK: *Any task that prevents maintenance rehearsal or prevents memories from being transferred to LTM.*

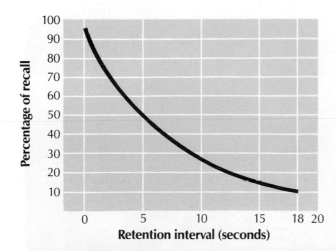

Figure 7.2 Rate of forgetting when an interference task prevents retention of words in STM.

Capacity of short-term memory   Our capacity for holding information in STM is limited to about 7 items, compared to at least 360,000 items (bits) stored by modern microcomputers such as the IBM PC. This limited capacity of working memory can be a serious disadvantage unless you know how to use STM effectively.

For a long time, researchers were puzzled about exactly how much information could be contained in short-term memory. Psychologist George Miller described his grapplings with the problem in a famous 1956 journal article titled "The Magical Number Seven, Plus or Minus Two":

> My problem is that I have been persecuted by an integer. For seven years this number has followed me around, has intruded in my most private data, and has assaulted me from the pages of our most public journals. This number assumes a variety of disguises, being sometimes a little larger and sometimes a little smaller than usual, but never changing so much as to be unrecognizable. . . . Either there really is something unusual about the number or else I am suffering from delusions of persecution. (p. 81)

Miller noted that the findings of research studies on the capacity of STM were not entirely consistent. For example, when subjects memorized nonsense syllables composed of three letters, like ZIQ or MUZ, they could usually keep only three syllables at a time in short-term memory. On the other hand, when subjects memorized words, they could usually remember up to seven words.

To explain this apparent inconsistency, Miller concluded that information in STM is grouped into units and that the capacity of STM is between five and nine *units* (the magical number 7, plus or minus two). Thus, the reason that only about three nonsense syllables are remembered at a time is that each of the letters of a nonsense syllable is processed in STM individually, so that three of the three-letter syllables comprise nine units. In contrast, a word is one unit regardless of the number of letters in it, so that up to nine complete words can be held in STM. Telephone numbers are easily held in short-term memory because they universally contain seven numbers. (Numbers are like the letters of nonsense syllables; they need to be processed individually.)

Question: Doesn't this "magical number" severely limit our short-term memories?   Yes, but under normal circumstances we need to retain only a few items in our short-term memories. Having too many items in STM is like having a horribly cluttered desk. If we wish to expand the number of items that we can hold in STM, there are several ways to do this. One technique is to group information into units, or chunks, a process known as **chunking**. Organizing letters into words and thinking of a telephone area code as a unit are examples of chunking. In reading-improvement courses, students are taught to chunk groups of words into phrases so that fewer eye movements are required and the brain can process the phrases as *units* rather than individual words.

CHUNKING: *The process of grouping information into units in order to be able to store more information in short-term memory.*

Good chess players are able to remember groups of pieces by chunking them into meaningful patterns.

The fact that expert chess players also use chunking to organize the information on a game board into meaningful patterns or units was discovered by researchers interested in comparing expert players' memory skills to those of novice players (Chase and Simon, 1973). In these studies, a chess board was set up as it would appear during a game. Novice players who looked at the board for five seconds could remember the positions of only a few pieces, but expert chess players could frequently remember all the positions because they saw the pieces in typical groups that occur during a game. To the expert players, these groups formed meaningful patterns, just as readers see words instead of individual letters. When chess pieces were arranged randomly on the board in ways that would not occur during a game, the expert players did no better than novices in remembering the positions.

Using short-term memory effectively

Question: Why do some people have only five units in STM whereas others have nine? Memory research has shown that people who at first seem to have fewer spaces in STM actually have just as much STM capacity as anyone else, but they have not been using this stage of memory efficiently. With attention to the limitations of STM, this stage of memory processing can be improved (Brown, Campione, and Barclay, 1978). For example, in one study, first-grade children were shown seven pictures. The teacher pointed to three of the pictures and then covered all of them. After 15 seconds, the children were asked to recall which of the pictures the teacher had pointed to and in what order. The children who had kept thinking about what had happened were able to remember the order, whereas the children who forgot the order had paid attention during the pointing but had then thought about other things. When the latter children were taught how to keep the information in STM after the presentation, they were able to remember it as well as the children who had spontaneously used this strategy. In a later test, only those children who went back to thinking about other things forgot the order again (Keeney, Cannizzo, and Flavell, 1967). This research points out the importance of paying attention to the things we are attempting to learn and organizing the information efficiently in STM in order to recall it later on.

Question: If I have room for at least seven units, why do I have so much trouble remembering even three or four names during introductions? The limited capacity and brief duration of STM both work against you in this situation. To be remembered, the name you have just heard must be selected as important enough for attention, and other things must not be selected as more important. If you want to remember a name long enough to carry on a conversation, you need to get it into your long-term memory. Because the name cannot be processed for transfer to LTM if other things occupy the STM spaces and cause interference, it helps to deliberately concentrate on the name and repeat it to improve its chances of being remembered.

When you are being introduced to people at a party, you may find that instead of concentrating on the names, you are using all the spaces in your short-term memory for wondering how you look and for rehearsing the brilliant things you will say. As you are being introduced to people, you might even notice that you have already forgotten some of the names, in which case you may fill your STM worrying about the fact that you haven't remembered them!

People who get anxious during introductions often occupy all their STM spaces with self-talk about how terrible it is not to be able to remember. People who are good at remembering names often repeat the name of each person out loud or to themselves to keep it entered in STM. They also make sure that other thoughts don't intrude until they have tested their ability to remember the name.

Question: I seem to remember things better if I see them rather than hear a description of them. Is visual memory usually better? Visualization is a highly effective way of processing certain kinds of information but we also have a verbal "chan-

You will be able to better remember the name of a person you have just been introduced to if you can relate the name to something unique about the person.

DUAL-CODING SYSTEM: *The process of coding information by both visual and verbal means.*

nel" for processing information contained in words and ideas. Allen Paivio (1982) refers to this two-part division of STM as a **dual-coding system.** Let's look at how this dual coding works.

We use the visual transfer system when we look at an object such as a tree. Information about the tree is processed through STM as a visual image, and we can later remember what the tree looks like in the form of a picture. Try to remember how many doors there are in the place where you live. If you visualize what the rooms look like, you can mentally walk through them to count the doors. This visual imagery system is vivid for many people. On the other hand, we use the verbal transfer system for processing words regardless of whether we hear them or see them. The word "tree" enters STM as a word pattern rather than a picture of this object. This verbal channel appears to operate separately from the visual imagery system.

Since we have both visual and verbal pathways for STM information, it is advantageous to use both systems for remembering information rather than just one. Research has shown that subjects remember a word they have heard or read better when they also think of a visual image of the object that word represents (Paivio, 1969, 1971).

Another way of using STM effectively is to analyze the deeper meaning of information as opposed to simply focusing on superficial characteristics (Craik and Tulving, 1975; Morris, Bransford, and Franks, 1977). For example, if when meeting people at a party you just paid attention to their names, noted whether they were male or female, and concentrated on their appearance, you would be doing a superficial analysis. However, if you discussed their political or religious beliefs and found out what they like to do with their spare time, you would be doing a deeper analysis and would be more likely to remember them the next time you meet.

LEVELS OF PROCESSING: *The depth to which STM contents are processed during consolidation to LTM.*

According to this **levels of processing** approach, a deeper analysis of meaning enables us to remember information better because we store it in LTM more efficiently. In research on levels of processing, when subjects are instructed to look at each word on a list and think of a word that rhymes with it or notice whether the word is capitalized, they are performing a superficial analysis. When subjects are told to think of other words that have similar meanings, they are using a deeper level of processing that associates the information to be learned into the organization of LTM more effectively (Hyde and Jenkins, 1969). Similarly, when you think about the meaning of the course materials you are studying, you are processing at a deeper level—a strategy that helps transfer the information more efficiently to LTM (Jacoby, 1974; Tulving and Thomson, 1973).

Review Questions

1 The three types of memory that are part of the memory model are
_____ _____, _____ _____, and
_____ _____.

2 The temporary memory that lasts for about ½ second is _____ memory.

3 The type of memory used when remembering a telephone number just long enough to dial the number is _____ memory.

4 To keep something in STM, we use _____ _____.

5 The process of _____ enables us to store more information in STM by grouping things into separate units.

6 Processing of information both visually and verbally is called a _____ system.

Answers: 1 sensory memory, short-term memory, long-term memory; *2* sensory; *3* short-term; *4* maintenance rehearsal; *5* chunking; *6* dual-coding

Long-term memory: The memory storage system

Unlike the sensory memory and STM stages, LTM is not limited in capacity or duration. Information in LTM can last as long as we live and we never run out of places to store new information (Klatzky, 1984). However, for this stored information to be useful, it must be organized so that it will be available for future reference and can be updated by new information.

During the transfer of information from STM to LTM, incoming information is "tagged" to be filed in the appropriate place. If it is not properly tagged and stored, it might not be accessible later. This storage process can require considerable time and effort. It is like organizing and filing away real items such as class notes, record albums, or tools so that they can be retrieved quickly and easily sometime in the future.

Some of the job of memory organization and filing apparently occurs during sleep. Some researchers believe that during REM sleep, our recent additions to long-term memory are reviewed, improved, and systematically tagged (Crick and Mitchison, 1983).

Question: Is it possible for me to learn something by listening to a tape while I'm asleep? Apparently not. Any learning from listening to a tape would occur during the "prime time" for remembering things just *before* falling asleep. Recordings of brain waves were used to determine whether subjects listening to sleep learning machines were really sleeping. It was found that subjects who had heard tapes while in a drowsy state could answer 50 percent of the questions they were asked about the information they heard. When they had been in a transition state between drowsiness and light sleep, they could answer only 5 percent of the questions. When they had been fully asleep during the tape playing, they did not remember any of the information (Simon and Emmons, 1956). This research would also suggest that you don't store information efficiently when you listen to lectures or study in a drowsy state. Proper tagging and storage of information requires an alert mind.

Question: Sometimes, I'm certain that I've remembered something accurately but someone else has a different recollection and is just as certain he or she is correct. What causes these disagreements? Because of the nature of LTM, our memories can include additions to, omissions from, and revisions of the original event. It always seems amazing to us when we are shown that what we remembered is not a perfect copy of the original event, especially if the memory seems vivid. The witnesses in Father Pagano's trial were probably startled to discover how little the real Gentleman Bandit resembled the man they had identified. Psychologists studying the memory process have been able to identify how some stored memories are altered from the original versions while they are being tagged, filed, and stored (Loftus and Loftus, 1980; Ward, 1987).

Sensory memory and short-term memory both tend to be like tape recordings or movies that replay information exactly, but transfer into long-term memory changes the form of the recording. For example, when subjects are given sentences to read, they can remember the exact wording if they are tested within 30 seconds. This information is coming from STM. However, when subjects are tested after 30 seconds and are prevented from using rehearsal to keep the information in STM, they often identify a sentence with the same meaning (but not the same wording) as the one they saw (Sachs, 1967). In the course of consolidating and storing the information in LTM, the exact wording has been lost.

Question: Why isn't the original version stored in long-term memory? The answer seems to be that when information is tagged for filing in long-term storage, the meaning of the item is more important than its exact physical form. To store or catalog the information, an analysis is performed to determine how it can be added to the things that are already stored. In this analysis, things can be added, left out, or rearranged. Most often, a rearranged memory is just as useful as the original version. We don't always need to remember something exactly, but we do need to know what it means. On the other hand, there are times when an exact duplicate is required of memory. When we memorize a poem or lines in a play, for example, we are making a special request of our memory processes to preserve the exact wording. It is difficult for most people to memorize exactly, since this isn't what long-term memory is designed to do.

Another reason we store an altered version of the original event is that during our analysis of incoming information, we make assumptions or inferences about the information. These assumptions occupy STM for a while and are filed along with the information being analyzed. Later, we can't accurately separate what we *assumed* from what we were given. For example, if your friend looks sad and tells you, "Fido was chasing a cat and was hit by a truck," you might assume that:

1. Fido is a dog, since this is a common name for dogs and dogs often chase cats.
2. Fido ran into the street.
3. Fido was injured or killed.

Later, you might remember your friend having said, "My dog Fido was killed by a truck when he ran into the street."

Another potential source of error that occurs during the storage phase of LTM is that the sources of information do not seem to be filed very carefully. That is, you may remember *what* you heard but not necessarily *where* you heard it. This can be a problem if you pay attention to both dependable and undependable sources of information. Suppose, for example, a famous movie star is interviewed on a television talk show and offers an opinion about a weight-loss diet. You might later recall that the information was presented by a dietary expert rather than a movie star with questionable credentials. A related phenomenon is known as the "sleeper effect." It occurs when a discounted previous message gains credibility or persuasiveness over time (Pratkanis et al., 1988). You've probably experienced this effect when a friend tells you about an innovative idea that is completely foreign to your way of thinking. At first, you reject the idea outright; but after a few weeks of consideration, the idea begins to seem quite plausible.

Semantic and episodic memory

Question: Why do we have so much difficulty remembering where information comes from if we can do an analysis of the meaning so well? Psychologists studying memory have concluded that determining the meaning of something involves one type of memory and knowing where or when we learned about it involves a different type of memory. Why one type of memory is easier to use than the other is not known (Tulving, 1985).

The first type of long-term memory, knowledge of facts and how they relate to each other, is called **semantic memory.** It is like a dictionary or encyclopedia in which a large amount of factual information (such as the names of the months or mathematics skills) is stored. Once something is entered into semantic memory, it is durable and available for comparison to incoming information. The second type of long-term memory, called **episodic memory,** contains "autobiographical" information: when and where a specific event or episode happened (Tulving, 1972, 1985). For example, when you first learned to read the word "cat" years ago, it took some effort to relate that word to particular animals. By now, you have had numerous experiences with the word and it has many meanings for you stored in your semantic memory. These meanings are available to you any time you deal with the word. However, if you were asked to describe the exact time, date, and location of each of your experiences with the word, you would have to refer to your episodic memory and you would have a difficult time locating the information in LTM. Several researchers have tried unsuccessfully to experimentally separate these two types of memory (McKoon et al., 1986; Neely & Durgunoglu, 1985; Richards and Goldfarb, 1986). In explanation, Tulving (1985, 1986) has suggested that episodic memory may actually be a subsystem of semantic memory. Even if this is so, the distinction between semantic and episodic memory has proven quite useful in studying and discussing human memory.

SEMANTIC MEMORY: *A type of LTM in which facts and relations between facts are stored.*

EPISODIC MEMORY: *A type of LTM in which memories for events are stored.*

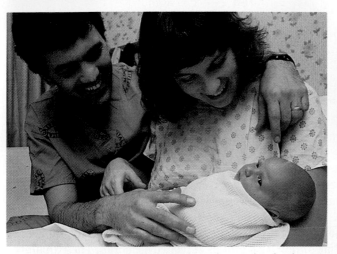

Graduation, marriage, the birth of a child, and a couple's first house are landmark events that enable us to locate other events in episodic memory.

Question: I've noticed that I can remember certain details such as what I had for dinner on the night of my high school graduation, but I can't remember what I ate just a few nights ago. Why is this?   Events that are important to us — graduation, going into the Army, getting married, having a child — act as landmarks for our memory and in fact are known as **landmark events.** We can use these events to search backward and forward in our memory to locate details about other events that occurred at about the same time. Without a specific landmark event, it is often difficult to retrieve details from episodic memory about such common everyday occurrences as meals (Lindsey and Norman, 1977).

LANDMARK EVENTS: *Events that are important to us, such as high school graduation or getting married, that can be used as an aid in memory.*

Organization of long-term memory   The diagram in Figure 7.3 illustrates one way concepts are thought to be arranged in LTM. Psychologists studying the organization of LTM have concluded that information is filed in categories and subcategories as a network with several pathways to reach a piece of information (Collins and Quillian, 1969).

You can become aware of the ways your own long-term memory is organized by associations and linkages whenever you experience the **tip-of-the-tongue (TOT)** phenomenon — the feeling that any second a word you are trying to remember will pop out from the tip of your tongue (Brown and McNeill, 1966; Read and Bruce, 1982). The gap in memory of a TOT state is an unusual case of forgetting because even though you can't say the word, you can often tell how many syllables it has, the beginning and ending letters, or what it rhymes with. When you try to remember a person's name or an unfamiliar word such as "sextant" or "ambergris" that is on the tip of your tongue, you can frequently eliminate words that are incorrect because they don't have the proper sound or length. Psychologists have studied the things that subjects know about a word while they are in the TOT state to identify the associations and linkages of items in LTM that form categories and hierarchies.

TIP-OF-THE-TONGUE (TOT): *The feeling that a word you are trying to remember is just barely inaccessible.*

Figure 7.3 A hierarchy of concepts in long-term memory (LTM).

Retrieval from Semantic Memory

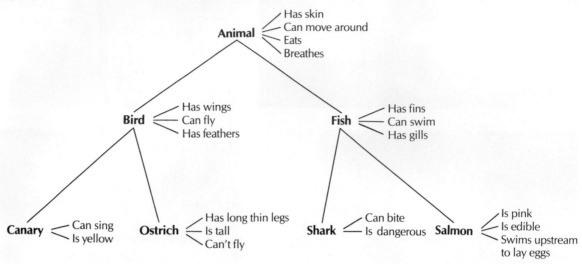

Another common experience that provides clues about the organization of LTM is **redintegration,** a type of remembering that occurs when something unlocks a rapid chain of memories. For example, hearing a particular song or name can create a flood of memories and emotions, and rereading a diary or journal or looking at photographs of significant events will sometimes bring back groups of related memories. These thoughts and emotions seem to be connected through a chain of associations that illustrate the ways our long-term memories are organized in time and place and interconnected by meaning (Bower, 1976).

Retrieval processes Whatever system is used to organize stored information, the purpose of memory storage is to be able to use the information later on. The process of returning long-term memory contents to short-term memory for analysis or awareness is called **retrieval.** Being able to retrieve information stored in LTM is one important key to having a "good" memory.

Question: The other day, I went from my bathroom to the kitchen to do something and when I got there, I couldn't remember what it was. I had to go back to the bathroom to remember. Why is that?   In a situation like this, something in the bathroom acted as a cue or signal for you to remember something you wanted to do and that cue wasn't present in the kitchen to remind you. While you were walking to the kitchen, you were probably thinking of other things, which kept the idea generated in the bathroom from remaining in STM. A **cue** is a stimulus that can begin a retrieval process from LTM (Klatzky, 1984). Being asked a question is an example of a cue. Some cues are more subtle than direct questions and might not even be noticed as memory joggers. The smell of perfume or after-shave lotion or the look on someone's face can trigger a group of memories that seem to appear out of nowhere.

The effect of environmental cues is illustrated in the research of anthropologist Margaret Mead (1964). When she lived with the aborigines of south Australia, she learned that some important aspects of their culture are transmitted through the storytelling of an oral tradition. Stories of significant events are memorized so that the next generation can learn about their cultural past. These stories are sometimes long and contain many important details. Mead found that in order to be able to tell a long story correctly, the natives had to walk through the places involved in the story. If the storytellers were tested in a laboratory without the retrieval cues of their physical environment, their memories would not be so remarkable.

Tribal storytellers often use specific cues in the environment to help them remember details of their complex stories.

Question: Why do I have so much trouble remembering names but I never seem to forget a face? When you know that you have seen a face before, you are using a retrieval strategy called **recognition** (Mandler, 1980). The operation you perform in recognition is to take the stimulus cue (the face) and check your long-term memory contents to see whether you have something there that matches the stimulus cue. When you use a recognition strategy, you are very accurate in judging whether you've seen something before. When you attempt to remember a name, you are using another type of retrieval process called **recall**, which is a more difficult task (Bransford, 1979). To recall information, you must use a more general cue than the exact information to be located and must find material in LTM *associated with* that cue. When you look at a face, for instance, it is a general cue for the person's name. This general cue often isn't specific enough to find the appropriate name among the many stored in long-term memory.

When you answer an essay question, you use a recall strategy to remember the information that is associated with the words of the question. For example, an essay question that asks you to compare recognition and recall strategies would require you to produce the pertinent information you have learned about these two terms. On the other hand, when you answer multiple choice items, you are given pieces of information to identify the ones that match the information you have already stored, which is a recognition task.

The ability to recognize faces and pictures of objects has been studied extensively. Humans seem to have a remarkable ability to recognize the things they have previously encountered (Shepard, 1967; Standing, Conezio, and Haber, 1970). In studies of recognition, subjects have looked at 10,000 slides (which takes five days) and later, when shown a pair of slides containing a new picture and an original, have been able to identify the original 98 percent of the time (Standing, 1973). In another study (see Figure 7.4), subjects were shown five pictures from yearbooks, one of which was a person from their

RECOGNITION: *Process of matching a specific stimulus cue to an appropriate item in LTM.*

RECALL: *Process of using a very general stimulus cue to search the contents of LTM.*

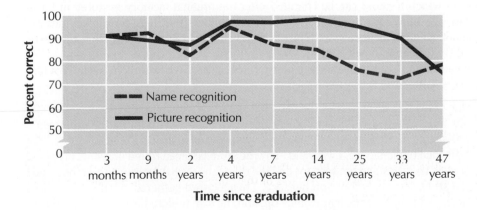

Time since graduation

Figure 7.4 Results from a study of recognition memory (Bahrick, Bahrick, and Wittlinger, 1975) in which subjects were asked to identify pictures of their high school classmates.

high school graduating class. Fifteen years after graduation, subjects were accurate in identifying 90 percent of their classmates. Even subjects who had been out of high school for more than 40 years could still identify 75 percent of their classmates (Bahrick, Bahrick, and Wittlinger, 1975).

RELEARNING: *Learning material a second time. Relearning usually takes less time than original learning.*

In addition to testing for recognition and recall, researchers have used measurements of **relearning** to study memory. One way of measuring relearning is to compare the amount of time it takes subjects to learn material again after they can no longer recognize or recall it. If relearning takes less time than the original learning, then some information must have been stored.

The relearning method was introduced to experimental psychology in 1885 by Hermann Ebbinghaus, a pioneer memory researcher who often used himself as his only subject. To measure memory performance, he calculated the amount of time it took for him to first learn and then to relearn a list containing nonsense syllables such as SIM or RAL. Ebbinghaus used three-letter nonsense syllables because he wanted to avoid the complications of previous learning. He wanted to learn materials that were as equal to each other as possible so that he could calculate the amount of time it took to learn similar materials. Nonsense syllables were useful because they do not have the previous meanings and associations that words do.

According to Ebbinghaus's research findings, we often have some memory for things we have learned, even when we seem to have forgotten them completely. This finding should be encouraging to you if you studied a foreign language many years ago but can no longer recall or recognize the vocabulary. If you need to pass a proficiency examination in the language someday, you could study the material again and expect to learn it more rapidly the second time.

ZEIGARNIK EFFECT: *Process of working unconsciously on a problem until it is solved.*

Question: Why do I sometimes remember something I thought I had forgotten, when I don't seem to be trying to remember it anymore?   Research has found that when thinking is left "unfinished," the brain will keep working on the problem unconsciously until an answer is obtained. Psychologists call this the **Zeigarnik effect** (Bonello, 1982; Zeigarnik, 1927). Apparently, an unfinished problem motivates us to find a solution. Our perceptual processes continue to select things that give us further information about the problem and we continue to search the categories of our memories until we find the information we need. If, for example, you had been trying to remember the names of the Seven Dwarfs, you might suddenly think of the name "Sleepy" as you sit in your chemistry class.

The alteration of stored memories

Until recently, short-term memory had been compared to wet cement that is still pliable and long-term memory to hardened cement that retains permanent impressions (Houston, Bee, and Rimm, 1983). Writing or drawing on this surface can be erased or changed only while the cement is still wet. As we shall see later in the chapter, memories in STM are indeed fragile and can be erased (amnesia) or altered before a permanent memory is created. However, research has revealed a number of ways in which memory can be changed *after* the original memory is stored in LTM. Such findings have convinced many memory researchers that long-term memories are easily modified after they are stored, rather than being permanent records that cannot be changed (Loftus and Loftus, 1980).

As an example of the pliability of memory, consider this account offered by psychologist Jean Piaget (1951):

> One of my first memories would date, if it were true, from my second year. I can still see, most clearly, the following scene, in which I believed until I was about fifteen. I was sitting in my pram, which my nurse was pushing in the Champs Elysees, when a man tried to kidnap me. I was held in by the strap fastened round me while my nurse bravely tried to stand between me and the thief. She received various scratches, and I can still see vaguely those on her face. Then a crowd gathered, a policeman with a short cloak and a white baton came up, and the man took to his heels. I can still see

The events that occurred in Tiananmen Square during 1989 created a vivid flashbulb memory for many people.

the whole scene, and can even place it near the tube station. When I was about fifteen, my parents received a letter from my former nurse saying that she had been converted to the Salvation Army. She wanted to confess her past faults, and in particular to return the watch she had been given as a reward on this occasion. She had made up the whole story, faking the scratches. I, therefore, must have heard, as a child, the account of this story, which my parents believed, and projected into the past in the form of a visual memory, which was a memory of a memory, but false. (pp. 187–188)

As this example illustrates, we can't always count on the vividness of a memory as proof that it actually happened. Psychologists have studied such feelings of certainty about the accuracy of memories in several ways. One of the most popular research topics has been to study **flashbulb memories**—vivid images of circumstances associated with surprising or strongly emotional events. These memories are like action pictures taken with a flash camera. One event that created flashbulb memories for many people was the assassination of President John F. Kennedy in 1963. The news of his death was sudden and startling, and many people have vivid memories of where they were when they first heard it. Ten years after the assassination, for example, Billy Graham could remember having been on the golf course when he heard the news. Julia Child could visualize being in the kitchen and could remember what she was eating at the time (Loftus, 1980). Indeed, it is events such as sudden disasters and assassinations of important political or religious figures that have lasting effects on memory (Brown and Kulik, 1977). People relive such events in their minds over and over again. This increase in rehearsal affects the number and quality of associations with the event, which lead to more vivid memories.

One psychologist studying flashbulb memories of Kennedy's assassination found evidence that some people were remembering inaccurately, even though, like Piaget, they were certain they remembered the event vividly. One person interviewed by psychologist Marigold Linton (1979) had a vivid memory of being interrupted by a friend while studying in the library and being told all about Kennedy's death. Yet the friend who supposedly described the events to her was actually attending a different school in a different state at the time of the assassination.

Question: How do memories get altered like this?   Several factors alter memories. As we discussed in the previous section, long-term memories (unlike sensory and short-term memories) are not exact duplicates of information. In our attempt to catalog and store memories in LTM, we often rearrange facts, leave out certain details, and

FLASHBULB MEMORIES: *Vivid images of circumstances associated with surprising or strongly emotional events.*

add other information to allow it to be stored with related topics. In addition, we have difficulty in separating what was *assumed* from what was actually presented and with remembering whether the original source was reliable or not.

Researchers have also discovered that information that is presented after the original event can have an important influence on our memory processes. In one study, for example, subjects were shown a film of a car driving through the countryside. Members of one group were then asked to estimate how fast the car was going when it passed *the barn*. Subjects in the other group who saw the same film were also asked to estimate the car's speed, but a *barn* was not mentioned. When all subjects were later asked if they saw a barn in the film, six times as many subjects in the group given the misinformation about the barn reported having seen it, even though it never appeared in the film (Loftus, 1982).

In a series of related experiments, subjects saw slides showing a red car drive down a street, approach an intersection, make a turn, and hit a pedestrian. The subjects in one group were asked the following question after viewing the slides: "Did another car pass the red car while it was stopped at the stop sign?" The sign at the corner was actually a "yield" sign, but 80 percent of the subjects were influenced by the misinformation they were given about the stop sign. They altered their long-term memories to include a memory of a stop sign that they never saw (Loftus, 1982).

Given these rather unsettling facts from research studies, how much weight do you think should be given to eyewitness testimony? If you were a juror for Father Pagano's trial, how much do you think you would be influenced by the testimony of eyewitnesses about the guilt of the defendant? Keeping in mind the results of eyewitness research, it is alarming to consider the influence of eyewitness testimony in court cases. The British government authorized a study of court cases in England and Wales involving police lineups. In the 347 cases where the *only* evidence presented against the defendant was the sworn statement of one or more eyewitnesses, the conviction rate was 74 percent (Loftus, 1980).

In laboratory experiments where variables can be controlled completely, the powerful influence of eyewitness testimony has been demonstrated repeatedly. In one mock trial experiment, the subjects acted as jurors in a robbery–murder case. Of the jurors who heard only circumstantial evidence, only 18 percent found the defendant guilty. Of subjects presented with exactly the same case except for the addition of the testimony of one eyewitness who identified the defendant as the guilty person, 72 percent found the defendant guilty (Loftus, 1980).

Even though eyewitnesses are often mistaken, Elizabeth Loftus (1980) has found that a discredited witness may be as effective as a nonchallenged witness. Bernard Whitley (1987) disagrees slightly with Loftus's findings. Still, he agrees that a discredited eyewitness can be more influential than no witness at all, and the unchallenged eyewitness is the most influential of all.

How often eyewitnesses are *mistaken* in their recollections of events is impossible to determine, but experimental evidence indicates that the amount of inaccuracy might be disturbingly high. For example, in an experiment at the University of Nebraska, subjects watched people committing a staged crime. About an hour later, they looked at "mugshots." A week later, they attempted to pick the suspects from a "lineup." In this experiment, *none* of the participants in the staged crime appeared in the mugshots or lineups, yet subjects identified 20 percent of the innocent people in the mugshots as participants in the crime and 8 percent of the people in the lineups as guilty parties (Brown, Deffenbacher, and Sturgill, 1977).

Question: How could the subjects have been so mistaken? It would seem that at least two properties of memory could combine to create the type of mistaken identity that occurred at the lineup stage. First, according to research on recognition, seeing a face in the mugshots would give witnesses a sense of familiarity with the person's face when he or she was later seen in the lineup. Second, according to research on episodic memory, it would be difficult for witnesses to be certain about where they had seen the person before, which might have led to the assumption that they saw this person committing the crime.

Review Questions

1 The permanent memory system is called _____ memory.

2 Knowledge of facts and how they relate to one another are stored in a special LTM called _____ memory.

3 A second type of LTM that contains autobiographical information is called _____ memory.

4 When we know the answer to a question, but can't quite get it out of our mouth, we are experiencing the _____ phenomenon.

5 The process of returning LTM contents to STM for analysis or awareness is called _____.

6 When people are asked to pick an assailant out of a police lineup, they are using a retrieval strategy called _____.

7 Vivid images of circumstances associated with surprising or strongly emotional events are called _____ memories.

8 The fact that memories can be _____ has called into question the validity of eyewitness testimony in courts of law.

Answers: 1 long-term; *2* semantic; *3* episodic; *4* tip-of-the-tongue; *5* retrieval; *6* recognition; *7* flashbulb; *8* altered

THE PROBLEM OF FORGETTING

Some memory research has focused specifically on the circumstances involved in forgetting, a familiar process that can be either helpful or disturbing. Even though there are times when we would rather not remember something disturbing or embarrassing, most of the time forgetting is an inconvenience we would like to avoid. What causes forgetting and how can we prevent it when we want to?

These questions have been important issues in psychology ever since Hermann Ebbinghaus emphasized the process of forgetting in memory studies over 100 years ago. As we discussed in the previous section, Ebbinghaus memorized lists of nonsense syllables until he knew them perfectly and then would continue to retest his memory of the list at regular intervals. He found that one hour after he knew a list perfectly, he remembered only 44 percent of the syllables. A day later, he recalled 35 percent, and a week later only 21 percent. Figure 7.5 is his famous and depressing "forgetting curve."

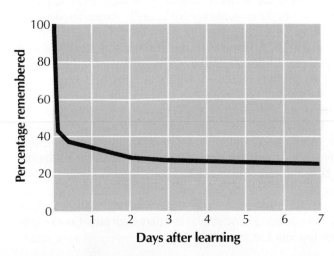

Figure 7.5 Ebbinghaus's forgetting curve. Nonsense syllables are forgotten rapidly.

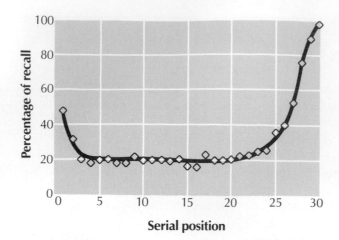

Figure 7.6 The serial position effect—immediate testing.

Serial position

> *Question:* Is everything forgotten this fast? If you were to forget textbook materials and lecture notes this rapidly, you would be able to pass a test only if you took it immediately after memorizing the information. An hour later, you would fail the test because you would remember less than half of what you had studied. Keep in mind, however, that the forgetting curve in Figure 7.5 applies to meaningless nonsense syllables. Meaningful material is much less likely to be forgotten.

Research on forgetting: Factors that affect remembering

SERIAL POSITION EFFECT: *The effect that occurs when a person remembers the material at the beginning and the end of a list better than the material in the middle.*

How interference creates forgetting is revealed in studies of the **serial position effect.** When subjects are given lists of words to learn and are allowed to recall them in any order they choose, it has been found that the words at the beginning and end of the list are remembered better than those in the middle (see Figure 7.6). The middle words are quite often forgotten.

The first words on the list are better remembered because they are processed into LTM without as much interference as later words receive. Because most subjects want to do well on a memory task, they concentrate on and rehearse each word as it appears. Thus, the first words to be remembered are processed and transferred to LTM. But, when subjects get to about seven words, they can't continue to rehearse all of them. At this point, they will often take up some of their STM by trying to decide what they will do to try to remember more words than they have spaces for. During this time, the next words on the list do not get as much analysis and attention.

> *Question:* Why are the words at the end of the list remembered so well? When subjects are allowed to recall the words they learned in any order they choose, they often use maintenance rehearsal to keep the words at the end of the list in STM until they are written down. Thus, in the long run, these words are not actually remembered as well as the words at the beginning of the list because they have not been stored. To find out how well these word lists are stored in LTM, subjects are retested on word recall at a later time. If subjects have not been told that it will be important to try to remember these words again later, they don't transfer all the final words on the list to LTM, and on the later surprise test these words are remembered only as well as the middle words (see Figure 7.7). On the other hand, if subjects are told before they memorize the word list that they will be retested at a later time, the final words are remembered as well as the beginning words because subjects make an effort to transfer them to LTM. This serial position phenomenon also explains why students tend to remember the material at the beginning and end of the chapter better than the contents in the middle.

Strategies for studying Despite their best intentions, students often study in ways that encourage forgetting. In addition to studying in noisy places where their attention is easily diverted, they often try to learn too much at one time.

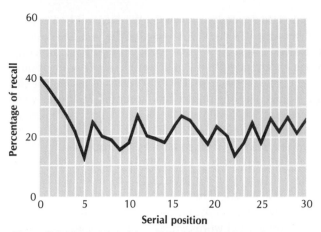

Figure 7.7 The serial position effect — later testing.

"Cramming" for an examination is an attempt to learn too much at one time, and it is less effective than spacing your studying over several days or weeks.

Question: I've heard that it isn't a good idea to "cram" for an examination. Is that true? Yes, it's true. Cramming is such a common approach to studying that we feel it is important to discuss the research in this area. Whether you are learning verbal materials such as the content of this textbook or motor skills such as typing, you are better off spacing your learning periods, with rest periods between practice sessions. Psychologists call this learning strategy **distributed practice**. "Cramming" is called **massed practice** because the time spent learning is massed into long, unbroken intervals. An early study of these learning strategies found that fewer nonsense syllables were forgotten when subjects were given a 126-second rest period between trials (distributed practice) compared to a 6-second rest period (massed practice) — see Figure 7.8 (Hovland, 1938). Similar benefits of distributed practice have been found for the learning of motor skills such as typing (Jones and Ellis, 1962).

DISTRIBUTED PRACTICE: *A learning technique in which practice sessions are interspersed with rest periods.*
MASSED PRACTICE: *A learning technique in which time spent learning is massed into long, unbroken intervals; cramming.*

State-dependent memory   Have you ever had trouble remembering the details of the information you studied when you are anxious during a test you're taking? When you are sad, do you tend to remember things that made you sad in the past? Such experiences are common because human memory systems are connected to emotional arousal level and feelings. Memory research has shown that the arousal level of the nervous system and the emotions that occur during learning have an important effect on memory for the learned

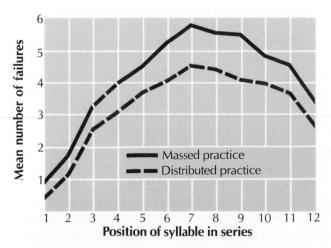

Figure 7.8 Comparison of massed and distributed practice effects.

STATE-DEPENDENT MEMORY: *Memory that is connected to a state of emotional arousal.*

material. This relationship is called **state-dependent memory.** We have all had experiences that are remembered vividly because we were very aroused at the time and concentrated on what was happening. Research has shown that people often have difficulty remembering something if they are experiencing a different arousal level or emotional state from the one they were in at the time they learned the information. This may be the reason why some of Father Pagano's accusers identified him inaccurately. If they were frightened during the robbery and relaxed when viewing the police lineup, their memory of the real robber might have been somewhat impaired.

The *arousal level* of the nervous system — how serene or excited one is — has been studied as an important element in forgetting (Fischer, 1976). Arousal level can be altered by emotions like anxiety or by use of psychoactive drugs such as alcohol, caffeine, nicotine, or marijuana (see Chapter 5). Caffeine and nicotine raise arousal level, whereas alcohol and marijuana lower it. In one research study, arousal level was altered through alcohol use. Subjects were asked to learn a list of words while either intoxicated or sober. It was found that subjects recalled the words best when they were in the same state as when they had learned the words, *either* intoxicated *or* sober (Weingartner et al., 1976). Marijuana has been shown to decrease reading comprehension, short-term memory processing, and ability to recall what was learned (Nicholi, 1983). Even though caffeine and nicotine are psychoactive drugs that make people feel more alert while they study or take tests, both of these drugs have been shown to decrease performance on complex memory tasks (Anderson, 1983; Mangan and Golding, 1983).

In addition to the effects of overall arousal level on memory, Gordon Bower (1981) has shown that *particular types* of emotions create state-dependent effects. In one of his studies, subjects learned lists of words while they were hypnotized to feel either happy or sad. When they attempted to recall the words, some subjects were hypnotized to be in the same emotional state as when they were learning, whereas others were put in the opposite state. Subjects who had been sad during learning remembered better when they were also sad during recall. Subjects who had been happy during learning remembered better when they were happy during recall. Learning was better when the acquisition and retrieval emotional states matched.

Question: Does this mean that if I'm going to be anxious during a test, I should be anxious while I study?   Absolutely not. According to Johnson and Hasher (1987), state-dependent effects on memory are almost always small. Therefore, conscientious studying is always more important than matching physiological and psychological states when trying to get a good grade on a test. However, if you want to try to match your arousal levels, you could try to reduce the differences in both directions rather than just changing your emotions during studying. If you know from past experience that you are anxious and aroused during tests, you could increase your arousal level during studying without having to resort to creating anxiety. You might try exercising during study breaks and checking frequently during study time to make sure you are not drowsy or bored. Perhaps you could figure out ways to make the information more interesting or personally relevant and thus increase your excitement level.

There are also several ways to decrease arousal level and anxiety during a test. You might set aside a few minutes before the examination for meditation or self-hypnosis to improve your relaxation and concentration abilities. In addition, you might also avoid using stimulants such as coffee or caffeine-containing drinks just before the test that would add to your arousal level.

Theories of forgetting: Why we don't remember everything

Four major theories have been offered to explain why forgetting occurs. Each theory focuses on a different stage of the memory process or on a particular type of problem in processing information.

INTERFERENCE THEORY: *The theory that claims we forget something because other information blocks its storage or retrieval.*

According to **interference theory,** we forget something because other information blocks its retrieval (McGeoch, 1942). Just as interference from other contents will disturb the processing of information in STM, other information can interfere with our ability to remember information stored in LTM (Dempster, 1985). If you have studied two foreign languages, for instance, you might have found that you remember words from the first language instead of the second one when you attempt to communicate. Forgetting something because information learned *previously* interferes with it is called **proactive interference**. Forgetting something because information learned *afterward* interferes is called **retroactive interference**. (*Retro* means "behind," so in retroactive interference something learned behind, or after, something else causes forgetting of the material learned first.) If you've ever changed phone numbers, the new number might have caused retroactive interference for recall of the old one.

PROACTIVE INTERFERENCE: *Effect that occurs when previously learned information interferes with new information.*

RETROACTIVE INTERFERENCE: *Effect that occurs when new information interferes with previously learned information.*

Decay theory is based on the commonsense assumption that memory, like all biological processes, deteriorates as time passes. If memory is processed and stored in a physical form, the vitality of the representation could be expected to decrease over time. As appealing as this explanation seems, it appears not to be the case that long-term memories decay once they are stored (Waugh and Norman, 1965). Experimental support for decay theory has been difficult to obtain because it is hard to control for interference effects when trying to test for the decay of memories.

DECAY THEORY: *The theory that memory, like all biological processes, deteriorates with the passage of time.*

A third theory of forgetting focuses on the fact that we sometimes unconsciously wish to forget something unpleasant. According to the **motivated forgetting theory**, people are blocked from remembering something that would cause pain, threat, or embarrassment. In such cases, the information is not "forgotten," because it is still in LTM and could be remembered if the protective mechanisms were overcome. Sigmund Freud claimed that people use protective defense mechanisms to keep painful memories from becoming conscious and creating anxiety. We will describe his theories of motivated forgetting in Chapter 14.

MOTIVATED FORGETTING THEORY: *The theory that people forget things that cause pain, threat, or embarrassment.*

Anyone who has ever "blanked out" during an examination or a conversation only to remember that "forgotten" information later has had a first-hand experience with the **retrieval failure theory** of forgetting. According to this theory, memories stored in LTM are never really "forgotten" but rather are momentarily inaccessible as a result of such things as interference or emotional states.

RETRIEVAL FAILURE THEORY: *The theory that forgetting is a problem with retrieval, not a problem with long-term storage of information.*

Question: How can I make information more accessible?   One way to avoid retrieval failure is to use the visual and verbal channels more effectively while learning so that the information can be more easily retrieved. Several memorizing strategies that can help will be described in the last section of the chapter.

Review Questions

1 The _____ _____ _____ is the effect experienced when we remember things at the ends of a list but forget things in the middle of the list.

2 The best way to study more material is to space learning periods with rest periods in between. This is called _____ practice.

3 "Cramming" for an examination is an example of _____ practice.

4 Memories that are associated with a particular level of emotional arousal are called _____ memories.

5 Proactive interference occurs when _____ learning interferes with _____ learning.

6 Retroactive intereference occurs when _____ learning interferes with _____ learning.

7 The theory of forgetting that is based on the assumption that memory deteriorates as time passes is the _____ theory.

Answers: 1 serial position effect;   *2* distributed;   *3* massed;   *4* state-dependent;   *5* old, new;   *6* new, old;   *7* decay

THE BIOLOGY OF MEMORY

What happens in the nervous system when we learn something? Where are long-term memories physically stored? A great deal of research has been done to try to answer these questions, and psychologists have developed theories of memory based on these physiological findings.

Theories of memory: Changes in the nervous system

REVERBERATING CIRCUITS: *The firing of a set of neurons over and over again during memory processing.*
ELECTROCONVULSIVE SHOCK (ECS): *Electrical shock applied to the brain such that it causes convulsions.*

Physiological psychologists such as Donald Hebb have approached the biology of memory by studying the reactions of neurons to incoming stimuli. By measuring the electrical activity of the brain during learning, Hebb (1949, 1961) discovered that neurons fire in **reverberating circuits** — that is, a set of neurons firing over and over during the short-term memory process. Any disruption of this electrical event, such as by brain trauma or the passage of electrical current through the brain (**electroconvulsive shock** or **ECS**), interferes with memory storage processes. Hebb has shown that when a particular stimulus enters the brain, it causes a specific pattern of neurons to become active. If an electrical current is passed through the brain at the same time, neurons throughout the brain will fire erratically and create a convulsion. As a result, the specific pattern created by the incoming stimulus cannot be consolidated and processed into a permanent memory. Hebb's theory accounts for the fragile nature of STM.

To transfer information into LTM, the temporary firing of neuron circuits initiates a permanent change in the nervous system. How this happens was described by Hebb in 1949:

> When an axon of cell A is near enough to excite a cell B and repeatedly or persistently takes part in firing it, some growth process or metabolic change takes place in one or both cells such that A's efficiency, as one of the cells firing B, is increased.

Thus, during the process of a short-term memory becoming a long-term memory, groups of neurons repeatedly fire in reverberating circuits, resulting in some chemical or physical modification of the neurons making up the circuits. One of the major theories used to explain this modification involves a process known as long-term synaptic potentiation (LTP) (Barnes and McNaughton, 1985; Brown et al., 1988; Lynch, Halpin, and Baudry, 1983).

LTP is a persistent increase in the efficacy of a synapse that can be induced relatively quickly. Quite simply, it is explained in this way: Repeated stimulation of a synapse causes a change in the dendrite of a neuron, which in turn causes an increase in the permeability of the cell to calcium ions. The movement of these calcium ions into the cell activates proteins that increase the sensitivity of the neuron to excitatory stimulation. This change in sensitivity is reasonably permanent (Barnes and McNaughton, 1980; Lynch, 1988; Lynch, Halpin, and Baudry, 1983).

Some researchers have found chemical and physical changes in the synapses (Deutsch, 1983). During the period of memory storage, the receiving dendrite membranes become more sensitive to the neurotransmitter acetylcholine. (Later, in the section on Alzheimer's disease, we will describe how this chemical is an important part of memory processing.) Other researchers have found evidence of physical changes occurring in the structure of the neurons themselves when something is learned (Crick, 1982; Lynch, 1984; Sokolov, 1977). These structural changes have been demonstrated dramatically in research on the effects of enriched and deprived environments on the brains of rats. Mark Rosenzweig (1972) et al. raised rats in enriched environments where they had many opportunities to learn. Later, he found that neurons in the rats' brains had developed more sprouts on their dendrites compared to the neurons of rats raised without as many learning experiences. Such changes in the structure of neurons enable them to transmit impulses differently. Figure 7.9 shows some of the effects of learning on neurons.

Another way that memory could be preserved is through changes in the genetic

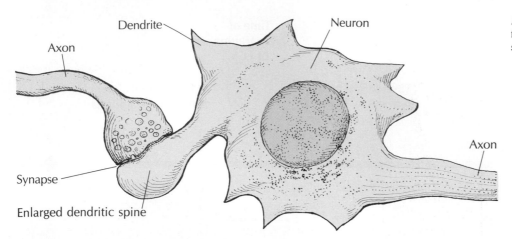

Axon

Dendrite

Neuron

Axon

Synapse

Enlarged dendritic spine

Figure 7.9 Changes in neurons from learning. A dendritic spine swells after long-term potentiation.

mechanisms of neurons. That is, memories may be stored in the form of alterations in the DNA of the neuron nucleus or in the activity of RNA when it manufactures proteins.

The genetic approach to the biology of memory was popularized as a result of a series of experiments conducted on planaria (a type of flatworm) in the 1960s by James McConnell (1962, 1968). He classically conditioned planaria to learn to fear a light. When a light was flashed, it was followed by a painful electric shock. Pain caused the planaria to scrunch their bodies, so observers could see when the animals had learned to associate the light with the shock. The animals that learned this response then became "donors." Their brain cells — containing the DNA, RNA, and proteins that might have been altered by the conditioning — were fed to planaria that had not been conditioned to fear a light. When these untrained worms were exposed to the light, they scrunched their bodies, indicating that the "memories" of the trained planaria had somehow been transferred to them. Improvements in performance with transfer of brain material from donors have also been demonstrated in rats and hamsters (Adam and Faiszt, 1967; Gay and Raphelson, 1967). This entire research area is controversial since other research studies have not been able to obtain the same results (Bennett and Calvin, 1964; Chapouthier 1973).

Question: Would it be possible to improve your memory by changing your diet or by injections of certain chemicals? At this moment the answer to that question is no. It is not currently possible to use drugs to significantly improve memory or the ability to learn new material. So far, memory enhancement through chemicals and drugs or through brain transplants remains in the realm of science fiction. But as the research into the neural basis of memory continues we may eventually have drugs that will enhance memory by, for instance, enhancing long-term synaptic potentiation and therefore allowing a person to more efficiently move information from short-term memory to long-term memory.

Amnesia: Trauma and shock effects

Some of our knowledge of memory has come from studies of people who have suffered memory problems as the result of brain trauma or electroconvulsive shock. Forgetting as a result of such brain insults is called **amnesia.** In **retrograde amnesia,** the person has difficulty remembering events that occurred *before* the brain disruption. In **anterograde amnesia,** the person has difficulty processing memory of events occurring *after* the traumatic incident, because the memory processes are not working efficiently. Fortunately, this type of forgetting is often temporary. Figure 7.10 illustrates the two types of amnesia.

In the case of serious automobile accidents or other forms of head trauma, the jarring of the brain can cause a loss of memory for events before and after the impact. Sometimes whole days or months cannot be remembered, particularly if the person is

AMNESIA: *Forgetting that results from brain injury or from physical or psychological trauma.*
RETROGRADE AMNESIA: *Difficulty in remembering previously learned material.*
ANTEROGRADE AMNESIA: *The inability to form new memories.*

Figure 7.10 Comparison of retrograde and anterograde amnesia.

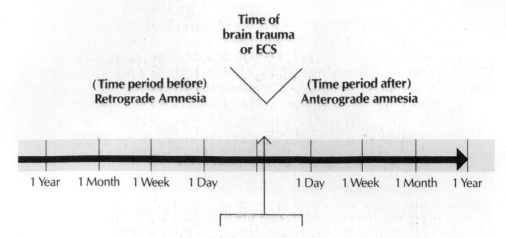

unconscious for a period of time. Eventually, any permanent memory loss is usually confined only to the contents of STM during the time of the trauma since this information was never stored in LTM (Whitty and Zangwill, 1977). An example of this type of memory loss can be seen in the case of a stewardess who managed to survive a fall from a Yugoslavian airplane that was exploded by a terrorist bomb. She suffered brain damage and spinal injuries and was paralyzed from the waist down after falling 30,000 feet. After regaining consciousness, she remembered getting on the airplane and waking up in the hospital, but had no memory of the events in between (Loftus, 1980).

Retrograde amnesia has been created in rats by administering electroconvulsive shock (ECS) during the time something to be learned is in short-term memory (Deutsch, 1969). For example, if rats are punished whenever they step off a platform, they learn to stay on the platform. However, if they receive ECS before the memory of the punishment has had time to be stored in long-term memory, they will continue to step off the platform and receive punishment. If ECS is administered *after* the memory of the punishment has had time to be stored, the rats remain on the platform to avoid the consequence of punishment because they are able to remember that this happened in the past.

Memory impairment: Brain damage

Damage to certain parts of the brain by tumors, strokes, or surgery can produce various types of memory impairment. Consider the memory problems of patient H.M., who had portions of his temporal lobes surgically removed in an attempt to control severe epileptic seizures. After the surgery he had fewer seizures, but he had also lost the ability to transfer any new information into LTM (Scoville and Milner, 1957).

Because H.M. could no longer store permanent memories, it was a difficult challenge to test his mental abilities. One problem was that he forgot that he was being tested as soon as this information was gone from his STM. H.M. could carry on a conversation with the psychologists who tested him and use their names as long as he was using maintenance rehearsal to keep this information in STM. However, if he looked away or didn't talk to them for a few minutes, he couldn't remember having seen them before or remember what he was doing. With such a serious memory problem, it is remarkable to realize that H.M. still had the same IQ scores after the surgery as before. Since his LTM was still intact and he could retrieve memories of things he had experienced before the surgery, he could perform LTM tasks as well as he ever did. Research with monkeys has demonstrated that H.M.'s inability to preserve memories must have been caused by removal of the hippocampus and amygdala in the subcortex when the temporal lobes were removed (Zola-Morgan, Squire, and Mishkin, 1982).

Damage to structures involved in memory can be caused by brain tumors, strokes, alcoholism, or activities such as boxing that create brain trauma. Since a punch thrown by a heavyweight boxer can land at a force exceeding 1000 pounds, nerve cells and blood

"Punch drunk" behavior in boxers is often due to brain damage resulting from years of this type of punishment.

vessels in the fragile brain tissue can be twisted, stretched, and ruptured, causing the "punch drunk" symptoms often seen in boxers. One study that examined the brain tissues of 15 boxers at autopsy found brain damage in all of them of the type that could interfere with memory processes (Corsellis, Bruton, and Freeman-Brown, 1973).

Although public awareness of boxing's potential for creating brain damage has been increasing through studies such as these, media attention was most sharply focused on this issue in 1984 when Muhammad Ali developed symptoms of impaired eye–hand coordination and often unintelligible speech. Ali's symptoms have decreased as a result of treatment with drugs ordinarily given to patients with Parkinson's disease, a disorder that occurs when the brain stops making adequate amounts of the neurotransmitter dopamine. Ali's doctors claim he does not have Parkinson's disease and that his symptoms are more likely the result of 30 years of brain trauma from boxing (Stoler, 1984). Instances such as these have led the legislative council of the American Psychological Association to resolve to work toward the eventual elimination of amateur and professional boxing (Mervis, 1985).

Alzheimer's disease: Progressive memory loss

An extreme example of memory impairment occurs in **Alzheimer's disease,** a progressive mental deterioration that occurs most commonly in old age. The most noticeable early symptoms of Alzheimer's disease are disturbances in memory, beginning with typical incidents of "forgetfulness" that everyone experiences from time to time. In this case, however, the forgetfulness progresses to the point where affected persons are

ALZHEIMER'S DISEASE: *A progressive mental deterioration that occurs most commonly in old age. It is characterized by severe memory loss.*

In the United States over one million people suffer from Alzheimer's disease. The most noticeable early symptoms of Alzheimer's disease are disturbances in memory.

unable to remember how to communicate or to take care of themselves. In the final stages of Alzheimer's disease, the afflicted person fails to recognize loved ones and needs to have total nursing care.

In the United States, over 1 million people (5 percent of the population over age 65) have this fatal brain disorder (Shodell, 1984). Although Alzheimer's disease does afflict people under 65, the incidence rises dramatically past middle age, and affects an estimated 20–30 percent of the people who reach their mid-80s (Heston and White, 1983). Since more people are living longer, it is estimated that by the year 2000, about 10 percent of the population of the United States (3 to 4 million people) will be victims.

Question: What is the difference between "normal" loss of memory as one gets older and Alzheimer's disease?   Autopsies of persons with Alzheimer's disease reveal shrinking of the cerebral hemispheres and neuron damage in a specific brain stem area called the *nucleus basalis* near the hippocampus. When the neurons in this area are functioning normally, they produce an important neurotransmitter called *acetylcholine,* which is used throughout the nervous system. In Alzheimer's disease, the damaged nucleus basalis is deficient in an important enzyme for making this neurotransmitter. Without enough acetylcholine, a person's brain cannot function normally. So far, medical efforts to replace acetylcholine have not proven successful.

Also of interest to psychologists is the pattern of memory loss in Alzheimer's patients. Not all types of memory are affected equally. One of the major differences between normal people and Alzheimer's patients is the latter's extreme decrease in episodic memory. Although nearly as good as normals at recalling information from semantic memory, Alzheimer's patients are greatly inferior when tested on tasks that require retrieval of information from episodic memory (Nebes et al., 1984). This problem may be due to a reduced control over their working memory (Morris and Baddeley, 1988). Because Alzheimer's patients are easily distracted, it may be harder for them to retrieve information from episodic memory, as episodic memories may be more complicated and take longer to retrieve.

The cause of the brain changes in Alzheimer's disease is not known, although there are several theories as to why it occurs. Some experts claim the cause is genetic. Others blame it on a slow-acting virus. Because unusual amounts of aluminum have been found in the brains of some people who have died from Alzheimer's disease, theorists have suggested that the brain damage is caused by environmental pollution that builds up toxic mineral deposits in the brain tissue (Heston and White, 1983). Since Alzheimer's disease is fatal and relegates its victims to years of inability to remember what they have learned, research studies are actively searching for a cause and a cure.

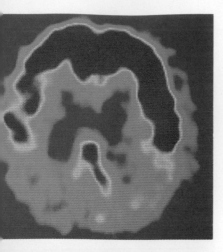
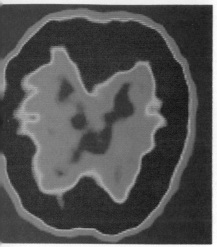

These PET scans show decreased blood flow in a brain with Alzheimer's disease (above) compared to a normal brain (below). Reduced blood flow in the temporal and parietal lobes in the Alzheimer's patient indicates decreased brain activity in these areas.

EXCEPTIONAL MEMORIES

In striking contrast to the problems of memory defects are people with exceptional memories. If you enjoy playing Trivial Pursuit, you have probably been impressed by how well some people can remember seemingly insignificant details. One man who can do well on the category of "facts about the United States" is Michael Barone, who started memorizing facts such as census figures when he was eight years old. He knows the population for major cities during different years (he can tell you that St. Louis had 750,026 inhabitants in 1960, for example) and the boundaries of every congressional district in the United States.

Some people are able to remember things so vividly that they are said to have a "photographic memory." The scientific name for this ability is **eidetic imagery.** People who have this type of memory are sometimes able to visualize things like a page of a textbook so vividly that it is very similar to a photograph (Klatzky, 1984; Neisser, 1982). They can tell you that a specific fact is located in the fourteenth line of the twentieth page of a book they have studied and cite the exact wording of the paragraphs. One example of a person with eidetic imagery is Elizabeth, a teacher at Harvard. Years after reading a

EIDETIC IMAGERY: *The ability to recall memories—especially visual memories—that are so clear they can be viewed like a clear picture; photographic memory.*

$$N \cdot \sqrt{d^2 \times \frac{85}{vx}} \cdot \sqrt[3]{\frac{276^2 \cdot 86x}{n^2 v^= \cdot \pi 264}} \, n^2 b = sv \frac{1624}{32^2} \cdot r^2 s$$

Figure 7.11 The formula Luria's subject remembered 15 years after learning it.

poem in a foreign language, she can retrieve an image of the page it was printed on and copy the poem from the bottom line to the top line as fast as she can write. When she looks at a computer-generated pattern of 10,000 dots with her right eye, she is later able to combine this pattern with another one she had seen with her left eye. She can line up the remembered image so perfectly that she can see a three-dimensional image from the two patterns (Stromeyer, 1970).

Another person with a remarkable memory was a Russian newspaper reporter tested by psychologist Alexander Luria (1968). When the man looked at a chart of 50 numbers, he could remember the rows or columns perfectly after 3 minutes of study. He memorized a meaningless formula (see Figure 7.11) by using visual images that he linked together into a story. Even though he was not warned that he would be tested on his recall of this formula, he reproduced it perfectly 15 years later. If you are wishing you had this type of exceptional memory, think again. This man had great difficulty paying attention to important details. He even had trouble figuring out the meaning of what he was reading, since as he was reading his mind would be flooded with visual images of all his previous experiences.

Photographic memory is a rare ability that seems to disregard the limitations to remembering imposed by short-term memory. Instead of using a selection process that concentrates on the most important aspects of incoming information, the person with a photographic memory stores all the information.

Even though this type of exceptional memory cannot be acquired, most people can improve their memory skills dramatically when they study memory processes and apply what they have learned. One way to improve memory is to use a mnemonic strategy.

Improving memory: Using mnemonics

Do you ever use a memory strategy to remember how many days there are in a particular month? If you don't have a calendar in front of you, do you resort to saying, "Thirty days hath September . . ."? This strategy is a **mnemonic device** that helps you remember something by organizing or "tagging" information visually or verbally while you are learning it or by giving you a system for retrieving information (Glass and Holyoak, 1986). Two mnemonic devices that use visualization to improve memory are the method of loci and the peg-word system (Bellezza, 1982; Roediger, 1980). A third strategy, the method of word associations, uses verbal organization.

The **method of loci** is a mnemonic device that was developed by early Greek and Roman orators to keep track of the parts of their long speeches. *Loci* is the Latin word for physical places. To use this method, the orators would imagine the parts of their speeches being attached to places inside a building or outside in a place like a courtyard. For example, if an opening point in a speech was the concept of "justice," they might visualize a courtroom placed in the first corner of their garden to remind them of this point. As they mentally walked around their garden during their speech, they would encounter each of the points to be made in their appropriate order.

To use the method of loci to help you remember things in a specific order you could use the places in your apartment or house as a sequence that you can visualize. Form a visual image for each of the items on your list and imagine them placed in order in specific areas as you mentally walk through the room. In one research study, college students associated lists of 40 nouns with 40 campus locations. When tested immediately, they

MNEMONIC DEVICES: *Memory strategies in which information is organized or "tagged" visually or verbally.*

METHOD OF LOCI: *A mnemonic device in which an idea is associated with a place or a part of a building.*

remembered an average of 38 items. When tested a day later, they still remembered an average of 34 of them (Ross and Lawrence, 1968).

To use the second visualization strategy, the **peg-word mnemonic system,** you need to memorize a set of visual images of objects to represent numbers. When you memorize a sequence of visual images to represent the numbers from 1 to 10, you can use these images as pegs or markers to "hang" ideas on. The easiest system of peg-words to learn is 10 objects that rhyme with the numbers they stand for. Try to imagine a graphic image for each of these objects.

one is a bun	six is sticks
two is a shoe	seven is heaven
three is a tree	eight is a gate
four is a door	nine is a line
five is a hive	ten is a hen

When you can produce the peg-word image for each number, you are ready to use these images as pegs to hold the items of any list. Try it with a group of items you might want to buy on your next trip to the grocery store: milk, eggs, bread, razor blades. The first item (milk) should be visualized with the picture of a bun, the second (eggs) with a shoe, and so on. Imagine a bun lying all soggy in a bowl of milk. Imagine a giant shoe stepping on a carton of eggs, slices of bread hanging on a tree, and a giant razor blade as a door complete with doorknob. The peg-word device enables you to remember the whole list in order or to find any item according to its number. To remember the third item, for instance, you would recall the image that is attached to *tree* (Bransford, 1979).

Question: But what if I need to remember words that can't be visualized? Since it is often the case that words we want to remember cannot be visualized as an object (words such as *occipital* or *parietal*), there are two approaches that enable you to still be able to use a mnemonic device. The first approach uses substitute words that can be visualized and the second uses verbal associations for the words to be learned, the method of word associations.

To use the substitute word system (Lorayne and Lucas, 1974; Lorayne, 1985), break the word to be remembered into parts or use words that sound similar that can be visualized. For example, the word *occipital* can be converted into *ox, sip it, tall* or *exhibit hall.* Make a vivid image of either of these. You might see an ox on stilts sipping something through a straw or an exhibit hall displaying paintings (of brains with the occipital lobes emphasized). Try creating substitute words for *parietal* (*pear* or *pair, eye, it tall*). If you practice this substitute word technique, you will find that it is fun to convert words that can't ordinarily be visualized into memorable visual images.

The **method of word associations** is a mnemonic device that creates verbal associations for items to be learned. You have used this method if you remember the order of colors in the rainbow or color spectrum by relating them to a man's name, "Roy G. Biv" (red, orange, yellow, green, blue, indigo, violet), or if you recall the names of the Great Lakes by relating them to the phrase "*homes* on a great lake" (Huron, Ontario, Michigan, Erie, Superior). Students of music use this verbal association technique to remember that the notes of the spaces of the treble clef spell FACE, or that the notes of the lines form a sentence: "Every good boy does fine" (E, G, B, D, F).

To use the method of word associations, you can form words or sentences with the first letters of items to be remembered as in the preceding example, or you can make up a story that will link items to be remembered into sentences that will tie them together. If, for example, you wanted to remember the words ostrich, bus, wind, sidewalk, and coffee, you might create a story beginning at the zoo: "The *ostrich* was the first animal we saw from the *bus.* When the ride was over, the *wind* was so chilly that we hurried to the *sidewalk* cafe for *coffee* to warm us." In one research study, subjects who used this story-creation method remembered six times as much as subjects who learned by repeating the words to themselves (Loftus, 1980).

PRACTICING REFLECTIVE THINKING
Exploring Your Early Childhood Memories

Reflective thinking, also known as recursive thinking, is the ability to review and analyze your own mental processes — to "think about thinking." Reflective thinking is an important component of critical thinking. It is the ability to objectively examine your thoughts and cognitive strategies and to evaluate their appropriateness. If you were watching television and suddenly decided to go to the kitchen for a snack, for example, reflective thinking would allow you to recognize that your "hunger" was prompted by the food commercials you were just watching. In the context of this chapter, reflective thinking would involve recalling and analyzing your own memory processes.

To practice your own reflective thinking:

1 Take out a clean sheet of paper and write down three of your early childhood memories, including the feelings and thoughts that accompanied these incidents. Choose only those occurrences that you can remember in clear detail and those that actually happened to you, not something you were told about.

2 Now, closely examine your memories by looking for dominant themes and overall patterns. Are you generally an observer or a participant? Are you alone or with others? What are your most frequent feelings? Fear? Sadness? Frustration?

3 According to some psychologists (see Adler, 1964), these early recollections offer important clues to adult personality. They believe that the study of these memories provides important insights into our self-perceptions, how we see the world, what our life goals are, what motivates us, what we believe in, and what we value (Corey, 1986). Using your previous examples of early memories, look for specific insights into your own self-perception, world view, and so on. Do your dominant themes (being an "observer" or "participant") and feelings ("sadness" or "frustration") correspond to your adult experiences? Do you think this is a valid or useful way to study personality? Are there simpler ways of explaining why you chose these specific childhood memories? *If* childhood memories are important to adult personality, what type of therapy or self-help techniques could be used to change these early memories?

Everyone can improve his or her memory. The major ingredient in any memory improvement scheme is effort. No matter how you try to improve your memory, the harder you work at it, the better your memory will become. You can learn to remember the names of the people you meet or the contents of a textbook if you apply yourself and use some of the techniques discussed in this chapter.

Review Questions

1 Circuits of neurons that fire over and over to process a memory are called _____ circuits.

2 Forgetting that results from brain damage or trauma is called _____.

3 In retrograde amnesia, a person has difficulty remembering events that occurred _____ the brain disruption.

4 When people have difficulty making new memories, they have _____ amnesia.

5 _____ disease is a progressive mental deterioration that occurs most commonly in old age.

6 The scientific name of a photographic memory is _____ _____.

7 Strategies that help us remember by organizing information are called _____ _____.

Answers: *1* reverberating; *2* amnesia; *3* before; *4* anterograde; *5* Alzheimer's; *6* eidetic imagery; *7* mnemonic devices

REVIEW OF MAJOR CONCEPTS

A THREE-STAGE MEMORY MODEL

1 Humans have at least three different kinds of memory: sensory memory, short-term memory (STM), and long-term memory (LTM).

2 Sensory memory is the memory that occurs within a sensory modality while incoming messages are being transmitted to the brain.

3 Short-term memory involves memory for current thoughts. Short-term memory can hold about seven items and can store them for about 30 seconds; however, its capacity can be increased by chunking and maintenance rehearsal can retain information at this stage. Dual-coding refers to the visual and verbal input channels of STM. During the storage process between STM and LTM, the way information is processed affects its ability to be retrieved from LTM.

4 Long-term memory is a more permanent memory where information and ideas are stored for future use. The type of LTM in which facts and their relation to one another is stored is called semantic memory. Memories of specific events are stored in episodic memory. Information in LTM is organized into categories and subcategories that form a network. If it is necessary to retrieve a particular piece of information, there are several pathways within the network that will lead to that information, but stored memories are not always retrievable.

5 Retrieval is the process of getting information out of LTM. The two types of retrieval are recognition and recall. Studies of eyewitness testimony have shown that memory can be modified and that the retrieval process is not always accurate.

THE PROBLEM OF FORGETTING

6 One technique that can be used to minimize the effects of forgetting is distributed practice, in which short practice or study sessions are interspersed with rest periods. The worst way to study or try to remember information is to use massed practice, in which a person studies large amounts of information without rest.

7 Some memories are state-dependent and are affected by states of arousal. These memories are easier to remember if

people are in a state similar to that in which the learning took place.

8 The interference theory of forgetting states that memories are forgotten because of either proactive or retroactive interference. Proactive interference occurs when previously learned information interferes with newly learned information. Retroactive interference occurs when newly learned information interferes with previously learned information. One illustration of these two types of interference is the serial position effect, in which it is easiest to remember items at the beginning and at the end of a list.

9 The decay theory of forgetting simply states that memory, like all biological processes, deteriorates as time passes.

10 The motivated forgetting theory states that people forget things that are painful, threatening, or embarrassing.

11 The retrieval failure theory of forgetting claims that information stored in LTM is never forgotten but may at times be inaccessible.

BIOLOGY OF MEMORY

12 Researchers have shown that learning can cause physical changes within the brain neurons and their circuits. Research on amnesia caused by electroshock, the learning and memory deficits found in brain-injured patients, and the deterioration of memory in Alzheimer's disease support several biological theories of memory. The case of H.M. illustrates the fact that damage to specific parts of the brain can cause disruption in the formation of new memories.

EXCEPTIONAL MEMORIES

13 There are only a few cases of people who have eidetic imagery or photographic memory. These people are able to retrieve a detailed copy of the original visual image from LTM. For most people, retrieval can be greatly improved by more effective use of memory processes.

14 The most effective strategies to use to keep from forgetting are mnemonic devices, which are used to organize or tag information visually or verbally. The method of loci, the peg-word system, and the method of word associations are examples of mnemonic memory systems.

SUGGESTED READINGS

BRANSFORD, J. D. (1979). *Human cognition: Learning, understanding, and remembering.* Belmont, CA: Wadsworth. A presentation of the research literature on memory processes (including Bransford's own research on levels of processing) and practical suggestions for benefitting from it.

KELLETT, M. (1983). *How to improve your memory and concentration.* Monarch Press, New York. Practical examples for improving concentration and organization of information in lectures and reading; analysis of how emotions and personality factors relate to memory.

LOFTUS, E. (1980). *Memory*. Reading, MA: Addison–Wesley. Loftus describes the findings of her active research studies and illustrates the processes of forgetting and efficient memory.

LORAYNE, H., & LUCAS, J. (1974). *The memory book*. New York: Ballantine Books. Lorayne and Lucas present techniques from their memory course for remembering abstract information, with specific examples and exercises for converting difficult items into substitute words that can be visualized.

chapter eight

Thinking and Intelligence

"E R — Dave, I have a report for you."

"What's up?"

"We have another bad AE-35 unit. My fault predictor indicates failure within twenty-four hours."

Bowman put down his book and stared thoughtfully at the computer console. He knew, of course, that Hal was not really *there*, whatever that meant. If the computer's personality could be said to have any location in space, it was back in the sealed room that contained the labyrinth of interconnected memory units and processing grids, near the central axis of the carrousel. But there was a kind of psychological compulsion always to look toward the main console lens when one addressed Hal on the control deck, as if one were speaking to him face to face. Any other attitude smacked of discourtesy.

"I don't understand it, Hal. *Two* units can't blow in a couple of days."

"It does seem strange, Dave. But I assure you there is an impending failure . . . ."

"Have you any idea," he said, "what's causing the fault?"

It was unusual for Hal to pause so long. Then he answered:

"Not really, Dave. As I reported earlier, I can't localize the trouble."

"You're quite certain," said Bowman cautiously, "that you haven't made a mistake? . . . Anyone can make mistakes."

"I don't want to insist on it, Dave, but I am incapable of making an error."

"All right, Hal," he said, rather hastily. "I understand your point of view. We'll leave it at that."

He felt like adding "and please forget the whole matter." But that, of course, was the one thing that Hal could never do.

Arthur C. Clarke, 2001

In this excerpt from the novel *2001: A Space Odyssey* (based on the movie of the same name), Dave Bowman, astronaut on the spaceship *Discovery*, is talking to Hal, the ship's computer brain and guiding force on the mission. The excerpt is quite representative of the film, during which the audience has the overwhelming feeling that Hal the computer is quite humanlike, that "he" is an intelligent, thinking being. Even in this short segment, it sounds like Bowman is talking to another person instead of a computer. What is it about Hal that makes Bowman, as well as us, feel that the computer is nearly human?

Above Photo: Astronaut Dave Bowman and HAL.

One of the first human qualities we notice about Hal is his ability to converse so freely. He not only has the ability to use language but uses it in a way that is both spontaneous and accurate. He listens to Dave, processes what he hears, then responds accordingly. We notice other humanlike qualities about Hal. He takes time to analyze what is causing the failure of the AE-35 units. He patiently reasons with Dave. He even knows how to go about solving problems. Hal detects a malfunction within his computer unit and knows that he will be disconnected if the astronauts discover it. His solution to this problem: to subtly and systematically cause the death of each of the astronauts.

These humanlike qualities we observe in Hal — language usage, information processing, reasoning, problem solving — are known as cognitive abilities. **Cognition** refers to the process of "coming to know," and includes our abilities to sense, perceive, learn, remember, and think. In short, our cognitive abilities enable us to know our world and thereby function in it. Most cognitive psychologists approach the study of cognition by viewing people, as well as computers, as information processors. In other words, information is, by various means, "input" into humans or into computers and is then processed so that it can be put to some productive use. One particularly intriguing field of study that we will discuss later in the chapter involves the creation of artificial intelligence. In this field, psychologists and computer specialists formulate computer models of human intelligence and program computers to perform cognitive tasks, from solving complex math problems to making medical diagnoses.

COGNITION: *The mental activities involved in acquiring, storing, retrieving, and using knowledge; it includes such mental processes as perceiving, learning, remembering, using language, and thinking.*

THINKING

From the point of view of cognitive psychology, we come to know things by gathering and processing information. This is accomplished through sensation and perception, learning and memory, and thinking. **Thinking** involves mentally acting upon the information that has been sensed, perceived, learned, and stored.

THINKING: *Using knowledge that has been gathered and processed; mentally manipulating concepts and images to perform such mental activities as reasoning, solving problems, producing and understanding language, and making decisions.*

Question: What do you mean when you say that we mentally act on information? Suppose you are Dave Bowman and, upset by the death of your fellow astronauts, you cloister yourself and a colleague inside a cubicle, away (so you assume) from the discerning ear of Hal. (Unfortunately, unbeknownst to you, Hal also has a discerning eye that is adroit at lip-reading.) Immediately, you start discussing the astronauts' deaths and other computer-related problems. In so doing, you bring to mind mental pictures of Hal's computer console and of the countless wires, computer chips, and other electronic hardware comprising Hal. You recall strange events and snatches of conversations you've seen and heard in the past few days and start drawing connections between them. You trace the problems to Hal. Ultimately, you discuss ways to remedy the problems and decide on one: disconnect the source of the problems.

What have you been doing? You have been thinking. You have been using information that was previously gathered and stored, and have been mentally acting on it by forming ideas, reasoning, solving problems, drawing conclusions, making decisions, expressing your thoughts, and comprehending the thoughts of others. Thinking involves a variety of mental processes and operations. The ones we will be examining here are mental imagery, concept formation, problem solving and creativity, and language. But before we get to these topics, we must address the larger issue of *how* we think. By what means do we encode incoming information so that we can think about it?

How we think: Pictures and words

Think about these two very different sentences:

1. The bulbous blue hippopotamus, reeking from the odor of stale fishy brine, waddled into the room and plopped onto the floor with a self-satisfied grin spreading over its face.

The Thinker *by Rodin.*

All (except one) of these animals fit the concept of "dog".

2. Our nation was conceived in a spirit of unity for all time, freedom from persecution, equality for the populace, and justice unequivocable.

After reading the first sentence, could you just "see" the hippo walking through the room? Were you almost disgusted at the fish odor? Could you "feel" the vibrations when the hippo plopped to the floor? How about the second sentence? Could you "see" unity? freedom? justice? How *do* we represent information in our minds? Do we think in pictures? As the sentence about the blue hippo illustrates, the answer seems to be yes. But most of us probably didn't call to mind any mental pictures when we read about the abstract concepts of justice and equality.

There is some controversy over how information is represented in our minds. Some experts suggest that we encode information about real objects and events into mental representations of those objects and events. When we think, we mentally manipulate these **mental images.** Others believe that we encode information in terms of verbal descriptions called *propositions* and that mental images are sometimes added to the propositions after they are retrieved from memory (Pylyshyn, 1979). But the majority of the evidence is pointing to a combination of the two views into a theory developed by Allan Paivio (1971) known as the dual-coding hypothesis.

According to the **dual-coding hypothesis,** information is encoded via both an imagery system and a verbal system, each working independently. We use the imagery system for processing real, concrete items and pictures, such as blue hippos and a painting of the Mona Lisa. We use the verbal system for more abstract items, such as spoken or written words and descriptions of abstract concepts such as liberty. So the imagery system is specialized for processing information about nonverbal objects and events, whereas the verbal system is specialized for processing linguistic information and generating speech (Sherman, Kulhavy, and Burns, 1976). The two systems are interconnected to a degree, as shown by the fact that we can convert verbal information like the description of the blue hippo to a mental image. Conversely, when we form a mental image of something — say, a juicy hamburger — we can access our verbal system to find its name when we want to place an order at our favorite restaurant. A considerable amount of research in recent years has focused on mental imagery and is yielding a number of interesting findings, as we will see in the following section.

Mental imagery: Thinking in pictures, sounds, smells . . .

One of the leading researchers in mental imagery, Stephen Kosslyn, wrote: "Having a visual mental image produces the conscious experience of 'seeing,' but with the 'mind's eye' rather than with real ones" (Kosslyn, 1987, p. 149). To amplify on this analogy, we also hear with our "mind's ear," smell with our "mind's nose," and so on with our various other senses. In a survey of 500 adults, McKellar (1972) found that the overwhelming majority experienced not only visual and auditory imagery but also tactile, motor, gusta-

MENTAL IMAGES: *Mental representations of objects and events that are not physically present; they are used during the thinking process to solve problems, express ideas, and so on.*

DUAL-CODING HYPOTHESIS: *The theory proposing that information is encoded into two separate but interacting systems: an imagery system for concrete items and pictures and a verbal system for abstract ideas and spoken and written words.*

232

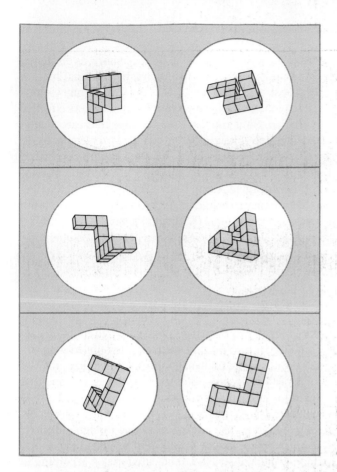

Figure 8.1 By using mental rotation and a watch with a second hand, see how long it takes you to figure out whether each pair is the same or different.

tory, and olfactory imagery. (For instance, it is probably easy to imagine sinking your hand into a sheep's woolly fleece or tasting a too-salty pretzel.)

Much of the research on imagery has demonstrated the similarity between actual physical objects and their mental representations. In one well-known study, Shepard and Metzler (1971) measured the amount of time subjects took to judge whether each pair of figures shown in Figure 8.1 is the same. Try it; all you need is a watch with a second hand. Which pair takes longer to judge? It should be C. Here's why: Before you could judge whether both members of a pair were the same, you had to mentally rotate one of the objects, then compare the rotated image with the other object to see whether they match. Shepard and Metzler found that the angle of rotation — the amount the object had to be tilted or turned — had a strong influence on the decision time. Therefore, when we mentally rotate an object only 20 degrees, it takes less time to compare it with another object than if we rotate it, say, 150 degrees. This is also true with real objects, where it takes less time to turn something part way around than to turn it all the way around.

Other studies have shown a correspondence between our actual perceptions and mental images. Just as a real elephant looks bigger than a real rabbit, an image of an elephant is bigger than the image of a rabbit. Furthermore, the details of an elephant's anatomy are easier to see if its image is large than if it is small (Kosslyn, 1975). Not only are sizes of objects held constant in our mind's eye but so are their shapes, such as outlines of states (Shepard and Chipman, 1970).

Question: Why do we have mental images? What good are they?   Very simply, mental images ease the thinking process. For instance, if you think about a dog, you almost inevitably picture one in your mind. Much of our thinking is done with mental images. Often we solve problems by mentally manipulating images of the problem situation. Sometimes our most creative moments come when we're forming mind pictures of puzzling situations. In fact, Albert Einstein claimed that his first insight into relativity theory occurred when he pictured a beam of light and imagined himself chasing after it at its own speed.

Mental imagery has also been shown to be an invaluable aid to memory, as discussed in Chapter 7. In reviewing the literature, Paivio (1982) maintains that material high in imagery is remembered better than abstract material. In a study comparing various memory techniques, Richardson (1978) concluded that mental imagery was more effective than all other memory techniques studied. So if you can take the time to create mental images of the material you are studying, you'll have a better chance of remembering it. Related to this is a fact that writers have discovered. By painting word pictures and thereby creating images in the reader's mind, they succeed not only in capturing interest but also in aiding comprehension of the written material. It has even been found that it is easier to learn new concepts when they are easy to image and particularly when people are instructed to use imagery when learning the concepts (Katz and Paivio, 1975). This is a noteworthy finding considering how much our thinking processes depend on our conceptual abilities.

Concepts: How we organize knowledge

Suppose you are suddenly transported to an exotic land somewhere in the Eastern Hemisphere. Although the people are friendly, you find it extremely hard to communicate because their language is totally unlike yours. You find yourself surrounded with unusual, sometimes bizarre artifacts. How are you to manage in this unfamiliar environment? For a few days, you are completely disoriented, but after only a week you find that you have learned the names and uses for many of the common items and animals. How could this happen? How could you adapt so quickly?

The fundamental factor underlying your ease in mastering this foreign culture is your ability to form and use concepts. When we see a new item or encounter a new situation, we relate it to our existing conceptual structure and categorize it according to where it fits. If in this alien land you see someone blow into an elongated pipelike object and produce a haunting melodious sound, you will probably categorize the pipe as something musical. It has characteristics that correspond to your concept of a musical instrument.

CONCEPT: *A mental structure used to categorize things that share similar characteristics.*

ATTRIBUTES: *Characteristics such as color, shape, and size that can change from one stimulus to another.*

When we form **concepts,** we mentally group items or events into the same category if they have certain characteristics, or **attributes.** The attributes of any particular concept are related to one another according to certain rules. One such rule is the *conjunctive* rule (Haygood and Bourne, 1965), in which attributes are combined with the word *and.* Thus, one person's conception of a children's book might be "It has easy-to-read words *and* it contains pictures." Slightly different is the *disjunctive* rule, in which attributes of a concept are related with the word *or.* Thus, someone else's concept of a children's book may be "It has easy-to-read words *or* it contains pictures." We tend to learn concepts employing the conjunction rule more easily than those formed by other rules, because we often use this rule in our everyday experiences (Bourne, 1974).

Question: So how do we learn new concepts?   Because there is no way to directly observe people think or conceptualize, psychologists have had to be especially creative in designing experiments to study concept formation. Methods vary from one study to another, but typically subjects are asked to choose which of several items conform to a particular concept. From the research, two main theories have emerged: the hypothesis-testing theory and the prototype theory.

HYPOTHESIS: *An educated guess about the answer to a question or the solution to a problem.*

According to the *hypothesis-testing theory,* people focus on some attribute or attributes, and formulate a **hypothesis** (a tentative guess) about how the attribute contributes to the concept. They then test this hypothesis. If it is wrong, they change to a new hypothesis that may incorporate different attributes or the same attributes but with different rules. One of the most common strategies we use in hypothesis testing is to systematically alter a hypothesis by one attribute at a time until we find the combination of attributes that fits the concept (Bruner, Goodnow, and Austin, 1956). Marvin Levine

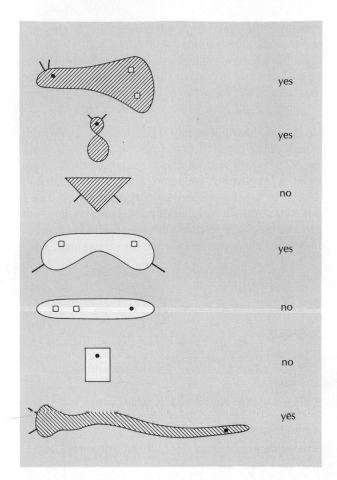

yes

yes

no

yes

no

no

yes

Figure 8.2 See if you can figure out what a glibbit is. Note how the feedback helps, which rule you use to combine attributes, and which attributes are the most relevant and noticeable.

(1975) proposed that people develop a pool of hypotheses. They select one of these and test it; if it is consistent with the feedback and with other feedback received in the past, they stick with it. If not, they choose another hypothesis from the pool that is consistent with the feedback.

Another current theory in concept formation, the *prototype theory,* was developed by Eleanor Rosch (1973). She proposed that in real life our concepts are organized in terms of **prototypes,** or best examples. When we are confronted with a new item, we decide whether it is part of any particular concept by comparing it with a prototype of that concept. For example, suppose that while wandering along the sands of your exotic land, you stumble upon a small, round, metal disk with a symbol imprinted on each side. You probably figure it is some type of money because it resembles your prototype of a coin.

PROTOTYPE: *A model or best example of items belonging to a particular category.*

The activity in Figure 8.2 is designed to let you experience the formation of a concept. You are to figure out what a *glibbit* is. While you're doing so, pay attention to how you form the concept (do you use a certain strategy?). Try to notice any rules you use to combine attributes, which attributes seem to be the important ones, and so on.

As, hopefully, you discovered, a glibbit is a creature with a curved contour *and* two antennae. These are the only *relevant* attributes; all other attributes—color, freckles, shape, and so on—are *irrelevant.* Using activities such as this, researchers have identified a number of other factors, in addition to relevance, that affect concept learning. Some of them are:

Number of attributes It is easier to learn a concept if there are only one or two relevant attributes or only a few irrelevant attributes than if there are several.

Salience It is easier to learn a concept if the relevant attributes are salient, or obvious.

Positive versus negative examples If we tell people what something *is*, they are more able to use that information than if we tell them what *isn't*. Although it is sometimes helpful and even necessary to have some negative feedback, people tend to learn faster if they are given more positive examples. Thus, you would learn about a glibbit faster if you were told that a glibbit has a curved contour and two antennae than if you were told that a glibbit doesn't have horns and doesn't have legs.

Without our ability to form concepts, it would be impossible to think like we do. Every time we encountered something a little different from something else, we would have to learn about it just as if it were a totally new item. As a result, we would have to have a separate storage system for every bit of information, and none of it would be related to anything else. We would basically be able to function only on instinct because we wouldn't be able to relate prior learning to new situations. To manipulate mental information — to reason, to make decisions, to comprehend language, to communicate information to other people, to solve problems — would be virtually impossible without our conceptual abilities.

Review Questions

1 _____ refers to the process of "coming to know" and includes sensation, perception, learning, memory, and thinking.

2 There is quite a controversy over how we think, but research tends to support the _____ _____ _____, which proposes that information is coded via both an imagery system and a verbal system.

3 Research on mental operations has found a marked similarity between real perceptions and real objects and the _____ _____ of those objects.

4 Our ability to form _____ enables us to categorize new information according to where it fits in our mental structure.

5 When forming concepts, we pay attention to the relevance, the salience, and the number of an item's characteristics, which are known as _____.

Answers: 1 cognition;   *2* dual-coding hypothesis;   *3* mental images;   *4* concepts;   *5* attributes

Problem solving: Moving from a given state to a goal

Several years ago, a bridge 11 feet, 6 inches high was being constructed over a Los Angeles freeway. A 12-foot-tall tractor–trailer rig tried to pass under it. As you might expect, the truck got stuck tightly under the bridge and caused a large traffic jam. After several hours of towing, tugging, and pushing the rig, the police and transportation workers were totally stumped. Finally, a young boy happened upon the scene and made a simple suggestion: "Why don't you let some air out of the tires?" This was a simple, unique, and creative suggestion that really worked.

PROBLEM SOLVING: *A series of thinking processes that are used when we want to reach a goal that is not readily attainable.*

Our everyday lives are filled with problem-solving dilemmas that may not be on as large a scale as this one but are problems just the same. **Problem solving** consists of moving from a given state, or problem, to a goal state, or solution. We are all familiar with mathematical problems, in which there are given states and goals that are clearly defined, such as the following:

Given that $x = 5$, what is $x + 3$?

However, even such mundane dilemmas as deciding what to eat for dinner or which TV show to watch constitute problems that need to be solved. Some problems have solutions that are easily reached; others, like the tractor–trailer problem, are not so evident.

Question: Why was the boy able to find a solution to free the tractor–trailer rig when so many "experienced" workers couldn't? It seems that we all follow certain steps when we attempt to solve problems and that we sometimes get stumped, like these workers did. The policemen and other workers probably tried to solve the problem by applying methods that had worked previously. The young boy, however, was able to go through the steps of problem solving with a fresh approach and was not hindered by having to rely on "tried-and-true" solutions. In this section we will explain the steps normally used in problem solving and will discuss the barriers that sometimes prevent effective problem solving; we will also discuss how incubating a problem — withdrawing from it for a time while engaging in another activity — can lead to sudden insights into the problem's solution.

Steps in problem solving Psychologists have identified three stages of problem solving: preparation, production, and evaluation (Bourne, Dominowski, and Loftus, 1979). As we examine each stage in depth, we will refer to the following problem:

> A woman has constructed a lily pond in her backyard. She goes to the local lily pad store to purchase lilies for her pond. There, the salesperson tells her that a special type of lily is on sale that is so prolific that each day it will double in number until the pond is full of lilies. After asking for the dimensions of the pond, the salesperson tells the woman that if she purchases one lily, it will take only 30 days to fill the pond (the frogs won't have to hop from pad to pad; they'll be able to walk!). Because the lilies are on sale, the woman buys two. How long will it take the two lily pads to fill the pond if it takes one pad 30 days?

Take a while to try to solve the problem. Write down your answer, and then continue reading. The answer is somewhere in the next few pages.

The first stage in problem solving is **preparation,** in which all the groundwork is laid for a successful solution to the problem. During this stage, we identify the given facts, separate the relevant facts from the irrelevant, and define the ultimate goal. Solving a problem often depends on how carefully we scrutinize the critical facts and on how broadly we define the goal. This latter point is illustrated by the stuck truck example. When the goal was thought of in terms of somehow pulling the truck from under the bridge, attempts were unsuccessful. It was only when the boy thought of the goal in broader terms of somehow freeing the truck that a successful alternate solution became evident.

PREPARATION: *The first stage in problem solving, in which the given facts are identified, relevant facts are distinguished from irrelevant facts, and the ultimate goal is identified.*

Let's apply the steps of preparation to the lily pad problem. First, we need to determine the given facts. Which facts are relevant, and which can be ignored? Relevant facts: (1) the pads double in number each day; (2) if the woman starts with one pad, it will take 30 days to fill the pond. Next, we need to identify the goal. Goal: To determine how long it will take to fill the pond if the woman starts with two pads. If you've had previous experience with this type of problem, this stage will probably be easy. If not, it may take more time and thought.

During the **production** process, the problem solver produces possible solutions, called *hypotheses,* to problems. Under normal circumstances, the more hypotheses generated, the better chance of solving the problem, since a large number of hypotheses provide a wide choice of alternatives during the evaluation stage.

PRODUCTION: *The problem-solving state during which possible solutions to the problem are generated.*

There are two major ways of generating hypotheses — by using algorithms and by using heuristics. An **algorithm** is a procedure that, if appropriate to the problem, will *always* eventually lead to the solution. Math problems are ideal for demonstrating algorithms: An algorithm for solving the problem 2×10 is $2 + 2 + 2 + 2 + 2 + 2 + 2 + 2 + 2 + 2$. As you can see, algorithms will eventually lead to the correct answer, but they may take a long time. Can you develop an algorithm for the lily pad problem?

ALGORITHM: *A problem-solving strategy that always eventually leads to a solution; it often involves trying out random solutions to a problem in a systematic manner.*

One approach would be first to calculate how many lilies there will be after 30 days if the lady starts with one pad (1, 2, 4, 8, 16, 32 . . . and so on, till we reach the thirtieth number, which is 536,870,912 lilies), then do the same thing starting with two lily pads (2, 4, 8, 16, 32, . . .) until we arrive at 536,870,912 and see how many days it took to get to that number. It may be obvious, after seeing the large numbers involved, that people don't generally rely too heavily on algorithms for problems other than simple mathematics like addition. Because computers work at fantastic speeds and don't make arithmetic errors, however, working with algorithms presents no problem for them.

The other major approach to forming hypotheses is using heuristics, a much faster method — if it works. **Heuristics** are rules of thumb or educated guesses that are usually developed from experience with similar problems. The disadvantage of heuristics is that using them does not guarantee a solution — they work most of the time, but not always. There are many different types of heuristics. We will describe the three most valuable: means–end analysis, working backward, and creating subgoals.

In using a *means–end analysis,* a problem solver tries to take measures that will reduce the difference between the given state and the goal. Suppose you sit down to do some studying and discover that the table is wobbly because one leg is shorter than the others. Your goal is somehow to extend the length of the short leg, so you place a book under the table. The book is too small, so you try a larger one, which is just right. You have succeeded in reducing the difference between the given state and the goal: You can now study at a stable table.

Working backward is a heuristic that is most often used in solving complex problems, such as mathematical proofs. This technique involves starting at the goal and working back toward the given state, rather than the more obvious method of working from the given state to the goal. A good example is explaining how a magician pulls a rabbit out of a hat. This is a rather difficult problem to solve if you start from the given, an apparently empty hat. But if you start from the goal state, the emergence of the rabbit from the hat, it becomes more apparent that the rabbit must be placed in the hat either before or during the magician's act. Because it would be difficult and risky for the magician to place it there during the show, the rabbit must be put there beforehand. If this is the case, then the hat must contain a compartment to hold the rabbit. As you can see, sometimes possibilities for a solution become more evident if you begin working on a problem from the end, or the goal state.

Another technique to use in solving more complex problems is to *create subgoals* that lead to the accomplishment of the main goal. In 1962, President John F. Kennedy stated that the goal of the U.S. Space Program was to have an American on the moon by the end of the decade. The National Aeronautics and Space Administration didn't just build a large rocket and send a crew to the moon; it set up subgoals consisting of several smaller missions that increased in complexity. First NASA created the Mercury series, in which it conducted suborbital and orbital flights with one astronaut; then it set up the Gemini series, which involved two astronauts in orbital flights; finally, it inaugurated the Apollo series, which involved three-person orbital flights, flights orbiting the moon, and ultimately the landing of astronauts on the moon.

See whether you can use subgoals in solving the following problem developed by Bartlett (1958). Try to determine which of the numerals 0 through 9 are represented by the letters, with each letter representing a separate, distinct number. You get one hint before you start: D = 5. The answer is at the bottom of the next page.

```
  D O N A L D
+ G E R A L D
  R O B E R T
```

Can you see how this problem would be too difficult to solve in a reasonable amount of time using an algorithm? There are 362,880 possible combinations of letters and numbers. At the rate of 1 per minute, 8 hours per day, 5 days a week, 52 weeks a year, it would take nearly 3 years to try all the possible combinations. A heuristic approach is much easier and quicker. When you worked on the problem, you probably used your knowledge of arithmetic to set subgoals, such as determining what number "T" represents (if D = 5, then D + D = 10; so T = 0, with a carryover of 1 into the tens' column).

The **evaluation** stage begins when one or more possible solutions have been generated. These hypotheses are then evaluated to determine whether they meet the necessary

---

HEURISTICS: *Problem-solving strategies using techniques that generally work; they involve selective searches for an appropriate solution to a problem and, although less time-consuming than algorithms, may or may not lead to a solution.*

EVALUATION: *The final stage in problem solving during which hypotheses are appraised to see whether they satisfy the conditions of the goal as it was defined in the preparation stage.*

Problem	Given Jars of the Following Sizes			Obtain the Amount
	A	B	C	
1.	29	3		20
2.	21	127	3	100
3.	14	163	25	99
4.	18	43	10	5
5.	9	42	6	21
6.	20	59	4	31
7.	23	49	3	20
8.	15	39	3	18
9.	28	76	3	25
10.	18	48	4	22
11.	14	36	8	6

Figure 8.3 Complete all 11 water jug problems as quickly as possible (after Luchins & Luchins, 1950).

criteria defined in the preparation stage. If one of the hypotheses meets the criteria, then the problem is solved. If none of them fulfills the criteria, then you must return to the production stage and produce more possible solutions. In the lily pad problem, one hypothesis would be that if the woman begins with two lilies, it will take only half as long—that is, 15 days—to fill the pond. This is a logical assumption, but it is not correct, so other hypotheses must be generated. How do you know when your hypotheses are wrong? You try them out to see whether they work.

Barriers to problem solving

Question: Why is it that I can solve some problems easily, yet seem to have a mental block when it comes to solving others? We all encounter barriers that prevent us from effectively solving problems. Two of the three major barriers are problem-solving set and functional fixedness.

You've undoubtedly heard that as people grow older, they get "set in their ways." They tend not only to become more unbending in their opinions, to use the same familiar products, and to engage in activities they've enjoyed in the past, but also to become "set" in the ways they go about solving problems. They rely on tried-and-true methods instead of searching for innovative and perhaps better solutions.

The first researchers to demonstrate that previous experience can affect problem-solving approaches were A. S. and E. H. Luchins (1950). They presented problems such as the following:

If you have one jug that holds 25 liters of water, another jug that holds 5 liters, and a third that holds 2 liters, how can you obtain exactly 16 liters of water?

The answer? Fill the 25-liter jug, then fill the 5-liter jug from the 25-liter jug, leaving 20 liters in the large jug; then fill the 2-liter jug from the largest jug, pour out the 2 liters and fill it again, leaving 16 liters in the 25-liter jug. Before reading any further, go to Figure 8.3 and try to solve all the water jug problems presented there.

Luchins (1942) found that over 70 percent of his subjects, whether children or adults, solved all the problems by using the same algorithm: B − A − 2C. They did not notice that problems 6 and 10 can be solved simply by subtracting C from A, or that

723970
+197485
526485

Solution to the DONALD + GERALD = ROBERT problem on the preceding page:

problems 7 and 9 can be solved merely by adding A and C. They failed to discover the shorter, easier solutions because their experience with the first five problems caused them (and probably you as well!) to develop a set problem-solving strategy.

Such a **problem-solving set** can be helpful if all the problems are of the same type. But it can also cause people to overlook other sometimes simpler solutions and prevent them from developing new strategies necessary for solving new types of problems. For example, one major difficulty people have when trying to solve the DONALD + GERALD problem is the habit of working arithmetic problems from the right (ones) column to the left. If you were persistent in trying to solve the problem by using that set, you probably ran into a lot of trouble.

People can get stuck in their own rigid sets when trying to solve any type of problem. For example, a few years ago one of the authors needed to paint something with a spray gun and couldn't find a little round quart can that fits onto the bottom. He searched endlessly for the can, but with no avail, so was forced to borrow one from a friend. Later, he told his wife about the lost can and she said, "Do you mean the can in that box on your workbench?" There it was, on the workbench. He hadn't noticed it because he was looking for a can instead of a box.

Suppose you were given the objects shown in the photograph on page 240 and were asked to mount the candle on the wall so that it could be easily lit in the normal fashion, with no danger of toppling (Duncker, 1945). How would you do this? The solution is to empty the box, use the tacks to attach it to the wall, light the candle and drop some wax on the bottom of the box, then set the candle in the dripped wax. Duncker found that his subjects had a much more difficult time solving the problem when the box was filled with matches than when it was presented with the matches separately. In the former situation the subjects saw the box as a container and thus had difficulty perceiving it as a useful item in itself. This tendency to see only familiar uses for well-known objects is known as **functional fixedness.**

Set and functional fixedness are only two of the many obstacles to effective problem solving. From experience, you know that the longer you're blocked from finding the correct solution to a problem, the more frustrated you become. One way to help overcome these obstacles to problem solving and to alleviate the frustration is to take a time out from solving the problem.

Incubation   Have you ever noticed that if you leave an especially difficult problem and return to it after doing something else, the solution suddenly pops into your head? It seems for some problems that a period of **incubation,** or time out, is necessary for the facts and possibilities to come into better focus. Köhler (1925) observed this type of incubation in his chimpanzee Sultan. As described in Chapter 6, Sultan was presented with the

PROBLEM-SOLVING SET: *A mental barrier to problem solving that occurs when people apply only methods that have worked in the past rather than innovative ones for solving problems.*

FUNCTIONAL FIXEDNESS: *A barrier to problem solving that occurs when people are unable to recognize novel uses for an object because they are so familiar with its common usage.*

INCUBATION: *A period of time during which active searching for a problem's solution is set aside; this is sometimes necessary for a successful solution of the problem.*

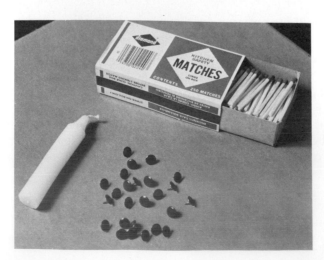

How would you mount the candle on a wall so that it could be lit in a normal way?

problem of how to reach a distant banana with only two short sticks at his disposal. Initially, the chimp was stumped. After a few weeks' incubation period, however, the solution came to him in a flash of "insight." He fit the two sticks together and successfully reached his banana.

If you had difficulty with the lily pad problem, perhaps you can come up with the solution after letting the problem incubate for awhile. The correct answer is 29 days. The solution is simple, if you begin by thinking about what happens with one pad: On the second day, it divides and there are two pads. So, if the woman starts with two lilies, she is just one day ahead of starting with one lily and it will therefore take 29 days to fill the pond.

In solving this problem, you may have started with an algorithm (1, 2, 4, 8, . . . for starting with one pad, and 2, 4, 8, . . . for starting with two pads) and recognizing the duplications in the pattern, switched to the heuristic approach. People often begin solving a problem with one method and then switch to another method when they recognize that it may be more useful or when their original method is unsuccessful.

Flexibility in approaching problems is a valuable asset. Set and functional fixedness lead to rigidity in problem solving; to be effective problem solvers, people need to be creative in their problem-solving approaches and to develop techniques that allow for flexibility, rather than rigidity, in their thinking.

Review Questions

1 The three stages that a person must pass through in order to solve a problem are _____ , _____ , and _____ .

2 During the production stage, we produce possible solutions called _____ .

3 A procedure that, if appropriate to the problem, will always eventually lead to the solution is called a(n) _____ .

4 Rules of thumb, or educated guesses, that are usually developed from experience with a type of problem are called _____ .

5 When we try to take measures that will reduce the difference between the given state and the goal, we are using _____ _____ _____ .

6 If we solve a problem by working from the goal to the given state, we are _____ _____ .

7 We are creating _____ when we solve a complex problem by breaking it into several smaller problems.

8 The two major barriers to the solution of a problem are _____ and _____ .

9 When a person is having trouble finding a solution to a problem, it sometimes helps to take a time out for a period of _____ .

Answers: *1* preparation, production, evaluation; *2* hypotheses; *3* algorithm; *4* heuristics; *5* means – end analysis; *6* working backward; *7* subgoals; *8* set, functional fixedness; *9* incubation

Creativity: Finding unique solutions to problems

Are you a creative person? We normally think of painters, dancers, and composers as being creative, but don't we all have a certain amount of creativity? Even when doing such mundane things as taking notes, you probably use some amount of creativity. You certainly organize them in your own unique way, and you probably use some unusual and unique abbreviations for common words that are different from the person's next to you. To a greater or lesser degree, everyone exhibits a certain amount of creativity in some aspect of life (Richards et al., 1988).

The solution to the candle problem: Use the tacks to mount the matchbox tray to the wall, and stand the candle on the mounted tray and light the candle.

CREATIVITY: *The ability to originate unique solutions to a problem that are also practical and useful.*

What is **creativity**? It is generally agreed that it is a special way of solving problems that involves combining new or unusual elements in ways that are practical, useful, and meaningful. It seems that creative ability is not limited to humans. As just described, the chimpanzee Sultan found a creative solution to his banana problem. Moreover, just as Hal was able to come up with a creative plan to prevent his shutdown, today's computers have been designed to generate unique and useful solutions to problems they are not specifically programmed to solve (Waldrop, 1988).

In Figure 8.4 are examples of items typically found on creativity tests. Take a couple of minutes to work them, and see if you can determine which traits or abilities are being measured.

According to J. P. Guilford (1959, 1967), a psychologist who has done extensive study of thought processes, creative thinking is associated with the following abilities:

1. *Fluency.* The ability to generate large numbers of possible solutions to problems.
2. *Flexibility.* The ability to shift with ease from one type of problem-solving strategy to another.
3. *Originality.* The ability to see unique or different solutions to a problem.

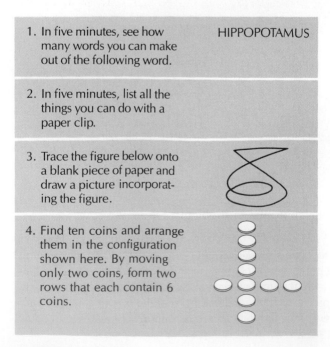

1. In five minutes, see how many words you can make out of the following word.   HIPPOPOTAMUS

2. In five minutes, list all the things you can do with a paper clip.

3. Trace the figure below onto a blank piece of paper and draw a picture incorporating the figure.

4. Find ten coins and arrange them in the configuration shown here. By moving only two coins, form two rows that each contain 6 coins.

Figure 8.4 Take some time to complete these creativity tasks.

Guilford has also suggested that there are two distinct types of thinking, convergent and divergent. In **convergent thinking**, we select, or *converge* on, a single correct answer or solution from among several alternatives. We used convergence in the DONALD + GERALD problem, where we had to find the one correct number that was represented by each letter. Divergent thinking is quite the opposite. In **divergent thinking** we generate as many different, or *divergent,* solutions as possible, such as listing all the possible uses for a paper clip. Divergent thinking is the type of thinking most often associated with creativity. Thus, most tests of creativity and most techniques used to improve creative thinking focus on divergent thinking.

CONVERGENT THINKING: *The type of thinking needed when there is only one correct answer or solution to a problem.*
DIVERGENT THINKING: *The type of thinking needed when it is necessary to generate as many ideas as possible.*

Question: Can I learn to be more creative?   There are several books available that claim to train people to be more creative. Most of the data on creativity point to the fact that the more a person knows about a particular type of problem, the more likely that person is to find a solution to such a problem. Thus, self-help books will likely help you to develop a wider range of problem-solving techniques. However, there is no substantive body of research indicating that a person can be trained to be more *creative,* although there have been some training programs, used especially in industry, that claim to stimulate creative production and reduce rigidity in thinking. One such approach is brainstorming.

A. F. Osborn (1963), the man responsible for the popularity of this technique, describes **brainstorming** as a group problem-solving situation in which four rules are followed:

BRAINSTORMING: *A group problem-solving technique in which participants are encouraged to generate as many unique solutions to a problem as possible by building upon others' ideas and disregarding whether the solutions are practical.*

Rule 1 No criticism. Postpone all judgments until after the brainstorming session.

Rule 2 Generate as many solutions to the problem as possible — the more, the better.

Rule 3 Encourage originality. The more unique and original the idea, the better. Do not consider whether the idea is practicable.

Rule 4 Try to build on previous ideas.

Osborn claims that it is possible to generate double the normal amount of useful ideas in the same amount of time when brainstorming techniques are used (Vervalin, 1978).

There has been some controversy over the effectiveness of brainstorming when compared to other creativity techniques. For example, Taylor, Berry, and Block (1958) showed that four people working independently were able to develop a greater number of unique and creative ideas than four people working together. It has also been shown that people are more productive when they are provided with instructions that stress creation of practical rather than unusual ideas (Weisskopf-Joelson and Eliseo, 1961). Currently, creativity programs are being offered, including some at the university level, that claim to improve creativity, although research data have not proven them to be effective.

Review Questions

1 The ability to originate new or unique successful solutions to a problem is _____ .

2 According to J. P. Guilford, creative thinking is associated with _____ , _____ , and _____ .

3 In _____ thinking, a person tries to generate many solutions to a problem.

4 The problem-solving technique in which a group of people tries to generate as many solutions as possible to a problem is called _____ .

Answers: 1 creativity;   *2* fluency, flexibility, originality;   *3* divergent;   *4* brainstorming

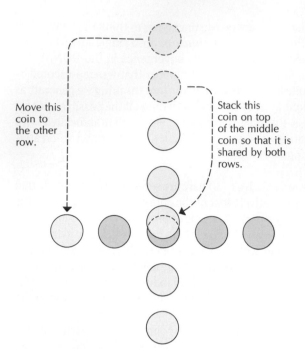

The solution to the coin problem in Figure 8.4.

Move this coin to the other row.

Stack this coin on top of the middle coin so that it is shared by both rows.

Language and thought: A complex interaction

Our cognitive processes are intricately related with one another. When solving any problem, from the simplest to the most complicated, we bring to bear our previous knowledge, our conceptual framework, our mental imagery talents, and even our ability to use language. When trying to solve the lily pad problem, did you find that you were talking to yourself? To some extent or other, most of us do talk to ourselves when we're thinking. In fact, if you recall, one way to encode information is by verbal description.

There are even some experts, led by Benjamin Whorf (1956), who believe that language influences the way people think and approach problems. Whorf proposed that the structure of our everyday language determines the structure of our thought — our vocabulary determines how we perceive and categorize the world around us. For example, Eskimos have several words for snow, such as hard-packed snow and wet snow. According to Whorf's hypothesis, Eskimos are able to think about distinct types of snow in ways different from people who don't have these terms in their vocabulary.

Whorf's view is intriguing; however, most psychologists currently agree that, although language and thought are definitely related and may influence one another, language does not dictate what we think.

Question: What do you call "language": Isn't it just a way of communicating? Yes, it is a form of communication, but it is a specialized type of communication. Other forms of life — bees, beavers, bluebirds — communicate, but they do it in a ritualistic manner dependent on instincts. Human **language** is a creative form of expression whereby we put together certain sounds and symbols in a systematic manner according to specified rules. We use language to convey our thoughts and feelings to other people or listen to others convey their thoughts and feelings to us. We use it to impart knowledge to others or to gain knowledge from them. We use it to persuade or convince other people to do something or to see our point of view; and others use it to persuade us.

LANGUAGE: *A creative form of expression in which sounds and symbols are combined according to specified rules.*

The elements of language All languages, from English to Japanese, have their own unique elements built from basic speech sounds and combined in certain prescribed ways.

These girls are communicating in American Sign Language, which consists of hand formations and facial expressions put together according to an agreed-upon set of grammatical rules.

The basic speech sounds are called **phonemes.** Each phoneme has some distinctive feature that distinguishes one from another, such as a voiced versus unvoiced component in the sounds /s/ and /z/. (When we say /s/ we merely hiss; /z/ is formed the same way, but we add the voice.) Our English language has some 40 to 50 phonemes. Here are some examples:

/p/	as in	*p*ansy
/ch/	as in	*ch*ariot
/oi/	as in	v*oi*ce
/ng/	as in	sti*ng*

PHONEME: *The most basic unit of speech; an individual speech sound.*

Phonemes are combined together to make up basic units of meaning, called **morphemes.** These are the smallest meaningful units of language. They include "root words" such as *think, play,* and *blanket,* as well as suffixes and prefixes such as *un, able, ed,* and *ing.* Thus, in the word *unthinkable* there are three morphemes, *un, think,* and *able;* in the word *playing* there are two morphemes, *play* and *ing.*

MORPHEME: *The smallest meaningful unit of language, formed from a certain combination of phonemes.*

Phonemes, morphemes, words, and phrases are put together by rules of **grammar,** which differ from one language to another. These rules govern combinations of phonemes into words, changes in the forms of words (from singular to plural, present tense to past tense, etc.), and the order of words or phrases in a sentence. For instance, rules of English grammar prohibit placing the phonemes /n/ and /g/ (which are different from the phoneme /ng/) side by side. In some of the African languages, however, such a combination is common, as in the African name Ngugi, who was an Olympic gold-medal runner from Kenya.

GRAMMAR: *The rules of a language that specify how phonemes, morphemes, words, and phrases should be combined to express meaningful thoughts.*

One branch of grammar, known as **syntax,** consists of the arrangement of words and phrases in a sentence. The syntax of a sentence is particularly important because changing the order of a few words or phrases can change the entire meaning of a sentence. See how the meaning of the following sentence is altered merely by changing the syntax:

SYNTAX: *The grammatical rules that specify in what order the words and phrases should be arranged in a sentence in order to convey meaning.*

I just took a shower because I was dirty.

I was dirty because I just took a shower.

The noted linguist Noam Chomsky (1968), in his study of language structure, has developed a set of *transformation rules* that we use when forming sentences. Any one thought can be expressed by using various combinations of words in a great variety of word orders by using these rules. According to Chomsky, there is a difference between a sentence's *surface structure* (its actual wording) and the sentence's *deep structure* (its real meaning). We can use the rules of transformation to convey a single deep structure by using a variety of surface structures:

245

Dave Bowman suspected a problem with Hal.

A problem with Hal was suspected by Dave Bowman.

"Is there a problem with Hal?" Dave Bowman wondered.

Dave Bowman suspected that there was a problem with Hal.

Language and cognition Psycholinguists are scientists who study the role played by the structure of language in its comprehension and production. They also study the cognitive processes involved in using language, both in producing our own language and in understanding the language of others. In trying to understand what others are saying, we hear the phonemes they produce and combine them together so that what we hear makes sense. This may not seem so hard, but think about it. When we talk, we produce a continuous stream of sounds — phonemes get all jumbled together and are even modified to some degree by the other sounds around them (Liberman, 1970). This is particularly evident when we listen to people speaking a foreign language.

Question: Then how do we ever make sense out of the jumbled sounds we hear? We use a number of cognitive devices. We call on our previous knowledge to help us interpret the phonemes, organize the sounds into words, and figure out the boundaries between the words. We keep in mind the context surrounding the sounds we hear (the other words) to help us figure out individual words (Cole and Jakimik, 1980). We can even figure out a word when a sound is missing just by using the context of the other words in the sentence. This was demonstrated by Warren (1970). He played a recording of a sentence such as the following and substituted a cough for the *s* in *legislatures: The state governors met with their respective legi*latures convening in the capital city.* Only one of his 20 subjects detected the missing *s.*

Another aid to understanding speech is our ability to organize what we hear into constituents, which are phrases or basic units of a sentence. The sentence *The excited fans in the bleachers cheered loudly* can be broken down into the constituents *the excited fans, in the bleachers,* and *cheered loudly.* Margaret Matlin (1983) summarizes the steps we use to understand a sentence:

1. We hear the speech sounds.
2. We store a representation of the sounds in short-term memory.
3. We locate the meaning of words in semantic memory.
4. We organize the representations of the speech sounds into constituents.
5. We determine the meaning of the constituents.
6. We combine the constituents to determine the sentence meaning.
7. We forget the exact wording and remember only the gist of the sentence.

Producing language is quite another thing. Planning what we want to say involves quite a bit of problem solving (Clark and Clark, 1977). We must gather all the relevant information from our knowledge bank and organize it so that it will be meaningful. We need to guess what our audience already knows and decide what background information they need. Not only do we plan what we want to say, we decide what form of speech to use, whether formal or colloquial. Finally, we translate the mental representation of what we want to say into the motor experience of saying it.

Animals and language

Question: This sounds pretty complicated. Can animals do all this? Do they have the ability to use language? There is quite a heated controversy over whether animals are capable of using language. Certainly it has not been demonstrated that they are capable of the complicated forms of communication used by humans. But there has been considerable research in an attempt to see whether animals, particularly apes and dolphins, can learn a human-designed language.

"ALTHOUGH HUMANS MAKE SOUNDS WITH THEIR MOUTHS AND OCCASIONALLY LOOK AT EACH OTHER, THERE IS NO SOLID EVIDENCE THAT THEY ACTUALLY COMMUNICATE WITH EACH OTHER."

Lana communicating with a computer.

The first attempts to teach animals to speak resulted in failure. Winthrop and Luella Kellogg (1933) brought up a baby chimpanzee named Gua with their own human baby, Donald. They raised their two "children" in much the same way, but although they tried for months to teach Gua to say the word "Papa," they never succeeded. Cathy and Keith Hayes (1951) undertook a similar project with a chimp named Viki, in hopes of raising her in a stimulating environment and teaching her to speak human language. Although they spoke to her as much as they would their own child, Viki never voluntarily tried to speak. After intense training the Hayeses eventually succeeded in teaching her to say "Mama," "Papa," "cup," and "up," but these words were uttered in a rasping voice and were produced only with much struggling and straining.

After analyzing these early studies, researchers concluded that the reason for their failure may have been the inability of apes to use vocal language. Thus, subsequent studies have involved attempts to teach apes nonvocal languages. One of the most successful and well-known was a study by Beatrice and Allen Gardner (1969), who recognized the manual dexterity of chimpanzees and their ability to imitate gestures. The Gardners decided to use American Sign Language (ASL), a language used by many deaf people, in working with a chimp named Washoe. Their success story speaks for itself. By the time Washoe was four years old, she had learned 132 signs and was able to combine them into simple sentences such as "Hurry gimme toothbrush" and "Please tickle more."

Since the Gardners' success with Washoe, several other language projects have been conducted with apes. David Premack (1976) taught a chimp named Sarah to "read" and "write" by placing plastic symbols on a magnetic board. She learned not only to use the symbols Premack had invented but also to follow certain grammatical rules in communicating with her trainers. Among many other studies was one involving a chimp named Lana. She learned to depress symbols attached to a computer in order to receive the things she wanted, such as food, a drink, a tickle from her trainers, or her curtains opened (Rumbaugh et al., 1974). In another study (described in the Chapter 6 preview) Penny Patterson (1981) taught the gorilla Koko over 600 signs in American Sign Language.

A number of studies have also focused on the comprehension of language by dolphins, particularly at the University of Hawaii. A typical dolphin study involves communicating with dolphins via hand signals and gestures or auditory commands, either spoken by the trainers or generated by computers and presented via an underwater speaker. In a study by Herman, Richards, and Wolz (1984), dolphins were given various commands made up of sentences of from two to five words. The words represented agents, objects, object modifiers, and actions and were combined in ways that were novel to the dolphins. Syntax was varied in a number of ways so that the meaning of a sentence could be changed merely by changing the word order. Results of the study demonstrated that dolphins could indeed carry out a great variety of commands that varied in meaning and syntax.

Question: All this research sounds pretty impressive. Why did you say there was a controversy over whether animals can learn language?   The research does indeed sound impressive. But a question still remains whether these animals are truly using language like humans do. Many psychologists criticize these studies on the grounds that true language consists of sentences that are put together creatively and meaningfully according to definite grammatical rules. Moreover, the average length of sentences produced or understood by humans is significantly more than the two- to five-word sentences used by animals. Critics claim that animals cannot possibly learn the countless rules of grammar, particularly those of syntax, that humans use in conveying subtle differences in meaning. They question whether animals can use language in ways that are considered creative or unique. Furthermore, they argue that, rather than gaining a conceptual understanding of the signs and symbols of language, animals merely learn to imitate the symbols in order to receive rewards. In short, they are not really trying to communicate but are simply performing operantly conditioned responses (Savage-Rumbaugh et al., 1980; Terrace, 1979).

To counter these attacks, proponents of animal language are quick to point out that chimpanzees and gorillas do use language creatively and have even coined some creative terms of their own. For example, Washoe called a refrigerator "open eat drink" and she called a swan a "water bird" (Gardner and Gardner, 1971). Koko signed "finger bracelet" to describe a ring and "eye hat" to describe a mask (Patterson and Linden, 1981). Proponents also argue that, as demonstrated by the dolphin studies, animals can be taught to understand basic rules of sentence structure and syntax.

Although there has been a substantial amount of success in teaching language to animals, the fact remains that the discrepancy between language as spoken and understood by humans and that generated and understood by other animals is considerable. Evidence of animals using language creatively is extremely sparse, whereas nearly every sentence we humans write or speak is unique. Furthermore, the vocabulary of children as young as four years old far exceeds that of the most verbal ape. All the evidence seems to point to the fact that animals can learn language at a rudimentary level but that this language is a far cry from the complex, creative, rule-laden language used by humans.

Review Questions

1 Benjamin Whorf proposed that the structure of our language influences the way we _____.

2 Human language differs from the instinctive communication of other animals because it is a _____ form of expression.

3 The basic speech sounds /ch/ and /v/ are known as _____; the smallest meaningful units of language such as "ing" and "book" are known as _____.

4 Specialized rules of grammar that have to do with word order are known as _____.

5 We are able to make sense of the jumbled sounds we hear in ordinary speech because we: call on previous _____; use the _____ of the surrounding words; and organize what we hear into _____, which are phrases or basic units of a sentence.

6 Because they concluded that apes were unable to use verbal language, the Gardners taught a chimp named ———————— to use ————————— ————————— ————————— .

7 Studies have shown that dolphins can understand sentences that vary in ———————— and ———————— .

Answers: 1 think; *2* creative; *3* phonemes, morphemes; *4* syntax; *5* knowledge, context, constituents; *6* Washoe, American Sign Language; *7* meaning, syntax

INTELLIGENCE AND INTELLIGENCE TESTING

For almost 200 years, researchers have been trying to define and measure human intelligence. But intelligence cannot be measured without first defining what is to be measured, and herein lies the problem. For intelligence is a rather vague concept referring to qualities and abilities that cannot be directly observed. Sometimes people do things — a professor eruditely discusses her newest findings in microbiology or a judge pronounces an astoundingly sensible decision — and we say that they are *so* intelligent. But what are the talents and abilities that make up that hidden and elusive "intelligence"?

Researchers have made innumerable attempts at defining intelligence and each has come up with his or her distinct definition. Charles Spearman (1927) proposed that intelligence is a single factor, a general cognitive ability that enables people to reason, solve problems, and do well in all areas of cognition. He called this factor "g," and maintained that it was responsible for an individual's performance on tests of mental ability. L. L. Thurstone (1938) proposed that there are actually seven distinct primary mental abilities, such as verbal ability, memory, numerical ability, and so on. Still another researcher, J. P. Guilford (1967), proposed as many as 120 factors that influence intelligence.

Howard Gardner (1983) proposed a theory of multiple intelligences. He claims that there are at least six different types of intelligence: linguistic, musical, logical–mathematical, spatial, bodily–kinesthetic, and personal. According to Gardner, any individual may exhibit one or more of these intelligences and attempts to define or measure intelligence must take these intelligences into account. More recently, Robert Sternberg (1985) has developed a model of intelligence in terms of information processing. Sternberg has defined intelligence as those mental functions that are used to adapt to, shape, and select real-world environments.

By incorporating these separate ideas, we have come up with the following concise definition: **Intelligence** is the capacity to solve problems and to adapt readily to a changing environment. Inherent in this definition are two notable points: (1) Solving problems implies a great variety of problems, from where to go for dinner to how to combat world hunger, from how to get your lab partner to help with cleanup to how to deal with the depletion of the ozone layer. (2) Adapting to the environment refers to the ability to apply knowledge gained from prior problem solving to new situations.

INTELLIGENCE: *The capacity to solve problems and to readily adapt to a changing environment.*

Many people make the mistake of assuming that overall intelligence can be accurately measured by an IQ test. It cannot. No single test can accurately measure the wide span of intellectual abilities humans possess. An IQ score is a score on a test that is intended to measure verbal and quantitative abilities necessary to succeed in a normal public school system. IQ scores do not measure overall intellectual abilities and do not necessarily predict success in the "real world."

Even though they should not be considered the only measure of intelligence, intelligence tests have traditionally been used by psychologists to estimate the overall intelligence of individuals. We will examine intelligence tests in depth in the next section, but first we need to introduce some general principles about testing that are essential to all kinds of psychological testing.

Toni Morrison

Gabriel García Márquez

Sally Ride

Meryl Streep

Stevie Wonder

Jonas Salk

Steve Jobs

Janet Evans

Mikhail Gorbachev

Some psychologists have claimed that there are many different kinds of intelligence and creativity. Award-winning authors Gabriel García Márquez and Toni Morrison, for example, represent literary intelligence, Sally Ride, Steve Jobs, and Jonas Salk represent the intelligence and creativity associated with scientific inquiry, Meryl Streep and Stevie Wonder illustrate the intelligence and creativity associated with music and performance art, Mikhail Gorbachev represents the type of intelligence necessary to succeed in politics, whereas Janet Evans represents the high level of motor intelligence required of world-class athletes.

Critical Thinking

EXPLORING YOUR OWN THINKING PROCESSES
What Kind of Critical Thinker Are You?

Throughout this text we have provided various exercises to foster critical thinking skills. In this chapter on thinking and intelligence, we felt that readers might be interested in a brief test of their overall critical thinking abilities (adapted from Moore and Parker, 1989, and Ruggiero, 1988).

Place a check mark next to each item that you believe is true (most of the time) of your personal thinking patterns.

_____ I think for myself and am not easily manipulated by others.

_____ I recognize my own values and perspectives, and I can talk insightfully about the influences on my beliefs.

_____ I do not simply accept conclusions; I evaluate and critique the underlying reasons.

_____ I recognize irrelevant facts and false assumptions, and I discount them.

_____ I am able to consider the strengths and weaknesses of my own point of view and that of opposing positions.

_____ I admit my tendency toward egocentrism and my capacity for self-deception; and I work to overcome them.

_____ I am able to distinguish what I know from what I don't know; and I am not afraid of admitting when "I don't know."

_____ I am willing to consider all available information when working on problems or making decisions; and I am also flexible and willing to try any good idea whether it has been done before or not.

_____ When evaluating the behavior of myself and others, I am conscious of the standards I use, and I am especially concerned with the consequences of actions.

_____ I am a good questioner. I like to probe deeply into issues, to get down to root ideas, to find out "what's really going on."

_____ I am comfortable being questioned, and I do not become defensive, confused, or intimidated. I welcome good questions since they help to clarify my thinking.

_____ I am a critical reader. I read with healthy skepticism, while reserving judgment until I fully understand the author's perspective.

How did you do? Although checklists such as these can provide important feedback, it is important to realize that critical thinking is a skill with no end point. Rather than focusing on a specific score, you should use this list to identify problem areas that you need to develop further.

Standardization, reliability, validity: Important requirements in testing

For a test to be useful, it must satisfy three major criteria: standardization, reliability, and validity.

Standardization   There are two major meanings of the term **standardization** as it applies to testing. First, every test must have established norms; that is, it must be given to a large number of people to determine which scores are average scores, which scores are above average, and which are below average. This type of standardization is necessary to discover the statistical properties of the test and is especially important when the test is to be used in testing thousands of people. Most tests found in popular magazines are not standardized and are therefore not accurate for determining the "normalcy" of people's behavior on the dimension being tested.

Second, it is necessary to assure standardization of testing procedures. The conditions under which the test is administered must be clearly and completely specified in the test manual. Everyone taking the test must be treated equally by receiving the same instructions and questions under identical conditions. This is so that any differences in scores can be attributed to differences in test-takers' abilities or characteristics rather than to the testing procedures. Also, scoring procedures should be specifically detailed in the testing manual for similar reasons.

The importance of standardization of testing procedures can be illustrated by the nationwide college entrance exams, the Scholastic Aptitude Test (SAT) and the American

STANDARDIZATION: *The process of establishing the norms of a test in order to assess which skills, knowledge, or characteristics are representative of the general population. Also, the development of standard procedures for administering and scoring a test to ensure that the conditions are the same for everyone taking the test.*

In standardized tests, everyone is read identical instructions and takes the test under similar conditions.

College Test (ACT). Normally, these are given on the same day and at the same time of day to graduating high school seniors, who take the same test under identical conditions. If the conditions varied from one test center to another, the individual test scores might also vary as a result of the change in conditions rather than differences in students' abilities. For example, suppose the test center at High-Tech High School permitted students to use electronic calculators for the math section of the test and the center at Manual Arts High did not. The High-Tech students with the calculators would have an unfair advantage over those at Manual Arts. Standardization, therefore, is a necessary requirement for a good, useful test. However, tests must also be reliable and valid.

Reliability and validity **Reliability** is a measure of the stability of test scores over time. The reliability of a test is usually determined by retesting subjects at a later date to determine whether their test scores have changed significantly. If a test were 100 percent reliable, any person taking it would get the same score every time he or she took it. In reality, this is never the case, but a good test must be relatively reliable over at least short periods of time. For example, if you took the SAT on one day and scored 475, then took the same test a week later and scored 250, it would definitely not be reliable and the test would be useless.

Validity refers to whether a test actually measures what it is intended to measure. There are several types of validity. The most important is *criterion-related validity,* or the accuracy with which test scores can be used to predict another variable of interest, the criterion. Criterion-related validity is assessed by determining the correlation between the test score and the criterion. As we saw in Chapter 1, a *correlation* is a standard measure of how two variables are related. A high correlation indicates that the two variables are closely related, and low or zero correlation indicates that there is little or no relationship between them. If two variables are highly correlated, then one variable can be used to predict the other. Thus, if a test is valid, its scores will be useful in predicting people's behavior in some other specified situation. For example, a test that is given to prospective job applicants is valid if it predicts job performance, and the SAT is valid if it predicts grades in college.

Without being valid, a test is totally useless, even though it may be standardized and reliable. Suppose you are giving someone a test of skin sensitivity. Such a test may be easy to standardize (the instructions specify the exact points on the body to apply the test) and it may be reliable (similar results are obtained on each retest), but it would certainly not be valid for predicting grades in college, since the test results would be correlated with criteria other than success in college.

Most major psychological tests have been carefully standardized, although they vary widely as to their reliability and validity. Much of the controversy concerning testing, in the United States and elsewhere, revolves around what is actually being tested by psychological tests, especially IQ tests.

IQ tests: Predictors of school performance

Question: What do IQ tests actually measure? There are many different types of IQ tests, and each approaches the measurement of intelligence from a slightly different perspective. Most, however, attempt to measure abilities that allow the test to be

RELIABILITY: *A measure of the consistency and stability of test scores when the test is readministered over a period of time.*

VALIDITY: *The ability of a test to actually measure what it is intended to measure.*

Review Questions

1 The capacity to solve problems and to readily adapt to a changing environment is the definition of _____.

2 If a test is given by many different people to hundreds of children, the instructions for giving the test must be _____.

3 A test is _____ if a person scores the same on a retest as he/she did on the first test.

4 If a test measures what it is supposed to measure, it is _____.

Answers: *1* intelligence; *2* standardized; *3* reliable; *4* valid

a valid predictor of academic performance. In other words, most IQ tests are designed to predict grades in school. To see how that's done, let's take a look at the most commonly used IQ tests.

Individual IQ tests The first IQ test to be widely used in the United States was the Stanford–Binet Intelligence Scale. It was loosely based on the very first IQ tests, developed in France around the turn of the century by Alfred Binet. Lewis Terman (1916) developed the Stanford–Binet (at Stanford University) to test the intellectual ability of U.S.-born children ages 3 to 16. The test is revised periodically—the latest revision was made in 1985. The test items are administered individually and consist of such tasks as copying geometric designs, identifying similarities, and repeating a sequence of numbers. Results of the test are expressed in terms of a *mental age.* For example, if a seven-year-old's score equals that of the average eight-year-old, the child is considered to have a mental age of eight, as measured by the test. To determine the child's **intelligence quotient (IQ),** mental age is divided by the child's chronological age (actual age in years). The usual formula for an IQ is as follows:

INTELLIGENCE QUOTIENT (IQ): *A score on a test that is intended to measure verbal and quantitative abilities. On the Stanford–Binet Intelligence Test, the IQ is the ratio of mental age to chronological age, times 100.*

$$IQ = \frac{MA}{CA} \times 100$$

(The ratio is multiplied by 100 to eliminate decimals or fractions.) Thus, a seven-year-old with a mental age of eight would have an IQ of 114. A "normal" child should have a mental age *equal* to his or her chronological age. ("Normal" in this case refers to the norms or statistics used to standardize the test. There is no child labeled as "The Normal Child" locked up in a vault at the National Bureau of Standards.) On a standardized IQ test, the majority of children will score within 16 points above or 16 points below 100. Figure 8.5 illustrates the typical distribution curve of scores on the Stanford–Binet: The majority (68 percent) of the children taking the test score within this normal range, whereas approximately 16 percent score above 116 and approximately 16 percent score below 84.

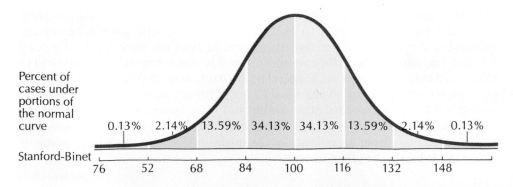

Percent of cases under portions of the normal curve

0.13%   2.14%   13.59%   34.13%   34.13%   13.59%   2.14%   0.13%

Stanford-Binet
76   52   68   84   100   116   132   148

Figure 8.5 Distribution of scores on the Stanford–Binet Intelligence Test.

The Wechsler Intelligence Scale, unlike the Standford-Binet, includes nonverbal performance measures such as the block design task being completed by this child.

Because scores on the Stanford–Binet are meant to predict grades in school, a high IQ should be related to higher grades or to higher scores on achievement tests. In fact, the correlations between the Stanford–Binet and other tests of academic ability were found by Bossard et al. (1980) to be between .70 and .82, which is considered to indicate a relatively high relationship between IQ and academic ability. Thus, the Stanford–Binet can be said to be a valid predictor of school grades.

The other major IQ tests that are individually administered are the Wechsler tests. In 1939, David Wechsler, a clinical psychologist at Bellevue Hospital in New York, developed his own intelligence scale, taking a different approach than Terman. Terman's Stanford–Binet test consists of a set of various age-level items, and subjects must complete one age level before advancing to the next. Wechsler's scale consists of three *separate* tests: the Wechsler Preschool and Primary Scale of Intelligence (WPPSI), for ages 3 to 6; the Wechsler Intelligence Scale for Children–Revised (WISC-R), for ages 5 to 15; and the Adult Intelligence Scale–Revised (WAIS-R), for adults.

The other major difference between the Stanford–Binet and the Wechsler tests is the degree to which verbal abilities are measured. Whereas the Stanford–Binet (above age 6 or 7) is primarily designed to measure verbal abilities, the Wechsler scales are designed to be half verbal and half nonverbal. This approach has two main advantages: The different abilities can be evaluated either separately or together, and people who are unable to speak or understand English can still be tested. The verbal portion of the tests doesn't have to be administered, since each subtest yields its own score.

In response to criticisms that individually administered tests are biased against certain cultural and ethnic groups, Alan and Nadeen Kaufman have constructed the Kaufman Assessment Battery for Children (K-ABC). The K-ABC is an individually administered test of achievement and aptitude that has been standardized to evaluate all students, including minority, hearing impaired, speech- and language-disordered, and non-English-speaking children. In developing the test, the Kaufmans attempted to sample problem-solving ability as well as general knowledge. The test battery evaluates children from 2½ to 12½ years of age on four major scales: sequential processing, simultaneous processing, mental processing composite (a combination of the first two scales), and achievement. The three processing scales are based on psychological theory dealing with different styles of problem solving (Kaufman and Kaufman, 1983). Sequential processing involves solving problems in a step-by-step fashion, whereas simultaneous processing involves integrating all parts of the problem into a gestalt, or whole, at one time in order to solve the problem. The achievement section of the test is similar to other tests of general knowledge.

The K-ABC is a relatively new test. Some studies have found the reliability and predictive validity of the test to be high (Childers et al., 1985; Siegel and Piotrowski, 1985), while others have suggested that the test is less valid than the Stanford–Binet or the WISC-R (Bracken, 1985; Jensen, 1984). Still others (Naglieri and Anderson, 1985; Van Melis and Strein, 1986) have objected to its lack of difficult items. They question its validity in testing "gifted" or high-IQ children. Much more research will be necessary before the K-ABC can make a significant contribution to psychology and education.

Group IQ tests

Question: I don't remember ever taking an IQ test like the ones you have discussed. Did I miss out as a child?   Probably not. Most IQ tests given today are not individual tests; they are group tests. Individual IQ tests are more useful in making diagnostic decisions because they are administered by psychologists who are trained to monitor not only right and wrong answers but also frustrations, points of difficulty, and so on. However, administering an individual IQ test is time-consuming (each test takes an average of one to two hours) and expensive (because of the amount of educational training and practice required of psychologists, they are paid quite a high wage). A faster and less expensive way to obtain an estimate of the intellectual abilities of a large group of individuals is to use the group IQ test.

Group IQ tests were first given to inductees into the U.S. Army during World War I. Individual tests would have taken too much time and would have been too expensive a method for determining the intellectual abilities of the nearly two million men recruited for the war. So a team of psychologists headed by Robert Yerkes developed the first group test of intelligence, the Army Alpha. The first paper-and-pencil IQ test, it measured such cognitive abilities as mathematical reasoning, analogies, and practical judgment.

Since the Army Alpha, many types of group tests have been developed. Group achievement tests are designed to measure what a person has already learned. Group aptitude tests measure a person's aptitude, or capability, to learn a certain skill. If you grew up in the United States and attended a public school, you probably took a group achievement test once a year. And when you were in high school, you and your friends probably took the SAT or the ACT, both of which are group aptitude tests required by four-year colleges and universities to measure prospective students' academic aptitude. Although the scales of these two tests and the actual items differ, the SAT and the ACT are about equally valid in their ability to predict college grades (Aleamoni and Oboler, 1978; Halpin et al., 1981).

Cultural bias   Employers and educators alike have come to rely on group tests for assessment purposes. Many employers routinely use ability tests as part of their hiring and promoting procedures, and 95 percent of U.S. schools use group IQ tests to determine student needs and abilities (Haney, 1981). Yet sole reliance on group tests is not warranted in making such critical decisions as whether to withhold a promotion or assign a child to slow learner status. A key controversy in such reliance on tests revolves around the fact that there are distinct racial differences in average IQ scores. For example, it has been well documented that blacks in the United States score an average of 15 points lower on IQ tests than whites (Block and Dworkin, 1976; Eckberg, 1979; Eysenck and Kamin, 1981). A significant reason for this discrepancy seems to be that both individual and group IQ tests carry a built-in **cultural bias.** Many black and other ethnic minority children are raised in a subculture that may systematically preclude them from learning information found on IQ tests. This cultural bias also applies to people raised in a country different from that in which the test was standardized. For example, people who were not born and raised as U.S. citizens may not know the answers to items like, "Who invented the telephone?" and "What are the advantages of having a president and a Congress?" It should be kept in mind when interpreting test results that any test is standardized on members of a particular culture and that the test is valid only when used for predicting behaviors of members of that culture.

CULTURAL BIAS: *The tendency of a test to give a lower score to a person from a culture different from the culture on which the test was standardized.*

Individual differences in IQ — Heredity versus environment

Question: Why are some people more intelligent than others?   This brings up one of the most hotly debated issues in psychology: Are individual differences in intelligence due primarily to genetic factors or primarily to environmental factors? Psychologists agree that both factors play a part in determining intelligence; indeed, a review of the data clearly indicates that both heredity and environment influence IQ scores as well as general intelligence (Eysenck and Kamin, 1981). It is the extent of their influence that is the source of controversy. Some psychologists, such as Arthur Jensen (1969), suggest that these differences are due chiefly to genetic factors, whereas other psychologists, such as Leon Kamin (1974), feel that these differences are due chiefly to environmental factors.

Adoption studies and twin studies are often used to argue the heredity side of this issue. Adoption studies have shown that IQs of children are more closely related to those of their biological parents than to those of their adoptive parents. Other studies have investigated this issue by studying IQ correlations of family members. As would be expected, studies show moderate correlations in IQ scores between parent and child and between sibling and sibling. Similarly, IQ scores of fraternal twins (who develop from different eggs) are correlated at about the same level as those of nontwin brothers and sisters. What is remarkable is that IQ correlations between identical twins (who develop from the same egg) are exceptionally high when they are raised together and only slightly less when they are reared apart (Eysenck and Kamin, 1981). Heredity proponents point to this similarity as proof of the high influence of heredity on intelligence.

Environment proponents argue that sample sizes in these studies were particularly small and that the method of testing IQs was in question. Furthermore, they say that the environment of identical twins is similar, people tend to treat them alike, and even when separated, they tend to be placed in homes with similar environments. Indeed, as Leon Kamin (1981) points out, in studies of identical twins "reared apart," twins were not actually separated: In one instance, the twins were best friends in the same school classroom and, in another, the twins lived next door to each other.

Environmentalists point to several studies that indicate the effects of environment on the development of intelligence. A classic study by Skeels and Dye (1939) involved a group of orphans living in overcrowded, deprived conditions in an orphanage who, labeled mentally retarded and therefore unadoptable, were transferred to a women's ward in a state mental institution. Here each child was "adopted" by a mildly retarded woman who lavished her charge with love and attention in a stimulating environment full of toys and plenty of space for play — quite a contrast to the impoverished and neglectful conditions in which the children had previously lived. The IQ scores of these children showed a marked improvement (in fact, their scores placed them within the normal range of intelligence). Scores of a control group of children remaining in the orphanage showed a marked drop. Furthermore, a follow-up study conducted over 20 years later revealed that most of the children in the retarded women's care had finished high school and were leading normal, productive lives. On the contrary, most of the children who had remained at the orphanage had not gone beyond the third grade and were unable to fully support themselves (Skeels, 1966).

Although there is evidence supporting both sides, psychologists tend to agree that the genetic component predetermines the upper and lower limits of a person's intellectual capacities, whereas environment has a large affect over whether people will reach their potential. Because it is the environment that we as psychologists, parents, and citizens can change, it is the environment that should be improved to maximize the intelligence of all children.

Review Questions

1 Most IQ tests attempt to measure abilities that enable them to be valid predictors of _____ _____.

2 An intelligence quotient (IQ) is the ratio of a child's _____ age to a child's _____ age, times 100.

3 A 12-year-old child with a mental age of 15 will have an IQ of _____.

4 One major difference between the Stanford–Binet and the Wechsler intelligence tests is that the Wechsler tests give both a _____ and a _____ score.

5 A new test that is designed and standardized to evaluate all students, including, among others, minorities and hearing impaired, is the _____.

6 The Army Alpha and the SAT are examples of _____ IQ tests.

7 The best predictor of college grades is _____ _____ _____.

8 Since many tests are designed to test or are standardized on only one group of people, these tests may be culturally _____.

Answers: 1 academic performance (school grades); *2* mental, chronological; *3* 1125; *4* verbal, performance; *5* K-ABC; *6* group; *7* high school grades; *8* biased

Artificial intelligence: Creating machines that behave like humans

At the beginning of this chapter, we provided an excerpt from *2001* featuring a conversation with the computer Hal. In the book we discover that the letters "HAL" stand for *h*euristically programmed *al*gorithmic computer, since Hal was programmed to learn and solve problems using both heuristic and algorithmic methods. Hal could store information, solve problems, and run a large spacecraft, and by most definitions we would have to say he was intelligent. In real life, attempts are being made to develop computers that, like Hal, will be able to solve problems in intelligent, new, or unique ways. This avenue of research is referred to as **artificial intelligence.**

To create intelligent machines, scientists have used two major approaches: a *cognitively* oriented approach based on human thinking processes, and a *behavioristic* approach based on human behavior. In most computer intelligence projects, the behavioral approach has been used, with the end result, the targeted behavior, being the most important factor. For example, a good chess-playing program would not necessarily be one that models the thinking processes of a human chess player; it would be one that wins chess games.

Developing intelligent computer programs without concern for copying human brain function takes advantage of the computer's ability to use algorithms, with which it can solve problems in a reasonable amount of time. This behavioristic approach leads to usable results, but there is controversy whether it can be used to produce computers that will simulate human capabilities.

The alternative to the behavioral approach is to try to develop computers that simulate human cognitive processes. Some psychologists are interested in using these computer models to better understand how humans think. Others believe that this approach will prove more valuable in designing supercomputers of the future. They envision that the next generation of computers will be designed in such a way that humans will be able to interact and converse with them and be as comfortable with them as they are with their refrigerators, vacuum cleaners, or television sets. It is foreseen that such computers will be present in almost every household and will perform all sorts of menial tasks when given the appropriate voice commands — in short, they'll become more and more like Hal.

To reach this level of computer sophistication, however, a lot of work remains to be done. It is first necessary for psychologists to have a better knowledge of how humans solve the types of problems that they want computers to solve. For instance, to have a computer solve the DONALD + GERALD problem in a humanlike manner, it is first necessary to research and collect data on how humans solve the problem. These data would then be used to build a model of human thinking, on which a computer program could be based.

Sounds pretty easy, doesn't it? But such data on internal thinking processes are difficult to collect. One way psychologists have alleviated this difficulty is to ask their human subjects to *think aloud* as they solve the problem. The statements that are generated by the subjects are recorded and later analyzed. Newell and Simon (1972) devote an entire chapter of their book *Human Problem Solving* to the verbal responses of *one* subject who was trying to solve the DONALD + GERALD problem. After analyzing human subjects' responses, psychologists build a model and then develop a computer program that simulates human performance. If the program works, it is assumed that the model and the means of arriving at the model are valid.

Question: Is it possible to create a computer program that can learn like a human? Yes, it is. Allen Newell, John Laird, and Paul Rosenbloom have developed a computer program called "Soar" that embodies their theory of cognition (Waldrop, 1988). According to this theory, all our cognitive processes ultimately involve some form of problem solving. Soar is designed to tackle any cognitive task by applying a set of problem-solving rules in an "if – then" manner: *If* this situation pops up, *then* do this. The rules it uses are the same heuristics commonly used by people, such as means – end

ARTIFICIAL INTELLIGENCE: *The creation of computer programs that enable computers to solve problems either by using algorithms or by simulating human thought processes.*

Someday, as the result of research into artificial intelligence, we may be as comfortable with robots serving lunch as we are today with refrigerators and television sets.

analysis and creating subgoals. If the computer is faced with an impasse where it can't figure out what to do next, it sets up a subgoal, which consists of solving the impasse. This consists of considering every rule and selecting the appropriate one. When it reaches its subgoal, Soar stores the solution, which is called a "chunk," as a new "if–then" rule. Soar thus *learns* in the same way we humans learn how to solve problems we have never encountered before. And if it runs across a similar problem in the future, it "remembers" this chunk and doesn't have to start from ground zero to solve the problem.

The Soar project is the culmination of attempts spanning four decades to simulate, by computer, human cognitive processes. Among these projects are ones that simulate human learning in such areas as vision, language, scientific problem solving (Good, 1984), and memory (Fiegenbaum, 1961; Gillund and Shiffrin, 1984).

Although there have been many successful attempts to simulate human learning and human thought processes, none of them approaches the diverse and complex abilities of a real human being to learn and process information. Humans have a distinct advantage over computers — we have sensory systems that are extremely adaptable and able to input information through multiple modes. In addition, human sensory systems are available to input this information even before we are born. And because sensory systems are constantly functioning, people are *constantly* learning over a life span greater than 70 years. No computer in existence can approach this kind of base of knowledge and experience. Not even Hal.

Review Questions

1 The attempt to develop programs that enable computers to solve problems in intelligent, new, or unique ways is an attempt to create _____ _____.

2 The _____ approach to artificial intelligence focuses only on the output of the computer.

3 The _____ approach to artificial intelligence uses computers to model human thought.

4 One approach that has been used in trying to build computer models of human thinking has been to ask subjects to _____ _____ when solving problems.

Answers: 1 artificial intelligence; *2* behavioristic; *3* cognitive; *4* think aloud

---

REVIEW OF MAJOR CONCEPTS

THINKING

1 Cognition refers to the process of "coming to know" and involves the processes of gathering and processing information, including sensation, perception, learning, memory, thinking, and problem solving.

2 Thinking is the mental manipulation of information that has been gathered and processed. It involves creating mental images, forming concepts, solving problems, and using language. There is some controversy regarding how we think, but the latest evidence supports a dual-coding theory proposing both an imagery system and a verbal system.

3 Mental images are mental representations of objects and events. Research in the areas of mental rotation and relative size and shape of objects has demonstrated the similarity of real objects and our mental representations of them.

4 Concepts are ideas or notions about groups of objects or situations that share similar characteristics known as attributes. We form concepts by combining attributes according to various rules and by noting their relevance and their salience. Two theories of concept formation are the hypothesis-testing theory and the prototype theory.

5 There are three major steps in problem solving: preparation, production, and evaluation. During the preparation stage, the facts are identified, the relevant facts are sifted from the irrelevant, and the ultimate goal is determined.

6 During the production stage, possible situations, called hypotheses, are generated. There are two major procedures for generating hypotheses: using an algorithm, which is any procedure that guarantees a solution; or using heuristics,

which are educated guesses that may or may not lead to a solution but that are quicker and easier than algorithms. Three major types of heuristics are means–end analysis, working backward, and creating subgoals.

7 The evaluation stage begins when one or more hypotheses have been generated. These hypotheses are then evaluated, and if one of them meets the criteria set down in the preparation stage, the problem is solved.

8 Among the barriers to successful problem solving are problem-solving set and functional fixedness. Problem-solving set is trying to apply a previously successful but inappropriate solution to a new problem. Functional fixedness is the failure to see new or unique uses for common objects. To break these barriers, it is sometimes helpful to take a time out from a problem and let it incubate before attempting to solve it.

9 Creativity is the ability to originate new or unique solutions to a problem that are also practical and useful. Creative thinking is associated with fluency, flexibility, and originality. J. P. Guilford has identified two distinct types of thinking: convergent, in which the person works toward a single solution to a problem; and divergent, in which the person tries to generate as many solutions as possible. Brainstorming is an example of divergent thinking.

10 Language is a creative form of communication consisting of a group of symbols that are put together by using an agreed-on set of rules. Phonemes are the basic speech sounds; they are combined to form morphemes, the smallest meaningful units of language. Phonemes, morphemes, words, and phrases are put together by rules of grammar and syntax, or word order. Psycholinguists study both language structure and the cognitive processes involved in language comprehension and production.

11 Researchers have investigated the ability of animals to learn human or humanlike language. The most successful of these studies have included the use of American Sign Language by apes and the comprehension of sentences that vary in syntax and meaning by dolphins. Although many psychologists believe that animals can truly learn a human language, skeptics suggest that the animals are being trained merely to respond for rewards.

INTELLIGENCE AND INTELLIGENCE TESTING

12 Intelligence is the capacity to solve problems and to readily adapt to a changing environment. IQ tests do not, and are not intended to, measure overall intelligence; rather, they are designed to measure verbal and quantitative abilities necessary to succeed in school.

13 For any test to be useful, it must be standardized, reliable, and valid. Standardization refers to (a) the process of giving a test to a large number of people in order for its norms to be developed; and (b) the use of identical procedures in administering a test so that everyone taking the test will do so under the same conditions. Reliability is a measure of the stability of test scores over time. Validity refers to how well the test measures what it is intended to measure.

14 There are several individual IQ tests. The Stanford–Binet measures primarily verbal abilities of children ages 3 to 16. The Wechsler tests, consisting of three separate tests for three distinct age levels, measures both verbal and nonverbal abilities. The K-ABC samples both problem-solving ability and general knowledge and was standardized to evaluate a large variety of students, including minority, hearing-impaired, and language-disordered children.

15 Group IQ tests can be given to large numbers of people at one time. The group test with which most college students are familiar is the Scholastic Aptitude Test.

16 All IQ tests may carry a built-in cultural bias because they were standardized on members of one particular culture. This bias must be kept in mind when generalizing test results to members of other cultures.

17 There is a heated controversy regarding individual differences in intelligence. Although there is evidence supporting both sides, it is generally agreed that heredity seems to determine a person's capacity but that environment determines whether people will reach their full potential.

18 Artificial intelligence refers to the attempt to develop programs that enable computers to solve problems in intelligent, new, or unique ways. To create more intelligent machines, scientists have used two different approaches: a behavioristic approach that focuses only on the output of the computer, and a cognitive approach that uses computer programs to model human cognitive processes.

SUGGESTED READINGS

EYSENCK, H. J., & KAMIN, L. (1981). *The intelligence controversy*. New York: Wiley. A debate between two well-known authorities on the nature of intelligence.

GARDNER, H. (1983). *Frames of mind*. New York: Basic Books. A book that outlines Gardner's theory of multiple intelligences.

GARDNER, M. (1982). *Aha! Gotcha: Paradoxes to puzzle and delight*. New York: Freeman. The title of this wonderful book says it all.

MATLIN, M. (1983). *Cognition*. New York: Holt, Rinehart & Winston. A comprehensive overview of cognition that is reasonably easy to read and contains ample illustrations and demonstrations of the concepts presented.

MAYER, R.E. (1983). *Thinking, problem solving, cognition*. New York: Freeman. An introduction to the study of cognition.

chapter nine
Early Development

I slip quietly into the back of the room, sit on the floor, lean back against the wall, and I watch the world's most important and most gentle revolution taking place. A beautiful little blonde two-year-old girl is reading aloud. So absorbed is she in reading that she sometimes giggles as she reads a phrase that touches her sense of humor. The humor is lost on me because she is reading in Japanese.

When I arrived at the math class, Suzie and Janet were presenting math problems to the tiny kids faster than I could assimilate the problems. Their answers were correct—not nearly right but exactly right.

"What," Suzie asked, "is 16 times 19, subtract 151, multiply by 3, add 111, divide by 4 and subtract 51?" "How far is it from Philadelphia to Chicago?" asked Janet. "And if your car gets 5 miles to the gallon, how many gallons of gas will it take to drive to Chicago?"

Doman, 1979, pp. 25–29

In contrast to Glen Doman's belief in the power of early education, Robert Klark Graham believes that child prodigies are largely the result of genetic contributions from the best and brightest parents (Tedrick, 1985; Lowry, 1987). To encourage selective breeding for such children, Graham established an exclusive sperm bank in 1980 and invited Nobel Prize winners, and others possessing high IQs, to contrib-

ute their sperm. Although the children produced from this sperm bank are showing some early signs of "giftedness," the proliferation of exclusive sperm banks such as Graham's has raised concerns. Author Jeremy Rifkin warns us that "a new **eugenics** has slipped in the back door. We not only want perfect plants and animals, we want perfect babies. And while there's no evil intent here, the road to the Brave New World is paved with good intentions" (cited in Lowry, 1987, p.8).

What do you think? Should academic instruction begin in the first few months of life? Should parents be encouraged to use "exclusive" sperm to increase the IQ of their offspring? In recent years many important social, legal, religious, personal, and ethical questions have been raised by scientific research into the areas of early childhood development. Given recent evidence of fetal learning before birth and the existence of artificial insemination, frozen sperm banks, and surrogate motherhood, some of Aldous Huxley's *Brave New World* imaginings of 1932 no longer seem so farfetched. We are quickly moving beyond the time when we have to rely exclusively on chance for securing the maximum development of our children. If you want to increase your child's "giftedness," for example, experts now encourage you to play classical music for and read to your developing fetus, and to

---

EUGENICS: The biosocial movement endorsing the selection of certain human traits for improvement of the species.

present vocabulary and math flash cards within the first few months of life (Engelmann and Engelmann, 1988; Field, 1987). This advice, like the technological advances in reproduction, has become controversial. Some researchers argue that facilities like Graham's sperm bank are just another form of dangerous eugenics where one group decides which characteristics should be preserved and which should be eliminated (Elias and Annas, 1986; Francoeur, 1985). Similarly, some experts believe that Doman's type of early "miseducation" can cause long-term damage to the child's motivation, intellectual growth, and self-esteem (Elkind, 1987, 1988; Shell, 1989; Spock, 1984, 1988).

As you might imagine, psychologists are some of the major advisors and experts in the area of child development. They not only seek answers to questions about ideal child-rearing techniques but also look for ways to maximize individual potential in all areas of development — physical, cognitive, language, personality, social-emotional, and so on.

The field of **developmental psychology** is concerned with the description, explanation, prediction, and modification of age-related behaviors during not just childhood but the full life span, from conception to death (see Table 9.1). Some developmental psychologists emphasize specific ages (such as infancy, adolescence, or old age), whereas others concentrate on specific areas (such as physical or cognitive development).

The period from conception to death is so large that it is impossible to adequately summarize it in just one chapter. We will therefore cover development in two phases: This chapter will focus on the time from conception to adolescence, and Chapter 10 will examine developmental issues in adolescence, adulthood, and aging. We begin now with a brief look at the "development" of developmental psychology.

DEVELOPMENTAL PSYCHOLOGY: *The branch of psychology that involves describing, explaining, predicting, and modifying age-related behaviors from conception to death. This field emphasizes maturation, early experiences, and various stages in development.*

STUDYING DEVELOPMENT

Today the idea of qualitatively different life stages — infancy, childhood, adolescence, midlife, and so on — is taken for granted. Yet this is a relatively recent concept. Prior to the fifteenth century, the general public believed that there were only two stages in life: infancy and adulthood. If you have ever looked at old paintings that included children, you may have noticed that the children were typically portrayed as miniature adults, with adultlike facial features and bodily proportions. During this time, children often held down full-time jobs and could also be found drinking in taverns alongside adults. It was not until the seventeenth and eighteenth centuries that childhood came to be acknowledged as a separate period (Aries, 1962). English philosopher John Locke (1632–1704)

TABLE 9.1
Life-Span Development

Stage	Approximate Age
Prenatal	Conception to birth
Infancy	Birth to 18 months
Early childhood	18 months to 6 years
Middle childhood	6 to 12 years
Adolescence	12 to 20 years
Young adulthood	20 to 45 years
Middle adulthood	45 to 60 years
Later adulthood	60 years to death

Before the seventeenth and eighteenth centuries, children were considered "miniature adults." Note the adult-like clothing, facial features, and body proportions of the children in this painting.

was one of the first to acknowledge the importance of childhood to later adult characteristics. He suggested that the creation of rational and ethical adults resulted from careful teaching and guidance during the first few years of life.

Building on Locke's ideas, later philosophers and psychologists proposed that childhood is a distinct *stage,* qualitatively different from adulthood. As we will see, the concept of stages remains as a primary emphasis of modern developmental psychology. According to *stage theory,* people all over the world experience predictable and distinct changes in behavior as they move through the life cycle. Each individual is believed to go through the same stages in the same order, and each stage builds on the preceding one. Whether such stages do exist, and whether they are universal, remains an ongoing debate among developmental psychologists. This type of persistent controversy can also be found in the area of research.

Research issues: Stability versus change and nature versus nurture

In all fields of psychology, certain theoretical issues seem to guide the basic direction of research. In the field of development, the two most common themes are stability versus change and nature versus nurture.

Development, by definition, automatically involves change. Given the fact that all people do change or "develop" over the life span, one task of developmental psychology is to study whether these changes are regular and consistent with earlier patterns or are relatively unstable and inconsistent. Do happy babies make happy adults? Is the child truly "father to the man"? Or does each individual have a pliable personality and fluctuating attitudes, values, and beliefs? Psychologists who tend to emphasize stability in development would suggest that measurements of personality taken during childhood are important predictors of adult personality (Costa and McCrae, 1988; Thomas and Chess, 1977). The baby who is happy and sociable as an infant, for example, would be expected to be outgoing and popular as an adult. Other psychologists tend to emphasize the dissimilarities among individuals, and the capacity for unique changes across the entire life cycle (Goldsmith et al., 1987; Kagan, 1984, 1987). Can you see how the stage theorists would support the *change* side of this debate?

The second major research issue in developmental psychology is whether behaviors are primarily inborn or learned—the old nature versus nurture controversy (Plomin, 1989). As we discovered in the discussion of intelligence in Chapter 8, nativists tend to emphasize the role of genetic inheritance in development. They believe that changes are largely due to the processes of **maturation**, in which development is governed by automatic, genetically predetermined signals. On the other side of the debate, the nurturists

MATURATION: *Changes in development that result from automatic, genetically determined signals.*

argue that the primary focus in development is learning through interactions with the environment. Glen Doman's belief in the superiority of his method of childhood education reflects a strong adherence to the nurturist side of this debate.

Question: Which position on each debate is most correct? There is ample research evidence for stability and for maturation effects, but there is also evidence for the opposing positions of individual change and environmental effects. Like most debates, the one correct position is somewhere in the middle. Most psychologists today believe that certain traits, such as height and weight, are relatively stable and genetically determined. On the other hand, less obvious traits, such as personality, are believed to be subject to change and a result of the *interaction* of both nature and nurture.

Research methods: Biographies and cross-sectional versus longitudinal data

The famous biologist Charles Darwin was one of the first persons to use scientific methods to study development. Darwin saw children as a natural microcosm of human development, and he kept detailed, systematic records of the day-to-day changes in his firstborn child. He gave scientific respectability to **baby biographies,** which are still widely used today.

BABY BIOGRAPHY: *A detailed journal or account of important changes in a child's development.*

In recent times, the biographical technique has been extended to the study of adult development (Datan et al., 1987). One of the best examples of this approach is the **personal narrative** (Cohler, 1983; Freeman, 1984). It consists of an individual telling his or her life story, with the psychologist interpreting the account and incorporating it into a larger narrative. The psychologist typically weaves together facts and inferences from interviews and the individual's social history to form the interpretation. In addition to baby biographies and personal narratives, developmental psychologists also use observation, experiments, surveys, and the other basic methods of research discussed in Chapter 1.

PERSONAL NARRATIVE: *A research technique based on an individual's recounting of his or her life story while the psychologist elaborates on the narrative with professional interpretations.*

When studying development, psychologists must first decide which technique they will use to *gather* the data (biographies, experiments, etc.) and then must choose whether to use the *cross-sectional* or the *longitudinal* method. The **cross-sectional method** examines individuals of various ages at one point in time and gives information about age *differences.* The **longitudinal method** follows a single individual or group of individuals over an extended period of time and gives information about age *changes* in development (see Figure 9.1). Both methods offer important insights into developmental issues, but it is important to recognize that they also have inherent differences that can sometimes produce contradictory results (see Figure 9.2). Cross-sectional studies, for example have traditionally reported that intelligence reaches its peak in early adulthood and gradually declines during adulthood (Horn and Donaldson, 1980), whereas longitudinal studies show an *increase* in intelligence until age 55 or 60 with a modest decline in the following years (Schaie, 1984).

CROSS-SECTIONAL METHOD: *A technique of data collection that measures individuals of various ages at one point in time and gives information about age differences.*
LONGITUDINAL METHOD: *A data collection technique that measures a single individual or group of individuals over an extended period of time and gives information about age changes.*

Question: How can these differences be explained? Because results from cross-sectional studies reflect group averages rather than individual developmental patterns, their results often confuse genuine age differences with **cohort effects** — differences that result from specific histories of the age group studied (Rosenfeld and Stark, 1987; Schaie, 1988). In the case of intelligence, cross-sectional studies overlook the fact that older subjects have generally received less formal education than younger subjects, which would be correlated with lower test scores. In addition, older subjects tend to have different beliefs and values concerning the general ideas of intelligence testing.

COHORT EFFECTS: *Statistical differences between research groups as a result of their specific histories rather than because of genuine age differences.*

Question: If cross-sectional studies are subject to such misleading effects, why don't researchers design only longitudinal studies? Longitudinal studies have their own set of problems. Not only are they expensive in terms of time and money, but their results are also restricted in generalizability. Since only a small number of subjects can realistically be tested, and since many of them will drop out or move away during the

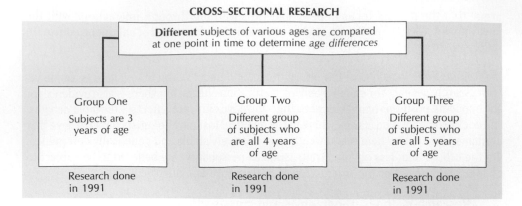

CROSS–SECTIONAL RESEARCH

Different subjects of various ages are compared at one point in time to determine age *differences*

Group One	Group Two	Group Three
Subjects are 3 years of age	Different group of subjects who are all 4 years of age	Different group of subjects who are all 5 years of age
Research done in 1991	Research done in 1991	Research done in 1991

LONGITUDINAL RESEARCH

Same subjects are studied at various ages to determine age *changes*

Study One	Study Two	Study Three
Subjects are 3 years of age	Same subjects as in Study #1, but they are now 4 years of age	Same subjects as Studies 1 and 2, but they are now 5 years of age
Research done in 1991	Research done in 1992	Research done in 1993

Figure 9.1 A comparison of cross-sectional and longitudinal research. Note that cross-sectional research uses *different* subjects and is interested in *age differences*, whereas longitudinal research uses the *same* subjects to study *age changes*.

COHORT-SEQUENTIAL RESEARCH: *A technique of data collection in which groups of people are repeatedly tested over time while new cohorts are added to allow age comparisons.*

extended test period, the experimenter ends up with a self-selected sample that may differ from the general population in important ways.

In response to these problems, Schaie (1983) developed the method of **cohort-sequential research,** which combines the strengths of both longitudinal and cross-sectional studies. Using this method, groups of people are repeatedly tested over time (longitudinal research), while new cohorts are added to allow age comparisons (cross-sectional techniques). This method shows promise for future research in developmental psychology, but the drawbacks of time and financial costs still apply. As you can see, each method of research has its own strengths and weaknesses. It is important to keep these differences in mind as you study the findings of developmental research in the following areas of physical, language, cognitive, and personality development.

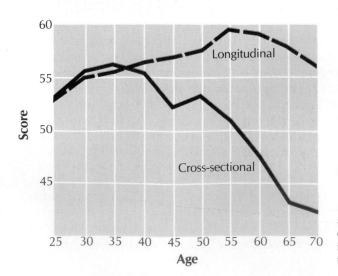

Figure 9.2 A comparison of the results of cross-sectional and longitudinal research on a typical measure of intelligence, the "verbal meaning" test.

Review Questions

1 _____ _____ involves the description, explanation, prediction, and modification of age-related behaviors from conception to death.

2 The debate over whether behavior is primarily learned or inborn is known as the _____ _____ _____.

3 Charles Darwin's detailed records of his firstborn child were a forerunner to the research method now known as _____ _____.

4 _____ studies of intelligence often find a peak in adolescence and a gradual decline in adulthood.

5 _____ studies are often expensive and restricted in generalizability because of the self-selected sample.

Answers: 1 developmental psychology; *2* nature versus nurture controversy; *3* baby biographies; *4* cross-sectional; *5* longitudinal

PHYSICAL DEVELOPMENT

Perhaps the most obvious aspect of development, at least in the first 15 to 20 years of life, is physical growth and alterations in body proportions and size. This process begins long before we are born.

Prenatal development: From conception to birth

Conception occurs when a male sperm fertilizes a female egg, or ovum. At the moment of conception, only *one* of the 200–400 million sperm contained in an average ejaculation actually fertilizes the ovum (each ejaculation contains enough sperm to more than repopulate the United States). Each of the three major stages of **prenatal development,** from conception to birth, has its own mysteries and marvels (see Figure 9.3).

During the **germinal period** (Figure 9.3*a*), which lasts from fertilization until about 14 days later, the original fertilized single cell undergoes repeated divisions at an astronomical rate of change. At the same time, the cells are beginning to form into distinct groups that will perform new and specialized functions. One major group of cells, for example, will become parts of the embryo, while others divide to become protective membranes and the placenta, which provides nourishment. The germinal period ends when the ball of cells implants in the wall of the uterus.

During the **embryonic period** (Figure 9.3*b*), which lasts from implantation to the eighth week of pregnancy, all the major organs are being developed and the basic plan of the body emerges. During embryonic development and later stages, growth at first proceeds from the head downward, in a sequence known as **cephalocaudal development** ("head-to-tail"). Among other things, this type of development results in the embryo having a head larger than its body. Subsequently, growth follows **proximodistal development** ("near-to-far"), meaning that it proceeds from the inside outward. Thus, the heart and lungs will develop before the hands and fingers. The embryonic period is also a **critical period**—an optimal or sensitive time in development when the organism is most easily affected by environmental events. As we will see in the next section, any serious interference during this period may result in permanent and irreversible damage.

The final stage of development, the **fetal period** (Figure 9.3*c*), lasts from the end of the second month to birth. During this period, the fetus continues its rapid rate of growth and the organs and muscles begin to function. As the fetus develops, it becomes increasingly active inside the uterus. Although most women report sensations of fetal movement

CONCEPTION: *The fertilization of the female ovum or egg by the male sperm.*

PRENATAL DEVELOPMENT: *Changes that occur from the point of conception to the moment of birth.*

GERMINAL PERIOD: *The first stage of pregnancy (conception to 2 weeks), characterized by rapid cell division.*

EMBRYONIC PERIOD: *The second stage of pregnancy (from uterine implantation to the eighth week), characterized by development of major body organs and systems.*

CEPHALOCAUDAL DEVELOPMENT: *A general pattern of physical growth in which the greatest growth occurs first in the region of the head and later in lower regions.*

PROXIMODISTAL DEVELOPMENT: *A general pattern of physical growth in which development starts at the center of the body and moves toward the extremities.*

CRITICAL PERIOD: *An optimal or sensitive time in development when the organism is most easily affected by environmental events.*

FETAL PERIOD: *The third, and final, stage of prenatal development (8 weeks to birth), characterized by rapid weight gain in the fetus and the fine detailing of body organs and systems.*

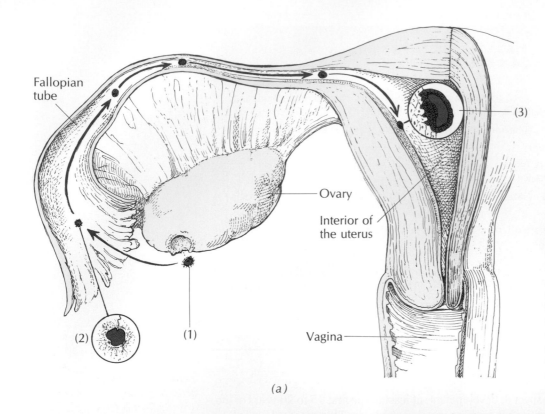

Fallopian
tube

Ovary

Interior of
the uterus

Vagina

(3)

(2)   (1)

(a)

Figure 9.3 *(a)* (LEFT) (1) After discharge from the ovary (ovulation), the ovum travels to the opening of the fallopian tube. If fertilization occurs (2), it normally takes place in the first third of the fallopian tube. The fertilized ovum is referred to as a *zygote*. When the developing organism reaches the uterus, it implants itself in the wall of the uterus (3) and begins to grow tendrils that intertwine with the rich supply of blood vessels located there. After this implantation, the organism is known as an *embryo*.

(b) (ABOVE) Embryonic Period. At eight weeks of age, the major organ systems have become well differentiated. As you can see from the apparently oversized head, growth of the head takes precedence over growth of the lower parts of the body.

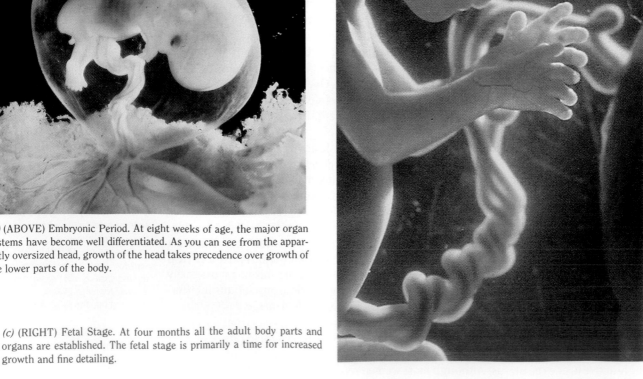

(c) (RIGHT) Fetal Stage. At four months all the adult body parts and organs are established. The fetal stage is primarily a time for increased growth and fine detailing.

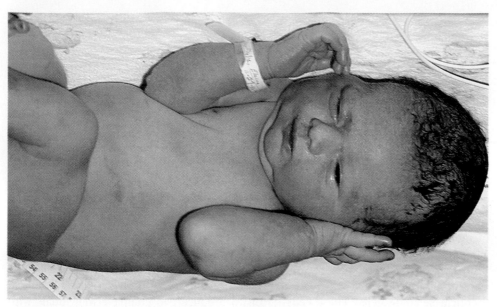

Figure 9.3 *(d)* Newborn baby approximately 10 minutes after birth.

by the third or fourth month, during the last three months these movements become progressively stronger and more distinct.

Genetic influences on physical development Many of the characteristics that make us unique — hair color, eye color, body build, and so on — are inherited at the moment of conception. As you may remember from biology courses, the nucleus of every cell in the body (except sperm and egg cells) contains 23 pairs of **chromosomes,** which carry the **genes,** or transmitters of hereditary information. The genes you inherit play a very important role in your development. Three of the most basic influences of genes are:

1. *Dominant–recessive characteristics.* Most genes occur in pairs, one on each matching chromosome. Some hereditary traits are governed by single gene pairs. The two genes may be identical, or one may be dominant while the other is recessive. When one or both genes are **dominant,** the characteristic they govern (such as brown eye color) will always be expressed. For a **recessive** trait (such as blue eye color) to be expressed, two recessive genes for that trait must be paired (see Figure 9.4).

CHROMOSOMES: *Microscopic threadlike structures in the nucleus of every living cell; they carry genes, the transmitters of inheritance.*
GENE: *The basic unit for the transmission of hereditary information.*

DOMINANT GENES: *In the process of genetic transmission, a dominant gene is one that exerts its full characteristic effect regardless of its gene partner.*
RECESSIVE GENES: *During genetic transmission, a recessive gene is one whose code is masked by a dominant gene and is only expressed when paired with another recessive gene.*

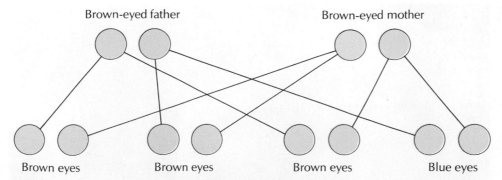

Figure 9.4 As you can see from this diagram, your chances of having either a blue-eyed or brown-eyed child depend on the dominant (brown-eyed) or recessive (blue-eyed) genes for both you and your mate. The circles represent the genes for the eye color.

SEX-LINKED TRAITS: *Traits that are inherited through genes found on the sex chromosomes.*
SEX-INFLUENCED TRAITS: *Traits that are governed by genes on the sex chromosomes but are expressed in the presence of other biological factors.*

2. *Sex-linked or sex-influenced characteristics.* Some **sex-linked** traits (such as color blindness and hemophilia) are controlled by genes carried on the X chromosome. **Sex-influenced** characteristics (such as baldness) are governed by genes on the sex chromosomes but are expressed in the presence of certain other biological factors. In the case of baldness, for example, both women and men inherit the genetic predisposition but it normally only shows up in the male because of his body's production of male hormones.

3. *Polygenic characteristics.* Although some traits are controlled by single gene pairs, most hereditary characteristics are the result of a complicated combination of genes and the interaction of genetic inheritance with environmental influences. Intelligence (Chapter 8) and the mental disorder of schizophrenia (Chapter 15) are but two of the many psychological characteristics thought to be polygenic (Plomin, 1989).

Each chromosome bears literally thousands of genes, which can occur in almost unlimited combinations. Because we each receive a different combination of genes, we are all truly biologically unique. The one exception to this genetic uniqueness occurs in the case of **identical twins,** which result when a fertilized ovum divides and forms two identical separate cells. These cells go on to produce two complete individuals with identical genetic information. **Fraternal twins,** on the other hand, result from the fertilization of two separate eggs by different sperm. These two "womb mates" are genetically no more alike than brothers and sisters born at differing times. In light of the nature–nurture controversy, you can understand why the study of identical and fraternal twins occupies a large part of the research in developmental psychology. Twins offer a unique and invaluable opportunity to evaluate the relative contributions of both genetic and environmental forces to development.

IDENTICAL TWINS: *Twins who share the very same genetic inheritance as the result of the splitting of an already fertilized egg.*
FRATERNAL TWINS: *Twins that develop from two eggs fertilized at the same time. From the point of heredity, they are no more alike than ordinary siblings.*

Question: How is the sex of a child determined? In contrast to other body cells, the sex cells — the sperm and the ovum — contain only 23 *single* chromosomes. These sex cells must be joined together during the process of conception to provide a complete set of chromosomes for the new individual. At conception, the sperm's 23 single chromosomes are matched with the 23 chromosomes of the ovum, and the sex of the future child is determined by the combination of *sex chromosomes*. Females have two X chromosomes, whereas males have one X chromosome and one Y chromosome. Because each ovum has an X chromosome, sex is determined by whether the fertilizing sperm has an X or a Y. If an X-bearing sperm fertilizes the ovum, the child will be female (XX), and if a Y-bearing sperm does so, the child will be male (XY).

Question: I've heard of ways to determine ahead of time whether the child will be male or female. Do they work? Although there have always been folk beliefs

Since identical twins share the same genetic inheritance, they are often of great interest to developmental psychologists.

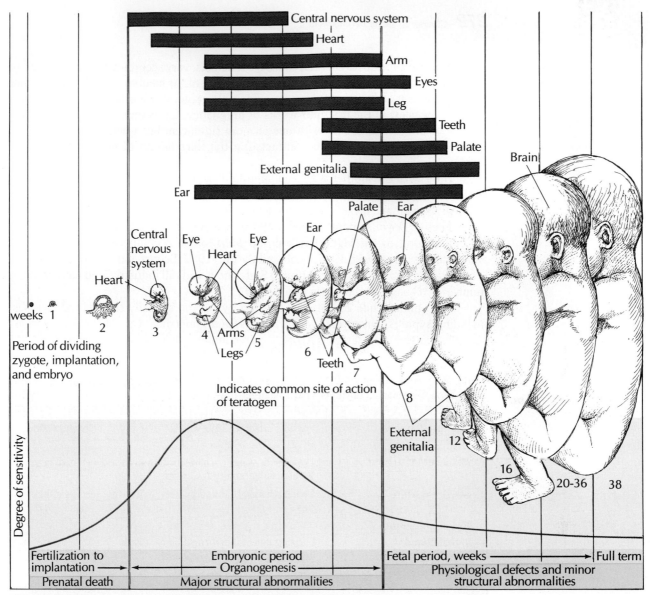

Figure 9.5 The specific effects of teratogens vary according to the stages of pregnancy. As you can see, major body systems form during the first eight weeks, and this period is probably the most critical time for the occurrence of major birth defects.

claiming to allow preselection of the sex of the unborn child, there is little reliable scientific evidence that such methods work (Jancin, 1989). There *are* more accurate methods, such as mechanically separating "male" and "female" sperm followed by artificial insemination, but many researchers question the value of being able to choose a baby's sex. Since many couples tend to have strong preferences for one sex or the other (Hyde, 1986), scientists are concerned about possible imbalances in the sex ratio in future generations. They are also worried that the emphasis on sex selection may overshadow more important benefits of genetic research, such as help for infertile couples or the prevention of genetic abnormalities.

Environmental influences on physical development Some genetic problems in development can occur as a result of defective genes, such as in Huntington's chorea, a progressive degeneration of the nervous system. Other problems can result from abnormalities in the chromosomes, such as in Down's syndrome, which produces various levels of mental and motor retardation, hearing defects, protruding tongues, small heads, and so on. However, the environment can also exert a powerful influence on development even before a child is born. As you can see in Figure 9.5, the specific effects of **teratogens**, or

TERATOGEN: *An external, environmental agent that may cross the placental barrier and disrupt development, causing minor or severe birth defects.*

271

environmental substances that can cause birth defects, vary according to the time they're encountered during the prenatal period in development. As mentioned earlier, in the first eight weeks the embryo is at its most vulnerable stage. If a mother contracts rubella (German measles) in the first four weeks of pregnancy, for example, the baby has a 50 percent chance of being born with one or more significant birth defects, but only a 17 percent chance if the disease is contracted in the third month of pregnancy (Rhodes, 1961).

The age of the mother is also an important factor in birth defects. Although most people are aware that older women are at greater risk for certain fetal abnormalities such as Down's syndrome, there is less awareness of the fact that women under 35 actually bear 80 percent of Down's infants (Kolata, 1988). It is important to recognize that teenage mothers belong to the highest risk group *both* for birth complications and for fetal abnormalities (Brylawski, 1987; Scott and Carran, 1987; Schorr and Schorr, 1990). This is of increasing concern since the United States now leads all industrialized nations in the number of teenage mothers (see Chapter 10).

The unborn child can also be affected by several sexually transmitted diseases, including syphilis, chlamydia, genital herpes, and gonorrhea. One of the most serious sexually transmitted diseases is AIDS (acquired immune deficiency syndrome). The AIDS

TABLE 9.2
Some Environmental Conditions That Endanger the Child

Maternal Behavior	Possible Effect on Embryo, Fetus, Newborn, or Young Child
Malnutrition	Low birth weight, malformations, less developed brain, greater vulnerability to disease
Stress exposure	Low birth weight, hyperactivity, irritability, feeding difficulties
Use of hormones:	
thalidomide	Hearing defects, deformed limbs, death
androgens	Masculinization of female fetus
diethylstilbestrol	Uterine and vaginal abnormalities in female fetus, possible carcinogenesis in male and female fetus, infertility
Excessive use of vitamin A	Cleft palate, congenital anomalies
Use of analgesics	Respiratory depression
Use of aspirin in large doses	Respiratory depression
Use of tetracycline	Inhibition of bone growth, discolored teeth
Use of streptomycin	Hearing loss
Narcotic addiction	Growth deficiency, withdrawal syndrome, central nervous system and respiratory depression, death
Heavy smoking	Low birth weight, increased fetal heart rate, prematurity, increased risk of spontaneous abortion, fetal death
Alcohol consumption	Fetal alcohol syndrome (growth deficiency, developmental lag, mental retardation); increased risk of spontaneous abortion, fetal death, attentional deficits in childhood
Cocaine consumption	Increased risk of spontaneous abortion, withdrawal syndrome, erratic emotions in infants
Exposure to X rays	Malformations, cancer
German measles (rubella)	Blindness, deafness, mental retardation, heart malformations
Herpes, AIDS, other STDs	Brain infection, death, spontaneous abortion, premature birth, mental retardation

(*Source:* Bower, 1989b; Kopp and Kaler, 1989; Lozoff, 1989; Scott and Carran, 1987; Shiono, Klebanoff, and Rhoads, 1986; Witters, 1988.)

virus can be passed from mother to child before birth, during the birth process, and after the child is born (perhaps through breast milk) (Novick, 1990; Spotkov and Anderson, 1988). The most likely route of transmission from mother to child is the blood. Former Surgeon General C. Everett Koop (1987, 1988) recommends that women considering pregnancy have blood tests to determine whether they have been exposed to the AIDS virus. Pregnant women who have AIDS or other sexually transmitted diseases should discuss their disorders with their physicians. In some instances, measures can be taken that will improve the chances for a healthy birth.

Because there are innumerable environmental hazards to the unborn child (a partial listing is provided in Table 9.2), we will concentrate on the two areas that are most easily controlled by the individual: nutrition and drugs.

Poor nutrition, both before and during pregnancy, can seriously affect the developing fetus. Inadequate maternal nutrition can lead to miscarriage, stillbirths, infant deaths, fewer neurons in the developing fetal brain, cerebral palsy, epilepsy, mental retardation, minor school and learning difficulties, premature birth, and low birth weight (Conger, 1988; Hui, 1985; Lozoff, 1989). As you can see in Figure 9.6, the United States has a higher infant mortality rate than 22 other nations, including Singapore, Malta, and most of Northern Europe. Each year more than 40,000 U.S. babies die before they reach their first birthday ("Health care," 1988). Maternal malnutrition and the lack of universal access to prenatal and early pediatric care are two of the most important factors in the high number of infant deaths.

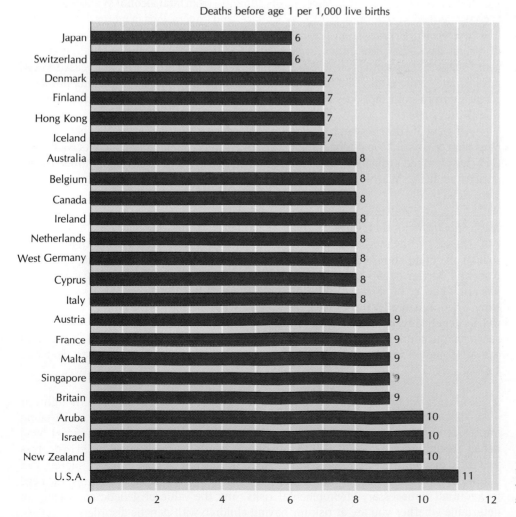

Deaths before age 1 per 1,000 live births

Japan	6
Switzerland	6
Denmark	7
Finland	7
Hong Kong	7
Iceland	7
Australia	8
Belgium	8
Canada	8
Ireland	8
Netherlands	8
West Germany	8
Cyprus	8
Italy	8
Austria	9
France	9
Malta	9
Singapore	9
Britain	9
Aruba	10
Israel	10
New Zealand	10
U.S.A.	11

Figure 9.6 An infant born in the United States has less chance of surviving to its first birthday than he or she would if born in 22 other nations.

Question: Why is nutrition such a problem in the United States? Many women are simply unaware of the importance of the prenatal stage of development and of the need for adequate nutrition. Others may choose an inadequate or improper diet during pregnancy in an attempt to minimize weight gain, stretch marks, and so on. However, many women do not "choose" to be malnourished during pregnancy but rather are forced into inferior diets for economic reasons. Given the fact that one of the major causes of fetal death and deformity could generally be avoided with adequate nutrition (Lozoff, 1989; Susser, 1981), it is important to look for ways to modify the economic, medical, and educational experiences of pregnant women.

In addition to poor nutrition, many drugs consumed before or during pregnancy are potential teratogens. Many drugs consumed by the mother — both legal and illegal — can cross the placenta and harm the developing child (Fackelmann, 1989; Witters, 1988). The most notorious example of drug-related birth defects came in the 1960s, when a drug known as thalidomide was prescribed for several hundred European women to counteract morning sickness or as a mild tranquilizer. These women subsequently gave birth to infants with a variety of birth defects, including stunted limbs. Before this tragedy occurred, it was widely believed that the only drugs that could harm the fetus were narcotics such as heroin. Thalidomide changed all this. Today doctors avoid prescribing all nonessential drugs and even warn their patients against taking common nonprescription drugs such as aspirin or antihistamines.

Nicotine and alcohol are also coming under heavy attack as potential teratogens. Mothers who smoke, for example, have significantly higher rates of premature births, low-birth-weight infants, and increased fetal deaths (Bower, 1989c; McIntosh, 1984). Alcoholic mothers are likely to have infants suffering from **fetal alcohol syndrome,** which is characterized by deformities of the heart, face, and fingers, lags in motor development, and severe mental retardation (Rawat, 1982). Even moderate drinking — less than one drink per day — has been found to be related to attentional deficits in children at four years of age (Streissguth et al., 1984, 1989), decreased fetal growth, and increased risk of miscarriage (Mills et al., 1984). Results of animal studies also show serious problems resulting from single episodes of heavy alcohol consumption around the time of conception (Furey, 1984).

In view of these research findings, the Surgeon General has warned that all pregnant women should avoid tobacco and alcohol entirely. Some areas, such as New York City, have passed ordinances that require all bars, restaurants, and liquor stores to post notices such as "Warning: Drinking alcoholic beverages during pregnancy can cause birth defects."

Question: Is there anything that the father does that can affect the health of the fetus? The mother obviously plays the primary role, since her health influences that of the child she is carrying and since almost everything she ingests can cross the placental barrier between the mother and fetus. (Some have suggested that the term placental barrier be replaced with "placental sieve.") But the father can also affect the baby, environmentally (the father's smoking may pollute the air the mother breathes) as well as genetically. It has been discovered, for example, that problems in cell division in the sperm may account for 20 to 25 percent of the cases of Down's syndrome, and the disorder is more common when the father is under 21 or over 55 years of age (Arehart-Treichel, 1979).

Question: What are my chances of having a "normal" baby? Although our discussion of genetic and environmental factors may have created a misleading impression of the dangers involved, the odds of having a child with a significant birth defect are only about 7 in 100. Our focus on the hazards has not been intended to depress you or to discourage you from having children. But if you do plan to have children, you should be aware of the importance of maternal nutrition and prenatal checkups, the need to avoid all unnecessary environmental risks, and the value of genetic counseling to determine whether you are at risk for having children with genetic disorders.

FETAL ALCOHOL SYNDROME: *A combination of birth defects, including organ deformities and mental, motor, and/or growth retardation, that results from maternal alcohol abuse.*

Review Questions

1 The three major stages of prenatal development are the _____
_____, the _____ _____, and
the _____ _____.

2 Color blindness is a _____ characteristic, whereas baldness is _____.

3 _____ _____ are the one exception to genetic uniqueness because
they develop from the same fertilized ovum.

4 Environmental substances that can cause birth defects are known as _____.

5 One of the major reasons for the high infant mortality in the United States
is _____ _____.

6 Alcoholic mothers may give birth to babies with the _____
_____ _____.

Answers: 1 germinal period, embryonic period, fetal period; *2* sex-linked, sex-influenced; *3* identical twins; *4* teratogens; *5* maternal malnutrition; *6* fetal alcohol syndrome

Early development: Brain, motor, and sensory/perceptual

At the time of birth the infant is at its most dependent and helpless stage of life. Although Shakespeare described newborns as capable of only "mewling and puking in the nurse's arms," they are actually capable of much more. In this section we will explore the newborn's physical capabilities and how he or she grows and develops in the first few years of life.

Brain development The brain and other parts of the nervous system grow faster than any other part of the body during both prenatal development and the first two years of life. A newborn baby's brain is one-fourth its full adult size and will grow to about 75 percent of its adult weight and size by the age of two. At five years of age, the brain is nine-tenths its full adult weight (see Figure 9.7).

It is generally believed that the newborn baby's brain contains most of the neurons it will ever have (Chugani and Phelps, 1986). Further brain development and learning occur primarily through an increase in the number of dendrites and synapses and with the

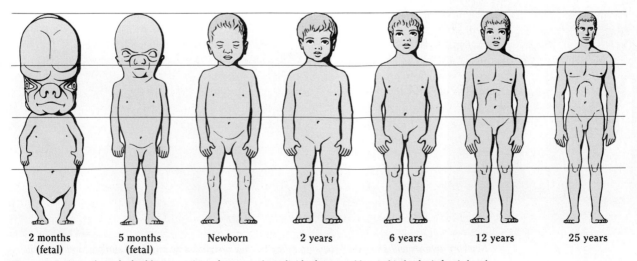

| 2 months (fetal) | 5 months (fetal) | Newborn | 2 years | 6 years | 12 years | 25 years |

Figure 9.7 Notice how the bodily proportions change as the individual grows older. At birth, the infant's head is one-fourth its full adult size.

development of myelin sheaths (see Chapter 2). Although some areas of the brain continue adding myelin up to age 60 or beyond, 90 percent of **myelination** is complete by age three (Thatcher, Walker, and Guidice, 1987).

MYELINATION: *The accumulation of myelin (a fatty tissue that coats the axons of nerve cells) in the nervous system, thereby increasing the speed of neural messages.*

Understanding brain development can contribute to our knowledge of children's learning abilities. Myelination, for example, can account for several instances of unsuccessful toilet training. Few parents realize that a child's nervous system must achieve a certain level of myelination before he or she can recognize the signals of a full bladder — a necessary prerequisite to toilet training. The parts of the brain involved in prolonged attention span and the perceptual ability to screen out distracting stimuli also become increasingly myelinated between the ages of four and seven (Higgins and Turnure, 1984). As a consequence, most children first become ready to read and focus on schoolwork at some time between these ages (Rathus, 1988).

Question: Doesn't this invalidate Glen Doman's claim about babies reading at 11 months? Wouldn't their nervous system be too immature at this age?   Although Doman generally ignores this type of question from his critics, many psychologists recognize these physiological limitations and do not advocate formal instruction for infants and young children. In terms of psychological damage, David Elkind (1981, 1988) warns that the current trend toward academic training in early childhood puts children at risk for short-term stress disorders and long-term personality problems. Signs of stress in two- and three-year-olds, such as pulling out their eyelashes or clumps of their hair, are frequently reported by pediatricians (Langway et al., 1983) and personality disturbances are becoming commonplace. One extreme example is that of the six-year-old who, while doing her homework, asked her mother, "If I don't get these right, will you kill me?" (Elkind, 1987).

Motor development   Compared to the hidden, internal changes in brain development, the orderly emergence of active movement skills, known as *motor development,* is easily observed and measured. The newborn's first motor abilities are limited to **reflexes,** involuntary responses to stimulation (see the photograph below), but the infant soon begins to show voluntary control over movements of the various body parts. In a matter of a few short months, a helpless newborn who can't even lift his head is transformed into an active toddler capable of crawling, walking, and climbing (see Figure 9.8). This transformation

REFLEXES: *Unlearned, involuntary responses of a part of the body to an external stimulus.*

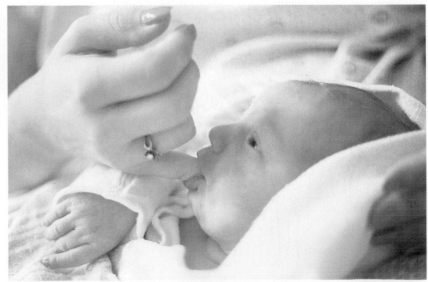

Newborn infants will show the "stepping reflex" if they are placed on any hard surface, and they will suck on any object that is placed in their mouth due to the sucking reflex.

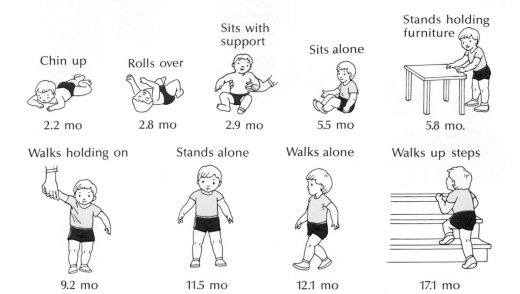

Chin up
2.2 mo

Rolls over
2.8 mo

Sits with support
2.9 mo

Sits alone
5.5 mo

Stands holding furniture
5.8 mo.

Walks holding on
9.2 mo

Stands alone
11.5 mo

Walks alone
12.1 mo

Walks up steps
17.1 mo

Figure 9.8 The "typical" progression of motor abilities from birth to 17 months. It is important to remember that no two children are alike and many will follow their own individual timetable for physical development. (Adapted from Frankenburg and Dodds, 1967.)

seems to be largely the result of maturation, since practice of basic motor skills does not seem to improve their performance. For example, Hopi Indian infants spend a great deal of their first year of life being carried in a cradleboard on their mother's back, yet they show no impairment in their motor development (Dennis and Dennis, 1940).

The important role of maturation extends beyond the obvious major milestones of crawling and walking. For example, a two-year-old can walk fairly well but has trouble hopping, standing on one foot, or even walking up and down stairs, one foot to a step. Each of these skills, and many more, will be naturally acquired through the simple process of growing older and becoming more physically mature. Although practice may improve a child's ability to ride a bike or throw a ball, it does not accelerate the time at which these abilities first become possible — an important distinction that many parents and athletic coaches should realize as they try to push children toward ever higher levels of achievement.

Infants from some tribes of native American Indians spend a great part of their first year of life bound to cradleboards, yet they walk at about the same age as babies who have had extensive practice in crawling and standing.

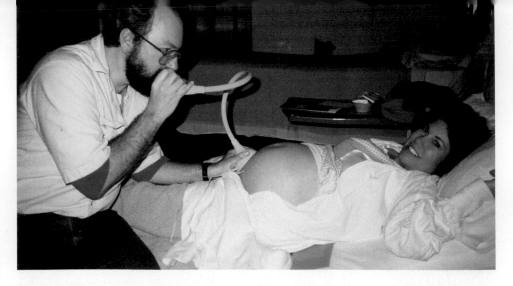

A father uses the pregaphone to talk to his infant right before delivery.

Question: Is it true that children who walk earlier turn out to be more intelligent later on?   Some people do believe this and point with pride to their children's physical achievements. However, there is no real correlation between physical and intellectual achievements, except in cases of severe motor development lags, which *are* associated with mental retardation (Hilton, 1987; Illingworth, 1974).

Sensory and perceptual development   William James (1890) believed that infants are so "assailed by eyes, ears, nose, skin, and entrails at once" that they view the world as "one great blooming, buzzing, confusion." Modern research, however, has demonstrated that at birth virtually all human senses are functional (Hall and Oppenheim, 1987). Research has also shown that even before birth the fetus will respond to sounds within the uterus (e.g., the mother's heartbeat) as well as to sounds outside the mother (Birnholz and Benacerrof, 1983). The fact that newborn infants easily recognize their own mother's voice and show preferences for children's stories that were read to them before birth (De Casper and Fifer, 1980; Trotter, 1987) lends experimental support to the popular belief in fetal learning. In response to this popularity, devices such as the "pregaphone" have been developed to help parents talk to their babies before birth (see the photograph above).

The sense of vision is poor immediately after birth but quickly improves. Within a short time infants can track a moving object and show a preference for complex patterns and curved contours (Maurer and Young, 1983). Newborns can also smell most odors and can distinguish between sweet, salty, and bitter solutions (Ganchrow et al., 1983). Breast-fed newborns also distinguish and show preference for the odor of their mother's milk over that of another mother's milk (Russell, 1976).

Question: How can scientists measure the "preferences" and abilities of such young babies?   Since newborns and infants obviously cannot talk or follow directions, researchers have been forced to design ingenious experiments to discover perceptual skills in infants. One of the earliest experimenters, Robert Fantz (1956, 1963), designed a special looking chamber in which infants lie on their backs and look at visual stimuli. The researcher stands over the baby and measures the length of time the visual stimuli are reflected in the baby's cornea. With this technique Fantz discovered that infants "prefer" (as measured by their longer visual contact) complex versus simple patterns, color versus black and white, and pictures of faces rather than nonfaces.

In addition to such specialized equipment, researchers also use the newborn's innate abilities, such as the sucking reflex or heart rate, to study how infants learn and how their perceptual abilities develop. Researchers might, for example, present two stimuli (the mother's voice and a stranger's voice) and then determine whether the baby will suck harder on a special nipple attached to a recording of the mother's voice than to a nipple with a recording of the stranger's voice. Similarly, the researchers might measure changes in the infant's heart rate when different odors are presented; presumably, if they can smell one but not the other, their heart rate will change in the presence of the first, but not the second. From research such as this, we now know that the senses develop very early in life.

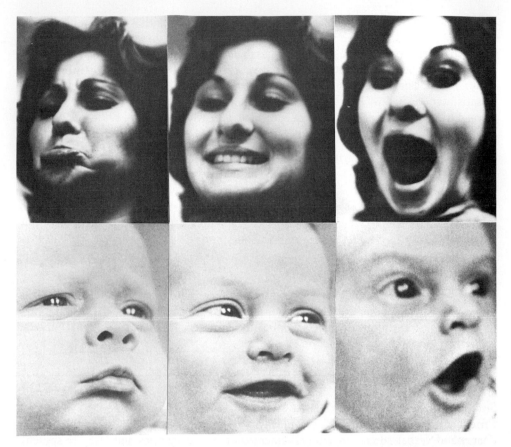

Infants as young as three weeks of age show a remarkable ability to imitate the facial expressions of adults.

As infants grow older their senses become even more fully developed, and they move toward improved perceptual abilities through interactions with the environment. Young children, for example, often have difficulty in learning to read because they are unable to distinguish between the letters "p" and "q" and "b" and "d" or between the words "was" and "saw." This is often explained by the fact that a child's perception is generally more flexible and less bound by a left-to-right and vertical – horizontal orientation. In time, the child gains perceptual experience, and reading, like other tasks, becomes easier to achieve.

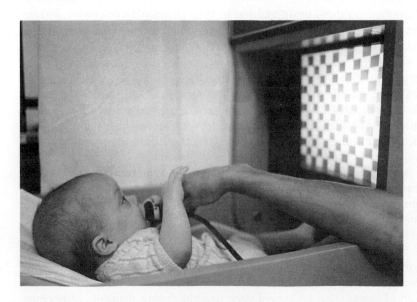

Using the sucking reflex, scientists have discovered that infants will suck harder to keep a complex pattern or color design in focus than a simple black-and-white design.

Question: How did Glen Doman's babies read and do math if young children have trouble distinguishing letters? This is a question that many of Doman's critics would like answered. When asked for studies to document his fantastic claims, Doman has replied that he lacks sufficient data and that a control study would be too costly (Langway et al., 1983). These answers obviously fail to satisfy scientific standards. They are also unsatisfactory when we look at problems that sometimes result from pressuring children to read before they are ready. The case of Victor, provided by David Elkind (1981), is a good example:

> Victor was a slow starter when reading instruction began in kindergarten and first grade. He was eager . . . [and] tried hard at first, but . . . the more he failed the more reluctant to try he became . . . By second grade, although he participated eagerly in music and art, when reading came around he became sullen . . . By this time he might have been ready to read, but simply seeing a word card or a spelling book would set off a tantrum of sullenness or of defiant aggression. This attitude began to spread to the rest of his school day. He vacillated between being dependent and being a hellion. (pp. 176–177)

As you can see, studies of physical development are important not only for the understanding they offer into the abilities of various ages but also for the insights they offer into possible problems when individual development fails to match external expectations.

LANGUAGE DEVELOPMENT

From birth the child has a multitude of ways to communicate. In addition to the obvious channel of verbal communication (characterized at first by cries and later by speech), babies possess a "silent language" that is perhaps an even more powerful form of communication. Through such nonverbal means as facial expressions, eye contact, and body gestures, babies only hours old begin to "teach" their parents and caregivers when and how they want to be held, fed, and played with.

Nonverbal communication: The earliest form of language

In the late 1800s Charles Darwin proposed that most emotional expressions, such as smiles, frowns, and looks of disgust, are universal and innate. Darwin's contention is supported by the fact that children who are born blind and deaf exhibit the same facial expressions for emotions as those of sighted and hearing children. Furthermore, infants only a few weeks old show distinct expressions of anger, joy, disgust, and so on (Field, 1987; Izard et al., 1980; Tronick, 1989) (see the photograph on p. 281).

Question: Aren't these expressions really just haphazard and sometimes due to physiological things like "gas"? Apparently not. In a long series of studies, Carroll Izard and his associates (1980) exposed infants from one to nine months of age to a variety of situations (such as being separated from and reunited with their mothers, having balloons popped in their faces, and so on). They then spent thousands of hours carefully studying, videotaping, and analyzing the infants' reactions. They found that the infants showed facial expressions very similar to those of adults in comparable circumstances. Many parents seem to be unaware of the complexity of expression in their baby's nonverbal communication, however.

In addition to facial expressions, children often communicate through gestures, movements, and bodily postures (Bower, 1989a). Lewis (1980) has noted that infants will use their entire body to communicate. For example, the head is often tilted to invite friendship or turned to reject an approach, whereas uplifted arms are a clear gesture to encourage approach or to request an adult's help. The trunk of the body is sometimes bent forward as a sign of domination or is held very straight during moments of nervous

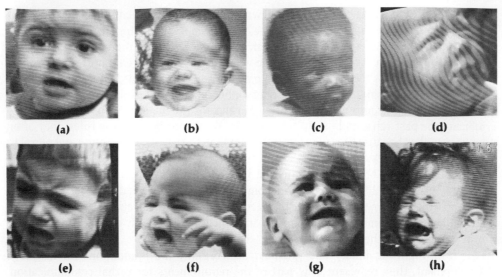

Note the striking similarity of these infant expressions to those of adults — (a) interest, (b) joy, (c) surprise, (d) sadness, (e) anger, (f) disgust, (g) fear, (h) physical distress.

hesitation. Limp hands generally indicate fatigue while rapidly moving arms show frustration, rage, or joy.

Verbal communication: The development of "official" language

Most researchers tend to agree that a baby's early cries, grunts, and "prompted" words are simple responses to the internal or external environment and do not qualify as true language. Therefore this stage is referred to as *prelinguistic.* "Official" language, or the *linguistic stage,* is said to begin when children are able to use novel or creative expressions that have meaning for them while attempting to communicate with others.

Stages of language development   The prelinguistic stage begins with the newborn baby's first reflexive cry. Within a short time, crying becomes more purposeful. At least three distinct patterns have been identified: the basic hunger cry, the angry cry, and the pain cry (Wolff, 1969). Although many child-care texts suggest that each of these cries can be easily identified and responded to by the primary caregivers (Hostetler, 1988a), most parents find that they must learn through a process of trial-and-error what actions will satisfy their child.

After "mastering" crying, children at about two months of age begin to *coo*—to produce vowel sounds ("ooh," "aah," and "eee")—and at about six months they begin to *babble*—adding consonants to their vowels ("bababa" and "dadada"). Some parents mark **babbling** as the beginning of language and consider their child's vocalizations as "words" even though the child typically does not associate a "word" with a specific object or person, and despite the fact that all children the world over babble in the same fashion.

The true linguistic stage begins toward the end of the first year of life, when babbling begins to sound more like the specific language of the child's home and when the child seems to understand that sounds are related to meanings. At the beginning of this stage, the child is generally limited to a single-utterance vocabulary such as "mama," "go," "juice," or "up." Children manage to get a lot of mileage out of these singular utterances ("mama" can be used to say "I want you to come and get me," "I'm hurt," or "I don't like this stranger"). However, their vocabulary more than doubles once they begin to express themselves by joining words into two-word phrases such as "Go bye-bye," "Daddy milk," and "Dog bite."

BABBLING: *An early stage of speech development in which infants emit virtually all known sounds of human speech.*

By the time "average" children are two years of age, they are able to create short but intelligible sentences by linking two, three, four, or more words together. Just as adults tend to leave out nonessential words when sending a telegram, the young children use **telegraphic speech** (short two- or three-word sentences that contain only the most necessary words) — "No sit there," "Tommy want milk," "What doing?" and so on.

While increasing their vocabulary at a phenomenal rate during these early years, children are also acquiring a wide variety of rules for grammar, such as adding "ed" to indicate the past tense and "s" to form plurals. While practicing these rules, they often make mistakes because they **overgeneralize** (extend the rules for past tense and plural to irregular forms), resulting in novel sentences like "I goed to the zoo" and "My foots hurt." By the age of five, most children have mastered major rules of grammar and typically use about 2000 words — an accomplishment that is considered by many foreign language instructors to be adequate for "getting by" in any given culture. Past this point, vocabulary and grammar acquisition generally progress through gradual stages of improvement during the entire life span.

Although vocabulary and grammar are certainly the foundations for language development, they represent only part of the requirements for verbal communication. Have you ever called someone and asked the child who answered the phone "Is your mommy at home?" The child probably answered "Yes" and then hung up! This response reflects the fact that children must also learn the implied messages of words.

Theories of language development   Numerous theories have been proposed to explain how children manage to acquire language. Some theorists suggest that the capability is inborn and innate, whereas others claim that it is totally learned through imitation and reinforcement (the nature versus nurture controversy again). Although there are staunch supporters of both sides, most psychologists find neither of these extreme positions satisfactory. They believe that language acquisition is probably a combination of both nature and nurture — the *interactionist* position (Rice, 1989).

According to the nativist position, the acquisition of language is primarily a matter of maturation. The most famous advocate of this viewpoint, Noam Chomsky (1968, 1980), suggests that children are born "prewired" to learn language. He believes they possess a type of **language acquisition device (LAD)** that needs only minimal exposure to adult speech to unlock its potential. The LAD enables the child to analyze language and unconsciously extract the basic rules of grammar. To support his viewpoint, Chomsky points to the fact that children all over the world go through similar stages in language development at about the same age and in a pattern that parallels that of motor development. He also cites the facts that babbling of babies is the same in all cultures and that deaf children babble just like hearing children.

Although the nativist position enjoys considerable support, it fails to adequately explain the individual differences that do exist among children. Why does one child learn the rules for English, for example, while another learns those for Spanish? The "nurturists" *can* explain individual differences and distinct languages because from their perspective children learn language through a complex system of rewards, punishments, and imitation. For example, any vocalization attempt from the young infant is quickly rewarded with smiles and other forms of encouragement. When the infant later babbles "mamma" or "dada," the proud parents are even more enthusiastic in their response. (By the way, if you ever observe such an interaction occurring, restrain yourself from pointing out that the baby also uses "mama" or "dada" for the teddy bear and other objects in the room. The parents will be busy ignoring these "minor details" — which also probably discourages the "inappropriate" labels for the teddy bear and further sharpens the infant's language skills.) Once children are old enough to form words and sentences, parents serve as models for language, and imitations of adult language are then rewarded.

Question: Why do children say things like "My foots hurt" if they've never been rewarded for doing so and are not imitating others?   Cognitive psychologist George Rebok (1987) suggests that imitative learning cannot explain these errors. Such

---

TELEGRAPHIC SPEECH: *The two- or three-word sentences of young children that contain only the most necessary words.*

OVERGENERALIZE: *A common error in a child's language acquisition where the rules for past tense and plurals are extended to irregular forms.*

LANGUAGE ACQUISITION DEVICE (LAD): *In Noam Chomsky's view, the child's inborn brain capacity to analyze language and unconsciously understand essential grammatical rules.*

mistakes in grammar are actually an important argument in favor of the innate or nativist position on language. While learning language, children apparently go through a regular and predictable sequence: (1) correct imitation, (2) rules of grammar acquisition, (3) errors in grammar, and (4) corrections in grammar. After first imitating the correct expression ("My feet hurt"), children then begin to observe and understand the basic rules of grammar and to overregularize them, producing sentences such as "My foots hurt." Since these sentences are seldom used by adults, it is difficult to explain such errors from a learning perspective. In addition, parents often tend to ignore imperfections in their children's grammar and actually reward some mistakes for being "cute." This tends to support the idea that a great part of language acquisition is self-generated and not a reflection of the environment.

Question: Isn't it wrong to encourage a child's mistakes?   Although some parents could carry this "cuteness" too far, the love and acceptance of such mistakes is undoubtedly beneficial to a child. Research has also shown that "baby talk" from the parents to the child may augment the child's language development (Cross, 1977; Gelman et al., 1987). For example, the simplification of "stomach" to "tummy" and "restroom" to "potty" seems to help the child to grasp the language more easily. Can you imagine how difficult it would be to learn a foreign language if your instructors refused to shorten their sentences or slow their pattern of speech? The fact that baby talk (officially referred to as *caretaker speech* or *motherese*) is universal, and even shown by four-year-old children when talking to a younger child, suggests that it is important to the child's learning and perhaps an innate capacity of the teacher (Blewitt, 1983; Caporael, 1981).

Question: Is there anything that should be done to help a child learn language?   Researchers have found that the most effective ways to encourage language skills are not through direct instruction but through responding to the child's overtures and making the child a full partner in dialogue (Menyuk, 1983; Rice, 1989). By offering the child opportunities to participate in conversations and acknowledging his or her attempts to communicate (even when incomprehensible), parents provide a warm and favorable climate for conversational development. It is also important to recognize that attempts to instruct small children in the finer points of language require a great deal of patience and good humor, as the following shows:

Child Nobody don't like me.
Mother No, say, "nobody likes me."
Child Nobody don't like me. *(dialogue repeated eight times)*
Mother Now, listen carefully, say *"Nobody likes me."*
Child Oh! Nobody don't *likes* me. (McNeill, 1966)

In summary, it appears that language is both innate and environmental, and the best way to foster its development is through a gentle acceptance of the child and a responsiveness to his or her individual needs.

Review Questions

1 Early toilet training is often unsuccessful because the infant's nervous system lacks the proper level of _____ .
2 Infants begin to crawl or walk at a given age as a result of _____ and not practice.
3 Facial expressions, eye contact, and body gestures are all part of _____ _____ .
4 _____ involves adding consonants to the vowels produced during cooing.

5 Children make errors like "mouses" and "goed" versus "mice" and "went" because they _____ the rules of grammar.

6 Noam Chomsky believes we possess an inborn ability to learn language known as the _____ _____ _____.

7 Research has shown that _____ _____ (or "baby talk") may be an essential part of a child's language development.

Answers: 1 myelination; *2* maturation; *3* nonverbal communication; *4* babbling; *5* overgeneralize; *6* language acquisition device; *7* caretaker speech

COGNITIVE DEVELOPMENT

The following fan letter was written to Shari Lewis (1963), a puppeteer on a popular children's television program, regarding her puppet Lamb Chop:

> *Dear Shari:*
> *All my friends say Lamb Chop isn't really a little girl*
> *that talks. She is just a puppet you made out of a*
> *sock. I don't care even if it's true. I like the way*
> *Lamb Chop talks. If I send you one of my socks will*
> *you teach it how to talk and send it back?*
>
> *"Randi"*

Randi's knowledge of the world and her separation of fantasy and reality are certainly different from an adult's view. It is intuitively obvious that, just as their bodies and physical abilities change, so, too, do children's ways of knowing and perceiving the world grow and change. Many people tend not to recognize this. Early psychologists seemed to ignore children's cognitive development and to focus instead on physical, emotional, language, or personality development. There was one major exception: Jean Piaget (1895–1980).

Today Piaget is well known and highly respected for his study of the development of thinking processes in children. One of his most significant contributions was to prove for the first time that the intellect of the child is fundamentally different from that of the adult (Flavell, 1985). He explained that a baby begins at a cognitively "primitive" level and that all subsequent intellectual growth progresses in distinct stages motivated by an innate *need to know.*

Question: Why was Piaget interested in this topic when no one else was?   Although initially trained as a biologist, Piaget in his early years also worked at Alfred Binet's laboratory in Paris and helped with the development of the first intelligence tests. While performing the routine measurements required in developing these tests, he began to notice an intriguing pattern in the way children of certain ages routinely "passed" or "failed" various sections of tests. By asking them gentle, probing questions about their reasons for making certain responses and decisions, he uncovered some of the modes of thinking underlying their right and wrong test answers. (This method of verbal probing later became a hallmark of the Piagetian form of research.) By asking deeper questions, Piaget went beyond the simple measurement of a child's IQ and laid the foundation for his life's work, including a carefully constructed theory of cognitive development.

This elaborate and comprehensive theory has proven so useful and insightful that it remains the major force in the cognitive area of developmental psychology today. In view of this fact, we will outline Piaget's theory in some detail.

Piaget's theory: Major terms and concepts

Perhaps the best way to approach an understanding of Piaget is to recognize that his background was as a biologist. Thus, he saw human cognition as only one of the ongoing processes of biology. Piaget believed that we are all born with an innate *drive* toward knowledge as part of our overall need for survival. Just as food is taken in and then digested into forms that are useful for the organism's biological survival, information is taken in by the human brain and "digested" in ways that also help the individual to survive. The cognitive processes are the "digestive" mechanisms that help humans to *adapt* to their environment, and "intelligence" is the ability to make adaptive choices (Cowan, 1978).

To understand this process of **adaptation,** we need to consider three major Piagetian concepts: schemata, assimilation, and accommodation. **Schemata** (plural form of *schema,* which is used interchangeably with *scheme*) are the most basic units of intellect. They act as patterns that organize our interactions with the environment. Like an architect's drawings or builder's blueprints, the schemata are the guiding forces for the "construction" of the intellect. In the first few weeks of life, for example, the infant apparently has several schemata based on the innate reflexes of sucking, grasping, and so on. In these early days, the schemata are primarily motor and may be little more than stimulus and response mechanisms — the nipple is presented and the baby sucks. Soon, however, other schemata emerge. The infant develops a more detailed schema for the eating of solid food, a different schema for the concepts of "mother" and "father," and so on. These schemata, or tools for learning about the world, are enlarged and changed throughout our lives, thus enabling us to process the ever-increasing load of information gained from our interactions with the environment.

Assimilation is the process of taking in new information that easily fits into an existing schema. For instance, infants use their sucking schema not only in sucking nipples but also in sucking blankets, fingers, and so on. They gain information about new objects in their environment by applying a reflexive response to them and *assimilating* this information into their existing schemata (Wadsworth, 1981).

Accommodation occurs when new information or stimuli cannot be assimilated and new schemata are developed or when old schemata are *changed* to adapt to the new features. An infant girl's first attempt to eat solid food with a spoon provides a good example of accommodation. When the spoon first enters her mouth, her first reaction will invariably be to attempt to assimilate it by using her previously successful "sucking schema" — shaping her lips and tongue around the spoon as she does a nipple. After repeated trials, with food all over her mouth, feeding tray, and anyone who is in close proximity, the infant will eventually try another strategy for closing around the spoon and then swallowing the solid food.

In addition to improvements in motor skills, this infant girl's language development will also reflect the processes of assimilation and accommodation. Having learned the word "dada," for example, she will first assimilate and call every man "dada," but after repeated corrections from the environment she will accommodate and only call her father "dada."

Question: What makes the child want to make these adjustments?   According to Piaget, we are all born with an innate need for harmony or *equilibrium* between our internal schemata and input from the environment. When our schemata do not fit or match the data coming in, we experience a *drive* to reestablish balance through assimilation or accommodation.

Stages of cognitive development: Birth to adolescence

According to Piaget, each child starts off with only the simplest and most rudimentary cognitive abilities. As a child ages, his or her abilities undergo an orderly series of changes that result in increasing levels of complexity. These changes tend to cluster

ADAPTATION: *Structural or functional changes that increase the organism's chances for survival.*

SCHEMATA: *Cognitive structures or patterns consisting of a number of organized ideas that grow and differentiate with experience.*

ASSIMILATION: *The process of responding to a new situation in the same manner that is used in a familiar situation.*

ACCOMMODATION: *The process of adjusting existing ways of thinking (reworking schemata) to encompass new information, ideas, or objects.*

TABLE 9.3
Piaget's Stages of Cognitive Development

Age	Stage	Description
Birth to 2 years	Sensorimotor	Infant uses senses and motor skills to explore the world; object permanence develops
2 to 7	Preoperational	Child cannot think by operations but can think in images and symbols; thinking is also egocentric and animistic
7 to 11	Concrete operational	Child understands and applies logical operations, but only to concrete, external objects
From 11 on	Formal operational (see Chapter 10)	Adolescent or adult is able to think abstractly and about hypothetical concepts; adolescents often exhibit a special type of egocentrism

around a pattern of interpreting the world, and when enough changes have occurred, the individual responds with a large developmental shift in his or her point of view (Cowan, 1978). Piaget called these developmental shifts cognitive *stages* in development (see Table 9.3).

Piaget suggested that all children go through the same four stages, at approximately the same age, regardless of the culture in which they live. He also believed that the movement from one stage to another is the result of both maturation and interaction with the environment. No stage can be skipped, since the skills acquired at the earlier stages are essential to the mastery of the later stages. Let's take a closer look at each of the four stages.

SENSORIMOTOR STAGE: *The first of Piaget's stages (birth to age two), in which cognitive development is acquired through exploration of the world via sensory perceptions and motor skills.*

The sensorimotor stage   During the **sensorimotor stage,** which lasts from birth until the time of "significant" language acquisition, children explore the world and develop their schemata primarily through their senses and motor activities — hence the term *sensorimotor.* If you've ever spent time watching infants, you've probably noticed that they put literally everything into their mouths and will bang pots and pans together for what may seem like hours. They do this not because they're hungry or trying to drive you crazy but, as Piaget explained, because they are little "experimenters" who are eagerly searching the world for information.

OBJECT PERMANENCE: *The understanding that objects (or people) continue to exist even when they are out of sight or disappear from view. This ability gradually develops between six and 18 months of age.*

One of the most important concepts acquired during this stage is **object permanence.** At birth and for the next three or four months, children seem to have no schemata for objects that disappear from their vision — out of sight is truly out of mind. You can check this out by first letting an infant play with an attractive toy and then covering it with your hand. The infant will act as if the toy never existed. If you interact with the same baby when he or she is four to eight months old, the infant may visually search for the toy if part of it is showing and will follow the path of your hand if you put the toy behind your back. Between the ages of eight and twelve months, the baby will physically search for the toy by lifting your fingers if you're covering it with your hand or by reaching behind your back if you've hidden it there. By the end of the sensorimotor stage, children's schema for object permanence is well developed and they will search a number of locations in an attempt to find a hidden toy.

PREOPERATIONAL STAGE: *The second of Piaget's stages (ages two to seven), characterized by the child's ability to employ mental symbols, to engage in fantasy play, and to use words. Thinking is egocentric and animistic and the child cannot yet perform operations.*

Preoperational stage   The second period of cognitive development is called the **preoperational stage** (ages two to seven). At this stage children have acquired object permanence and can now understand that sounds can be used as symbols for objects (knowledge of objects *must* precede the use of language — you have to acknowledge an object before you can label it). As you may imagine, language has a powerful influence on all aspects of behavior, but in terms of cognitive development the acquisition of language is

While developing the concept of object permanence — the realization that an object (or brother) continues to exist even if it can no longer be seen — an infant will find great pleasure in games of "peek-a-boo."

of critical importance. Once the child truly grasps the fact that objects and events in the environment can be represented by words, a whole new world of learning opens up. In the story of Helen Keller (Chapter 4), the famous teacher who was both blind and deaf, it was clear that the crucial turning point in her cognitive development was the moment when she finally realized that the hand signals her loving teacher had so patiently repeated time after time were representational symbols. Following this recognition, she immediately ran around "asking" the label for everything she could touch, which is similar to the preoperational child's endless "What's that?" questions.

This stage is called "preoperational" because the child has not yet developed *operations*. According to Piaget, an **operation** is a set of rules for transforming or maneuvering knowledge — a "schema for schemata." For example, when shown a ball of clay that is first rolled out to form a "snake" and then rolled back into a ball, the preoperational child can repeatedly watch the transformation and each time say that the "snake has *more* clay than the ball. The child's cognitive understanding is blocked because he or she lacks the operation or rule that says things can be changed in shape while still retaining the same volume.

OPERATION: *A set of rules for manipulating or transforming information.*

During the preoperational stage children are also quite **egocentric.** By this Piaget did not mean that children are selfish, but rather that they are *unable* to take the perspective of others (Piaget and Inhelder, 1956). Children at this level of development tend to believe that the world is merely an extension of their own mind and that people and objects in the world exist only for their use and benefit. They therefore believe, for example, that the sun follows them around, shines on them to keep them warm, and goes away at night to make them go to sleep. If you ever notice a three-year-old child loudly talking to his father, who is desperately trying to carry on a conversation with someone on the phone, or standing in front of his mother as she tries to watch television, you can explain to them the concept of egocentrism.

EGOCENTRISM: *The inability to consider another's point of view or perspective, which Piaget considered a hallmark of the preoperational stage.*

In addition to an inability to perform mental operations and a tendency to be egocentric, preoperational children's thinking is also very **animistic.** They tend to believe that inanimate objects such as trees and teddy bears are alive and have feelings. Piaget once observed his son turning a rock around and asked him why. The child replied, "The rock must get bored seeing the same thing all the time."

ANIMISM: *Thinking that all things are living and capable of intentions, consciousness, and feelings.*

Question: Can't preoperational children be taught how to use operations? Piaget was always surprised at questions of this type. Since he believed so strongly in the child's innate drive toward knowledge and in a natural biological progression in development, he felt that "pushing" a child was neither possible nor wise. Although some people have reported success in accelerating the preoperational stage (e.g., Field, 1981), Piaget was annoyed by attempts to push children ahead of their own developmental schedule and believed children should be allowed to grow at their own pace, with minimal adult interference (Elkind, 1981). In view of the fact that Piaget saw Americans as particularly guilty of pushing children (calling it the "Great American Kid Race"), you can imagine what his opinion would have been of Doman's work with "superbabies" discussed at the beginning of this chapter.

"Look what I can do, Grandma!"

Reprinted with special permission of King Features Syndicate, Inc.

CONCRETE OPERATIONAL STAGE: *The third of Piaget's stages of cognitive development (ages 7 to 11), during which the child develops the ability to think logically but not abstractly.*

CONSERVATION: *The principle that a given quantity, weight, or volume remains constant despite changes in shape, length, or position.*

> *Question:* What about true "superstar" children? Shouldn't something be done to stimulate their talents?   In a systematic study of gifted and talented adults (concert pianists, sculptors, mathematicians, and scientists), Benjamin Bloom (1985) found that the critical factors in their development were the support and encouragement of parents and the intellectual climate in the home. Thus it seems that by providing opportunities for learning, offering warm reinforcement for both success and failure, and modeling personal enthusiasm for their own work, parents can play a crucial role in developing gifted children. As Piaget (1983) suggested, cognitive activity is basically self-reinforcing. Given exposure to educational materials, children will achieve when they are ready to achieve. From the Piagetian perspective, any attempts at education should be child-centered and based on the child's own interests, not on formal academic instruction (Elkind, 1988).

Concrete operational stage   In the **concrete operational stage** (ages 7 to 11), thought becomes logical, and the child has acquired a set of rules for relating symbols and making inferences. Although the child's schemata seem to be limited to "concrete" objects and situations, he or she can logically check symbols against reality. Thus, most children stop believing in Santa Claus and the Easter Bunny during this stage. They seem to use their newly acquired logic to reason that one man, even with the help of all those elves, couldn't possibly make all those presents and visit everyone's house in the whole world and that one bunny couldn't deliver that many colored eggs.

At this stage of development, the child also becomes capable of understanding **conservation,** the principle that a given quantity, weight, or volume of a substance remains the same regardless of its shape or configuration. In a typical test of conservation, a child is presented with two equal-sized glasses, each filled with the same amount of water (see Figure 9.9). After the water is poured from one glass into a taller glass, the child is asked whether the tall and short glasses both contain the same amount of water. The

In this test for conservation of area, preoperational children are often confused by the different spacing of the two lines of doll clothes, whereas concrete operational children easily recognize the two sets as equal.

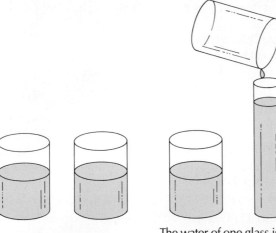

Two glasses are filled with the same amount of water. The subject sees that they contain an equal amount.

The water of one glass is poured into a tall glass. The subject is asked whether each glass contains the same amount of water.

Figure 9.9 A sample test for conservation of volume.

concrete operational child will immediately understand that there has been no change in quantity, but the preoperational child will typically judge the taller glass as having "more." If you have access to a child in this age group, you may enjoy testing his or her grasp of conservation by trying some of the experiments shown in Figure 9.10.

During the concrete operational stage, children also become less egocentric. They begin to realize that others have differing perspectives from their own and that they must share their own views if they hope to be understood. This realization leads to an improved type of communication pattern. Children at this stage are also capable of learning and operating under elaborate rules. If you've ever tried to play a card game or a board game such as Monopoly with a preoperational child, you can easily understand and *appreciate* the enormous improvement in the concrete operational child's ability to follow elaborate rules.

Such rules are important in formal education, since mastering basic language and math skills requires many rules (such as "*i* before *e* except after *c*," "When adding numbers always start in the 1's column," and so on). David Elkind (1981) suggests that we be careful not to underestimate the importance of this ability to comprehend and comply with rules. He notes that many parents see little difference in their child being able to count to ten and being able to do arithmetic, or between the ability to "sight read" a basic primer with one sentence per page and the ability to read a novel. This lack of understanding often leads to a pushing of preoperational children into math and reading far beyond their capabilities, which can result in damaging stress for the child.

During the final stage of cognitive development, the **formal operational stage,** the individual finally becomes capable of abstract reasoning, hypothetical thinking, and formulation of hypotheses. Because this stage occurs during the time of adolescence, we will save discussion of it for the next chapter.

FORMAL OPERATIONAL STAGE: *Piaget's final stage of cognitive development (age 11 and beyond), characterized by the ability to think logically, abstractly, and hypothetically.*

Piaget and his critics: Was he right or wrong?

Piaget's theory has recently received important support from physiological research that shows significant overlap between brain development and his stages of cognitive development (Thatcher, Walker, and Guidice, 1987). Piaget's theory has also been subject to a number of criticisms. One idea that has come under fire is that the stages of cognitive development occur in a rigid and invariant universal sequence. Several studies have found that children in fact vary a great deal in the acquisition of these skills: Some acquire them at ages other than those Piaget specified, some never acquire all the skills,

DEVELOPING INSIGHT INTO EGOCENTRICITY
Adult versus Childhood Egocentrism

Piaget asserted that preoperational children (ages two to seven) are *egocentric*. He proposed that children are unable to take the perspective of others because of their limited cognitive development. Although Piaget believed that most adults naturally outgrow such egocentric thinking, recent research suggests that a tendency toward egocentricity may persist throughout adulthood. It is difficult to outgrow our own egocentricity because we suppress facts that are inconsistent with our conclusions and we fail to notice when our behavior contradicts our self-image.

The best antidote to egocentricity is self-awareness and critical self-analysis. We must reflect on our reasoning, apply the same rules and standards for others to ourselves, and make our conclusions consistent with the evidence. To develop insight into your own egocentricity, you should use the following rating scale to first rate the personality traits of someone you find it hard to get along with. Then using the same scale, rate your best friend and then yourself.

1 = never behaves in this way
2 = seldom behaves in this way
3 = occasionally behaves in this way
4 = often behaves in this way
5 = always behaves in this way

	DISLIKED PERSON	BEST FRIEND	SELF
Is aggressive and irritable with others.	____	____	____
Is helpful and courteous to others.	____	____	____
Offers support and encouragement to others.	____	____	____
Takes advantage of others.	____	____	____
Is hardworking and reliable.	____	____	____

	DISLIKED PERSON	BEST FRIEND	SELF
Is sociable and fun to be with.	____	____	____
Dominates conversations.	____	____	____
Values advice from others.	____	____	____
Is interested in trying new things.	____	____	____
Tries to be fair and just with others.	____	____	____

Now check back over the values you assigned in the first and third column. Compare the positive and negative items. Do you think the "disliked person" would agree with your evaluation? Why or why not? Can you see how your own egocentrism, and that of your "disliked person," could explain the differences in perception?

Now compare the ratings you assigned for yourself and your best friend. If you are like most people, you will notice a strong similarity. An obvious, and somewhat egocentric, explanation for this is that similarity attracts — we like people who are like us. Further critical thinking, however, would explain this similarity as the result of *sociocentricity*—the extension of egocentrism to groups. The individual goes from thinking "I am right!" to "We are right!" When this egocentrism extends to ethnic groups, countries, and religions it is sometimes referred to as *ethnocentrism*. It is easy to recognize the egocentrism, sociocentrism, and ethnocentrism of opposing groups. Our belief in our own rightness is easy to maintain because we ignore the faults in our thinking and the contradictions in our behavior. The best antidote is to listen carefully and with an open mind to those with whom we disagree and to apply the full force of our critical thinking skills to our own behaviors.

---

and there is occasional overlapping between the abilities in each stage. (Chance and Fischman, 1987; Feldman, 1980; Flavell, 1985; Ralichman, in press). Second, many of the specific skills Piaget described as appearing at certain times within the stages have been demonstrated at much younger ages. For example, object permanence has been demonstrated in infants as young as five months (Baillargeon, 1982). And preschool children *do* show an ability to take another's point of view during the time of the preoperational stage when the testing situation is more familiar (Flavell, 1982; Sugar-

Type of Conservation	Step 1 of Experiment	Experimenter then . . .	Child is asked conservation question	Average age at which concept is grasped
Length	 Center two sticks of equal length. Child agrees that they are of equal length.	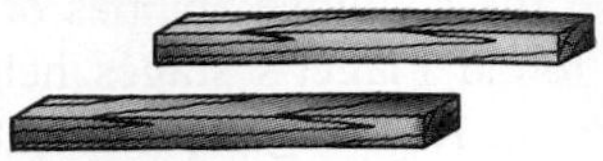 moves stick over.	*Which stick is longer?* Preconserving child will say that one of the sticks is longer. Conserving child will say that they are both the same length.	7–8
Substance amount	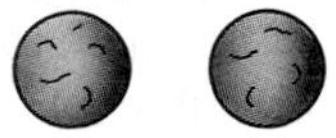 Center two identical clay balls. Child acknowledges that the two have equal amounts of clay.	 rolls out one of the balls.	*Do the two pieces have the same amount of clay?* Preconserving child will say that the long piece has more clay. Conserving child will say that the two pieces have the same amount of clay.	7–8
Area	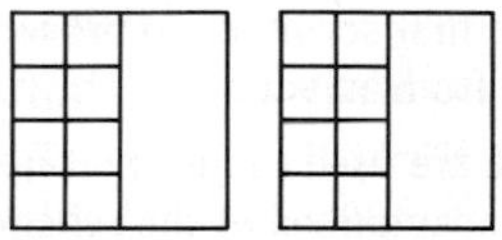 Center two identical sheets of cardboard with wooden blocks placed on them in identical positions. Child acknowledges that the same amount of space is left open on each piece of cardboard.	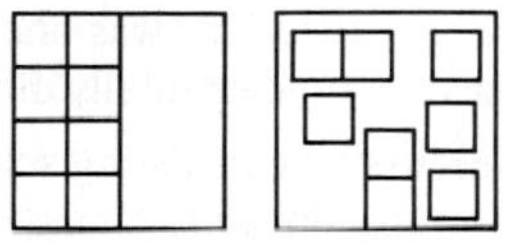 scatters the blocks on one piece of cardboard.	*Do the two pieces of cardboard have the same amount of open space?* Preconserving child will say that the cardboard with scattered blocks has less open space. Conserving child will say that both pieces have the same amount of open space.	8–9
Volume	 Center two balls of clay in two identical glasses with an equal amount of water. Child acknowledges that they displace equal amounts of water.	 changes the shape of one of the balls.	*Do the two pieces of clay displace the same amount of water?* Preconserving child will say that the longer piece displaces more water. Conserving child will say that both pieces displace the same amount of water.	14–15

Figure 9.10 A sample of the various experiments devised to test for Piagetian forms of conservation. You may want to try these tests on children of various ages.

man, 1987). In the familiar surroundings of home, for example, children as young as two or three will (occasionally) show empathy for a younger sibling and will also use different vocabulary when communicating with an adult versus another child. Thus, they show an ability to consider another's perspective—a quality thought to be lacking in the egocentric preoperational child.

Finally, Piaget has been criticized for overemphasizing the biological determinants of cognitive development and for his insistence on a rigid stage theory. Piaget insisted that cognitive development results from maturation (a naturist perspective) and that all human thinking proceeds through four qualitatively discrete stages. As we mentioned at the beginning of this chapter, the issue of stage theory and the related debates over stability versus change and nature versus nurture are continuing controversies in psychology.

Monkeys and humans differ in many ways, so caution is always advised in generalizing from animal experiments to the human experience. However, Harlow's findings suggest that physical contact (holding, caressing, rocking) might be an important factor in human attachment. Researchers such as Klaus and Kennell (1976) have, in fact, suggested that early skin contact and touching between human mother and child immediately after birth is an essential part of "bonding" (see Chapter 3). Although the importance of the first few hours of life on long-term attachment may have been overstated (see Chess and Thomas, 1986; Kennell and Klaus, 1984), children undoubtedly benefit from lots of cuddling and caressing, and attachment remains an important part of normal psychosocial development.

Question: What happens if a child doesn't form an attachment?   To investigate this question, many researchers have looked at children or adults who spent their early years in institutions. Although many institutions provide excellent child care, some are so poorly funded and understaffed that they can only meet the physical needs of the children. Research has generally found that infants raised in such impersonal surroundings without significant touching and individualized mothering suffer from a number of problems. They tend to show intellectual, physical, and perceptual retardation, increased susceptibility to infection, neurotic "rocking" and isolation behaviors, and in some cases death (Bowlby, 1973, 1982; Dennis, 1973; Spitz and Wolf, 1946).

While most children are never exposed to such harsh conditions, Mary Ainsworth and her colleagues (1967, 1978) have found significant differences in the *level* of attachment between infants and their mothers that can produce long-term differences in behavior. Using a method called the *strange situation procedure,* in which the researcher observes infants in the presence or absence of their mother and a stranger, these researchers found they could divide children into three groups:

1. *Securely attached.* The infant seeks closeness and contact with the mother, uses the mother as a safe base from which to explore, shows moderate distress upon separation, and is enthusiastic when the mother returns.
2. *Avoidant.* The infant does not seek proximity or contact with the mother, treats the mother much like the stranger, and rarely cries when the mother leaves the room.
3. *Anxious – ambivalent.* The infant becomes very upset as the mother leaves the room, but when she returns they seek close contact while also squirming angrily to get away.

In related studies, securely attached children have been found to be more sociable, enthusiastic, cooperative, persistent, curious, competent, and likely to have internalized controls versus controls by external, authority figures (Hartup, 1989; Jacobson and Wille, 1986; Pastor, 1981; Weston and Richardson, 1985). Such personality differences often persist into adulthood (Kobak and Sceery, 1988). An intriguing study conducted by Cindy Hazen and Phillip Shaver (1987) also found that adult love styles often show a striking resemblance to their infant pattern of attachment. According to their findings, romantic love is an attachment process, and a person who had an anxious – ambivalent attachment in infancy will tend to have adult romantic relations characterized by anxiety and ambivalence. In other words, we relive our early attachment patterns in our intimate adult relationships.

During their survey of adult love patterns, Hazen and Shaver discovered that *secure adults* find it relatively easy to establish intimate, trusting relations with others. *Anxious – ambivalent adults* on the other hand, experience volatile, jealous relationships and report a preoccupation with love and strong fears of rejection. *Avoidant adults* experience difficulty in getting close to others and describe their love relations as lacking in intimacy. The childhood recollections of these same three groups of adults were consistent with the idea that we relive our infant attachment experiences in our adult romances.

Although Hazen and Shaver's theory has generated a great deal of popular attention, it is important to remember that the results of a single survey should always be regarded as tentative. Further research is necessary before we can fully understand the link between infant attachment and adult intimate relations. Nonetheless, this research illustrates the potential importance of early social bonds and later adult development.

Personality development in childhood: The effects of child-rearing methods

How much of our personality comes from the way our parents treat us as we are growing up? Researchers since the 1920's have attempted to study the effects of different methods of child rearing on children's behavior, development, and mental health (Baldwin, 1949; Schaefer, 1960). Some of the most recent studies, by Diana Baumrind (1980), found that parenting styles could be reliably divided into three distinct patterns: authoritarian, permissive, and authoritative. *Authoritarian* parents value unquestioning obedience and mature responsibility from the child, while remaining aloof and detached. *Permissive* parents give their children lots of warmth, affection, and freedom, but since they also do not feel in control they administer lax and inconsistent discipline. *Authoritative* parents set firm limits and enforce them, while also encouraging increasing responsibility and being loving and understanding.

Is it better to wait until your 30's or 40's to have children? Given that a large number of couples are currently delaying parenthood, psychologists are actively researching this topic.

Question: How did these three styles affect the children?   As you might expect, children did best under the authoritative parents (Lewis, 1981). They became self-reliant, self-controlled, and high-achieving. They also seemed more content, friendly, and socially competent in their dealings with others. The children of the permissive parents, on the other hand, were the least self-reliant and controlled and seemed unhappy, immature, and overly dependent. The children of the authoritarian parents fell somewhere in between. Although they were confident and self-reliant, they also seemed discontent, distrustful, and socially withdrawn.

Based on Baumrind's studies it seems that children would benefit the most from parents who personally model the behavior they want from their children (if you want your child to knock before entering your bedroom, you should also knock on theirs). Parents should also seek out the child's opinion and give reasonable explanations when demanding compliance, and should frequently express love, warmth, and pride in the child's accomplishment.

Before you conclude that this is the only way to successfully raise children, you should know that other studies have found that even though permissive parents tend to produce difficult children, these children eventually become cooperative, caring adults (McClelland et al., 1978). Baumrind's findings have also been criticized on grounds that children's temperaments may also play a principal role in parenting styles (Lewis, 1981). The parents of mature and competent children may have developed the authoritative parenting style *because* of the child's behavior rather than vice versa. Although Baumrind (1983) refutes this, it is important to recognize that all behavior involves both the child and the parent, not to mention the situation and other social forces.

Question: Do fathers differ from mothers in their parenting style?   Until recently, the father's role in discipline and child care was largely ignored. But as more fathers have begun to take an active role in child rearing, there has been a corresponding increase in research. From these studies we now know that fathers are absorbed, excited, and responsive to their newborns (Greenberg and Morris, 1974; Lamb, 1977) and that there are few differences in the way children form attachments to either parent (Hartup, 1989). After infancy, the father becomes increasingly involved with his children, yet he still spends less overall time in direct child care than the mother (Campos et al., 1983; Collins and Russell, 1988; Hartup, 1989). Although the mother may remain the primary caregiver in most families, the father continues to be an important source of love and security for the developing child.

Theories of personality development: Psychoanalytic, learning, and cognitive

To what extent is personality influenced by genetics and to what extent is it influenced by environmental influences? In the classic nature versus nurture controversy, the nativists often point to studies that find a strong hereditary component in personality traits such as sociability, emotionality, and activity level (Pedersen et al., 1988; Plomin, 1989). Most developmental psychologists also accept the fact that infants are born with distinct and demonstrable differences in **temperament.** These inborn, dispositional qualities help to explain why some babies tend to smile and laugh almost all the time and eagerly approach strangers, whereas others are fussy or shy. Thomas and Chess (1977) found that approximately 60 percent of the babies they observed could be reliably separated into three categories:

1. *Easy children* who were happy most of the time, were relaxed and agreeable, and adjusted easily to new situations (approximately 40 percent).
2. *Difficult children* who were moody, easily frustrated, tense, and overreactive to most situations (approximately 10 percent).
3. *Slow-to-warm-up children* who showed mild responses, were somewhat shy and withdrawn, and needed time to adjust to new experiences or people (approximately 10 percent).

Follow-up studies of these infants found that these basic temperamental styles tended to be consistent and enduring into childhood and even adulthood—an indicator that at least some aspects of personality are inborn.

One of the strongest arguments for the influence of inborn, biological forces in personality development comes from the work of Sigmund Freud (1856–1939) and the psychoanalytic tradition.

The psychoanalytic perspective   Freud (1905) believed that personality develops during childhood in five distinct *psychosexual stages.* These stages are examined in detail in Chapter 14. Although many of Freud's specific beliefs about the stages of childhood have been criticized (e.g., Masson, 1983), his theories revolutionized our concept of children and the importance of early childhood experiences.

The work of Erik Erikson is probably the best example of the continuing influence of Freud's ideas on modern-day psychology. Like Freud, Erikson believes that human development progresses through a sequence of stages. At each stage the individual faces a developmental crisis or conflict that must be resolved before advancement to the next stage. But whereas Freud thought that personality was pretty much set by age five or six, Erikson suggests that personality development continues throughout the life span. He also believes that Freud underestimated the power of many social and cultural influences on human behavior. To reflect these changes, he developed a life-span, eight-stage **psychosocial theory** of development, with separate psychosocial conflicts at each stage (Table 9.4).

Erikson's first stage, **trust versus mistrust,** occurs from birth to approximately one year. During this period of development, the infant is almost completely dependent on the external world for basic survival and satisfaction of needs. When and how these needs are met will determine whether the infant decides that the world is a good and satisfying place to live in or a source of pain, frustration, and uncertainty. If caregivers respond with warm affection and reasonable regularity, the infant will develop a feeling of trust toward the world. But if the infant receives erratic care from an impatient, hostile, anxious, or tense adult, he or she may develop a lifetime sense of mistrust.

Autonomy versus shame and doubt, the second of Erikson's stages, covers the years from one to three. The infant is moving away from babyhood and approaching childhood by developing a sense of self-awareness and a need for independence. In this search for autonomy, the child begins to gain control over bowels and bladder and to show strong preferences for certain clothes, foods, and bedtime rituals. The toddler begins to

TEMPERAMENT: *A basic, inborn dispositional quality that appears shortly after birth and characterizes an individual's style of approaching people and situations.*

PSYCHOSOCIAL THEORY: *Erikson's theory that individuals undergo a series of eight developmental stages and that adult personality reflects successful or unsuccessful resolution of the distinct challenges or crises at each stage.*

TRUST VERSUS MISTRUST: *The first of Erikson's eight stages of psychosocial development (from birth to 12–18 months), in which the infant must determine whether the world and the people in it can be trusted.*

AUTONOMY VERSUS SHAME AND DOUBT: *Erikson's second psychosocial stage (from 12 months to three years), in which the child's crisis or challenge is to develop independence and self-assertion.*

During Erikson's first stage of development (trust versus mistrust), infants pick up important cues about the world from the way they are handled and cared for by adults.

TABLE 9.4
Erikson's Stages

Approximate age	Stage	Description
Birth to 1 year	Trust versus mistrust	Infants learn to trust that their needs will be met by the world, especially by the mother; if not, mistrust develops
1 to 3 years	Autonomy versus shame and doubt	Children learn to exercise will, to make choices, to control themselves; if not, they become uncertain and doubt that they can do things by themselves
3 to 5 years	Initiative versus guilt	Children learn to initiate activities and enjoy their accomplishments, acquiring direction and purpose; if they are not allowed initiative, they feel guilty for their attempts at independence
6 years through puberty	Industry versus inferiority	Children develop a sense of industry and curiosity and are eager to learn; if not, they feel inferior and lose interest in the tasks before them
Adolescence	Identity versus role confusion	Adolescents come to see themselves as unique and integrated persons with an ideology; if not, they become confused about what they want out of life
Early adulthood	Intimacy versus isolation	Young people become able to commit themselves to another person; if not, they develop a sense of isolation and feel they have no one in the world but themselves
Middle age	Generativity versus stagnation	Adults are willing to have and care for children, to devote themselves to their work and the common good; if not, they become self-centered and inactive
Old age	Integrity versus despair	Older people enter a period of reflection, becoming assured that their lives have been meaningful, and they grow ready to face death with acceptance and dignity; if not, they despair for their unaccomplished goals, failures, and ill-spent lives

(*Source:* Adapted from Clarke-Stewart, A.; Friedman, S.; and Koch, J., 1985. *Child development: A topical approach.* Copyright © 1985 by John Wiley & Sons, Inc. Reprinted by permission of John Wiley & Sons, Inc.)

This type of exploration and "initiative" is normal and expected behavior. If this little girl's parents are overly harsh and critical, however, she may develop lasting feelings of guilt and self-doubt.

insist on trying to dress himself or herself, to pick out clothes to wear, to push the stroller rather than ride in it, and to refuse parental offers to help or parental commands and requests. If the parents handle these beginning attempts at independence with patience and good-humored encouragement, the toddler will develop a sense of autonomy: conversely, if the child faces ridicule, impatience, or strong parental insistence on control, feelings of shame and doubt will develop.

During the stage of **initiative versus guilt** (ages three to five), the major conflict is between a child's desire to initiate activities and the guilt that comes from unwanted or unexpected consequences. Erikson believed that during this stage children may begin to incorporate criticism and punishment into their self-images, learning to experience not only shame but also guilt. According to Erikson, children need to discover various activities and outlets for their frustrations that will also provide opportunities for growth and accomplishment. If loving adults provide an environment that encourages the ever-increasing need for independence and provide opportunities for interaction with other children, the child will develop feelings of power and initiative rather than of guilt and doubt. (Can you see how the training offered by Doman might lead to doubt in the previous stage and guilt in this stage unless the trainers are patient, are supportive, and provide challenges that won't frustrate or discourage the child?)

INITIATIVE VERSUS GUILT: *The third stage in Erikson's psychosocial theory of development (ages three to six), in which the child must overcome feelings of guilt and doubt and develop feelings of power and initiative.*

INDUSTRY VERSUS INFERIORITY:
Erikson's fourth psychosocial stage of development (ages 6 to 11), in which the child faces the challenge of mastering the skills needed to succeed in his or her culture.

During the stage of **industry versus inferiority** (six years through puberty), the child is primarily involved in an elaborate development of intellectual and physical skills. This development naturally includes lots of competition and skill comparisons. How the child's successes and failures are handled by the external world will determine whether she or he develops feelings of competency and industriousness or feelings of insecurity and inferiority.

Because the final four stages of Erikson's psychosocial theory deal with adolescence and adulthood, we will describe them in the next chapter.

Learning theories   In contrast to the psychoanalytic theorists, learning theorists emphasize the power of the immediate situation and observable behavior rather than "stages" and inferred mental processes (such as feelings of initiative and guilt). They also object to theories that consider personality to be a stable, consistent core of an individual that is somewhat evident at birth (e.g., Block, 1982; Costa and McCrae, 1988). According to the learning perspective, children develop certain personality "habits" as a result of particular patterns of rewards and punishments they experience. Individual differences occur because each of us grows up in a slightly different environment and is rewarded for different behaviors. The social learning theorists expand on this idea and suggest that personality develops as a result of imitating models. This approach is described in greater detail in Chapter 14.

GENDER ROLE: *The set of behaviors that a given culture expects of each sex.*

One of the most important contributions made by learning theory to our understanding of development is in the area of **gender roles** — the behaviors expected of individuals on the basis of their maleness or femaleness. Learning theorists suggest that children generally imitate the same-sex parent because they receive rewards for doing so. Once the gender identity is formed, social forces condition the child toward acquiring the behaviors of their gender role — girls are rewarded for feminine behavior, and boys are rewarded for masculine behavior. For learning theorists, all male – female differences in behavior can be explained by cultural training.

Cognitive theories   At this point in our discussion, it may seem that children play a rather minor role in their own personality development. They become distrustful, for example, as a result of inconsistent parental treatment or they develop behaviors in response to rewards and punishment. One of the best perspectives to offset this rather

To overcome the limits of traditional sex roles, many parents and preschools now encourage children to engage in activities that were once reserved for one sex or the other.

passive view of the child comes from the cognitive developmental theory. According to this viewpoint, children actively observe, interpret, and judge the world around them and from this develop their own unique explanations and personalities.

Question: How would cognitive theory explain gender role development? One cognitive theorist, Lawrence Kohlberg (1966), suggests that children identify with and imitate same-sex parents, and others of their same gender, because they recognize that these individuals belong to the same category they do (male or female). According to his view, children's understanding of gender advances in concert with their general cognitive development. They first develop a concept of what sex category they belong to *(gender identity)* and only later come to realize that their gender and that of others does not change with age, dress, or behavior *(gender constancy).* Although a three-year-old child can easily tell you, "I am a boy" or "I am a girl," it isn't until they are five or six that they understand that they will always be male or female and that their sex will not change if they wear clothing of the opposite sex (Wehren and De Lisi, 1983). When three-year-old children label the gender of others, they appear to rely on external appearances such as hairstyles and clothing rather than on genital anatomy. For example, after watching the neighbor bathe her newborn, one preschool girl couldn't answer whether the child was male or female. "I don't know," she replied, "it's so hard to tell at that age, especially when it's not wearing clothes" (Stone and Church, 1973).

According to the cognitive perspective, children should not begin to show a preference for masculine or feminine behaviors until they have a well-developed sense of gender identity and gender constancy. Although several studies do support this contention (e.g., Ruble et al., 1981), others have found differences in behavior and preferences in sex-appropriate toys within the first two years of life (Maccoby and Jacklin, 1974; Weinraub et al., 1984). This would seem to indicate an earlier sense of gender identity.

Question: Does this mean that learning theory is a better explanation for gender role development? Many researchers now suggest that the acquisition of gender roles can be best explained by combining elements of both the learning and cognitive perspectives (Jacklin, 1989; Liben and Signorella, 1987). Sandra Bems' (1981, 1985) **gender schema theory** provides this combination. Her theory suggests that children acquire gender-specific behaviors through social learning and conditioning but that cognitive processes help them to organize and integrate gender-related information. Like Kohlberg, Bem asserts that concepts of maleness and femaleness are among the earliest schemata children form. (Recall from our previous discussion of Piaget that schemata are cognitive frameworks for organizing and guiding perceptions.) Rather than simply imitating the gender model that provides the most reinforcement (learning theory), these male or female schemata allow children to shape their own attitudes and beliefs about what is gender-role appropriate.

GENDER SCHEMA THEORY: *A theory developed by Sandra Bem that suggests that children learn gender-specific behaviors and that cognitive processes help them to interpret gender-related information.*

Although developmental psychologists have provided several intriguing theories regarding gender role development, research by psychological anthropologists also provides an important cross-cultural perspective. In a landmark study, Whiting and Edwards (1988) analyzed eleven separate cultures for sex differences and concluded that children's gender role development is largely the result of "the company they keep." Nurturing behavior, for example, is largely due to spending time with an infant. The infant itself seems to bring forth nurturing responses. According to Whiting and Edwards, many cultures, but not all, assign greater child-care responsibilities to young girls. As a function of those responsibilities, females are more likely to become nurturant.

The hypothesis that "we are the company that we keep" is an important contribution to our understanding of gender role development. It also demonstrates the fruitfulness of combining psychological and anthropological research. There is a growing need to combine psychology and anthropology, psychology and sociology, and other disciplines in the search for knowledge of early childhood development. This interdisciplinary approach will also increase our understanding of adolescent and adult development—the topic of our next chapter.

Review Questions

1 An active, intense, emotional bond between two people is known as _____.

2 Harry Harlow's research with cloth and wire mothers found that _____ _____ may be the most important variable in attachment.

3 Mary Ainsworth found _____ _____ children to be more sociable, curious and competent than children who were at a lower level of attachment.

4 _____ parents require obedience and responsibility from their children, _____ parents feel out of control and administer lax or inconsistent discipline, and _____ parents combine the best of both these parenting styles.

5 An infant's inborn, dispositional qualities are known as _____.

6 According to Erikson, the major psychosocial crisis in the first year of life is that of _____ versus _____.

7 _____ theory suggests that gender role behaviors develop as a result of reward and punishments.

8 _____ _____ theory integrates the learning and cognitive perspectives on gender roles.

Answers: 1 attachment; *2* contact comfort; *3* securely attached; *4* authoritarian, permissive, authoritative; *5* temperament; *6* trust, mistrust; *7* learning; *8* gender schema

---

REVIEW OF MAJOR CONCEPTS

STUDYING DEVELOPMENT

1 Developmental psychology is concerned with describing, explaining, predicting, and modifying age-related behaviors across the entire life span. Before the seventeenth century, childhood was not considered to be a separate stage in life with special characteristics different from those of adulthood.

2 The research of developmental psychologists is often directed toward the issues of stability versus change and nature versus nurture. They want to know to what extent you can predict adult behaviors from childhood observations ("Is it stable?"), and whether observed differences between individuals result mostly from biology or from the environment.

3 Researchers in this field use basic scientific methods such as surveys, experiments, and so on, as well as employing baby biographies and personal narratives. Two of the most widely used methods of data collection are cross-sectional and longitudinal studies, each with its own advantages and disadvantages. These disadvantages are largely offset by the newer techniques of cohort-sequential research.

PHYSICAL DEVELOPMENT

4 The prenatal period of development involves three major stages: the germinal period, the embryonic period, and the period of the fetus. The embryonic period is a true critical period in development and the embryo is at particular risk for major birth defects.

5 Physical development is often affected by genetic influences. Some characteristics such as eye color result from dominant or recessive genes, whereas other traits like color blindness and baldness are sex-linked or sex-influenced. Most genetic influences on development are polygenic—the result of a combination of genes and interaction with the environment.

6 Physical development also results from environmental influences. Poor prenatal nutrition is a leading cause of birth defects, and most drugs (both prescription and over-the-counter) are potentially teratogenic (capable of producing birth defects). Doctors advise pregnant women to avoid all unnecessary drugs, especially nicotine and alcohol. The father's behavior may also contribute to birth defects.

7 During the prenatal period and the first year of life, the brain and nervous system grow faster than all other parts of the body. Early motor development (crawling, standing, and walking) is largely the result of maturation. Early physical abilities are not connected with higher intelligence and practice will not cause some children to walk sooner than others.

8 Contrary to earlier beliefs, psychologists now know that the sensory and perceptual abilities of newborns are relatively well developed.

LANGUAGE DEVELOPMENT

9 Language development involves both verbal and nonverbal channels. Through facial expressions, eye contact, and body gestures, infants communicate many things long before their first verbal skills appear.

10 Children go through two stages in their acquisition of language: prelinguistic (crying, cooing, babbling) and linguistic (which includes single utterances, telegraphic speech, and the acquisition of rules of grammar).

11 Nativists believe that language is an inborn capacity and develops primarily from maturation. Noam Chomsky suggests that humans are "prewired" for language and possess a language acquisition device that needs only minimal environmental input.

12 Nurturists emphasize the role of the environment and suggest that language development results from rewards and punishments and imitation of models. Although this position does explain why a child learns a specific language, it fails to explain novel speech or the fact that children around the world go through predictable stages at relatively the same age.

COGNITIVE DEVELOPMENT

13 Jean Piaget, perhaps more than any other researcher, has demonstrated the unique cognitive processes of children. He believed that children are driven toward knowledge because of their biological need for adaptation to the environment. During adaptation, the child uses schemata (mental patterns or blueprints) to interpret the world. Sometimes existing schemata can be used "as is" and information is assimilated, but on other occasions the situation requires modification of existing schemata, which calls for accommodation.

14 In Piaget's view, cognitive development occurs in an invariant sequence of four stages: sensorimotor (birth to 2 years), preoperational (from 2 to 7 years), concrete operational (from 7 to 11 years), and formal operational (from 11 and over).

15 The sensorimotor stage is characterized by the acquisition of object permanence — the realization that objects (or people) continue to exist even when they are out of sight. During the preoperational stage, children are better equipped to use symbols, but their thinking is also egocentric and animistic. The concrete operational stage is characterized by the acquisition of operations and increased logic. During the formal operational stage, the adolescent is able to think abstractly and deal with the hypothetical.

16 Although Piaget has been criticized for his insistence on the invariance of his stages and his biological emphasis, he remains one of the most respected psychologists in modern times.

PSYCHOSOCIAL DEVELOPMENT

17 Nativists believe that attachment is innate, whereas nurturists believe it is learned. Harlow's experiment with rhesus monkeys raised by cloth or wire surrogate mothers found that contact comfort may be the most important factor in attachment.

18 Infants who fail to form attachments may suffer serious effects. When attachments are formed, there may be differences in the level or degree. Research on securely attached, avoidant, and ambivalent children found significant differences in behaviors that often persist into adulthood.

19 Investigations of various styles of parenting found three major patterns: authoritarian, permissive, and authoritative. Each method had varying effects on the child's development.

20 Nativist theories of personality development emphasize the genetic component of certain traits (such as sociability) and the fact that babies often exhibit differences in temperament shortly after birth.

21 Erik Erikson expanded on Freud's ideas and developed eight psychosocial stages that cover the entire life span. The four stages that occur during childhood are trust versus mistrust, autonomy versus shame and doubt, initiative versus guilt, and industry versus inferiority.

22 Learning theories emphasize the importance of the environment on personality. Through rewards, punishments, and imitation of models the child develops certain personality "habits." Whereas psychoanalytic theory sees gender role behavior as a result of identification, learning theory suggests that children develop masculine or feminine traits because they are rewarded for imitating the same-sex parent.

23 The cognitive theory of personality development emphasizes the active, thinking processes of the individual. Kohlberg explains gender roles as a result of the development of the concepts of gender identity and gender constancy. Sandra Bem integrates the learning and cognitive perspectives with her gender schema theory.

SUGGESTED READINGS

CLARKE-STEWART, A., FRIEDMAN, S., & KOCH, J. (1988). *Child development: A topical approach* (2nd ed.). New York: Wiley. A comprehensive, current, and engrossing general textbook that discusses the major developmental changes from conception through adolescence.

DOMAN, G. (1979). *Teach your baby math.* New York: Pocket Books. Glen Doman's personal account of his daily learning program designed to teach math to very young children.

ELKIND, D. (1981). *The hurried child: Growing up too fast too soon.* Reading, MA: Addison–Wesley. In sharp contrast to the positive reports of Glen Doman, David Elkind warns that introducing children to formal education at too young an age may lead to dangerous physical, educational, and psychological damage.

FLAVELL, J. H. (1985). *Cognitive development* (2nd ed.). Englewood Cliffs, NJ: Prentice–Hall. An in-depth analysis of cognitive growth from infancy through adolescence.

LEWIS, D. (1978). *The secret language of your child.* New York: Berkley Books. A book that shows adults how to improve their interactions with small children by learning to interpret the child's nonverbal messages.

chapter ten
Later Development

A T 17, Richard H. is ambivalent about his age. On some days he feels happy to be so young and just starting life, but at other times he complains that his age limits his access to alcohol, makes him pay too much for car insurance, and encourages some adults to treat him with less respect than he feels he deserves. His 20-year-old sister, Kandis H., also experiences ambivalence about her age. Although she often daydreams about all the exciting possibilities ahead of her ("Do I want to be a model, an actress, an obstetrician, or even governor?"), she also worries that she hasn't finalized her career plans. One of her strongest fears is that at middle age (which she feels begins around age 30 or 35) she will find herself locked into a career or marriage that she doesn't enjoy and that she'll regret not choosing another alternative.

At 43, William B. (stepfather to Richard and Kandis) is concerned about his age. He appreciates the greater wisdom that has come with life experience, but he also worries about recent physical reminders of aging. "I can't run as far as I did ten years ago," he says. "I also don't enjoy late night parties like I once did, and I wonder if I'll be able to work as long as I had planned."

At 80, Maggie Kuhn is proud of her age—"My wrinkles are a badge of distinction. I earned them" (*New York Times*, 1984). She notes that people spend a large portion of their life worrying about growing old and covering all signs of aging with hair colors, "line preventors," makeup, and so on. But once they reach retirement age and older, people are often pleasantly surprised at the many pleasures of this stage of life. As founder of one of the most active lobbyist groups in America, the Gray Panthers, Maggie Kuhn works long hours and travels all over the world to educate others about the real and imagined problems of growing old.

Above Photo: William B., Kandis H., and Richard H. during a family celebration.

Of these four individuals, who are you most like? Like Richard or Kandis, are you just beginning your college education and worrying and dreaming about potential careers? Or are you more like William or Maggie Kuhn and perhaps taking this course in hopes of a career change, as part of continuing education, or just for personal enrichment? Although you are undoubtedly different from each of these individuals, you also share some important similarities with those who are in your own age group. The exact nature of these differences and similarities is of prime interest to developmental psychologists. As we discussed in Chapter 9, *developmental psychology* is devoted to the study of age-related behaviors from conception to death. This chapter continues our study beyond childhood by looking at physical and behavioral changes that occur during adolescence and adulthood.

PHYSICAL DEVELOPMENT

The physical changes that occur with the onset of adolescence are noticeable and dramatic. Physical changes beyond adolescence are more gradual but nevertheless significant.

Adolescence: A time of rapid physical change

Think back for a moment to the start of your own adolescence. Did you have many concerns about the physical changes you were going through? Did you worry about how you differed from your classmates? Differences in height and weight, the growth of breasts and menstruation for girls, and the deepening of voices and growth of beards for boys are all important milestones for adolescents. **Puberty,** the period of life when a person becomes capable of reproduction, is a major physical milestone in everyone's life. It serves as a clear biological signal of the end of childhood. Although commonly associated with puberty, **adolescence** is the loosely defined psychological period of development between childhood and adulthood. In the United States, it roughly corresponds to the teenage years. It is important to recognize that adolescence, like childhood, is not a universal concept. Some nonindustrialized countries have no need for such a slow transition, and children simply assume as many adult responsibilities as soon as possible.

The clearest and most dramatic physical sign of both puberty and adolescence is the *growth spurt,* which is characterized by rapid increases in height, weight, and skeletal growth. Do you remember feelings of awkwardness, anxiety, and confusion at this time in your life? Growth during early stages of development is *proximo-distal* (near to far), with the head and upper body developing before the lower body. Growth at puberty, however, is **distal-proximo** (far to near), which results in faster development of hands, feet, nose, lips, and ears. This type of development, along with the characteristically unequal development of the two halves of the body (one foot, breast, or hand can be temporarily larger than the other), often explains adolescent awkwardness.

Adolescence also is a time for rapid changes in reproductive structures and sexual characteristics. As a result of maturation and the secretion of hormones, the adolescent female body experiences rapid development of the ovaries, uterus, and vagina and undergoes the *menarche* (the onset of the menstrual cycle). At the same time the adolescent male experiences development of the testes, scrotum, and penis. The ovaries and testes are then responsible for producing the hormones that lead to the development of **secondary**

PUBERTY: *The period in life during which the sex organs mature to a point where sexual reproduction becomes possible. Puberty generally begins for girls around 8 to 12 years of age, and for boys about two years later.*

ADOLESCENCE: *The psychological period of development between childhood and adulthood, which in the United States roughly corresponds to the teenage years.*

DISTAL-PROXIMO: *Physical development in an outer to inner direction, such that peripheral development outdistances that along the central axis.*

BLOOM COUNTY   **by Berke Breathed**

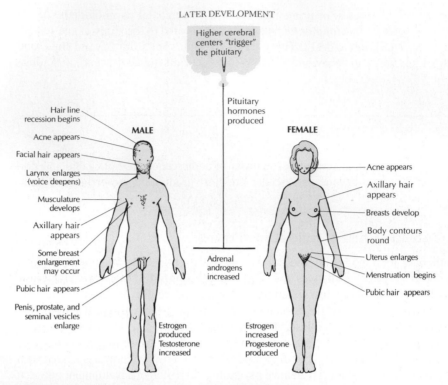

LATER DEVELOPMENT

Higher cerebral centers "trigger" the pituitary

Pituitary hormones produced

MALE

FEMALE

Hair line recession begins

Acne appears

Facial hair appears

Larynx enlarges (voice deepens)

Musculature develops

Axillary hair appears

Some breast enlargement may occur

Pubic hair appears

Penis, prostate, and seminal vesicles enlarge

Adrenal androgens increased

Estrogen produced Testosterone increased

Acne appears

Axillary hair appears

Breasts develop

Body contours round

Uterus enlarges

Menstruation begins

Pubic hair appears

Estrogen increased Progesterone produced

Figure 10.1 Secondary sex characteristics. The effects of hormones on physical changes at puberty are complex. Hormones are secreted not only from the ovaries and testes but also from the pituitary gland in the brain and the adrenal cortex.

SECONDARY SEX CHARACTERISTICS: *Hormonally generated sexual characteristics, secondary to the sex organs, that are not necessary for reproduction.*

sex characteristics, such as pubic hair, deepening of the voice, facial hair, breasts, and so on (see Figure 10.1).

How these physical changes affect an individual's psychological adjustment may depend on how quickly he or she matures. Early maturation for boys has been found to be correlated with higher school achievement, positive body image, positive moods, and higher regard from both peers and adults (Petersen, 1988; Tanner, 1982). In addition, most boys are about two years behind most girls in the pubertal growth spurt (see Figure 10.2). Thus, early-maturing males may also enjoy an important social advantage over other boys because of their increased height and physical abilities.

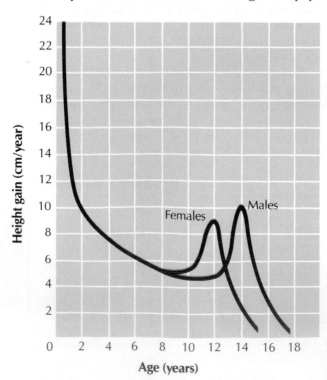

Figure 10.2 The adolescent growth spurt. Notice how the female spurt precedes the male one, so that girls tend to be taller than boys from the ages of 10 to 14.

Normal male and female differences in height during adolescence are particularly apparent during social activities.

The effects of early or late maturation for girls are less clear. Although early-maturing females do seem to have higher school achievement and show more independence, they also tend to have a lower self-esteem, poorer body image, and more conflicts with their parents (Blyth et al., 1981; Petersen, 1987).

Question: Why is early maturation not as positive for girls?   Anne Petersen and her colleagues have speculated that academic success may come at a high social cost for adolescent girls. They found that when early-maturing girls lowered their academic achievement, their popularity and self-image increased (Petersen et al., 1987). In addition, the poor body image of these girls may be due to their increased levels of estrogen. Given that estrogen inhibits long bone growth and increases the percentage of fatty tissue, early-maturing females tend to be shorter and stockier than late-maturing females. In a society that values tallness and slimness in females, it is not surprising that early-maturing females tend to have a poorer body image. Finally, parents of early-maturing girls tend to increase their viligance and restrictiveness, which may explain increased parent – child conflicts (Savin-Williams and Small, 1986).

All is not entirely rosy for the early-maturing boy, however. He may enjoy his early height advantage and greater strength, but he lacks a comparison group to reassure him that some changes (such as acne and the temporary enlargement of the breasts) are also normal and transitory. The desire to be "normal" is perhaps the one element that is common to almost all adolescents. Even when early development results in culturally valued changes, such as beards and deepened voices in males, these changes are sometimes disadvantageous, since they may lead to teasing or exclusion from the group that has not developed at the same rate.

Adulthood: The process of aging

Once the large and obvious pubertal changes have occurred, further age-related physical changes are less dramatic. Beyond some continued increase in height and muscular development during the late teens and early twenties, most individuals experience only minor physical changes until middle age. For the female, **menopause,** the cessation of the menstrual cycle, which occurs somewhere between the ages of 45 and 55, is the second most important milestone in physical development. Although the decreased production of the female hormone *estrogen* does lead to certain physical changes, the popular belief that menopause (or "the change of life") causes serious psychological mood swings, loss of sexual interest, and depression is not supported by current research (Davis, 1989; McKinlay and McKinlay, 1986). The menopause, like most developmental changes, is

MENOPAUSE: *The gradual cessation of menstruation that occurs between the ages of 45 and 55; sometimes referred to as the climacteric or change of life.*

Note the age-related changes in the size of the nose and lips and the relative prominence of the chin and forehead.

associated with both advantages and disadvantages and with a wide variation in individual responses.

Beginning in middle adulthood, males experience a gradual decline in the production of sperm and *testosterone* (the male hormone), although they may remain capable of reproduction well into their eighties or nineties. Physical changes such as unexpected weight gain, loss of muscle strength, and graying or loss of hair may lead some men (and women as well) to feel depressed and to question their life goals, since they see these changes as a biological signal of aging and mortality. Such physical and psychological changes in males are known as the **male climacteric.** Whether all of these changes are an inevitable part of biological aging is called into question by the outstanding physical achievements of some older individuals, such as fitness guru Jack La Lanne. At the age of 45, La Lanne did 1000 push-ups and 1000 chin-ups in 82 minutes, at 60 he swam almost a mile in San Francisco Bay towing a 1000-pound boat while wearing handcuffs and leg shackles, and at the age of 70, again while shackled, swam a mile while towing 70 manned rowboats (Dorman, 1986).

MALE CLIMACTERIC: *A term used to describe the physical and psychological changes associated with the male's movement into midlife.*

Other changes with age include alterations in the heart and arteries, nervous system, and sensory receptors. As the circulatory system ages, cardiac output (the volume of blood pumped by the heart each minute) decreases, and blood pressure increases because of the thickening and stiffening of arterial walls. Studies of the central nervous system (the brain and spinal cord) show that with age the brain appears to shrink, the number of neurons stabilizes, and some simple reflexes (such as the knee jerk) may weaken or disappear (Rakic, 1985; Rockstein and Sussman, 1979). As sensory systems age, visual acuity and depth perception decline, hearing acuity lessens, especially for high-frequency sounds, and smell sensitivity decreases (Cunningham and Brookbank, 1988).

Such physical changes have several important psychological implications. Although the progressive deterioration of vision may cause a middle-aged man such as William B. to hold his reading at arm's length or to begin to wear glasses for the first time in his life, the problems are much more serious for the elderly. Poorer vision means that pleasures such as reading and television viewing are limited and that they are at greater risk as pedestrians and drivers. Similarly, hearing losses can restrict conversations with others, which often results in a sense of increasing social isolation.

Perhaps the most frightening aspect of aging is the increased risk of developing diseases that attack the brain and nervous system. These age-related disorders include

Alzheimer's disease and Parkinson's disease. **Alzheimer's disease** is a progressive deterioration of the brain characterized by loss of memory, confusion, and personality deterioration (see Chapter 7). **Parkinson's disease** is a neurological disorder characterized by rigidity, tremor, and difficulty in controlling movements.

Question: This all sounds pretty depressing. Can anything be done about it? Since many declines in ability are gradual, people generally have time to adjust and adapt to the changes. Some sensory problems, such as reduced visual acuity and certain types of hearing loss, can also be improved with eyeglasses and hearing aids. One of the most exciting ideas for the possible treatment of Alzheimer's or Parkinson's disease is the use of brain grafts. After initial success in Sweden with tissue transplanted from the adrenal glands to the brain in four patients with Parkinson's, later researchers attempted similar transplants and reported conflicting results (Davies, 1988; Lindvall et al., 1990). Freed (1988) suggests that only time and further investigation will resolve the questions surrounding this controversial procedure.

Many supposedly "inevitable" age-related changes, such as reduced lung capacity, increased blood pressure, loss of muscle mass, and even some wrinkling of the skin, may be the result of environmental factors and individual lifestyles (Rodin and Salovey, 1989). Exposure to the sun, wind, and abrasion, for example, is an important factor in skin damage. Personal factors such as nutrition, smoking, exercise, and degree of stress (see Chapter 13) may also affect physical health (Toufexis, 1988). Changes in lifestyles (e.g., decreased smoking, increased leisure activities and exercise, and changed eating habits) have allowed older people to maintain most of their physical and mental abilities (Horn and Meer, 1987).

It is also important to recognize that not all body systems age at the same rate — someone might have poor vision or hearing but have a sturdy heart and circulatory system. Furthermore, there is considerable variation among individuals (Meaney et al., 1988). Some people may get their first gray hairs or signs of balding as teenagers, whereas others may go their entire life with no signs of either. Despite the inevitable nature of some physical changes, individuals from many different walks of life continue to be active and productive throughout their entire life span (see Figure 10.3).

Question: What causes us to age and eventually die? If we set aside considerations of **secondary aging**, which results from disease, disuse, or abuse through certain lifestyles and environmental factors, we are left with the gradual changes that constitute **primary aging**. Although scientists do not really know what causes primary aging, there are two main theories that account for it. According to *programmed theories,* aging is genetically controlled (Cunningham and Brookbank, 1988). Once the ovum is fertilized, the program for aging and death is set and begins to run. Researcher Leonard

ALZHEIMER'S DISEASE: *An irreversible, progressive deterioration of the brain characterized by serious loss of memory.*
PARKINSON'S DISEASE: *A neurological disorder characterized by rigidity, tremor, and difficulty in controlling movements, believed to be caused by a dopamine deficiency.*

SECONDARY AGING: *Acceleration in the normal physical changes associated with aging as a result of abuse, neglect, disuse, or disease.*
PRIMARY AGING: *Gradual changes in physical and mental processes that inevitably occur with age.*

Throughout the lifespan, physical exercise is one of the best ways to insure a healthy and productive life.

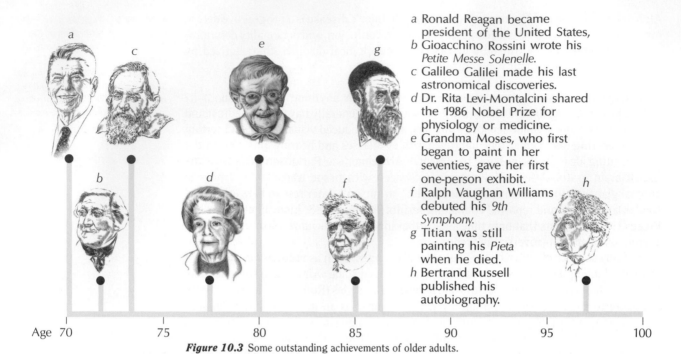

a Ronald Reagan became president of the United States,
b Gioacchino Rossini wrote his *Petite Messe Solenelle.*
c Galileo Galilei made his last astronomical discoveries.
d Dr. Rita Levi-Montalcini shared the 1986 Nobel Prize for physiology or medicine.
e Grandma Moses, who first began to paint in her seventies, gave her first one-person exhibit.
f Ralph Vaughan Williams debuted his *9th Symphony.*
g Titian was still painting his *Pieta* when he died.
h Bertrand Russell published his autobiography.

Figure 10.3 Some outstanding achievements of older adults.

Hayflick (1977, 1980) found that human cells seem to have a built-in life span. After about 50 doublings of laboratory-cultured cells, they cease to multiply — they have reached *the Hayflick limit.* Other theorists suggest that the programming is in the immunological system, which, with age, begins to lose its ability to recognize and fight off foreign substances and may begin to self-destruct (Walford, 1983).

The second approach to explaining primary aging is the *wear-and-tear theory,* which proposes that everyday life damages biological systems and limits their ability to repair themselves. Internal and external stressors gradually wear out the cells and they stop dividing. Whichever theory is correct, human beings appear to have a maximum life span of about 110 to 120 years. Although we can try to control secondary aging in an attempt to reach that maximum, so far we have no means to control the inevitability of primary aging.

Review Questions

1 The period of life when an individual first becomes capable of reproduction is known as _____.

2 During the early stages of development, growth is _____ (from near to far), whereas growth during adolescence is _____ (from far to near).

3 _____ _____ _____ (such as deepening of the voice, pubic hair, and breasts) are primarily produced by hormones from the ovaries and testes.

4 The psychological equivalent to the female menopause for the male is the _____ _____.

5 With aging, cardiac output, some simple reflexes, vision acuity, depth perception, and smell sensitivity all _____.

6 Aging due primarily to disease, disuse, or abuse is known as _____ aging.

COGNITIVE DEVELOPMENT

In Chapter 9 we introduced Piaget's stage theory of cognitive development and described his first three stages: sensorimotor (birth to age 2), preoperational (ages 2 to 7), and concrete operational (ages 7 to 11). Here we will examine Piaget's fourth stage, formal operations. We will then explore the possibility of a fifth stage that reflects the continued growth of cognitive abilities in adulthood.

The formal operational stage: Piaget's final stage of development

During Piaget's **formal operational stage** (age 11 to adult), adolescents become capable of abstract reasoning, hypothetical thinking ("what if?"), deductive reasoning ("if . . . then"), and systematic formulation and testing of concepts. Using this advanced type of thinking, those who have achieved formal operations can easily solve the following problem:

If Tom is taller than Jim and Jim is taller than Bill, who is taller, Tom or Bill?

FORMAL OPERATIONAL STAGE: *Piaget's fourth stage of cognitive development characterized by logical thinking, abstract reasoning, and conceptualization.*

Children in the earlier concrete operational stage often have significant difficulty with problems of this sort. They can only solve such problems when presented with concrete objects, such as three sticks of different sizes that can be readily seen. Formal operational thinking also allows the adolescent to construct a well-reasoned argument based on hypothetical concepts, such as "What if dinosaurs were alive today?" Given the same task, the preoperational child would have difficulty separating fantasy and reality, whereas a concrete operational child might respond with a limited argument such as, "They can't; they died a long time ago."

Although some researchers have suggested that formal operational thought may never appear in many adults (Datan et al., 1987; Kohlberg and Gilligan, 1971), the attainment of this level of cognition, when it does occur, has important benefits. For the first time in their cognitive developmental history, individuals are able to handle the abstract reasoning necessary for complete comprehension of algebra and of difficult grammar concepts (both of which involve manipulating symbols for symbols). Their ability to think about thinking also allows formal operational thinkers to explore their own values and beliefs and compare them to those of their friends, teachers, and parents. And the fact that they can deal with the hypothetical means that they can reason from the real to the possible, which often results in an intense type of *idealism*. There is an increased interest in thinking about what "should be" or "could be" rather than just "what is."

Along with the many benefits of this style of cognition comes several problems. For example, just as two-year-olds will hop everywhere for a while after they first learn this new motor skill, newcomers to the formal operational style of thinking often become fascinated with their newly acquired cognitive skills. Have you ever heard parents complaining about their teenager who wants to argue with everything they say? If the parents recognized that these debates and arguments are basically a form of "cognitive exercise" similar to the two-year-old's hopping, they could probably relax and maybe even enjoy the

During Piaget's fourth stage of development (formal operational), a strong sense of justice and idealism often motivates adolescents to participate in charitable drives and social protests.

interactions. It is also important to realize that improving cognitive skills may allow the adolescent to successfully challenge weak or arbitrary rules that may be difficult for adults to justify.

During the formal operational period, the adolescent begins to understand that others have unique thoughts and perspectives. However, they often fail to differentiate between what others are thinking and their own thoughts. This **adolescent egocentrism** may help to explain what seems like extreme forms of self-consciousness and concern for physical appearance ("Everyone is watching me," "Everyone knows that I don't know this answer," "They're noticing how fat I am and this awful haircut"). David Elkind (1981, 1984) believes that the adolescent's strong potential for embarrassment, affinity for mirrors, and preoccupation with grooming result from a characteristic cognitive error. Given the dramatic changes that are occurring both physically and cognitively, adolescents often erroneously assume that everyone else is just as aware of their appearance, thoughts, and feelings as they are. They construct an *imaginary audience* whose eyes are all focused on their behavior. The brother and sister in our introductory incident, Richard and Kandis, both remember times in high school when they would rather go thirsty than have the whole class watch them get up and leave the room. You can see how this style of thinking could also explain the passion for privacy that is often observed in adolescents. If everyone is watching and evaluating you, then closed doors and time alone provide an important means of escape.

A teenager's "mirror fixation" may be due to adolescent egocentrism — a belief that they are the focus of other's thoughts and attention.

Adolescent egocentrism and the imaginary audience also lead to a closely related problem: the *personal fable*. The personal fable is the belief that what one is thinking and experiencing is original and special and that one is a unique individual and therefore an exception to the rule. Kandis (our young adult in the introductory incident) remembers how upset she once was when her mother tried to comfort her over the loss of an important relationship. "I felt like she couldn't possibly know how it felt, no one could. I couldn't believe that anyone had ever suffered like this or that things would ever get better." Several forms of risk-taking, such as engaging in sexual intercourse without benefit of contraception, driving dangerously, or experimenting with drugs, also seem to arise from

312

the personal fable (Kegeles, Adler, and Irwin, 1988). The adolescent has a sense of uniqueness, invulnerability, immortality, and other special abilities.

The personal fable, imaginary audience, and related forms of egocentric thinking tend to decrease in later adolescence, when the individual has made the full transition to the formal operational period. This is Piaget's final stage of cognitive development.

Question: Is this really the final cognitive stage? Don't adults think differently than adolescents?   Although Piaget never described postadolescent thinking in much detail, several neo-Piagetians have suggested that some adults may enter a fifth or later cognitive stage (Arlin, 1984; Commons et al., 1986). These researchers have suggested that thinking during the formal operational period is primarily a passive, intellectual exercise whereas thinking in later years is active and employs the rules of logic to tackle problems in the real world. Thinking becomes a means to understanding the world, rather than just an end in itself. Information and insights from several sources are synthesized or combined with actual experience and applied to actual problems in the individual's life or to problems in society.

Although it seems intuitively obvious that cognitive changes continue throughout the life span and that the thinking of adults differs from that of adolescents, the exact nature of such changes and differences will remain a mystery without further research. One area of cognitive changes in later adulthood that has received extensive research is the topic of intelligence. For many years it was believed that general intelligence peaks at late adolescence and then declines. This pessimistic picture of aging was largely based on findings from cross-sectional studies and was later contradicted by longitudinal studies. We now know that certain types of intelligence actually continue to improve and develop with time.

Many adolescents have an intense desire for privacy and a need for self-reflection.

Fluid versus crystallized intelligence: Age-related changes

On the basis of a series of tests by Cattell (1965, 1971) and Horn (1970, 1978), researchers now distinguish between two types of intelligence: fluid and crystallized. **Fluid intelligence** involves pattern recognition, spatial orientation, memory, speed of information processing, and the abilities of reasoning and abstraction. This type of intelligence appears to remain stable through middle adulthood and then declines. **Crystallized intelligence,** on the other hand, involves vocabulary, accumulation of general knowledge, and the application of knowledge to problem solving and judgments. This type of intelligence continues to increase until the mid-sixties.

FLUID INTELLIGENCE: *A relatively culture-free type of intelligence that includes pattern recognition, spatial orientation, memory, reasoning, and abstraction.*
CRYSTALLIZED INTELLIGENCE: *A largely cultural and educationally related intelligence that involves general knowledge, vocabulary, and the application of knowledge.*

Question: What causes one ability to decline while the other improves?   Fluid intelligence is generally considered to be an innate, biological capacity, and age-related declines are seen as a response to neurological problems and perceptual slowing. Conversely, crystallized intelligence is primarily a measure of education and cultural experiences; older people do better on tests of this type of intelligence because they have more information available and have organized their information so that it is more cohesive and accessible (Horn, 1982). These differences are not clear-cut, however. Environmental influences may also affect fluid intelligence. It was found in one longitudinal study, for example, that lowered scores on fluid intelligence may reflect the rigid personality and lifestyle of some individuals that lead to disuse of intellectual abilities (Schaie, 1984).

Question: What about memory? Aren't older people more forgetful?   As you may recall from Chapter 7, memory can break down for a variety of reasons. Although many people tend to associate aging with "senility" and forgetfulness, psychologists have criticized earlier studies of memory deficits in the elderly and have concluded that much of memory ability is largely unaffected by the aging process (Meer, 1986b; Poon, 1985; Schaie, 1988). Memory deficits in older adults are largely confined to problems in *encod-*

Although many people believe that intelligence declines with age, recent research shows that this is largely a myth.

AGEISM: *A discriminatory attitude (prejudice) against older adults.*

ing (putting information into long-term storage) and *retrieval* (getting information out of storage) (Erber, 1982). If memory is like a filing system, older people just have more filing cabinets and it takes them longer to initially file and later retrieve information. This increase in filing and retrieval time is often misinterpreted as a loss of intelligence. In our fast-paced technological society where computer advances are often measured in comparison to human memory capacity and speed of information processing, the elderly's need for greater time for encoding and retrieval takes on an unreasonably negative connotation. How these misconceptions and other problems associated with **ageism** (prejudice based on age) can be reduced will be discussed at the close of this chapter.

Review Questions

1 During the _____ _____ period, adolescents first become capable of abstract reasoning and hypothetical thinking.

2 The belief that one is the focus of everyone else's thoughts and attention is known as _____ _____.

3 The belief that one is unique and special and therefore exempt from the normal rules of safety and precautions is known as the _____ _____.

4 _____ intelligence declines after middle adulthood and is primarily biological, whereas _____ intelligence increases until the mid-sixties and is primarily environmental.

5 Memory losses in old age are primarily problems of _____, taking more time to store the information, and in _____, taking more time to find the information.

Answer: 1 formal operational; *2* adolescent egocentrism; *3* personal fable; *4* fluid, crystallized; *5* encoding, retrieval

MORAL DEVELOPMENT

What do you consider moral behavior? Is morality "in the eye of the beholder," where everyone simply argues for his or her own self-interest, or are there universal truths and principles that *should* serve as rules and guideposts for all human behavior? Regardless of your answer, the very fact that you are able to think, reason, and eventually respond to this question demonstrates another type of development that is very important to psychology: moral development. How each individual develops his or her own sense of right and wrong and personal standards for behavior has fascinated scientists for many years. Whereas some researchers have suggested that the components of morality (such as empathy and sensitivity) are present at birth (Zuckerman, 1985; Radke-Yarrow, Zahn-Waxler, and Chapman, 1983), psychoanalysts typically believe that it results from the internalization of parental and societal values in the form of the superego (see Chapter 14). In this section we will look at morality from a developmental perspective. We will first explore two major theories that explain the major stages in moral development and then discuss how psychological principles may be used to encourage higher levels of moral thinking and behavior.

Theories of moral development: Explaining differences in morality

The foremost theorist of moral development, Lawrence Kohlberg (1964, 1984), built his approach on a foundation laid by Jean Piaget (1932). Kohlberg's theory has more recently been criticized and modified by Carol Gilligan.

Kohlberg's stage theory   Using the research techniques first developed by Piaget, Kohlberg presented subjects with descriptions of moral dilemmas and asked them to explain what they would do in the same situation. Before we continue, take a moment right now to read one of Kohlberg's most famous dilemmas and then jot down what you would do in this situation.

> In Europe, a woman was near death from a special kind of cancer. There was one drug that the doctors thought might save her. It was a form of radium that a druggist in the same town had recently discovered. The drug was expensive to make, but the druggist was charging ten times what the drug cost him to make. He paid $200 for the radium and charged $2,000 for a small dose of the drug. The sick woman's husband, Heinz, went to everyone he knew to borrow the money, but he could only get together about $1,000, which is half of what it cost. He told the druggist that his wife was dying and asked him to sell it cheaper or let him pay later. But the druggist said, "No, I discovered the drug and I'm going to make money from it." So Heinz got desperate and broke into the man's store to steal the drug for his wife. Was Heinz morally right or wrong in stealing the drug? Why?
>
> *Kohlberg (1964), pp. 18–19)*

Question: What would be the right answer to this problem?   Kohlberg was interested *not* in whether subjects judged Heinz as right or wrong but in the reasons they gave for their decision. On the basis of the responses of his original subjects, he proposed that there are three broad levels in the evolution of moral reasoning, as shown in Table 10.1. Each level consists of two stages, making six stages in all. (Can you find your own stage of development according to your response to the Heinz dilemma?)

Like Piaget's stages of cognitive development, Kohlberg's stages of moral development are assumed to be universal and invariant. That is, because abilities gained at a lower stage are required for advancement to the next, everyone goes through the stages in an orderly fashion. But unlike Piaget's cognitive stages, there are no specific ages associated with particular levels of morality, and both children and adults can sometimes be at the same stage. The few age trends that *are* noticed tend to be rather broad and nonexclusive. For example, until adolescence most children tend to respond at the **preconventional level**. At this level, morality is based on the consequences of an act — it is moral if it feels good and is not punished. During adolescence, however, there is an advancement to the **conventional level** of morality, where moral reasoning is based on compliance with the rules and values of society. When first entering this level, individuals are at Stage 3, and their primary moral concern is with being "nice" and gaining approval through obedience to authority — the "good child" morality. As this stage is mastered, a respect for author-

PRECONVENTIONAL LEVEL: *Kohlberg's first level of moral development, characterized by moral judgments based on fear of punishment or desire for pleasure.*

CONVENTIONAL LEVEL: *Kohlberg's second level of moral development, where moral judgments are based on compliance with the rules and values of society.*

TABLE 10.1
Kohlberg's Stages of Moral Development

| | | Heinz's Dilemma Responses | |
Moral Reasoning	What Is Right	Pro	Con
Preconventional level			
Stage 1 "Punishment–obedience" orientation	Obedience to rules so as to avoid punishment	If you let your wife die, you will get in trouble. You'll be blamed for not spending the money to save her and there'll be an investigation of you and the druggist for your wife's death.	You shouldn't steal the drug because you'll be caught and sent to jail if you do. If you do get away, your conscience would bother you thinking how the police would catch up with you at any minute.
Stage 2 "Instrumental-exchange" orientation	Obedience to rules so that rewards or favors may be obtained	If you do happen to get caught, you could give the drug back and you wouldn't get much of a sentence. It wouldn't bother you much to serve a little jail term, if you have your wife when you get out.	He may not get much of a jail term if he steals the drug, but his wife will probably die before he gets out so it won't do him much good. If his wife dies, he shouldn't blame himself, it wasn't his fault she has cancer.
Conventional level			
Stage 3 "Good-child" orientation	Seeking and maintaining the approval of others	No one will think you're bad if you steal the drug, but your family will think you're an inhuman husband if you don't. If you let your wife die, you'll never be able to look anybody in the face again.	It isn't just the druggist who will think you're a criminal, everyone else will too. After you steal it, you'll feel bad thinking how you've brought dishonor on your family and yourself, and you won't be able to face anyone again.
Stage 4 "Law-and-order" orientation	Conforming to norms so as to avoid censure or reprimands by authority figures	If you have any sense of honor, you won't let your wife die because you're afraid to do the only thing that will save her. You'll always feel guilty that you caused her death if you don't do your duty to her.	You're desperate and you may not know you're doing wrong when you steal the drug. But you'll know you did wrong after you're sent to jail. You'll always feel guilty for your dishonesty and lawbreaking.
Postconventional level			
Stage 5 "Social-contact" orientation	Obedience to democratically ac-cepted laws and contracts	You'd lose other people's respect, not gain it, if you don't steal. If you let your wife die, it would be out of fear, not out of reasoning it out. So you'd just lose self-respect and probably the respect of others too.	You would lose your standing and respect in the community and violate the law. You'd lose respect for yourself if you're carried away by emotion and forget the long-range point of view.
Stage 6 "Universal ethics" orientation	Morality of individual con-science	If you don't steal the drug and let your wife die, you'll always condemn yourself for it afterward. You wouldn't be blamed and you would have lived up to the outside rule of the law, but you wouldn't have lived up to your own standards of conscience.	If you stole the drug, you wouldn't be blamed by the other people but you'd condemn yourself because you wouldn't have lived up to your own conscience and standards of honesty.

Sources: Kohlberg (1967, 1969); Rest et al. (1969).

ity and "doing one's duty" become more important, and moral development moves on to Stage 4 — a "law and order" orientation. Kohlberg believed that most adults remain at either Stage 3 or 4 in their moral development (see Figure 10.4).

For those few adults who do make it to the **postconventional level**, morality transcends the need for approval and the fear of censure (characteristic at the previous level), and individuals develop personal standards for right and wrong according to their own principles and values (Stages 5 and 6). In his later studies Kohlberg questioned

POSTCONVENTIONAL LEVEL: *Kohlberg's highest level of moral development, which occurs when individuals develop personal standards for right and wrong.*

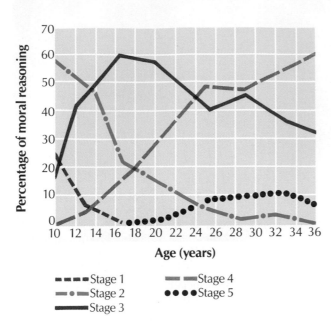

Figure 10.4 Variations in percentages of boys and men who achieve Kohlberg's first five stages of moral reasoning.

whether Stages 5 and 6 are actually two separate stages and also suggested that there may be an additional stage of moral development (Stage 7) that is more commonly found among the elderly and involves a spiritual and cosmic perspective (Kohlberg, 1969, 1981). Kohlberg believed that the moral principles of individuals like Martin Luther King, Jr., Mother Teresa, and Mahatma Gandhi are characteristic of a Stage 7 orientation.

Question: Are the people who achieve higher stages on Kohlberg's scale really more moral than others, or do they just "talk a good game"?   Although we often assume that moral reasoning is automatically related to moral *behavior,* there is considerable debate over whether Kohlberg's stages can accurately predict an individual's actions. Some studies *have* found a positive correlation between higher stages of reasoning and higher levels of morality (Langdale, 1986), whereas others have found that the pressures of the situation are better predictors of moral behavior (Haan, Aerts, and Cooper, 1985; Hartshorne and May, 1928; Wynne, 1988).

In addition to this questionable correlation between moral reasoning and behavior, critics have also suggested that Kohlberg's stages are culturally biased in favor of Western ideas of what is morally "advanced" and that they are politically biased so that liberals tend to be more "moral" than conservatives (Hogan and Schroeder, 1981; Rogoff and Morelli, 1989; Snarey, 1985).

Gilligan's theory of sex differences in moral reasoning   Perhaps one of the most intriguing criticisms applied to Kohlberg's theory is Carol Gilligan's accusation of sexual bias. Gilligan has criticized Kohlberg's stages of moral development because they were originally developed from the responses of only male subjects. She suggests that this initial sampling bias explains why women generally score lower than men on Kohlberg's scale. On the basis of separate research that included both men and women who were involved in a personal moral decision for or against abortion (Gilligan, 1977, 1982, 1986) Gilligan has concluded that males and females actually have "separate-but-equal" paths for moral development.

Question: If men and women are equal, why do men score higher on Kohlberg's scale?   According to Gilligan, Kohlberg's "higher" stages of development (Stages 5, 6, and 7) are based on traditional male values of independence and individual rights, so

Mother Theresa and her selfless dedication to others is a good example of Kohlberg's highest level of moral development.

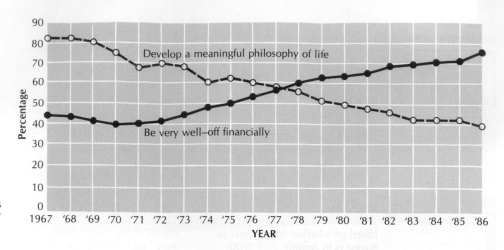

Figure 10.5 Changing of life goals among college freshmen from 1967 to 1986.

Among high school seniors, there has been a similar increase in the number who rate "a chance to earn a good deal of money" as very important in a job (Bachman, 1971; Bachman, Johnston, and O'Malley, 1981, 1987). In addition, fewer than one out of six college-bound seniors consider "making a contribution to society" or "working to correct social and economic inequities" to be a very important value (Bachman et al., 1987; Johnston et al., 1986).

Question: Is there any reason for this change in moral values?   One possible explanation is that these youth are simply mirroring larger societal values. According to researcher John Conger (1988), our twin legacies from the 1970s and early 1980s (self-preoccupation and materialism, mixed with lingering fears of recession, inflation, and unemployment) have made many of us reluctant to worry about the needs of others or to make their problems our own. He suggests that these current trends in social values have "failed to provide an effective model to sustain young people in their own search for values and a stable, consistent sense of their own identity" (Conger, 1988, p. 291).

As you might imagine, others dispute the charge of "declining youthful values" (e.g., Kennedy, 1988). Although this issue, like Kohlberg's general theory, remains open to question, it is clear that moral development is an important aspect of social and personality development — the topic of our next section.

Review Questions

1 According to Kohlberg, individuals at the _____ level of morality tend to judge right and wrong on the basis of the consequences (reward or punishment), whereas those at the _____ level tend to comply with the rules of society in an attempt to please others or to "do one's duty."

2 People who have developed their own standards for right and wrong are considered by Kohlberg to be at the _____ level.

3 According to Gilligan, Kohlberg's theory emphasizes the _____ perspective and underplays the _____ perspective.

4 Parents who use lots of punishment and fear to induce moral behavior are likely to produce children with an _____ moral orientation.

5 Kohlberg advocated a _____ or "time off" in which one can explore his or her values and identity before making final commitments.

Answers: 1 preconventional, conventional;   *2* postconventional,   *3* Justice, care;   *4* external;   *5* moraturium

PERSONALITY AND SOCIAL DEVELOPMENT

As we saw in Chapter 9, one of the fundamental issues that guides developmental research is that of stability versus change. Nowhere is this issue more evident than in the area of personality and social development. When we look around us, we can find numerous examples of people who demonstrate a dramatic difference between their child and adult personalities, physiques, and lifestyles. Jack La Lanne, for example, not only transformed his scrawny, teenage body into an internationally famous symbol of strength but also changed from an insecure, suicidal adolescent into an outgoing adult who at 76 runs a $30-billion business and is known for his inexhaustible energy and passionate zest for life. On the other hand, we also see people like 43-year-old William, whose adult life and personality, according to both self-report and others' observations, is very stable and reflective of his early childhood. Even Gray Panther Maggie Kuhn's dramatic rise to fame as a political activist and writer is not that surprising given her early work as a U.N. observer and editor for her church magazine (Marshall, 1985).

Whereas many personality theorists have focused on the innate versus situational factors in personality (see Chapter 14), most developmental theorists assume that personality is the result of built-in, preprogrammed sequential stages that are brought about through maturation. They see the individual as having a biological predisposition to progress through these stages, and they see personality as resulting from how the individual meets the challenges at each stage. Freud, for example, saw personality as resulting from successful and unsuccessful resolution of the various psychosexual crises that occur early in life (see Chapter 14). Two major theorists who have extended the idea of developmental stages past adolescence into adulthood are Erik Erikson and Daniel Levinson.

Erikson's psychosocial stages: Adolescence and adulthood

According to Erikson (1968; 1987), the most important challenge of *psychosocial development* in adolescence is the search for identity. His fifth stage of development (the first four were described in Chapter 9) is the period of **identity versus role confusion.** Erikson believes that each individual's personal identity develops from a period of serious questioning and intense soul searching. During this **identity crisis,** adolescents attempt to discover who they are, what their skills are, and what kinds of roles they are best suited to play for the rest of their lives. The "Who am I?" question that characterizes this stage is most easily resolved by the selection of a career, but adolescents must also discover their own personal philosophy and individual values during this time in order to firmly establish a sense of who they are. While searching for their own values, most adolescents begin to emotionally separate and withdraw from their parents. Erikson believes this is a natural and desirable reaction. If adolescents are to function as adults, they must learn to make their own decisions based on their individual wants, needs, and aspirations. Failure to resolve the identity crisis can lead to a lack of a stable identity, delinquency, or difficulty in maintaining close personal relationships in later life (Kahn et al., 1985).

Once a firm sense of identity is established, Erikson believes the individual (now in young adulthood) is ready to meet the challenges of the **intimacy versus isolation** stage of development. The establishment of close interpersonal bonds is the major task of this stage. If these bonds are made, a basic feeling of intimacy with others will result. If not, the individual may avoid interpersonal commitments and experience feelings of isolation. Erikson has commented that the current trend toward casual sex may lead to feelings of intense loneliness because it lacks mutuality—real intimacy. According to Erikson, "Real intimacy includes the capacity to commit yourself to relationships that may demand sacrifice and compromise. The basic strength of young adulthood is love—a mutual, mature devotion" (cited in Hall, 1983, p. 25).

IDENTITY VERSUS ROLE CONFUSION: *Erikson's fifth stage of psychosocial development; the adolescent may become confident and purposeful through discovery of an identity, or may become confused and ill-defined.*
IDENTITY CRISIS: *According to Erikson, a period of inner conflict during which an individual examines his or her life and values and makes decisions about life roles.*

INTIMACY VERSUS ISOLATION: *Erikson's sixth stage of psychosocial development; the young adult must develop a capacity for close interpersonal bonds or face isolation and loneliness.*

According to Erikson, the task of early adulthood is to develop close interpersonal bonds with others.

GENERATIVITY VERSUS STAGNATION: *The seventh stage in Erikson's theory of psychosocial development. To avoid stagnation, the adult must "generate" or give something back to the world beyond the concern and care for the immediate family.*

EGO INTEGRITY VERSUS DESPAIR: *During this eighth and final stage of psychosocial development, adults review their accomplishments and feel either satisfaction or regret.*

The stage of **generativity versus stagnation,** which characterizes middle adulthood, involves expanding the individual's love and concern beyond the immediate family group to include all of society. Generativity involves concern about the welfare of the next generation, and individuals who are successful at this stage work to make the world a better place to live. If this expansion and effort does not occur, an individual may stagnate and become concerned with only material possessions and personal well-being.

An understanding of the generativity versus stagnation stage may ease the tension that sometimes develops between college professors and the increasing number of older college students. Whereas professors have typically experienced satisfying feelings of generativity through their caring for the younger generation, older students share the professor's need for generativity and may find the professor's caring condescending. In turn, the professor may feel threatened when older students, who have the real-world expertise to do so, challenge his or her academic material (Datan et al., 1987).

In the final years of life, adults enter the period of **ego integrity versus despair.** The central developmental task of this stage is the maintenance of a sense of who one is and what one stands for (ego integrity) in the face of physical deterioration and impending death. During this stage, those who have been successful in resolving their earlier psychosocial crises will tend to look back upon their lives with feelings of accomplishment and satisfaction. Those who have resolved their earlier crises in a negative way or who have lived fruitless, self-centered lives may deeply regret their lost opportunities. They may also experience feelings of gloom and despair since they realize that it is too late to start over.

Question: Do most researchers agree with Erikson's theory? Can I count on these ideas as predictive of my own future?   Like most psychoanalytically based theories, Erikson's is subjective, coming from his own experiences, the recollections of his patients, and classic literature (Berger, 1988). This subjectivity, along with the vague terminology, makes objective evaluation difficult. The one area that has received the most research attention — and support — is that of the development of identity in adolescence (Waterman, 1982). In one study of psychological adjustment, for example, male and female adolescents who had established a clear identity also possessed a sense of trust and industry and good self-concepts, whereas adolescents who had not yet established firm identities showed greater maladjustment (La Voie, 1976). A study by Tesch and Gennelo (1985) has also given tentative support to Erikson's stage of intimacy versus isolation.

Like Kohlberg's stages of moral development, Erikson's theory *has* been criticized for its male-biased pattern. Marcia (1980) has discovered that identity and intimacy develop simultaneously in females, and Gilligan (1982) has found that a woman's identity is based more on her relationships with other people and less on her achievement of a separate identity. Despite the questionable "universality" of Erikson's stages, his theory has been an important contribution to the study of adult psychosocial development. Erikson was among the first to suggest that development continues past adolescence, and his theory was an important stimulant to further research. Given the limited nature of the scientific support of his theory, however, most researchers caution against using it as a predictor of individual lives.

Levinson's conception of development: The "seasons" of life

Like Erikson, Daniel Levinson and his colleagues (1977, 1986a, 1990) have arrived at a theory of development that emphasizes the effects of various developmental tasks at separate "seasons" throughout a person's life. Just as the calendar year goes through predictable phases or seasons, so, too, does human life. But unlike Piaget's hierarchical stages of cognitive development and Kohlberg's stages of moral development, which become higher and "better" with age, none of Levinson's stages is better or more important than any other. "Each has its necessary place and contributes its special character to the whole" (Levinson, 1986b, p. 4).

In his book *The Seasons of a Man's Life* (1978), Levinson discusses in-depth interviews conducted with 40 men from a wide variety of occupations, religions, and incomes. On the basis of these interviews, as well as the biographical accounts of over 100 men and women and interviews with 45 women, Levinson (1986b) has developed his concept of the **life structure**. Each individual's life structure contains internal values, dreams, and aspirations and external realities such as work, family, religion, and so on. As people go through life, the integration of the internal and external is continually affected and modified by life circumstances.

According to Levinson, major modifications to the life structure tend to occur during four major *eras* in the life cycle and during *cross-era transition periods* that help to terminate the outgoing era and initiate the new (see Figure 10.6). Levinson believes that the transition phase between each period in life is an important time in development. The characteristic upheaval that comes from questioning and examining one's life during these transitions can be an important stimulus for growth.

LIFE STRUCTURE: *According to Levinson, the internal and external aspects of an individual's psychosocial development that are built up during the four eras of development and modified during periods of transition.*

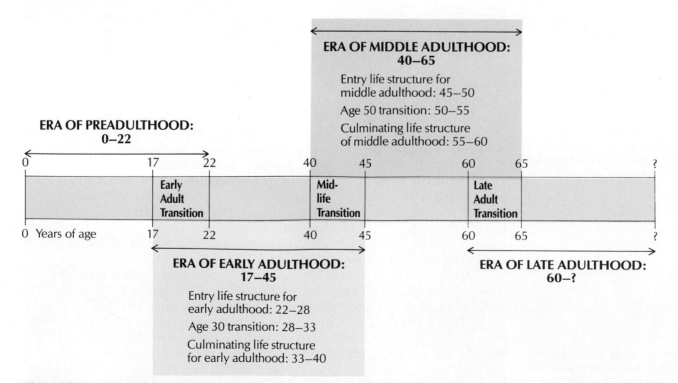

Figure 10.6 Levinson's adult stages. He believes that each of the four major eras of life has a profound influence on development, as does each of the major transition phases.

In Levinson's schema, the first three eras and corresponding transitions are:

1. The *era of preadulthood* (conception to age 22). Development during the formative years is largely a process of biological and psychological separation and individuation. The child moves from a highly dependent and undifferentiated infant into a more independent and responsible adult.

    During the *early adult transition period* (ages 17 to 22), the young adult examines and modifies his or her family relationships and other aspects of childhood to begin to form a place in the adult world.

2. The *era of early adulthood* (ages 17 to 45). The major developmental tasks of this period are to form and pursue youthful dreams, establish a niche in society, raise a family, and as the era ends, reach a "senior" position in the adult world. Although this can be a time of rich satisfaction and rewards, Levinson warns that the costs often equal or even exceed the benefits.

    During the *midlife transition* (ages 40 to 45), early adulthood ends and middle adulthood begins. This midlife transition was a time of major crisis for 80 percent of the men in Levinson's original study (1977, 1978). During the so-called *midlife crisis,* these men began to appraise their lives and usually discovered that they had failed to fulfill the dreams established in early adulthood. Forced to deal with the loss of their youth and the unfulfilled expectations, many men made drastic choices: They divorced, remarried, changed jobs, or moved to another city.

3. The *era of middle adulthood* (ages 40 to 65). For those men who successfully resolve the midlife transition phase, the years of middle adulthood may be some of the happiest and most fulfilling. (Because none of the men studied by Levinson in his original study was older than 47 at the last contact, his description of life past this point is speculative and is not discussed here.)

MIDLIFE CRISIS: *A time of psychological and emotional turmoil that supposedly occurs around the age of 35 for women and 40 for men.*

Question: How common is the midlife crisis? The idea of the **midlife crisis** achieved a great deal of public attention largely as the result of the publishing of Gail Sheehy's book *Passages* (1976). In this national best-seller, Sheehy drew upon the theories of Levinson and psychiatrist Roger Gould (1975), as well as her own interviews, and reported a "predictable crisis" at about age 35 for women and 40 for men. Although middle age *is* typically a time of reevaluation of one's values and lifetime goals, this phenomenally successful book has led many people to automatically expect a midlife *crisis* with drastic changes in one's personality and behavior. Other research has suggested such a severe reaction or crisis may actually be quite rare and not typical of what most people experience during middle age (Costa and McCrae, 1988; Schlossberg, 1987).

Just as the midlife crisis may turn out to be something of a myth, there is also considerable doubt as to the reliability of other common beliefs about age-related crises. One such belief is that parents whose last child leaves home experience the **empty nest syndrome** — a painful separation and time of depression for the mother, the father, or older parents. Like the midlife crisis, however, research suggests that the empty nest syndrome may be an exaggeration of the turmoil experienced by a few individuals and a downplaying of the commonly experienced positive reactions (Neugarten and Neugarten, 1987). For example, one major benefit of the empty nest is an increase in marital satisfaction (see Figure 10.7). It is also important to recognize that parent–child relationships do continue once the child leaves home (Gross, 1987). As one mother said, "The empty nest is surrounded by telephone wires" (Troll et al., 1979).

EMPTY NEST SYNDROME: *A painful separation and depression that parents supposedly feel when their last child leaves home.*

STORM AND STRESS: *The idea that emotional turmoil and rebellion are characteristic of all adolescents.*

Another potential myth of development that needs to be explored is the idea that adolescence is a period of turmoil and rebellion. Thanks to movies like *The Breakfast Club* and media reports of teenage drug use, runaways, prostitution, and pregnancy, many people have a grossly exaggerated view of the problems of adolescents. Until recently, most psychologists also shared this view. Adolescence was inevitably characterized as a time of **storm and stress,** during which young people experience strong emotional turbulence and psychological strain (Hall, 1904). Research within the last 20 years, however, has found that adolescence is just one of many life transitions and no stormier than any other (Petersen, 1988; Powers, Hauser, and Kilner, 1989).

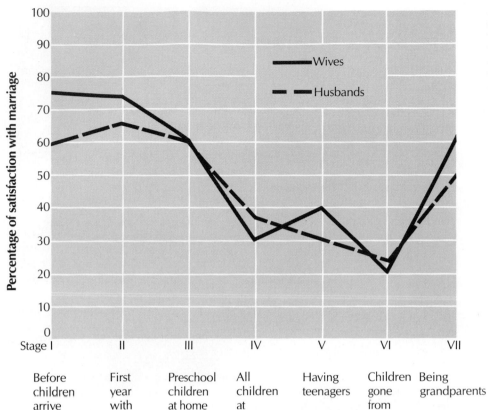

Stage | I | II | III | IV | V | VI | VII |
|---|---|---|---|---|---|---|
| Before children arrive | First year with infant | Preschool children at home | All children at school | Having teenagers | Children gone from home | Being grandparents |

(Source: Lupri and Frideres, Canadian Journal of Sociology, 1981, 6, 289.)

Figure 10.7 The relation of marital satisfaction to stage of married life. Contrary to the popular belief that children make a marriage happy and that parents experience a depressing "empty nest" when children leave, this graph shows that reported marital satisfaction is higher before children are born and after they leave.

![gray box]*Question:* If these concepts are so questionable, what accounts for their continued popularity? Joseph Adelson (1979) suggests that one reason for this persistence is the tendency for research to focus on atypical factions of the population — addicts, delinquents, and so on — and to generalize from these minorities to the group as a whole. In addition, we tend to "see" and remember examples of behavior that fulfill our expectations. Our beliefs may also act as subtle encouragement for the expected behavior. As 17-year-old Richard puts it:

> Most of my friends never tell their parents the truth about where they're going or what they're doing because they over-react. We're really pretty good. Parents would probably be bored by what we actually do on the weekends, but they worry all the time about drugs and pregnancies and stuff. They think we'll lie to them and we do, but not for the reasons they expect.

One additional possibility for the prevalence of these myths, especially that of the adolescent rebellion, lies in the acceptance of the related myth of **linear development.** In so many aspects of development change seems to be *cumulative*—the baby grows increasingly taller and larger, vocabulary increases, intelligence improves, and so on. We have little experience in dealing with "plateaus" or even reversals. Some problems experienced during the period of adolescence arise from the turmoil created as the teenager "flips" back and forth between adolescence and adulthood. As William (our middle-aged individual) notes in his teenagers, "Just when I get used to them being and acting like adults, they do a 180 on me and act like kids again. Won't they ever grow up?"

Although "growing up" may include some stabilizing of the personality, adults should also remember that adult life is not a simple plateau that continues to death. People grow and change and "flip" (the so-called midlife crisis?) many times in their lives.

LINEAR DEVELOPMENT: *The idea that development progresses in a fairly straight line, at a steady rate, and that each new development is built on the previous stages or abilities.*

Review Questions

1　Erikson suggests that the "Who am I?" question of adolescents characterizes the psychosocial stage of _____ _____ _____.

2　During young adulthood, Erikson believes that we must reach out to others and establish _____ or we experience deep feelings of loneliness and _____.

3　During middle adulthood, Erikson suggests that our major challenge for psychosocial adjustment is _____ _____ _____, and our challenge during the final years of life is that of _____ _____ _____ _____.

4　Unlike Piaget's hierarchical stages of cognitive development, _____ "seasons" of personality and social development are considered to be equally valued—none is higher or better than the other.

5　Levinson's first three eras of development are _____, _____ _____, and _____ _____.

6　Two common myths about adulthood are the _____ _____ and the _____ _____ _____.

7　The myth of _____ _____ assumes that development progresses in a steady, unbroken pattern with no plateaus or reversals.

Answers: 1 identity versus role confusion;　*2* intimacy, isolation;　*3* generativity versus stagnation, ego integrity versus despair;　*4* Levinson's;　*5* preadulthood, early adulthood, middle adulthood;　*6* midlife crisis, empty nest syndrome;　*7* linear development

Social development: The importance of family and occupation

Given the contradictory research concerning adolescent rebellion, empty nests, and so on, it is easy to see why there is a growing body of research that limits itself to specific issues in development. Two specific influences on social development are the role of families and the choice of occupation.

The effect of family on development　Psychologists such as Erikson and Levinson see one of the major tasks of adult development as establishing intimate relationships and beginning a family. Most people discover that these tasks are far from easy. Some take on these tasks before they are psychologically prepared (teenage pregnancy). Others find the tasks so frustrating or difficult that the family becomes a battleground (spouse abuse and child abuse). Many give up (divorce) and try again with someone new (remarriage). All these behaviors have ramifications for continued social and emotional development.

For better or worse, families exert an enormous influence on members' psychosocial development (Rodin and Salovey, 1989). Children and adolescents who experience physical, emotional, or sexual abuse, or who live in homes disrupted by parental schizophrenia, alcoholism, or major depression, are disrupted in their own personality and social development. They frequently show not only physical damage (from the assault, poor nutrition, and so on), but also display emotional disorders such as withdrawal, aggression, suicidal tendencies, anger, guilt, and distortion of the development of close, trusting, and overly dependent relationships (Emery, 1989; Hart and Brassard, 1987; Torrey, 1988). As adults these same children and adolescents are more likely to abuse their own children and to abuse their spouses (Kempe and Kempe, 1984).

"Why don't you grow up!"

Illustration by Bil Keane, © 1971 by Erma Bombeck and Bil Keane from *Just wait till you have children of your own.* Reprinted by permission of Doubleday & Company, Inc.

Question: Is there anything that can be done to interrupt this cycle? Attempts to deal with family violence have centered on two approaches. *Primary programs* attempt to identify "vulnerable" families and then try to prevent abuse. *Secondary programs* attempt to rehabilitate the families after abuse has occurred (Finkelhor and Hotaling, 1988; Kaplan, 1986). The aims of primary programs are to improve parenting and marital skills, teach people to recognize the signs of abuse, and encourage people to report suspected cases of abuse. Secondary programs involve improved social services, self-help groups such as Parents Anonymous and AMAC (Adults Molested as Children), and individual and group psychotherapy for both the victim and the abuser.

Abuse is just one of many important family influences that may affect development. Another is becoming a parent and starting a family at too early an age. At the current time, America has the highest rate of teen pregnancies among the major industrialized nations. Nearly one in six female adolescents becomes pregnant at least once before marriage (Conger, 1988). Pregnancy during adolescence carries with it considerable health risks for both the mother and child (see Chapter 9). In addition, teenage mothers — 90 percent of whom currently keep their babies — generally face significant problems in other areas (Conger, 1988; Furstenberg, Brooks-Gunn, and Chase-Lansdale, 1989; Hayes, 1987; Wallis, 1985a):

1. Lower educational achievement (pregnancy is the most common reason for dropping out of high school).
2. Reduced economic opportunities (teenage mothers are less likely to find employment, are more likely to become chronically dependent on welfare, and will generally spend their lives below the official poverty level).
3. Impaired marital opportunities (teenage mothers are less likely to marry, and if they marry they are more likely to divorce).

In view of these statistics, is it any wonder that teen mothers also report one of the highest levels of depression (see Figure 10.8)?

Question: What can be done to reduce the number of teen pregnancies? Conger (1988) recommends the following steps:

1. *Sex education and family-life planning.* Adolescents need facts about sexuality and help in learning to integrate this information into their lives and future (Edelman, 1987).

Ads such as this are now being used to combat the increasing number of unintended teenage pregnancies.

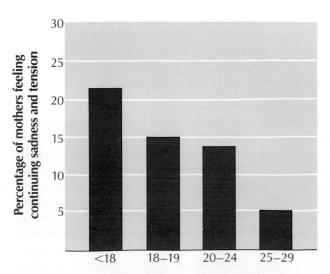

Age of mother at birth of first offspring

y-axis: Percentage of mothers feeling continuing sadness and tension

x-axis: <18, 18–19, 20–24, 25–29

Figure 10.8 The relation of negative feelings to maternal age.

DEVELOPING THE ABILITY TO EMPATHIZE
Abortion, Adoption, or Keeping the Child?

In view of the increasing number of teen pregnancies in America, it becomes ever more important to fully understand and appreciate the questions and conflicts a pregnant teenager must face. Should she have an abortion, give the baby up for adoption, or keep her child? Should her boyfriend or parents have a say in what she decides?

This exercise is designed to improve your critical thinking skills through empathizing, which is the ability to consider others' points of view. Begin by reading the following scenario.

Anne is an average American high school student. She is a 17-year-old senior who gets top grades and has an excellent chance of obtaining several academic scholarships. In addition to school, Anne works 15 hours a week and is saving for college, which she hopes to attend the following fall. She is also pregnant.

Anne's father, who is morally opposed to abortion, has warned her about premarital sex. He was very disappointed when he found out about her pregnancy, and would never accept an abortion. He would like to see Anne keep the baby and try to get her boyfriend to marry her. Anne's mother, on the other hand, does not want anything to prevent Anne from getting a college degree, and wants her to give the baby up for adoption. Anne's boyfriend does not want to marry her nor be financially responsible. He plans to enter college in the fall and wants Anne to have an abortion.

Anne knows that, realistically, her pregnancy would prevent her from attending college in the fall, and that this delay would seriously jeopardize her scholarship opportunities. Without the aid of a substantial scholarship, she would need to work full-time. Anne's parents cannot afford to help her with college expenses and are unable to offer significant help with child care. Anne does not want to marry her boyfriend, nor does she assume that he will provide much support should she decide to keep the child. Anne must make a decision on her own. (Adapted from Bernards, 1988.)

With a group of friends or alone:

1 Make a list of several possible arguments from each character's perspective — Anne, her father, her mother, and her boyfriend.

2 Decide which of these arguments are the most compelling for keeping the child, putting it up for adoption, and for having an abortion.

3 Decide what are the most persuasive arguments against each option.

4 If you, your girlfriend, or your child were pregnant and in a similar situation, how would you decide? Are your reasons different than those listed above? If so, explain why.

---

2. *Access to contraceptive methods.* Sexually active adolescents need easily accessible health services that provide comprehensive, high-quality care.
3. *The life options approach.* Motivation to avoid pregnancy is essential and can only be accomplished when young people feel good about themselves and have a "clear vision of a successful and self-sufficient future" (Edelman, 1987, p. 58).
4. *Broad community involvement and support.* Community support is the major reason why other industrialized nations have fewer pregnancies, abortions, and teenage mothers, despite comparable levels of sexual activity (Jones et al., 1985).

Another aspect of family life that greatly influences development is divorce. Contrary to the belief that "Time heals all wounds," 40 percent of divorced women and 30 percent of divorced men still feel rejected and angry at their former partners 10 years after breaking up (Fischman, 1986). In addition to the stress for the divorcing couple, their children also suffer both short-term and long-lasting effects on their development (Hetherington et al., 1989; Wallerstein and Blakeslee, 1989). Despite widespread beliefs that divorce is a short-term crisis, recent research has shown that divorce has a profound and lasting effect on all members of the family. Some children and parents exhibit remarkable adaptation and in the long term may be enhanced by the divorce experience, whereas others show severe developmental disruptions both initially and in the years that follow. Still others appear to adapt well in the early stages of divorce but show delayed effects that emerge at a later time (Hetherington, 1990; Wallerstein et al., 1988). Whether children

TABLE 10.3
Typical Reactions to Parental Divorce by Children of Varying Ages

Age (at time of divorce)	Initial Reaction	Later Reaction (2–10 years later)
Preschool (2½ to 6 years)	Blames self for divorce; fears abandonment; confused; fantasizes reconciliation; difficulty in expressing feelings	Few memories of either own or parents' earlier conflict; generally has developed close relations with custodial parent and competent step-parent; feels anger at unavailability of noncustodial parent
Elementary School (7 to 12 years)	Expresses feelings of fear, sadness, anger; divided loyalties; better able to take advantage of extrafamilial support	Least adaptable to step-parenting and remarriage; may challenge family rules and regulations; decreased academic performance; disturbed peer relations
Adolescence (13 to 18 years)	Difficulty coping with anger, outrage, shame, and sadness; reexamines own values; may disengage from family	Shares feelings of 7- to 12-year-olds, but may not be similarly expressed; fears long-term relations with others; more consciously troubled

Sources: Bray (1988); Hetherington et al. (1985); Wallerstein et al. (1988); Wallerstein and Blakeslee (1989).

become "winners" or "losers" from the divorce process depends on the individual attributes of the child, the qualities of the custodial family, and the resources and support systems available to the child (Forgath et al., 1988; Hetherington et al., 1985, 1989). As can be seen in Table 10.3, children's *initial* and *later* reactions to marital transitions also differ according to their age at the time of the divorce.

Although the family *does* have problems in our culture, it also is the major source for fulfillment of crucial social needs (Sagan, 1988). Beyond the basic survival needs that families provide, Weiss (1975) has identified at least six social needs that families are in a position to fulfill:

1. *Attachment.* A sense of security and comfort.
2. *Social integration.* A feeling of belonging and being a part of the community.
3. *Reassurance of worth.* Feedback on one's accomplishments and support for one's sense of being a competent and valued person.

Research has shown that the family provides important social needs for all its members.

Figure 10.9 The "normal" developmental sequence for attachment. (*Source:* Kinsey, 1948; Kinsey et al., 1953.)

4. *A sense of reliable alliance.* A feeling that there are others around who can be counted on for assistance in times of need.
5. *Guidance.* Availability of others who can provide reliable advice and information.
6. *Opportunity for nurturance.* A sense of being needed and important that arises out of being responsible for the well-being of another.

Although many people acknowledge at least some of these needs, few recognize how strong these needs are throughout the entire life span. Attachment, for example, apparently progresses through several predictable stages (see Figure 10.9). From the beginning stage of contact comfort (see Chapter 9) to the ending stage of heterosexual pair-bonding, attachment plays an important role in our sense of well-being and overall adjustment (Harlow and Harlow, 1966; Hazen and Shaver, 1987).

Question: Could this explain why some people feel so miserable after a divorce? Yes. Studies have consistently found that following divorce, admission rates to psychiatric facilities increase, illness and disability increase, and there are more suicides, homicides, and deaths from disease (Garvin et al., 1988; Hendrick, 1989; Wallerstein and Blakeslee, 1989). Numerous studies of divorced couples have found that the loss of the attachment figure is one of the major reasons for the severe reactions to divorce (Berman, 1988; Bowlby, 1988; Weiss, 1975, 1979). Even when love, friendship, admiration, and other positive feelings have been eroded from a relationship, recently divorced individuals sometimes experience a profound sense of sadness and confusion. They also report recurring thoughts and images of the ex-spouse, feelings of emptiness, attempts to contact or learn about him or her, and loneliness and panic when the ex-spouse is inaccessible. Weiss (1975) notes that just as young infants often go through a stage of *separation distress* when an attachment figure leaves, adults go through similar feelings when ending an important love relationship.

The importance of recognizing the nature of attachment throughout our lives may help us better understand lingering "after-effects" following the breakup of important relationships, as well as the normal mixed feelings we experience when we leave home after adolescence or as parents when our children leave. Besides our relationships with others, the major other influence on our social development is our work life.

Occupational choices Most working adults spend more time on the job than they do with their families. Erikson emphasized the importance of "generativity" to adult development — the need to accomplish something with one's life. Most people channel their accomplishment needs into their work or occupation.

Question: How can I find a rewarding career that best suits my personality and interests? Choosing an occupation is one of the most important decisions in our lives, and the task is becoming ever more complex as the number of career options increases as a result of specialization. The *Dictionary of Occupational Titles*, a government publication, currently lists more than 20,000 job categories. One way to gain more information about these job categories and potential careers is to visit your college career center. At such centers, career counselors will often suggest you take a group of vocational interest tests.

Question: Should young people be encouraged to find a job during high school and college as a way of preparing for a career? The research is contradictory. Although having a job does seem to earn parental respect and often eases the financial burden and household tension (Cole, 1980), it generally fails to provide the training

Recent research suggests that part-time work may have a negative influence on high school students.

necessary and useful in later life (Elkind, 1987). In addition, working teens are usually involved in boring, sex-stereotyped jobs and must give up not only time with their families but also time studying and in extracurricular activities (Garwad et al., 1989).

Whereas part-time work may be a negative influence on high school students, the effect on college students is less clear. One of the safest ways to help find the "right" career is to do volunteer work or internships in the actual field you propose to enter. This helps to gather on-the-job experience and exposure and often helps to avoid costly mistakes in career decisions. One rule of thumb may be to keep as many options open as possible and to delay making a final decision as long as possible. It is ironic that career decisions are encouraged during adolescence, when many young people are struggling with the crisis of identity, leaving home, and the establishment of love relationships. In addition, at this age they are new to the stage of formal operations, which, as you may remember, is a time of high idealism and adolescent egocentrism.

Once a career decision is made, careers, just like lives, can go through stages (Van Maanen and Schein, 1977). In the initial phases there is often a great deal of "job hopping," especially among younger workers. Men between the ages of 16 and 19 have a 74 percent chance of a job change within five years, whereas men in their twenties have a 56 percent chance (Sommers and Eck, 1977). Most experts tend to agree that job satisfaction and stability peak during middle age. Although work is often considered to be a primary source of pleasure, one study found that only about 12 to 13 percent of the workers in 1957 and 1976 mentioned work as a source of happiness (Veroff et al., 1981).

The overestimation of the importance of work is readily apparent when we look at the mythology that surrounds the final career stage: Retirement. Like the midlife crisis and empty nest syndrome, the loss of self-esteem and depression that is commonly assumed to accompany retirement may be largely a myth. Many workers are glad to retire and are primarily depressed at the change in their standard of living (Schaie and Geiwitz, 1982). Although Maggie Kuhn was personally outraged at her forced retirement at age 65, she also recognized that many people do want to retire. Her group, the Gray Panthers, is opposed to mandatory retirement and hiring policies that discriminate on the basis of age. Like many researchers (Maddox, 1970), she believes that the best way to enjoy a fulfilling old age is to remain active and involved as long as possible — the **activity theory** of aging. This approach is in sharp contrast to the **disengagement theory**, which suggests that the elderly naturally and gracefully withdraw from life because they seek relief from roles they are no longer able to fill (Cumming and Henry, 1961). Although the disengagement theory has been strongly criticized and generally discredited, it has helped stimulate research into some of the causes of social withdrawal, such as losses in sensory capacities and ostracism by a youth-oriented society. What may seem like natural and willing disengagement or "mellowness" may in fact reflect an older person's attempt to retreat to a smaller social world and to avoid further alienation from an ageist society (Blau, 1973). A more positive approach to coping with ageism, as well as specific techniques for dealing with death, is offered in the next section.

ACTIVITY THEORY: *A theory of aging that suggests that successful adjustment is fostered by a full and active commitment to life.*
DISENGAGEMENT THEORY: *A theory of aging that suggests that successful aging involves a natural and mutual withdrawal, in which both the individual and society gradually pull away from each other as a preparation for death.*

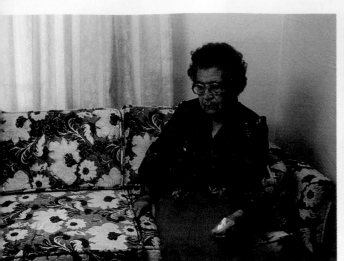 

Although some theorists suggest that the elderly naturally disengage and withdraw from life, others advocate active involvement as long as possible.

Special issues in development: Death and ageism

Throughout our entire life span, our understanding of death, dying, and the entire process of aging is limited by our culture's emphasis on youth, growth, strength, speed, and progress. Any evidence of a loss or decline in any of these qualities or capabilities is deeply feared, exaggerated, and/or denied (Butler and Lewis, 1982; Gatz and Pearson, 1988). How does this reaction to a normal and inevitable part of life affect our personal and societal adjustment? Like all forms of prejudice, ageism and the irrational fear of death punish both the victim and perpetrator. The victims in this case (the elderly and dying) are limited in their access to full support and respect from society, and the perpetrators are limited in their access to valuable information from "pilgrims" who journey on before them (Stoddard, 1978).

Question: What can be done to combat these prejudices and irrational fears? Education is one of the best antidotes to prejudice and misinformation. After spending hundreds of hours at the bedside of the terminally ill, Elizabeth Kübler-Ross developed a greater understanding of the psychological processes surrounding death (1969; 1983). Using extensive interviews with these patients, she proposed that most people go through a sequence of five stages while coping with death: *denial* of the terminal condition ("This can't be true, it's a mistake!"), *anger* ("Why me? It isn't fair!"), *bargaining* ("God, if you let me live I'll dedicate my life to you!"), *depression* ("I'm losing everyone and everything I hold dear"), and finally *acceptance* ("I know that death is inevitable and my time is near").

Critics of this "stage theory" of dying have stressed that each person's death is a unique experience and that emotions and reactions depend on the individual's personality, life situation, age, and so on (Kastenbaum, 1982). Others have worried that the popularization of her theory will cause further avoidance and stereotyping of the dying ("He's just in the anger stage right now"). In response to this, Kübler-Ross (1983, 1985) agrees that not all people go through the same stages in the same way, and regrets that anyone would use her theory as a model for a "good death."

In spite of the potential abuses of this theory, the work of Kübler-Ross has spurred important insight and research into a long-neglected topic. **Thanatology,** the study of death and dying, has become a major topic in human development. Many people now recognize that dealing with death can help a person to more fully enjoy everyday life. Thanks in part to this research, the dying are also being helped to die with dignity by the *hospice* movement, which has created special facilities and has trained staff and volun-

THANATOLOGY: *The study of death and dying. The term comes from* thanatos, *the Greek name for a mythical personification of death, and was borrowed by Freud to represent the death instinct.*

teers to provide loving support for the terminally ill and their families (Brand, 1988). Just as the shame, fear, and superstition that once surrounded pregnancy and "birthing" have been replaced with open discussion and loving celebration, death awareness leaders hope that "deathing" can become a similarly natural and positive part of the life cycle (Foos-Graber, 1985).

Through these efforts at education, research, and exposure to death, it is also hoped that ageism will decline. Once people recognize that their self-protective prejudices provide only short-term relief from their fears of an inevitable process, they may welcome information to help cope with their own aging and death and that of their loved ones. Any form of discrimination or prejudice that limits the elderly from full participation is a cost to all of society. Maggie Kuhn offers this important advice concerning our attitudes toward aging:

> There are many stereotypes about growing old. We are not useless, toothless, and sexless. In fact, old people have a special place in society. My generation has been part of more changes than any other. We have to share that knowledge. We are the whistle blowers, the social critics. We are the ones who must be advocates for disarmament and safe, renewable sources of energy (cited in Conniff, 1984, p. 273).

Gray panther activist Maggie Kuhn is an important role model in the battle against ageism.

Review Questions

1 Family violence is often treated by _____ programs that attempt to identify and then prevent abuse, whereas _____ programs attempt to rehabilitate the family after abuse has occurred.

2 _____ is the most common reason for teenage females to drop out of school.

3 Loss of _____ is a common reason why adults experience severe reactions to divorce.

4 Research has shown that part-time jobs in high school generally have a _____ influence on adolescent development.

5 The _____ theory of aging suggests that you should remain active and involved until death, whereas the _____ theory suggests that you should naturally and gracefully withdraw from life.

6 Elizabeth Kübler-Ross's five stages of dying are _____, _____, _____, _____, and _____.

Answers: 1 primary, secondary; *2* pregnancy; *3* attachment; *4* negative; *5* activity, disengagement; *6* denial, anger, bargaining, depression, acceptance

---

REVIEW OF MAJOR CONCEPTS

PHYSICAL DEVELOPMENT

1 Changes in physical development occur across the life span but are most noticeable in childhood and adolescence. At puberty, the adolescent first becomes capable of reproduction and experiences a sharp increase in height, weight, and skeletal growth as a result of the pubertal growth spurt.

2 The growth spurt and secondary sex characteristics (such as pubic hair, facial hair, and deepened voices) may be advantageous for early-maturing boys, but the effects of early or late maturation for girls are less clear.

3 Both men and women experience bodily changes in middle age. Many female changes are related to the hormonal changes of menopause; similar psychological changes in men have been called the male climacteric.

4 Although many of the changes associated with physical aging (such as decreases in the cardiac output, visual acuity, and so on) are the result of normal or primary aging, others are the result of abuse, disuse, and disease — secondary aging. Attempts to explain physical aging have suggested that aging is genetically built-in from the moment of conception (programmed theories) or that it results from the body's loss of ability to repair damage (wear-and-tear theories).

COGNITIVE DEVELOPMENT

5 Adolescents develop impressive advances in cognitive abilities, which Piaget referred to as formal operational thought. At this fourth cognitive stage, the adolescent is able to think hypothetically, to use abstract and deductive reasoning, and to systematically formulate and test concepts.

6 The major problems associated with the formal operational period are the desire for debate and arguments and adolescent egocentrism. Egocentric thinking leads adolescents to construct an imaginary audience and to believe in the personal fable.

7 Some research has suggested that there is a fifth stage of cognitive development that results from an active application of knowledge to the outside world.

8 Despite stereotypes of a declining intelligence with age, certain types of intelligence continue to increase throughout life. Whereas fluid intelligence generally begins to decline in middle adulthood, crystallized intelligence continues to improve until the mid-sixties.

9 Memory losses in old age occur primarily in the process of encoding (getting the information stored in long-term memory) and retrieval (getting information out of storage). The extra time needed for storage and locating information is often misinterpreted as lower intelligence.

MORAL DEVELOPMENT

10 According to Kohlberg, morality progresses through three levels, with each level consisting of two subsets or stages. At the preconventional level, morality is based on the consequences of an act (either reward or punishment); at the conventional level, morality reflects the need for approval and the desire to avoid censure from authority figures; and at the postconventional level, moral reasoning comes from the individual's own principles and values.

11 One major criticism of Kohlberg's theory of moral development has come from Gilligan's research, which suggests that women have a "separate-but-equal" type of moral development. According to Gilligan, women go through three stages of development, from focusing on a selfish, individual survival morality, to an all-giving, self-sacrificing style, to a final stage of caring for herself as well as others.

12 Research shows that moral development can be enhanced by parents and adults who set good examples for children and who avoid harsh disciplinary methods that focus on fear of punishment. Direct instruction in school, in the form of moral education programs, has also helped to improve students' moral reasoning.

PERSONALITY AND SOCIAL DEVELOPMENT

13 Erikson suggests that the major psychosocial crisis of adolescence is the search for identity versus role confusion. During young adulthood, the individual's task is that of establishing intimacy, and during middle adulthood the person must deal with generativity versus stagnation. At the end of life, the older adult must establish ego integrity, which depends on the acceptance of the life that has been lived, or face overwhelming despair at the realization of lost opportunities.

14 Levinson outlined four eras of development, during which people continuously build or modify their life structure, and four transition periods, during which people question and reevaluate their choices.

15 From Levinson's emphasis on the midlife transition, there has been a popularization of the "midlife crisis." Many researchers now suggest that the midlife crisis, empty nest syndrome, and adolescent "storm and stress" may all be exaggerated accounts of a few people and may not reflect the experience of most people.

16 Families play an important role in development. In addition to the negative influences of abuse, teenage pregnancies, and divorce, families also provide several positive contributions to adjustment: feelings of attachment, social integration, reassurance of worth, reliable alliance, guidance, and opportunities for nurturance.

17 The kind of work people do and the occupational choices they make can play an important role in their lives. Career decisions can be improved through research into possible alternatives and interest inventories. Part-time jobs, at least in high school, seem to have a negative influence on school and family relations.

18 Careers tend to go through stages — from initial "job-hopping" to retirement. After retirement there are two major theories of successful aging. According to activity theory, people should remain active and involved throughout the entire life span. According to disengagement theory, the elderly naturally and gracefully withdraw from life because they welcome the relief from roles they can no longer fulfill.

19 Two of the most important issues in adult development are the damage done by ageism and the irrational fear of death. Kübler-Ross's theory of the five-stage process of dying offers important insight and education concerning death. It is hoped that by confronting our fear of death, prejudice against the elderly will also decline.

SUGGESTED READINGS

GILLIGAN, C. (1982). *In a different voice: Psychological theory and women's development.* Cambridge, MA: Harvard University Press. An interesting and controversial discussion of a recent theory that contrasts the stages of moral development in women with traditional theories based largely on male subjects.

KÜBLER-ROSS, E. (1969). *On death and dying.* New York: Macmillan Co. The book that paved the way for the latest interest in the psychological experiences surrounding the "final stage" of development.

LICKONA, T. (1985). *Raising good children.* New York: Bantam Books. Using Kohlberg's basic theory of moral development, Thomas Lickona offers "how-to" advice on improving a child's level of morality.

PERLMUTTER, M., & HALL, E. (1985). *Adult development and aging.* New York: Wiley. A basic, engagingly written general text that covers the developmental changes from young adulthood through middle and late adulthood.

chapter eleven

Human Sexuality

IT was an unusual circumcision. The identical twin boys were already seven months old when their parents took them to the doctor to be circumcised. For many years in the United States, most male babies have had the foreskin of their penis removed during their first week of life, when it is assumed they will experience less pain. The most common procedure is cutting or pinching off the foreskin tissue. In this case, however, the doctor used an electrocautery device, which applies an electrical current that is used to burn off moles or small skin growths. The electrical current used for one of the brothers was too powerful, and the entire penis was accidentally removed or ablated.

After this tragedy, the parents continued to raise their sons as identical twin boys while undergoing considerable personal anguish and repeated consultations with medical experts. Following discussions with John Money and other specialists at Johns Hopkins University, the parents and doctors made an unusual decision—the twin with the ablated penis would be raised as a girl.

The first step in the "reassignment" process occurred at 17 months of age, when the child's name was changed. "She" was then dressed in pink pants and frilly blouses and the parents let "her" hair grow long. At 21 months of age, plastic surgery was performed to create external female genital structures. Further plastic surgery to create a vagina was planned at the beginning of adolescence, when the child's physical growth would be nearly complete. At this time she would also begin to take female hormones to complete the boy-to-girl transformation.

By age three, the child wore nightgowns and dresses almost exclusively and was given bracelets and hair ribbons. She clearly preferred dresses over slacks and took pride in her long hair. Her mother was surprised and pleased by the striking differences that had developed in her two children. By age four and one-half, the daughter was much neater than her brother and, in contrast to him, disliked being dirty. The mother reported, "She likes for me to wipe her face. She doesn't like to be dirty, and yet my son is quite different. I can't wash his face for anything. . . . She seems daintier. Maybe it's because I encourage it" (Money and Ehrhardt, 1972, p. 119).

During the preschool years, the girl preferred playing with "girl-type" toys and asked for a doll and carriage for Christmas. Her brother asked for a garage with cars, gas pumps, and tools. By age six, the brother was accustomed to defending his sister whenever anyone threatened her. The daughter copied the mother in tidying and cleaning up the kitchen, whereas the boy did not. The mother agreed that she encouraged her daughter when she helped with the housework and expected the boy to be uninterested.

What do you think about the outcome of this surgery? Is it possible that the only thing that makes you male or female is how your parents or others treat you? Could surgery and the administration of opposite-sex hormones change your sexuality? How about dating and marriage? Would you still be attracted to the same type of person, or would this change with the administration of opposite-sex hormones? As you can see, the concepts of sex, attraction, and one's personal sense of maleness and femaleness are not as simple as we usually imagine.

In spite of this complexity, scientists interested in the field of human sexuality have made several exciting discoveries that you will find useful in your interpersonal relationships. The background of these scientists and their methods of study are the topic of the first section of this chapter. The second section will focus on *gender,* the basic concept of maleness and femaleness, and how it relates to specific issues in sexuality, such as transsexualism and homosexuality. We will also discuss how people come to identify themselves as men and women, and how males differ from females anatomically, hormonally, cognitively, and behaviorally. Next, we will describe sexual arousal and response, some common myths surrounding sexual behavior, and the role of sex therapy in the treatment of sexual problems or dysfunctions. Finally, we will look at the general field of interpersonal attraction, examining such issues as what factors determine liking or loving and how romantic love differs from companionate love.

Before we begin, you may be interested in sampling your current level of sex knowledge with the quiz in Table 11.1. The answers are provided at the bottom of the quiz, and expanded explanations can be found throughout the chapter.

THE STUDY OF HUMAN SEXUALITY

Sex is used and abused in many ways: as a major theme in literature, movies, and music; to satisfy sexual desires; to gain love and acceptance from partners and peer groups; as a way of expressing love or commitment to a relationship; as a way of ending relationships

TABLE 11.1
Test Your Sexual IQ

Do you know which of the following statements are true and which are false?

1 The breakfast cereal, Kellogg's Corn Flakes, was originally developed to discourage masturbation.

2 Nocturnal emissions and masturbation are signs of abnormal sexual adjustment.

3 AIDS can be spread through swimming pools.

4 Transsexuals are basically homosexual.

5 If a developing male fetus fails to get sufficient testosterone during prenatal development, he may develop female genitals.

6 Women are less aroused by explicit sexual material than men.

7 There are documented physical differences between male and female brains.

8 Sexual skill and satisfaction are learned behaviors and can be increased through education and training.

9 Sexual arousal is largely the result of reflexes and the parasympathetic nervous system.

10 Women fail to achieve vaginal orgasms due to psychological immaturity.

11 Only women are capable of multiple orgasms.

12 "Looks" are the primary factor in our initial feelings of attraction, liking, and romantic love.

13 A stranger's compliments are often more rewarding than those of our spouse or long-term best friend.

14 Romantic love rarely lasts longer than 6 to 30 months.

Answers: 1. T *2.* F *3.* F *4.* F *5.* T *6.* F *7.* T *8.* T *9.* T *10.* F *11.* F *12.* T *13.* T *14.* T

Sexuality is an important part of everyone's life throughout their entire life cycle.

through affairs with others; to dominate or hurt others; and, perhaps most conspicuously, to sell products.

Although people have probably always been interested in understanding their sexuality, strong cultural forces have been exerted to suppress and control this interest. During the nineteenth century, for example, polite society avoided mention of all parts of the body covered by clothing (the breast of chicken became known as "white meat"), female patients were examined by male doctors in totally darkened rooms, and some people even considered it necessary to cover piano legs for the sake of propriety (Gay, 1983; Money, 1985a).

The medical experts of this same time warned that masturbation led to blindness, impotence, acne, and insanity. Believing that a bland diet helped to suppress sexual desire, Dr. John Harvey Kellogg and Sylvester Graham, respectively, developed and marketed the original Kellogg's Corn Flakes and Graham crackers in an attempt to prevent masturbation (Money, 1985a). One of the most serious concerns of many doctors was the problem of nocturnal emissions ("wet dreams"), which were widely believed to lead to brain damage and death. Thus, special devices were marketed for men to wear at night to prevent their sexual arousal (see Figure 11.1).

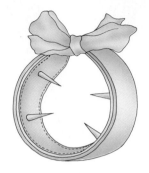

Figure 11.1 During the eighteenth century, men were encouraged to wear spiked rings around their penises at night to discourage nocturnal emissions (or "wet dreams"). If the wearer had an erection, the spikes would cause pain that would awaken the sleeper.

Question: Did men really wear these devices? In light of modern knowledge, it does seem hard to understand how anyone ever consented to such strange practices or believed these outrageous myths about masturbation and nocturnal emissions. One of the first physicians known to question these practices was Havelock Ellis (1858–1939). When he first heard of the dangers of nocturnal emissions, Ellis was extremely frightened, since he recognized that he himself had personal experience with this problem. His fear led him to a frantic search of the medical literature, but instead of a cure, he found predictions of a gruesome illness and eventual death. Although he initially reacted to these predictions by contemplating suicide, he eventually decided that he could give meaning to his life by keeping a detailed diary of his deterioration that he could later dedicate to science when he died. After several months of careful and detailed observation, he slowly began to realize that the books were wrong — he wasn't dying. He wasn't even sick. Angry that he had been so misinformed by the "experts," he dedicated the rest of his life to the search for reliable and accurate sex information. He is generally remembered today as one of the most important early pioneers in the field of sex research, and for his advancement of the method of the case study.

Using the case study technique (an in-depth study of a single research subject or of small groups of people), Ellis studied the actual sexual experiences of hundreds of people. From these case studies he found that nocturnal emissions and masturbation were normal, harmless, and commonly experienced. He also argued that homosexuality did not always involve pathology and that the sexual capacities and needs of women were equal to those of men (Brecher, 1969). These beliefs failed to receive general acceptance during Ellis's own time, but he is widely respected today for his courageous and surprisingly modern views.

Although the case study approach is still widely used in sex research (as with the case of the twin boy who was reassigned as a female), interviews and surveys are probably the most popular research techniques today. Among the earliest and most extensive studies in sexuality were those conducted by Alfred Kinsey and his colleagues (1948, 1953). Kinsey and his coworkers personally interviewed over 18,000 subjects, asking detailed questions about their sexual activities and sexual preferences (Pomeroy, 1972). Despite criticisms concerning his methodology and sample of subjects (mostly young, single, urban, white, and middle class), Kinsey's work is still widely respected, and his data are frequently used as a *baseline* for modern research. In recent years, hundreds of sex surveys and interviews have been conducted regarding such topics as contraception, abortion, premarital sex, and rape (Davis and Yarber, 1988; Weiss, 1989a). By comparing Kinsey's data to the responses found in later surveys, we can see how sexual practices have changed over the years.

In addition to case studies, surveys, and interviews, some researchers have em-

Havelock Ellis was one of the first sex researchers to celebrate eroticism and acknowledge female sexuality.

The survey results of Alfred Kinsey are still widely quoted today.

William Masters and Virginia Johnson are probably the best known and most widely quoted sex researchers.

ployed direct laboratory experimentation and observational methods. Interested in documenting the physiological changes involved in sexual arousal and response, William Masters and Virginia Johnson (1966, 1970) and their research colleagues enlisted several hundred men and women volunteers. After attaching them to intricate physiological measuring devices, the researchers then carefully monitored the subjects' bodily responses while masturbating or engaging in sexual intercourse. Masters and Johnson's research findings are hailed as a major contribution to our knowledge of sexual physiology, and some of their results will be discussed in later sections.

Some sex researchers also conduct cross-cultural studies by comparing the sexual practices, techniques, and attitudes of various societies (Beach, 1977; Reiss, 1986). Since most people are exposed only to the sexual practices of their own particular culture, such cross-cultural comparisons help to put sex in a broader perspective and to counteract the tendency to see one's own practices as the only "natural" pattern.

Although the methods of sex researchers may vary (from individual case studies to cross-cultural comparisons), all share the common desire to increase knowledge about the causes, correlates, and consequences of various sexual attitudes and behaviors. This shared goal will become apparent in the coming sections.

Review Questions

1 One of the earliest uses of the case study technique in the field of human sexuality came from _____.

2 Kinsey and his colleagues popularized the use of the _____ method in the study of human sexuality.

3 _____ and _____ pioneered the use of direct observation and physiological measurement of bodily responses during sexual activities.

4 _____ studies compare and contrast the sexual practices, attitudes, and techniques of different societies in an attempt to learn more about human sexuality.

Answers: 1 Havelock Ellis;   *2* survey;   *3* Masters, Johnson;   *4* cross-cultural

BECOMING AND BEING MALE OR FEMALE

Have you ever tried to imagine what life would be like if there were no divisions according to maleness or femaleness? Would your career plans or friendship patterns change? Why is it that the first question most people ask after a baby is born is "Is it a girl or a boy?" These questions reflect the great importance of **gender** in our lives. This section begins with a look at the various ways in which gender can be defined, followed by a discussion of the major biological and psychological differences between men and women and potential causes of these differences.

GENDER: *The state of being male or female.*

Gender dimensions: Defining "maleness" and "femaleness"

Before we can explore what is known about the differences between the sexes, we must clarify the terms "maleness" and "femaleness." In the case of the male twin who was reassigned as a female, do you still think of "her" as being basically male? Or do you think that her feminine dress and behavior patterns and her own personal identity as female are sufficient to label her female? As you can see, the general topic of gender can sometimes be very confusing. To improve our understanding, Money and Ehrhardt (1972) offer a useful categorization of the various dimensions of gender:

1. *Chromosomal gender or genetic sex.* Females have a chromosome pattern of XX, whereas males have the XY pattern (see Chapter 9).
2. *Gonadal gender.* The gonads are the sex glands. The female gonads are the ovaries, which produce the ova, or egg cells. The male gonads are the testes, which produce sperm.
3. *Hormonal gender.* Feminizing **estrogens** are hormones produced primarily in the ovaries; masculinizing **androgens** are produced primarily in the testes (testosterone is the most common androgen). The ovaries also produce small amounts of androgens, the testes produce small amounts of estrogens, and the adrenal glands of both sexes produce some androgens and estrogens. It is the relative proportion of these hormones that account for male–female differences in development.
4. *Genital sex.* The external sex organs of females include the vulva, clitoris, and vaginal opening. The external male genitals are the penis and scrotum (see Figure 11.2).
5. *Internal accessory organs.* The major internal organs for the female include the uterus, vagina, and fallopian tubes. The major internal structures for the male include the prostate gland, seminal vesicles, and vas deferens (see Figure 11.2).

ESTROGENS: *Hormones that stimulate maturation and functioning of the female reproductive system.*
ANDROGENS: *Hormones that stimulate maturation and functioning of the male reproductive system.*

In addition to these biological dimensions of gender, there are several psychological and behavioral dimensions to include in a definition of gender:

1. *Gender identity or psychosexual identity.* One's perception of oneself as being male or female.
2. *Gender role or sex role.* The differing societal expectations for the proper behavior of males and females. When these expectations are based on a firm belief in fundamental differences between the sexes and are rigidly applied to all members of each sex, they are known as *sex-role stereotypes.*
3. *Sexual orientation or sexual preference.* One's choice of same-sex (homosexual) or opposite-sex (heterosexual) persons as preferred sexual partners.
4. *Sexual behavior.* Behavior related to sexual desire, including both arousal and gratification. Masturbation and intercourse are examples of sexual behaviors.

Using the summary of these nine dimensions of gender found in Table 11.2, you can see why the case of the reassigned twin is considered such a classic in the field of human sexuality. Although born a chromosomal male, the child's genital sex was first altered by

about how their gender identity development differs from that of other children. One of the earliest theories suggested that transsexualism resulted from inappropriate roles of the parents. The mother and father were either too warm or too cold, were either domineering or ineffectual, or encouraged inappropriate behaviors (Green, 1975; Pauly, 1974; Stoller, 1969). Despite the lack of later research support, and other theories that suggest genetic or hormonal causes (Money, 1988), this "faulty parental role" theory is still widely accepted by the general public.

At the present time no one really knows what causes either transsexualism or homosexuality. Most transsexuals and homosexuals come to accept these labels as a result of their gender identity problems or because of their sexual preference for members of the same sex. As we have seen in the case of the reassigned twin, self-perception seems to be a very important part of sexuality. It is interesting to note that many people do engage in some form of homosexual behavior in their lifetime, ranging from a single, exploratory contact in adolescence to long-term repeated contacts. Yet most of these same individuals do not identify or define themselves as homosexual.

When scientists attempt to explain homosexuality, the answers are generally either biological or psychological. The *biological model* suggests that homosexuality is caused by a genetic predisposition, hormonal deficiencies, or prenatal biasing of the brain (Ellis and Ames, 1987; Money, 1988; Zuger, 1989). However, there is little research support for hormonal explanations (Gladue, 1987), and the data on genetic predisposition and prenatal biasing are conflicting.

The two major *psychological* causation theories are the psychoanalytic and the learning models. According to the psychoanalytic theory, male homosexuality develops from "close-binding intimate mothers" and emotionally, detached, hostile fathers (Bieber et al., 1962). Female homosexuality, on the other hand, is believed to result from rejecting or indifferent mothers and a silent or absent father (Wolff, 1971).

Although Freud originated most of the modern "disturbed family" theories, he also held a relatively benign view of homosexuality. He believed that we all begin life as *bisexuals*. Given the repressive nineteenth-century view of sexuality, Freud's advice to a mother who had written to him about her homosexual son can be seen as particularly sensitive and enlightened:

> *Dear Mrs. . . .*
> *I gather from your letter that your son is a homosexual. I am most interested by the fact that you do not mention this term yourself in your information about him. May I question you, why you avoid it? Homosexuality is assuredly no advantage, but it is nothing to be ashamed of, no vice, no degradation. It cannot be classified as an illness. . . . Many highly respectable individuals of ancient and modern times have been homosexuals, several of the greatest men among them (Plato, Michelangelo, Leonardo da Vinci, etc.). It is a great injustice to persecute homosexuality as a crime, and it is a cruelty too. . . .*

> *(Gay, 1988, p. 415)*

Learning theorists, like psychoanalysts, believe in the importance of the early years on later homosexual identification. But they emphasize the importance of reinforcement of differing sex-role behaviors. Whether one becomes predominantly homosexual or heterosexual is believed to result from early experiences and their consequences (Brody, 1985; Masters and Johnson, 1986).

In summary, research on the causes of homosexuality is inconclusive. Despite this lack of empirical evidence and the fact that many homosexuals are known to come from well-adjusted families (Siegelman, 1987; Zuger, 1988), many parents still feel guilty for "causing" their child's homosexual orientation. Such parental guilt, as well as the whole idea of looking for "causes" of homosexuality, may be a form of covert prejudice against this sexual orientation. Since parents never experience such negative feelings about having caused their children to be heterosexual, and since researchers are not actively seeking "causes" for heterosexuality, the implication is that homosexuality is a disorder

These protesters are demonstrating support for gay fathers and working to overcome prejudice against homosexuality.

and that a "cure" can be found. This belief among some mental health professionals, accompanied by the generally hostile public feelings, obviously creates serious problems for many who have a homosexual orientation.

Review Questions

1 The chromosomal patterns of XX and XY determine one's _____ _____ .

2 Males have a dominance of masculinizing hormones known as _____ , whereas females have a dominance of feminizing hormones known as _____ .

3 Societal expectations for behavior that differ for men and women are known as _____ _____ .

4 A _____ has a gender identity that is opposite that of his or her physical anatomy, whereas a _____ wears clothing of the opposite sex primarily for sexual arousal and gratification.

5 Being _____ refers to having sexual preference for members of the same sex.

6 Psychoanalytic explanations stress _____ _____ _____ as the most important cause of both homosexuality and transsexualism.

Answers: 1 chromosomal gender;   2 androgens, estrogens;   3 gender roles;   4 transsexual, transvestite;   5 homosexual;   6 faulty parental roles

Biological differences: Anatomy and hormones

Physical anatomy is the most obvious difference between males and females. The physique of male and female bodies differs from birth in composition, shape, and fat distribution. The average adult male is taller, heavier, and stronger than the average adult female. Males have larger hearts and lungs, which help them to recover more quickly from physical exertion, but men are also more likely to be bald, to be color-blind, and to have a shorter life expectancy. In addition, there are also major differences in the sexual and reproductive organs, as we noted in the discussion of gender dimensions. In Chapter 10, we also discussed how males and females differ in their secondary sex characteristics (facial hair, breasts, and so on), their signs of reproductive capability (the menarche for girls and the ejaculation of sperm for boys), and their psychological reactions to middle age or the end of reproduction (the female menopause and male climacteric).

In view of these obvious physical differences in later life, it may be surprising to learn that in the first six weeks after conception all embryos are anatomically identical (see

BEFORE THE 6TH WEEK—UNDIFFERENTIATED

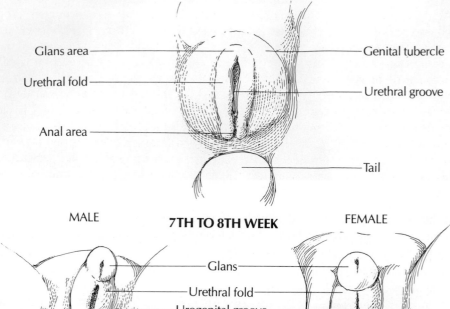

Glans area — — Genital tubercle

Urethral fold — — Urethral groove

Anal area

— Tail

MALE   **7TH TO 8TH WEEK**   FEMALE

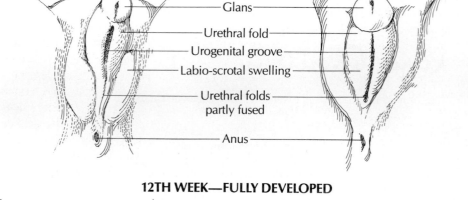

Glans
Urethral fold
Urogenital groove
Labio-scrotal swelling
Urethral folds
partly fused
Anus

12TH WEEK—FULLY DEVELOPED

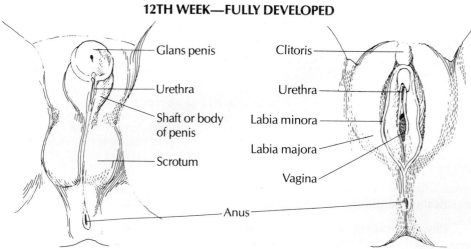

Glans penis   Clitoris

Urethra   Urethra

Shaft or body
of penis   Labia minora

Scrotum   Labia majora

Vagina

Anus

Figure 11.3 Prenatal stages of external genital development. Notice that before the sixth week there is no visible difference between the male and female genitals. As development continues, the same embryonic tissue differentiates to become distinctly male or female.

Figure 11.3). During this time, the gonads are *undifferentiated,* which means that they have the potential to develop into either testes or ovaries. If the embryo is genetically male (XY chromosome pattern), the gonads differentiate into testes and begin to produce the masculinizing hormones known as androgens. The most important androgen is testosterone, which stimulates the further differentiation into internal and external male sex structures. If the embryo is female (XX chromosome pattern), ovarian tissue forms and begins to produce estrogen. It is important to recognize that it is the *presence* or *absence* of testosterone that determines anatomical sex. Without the Y chromosome and testosterone, *all* fetuses would develop female reproductive organs and genitals. It seems that nature's basic blueprint is for a female fetus (Tavris and Wade, 1984).

Question: What happens if a male baby doesn't get enough testosterone or a female gets too much? Although genital development almost always matches the genetic sex, there are rare exceptions. As a result of hormonal or genetic problems, some children are born with both male and female genital structures or with ambiguous genitals. In chromosomal females (the XX pattern), "faulty" genital development is generally due to an oversecretion of androgens by the adrenal glands (**adrenogenital syndrome**) or to masculinizing synthetic hormones that entered the fetus from the mother's bloodstream during pregnancy. (Such hormones were at one time given to pregnant mothers to prevent miscarriage.) In chromosomal males (the XY pattern), male genitals may fail to develop if testosterone is absent or low at the critical time of six to twelve weeks after conception. Even when the testosterone is adequate and present, a genetic defect may prevent the cells of the body from responding to it (**androgen-insensitivity syndrome**). In this case, the male will develop normal-appearing external female genitals.

ADRENOGENITAL SYNDROME: *A masculinization of a chromosomal female as a result of an excessive amount of androgens being produced during fetal development.*
ANDROGEN-INSENSITIVITY SYNDROME: *A feminization of a chromosomal male as a result of a genetic defect in which androgens have no effect on the developing fetal tissues.*

Question: What happens to these babies who are not clearly male or female at birth? Most abnormalities can be corrected by surgery and the administration of extra hormones. The long-term physical and psychological adjustment of several such children has been closely followed, and the data have been used to support both sides of the ongoing nature–nurture controversy.

In the case of the reassigned twin, for example, we have seen that nurturists have used "her" successful reassignment as evidence of the primary importance of the environment in the development of gender identity. As the female twin entered adolescence, however, the "success" began to be questioned. The child's appearance and masculine gait led her classmates to taunt her, calling her "cavewoman." She also expressed ideas about becoming a mechanic, and her fantasies showed some discomfort with her female role (Diamond, 1982). Although these problems may have reflected a need for an adjustment in her estrogen dose or even just the normal pains and problems of adolescence that could occur in any female, they do make it more difficult to use this case as support for the environmental position.

The nativist (biological) position has been strengthened by the study of the later development of females who were affected by masculinizing hormones during prenatal development. Although their hormone balance became more female at birth and they were raised as girls, these individuals were more frequently described as "tomboys" during childhood, seemed to prefer the company of boys to girls, were more achievement oriented, and were more aggressive and athletic (Money, 1977).

Question: Couldn't this also be the result of the parents' treatment? Researchers who looked at this question found that the parents of these children were actually even more concerned about encouraging feminine behaviors than the average parent (Ehrhardt and Meyer-Bahlburg, 1981). However, it remains impossible to truly separate the effects of biological and environmental or social influences on sexual development.

Psychological differences: Innate or culturally produced?

Do you think there are inborn psychological differences between women and men? Do you believe that women are more emotional and more concerned with aesthetics, whereas men are naturally more aggressive and competitive? As a test of your personal attitudes about the psychological differences in men and women, stop for a moment and do the following exercise:

Imagine that you have just entered a room full of strangers. To your right is a group of five females and to your left is a group of five males. Which group would you join? Jot down the first five reasons that come to mind for your joining one group over the other.

cathy® by **Cathy Guisewite**

SEX-ROLE STEREOTYPES: *Rigid, preconceived beliefs about the characteristics of males and females.*

Regardless of your choice of groups, either male or female, your reasons for the choice are based on the existence of your personal **sex-role stereotypes,** or fixed ways of thinking about and perceiving men and women. Although your list probably contains general statements like "I feel more comfortable with . . ." or "I'm more attracted to . . . ," the underlying reasons for your comfort or attraction are based on your assumptions (stereotypes) about the "average" male or female—"I feel more comfortable with women because they're not so competitive."

Question: What if I had positive reasons for joining the group? Aren't stereotypes negative? Although the term "stereotype" *is* generally used in a negative manner, we also hold "positive" stereotypes, such as "women are warm and sensitive" and "men are independent and ambitious." The fact that men and women hold both positive and negative sex-role stereotypes was demonstrated by Broverman and her colleagues (1970). After listing the characteristics, attributes, and types of behavior in which they thought men and women differed, subjects were asked to indicate which traits were most desirable. As you can see in Table 11.3, the list of desirable traits is much longer for males than for females. The fact that so many of the "masculine" traits (e.g., independence, ambitiousness, self-confidence) are also economically rewarded has serious implications for the financial future of "feminine" women. Furthermore, the so-called masculine traits of "hiding emotions" and "easily separating feelings from ideas" may conflict with the

TABLE 11.3
Male-Valued and Female-Valued Stereotypic Items

Female-Valued Items	Male-Valued Items
Very talkative	Very aggressive
Very gentle	Very independent
Very aware of feelings of others	Almost always hides emotions
Very interested in own appearance	Likes math and science very much
Very strong need for security	Not at all excitable in a minor crisis
Easily expresses tender feelings	Very competitive
	Very logical
	Very adventurous
	Can make decisions easily
	Almost always acts as a leader
	Very self-confident
	Very ambitious
	Easily able to separate feelings from ideas

Source: Adapted from Broverman et al. (1970). "Sex-role stereotypes and clinical judgments of mental health," *Journal of Consulting and Clinical Psychology, 34(1)*, 3. Copyright © 1970 by the American Psychological Association. Used by permission of the author.

feminine trait of "easily expressing tender feelings" and may create relationship problems.

Question: Aren't sex-role sterotypes sometimes true?　　Just as stereotypes can be both positive and negative, they can also be accurate and inaccurate. For example, the stereotype that men have a higher number of sexual outlets (through fantasy, masturbation, and intercourse) throughout their life span was supported by Kinsey's (1948, 1953) large-scale survey of American adolescents and adults. In contrast, the stereotype that women are "turned off" by explicit sexual material is *not* supported (Heiman, 1977; Morokoff, 1985).

Although some stereotypes are accurate, research has found few legitimate psychological differences between men and women (see Table 11.4). In fact, in almost all instances the overall variance between the sexes is less than 5 percent (Deaux, 1985). It is

TABLE 11.4
Research-Supported Sex Differences

Type of Behavior	More Often Shown by Men	More Often Shown by Women
Touching	Are touched, kissed, and cuddled less by parents	Are touched, kissed, and cuddled more by parents
	Exchange less physical contact with other men and respond more negatively to being touched	Exchange more physical contact with other women and respond more positively to being touched
	More likely to initiate both casual and intimate touch	Less likely to initiate either casual or intimate touch
Friendship	Have larger number of friends and express friendship by shared activities	Have smaller number of friends and express friendship by shared communication about self
Aggression	Are more aggressive from a very early age	Are less aggressive from a very early age
Personality	Are more self-confident of future success	Are less self-confident of future success
	Attribute success to internal factors and failures to external factors	Attribute success to external factors and failures to internal factors
	Achievement is task oriented; motives are mastery and competition	Achievement is socially directed with emphasis on self-improvement; have higher work motives
	Are more self-validating	Are more dependent on others for self-validation
	Have higher self-esteem	Have lower self-esteem
Intelligence	Are superior in mathematics and visual–spatial skills	Are superior in grammar, spelling, and perceptual speed
Sexual behavior	Begin masturbating sooner in life cycle and have higher overall occurrence rates	Begin masturbating later in life cycle and have lower overall occurrence rates
	Start sexual life earlier and have first orgasm through masturbation	Start sexual life later and have first orgasm from partner stimulation
	Are more likely to recognize their own arousal	Are less likely to recognize their own arousal
	Experience more orgasm consistency in their sexual relations	Experience less orgasm consistency in their sexual relations

Sources: Allgeier and Allgeier (1988); Basow (1986); Jacklin (1989); Katchadourian (1989); Masters and Johnson (1986); Rose (1985).

Figure 11.4 Variations in heights of males and females. Note the overlap between the sexes—some men are shorter than the average female and some women are taller than the average male.

Females   Males

Short   Tall

Approximate magnitude of sex differences in height

important to remember that variation *within* each sex is always greater than the average difference *between* the sexes. This can be understood by considering the obvious male/female physical difference in height. As can be seen in Figure 11.4, there is approximately a six-inch difference in height between the average male and the average female (5'10" minus 5'4"), but the range of heights within each sex is enormous. Just as knowing someone's gender doesn't allow us to predict how tall he or she is, we also cannot predict whether an individual will be good at math simply by knowing that the average male has higher math scores than the average female. The famous English author Samuel Johnson once gave a very appropriate response to the question on whether males or females are more intelligent. He responded, "Which man? Which woman?"

Question: What causes those differences that do exist between the sexes? Explanations for gender differences again reflect the nature – nurture controversy. For example, the fact that males tend to be more aggressive and to have greater spatial skills is considered by the nativists to be the result of inborn, genetic factors. The nativists also point out that the female brain is apparently more symmetrically organized than the male brain (Hopson, 1984). Furthermore, the corpus callosum (the structure that connects the two cerebral hemispheres) in the female brain is supposedly larger than in the male (de Lacoste-Utamsing and Holloway, 1982). This finding of a structural sex difference in the corpus callosum has been refuted by the work of Ruth Bleier (1987), a neuroanatomist at the University of Wisconsin. Whereas the earlier researchers had based their report on 14

From an early age, children are socialized toward the roles and values of either masculinity or femininity.

autopsied brains, Bleier used the magnetic resonance imaging technique (see Chapter 2) on 39 live subjects and found no evidence of a sex difference. Bleier criticized the methodology of the previous research and also suggested that there is no evidence that the size or shape of the corpus callosum has an effect on behavior.

One of the best-documented structural differences between male and female brains that does have measurable effects on behavior is in the synapses in the hypothalamus (Marx, 1988). During prenatal development, the presence of androgens stimulates the hypothalamus to develop in a male pattern (MacLuskey and Naftolin, 1981). At the time of puberty, this prenatal hormone programming controls the relatively constant level of sex hormones in males and the cyclic sex hormone production and menstruation in females.

As adults, the female's monthly ebb and flow of estrogen levels may explain recently reported fluctuations in her cognitive and behavioral skills. Researchers Elizabeth Hampson and Doreen Kimura (1988) have found that when a woman experiences low estrogen levels — during and immediately after menstruation — she does better at tasks involving spatial relationships. In contrast, peak estrogen levels — around the time of ovulation — are associated with improved performance of motor and verbal tasks.

Question: How does estrogen affect these skills? Estrogen has been found to enhance the function of the brain's left hemisphere, which would account for the improved performance in verbal skills, and sex hormones may also influence the release of specific neurotransmitters that play a role in motor coordination (Weiss, 1988).

In contrast to such biological arguments, the nurturists suggest that male – female differences can be explained by environmental effects. One of the best arguments for this position, and against the biological model, is the recent finding that cognitive gender differences have dramatically declined over recent years (Jacklin, 1989). Using meta-analysis (a statistical technique for estimating the size of effects and comparing large numbers of studies), Hyde and Linn (1988) found a significant reduction in male – female differences in verbal-ability scores. A similar reduction in differences between males and females on mathematic scores has also been observed (Feingold, 1988). The only exception to this trend of vanishing gender differences is at the upper levels of performance on high school mathematics, where males still tend to dominate.

Although cognitive gender differences seem to be disappearing, variations in personality factors like aggression seem relatively stable (Basow, 1986; Hyde, 1984). Nurturists typically explain these consistent personality differences by referring to environmental pressures that encourage "sex-appropriate" behaviors and skills. Elementary school teachers, for example, often inadvertently encourage aggressive behavior in boys and passivity in girls. Research by Sadker and Sadker (1985) found that boys talked three times as often as girls. Whereas boys tended to call out their answers to teacher questions, girls usually raised their hand and waited to be called on. When a girl called out her answer, the teacher generally told her that such behavior was inappropriate. Sadker and Sadker concluded that "The message was subtle but powerful: Boys should be academically assertive . . .; girls should act like ladies and keep quiet."

Parents and peers are also important forces in gender role **socialization** — the process of imparting societal expectations. During prenatal development, for example, mothers who have an active fetus that kicks and moves a great deal are more likely to assume it is a boy (Lewis, 1982). Within 24 hours after birth both parents often perceive strong sex-related differences in their newborn babies. Even when there is no physical difference in muscle tone, size, or reflexes, parents, especially fathers, perceive boy infants as stronger, more alert, larger, hardier, and better coordinated than girls (Rubin et al., 1974). Once children get older and go outside the home, the gender role training of the parents is generally reinforced by peer group pressure. Boys as young as three or four will often be ridiculed if they attempt to play "house" and "dolls" with the girls.

When we look at specific differences between the sexes that usually don't appear until adolescence, such as male superiority in quantitative and spatial tasks, we find that the parents' "silent" expectations of these traits in males may foster their development. In a study where parents were interviewed about their child's mathematical skills, for exam-

SOCIALIZATION: *The process of imparting the customs, habits, folkways, and mores of a given culture to a child or a newcomer to the society.*

ple, it was found that when boys did well the parents attributed it to their natural ability, but when girls did well the parents downplayed natural abilities and assumed that they had had to work very hard (Eccles et al., 1984). In addition, many parents believed that math is more important for boys and are more likely to encourage additional math courses for boys (Basow, 1986).

Subtle environmental forces may explain other male–female differences as well. For example, the purchase of elaborate building blocks and erector sets for boys and the encouragement of active, rough-and-tumble play (wrestling, throwing, climbing) may provide differential growth experiences for boys that are important to the development of visual–spatial skills. Certainly the case of the reassigned twin shows how differential treatment by parents can lead to feminine rather than masculine traits. How else would you explain the preference for dolls and ribbons in one twin and the preference for cars and tools in the other?

ANDROGYNY: *The combining of some characteristics considered to be typically male (e.g., assertive, athletic) with those that are typically female (e.g., yielding, nurturant); from the Greek* andro *meaning "male" and* gyn *meaning "female."*

It was very popular at one time to talk about encouraging **androgyny** (a combination of both male and female personality traits) as a possible "solution" to the problems created by male–female psychological differences (Bem, 1974, 1981; Spence, 1984). But further studies have suggested that it may not be the panacea that many anticipated (Carson, 1989). In addition to the basic problems with defining and measuring "masculinity" and "femininity," there are also disagreements over which are the "best" traits of men and women that should be encouraged for both sexes. Perhaps the most important criticism of the concept of androgyny is that it seems to advocate a specific combination of traits for "ideal" adjustment and such advocacy is generally seen as stepping beyond the bounds of scientific research (Deaux, 1984).

Review Questions

1. In the prenatal determination of anatomical sex, the presence or absence of _____ is all-important.

2. An oversecretion of androgens in the female fetus produces the _____ syndrome, whereas the _____ syndrome is produced when the developing male fetus's body fails to respond to testosterone.

3. The belief that most women are warm and sensitive or that most men are independent is an example of a _____ _____ .

4. In studies that compare the psychological differences between men and women, the overall variance is generally found to be less than _____ percent.

5. Gender role socialization by parents and peers is used by _____ to explain male–female differences.

6. _____ , a combination of both male and female personality traits in the same person, was once promoted as a way to overcome male–female differences.

Answers: 1 testosterone; *2* adrenogenital, androgen-insensitivity; *3* sex-role stereotype; *4* five; *5* nurturists (or environmentalists); *6* androgyny

SEXUAL BEHAVIOR

Did you know that in some cultures kissing is unknown, that sexual partners in some societies arouse each other by biting to the point of drawing blood, or that intercourse three to five times a night every night is not unusual in certain societies (Ford and Beach, 1951; Gregersen, 1983)? Most Americans are surprised to learn that their particular form of sexual arousal or frequency of response is very different from that in other cultures. Cross-cultural studies of human sexuality are important not only for their contributions to our basic knowledge of human behavior but also because they remind us that much of what we consider "typical" is simply a reflection of our specific cultural training. In this section we will explore what researchers have learned about sexual arousal and response patterns in American culture. As you read, you should also keep in mind that there are individual differences within our culture as well.

Sexual arousal: The role of biology and learning

All healthy men and women are biologically prepared to respond sexually to direct physical stimulation. Although the degree of sensitivity may vary among individuals, the various **erogenous zones,** such as the penis, the clitoris, the inside of the thighs, and so on, are particularly sensitive to touch because they have a higher concentration of skin receptors. The fact that these same biologically prepared individuals are *not* aroused by the stimulation of erogenous zones during a medical examination or while riding a bicycle demonstrates the powerful role of cultural learning and individual thoughts and expectations in sexual arousal. Many problems that are seen by sex therapists, such as **erectile dysfunctions** (the inability to get or maintain an erection firm enough for intercourse) and **orgasmic dysfunctions** (the inability to respond to sexual stimulation to the point of orgasm), are also clearly affected by the emotions and cognitions of the individual. Certain medical conditions such as diabetes, alcoholism, hormonal deficiencies, and circulatory problems also contribute to such problems. Most experts agree, however, that psychological causes (preoccupation with problems, fear of evaluation or consequences of the sexual activity, and early negative sexual experiences) are much more prevalent (Kaplan, 1987; "Sexual disorders," 1990). Our bodies are apparently biologically prepared to become aroused and respond to erotic stimulation, but learning is the over riding factor in how we actually respond.

EROGENOUS ZONES: *The areas of the body that elicit sexual arousal when stimulated.*

ERECTILE DYSFUNCTION: *The inability to get or maintain an erection firm enough for intercourse.*
ORGASMIC DYSFUNCTION: *The inability to respond to sexual stimulation to the point of orgasm.*

Question: How do we learn to become sexually aroused? From our earliest social interactions with others, according to John Gagnon (1977), we learn explicit **sexual scripts** that teach us "what to do, when, where, how, and with whom." In our culture, for example, societal messages seem to say that the "best" sex is sexual intercourse at night, in a darkened room, with the male on top, and between attractive young people of the opposite sex. Yet, most sexual behaviors and people fail to fit within these narrow definitions.

SEXUAL SCRIPTS: *Socially dictated descriptions of the sequences of behavior that are considered appropriate in sexual interactions.*

A less obvious difficulty with sexual scripts is that, though they do act as strong controls over sexual behavior, they are seldom discussed or examined. Many of our deepest fears and disappointments are a reflection of these unconscious scripts. Women who build their expectations for sexual interactions on the basis of romantic novels and men whose conceptions of the female body are based on photos in *Playboy* or *Penthouse* are often disappointed with real life. A major aim of sex therapy is to encourage individuals to examine their sexual scripts and then to explore openly how these expectations may be interfering with their relationships.

Question: Aren't there some parts of arousal that are automatic and unlearned? Yes. Although many people may consider it unromantic, some parts of sexual arousal are clearly the result of automatic processes. Most people would consider a romantic evening, with a blazing fire and soft music, to be a "recipe" for sexual arousal, but few people recognize the role of reflexes and the autonomic nervous system in sexual desire.

As discussed in Chapter 2, several aspects of human behavior are reflexive — that is, unlearned, automatic, and occurring without conscious effort or motivation. Sexual arousal for both men and women is partially reflexive and somewhat analogous to simple reflexes like the eye blink response to a puff of air. Just as the puff of air produces an automatic response of closing the eye, certain stimuli, such as stroking of the genitals, *can* lead to automatic arousal. In both situations, nerve impulses from the receptor site travel to the spinal cord, which responds by sending messages to target organs or glands.

In the case of sexual arousal, the spinal cord responds to stroking messages by telling the valvelike channels in genital arteries to relax. When these valves relax, blood is allowed to flow into the area, and this increased blood volume results in the erection of the penis in the male and the engorgement of the clitoris and surrounding tissues in the female.

Question: If this is so automatic, why do some people have difficulty in getting aroused?   Unlike simple reflexes such as the eye blink, sexual arousal may be blocked by competing thoughts, expectations, and high emotional states. As you may remember from Chapter 2, the autonomic nervous system (ANS) is intricately involved in emotional (and sexual) responses. The ANS is composed of two subsystems: the *sympathetic,* which prepares the body for "fight or flight," and the *parasympathetic,* which is responsible for maintaining bodily processes at a steady and even balance. The parasympathetic branch of the nervous system is in dominance during sexual arousal (the body must be relaxed to allow the blood flow to the genital area), and the sympathetic branch is dominant during *ejaculation* and *orgasm.*

Problems with arousal are sometimes explained by the fact that strong emotions, like fear or anxiety, place the individual in sympathetic dominance, which would block the initial arousal. This fear or anxiety also explains why young women often have difficulty with sexual arousal. The secretive and forbidden conditions of many early sexual experiences create strong anxieties over fear of discovery, loss of respect, and fear of pregnancy. Many women discover that they need locked doors, committed relationships, and reliable birth control to enjoy sexual relations.

Question: What about men?   Males often have difficulty with arousal if they drink too much alcohol, are fatigued, or experience **performance anxiety.** These same factors have similar effects on female arousal, and many men also share the female's desires for privacy, commitment, and freedom from pregnancy concerns.

In spite of the many similarities in male–female physiological responses to arousal, men often seem more "interested" in sex and more easily aroused, at least during adolescence and early adulthood. Sex therapists have often attributed this difference to the male's superior ability to fantasize (Barbach, 1975, 1982; LoPiccolo, 1980). Since men are more encouraged to think about sex, they are more easily aroused through their own cognitive activities — erotic thoughts send messages from the brain to the spinal cord. The sexual scripts for men and women also reflect some aspects of the **double standard,** which helps to explain some male–female differences in arousal. According to this standard, women are responsible for stopping male advances and are expected to refrain from sexual activity until marriage. Men, on the other hand, are often encouraged to explore their sexuality and to bring a certain level of sexual knowledge into the marriage (Doyle, 1985). Overt examples of this double standard are less evident in modern times, but you can still see how covert or hidden traces of this belief may cause many problems (like differences in arousal) between men and women.

Sexual response: The physiology of orgasm

Now that we have examined some of the many influences on sexual arousal, let us turn our attention to the bodily processes involved in the complete **sexual response cycle** identified by William Masters and Virginia Johnson. As we mentioned in the initial section of this chapter, Masters and Johnson (1966) were among the first scientists to study human sexual responses through systematic observation in a laboratory setting. Out of their work came a widely publicized model for describing the basic physiological and biological processes that occur from initial arousal to orgasm and back to the unaroused state. Masters and Johnson's model divided the typical sexual response into four phases: excitement, plateau, orgasm, and resolution (see Figure 11.5).

In the **excitement phase,** which can last from a few minutes to several hours, arousal is initiated through physical factors, such as touching or being touched, or through psychological factors, such as fantasy or erotic stimuli. During this stage, heart

PERFORMANCE ANXIETY: *A fear that one will be unable to meet the expectations for sexual "performance" of one's self or one's partner.*

DOUBLE STANDARD: *The belief that different rules for sexual behavior should be applied to men and women.*

SEXUAL RESPONSE CYCLE: *Masters and Johnson's description of the bodily response to sexual arousal. The four stages are excitement, plateau, orgasm, and resolution.*

EXCITEMENT PHASE: *The first phase of the sexual response cycle, characterized by increasing levels of muscle tension and contraction and increased amounts of blood concentration in the genitals.*

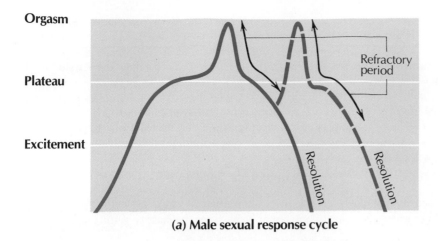

(a) Male sexual response cycle

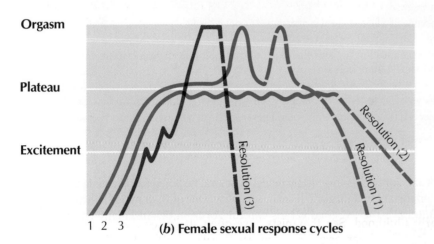

(b) Female sexual response cycles

Figure 11.5 Masters and Johnson's view of the male and female sexual response cycles. *(a)* A "typical" male pattern of arousal from excitement through resolution is shown by the solid line. The dotted line represents the possibility of a second orgasm after the *refractory period* (the time immediately following ejaculation when a further orgasm is believed to be impossible). Males may also have cycles that resemble lines 2 and 3 in the female. Some researchers also believe that males have multiple orgasms, which would resemble the female's line 1. *(b)* Three possible variations on the female pattern of arousal during the sexual response cycle. Line 1 shows a multiple orgasm pattern, line 2 shows a prolonged arousal at the plateau stage that does not end in orgasm (note the longer time in resolution associated with this lack of orgasm), and line 3 shows several minor drops in arousal during the excitement phase and a rapid resolution.

rate and respiration increase, and blood flows to the pelvic region, causing engorgement of both the penis and the comparable blood-storing spaces in the female. Both male and female nipples may become erect, and both may experience a *sex flush,* or reddening of portions of the upper torso and face.

If stimulation continues, the individual enters the **plateau phase,** where there are further increases in heartbeat, respiration rate, and blood pressure. In the male, the penis becomes even more engorged and erect, while the testes swell and pull up closer to the body. In the female, the clitoris pulls up under the clitoral hood, and the entrance to the vagina contracts while the uterus rises slightly. This movement of the uterus causes the upper two-thirds of the vagina to "balloon" or expand. As excitement reaches its peak, some fluid, which may contain live sperm, may seep out the opening of the penis and both sexes may experience a feeling that orgasm is imminent and inevitable.

During the **orgasm phase,** the individual experiences a highly intense and pleasurable sense of release of tension. This sensation results from muscular contractions that force the blood that has been collecting in the genitals back into the bloodstream. In the female, muscles around the vagina push the vaginal walls in and out and the uterus pulsates. Muscles in and around the penis also contract in the male, causing **ejaculation,** the discharge of semen or seminal fluid.

Both male and female bodies gradually return to their preexcitement state during the **resolution phase.** After one orgasm, most men enter a **refractory period,** during which further excitement to orgasm is impossible. Most women, however, are generally capable of multiple orgasms in fairly rapid succession.

PLATEAU PHASE: *The second phase of the sexual response cycle, characterized by maintenance and intensification of sexual tensions.*
ORGASM PHASE: *The third phase of the sexual response cycle, during which pleasurable sensations peak and the body suddenly discharges its accumulated sexual tension in the process of orgasm or climax.*
EJACULATION: *The discharge of semen from the penis at orgasm.*
RESOLUTION PHASE: *The final stage of the sexual response cycle, characterized by continued relaxation as the body returns to its unaroused state.*
REFRACTORY PERIOD: *The period after orgasm during which further orgasm is considered physiologically impossible. This stage is believed to be absent in the female.*

TABLE 11.5
Widely Accepted Myths about Sexual Behavior

1 Simultaneous orgasms are better than those experienced separately and should be worked for.

2 In a mutually satisfying sex life, there is no need for masturbation.

3 A male's effectiveness as a sexual partner is dependent upon penis size.

4 Men over 55 have an increased risk of heart attacks if they maintain an active sex life.

5 When a man and woman really love each other, they will intuitively know how to sexually please each other.

6 If a man is sexually aroused and fails to climax, he will experience strong pain for several hours.

7 Sexual activity the night before an athletic competition will reduce athletic performance.

8 If a man or woman lacks sexual interest at home, he or she must be getting sex somewhere else.

9 To have a satisfactory sex life, individuals should have sexual intercourse at least three times a week.

10 The absence of a hymen proves that a girl is not a virgin.

11 Alcohol is a stimulant for sexual activity.

12 General sex education and knowledge about contraception lead adolescents into premature experimentation with sex.

13 Blacks have stronger sex drives than other races.

14 Couples who live together before marriage have a better chance for marital happiness.

15 A partner in a loving relationship should never say no to requests by his or her partner for sex.

Masters and Johnson's four-stage model of sexual responses in the male and female has provided important insights into human sexuality. One of their major contributions is in the discounting of the "vaginal versus clitoral" orgasm debate. Many couples seek therapy or help in acquiring the "right" kind of orgasm, which they interpret as a vaginal response to intercourse. This preference is largely the result of the early pronouncements of Freud and his followers. One of the major tenets of psychoanalytic theory was that women who had orgasms only through direct clitoral stimulation were developmentally immature and were rejecting their femininity. Vaginal orgasms through intercourse were considered the hallmark of sexually mature women. Masters and Johnson found, however, that the orgasms women achieved from breast, clitoral, or vaginal stimulation (or even fantasy alone) are not qualitatively different. A number of other myths about sex that researchers such as Masters and Johnson have been working to dispel are listed in Table 11.5.

Although the work of Masters and Johnson is widely accepted and respected in the field of human sexuality, there has also been considerable criticism. Helen Singer Kaplan (1974, 1987) has questioned the existence of the separate plateau cycle or the need to describe a "nonstate" like the refractory period. She suggests that sexual response consists of only three phases: desire, excitement, and orgasm. Masters and Johnson have also emphasized that the major differences between men and women are that women have multiple orgasms and only men ejaculate, but this assertion has been disputed. Some researchers have found that some men experience multiple orgasms (Hartman and Fithian, 1984; Robbins and Jenson, 1978), and certain studies have presented highly controversial evidence of *female ejaculation* (an expulsion of fluid from the urinary opening during orgasm) (Perry and Whipple, 1982; Zaviacic et al., 1988). This ejaculation is said to occur in approximately 10 percent of the women who have experienced direct stimulation of the **Grafenberg spot** (or "G Spot")—a region in the front wall of the vagina that supposedly has a special sensitivity to erotic stimulation. Although some researchers question this "G Spot" and ejaculatory response (Alsatc, 1985) the idea of such a spot has received considerable media attention and public acceptance. Sex educators and therapists are concerned that this type of public attention gives further fuel to the "vaginal

GRAFENBERG SPOT: *A region in the front wall of the vagina that supposedly has a special sensitivity to erotic stimulation.*

versus clitoral" orgasm debate and might also lead to one more goal for couples to achieve. As we will see in the next section, this type of goal setting is one of the primary causes of sex problems.

Sex therapy: Help for sexual dysfunctions

When sexual functioning is working well, we tend to ignore it and take it for granted. But what happens when things don't go smoothly? What causes normal functioning to stop for some people and never begin for others? Some problems in sexual responsiveness, as we have just seen, result from temporary, situational factors — the need for privacy, protection from pregnancy, too much alcohol, fatigue, and so on. Many sexual problems, however, are much more complex. As shown in Table 11.6, there are a wide variety of **sexual dysfunctions,** or difficulties in sexual functioning, that may lead people to seek professional help from a sex therapist.

Of course, what is considered "dysfunctional" sexual behavior can vary from era to era, from culture to culture, and even from therapist to therapist. During the nineteenth century, for example, Western European married women who actively enjoyed sexual intercourse, rather than just enduring their husbands attentions or "fulfilling the obligations of maternity," were considered abnormal and impure (Money, 1985a). Today the woman who simply endures intercourse is considered to be the one with the problem. Cultural differences in definitions of "normal" sexual behavior can be seen in a comparison of Soviet and American attitudes about male ejaculation. In the Soviet Union, for example, it is believed that men should not delay their orgasms, and one Soviet medical journal suggests that the ideal duration of the "sexual act" is two minutes (Stern, 1980). This same behavior would be classified as **premature ejaculation** by most Western sex therapists. Even Western therapists, however, vary in their definitions of premature ejaculation; many relate it to the partner's satisfaction (frequency of orgasm), which doesn't take into account possible female orgasmic difficulties.

In addition to the problems created by historical, cultural, and inter-therapist variations in defining sexual dysfunctions, there are also labeling and definitional problems within specific sexual relationships. Not only is it difficult to separate "his" problem (premature ejaculation) from "hers" (orgasmic dysfunction), but many couples often disagree with each other and with therapists as to what constitutes a sexual dysfunction. Once a dysfunction is diagnosed they may look to each other for blame and responsibility for the problem. After the problem is labeled, some individuals may also experience a loss of self-esteem and perceive the label as a threat to their masculinity or femininity (Goldberg, 1983).

Question: How do therapists work with sex problems? For many years the major treatment for sexual dysfunctions was long-term **psychoanalysis,** based on the assumption that sexual problems result from deep-seated personality conflicts that originate in childhood experiences. During the 1950s and 1960s, **behavior therapy,** which focuses on learning through rewards and punishments as the cause of sexual dysfunctions, was also a method of treatment (see Chapter 15 for a more complete description of both psychoanalysis and behavior therapy). It wasn't until the early 1970s, and the publication of Masters and Johnson's *Human Sexual Inadequacy,* that sex therapy gained national recognition. Because the model of therapy that Masters and Johnson developed is still popular and used by many sex therapists, we will use it as our example of how sex therapy is conducted.

Masters and Johnson's sex therapy program Masters and Johnson's approach is founded on four major principles:

1. *A relationship focus.* Unlike forms of therapy that focus on the individual, their sex therapy focuses on the relationship between two people. To counteract any "blaming" tendencies, each partner is considered to be fully involved and affected by sexual problems.

SEXUAL DYSFUNCTIONS: *Conditions in which the normal physiological processes of arousal and orgasm are impaired.*

PREMATURE EJACULATION: *Ejaculation that takes place too quickly for the pleasure of one or both partners.*

PSYCHOANALYSIS: *A type of psychotherapy originated by Sigmund Freud that is designed to bring relief from anxiety created by unconscious desires and motives.*
BEHAVIOR THERAPY: *A psychotherapeutic approach based on learning principles and used to overcome maladaptive patterns of behavior.*

TABLE 11.6
The Major Male and Female Sexual Dysfunctions

Type of Dysfunction	Description	Causes
Male		
Erectile dysfunction (impotence)	Inability to have or maintain an erection firm enough for intercourse	*Physical*—diabetes, circulatory conditions, heart disease, drugs, extreme fatigue, alcohol consumption, hormone deficiencies
		Psychological—performance anxiety, guilt, difficulty in expressing desires to partner, severe antisexual upbringing
Primary erectile dysfunction	The male has never been able to have sexual intercourse	
Secondary erectile dysfunction	Erection problems occurring in at least 25 percent of sexual encounters	
Premature ejaculation	Rapid ejaculation that is beyond the male's control and his partner is non-orgasmic in at least 50 percent of their intercourse episodes	Almost always *psychological*—the male has learned to ejaculate quickly due to guilt, fear of discovery while masturbating, hurried experiences in cars or motels, and so on
Both male and female		
Dyspareunia	Painful intercourse, more frequent in females but also occurs in males	Primarily *physical*—irritations, infections, or disorders of the internal or external genitals
Inhibited sexual desire (sexual apathy)	Lack of willingness to participate in sexual relations due to disinterest	*Physical*—hormone deficiencies, alcoholism, drugs, chronic illness
		Psychological—depression, prior sex trauma, relationship problems, anxiety
Sexual aversion	Lack of participation in sex due to overwhelming fear or anxiety	*Psychological*—severe parental sex attitudes, prior sex trauma, partner pressure, gender identity confusion in men
Female		
Orgasmic dysfunction (anorgasmia, frigidity)	Inability or difficulty in reaching orgasm	*Physical*—chronic illness, diabetes, extreme fatigue, drugs, alcohol consumption, hormone deficiencies, pelvic disorders, lack of appropriate or adequate stimulation
Primary orgasmic dysfunction	The female has never had an orgasm	
Secondary orgasmic dysfunction	The female was regularly orgasmic at one time, but no longer is	*Psychological*—fear of evaluation, poor body image, relationship problems, guilt, anxiety, severe antisexual upbringing, difficulty in expressing desires to partner
Situational orgasmic dysfunction	Orgasms occur only under certain circumstances	
Vaginismus	The muscles around the outer one-third of the vagina have involuntary spasms and penile insertion is impossible or difficult and painful	Primarily *psychological*—the woman has learned to associate pain or fear with intercourse due to prior sexual trauma, severe antisexual upbringing, guilt

Source: Adapted from Masters and Johnson (1970); Masters et al. (1988).

2. *An integration of physiological and psychosocial factors.* Because medication and many physical disorders can cause or aggravate sexual dysfunctions, Masters and Johnson's emphasize the importance of medical histories and exams. They also delve into such psychosocial factors as how the couple first learned about sex, what their current attitudes and values are, and so on.

3. *An emphasis on cognitive factors.* Recognizing that many problems result from fears of performance and *spectatoring* (a mental watching and evaluation of re-

sponses during sexual encounters), couples are discouraged from "goal setting" and from judging sex in terms of "successes" or "failures."

4. *An emphasis on specific behavioral techniques.* Couples are seen in an intensive two-week program that consists mainly of discussions (to explore their values and misconceptions) and specific behavioral exercises, or "homework assignments." In these exercises, couples often begin with the *sensate focus assignment* where each partner takes turns gently caressing the other, communicating what is pleasurable, but with *no* goal or performance demands. After this exercise is completed, couples are then given special assignments tailored to their particular sex problem.

Other therapies   Important contributions to the field of sex therapy have also been made by individuals like Helen Kaplan (1974, 1987), who suggests that Masters and Johnson's program works mainly with milder sex problems and that some problems require extensive therapy at a deeper level of insight. In partial response to the expense of the Masters and Johnson's program (in 1984 the two-week program was $5000), other therapists have offered group therapy to treat sexual dysfunctions (Zilbergeld, 1986). One of the most controversial treatments, once offered by Masters and Johnson and others, involves the use of a "surrogate partner"—a stranger who is paid to serve as a sexual partner during the course of therapy. There are obvious ethical and legal questions that surround this practice.

Question: How effective is sex therapy?   Just as there are disagreements concerning what constitutes a sexual dysfunction, there are also disagreements over what constitutes success in therapy (Kolodny, 1981; "Sexual disorders," 1990). Although the high success rates reported by Masters and Johnson have been seriously questioned (Lo Piccolo, 1989; Zilbergeld and Evans, 1980), a variety of studies show that sex therapy can be quite effective for many people. With further research, therapists may find ways to clearly document which elements of therapy are most successful with specific clients and specific disorders.

Work in sex therapy has provided several useful guidelines to improve general sexual functioning and to avoid future sexual dysfunctions:

1. *Sex education should begin as early as possible.* Children should be given positive feelings about their bodies and an opportunity to discuss sexuality in an open, honest fashion.
2. *Goal- or performance-oriented approaches should be avoided.* Therapists often remind clients that there really is no "right" way to have sex. When couples or individuals attempt to judge or evaluate their sexual lives or to live up to others' expectations, they risk making sex "work" rather than pleasure.
3. *Couples need to learn clear communication skills.* "Mind reading" belongs in the circus, not the bedroom. Partners need to tell each other what feels good, and what doesn't. A sexual problem should be openly discussed without blaming, and if the problem does not improve with discussion and the reading of self-help books, professional therapy may be necessary.

The general guidelines for choosing a therapist provided in Chapter 15 can also be used to select a responsible sex therapist.

Sexually transmitted diseases: The problem of AIDS

The suggestions for early sex education and improved communication also apply to one of our most serious sexual problems—that of sexually transmitted diseases (STDs). Each year millions of Americans contract one or more STDs, and by the age of 25 more than half of America's youth have been infected (Allgeier and Allgeier, 1988).

Although STDs such as genital warts and chlamydial infections have reached epidemic proportions on college campuses (Bowie and MacDonald, 1989; Ismach, 1988), **AIDS** (acquired immune deficiency syndrome) has received the largest share of public

AIDS (ACQUIRED IMMUNE DEFICIENCY SYNDROME): *A catastrophic illness in which a virus destroys the ability of the immune system to fight disease. Although the term "AIDS" continues to be used, the President's Commission in 1988 recommended the use of the term* human immunodeficiency virus infection *(HIV infection). They believe that this term more correctly defines the problem and places proper emphasis on the entire spectrum of the epidemic.*

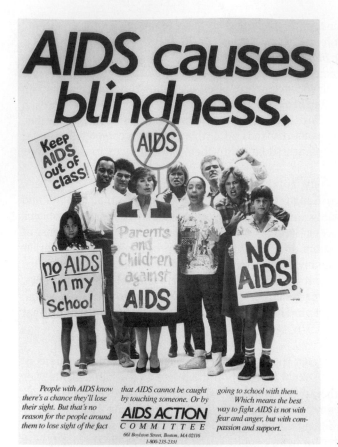

AIDS causes blindness.

Keep AIDS out of class!

AIDS

Parents and Children against AIDS

no AIDS in my School!

NO AIDS!

People with AIDS know there's a chance they'll lose their sight. But that's no reason for the people around them to lose sight of the fact that AIDS cannot be caught by touching someone. Or by

AIDS ACTION
C O M M I T T E E
661 Boylston Street, Boston, MA 02116
1-800-235-2331

going to school with them.
Which means the best way to fight AIDS is not with fear and anger, but with compassion and support.

Ads such as this are currently being used to combat prejudice and misinformation concerning AIDS.

attention. Former Surgeon General C. Everett Koop has stated that "AIDS is one of the most serious health problems that has ever faced the American public" (1988, p. 2). AIDS is a tragic illness that destroys the body's natural defenses against disease and infection. People with AIDS are vulnerable to a number of opportunistic infections that would not be a threat if their immune systems were functioning normally. The AIDS virus may also attack the brain and spinal cord, creating severe neurological deficits. These deficits (known as AIDS dementia) may produce impaired coordination, forgetfulness, difficulty in concentrating, personality changes, and even seizures and spasms (Joyce, 1988).

AIDS is transmitted only through sexual contact or by exposure to infected blood. All known cases of AIDS have been contracted by one of five routes:

1. *Sexual intercourse.* Having sex—oral, anal, or vaginal—with someone who is infected with the AIDS virus.
2. *Intravenous drug use.* Sharing needles or syringes with an infected drug user (Fackelmann, 1989).
3. *Blood transfusions.* Receiving blood from an infected donor. The risk of infection from transfusions has been minimized as a result of rigorous screening. There is absolutely NO risk of contracting AIDS by donating blood. Since blood banks use sterile, throwaway needles and collection equipment, there is no way a donor can be exposed ("AIDS and blood donation," 1988).
4. *Mother and child.* Transmitting AIDS from an infected mother to her child before birth, during the birth process, or after the child is born (perhaps through breast milk) (Spotkov and Anderson, 1988). AIDS-infected infants have also transmitted the virus to noninfected mothers while nursing (Weiss, 1989b).
5. *Patient-to-medical personnel.* Inadvertently exposing medical personnel to the contaminated blood of infected patients. This is an extremely rare occurrence.

Despite alarmist claims from the highly sensationalized book *Crisis,* you *cannot* get AIDS by everyday contact such as kisses, insect bites, or contaminated toilet seats (Koop,

1988). The primary authors of this book, William Masters and Virginia Johnson, bear the best-known names in sexual research, but this book has greatly damaged their scientific reputation. Instead of focusing attention on the steps most likely to control the disease (like using condoms and limiting one's sexual partners), Masters and Johnson have increased the public's general hysteria and misinformation about AIDS. In a 1988 survey, 30% of Americans believed that insect bites could transmit the disease, 29% thought you could get AIDS from a drinking glass, and 25% saw a risk in being coughed or sneezed on (Gallup and Gallup, 1988).

Question: Didn't the federal government send a special AIDS pamphlet to every home in the United States? Why aren't these extensive education efforts changing these misconceptions? One major reason for the public's confusion is the publication of conflicting data such as that of Masters and Johnson. In addition, psychologists have found that passive forms of education, such as the mailing of the AIDS brochure, are much less effective than face-to-face communications (Hostetler, 1988b). A third factor in the continuing controversy is the irrational nature of prejudice (see Chapter 17). Given that the majority of AIDS victims are gay or bisexual men, people who are **homophobic** may avoid information about the disease and react negatively to AIDS-infected persons because AIDS symbolizes something they are against (McManus, Pryor, and Reeder, 1988; Newell and Newell, 1988). Some antigay groups have also exploited public misinformation and fears of the "gay plague" and sought criminal punishment or quarantine of gay men (Fitzpatrick, 1988; Melton and Gray, 1988).

HOMOPHOBIA: *Irrational fears of homosexuality; the fear of the possibility of homosexuality in oneself, or self-loathing toward one's own homosexuality.*

Partially in response to the harmful effects of this type of fear and prejudice, public health officials are currently downplaying the statistics about "high-risk" groups and are focusing instead on specific behaviors that increase the risk of exposure. In a similar way, psychologists are conducting research and implementing educational projects that may help reduce misinformation and discrimination (Aroesty et al., 1986; McManus, Pryor, and Reeder, 1988).

Although AIDS and other STDs are important to the study of human sexuality, many believe that the "finest" use of sex is as an expression of deep love and commitment. A 1983 survey of *Psychology Today* readers (Rubenstein, 1983) found that 29 percent of the males and 44 percent of the females believed that sex without love was either unenjoyable or unacceptable. In view of such beliefs, the topics of our next section — liking and loving — are especially relevant to many readers.

Review Questions

1. Areas of the body that are known to be particularly sensitive to touch and arousal are known as _____ _____.

2. Socially dictated descriptions of the sequences of behavior that are considered appropriate in sexual interactions are known as _____ _____.

3. Like the eye blink response to a puff of air, some aspects of sexual arousal are _____.

4. The _____ branch of the autonomic nervous system dominates during sexual arousal, whereas the _____ branch dominates during ejaculation and orgasm.

5. Society's separate expectations for female and male sexual behavior are known as a _____ _____.

6. Masters and Johnson's four stages of the male and female physiological changes during sexual activity are known as the _____ _____ _____.

7. During the male's _____ _____, further stimulation to orgasm is believed to be impossible.

8 Before the 1970s and the popularization of Masters and Johnson's program for sex therapy, _____ and _____ _____ were the primary methods for treating sexual dysfunctions.

9 The mental watching and evaluation of responses during sexual encounters is known as _____ .

10 _____ is a catastrophic illness that destroys the body's immune system.

Answers: 1 erogenous zones; *2* sexual scripts; *3* reflexive; *4* parasympathetic; sympathetic; *5* double standard; *6* sexual response cycle; *7* refractory period; *8* psychoanalysis, behavior therapy; *9* spectatoring; *10* AIDS

INTERPERSONAL ATTRACTION

One of the most common criticisms of the scientific study of human sexuality is its heavy emphasis on the biological and rather mechanical aspects of sexual behavior. Although researchers like Alfred Kinsey and Masters and Johnson have provided invaluable insights, we want to know more about sex than just the frequencies of sexual behaviors, the exact physiological responses during sexual intercourse, or the treatment for sexual dysfunctions. We want to know how to "connect" with others — how to attract others, how to find and keep "meaningful relationships," how to keep the romance alive. What do men and women really want of the opposite sex? Is there really a "Mr. Right" or "Ms. Right" out there somewhere for each of us to discover? Psychologists have arrived at many answers to such questions, and in this section we'll look at some of these.

Liking: Factors and theories in friendship

Just as we have clear preferences for one food over another, we also have clear preferences for certain people. Psychologists have examined many of the variables associated with liking, or "people preferences." We'll look at three of the most influential factors — attractiveness, proximity, and similarity — and then discuss some major theories of why we like some people and not others.

Physical attractiveness Can you remember what first attracted you to your best friend? Was it his or her warm and sparkling personality, intelligence, or sense of humor? Or was it his or her looks? Although you may not want to admit it, looks probably were the main factor at first. Research has consistently shown that **physical attractiveness** (size, shape, facial characteristics, and manner of dress) appears to be one of the most important factors in our liking (and even our loving) of others (Snyder et al., 1988).

PHYSICAL ATTRACTIVENESS: *Having the physical properties (size, shape, facial characteristics, and so on) that elicit favorable evaluations from others.*

Question: But isn't there a wide range in what different people find attractive? Standards of attractiveness have varied considerably from era to era and from culture to culture. In the fairly recent past it was considered desirable in our culture for both men and women to have fair skin, rounded bodies, and no evidence of muscles, whereas today the emphasis is on tans, thinness, and well-defined muscles. In some cultures people place large pieces of wood in their lips to make them protrude, whereas people in our culture spend lots of time and money for orthodontics or even surgery to correct even the smallest amount of protrusion.

In spite of such historical and cultural variations, there is usually a great deal of agreement on the ideals of beauty within a culture (Kopera et al., 1971). In our society, for example, "babyish" characteristics (large eyes and head, small nose, rounded features, and soft skin) are considered attractive for women (Keating, 1985), whereas strong, jutting chins and facial hair (mustaches, beards) are desirable in men. Men with "baby faces" are seen as naive but also unusually warm and kind (Berry and McArthur, 1985).

The soft, "generous" figure of the Renaissance women and the "hourglass" ideal of the 1950s are surprising, compared to the lean, athletic body of today's standard for attractiveness.

Physical attractiveness plays an incredibly important role in our perceptions of others throughout the entire life span. As early as nursery school, for example, beautiful children are more popular with their classmates and are judged to be more intelligent and well adjusted by their teachers (Felson, 1980). By the time they reach adulthood, attractive individuals are seen by both men and women as being more poised, interesting, sociable, independent, exciting, and sexually warm (Brigham, 1980; Hatfield and Sprecher, 1986).

Question: Aren't these beliefs similar to stereotypes? Yes. Just as we often form impressions and stereotypes of others on the basis of their sex or race, we also form stereotypes on the basis of physical attractiveness. Because of our attractiveness stereotypes, we have certain expectations about people's other characteristics that lead us to interact with them in such a way that they actually *exhibit* those characteristics. This process is referred to as a **self-fulfilling prophecy.** An interesting study that documents this type of self-fulfilling prophecy was done by Snyder, Tanke, and Berscheid (1977). In this experiment, male students engaged in microphone and headphone conversations with a female student after being shown a photo showing her to be either very attractive or

SELF-FULFILLING PROPHECY: *A sequence in which an individual's or other's expectations lead to behaviors that cause the expected events to occur.*

somewhat unattractive. When the male thought he was talking to an attractive female, he was judged by student observers to be friendlier, more outgoing, and overall more sociable. The female students, who were actually equal in their physical attractiveness and did not know of the impression the males had been given, tended to respond in a manner that *fulfilled* the expectations of the caller. That is, those women who talked with men who believed them to be attractive were also judged by observers to be more poised, humorous, and sociable.

Although such studies can serve as a useful caution against the excessive emphasis on physical attractiveness, they also tend to depress anyone who happens to fall outside the rather narrow range of our culture's current standard of beauty. It is therefore comforting to know that research has also shown that physical attractiveness loses its importance once a relationship goes beyond its initial stages. According to Hatfield and Sprecher (1986), perceived attractiveness increases with repeated exposure — we generally find familiar people more attractive than strangers. Attractiveness is also related to shared values and interests. If you're a surfer, you'll find other surfers more attractive. Both of these factors — exposure and similarity — also affect interpersonal attraction in other ways.

PROXIMITY: *Physical closeness, a factor that leads to increased attraction.*

Exposure through proximity   Just as it is hard to admit that attractiveness often governs our *initial* liking for others, it is also difficult to recognize the role of simple nearness, or **proximity** in liking. In other words, the nearer you live to or work with someone, the more likely it is that you will like that person. One of the classic studies of the proximity effect showed that simple distance between apartments seemed to determine who became friends with whom (Festinger et al., 1950). Similarly, a study of friendship in college dormitories found that the person next door was more often liked than the person two doors away, the person two doors away was liked more than someone three doors away, and so on (Priest and Sawyer, 1967). This closeness effect can also be found in the classroom — when students are assigned seating according to alphabetical order, their friendships reflect the alphabetical listing (Segal, 1974). Those of us who remember begging our grade school teachers to let us sit by certain people probably had an early intuitive understanding of this principle of proximity.

Question: How does proximity promote attraction?   One of the major reasons seems to be *mere exposure*. Repeated exposure to all sorts of stimuli apparently increases liking. You've no doubt observed that you gradually come to accept and eventually like outrageous changes in fashions or hairstyles. Research has also shown that liking for presidents and actors or actresses is strongly correlated to the number of times they appear in the mass media (Harrison, 1977).

SIMILARITY: *A sharing of common interests, values, and beliefs — an important factor in long-term attraction.*

Similarity   Once we've had the repeated opportunity to get to know someone through simple physical proximity, and assuming we find him or her attractive, we then need something to hold the relationship together over time. This major cementing factor for long-term relationships, whether liking or loving, is **similarity.** We tend to prefer, and stay with, those people who are most like us — those who share our ethnic background, social class, interests, and attitudes (Byrne, 1971; Hendrick et al., 1988). In other words, "Birds of a feather flock together."

NEED COMPLEMENTARITY: *The tendency to seek out and be attracted to people whose qualities we admire but personally lack.*
NEED COMPATIBILITY: *A sharing of similar needs.*

Question: What about the old saying, "Opposites attract"?   Although it does seem that these two pieces of common folklore are contradictory, the term "opposites" here probably refers to personality traits rather than to social backgrounds or values. An attraction to a seemingly opposite person is more often based on the recognition that in one or two important areas that person offers us something we lack. If you are a talkative and outgoing person, for example, your friendship with a rather quiet and reserved individual may endure because each of you provides important resources for the other. Psychologists refer to this as **need complementarity,** as compared to the **need compatibility** represented by similarity.

Theories of liking At this point in our discussion you are undoubtedly beginning to wonder how each of these different, and sometimes disparate, factors in liking can all be integrated or related. Once scientists have established that several variables seem to be operating in a specific field, they generally attempt to integrate these findings into comprehensive theories — to go beyond the "whats" to the "whys" and "hows." Four of the most important theories in liking are reinforcement theory, equity theory, social exchange theory, and gain–loss theory.

According to **reinforcement theory,** we come to like or dislike others as a result of learning (Byrne, 1971). Through a system of rewards and punishments, attractiveness, proximity, and similarity work individually and in combination to create our preferences for certain people. That is, we tend to obtain the greatest rewards from those who are near us and who share similar backgrounds and values. One interesting combination effect is seen in the fact that repeated exposure through proximity makes some people become more physically attractive to us. It has also been found that we tend to judge attractive people as being more similar to us than nonattractive persons (Beaman and Klentz, 1983).

REINFORCEMENT THEORY: *The theory that attraction results from a positive emotional arousal. We like those who make us feel good and dislike those who make us feel bad.*

If rewards were the only reason for liking, we would logically prefer those who did the most for us. But since we have also learned that it is important to be fair with others, we tend to feel most comfortable and satisfied with relationships that are *equitable.* According to **equity theory,** we like people and relationships where the output is proportional to the input. Research has shown that the partner who feels that the relationship is out of balance will become distressed and try to restore equity. He or she attempts to rebalance the relationship by altering inputs and outcomes or by psychologically altering his or her perception of the gains and costs.

EQUITY THEORY: *The theory that people are highly motivated to seek a fair share of the rewards and that they prefer a balanced relationship.*

One of the interesting predictions of equity theory is that people will become dissatisfied whether they are overbenefited or underbenefited in comparison to their partner. There are some sex differences in this dissatisfaction. When men feel overbenefited they are more likely to express anger, whereas women report feelings of guilt. In the case of underbenefits, women report feeling depressed whereas men feel angry (Sprecher, 1986). Regardless of the male–female emotional responses to imbalances, relationships that are considered equitable are most likely to endure (Davidson, 1984).

According to the third major theory of liking, **social exchange theory,** friendships must not only be fair and equitable but must also show a net profit to both parties. Liking is said to result from a type of "interpersonal marketplace" where the traders exchange certain "commodities." If the relationship becomes too costly it is terminated. Have you ever heard someone explain the end of a relationship because he or she "just wasn't getting anything out of it anymore" or because "the costs were outweighing the benefits"? Such comments show exchange theory at work.

SOCIAL EXCHANGE THEORY: *The theory that interpersonal interactions are governed by the costs and benefits each person gives and receives.*

Question: If the reinforcement, equity, and social exchange theories are correct, how would you explain the case of a husband running off with his secretary? This is an interesting exception. Although it *should* be more reinforcing, fairer, and less costly for the husband to stay in his marriage, it is also true that human beings tend to **habituate** to unchanging stimuli — to become less responsive with repeated exposure. After spending many years together, people sometimes tend to accept and take each other for granted and are more responsive to the attention of new friends.

HABITUATE: *To become less responsive to a stimulus as the result of repeated exposure.*

Experimental evidence of this effect in even short-term relationships was offered by a study in which college students were allowed to "accidentally" overhear the conversations among other students who discussed their "honest opinion" of the student subject. These conversations were actually staged by the experimenter and arranged so that the subject heard a consistently positive personal evaluation, a consistently negative evaluation, a negative turning to positive evaluation, or a positive turning to negative evaluation (Aronson and Linder, 1965).

Which evaluation do you think you would prefer? Although it seems like we ought to prefer the consistently nice comments, the researchers found that the subjects responded most favorably to the subject who initially expressed negative attitudes and then changed to positive ones. They responded least favorably to the subject who first gave positive comments and then became negative. According to the fourth principle of attraction, **gain–loss theory**, unexpected gains in liking or approval are more rewarding than constant liking; conversely, sudden losses are more punishing than constant dislike.

It is ironic that in long-term relationships we're really operating in a *double-bind* or no-win situation. That is, since our attention and approval no longer offer a gain to our friends or partners, we have little rewarding power, but if we withdraw our affections we have an increased potential to hurt (lending some truth to the old saying, "you always hurt the one you love"). In contrast, a stranger's attention is powerfully reinforcing, since it represents an unexpected gain, and his or her withdrawal is less punishing, since little was expected.

Question: Isn't there any way to counteract this tendency?   Fortunately, there is. Although we *are* attracted to changing stimuli, we also have memories for the benefits of old relationships and apprehension about the costs of replacement. Simply being aware of the dangers of habituation and the limited nature of the "gain" from a stranger's flattery should help us to be less vulnerable to the lure of a stranger's attentions. Awareness of the gain–loss theory can also help us when it is our partner or friend who is losing interest in us. The strong sensitivity we apparently have to any signs of reduced feelings in a long-term relationship can be used as an important warning signal. Just as detour signs and red traffic lights alert us to possible hazards, so too does the anxious feeling we experience when others show a reduced interest. At the risk of encouraging people to be overly anxious about their relationships, it is important to point out that long-term relationships (husband–wife, parent–child, friend–friend, and so on) often go through cycles of more or less interest, loving, liking, and even disliking at times. However, most relationships do survive because of the overriding factors identified by reinforcement, equity, and social exchange theory.

Question: If this is so, why are there so many divorces in our society?   There is no easy answer to this question, since so many factors are involved. But in the context of the current chapter, it's important to recognize that romantic love, which is the most popular basis for American marriages, is a unique type of love that has interesting problems and qualities that are directly related to divorce. Romantic and companionate love are central topics of the next section.

Loving: The many faces of love

Is love an appropriate area for research? Not everyone thinks so. One of the strongest critics of love research has been Senator William Proxmire. When Proxmire discovered that the National Science Foundation had awarded a grant to psychologists interested in studying romantic love, he called it a big waste of taxpayer's money. He went on to say, "I believe that 200 million Americans want to leave some things in life a mystery, and right at the top of things we don't want to know about is why a man falls in love with a woman and vice versa" (Walster and Walster, 1978, p. 8).

Given the high percentage of marriages that end in divorce and the strong emphasis on love as a basis for marriage in our society, Senator Proxmire's complaint is particularly surprising. The reason for his complaint, as well as the relative lack of research in this area, may be due to the fact that love is so difficult to define and measure. Some attempts to study love have concluded that we label certain feelings as love when we experience the appropriate combination of strong physiological arousal (from sexual attraction, excitement, fear, and so on) plus the availability of an appropriate love object (see Chapter 12). For most of us, however, love seems more than just an "aroused label." Since love relationships often develop from friendships and initial feelings of liking for another, many people define love as an intense form of liking.

One attempt to define and understand both liking and loving has come from the work of Zick Rubin (1973). Using items such as those shown in Figure 11.6, Rubin asked

---

LOVE SCALE

1 I feel that I can confide in _____ about virtually everything.

2 I would do almost anything for _____ .

3 If I could never be with _____ , I would feel miserable.

LIKING SCALE

1 I think that _____ is unusually well adjusted.

2 I would highly recommend _____ for a responsible job.

3 In my opinion, _____ is an exceptionally mature person.

Figure 11.6 Sample items from Rubin's love and liking scales. The person taking this test is asked to fill in the blanks first with the name of their dating partner and then with the name of their best friend of the same sex. (*Source:* Rubin, Z. (1970). "Measurement of romantic love," *Journal of Personality and Social Psychology, 16,* 265–273. Copyright © 1970 by the American Psychological Association. Reprinted by permission of the author.)

158 dating couples to complete both the love scale and the liking scale with respect to their dating partner and then with respect to a close friend of the same sex. Rubin found that while the couples tended to match each other on their love scores, women liked their dating partners significantly more than they were liked in return. These couples also reported *liking* their same-sex friends similar amounts, but women reported *loving* their same-sex friends more than men did.

■ *Question:* How does love differ from liking on Rubin's scales? Although Rubin noted that liking involves a favorable evaluation of another, as reflected in greater feelings of admiration and respect, he found love to be not only more intense than liking but to be composed of three basic elements: *caring,* or the desire to help the other person, particularly when help is needed; *attachment,* or the need to be with the other person; and *intimacy,* or a sense of empathy and trust that comes from close communication and self-disclosure from another.

Each of these three elements can present problems for love relationships. When there are differences in each partner's definition of these elements, or if one feels that he or she is more caring, more attached, or more desiring of intimacy than the other, the relationship may be jeopardized (Hendrick, Hendrick, and Adler, 1988). Caring, for example, is an area where women are often assumed to give more and to do more than men, but research has often failed to support this assumption (Tavris and Wade, 1984). Perceived differences may be a reflection of how males and females are trained to express caring. For example, a woman might be socialized to assume primary responsibility for caring for her partner's feeling and for the well-being of the relationship itself. If she marries, she might be expected to assume the major responsibility for the primary care of the children. A man, on the other hand, is more likely to be socialized toward caring about the safety of his love partner. If he marries, he might assume primary responsibility for the family's economic well-being. Though these gender role expectations are becoming less rigid today, they often remain as a part of our unconscious scripts and definitions of love. Males may welcome a sharing of financial responsibilities while also experiencing some anxiety over a partner's independence ("Does she still love me if she doesn't need me?"). Females, on the other hand, may also value the shared independence of the newer relationships but still have some unfulfilled scripts for protection ("Why doesn't he offer to go investigate the strange noise in the basement?")

Attachment and intimacy also present problems for relationships. Attachment, for example, can be so powerful that people often stay in, or go back to, destructive relationships because they desperately "need" the other person. And in the search for intimacy, many people look to sex for fulfillment and are confused and disappointed when physical intimacy leaves them empty and sad. Each of us apparently has a deep need for the trust and shared communication in an intimate love relationship. The fact that women tend to

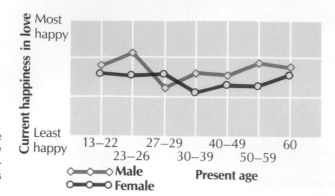

Figure 11.7 Happiness in love throughout the life cycle. Contrary to popular opinion, men generally report higher levels of love happiness than women.

have overall lower scores in love happiness (see Figure 11.7) is sometimes attributed to their unfulfilled needs for intimacy from men (Rubenstein, 1983).

Question: Why do women seem to value intimacy more than men? Women do tend to disclose more intimate information than men and do so earlier in the relationship, but men may simply define intimacy differently than women (Hays, 1985). Men's need for intimacy appears to be greatly satisfied through physical presence, whereas women tend to need close talk (McGill, 1985; Rubin, 1983). Fear of intimacy, however, seems to be shared by both males and females, and Elaine Hatfield (1988) suggests that this fear may be justified. She argues that many people have suffered from instances in which their trust and disclosure of personal information have led to rejection by the other person. Their trust may also have been exploited and the information used against them. Such violations of trust make people fearful of again opening themselves to others. Can you imagine the problems of self-disclosure and intimacy for the twin with the

Women tend to disclose more intimate information than men, which may explain some frustrations associated with male/female relationships.

sex reassignment? Transsexuals also have serious relationship problems due to rejection and violations of trust after self-disclosure (Martino, 1977; Patton, 1986).

Findings about intimacy have important implications for our individual lives. Not only should we be careful to honor the trust and disclosures of others, but we should also take care to protect ourselves. Since research shows that liking seems to be maximized in situations where there is an equal and shared amount of disclosure (Cunningham and Strassberg, 1981), we can protect ourselves and others by giving relationships time to develop. By waiting for shared trust to evolve and matching our disclosures to those of our partner, we may avoid the pitfalls of unequal intimacy and also help to minimize the male–female differences. The time factor should also be kept in mind if we want to use physical intimacy or sex as a way to feel closer and more bonded to another.

Question: Are caring, attachment, and intimacy all there is to love? What about the "magic" and passion? What is typically experienced as magic or passion is the basic components of a special type of feeling — that of "falling in love." This **romantic love,** also called passionate love or limerence (Tennov, 1979), "is a widely emotional state: tender and sexual feelings, elation and pain, anxiety and relief, altruism and jealousy coexist in a confusion of feelings" (Berscheid and Walster, 1978, p. 177). It is the stuff of which most novels, plays, films, and popular songs are made, and is probably the type of love Senator Proxmire objected to studying, since it also relies on mystery and uncertainty. If romantic love were only used as a basis of entertainment, as was true in the Middle Ages, it might *not* be a worthy subject for study. But since both males and females overwhelmingly regard this form of love as very important to their relationships (Rubenstein, 1983), it is important that we understand it.

ROMANTIC LOVE: *An intense feeling of attraction to another person that is characterized by high passion, obsessive thinking, and emotional fluctuation.*

Romantic love One of the major components of romantic love, which also leads to its inevitable decline, is its intensity of feeling. Whereas no one expects other intense emotions like anger or elation to go on forever, we often secretly hope that our love is special and that its excitement will be eternal. But the very desire that leads couples to want to be together every possible moment also carries with it the seeds of destruction for romantic love. Since romance is largely dependent on mystery and fantasy, the illusions are difficult to maintain in everyday interactions and long-term exposure. Our "beautiful princess" or "knight-in-shining armor" is hardly romantic when we hear her snore while she sleeps, when we watch him brush or floss his teeth, or when he or she criticizes us for our shortcomings.

Question: Is there any way to keep love alive? If you mean romantic love, one of the best ways to fan the flames is through *interference,* or some form of frustration that keeps you from fulfilling your desire for the presence of your love. Researchers have found that interference, such as that provided by the parents in Shakespeare's *Romeo and Juliet,* may serve to increase the feelings of love (Driscoll et al., 1972). Similarly, the case of a married man who runs off with his secretary could be seen as an example of this same "Romeo and Juliet effect," since the marriage would act as an interference in intensifying any feelings of attraction toward the secretary.

Because romantic love depends on uncertainty and fantasy, it can also be kept alive by situations in which we never really get to know the other person. This may explain the old saying "Absence makes the heart grow fonder," and why old high school romances and unrequited loves have such a tug on our emotions. Since we never really get to test these relationships, we can always fantasize about what might have been.

One of the most constructive ways of keeping romantic love alive is to recognize its fragile nature and to nurture it with carefully planned "surprises," flirting and flattery, and special dinners and celebrations. In the long run, however, romantic love might serve its most important role as the glue that keeps us attached long enough so that we can move on to companionate love.

DEVELOPING ONE'S PERSPECTIVE
Clarifying Your Sexual Values

One of the most important ingredients of critical thinking is the ability to closely examine one's own *values* (ideals, mores, standards, and principles that guide behavior). Are the values you currently hold a simple reflection of the values of your family or peer group? Or are they the result of careful, deliberate choice? Have you listened carefully to opposing values and compared the relative costs and benefits? Since values have such a powerful influence on thinking, you should critically evaluate each of your personal values.

To help you explore your values regarding sex and love, we offer the following exercise. Below are listed five value statements. In the space to the right, simply check whether you agree or disagree.

	AGREE	DISAGREE
1. Anyone who wants to prevent pregnancy should have easy access to reliable methods of contraception; it doesn't matter whether a person is married or single, young or old.	____	____
2. Gay couples should be allowed the same legal protections (property inheritance, shared pension plans, shared medical benefits) as heterosexual married couples.	____	____
3. Abortion in the first four months of pregnancy should be a private decision between the woman and her doctor.	____	____

	AGREE	DISAGREE
4. Premarital sex is morally wrong and should be discouraged.	____	____
5. Extramarital sex is morally wrong and should be discouraged.	____	____

Each person's sexual values come from a host of sources, some internal and others external to the individual. The second part of this exercise is designed to give you an opportunity to examine some of these sources.

Using the table on the next page, review your agree or disagree responses to the previous five statements. Indicate the degree to which each of the sources listed in the left-hand column has influenced your beliefs by placing a check mark in the appropriate column.

Now reexamine the checks you made for each of your five sexual values and their source of influence. Do you notice any patterns in your check marks? Which source has been most influential in the development of your sexual values? Do you think this source is the most appropriate and most justifiable? Why or why not? Which source has been least influential in the development of your sexual values? How do you explain this? Did you notice any inconsistencies in your choice of sources? In what cases did personal experience play a more significant role than family patterns, peer standards, and so on?

To further clarify your sexual perspective and sharpen your critical thinking skills, your answers to each part of this exercise should be shared with a close friend, dating partner, and/or spouse.

Unlike romantic love, which rarely lasts longer than 6 to 30 months, companionate love lasts an entire lifetime.

Sexual Values

Sources	Contraception			Homosexuality			Abortion			Premarital Sex			Extramarital Sex		
	VS	SS	NS	VS	SS	NS	VS	SS	NS	VS	SS	NS	VS	SS	NS
Personal experience															
Family patterns															
Peer standards															
Historical events															
Religious views															
Research findings															

VS = Very Significant Influence

SS = Somewhat Significant Influence

NS = Not a Significant Influence

Companionate love   **Companionate love** is based on admiration and respect (liking) combined with deep feelings of caring and commitment to the relationship. Unlike romantic love, which rarely lasts longer than six to thirty months (Ebersole and De Paola, 1988; Walster and Walster, 1978), companionate love seems to grow stronger with time and often lasts an entire lifetime. Studies of close friendships have found that satisfaction seems to grow with time as we come to recognize the value of companionship and of having an intimate confidante (Hays, 1984, 1985).

Even though we often feel companionate love for our best friends, the combination of the sexual attraction and passion of romantic love with the deep caring of companionate love can be the basis for a strong and lasting marriage. To maintain this relationship, it is important to remember the influence of each of the theories of friendship—reinforcement, equity, social exchange, and gain–loss. It is also important to avoid the pitfalls associated with romantic love. Since many of our expectations for love are based on romantic fantasies and unconscious programming from fairy tales and television shows

COMPANIONATE LOVE: *A strong feeling of attraction to another person characterized by trust, caring, tolerance, and friendship. It is believed to provide an enduring basis for long-term relationships.*

Childhood stories and modern movies often perpetuate romantic messages, such as that "Prince Charming" will rescue women from meaningless lives; they proceed to fall in love, get married, and live "happily ever after."

where everybody lives "happily ever after," we are often ill-equipped to deal with the hassles and boredom that come with any long-term relationship.

The old adage "love is blind" also has some insights to offer couples who seek a long and lasting relationship. Although the need for similarity and the costs of attitudinal dissimilarity often help guide our choice of friends, it seems that the arousal that occurs with romantic love may cause us to ignore the dissimilarities in our partners and to exaggerate any shared interests (Hendrick and Hendrick, 1989; Rusbult, 1983). According to Gold and his colleagues (1984), the "highly emotional state [of romantic love] may lead to a suspension of the typical discriminations employed in judging others and consequently may result in attraction to a dissimilar other" (p. 359).

In the final analysis, many problem areas in love and human sexuality—intimacy, romantic love, unwanted pregnancies, and sexual dysfunctions—may be the result of "faulty programming." After a lifetime of socialization into a world of "the pinks and the blues" (where parents, teachers, and general society expect different behaviors on the simple basis of gender) and into marriages and relationships that are built on the shaky foundation of romantic love, it is any wonder that people have problems? Some researchers have suggested that a greater acceptance of the "masculine" and "feminine" parts in each individual might eliminate some problems (men could be more self-disclosing and intimate, and women could be more sexually assertive and communicative about their desires). In addition, male–female and individual differences in friendships and love may be improved by developing a wider variety of friends and social resources. Romantic lovers need to be reminded that no single relationship can provide all their social needs. People can fulfill a variety of needs through significant relationships with relatives, through casual acquaintances and coworkers, and through both same-sex and opposite-sex friendships, as well as sexually intimate relationships. Good psychological adjustment seems to depend on having a wide network of over-lapping social relations.

Review Questions

1. _____ _____ seems to be one of the most important factors in our initial liking of others.
2. Proximity seems to be an important factor in attraction primarily because of the increased opportunities for _____.
3. The attraction to similar others is known as _____ _____, whereas the attraction to those who possess opposite traits that we lack is known as _____ _____.
4. _____ theory suggests that attraction results from learning through rewards and punishments.
5. Our preference for fair relationships where people put in as much as they get out is known as _____ theory.
6. _____ _____ theory suggests that relationships must show a net profit for both parties.
7. The fact that we are often more attracted to the compliments of a stranger versus those from an old friend is explained by the _____ theory.
8. The three factors of loving found in Rubin's scale are _____, _____, and _____.
9. _____ love seems to place heavy emphasis on mystery and fantasy, whereas _____ love seems to be based on mutual respect, trust, and friendship.

Answers: *1* physical attractiveness; *2* exposure; *3* need compatibility, need complementarity; *4* reinforcement; *5* equity; *6* social exchange; *7* gain–loss; *8* caring, attachment, intimacy; *9* romantic, companionate

REVIEW OF MAJOR CONCEPTS

THE STUDY OF HUMAN SEXUALITY

1 Although sex has always been an important part of human interest, motivation, and behavior, it received little scientific attention before the twentieth century. Using the case study technique, Havelock Ellis was among the first to attempt to study human sexuality in the face of heavy repression and secrecy from nineteenth-century Victorian standards.

2 Alfred Kinsey and his colleagues were the first to conduct large-scale, systematic surveys and interviews of the sexual practices and preferences of Americans during the 1940s and 1950s. The research team of Masters and Johnson pioneered the use of actual laboratory measurement and observation of human physiological response during sexual arousal. Cross-cultural studies are also important sources of scientific information in human sexuality.

BECOMING AND BEING MALE OR FEMALE

3 Maleness and femaleness (gender) can be differentiated along several biological dimensions: chromosomal gender, gonadal gender, hormonal gender, genital sex, and internal accessory organs. There are also four psychological and behavioral dimensions to gender: gender identity, gender role, sexual orientation, and sexual behavior.

4 These gender dimensions can be used to explain several misunderstandings. Transsexuals, for example, have problems in gender identity (their anatomy fails to match their personal sense of being male or female), whereas transvestites cross-dress for the purpose of sexual arousal.

5 The causes of both transsexualism and homosexuality are seen by some to be environmental (parental modeling or treatment and learning through rewards and punishments), but others suggest that their origins are biological (either genetically transmitted or due to hormonal imbalances).

6 Males and females have several obvious physical differences, such as height, body build, and reproductive organs, but during the first six weeks of prenatal development all embryos are anatomically identical. The presence of testosterone allows the male embryo to develop male genitals, and disruptions in this hormone can lead to problems in the development of both male and female genitals.

7 The belief in rigid, psychological differences in males and females is known as sex stereotyping. Although some actual differences have been documented (such as in aggression and verbal skills), the cause of these differences (either nature or nurture) is hotly debated.

SEXUAL BEHAVIOR

8 Several aspects of sexual arousal an be explained from a biological perspective. Erogenous zones contain increased sensory receptors, and ejaculation and orgasm are partially reflexive. Dominance of the parasympathetic nervous system allows for sexual arousal, but dominance of the sympathetic nervous system is necessary for orgasm to occur.

9 Arousal is also learned. Sexual scripts teach us what to consider the "best" sex, and these scripts may create problems if they are based on unrealistic expectations.

10 Arousal is increased through sexual fantasies and exploration. Since females are discouraged from both fantasy and exploration (part of the double standard), they may seem to have a slower arousal time.

11 Masters and Johnson identified a four-stage sexual response cycle during sexual activity—excitement, plateau, orgasm, and resolution. Although this model has received some criticism, it is still widely used and has helped to dispel several myths, such as that of the superiority of the vaginal orgasm.

12 Sexual problems or dysfunctions are sometimes treated by sex therapists. Although the labeling or defining of these problems creates difficulties, many people have been helped by sex therapy. Masters and Johnson's two-week intensive approach is the most popular therapy technique. Their program emphasizes the relationship, an integration of physiological and psychosocial factors, cognitions, and specific behavioral techniques (such as sensate focus exercises). Professional sex therapists offer important guidelines for everyone: Sex education should be early and positive, a goal or performance orientation should be avoided, and communication should be improved and emphasized.

13 Sexual behavior is also affected by the problem of AIDS and other sexually transmitted diseases (STDs). Although AIDS is known to be transmitted only through sexual contact or exposure to infected blood, many people have irrational fears of contagion.

INTERPERSONAL ATTRACTION

14 Physical attractiveness is very important to initial attraction. Physically attractive people are often perceived as being more intelligent, sociable, and interesting than less attractive people.

15 Physical proximity increases one's attractiveness, and similarity and need complementarity are also important to long-term relationships.

16 The four major theories of liking are: reinforcement theory, which sees attraction as resulting from learning through rewards and punishments; equity theory, which suggests that people prefer a balanced relationship, with outputs matching inputs; social exchange theory, which holds that each partner must show a "net profit" for a relationship to succeed; and the gain–loss theory, which suggests that unexpected increases in approval from others are particu-

larly rewarding and that losses of approval are particularly punishing.

17 Rubin's research on liking and loving found that love can be defined in terms of caring, attachment, and intimacy. Each of these three dimensions may present problems if there are real or perceived imbalances.

18 Romantic love is highly valued in our society, but because it is based on mystery and fantasy it is hard to sustain in long-term relationships. Companionate love relies on mutual trust, respect, and friendship and seems to grow stronger with time.

SUGGESTED READINGS

CALDERONE, M. J., & JOHNSON, E. W. (1988). *The family book about sexuality.* New York: Harper & Row. This text provides an excellent introduction to sex education, especially for parents who have had minimal exposure to academic discussions of sexuality.

LURIA, Z., FRIEDMAN, S., & ROSE, M. (1988). *Human sexuality* (2nd ed.). New York: Wiley. Students interested in an expanded discussion of the topics in this chapter, as well as related areas such as birth control and sexually transmitted diseases, will find this introductory text highly readable and interesting.

MONEY, J. (1985). *The destroying angel.* New York: Prometheus Books. A well-written, historical look at America's "antisex" attitudes, both past and present. Discusses eighteenth- and nineteenth-century attempts to control sex through bland diets (Kellogg's Corn Flakes) and general health reform.

PERPER, T. (1985). *Sexual signals: The biology of love.* Philadelphia: ISI Press. This book provides fascinating insights for those who wish to learn more about relationship initiation and maintenance.

chapter twelve
Motivation and Emotion

OUTLINE

I N Chapter 6 we introduced you to Koko, the gorilla who "speaks" more than 800 words in American Sign Language (the hand language of the deaf). The ability of Koko and other primates to use sign language raised many questions about whether language is unique to the human species. Now, subsequent behavior on Koko's part has raised additional questions about what many consider to be uniquely human behaviors: the need for companionship, feelings of love, and emotions of sadness and grief.

During her years of language training with Penny Patterson, Koko learned to use signs in a variety of ways — to converse with others, talk to herself, rhyme, joke, and even lie (Patterson and Goodreau, 1987). Through this language ability, Koko was also able to communicate about her personal preferences, such as her strong attraction for cats. During training sessions, she often "talked" of cats, and "The Three Little Kittens" and "Puss in Boots" came to be two of her favorite stories. When Koko asked for a cat for Christmas in 1983 and was given a stuffed toy one, she "pouted" (Vessels, 1985).

In June 1984, a litter of three real kittens was brought to visit Koko. She selected one as her favorite and named him "All Ball" (based on his lack of a tail and her love of rhymes). After repeatedly requesting a cat for her birthday present, Koko finally got her wish — All Ball. In their initial encounters, Koko treated the kitten as she would a baby gorilla — sniffing him, tucking him into her thigh, and trying to get him to nurse. She also behaved like a human child with a pet — dressing him in linen napkins and hats and playing chase games. At the same time, Koko demonstrated extreme gentleness and patience with her pet. When All Ball demonstrated his natural kittenlike behavior by biting Koko, for example, she sometimes laughed but usually just signed "obnoxious" (Vessels, 1985).

If all of this seems too "humanlike," you will surely have trouble with the description of Koko's reaction to the loss of her pet. According to media reports (Stone, 1988; Zimmerman, 1985), when Koko was told that her cat had wandered off one night and had been killed by a car, she showed typical signs of bereavement. When first told, she acted as if she hadn't heard, but later she "broke down" and wept the tearless hooting cry typical of lowland gorillas. When asked if she wanted to talk about her cat, she signed "cry" by running her finger from each eye down her cheeks.

Does Koko's behavior surprise you? Or are you skeptical that a gorilla can really become attached to a "pet" and feel grief at its loss? If so, you are not alone, for many people wonder whether animals can really experience emotions similar to those of humans. They question whether the reports on Koko aren't just another example of the common problem of **anthropomorphism** — attributing human characteristics to animals, gods, or inanimate objects.

Although the possible motives and emotions of animals such as Koko are of interest to both scientists and the general public, we tend to be more concerned with the motives and emotions of human beings. Have you ever wondered, for example, why some individuals eat themselves into obesity whereas others starve themselves to death, or why some people seem "addicted" to dangerous sports like parachute jumping or to painful love relationships? Have you ever asked yourself whether your emotions of anger and jealousy could, or should, be better controlled? These are the sorts of questions addressed in the research field known as motivation and emotion. **Motivation** refers to factors within an individual (such as needs, desires, and interests) that arouse, maintain, and channel behavior toward a goal. **Emotion** refers to feelings or affective responses that result from physiological arousal, thoughts and beliefs, subjective evaluation, and bodily expression (frowns, smiles, gestures, and so on). In other words, motivation energizes and directs behavior, whereas emotion is the "feeling" response or reaction.

The topics of motivation and emotion often overlap. When you see your loved one in the arms of another, for example, you may react with a variety of emotions (jealousy, fear, sadness, disbelief), and a corresponding variety of possible motives may determine how you act in the situation. Your desire for safety and security may cause you to ignore the situation, while your need for love and belonging may motivate you to look for ways to excuse the behavior or to protect your relationship. Although there is some inescapable overlap between motivation and emotion, and indeed with other areas of psychology, in this chapter we'll treat the topics separately and will look at specific theories and problems related to each topic.

UNDERSTANDING BASIC MOTIVATIONAL CONCEPTS

When we begin to ask the "why" questions about human and animal behavior (Why did you spend hours playing with a new computer game instead of studying for a major exam? Why did Koko dress up her pet in hats and napkins?), we quickly realize that there are many *motives,* or internal factors, that energize and direct behavior. Such motives include hunger, thirst, sex, approval, love, curiosity, achievement, and so on.

One of the most ambitious attempts to categorize and prioritize motives was made by Abraham Maslow (1954, 1970). According to Maslow, motives differ primarily on the basis of *prepotence,* or relative strength. In his view, the stronger needs (such as hunger and thirst) must be satisfied before one can move on to the higher needs, such as safety, belonging, and self-esteem. As shown in Figure 12.1, Maslow developed a five-level **hierarchy of needs,** with basic physiological needs at the bottom and self-actualization at the top. Although he saw "higher" motives as weaker than the more prepotent biological drives, Maslow believed that once freed from the "lower" needs, humans are drawn to satisfy those needs that will help them to grow and develop.

Maslow's hierarchy of needs seems intuitively correct in many situations — a starving person would first look for food, then worry about safety, then seek love and friendship, and so on. Critics have argued, however, that Maslow's choice of needs was somewhat arbitrary and that the order of progression is not universally fixed. For example, some people may starve themselves to make a political statement, or risk their own life for a loved one.

Maslow's arrangement of needs offers us a general overview of the major motives, but scientists have also developed several biological and psychological theories to explain the larger process of motivation.

How would you explain the motives of this skier and those of the wild-water rafter?

Figure 12.1 Maslow's hierarchy of motives or needs. According to Maslow, the basic, physical necessities must be satisfied before higher growth needs can be expressed.

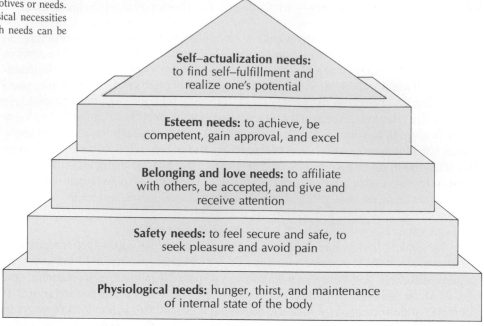

Self–actualization needs: to find self–fulfillment and realize one's potential

Esteem needs: to achieve, be competent, gain approval, and excel

Belonging and love needs: to affiliate with others, be accepted, and give and receive attention

Safety needs: to feel secure and safe, to seek pleasure and avoid pain

Physiological needs: hunger, thirst, and maintenance of internal state of the body

Biological theories: Looking for internal "whys" of behavior

Many theories of motivation take a biological approach—that is, they look for inborn processes that control and direct behavior. Among these biologically oriented theories are instinct and drive theories (discussed here) and psychoanalytic theory (discussed in Chapter 14).

INSTINCTS: *Behavioral patterns that are (1) unlearned, (2) uniform in expression, and (3) universal in a species.*

Instinct theories   A biological approach to the study of motivation would logically begin with a study of **instincts**. These are rigid and fixed motor response patterns that are not learned, are characteristic of all members of a species, and have an inherited, genetic foundation derived from the process of evolution. Instinctual behaviors are obvious in many animals: birds building nests, salmon swimming upstream to spawn, and so on. Such instinctive behaviors have been of prime interest to *ethologists*—scientists who study animals in their natural habitat. From their studies, ethologists have suggested that behaviors such as the fighting instinct have developed over the course of evolution because they increase chances for survival (Dewsbury, 1989; Lorenz, 1966, 1974).

Nest building and feeding of the young seem to be instinctual behaviors for birds.

Question: Do humans have instincts? In the earliest days of psychology the definition of instinct was not as rigorous as the one we have presented. At that time, researchers like William McDougall (1908) proposed that humans had numerous "instincts," including, repulsion, curiosity, self-assertiveness, parenting, and so on. Other researchers added their favorite "instincts," and the list eventually became so long that it was virtually meaningless — one account found listings for over 10,000 human instincts (Bernard, 1924). Some authors have jokingly referred to this as an example of the "instinct to believe in instincts" (Weiner, 1985).

In addition to the problem of a never-ending list of possibilities, the label "instinct" has produced circular types of explanations that can still be seen today. Have you ever heard someone say that men are just naturally or instinctually aggressive, or that all women have a maternal instinct? When asked for evidence of these instincts, the person (like the researchers did in McDougall's time) will most likely point to examples of male aggression or female nurturing. Thus, the explanation *of* the behavior *is* the behavior: "They act that way because they naturally act that way."

In more recent times, a case for human instincts has been made by the *sociobiologists* (Daly and Wilson, 1988; Wilson, 1978). They propose that much of human social behavior can be explained by the principle of *natural selection* — that is, behaviors that contribute to the preservation and promotion of one's genes are favored for survival. In the case of altruism (helping behavior), for example, sociobiologists suggest that parents protect their own children often at great personal risk not necessarily out of feelings of love but because of "genetic selfishness." In other words, parents may risk their own lives for those of their children because they "instinctively" know that this will improve the chances for survival of their own genes.

Both ethological and sociobiological theories have been criticized as being narrow and overly simplified (Gould, 1977, 1983; Kitcher, 1985). Furthermore, critics say these theories contribute support to those who believe that human nature is fixed and that efforts to solve social problems are therefore doomed to failure (Kriegman and Knight, 1988).

Such critics have been criticized in turn for ignoring the relevance of biology to human behavior. Nevertheless, most psychologists agree that according to the strict definition of instinct, it plays less and less of a role as we move up the evolutionary scale. The nurturing behavior of female rats, for example, seems to be primarily instinctual (Fahrbach and Pfaff, 1982), whereas nurturance among primates seems to reflect modifiable, flexible behavior response patterns. Male members of the lowland gorillas have been observed engaging in nurturing behaviors of orphaned animals. They apparently learned these behaviors from trial-and-error interactions with the infant animals or from watching the behavior of female gorillas (Fossey, 1983; Goodall, 1986). Even in the case of Koko and her attempts to nurse All Ball, it is hard to say that this behavior was instinctual, as Koko's trainers encouraged visits from nursing human mothers in an attempt to provide role models and learning experiences.

Drive-reduction theory Beginning in the 1930s, the concepts of drive and drive reduction began to expand and replace the theory of instincts. According to **drive-reduction theory** (Hull, 1952; Spence, 1951), motivation begins with a physiological *need* (a lack or deficiency). The need elicits a mobilization of psychological energy, known as a *drive,* that is directed toward behavior that will satisfy the original need (see Figure 12.2). Although "need" and "drive" are often used interchangeably, it is important to keep in mind that needs seem to increase in intensity over time, whereas the drive to satisfy them can be psychologically "ignored" and even forgotten on some occasions. Your need for food, for example, may increase between breakfast and lunch, but if you run into a friend while walking toward the cafeteria, your hunger drive may be easily diverted by the chance to talk.

> **DRIVE-REDUCTION THEORY:** *Theory that motivation begins with a physiological need (a lack or deficiency) that elicits a psychological energy or drive directed toward behavior that will satisfy the original need.*

Question: How does drive-reduction theory differ from instinct theory? Although drive-reduction theory does rely on innate, biological needs for the original impetus or "push," it also suggests that the original arousal (drive) is nonspecific and that

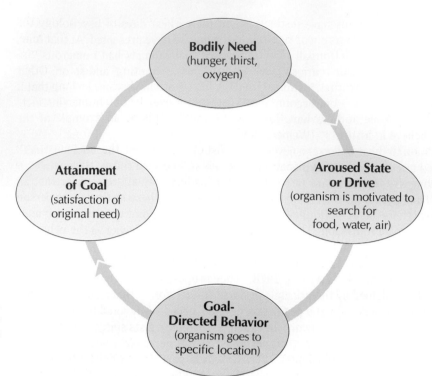

Figure 12.2 According to drive-reduction theory, our basic bodily needs drive us to look for specific methods of satisfaction.

the organism must *learn* which specific action to take to satisfy this need. Motivation is therefore a combination of biology and learning—your hunger "drives" you to search for food and you learn to go to the cafeteria.

Question: If drives can be ignored, why can't needs? All animals must eat, drink, take in oxygen, maintain body temperature, and avoid painful injuries in order to survive. Strong feelings of biological "pushing" or tension are created by the body's demand for constancy or balance in the internal environment—a process known as **homeostasis.** When this balance is disrupted by deprivation of food or water or by changes in body temperature, the brain sends strong signals that direct activity designed to restore homeostasis (see Figure 12.3).

HOMEOSTASIS: *Balance or equilibrium of the internal environment, which is accomplished through constant adjustments of the nervous system.*

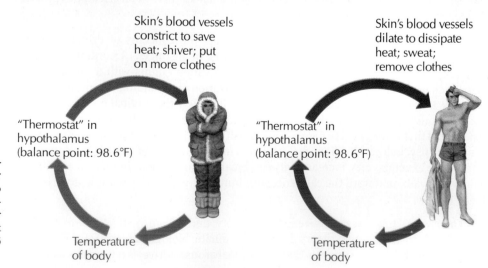

Figure 12.3 The concept of *homeostasis.* Like the thermostat in your home that adjusts the furnace to maintain a relatively stable room temperature, the "thermostat" in your hypothalamus sends messages that adjust your internal bodily heat (98.6 degrees Fahrenheit).

Drive theorists note that there are also *nonhomeostatic* motives that influence behavior. Sex and reproductive desires, for example, do not contribute to individual balance or survival, but they *are* necessary to species survival. Each of us can freely choose whether to respond to these nonhomeostatic drives. Although in many animals the sex drive is a powerful determinant of behavior and parenting of offspring is paramount, among humans the needs of sex and nurturing are less evident. As we discovered in Chapter 11, human sexual behaviors primarily reflect individual learning experiences.

The problem of explaining nonhomeostatic drives is one of the major limits of drive-reduction theory. For example, how would this theory explain why we continue to eat even when our biological needs are completely satisfied? Or why someone continues to work overtime when his or her salary is sufficient to meet all basic biological needs? The answers to these questions can be better answered by theories that emphasize incentive or cognitive factors.

Psychological theories: The role of incentives and cognitions

Psychologically oriented theories emphasize external, environmental factors (incentives) and the role of thoughts, attributions, and expectancies (cognitions) in motivation.

Incentive theory   Incentive theory plays down biological forces in motivation that "push" behavior and focuses instead on external stimuli in the environment that "pull" the organism in certain directions (Bolles, 1970, 1975; Pfaffmann, 1982). Because of certain characteristics of the external stimuli, the individual is motivated to perform some action to obtain desirable goals or to act in ways that avoid or eliminate undesirable events. People continue to eat even when they no longer feel hungry, for example, because the sight of a piece of their favorite pie or cake "pulls" them toward further food intake. Conversely, the sight of the mound of dirty dishes in the kitchen will "push" them toward the living room couch to avoid the disagreeable task of dishwashing.

INCENTIVE THEORY: *Theory that motivation results from environmental stimuli that "pull" the organism in certain directions, as opposed to internal needs that drive the organism in certain directions.*

Cognitive theories   The cognitive perspective on motivation emphasizes the importance of mental processes in goal-directed behavior. If you receive a high grade in your psychology course, you can interpret this grade in a variety of ways: you earned it because you really studied, you "lucked out," or the textbook was exceptionally interesting and helpful (our preferred interpretation!). Researchers who study such *attributions,* or explanations for the causes of behavior, have found that how we interpret our own behavior and that of others often has a strong effect on motivation (see Chapter 17). People who attribute their own successes to personal ability and effort tend to work harder toward their goals, for example, than people who attribute their successes to luck (Weiner, 1972, 1982). *Expectancies* are also important to motivation. Your anticipated grade on the test obviously affected your willingness to read and study the material.

Instinct, drive-reduction, incentive, and cognitive theories are four of the most popular scientific attempts to answer the original "why" questions that surround behavior. We should emphasize, however, that no one theory has been proven "correct" — each has elements that offer insights into what motivates behavior.

Can you see how both incentive theory and cognitive theory could be used to explain the motivation for a brand new sports car?

Review Questions

1 The act of attributing human characteristics to animals, gods, or inanimate objects is known as _____ .

2 _____ refers to internal factors that energize and direct behavior, whereas _____ refers to feelings or affective responses.

3 According to Maslow's _____ __ _____, basic survival and security needs must be satisfied before one can move on to the higher needs such as self-actualization.

4 Contemporary supporters of the instinct theory include _____, who suggest that instincts have survived because they increase chances for survival, and _____, who believe that much of human social behavior is due to natural selection and "genetic selfishness."

5 _____ theory suggests that biological needs "push" the organism to look for satisfaction and that the specific action taken results from learning, whereas _____ theory proposes that external, environmental stimuli "pull" the organism toward certain goal-directed behaviors.

6 _____ theories emphasize the importance of thoughts, attributions, and expectancies in motivated behaviors.

Answers: 1 anthropomorphism; *2* motivation, emotion; *3* hierarchy of needs (or motives); *4* ethologists, sociobiologists; *5* drive-reduction, incentive; *6* cognitive

THE NATURE OF SPECIFIC MOTIVES

Now that we have outlined some major motivation theories, let us look at three categories of specific motives: primary (biological), stimulus-seeking, and learned.

Primary motives: Hunger and the regulation of food intake

PRIMARY MOTIVES: *Motives that arise from innate, biological needs, such as hunger, thirst, pain avoidance, and sleep.*

Primary motives are generated from innate, biological needs that must be met for survival. These motives include hunger, thirst, pain avoidance, sleep, elimination of wastes, oxygen, and so on. In this section, we will focus on hunger as an example of a primary motive.

How do you know when you are hungry? One of the earliest attempts to understand the sensation of hunger was an experiment conducted by Cannon and Washburn (1912). In this study, Washburn swallowed a balloon and then inflated it in his stomach. His stomach contractions and subjective reports of hunger feelings could then be simultaneously recorded (see Figure 12.4). Since each time Washburn reported having stomach pangs (or "growling") the balloon also contracted, the researchers naturally concluded that it was the stomach movements that caused the sensation of hunger.

What do you think is wrong with this conclusion? As you may remember from Chapter 1, researchers must always control for the possibility of *extraneous variables,* or factors that contribute irrelevant data that confuse the results. In this particular case, it was later found that an empty stomach is relatively inactive and that the stomach contractions experienced by Washburn were an experimental artifact resulting from the presence of the balloon—his stomach had been "tricked" into "thinking it was full" and was responding by trying to digest the balloon.

Further evidence for the lack of connection between stomach stimuli and feelings of hunger was provided in experiments in which rats had their stomachs removed or their nerve pathways to and from the stomach severed. The hunger behavior of these rats was essentially the same as that of the control rats (those with intact stomachs or nonsevered nerves) (Morgan and Morgan, 1940). Similarly, human patients who have had their stomachs removed in ulcer or cancer operations report normal feelings of hunger (Janowitz, 1967). The recent introduction of the *gastric bubble* as a weight-reduction technique provides further data on the limited role of stomach sensations on hunger (Seligman and Gosnell, 1986). Despite having a fully inflated small balloon in their stomachs, gastric bubble patients still report feelings of hunger.

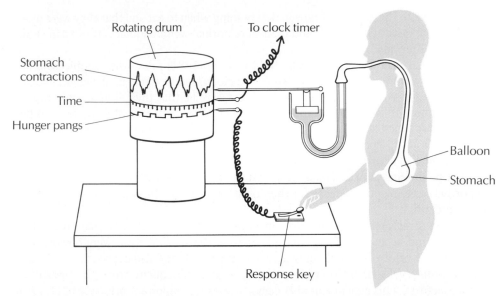

Rotating drum — To clock timer

Stomach contractions

Time

Hunger pangs

Balloon

Stomach

Response key

Figure 12.4 Cannon and Washburn's technique for measuring hunger. The subject first swallowed a balloon designed to detect stomach movements. These stomach movements were automatically recorded, and the recordings were compared to the voluntary key presses that the subject made each time he or she experienced a feeling of hunger. (*Source:* Cannon and Washburn, 1912.)

Question: If stomach sensations aren't necessary for hunger, what does explain it? As we noted in Chapter 2, a part of the brain known as the *hypothalamus* contains areas that regulate eating, drinking, and body temperature. In specific reference to hunger, research has shown that one area of the hypothalamus, the **lateral hypothalamus (LH),** seems to stimulate eating (Anand and Brobeck, 1951). Another area, the **ventromedial hypothalamus (VMH),** creates feelings of satiation or satisfaction and signals the organism to stop eating (Hetherington and Ranson, 1942). The LH has been called the "start eating" center, whereas the VMH has been identified as the "stop eating" center. So important is the VMH area that when it is destroyed in rats, they will overeat to the point of extreme obesity (see photograph on this page). Similarly, when the LH area is destroyed, animals stop eating and some may starve to death if they are not force-fed. With time, LH-damaged rats will resume eating but they maintain their weight well below normal. Humans with tumors in the LH or VMH area show similar weight reactions.

Question: How do these parts of the hypothalamus know when to turn "on" and "off"? Further research on the role of the LH and VMH in the control of eating has shown that these areas are not simple on–off switches for the control of eating. Keesey and Powley (1975, 1986) have found that the LH area is responsible for establishing a **set point** for body weight. Damage to this area results in a lower set point and the animal adjusts its eating behavior to maintain the lower level. (The applications of set point theory to obesity in humans is discussed at the end of this chapter.) Keesey and Powley have also found that the VMH is responsible for basal metabolism and the obesity that results from damage to the VMH is believed to be caused by below average energy expenditure.

Although the LH and VMH areas of the hypothalamus are important determinants of food consumption, other areas of the brain (such as the brain stem) are also involved (Schwartz, 1984). In addition, the level of sugar in the blood may serve as a trigger or signal to start or stop eating (Davis, Gallagher, and Ladove, 1967; Novlin et al., 1983), and the level of body fat affects food intake as well (Bennett and Gurin, 1982). One intriguing finding is that many forms of simple stimulation, such as noise, the presence of others, and (for rats) a pinch on the tail, initiate eating behaviors (Valenstein et al., 1982).

This idea that external, nonphysiological factors also affect hunger has been of prime interest to psychologist Stanley Schachter (1971). He and his colleagues conducted a series of ingenious experiments in which normal-weight and overweight individuals were provided with a variety of external cues to eating (such as the presence of food or a clock that indicated "dinner time"). The researchers found that overweight subjects were

LATERAL HYPOTHALAMUS (LH): *Area of the hypothalamus responsible for stimulating eating behavior.*

VENTROMEDIAL HYPOTHALAMUS (VMH): *Area of the hypothalamus responsible for signaling the organism to stop eating. If destroyed, the organism will overeat and become obese.*

SET POINT: *An organism's personal homeostatic level for a particular body weight that results from factors such as early feeding experiences and heredity.*

The ventromedial area of the rat on the left has been destroyed. Note the extreme obesity compared to the normal rat on the right.

more attentive to the passage of time in determining when to eat and that they were more excited by the taste and sight of food than were normal-weight subjects (Goldman et al., 1968; Schachter and Gross, 1968).

In a follow-up on this research, Judith Rodin (1981) found that people who are responsive to external cues to eating (such as a clock) can be found in all weight categories. One reason why some "externals" overeat may be that they experience a higher insulin response to the sight of food. When Rodin (1984, 1985) invited subjects to her laboratory for lunch after they had first endured 18 hours without food, she found that insulin levels in the blood samples of the "external" subjects were stimulated by the mere sight and smell of a sizzling steak. If you've ever heard friends complain that they can "get fat" just by looking at or smelling food, you can now tell them that there may be some supportive experimental evidence for their observation — the increase in insulin encourages overeating.

Rodin's research illustrates how incentives and drive reduction may interact to motivate eating behaviors. The sight and sound of the sizzling steak were obviously of high incentive value (the "pull" of a desirable goal), and they also caused an increase in blood insulin level that led to a biological need and subsequent drive (the "push" of internal factors). This experiment also demonstrates the important principle of classical conditioning (see Chapter 6). Like Pavlov's dogs who learned to salivate to the sound of the bell, "external" eaters learn to increase their insulin levels at the sight and smell of desirable food.

Stimulus-seeking motives: The need for novel stimulation

When you see a box sitting on a table, do you peek to see what's in it? If you hear an unusual sound, do you explore to find out what caused it? Have you ever wondered why you sometimes stand in line for hours for a chance to ride a "killer" roller coaster or to see a horror film? Certainly there is no biological need that will be satisfied by such behaviors, yet you are still driven by a "need to know" and by desires for physical or emotional stimulation. Like the primary motives, such **stimulus-seeking motives** appear to be innate, yet they are unnecessary for basic survival. Our nervous sytem is apparently "driven" to search for *novel* cognitive, physical, and emotional stimulation.

Examples of such stimulus-seeking behavior are easily found. Shortly after birth, infants show a marked preference for complex versus simple visual stimuli (see Chapter 9). Adults also pay more attention, and for a longer period of time, to complex and novel stimuli. Similarly, research with animals has shown that monkeys will learn discrimination tasks for the simple "reward" of a brief look around the laboratory (Butler, 1954). As can be seen in the photograph on p. 389, they will also learn to open latches for the sheer pleasure of curiosity and manipulation (Harlow, Harlow, and Meyer,1950).

In the case of Koko, the need for physical and emotional stimulation was clearly seen in her excited preference for a game of "Spin." In this game, Koko would lie on her back and Patterson would spin her around by the hand or foot — often at high speed due to the frictionless ride provided by her fur. In addition, Koko's strong curiosity drive (cognitive stimulus seeking) helped motivate her to learn sign language — although it also occasionally got her into trouble. For example, when she was caught "exploring" (and destroying) a window screen with a chopstick, she compounded the damage by lying! Asked what she was doing, Koko tried to cover up by placing the stick in her mouth (simulating cigarette smoking) and signing "smoke mouth."

Intrinsic versus extrinsic motivation   Koko's lies, the monkeys' "working" for a look around the laboratory, and humans standing in long lines for the "reward" of riding roller coasters are all examples of the strength of the internal, stimulus-seeking motives. What do you think would happen to the level of motivation if someone added an external payoff or reward? Would motivation increase or decrease? Researchers who have studied the effects of **extrinsic** (external) **rewards** versus **intrinsic** (personally satisfying) **rewards** have discovered that people who are paid or rewarded for doing a task that they had

STIMULUS-SEEKING MOTIVES: *Innate, internal needs for novel cognitive, physical, and emotional stimulation.*

EXTRINSIC REWARDS: *External reinforcers that often work to undermine personal interest, enjoyment, and satisfaction since the person is doing it for someone else.*
INTRINSIC REWARDS: *Internal, personally satisfying reinforcers that motivate individuals to perform certain activities because of personal enjoyment and interest.*

Monkeys will "work" very hard at opening latches for the sheer pleasure of satisfying curiosity and the need for novel stimulation.

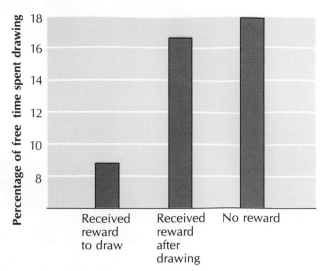

Figure 12.5 Intrinsic versus extrinsic motivation. When children were given free time to draw, those who had previously received a reward for drawing were less likely to later freely choose to draw. (*Source:* Lepper et al., 1973.)

previously done for the sheer fun of it actually lose enjoyment and interest in the task (Amabile, 1985; Fabes, 1987). In one study, preschool children who liked to draw were given artist's paper and felt-tipped pens (Lepper, Greene, and Nisbett, 1973). One group of children were promised a reward of a "Good Player" certificate and a gold seal and ribbon for their drawings. A second group were asked to draw and then received an unexpected reward when they were done. A third group received no promise of reward and were given none. A few weeks later, these same children were placed in a situation where they could draw if they wanted to, and the amount of time they spent drawing was recorded. As can be seen in Figure 12.5 having received rewards on the first occasion seemed to undermine the children's subsequent interest in drawing. In a similar study with college students, McNeill and Kimmel (1988) found that offering money for problem solving dramatically decreased the students' intrinsic motivation and detrimentally affected their performance.

Question: Can you explain this? The critical factor in enjoyment of a task seems to be in how we explain our motivation to ourselves. When we perform a task for no apparent reason, we seem to use internal, personal reasons ("I like it," "It's fun"). But

Children seem to have an intrinsic love of drawing. Will grades and other forms of extrinsic motivation affect this behavior?

When rewards are contingent on competent or outstanding performance, they are less likely to reduce intrinsic motivation.

when extrinsic rewards are added, the explanation seems to shift to external, impersonal reasons ("I did it for the money," "I did it to please the boss"). This shift generally causes us to experience a decrease in enjoyment and performance of the behavior.

Question: But how does this theory explain situations where getting a raise, or receiving a gold medal, seems to increase enjoyment or productivity?   Researchers such as Deci and Ryan (1985) and Rosenfeld, Folger, and Adelman (1980) explain that rewards will not invariably reduce intrinsic interest in an activity if the reward is based on competent or outstanding performance rather than on merely engaging in the behavior. Rewards for competency actually seem to produce a greater feeling of pride that may help to intensify the desire to do well again (Harackiewicz and Manderlink, 1984).

The concept of intrinsic and extrinsic motivation has important implications for business, education, and everyday interactions with others. Manufacturers who offer a substantial rebate for buying a product, for example, may find that the gimmick works well for initial purchases but may also reduce "brand loyalty" (the tendency to repeat the purchase) once the rebate is withdrawn (Dodson, Tybout, and Steinthal, 1978). Similarly, educational institutions that use extrinsic rewards for school attendance may see an increase in overall absenteeism once the rewards are removed. It is important to remember in each case that the reward must come *after* the behavior is performed (see Chapter 6) and must be given only as a way to provide feedback on achievement.

In the long run, reward should probably be saved for truly outstanding performance or as a way of maintaining interest long enough for a task to become intrinsically interesting. When children are first learning to play a musical instrument, for example, it may help to provide some rewards until they gain a certain level of mastery. But once the child is working happily or practicing for the sheer joy of it, it may be best to leave him or her alone. There's an old saying that seems appropriate: "When funds come in, fun goes out!"

Optimal level of arousal   Although research has shown that both animals and humans tend to prefer complex and changing stimuli, some research also suggests that there is an ideal and **optimal level of arousal** that an organism is motivated to maintain (Berlyne, 1971; Hebb, 1955, 1966). Similar to the need for physiological homeostasis is a need for homeostasis in stimulus seeking. When arousal is too low or too high, performance is negatively affected (see Figure 12.6). In the classroom, you may have noticed that both extremes of arousal (being too relaxed or too anxious) can be detrimental to your test-taking abilities.

OPTIMAL LEVEL OF AROUSAL: *Idea that there is an ideal or optimal level of excitement that is maintained through the body's need for homeostasis in stimulus seeking.*

Question: Don't some people seek more stimulation than others?   Just as there are "homebodies" who prefer familiarity, stability, and a good book in front of a warm fire, there are also people who find these activities boring and who will actively seek

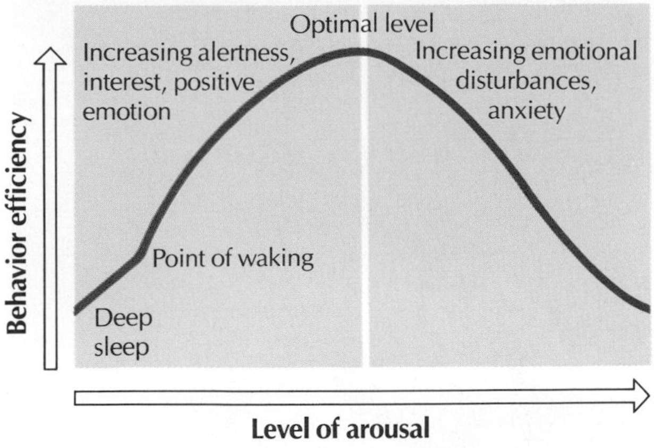

Figure 12.6 What is the best level of arousal for maximum efficiency? According to the optimal level of arousal theory, overall production is highest with moderate arousal.

out high adventure and risks. These two extremes represent differing optimal arousal levels and could be classified as low and high "sensation seekers" according to some psychologists (Zuckerman et al., 1974, 1978). To find out where you would fit on this sensation-seeking dimension, you can score yourself using Marvin Zuckerman's scale in Table 12.1.

Research based on longer versions of this scale does support the idea of strong differences among individuals in their desire for stimulation and varied experiences. High sensation seekers are more likely to experiment with drugs, to have more varied sexual

TABLE 12.1
Abbreviated Test to Determine Sensation Seekers

Are you a high or a low sensation seeker?

To test your own sensation-seeking tendencies, try this shortened version of one of Marvin Zuckerman's earlier scales. For each of the 13 items, circle the choice A or B that best describes your feelings.

1 A I would like a job that requires a lot of traveling.
　B I would prefer a job in one location.

2 A I am invigorated by a brisk, cold day.
　B I can't wait to get indoors on a cold day.

3 A I get bored seeing the same old faces.
　B I like the comfortable familiarity of everyday friends

4 A I would prefer living in an ideal society in which everyone is safe, secure, and happy.
　B I would have preferred living in the unsettled days of our history.

5 A I sometimes like to do things that are a little frightening.
　B A sensible person avoids activities that are dangerous.

6 A I would not like to be hypnotized.
　B I would like to have the experience of being hypnotized.

7 A The most important goal of life is to live it to the fullest and experience as much as possible.
　B The most important goal of life is to find peace and happiness.

8 A I would like to try parachute-jumping.
　B I would never want to try jumping out of a plane, with or without a parachute.

9 A I enter cold water gradually, giving myself time to get used to it.
　B I like to dive or jump right into the ocean or a cold pool.

10 A When I go on a vacation, I prefer the comfort of a good room and bed.
　B When I go on a vacation, I prefer the change of camping out.

11 A I prefer people who are emotionally expressive even if they are a bit unstable.
　B I prefer people who are calm and even-tempered.

12 A A good painting should shock or jolt the senses.
　B A good painting should give one a feeling of peace and security.

13 A People who ride motorcycles must have some kind of unconscious need to hurt themselves.
　B I would like to drive or ride a motorcycle.

Scoring
Count one point for each of the following items that you have circled: 1A, 2A, 3A, 4B, 5A, 6B, 7A, 8A, 9B, 10B, 11A, 12A, 13B. Add up your total and compare it with the norms below.

0–3	Very low
4–5	Low
6–9	Average
10–11	High
12–13	Very high

Source: Zuckerman, M. (1978) "The search for high sensation," *Psychology Today,* February, 1978, *pp.* 38–46. Copyright © 1978 by the American Psychological Association. Reprinted by permission.

Can you see how personality differences in high and low sensation seekers may explain certain occupational choices or feelings of job dissatisfaction?

experiences with a larger number of partners, to have been convicted of assaultive offenses, and to prefer higher-risk sports and professions (Berman and Paisey, 1984; Zuckerman, 1979, 1983). Zuckerman also suggests that large differences in desire for sensation seeking may lead to relationship problems between husband and wife, therapist and patient, and parent and child. Such differences might also create job difficulties for the person who is ill matched for either routine assembly-line work or a highly challenging and variable occupation.

Question: Is there any way to change one's optimal arousal level? Considerable evidence suggests that varying needs for sensation cannot be changed, since they are a basic part of personality that may be genetically determined through brain chemistry and gonadal hormones (Zuckerman et al., 1980). Other research, using a related test for "thrill seeking," has suggested that instead of attempting to change sensation-seeking needs, high sensation seekers should be identified early in life so that appropriate measures can be taken to funnel their energy toward constructive outlets (Farley, 1986).

Learned motives: Explaining unexpected behaviors

Although some aspects of sensation seeking or risk taking may be innate or part of an exaggerated need for novel stimulation, there is also evidence that such behavior may be learned. It is relatively easy to see how most **learned motives,** such as needs for achievement, power, approval, and affiliation (being with others), are the direct result of simple reinforcement and of observation of others (see Chapter 6). But how would we account for the desire to engage in scary behaviors such as parachute jumping or destructive and expensive drug habits?

The motivation is partially explained by a combination of learning and the body's natural desire for homeostasis (Piliavin, Callero, and Evans, 1982; Solomon, 1980, 1982). According to the **opponent-process theory** (not to be confused with the opponent-process theory of color vision, Chapter 4), whenever an intense emotional experience upsets psychological and physiological balance, a compensating force (the opponent-process mechanism) starts to work to restore equilibrium. In other words, if one set of activities

LEARNED MOTIVES: *Motives that are acquired through direct experience with rewards and punishments, or through the observation of others. These motives include the needs for affiliation, power, achievement, and so on.*

OPPONENT-PROCESS THEORY OF EMOTIONS: *Idea that an intense emotional experience elicits an opposite (opposing) emotion. With repeated experiences, the second emotion becomes stronger than the first.*

A love of skydiving may result from the learned contrast between initial terror and postjump elation.

goes too far in one direction (a process), the brain responds with an opposite (opposing) emotional state that offsets the first emotion. During the initial experience, the individual apparently watches and learns to associate a particular *range* of emotional response with the behavior. When this behavior is repeated many times, however, the initial emotional reaction diminishes in intensity because of simple habituation (see Chapter 6). Since the individual has learned a certain range of response, the intensity of the first emotion is shifted to the second, opposing emotion (see Figure 12.7).

In the example of skydiving (the dotted line in Figure 12.7), the first jump elicits an initial reaction of sheer terror in virtually everyone. After a few moments, however, the terror is replaced by a sense of relief and well-being (notice the slight rise in positive feelings). After repeated jumps (the graph on the right), the jumper gradually habituates

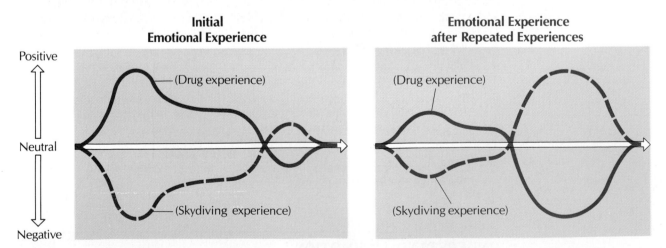

Figure 12.7 How does someone become "addicted" to drugs or skydiving? According to the opponent-process theory of emotion, each individual's first emotional reaction is soon replaced with an opposing (opposite) emotion. As a result of the body's need for balance, combined with the psychological effects of learning, the person soon needs more and more of the original stimulus. The drug addict needs more of the drug to relieve the increasingly negative feelings, whereas the skydiver desires more frequent jumps to obtain the rising feelings of pleasure.

to the initial emotional reaction and the terror diminishes. The previously learned contrast and range of emotions remain constant, however. As the terror decreases, the postjump elation increases. Thus, sky divers may become "addicted" to the sport because of the pleasurable aftereffects.

The opponent process is also active in situations that start with positive emotional states. In the case of drug taking (the solid line in Figure 12.7), the initial emotional experience is often one of euphoria, insight, and feelings of omnipotence (depending on the drug taken). But as time passes and the drug wears off, the opponent process of boredom, confusion, or worthlessness is experienced. After repeated drug-taking experiences, the drug user habituates to the initial stimulus (the drug) and the negative aftereffect gains strength. The drug taker soon learns that another joint or shot or snort will ease the bad feelings, even if it doesn't bring back the original good feelings. Thus, the drug "addict" takes the drug to combat the undesirable opponent process even after the drug no longer gives the positive benefits that provided the original motivation. This same opponent-process theory helps to explain why some people might stay in destructive love relationships long after the original joy and pleasure have gone. Can you see how someone might become "addicted" to the high of the beginning stages of love and then find it painful to "withdraw"? Although complex behaviors such as skydiving, drug use, and love relationships obviously encompass more than just opponent processes, this theory does help to explain some of the more puzzling aspects of "addictive" behaviors.

Review Questions

1 _____ motives are innate, biological needs (such as hunger and thirst) that are necessary for basic survival; _____ motives are innate needs for novel stimulation; and _____ motives result from reinforcement and observation of others.

2 The _____ _____ is the area of the brain that stimulates eating behaviors, whereas the _____ signals the organism to stop eating.

3 According to Stanley Schachter, overweight individuals are more responsive to _____ _____ for eating, but Judith Rodin found that overeating can be explained by a higher _____ level in the blood that results from the sight of food.

4 _____ rewards have been found to decrease motivation because they shift the individual's internal explanations for their behavior to an external source.

5 The _____ _____ ___ _____ theory suggests that there is an ideal level of stimulation that the organism is motivated to maintain.

6 The _____ theory of emotions suggests that an intense emotional experience is initially followed by a slight rise in the opposite emotion, but with repeated experience the second emotion replaces the first.

Answers: 1 primary, stimulus-seeking, learned; *2* lateral hypothalamus, ventromedial hypothalamus; *3* external cues, insulin; *4* extrinsic; *5* optimal level of arousal; *6* opponent-process

UNDERSTANDING EMOTION

Have you ever used the expression, "I was so excited, I thought I would die?" Although this is a common use of words in casual conversation, for some people the expression is anything but casual. Consider the following: "Upon meeting his 88-year-old father after a 20 year separation, a 55-year-old man suddenly died. The father than dropped dead. A

75-year-old man, who hit the twin double for $1683 on a $2 bet, died as he was about to cash in his winning ticket" (Engel, 1977, p. 153).

The idea that sudden death can result from emotional trauma has been around for a long time, but only in the last few years have we been able to scientifically document the connection between emotions and physical health. A National Academy of Sciences panel in 1984 found that grief over the death of a family member may substantially raise the risk, especially among men, of contracting an infectious disease or of dying of a heart attack or stroke (Maranto, 1984). It has also been suggested that the inhibition of emotions (particularly anger and hostility) can lead to ulcers, high blood pressure, obesity, heart disease, and cancer (Eysenck, 1988).

The study of the interrelationship between psychological factors and physical health has resulted in an exciting new field of psychology, known as health psychology or behavioral medicine (see Chapter 13), and has renewed interest in the basic study of emotions. Emotions play an important role in our lives. They color our dreams, memories, and perceptions, and when they are disturbed they contribute significantly to psychological disorders (see Chapter 15).

But what exactly are emotions? Where do they come from? And why do some people seem to be more "emotional" than others? In this section, we will discuss several aspects of emotions, including their basic components, their origins, and the major theories.

The components of emotions: What are the basic ingredients?

As mentioned earlier, the term "emotion" refers to feelings or affective reactions. These reactions result from the combination of four basic components:

1. The *physiological* aspect, which involves active changes in the physical body. When the body is emotionally aroused, the heart rate accelerates, pupils dilate, respiration increases, and so on.
2. The *cognitive* component, which emphasizes the importance of thoughts, beliefs, and expectations in determining the type and intensity of emotional response.
3. The *behavioral* component, which involves the various forms of expression that emotions may take. Facial expressions, bodily postures and gestures, and tone of voice vary with anger, joy, sorrow, fear, and so on.
4. The *subjective experience,* which includes elements of pleasure or displeasure, intensity of feeling, and complexity. What one person experiences as intensely pleasurable may be boring or aversive for another.

Psychologists generally use *subjective* self-report techniques to study the cognitive and subjective components and *objective* physical measurements to study the physiological and behavioral components.

To learn how people feel about something, psychologists tend to simply ask subjects to "self-report" by labeling their emotion and describing what it feels like. Because Koko was trained to communicate through sign language, researchers attempted to explore gorilla emotions by asking her about her feelings. When Koko was directly asked, "How do gorillas feel when they die — happy, sad, afraid?" Koko responded, "Sleep." But when death questions became more personal, Koko apparently got very upset. When asked, "Do you think Penny [her primary trainer] will die?" Koko noticeably fidgeted and then signed, "Damn!" (Patterson and Linden, 1981).

As you may imagine, there are numerous problems with the self-report technique. First, emotions are difficult to describe. People (and animals?) differ not only in their subjective experiences and expressions of emotions but also in their ability to accurately identify and describe their emotions. This is a particular problem when studying children or animals. How do the emotional experiences of Koko, for example, compare with those of humans? Some people see Koko's use of sign language as a unique opportunity to obtain valid self-report data on animal emotions, but others believe that ape language

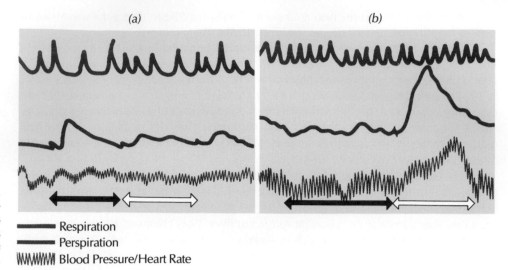

(a) (b)

▬▬▬ Respiration
▬▬▬ Perspiration
〰〰〰 Blood Pressure/Heart Rate

Figure 12.8 Polygraph testing. The printouts with the three lines represent typical responses to various questions. The lines in *(a)* represent a "truthful" response, whereas the line in *(b)* represent a "lie" response.

POLYGRAPH: *Instrument that measures emotional arousal through various physiological reactions, such as heart rate, blood pressure, respiration rate, and electrodermal skin response.*

During administration of a polygraph, or lie detector test, measurements are taken of the subject's breathing rate, blood pressure, and electrodermal response (a measure of skin resistance to a very weak electric current).

capabilities are exaggerated and that trainers often interpret ape signs rather imaginatively (Savage-Rumbaugh, 1986; Terrace, 1979).

Second, some subjects may lie or hide their feelings because of social expectations or as an attempt to please the experimenter. Most people have learned, for example, that certain emotions are inappropriate to express ("Big boys don't cry"). Similarly, Koko lied about the destruction of her window screen in an attempt to avoid disapproval. Finally, memories of past emotions may be inaccurate, and it is often impractical or unethical to artificially create conditions that will elicit strong feelings of fear, anger, love, and so on in the present.

To get around problems with self-reports, psychologists use a variety of more direct research techniques. When subjects are angered, for example, systematic observations of their external bodily expressions can be recorded (clenched teeth, furrowed eyebrows, and so on). Researchers can also study changes in the level of *internal* physiological arousal by measuring variations in heart rate, electrodermal response (the resistance of the skin to passage of a weak electric current), respiratory rate, and blood pressure.

Out of a desire to monitor bodily changes during emotional arousal has come one of the most widely publicized and controversial scientific tools: the **polygraph,** or "lie detector" (see Figure 12.8). In police work the polygraph has been used for many years on the assumption that while guilty individuals may lie about their activities, they cannot control their internal emotional reactions, which the polygraph is designed to detect. In recent years the use of polygraphs has been extended to security agencies, to national government jobs, and to general employers who are interested in screening potential job applicants or in detecting employee theft (Meyer, 1982).

Question: Do lie detectors really work? Psychologists have serious doubts about the use of the polygraph for "lie detector" purposes (Bales, 1988; Hyman, 1989). Although the polygraph does detect major changes in emotionality, it doesn't indicate whether subjects are aroused because they're lying, because they're afraid, or because they've taken certain drugs. Laboratory tests have demonstrated several ways in which polygraph tests can be "fooled" by people who are taking tranquilizers, who have consumed high levels of alcohol, or who are *psychopathic* individuals (see Chapter 15) who seem to experience little or no emotional reactions to their crimes (Bradley and Ainsworth, 1984; Waid and Orne, 1982). Waid and Orne found that test results could also be affected by the ethnic background of the examiner and respondent, by birth order (later-born children could lie more effectively), and by whether or not the respondent was depressed.

Although proponents often claim polygraph accuracy rates of 90 percent or higher (Lykken, 1981), actual tests show about 20 percent of the guilty people are misclassified as innocent, and up to 90 percent of the innocent are judged to be guilty (Kleinmuntz and Szucko, 1984; Lykken, 1984). Even though many people have heard that the innocent have nothing to fear from a polygraph test, this research would suggest otherwise.

Several methods have been suggested for solving some problems associated with the use of the polygraph. One suggestion has been to use "guilty knowledge" questions based on specific information that only a guilty person would know (such as the name of the bank teller who the defendant allegedly robbed). Lykken (1984) suggests that a guilty person would recognize these specific cues and respond in a different way than a nonguilty person. Other psychologists have suggested the use of computers and statistical analyses as means to improve the reliability of the polygraph (Kleinmuntz and Szucko, 1984).

In spite of these improvements, many psychologists still strongly object to the use of polygraphs by untrained administrators or for the purpose of establishing guilt or innocence. In response to the growing concern over the use of lie detector tests, the U.S. Senate passed a bill in 1988 that limits their use in job screening for all workers except security guards and those with access to controlled substances ("Ask Me No Questions," 1988). The increased restrictions on the polygraph have led to a proliferation of a new form of employment screening known as *integrity tests*. Some of these paper-and-pencil self-report tests measure a person's general attitude about dishonesty, whereas others are more broadly based and measure personality traits such as dependability, deviance, social conformity, and hostility to rules. Responding to the increasing number of tests and their widespread use, the American Psychological Association has created a task force to review the use of integrity tests in employment decision-making (Adler, 1989). Even if these tests are eventually shown to be scientifically sound, their use, like that of the polygraph, will be open to exploitation and abuse.

The origins of emotions: Inborn or learned?

Although there are obvious differences in their emphasis and perspectives, psychologists generally believe that emotions are a complex combination of both environmental and genetic factors. Adult expressions of emotion appear to depend largely on the cultural training of the individual, but there seem to be several compelling arguments for the idea that *basic* emotions are inborn and biologically inherited:

1. As we discovered in Chapter 9, infants only a few hours old show distinct expressions of emotion that closely match those of adults (Field et al., 1982).
2. All infants, even those that are born deaf and blind, show similar facial expressions in similar situations (Eibl-Eibesfeldt, 1980b; Feldman, 1982).
3. Infants are able to recognize facial expressions in others at a very young age (Nelson, 1987).
4. There is a striking similarity in the expression of emotions across a wide variety of cultures (see the photograph on p. 401).

Such infant and cross-cultural similarities in emotional expressions give obvious support to the evolutionary theory of emotions first advanced by Charles Darwin in 1872. In his classic book *The Expression of the Emotions in Man and Animals,* Darwin proposed that emotional displays evolved as a means of communication and that they contribute to species survival.

Some modern theorists also stress the importance of evolution on emotions (Blanchard and Blanchard, 1988; Brothers, 1989). Psychologist Robert Plutchik (1980) has suggested that emotions evolved because they help species survive. Fear, for example, serves the obvious function of protection for the organism. From his research, Plutchik has classified emotions into two basic categories — *primary* and *secondary* (see Figure 12.9). Like colors on a color wheel, the primary emotions (fear, anger, sadness, and so on)

Figure 12.9 Plutchik's wheel of emotions. The inner circle represents the eight primary emotions. The outer circle demonstrates how emotions can be combined to form secondary emotions.

can be combined to produce secondary emotions (aggression, contempt, remorse, and so on). Again like the color wheel, emotions that lie next to each other are more alike than those that are located farther away. For example, anger is similar to disgust, and both are very different from acceptance.

Although this evolutionary emphasis and the classification of primary and secondary emotions are important to our understanding of the behavioral and subjective components of emotions, we also need to understand the physiological aspects of emotions.

The physiology of emotions: How emotions affect the body

Pretend for the moment that you're walking alone on a dark street in a dangerous part of town. You suddenly see someone jump from behind a stack of boxes and start running toward you. How do you respond? Like most of us, you would undoubtedly interpret this situation as threatening and would run to escape. Your accompanying emotion of fear would involve many of the following physiological experiences: increased heart rate and blood pressure, dilated pupils, perspiration, dry mouth, rapid or irregular breathing, increased blood sugar, trembling, decreased gastrointestinal motility, and piloerection ("goose bumps"). Such physiological reactions are triggered by several areas of the nervous system, including the frontal lobes of the cerebral cortex, the autonomic branch of the nervous system, and the limbic system (see Figure 12.10).

As we noted in Chapter 2, the limbic system seems to play an important role in the more "primitive" types of emotion, such as fear, anger, and sexual desire. For example, electrical stimulation of separate areas in the limbic system (in particular the *hypothalamus*) can produce a "sham rage" that turns a cat into a hostile, hissing, and slashing animal. Stimulation of adjacent areas can cause the same animal to purr and lick your fingers. (The rage is considered "sham" since it occurs in the absence of provocation and disappears immediately.)

If you felt threatened on the dark street, your limbic system would undoubtedly be aroused. Your emotion of fear would also lead to a behavioral reaction of hiding, running, or preparing to fight. This motor response would be "programmed" by your frontal lobes, which organize and orchestrate responses to the hypothalamus.

Question: How does this explain why my heart pounds or why my hands tremble when I'm afraid? Although the limbic system and frontal lobes play extremely important roles in the production of emotion, the most obvious and easily recognized

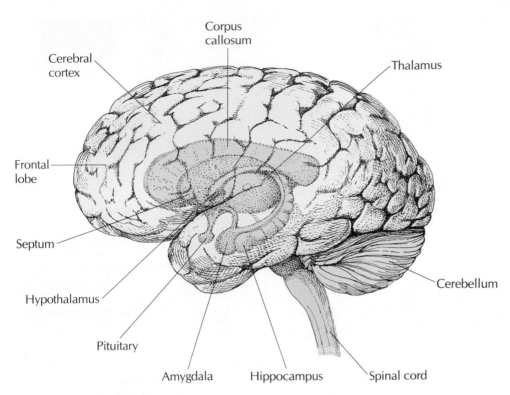

Corpus
callosum

Cerebral
cortex

Thalamus

Frontal
lobe

Septum

Cerebellum

Hypothalamus

Pituitary

Amygdala   Hippocampus   Spinal cord

Figure 12.10 Brain areas involved in emotions. The limbic system is not specifically labeled because it consists of a number of small structures, including the amygdala, septum, hypothalamus, thalmus, and hippocampus.

signs of arousal (increased heart rate, fast, shallow breathing, trembling, sweating, dry mouth) are produced by the autonomic nervous system (ANS). These largely automatic responses result from the interconnections of the ANS with various glands and muscles (it is these responses that the polygraph attempts to monitor and record).

The ANS has two major subdivisions: the **sympathetic nervous system** and the **parasympathetic nervous system.** When you are emotionally aroused, the *sympathetic* branch works to increase heart rate, blood pressure, pupil dilation, salivation, and so on. When you are relaxed and resting, the *parasympathetic* branch tends to reverse these effects — heart rate decreases and blood pressure drops. The combined action of both these systems allows you to respond appropriately to emotional arousal.

Question: Where does adrenalin fit into this picture?   Adrenalin, or more properly **epinephrine**, is a hormone secreted from the adrenal glands after messages are received from the hypothalamus. Whereas the sympathetic nervous system is almost instantaneously "turned on" along with the limbic system and frontal lobes, secretion of both epinephrine and another adrenal hormone, norepinephrine, works to keep the system in sympathetic control until the emergency is over. The damaging effects of too much sympathetic arousal as a result of stress are discussed in Chapter 13.

Theories of emotion: How emotions are activated

How are emotions activated? What causes us to experience particular emotions? Over the years three major approaches to answering these questions have dominated the field: the James–Lange theory, the Cannon–Bard theory, and the cognitive labeling theory. In this section, we will discuss each of these theories, as well as the most recent facial feedback hypothesis. As you read about each of these theories, you may find it helpful to refer to Figure 12.11.

James – Lange theory   According to ideas originated by psychologist William James and later expanded by physiologist Carl Lange, emotions depend on feedback from the body (see Figure 12.11*a*). Contrary to popular opinion, which suggests that we cry

SYMPATHETIC NERVOUS SYSTEM: *A subdivision of the autonomic nervous system that mobilizes the body's resources toward "fight or flight."*
PARASYMPATHETIC NERVOUS SYSTEM: *A subdivision of the autonomic nervous system that restores the body to its "status quo" after sympathetic arousal.*

EPINEPHRINE: *Hormone secreted by the adrenal glands in response to messages from the hypothalamus. Secretion is associated with emotional arousal, especially fear and anger.*

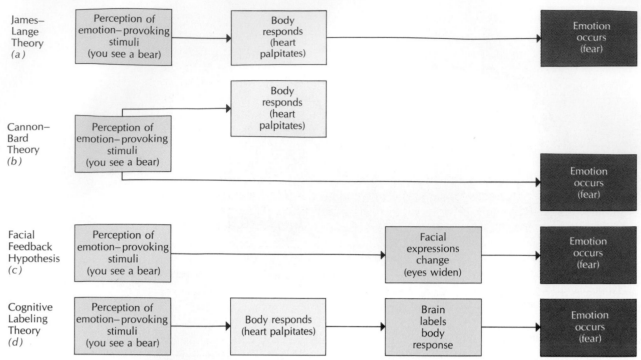

Figure 12.11 A comparison of the four major theories of emotion. In the James–Lange theory *(a)*, the emotion occurs *after* the body is aroused. The Cannon–Bard theory *(b)* suggests that arousal and emotion occur *simultaneously.* Whereas the facial feedback hypothesis *(c)* proposes that changes in facial expression *produce* emotions, the cognitive labeling theory *(d)* suggests that autonomic arousal within the body causes the brain to search and find the reasons for the arousal. Once the arousal is labeled, the emotion occurs.

because we're sad, James suggests: "We feel sorry *because* we cry, angry *because* we strike, afraid *because* we tremble" (James, 1890).

JAMES–LANGE THEORY: *Theory that emotion is the perception of one's own bodily reactions and that each emotion is physiologically distinct.*

> *Question:* This doesn't make sense. Why would I tremble unless I first felt afraid? According to the **James–Lange theory,** your bodily response of trembling is a reaction to a specific stimulus such as seeing a large bear in the wilderness. This theory proposes that you first perceive an event, your body reacts, and *then* you interpret the bodily changes as a specific emotion (see Figure 12.11*a*). William James suggested that your PERCEPTION of autonomic arousal (palpitating heart, sinking stomach, flushed cheeks) as well as actions (running, hitting, yelling) and changes of facial expression (crying, smiling, frowning) all produce what we refer to as "emotions." In short, emotion IS the perception of one's own bodily reactions.

Cannon–Bard theory Walter Cannon (1927) and Philip Bard (1934) objected to the James–Lange approach. They proposed that during perception of the emotion-provoking stimuli (seeing the bear) the thalamus sends *simultaneous* messages to both the general body and to the cerebral cortex (see Figure 12.11*b*). Messages to the cortex produce the *experience* of emotion (fear), whereas other messages from the thalamus produce bodily changes (heart palpitations, running, eyes widening, and mouth opening). A major point in the **Cannon-Bard theory** is that the body's response is not a necessary or even major factor in emotion. Cannon supported his position with several experiments in which animals were surgically prevented from experiencing physiological arousal, yet they still showed emotional reactions (Cannon, Lewis, and Britton, 1927).

CANNON-BARD THEORY: *Theory that the thalamus responds to emotion-arousing stimuli by sending messages simultaneously to the cerebral cortex and the autonomic nervous system. In this view, all emotions are physiologically similar.*

Whereas the James–Lange theory argues that each emotion has its own distinct physiological reaction, the Cannon–Bard theory suggests that all emotions are physiologically similar. Cannon also argued that emotions occur faster than changes in the internal organs and that bodily changes are not enough to produce emotion.

Question: Which theory is correct?   The Cannon–Bard theory received a great deal of scientific support during the first part of the twentieth century. More recently, however, the pendulum of scientific opinion has begun to swing the other way. The James–Lange theory has substantial support on two major points. First of all, the James–Lange idea that different emotions are associated with different patterns of physiological activity has received research support (e.g., Davidson, 1984; Panskepp, 1982). Second, both the suggestion of distinct emotions and the idea that bodily reactions *precede* emotional experiences are partially supported by the recent development of a third major explanation of emotion—the **facial feedback hypothesis.**

Facial feedback hypothesis   In its initial stages of development, the facial feedback hypothesis proposed that changes in facial expression provide information about what emotion is being felt (Gelhorn, 1964; Izard, 1971; Tomkins, 1962). Thus, when you find yourself smiling, you must be happy. Whereas these early researchers believed that facial expressions were involuntary and that movement only directed further emotional response, later research found that when professional actors were asked to make various facial configurations, their autonomic responses were similar to those normally accompanying emotions (Ekman, Levenson, and Friesen, 1983). According to this revised form of the facial feedback hypothesis, facial changes not only correlate with and intensify emotions, but also *cause* or initiate the emotion itself (Adelman and Zajonc, 1989; Strack, Martin, and Stepper, 1988). Contractions of the various facial muscles send specific messages to the brain, identifying each basic emotion (see Figure 12.11*c*). Like James, these researchers suggest that we don't smile because we are happy; rather, we feel happy because we smile. This facial feedback hypothesis also supports Darwin's (1872) original

FACIAL FEEDBACK HYPOTHESIS: *Proposal that movements of the facial muscles* produce or intensify *emotional reactions.*

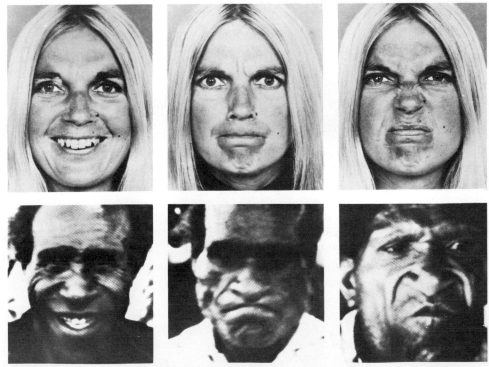

To demonstrate that emotional facial expressions are universal rather than learned, Paul Ekman traveled to remote areas of New Guinea and found that members of the Fore tribe could easily identify the emotions on a Westerner's face (top line of photos). He also found that American college students had no difficulty in identifying similar expressions in the Fore (bottom line of photos). (Top: Copyright, Paul Ekman, 1975; bottom: Copyright, Paul Ekman, 1972.)

evolutionary proposal that freely expressing an emotion intensifies it, whereas suppressing outward expressions of an emotion diminishes it.

If the expression of an emotion *produces* subsequent emotional reactions, this may help explain several common experiences. Have you ever felt depressed after listening to a friend's problems? Your unconscious facial mimicry of their sad expression may have created similar physiological reactions in your own body. This theory could have important implications for therapists who constantly work with depressed clients and for actors who depend on simulation of emotions for their livelihood. If Darwin is right that expressing an emotion intensifies it, we also must question some theorists who advocate the expression of anger and aggression as a way of *relieving* built-in tension (see Chapter 17).

Cognitive labeling theory   Although each of the three previous theories provides some insight into the experience of emotions, they give little attention to the role of cognition and interpretation. According to Schacter and Singer's **cognitive labeling theory** (1962), an individual's interpretation or label for physiological arousal determines the emotion experienced. If we are crying at a wedding, for example, we often interpret our emotion as joy or happiness, but if we cry at a funeral we label it as sadness (see Figure 12.11d).

In Schacter and Singer's classic study, subjects were given shots of epinephrine, disguised as a type of "vitamin," and their subsequent arousal and labeling were investigated (see Figure 12.12). One group of subjects were *correctly* informed about the expected effects from an injection of epinephrine (hand tremors, excitement, and heart palpitations), and a second group were *misinformed* and told to expect itching, numbness, and headache. A third, *uninformed,* group were told nothing about the possible side effects.

Following the injection, each subject was placed in a room with a *confederate* (a "stooge" who was part of the experiment but pretended to be a fellow volunteer). The

COGNITIVE LABELING THEORY: *Theory that the cognitive (thinking), subjective (evaluating), and physiological arousal components are all necessary to emotional experiences.*

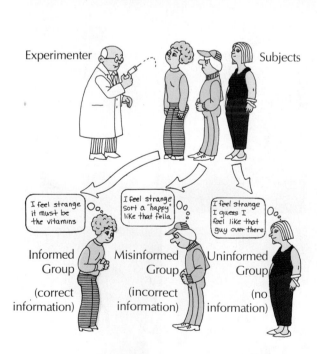

Figure 12.12 Cognitive labeling theory. A comparison of "informed," "misinformed," and "uninformed" subjects in Schacter and Singer's classic experiment demonstrates the importance of cognitive labels in the experience of emotions.

confederate was told to act either happy and cheerful (throwing paper airplanes around the room and shooting wads of paper into the wastebasket) or unhappy and angry (complaining about the questionnaire and expressing general dissatisfaction with the entire experiment).

The results of the study confirmed the experimental hypothesis: Those subjects who did not have an appropriate cognitive label for their emotional arousal (the misinformed group and the uninformed group) tended to look to the situation for an appropriate explanation. Thus, those placed with a happy confederate became happy, whereas those with an unhappy confederate were unhappy. Subjects in the informed group, on the other hand, knew their physiological arousal was the result of the shot, so their emotions were generally unaffected by the confederate.

Although some researchers have been unable to replicate these specific findings (Marshall and Zimbardo, 1979; Reisenzein, 1983), indirect support can be found with studies of *misattribution,* where a person mistakenly believes that the cause of an emotion is something other than it really is (Olson, 1988). For example, studies have found that severely shy students or children can be helped by providing a handy (but false) explanation for their normal symptoms of shyness (dry mouth, trembling, heart palpitations, and so on) (Zimbardo, 1977; Zimbardo and Radl, 1981). When given a logical reason for their symptoms, shy subjects often become less anxious and self-conscious. Philip Zimbardo suggests that creating such conditions may serve as a valuable first step in demonstrating to shy people that they can interact successfully with others, which may then lead to further successful attempts at interaction.

Review Questions

1 The four basic components of emotions include the _____, _____, _____, and _____.

2 _____ techniques attempt to study the subjective elements of emotions, whereas _____ physical measurements study the physiological and behavioral aspects of emotions.

3 Proponents of _____, or "lie detector," tests have claimed accuracy rates as high as 90 percent, but this is contradicted by other research.

4 The most obvious signs of emotional arousal (trembling, sweating, increased heart rate) result from action from the _____ nervous system, which is further subdivided into the _____ and _____ branches.

5 The hormone _____ helps to keep the sympathetic nervous system in action until the emergency is over.

6 According to the _____ theory of emotions, the physiological arousal precedes experiencing of the emotion, whereas the _____ theory suggests that emotions result from simultaneous stimulation of the cortex and the autonomic nervous system.

7 The _____ _____ hypothesis suggests that facial expressions produce emotional responses.

8 Proponents of the _____ _____ theory believe that emotions result from a combination of the subjective, cognitive, and physiological arousal components of emotion.

9 Through the use of _____, false explanations for emotional arousal, shy people have been helped to reduce their anxiety and self-consciousness.

Answers: *1* physiological, cognitive, behavioral, subjective experience; *2* self-report (or subjective), objective; *3* polygraph; *4* autonomic, sympathetic, parasympathetic; *5* epinephrine; *6* James–Lange, Cannon–Bard; *7* facial feedback; *8* cognitive labeling; *9* misattributions

Critical Thinking

RECOGNIZING ILLEGITIMATE APPEALS TO EMOTION:
Ads and Everyday Attempts to Persuade

Advertisers spend billions of dollars each year hiring highly trained professionals who understand our deepest fears and desires and use them to motivate us to buy specific products and services. Our closest friends and family members also use similar emotional appeals. Although critical thinkers accept emotional appeals in some cases (e.g., public safety warnings about seat belts), they recognize that many attempts at persuasion are based on illegitimate exploitation of emotions.

Below are a few common examples of illegitimate emotional appeals.

(a) Appeal to self-esteem—an approach that manipulates our need to feel good about ourselves ("Fine wine drinkers prefer . . ." or "Mothers who care . . .").

(b) Appeal to social fears—an approach that carries an implied threat of ostracism or social rejection ("Not even your best friend will tell you . . .").

(c) Appeal to authority or experts—quoting or using authority figures to prove a point. Although some authorities have legitimate expertise in the area in which they are advising (a qualified mechanic diagnosing a problem with a car), people often use "authorities" who are not qualified to give an expert opinion (a respected newscaster selling life insurance).

(d) Appeal to pity—a person attempts to persuade you to do or buy something because he or she will be hurt if you don't agree.

(e) Appeal to force—a person attempts to persuade you to do or buy something because he or she will hurt you if you don't agree.

(f) Plain folks—an approach based on the similarity principle. If you think the persuader is "like you," "just one of the guys," or "regular folk," you will be persuaded more easily.

(g) Associations—using a positive symbol to endorse whatever the persuader wants you to "buy." The idea is that through classical conditioning (see Chapter 6) you will transfer the positive qualities of the endorser to the product.

The following activity will sharpen your skills in recognizing illegitimate emotional appeals. Beside each statement, mark the letter of the illegitimate appeal being used. More than one type of tactic may be applicable.

_____ 1 A Bell telephone ad shows a small, sweet grandmother sitting patiently by the phone waiting for her loved ones to call.

_____ 2 A teenager argues against the family's vacation plans, and the father responds by saying, "When you pay the bills, you can make the decisions."

_____ 3 Peanut butter ads suggest that "Choosy mothers choose Jif."

_____ 4 Scope mouthwash commercials show two people just waking up in the morning with the words "Yech! Morning breath, the worst breath of the day."

_____ 5 A college student asks his professor to accept a late paper: "I've worked all weekend on this report. I know that it's past your deadline, but I have to work full-time while also attending college."

_____ 6 While showing a very expensive home to a young couple, the realtor says "You owe it to yourself and your family to buy the very best."

_____ 7 Actor Robert Young, former star of "Father Knows Best" and "Marcus Welby, M.D.," "prescribes" Sanka coffee for people who are nervous, irritable, or in stressful situations.

_____ 8 A political ad shows George Bush wearing a hard hat at the steel workers' company picnic and pitching horseshoes in his backyard.

_____ 9 A Marlboro cigarette ad shows a strong, ruggedly handsome cowboy riding alone on the range.

_____ 10 After making it clear that he values employee "loyalty," a supervisor asks for "volunteers" to help a fellow supervisor move on the weekend.

ANSWERS: 1 D; 2 E; 3 A; 4 B; 5 D; 6 A; 7 C; 8 F; 9 G; 10 E. Although we are providing a list of possible answers, we encourage you to discuss your responses with your classmates. Comparing answers to each alternative helps to further your critical thinking skills.

PROBLEMS IN MOTIVATION AND EMOTION

As you were reading about the theories connected with motivation and emotion, you undoubtedly had questions concerning specific problems related to these areas. In this section we will attempt to show you how research in motivation and emotion can be used to understand and control three common problems: eating disorders, jealousy, and grief.

Eating disorders: Obesity, anorexia, and bulimia

Before we begin this section, jot down your answers to the following questions:

1. If you had weighed yourself exactly 12 months ago today, how much would you have weighed? How much do you weigh today? How many times have you dieted in these 12 months (please estimate)?
2. Binge eating is defined as any eating episode in which you are unable to control the amount of food you eat and consume large quantities. Do you ever binge eat? Do you ever feel guilty, depressed, or disgusted after such binges? Do you attempt to hide these binges from others?
3. How often do you think about food? When you first wake up in the morning, do you think about what you will "allow" yourself to eat during the day? Has your weight ever stopped you from attending or fully enjoying certain social functions, such as dances or swim parties?

If your answers to these questions show repetitive dieting, uncontrollable and frequent binging, or obsessive thinking about food and planning of meals, you *may* have an eating disorder. Although many people think of eating disorders as including only the extremes of obesity and anorexia, problems in eating, like almost every aspect of human behavior, exist along a continuum. One of the major "definitions" of anorexia, for example, is the loss of 20 to 25 percent of body weight, but many of the signs and symptoms of this type of disturbed eating pattern are present long before this drastic criterion is met. So although we will be confining our discussion to the extremes, keep in mind that many of the causes (and solutions) for severe eating disorders also offer useful insights and suggestions for less critical cases.

Obesity   Despite repeated attempts to precisely define obesity through height and weight charts or skin-fold tests, there is still widespread disagreement about what constitutes "ideal," "normal," "obese," or "problem" weights. The very fact that these terms are so often written with quotation marks around them is evidence of the social nature of the labels (Schwartz, 1984).

By looking at your own eating behavior and that of your friends, family, and acquaintances, you have undoubtedly discovered that many people have accepted some standard for "ideal" weight and that they spend a great deal of time and energy in a continual struggle to achieve or control that weight. And although dieting has developed into what amounts to a national hobby for Americans, it doesn't seem to work — the failure rate has been estimated somewhere between 65 and 99.5 percent (Corcoran, 1988; Meyer, 1984; Schwartz, 1982).

Question: Why is weight control such a problem for so many people?   Some researchers have suggested that biology may play the biggest role. Did you know, for example, that if neither of your parents is obese you have only a 10 percent chance of becoming obese yourself? Your odds increase to 40 percent, however, if one of your parents is obese and to 70 percent if both your parents are obese (Logue, 1986). These percentages obviously reflect some learning of eating habits from parental models. However, researchers also believe that some people are genetically predisposed toward obesity because their inherited *set point* is higher than average (Foreyt and Kondo, 1984;

**How the set point interferes
with both losing and gaining weight.**

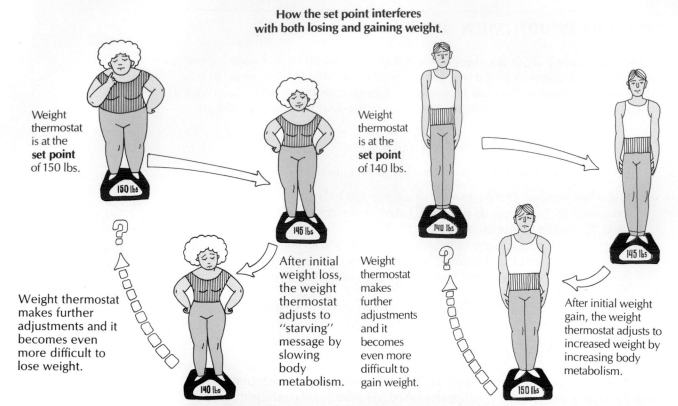

Weight
thermostat
is at the
set point
of 150 lbs.

Weight thermostat
makes further
adjustments and it
becomes even
more difficult to
lose weight.

After initial
weight loss,
the weight
thermostat
adjusts to
"starving"
message by
slowing
body
metabolism.

Weight
thermostat
is at the
set point
of 140 lbs.

Weight
thermostat
makes
further
adjustments
and it
becomes
even more
difficult to
gain weight.

After initial weight
gain, the weight
thermostat adjusts to
increased weight by
increasing body
metabolism.

Figure 12.13 Set point theory. If your set point is 150 pounds, your weight will remain within a relatively narrow range—145 to 155 pounds. Your body responds to increased calorie intake with increased metabolism that "burns off" the calories. Decreased calorie intake leads to decreased metabolism and increased difficulty in losing weight.

Roberts et al., 1988). According to set point theory, the body has a predetermined "weight thermostat" that adjusts to changes in food consumption by burning off more calories if the weight goes above the set point and burning off fewer calories if the weight drops (see Figure 12.13). The particular set point for any individual appears to be the result of a number of factors, including early feeding experiences and heredity. Many people have been taught that obesity is a simple matter of consuming too many calories, but set point research has suggested that two people of the same height, age, activity level, *and* caloric consumption can be either fat or thin depending on their individual biological set point.

Although the theory of set points is currently receiving a great deal of attention, critics question whether a set point actually exists and argue that the concept has been overstated (Brownell and Venditti, 1982; Grinker, 1982). In addition, some researchers have criticized the overemphasis on biological factors, noting that psychological factors generally interact with biology to produce obesity (Hermann and Polivy, 1984; Schwartz and Inbar-Saban, 1988). As discussed earlier, obese individuals may be more responsive to external cues for food (Schachter, 1981) and may actually ignore internal, biological signals for eating (Simmons, 1987). Research has also found that many people overeat when they are anxious (Schwartz, 1982) or binge when they are tense, lonely, or bored (Abraham and Beaumont, 1982; Wurtman, 1987).

Question: Isn't there any way to counteract these effects and successfully lose weight?   Since most cases of obesity result from consuming more calories than the body can metabolize, or burn up, the safest and most reliable way to lose weight is to follow a *sensible* diet and to exercise regularly (Grady, 1988). Daily, sustained exercise

Does the sight of food in this photograph make you feel hungry? Control of your reactions to external cues is an important tool in weight management.

seems to lower the body's set point, making it easier to lose weight (Remington, Fisher, and Parent, 1984; Thompson et al., 1982). In addition, newly developed drugs, such as *dextrofenfluramine,* may help control obesity by controlling the cravings for carbohydrates. Other drugs are being tested to help correct metabolic defects that cause some obese people to burn fewer calories than normal-weight individuals.

There are problems, of course, with taking any drug for any length of time, and there are healthy and effective alternatives. In conjunction with diet and exercise, it is important to pay attention to psychological factors. Weight control specialists have had lasting results by incorporating basic behavior modification principles (see Chapter 16) with the motivation and emotion concepts presented in this chapter. If you would like to try to "put psychology in action" for your own weight management, there are three basic steps:

Step 1. *Identify destructive thoughts, emotions, and behaviors.* Become aware of what you think, feel, and do each time you eat. Many people fail to recognize how many self-defeating thoughts they have about eating ("I can't control myself," "I'll go on a diet tomorrow," "Since I already went a little over my limit today, I might as well go whole hog"). We also fail to recognize how we use food and drink to improve our moods. Coffee and doughnuts perk us up in the morning, lunch and break times allow us to escape boring work, and dinner and drinks provide us with entertainment and a chance to socialize.

Step 2. *Identify and control food-related stimuli.* Because external cues can trigger eating behavior, you should arrange your environment to minimize such cues. Remove (or hide) tempting foods, throw out or freeze leftovers, stand away from the food tables at parties, and so on. You can also use an "eating habits" diary to locate and correct certain stimuli that induce overeating. If you find that you consume a large portion of your daily calories while reading, studying or watching television, for example, you may find it helpful to restrict your eating to one place (such as the kitchen or dining room table) and to not do anything else (such as watching television or reading) while eating. The "mindless" eating that is associated with food-related stimuli ("I see peanuts and I want them") and the automatic associations you build around certain activities (television = snacks, movies = popcorn, baseball games = hotdogs, and so on) can be highly destructive to your desire for weight control. You need to avoid or control such stimuli.

Step 3. *Change destructive cognitions, emotions, and behaviors.* Instead of eating when you're depressed, bored, or tense and indulging yourself in self-defeating thoughts, try substituting healthier activities for eating (such as jogging) and healthier thoughts ("I *can* control myself"). When you do eat, use behavioral techniques such as eating slower, using smaller serving plates, and so on. While

Exercise is an important component of long-term weight control.

Popular singer Karen Carpenter died in 1983 from complications associated with anorexia nervosa.

changing your behavior, be sure to incorporate small rewards to reinforce yourself. To avoid the problems associated with extrinsic motivation, these rewards should be given only *after* the appropriate behavior, and only during the initial part of your weight-management program.

Before we leave this topic, it is also important to recognize that there *are* other options to this whole problem of dieting and the national preoccupation with weight control. Although some people do need to reduce for physical health reasons, a large number of people in our society needlessly operate on a destructive cycle of diets and relapses, followed by guilt, depression, and new rounds of dieting. Given that each relapsed dieting episode makes future dieting more difficult, some people may be healthier and happier if they simply accept a certain level of "chubbiness" in themselves and others (Brownell, 1988; Rodin and Salovey, 1989).

Anorexia and bulimia   Two of the most "costly" disorders directly related to the fear of obesity are **anorexia nervosa** (a disorder involving self-starvation and extreme weight loss) and **bulimia nervosa** (intense, recurring episodes of binge eating followed by efforts to avoid weight gain, such as vomiting and using laxatives).

Anorexia nervosa is a perplexing disorder characterized by prolonged and severe refusals to eat, resulting in a loss of 20 to 25 percent of the original body weight. The anorexic's overwhelming fear of becoming obese does not diminish even with radical and obvious weight loss. The person's body image is so distorted that he or she still perceives the skeletonlike body as too fat. This "disease" often causes irreversible physical damage and if not corrected may lead to death. The disorder primarily affects white, middle- and upper-class female adolescents and young adults, but there is growing evidence that the problem may begin as early as seven or eight years of age and that males may also be affected (Margo, 1987; Palmer, 1983).

Many anorexics are also bulimic. Some bulimics can ingest well over 6000 calories in a single sitting. This is not only expensive but can lead to serious physical problems, such as hair loss, the erosion of tooth enamel and tooth loss, and digestive irritation and disease (Levenkron, 1982). Table 12.2 lists the foods that one bulimic consumed on a typical binge.

Question: How prevalent is bulimia on college campuses?   Estimates range from 5 percent of the general population (Nagelman, Hale, and Ware, 1983) to 4 to 67 percent of the college population (Halmi, Falk, and Schwartz, 1981). The wide variation in percentages is the result of varying definitions of bulimia. If bulimia is defined as binge eating ("any eating episode when you do not feel able to control the amount of food you eat and when a large amount of food is eaten"), one study found 42 percent of the college female sample would qualify. But if the definition includes feeling disgusted, binging once a week or more, feeling depressed, and so on, only 4.4 percent would qualify (Sinoway, Raupp, and Newman, 1985).

Question: What causes anorexia or bulimia?   There are almost as many suggestions for causes as there are victims. Some theories focus on potential physical causes, such as hypothalamic disorders, lowered levels of various neurotransmitters, and

TABLE 12.2
One Bulimic's Typical Binge (lasting 3–5 hours)

2 pounds of vanilla sandwich cookies with vanilla filling
1 pint of vanilla ice milk
1 pint of butter pecan ice cream
2 quarts of skim milk
4 waffles
1 loaf of white bread ⎫
½ pound of butter ⎬ for French toast
6 eggs ⎭
1 bottle of maple syrup
1 pound of Ritz crackers
½ pound of potato salad
½ pound of bakery cookies, assorted
  a packaged crumb coffee cake (one pound)
2 ice cream sandwiches
2 yogurts
10 cream-filled chocolate cupcakes

Source: Levenkron, S. (1982). *Treating and overcoming anorexia nervosa.* New York: Scribner's.

genetic or hormonal disorders. Other theories emphasize psychological or social factors, such as perceived loss of control, depression, family malfunctioning, distorted body images, and societal pressures for thinness (Bennett and Gurin, 1982; Margo, 1987; Scott, 1986; Underwood and Alexander, 1988).

Although there are few definitive statements at the present time concerning anorexia and bulimia, it is important to recognize the symptoms (see Table 12.3) and to seek therapy if the symptoms apply personally to you. In spite of the wide diversity of opinion as to the cause, there is general agreement that both disorders are potentially life-threatening and require treatment. [For immediate information you can call the new 24-hour eating disorders hotline at (800) 382-2832 — within New York State call (212) 222-2832.]

Jealousy: Protective or destructive?

Are you a jealous person? Then you probably wouldn't fit into the Eskimo culture, where good manners dictate that a host invite his dinner guest to have sex with his wife. Neither would you make a good member of the Kerista Village in San Francisco, California, where individuals are sexually faithful to the group but believe in "nonpreferential" and "rotational" sleeping patterns within the group. As one female member puts it: "To me, the erotic fantasy of sleeping with a variety of men — all of whom I love — and living with a number of other marvelous female partners who are sleeping with the same people is extremely exciting. It is also very 'homey'" (Adams, 1980, p. 42).

Although many people believe that jealousy is a "natural" and inescapable part of living, these two examples demonstrate the fact that jealousy, like anger and other emotions, is greatly affected by both cultural standards and individual belief systems (Reiss, 1986). As recently as the early 1960s, for example, most Americans saw jealousy as "proof of love," but today it is often considered a sign of personal insecurity or low self-esteem (Brody, 1987; White, 1981).

Question: How are you defining "jealousy" in this case? Jealousy has been a particularly difficult emotion to define because it is so often confused with other emotions, such as anger, love, and depression. One definition that avoids this problem is that **jealousy** refers to the thoughts and feelings that arise when an actual or desired

JEALOUSY: *Thoughts and feelings that arise when an actual or desired relationship is threatened.*

TABLE 12.3
Symptoms of Anorexia and Bulimia

Symptoms of Anorexia Nervosa
20–25% body weight loss
Hyperactivity
Distorted body image
Amenorrhea (in females)—loss of menstruation
Excessive constipation
Depression
Loss of hair (head)
Growth of fine body hair (called lanugo)
Extreme sensitivity to cold temperatures
Low pulse rate

Symptoms of Bulimia Nervosa
Difficulty swallowing and retaining food
Swollen and/or infected salivary glands
Damage to esophagus, sometimes causing pain and/or internal bleeding.
Bursting blood vessels in the eyes
Excessive tooth decay, loss of tooth enamel (an irreversible condition)
Weakness, headaches, dizziness
Inconspicuous binge-eating
Frequent significant weight fluctuations due to alternating binges and fasts
Fear of inability to stop eating voluntarily

Source: B.A.S.H.SM, Inc. St. Louis, MO.

THE FAR SIDE By GARY LARSON

"Not that hand, the other hand!.. And if you've got another woman in it you're *dogmeat!*"

The Kongs at home

ENVY: *Thoughts and feelings that arise when one's personal qualities, possessions, or achievements do not measure up to those of someone relevant to us.*

relationship is threatened (Salovey and Rodin, 1988). Jealousy is also commonly confused with "envy," but they are quite different emotions. **Envy** refers to thoughts and feelings that arise when one's personal qualities, possessions, or achievements do not measure up to those of someone relevant to us, whereas jealousy emphasizes the fear of loss. By these definitions a child can be envious of her brother's new toy but may also feel jealous if she believes the toy means her parents like her brother more than her.

Question: Aren't some people more likely to see threats and react with more jealousy than others? Several personality characteristics have been found to be highly correlated with jealousy, including negative self-image, personal insecurity, and general life dissatisfaction (Aronson and Pines, 1980; Manges and Evenbeck, 1980). It has also been found that couples who have been in a relationship fewer than five years experience more jealousy (Pines and Aronson, 1983). Furthermore, women are more likely to try to induce jealousy in their partner, particularly when they feel more involved in the relationship and are in a lower position of power (White, 1980).

Question: Aren't women generally more jealous than men? Although research subjects say they agree with the popular belief that women are more jealous, when men and women are asked to report on their own jealous feelings no sex differences are found (Aronson and Pines, 1980). Women, however, do report more physical and emotional distress when they feel jealous, but they are less likely to end an ongoing relationship because of it. Other researchers have found that men tend to manage their jealous feelings by blaming their partner and by making efforts to protect their self-esteem. Women, on the other hand, tend to blame themselves and to try to protect the relationship (Bush et al., 1988; Shettel-Neuber et al., 1978).

TABLE 12.4
How Jealous Are You?

Use the scale below to indicate how frequently you have engaged in the following types of behavior:

5 frequently, 4 somewhat often, 3 sometimes, 2 rarely, 1 never

How often have you:

1 Taken advantage of unplanned opportunities to look through a spouse or lover's belongings for unfamiliar names, phone numbers, etc.? _____

2 Intentionally looked through a spouse or lover's personal belongings for unfamiliar names, phone numbers, etc? _____

3 Called a spouse or lover unexpectedly just to see if he or she is there? _____

4 Listened in on a telephone conversation of a spouse or lover or secretly followed him or her? _____

5 Extensively questioned a spouse or lover about previous or present romantic relationships? _____

Compare your responses to the average of approximately 25,000 readers who replied to this survey in the February 1985 issue of *Psychology Today.*

1	2.1	4	1.4
2	1.8	5	2.2
3	2.0		

If you answered "3," "4," or "5" on any of the five questions, you would be considered above average in your jealous feelings.

Source: Salovey and Rodin (1985).

Question: Both of these methods sound destructive. Isn't there a healthy way to handle jealousy?   As a first step it is important to recognize that just as we need to become aware of and accept our feelings of anger, so too must we acknowledge and accept our feelings of jealousy (Friday, 1985). In addition, we must also recognize that jealousy, like all emotions, has many gradations. At one end of the scale it can be a perfectly natural "protective" reaction to a potential threat. But at the other extreme, jealousy can be an irrational, obsessive, and potentially lethal response. Even though our culture often glamorizes this obsessional type of jealousy, researchers have cautioned against using jealousy as a barometer of love — to "kill for love" is a contradiction in terms. To get a feeling of how your feelings of jealousy compare with those of others in our culture, you may want to stop and take the quiz in Table 12.4.

When jealousy falls within the "normal" range, it can still be painful and humiliating. To manage it more effectively you may want to follow the advice of a primary researcher in the field, Gordon Clanton (1981):

1. Relearn or reframe your unrealistic perceptions of the "ideal" relationship.
2. Gather more information to determine whether the perceived threat is real or imaginary.
3. Learn constructive ways to express your concern and to nurture your relationship so that jealous reactions are less likely.

If jealousy is severe and seriously disrupting your life, you may want to seek professional help. This assistance may be directed toward helping the jealous individual understand and modify his or her behavior, or it may be defined as a couple problem, with efforts directed toward helping both partners (Beck, 1989).

Grief: How to survive a loss

What do I do now that you're gone? Well, when there's nothing else going on, which is quite often, I sit in a corner and I cry until I am too numbed to feel. Paralyzed motionless for awhile, nothing moving inside or out. Then I think how much I miss

CALVIN AND HOBBES © 1987 Universal Press Syndicate. Reprinted with permission. All rights reserved.

you. Then I feel fear, pain, loneliness, desolation. Then I cry until I am too numbed to feel. Interesting pastime.

Colgrove, Bloomfield, and McWilliams, How to Survive the Loss of a Love, 1976

Can you identify with these feelings? Have you ever shared this kind of incredible and unrelenting pain? Although losses (such as the death of a loved one, divorces, breakups of relationships, loss of a job, and so on) are a natural and inevitable part of life, many people may wonder why it has to be so painful.

The function and stages of grief   These feelings of desolation, loneliness, and "heart-ache" associated with loss, disaster, or misfortune are all characteristic of the emotion we call **grief** (Sanders, 1989). The need for pain during the grief process has been explained as an adaptive mechanism for both social animals and humans. Since the outward signs of grief are primarily an attempt at reunion, the pain may serve to motivate parents and children or mates to search for one another. Such obvious signs of distress may also be adaptive since they bring the group to the aid of the bereaved individual (Averill, 1969).

GRIEF: *Feelings of desolation, loneliness, and painful memories associated with loss, disaster, or misfortune.*

Question: What does it mean if someone doesn't show any signs of emotion after an important loss?   Although these outward signs of strong emotion may be the most obvious expression of grief, they represent only one of four theoretical stages in the "normal" grieving process (Parkes, 1972; Parkes and Weiss, 1983). In the initial phase of grief, the *numbness* stage, the individual often seems dazed or shocked and may show little emotion other than numbness or emptiness. He or she may also exhibit some signs of denial or disbelief and insist that a mistake has been made. Following this stage of protective numbness, the yearning stage appears. This is a period of acute and obvious distress. The individual experiences sharp pangs of yearning, as well as guilt, anger, and resentment. After the death of a loved one, the survivor often experiences illusions (they "see" the deceased person in his or her favorite chair or in the face of a stranger), has vivid dreams in which the deceased is still alive, and often reports feeling the presence of the dead person. The person also experiences strong feelings of guilt ("If only I had gotten her to a doctor sooner," "I should have been more loving") and anger or resentment ("Why wasn't he more careful?" "It isn't fair that I'm the one left behind").

Once these powerful feelings of acute yearning (or guilt and anger) subside, the *depression* stage follows. The survivor often feels isolated and disorganized. Life seems to lose much of its meaning. The mourner feels listless, apathetic, and submissive. As time goes by, the survivor gradually begins to accept the loss both intellectually (the loss makes sense) and emotionally (memories are both pleasurable as well as painful). This acceptance, combined with the building of a new identity ("I am a single parent," "We are no longer a couple"), characterizes the final state of grief — the *resolution* or reorganization stage.

Question: So what is the best way to help someone who is grieving?   Most bereaved individuals want sympathetic company, reassurance, and a willingness to listen. They are generally annoyed by platitudes such as "Time heals," "It is the will of

Grief is a natural reaction to losses such as death and divorce.

God," and by vague offers of help. Don't be afraid to simply admit "I don't know what to say," and try to be specific in your personal offers of assistance (Osterweis, Solomon, and Green, 1984).

Although the description of these four stages may help you to understand another's grief, as well as your own, it is not a prescription for the best or only way to grieve. Grief is obviously not the same for everyone. Just as people show a wide variation in their "stages" of dying (see Chapter 10), there is also considerable variety in the "stages" of grief. Whatever style individuals choose, they should be allowed and encouraged to do their "grief work" and not to suppress their emotions. It is also important to remember that there is no set time limit for grief. Depending on the individual and specific environmental factors, grieving can be a matter of a few days or weeks or can sometimes last a lifetime.

When it comes to dealing with our own losses, psychologists offer several self-help techniques related to these stages of grief that you may find helpful (Colgrove, Bloomfield, and McWilliams, 1976; Stroebe and Stroebe, 1987).

1. *Recognize the loss and allow yourself to grieve.* Despite feelings of acute loneliness, remember that loss is a part of everyone's life and accept comfort from others. Pamper yourself by avoiding any unnecessary stress, getting plenty of rest, and giving yourself permission to enjoy life whenever possible.
2. *Control your dysfunctional thoughts.* Begin by keeping a record of the situation that led to a sad or anxious feeling and the thought that accompanied the feeling. By using the thought stopping and cognitive restructuring techniques described in Chapter 15, you can then learn to eliminate your negative thoughts or replace them with more positive ones.
3. *Set up a daily activity schedule.* One of the best ways to offset the lethargy and depression of grief is to force yourself to fill your time with useful activities (studying, washing your car, doing the laundry, and so on).
4. *Join a support group.* Several official groups offer mutual support during bereavement (Theos, Widow to Widow, Parents of Murdered Children, Mothers Against Drunk Drivers, Survivors of Suicide and Seasons, and so on). If these groups do not exist in your area or if they seem inappropriate to your particular case (such as the loss of a relationship or a job), you may want to start your own informal group. Meeting on a regular basis with others who share your experiences can be an important adjunct to the healing process.

Beyond allowing yourself to grieve in your own way and using these self-help strategies, it is important to recognize that professional counseling may sometimes be necessary in cases of extreme or prolonged numbness, anger, guilt, or depression (see Chapters 15 and 16).

Before leaving this chapter, we would like to leave you on a happier note and update you on Koko and her sadness over the loss of All Ball. In April 1985, she was given a new kitten and quickly formed a new attachment (Stone, 1988). Her major problem then came from Michael, a male gorilla companion who also knows sign language, who laid claim to her kitten. (Newspapers reported that Michael was "jealous," but can you see why this is more appropriately labeled envy?) The problem was eventually resolved by allowing both Koko and Michael to each have their own kitten.

Trainer Penny Patterson is presenting Koko with her new kitten Smokey.

Review Questions

1 _____ _____ theory suggests that one reason people are over-weight is that they have a higher homeostatic level that maintains a certain weight that is difficult to change.

2 Both _____ _____ (self-starvation and extreme weight loss) and _____ _____ (binges of eating followed by purging) are directly related to an intense fear of obesity.

3 _____ refers to feelings of threat to a relationship, whereas _____ refers to beliefs and feelings that one's personal qualities, possessions, or achievements don't measure up.

4 Feelings of desolation, loneliness, and sadness associated with loss, disaster, or misfortune are known as _____.

5 The four major stages of grief are _____, _____, _____, and _____.

Answers: *1* set point; *2* anorexia nervosa, bulimia nervosa; *3* jealousy, envy; *4* grief; *5* numbness, yearning, depression, resolution

REVIEW OF MAJOR CONCEPTS

UNDERSTANDING BASIC MOTIVATIONAL CONCEPTS

1 Motivation is essentially the study of the "whys" of behavior, whereas emotion is the study of the feelings. Because motivated behaviors are often closely related to emotions, these two topics are frequently studied together.

2 Abraham Maslow proposed a hierarchy of needs or motives. He believed that the basic physiological and survival needs must be satisfied before a person can attempt to satisfy higher needs.

3 There are basically two approaches to the study of motivation: biological theories (which include instinct theory and drive-reduction theory) and psychological theories (which include incentive theory and cognitive theories).

4 Instinct theories suggest that there is some inborn, genetic component to motivation. Although the original interest in this theory declined because of the unwieldy list of possible instincts, interest has been revived in recent years by the work of ethologists and sociobiologists.

5 Drive-reduction theory suggests that internal tensions (produced by the body's demand for homeostasis) "push" the organism toward satisfaction of basic needs, and that the organism learns which specific actions to perform to meet this goal. According to incentive theory, motivation results from the "pull" of external environmental stimuli. Cognitive theories emphasize the importance of thoughts, attributions, and expectations.

THE NATURE OF SPECIFIC MOTIVES

6 There are three basic categories of motives: primary (innate, unlearned motives that are basic to survival), stimulus-seeking (innate needs for novel stimulation), and learned (acquired motives that result from experience).

7 Hunger is a complex primary motive. Studies have found that stomach contractions are generally unrelated to feelings of hunger and that the lateral hypothalamus apparently stimulates eating behavior, whereas the ventromedial hypothalamus signals the organism to stop eating. Other areas of the brain, the level of sugar in the blood, and the sight of external cues for eating all seem to play a role in hunger.

8 People will apparently work very hard to satisfy their need for novel stimulation (stimulus-seeking motives), but if they suddenly begin to receive extrinsic rewards for this behavior their interest and motivation often decline.

9 Although there seems to be an optimal level of arousal that is necessary for maximum performance, there are individual differences in this ideal level. According to Zuckerman's theory, high sensation seekers are biologically "prewired" to need a higher level of stimulation, whereas the reverse is true for low sensation seekers.

10 Whereas some researchers emphasize the biological component of sensation seeking, others suggest that activities such as skydiving and drug taking may be among the learned motives. According to opponent-process theory, the individual first experiences a strong emotional reaction to certain activities like skydiving, which is then followed by an opposing (opposite) emotion that the individual learns to associate with the original activity.

UNDERSTANDING EMOTION

11 There are four basic components of all emotions: the physiological component (increased heart rate, respiration rate, and so on); the cognitive component (thoughts, beliefs, and

expectations); the behavioral component (facial expressions and bodily gestures); and subjective experience (evaluations of intensity, pleasure versus displeasure, and so on).

12 The cognitive and subjective components are generally studied through self-report techniques, whereas the bodily expressions and physiological arousal components are measured more directly through observation of overt behavior or through the use of a polygraph.

13 The polygraph is a mechanical measurement of changes in emotional arousal (increased heart rate, blood pressure, and so on). Although the polygraph is being extensively used in police work and for employment purposes, psychologists generally object to this practice because they find the polygraph to be a poor predictor of guilt or innocence or of truth or lies.

14 Most psychologists believe that emotions result from a complex combination of both inborn and learned reactions. Studies that attempt to discover how emotions are activated have found that most emotions result from a general, nonspecific arousal of the nervous system. This arousal reflects a combination of factors, including the cerebral cortex, the limbic system, and the frontal lobes of the brain. The most obvious signs of arousal (trembling, increased heart rate, sweating, and so on) result from activation of the sympathetic nervous system, a subdivision of the autonomic nervous system.

15 There are four major explanations for the activation of emotions. The James–Lange theory suggests that we interpret the way we feel on the basis of physical sensations such as increased heart rate, trembling, and so on. The Cannon–Bard theory suggests that feelings are created from independent and simultaneous stimulation of both the cortex and the autonomic nervous system. The facial feedback hypothesis asserts that facial movements elicit specific emotions. The cognitive labeling theory of Schachter and Singer maintains that emotions result from a combination of cognitive, subjective, and physiological components. People note what's going on around them, as well as their own bodily responses, and then attempt to label the emotion accordingly.

PROBLEMS IN MOTIVATION AND EMOTION

16 A large number of people show evidence of one or more eating disorders. Obesity seems to result from a variety of biological factors, such as the individual's set point, which tends to maintain a given level of body fat, and from psychological factors, such as sensitivity to external cues. The most effective way to lose weight seems to be a combination of exercise, diet, and behavioral principles (such as removing or managing food-related cues, changing the reinforcers, and so on).

17 Anorexia nervosa (extreme weight loss due to self-imposed starvation) and bulimia (excessive consumption of food followed by vomiting or laxatives) both seem to be related to an intense fear of obesity.

18 Jealousy (thoughts or feelings associated with a threat to relationships) is often confused with the emotion of envy (thoughts or feelings that one's abilities, possessions, or characteristics do not "measure up" to those of others). Although jealousy has been seen as a proof of love, as a sign of personal insecurity, and as a natural "protective" response to feelings of threat, others have worried about the uncontrollable, obsessive type of jealousy that may lead to dangerous acts of retaliation. Researcher Gordon Clanton offers specific techniques for managing jealousy, which include examining one's expectations for relationships, gathering more information, and learning more constructive ways to express concern and nurture relationships.

19 Grief is a natural and painful reaction to any type of important loss. For most people, grief consists of four major stages—numbness, yearning, depression, and resolution. Although people do grieve in different ways, they share the common need to express their feelings, to do their "grief work."

SUGGESTED READINGS

IZARD, C., KAGAN, J., & ZAJONC, R. (1984). *Emotions, cognition, and behavior.* New York: Cambridge University Press. This text, written by three of the top researchers in the field of emotion, provides an engaging summary of recent developments and controversial issues.

LEVENKRON, S. (1982). *Treating and overcoming anorexia nervosa.* New York: Scribner's. A fascinating account of the lives and treatment of six anorexic females.

PETRI, H. L. (1985). *Motivation: Theory and research* (2nd ed.). Belmont, CA: Wadsworth. A comprehensive and up-to-date discussion of the major research interests in motivation.

REMINGTON, D., FISCHER, G., & PARENT, E. (1983). *How to lower your fat thermostat.* Provo, UT: Vitality House International. Intended for nonprofessional readers, this paperback offers a "scientific" explanation for the "setpoint theory" and a step-by-step method for weight reduction.

chapter thirteen

Health Psychology

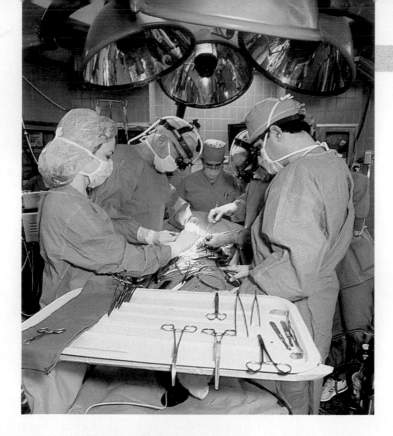

THAT noise — sounds like hundreds of explosions! I can't see — the light — too bright — hurts. Am I dead? I must be — can't breathe. I can't breathe! Gotta get this tube out of my throat. Can't — arms strapped down. What? Who's that? Nurse. Says my throat tube is hooked up to a respirator. Does my breathing for me. Okay. Also says the noise is from life-support machines and monitors . . .

I must have dozed off. Where am I? Can't think — so groggy . . . I remember now. I had a heart attack. After running tests, the doctors decided I needed bypass surgery. It must be over now. Well, I seem to have come out of it all right. What an agonizing decision, to agree to let a surgeon actually open up my chest and work on my heart. How scary, to think that my whole life depended on that heart–lung machine to pump and cleanse my blood. Glad they had that psychologist working with us: the decision was a lot easier, with him supporting us, answering Carol's and my questions, and showing those movies so that we would know what to expect.

Here's Carol. I have to tell her how much I — drat, I can't talk — the throat tube. How good it is to feel her hand in mine. We haven't held hands since our kids were babies. We'll have to do more of that when — if — I ever get out of here. What's that? Oh, the nurse says most people have their tubes out by now, but because of my heavy smoking I need the respirator for a longer time. Guess I should have tried harder to stop smoking. There are a lot of things the doctor told me to stop, but I didn't listen. She said that with my father dying of a heart attack at 55, I was a likely candidate for heart disease. She said that, besides stopping smoking, I should change my eating habits, lose weight, exercise, and try to reduce sources of stress. Reduce stress? How could I? At work, there are always deadlines to make, meetings to attend, clients to court. How is the company going to get along while I'm in the hospital? And who's going to coach Elizabeth's soccer team? No one can coach those kids like I can — I coach them to win, and win I always do! And Jimmy's Boy Scout trip next weekend: Who's going to take them if I don't? And who'll preside over the Lion's Club meeting next week? . . . Wait a minute. The doctor told me to take it easy, but I didn't. That's why I'm here. Maybe I should stop worrying about who will take over for me and concentrate on how to change my life. This heart attack thing sure is scary. Carol said I nearly died. Well, I'm gonna change. I'm never going to light up another cigarette. I'm going to have to bow out of most of my extra activities, just volunteer for one thing at a time. As for watching my diet and exercising — well, maybe it's time for those now, too.

418

Do you know someone like our heart attack victim? Your father? An aunt? A friend? Or maybe even yourself? Although the person we have portrayed is completely fictitious, his personality is a composite of real, ordinary people. This description illustrates some of the issues that are dealt with in health psychology. Because he was "at risk" for heart disease, our heart attack patient's doctor made several recommendations based on research findings from this relatively new field.

In this chapter, we will discuss many research findings that can have quite an impact on your physical well-being. For example, did you know that according to some sources, smoking is the most preventable contributing factor in the development of serious disease, such as heart disease and lung cancer? That people with certain types of personalities are more prone to heart disease than others? That excess stress can lower your body's resistance not only to minor illnesses such as colds and the flu but also to major illnesses such as cancer and heart disease? That people who feel in control of themselves and their environment tend to handle stress better than those who feel helpless in most situations? And that today, causes of death stem more from our behavior patterns than from viral or bacterial disease? These and many other findings will be examined in this chapter.

THE NATURE OF HEALTH PSYCHOLOGY

Health psychology is the study of the relationship between psychological behavior and physical health and illness, with an emphasis on "wellness" and the prevention of illness. Health psychologists study how people's lifestyles and activities, emotional reactions, ways of interpreting events, and personality characteristics influence their physical health. Some health psychologists are involved primarily in research, whereas others work directly with physicians and other health professionals in implementing research findings to prevent and treat illness.

HEALTH PSYCHOLOGY: *The study of the relationship between psychological behavior and physical health and illness, with an emphasis on wellness and the prevention of illness.*

Health psychology is a field that has only recently become recognized. The relationship between the mind and physical health had been a widely accepted fact from ancient times and throughout most of history. However, the discovery of specific physiological causes for infectious diseases such as typhoid and syphilis in the late 1800s led doctors to search for *only* physiological causes of disease and to virtually ignore the psychological factors in physical health. This attitude prevailed until only recently, as doctors and other health professionals have begun to work with health psychologists and have begun putting research from this field into practice (Myerowitz, Burish, and Wallston, 1986).

Researchers in health psychology study practical problems encountered by health professionals, such as patients failing to adhere to their doctors' recommendations (Davis, 1966). They also study health problems, from cancer to obesity, to try to determine their causes and contributing factors and discover optimum methods of treatment or ways of coping with the problems.

Other health psychologists work in the medical field, in such settings as hospitals and clinics. Astounding technological advances have been made in medicine in the last few years, including heart transplants and bypass surgery. When hearing of such advances, we tend to jump to the conclusion that people with severe medical problems need only have operations and their problems will disappear. But this is just not so. According to Jack Copeland, a cardiothoracic surgeon, patients almost uniformly have accompanying psychological problems—extreme guilt in the case of transplant patients, plus worry over changes in appearance, adjustment to dietary restrictions, changes in activity level, and so on (Rodgers, 1984). Health psychologists often work hand-in-hand with physicians, nurses, anesthesiologists, and others in helping patients with such problems. They assist patients and their families in making critical decisions and in knowing what to expect during and after surgery or other treatment. For example, before recommending bypass surgery, cardiologists often order several tests that can be frightening and painful. By discussing the purpose of the tests and suggesting ways to cope with them, psychologists can help patients through some stressful situations.

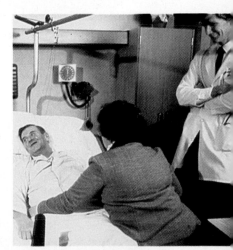

Health psychologists can help patients like Bill Schroeder, one of the first artificial heart recipients, to adjust to the changes in lifestyle associated with heart surgery.

Health psychologists also educate patients and the general public regarding health maintenance. They provide information about the effects of stress, smoking, lack of exercise, and other factors on their health. They also develop and administer programs to help people learn how to cope with existing problems, such as high blood pressure, as well as unhealthful behaviors, such as hostile reactions. In the next sections we will examine how health psychologists help people cope with problems and problem behaviors. By focusing on two problems that are among the most prevalent, chronic pain and smoking, we will illustrate techniques commonly used by health psychologists.

Chronic pain: The role of psychologists in helping patients cope

CHRONIC PAIN: *Long-lasting pain that often is recurring.*

If you've ever had your back "go out" or had a headache that lasted for days, you have an idea of the suffering of people experiencing **chronic pain** from arthritis, cancer, migraine or tension headache, neuralgia, and other sources of pain. They experience the same kind of pain that you feel from your bad back or your headache, except that their pain doesn't go away. Because their pain is always with them, they become irritable, easily angered, anxious, depressed, and dependent on others, with a consequent loss of self-esteem. Their social lives and personal relationships are profoundly affected, their sporting and other activities are considerably curtailed, and some are forced to quit their jobs (Olshan, 1980; Egan and Keaton, 1987). In being shuffled from one doctor to another, they are sometimes rebuffed with such statements as "I just don't know how to help you" or "It's all in your head" (which, of course, it is, since it's in our brain that we perceive pain). Doctors often prescribe a variety of pain medications, to which the patients can become addicted, and in some cases may perform surgery, which may not successfully relieve the pain.

Question: Is chronic pain very common? It has been estimated that as many as one-third of all Americans have, at one time or another, suffered from some sort of chronic pain (i.e., pain that continues for six months or more) (Bonica, 1977). In recent years, doctors have begun teaming up with or referring patients to health psychologists who can help them deal more effectively with pain. (Today, there are over 250 pain clinics in the United States.) The psychologist may recommend an increase in activity and exercise levels or suggest changes in diet, since chemicals such as monosodium glutamate and caffeine can contribute to pain, particularly headache. The psychologist may also use specific treatment methods that include operant conditioning techniques, biofeedback, relaxation techniques, and hypnosis.

Operant conditioning techniques Working with chronic pain patients is no easy matter, for there are countless factors that may tend to reinforce the pain. For example, talking about the pain tends to focus attention on it, and anxiety tends to increase its perception, which further increases the anxiety. Often, the patient learns inappropriate behaviors, such as inactivity, that come to be associated with the pain. Contrary to popular belief, an increase in activity and exercise levels can be quite beneficial for pain patients. Exercise increases the release of **endorphins,** the chemicals that attach themselves to nerve cells in the brain and act to block the perception of pain. Pain patients, however, tend to *decrease* their activity levels and to stop exercising altogether. Well-meaning friends and relatives reinforce this inactivity by doing things for the patients when they complain. In this way, some patients have been operantly conditioned to inactivity and other disadvantageous behaviors, such as complaining about their pain, by being reinforced for them. In such cases, psychologists may initiate a behavior modification program not only for the patients but also for their families and friends.

ENDORPHINS: *Morphinelike chemicals occurring naturally in the brain that can lessen the perception of pain.*

Cairns and Pasino (1977) conducted the first controlled study on the effectiveness of operant conditioning techniques in the treatment of chronic pain. The researchers provided reinforcement by congratulating pain patients when they followed through with their pain treatment programs (daily exercise, use of relaxation techniques, and so on) and by charting their adherence to the program. The researchers found that both of these techniques were effective in reducing the subjective pain experienced by their patients. Thus, many pain control programs now incorporate an operant conditioning component, in which patients are reinforced for carrying through with changes in behavior.

Biofeedback   Biofeedback (see Chapter 6) with patients suffering from chronic pain has been done chiefly with the **electromyograph (EMG)**. This is a device that measures muscle tension by recording the amount of electrical activity in an area of skin to which electrodes have been attached. Pain therapists use the EMG to help people whose pain has an exaggerated muscle tension component, such as tension headache and lower back pain. When the EMG is used, electrodes are attached to the site of the pain and the patient is instructed to relax. When sufficient relaxation is achieved, a signal such as a tone or a light is given by the machine. This signal serves as feedback to the patient.

The effectiveness of such therapy has been demonstrated in a study in which subjects suffering from tension headaches received either accurate EMG biofeedback or pseudofeedback (inaccurate biofeedback). It was found that patients receiving accurate biofeedback experienced greater reduction in headache intensity and needed medication less frequently than did patients receiving the pseudofeedback (Philips, 1977). It appears that although biofeedback does not reduce the number or frequency of tension headaches, it does reduce the severity.

A study conducted by Nouwen and Solinger (1979) indicates that a major contribution of biofeedback is that it helps people feel they have some control over their pain. Subjects with lower back pain who received EMG biofeedback showed a significant decrease in their tension levels and in subjective reports of pain, as compared to controls. What is remarkable about this study is that when the same patients were studied three months later, their tension levels had returned to pretreatment levels, but they still reported lowered levels of pain. These results suggest that the EMG training was successful at teaching the patients that they need not accept the pain as uncontrollable. They could assume an **internal locus of control** over their pain and therefore cope more effectively with it.

Several researchers have attempted to use EEG (brain wave) biofeedback to alleviate pain (Gannon and Sternbach, 1971; Melzack and Perry, 1975; Pelletier and Peper, 1977; Sternbach, 1974). Subjects try to produce *alpha* brain waves, which tend to be associated with relaxed states. Although some success has been achieved with this type of biofeedback, there are no solid conclusions about its effectiveness in alleviating chronic pain. Biofeedback has been shown to be effective in learning to cope with chronic headache pain, but not with other kinds of chronic pain.

Altered attention — relaxation techniques and hypnosis   Because the pain always seems to be there, chronic pain sufferers tend to talk and think about their pain whenever they're not thoroughly engrossed in other activities. Thus, any attempt to divert their attention — watching TV shows or films, attending parties, or exercising — might help to reduce their discomfort. Attention can be diverted with relaxation techniques and hypnosis, which have the added advantage of easing the tension and anxiety components of pain. The goal of one of the most widely used relaxation techniques is to achieve complete relaxation through focusing attention on each part of the body.

Question: Are these like the relaxation techniques used in natural childbirth?
Yes. **Relaxation techniques** are used in conjunction with breathing techniques as a way of reducing the anxiety and pain of childbirth. They work by focusing attention on the relaxation process rather than on the uncertainty and fear of the birthing process and by helping relieve the muscle tension that aggravates the pain perceived during childbirth. These same techniques can be used to try to relieve other kinds of pain. Again, these techniques do not eliminate the pain; they merely allow the person to ignore it for a time. A progressive relaxation exercise is described at the end of this chapter.

ELECTROMYOGRAPH (EMG): *Biofeedback device that can measure muscle tension by recording the amount of electrical activity in an area of skin to which electrodes are attached.*

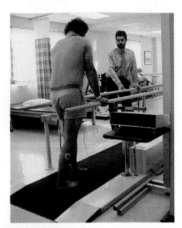

Pain clinics often use biofeedback to help patients learn to control muscle tension and blood flow.

INTERNAL LOCUS OF CONTROL: *The belief that one has significant control over the events in one's life.*

RELAXATION TECHNIQUES: *Procedures used to relieve the anxiety and bodily tension accompanying such problems as stress and chronic pain.*

Relaxation techniques are often taught as part of natural-childbirth classes.

SELF-HYPNOSIS: *An alternate state of consciousness induced by oneself during which one is more relaxed, more alert, and more open to suggestion than in the normal state.*

Another approach used to alter people's focus on pain is hypnosis. As we saw in Chapter 5, *hypnosis* is an alternate state of consciousness in which the brain is highly alert and more open to suggestion. The hypnotic state can be induced by focusing the attention on something like the drone of a soft voice, the ticking of a watch, or the process of totally relaxing the body. Hypnosis can be either self-induced, in which case it is referred to as **self-hypnosis,** or it can be induced by a specially trained person. In the treatment of pain, the hypnotized individual can learn to ignore the pain or to experience it in a different way.

The effectiveness of hypnosis in pain relief is controversial, since not all research results are conclusive. But there are a few studies that have shown definite benefits (Elton, Burrows, and Stanley, 1980). Paul Sacerdote (1978) found that hypnosis brought some degree of relief to 90 percent of pain patients, and in the 25 percent of those patients who had "high hypnotic talent" there was a highly significant degree of pain relief. In another study, Sachs, Feuerstein, and Vitale (1977) concluded that patients using self-hypnosis experienced reductions in pain intensity, life dissatisfaction and suffering, unpleasant personality characteristics associated with chronic pain (such as irritability), amount of pain medication used, and the amount that pain interfered with daily activities such as social life and sleep.

Whatever pain relief technique is used, one of the most important components for success is the patient's conviction that the pain *can* in fact be controlled. This brings us back to the importance of an internal locus of control. Weisenberg (1980) has suggested that without this feeling of control, the effectiveness of any attempt at pain control would be substantially reduced. Melzack and Perry (1975), in whose study over half of the patients achieved at least a 33 percent reduction in pain through a program that included both biofeedback and hypnosis, attributed the success of their program to four factors: distraction of attention, suggestion, relaxation, and the sense of control over the pain.

The techniques used in treating chronic pain patients can also be used in treating people who are suffering from excessive stress. Later in the chapter we will thoroughly discuss the nature, causes, and effects of stress. First, however, we will discuss another major health problem: smoking.

Review Questions

1 Health psychology is the study of the interrelationship between _____ and _____ .

2 Long-term pain that never goes away is called _____ pain.

3 Health psychologists have used _____ conditioning to remove behaviors that tend to reinforce or aggravate long-term pain.

4 Biofeedback has been used to help chronic pain patients by allowing them to learn to relax muscles and teaching them an _____ locus of control.

5 Techniques such as _____ and _____ have been used with chronic pain patients to help them focus their attention on something other than their pain.

Answer: 1 medicine, psychology; *2* chronic; *3* operant; *4* internal; *5* relaxation, hypnosis

Smoking: Hazardous to your health

According to the U.S. Department of Health and Human Services, cigarette smoking is the single most preventable cause of death and disease in the United States. It will adversely affect the health of one out of every three people who smoke cigarettes. Like our heart attack patient, most people know that smoking is bad for their health and that the more they smoke, the more at risk they are. It is therefore not surprising that most professionals in the medical field are concerned with the prevention of smoking and with encouraging those already smoking to stop.

Smoking prevention   The first puff on a cigarette is rarely pleasant. Why, then, do people ever start smoking? The answer is complex, since the decision involves psychological, social, and biological factors. Although for some people smoking is an expression of rebellion against their parents or society. (Krantz, Grunberg, and Baum, 1985), most people begin to smoke in response to social pressures from peers or in imitation of role models such as family members, movie stars, and athletes (Bowen and Peterson, 1988). Once a person begins to smoke, there is additional biological pressure to continue smoking because of the addictive effects of nicotine. Therefore, one way to reduce the number of smokers is to prevent people from taking their first puff (Biglan et al., 1987).

Those concerned with the prevention of smoking face a tough uphill battle in having to contend with the effects of peer pressure and the advertising budgets of the large tobacco companies. Smoking provides adolescents with immediate short-term reinforcements from their peers, whereas the long-term health disadvantages do not seem at all relevant to them. Therefore, the most successful techniques geared toward prevention of smoking in young people have focused on the short-term detrimental effects of tobacco use, such as coughing, bad breath, difficulty in breathing, dependence on an addictive-substance, and the effects on personal appearance and hygiene (Murray et al., 1984). Most young people do not realize that smoking makes them smell as well as taste like cigarette smoke until the facts are converted to down-to-earth terms like, "Who wants to kiss a dirty ashtray?" Another successful technique involves using peer role models to teach specific social skills that enable young people to resist the social pressure to start smoking (Evans et al., 1981).

The single most preventable cause of death and disease in the United States is cigarette smoking. Posters like this one with Brooke Shields attempt to get young people to quit smoking by pointing out that smoking is also unattractive.

Cessation of smoking

Question: What's the best way to stop smoking?   It is difficult for many people to quit smoking, since the same social pressures that help initiate the habit also help maintain it. These social pressures, combined with the fact that smoking is now part of their everyday behavior and the fact that they are now addicted to the nicotine, make smoking an especially hard habit to break. The maintenance of smoking behaviors can be viewed as the result of both positive and negative reinforcement. Most smokers tend to associate smoking with pleasant things, such as good food, friends, and sex, as well as the "high" that nicotine gives them, so smoking is positively reinforced by these factors. When smokers are deprived of their cigarettes for a few hours, they start to go through an extremely unpleasant physical withdrawal. When they are finally able to smoke, the nicotine reduces these symptoms, and smoking is thereby negatively reinforced

(Schachter, 1978). Any program designed to help smokers break their habit must therefore combat both the positive and the negative reinforcement obtained from smoking.

Several approaches are currently being used to help people quit smoking. In addition to ad campaigns designed to alert the general public to the dangers of cigarette smoking, both cognitive and behavioral techniques have been developed.

One cognitive approach used to break the smoking habit is **covert sensitization,** a form of cognitive classical conditioning. With this technique, smokers are asked to mentally associate something extremely unpleasant with smoking. For example:

> Imagine that your favorite brand of cigarettes is sitting on a table in front of you. Now imagine that a housefly lands on the cigarettes and lays her eggs inside the cigarettes. The eggs hatch and little maggots begin to crawl around inside each cigarette. You now pick up the cigarette and put it in your mouth. You light up and draw in your first breath with the maggots still inside. The heat of the cigarette forces the maggots to crawl into your mouth and down your throat and start to eat at your body from the inside out.

If smokers used this imagery every time they felt like having a cigarette, there is a good chance they would be able to combat some of the positive associations of cigarette smoking.

Another approach used in eliminating the positive reinforcement of smoking is **stimulus control.** With this technique, smokers are made aware of stimuli leading to the unwanted behaviors so that they can control or reduce these stimuli. The smoker is asked to make a list of the situations in which he or she normally smokes. By doing so, the individual is made aware of the specific situation or stimuli that trigger smoking behavior. Once the smoker is aware of these specific situations, he or she can be extra aware of the tendency to smoke at these times and more able to combat the urge to smoke. Or the smoker can substitute another behavior (preferably something that is not equally "addicting") or can try to avoid the situations altogether. For example, if a smoker tends to light up right after meals and snacks, he or she could reduce the number of meals per day or could have a pencil handy after meals and doodle on a napkin instead of smoking.

Although covert sensitization and stimulus control have been used successfully in reducing the number of cigarettes smoked each day, they have not been very successful in helping people quit completely (Flaxman, 1978). More successful strategies have included reinforcement for not smoking, aversion therapies, and slow withdrawal using nicotine gum.

If an appropriate reinforcer can be found, reinforcement for *not* smoking can be very effective. Basically, this technique involves choosing one or several alternative behaviors to smoking and trying to reinforce those behaviors. Ideally, these behaviors should be incompatible with smoking. Many forms of physical exercise fit this criteria—you certainly can't smoke when you're swimming. The most common reinforcer used is money. The subject makes a large monetary deposit and is then paid for doing things other than smoking. This type of approach has been successful for some people (Winett, 1973).

Question: Is this how they help smokers stop smoking in smoking clinics like the Schick centers?   Most commercial smoking clinics use **aversion therapy** (see Chapter 16) to help people stop smoking. In this approach, smoking behavior is paired with some kind of aversive stimulus, such as electric shock or an abundance of cigarette smoke. In typical electrical shock aversion therapy, electrodes are attached to smokers' hands or wrists. The smokers are then asked to begin smoking cigarettes. Each time they take a puff, they receive an unpleasant shock. The electrical shock becomes paired with the cigarette, and the smoker is classically conditioned to feel uncomfortable around cigarettes. Some researchers using this method have reported up to 70 percent abstinence after one year (Pope and Mount, 1975). However, most controlled research on smoking

COVERT SENSITIZATION: *Cognitive approach used in behavior control in which the individual learns to associate an aversive stimulus with the undesired behavior.*

STIMULUS CONTROL: *A technique used in behavior control in which the individual becomes aware of the stimuli leading to the undesired behavior in order to control them by such means as avoiding them or substituting other stimuli.*

AVERSION THERAPY: *A classical conditioning technique used in behavior control in which the undesired behavior is paired with some kind of aversive, or intensely displeasing, stimulus.*

and electrical shock has found no difference between the shock group and a control group (Russell, Armstrong, and Patel, 1976). This has been attributed to the fact that once smokers are no longer hooked up to the shock device, they know that they won't get a shock if they smoke. In conditioning terms, they have failed to generalize the associations learned in the laboratory to the real world.

A type of aversion therapy that gets around this generalization problem uses cigarette smoke as the aversive stimulus. The most widely used technique is called "rapid smoking," in which the smoker takes a puff every 6 seconds (10 puffs per minute) while concentrating on the negative sensations produced by the rapid smoking. If the smoker gets sick, so much the better. Rapid smoking, accompanied by long-term support or therapy, has been a highly successful cessation technique (Lichtenstein and Penner, 1977; Suedfeld and Baker-Brown, 1986). The one major drawback is that it can produce a moderate amount of stress on the heart and lungs; it should therefore be used only under the supervision of a physician.

Another cessation strategy is to deal with the physical addiction to nicotine experienced by cigarette smokers. If they can become less dependent on this substance, they will have a better chance at quitting smoking altogether. Use of nicotine gum is one way to slowly withdraw smokers from the dependency on nicotine (Gottlieb, Killen, Marlatt, and Taylor, 1987).

Freedom from dependence on nicotine is, of course, not enough to prevent former smokers from wanting to smoke; both nicotine gum and sheer willpower must be used in conjunction with other techniques to help smokers eliminate their psychological need for cigarettes. For instance, two common problems faced by those trying to kick the habit are fear of weight gain and lack of replacements for the rituals associated with smoking. They often find themselves wondering, "What can I put in my mouth?" and "What can I do with my hands?" Therefore, an effective smoking cessation program must include not only techniques for physically kicking the habit but also suggestions for controlling weight, countering social pressures, and replacing the rituals associated with smoking.

Rapid smoking, which involves smoking several cigarettes in a very short period of time, is one type of aversion therapy used to help people stop smoking.

Review Questions

1 The single most preventable cause of death and disease in the United States is _____ _____ .

2 Smoking prevention campaigns usually are more effective if they counter tobacco advertising by focusing on the _____-term effects of smoking rather than on the _____-term effects.

3 The maintenance of smoking behaviors can be viewed as a combination of both _____ and _____ reinforcement.

4 When people try to quit smoking by imagining that their cigarettes are infested with maggots, they are using _____ _____ .

5 When using the technique of _____ _____ , people try to quit smoking by controlling or reducing the number of stimuli that normally lead up to the smoking behavior.

6 Most commercial centers for smoking cessation use _____ therapy.

7 Gum laced with _____ has recently been used to help smokers withdraw from the physical addiction to the chemicals in cigarette smoke.

Answers: 1 cigarette smoking; *2* short, long *3* positive, negative; *4* covert sensitization; *5* stimulus control; *6* aversion; *7* nicotine

STRESS AND ITS ROLE IN HEALTH

The study of stress and its effects on humans and animals has resulted in many different definitions of stress. We will use the definition proposed by Hans Selye (1974), a physiologist who has done a significant amount of research and writing in the area of stress since the 1930s. Selye defines **stress** as the nonspecific response of the body to any demand made on it. For example, a child who has been outside for hours in the cold will have goose bumps, the shivers, and an increased heart rate. That same child, when awakening from a terrifying nightmare, may experience identical stress responses, even though they are triggered by completely different stimuli. Thus, "stress" is a bodily reaction that can occur in response to either internal, cognitive stimuli or external, environmental stimuli. A stimulus that causes stress is known as a **stressor**.

STRESS: *According to Selye, the nonspecific response of the body to any demand made on it.*

STRESSOR: *Any stimulus that causes stress.*

To clarify the terms *stress* and *stressor,* imagine you are taking a public speaking class and have just been asked to give an extemporaneous speech on a topic you know little about. The *stress* you experience consists of your bodily responses — increased heart rate and blood pressure, "butterflies" in your stomach, dry mouth, rapid breathing, and so forth. The *stressors* producing these responses are the stares and reactions of your classmates, your own internal self-criticism, and the comments and reactions of your instructor.

Question: It seems then that stress is something you should always avoid. Is this true?   No, stress is not necessarily something to avoid. If you think back to Selye's definition of stress, it states that anything placing a demand on the body can cause stress. That means that almost all external stimuli can cause some stress. In fact, much of our stress is pleasant and beneficial. Exercise, for instance, is a beneficial stressor, in that it helps increase the efficiency of the cardiovascular system. Selye (1974) distinguishes between *eustress* (pleasant, desirable stress such as that produced by reasonable exercise) and *distress* (unpleasant, objectionable stress such as that produced by prolonged illness). The body is nearly always in some state of stress, whether pleasant or unpleasant, mild or severe. The total absence of stress would mean the total absence of external stimulation, which would eventually lead to death. Because health psychology has been chiefly concerned with the negative effects of stress, we will adhere to convention and use the word "stress" to refer primarily to harmful or unpleasant stress (Selye's "distress") even though stress has its positive side.

Causes of stress: From major life changes to minor hassles

Although stress is pervasive in our lives, some things cause more stress than others. The major causes of stress include life changes, chronic life stress, hassles, frustration, and conflicts.

Life changes   Significant life events, such as marriage, death of a family member, or moving to a new home, tend to disrupt our lives and cause more stress than normal. Thomas Holmes and Richard Rahe (1967) have postulated that exposure to numerous stressful life events within a short period of time may have a detrimental effect on health. Such events might be joyous as in the case of a marriage, grievous as in the case of a family member's death, or apparently neutral as in the case of a change in work hours, yet all such events do cause extra stress, and an inordinate amount of such stress will exceed the body's ability to cope and may lead to moderate or serious illness.

Holmes and Rahe developed a scale on which they listed 43 life events and ranked them according to their relative importance in contributing to health problems. They assigned to each event a value in terms of life change units (LCUs) and developed a *Social Readjustment Rating Scale,* which is presented in Table 13.1. Look through the scale and add up the life change units for the events you have experienced in the last year. What is your total? A score of less than 200 LCUs is considered low, 200–300 LCUs is

TABLE 13.1
Social Readjustment Rating Scale

Rank	Life Event	Life Change Units (LCUs)
1	Death of spouse	100
2	Divorce	73
3	Marital separation	65
4	Jail term	63
5	Death of close family member	63
6	Personal injury or illness	53
7	Marriage	50
8	Fired at work	47
9	Marital reconciliation	45
10	Retirement	45
11	Change in health of family member	44
12	Pregnancy	40
13	Sex difficulties	39
14	Gain of new family member	39
15	Business readjustment	39
16	Change in financial state	38
17	Death of close friend	37
18	Change to different line of work	36
19	Change in number of arguments with spouse	35
20	Mortgage over $10,000	31
21	Foreclosure of mortgage or loan	30
22	Change in responsibilities at work	29
23	Son or daughter leaving home	29
24	Trouble with in-laws	29
25	Outstanding personal achievement	28
26	Wife begins or stops work	26
27	Begin or end school	26
28	Change in living conditions	25
29	Revision of personal habits	24
30	Trouble with boss	23
31	Change in work hours or conditions	20
32	Change in residence	20
33	Change in schools	20
34	Change in recreation	19
35	Change in church activities	19
36	Change in social activities	18
37	Mortgage or loan less than $10,000	17
38	Change in sleeping habits	16
39	Change in number of family get-togethers	15
40	Change in eating habits	15
41	Vacation	13
42	Christmas	12
43	Minor violations of the law	11

Source: Holmes and Rahe (1967).

moderate, and above 300 LCUs is high. According to Holmes and Rahe, people scoring high on the scale are more likely to experience problems such as heart disease, depression, and cancer than those scoring in the low to moderate range. Rahe and Arthur (1978) have also noticed that increases in LCUs are predictive of an increase in many types of accidents.

Stressful life events such as moving may have a detrimental effect on a person's health.

Question: Many events included on the scale do not seem particularly stressful to me. Is this approach accurate for everyone? Many people have criticized this approach to stress measurement. Lazarus and Folkman (1984) have pointed out three main defects in the assumptions underlying the life events approach to stress measurement. First, they question the assumption that change alone — any change — is stressful. They cite research on aging that suggests that life events such as menopause and retirement do not pose serious problems for most people (Neugarten, 1970; Rosow, 1963).

The second assumption discredited by Lazarus and Folkman is that a life change must be major to create stress great enough to cause illness. They point out that individual perceptions of an event differ and that what may be highly stressful for one person may be minimally stressful for another. For example, whereas one person may view moving to another state as a terrible sacrifice and experience a great amount of stress in doing so, another person may see the move as a wonderful opportunity to explore a new region of the country and experience only a minimal amount of stress. Thus, Lazarus and Folkman believe that the way in which each individual *interprets* an event is more important than the event itself.

The third assumption they challenge is that significant life changes in themselves constitute a major factor in causing illness. It is true that *stress* is a major factor in many different types of illness. But the correlation between LCUs and illness is very small — around .12 (Rabkin and Struening, 1976; Tausig, 1982). Given this low relationship, it appears that the number of LCUs by itself is not especially valid in predicting potential illness. Lazarus and Folkman feel that more important than the number of life changes is the way in which the individual appraises these changes.

Chronic stress Not all stressful situations are single, short-term events such as the death of a loved one or the birth of a child. A bad marriage, poor working conditions, and an intolerable political climate can serve as *chronic* stressors. However, just as people react individually to significant life changes, so too do they react to chronic stressors in various ways. Whereas one person might spend years working under an obnoxious, abusive supervisor and be able to ignore the verbal abuse, another worker might suffer considerable amounts of stress and take it out on his or her family at home.

How we react to chronic stressors in our everyday lives depends on our cognitive appraisal of situations we encounter in our private lives, our social lives, and our work lives. In our private lives, family problems such as divorce, child abuse, spouse abuse,

Air traffic controllers are chronically exposed to stress on the job.

alcoholism, and money problems can place severe stress on all members of a family (Wallerstein and Kelly, 1980). Our social lives can also be very stressful, since making friends and maintaining friendships can involve a considerable amount of thought and energy. This is especially true for people who tend to be shy or ill at ease with people they don't know well. Even old, rewarding friendships can be hard to maintain when distance separates the friends or when other involvements like marriage or a career limit the amount of free time.

Much research on chronic life stressors has focused on work-related stress, since most people spend a large percentage of their life at work. People may experience stress associated with keeping and moving their careers, with job performance, or with interactions with coworkers (Gross, 1970).

The most stressful jobs make great demands on performance and concentration while allowing little creativity and job advancement, such as assembly-line work. Recently Chaya Piorkowske and Evan Stark (1985) documented that stress at work can also cause serious stress at home for other family members. Their research showed that if a father reported job stress, his son was more likely to report conflicts with the father, who tended to reject him. Also, the son was often depressed and expressed dissatisfaction about his relationships with his peers.

Hassles   In addition to chronic types of stress, much daily stress is in the form of little problems that themselves are not necessarily significant. These **hassles,** whether they involve trying to find a parking place, having to run to the store for an essential dinner item, or not being able to get a computer program to work, are a part of living. But when hassles pile up, they can become a major source of stress (deLongis et al., 1988).

HASSLES: *Minor daily problems that, when they mount up, can be a major source of stress.*

When daily hassles accumulate, they can become a major source of stress.

MAKING SOUND DECISIONS
Recognizing the Role of Personal Values in Conflict Resolution

After reading about approach–approach, avoidance–avoidance, and approach–avoidance conflicts, most students quickly recognize their own experiences with each of these forms of conflict. When faced with a conflict, we often turn to others for advice in resolving our conflicts. Although others' opinions are valuable, critical thinkers recognize that the most successful decision is one that is guided by the decision maker's own personal values and goals. Good decision makers take full responsibility for their own future. They realize that they are the only ones who can truly evaluate the merits of each alternative. A critical thinker also recognizes that decisions are often stressful, but that they cannot be avoided. Avoiding a decision is, in fact, making one without the benefit of a careful analysis of the problem.

To improve your decision-making skills, we offer the following chart that may help to clarify some of your current conflicts (adapted from Seech, 1987):

1 At the top of the chart, identify your specific conflict (approach–approach, avoidance–avoidance, and approach–avoidance).

2 On the lines in the left-hand column, list all possible alternatives or possible courses of action. Although the wording of the "approach–approach" discussion may imply only two choices, most conflicts involve several op-

tions or alternatives. The identification of options will require a good deal of homework. Read up on your problem. Talk to as many people as you can.

3 Now list the logical outcome or consequence of each alternative, regardless of whether the consequence is significant or insignificant and regardless of whether it is a certain or a possible outcome.

4 Your next step is to assess both the probability and significance of each outcome. Using a 0 to 5 rating scale (0 = won't occur and 5 = certain to occur), assign a numerical rating for the likelihood that each consequence will actually occur. Using a similar 0 to 5 rating scale (0 = no significance and 5 = high significance), assess the importance you place on each consequence.

5 Now review the chart. In some cases, you may find it helpful to multiply your probability and significance ratings and then compare your results for the various alternatives. In other cases, you will find it difficult to assign numerical values to complex issues and feelings. Even in the most difficult decisions, however, the thinking and evaluation elicited by this chart may provide useful insights to your conflict. Be careful to also note your feelings associated with each alternative. Careful decision making involves integrated consideration of both feelings and cognitions.

6 Once you've reviewed each alternative, ask yourself

Some authorities, including Pearlin (1980), believe that hassles can be more significant than major life events. In fact, the reason people are so affected by major life events may be because the number of hassles increases greatly at such times (deLongis et al., 1982). For example, a change in residence has a moderate LCU of 20, whereas a divorce has a high LCU of 73. Both of these life changes create an increase in hassles, but the divorce may mean a long-term increase in the number of hassles, including taking on extra chores and other hassles previously assumed by the spouse. It may also be true that preparing to move or having your house up for sale for an extended period of time can be more stressful than the actual move itself.

Frustration

Question: I feel "stressed out" when something prevents me from doing what I want. Is this a common form of stress?   Yes. Whenever we set a goal and are prevented from attaining it, we feel frustrated, and this leads to stress. **Frustration** is a negative emotional state that is generally associated with a blocked goal, such as being refused a loan after having found just the right car, or not being accepted for admission to the college that was your first choice.

Frustration is closely associated with motivation. We wouldn't be frustrated if we had not been motivated to achieve a particular goal. Furthermore, the more motivated we

FRUSTRATION: *An unpleasant state of tension, anxiety, and heightened sympathetic activity resulting from the blocking or thwarting of a goal.*

430

TYPE OF CONFLICT _____

ALTERNATIVES	LOGICAL OUTCOME			PROBABILITY	SIGNIFICANCE

which choice is most in line with your overall goals and values. Some alternatives may look different when they are weighed against long-term relationship plans, career goals, and personal belief systems. As a final check on your decision, you may want to share your chart with a trusted friend and ask for their input.

Once a decision is made commit yourself and give it all you've got. Throw away your expectations. Many decisions don't turn out the way we imagined, and if we focus on the way it is supposed to be we miss enjoying the way it is. If the decision doesn't work out, don't stubbornly hang on for dear life. Change or correct your course.

are, the more frustration we experience when our goals are blocked. For example, suppose you got stuck in traffic on the way to school. If the delay caused you to be late to an important exam, you would be quite frustrated. On the other hand, if it caused you to be five minutes late to a boring lecture, your frustration level would be practically nil.

Conflicts   A final major source of stress is conflict. **Conflicts** arise when people are forced to make a choice between at least two different alternatives. The amount of stress produced by a conflict depends on the complexity of the conflict and on the difficulty involved in resolving it. Three basic types of conflicts that can lead to varying levels of frustration and stress are approach–approach, avoidance–avoidance, and approach–avoidance.

CONFLICT: *A negative emotional state caused by an inability to choose between two or more incompatible goals or impulses.*

An **approach–approach conflict** is one in which a person must choose between two or more favorable alternatives. Thus, no matter what choice is made, the result will be desirable. At first it might seem that this type of conflict shouldn't create any stress, but consider the following example. Suppose you have to choose between two summer jobs. One job involves working at a resort where you are likely to meet interesting people and have a good time; the other job will provide you with valuable experience and might be helpful in a future career. No matter which job you choose, you will benefit in some way. In fact, you would like to take both jobs at once but you can't, and herein lies the source of stress.

APPROACH–APPROACH CONFLICT: *Conflict in which a person must choose between two alternatives that will both lead to desirable results.*

431

AVOIDANCE–AVOIDANCE CONFLICT: *Conflict in which a person must choose between two or more alternatives that will both lead to undesirable results.*

APPROACH–AVOIDANCE CONFLICT: *Conflict in which a person must make a choice that will lead to both desirable and undesirable results.*

An **avoidance–avoidance conflict** involves making a choice between two or more unpleasant alternatives that will lead to negative results, no matter which choice is made. The film (and book) *Sophie's Choice* provides a good example of an avoidance–avoidance conflict. Sophie is taken to a German concentration camp, along with her son and daughter. Upon her arrival in the camp, a soldier demands that she make the decision to give up (apparently to be killed) either her daughter *or* her son, or they both will be killed. Obviously, neither alternative is acceptable; both will have tragic results. Although this is an extreme example, you can see that avoidance–avoidance conflicts can lead to intense, and in Sophie's case long-lasting, stress.

An **approach–avoidance conflict** occurs when a person must choose whether to do something that will have both desirable *and* undesirable results. For example, we have all been faced with decisions like, "Should I become more involved with my girlfriend? If I do, I will enjoy the benefits of a close relationship, but I will also miss out on activities with my old friends." This conflict thus leads to a great deal of ambivalence. In an approach–avoidance conflict, we will experience both good and bad results from any alternative we choose.

The longer the conflict exists or the more important the decision, the more stress a person will experience. Generally, the approach–approach conflict is the easiest to resolve because no matter what choice is made, we will benefit in some way. The avoidance–avoidance conflict, on the other hand, is usually the most difficult to resolve because all choices will lead to unpleasant results. Approach–avoidance conflicts are somewhat less stressful than avoidance–avoidance conflicts, since they are usually moderately difficult to resolve.

Results of stress: How the body responds

When you are stressed, whether from psychological or physiological causes, your body undergoes several major and minor physiological changes, some of which we have already mentioned. The most significant changes are those controlled by the autonomic nervous system (see Chapter 2). These changes are particularly important because they can lead to a reduction in the body's resistance to disease.

Physiological effects of stress   Under normal, everyday low stress conditions, the parasympathetic part of the autonomic nervous system tends to lower heart rate and blood pressure while increasing the movement of muscles in the stomach and intestines. This allows the body to conserve energy, absorb nutrients, and maintain normal functioning. Under stressful conditions, the sympathetic part of the autonomic nervous system takes control, increasing heart rate and blood pressure, decreasing the movement of stomach muscles, and causing the release of several hormones into the bloodstream, the most significant of these being epinephrine (adrenalin).

There is a good reason for all this sympathetic activity. At the beginning of human evolutionary history, the autonomic nervous system could be easily characterized as the fight/flight system. Back then, when a person was under extreme stress—when she was being confronted by a bear or when he was being faced with a larger person encroaching on his territory—there were only two reasonable alternatives: fight or flee. Our ancestors, when faced with such stressors, needed the physiological boosts supplied to them by their sympathetic nervous system.

Today we retain the same autonomic responses of our ancient ancestors, but our world and our culture are quite different. When we encounter stressful situations, we rarely jump into action, so we have little need for increased heart rate, blood pressure, and hormone levels. In our culture we are taught not to fight or to flee but to attempt to stay calm and resolve stressful situations rationally. To comply with these cultural rules, we are left with no physical outlet for the physical changes caused by stressors. Thus, in our culture, the fight/flight response of the autonomic nervous system might even be *mal*-adaptive (Gill, 1983). It causes physiological changes that in the long run can be detri-

The fight/flight responses of the autonomic nervous system were necessary for a hunting and gathering society, but they may be less necessary for a modern society.

mental to health, contributing to such serious illnesses as heart disease and cancer (as we will see later in this chapter).

Hans Selye began investigating the body's reactions to stress over 50 years ago. In 1936, he described a generalized physiological reaction to severe stressors that consisted of three phases, which he called the **general adaptation syndrome** (see Figure 13.1). In the initial phase, called the *alarm reaction,* the body reacts to the stressor by activating the sympathetic nervous system (with increases in heart rate, blood pressure, secretion of epinephrine and other hormones, and so on). Because of this, the body has abundant energy and is highly alert and ready to deal with the stressor but is in a lowered state of resistance to illness. If the stressor remains, the body enters the *resistance phase.* In this phase, the alarm reaction subsides and the body adapts to the stressor, with resistance to illness increasing above normal levels. However, this period of adaptation and resistance requires considerable energy and is very taxing, and long-term exposure to the stressor will eventually lead to the *exhaustion phase.* During this final stage, the signs of the alarm reaction reappear, resistance to illness decreases, all adaptation energy becomes depleted, and the eventual result is death. Thus, Selye characterized long-term exposure to stressors as life-threatening.

GENERAL ADAPTATION SYNDROME: *As described by Selye, a generalized physiological reaction to severe stressors consisting of three phases: the alarm reaction, the resistance phase, and the exhaustion phase.*

Stress and the immune system   The physiological changes caused by stress can contribute to serious illness in a fundamental way by suppressing immune system functioning (Baum et al., 1982). Normal functioning of the immune system includes detecting and defending against disease. Therefore, suppression of the immune system can render the body susceptible to any number of diseases. Several studies have shown that significant stress, such as occurs with bereavement, surgery, and sleep deprivation, is related to changes in the immune system (Jemmott and Locke, 1984; Schleifer et al., 1980). These changes have been linked to high levels of such stress-related hormones as epinephrine, norepinephrine, and cortisol in the bloodstream. Recent research has shown that increases in these hormones often precede suppressed immune system function (Stein, 1983) and the appearance of infectious diseases (Jemmott and Locke, 1984).

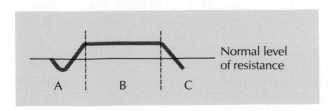

Normal level of resistance

A   B   C

Figure 13.1 The three phases of the general adaptation syndrome.

Question: So you're telling me that I might get a cold or the flu just because I've been under a lot of stress? You would be *more likely* to get a cold or the flu when under a lot of stress, since one stress reaction would be a suppression of your immune system. But a more noteworthy concern is that your stress may set the stage for your contracting more serious diseases, such as cancer and heart disease.

Review Questions

1. _____ is defined as the nonspecific response of the body to any demand made on it.

2. Any stimulus causing stress is known as a _____.

3. The Social Readjustment Rating Scale measures the amount of _____ in a person's life.

4. Long-term stressful situations such as a bad job or a bad marriage may result in _____ stress.

5. Stressful problems that are just part of daily living are called _____.

6. Frustration is a source of stress that occurs when a person is prevented from reaching a _____.

7. _____ arise when people are forced to make a choice between at least two alternatives.

8. The part of the autonomic nervous system that is activated under stressful conditions is the _____ nervous system.

9. The three-phase bodily response to chronic stress that includes the alarm reaction, the phase of resistance, and the stage of exhaustion is the _____ _____ _____.

10. People may be more likely to get a cold or flu if they are under a lot of stress because stress can suppress the _____ system.

Answers: 1 stress; *2* stressor; *3* change; *4* chronic; *5* hassles; *6* goal; *7* conflicts; *8* sympathetic; *9* general adaptation syndrome; *10* immune

STRESS AND SERIOUS ILLNESS

Psychological factors play a role in the development of a number of physical disorders, including heart disease, cancer, rheumatoid arthritis, bursitis, migraine headache, asthma, and gastrointestinal problems such as ulcers and colitis. We will discuss how stress caused by such psychological factors leads to physical ailments, but we will limit discussion to our society's two major killers: cancer and heart disease.

Cancer: A variety of causes — even stress

The word "cancer" strikes fear into the heart of nearly everyone. There is good reason for this: Cancer is the second major cause of death in North America. Cancer occurs when a body cell begins to replicate out of control, producing many more of this type of cell than there should be. These cells then begin to invade areas of healthy cells and, unless destroyed or removed, eventually cause damage to tissues and organs, resulting in death. To date, over 100 types of cancers have been identified. They appear to be caused by an interaction between hereditary predispositions, environmental factors, and changes in the body's immune system. Although we can do nothing about heredity, we can reduce the risk of cancer by making changes in our behavior.

When it was announced that Love Canal was the source of cancer causing pollution, people living near the canal chose to lessen their chances of exposure to the cancer-causing agents by moving away from the area.

Question: How can our behavior cause cancer?   Sometimes it seems like nearly everything causes cancer. Some familiar causes of cancer are substances found in our environment, such as cigarette smoke and harmful chemicals. Other major causes are internal biochemical (body chemistry) changes that may affect how cells replicate. What many people don't realize is that their behavior can affect both these factors. Your overt behavior can certainly put you in contact with environmental carcinogens. If you smoke you expose yourself to the cancer-causing substances in tobacco, if you work in an old building you may be exposed to asbestos fibers, and so on. To reduce environmental risk factors, you can simply avoid known carcinogens (which may not be so simple if you have to change your way of life, such as quitting smoking or finding a new job). How your behavior affects internal biochemistry is much more complex, however, and not so easily changed.

To comprehend the relationship between behavior and body chemistry, it helps to understand what normally happens to cancerous cells. Whenever cancer cells start to multiply, the immune system normally acts to check the uncontrolled growth by attacking the cancerous cells and bringing the growth under control (see the photograph on this page). This type of fight goes on constantly within the body, and in a normal, healthy person, the immune system manages to keep cancer cells in check.

Something different happens when the body is stressed. As we saw earlier, the stress response involves release of adrenal hormones that suppress immune system functioning. This suppression reduces the body's ability to resist not only disease organisms but cancer cell growth as well. Specifically, Riley (1981) has found that stress in animals can inhibit immune system defenses against cancer and can lead to enhanced tumor growth. This may indicate that, once a person has cancer, additional stress may further the growth of the tumor. Solomon, Amkraut, and Kasper (1974) have presented evidence suggesting that stress can also directly affect lymphocytes, the main cells that are used by the immune system to control cancer.

Stress is not the only way psychological factors influence immune function and possible cancer development. Ader and Cohen (1984) have shown in a classical conditioning experiment that suppression of immune function can be learned. They paired a neutral stimulus (saccharin) with drugs that suppress the normal functioning of the immune system. (The drug was the UCS and the suppressed immune function was the UCR.) Later, when the subjects were exposed to saccharin alone, they showed decreases in antibody response, an indication that the saccharin had become a conditioned stimulus and that there was a *learned* decrease in the immune system response. It is possible, then, that people can somehow inadvertently learn to lower their immunity to certain environmental carcinogens and therefore be more susceptible to cancer formation.

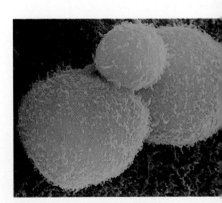

The smaller lymphocyte attacks and destroys two larger cancer cells.

Cardiovascular disorders: The leading cause of death in the United States

Cardiovascular disorders—specifically, hypertension and heart disease—are the major causes of over half of *all* deaths in the United States (Krantz, Grunberg, and Baum, 1985). Health psychologists are especially concerned with studying the effects of stress and other risk factors that have been identified as major contributors to these disorders.

HYPERTENSION: *Excessive muscular tension and high blood pressure.*

Hypertension   **Hypertension** is a state of chronically elevated blood pressure. In a small percentage of the cases of hypertension (about 10 percent), the increased blood pressure is caused by some physical ailment, such as kidney disease, but in the vast majority of cases there is no medical cause. In these latter cases, the disorder is called **essential hypertension.**

ESSENTIAL HYPERTENSION: *State of chronically elevated blood pressure that has no detectable medical cause.*

It is not clear whether stress can actually cause essential hypertension, but it is clear that people with essential hypertension tend to react to stressful situations with more exaggerated and prolonged blood pressure increases (Goldstein, 1981). These exaggerated reactions have been demonstrated in response to cold (Hines and Brown, 1936), to breath holding (Ayman and Goldshine, 1939), to exercise (Alam and Smirk, 1938; Groen et al., 1977), and to mental stressors such as doing arithmetic problems (Brod, 1970; Faulkner et al., 1979).

Question: Why should people with high blood pressure be concerned?   Because their blood pressure reactions are more intense and last longer, hypertensive people are more likely to be susceptible to the negative effects of stress. Hypertensives are also good candidates for stroke, since the extra pressure in brain blood vessels could cause weakened or clogged vessels to burst. In addition, high blood pressure places undue stress on the heart, causing it to work harder, which could ultimately lead to heart attack. Therefore, it is a good idea to follow a doctor's advice if he or she tells you, as our heart attack patient's doctor told him, to reduce your salt intake or to lose weight. Excess sodium increases the amount of water in the blood, making the heart pump faster to supply the body with enough oxygen. Excess weight means excess tissue that needs to be oxygenated.

HEART DISEASE: *General term used to include all disorders that in some way affect the heart muscle and can ultimately result in heart failure.*

Heart disease   **Heart disease** is a general term used to include all disorders that eventually affect the heart muscle and lead to heart failure, such as clogged arteries and simple overtaxing of the heart. Researchers have pinpointed certain factors that contrib-

"Wow! What a day to be a workaholic!"

Drawing by Ross; © 1986 The New Yorker Magazine, Inc.

ute to heart disease: smoking, stress, certain personality characteristics, obesity, a high-fat diet, and lack of exercise.

Question: I understand how stress can be a contributor to cancer, but how does it contribute to heart disease? You may remember that one of the major results of the autonomic nervous system fight/flight reaction is to release the hormones epinephrine and cortisol into the bloodstream. Epinephrine and cortisol act together to increase the heart rate and remove fat from the body's stores so that the muscles can have a quickly available source of energy. If some physical action is taken, such as fight or flight, the fat is used as an energy source and there are no ill effects. If, on the other hand, no physical action is taken (and this is most likely to be the case in our modern lives), the fat that is released into the bloodstream may begin to form fatty deposits on the walls of the blood vessels (see the photograph on the right). These fatty deposits are a major cause of the blood supply blockages that cause heart attacks (Lee, 1983). In fact, the heart attack of the patient in our opening example could very well have been caused in this way, since he was a person who was continually under a lot of stress.

The effects of stress may be amplified if an individual tends to be hard-driving, competitive, ambitious, impatient, and hostile. People with such **Type A personalities** are chronically on edge, tend to talk rapidly, and like our heart attack patient, are constantly preoccupied with responsibilities and feel an intense time urgency. The antithesis of the Type A personality is Type B. People with a **Type B personality** have a laid-back, calm, relaxed attitude toward life.

The Type A personality was first described by two cardiologists, Meyer Friedman and Ray Rosenman (1959). The idea for the Type A personality may have been planted in the mid-1950s, when an upholsterer who was recovering the waiting room chairs in Friedman's office noticed an odd wear pattern. He mentioned to Friedman that all the chairs looked like new except for the front edges, which were badly worn, as if all the patients sat only on the edges of the chairs. Initially, this didn't seem too important to Friedman, but he has since changed his mind. He and Rosenman formulated a theory that the Type A personality may be a contributing factor to heart disease and essential hypertension.

Question: How can I tell whether I'm a Type A? Psychologists assess personality types by using a questionnaire in an interview situation. You can probably get an idea of whether you are Type A, Type B, or some combination of the two by looking over Table 13.2, which provides profiles of both Type A and Type B personalities as they are revealed in such interviews.

Initial research into Type A behavior suggested it was a prominent risk factor in both heart disease and hypertension. However, more recent research has not found such a strong relationship (Mathews, 1984; Williams, 1984). The reason seems to be that not all the Type A personality characteristics contribute to heart disease; perhaps only certain characteristics — hostility, anger, and vigorous speech — are contributors (Dembroski et al., 1985).

Redford Williams (1984) isolated hostility and cynicism as contributing factors. In his research, he has concluded that Type A's with a cynical, hostile outlook on life are at an *increased* risk for heart disease, whereas Type A's with a positive outlook on life actually are at *lowered* risk.

Question: Why is it that cynicism is related to heart disease? By possessing a negative attitude toward the world in general, cynical people feel as if they must be constantly on the alert to foresee problems and to work to avert those problems. This attitude produces a nearly constant state of stress. In addition, Type A people also tend to have a more pronounced and longer-lasting reaction to stressful situations (Williams, 1984).

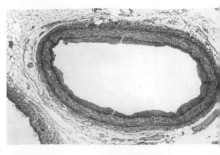
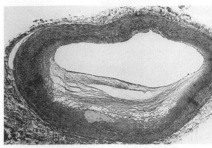
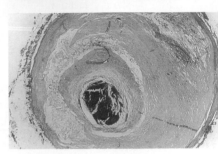

One major cause of heart disease is the blockage of arteries that supply blood to the heart. The artery on the top is normal, the one in the center is partially blocked by fatty deposits, and the one on the bottom is completely blocked. Stress is thought to contribute to such fatty build-up.

TYPE A PERSONALITY: *Set of behavior characteristics that includes intense ambition, competition, drive, constant preoccupation with deadlines, a sense of time urgency, and a cynical, hostile outlook.*

TYPE B PERSONALITY: *Set of behavior characteristics consistent with a calm, patient, relaxed attitude toward life.*

TABLE 13.2
Profiles of the Type A and Type B Behavior Patterns

Characteristics	Type A	Type B
Speech		
Rate	Rapid	Slow
Word production	Single-word answers; acceleration at the end of sentences	Measured; frequent pauses or breaks
Volume	Loud	Soft
Quality	Vigorous, terse, harsh	"Walter Mitty" monotone
Intonation/inflection	Abrupt, explosive speech, key word emphasis	
Response latency	Immediate answers	Pauses before answering
Length of responses	Short and to the point	Long, rambling
Other	Word clipping, word omission, word repetition	
Behaviors		
Sighing	Frequent	Rare
Posture	Tense, on the edge of the chair	Relaxed, comfortable
General demeanor	Alert, intense	Calm; quiet attentiveness
Facial expression	Tense, hostile; grimace	Relaxed, friendly
Smile	Lateral	Broad
Laughter	Harsh	Gentle chuckle
Wrist clenching	Frequent	Rare
Responses to the interview		
Interrupts interviewer	Often	Rarely
Returns to previous subject when interrupted	Often	Rarely
Attempts to finish interviewer's questions	Often	Rarely
Uses humor	Rarely	Often
Hurries the interviewer ("yes, yes," "m-m," head nodding)	Often	Rarely
Competes for control of the interview	Wide variety of techniques—interruptions, verbal duets, extraneous comments, lengthy or evasive answers, questioning or correcting the interviewer	Rarely
Hostility	Often demonstrated during the interview through mechanisms such as boredom, condescension, authoritarianism, challenge	None
Typical content		
Satisfied with job	No, wants to move up	Yes
Hard-driving, ambitious	Yes, by own and others' judgments	Not particularly
Feels a sense of time urgency	Yes	No
Impatient	Dislikes waiting in lines, will not wait at a restaurant, annoyed when caught behind a slow-moving vehicle	Takes delays of all kinds in stride and does not become frustrated or annoyed
Competitive	Enjoys competition on the job, plays all games (even with children) to win	Does not thrive on competition and rarely engages in competitive activities
Admits to polyphasic thinking and activities	Often does or thinks two (or more) things at the same time	Rarely does or thinks two things at once
Hostility	In content and stylistics—argumentative responses, excessive qualifications, harsh generalizations, challenges, emotion-laden words, obscenity	Rarely present in any content

Source: Chesney, Eagleston, and Rosenman (1981).

438

Question: Is it possible to change a Type A into a Type B? Since Type A personality (or at least aspects of it) is a significant risk factor in heart disease, it would be advantageous for Type A people to modify some of their behavior characteristics. Type A's with a positive outlook on life may not need to change their behavior, but cynical Type A's would be well advised to slow down and smell the roses. Health psychologists have developed two approaches to Type A behavior modification, the shotgun approach and the target behavior approach.

In the **shotgun approach,** the attempt is made to alter all the behaviors that relate to the Type A personality. Type A people are encouraged to slow down and to perform tasks that are incompatible with their personality. For example, Type A people might be asked to try to *listen* to other people without interrupting, plan quiet times when they just try to relax and do nothing, stand in the *longest* bank line on purpose, and so on. According to Williams's research, however, this shotgun type of approach may eliminate many desirable Type A traits. More effective is the **target behavior approach,** which focuses on only those Type A behaviors that are likely to cause heart disease, especially those that lead to a cynical and hostile outlook on life. By modifying these targeted behaviors, the person will more than likely reduce his or her risk of heart disease.

Stress and Type A behavior are not the only risk factors associated with heart disease, of course. As we mentioned previously, other major risk factors include smoking, obesity, a high-fat diet, and lack of exercise. Obesity can place direct stress on the heart itself because excess weight causes the heart to have to pump more blood to the excess body tissue. A high-fat diet, especially one high in cholesterol, can contribute to the fatty deposits that clog blood vessels. Lack of exercise contributes to weight gain and prevents the body from obtaining important exercise benefits, including strengthening of heart muscles, increased heart efficiency, and utilization of stress-related hormones and the fatty acids those hormones cause to be released.

In summary, to minimize the chances of developing cancer or heart disease, we should eat properly, exercise regularly, try to have a positive outlook on life, and try to avoid all environmental factors known to be contributors to disease. We should also try to learn how to deal with stressful situations in a way that will minimize negative physiological effects.

SHOTGUN APPROACH: *The technique used in behavioral change whereby there is an attempt to change all the behaviors constituting the Type A personality.*

TARGET BEHAVIOR APPROACH: *The technique used in behavioral change whereby there is an attempt to change only Type A behaviors that have specifically been found to lead to heart disease, particularly those accompanied by a hostile and cynical attitude.*

"TYPICAL 'TYPE A' BEHAVIOR."

Review Questions

1. Stress can contribute to cancer by _____ the immune system.

2. Chronic high blood pressure is called _____.

3. Stress can have a major effect on essential hypertension because hypertensives tend to _____ to stressful situations.

4. Stress can contribute to heart disease by releasing the hormones _____ and _____, which cause an increase in the level of fat in the blood.

5. People who are ambitious, competitive, and hurried may have a _____ personality.

6. People who have a laid-back, calm, relaxed attitude are considered to have a _____ personality.

7. The factor within the Type A personality that is most related to heart disease is _____.

8. The two major approaches to modifying Type A behavior are the _____ approach and the _____ _____ approach.

Answers: 1 suppressing; *2* hypertension; *3* overreact; *4* cortisol, epinephrine; *5* Type A; *6* Type B; *7* hostility or cynicism; *8* shotgun, target behavior.

COPING WITH STRESS

In light of all the adverse effects of excess stress, you may feel by now that you should try to avoid all stressful situations. However, this is virtually impossible. Everyone is bound to occasionally encounter some type of stress in the form of pressure at work, daily hassles, the death of a family member, and so on. The way to escape the adverse effects of stress is to learn how to effectively deal with various types of stressors.

COPING: *Attempting to manage stress in some effective way.*

Traditionally, effectively dealing with stress has been called **coping**. But coping does not always lead to what most people consider successful outcomes. For example, one way to cope with extreme stress is to totally withdraw from the real world. This complete withdrawal, although effective in reducing the body's stress reactions, is otherwise maladaptive.

Lazarus and Folkman (1984) define coping as "constantly changing cognitive and behavioral efforts to manage specific external and/or internal demands that are appraised as taxing or exceeding the resource of the person." In simpler terms, *coping* is an attempt to manage stress in some effective way. It consists not of one single act but is a process that allows us to deal with various stressors. This process can take two main forms: It can focus on the emotional effects of the stressor, or it can focus on solving the problem causing the stress.

Emotion-focused forms of coping: Reappraising the situation

EMOTION-FOCUSED FORMS OF COPING: *Coping strategies that lead to changes in one's perceptions of stressful situations.*

Emotion-focused forms of coping are emotional or cognitive strategies that lead to changes in how one views or appraises stressful situations, rather than strategies for changing the situation themselves. For example, suppose you are turned down for a job you wanted very much. You might reappraise the situation and decide that the job wasn't for you in the first place. [Or if your current significant other (husband, wife, boyfriend, girlfriend, dog, horse, or whatever) just ran off with someone else, you might decide that he/she/it was not your type after all.]

Often, as a means of coping, people use psychological *defense mechanisms,* strategies that are unconsciously employed to protect the ego and avoid anxiety while distorting reality (see Chapter 14). Although defense mechanisms may alleviate feelings of anxiety and guilt, they may not be beneficial in the long run. For instance, people often use *rationalization,* the fabrication of excuses, when they are frustrated in attaining particular goals, such as concluding that they didn't get a job because they didn't have the right "connections." Defense mechanisms, as well as other emotion-focused forms of coping, can sometimes lead to dangerous results. For example, an oft-used coping method is *denial,* in which a person refuses to acknowledge that a problem exists. When our heart attack patient was diagnosed as suffering from essential hypertension, he refused to accept the upsetting fact that the disease might lead to his death. This denial led to a failure to take his medication and follow the doctor's other recommendations, an all too common problem today.

Although emotion-focused forms of coping can at times distort reality, they can be used successfully as positive coping strategies when they are accurate reappraisals of stressful situations. Many times, however, it is necessary and more effective to confront the stressor directly.

Problem-focused forms of coping: Putting problem-solving skills to work

Problem-focused forms of coping are strategies that deal directly with the situation or the stressor in ways that will eventually decrease or eliminate it. Generally, these approaches are the same as problem-solving strategies (see Chapter 8). Thus, the better a person is at solving problems, the more likely he or she will develop effective coping strategies. These strategies consist of identifying the stressful problem, generating possible solutions, selecting the appropriate solution, and applying the solution to the problem, thereby eliminating the stress.

To illustrate the difference between the two forms of coping, let's suppose that your professor loses your term paper and threatens to give you an "F" for the semester. You could cognitively reappraise the situation and decide that one "F" won't hurt you (emotion-focused approach). Or you could generate ideas and decide on a course of action that would compel the professor to take the responsibility for the loss and thereby avoid the "F" (problem-focused approach).

Question: It sounds like emotion-focused forms of coping are really just "copping out." Is this right?   Many people think of problem-focused coping as true coping and of emotion-focused coping as copping out. However, it is not necessary to master a problem or stressor in order to relieve stress, and at times emotion-focused coping may be the only way to deal with a problem. Under many situations, dealing with emotions can even lead to mastery of the problem. Imagine that you are about to take your first exam in a difficult course. You are especially anxious, since you don't know whether you studied enough, you don't know what kind of test the professor gives, and you feel that you may forget everything that you've learned once the test is in front of you. Exams can be extremely stressful for many students. If you take an emotion-focused approach to this situation, you will first try to calm your fears. You might say to yourself, "Relax and take a deep breath; it can't be as bad as I imagine." If this strategy proves effective at reducing your anxiety, you can then use problem-focused coping techniques and focus on answering the questions on the test, thereby dispelling both your stress and your problem. As this example illustrates, both types of coping can be used together in certain situations.

Resources for effective coping: From good health to money

A person's ability to cope effectively depends on the stressor itself — its complexity, intensity, and length of duration — and on the type of coping strategy used. It also depends on what resources are available to provide "background support" for the individual. Lazarus and Folkman (1984) list several major types of coping resources: health and energy, positive beliefs, problem-solving skills, social skills, social support, and material resources.

PROBLEM-FOCUSED FORMS OF COPING: *Coping strategies in which one views stressful situations as problems and uses problem-solving strategies to decrease or eliminate the source of stress.*

Health and energy All stressors cause some type of physiological changes. Therefore, the health of an individual under stress significantly affects his or her ability to cope. If you refer back to Figure 13.1, depicting the general adaptation syndrome, you can see that the stage of resistance is a coping stage. The stronger and healthier people are, the longer they can cope without entering the stage of exhaustion.

Positive beliefs A positive self-image and a positive attitude can be especially significant coping resources. Hope can sustain a person in the face of severe odds, as is often documented in news reports of people who have triumphed over seemingly unbeatable circumstances. According to Lazarus and Folkman, such hope can come from a belief in oneself, which can enable us to devise our own coping strategies; a belief in others, such as medical doctors, whom we feel can effect positive outcomes; or a belief in a just and helpful God. In his book *Anatomy of an Illness* (1979) Norman Cousins describes how he attributes his recovery from a usually fatal disease to an overall positive outlook and to such positive emotions as laughter, hope, confidence, and the will to live. Having read Hans Selye's (1956) account of how negative emotions can lead to negative effects on body chemistry, Cousins pondered the effects of positive emotions. This led him to initiate, in partnership with his physician, a self-prescribed recovery program that, he claims, proves true the saying "Laughter is the best medicine." Along with a determined will to live and a swearing off of many traditional methods for treating similar illnesses, he took liberal doses of movie comedies, including Marx Brothers films, and read several humorous books. Nezu et al. (1988) provide research support for this idea.

It has been found that people who feel that they have an internal locus of control — or a feeling that they have significant control over the events in their lives — tend to cope more successfully than those who feel that they have no control (Strickland, 1978). For example, when faced with severe illness, people with an internal locus of control are more likely to collect information about their disease and to stay on a program of health maintenance than those who have an external locus of control (Wallston, Maides, and Wallston, 1976).

Social skills Social situations — meetings, discussion groups, parties, dates, and so on — are often a source of pleasure, but they can also be a source of stress. Merely meeting and talking to a stranger, an acquaintance, or even a friend can be stressful if we don't know what to say or how to act. The more social skills we possess, the less stress we will experience in these situations. Our social skills also help us to communicate our needs, enlist help, and decrease hostility.

Social support An important resource for coping is social support from friends, families, and social organizations such as fraternal organizations and churches (de Longis et al., 1988). In recent years, support groups for specific problems have arisen, such as hospices for terminally ill people and their families, Alcoholics Anonymous and related groups for families of alcoholics, support groups for former drug addicts and for families of drug addicts, support groups for divorced people or for single parents, and so on. Support groups help people cope not only because they provide other people to lean on but also because people can learn techniques for coping when around others with similar problems. The idea of community support maintenance organizations providing psychological and social support has been suggested by Leff and Bradley (1986). Support groups can prove invaluable, especially for those people who are faced with long-term stressful situations such as illness or poverty (House, Landis, and Umberson, 1988).

Material resources We've all heard the saying, "Money isn't everything." But when it comes to coping with stress, money and the things that money can buy can be very real resources, since they increase the number of options available to eliminate sources of stress or to reduce the effects of stress. When people have sufficient income, they can afford to eat a balanced and healthful diet, seek needed medical or psychological help, or quit a job that is detrimental to their health and reeducate themselves for another. They

These women recently widowed have realized that an important resource for coping with stressors such as the death of a spouse is social support from friends, families, and social organizations.

Even mild forms of exercise, such as walking, can help reduce the negative effects of stress.

can afford to join health spas or other exercise programs, live in a relatively crime-free neighborhood, buy a house that was built according to current fire, earthquake, and other safety standards, and so on. Whether they are faced with the minor hassles of everyday living, with chronic stressors, or with major catastrophes, people with money who have the skills to effectively use that money generally fare much better and experience much less stress that those without money (Lazarus and Folkman, 1984).

Specific coping strategies: How you can reduce stress

Question: What are the specific things I should do, then, to reduce stress in my life? Many ways to successfully cope with stress have already been discussed: appraising situations rationally and realistically, maintaining the conviction that you are in control of your life and have control over how you deal with your stress, focusing on the positive rather than on the negative aspects of stressful situations, and learning as much as you can about how to solve problems and problem situations in order to resolve them quickly and easily.

In addition to these cognitive coping methods, there are a number of other active methods, including relaxation and exercise. Active coping methods "provide more direct and deliberate means of controlling and reducing the impact of stress . . . [and] prepare us to deal with unexpected stress and keep us in stress-ready condition" (Gill, 1983, p. 84).

Relaxation One of the most effective means of dealing with physical stress reactions is to relax during stressful situations. You can learn to relax through a variety of techniques, including biofeedback, self-hypnosis, meditation, and progressive relaxation. Perhaps the easiest of these techniques is *progressive relaxation*. Here's how to do it:

1. Make sure you are sitting in a comfortable position, with your head supported.
2. Start breathing slowly and deeply.
3. Let your entire body go limp and try to let go of any tension that remains. Try to visualize your body getting more relaxed.
4. Systematically tense and release each part of your body, beginning with your toes. Focus your attention on your toes and try to visualize what they are doing. Curl them tightly while counting to 10, then release them and feel the difference between the tense state and the relaxed state. Next, tense your feet to the count of 5, then relax them and feel the difference between the two states. Continue with your calves, thighs, buttocks, abdomen, back muscles, shoulders, upper arms, forearms, hand and fingers, neck, jaws, facial muscles, and forehead.

This technique is much more effective if you remember to use visual images of your body relaxing. After practicing progressive relaxation twice a day for about 15 minutes per session, you will be able to relax within a short time. You should be able to use these techniques whenever you are feeling stressed, such as after driving to work through traffic or while waiting in class to begin an exam.

Exercise   Exercise plays several roles in reducing the negative effects of stress. First, it utilizes the hormones secreted into the bloodstream during stress, thereby reducing the chances of their inhibiting immune system functioning. Second, exercise can help work out tension that has built up in muscles. Third, exercise increases strength, flexibility, and stamina for encountering future stressors and increases the efficiency of the cardiovascular system. The best exercise for these purposes is *aerobic exercise*—regular strenuous activity that heightens cardiovascular functioning, such as brisk walking, jogging, bicycling, swimming, dancing, and so on.

Health psychologists have found that by minimizing the amount of stress in our lives, we help our bodies stay well and fight off disease. We can further help to maintain wellness by avoiding smoking, eating nutritionally balanced diets, exercising regularly, and, among other factors, adopting an internal locus of control and a positive attitude toward life.

Review Questions

1 The attempt to manage stress in some effective way is known as _____ .

2 The two major forms of coping with stress are _____ and _____ .

3 Rationalization and denial are examples of _____ _____ .

4 People are better able to cope with stress if they have an _____ locus of control.

5 Two specific techniques used to reduce stress are _____ and _____ .

Answers: 1 coping;   *2* emotion-focused, problem-focused;   *3* defense mechanisms;   *4* internal;   *5* relaxation, exercise

---

REVIEW OF MAJOR CONCEPTS

THE NATURE OF HEALTH PSYCHOLOGY

1 Health psychology can be defined as the study of the relationship between psychological behavior and physical health and illness, with an emphasis on "wellness" and the prevention of illness.

2 Health psychologists work with patients who are about to undergo complex surgical procedures by teaching them what to anticipate during and after the operation and provide them and their families with methods and suggestions for dealing with psychological problems that may develop following surgery.

3 Health psychologists help chronic pain patients by teaching them to cope with their pain through such techniques as operant conditioning, biofeedback, and altered attention techniques such as relaxation and self-hypnosis.

4 Because smoking is the single most preventable cause of death and disease in the United States, prevention and cessation of smoking are of primary importance to all health practitioners, including health psychologists.

5 Smoking prevention programs involve educating the public about short- and long-term consequences of smoking, try-

ing to make smoking less socially acceptable, and helping nonsmokers resist social pressures to smoke.

6 Approaches to help people quit smoking include behavior modification techniques such as covert sensitization, stimulus control, and aversion therapy; techniques to aid smokers in their withdrawal from nicotine; and techniques for dealing with social pressures.

STRESS AND ITS ROLE IN HEALTH

7 Stress is the nonspecific response of the body to any demand made on it. Any stimulus that causes stress is called a stressor. There are both beneficial and nonbeneficial types of stress.

8 Among the many causes of stress are life changes, chronic stress, hassles, frustration, and conflicts.

9 When stressed, the body undergoes several physiological changes. The sympathetic part of the autonomic nervous system is activated, increasing heart rate and blood pressure. This sympathetic activation is beneficial if people need to fight or flee, but it can have negative consequences if they do not.

10 Hans Selye described a generalized physiological reaction to severe stressors, which he called the general adaptation syndrome. The general adaptation syndrome has three phases: the alarm reaction, the resistance phase, and the exhaustion phase.

11 Prolonged stress can cause suppression of the immune system, which can render the body susceptible to any number of diseases, including colds, flu, and even such serious diseases as cancer.

STRESS AND SERIOUS ILLNESS

12 Cancer can be caused by environmental factors, such as cigarette smoke or asbestos, or by changes in body chemistry that affect how certain cells within the body replicate. During times of stress, the body may be less able to check cancerous tissue growth because of suppression of the immune system.

13 The leading cause of death in the United States is cardiovascular disease. The two major cardiovascular diseases are essential hypertension and heart disease. Essential hypertension is an increase in blood pressure that does not have a medical cause. Hypertension can cause the heart to work harder, making the individual more prone to stroke and heart attack. Heart disease includes all illnesses that eventually affect the heart muscle and lead to heart failure.

14 Risk factors in heart disease include smoking, stress, obesity, a high-fat diet, lack of exercise, and Type A personality traits. The two main approaches to modifying Type A behavior are the shotgun approach and the target behavior approach.

COPING WITH STRESS

15 The two major forms of coping with stress are emotion-focused and problem-focused. Emotion-focused forms of coping are strategies that lead to changes in how we view or appraise stressful situations, rather than strategies for changing the situations themselves. Problem-focused forms of coping involve strategies that deal directly with the situation or the factor causing the stress in ways that will eventually decrease or eliminate it.

16 The ability to cope with a stressor also depends on the resources available to help people cope with the stress. Such resources include health and energy, positive beliefs, social skills, social support, and material resources.

17 Relaxation techniques and exercise are specific behaviors that can help people cope effectively with stress.

SUGGESTED READINGS

GREENBERG, J. S. (1983). *Comprehensive stress management* Dubuque, IA: Wm. C. Brown. Written in a personal, informal style, this book provides a comprehensive view of stress and stress management.

LAZARUS, R. S., & FOLKMAN, S. (1984). *Stress, appraisal, and coping.* New York: Springer. A detailed theory of the psychology of stress.

MATARAZZO, J. D., WEISS, S. M., HERD, J. A., MILLER, N. E., & WEISS, S. M. (EDS.) (1984). *Behavioral health.* New York: Wiley. A collection of some of the most significant findings in health psychology.

SELYE, H. (1974). *Stress without distress.* Signet. A short book outlining how to use stress as a positive force in your life.

chapter fourteen
Personality

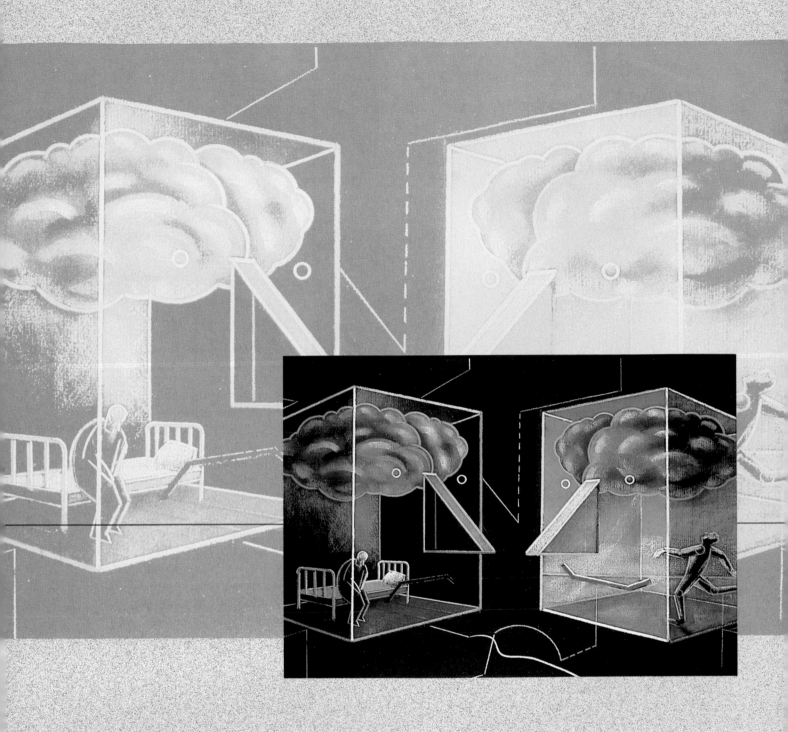

IN 1909, the Austrian psychoanalyst Sigmund Freud was invited to deliver a lecture series in the United States to describe his observations of personality development and to explain his therapy methods. Freud had become accustomed to reactions of skepticism and anger whenever he described his ideas. When he lectured, his physician colleagues in Europe were shocked by his emphasis on the importance of sexual and aggressive impulses in creating behaviors. The professor who presided over one such lecture in 1896 had dismissed Freud's theory as a "scientific fairy tale" (Jones, 1961, p. 167). In a letter to one of his friends describing the icy reception he had received at that meeting, Freud said, "I innocently addressed a meeting of the Vienna Society for Psychiatry and Neurology, expecting that the material losses I had willingly undergone would be made up for by the interest and recognition of my colleagues" (Freud, 1914/1963, p. 21). When these people he wanted to impress rejected his views, Freud said, "They can all go to hell."

Freud's own personality development had apparently been influenced by the fact that he was a Jew living in Austria, a country where Jews were heavily discriminated against and persecuted. The Vienna that was to teach Adolf Hitler his passionate hatred of Jews was his social environment. His family's poverty may have left indelible impressions on him as well.

Despite the social barriers of this time and place, Freud did well in school and entered the University of Vienna as a medical student at the age of 17. He enjoyed laboratory research and wanted to become a professor. But when one of his favorite professors told him that he would have little chance of advancing in that profession because he was poor and Jewish, he studied neurology and entered private practice. As a neurologist, treating nervous system problems, he became interested in patients whose physical problems (such as paralysis or blindness) seemed to be psychologically caused and were not curable by the usual medical treatments. In Freud's day, this kind of problem was called **hysterical neurosis,** and he found that the symptoms could often be treated through the use of hypnosis. Eventually, Freud limited his practice to patients whose problems were assumed to be psychological. He spent his days listening to patients relate their childhood experiences, often reliving with them their memories of sexual assault and betrayal.

Sharing the unpleasant experiences of his patients may have deepened Freud's own cynicism about human nature. From his letters to friends and his descriptions of himself, we have a picture of a man wrestling with pain, one who suffered from periodic depressions, apathy, and fatigue. He sometimes had attacks of anxiety and dwelt on fears of dying. He was moody and alternated between periods of excitement when he felt confident and periods of depression when he doubted

HYSTERICAL NEUROSIS: A disorder with physical symptoms created by psychological factors.

448

himself and could neither write nor concentrate. When he was 29, he wrote in a letter, "I never felt so fresh in my life," and then the following day wrote, "I can't stand it much longer" (Jones, 1961, p. 112). Freud suffered migraine headaches, indigestion, and constipation, and he was afraid of traveling by railroad. He used cocaine to raise himself out of his moods of depression and became dependent on cigars (the smoking of which eventually killed him).

During his self-analysis, he attempted to make sense out of the contradictions of his behavior by looking for hidden causes from his past. By concentrating on this task, he became aware of some painful memories from his childhood that he had seemingly forgotten. For example, he recalled seeing his mother naked and feeling sexually aroused. Even though he had grieved

deeply over the death of his father, his self-analysis revealed intense feelings of hostility toward his father that he had buried deeply. He remembered a time when he had deliberately urinated in his parents' bedroom at the age of seven or eight. His father had punished him and said, "That boy will never amount to anything" (Jones, 1961, p. 15).

Despite this harsh prediction, Freud's parents were actually quite supportive of his efforts and expected great things of him. Their "Golden Siggy" proved them correct (Gay, 1988). Arising from a modest family background and an anti-semitic culture, Freud eventually founded an entire school of psychology and became such an eminent therapist that Hollywood's Samuel Goldwyn offered $100,000 for his consulting services (Sheppard, 1988).

Like all of us, Sigmund Freud was a complex and unique individual with a distinctive personality. It is difficult to describe or explain how each of us, from famous psychologists like Freud to the person who lives next door, has developed particular ways of interacting with the world. Despite the problems involved, people find it fascinating to try to understand what makes us the persons we are. For instance, when we read a good novel or biography, we can get engrossed in the descriptions of the characters. We can often form a clear mental picture of what the person must look like and try to predict how that person would behave in new situations. When we have become absorbed in a murder mystery, this kind of character analysis often allows us to figure out "who done it" long before the author tells us.

It is an interesting form of entertainment to attempt to understand people. It is also useful in our personal interactions to be able to figure out what people are like, to understand what "makes them tick," and to be able to anticipate their reactions.

It is not always possible in real life situations, however, to be able to predict with certainty how a person will behave, even when we know that person well. Sometimes people do things we don't expect or understand. How can we explain the behaviors of serial murderers who seem to enjoy the repeated luring and murdering of unsuspecting victims? At the other end of the human spectrum, how do we account for the actions of people who go out of their way and even risk their lives to help others they don't even know? Psychologists who attempt to describe and explain such differences in human behavior from a scientific perspective are concerned with the study of personality, or what makes each person unique.

Question: What exactly is personality? As with other abstract concepts such as "motives" or "intelligence," the term personality has many meanings. In fact, Gordon Allport (1937) identified more than 50 different definitions of the word. For our purposes, **personality** is defined as an individual's characteristic pattern of thoughts, emotions, and observable behaviors. Psychologists studying personality are interested in describing and measuring individual differences in all kinds of behavior and analyzing how those differences came about. They are also concerned with describing a personality as an integrated whole rather than as a collection of bits and pieces.

The approaches that personality researchers take and the conclusions they reach depend greatly on their theoretical orientation (Ewen, 1984). That is, psychologists who start with different assumptions about basic human nature will reach different conclu-

PERSONALITY: *An individual's characteristic pattern of thoughts, emotions, and behaviors, which make him or her unique.*

Are you a good judge of character and personality? Which of these five individuals is a vicious serial killer, which an attempted assassin, and which an author of this text? The answers appear at the bottom of this page.

sions about how personality develops. For example, psychologists with a behaviorist orientation might conclude that Sigmund Freud became a successful doctor rather than a lawyer, merchant, or thief because of the patterns of rewards he received during his lifetime. Other psychologists might claim that Freud's motivation to succeed came from inborn drives that were strongly influenced by his early family experiences. Still others would emphasize the importance of the self-concept he developed as he dealt with other people. In this chapter, we will examine each of the major theoretical approaches to personality, both classical and contemporary. We will then describe how psychologists use various kinds of tests to assess personality.

CLASSICAL THEORIES OF PERSONALITY

Prior to the 1960s, three approaches to the study of personality provided our core assumptions for understanding individual differences: type theories, trait theories, and psychoanalytic theories (Mischel, 1984). Each of these approaches assumed that people can be analyzed and understood by using physical or behavioral signs as a means of describing their current behavior and predicting their future behavior. Because of their important impact on the study of personality, we will begin by examining these three classical approaches.

Type theories: Pigeonholing people into categories

One of the simplest and oldest ways of describing personality differences is to categorize people into "types" on the basis of a major characteristic (Coan, 1984). A **typology** is a system used to classify individuals according to certain criteria. A typology looks at a broad aspect or characteristic and relates the differences in people to that aspect. As we saw in the previous chapter, for example, people who are competitive and hard-driving have been classified as Type A's, whereas people who are relaxed and easygoing are often categorized as Type B's.

The desire to quickly understand and categorize people into a few basic personality types has great appeal. For example, three of the individuals in the photographs above are authors of this text and the other two are either an attempted assassin or a rapist and serial killer. Can you identify the authors versus the criminals? To make this type of decision, most people rely on individualized typing systems, which reflect their unique life histories and personal stereotypes (Deaux and Wrightsman, 1988). (If you want to check how well you did in categorizing these individuals, the answers are provided at the bottom of this page.)

TYPOLOGY: *A system used for classification of individuals according to certain criteria.*

Answers to "personality quiz" in the photographs above: Photo 1 *Ken Bianchi (convicted rapist and serial killer),* Photo 2 *Mark Vernoy (an author of this text),* Photo 3 *Judy Vernoy (another author of this text),* Photo 4 *"Squeaky" Fromme (an attempted assassin),* Photo 5 *Karen Huffman (a third author of this text).*

TABLE 14.1
The Four Humoral Personality Types

Personality Type	An Excess of	Personality Description
Sanguine	Blood	Warm, passionate, cheerful, confident, optimistic, hopeful
Melancholic	Black bile	Gloomy, irritable, depressed, pensive, sad
Phlegmatic	Phlegm	Hard to rouse to action, sluggish, dull, calm, cool, imperturbable, not easily disconcerted or aroused
Choleric	Yellow bile	Easily angered, quick tempered, volatile

Just as individuals tend to develop discrete categories for classifying people, every science has found it necessary to develop classifications of its basic phenomena, whether stars, species of animals, or psychological attributes (Zuckerman, Kulman, and Camac, 1988). One of the earliest attempts to classify personality types came from the Greek physician Hippocrates during the fifth century B.C. Hippocrates believed that people's differences in activity level and emotional expression were due to an imbalance of the four humors or body fluids: blood, phlegm, yellow bile, and black bile. An excess of each humor was said to create specific personality characteristics. This humoral theory of personality types was further popularized in the second century A.D. by another Greek physician, Claudius Galen (see Table 14.1).

As you may imagine, type theories have received a fair share of criticism. Just as our own "pet" theories of personality types are often faulty and reflective of our personal prejudices, Hippocrates and Galen's humoral theories reflected their limited information and neither theory was substantiated by later research. One of the most common complaints about modern-day typologies (such as Type A's and Type B's) is that the full range of human personality is difficult to compress into a few, discrete types. It is also common observation that people are not always clearly one type or another but actually represent a blend between types. To avoid such problems, many psychologists have instead used a *trait* approach to studying personality. This perspective recognizes a range or combination of possibilities for differences in people.

Trait theories: Identifying important characteristics

Whereas typologies classify people as *either* Type A's *or* Type B's *or* melancholic or sanguine, trait theorists suggest that personality characteristics exist along a continuum. Instead of thinking that people possess exclusively one characteristic or another, they are perceived as having varying degrees of **traits**. An easy way to understand the difference between types and traits is to think about the physical characteristic of height. If height were a personality characteristic, we would have two *types*—tall people and short people. With trait theory, however, we recognize that height varies along a continuum (from very short to very tall), and we can describe each person according to his or her specific height. Trait theorists reject the notion of discrete categories of personality. They are interested in first discovering *how* people differ (which key traits best describe them), and then measuring *how much* they differ.

As you may imagine, this task sounds easier than it actually is. Each individual differs from another on a wide variety of personality traits. An early study of dictionary terms found almost 18,000 specific words for personality traits (Allport and Odbert, 1936). Faced with this enormous list of potential traits, Gordon Allport (1937) believed that the best way to understand personality was to study each individual and then group his or her unique personality traits into a hierarchy. Allport's hierarchy placed the most important and descriptive traits on top and the least important on bottom. He developed three names for these groups of traits: cardinal, central, and secondary. **Cardinal traits** are at the very top of the hierarchy. Allport believed that some individuals' personalities are

TRAIT: *An enduring predisposition to respond in a particular way, distinguishing one individual from another. People can vary in their personality traits along a wide range of values.*

CARDINAL TRAITS: *In Allport's theory, a pervasive, all-encompassing personality characteristic that seems to influence most areas of a person's life. Cardinal traits are relatively uncommon and are observed in only a few people.*

organized around only one or two fundamental (*cardinal*) characteristics and that these traits influence all or nearly all areas of their lives. Abraham Lincoln's honesty, Adolf Hitler's hatred, and Albert Schweitzer's and Mother Teresa's humanitarianism may be examples of cardinal traits. Few individuals are believed to possess such dominant and pervasive traits.

In contrast to cardinal traits, *everyone* possesses **central traits,** specific behavioral tendencies that are highly characteristic of an individual. Central traits are the five to ten traits your friends would agree describe you — outgoing, intelligent, ambitious, and so on. According to Allport, each of us possesses only a few central traits and these are easily identified by others.

All other traits within an individual are called **secondary traits.** These traits are far less enduring and general than central or cardinal traits, and are generally less important in personality descriptions. Examples of secondary traits might be liking the outdoors or enjoying foreign films.

Allport believed that no two people have exactly the same traits. Indeed, one hallmark of Allport's trait theory was his emphasis on the uniqueness of the individual. In contrast, two other prominent trait theorists have emphasized the universality of basic traits.

Raymond Cattell (1965) and Hans Eysenck (1967) developed a cluster of traits they believe represent the core of each of our personalities. Using the mathematical technique of **factor analysis,** they reduced the large number of traits to a manageable size. Cattell found sixteen basic personality dimensions, which he calls **source traits** (see Table 14.2). Eysenck, on the other hand, found that the traits of introversion–extroversion and stability–instability could explain most personality differences. An introverted person is quiet, passive, unsociable, and careful; an extroverted person is sociable, active, outgoing, and optimistic. An unstable personality is moody, touchy, anxious, and restless; a stable personality is calm, even-tempered, carefree, and has leadership qualities.

The trait approach has contributed much to the study of personality. Cattell's theoretical structure and research strategies, for example, have generated a great deal of empirical research (Wiggins, 1984). On the other hand, trait theory has also been heavily

CENTRAL TRAITS: *For Allport, a small number of traits that are highly characteristic of a given individual and easy to infer.*

SECONDARY TRAITS: *In Allport's theory, these traits are not as important as central traits for describing personality since they influence few situations or behaviors.*

FACTOR ANALYSIS: *A mathematical procedure used to determine the basic units or factors that constitute personality or intelligence.*
SOURCE TRAITS: *Cattell's term for the basic personality traits he believed were shared by most individuals.*

TABLE 14.2
Cattell's End Points on Sixteen Source Traits Obtained by Factor Analysis

Description of High Scorers	Description of Low Scorers
Warm, easygoing	Cool, reserved
Abstract thinking	Concrete thinking
Calm, stable	Easily upset
Dominant	Not assertive
Happy-go-lucky	Sober, serious
Conscientious	Expedient
Venturesome	Shy, timid
Tender-minded	Tough-minded
Suspicious	Trusting
Imaginative	Practical
Shrewd	Forthright
Apprehensive	Self-assured
Experimenting	Conservative
Self-sufficient	Group-oriented
Self-disciplined	Undisciplined
Tense, driven	Relaxed

Source: Adapted from the Administration's Manual for the 16 PF. Copyright © 1972, 1979, 1986.

criticized. Researchers have questioned whether childhood personality traits remain consistent into adulthood, or if personality changes according to the situation (Carson, 1989; Mischel, 1968, 1984; Mischel et al., 1989; Pervin, 1987).

To determine whether personality traits remain consistent over time, psychologists often do *longitudinal studies*. This type of research tests the same individuals at regular intervals as they get older. In one longitudinal study, Alexander Thomas and Stella Chess (1977) measured the traits of activity level, intensity of response, and persistence in infants and then reexamined the children as they got older. The researchers found that individual patterns of behavior tended to be consistent and enduring. Other longitudinal studies have verified that babies' differences in activity level and sensitivity to stimulation tend to persist (Kagan, 1987). In one of the most comprehensive longitudinal studies of adult personality, Paul Costa and Robert McCrae (1988) found that on five of the major dimensions, personality traits are extremely stable after age 30. They suggest that a person who was agreeable and outgoing at 30 years of age would remain so at 65, whereas a person who was irritable and introverted at 30 would be about the same at 65.

Researchers have found that shyness tends to be one of the more enduring and stable personality traits.

Question: Are people really that predictable?   Whether we can depend on the fact that people have such enduring personality traits has been the subject of much debate among personality psychologists. When observers measure traits and then attempt to predict future behaviors, they are often inaccurate, which seems to mean that people are unpredictable. One early study that brought the trait concept into question was conducted by Hartshorne and May (1928). They gave children opportunities to be dishonest in a variety of circumstances, such as taking an examination and being left with a tempting object they would like to have. The experimenters found that the same child would be honest in some situations but not in others, which led them to question the existence of a consistent trait of "honesty." Other researchers have also failed to find dependable consistencies in a number of other traits.

Failures to find consistency in predicting behavior led personality theorists in the 1960s to challenge the entire trait approach. In 1968, Walter Mischel published a landmark book in the field of personality, *Personality and Assessment.* Rather than seeing personality as consistent, internal traits of the individual, he suggested that personality changes according to the situation. Citing research such as Hartshorne and May's, Mischel argued that people will behave honestly or dishonestly according to factors and conditions in the external environment.

Mischel's arguments were persuasive. Many scientists joined his camp, whereas others held out for the existence of stable traits that cause individuals to behave consistently across a wide range of settings. For years a heated debate, known as *trait versus situationism* or the *person-situation controversy,* existed in psychology. After nearly two decades of continuing debate and research, the current consensus seems to be that relatively stable traits do exist but they are also affected by situational pressures (Kenrick and Funder, 1988). This *interactionist* position is not a compromise but a blending of views based on research findings. It is important to realize that scientific progress often results from this type of ongoing critical debate and the research it provokes (Houts, Cook, and Shadish, 1986). (We will return to the topic of interactionism at the end of this section.)

Review Questions

1 Psychologists studying personality focus on individual _____ in behavior.

2 _____ theories of personality pigeonhole people into categories based on prominent, consistent behavioral characteristics.

3 _____ theories of personality suggest that people can vary in their personality characteristics along a wide range of values.

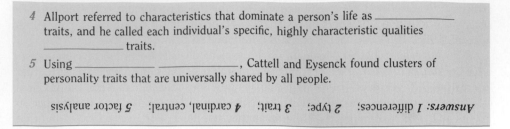

4 Allport referred to characteristics that dominate a person's life as _____ traits, and he called each individual's specific, highly characteristic qualities _____ traits.

5 Using _____ _____, Cattell and Eysenck found clusters of personality traits that are universally shared by all people.

Answers: 1 differences; *2* type; *3* trait; *4* cardinal, central; *5* factor analysis

Psychoanalytic theory: Freud's developmental approach

In contrast to type and trait theories, which generally *describe* personality as it currently exists, developmental theories of personality attempt to account for individual uniqueness by examining the development and changes within people as they mature from infancy to adulthood and are influenced by their environments.

Freud's **psychoanalytic theory** of personality evolved from his thinking as he worked with psychologically disturbed patients in therapy (Gay, 1988). He was deeply impressed by the fact that while under hypnosis, his patients would often reveal an apparent connection between a current behavioral or emotional problem and a sexual incident that had occurred earlier in their lives. In his later published writings, Freud either deemphasized the importance of *actual* sexual traumas or claimed that much of what patients told him was factually untrue. They were describing things *as if* they had happened, but these events were fantasies or wishes rather than actual events (Masson, 1984a). Whether his patients were fantasizing or remembering actual events was probably not the important issue. What counted to Freud was the power of these images. He continued to explore his patients' revelations and found repeated examples of traumatic and disturbing childhood experiences (real or imagined). From these examples, he concluded that we all have stored memories in our unconscious minds that influence our present behavior.

Question: What exactly is the unconscious mind? Freud called the mind the *psyche* and saw it as containing both conscious and unconscious components (see Figure 14.1). The **conscious** mind includes information we are currently aware of or are remembering. Below consciousness are the thoughts we are not aware of at the moment but that could be rather easily remembered (the **preconscious**) and ideas that we actively

PSYCHOANALYTIC THEORY: *Freud's theory focusing on unconscious motivation of behavior.*

CONSCIOUS: *In Freudian terms, thoughts or information one is currently aware of or is remembering.*
PRECONSCIOUS: *Freud's term for thoughts or information one can become aware of easily.*

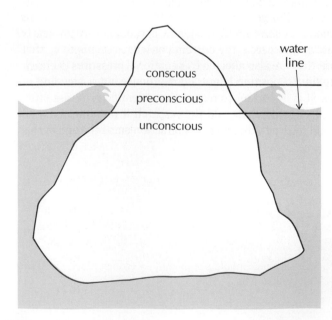

water line

Figure 14.1 Freud's view of the levels of consciousness. The parts of the mind can be compared to an iceberg in the ocean. The tip of the iceberg is similar to the *conscious* mind —open to easy inspection. Directly below the conscious mind is the *preconscious,* whose contents can be viewed with a little extra effort. Like the base of the iceberg, the *unconscious* mind is the largest area, and it is completely submerged and hidden from personal inspection.

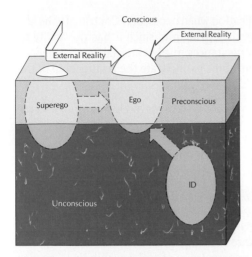

Figure 14.2 Freud's view of the three parts of the personality. The *id* is completely submerged in the unconscious mind and is motivated by the *pleasure principle*. The *superego* and *ego* possess all three levels of consciousness—unconscious, preconscious, and conscious. The ego operates according to the *reality principle*, whereas the superego is guided by the *conscience* and *ego-ideal*.

resist bringing into awareness, the **unconscious**. Freud did not use the term "subconscious" mind, since he disliked its implication of an inferior status compared to conscious thinking (Freud, 1900/1953). He considered the unconscious mind to be the most important influence on behavior.

One way Freud claimed that people revealed their unconscious thoughts is through **Freudian slips** (seemingly unintended errors in speech, memory, or behavior). For example, when a flight attendant says, "It has been a real *job* serving you . . . I mean, *joy!*" she might be unintentionally allowing her true thoughts to be expressed.

Personality structure   Freud's personality theory is called **psychodynamic** because it emphasizes dynamic or active interactions within the psyche. These interactions occur among three components of the psyche: the id, the ego, and the superego (see Figure 14.2).

The **id** is the original part of the psyche that is present at birth. Like a newborn child, the id is immature, impulsive, and irrational. The id is the reservoir of mental energy. When the forcefulness of its primitive drives builds up, the id seeks immediate gratification in order to relieve the tension. Thus, the id functions according to what Freud called the **pleasure principle,** which is the immediate and uninhibited seeking of pleasure and avoidance of discomfort.

Because it is such a primitive and completely unconscious part of the psyche, the id operates without any consideration for logic or the demands of reality. The id *can,* however, obtain partial gratification for its instinctual energy by forming mental images of desired objects. Freud called this *wish-fulfillment.* According to this concept of the id, a hungry person can obtain partial satisfaction by imagining a delicious pizza or hamburger, but obtaining the object that satisfies the drive brings greater pleasure.

Question: Did Freud mean that people only seek pleasure?   If the id were the only part of the psyche, we would always seek pleasure and avoid pain in illogical and impulsive ways, since this is what the id urges us to do. However, Freud postulated that there are two other parts of the psyche that act to control and channel the id's potentially destructive energy. These parts, the ego and the superego, keep us from always seeking immediate gratification.

The ego is the second part of the psyche to develop. The **ego** is the executive of the psyche. It is capable of planning, problem solving, reasoning, and controlling the id. In Freud's system, the ego corresponds to the "self" — our conscious identity of ourselves as persons. Unlike the id, the ego contains a conscious level in addition to unconscious contents.

Once it has developed as the second part of the psyche, the ego's task is to channel and release the id's energy in ways that are consistent with the external environment.

UNCONSCIOUS: *Freud's term for thoughts or information shoved far beneath our level of awareness.*

FREUDIAN SLIPS: *Seemingly unintended errors in speech, memory, or behavior, thought to reveal unconscious motivational forces.*

PSYCHODYNAMIC: *Pertaining to processes undergoing change or development.*

ID: *In psychoanalytic theory, the reservoir of psychic energy and instincts that perpetually presses us to satisfy our basic needs.*

PLEASURE PRINCIPLE: *According to Freud, the id's strategy of seeking immediate and uninhibited pleasure and avoiding discomfort.*

EGO: *In psychoanalytic theory, the rational part of the psyche that deals with reality and attempts to control the impulses of the id, while also satisfying the social approval and self-esteem needs of the superego.*

REALITY PRINCIPLE: *According to Freud, the principle on which the conscious ego operates as it tries to meet the demands of the unconscious id and the realities of the environment.*

Thus, the ego is responsible for delaying gratification when necessary. Contrary to the id's pleasure principle, the ego operates on the **reality principle,** since it has the ability to understand and deal with the objects and circumstances in the external environment.

Freud used the example of a rider and his horse to illustrate the relationship of the ego and id:

> In its relation to the id [the ego] is like a man on horseback, who has to hold in check the superior strength of the horse. . . . Often a rider, if he is not to be parted from his horse, is obliged to guide it where it wants to go; so in the same way the ego is in the habit of transforming the id's will into action as if it were its own.
>
> *Freud (1923/1961), p. 25*

SUPEREGO: *In psychoanalytic theory, the part of the personality that incorporates parental and societal standards for morality.*

The final part of the psyche to develop is the **superego.** It originates as a part of the ego but separates from it to become an overseer or moral censor for the psyche. The separation of the superego occurs when children have learned the rules and values of their parents. The superego is a set of ethical standards or rules for behavior. It has two parts, the conscience and the ego-ideal. The *conscience* is a group of social prohibitions, similar to a penal code or legal statutes. It lists the things we should *not* do. The *ego-ideal* is a list of things we *should* do to feel proud of ourselves.

According to Freud, each of us has a unique superego that is the result of our early experiences with our parents. For example, our parents may have taught us that walking around naked is improper, that loving other people is "good," that hitting and stealing are "wrong," and that expressing appreciation is "nice." Out of these specific learning experiences, we have developed a superego that continues to urge that our behavior match our internalized standards of right and wrong. Even though it is the ego that judges which behavior will satisfy the urgings from the id and still meet the demands of the environment at the moment, it is the superego that constantly pressures the ego into acting justly.

Like the ego, the superego contains both conscious and unconscious parts. For example, whenever you are tempted to hurt another person or steal something, you are probably conscious of your superego's rules against these behaviors (i.e., if you have them as rules). You might not, on the other hand, be aware of your rule for getting revenge ("I *should* make people pay for hurting me") if this standard is part of your *unconscious* superego (refer to Figure 14.2).

Freud provided many examples of ways in which conflicts can occur between the three parts of the psyche over the course of development. Not surprisingly, these problems are termed *intrapsychic conflicts.* For instance, if the rules contained in the superego are different from the rules of society, the ego will not get appropriate guidance. The ego then might choose a behavior that could get the person in trouble. On the other hand, if the superego's regulations are too critical of id impulses, the ego may not be able to find ways to gratify the id's needs. Pressure will build up in the system if the id's energy is not relieved. If too much pressure builds up, the ego can be completely overpowered, leaving the id forces uncontrolled. The result would be what is commonly described as a "mental breakdown."

Question: It sounds like these conflicts are relatively common. If so, why doesn't everyone have a breakdown at some point?   Normally, before the ego is overpowered or damaged, it experiences a signal or perception of danger in the form of feelings of anxiety. According to Freud, there are three types of anxiety that warn the ego of problems with the id, the superego, or the environment (Coleman, Butcher, and Carson, 1984). *Neurotic anxiety* occurs when the strength of the id impulses has built up to become so forceful that the ego is in danger of being overwhelmed. For example, extreme anger or intense sexual desire could overpower the ego's ability to keep rational control over behavior. *Moral anxiety* occurs when the superego is critical of the choices the ego makes. The guilt or shame of moral anxiety acts as encouragement for behavior change, since it conflicts with our internal values. *Realistic anxiety* occurs when one is appropriately afraid of something in the environment. This signal helps alert the individual to do something about the danger.

When any type of anxiety occurs, the ego must protect itself by solving the problem that has created the discomfort. Sometimes, however, the ego takes shortcuts and uses defense mechanisms to relieve unpleasant feelings of anxiety rather than cope with the original problem.

Defense mechanisms   **Defense mechanisms** are strategies that the ego ordinarily uses unconsciously to distort reality and thereby escape or avoid anxiety. Freud suggested that **repression** is the single most powerful and pervasive defense mechanism. It works to push unacceptable, unwanted thoughts and impulses out of our awareness and back into our unconscious mind. Given that the major goal for every defense mechanism is to push threatening impulses out of awareness, repression is considered the foundation of all defense mechanisms. Repression and several other Freudian defense mechanisms are summarized in Table 14.3.

Question: My friends and I often use some of these defense mechanisms. Is this bad?   Although defense mechanisms do twist the truth and distort reality, recent research has supported Freud's belief that some misrepresentation seems to be necessary for our psychological well-being (Snyder, 1988; Taylor et al., 1988). During a gruesome surgery, for example, physicians and nurses may *intellectualize* the procedures as an unconscious way of dealing with their personal anxieties. By focusing on abstract thoughts, words, or ideas, they do not become emotionally overwhelmed by the horrifying situations they sometimes encounter. Most psychologists agree that the use of defense mechanisms is healthy as long as it does not become extreme.

Psychosexual stages of development   Freud believed that experiences during early childhood were important predictors of later adult personality. According to him, each

Graduation represents a major turning point in life and the anxiety it creates may lead to the use of certain defense mechanisms.

DEFENSE MECHANISMS: *In psychoanalytic theory, unconscious strategies used by the ego to attempt to avoid anxiety and resolve conflict. These mechanisms are commonly used and only cause serious problems when they are excessively used.*
REPRESSION: *Freud's most important defense mechanism that involves unconscious blocking of unacceptable impulses to keep them from awareness.*

TABLE 14.3
Six Sample Psychological Defense Mechanisms

Defense Mechanism	Description	Example
Repression	Freud's most fundamental mechanism, also called "motivated forgetting"	Forgetting an appointment with someone you dislike
Rationalization	Socially acceptable reasons are substituted for thoughts or actions based on unacceptable motives	Justifying cheating on an exam by saying "everyone else does it"
Intellectualization	Repressing the emotional aspects of a painful experience by focusing on abstract thoughts, words, or ideas	Repressing your hurt, while academically discussing the major reasons for your divorce
Projection	Unacceptable motives or impulses are transferred to others	Repressing your own temptations, while becoming unreasonably jealous of your mate
Reaction formation	Repressing unacceptable urges, thoughts, or feelings by exaggerating the opposite state	Being domineering, loud, and boastful when you feel inferior and low in self-esteem
Regression	Responding to a threatening situation in a way appropriate to an earlier age or level of development	Throwing a temper tantrum when a friend refuses to meet your demands

TABLE 14.4
Summary of Freud's Five Stages of Psychosexual Development

Stage	Approximate Age	Erogenous Zone	Key Conflict or Developmental Task
Oral	0–1	Mouth	Weaning (from breast or bottle)
Anal	1–3	Anus	Toilet training
Phallic	3–6	Genitals	Overcoming the Oedipal or Electra complex (by identifying with same-sex parent)
Latency	6–12	None	Expanding interests and social contacts
Genital	12–adult	Genitals	Establishing intimate relationships

PSYCHOSEXUAL STAGES: *In psychoanalytic theory, a developmental period in which individual pleasures must be gratified if personality development is to proceed normally.*

ORAL STAGE: *Freud's psychosexual stage (from birth to 12–18 months) during which the mouth is the center of pleasure and feeding is an important source of conflict.*

ANAL STAGE: *Freud's psychosexual stage (from 12–18 months to 3 years) during which the anal area is the center of pleasure and toilet training is an important source of conflict.*

PHALLIC STAGE: *Freud's psychosexual stage (ages 3 to 6) during which the child experiences either the Oedipus or Electra complex, which can only be resolved through identification with the same-sex parent.*

OEDIPUS COMPLEX: *The Freudian term for the sexual attachment of a boy to his mother and his desire to replace his father.*

ELECTRA COMPLEX: *The Freudian term for the sexual attachment of a girl to her father and her desire to replace her mother.*

According to Freud, toilet training is a critical factor in a child's psychosexual development. Difficulties in training may explain later personality traits.

person passes through five **psychosexual stages** during the first twelve or so years of life. The term "psychosexual" reflects Freud's major emphasis on the importance of *infantile sexuality*—his belief that children experience sexual feelings from birth (although in different forms than those of adolescents or adults). Four of his stages are named for the area of the body (or *erogenous zone*) that corresponds to the primary source of pleasure at these stages—the mouth, anus, phallus, or genitals (see Table 14.4).

Freud believed that movement through all five stages is motivated by strong biological drives, but he also believed that if a child's needs are not met or are overindulged at one particular stage the child may *fixate* and a part of the personality will remain at that stage. Even if they make it through all five stages, some people may return (or *regress*) to a stage that represented either major frustrations in needs or overgratification.

During the **oral stage** (birth to 12–18 months), the erogenous zone is the mouth and the infant receives satisfaction through sucking, eating, biting, and so on. Because the infant is highly dependent on parents and caregivers to provide opportunities for oral gratification, fixation at this stage can easily occur. According to Freud, if the mother overindulges her infant's oral needs, the child may fixate and as an adult become gullible ("swallowing" anything), dependent, and overly passive. The underindulged child, however, will develop into an aggressive, sadistic person who exploits others. Orally fixated adults may also orient their life around their mouth—overeating, drinking, smoking, talking a great deal, and so on.

During the **anal stage** (from 12–18 months to 3 years), the child's erogenous zone shifts to the anus and the child receives satisfaction by having and retaining bowel movements. Since this is also the time when most parents begin toilet training, the child's desire to control his or her own bowel movements often leads to strong conflict. Adults who fixated at this stage may display an *anal-retentive* personality and be compulsively neat, stingy, orderly, and obstinate. Or they may become disorderly, rebellious, and destructive—the *anal-expulsive* personality. (It may help you to remember these two personalities types by thinking of *The Odd Couple*—Felix would be the anal-retentive and Oscar the anal-expulsive.)

During the **phallic stage** (from 3 to 6 years), the major center of pleasure becomes the phallus (penis) for the boy and the clitoris for the girl. Children develop a desire for the opposite-sex parent and a wish to displace the same-sex parent. This attraction creates a conflict (the **Oedipus complex** for boys and **Electra complex** for girls) that must be resolved. Freud based his name for these complexes on characters in Greek plays: King Oedipus, who killed his father and married his mother, and Electra, a character from the Greek play *Agamemnon*, who induces her brother to kill her mother. In Freud's view, young boys desire their mother and unconsciously want to replace their father, but, recognizing the father's power, they fear he will punish them by castration. This *castration anxiety* and the Oedipus conflict are resolved when the boy represses his sexual drives, gives up his rivalries with his father, and begins to *identify* with him. If the resolution of this stage is not complete or positive, the boy will grow up resenting his father and generalize this feeling to all authority figures (Nye, 1975).

In the case of young girls, Freud suggested that the discovery that she lacks a penis causes a girl to develop *penis envy*. The Electra conflict is resolved when the girl suppresses her desire for her father, gives up her rivalries with her mother, and identifies with her. Freud believed that most young girls never really overcome penis envy and fully identify with their mothers. This belief led him to suggest that women generally have a lower level of morality than men — one of the many Freudian ideas that have been criticized in modern times.

Following the phallic period is the **latency stage** (from 6 years to puberty). Freud believed that the individual's personality is generally completed by this stage, a time of relative sexual calm. Sexual energy this period is directed toward schoolwork, hobbies, and same-sex friendships.

With the beginning of adolescence comes the **genital stage**. The genitals are once again erogenous zones and individuals receive satisfaction through heterosexual matings outside the family.

LATENCY STAGE: *Freud's fourth psychosexual stage (age 6 to puberty), characterized by the relative lack of sexual interests.*

GENITAL STAGE: *The stage of psychosexual development that begins in puberty and represents mature adult sexuality and personality development.*

Question: Why was Freud so "hung up" on sex? It seems like his entire theory revolves around it.   Freud has been widely criticized for his overemphasis on sex, perhaps for the wrong reasons. Since Freud generally used the term "sex" to include all forms of pleasure, many people have misinterpreted his theories. From his biological perspective, he saw children as operating on their need to satisfy basic biological drives, including the drive for pleasure. It is also important to recognize that Freud was a product of his times. During the time he was writing and seeing patients, the Victorian society he lived in was probably the most sexually repressive in all of history. Freud's basically negative perception of women and their sexuality was a part of Victorian beliefs (Gay, 1988).

In addition to his personal biases, Freud has been criticized for emphasizing processes that are difficult to test. How do you conduct experiments on an unavailable, unconscious mind (Silverman, 1976)? Since Freud's observations of personality development were limited to patients with serious problems rather than including people with more normal behavior, his sampling techniques are also subject to criticism.

On the most fundamental level, Freud's theory has been criticized for assuming that unconscious impulses and operations are more important than the things we are consciously aware of (Skinner, 1988). Freud assumed the thoughts and behaviors of our dreams to be more accurate examples of our "real" personality than what we consciously feel or express.

Neo-Freudian theories: Revising Freud's approach

Freud's early colleagues originally supported his views, but frequent and intense disagreements among the psychodynamic analysts led to a dramatic severing of friendships and allegiances. Two of Freud's early supporters who later developed their own psychodynamic theories were Alfred Adler and Carl Jung. Other analysts who disagreed with Freud and devised their own approaches included Karen Horney, Harry Stack Sullivan, and Erich Fromm. These theorists are often grouped together as the **neo-Freudians** (The prefix *neo-* means *recent* or *latest*.)

To neo-Freudians one bothersome aspect of Freud's theory was his emphasis on the importance of unconscious sexual impulses in creating normal and abnormal personality characteristics. The neo-Freudians instead preferred to emphasize the importance of social and cultural influences in shaping personality.

Adler, the first to leave Freud's inner circle of followers, developed a theory he called "individual psychology" (Mosak, 1984). Instead of seeing behavior as motivated by unconscious forces, he claimed that behavior is purposeful and goal-directed. Unlike Freud, he felt that *consciousness* is the center of personality. He believed that each of us

NEO-FREUDIANS: *Contemporaries of Freud who both supported and criticized his theory.*

has the capacity to choose and to create. According to Adler (1979), our goals in life provide the source of our motivation — especially those goals that aim to obtain security and overcome inferiority feelings.

Question: Doesn't everyone have inferiority feelings? Yes, in Adler's view, we all have inferiority feelings because we begin life as completely helpless infants. During the early years of life, each child feels small, incompetent, and helpless when dealing with skilled adults. These early feelings of inadequacy result in a *will-to-power* that causes children to strive to be superior to others or to develop their own capacities fully. As you can see, this early "inferiority complex" can lead to negative personality traits of dominance, aggression, or envy of others or it can be positively directed as a *social interest*— identifying with others and cooperating with them for the social good. In stressing social interest, Adlerian theory is more optimistic than Freudian theory. Adler claimed that unpleasant and potentially harmful feelings can motivate us to strive for mastery and control in our lives and can encourage us to be creative (Adler, 1964).

Another early dissenter, Carl Jung, is perhaps best known for his ideas about the unconscious mind and its influence on dream processes (Haynie, 1984). Jung claimed that the unconscious mind contains positive and spiritual motives as well as sexual and aggressive forces. He also presented the view that each of us has two types of unconscious mind, the personal unconscious and the collective unconscious. The **personal unconscious** is created from our experiences, whereas the **collective unconscious** is identical in each person and is inherited (Jung, 1936/1969). It consists of images and patterns for thought, feeling, and behavior that Jung called **archetypes**. He claimed that the collective unconscious is the ancestral memory of the human race that gives people of different cultures their similarities in religion, art, symbolism, and dream imagery. The archetype patterns contained in the collective unconscious cause us to perceive and react in certain predictable ways. One set of archetypes deals with sexual roles. Jung claimed that both males and females have patterns for feminine aspects of personality *(anima)* and masculine aspects *(animus)*.

Karen Horney was originally trained as a Freudian psychoanalyst in Berlin (Lunden, 1984). Her writings emphasized the importance of powerful unconscious conflicts in shaping personality and described the role of anxiety in creating a basic drive for safety and security (Horney, 1939, 1945). This striving for security can create movements toward, against, or away from people and can cause us to deny our true needs and desires for affection and personal growth. The drive created by anxiety over unconscious conflicts is painful and pushes us into unrealistic goals that Horney called "the tyranny of the should." Like Adler and Jung, Horney emphasized the importance of social forces. She criticized Freud's view that women inevitably feel inferior to men and always develop penis envy. Horney claimed that when these views exist at all, they are the result of cultural forces rather than the consequence of alleged biological inferiority (Pervin, 1989).

In recent years, there has been increased interest in neo-Freudian viewpoints, quite possibly because the writings of therapists such as Adler, Jung, and Horney encourage people to find ways to be creative and accomplish their potential despite any difficult experiences they have encountered. This perspective is consistent with several contemporary approaches to personality that will be discussed in the next section.

PERSONAL UNCONSCIOUS: *Jung's concept of unconscious memories created from one's own experiences.*
COLLECTIVE UNCONSCIOUS: *Jung's concept of an inherited portion of the unconscious that all humans share.*
ARCHETYPES: *Jung's concept of images or patterns for thought, feelings, and behavior that reside in the collective unconscious.*

Review Questions

1 Freud's developmental theory of personality is known as _____ or _____ theory.

2 The id operates on the _____ principle, seeking immediate gratification.

3 The superego contains the _____ and the _____ that provide moral judgments for the ego.

4 The ego operates on the _____ principle, attempting to meet the external demands of reality.

5 A(n) _____ conflict occurs when the three parts of the psyche are not interacting appropriately.

6 Repression and projection are examples of _____ _____ used to escape or avoid anxiety.

7 Freud believed that an individual's adult personality resulted from his or her movement through five _____ _____ of development.

8 The Oedipus and Electra complexes occur during the _____ stage of development.

9 The inferiority complex is a central idea in the theory of _____ _____.

10 According to Jung, _____ are patterns for behavior that reside in the collective unconscious.

Answers: 1 psychoanalytic, psychodynamic; *2* pleasure; *3* conscience, ego-ideal; *4* reality; *5* intrapsychic; *6* defense mechanisms; *7* psychosexual stages; *8* phallic; *9* Alfred Adler; *10* archetypes

CONTEMPORARY THEORIES

Contemporary theoretical orientations provide us with views of personality that contrast dramatically with the previous classical theories and with each other in a number of ways. These alternative orientations include the learning, humanistic, cognitive, and biological theories of personality.

Learning theories: Behaviorist and social learning approaches

In the type, trait, and psychodynamic approaches discussed so far, personality is seen as an abstract, *internal* part of each individual that may or may not be related to external behavior. From the learning perspective, personality is viewed from the *outside* by measuring observable behaviors, such as aggressive acts or kindly overtures. The term "personality" is seen as a label for the sum total of a person's behavioral patterns. Personality and behavior are basically the same thing.

Question: What motivates certain behaviors if it isn't the person's internal personality? Motivation for behavior is assumed to come from each individual's history of learning. People act aggressively or kindly because they expect a reward or desire to avoid punishment.

Behaviorist theory The most extreme learning theorists are called *behaviorists*. They believe an infant is born as a *tabula rasa,* or "blank slate," to be written on by learning experiences. John Watson, one of the most radical behaviorists, believed that simple conditioning (see Chapter 6) is the primary factor in the development of personality. On one occasion he went so far as to say:

> Give me a dozen, healthy infants, well-formed, and my own specified world to bring them up in, and I'll guarantee to take any one at random and train him to become any type of specialist I might select — doctor, lawyer, artist, merchant-chief, and, yes, even beggar-man and thief, regardless of his talents, penchants, tendencies, activities, vocations, and race of his ancestors.
>
> *Watson (1930), p. 65*

Can you see how the family and childhood experiences can have lasting effects on personality?

Following in Watson's footsteps, modern-day behaviorist B. F. Skinner believes we do not need to resort to biological or internal aspects of the person to explain personality, rather we need only look at relations between stimuli and responses. If you are a shy individual who is afraid to approach others for dates or friendship, Skinner would suggest that you have *learned* to behave in this fashion as a result of previous interactions with family members, friends, teachers, and others. Behaviorists have been criticized for taking the *person* out of personality and viewing the organism as "empty" (Phares, 1984).

Social learning theory   Social learning theorists agree with behaviorists that personality is learned and influenced by environmental experiences, but they also emphasize the importance of less observable phenomena, such as thinking and observation of others.

Question: How does observation of others influence personality?   When you observe another person doing something, you evaluate and interpret his or her behavior. You not only see the consequences of that person's actions, you also think about whether that particular behavior would be appropriate for you. For example, children observe the behavior of both male and female adults, but they tend to imitate the adults who are judged to be most "like themselves." When a little girl dresses up in her mother's dress and puts on makeup, she tends to get attention: "Isn't she cute? She's such a little lady. She'll grow up to be a real charmer someday, just like her mother." If a boy does the same kind of dressing up, his parents react quite differently. Worried that he will grow up to be "strange," they do not praise him for imitating his mother's behavior and may even punish him. Thus, children are rewarded for imitating sex-appropriate behaviors, and their personalities become "feminized" or "masculinized."

Because of their emphasis on imitation, social learning theorists are particularly concerned about children having appropriate role models. These psychologists are among the strongest critics of the prevalence of models for aggression in movies and on television. Research tends to support this criticism. As we saw in Chapter 6, experiments have shown that children who watch aggressive behaviors on film behave more aggressively themselves compared to children who have not seen aggressive acts modeled (Bandura, 1969, 1973; Huesmann and Eron, 1986; Huston et al., 1989).

Learning and environmental influences are obviously important to personality development. Critics of the learning theory point out, however, that people are more than the sum of what they have learned. The individual personality, they argue, also reflects unique perceptions, values, beliefs, and intentions. These factors are the focus of the humanistic theories discussed next.

Children frequently imitate the behaviors they observe.

Humanistic theories: Understanding the person

The humanistic orientation is known as the "third force" in psychology since it developed as a reaction to both Freudian and learning theories. The humanistic perspective on personality offers a distinctly different approach from the pessimism of Freudian views and the "mindless" approach of behaviorism (Rogers, 1980). These theories approach the study of personality from the "inside out," emphasizing internal experiences —feelings and thoughts—and the basic worth of the individual human being.

From a humanistic perspective people are seen as basically good (or, at worst, neutral), and they possess a positive drive toward self-fulfillment. Humanistic approaches to personality are sometimes referred to as the **phenomenological perspective.** This means that each individual's personality is created out of his or her unique way of perceiving and interpreting the world. Behavior is controlled by the individual's perception of reality, not by traits, unconscious impulses, or rewards. Since there is no external, objective *reality,* to fully understand another human being you must know how he or she perceives the world. Humanistic psychology was developed largely through the writings and efforts of Carl Rogers and Abraham Maslow.

PHENOMENOLOGICAL PERSPECTIVE: *The view that understanding another person requires knowing how he or she perceives the world. The term comes from philosophy, where the mental experiencing of the environment is called a phenomenon, and the study of how each person experiences reality is phenomenology.*

Carl Rogers's self-concept theory To humanistic psychologist Carl Rogers (1902–1987), the most important component of personality is the *self,* that part of experience

Carl Rogers, on the right, is one of the major figures in humanistic theories of personality.

that a person comes to identify early in life as "I" or "me." Rogers was very concerned with the match between two parts of the self: the *actual self* and the *ideal self*. The actual self is the self-concept, or self-perception, of the individual, whereas the ideal self is the self-concept to which the individual aspires. When the fit between the two selves is good, a person experiences high self-esteem, but when the match is off, the person has low self-esteem.

Incongruence between the actual and ideal self is especially likely when parents and teachers suggest to a child that his or her worth as a person is dependent on displaying the "right" attitudes, beliefs, and/or behaviors. Subjected to such a system of manipulation, children's self-concepts come to include the idea that love from others is *conditional*. For children's uniqueness and positive self-concept to unfold naturally, they need **unconditional positive regard**. According to Thomas Gordon:

> Acceptance is like the fertile soil that permits a tiny seed to develop into the lovely flower it is capable of becoming. The soil only *enables* the seed to become the flower. It *releases* the capacity of the seed to grow, but the capacity is entirely within the seed. As with the seed, a child contains entirely within this organism the capacity to develop. Acceptance is like the soil — it merely enables the child to actualize his potential.
>
> *Gordon (1975), p. 31*

Question: Does acceptance mean that we should allow people to do whatever they please? Humanists are often misinterpreted as being advocates of wholesale acceptance of all behaviors, good and bad. Actually, however, humanists separate the value of the person from his or her behaviors. They still accept the person's positive nature while believing that specific self-destructive or hostile behaviors of the person should be limited, not encouraged. Hitting a playmate or grabbing a friend's toy is contrary to the child's positive nature as well as offensive to others. Such actions reveal that the child has not learned effective ways to behave. To remedy the situation, the child needs appropriate guidance in order to be kept safe and to develop a healthy self-concept as well as healthy relationships with others. One way to provide such guidance is to enable individuals, at whatever age, to communicate their frustrations to someone who takes time to listen and appreciate their experiences. In Chapter 16, we will describe the humanistic therapy approach that illustrates this process.

Abraham Maslow's humanistic approach to personality Like Rogers, Abraham Maslow believed there is a basic goodness to human nature and a natural tendency toward self-actualization. He saw personality as the expression of this tendency.

UNCONDITIONAL POSITIVE REGARD: *Rogers's term for how we should behave toward someone to increase their self-esteem; positive behavior shown toward a person with no contingencies attached.*

Can you guess how each of the five major approaches to personality would explain this type of aggression?

TABLE 14.5
Characteristics of Self-Actualized People

1. Perceive reality efficiently and are comfortable with uncertainty.
2. Accept themselves and others for what they are.
3. Spontaneous in behavior, motivated by the attempt to develop their own style.
4. Problem-centered rather than self-centered, focusing on accomplishing unselfish tasks.
5. Enjoy solitude and privacy for making decisions.
6. Maintain an inner serenity in unpleasant circumstances and when dealing with social pressures.
7. Have a continued freshness of appreciation rather than taking things for granted.
8. Occurrence of peak experiences, feeling transcendence and intense joy in basic experiences of life.
9. Affectionate identification with other people.
10. Establish deep, satisfying interpersonal relationships with a few, rather than many, people.
11. Democratic and unprejudiced in dealing with others.
12. Strongly ethical in behavior as well as attitudes.
13. A spontaneous, unhostile sense of humor.
14. Creativity.
15. Resistant to enculturation, although not purposely unconventional.

Source: Maslow (1970).

Question: What exactly is "self-actualization"? According to Maslow, **self-actualization** is the inborn drive to develop all one's talents and capacities. It involves the mental processes of understanding one's own potential, accepting oneself and others as unique individuals, and using a problem-centered approach to situations (Maslow, 1970). Self-actualization is an ongoing process of growth rather than an end-product or accomplishment—such as winning a trophy or graduating from college. Table 14.5 summarizes the characteristics of self-actualized people.

SELF-ACTUALIZATION: *According to humanistic theories, an innate tendency toward growth that motivates all human behavior and results in the full realization of a person's highest potential.*

Although Maslow believed that only a few, rare individuals, like Abraham Lincoln, Albert Einstein, and Eleanor Roosevelt, ever fully achieve self-actualization, he saw it as part of every person's basic hierarchy of needs. As we discussed in the chapter on motivation and emotion, self-actualization is the highest need and should be seen as more of a journey or a way of life rather than as a final goal.

The humanistic orientation is not without its critics. Some psychologists feel that humanism is too optimistic in its approach to human nature. Others feel that its emphasis on therapy and human development limits its usefulness. A significant criticism is that this perspective lacks extensive experimental research to support it because it is difficult to evaluate subjective qualities such as self-actualization or the development of human potential (Maddi, 1980).

The cognitive approach to personality: The importance of interpretations

According to the cognitive perspective, each of us has a unique personality because we think about the world and the things that happen to us in our own unique ways. We *interpret* the things we experience. This emphasis on interpretation has been summarized by psychologist Albert Ellis (1983), who claims that the things that occur do not upset us, but our analysis of those things does. Ellis and other cognitive psychologists assume that psychological problems are created when people interpret their experiences in particular ways that Ellis calls *misconceptions*. He claims these disturbed ways of interpreting events are readily available for examination rather than being buried deep in the unconscious mind.

You can become aware of some of your own misconceptions by paying attention to what you say to yourself about events. For example, when someone is rude to you, what do you tell yourself about the situation? Do you think, "What did I do wrong?" Or do you tell yourself, "This person has no right to treat me like this." According to Ellis, how we talk to ourselves with such internalized sentences, or *self-talk,* affects both our emotions and our behavior. If we say to ourselves, "I can't do well on examinations and I'll always be a failure," we will feel anxious or depressed and we will most likely fail on exams. Similarly, when people tell themselves that it is unfair to have a parent who rejects them or who drinks excessively, they can view themselves as victims rather than as capable persons. If, on the other hand, they tell themselves that they are capable of making important changes in their lives, they often begin the process of making those changes.

Self-talk arises out of each person's *belief system,* an organized group of interpretations of reality. This belief system is an important personality structure in the cognitive approach to personality. Ellis agrees with Freud and Rogers that some unconscious beliefs can still influence behavior. He also agrees that it is important to get unconscious beliefs into current awareness to determine whether they are beneficial or harmful.

Question: How do you get unconscious beliefs into awareness? During actual therapy sessions, Ellis uses specific, therapeutic techniques known as rational-emotive therapy (see Chapter 16). When dealing with everyday misconceptions, he recommends that people examine their own belief systems by simply asking themselves what they are thinking about when a particular person or situation disturbs them. In the example of someone who does poorly on exams, the unconscious beliefs might include "I don't belong in college" or "I will certainly fail at anything I attempt." By making such beliefs conscious the person can do something about changing those that are unrealistic or inaccurate.

Biological theories: Body shape and genetics

Have you ever heard that redheads have fiery tempers, that tall, thin people are "eggheads," or that fat people are jolly? Descriptions of personality based on physical, biological characteristics have been popular for many years. One of the oldest and most controversial biological explanations for personality came from William Sheldon, a psychologist and physician.

SOMATOTYPES: *Sheldon's theory that body shape is associated with distinct personality patterns.*
ENDOMORPH: *Sheldon's term for the soft, round, large-stomached individual who is believed to be sociable, relaxed, and affectionate.*
MESOMORPH: *Sheldon's term for the strong, athletic, and muscular individual who is said to be energetic, competitive, and aggressive.*
ECTOMORPH: *Sheldon's term for the tall, thin, fragile individual who is believed to be fearful, introverted, and restrained.*

Sheldon's body somatotypes After viewing photographs of 4,000 men, Sheldon proposed three basic body types, or **somatotypes,** each associated with a specific personality style (Sheldon and Stevens, 1942). Figure 14.3 illustrates Sheldon's three somatotypes — **endomorph, mesomorph,** and **ectomorph.** Below each drawing is a description of the supposed personality of individuals with that particular body type. According to this drawing, how would you classify your own body type? Does the associated personality type match your self-concept?

Sheldon's personality system has been strongly criticized as both biased and inaccurate. Since Sheldon personally made the subjective ratings of body builds and corresponding personality traits, his own preconceived ideas could have easily influenced his judgments. Critics have also suggested that instead of body shape controlling personality, certain personality types could create specific physical attributes — competitive, aggressive people might naturally exercise and become more muscular, for example.

Genetics and personality Although Sheldon's theory failed to generate the necessary scientific data, later biological theories have garnered substantial research support. Biological studies on shyness, for example, have found that shy children show intense physiological responses to unexpected changes in the environment (Asher, 1987; Kagan, Reznick, and Snidman, 1988). Such responses are believed to be due to an inherited

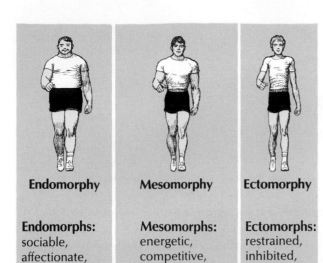

Endomorphy	Mesomorphy	Ectomorphy
Endomorphs: sociable, affectionate, self-indulgent, approval seeking	**Mesomorphs:** energetic, competitive, assertive, daring	**Ectomorphs:** restrained, inhibited, sensitive, like solitude

Figure 14.3 Sheldon's somatotype theory. According to Sheldon, you can understand personality types by looking at body shapes. For example, a round, overweight person is said to be sociable and relaxed; whereas the thin, underweight person is supposedly introverted and tense.

variation in the threshold of arousal, which may contribute to shyness in both children and adults.

The suggestion that psychological characteristics like shyness may be inherited has gained considerable attention as a result of research being done at the Minnesota Center for Twin and Adoption Research. Since 1979 literally hundreds of sets of twins have been tested at this center. The most recent findings of Tellegren and his colleagues (1988) suggest that the old nature versus nurture debate may have taken a decisive turn. Using a test of 11 traits, the researchers found that about 50 percent of the variation in personality was attributable to heredity, whereas nurture or the environment accounted for only about 20 to 35 percent. Heritability was the primary predictor of the personality traits of aggressiveness, need for achievement, vulnerability to stress, and proneness to imaginative activities. It was particularly surprising to find that *traditionalism,* or commitment to traditional moral and family values, did not show a familial or environmental effect.

Although researchers are cautious about overemphasizing the genetic basis of personality (Plomin, 1989; Rose et al., 1988), some people fear that this latest research on "genetic determinism" could be misused to "prove" that some races are inferior, that male dominance is natural, and that social progress is impossible (Wellborn, 1987). There is no doubt that genetic discussions have produced some of the most exciting and controversial results, but it is also clear that more high-quality research is necessary before we will have a cohesive biological theory of personality.

Interactionism: Putting the perspectives together

Question: Is the biological theory more "correct" than the other theories you've talked about? When it comes to personality, no one theory has been shown to be more accurate or correct than the others. Each provides a different perspective and offers different insights into how each person tends to develop a distinctive set of characteristics. Instead of adhering to any one theory, some psychologists urge the use of an approach called *interactionism.* As we discussed in the trait theory section, both individual (inside) and situational (outside) factors must be taken into account when trying to explain people's behaviors. According to the interactionist approach, a person's response depends on *external,* environmental factors, as well as *internal* factors such as thoughts and interpretations (cognitive theory), previous learning (psychoanalytic and learning theory), the individual's self-concept (humanistic theory), and genetic determinants (biological theory).

Review Questions

1 Learning theories include _____ and _____ _____ approaches that focus on conditioning and observational learning.

2 _____ _____ theories emphasize the effects of observation of others on personality development.

3 Humanistic theories emphasize thoughts and feelings that create one's _____.

4 Abraham Maslow's belief that all people are motivated toward personal growth and development is known as _____.

5 Albert Ellis stresses the importance of _____ of events in his cognitive view of personality.

6 _____ theories emphasize the importance of heredity and other genetic determinants of personality.

7 Interactionism stresses the combination of both internal and _____ factors.

Answers: 1 behaviorist, social learning; *2* social learning; *3* self-concept; *4* self-actualization; *5* interpretation; *6* biological; *7* external

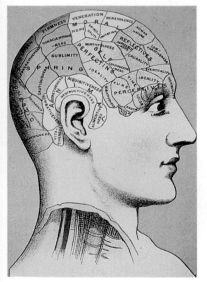

Franz Gall, founder of phrenology, believed that areas of the skull represented different personality traits.

PHRENOLOGY: *Pseudoscience that measures the skull to determine personality characteristics.*

RELIABILITY: *A measure of the stability of test scores over time.*

VALIDITY: *The ability of a test to actually measure what it is intended to measure.*

PERSONALITY ASSESSMENT

Back in the 1800s, if you wanted to have your personality assessed, your best bet was to go to a phrenologist. This highly respected person would carefully measure your skull, examine the bumps on your head, and then give you a psychological profile of your unique qualities and characteristics (Reuder, 1984). The phrenologist would rely on a **phrenology** chart to determine which personality traits were associated with bumps on different areas of the skull. Today personality differences are no longer assessed by taking skull measurements. Instead, personality assessment involves interviews, observational methods, self-report measures, and projective tests.

Question: How can we be sure that these modern methods are any better than phrenology? You might very well be suspicious of the accuracy of current testing methods in light of the fact that there are so many differing theories of personality. You have no doubt also been bombarded with so-called personality tests in popular magazines and supermarket tabloids. You may even have taken some official tests as part of a job or school selection process. Fortunately, there are some standards to judge the value of any type of psychological test.

The standards for evaluating tests include reliability and validity. As explained in Chapter 8, **reliability** is a measure of the stability of test scores over time. Reliability measures the extent to which a test gives similar scores with retesting. If an individual's score on a given personality test varies significantly from one testing to another, the test is considered *un*reliable. **Validity** is the extent to which a test measures what it was designed to measure rather than some other dimension. If we develop a new test of extroversion, for instance, we have to provide some evidence that it really measures outgoingness and sociability rather than assertiveness or aggressiveness. For each type of personality assessment technique, psychologists hve measured reliability and validity and have obtained other evidence of the usefulness of these modern-day methods of personality testing.

Interviews and observational methods:
Listening and watching

When you want to know more about people's personalities, you talk to them or watch them in action. Psychologists use these same methods, but on a more sophisticated level.

Psychological interviews may be structured or unstructured. Unstructured interviews are often used for job and college selections and for diagnosing psychological problems. In an unstructured format, interviewers are able to get impressions and pursue hunches or let people expand on promising information. The people being interviewed have a chance to explain their unique qualifications in their own words. Structured interviews ask specific questions and follow a set procedure so that the people being evaluated can be compared more directly. The results of a structured interview are often charted on a rating scale to standardize the evaluations for comparison purposes.

Interviews are an important tool in accurate personality assessment.

Question: But are interviews really fair? Don't some people get too nervous to make a good impression?   Most people being interviewed experience the situation as artificial and stressful if there are important consequences, such as being selected for a job or a college. Interviewers expect this reaction. Most often, an interview is only one part of an assessment process, and it is performed to evaluate the way a person is able to communicate under less than ideal circumstances.

Structured interviews have gained popularity as a way to select prospective jurors. Since both the defense and the prosecution can exclude any potential jurors who might be biased, attorneys have turned to psychologists for assistance in determining the characteristics of jurors that will be useful as well as harmful to their cases. In several prominent trials, interview techniques have been used to measure such juror attributes as attitudes toward authority and flexibility in making decisions (Werner, Kagehiro, and Strube, 1982).

In addition to structured or unstructured interviews, psychologists also use direct behavioral observations to assess personality. Many individuals enjoy "people watching" on college campuses, at airports or subway stations, and in other public places. When used as an official assessment procedure, however, the psychologist is looking for examples of specific behaviors and following a careful set of guidelines. For instance, a psychologist might arrange to observe a schizophrenic client's interactions with his or her family. Does the client become agitated by the presence of certain family members and not others? Does he or she become passive and withdrawn when asked a direct question? By careful observations, the psychologist gains valuable insights into the client's problems and personality characteristics.

Self-report tests: Describing yourself to others

Another type of personality assessment relies on self-reports by asking people to describe themselves on a paper and pencil questionnaire, rating scale, or other measuring device.

One widely used self-report personality test is the Sixteen Personality Factors Questionnaire (16 PF) developed by Raymond Cattell (1973). Analysis of 16 PF test results has provided some interesting insights into how people behave and relate to each other. Couples with stable marriages, for example, have greater similarities in their personality profiles than couples with unstable marriages. Even though it is often assumed that opposites attract, Cattell's research indicates that differences in characteristics such as warmth versus aloofness, trust versus suspiciousness, and self-sufficiency versus dependency create instability rather than permanence in a marriage.

Question: On self-report tests, couldn't people just lie about themselves?   Some tests have a built-in *lie scale* to detect instances when people are deliberately faking their responses. If you have ever taken a test that seemed to repeat items or to ask the same

RECOGNIZING DECEPTIVE APPEALS
The Problem with Popularized Personality Tests

Newspapers and magazines often present personality tests that claim to measure "your chances for business success," "what's wrong with your style of loving," or "your marriageability quotient." Why are so many people attracted to these tests? One answer is that they fail to think critically about the concept of personality and the problems with its assessment.

Consider the following personality description. How well does it describe your own personality?

You have a strong need for other people to like you and admire you. You have a tendency to be critical of yourself. You have a great deal of unused capacity that you have not turned to your advantage. Although you have some personality weaknesses, you are generally able to compensate for them. You pride yourself on being an independent thinker and do not accept other opinions without satisfactory proof. Disciplined and self-controlled outside, you tend to be worrisome and insecure inside. At times you have serious doubts whether you have made the right decision or done the right thing. (Adapted from Ulrich, Stachnik, and Stainton, 1963.)

If you are like most college students, you probably found this description to be a fairly accurate portrayal of your personality. When students are told that the description is written specifically for them on the basis of previous psychological tests or astrological data, a high percentage will judge the description to be *very* accurate. In fact, when given a choice between this type of fake assessment and a bona fide personality description based on scientifically designed tests, most people prefer the phony assessment (Hyman, 1981).

Why are people so gullible? There are four major reasons: the *Barnum Effect*, the *Fallacy of Positive Instances*, the *Self-Serving Bias*, and *Ad Hoc Explanations*. The "Barnum effect" is named after P. T. Barnum, the legendary circus promoter, who is remembered for his famous sayings: "Always have a little something for everybody" and "There's a sucker born every minute." Reread the description and you will see that it offers several ambiguous statements that are stated in such general terms that they fit almost everyone. Given the human tendency to overestimate one's own uniqueness, such general statements are accepted as being unique and special.

Now reread the description and notice the number of times it contains both sides of several personality dimensions ("You have a strong need for other people to like you . . . You pride yourself on being an independent thinker . . ."). As we discussed in Chapter 4, the "fallacy of positive instances" allows people to remember or notice instances that confirm their expectations and ignore the rest. People who believe in horoscopes can always find "Gemini" characteristics in a Gemini, but they fail to notice the times when the Gemini predictions "miss" or when the same Gemini traits appear in Scorpios, Leos, etc.

Review the original description once again and compare it to any daily newspaper's horoscope predictions. Do you notice an overall positive tone? Most nonscientific personality tests are composed primarily of *flattering* personality traits. The "self-serving bias" (see Chapter 18) generally refers to the personal tendency to prefer information that maintains a positive self-image. Research has shown that the more favorable a personality description is, the more people believe it, and the more likely they are to perceive it as unique to themselves (Shavit and Shouval, 1980).

Finally, the use of "ad hoc explanations," or special-purpose interpretations, works to maintain the belief in astrology. For example, an astrologer who wrongly describes an outgoing, extroverted person as shy will explain that the individual's extroversion is just a cover-up for their true shy nature. As you can see, ad hoc explanations make it impossible to logically refute astrological claims — even when they're wrong, they're right!

The goal of this discussion has been to make you a more critical consumer of popularized personality tests. Now that you can recognize the "Barnum effect," the "fallacy of positive instances," the "self-serving bias," and "ad hoc explanations" you will be more alert to the use of these particular types of deceptive appeal. The best antidote to any form of nonscientific personality assessment is the active application of critical thinking.

A person taking the Rorschach test is instructed to tell what each blot looks like or might be. On the average, subjects give about 30 to 40 responses to the card series. These responses are then evaluated on several dimensions, including content, areas of the cards described, and appropriateness. Because subjects can reply in any way they wish, their responses are often difficult to interpret, so the reliability and validity of the Rorschach are low (Anastasi, 1982). Despite these problems, some therapists, especially Freudians, continue to use the inkblot on the assumption that they reveal unconscious processes unable to be evaluated in other ways.

This is one of the picture cards from the Thematic Apperception Test. If you were taking the test, you would be asked to describe the events leading up to the pictured situation, what is happening now, and what will happen in the future.

The Thematic Apperception Test   The **Thematic Apperception Test (TAT)** consists of 29 picture cards like the one on the right. Subjects are shown several cards, one at a time, and are instructed to tell a story about the events that led up to the scene, what the people are currently thinking and feeling, and how the story will end. Some common themes that emerge in these stories are needs for achievement, dependency, and hostility.

The reliability and validity measures of the TAT are low (Weinstein, 1969). In addition, the interpretation of projective tests might also be considered a projective test of the evaluator, since patients reveal parts of themselves when they compose a story to explain the picture but evaluators may also reveal parts of themselves when they evaluate the patient's story.

The various personality measures we have described in this section help psychologists to measure people's differences and attempt to understand them in scientific ways. As can be seen in Table 14.7, psychologists from differing orientations also use different measures of personality assessment. Personality tests also give insights into abnormal personality patterns, as we will see in the next chapter.

THEMATIC APPERCEPTION TEST (TAT) *A projective personality test requiring subjects to tell stories about pictures shown on cards. Presumably, the subjects will "project" themselves into the story, and their narrative will reflect their hidden needs.*

TABLE 14.7
A Comparison of Major Personality Theories

Theory	Major Figures	Determinants of Personality	Major Concepts	Methods of Assessment
Type and trait	Hippocrates Allport	Individual characteristics	Bodily humors; common, central, cardinal, and unique traits	Self-report tests
Psycho-analytic	Freud, Adler, Jung, Horney	Unconscious drives, intrapsychic conflicts, and psychosexual development	Id, ego, superego; defense mechanisms; will-to-power; collective unconscious; archetypes	Interviews; projective tests; self-report tests
Learning	Watson, Skinner, Bandura	Learning from direct experiences and specific situations	Rewards, punishments, modeling	Interviews; self-report tests; observation
Humanistic	Rogers, Maslow	Subjective perception of reality	Self-concept, conditions of worth, unconditional positive regard, self-actualization	Interviews and tests
Cognitive	Ellis	Cognitive interpretation of events	Self-talk, belief systems	Interviews and tests
Biological	Sheldon, Kagan et al., Tellegren et al.	Body shape; bodily responses; inheritance	Somatotypes; genetics	Observation; self-report tests; biological tests

473

Review Questions

1 Interviews can be _____ or _____ in format, enabling the interviewer to obtain informal impressions or comparative ratings on interviewees.

2 _____ tests enable people to describe themselves.

3 The MMPI measures _____ personality characteristics.

4 The Rorschach inkblot test and the Thematic Apperception Test are _____ tests that use neutral or ambiguous stimulus materials.

Answers: 1 structured, unstructured; *2* self-report; *3* abnormal (or disturbed); *4* projective

---

REVIEW OF MAJOR CONCEPTS

STUDYING PERSONALITY

1 Personality is defined as an individual's characteristic pattern of thoughts, emotions, and behaviors. Psychologists describe and explain personality differences within their differing theoretical orientations.

CLASSICAL THEORIES OF PERSONALITY

2 Type theories categorize people into typologies or categories according to physical or behavioral characteristics.

3 Trait theories use personality characteristics to describe and predict behaviors. Allport distinguished cardinal, central, and secondary traits. Consistency of traits has been demonstrated in some cases.

4 Freud's psychoanalytic or psychodynamic theory of personality is a developmental theory that focuses on early childhood experiences. Freud found connections between unconscious childhood instances of sexual trauma or fantasies and adult problems.

5 According to Freud, the psyche is composed of the ego, the superego, and the id. The id contains life and death instincts and seeks immediate gratification of sexual and aggressive impulses, operating on the pleasure principle. The superego is the set of rules for guiding behavior, containing the conscience and the ego-ideal. The ego is the reasoning executive of the psyche, responsible for controlling the id, satisfying the superego, and meeting the expectations of society.

6 An intrapsychic conflict occurs when the three parts of the psyche do not function effectively. If conflict is continued and severe, the ego can be overpowered, causing anxiety. Defense mechanisms are temporary and unconscious strategies used to protect the ego from anxiety.

7 Freud believed that adult personality results from the successful passage through five psychosexual stages. If needs are not met or are overindulged at any particular stage, the person may get stuck (fixated) at that stage or they may regress to a previous stage under times of stress.

8 During the oral stage, the erogenous zone is the mouth and feeding is an important issue. In the anal stage, the anal region is erogenous and toilet training may be an important source of conflict. In the phallic stage, the erogenous zone shifts to the genitals and the child must resolve either the Oedipus or Electra conflict through identification with the same-sex parent. The latency stage is a relatively calm "holding pattern" in which sexual interests are suppressed. Adolescence marks the entrance to the genital stage.

9 The neo-Freudians Jung and Adler emphasized the importance of social and cultural influences on personality development. Adler claimed that inferiority feelings can be overcome. Jung described a personal and collective unconscious and archetypes or patterns for behavior.

CONTEMPORARY THEORIES

10 Learning theories include behaviorist and social learning approaches. They assume human nature to be neutral and claim that individuals are unique because of significant learning experiences.

11 Humanistic theories emphasize internal experiences, thoughts and feelings, that create the individual's self-concept. Humanists such as Carl Rogers and Abraham Maslow emphasize the potential for self-actualization when people receive acceptance or unconditional positive regard.

12 Cognitive theories, such as that of Albert Ellis, stress the importance of interpretation of events in creating individual differences.

13 One of the early biological theorists, William Sheldon, classified people according to three basic body types, or somatotypes: ectomorph (thin), endomorph (overweight), and mesomorph (muscular). He correlated these body types with matching personality types. Although Sheldon's theory has not been substantiated, recent research on the biological components of shyness and the strong personality similari-

ties of twins has given support to the biological theory of personality.

14 Interactionism combines individual and situational factors to explain how people interpret and interact with their environment.

PERSONALITY ASSESSMENT

15 Reliability and validity are two measures used to judge the value of personality tests.

16 Structured and unstructured interviews enable raters to obtain impressions of subjects' personalities.

17 Self-report tests enable people to describe themselves, and include such information as beliefs or interpretations of events and traits. These tests sometimes contain a lie scale and can be constructed to reduce response bias inaccuracy. The MMPI is a widely used self-report test that determines the presence of disturbed personality characteristics.

18 Projective tests require subjects to interpret neutral or ambiguous stimulus materials such as inkblots. The Rorschach inkblot test and Thematic Apperception Test are most often used by researchers to study unconscious elements of personality.

SUGGESTED READINGS

ANASTASI, A. (1982). *Psychological testing* (5th ed.). New York: Macmillan Co. Personality and intelligence testing is described and details and interpretations of commonly used psychological tests are given.

FREUD, S. (1965). *The interpretation of dreams.* New York: Avon/Discus. One of Freud's most popular books, it presents his analysis of the meanings of dreams.

GAY, P. (1988). *Freud: A life for our time.* New York: Norton. A highly readable and entertaining biography of Freud. Given that Freud is one of the most widely known psychologists, this text should be required reading for students planning to major in psychology.

HALL, C. S., LINDZEY, G., LOEHLIN, J. C., MANOSEVITZ, M., & LOCKE, V. O. (1985). *Introduction to theories of personality.* New York: Wiley. A college-level textbook that offers in-depth descriptions and critiques of the major theories of personality.

ROGERS, C. R. (1961). *On becoming a person.* Boston: Houghton Mifflin. One of Carl Rogers's earliest books; an interesting and clear presentation of the humanistic orientation.

chapter fifteen
Abnormal Behavior

SUSAN, a 25-year-old legal secretary, was about to leave her office one evening when she was suddenly overwhelmed by intense feelings of anxiety. Believing that something dreadful and frightening was going to happen to her, she became flushed and found it difficult to breathe—almost as though she were choking. She stumbled outside for some fresh air and the feelings gradually subsided. As Susan later described her terror, "It could not be worse if I were hanging by my fingertips from the wing of a plane in flight. The feeling of impending doom was just as real and frightening."

Fishman and Sheehan (1985), pp. 26–32

Jim is . . . a third year medical student. Over the last few weeks he has been noticing that older men appear to be frightened of him when he passes them on the street. Recently, he has become convinced that he is actually the director of the Central Intelligence Agency and that these men are secret agents of a hostile nation. Jim has found confirmatory evidence for his idea in the fact that a heli-

copter flies over his house every day at 8:00 a.m. and at 4:30 p.m. Surely, this surveillance is part of the plot to assassinate him.

Bernheim and Lewine (1979), p. 4

Ken Bianchi, the "Hillside Strangler," terrorized the Los Angeles area for more than a year. Working with his cousin, Angelo Buono, Bianchi used phony police badges to lure victims into his car or home where they were later raped, systematically tortured, and then murdered. Bianchi and Buono killed 10 females aged 12 to 28. Bianchi killed two more after moving to Washington state. After the longest trial in Los Angeles history, Bianchi was sentenced to life in prison. Presiding Judge Ronald M. George stated: "If ever there was a case where the death penalty was appropriate, this is that case. Angelo Buono and Kenneth Bianchi . . . abducted children and young women, torturing, raping and, finally, depriving their family and friends of them forever as they slowly squeezed out of their victims their last breath of air and their promise of a future life. And for what? The momentary, sadistic thrill of enjoying a brief perverted sexual satisfaction and the venting of their hatred of women."

Magid and McKelvey (1987), pp. 15–18

PARANOIA: *A mental disorder characterized by delusions, or mistaken beliefs, of persecution or grandeur.*

Each of these three individuals has a severe psychological problem, and each case raises a series of interesting questions. What caused Susan's anxiety, Jim's **paranoia**, and Ken's cold-blooded murders? Was there something in their early backgrounds that could explain their later behaviors? Is there something medically wrong with each of them?

What about less severe forms of abnormal behavior? Would a person who dreams of airplane crashes and refuses to fly be considered "mentally ill"? Would the compulsively neat student who types all his lecture notes and refuses to write in any textbook qualify for psychiatric examination? What is the difference between being "eccentric" and very disordered? In short, how do we draw the line between normal and abnormal?

Although none of these questions can be answered simply, we will address the issues they raise in this and the following chapter. This chapter discusses the diverse definitions of abnormal behavior, examines the historical perspectives on the reasons for abnormal behavior, and provides an overview of the various categories of abnormal behavior. Using the classification system of mental health specialists, the chapter presents seven representative psychological disorders found in our culture (anxiety, substance abuse, mood disorders, schizophrenia, personality disorders, dissociative disorders, and organic disorders). The chapter concludes with a discussion of problems in classifying abnormal behavior and examines the issue of discrimination against the mentally disturbed. Chapter 16 is devoted to how various psychological disorders are professionally treated.

A cautionary note is in order before you read on. Talking about the symptoms for mental disorders and studying the details of specific categories of abnormal behavior sometimes creates a psychological version of *medical students disease* (the tendency of medical students to notice in themselves whatever symptoms they are studying in school). As psychology students learn about abnormal behaviors, it is typical for them to notice many of these abnormal characteristics in themselves and other people. When you read about depression, for example, you may wonder whether the depressions you sometimes feel are "abnormal." If you do become seriously concerned about any of the thoughts or feelings you have while studying this chapter, we suggest that you consider seeking the advice of your instructor or a counselor. It's easy to overreact and worry about yourself and the people you care about. On the other hand, studying about abnormal psychology also gives you an opportunity to evaluate the healthiness of your lifestyle and to adjust or change it when appropriate. As you will see here and in the next chapter, there are many effective ways to change problem behaviors.

DEFINING ABNORMAL BEHAVIOR

*Would this behavior be considered abnormal? Although it is not statistically "normal," psychologists generally restrict the term **abnormal behavior** to behavior that is maladaptive or that interferes with the individual's daily functioning.*

What does it mean when a psychologist describes someone's behavior as "abnormal"? The answer depends on the particular psychologist's approach since there is no one generally accepted definition of abnormality. There are in fact three main approaches or standards to determining whether specific behaviors are abnormal: the statistical, subjective discomfort, and maladaptive functioning approaches.

One way to judge whether a person's behavior is abnormal is to compare it to the ways other people in that culture behave. Although standards for normality vary from one culture to another, all cultures have expectations or norms for what is considered appropriate and inappropriate behavior. Individuals who do not adhere to these standards may be labeled mentally ill. When we use the model of "average" behavior in a given culture as our standard for deciding whether a behavior is abnormal, we are using a **statistical standard.** In our culture, for instance, it is considered abnormal for a man to wear a dress, bra, and nylons. Women, on the other hand, are allowed, and even encouraged by the "Dress for Success" standard, to dress in men's clothing. According to the statistical standard, the same overt behavior (cross-sex dressing) is deemed acceptable for women and deviant for men.

STATISTICAL STANDARD: *Evaluates behavior as abnormal when it deviates from average behavior in that particular culture.*

Given the "cultural relativity" found in the statistical approach, some mental health professionals prefer to concentrate on the individual's own judgment of his or her current level of functioning and feelings. This **subjective discomfort approach** allows people to define for themselves what they will individually accept as abnormal or normal. A moderate fear of snakes is statistically normal, for example, but a herpetologist might find this level of fear to be an obstacle to career advancement and might seek therapy to remove the fear. Since many alcoholics and most psychopaths don't see themselves as having psychological problems, however, the subjective discomfort standard, by itself, is not a sufficient basis for judgments of abnormality.

SUBJECTIVE DISCOMFORT APPROACH: *Evaluates behavior as abnormal when the individual is discontented with his or her own psychological functioning.*

Drawing by Sidney Harris

"WHAT A RELIEF. NOW I CAN FOCUS MY FREE-FLOATING ANXIETY ON TO SOMETHING SPECIFIC."

Although abnormal behavior has provided considerable material for cartoonists, the afflicted individual's pain and discomfort are no laughing matter.

ANXIETY DISORDERS: *Type of abnormal behavior characterized by unrealistic, irrational fear.*

Like this man and Susan (in our introduction), people with an **anxiety disorder** have a persistent feeling of threat in facing everyday problems. They feel anxious, ineffective, unhappy, and insecure in a world that seems to them to be dangerous and hostile. According to a 1988 National Institute of Mental Health (NIMH) study, anxiety disorders are the most widespread of all major mental disorders and are found about twice as often in women as in men (Regier et al., 1988).

Unreasonable anxiety: Five major anxiety disorders

Symptoms of anxiety, such as rapid breathing, dry mouth, and increased heart rate, plague all of us during major exams, first dates, and visits to the dentist. But some people experience unreasonable anxiety that is so intense and chronic that it seriously disrupts their lives. We will consider five major types of anxiety disorders: generalized anxiety disorder, panic disorder, phobia, obsessive-compulsive disorder, and post-traumatic stress disorder.

GENERALIZED ANXIETY DISORDER: *Type of long-term anxiety that is not focused on any particular object or situation.*

Generalized anxiety disorder, as the name implies, is a disorder characterized by long-lasting anxiety that is not focused on any particular object or situation *(free-floating anxiety).* The individual feels afraid of *something,* but he or she is generally unable to articulate the specific fear. Because of persistent muscle tension and autonomic fear reactions, individuals may develop headaches, heart palpitations, dizziness, and insomnia. These physical complaints, combined with the intense, long-term anxiety, make it difficult for the individual to cope with normal daily activities.

PANIC DISORDERS: *Type of anxiety disorder characterized by severe attacks of exaggerated anxiety.*

In **panic disorders,** anxiety is concentrated into specific episodes, or panic attacks, during which the person may have heart palpitations, breathing difficulties, dizziness, and fears of going crazy or doing something uncontrollable. A panic attack usually lasts several minutes but may last for hours.

Question: Was Susan's attack an example of a panic disorder?   Yes. Her sudden feelings of fear and breathing difficulties described at the beginning of this chapter are symptomatic of most panic attacks. Because of her worry about having these unpredictable attacks, Susan eventually curtailed her business and social activities to the point that she went on to develop *agoraphobia,* an exaggerated fear of open spaces. This pattern of initial panic attacks followed by later development of agoraphobia is very common (Chambless, 1988).

PHOBIA: *Mental disorder characterized by exaggerated fears of an object or situation.*

Agoraphobia, like other **phobias,** involves a strong, irrational fear of an object or

486

TABLE 15.3
Phobias

Type of Phobia	Object or Situation Feared
Acrophobia	High places
Agoraphobia	Leaving the house; fear of being afraid
Claustrophobia	Small or enclosed places
Cynophobia	Dogs
Cypridophobia	Sexually transmitted disease
Electrophobia	Electricity
Genophobia	Sex
Gynophobia	Women
Hydrophobia	Water
Kakorrhaphiophobia	Failure
Mysophobia	Dirt
Nyctophobia	Darkness
Social phobia	Observation or evaluation by others
Thanatophobia	Death
Zoophobia	Animals

For a person with a strong fear of heights (acrophobia), this photo would be very upsetting.

situation that should not cause such a reaction. Phobic disorders differ from generalized anxiety disorders and panic disorders because there is a specific stimulus that elicits the strong fear response. Imagine how it would feel to be so frightened by a spider that you would attempt to jump out of a speeding car to get away from it. This is how a phobic person feels. Phobics recognize that their fears are excessive and unreasonable but don't seem to be able to prevent their anxiety. People with phobias have especially powerful imaginations and can vividly anticipate severe consequences from encountering such feared objects as knives, bridges, blood, enclosed places, or certain animals (see Table 15.3 for examples of phobias and their official names).

So far we have been discussing only those fears that would qualify as *simple* phobias in the DSM-III-R classification system. *Social* phobias, the other major category, usually center on the fear of being negatively evaluated by others, or on the prospect of being publicly embarrassed because of one's impulsive acts. One of the most common types of social phobias is "stage fright." Although each of us experiences some anxiety when speaking or performing in front of a group, social phobics become so anxious that performance is out of the question. Their fears of public scrutiny and potential humiliation become so pervasive that normal life becomes impossible (Bower, 1988d; Yudolfsky and Silver, 1987).

Unlike phobias, where the anxiety is focused on specific objects or situations, **obsessive-compulsive disorders (OCD)** are characterized by diffuse anxiety created by obsessive thoughts or compulsive behaviors. An *obsession* is a persistent preoccupation with something, most often an idea or feeling. A *compulsion* is an irresistible impulse to perform ritualistic behaviors, such as handwashing, counting, or putting things in order. In OCD, individuals feel driven to think about certain things or to carry out some action against their will. The person generally recognizes that the behavior is irrational but cannot seem to control it. When they resist performing compulsive behaviors, they generally experience a feeling of mounting tension that can only be relieved by yielding to the compulsion.

OBSESSIVE-COMPULSIVE DISORDER (OCD): *Type of anxiety disorder characterized by persistent thoughts and repetitive, ritualistic behaviors.*

Question: I sometimes find myself checking and rechecking the stove burners before I leave my home. Would this be considered an obsessive-compulsive disorder? The difference between an OCD and milder forms of compulsion is that the

Survivors of natural disasters sometimes experience long-lasting emotional disturbances known as post-traumatic stress disorders.

behaviors are much more extreme, appear irrational to almost everyone, and interfere considerably with everyday life. OCD individuals sometimes wash their hands hundreds of times a day or spend hours performing senseless rituals of organizing and cleaning (Rapoport, 1989). The psychological problems of billionaire Howard Hughes provide an extreme example of obsessive-compulsive behavior:

> Due to his unreasonable fear of germs, he made people who worked with him wear white gloves, sometimes several pairs, when handling documents he would later touch. When newspapers were brought to him, they had to be in stacks of three so he could slide the middle one out by grasping it with Kleenex. To escape contamination by dust, he ordered that masking tape be put around the doors and windows of his cars and houses.
>
> *Fowler (1986)*

POST-TRAUMATIC STRESS DISORDER (PTSD): *Type of anxiety disorder that follows an overwhelming, traumatic event.*

Extreme feelings of anxiety are also the problem for victims of **post-traumatic stress disorder (PTSD).** The essential feature of this disorder is the development of characteristic symptoms following a traumatic event, such as rape, combat experiences, or sudden disasters. Symptoms include intense terror, fear, and helplessness during the trauma, and recurrent dreams, flashbacks, impaired concentration, and/or emotional numbing afterward (Davison and Neale, 1989). Although the disorder has received much attention, there is considerable controversy concerning its prevalence and diagnosis (Breslau and Davis, 1989; Helzer, Robins, and McEvoy, 1987; Roberts, 1988). For those individuals who do suffer from PTSD, the symptoms may continue for years after the initial traumatic incident. Rape victims and combat veterans, for example, may experience unpleasant emotional consequences for the rest of their lives (Buie, 1989).

Causes of anxiety disorders: Biology or learning?

As you may imagine, the exact cause of anxiety disorders is a matter of considerable debate, but recent research has focused primarily on the roles of learning and biology.

The learning perspective on anxiety disorders suggests that phobias and other reactions are the result of *classical* and *operant* conditioning (see Chapter 6). The original neutral stimulus (e.g., the office building in Susan's case) may be paired with a frightening event (the sudden panic attack) so that it becomes a conditioned stimulus-eliciting anxiety. After this type of classical conditioning, the phobia is typically maintained through the process of operant conditioning. Susan starts to avoid the anxiety-producing stimulus (her office) because of negative reinforcement—avoiding the stimulus leads to a reduction in the unpleasant feelings of anxiety. Susan's later development of *agoraphobia* could be explained by the process of stimulus generalization—her fear of having a panic attack spread from her office to all open places (McAllister et al., 1986).

Social learning theorists would propose that some phobias are the result of modeling and imitation. Overprotective, fearful parents may make their children more prone to developing phobias and other anxiety disorders. Howard Hughes, for instance, was raised by an extremely overprotective mother who worried constantly about his physical health (Fowler, 1986).

Question: How does biology contribute to anxiety disorders?   Recent research has found that certain individuals are more likely to develop anxiety disorders because of a genetic predisposition toward an overreaction of the autonomic nervous system (Foa and Kozak, 1986). These people apparently respond more quickly and intensely to stressful stimuli. The fact that drugs, like Valium, block or relieve symptoms of anxiety provides further evidence for a biochemical basis (Schatzberg, 1988; Yudolfsky and Silver, 1987). Researchers have also noted that sodium lactate and caffeine can provoke or exaggerate a panic attack (Bower, 1989c; Fishman and Sheehan, 1985).

If we look further into the biology of obsessive-compulsive disorders, we find considerable evidence for a genetic link and a brain abnormality (Rapoport, 1989). The disorder runs in families and studies have shown that individuals with OCD may be suffering from a disruption of the brain pathways that link the frontal lobes of the cerebral cortex to the basal ganglia. The good news is that sufferers of OCD have been helped with a combination of drug therapy and behavior therapy (Gelman, 1989).

DISSOCIATIVE DISORDERS

The most dramatic and popularized cases of psychological disorders are the **dissociative disorders**. The core element of these disorders is the splitting apart (dissociation) of critical elements of the personality. Individuals can separate themselves from the core of their personality by failing to recall or identify past experience *(psychogenic amnesia)*, by leaving home and wandering off *(psychogenic fugue)*, or by developing completely separate personalities *(multiple personality)*.

DISSOCIATIVE DISORDER: *Stress-related disorder characterized by amnesia, fugue, or multiple personality.*

Question: Why would someone want to separate from their basic personality? The major problem underlying all dissociative disorders is the need to escape from stress. By developing amnesia, running away, or creating separate personalities, the individual is able to cope (in a maladaptive way) with the stressors and is able to deny responsibility for unacceptable behavior. Children who are victims of incest, for example, often develop amnesia for the actual sexual episodes (Berkowitz, 1987). In cases where the incest was also violent or sadistic, the victim may block out all memories for long segments of time (Herman and Schatzow, 1987). Some researchers have also found that about 98 percent of people with multiple personalities were abused as children (Chance, 1986).

Despite the common appearance of these disorders in movies, television soap-operas, and novels, they are actually quite rare. Hence, our coverage of them will be relatively brief.

Psychogenic amnesia: Memory loss

Psychogenic amnesia is a partial or total inability to recall past experience. Although memory loss also occurs with brain damage, psychosis, and substance abuse, psychogenic amnesia is usually related to a failure to *recall.* The "forgotten" information is still there, but it is beneath the level of consciousness. People with this disorder tend to forget personal information such as their name and address and are unable to recognize parents and friends. They rarely forget impersonal facts like the name of their country or skills like driving a car and reading a book (Carson, Butcher, and Coleman, 1988).

PSYCHOGENIC AMNESIA: *Inability to recall the personal past as a result of psychological stress.*

During the period of amnesia, the person is often indifferent about the memory disturbance but may seem perplexed and disoriented, and may wander purposelessly. In movies, the return of memory often occurs when the person is hit over the head. But this is not the usual way that memories are regained in psychogenic amnesia. Termination is often spontaneous and abrupt. Complete recovery with no return of amnesia is the usual case.

Psychogenic fugue: Wandering off

PSYCHOGENIC FUGUE: *A type of amnesia in which people suddenly leave where they live and assume a new identity.*

Psychogenic fugue is a more unusual form of amnesia where the person retreats further from stress by going in what is called a *fugue* (Latin for "to flee") state. Individuals wander away from home and often assume a new identity. Although all personal memories from the former life are blocked, other abilities are unimpaired and the individual appears normal to others. After a period of time—days, months, or sometimes years—they suddenly "wake up" and find themselves in a strange place, not knowing how they got there and with complete amnesia for the period of the fugue. Recovery is usually complete, but people seldom recall experiences that happened during the fugue state.

Multiple personality: Changes in identity

MULTIPLE PERSONALITY: *Dissociative disorder characterized by the presence of two or more distinct personality systems within the same individual.*

A person with a **multiple personality** has two or more distinct personality systems that become dominant at different times. Each personality has unique memories, behaviors, and social relationships. Transition from one personality to another occurs suddenly and is often associated with psychological stress (Thigpen and Cleckley, 1957). Usually the original personality has no knowledge or awareness of the existence of the alternate subpersonalities, but all of "them" are aware of lost periods of time. Often, the alternate personalities are very different from the original personality and may be of the opposite sex or a different race or age.

Although multiple personalities are extremely rare, a few well-publicized cases have drawn attention to the disorder. The book and movie *The Three Faces of Eve* presented the story of Chris Sizemore, a young homemaker who discovered that she had three separate personalities: "Eve White," a mild, meek, and virtuous wife and mother; "Eve Black," an extroverted, seductive, adventurous woman who rejected her marriage and family; and a nameless third personality who seemed to blend the traits of the other two (Thigpen and Cleckley, 1957). The book and movie *Sybil* portrayed the case of Sybil Dorsett, a midwestern schoolteacher who experienced 16 personalities that would take turns controlling her body. Instead of thinking of herself as one person who behaved differently at times, Sybil had lapses of memory when she became "another person." When she was "Peggy Lou," she was aggressive and capable of anger. As "Peggy Ann," she could deal with fearful situations.

Question: What caused her to develop these other personalities? As a child, Sybil would escape from the cruel reality of physical and emotional abuse at the hands of her sadistic mother by becoming another person. She apparently resorted to this method of dealing with trauma and stress again and again, for she would often find herself regaining consciousness without any memories of the previous days or years. Eventually, she sought the help of a psychiatrist, who treated her for 11 years before she became *just* Sybil (Schreiber, 1973).

The classification of *multiple personality* is one of the most troublesome and controversial of all psychological disorders. First of all, the general public often confuses this disorder with *schizophrenia,* but as you'll see later, schizophrenic disorders are entirely different. In addition, mental health professionals have questioned whether this disorder actually exists. Is this a real psychological disorder or are the persons involved merely faking?

In the television drama Sybil, *actress Sally Field (right) won an Emmy Award for her sensitive portrayal of a woman suffering a multiple personality disorder. Joanne Woodward portrayed the psychiatrist who spent long hours helping Sybil.*

Some researchers suggest that many cases of multiple personality *are* faked and that other cases result from unconscious efforts by the persons involved to please the therapist (Levitt, 1988; Spanos, Weekes, and Bertrand, 1985; Thigpen and Cleckley, 1984). Such skeptics believe that therapists may be unintentionally encouraging and thereby overreporting multiple personalities. On the other side of the debate are psychologists who accept the validity of multiple personality and suggest that they are underdiagnosed (Kluft, 1987). At present, the debate is far from settled and probably won't be resolved without a great deal of additional research.

Review Questions

1 _____ are anxiety disorders with exaggerated, irrational fears of specific objects or situations.

2 In _____ disorders, there are anxiety-arousing thoughts and ritualistic behaviors.

3 In _____ stress disorder, the person has experienced an overwhelming stress.

4 Learning theorists suggest that anxiety disorders result from the processes of _____ and _____ conditioning.

5 The major, underlying problem for *all* dissociative disorders is the psychological need to escape from _____ .

6 Psychogenic _____ is a partial or total inability to recall the past, whereas psychogenic _____ is a "running away" from the previous residence and creating a new identity.

7 _____ _____ is a disorder characterized by two or more distinct personality systems.

Answers: 1 phobias;   *2* obsessive–compulsive;   *3* post-traumatic;   *4* classical, operant;   *5* stress;   *6* amnesia, fugue;   *7* multiple personality

SCHIZOPHRENIA

Imagine for the moment that you hear voices inside your head ordering you to "Be good," "Do bad," "Stand up," or "Collide with the Other World." These voices also repeatedly ask "Do you want a cigar?" How would you react if your visual world contained colored patterns floating in the air, if to you sneezes exploded into colorful designs, or if you believed that others could read your mind? These are the actual experiences that plagued psychiatrist Carol North for nearly two decades (Wells, 1988).

SCHIZOPHRENIA: *Group of psychotic disorders involving distortions in language and thinking, perception, emotion, and behavior.*

These symptoms are hallmarks of the disorder known as **schizophrenia.** Literally, *schizophrenia* means "split mind," but when Eugen Bleuler coined the term in 1911 he was referring to the fragmenting of thought processes and splitting of thoughts and emotions found in schizophrenic disorders (Neale, Oltmanns, and Winters, 1983). Unfortunately, "split mind" and "split personality" are often confused by the general public. One study of college freshmen found that 64 percent believed that multiple personality was a common symptom of schizophrenia (Torrey, 1988). As you have just discovered, *multiple personality disorder* is the correct term for the rare syndrome of having more than one distinct personality. Schizophrenia is a much more common, and altogether different, type of psychological disorder. What are the nature and symptoms of the disorder we call schizophrenia? What different forms does it take? What are its causes? These are the questions we will now address.

Symptoms of schizophrenia: Losing contact with reality

Schizophrenia is generally considered the most serious and severe form of mental disturbance. According to statistics, one out of every 100 people will develop schizophrenia and approximately half of all people admitted to mental hospitals are diagnosed as schizophrenic (Torrey, 1988). Schizophrenic disorders usually emerge during adolescence or young adulthood and only rarely after age 45 (Murphy and Helzer, 1986).

Schizophrenia is classified under the larger heading of *psychosis,* a category used primarily to describe lack of contact with reality. All the disorders we have considered so far are serious. They involve considerable pain and distress to the afflicted individual, but most sufferers *can* still function in their daily lives. Schizophrenics, like other individuals suffering from psychosis, are usually not capable of living ordinary lives, particularly during their schizophrenic episodes. During these episodes schizophrenics lose contact with reality to such an extent that they cannot relate to others, and they require institutional or custodial care.

Question: What are the signs or symptoms that indicate schizophrenia? Schizophrenia is characterized by psychological disturbances or disruptions in four major areas: perception, language and thought, emotions, and behavior.

Perceptual symptoms The senses of schizophrenics may be either enhanced (as in the case of Carol North) or blunted. The usual filtering and selection processes that allow most people to concentrate on whatever they choose seem to be impaired in schizophrenics, and sensory stimulation is jumbled and distorted. In the book, *I Never Promised You a Rose Garden,* a schizophrenic girl is described as having the following perceptual distortions:

> The laws of physics and solid matter were repealed and the experience of a lifetime of tactile sensation, motion, form, gravity, and light were invalidated. She did not know whether she was standing or sitting down, which way was upright, and from where the light, which was a stab as it touched her, was coming. She lost track of the parts of her body; where her arms were and how to move them. As light went spinning erratically away and back she tried to clutch at thoughts only to find that she had lost all memory of the English language.
>
> *Green (1964), p. 90*

A more organized type of mistaken perception experienced by schizophrenics is **hallucinations,** or perceiving things for which there are no appropriate external stimuli. Hallucinations can occur in any of the senses (visual, tactile, olfactory), but auditory hallucinations are most common in schizophrenia. As Carol North's case demonstrates, schizophrenics often hear voices speaking their thoughts aloud, commenting on their behavior, or telling them what to do. The voices seem to come from inside their own heads or from an external source such as an animal.

HALLUCINATIONS: *Sensory perceptions that occur in the absence of a real external stimulus.*

Question: Are schizophrenics dangerous?   Occasionally schizophrenics will hurt themselves or others in response to their distorted internal experiences or the voices they hear. These are the cases that are reported dramatically in the media and that create an exaggerated fear of "mental patients." In reality, schizophrenics are often withdrawn and gentle people who are statistically *less* likely to harm you than are members of your own family (Stedman, 1975).

Language and thought disturbances   For schizophrenics, words lose their usual meanings and associations, logic is impaired, and thoughts are disorganized and bizarre. For example, a schizophrenic patient gave this explanation for the meaning of the proverb "People who live in glass houses shouldn't throw stones":

> People who live in glass houses shouldn't forget people who live in stone houses and shouldn't throw glass.

In mild language and thought disturbances, schizophrenic speech is tangential, switching from one idea to another. In more severe disturbances, phrases and words are disconnected (referred to as *word salads*) and artificial words are created *(neologisms)*. Table 15.4 presents some examples of these language disturbances.

The thought process of schizophrenics often focus on remarkably unrealistic or distorted beliefs called delusions. Contrary to common mistaken beliefs that we all experience from time to time, such as thoughts that we can do no wrong or that someone is deliberately persecuting us, **delusions** are mistaken beliefs that are maintained in spite of strong evidence to the contrary. Carol North held the delusion that others could read her mind. In *delusions of grandeur*, people believe they are extremely important persons like Jesus Christ or the Queen of England. In *delusions of persecution*, individuals believe they are the target of a plot to harm or destroy them (as was the case with Jim, our introductory character who believed that "secret agents" were trying to assassinate him). In *delusions of reference*, unrelated events are given special significance (as when it is assumed that a radio program or newspaper article is giving a special message to the person).

DELUSIONS: *Mistaken beliefs maintained in spite of strong evidence to the contrary.*

Emotional symptoms   Changes in emotions (affect) are common in schizophrenia and follow a predictable pattern of abnormality. In the early stages, emotions can be exaggerated and often fluctuate rapidly in inappropriate ways. For example, extreme fear, guilt, or

Disorganized thoughts, emotions, and perceptions are often reflected in the artwork of schizophrenics. This picture of a tree-man holding a bleeding human head was drawn by a schizophrenic who described the scene as "humorous."

TABLE 15.4
Schizophrenic Language Problems

Problem	Examples
Word salads	"The same children are sent of a rose, sweet-smelling perfume that gives us peace and parts and whole." "The sad kind and peaceful valleys of the mind come beckoning under rivers."
Neologisms	"splisters" (combination of splinters and blisters) "smever" (combination of smart and clever)

The distortion of reality in schizophrenia can create bizarre behaviors.

euphoria may occur suddenly without any reasonable causes. In other cases, emotions may become blunted or decrease in intensity. In some extreme cases, schizophrenics have *flattened affect,* a serious decrease in emotional responses of any kind.

Behavioral disturbances The abnormal behaviors of schizophrenics are often related to the disturbances in their thoughts and feelings. For example, when they experience a flooding of sensory stimuli or feel confused, they often withdraw from social contacts and remain silent. Although they may appear bizarre to others, a schizophrenic's unusual actions sometimes have special meanings for them. One patient shook his head rhythmically from side to side to try to shake the excess thoughts out of his mind. Another massaged his head repeatedly "to help to clear it" of unwanted thoughts.

In place of the four previous categories of symptoms (perception, language and thought, emotions, and behavior) some researchers have suggested that schizophrenic symptoms naturally fall into one of two categories:

1. *Positive symptoms* involving excessive or distorted activity (e.g., bizarre delusions of persecution, hallucinations, inappropriate laughter and tears, and erratic behavior).
2. *Negative symptoms* involving behavioral deficits or loss of activity (e.g., toneless voices, flattened emotions, social withdrawal, and poverty of speech).

Under the proposed new form of classification, schizophrenics would be categorized as either Type 1 (positive symptoms) or Type 2 (negative symptoms). The distinction is promising, and researchers are now in the process of clarifying which symptoms are positive and which are negative (Crow, 1985; Kay, Fiszbein, and Opler, 1987).

Causes of schizophrenia: Nature and nurture theories

There are several theories that attempt to explain schizophrenia. Biological theories emphasize physical changes in the nervous system based on abnormal brain functioning or inherited predispositions. Other theories emphasize psychosocial factors such as disturbed family interactions or stressful experiences.

Biological theories An enormous amount of scientific research has been done concerning possible biological factors in schizophrenia. Most of this research can be grouped into three major categories: neurotransmitters, brain abnormalities, and genetics.

Neurotransmitters, primarily dopamine, have long been suspected of playing a major role in schizophrenia (Lucins, 1975; Miklowitz et al., 1986; Torrey, 1988). The

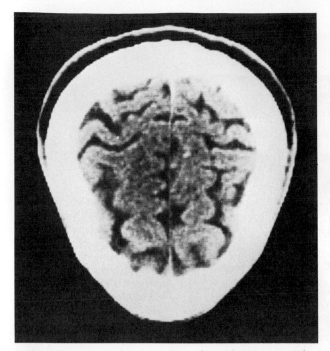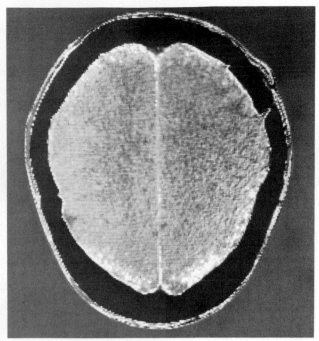

Following an attempted assassination of President Reagan, John Hinkley, Jr. was diagnosed as schizophrenic and CAT scans of his brain showed widened fissues or spaces (left). The fissures of most young adults are pressed together too tightly to be seen (right).

dopamine hypothesis suggests that excess dopamine or oversensitivity to dopamine is related to the onset and maintenance of schizophrenic episodes. This hypothesis is based on three facts:

DOPAMINE HYPOTHESIS: *A theory suggesting that schizophrenic episodes occur when there is an abundance of dopamine or an oversensitivity to its effects.*

1. Amphetamines are known to increase dopamine uptake and also to worsen the symptoms of schizophrenia.
2. Drugs that block the action of dopamine at receptors in the brain are known to eliminate the symptoms of schizophrenia.
3. Autopsies of brains of schizophrenics have discovered an increased number of dopamine receptors (Suinn, 1987).

Researchers have criticized the dopamine hypothesis because approximately 20 percent of schizophrenics do not respond to the dopamine-blocking drugs (Holden, 1987). Furthermore, these same drugs complete their work at the receptor level within hours, yet the symptoms of schizophrenia don't improve for weeks. Perhaps the most important criticism of the dopamine hypothesis is that it is based on correlational data and, as you may remember from Chapter 1, correlation does not establish causation. This means that dopamine has only been found to be *related* to schizophrenia. The current thought is that some other (unknown) factor causes schizophrenia, and this factor is also correlated with dopamine.

The second major biological theory for schizophrenia centers on the possibility of brain abnormalities. When studying the brains of schizophrenics, some researchers have found an abnormal enlargement of the brain's ventricles (the hollow areas filled with fluid) and other abnormalities of the central nervous system (Andreasen, 1988; Heinrichs and Buchanan, 1988). These structural changes do not seem to be related to medical treatments and drugs, and there is evidence that patients with the largest ventricles have the most severe symptoms. The enlarged ventricles may also explain why schizophrenics tend to show decreased activity in the frontal lobes of the brain (Weinberger, Berman, and Zec, 1986).

Question: How did researchers discover these enlarged ventricles and the decreased activity? One method they used was computerized axial tomography (CAT) scans, in which a computer analyzes X-ray pictures of specific brain sections. As can be seen in the photograph on this page, CAT scans often show physical changes in the brain structures of schizophrenics. Another technique, positron emission tomography

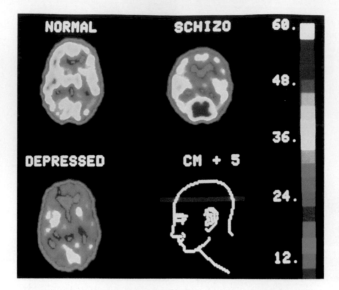

PET scans are being widely used in the diagnosis and treatment of several disorders. Note the variations in brain activity in the normal, schizophrenic, and depressed brain scans. Levels of brain activity correspond to the colors and numbers on the right-hand section of the photo. The higher numbers and "warmer" colors are associated with increased brain activity.

(PET), uses a computer to summarize the distribution of a radioactive sugar solution injected into the brain. PET scans have shown that the frontal lobes of schizophrenics tend to have decreased activity.

The significance of brain abnormalities, such as enlarged ventricles, is currently being debated by psychologists. As with the criticism of the dopamine hypothesis, critics have argued that it is difficult to sort out whether this brain abnormality is a cause or effect of schizophrenia (Weinberger et al., 1983). In view of our earlier distinction between *positive* and *negative* symptoms, it is interesting to note that increased dopamine seems to lead to positive symptoms and the enlarged ventricles are associated with negative symptoms (Crow, 1985).

The third biological theory, the genetic argument, suggests that certain people inherit a predisposing *vulnerability* to schizophrenia (Beatty, 1987; Loehlin, Willerman, and Horn, 1988). As noted earlier, the incidence of schizophrenia in the normal population is about 1 percent, but for people with two parents who are schizophrenic it is around 46 percent (Nichol and Gottesman, 1983). Family studies have shown that the incidence of this disorder among biological relatives increases with genetic similarity. The highest incidence occurs in identical twins (see Figure 15.3).

Figure 15.3 Heredity risks for schizophrenia. Your lifetime risk of developing schizophrenia is related to how closely you are genetically related to a schizophrenic individual. Although environmental factors also play a role in the development of schizophrenia, these statistics demonstrate the importance of genetic vulnerability. (*Source:* Bernheim and Lewine, 1979; Gottesman and Shields, 1982; Gottesman et al., 1988.)

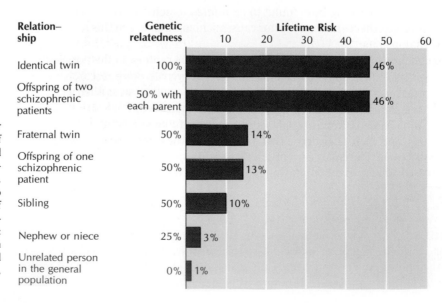

Question: Does that mean that identical twins become schizophrenic more often than usual?   No. Identical twins become schizophrenic at the same rate as nontwins—one person in every 100. However, if you have an identical twin who is schizophrenic, your likelihood of being schizophrenic yourself is the highest of any biological relationship.

In sum, there is evidence linking schizophrenia to neurochemistry (the dopamine hypothesis), abnormal brain structure, and heredity. Evidence for the first two factors is tentative, however. It is also clear that nonbiological, psychosocial factors contribute to schizophrenia.

Psychosocial theories   Many theorists believe that the causes of schizophrenia lie not in biological factors but in the environment. Stress, as we discovered in Chapter 13, has long been known to produce dramatic physical and psychological effects. Given the fact that identical twins share the same genes, researchers have suggested that when only one twin develops schizophrenia the cause might be differences in environmental stress. Supportive research finds that the twin who becomes schizophrenic has often been subjected to stressful experiences, such as serious illnesses and hospitalization (Parnas, Teasdale, and Schulsinger, 1985). Further evidence for the role of stress in schizophrenia comes from Hollingshead and Redlich's (1958) classic study on social class. These researchers found that individuals from the lowest socioeconomic class were at nine times greater risk of developing schizophrenia. This suggests that the stress of living in impoverished conditions may contribute to schizophrenia.

Another potential psychosocial source of schizophrenic symptoms is the child's family or social environment. According to this type of theory, a child who is subjected to rejection or mistreatment will fail to develop an adequate concept of reality and normal emotional responses (Roff and Knight, 1981). This "disturbed environment" theory is supported by several studies that evaluated the schizophrenic's family style of *expressed emotionality* (EE). By measuring the level of criticism and hostility aimed at the schizophrenic individual, as well as emotional overinvolvement in the schizophrenic's life, researchers found greater relapse and worsening of symptoms among hospitalized schizophrenics who go home to high-EE families (Brown, Birley, and Wing, 1972; Hooley, 1988; Vaughn et al., 1984).

Other researchers have questioned this "disturbed family" research, and advocacy groups for the families of the mentally disordered have argued that this is just one more attempt to blame families for what the organizations consider a biological brain disease (Bower, 1988b). At the present time, there is no one theory that adequately explains the cause of schizophrenia. Most psychologists agree that a combination of factors is probably involved.

Question: Do any schizophrenics get better?   Although no totally effective therapy has yet been devised, the outlook has improved over the last 25 years. According to estimates by the National Institute of Mental Health, approximately 25 percent achieve full recovery, 50 percent recover at least partially, and 25 percent require long-term care (Shore, 1986). Thus, despite the fact that schizophrenia is a serious disturbance, many individuals improve enough to lead independent, satisfying lives (Torrey, 1988). As we learn more about the causes and treatments, we should be able to help even more schizophrenics to achieve successful outcomes.

Review Questions

1 Schizophrenia is diagnosed in one person in every _____.

2 Schizophrenic symptoms include _____, a major loss of contact with reality.

3 _____ are perceptual distortions in any of the sensory modalities, such as hearing voices.

4 _____ are mistaken beliefs that persist, even when strong evidence to the contrary is presented.

5 Schizophrenic symptoms have been related to increased activity of _____ neurotransmitter circuits.

Answers: 1 100; *2* psychosis; *3* hallucinations; *4* delusions; *5* dopamine

MOOD DISORDERS

Ann had been divorced for eight months when she called a psychologist for an emergency appointment. Although her husband had verbally and physically abused her for years, she had had mixed feelings about staying in the marriage. She had anticipated feeling good after the divorce, but she became increasingly depressed. She had trouble getting to sleep, had little appetite, felt very fatigued, and showed no interest in her usual activities. She stayed home from work for two days because she "just didn't feel like going in." Late one afternoon she went straight to bed, leaving her two small children to fend for themselves. Then, the night before calling for an appointment, she took five sleeping tablets and a couple of stiff drinks. As she said, "I don't think I wanted to kill myself; I just wanted to forget everything for awhile."

Meyer and Salmon (1988), p. 312

Ann's case is a good example of a *mood disorder* (also known as an affective disorder). This category encompasses not only excessive sadness like Ann's but also excessive and unreasonable elation.

Question: Do you mean it is considered abnormal to be too happy? The key words in classifying a person's emotions as disordered are *excessive* and *unreasonable*. Both depression and euphoria are problematic reactions when they are extreme or when the person is not in touch with reality. There are two main types of mood disorders. In **major depression**, the person experiences a persistent depression. In **bipolar disorder**, the person experiences euphoric (manic) episodes that alternate with normal feelings or with normal and depressed periods. In both types of mood disorder, the person can have delusions or hallucinations. When these symptoms are accompanied by the psychotic loss of contact with reality it is referred to as an *affective psychosis*.

MAJOR DEPRESSION: *A lasting and continuous state of depression without apparent cause.*

All of us feel depressed from time to time, but people suffering from *major depression* are unusually or chronically depressed and often unable to function. As we saw in the case of Ann, depressed individuals typically lose interest in everyday activities and feel worthless and discouraged. They often have a hard time thinking clearly or recognizing their own problems. They are most often helped by family or friends who recognize the symptoms.

Question: What are the symptoms of serious depression? As can be seen in Table 15.5, there are numerous emotional, cognitive, and behavioral signs. If a friend exhibits several of these symptoms, you should encourage him or her to seek professional help.

BIPOLAR DISORDER: *An affective disorder characterized by manic episodes that alternate with normal feelings or with normal and depressed periods.*

Bipolar disorder is characterized by alternating appearance of two emotional extremes. Everyone experiences mood swings from time to time, but when someone shifts from mania to depression and back again, and especially when these moods are unrelated to external events, they are said to show a bipolar disorder.

During a manic episode, the person feels euphoric, with an inflated and unrealistic sense of his or her own importance. Irritability sometimes occurs suddenly, causing a shift

TABLE 15.5
Recognizing the Symptoms of Serious Depression

The following questions can help you decide if a friend is seriously depressed and may need help.

Does the person express feelings of
_____ Sadness or "emptiness"?
_____ Hopelessness, pessimism, or guilt?
_____ Helplessness or worthlessness?

Does the person seem
_____ Unable to make decisions?
_____ Unable to concentrate or remember?
_____ To have lost interest or pleasure in ordinary activities — like sports or talking on the phone?
_____ To have more problems with school, work, and/or family?

Does the person complain of
_____ Loss of energy and drive?
_____ Trouble falling asleep, staying asleep, or getting up?
_____ Appetite problems; is he or she losing or gaining weight?
_____ Headaches, stomachaches, or backaches?
_____ Chronic aches and pains in joints and muscles?

Has his or her behavior changed suddenly so that he or she
_____ Is restless or more irritable?
_____ Wants to be alone most of the time?
_____ May be drinking heavily or taking drugs?

Has the person talked about
_____ Death?
_____ Suicide — or has he or she attempted suicide?

Source: National Institute of Mental Health (1985).

to anger or depression. The manic person often makes plans for becoming rich and famous and may have delusions of grandeur. Manics are hyperactive and often go without sleep for days at a time without becoming fatigued. They have an unceasing and unselective enthusiasm for interacting with people and doing things. Thinking is speeded up and can change abruptly to new topics. Poor judgment is common. Manic episodes last a few days to a few weeks and often end abruptly.

During a depressive episode, the person's mood, thinking style, and activity level are reversed. The symptoms of moderate or severe depression take the place of the extreme behaviors of mania. A depressive episode may last for weeks or months (Papolos and Papolos, 1987).

Question: Are depression and mania physical or psychological? **Earlier biological** research suggested that depression was due to depletion of neurotransmitters, such as norepinephrine and serotonin, whereas mania was due to an excess of these same chemicals (Goodwin and Potter, 1979). Later research, however, failed to support such a straightforward mechanism (Thase, Frank, and Kupfer, 1985). Although the precise link between neurotransmitters and depression is still being investigated, it *is* known that the most effective antidepressant drugs work mainly on norepinephrine pathways (Sargent, 1986).

Whatever the primary physiological basis, there is some evidence that major depression, as well as bipolar disorders, may be inherited (Georgotas and Cancro, 1988; Wierzbicki, 1987). Twenty-five percent of patients with major depression and up to 50 percent of patients with bipolar disorder have a relative with some form of mood disorder ("Nature and Causes," 1988). In a highly publicized study of Old Order Amish families,

Studies of Amish families in Lancaster County, Pennsylvania, have suggested that bipolar disorders are at least partly a matter of genetic inheritance.

researchers discovered two genetic "markers" (on chromosome 11) common to family members suffering from bipolar disorders (Egeland et al., 1987). This study initially generated a great deal of enthusiasm since it supposedly discovered the "first genetic marker for a mental illness" (Kolata, 1987). However, other studies failed to support this research or reported other possible genes (Depue and Iacono, 1989; Mendlewicz et al., 1987). At the present time, psychologists are recommending caution concerning genetic markers for mood disorders. It is important to remember that genetic research is correlational, the findings are controversial, and the attention to biological factors may lead to a neglect of possible psychological causes.

Psychological theories of depression focus on disturbances in the person's interpersonal relationships, self-concept, and learning history. The psychoanalytic explanation of depression sees it as anger turned inward against oneself when an important relationship or attachment is lost. Anger is assumed to come from feelings of rejection or withdrawal of affection, especially when a loved one dies. A humanistic analysis assumes depression is created when a person's self-concept is overly demanding or when positive growth is blocked.

LEARNED HELPLESSNESS: *Seligman's theory that a personal sense of helplessness or resignation leads to depression.*

The **learned helplessness** theory of depression, developed by Martin Seligman (1975, 1988), is an outgrowth of research on avoidance learning in animals (see Chapter 6). Seligman has demonstrated that when animals or humans are subjected to pain they cannot escape, they may develop a sense of helplessness or resignation and thereafter not attempt to escape painful experiences. This expectancy of being unable to change things for the better leads to depression. Seligman also suggests that our general societal emphasis on individualism and diminished involvement with others makes us particularly vulnerable to depression. In a later revision of learned helplessness theory, a cognitive element was added involving the explanations people assign to their own and others' behavior (Abramson, Alloy, and Metalsky, in press; Peterson and Seligman, 1984). Once the individual perceives that his or her behaviors are unrelated to outcomes (learned helplessness), depression is most likely to occur when the person attributes failure to causes which are *internal* ("my own weakness"), *stable* ("this weakness is a long-standing and unchanging one"), and *global* ("this weakness is a problem in lots of settings") (Suinn, 1987). This type of reasoning is further discussed under the topic of attribution theory in Chapter 17.

Question: Is depression affected by the seasons? I've heard of people being treated by simply sitting under bright lights.   Some individuals do suffer from seasonal depression, also known as *seasonal affective disorder* (SAD). Although some researchers have found people whose depression occurred during the summer months, most SAD sufferers report winter depression followed by normal mood or even elevation in the spring and early summer (Bower, 1988a; Terman and Link, 1989; Wehr et al., 1986,

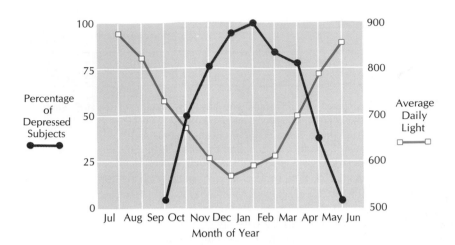

Figure 15.4 Seasonal affective disorder. Research has shown that some forms of depression are strongly correlated with the amount of daily light. As you can see in this graph, the months of lowest light are the highest months for depression. (*Source:* Adapted from Wurtman and Wurtman, 1989.)

1987). As can be seen in Figure 15.4, this second pattern of winter depression is closely correlated with the average daily light for each month. Studies with controlled periods of air-conditioning for summer depression and exposure to artificial lights for winter depression produced dramatic improvement in mood, and when treatment was discontinued relapses occurred (Bower, 1988a; Rosenthal et al., 1984). The possibility of a seasonal type of depression has been accepted to the degree that it is now listed as a subcategory in the DSM-III-R.

Whatever the causes of depression, one of the major dangers associated with it is the increased risk of suicide. Severely depressed people often become suicidal as a result of their feelings of hopelessness and helplessness. They may be unable to act on their suicidal feelings while deeply depressed. But in the period following the deepest depression, when others around them see them as "getting better," they may muster sufficient energy to carry out their wishes to die.

At the present time, suicide ranks among the top ten causes of death in most Western countries (Carson, Butcher, and Coleman, 1988). In the United States, there are over 25,000 suicides a year and as many as 200,000 suicide attempts. Statistics, however accurate, can never describe the full horror of suicide. If we look at the typical suicide victim, we find a depressed, lonely individual who is often undergoing a *temporary* crisis in his or her life. During this state of severe psychological distress, the person often makes the *permanent* decision to end his or her life because of an inability to see his or her problems objectively or to see an alternative course of action. Studies have shown that the vast majority of people who take their own lives are actually very ambivalent (Shneidman, 1987). They don't necessarily want to die, they're just unsure about how to go on living.

A second major tragedy associated with suicide is the lifelong sadness that is often experienced by the friends and relatives of the suicide victim. Children of parents who kill themselves are at particularly high risk of severe personality disturbances and of also committing suicide (Ojanlatua, Hammer and Mohr, 1987). As Shneidman (1969) suggests: "The person who commits suicide puts his psychological skeleton in the survivor's emotional closet" (p. 22).

Question: How can you tell if someone is suicidal? Because factors that precipitate suicide are complex, we have compiled a list of high-risk factors in Table 15.6. As a general rule of thumb, signs of depression and dramatic changes in behavior are good clues. People who attempt suicide often give suicidal threats or warnings, such as "I wish I were dead" or "I have nothing to live for." If you believe someone is contemplating suicide, act on your beliefs. Stay with the person if there is any immediate danger, and encourage him or her to talk to you rather than withdraw. Show the person that you care, but don't give false reassurances that "everything will be O.K."; this type of response encourages a sense of alienation in a suicidal person. Instead, openly ask if the person is

percent of the sons and 5 percent of the daughters of alcoholics become alcoholics themselves (Goodwin, 1988). These rates are about four or five times greater than those for the general population (Cloninger et al., 1986). Even when children are separated from their biological parents and raised by nonalcoholic parents they remain at higher risk of becoming alcoholic.

ORGANIC MENTAL DISORDERS

ORGANIC MENTAL DISORDERS: *Temporary or permanent physical effects on the nervous system resulting in abnormal behavior.* FUNCTIONAL DISORDERS: *Abnormal symptoms with psychological causes or for which no physical cause is known.*

In **organic mental disorders,** symptoms are caused by temporary or permanent physical effects on the nervous system. Organic disorders can be contrasted with **functional disorders,** which are psychologically caused or for which no physical cause is known. Organic mental disorders include conditions where symptoms are caused by drugs or toxic chemicals or by brain damage. In the case of drug-induced disorders, the effects can be temporary and the person often returns to normal functioning when the drug wears off or normal balance is restored. In the case of brain damage, the effects are usually permanent.

In excessive amounts, chemicals affecting the nervous system can cause abnormal behaviors that can be confused with functional disorders. For example, caffeine can cause agitation, disorganization of thinking, rambling speech, and other symptoms of manic episodes and generalized anxiety disorders. At high dosage levels, cocaine, PCP, and amphetamines cause delusions, hallucinations, and psychotic disorientation similar to the symptoms found in schizophrenic disorders (DSM-III-R, 1987).

Psychotic symptoms can also occur as withdrawal symptoms when a person has been drinking alcohol heavily for several days and then abruptly stops drinking. Because alcohol is a central nervous system depressant, the nervous system becomes hyperactive during withdrawal. This abrupt change causes tremors, perceptual distortions, confusion, delusions, and hallucinations (Victor and Wolfe, 1973).

Whenever brain tissue is damaged by trauma, hemorrhages or blood clots (strokes), the final stage of a syphilis infection, or tumors, the afflicted person can exhibit psychotic symptoms and serious personality deterioration. Half of the patients with brain tumors experience hallucinations such as seeing animals or hearing voices and conversations (Nicoli, 1988).

Since psychological problems can be caused by treatable physical conditions, it is important to examine a person with psychotic symptoms or anxiety for the presence of an organic, physical cause.

PROBLEMS WITH LABELING

Now that we have discussed seven major forms of abnormal behavior, it is important to consider two important issues: the dangers of classification and discrimination against mentally disturbed persons.

As we have seen, the DSM is a useful system for describing the symptoms of various forms of abnormal behavior, and it has helped standardize the terminology used for diagnosis (McReynolds, 1989). The benefits of the DSM system must, however, be balanced against some serious disadvantages. One of these is the fact that despite its detailed presentations of characteristics, disorders can still be misdiagnosed when the causes of a disorder are not known and cannot be specifically identified (Bower, 1989b). Kenneth Bianchi, for instance, was able to fool several psychiatrists into believing that he was actually suffering from multiple personality (Magid and McKelvey, 1987). Only when prosecutors brought in a fifth psychiatrist, Martin Orne, was Bianchi's ruse uncovered.

In addition to the possibility of misdiagnosis, the system of classification can be misused because of the tendency toward *labeling.* Once a diagnostic label is accepted, it can become self-perpetuating. That is, a person who is perceived by himself or herself and

EVALUATING ARGUMENTS
Do Diagnostic Labels of Mental Disorders Help or Hinder Effective Treatment?

You have just read a brief description of the various problems associated with diagnostic labels for mental disorders. Whereas researchers like David Rosenhan argue that diagnostic labels may create a dangerous self-fulfilling prophecy, other psychologists believe that diagnostic classification is necessary and valuable. As a reader, what do you think about this debate? Which argument do you believe is strongest? The evaluation of arguments is one of the most important elements of critical thinking. Rather than carelessly agreeing or disagreeing with arguments, critical thinkers analyze the relative strengths and weaknesses of each position. They are especially sensitive to the arguments with which they personally disagree because they recognize the natural human tendency to ignore or oversimplify opposing information. After carefully evaluating all arguments, the critical thinker develops his or her own independent position.

To help sharpen your critical thinking skills in the area of "argument evaluation," we offer the following guidelines.

1 Begin by listing the "points" and "counterpoints" of each argument. When all points and counterpoints are not explicitly stated, you will need to "read between the lines" and make your best guess of what each side might say. Here is an example of this process using the Rosenhan labeling debate:

POINT	COUNTERPOINT
Diagnostic labels are sometimes incorrectly applied.	Errors are a natural part of all human endeavors.
Labels can become a self-fulfilling prophecy for the doctor or patient.	This can be minimized by careful attention to correct diagnoses.

(Can you add your own additional points and counterpoints?)

_____   _____

_____   _____

_____   _____

_____   _____

2 After clarifying the points and counterpoints, you should attempt to use the following analytical tools:

(a) *Differentiating between fact and opinion.* As discussed in the critical thinking exercise for Chapter 5, the ability to recognize statements of fact versus statements of opinion is an important first step to successful analyses of arguments. After rereading the arguments regarding diagnostic labels, see if you can label at least two facts and two opinions on each side.

(b) *Recognizing logical fallacies and faulty reasoning.* Several chapters in this text and their corresponding critical thinking exercises can help you recognize faulty logic. For example, the problem of "incorrect assumption of cause/effect relationships" is discussed in Chapter 1, the issue of "deceptive appeals" is presented in Chapters 12 and 14, and the "incorrect or distorted use of statistics" is discussed in the Appendix.

(c) *Exploring the implications of conclusions.* Questions such as the following can help expand your analysis of arguments. "What are the conclusions drawn by proponents of each side of the issue?" "Are there other logical alternative conclusions?"

(d) *Recognizing and evaluating author bias and source credibility.* Ask yourself questions such as, "What does the author want me to think or do?" "What qualifications does the author have for writing on this subject?" "Is the author a reliable source for information?"

Although each of these steps do require additional time and energy, the payoff is substantial. Such exercises not only refine your critical thinking skills, but they also help make your decisions and opinions more educated and valuable.

by others as a "phobic" or a "schizophrenic" will tend to enact that role and will have trouble being perceived as something other than the label (Szasz, 1983, 1987).

A famous example of the problems of psychiatric labeling was a study in which David Rosenhan (1973, 1988) and seven of his colleagues faked the symptom of hearing voices in order to be admitted to mental hospitals. Because of this symptom, all were diagnosed as schizophrenic. Once admitted, they acted normally and never again mentioned hearing voices. Instead, they spoke normally with hospital personnel, interacted naturally with other patients, and kept extensive notes of their observations. Neverthe-

TABLE 15.8
Myths about Psychological Disorders

Myth #1 People with psychological disorders act in bizarre ways and are very different from normal people.

Fact: This is true in only a small minority of individuals and during a relatively small portion of their lives. As was the case in Rosenhan's study, even mental health professionals sometimes find it difficult to distinguish normal from abnormal behavior.

Myth #2 Mental disorders are a sign of personal weakness.

Fact: Psychological disorders are a function of many factors, such as exposure to stress, genetic disposition, family background, and so on. Mentally disturbed individuals can't be blamed for their problems any more than people who develop heart disease or other physical illnesses.

Myth #3 Mentally ill people are often violent and dangerous.

Fact: Only a few disorders, such as some paranoid and antisocial personalities, are associated with violence toward others. If anything, most mentally disturbed individuals may be dangerous to themselves. The stereotype that connects mental illness and violence persists because of selective media attention.

Myth #4 A person who has been mentally ill can never be normal.

Fact: The vast majority of people who are diagnosed as mentally ill eventually improve and lead normal productive lives. In addition, mental disorders are generally only temporary. A person may have an episode that lasts for days, weeks, or months and then may go for years — even a lifetime — without further difficulty.

Myth #5 Most recovered mentally ill persons can only work successfully at low-level jobs.

Fact: Recovered mentally disturbed persons are individuals. As such, their career potentials depend on their particular talents, abilities, experience, and motivation, as well as their current state of physical and mental health.

Source: Adapted from "Fourteen Worst Myths" (1985).

less, the hospital staff continued to think of them as patients and treated them as such, not challenging the diagnostic label of schizophrenia even though it did not match their daily behaviors. The fact that they spent a lot of time note taking, for example, was described in their charts as "paranoid" behavior. Critics of Rosenhan's study have pointed out that therapists tend not to suspect that patients will lie about experiencing symptoms such as hearing voices, and that patients do not always continue to describe such experiences if they are suspicious of the people around them (Davis, 1976; Spitzer, 1988). Despite these criticisms, the Rosenhan study does point out the tendency for labels — whether they are accurate or not — to be maintained.

Once a person leaves a mental institution, the problem of labels continues. The history of once having been a "mental patient" can lead to difficulty in obtaining employment and housing (Melton and Garrison, 1987). Even seeking help from a counselor or therapist has been a political liability for some candidates for national office (Buie, 1988). Table 15.8 addresses five of the most damaging myths that still persist concerning mental disorders.

As we conclude this chapter, you may be feeling overwhelmed by all the descriptions of abnormal behavior and the many ways to become disturbed. Are you also feeling discouraged about the negative aspects of psychotherapy? If so, then, it is important that we mention two final points. First of all, the vast majority of people manage to cope with their problems and never develop major psychological disorders. Second, despite the criticisms of psychotherapy, it is still a good idea to seek treatment for disorders if they *do* arise. Many effective treatments exist for both major and minor psychological problems. The various therapeutic methods used to treat people with problem behaviors are described in the next chapter.

Review Questions

1 Use of a psychoactive drug is classified as substance _____ when it interferes with social and occupational functioning and also causes tolerance and withdrawal symptoms.

2 Organic mental disorders are caused by a physical effect on the nervous system, whereas _____ disorders are presumed to be psychologically caused.

3 Drug abuse, strokes, and the last stages of syphilis can all create _____ disorders.

4 Rosenhan and his colleagues were admitted to mental hospitals with the diagnosis of _____ .

5 Failure of hospital staff to detect fake patients in David Rosenhan's study can be attributed to the effects of _____ .

Answers: 1 dependence; *2* functional; *3* organic; *4* schizophrenia; *5* labeling

REVIEW OF MAJOR CONCEPTS

DEFINING ABNORMAL BEHAVIOR

1 The statistical standard defines abnormality according to social practices in a culture. The subjective discomfort approach evaluates behavior as abnormal when the individual is discontented. The maladaptive functioning model considers behavior abnormal when it interferes with an individual's functioning within his or her own life and within society.

2 Belief that demons cause abnormal behavior was common in ancient times. The medical model, which emphasizes diseases and illness, replaced this demonological model.

3 During the Middle Ages, demonology returned and exorcisms were used to treat abnormal behavior. Asylums began to appear toward the close of the Middle Ages.

4 Critics of the medical model often use psychological perspectives, which emphasize unconscious conflicts, inappropriate learning, faulty cognitive processes, and negative self-concepts in the development of abnormal behavior. Modern biological theories, a continuation of the medical model, emphasize physiological causes for problem behaviors.

5 The *Diagnostic and Statistical Manual of Mental Disorders* (DSM-III-R) identifies categories of disorders and provides detailed descriptions useful for communication.

ANXIETY DISORDERS

6 People with anxiety disorders have persistent feelings of threat in facing everyday problems. Phobias are exaggerated fears of specific objects or situations, such as agoraphobia, a fear of being in open spaces. In generalized anxiety disorders, there is a persistent free-floating anxiety. In panic disorder, anxiety is concentrated into brief or lengthy episodes of panic attacks. In obsessive-compulsive disorder, persistent anxiety arousing thoughts (obsessions) are relieved by rituals (compulsions) such as handwashing.

7 In post-traumatic stress disorder, a person has experienced an overwhelming trauma, such as rape, which creates continued uncontrolled and maladaptive emotional reactions, such as exaggerated startle responses and sleep disturbances.

8 Two common explanations for anxiety disorders are learning and biology. Learning theorists suggest anxiety disorders result from classical and operant conditioning, as well as modeling and imitation. The biological perspective suggests that genetic predispositions, brain abnormalities, and heredity influence the development of anxiety disorders.

DISSOCIATIVE DISORDERS

9 In dissociative disorders, there is a splitting apart of critical elements of the personality. Individuals make this split by failing to recall or identify past experience (psychogenic amnesia), by leaving home and wandering off (psychogenic fugue), or by developing completely separate personalities (multiple personality).

10 Schizophrenia is a serious psychotic mental disorder that afflicts approximately 1 percent of the population. The four major disturbances are in perception, language and thought, emotions, and behavior.

11 Perceptual symptoms of schizophrenia include disturbances in filtering, selection, and judgment. Hallucinations are mistaken perceptions in any of the sensory modalities but auditory hallucinations are the most common type.

12 In schizophrenia, words lose their usual meanings and associations, logic is impaired, and speech is often tangential and disconnected. Thoughts can become disorganized and bizarre. Schizophrenics often have delusions, mistaken beliefs that are maintained in spite of strong evidence to the contrary. There are delusions of grandeur, persecution, and reference.

13 Emotional disturbances are common in schizophrenics and include extreme and inappropriate feelings.

14 The abnormal behaviors of schizophrenics are often related to disturbed thoughts and feelings. They often engage in bizarre and repetitive responses that seem crazy to others and interfere with their social relationships.

15 Biological theories of schizophrenia are based on findings of disturbed dopamine activity, abnormal brain scans, and hereditary transmission patterns. Psychosocial theories of schizophrenia focus on disturbed family relationships and stress.

MOOD DISORDERS

16 Mood disorders are disturbances of affect or emotion that may include psychotic distortions of reality. In major depression, there is a persistent depression. In bipolar disorder, there are manic episodes that alternate with normal or with normal and depressed periods.

17 Biochemical theories of affective disorders focus on neurotransmitter imbalances and genetic transmission. Psychological theories focus on disturbances in interpersonal relationships, self-concept, or learning history.

18 Suicide is a serious problem often associated with depression. By becoming involved and showing concern, individuals can help reduce the growing number of suicides.

PERSONALITY DISORDERS

19 Antisocial personality is a personality disorder characterized by egocentrism, lack of guilt, impulsivity, and superficial charm. Some research on this disorder has demonstrated defects in brain waves, arousal patterns, genetic inheritance patterns, and disturbed family relationships.

PSYCHOACTIVE SUBSTANCE USE DISORDERS

20 Psychoactive substance abuse is diagnosed when use of a psychoactive drug interferes with social or occupational functioning. Psychoactive substance dependence includes abuse and drug tolerance or withdrawal symptoms. Learning theories point to maladaptive learning in substance abuse. Genetic inheritance patterns occur for abuse of alcohol.

ORGANIC MENTAL DISORDERS

21 In organic mental disorders, symptoms are caused by temporary or permanent physical effects on the nervous system, including drug effects and brain damage.

22 Although DSM classification has many advantages, it also has some disadvantages. Misdiagnosis is possible, and once someone is labeled "mentally ill" the label often becomes self-perpetuating. The mentally disabled suffer from many myths and this prejudice often limits their social and economic opportunities.

SUGGESTED READINGS

BEAN, P. (Ed.). (1983). *Mental illness: Changes and trends.* New York: Wiley. A collection of essays on important aspects of classification, social and legal issues.

DAVISON, G. C., & NEALE, J. M. (1989). *Abnormal psychology.* (5th. ed.) New York: Wiley. A thorough, yet highly readable, presentation of diagnostic categories for abnormal behaviors, their diagnosis, and current treatment.

SZASZ, T. (1974). *The myth of mental illness.* New York: Perennial Library, Harper & Row. A classic critique of the existing views toward statistically infrequent behaviors, which Szasz describes as "problems in living."

TORREY, E. F. (1988). *Surviving schizophrenia: A family manual.* New York: Harper & Row. Describes the nature, causes, symptoms, treatment, and course of schizophrenia, with special attention to living with schizophrenia from both the schizophrenic's and the family's point of view.

chapter sixteen
Therapy

WHEN she was in college, Frances Farmer decided to become an actress. She eventually became a movie star, but in her efforts to achieve this goal, she managed to alienate many people. Frances made enemies on the movie set when she argued, screamed, and belittled everyone who disagreed with her. As one of her directors said, "The nicest thing I can say about Frances Farmer is that she is utterly unbearable." Like many other actresses consumed by their passion for acting, she had volatile confrontations with her directors and often worked herself into a state of exhaustion. Her assertiveness and lack of interest in making favorable impressions on people also deepened the conflicts she had always had with her mother, who eventually became her worst enemy. Frances learned to retreat from the stresses of her career and the loneliness of her life by drinking excessively. Unfortunately, she often became assaultive and verbally abusive during drinking bouts. When her anger was directed against a police officer and a judge, she was committed to a sanitarium. When her violence was directed against her mother, she was repeatedly admitted against her will to an asylum. Her final stay lasted eight years and was terminated only when her parents requested that she be allowed to come home to care for them in their old age.

While in the asylum, Frances was subjected to a number of treatments designed to calm her. One such treatment was hydrotherapy. She was bound with canvas straps that held her motionless in a cold bath for several hours at a time until she became semiconscious. After a few hydrotherapy treatments, she decided to be compliant and passive in order to avoid being subjected to this form of "therapy." However, she found she could not avoid angry outbursts entirely, and her fits of violence led doctors to give her the ultimate "calming" treatment: a frontal lobotomy.

After her eventual release, Frances described her institutionalization in an autobiography that has encouraged many people to examine the treatment of mental patients. Here are some of her words:

> For eight years I was an inmate in a state asylum for the insane. During those years I passed through such unbearable terror that I deteriorated into a wild, frightened creature intent only on survival.
> And I survived.
> I was raped by orderlies, gnawed on by rats, and poisoned by tainted food.
> And I survived.
> The asylum itself was a steel trap, and I was not released from its jaws alive and victorious. I crawled out mutilated, whimpering and terribly alone.
> But I did survive.
> The three thousand and forty days I spent as an inmate inflicted wounds to my spirit that could never heal. They remain, raw-edged and festering, for I learned there is no victory in survival — only grief.
>
> *Farmer (1972), p. 9*

Above Photo: In this scene from a movie based on Frances Farmer's life, actress Jessica Lange displays the type of angry outburst that caused Farmer to be committed to an institution.

Although the treatment Frances Farmer received seems barbaric, earlier approaches to dealing with disturbed persons were even more severe. As we discussed in Chapter 15, early treatment for abnormal behavior consisted of trephining (boring a hole in the skull), exorcisms, and burnings. Later, more advanced treatment involved hospitalization in asylums for the mentally ill. But conditions in these asylums were not always humane, as Frances Farmer's case graphically illustrates.

Today only people with the most severe disturbances are institutionalized. Most other people with psychological disorders can be helped without institutionalization by drug therapy or by **psychotherapy,** which is the application of psychological principles and techniques in an attempt to remedy psychological difficulties.

This chapter first examines the psychologically based forms of treatment. These include psychoanalysis, cognitive approaches, humanistic therapies, and behavioral approaches to therapy. Next, the chapter examines group therapies, where people are treated in small or large groups instead of using the traditional one-on-one approach. Following this, the chapter discusses **biological therapies,** which include drug treatments, electroconvulsive shock, and psychosurgery. The chapter concludes with a discussion of institutionalization for the severely disturbed and advice on how to choose an appropriate therapy and therapist.

As we examine the various forms of therapy, it is important to keep in mind that all psychotherapies share some common ground. Depending on the individual's specific complaint, each therapist will work on one or more of the following basic problem areas:

1. *Thoughts.* Troubled individuals typically suffer some degree of confusion, destructive thought patterns, or blocked understanding of their problems. Therapists work to change these thoughts, provide new ideas or information, or guide the individual toward finding his or her own solutions to problems.
2. *Emotions.* People who seek therapy generally suffer from extreme emotional discomfort. By encouraging free expression of feelings and by providing a warm, supportive environment, therapists help their clients replace feelings such as despair or incompetence with feelings of hope and self-confidence (Frank, 1986).
3. *Behavior.* Troubled individuals usually exhibit problem behaviors. Therapists help their clients to eliminate troublesome behaviors and guide them in ways to develop new and better approaches.

Although these three problem areas are addressed in all forms of therapy, the degree of emphasis varies. Psychoanalysts focus primarily on providing **insight** into blocked thoughts and troublesome emotions. Cognitive therapists work to eliminate their client's faulty thinking and belief patterns, whereas humanistic therapists attempt to alter the client's negative emotional responses. And as the name implies, behaviorists focus on changing maladaptive behaviors.

Psychotherapy is often misunderstood by the general public and many popular myths surround it (Buie, 1988). Before we begin our discussion of the first major form of therapy, psychoanalysis, you may want to check out some of these myths, which are presented in Table 16.1.

PSYCHOTHERAPY: *A general term for several methods of treating psychological disorders. All psychotherapies involve the application of psychological principles and techniques in an attempt to correct problems in thinking, emotion, or behavior.*

BIOLOGICAL THERAPIES: *Application of drugs and other medical procedures to correct a psychological problem or condition.*

INSIGHT: *In psychoanalysis, a bringing into awareness of motives, relationships, feelings, or impulses that had previously been poorly understood or of which the subject was totally unaware.*

PSYCHOANALYTIC THERAPY

Sigmund Freud was one of the first major theorists to go beyond the *medical model* of abnormality (see Chapter 15). He believed that abnormal behaviors are largely due to psychological rather than physiological problems. This belief led him to establish his own form of therapy, which later came to be known as *psychoanalysis.*

"Maybe it's *not* me, y'know? ... Maybe it's the *rest* of the herd that's gone insane."

TABLE 16.1
Common Myths about Psychotherapy

MYTH: There is one best therapy.

Fact: As we will discuss at the close of this chapter, many problems can be treated equally well with all major forms of psychotherapy.

MYTH: Therapists can "read minds."

Fact: Good therapists often seem to have an uncanny ability to understand how their clients are feeling and to know when someone is trying to avoid certain topics. This is not due to any special mind-reading ability, but is a direct reflection of their specialized training and daily experience working with troubled people.

MYTH: Most people who go to therapists are crazy or just weak individuals.

Fact: Most people seek counseling because they are experiencing some current stress in their life or because they realize that therapy can enrich their current level of functioning. Since most people find it difficult to be objective about their own problems, seeking therapy is not only a sign of wisdom but also one of personal strength.

MYTH: Only the rich can afford to go to therapy.

Fact: Although therapy *is* expensive, there are many clinics and therapists who charge on a sliding scale based on the client's income. Some insurance plans also cover psychological services.

The goal of psychoanalysis: Neutralizing the power of hidden conflicts

Psychoanalysis is based on the premise that the primary source of abnormal behavior is unresolved past conflicts and anxiety over the possibility that unacceptable unconscious impulses will enter the conscious part of a person's mind. Freud concluded that the only cure for disturbed behaviors is to obtain insight into the underlying conflicts.

Question: How can it change your behavior just to become aware of a conflict that is in your unconscious mind?   Freud explained that becoming aware of a painful conflict often permits a release of tensions and anxieties. He observed that when his patients relived a traumatic incident, complete with disturbing emotions, the conflict seemed to lose its power to control the person's behavior. Freud called this process of emotional release **catharsis.**

An example of the process of catharsis occurred during Dr. Cornelia Wilbur's psychoanalysis of Sybil, the woman with 16 personalities. Dr. Wilbur used both hypnosis and sodium pentothal injections to gain access to the contents of Sybil's unconscious mind. During their sessions, Sybil recalled many repressed traumatic experiences with her mother, like being subjected to painful enemas, and expressed great anger as she relived these abuses. On the days after the pentothal injections, Sybil was elated and often able to remember the activities of her "other personalities," which ordinarily were unknown to her (Schreiber, 1973).

Techniques of psychoanalysis: Exploring the unconscious mind

As Sybil's case suggests, psychoanalysis requires an expert analyst who can draw out and interpret the hidden conflicts of the psyche. Although modern-day psychoanalysts rarely use hypnosis and pentothal injections, they do use other techniques, including free association, interpretation of resistance, dream analysis, and transference.

PSYCHOANALYSIS: *A system of therapy developed by Freud that seeks to bring unconscious conflicts, which usually date back to early childhood experiences, into consciousness. Psychoanalysis is also Freud's theoretical school of thought, which emphasizes the study of unconscious processes.*

CATHARSIS: *In psychoanalytic theory, the release of tensions and anxieties through the reliving of a traumatic incident.*

When most people think of psychotherapy, they envision a scene such as this — a patient lying on a couch and a therapist providing important insights and interpretations. Although this scenario **would** be common to Freudian-style psychoanalysis, you'll discover in this chapter that this is just one of many approaches to psychotherapy.

Free association   Have you ever let your mind wander without attempting to monitor or control the direction of your thoughts? If so, you've probably discovered that some rather unexpected thoughts seem to pop up. This process of temporarily removing the conscious censorship over thoughts — called **free association** — often produces interesting and even bizarre connections that seem to spring into awareness. In psychoanalysis, the patient is told to say whatever comes to mind. Analysts use free association to overcome the ego's usual style of **repression** — keeping unconscious those thoughts that are embarrassing, irrational, or painful. To encourage free association rather than conversation, the patient reclines on a couch or sits in a comfortable chair while the analyst sits out of sight, often saying little or nothing during the sessions.

Question: Why doesn't the analyst say something?   The analyst speaks only to offer an **interpretation** or explanation of what the patient says or does. The rest of the time, the analyst listens closely in order to observe patterns and hidden meanings in the patient's seemingly disconnected ramblings. For example, if a patient's references to his or her father are often interspersed with expressions of anger or with descriptions of frustrating experiences involving various authority figures, the analyst might offer the interpretation that repressed feelings about the father are causing present-day symptoms.

Analysis of resistance   When observing the patient's behaviors and verbalizations, the analyst looks for examples of **resistance,** the tendency to block or prevent the free expression of unconscious material. For example, if the patient is late or cancels an appointment, the analyst assumes that the patient's ego defenses are attempting to keep unconscious conflicts from being revealed. Similarly, if the patient pauses in conversation or changes topics suddenly, the analyst will try to find out what is causing the resistance by pursuing the topic that preceded the block. Interpretation of resistance is similar to the conclusions you might reach if a friend were to suddenly change the subject or become evasive in discussing something with you.

Dream analysis   Freud called dreams "the royal road to the unconscious." Because the ego is not as efficient in defending itself against unconscious conflicts during sleep, these conflicts may be expressed in various ways in the form of dreams. As we saw back in Chapter 5, Freud felt that dreams could be interpreted on two levels. On a superficial level, interpretation can be based on the **manifest content** of the dream, or the dream's actual events. On a deeper level, dreams may be interpreted in terms of their **latent content,** or the hidden meaning that is expressed in dream symbols. Thus, Freudian therapists might interpret a dream of riding a horse or driving a car (the manifest content) as a desire or concern about sexual intercourse (the latent content).

FREE ASSOCIATION: *In psychoanalysis, reporting whatever comes to mind, regardless of how painful, embarrassing, or irrelevant it may seem. Freud believed that the first thing to come to a patient's mind was often an important clue to what the unconscious mind wants to conceal.*
REPRESSION: *Defense mechanism whereby the ego keeps unconscious impulses from reaching consciousness.*

INTERPRETATION: *A psychoanalyst's explanation of the significance of a patient's free associations and dreams.*

RESISTANCE: *A stage in psychoanalysis where the patient avoids (resists) the analyst's attempts to bring unconscious material to conscious awareness.*

MANIFEST CONTENT: *The surface content of a dream, containing dream symbols that distort and disguise the true meaning of the dream, according to Freudian dream theory.*
LATENT CONTENT: *The true unconscious meaning of a dream, according to Freudian dream theory.*

TRANSFERENCE: *The tendency of an individual in psychoanalysis to transfer his or her feelings and perceptions of a dominant childhood figure—usually a parent—to the psychoanalyst.*

Transference   **Transference** is the transfer of feelings from a previous relationship onto the therapist. The result is that the patient acts toward the analyst as though he or she were that other person. When transference occurs, the behavior of the patient includes carry-over feelings of unresolved conflicts from the previous relationship. Transference is assumed to have occurred if the patient falls in love with the analyst or accuses the analyst of being uncaring or demanding. Rather than assuming that these are realistic reactions, the analyst will interpret them as evidence of attachments or conflicts in a previous relationship.

Question: Couldn't it be true that the analyst really *is* seductive, uncaring, or demanding?   Freudian analysts are taught to avoid presenting their own personalities during sessions with their patients. Freud (1956) said an analyst should be "impenetrable to the patient, and, like a mirror, reflect nothing but what is shown him." When transference occurs it is used by the analyst as an opportunity to explore a previous pathological relationship and to change the effects created by carry-overs from this relationship. Analysts are also taught to identify and overcome their own reactions of **countertransference,** so they will not react toward patients as substitute people themselves (Jacobson and McKinney, 1982).

COUNTERTRANSFERENCE: *In psychoanalysis, the analyst's experience of transferring his or her feelings and perceptions of previous relationships onto the patient.*

When patients learn about transference reactions, they are often able to identify past situations that have been affecting a present relationship. Have you ever found, for example, that you were suspicious or anxious with someone because of some previous relationship with a person who had similar characteristics or a similar role? When you recognized the actual source of your feelings, you were no doubt able to respond more appropriately to the new person.

If a psychoanalyst had treated Frances Farmer to change her uncontrolled emotional outbursts and drug dependence, the analyst would have guided her to relive her experiences with her parents, probing her psyche to find childhood origins for her current problems. If you were to undergo psychoanalysis, you would feel an intense absorption in the process of analyzing your past relationships and attempting to relate them to your present behaviors. You would begin to look for meanings behind events that would ordinarily escape your attention.

Classical Freudian psychoanalysis is not as popular as it once was. Although it still enjoys considerable attention in academic circles, the number of patients seeking this form of therapy is rapidly declining (Gelman, 1988).

Question: Can you explain this?   There are several reasons that may help explain this decline. First, psychoanalysis is time-consuming (often lasting several years with sessions four to five times a week) and expensive (usually well over $10,000). Second, it seems to be suitable for a very select group of articulate individuals. Critics have facetiously suggested the YAVIS acronym to describe the perfect psychoanalysis patient: young, attractive, verbal, intelligent, and successful (Schofield, 1964).

Since the time, money, and verbal skills required make psychoanalysis unavailable for most people, a recent trend is toward short-term psychoanalysis (Gelman, 1988; Hellerstein, 1980). This brief version, generally limited to about 30 sessions, reduces many of the disadvantages of traditional psychoanalysis.

Review Questions

1 _____ is the use of psychological principles and techniques to change symptomatic behaviors.

2 Sigmund Freud developed _____ to alter unconscious conflicts that have been _____ by ego defense mechanisms.

3 The reliving of a traumatic incident to release the associated emotions is called _____.

4 In dream analysis, the _____ content is the apparent plot of the dream, whereas the _____ content is its symbolic meaning.

5 The psychoanalytic techniques of _____ _____ and _____ _____ attempt to bypass the censorship and control by the ego of unconscious conflicts.

6 In psychoanalysis, the patient's tendency to block or prevent the free expression of unconscious impulses is called _____ .

7 Freudian analysts avoid presenting their own personalities to patients in order to create _____ , a reflection of a previous relationship.

Answers: 1 psychotherapy; *2* psychoanalysis, repressed; *3* catharsis; *4* manifest, latent; *5* free association, dream analysis; *6* resistance; *7* transference

COGNITIVE THERAPY

Cognitive therapy assumes that problem behaviors and emotions are created by faulty thought processes and beliefs. For example, a cognitive therapist would say that feelings of depression are created by beliefs like "If I don't do everything perfectly, I am worthless" or "I'm helpless to change my life so that I could feel satisfied." When people have beliefs that are irrational, that are overly demanding, or that fail to match reality, their emotions and behaviors can become disturbed (Beck, 1985; Ellis, 1987).

Cognitive therapy is similar to psychoanalysis in that the therapist analyzes a person's thoughts and performs a cognitive restructuring, or alteration of destructive thoughts, to enable the person to think more productively (Sarason, 1982). Like psychoanalysts, cognitive therapists assume that many of the beliefs that create problem behaviors operate at the unexamined level. Cognitive therapists also agree that exploring an unexamined belief system can produce insight into the reasons for disturbed behaviors. However, instead of believing that a change in behavior occurs because of catharsis, cognitive therapists believe that insight into the sane and crazy things a person has been telling himself or herself gives the individual a chance to directly change maladaptive ways of interpreting events. That is, self-talk can be changed to sane statements like, "I can accept my faults" or "I can make constructive changes in my behavior." What sort of irrational ideas might a person like Frances Farmer be telling herself in a high-stress situation that would lead to emotional outbursts or alcohol abuse?

Whereas psychoanalysts focus primarily on childhood relationships within the patient's family, cognitive therapists emphasize the way that events and people both inside and outside the family influence beliefs. Events like going to college or boot camp, falling in love, or becoming a parent can change attitudes and beliefs in significant ways, and interactions with teachers, bosses, and friends can create disturbed as well as realistic ways of thinking.

One of the best-known cognitive therapists is Albert Ellis, a clinical psychologist who developed his approach, **rational-emotive therapy (RET)**, during the 1950s. Ellis calls RET an A-B-C approach, referring to the three steps involved in creating disturbed responses: (A) an activating event, which is some type of stimulus such as criticism from a boss or a failing grade on an examination; (B) the belief system, which is the person's interpretation of the meaning of the activating experience; and (C) the consequence, or the response the person makes (see Figure 16.1). Ellis claims that unless we stop to think about our interpretations of events, we will erroneously believe that we go automatically from A (the activating event) to C (the consequence).

Ellis's basic A-B-C model starts with his assumption that each person shares a fundamental drive for success, love, security, and so on. When these goals are blocked (the activating event), two categories of beliefs can be initiated:

COGNITIVE THERAPY: *Therapy that focuses on faulty thought processes and beliefs to treat problem behaviors.*

RATIONAL-EMOTIVE THERAPY (RET): *Cognitive therapy system developed by Albert Ellis to attempt to change the troubled person's belief system.*

1. *Rational beliefs,* such as "I don't like criticism or a failing grade, but it's not the end of the world" or "I have other ways to reach my goals."
2. *Irrational beliefs,* such as "I can't stand criticism and failure" or "I absolutely *must* perform well at all times."

Ellis believes the creation and activation of these irrational beliefs create "neurotic" behaviors. Convinced that they must achieve impossible goals and can't stand the normal frustrations of life, people become anxious, angry, and/or depressed. Ironically, once the negative feelings develop, they tend to perpetuate the faulty, irrational beliefs that caused them in the first place (part C of the model). Ellis calls this vicious cycle "the Catch-22 of human neurosis" (Ellis, 1987 p. 367).

Question: How can we change these irrational beliefs?   Although Ellis believes that most people require the assistance of a therapist to see through their defenses and force them to challenge their self-defeating responses, he claims that some people are able to change their own behaviors. If you want to try rational-emotive therapy techniques to improve your belief system, Ellis recommends the following steps:

1. *Evaluate the consequences.* Emotions such as anger, anxiety, and depression often seem reasonable and it seems "natural" for them to happen. Instead of perpetuating these negative consequences by assuming that they *must* be experienced, focus on whether such reactions help you live effectively and enable you to solve your problems.
2. *Identify your belief system.* Find out what your beliefs are by asking yourself *why* you feel the particular emotions you do. By confronting your beliefs, Ellis claims you can discover misconceptions or irrational assumptions that are creating the problem consequences. Some of the most common misconceptions in our culture are summarized in Table 16.2.
3. *Dispute the self-defeating beliefs.* Once you have identified an overly demanding or irrational belief, argue against it. For example, it is gratifying when people you cherish love you in return, but if they do not, continuing to insist that they must give you what you want will only be self-defeating.
4. *Practice effective ways of thinking.* Continue to examine your reactions to events and situations to create opportunities to dispute irrational beliefs and substitute more realistic perceptions. Practice more effective behaviors through acting them out at home and imagining more successful outcomes.

According to the cognitive perspective, an argument is an "activating experience" that can be interpreted in various ways by a person's belief.

After winning prizes or awards for top performances, some individuals tell themselves, "Now I must perform well at all times." This is the type of irrational thinking that interests cognitive therapists.

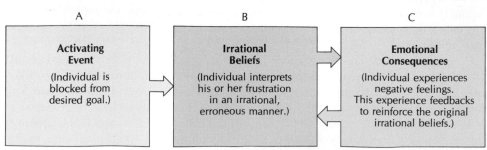

A	B	C
Activating Event (Individual is blocked from desired goal.)	**Irrational Beliefs** (Individual interprets his or her frustration in an irrational, erroneous manner.)	**Emotional Consequences** (Individual experiences negative feelings. This experience feedbacks to reinforce the original irrational beliefs.)

Figure 16.1 According to Ellis, people often experience frustrations from blocked goals (A). They then go on to interpret this event in an irrational way (B). Such beliefs lead to negative emotional responses, and these responses then sustain the irrational belief (C).

RECOGNIZING FAULTY REASONING
The Role of Logic in Cognitive Therapy

In this section we have just discussed Albert Ellis's approach to psychotherapy in which he states that illogical thinking is the basis for most human suffering. To improve your logical, critical thinking skills, we will briefly discuss the two basic tests for sound reasoning, and then give you a chance to apply these principles to Ellis's "irrational misconceptions."

Part I

Consider the following syllogism:

Premise 1   All dogs are animals.
Premise 2   All animals are blue.
Conclusion   Therefore, all dogs are blue.

Is this sound and logical reasoning? To determine whether an argument is sound and whether the conclusions should be accepted, critical thinkers ask two major questions: "Is the argument valid?" and "Are all premises true?" An argument is considered valid *if* the conclusion logically follows from the premises. The previous syllogism, for example, would be considered valid because *if* all dogs are animals, and all animals are blue, then *logically* all dogs *must* be blue.

Although the test for validity does not rest on the truth or falsity of the premises, the second step in evaluating the soundness of arguments *does* require an examination of the content of the argument. For an argument to be sound, each premise must also be true. This is where the previous syllogism falls apart. All dogs are obviously not blue.

Part II

After reviewing these two basic determinants of sound logic, can you recognize the faulty reasoning that underlies Ellis's "irrational misconceptions"? See if you can identify the problems with the following misconception.

Premise 1   I must have love or approval from all the people I find significant [in order to be happy].

Premise 2   I don't have approval from my mother.
Conclusion   Therefore, I am unhappy.

Is this argument valid? If not, why not? _____

_____

Are the premises of this argument true? If not, which ones are false and why? _____

_____

Think carefully now about your own personal irrational misconceptions (e.g., "I must make everyone happy," "Life must be fair," etc.). In the following spaces, analyze your "self-talk" about this misconception and try to put it in syllogism form by identifying your two basic premises and your conclusion.

Premise 1   _____
Premise 2   _____
Conclusion   _____

Now answer the following questions:

Is my argument valid? If not, why not? _____

_____

Are the premises of my argument true? If not, which one is false and why? _____

_____

For further practice on your reasoning skills, you may want to follow this same procedure and logically examine each of your irrational misconceptions. By actively applying your logical skills to your own thought processes, you will not only improve your basic critical thinking skills, but according to Ellis you will also be in a better position to subsequently change these self-distructive thought patterns.

TABLE 16.2
Common Misconceptions

> *1* I must have love or approval from all the people I find significant.
>
> *2* I must be thoroughly competent, adequate, and achieving.
>
> *3* When people act obnoxiously or unfairly, they should be blamed for being bad, wicked, or rotten individuals.
>
> *4* When I am seriously frustrated, treated unfairly, or rejected, I must view the situation as awful, terrible, horrible, and catastrophic.
>
> *5* Emotional misery comes from external pressures and I have little ability to control or change my feelings.
>
> *6* If something seems dangerous or fearsome, I must preoccupy myself with it and make myself anxious about it.
>
> *7* It is better to avoid facing my difficulties and responsibilities than it is to use self-discipline to obtain rewarding things.
>
> *8* My past experiences remain all-important. Since something once strongly influenced my life, it has to keep determining my feelings and behavior today.
>
> *9* It is awful and horrible if I do not find good solutions to life's grim realities.
>
> *10* I can achieve maximum human happiness by inertia and inaction or by passively and uncommittedly "enjoying myself."

Source: Ellis, A., & Harper, R. A. (1975). *A new guide to rational living.* Wilshire Book Co.: Hollywood, CA.

HUMANISTIC THERAPY

HUMANISTIC THERAPY: *Therapy approaches that assist individuals to become creative and unique persons through affective restructuring processes.*

As we noted in Chapter 14, humanists see human potential as including the freedom to become what one wants to be as well as the responsibility to make choices. **Humanistic therapy** assumes that people with problems are suffering from a blocking or disruption of their normal growth potential. This blocking creates a defective self-concept. When barricades are removed, the individual is free to become the self-accepting and genuine person everyone is capable of being.

Imagine for a minute how you feel when you are with someone who believes you are a good person with unlimited potential, a person whose "real self" is unique and valuable. These are the feelings that are nurtured in humanistic therapy approaches.

One of the best-known humanistic therapists, Carl Rogers (1961, 1980), developed a therapy approach that encourages people to actualize their potentials and to relate to others in genuine ways. His approach is generally referred to as **client-centered therapy**.

CLIENT-CENTERED THERAPY: *A type of psychotherapy developed by Carl Rogers that emphasizes the client's natural tendency to become healthy and productive; specific techniques include empathy, unconditional positive regard, and genuineness.*

Question: Why does Rogers use the term "client" instead of "patient"? Rogers believed that the label "patient" implies being "sick" or "mentally ill," rather than responsible and competent. Treating people as "clients" emphasizes the fact that *they* are the ones in charge of the therapy and focuses on the equality of the therapist–client relationship.

Client-centered therapy, like psychoanalysis and cognitive therapies, encourages exploration of thoughts and feelings in order to obtain insight into the causes for behaviors. For Rogerian therapists, however, the focus is on encouraging healthy emotional experiences, and client-centered therapy promotes an *affective restructuring,* or alteration of emotions. Clients are responsible for discovering their own maladaptive patterns and connections, while the therapist provides an accepting atmosphere in which the client is able to freely explore important thoughts and feelings.

Question: How does the therapist create such an atmosphere? Rogerian therapists learn how to create a therapeutic relationship by focusing on three important qualities of communication: empathy, unconditional positive regard, and genuineness (Davis, 1989).

Empathy and unconditional positive regard are important techniques in humanistic therapies.

Empathy is a sensitive understanding and sharing of another person's inner experience. When we put ourselves in other people's shoes, we explore their inner world, or *phenomenological experience,* with them. To express empathy, therapists watch body language and listen for subtle cues that will help them understand the emotional experiences of clients. When clients express feelings verbally, they are encouraged to explore them further. The therapist uses open-ended statements like "You found that upsetting . . ." or "You haven't been able to decide what to do about this . . ." rather than asking questions or offering explanations.

EMPATHY: *In Rogerian terms, an insightful awareness and ability to share another person's inner experience.*

Unconditional positive regard is genuine caring for people based on their innate value as persons. Since humanists assume that human nature is positive and each person is unique, clients can be respected and cherished without having to prove themselves worthy of the therapist's esteem. Unconditional positive regard allows the therapist to trust that clients have the "best" answers for their own lives. To maintain a climate of unconditional positive regard, the therapist avoids making evaluative statements such as "That's good" or "You did the right thing," which give the idea that clients need to receive approval. When people receive unconditional caring from others, they become better able to value themselves in a similar way.

UNCONDITIONAL POSITIVE REGARD: *According to Carl Rogers, the nonjudgmental attitude and genuine caring that a therapist should express toward the client.*

Genuineness, or authenticity, is being aware of one's true inner thoughts and feelings and being able to share them honestly with others. When people are genuine, they are not artificial, defensive, or "playing a role," Rogerian therapy is based on the belief that when a therapist is authentic, clients develop a feeling of trust in themselves and are then able to know and express themselves honestly, too.

GENUINENESS: *In Rogerian terms, authenticity or congruence; the awareness of one's true inner thoughts and feelings and being able to share them honestly with others.*

Review Questions

1 Cognitive therapy techniques assume that disturbed behaviors are created by faulty or irrational _____ .

2 Albert Ellis's therapy, called _____ , uses an A-B-C model.

3 Carl Rogers's therapy, called _____ , performs a(n) _____ restructuring.

4 A sensitive understanding and sharing of another person's inner or phenomenological experience is known as _____ .

5 Giving a person genuine respect that does not have to be earned is called

_____ _____ _____ .

6 Authenticity or _____ is the honest sharing of inner thoughts and feelings.

Answers: 1 beliefs;   *2* rational-emotive;   *3* client-centered, affective   *4* empathy;   *5* unconditional positive regard;   *6* Genuineness

BEHAVIOR THERAPY

Have you ever *understood* why you were doing something you would rather not do but continued to do it anyway? In such instances, having insight into a problem does not automatically solve it. Take the example of Mrs. D, an agoraphobic woman who had not left her house for 3½ years except with her husband. She had undergone 1½ years of insight therapy and had become well aware of the causes of her problem, but she did not change her behavior. She finally sought the help of a behavior therapist who, instead of continuing to obtain an understanding of her problems or attempting to restructure her feelings, systematically trained her to behave differently. Mrs. D's behavior therapist worked with her to "extinguish" the anxiety she felt about leaving her house. For several therapy sessions, she was guided by her therapist to visualize herself traveling alone to the clinic where she was treated. During these visualization exercises, she concentrated on keeping her body relaxed. Whenever she experienced anxiety, she thought the words "calm, no panic" to relax herself. After less than two months of behavior therapy, she was able to leave her house and travel alone to appointments (Lazarus, 1971).

BEHAVIOR THERAPY: *A group of techniques based on learning principles that are used to change maladaptive behaviors.*

As this example shows, **behavior therapy** (also known as behavior modification) uses conditioning and learning principles to change behaviors. Behavior therapists believe that it is generally unnecessary to obtain insight or restructure feelings *before* changes in behavior can occur. The focus in this approach is on the problem behaviors, rather than on any underlying causes or "disease" states, but the person's feelings and interpretations are not disregarded (Skinner, 1988).

Behavior therapists believe that abnormal or maladaptive behaviors are learned in the same way that adaptive behaviors are learned and that abnormal behaviors can also be "unlearned" if treated systematically. Just as any bad habit can be modified if subjected to systematic techniques for behavior change, abnormal behaviors can be eliminated using specific behavioral approaches.

Question: Do behavior therapists attempt to condition people like rats? Behavior therapists don't treat people like rats or robots. They attempt to make their clients feel understood and cared about. Like psychoanalysts and Rogerian therapists, they believe that underlying processes are the source of maladaptive behavior. In their view, these underlying processes consist of past associations between stimuli and responses, or between responses and rewards or punishments. However, rather than probing the past associations, the behavior therapist attempts to alter their resulting behavior, in the process creating *new* associations to replace the maladaptive ones.

In behavior therapy, the therapist diagnoses the problem by listing the maladaptive behaviors that occur and the adaptive behaviors that are absent. The therapist then attempts to *decrease* the frequency of maladaptive behaviors and *increase* the frequency of adaptive behaviors. To accomplish this type of change, a behavior therapist may draw on principles from classical or operant conditioning, observational learning, or cognitive behavior theory (Corsini, 1984).

Classical conditioning techniques: Changing associations

Classical conditioning techniques, based on Pavlov's model for associating two stimulus events (Chapter 6), are used to decrease maladaptive behavior by creating new associations to replace the faulty ones. Behavior therapy techniques based on classical conditioning principles include systematic desensitization and aversion therapy.

SYSTEMATIC DESENSITIZATION: *Behavior therapy counterconditioning technique used to extinguish a classically conditioned anxiety response through the use of a hierarchy and relaxation.*

Systematic desensitization   **Systematic desensitization** is a humane way of extinguishing a classically conditioned anxiety response such as Mrs. D.'s agoraphobia. Instead of repeatedly exposing a client to the feared situation in order to extinguish the anxiety, systematic desensitization uses a gradual process based on the learning principle of **counterconditioning**. In counterconditioning, the client learns to relax instead of feeling anxious in response to an anxiety-arousing stimulus (Wolpe, 1958, 1982, 1987).

The principle of counterconditioning was used by Mary Cover Jones (1924) to extinguish the anxiety response of a three-year-old boy named Peter, who was afraid of a rabbit. While Peter was relaxed and eating, the rabbit was slowly brought closer to him in gradual steps. Over time, the rabbit was increasingly associated with the pleasurable responses of eating and relaxation and the anxiety response was slowly extinguished. One of the authors used this technique to tame some wild kittens. She put out food for them and then gradually approached them while they were eating. Eventually, they enjoyed being held.

Based on these examples, do you think it might be possible for people to extinguish their anxiety responses to a frightening movie by eating something while they watch it? Could it be the case that some people have inadvertently conditioned themselves to use food as a way to reduce anxiety?

In systematic desensitization, the counterconditioning process uses pleasurable muscular relaxation of the body rather than the pleasurable response of eating as the new association to be learned. Desensitization is based on the opposite actions of the sympathetic and parasympathetic branches of the autonomic nervous system (see Chapter 2). Since the parasympathetic nerves control autonomic functions when we are relaxed and the sympathetic nerves are dominant when we are anxious, it is physiologically impossible to be both relaxed and anxious at the same time. The goal, then, is to replace an anxiety response with a relaxation response to particular stimuli.

Desensitization uses a three-step process for counterconditioning (Martin and Pear, 1983). First, a **hierarchy,** or ranked listing of anxiety-arousing images, is constructed. The therapist and client list about 10 scenes ranging from those that produce very little anxiety to those that arouse extreme anxiety (see Figure 16.2). In the second step, the client is taught how to maintain a state of deep relaxation that is physiologically incompatible with an anxiety response. As the final step, the client visualizes items of the hierarchy, beginning with the least anxiety-arousing image, while maintaining the relaxation state. If

COUNTERCONDITIONING: *A procedure that replaces an anxiety response to a stimulus with a pleasure or relaxation response.*

HIERARCHY: *Ranked listing of something; used in the behavior therapy systematic desensitization process.*

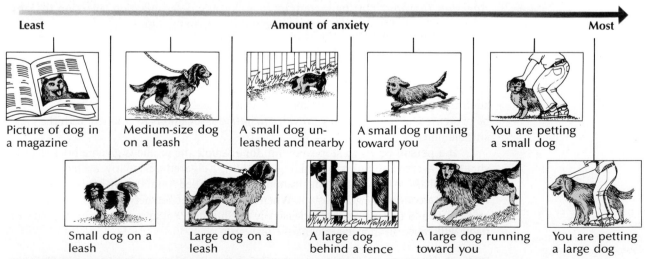

Least   **Amount of anxiety**   **Most**

Picture of dog in a magazine

Medium-size dog on a leash

A small dog unleashed and nearby

A small dog running toward you

You are petting a small dog

Small dog on a leash

Large dog on a leash

A large dog behind a fence

A large dog running toward you

You are petting a large dog

Figure 16.2 Sample hierarchy of items for a dog phobia. Each image is mentally visualized in conjunction with relaxation techniques until it no longer arouses anxiety.

During the final stages of desensitization, the phobic individual directly confronts the originally feared stimulus.

any image begins to create an anxious feeling, the client stops visualizing it and returns to a state of complete relaxation. The items are introduced in ascending order until all of them can be visualized without anxiety. Research has shown that this imagery technique helps reduce anxiety in actual situations outside the therapist's office (Goldfried and Davison, 1976).

In some cases, actual behaviors, such as climbing a ladder for fear of heights or approaching a feared animal such as a dog or snake, are performed instead of imagining the behaviors. In treating Mrs. D.'s agoraphobia, for example, she first visualized herself traveling unaccompanied to and from the clinic where she was treated and then gradually practiced leaving her home by herself.

A knowledge of systematic desensitization has many practical applications. If there is something that creates excessive anxiety for you, such as taking examinations or being in small spaces, try going through the three-step process described above to countercondition the anxiety response and develop more realistic and effective behaviors (Martin and Pear, 1983).

AVERSION THERAPY: *Behavior therapy counterconditioning technique that pairs an aversive stimulus with maladaptive behaviors.*

Aversion therapy   In sharp contrast to systematic desensitization, **aversion therapy** uses counterconditioning to *create* anxiety rather than extinguish it.

Question: Why would a therapist want to make someone feel anxious?   Aversion therapy techniques create anxiety in order to stop maladaptive behaviors, such as smoking and excessive drinking, that have built up a number of pleasurable associations, such as relaxation or relief of tension. Since these pleasurable associations cannot always be prevented, aversion therapy provides *negative* associations to compete with the pleasurable ones.

If a person wants to stop smoking, for example, he or she is given a brief electric shock (an aversive stimulus) on holding or lighting a cigarette. Similarly, aversion therapy for alcohol abuse involves administration of a drug called Antabuse that causes vomiting whenever alcohol enters the system. When the new connection between smoking and pain or alcohol and nausea has been classically conditioned, engaging in the once desirable habit will cause an immediate negative response.

Question: Isn't this also an example of operant conditioning, where punishment is used to decrease a response?   Yes. In addition to the classically conditioned associations that are learned in aversion therapy, voluntary behaviors such as smoking and drinking are also influenced by operant conditioning principles.

THE FAR SIDE   By GARY LARSON

Larson 11-27

Professor Gallagher and his controversial technique of simultaneously confronting the fear of heights, snakes and the dark.

Operant conditioning techniques: Changing the consequences of behaviors

Operant conditioning techniques use punishments and extinction to decrease maladaptive behaviors and shaping and reinforcement to increase adaptive ones.

Punishment and extinction   Application of punishment can take the form of **positive punishment,** in which an aversive stimulus is applied to an operant behavior to decrease its frequency, or **negative punishment,** in which a rewarding stimulus is removed whenever a maladaptive behavior occurs. In both cases, the result is a decrease in the problem behavior.

One of the most successful applications of punishment has been to reduce maladaptive behaviors in autistic children. **Autistic** children do not respond normally to other people, fail to develop effective speech, and frequently engage in self-mutilating behaviors, such as biting and head banging. In the past, such children had to be restrained in beds or chairs at all times to prevent injuries. However, use of positive punishment in the form of mild electric shocks whenever the children begin to injure themselves has been successful in eliminating the self-mutilating behaviors (Lovaas, 1977; Mikkelson, 1986).

Use of negative punishment in behavior therapy can also be seen in the procedure called **time out,** in which people are removed from sources of rewards whenever they behave inappropriately. In one mental hospital, for example, an overweight schizophrenic patient had resisted all attempts to keep her from stealing food from other patients (Ayllon, 1963). Finally, it was decided to remove the woman from the cafeteria whenever she attempted to take more food. The negative punishment of the time out procedure removed her from a reward (access to food), and within two weeks her food-stealing behavior was extinguished and she eventually attained a more normal weight.

The technique of **extinction** can also be used to eliminate maladaptive behavior. In the case of the overweight patient, the nurses had been inadvertently rewarding her with

POSITIVE PUNISHMENT: *Application of an aversive stimulus to an operant behavior to decrease its frequency.*
NEGATIVE PUNISHMENT: *Removal of a rewarding stimulus whenever a maladaptive behavior occurs to decrease the frequency of this operant behavior.*

AUTISM: *An abnormal condition in which an individual becomes immersed in fantasy to avoid communicating with others.*

TIME OUT: *Use of negative punishment through removal of people from sources of rewards whenever they behave inappropriately.*

EXTINCTION: *During operant conditioning, the elimination of maladaptive behaviors by removing the rewards that were previously connected with them.*

This type of social withdrawal is a common feature of autism and is directly confronted by behavior therapists.

attention whenever she misbehaved. Even without the time out approach, her food stealing might have decreased if the staff had completely ignored her behavior. When diagnosing problem behaviors, behavior therapists try to identify instances such as this in which inappropriate rewards should be discontinued.

Of course, getting rid of problem behaviors is only part of behavior therapy. It is also important to make sure that *appropriate* behaviors are learned in place of inappropriate ones. Behavior therapists use several approaches to increase adaptive behaviors.

Shaping and reinforcement   In behavior therapy, a behavior to be acquired is known as a *target behavior.* By being rewarded for successive approximations of the target behavior, the person is able to eventually perform the desired response. In one research study, for example, a schizophrenic patient who had not talked for 19 years was given gum as a reward to reacquire language (Isaacs, Thomas, and Goldiamond, 1960). At first the patient was rewarded for any sounds and then later only for words and sentences. Such **shaping** techniques are often necessary in helping patients acquire desirable behaviors, since the target behavior is not likely to appear on its own.

SHAPING: *During behavior therapy, target behaviors are acquired by rewarding successive approximations of the desired response.*

Shaping is also used in behavior therapy to help people acquire social skills, including such tasks as making a presentation to a group or asking for a date. One commonly used technique is *behavior rehearsal* in which clients practice different types of behaviors and are given reinforcement in the form of feedback about how well each approach works (Lazarus, 1971; Rimm and Masters, 1979). A popular application of behavior rehearsal is *assertiveness training,* which teaches people to express genuine feelings, improve their social skills, and obtain fair treatment from others (Lange and Jakubowski, 1976). Clients practice using effective verbal and nonverbal responses, beginning with simple situations and progressing to more complex circumstances where they must make an active response. In treating Mrs. D.'s agoraphobia, for example, her therapist shaped assertive behaviors such as standing up for her rights with her domineering father by using role playing.

TOKEN ECONOMY SYSTEM: *Use of secondary (conditioned) reinforcers to reward adaptive behaviors.*
TOKEN: *Tangible secondary (conditioned) reinforcer that can be exchanged for primary rewards.*

Adaptive behaviors can also be taught or increased using techniques that provide immediate reinforcement. One such technique that has proved successful in group situations is the **token economy system** (Allyllon and Azrin, 1968). **Tokens** are secondary (conditioned) reinforcers such as poker chips, "credit" cards, or other tangible objects that can be exchanged for primary rewards such as food, treats, watching television, a private room, or outings. In a token economy system at a treatment facility, patients are rewarded with tokens for socially desirable activities such as taking medication, attending group therapy sessions, or engaging in recreational programs. Patients can also be "fined" for inappropriate or symptomatic behaviors by having tokens taken away.

Question: Isn't this approach too dependent on the tokens to have lasting effects? Advocates of the token approach point out that tokens help people acquire beneficial behaviors that become rewarding in themselves. In a token economy system, a series of levels is usually employed so that increasingly complex adaptive behaviors are required to earn tokens. For example, mental patients would at first be given tokens for merely attending group therapy sessions. Once this behavior is established, they would be rewarded only for actually participating in the sessions. Eventually, the tokens could be discontinued when the patient receives the reinforcement of being helped by participation in the therapy sessions.

Cognitive behavior therapy: Changing both behavior and thought

The techniques used by the *cognitive* version of behavior therapy focus on altering the ways clients discuss things with themselves (their self-talk) in evaluating their own behaviors and observing others. In this approach, the therapist intervenes at the cognitive level to change the things the client is thinking in the problem situation.

Question: How is this different from the cognitive therapies such as rational-emotive therapy? Even though Ellis is often classified as a cognitive behavior therapist, the distinction can be made according to how self-talk is handled. **Cognitive behavior therapy** deemphasizes the expression of emotions and does not consider it important for the client to understand the underlying process that creates self-statements, whereas cognitive therapists and psychoanalysts encourage the expression of thoughts and feelings in order to gain insights into the origins of maladaptive behaviors. A cognitive behavior therapist judges self-talk to be useful if it leads to adaptive behaviors, such as satisfaction or self-confidence, and to be maladaptive if it creates negative symptoms, such as anger or depression. For instance, Mrs. D. (the agoraphobic client) referred to herself as "the height of mediocrity" and said, "I'm not especially intelligent, good-looking, well-educated, or knowledgeable. . . . I'm kind of blah!" These negative self statements were replaced in therapy sessions until she concluded, "If you want to *feel* useful, you have to *be* useful" (Lazarus, 1971, pp. 22–23). She then proceeded to work on an original idea to help the needy and started an organization to distribute food and clothing.

Once self-statements have been analyzed and determined to have negative consequences, the therapy process creates systematic changes in the client's type of thoughts through such behavior modification techniques as thought stopping.

COGNITIVE BEHAVIOR THERAPY: *A therapy that helps clients change the way they think as well as the way they behave.*

Thought stopping For the next five seconds, do not think of a yellow submarine. As you have just discovered, trying *not* to think of something is rarely effective as a way of avoiding it. The effort to forget or avoid unpleasant thoughts can act as a cue to trigger unwanted memories (Wegner, 1988). You may have noticed this effect when you try to forget an unpleasant experience or someone who no longer loves you. Instead of forgetting, you find that the memories are actually sharpened. You then not only feel frustrated at being unable to forget but also guilty for continuing to dwell on thoughts that make you unhappy.

A more effective way to remove unhappy or maladaptive thoughts is the two-step process called **thought stopping.** The first step is to construct a list of pleasurable scenes that do not involve the person or situation you wish to forget. The images can be funny, adventurous, or unusual but must be interesting and absorbing to you. Here are some examples (but you may want to create your own list):

THOUGHT STOPPING: *Behavior therapy technique for extinguishing maladaptive self-talk.*

Robert Redford and Tom Cruise (or their female counterparts) are giving you a wonderful massage at a poolside in the Bahamas.

You've won a million dollars in a lottery and are actively spending it.

When you have your list of positive thoughts ready, intentionally think about the person or situation you wish to forget. As soon as the thought enters your mind, yell "Stop!" as loudly as you can and immediately begin actively thinking about something from your list. (This technique can be performed with "private shouts" when others are around since yelling "Stop!" in public often attracts too much attention.) Continue to practice banishing unwanted thoughts and substituting rewarding ones.

Review Questions

1 _____ _____ changes associations through the classical conditioning technique of pairing deep relaxation with the visualization of a(n) _____ of anxiety-arousing images.

2 In counterconditioning, the client learns to _____ an anxiety response.

3 A behavior therapist attempts to decrease the frequency of _____ behaviors and to increase the frequency of behaviors.

4 _____ therapy creates a negative association to reduce the frequency of a maladaptive behavior.

5 A time-out procedure removes the person from sources of reward and is based on the principle of _____ punishment.

6 A behavior to be acquired in a shaping procedure is called a(n) _____ behavior.

7 _____ are conditioned reinforcers used to shape or increase the frequency of adaptive behaviors.

8 Cognitive behavior therapy alters _____, the things people say to themselves when they interpret events.

Answers: 1 systematic desensitization, hierarchy; *2* extinguish; *3* maladaptive, adaptive; *4* aversion; *5* negative; *6* target; *7* tokens; *8* self-talk

GROUP THERAPIES

Besides the four major therapy approaches we have just described, there are over 250 recognized forms of psychotherapy (Meredith, 1986). Some approaches are unconventional, such as *primal therapy,* where screaming is encouraged, and *rebirthing,* where nude participants snorkel in a tub of warm water in order to reexperience the panic of birth. Some experts suggest that it is possible to convert almost any activity into therapy, leading to such variations as jogging therapy, soap opera therapy, and past-lives therapy. Such approaches can sometimes create the impression that psychotherapy is a commercial venture with simplistic solutions to serious problems. Although that may indeed be the case with some types of "pop" psychology, most therapists seriously want to help people and use a variety of techniques to achieve this goal. One service that many therapists offer is treating people in groups.

▪ *Question:* Why would anyone want to be in a group instead of private individual therapy? Compared to individual therapy, group therapy is usually less expensive. Therapy groups also enable their members to exchange information and support each other's efforts in dealing with common problems under the expert guidance of a therapist. In particular, self-help groups such as Alcoholics Anonymous, Alanon, Survi-

Group therapy provides support from other people and the opportunity to assist one another with shared problems.

vors of Suicide, Compassionate Friends, Parents Anonymous, and Parents United provide unique opportunities for people to gain information and to plan and practice new responses in a supportive environment (Galanter, 1989).

Group therapy approaches can utilize techniques drawn from psychoanalysis, cognitive therapy, humanistic therapy, and behavior therapy. In addition, some therapy approaches have been specifically developed for the group setting — for example, transactional analysis, Gestalt therapy, and family therapy.

Transactional analysis: The parent – adult – child

Transactional analysis (TA) was developed as a group therapy approach by psychoanalyst Eric Berne, who described TA in his best-selling book *Games People Play* (1964). With TA people examine the roles they play in social interactions (transactions) in order to identify styles that are manipulative and self-defeating. Like Freud, Berne has identified three parts of the personality that he calls *ego-states:* the Parent, the Adult, and the Child (see Figure 16.3).

TRANSACTIONAL ANALYSIS (TA): *Group therapy approach that identifies the use of ego-state styles.*

🔲 *Question:* Are ego-states part of the ego? Although from the name that would seem to be the case, in fact these three parts of the personality match Freud's three parts of the psyche, rather than just the ego (Maddi, 1980). The *Parent* ego-state resem-

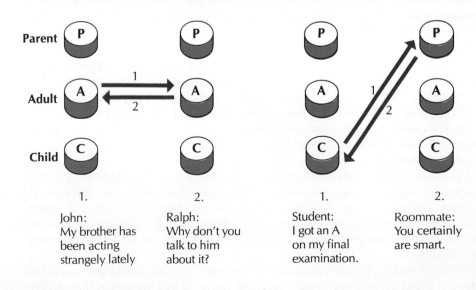

Complementary Transaction   Crossed Transaction

Figure 16.3 Complementary and crossed interactions in transactional analysis. According to Eric Berne, *complementary interactions* occur between two individuals when they are both operating on the same level. *Crossed interactions* occur when participants interact from different levels, recreating childhood needs.

Fritz Perls, the founder of Gestalt therapy.

bles the superego. It is the incorporation of parental standards that contains "shoulds" and "oughts." When people use their Parent mode to relate to others, they are supportive and compassionate or judgmental, critical, and domineering. The *Adult* ego-state deals with objective reality and matches Freud's concept of the ego. The Adult gathers information, evaluates, and makes decisions. When people use their Adult state in transactions, they are mature and logical. The *Child* consists of spontaneous feelings and impulses and is like the id, except that the Child state is not limited to sexual and aggressive impulses. According to Berne, the Child state is not only naive and impulsive but also playful and likeable. He suggests we should not take ourselves so seriously that our Child does not get to "play" occasionally.

In TA, the group members learn to identify the styles that are being used in social interactions by analyzing nonverbal responses such as facial expressions and gestures, as well as the things that are said. Berne assumes that as adults we are still influenced by unconscious parental messages (called "injunctions") and we continue to seek recognition (called "strokes") in the same way we sought attention from our parents as children.

In the group, members relive early childhood scenes to identify self-defeating styles of relating to others. These relating styles are part of people's "life script," the pattern they developed in childhood in order to obtain "strokes," and can be played as pathological games like "Carrying My Cross" or "Waiting For Santa Claus." Once the childhood problems are identified, a TA group member makes a *contract* or plan to behave differently (Berne, 1966).

Gestalt therapy: Help from the "hot seat"

GESTALT THERAPY: *Form of group therapy that obtains insights into one's current thoughts, feelings, and body sensations through the use of awareness exercises.*

The **Gestalt therapy** approach was developed by Fritz Perls (1969), an early leader of the human potential movement. Although Perls was trained as a Freudian psychoanalyst, his therapy techniques are more similar to the humanistic approach. Like client-centered therapists, Gestalt therapists enable group members to find their own meanings for behaviors rather than offering interpretations. The emphasis is on integrating present experiences into a whole ("gestalt") through a continuing awareness of one's current thoughts, feelings, and body sensations.

Question: But isn't my past a part of the whole?   Gestaltists believe that focusing on the past distracts people from the quality of their current reality (Polster and Polster, 1973). Past experiences are disregarded except when they reappear as current memories, at which time they can have an effect on the current situation. Instead of blaming their problems on the past or other people or the environment, Gestalt therapy group members are taught to understand and assume full responsibility for the ways they are behaving (Perls, 1969).

One technique in Gestalt therapy is the awareness exercise. In an *awareness exercise,* the therapist asks "what" questions ("What are you aware of right now?") instead of "why" questions that evaluate the past. During any exercises, the group members are taught to pay attention to their body cues, such as muscle tension, facial expressions, and gestures. They are told to repeat and exaggerate any gestures to discover their function or significance. Clenched hands, for instance, might be increased to a strangling motion when it is exaggerated.

A dramatic technique in Gestalt therapy is the "hot seat" or "empty chair" exercise. In this exercise, a group member volunteers to occupy the "hot seat," a chair in the middle of the group. Facing an empty chair, the client imagines another person, a part of the self, or an object in order to carry on a two-way conversation or dialogue. During the dialogue, the person in the hot seat moves back and forth between the chairs, acting out both parts of the interaction.

When a friend of the authors sat in the "hot seat" to work on her problem of test anxiety, she found herself surprisingly hostile as she acted out the part of the test. She said things like "I'm going to show people that you aren't really very smart. I'll fix it so

Gestalt therapists are particularly sensitive to "body language." Can you read this individual's non-verbal message?

In family therapy, each member of the family learns ways to improve his or her communication style and faulty interaction patterns.

you can't be a success in life." This hot seat exercise is a modification of the role-playing techniques of **psychodrama,** one of the earliest forms of group therapy.

Family and marital therapy: Helping families cope

Family therapy is group therapy that tries to assist families to function more successfully. A family could enter therapy for personal growth of its members, but most often families seek therapy when there is a serious possibility of divorce or when one member's problems (such as drug abuse) are disrupting the family (Allen, 1988; Duck, 1984). Because a family is a system of interdependent parts, the problems of any one of the members unavoidably affect the adjustment of all the others (Beck, 1989; Liberman et al., 1987).

Marital therapy, or marriage counseling, attempts to improve the interactions of a married couple by focusing on individual, couple, or parent–child issues. In family and marital therapy, improvement of communication skills is often a central issue. When more than one couple or family is treated in a group, the members have an opportunity to give support and receive it from others with common problems.

PSYCHODRAMA: *A diagnostic and therapeutic technique developed by J. L. Moreno that consists of having the individual act out on stage his or her relations with others around whom conflicts center.*
FAMILY THERAPY: *Group therapy method that attempts to assist families to function more effectively.*

MARITAL THERAPY: *Marriage counseling that attempts to improve the interactions of a married couple.*

Review Questions

1 In _____ _____, the group members examine the parent–adult–child communication pattern being used.

2 In TA, the child ego-state — spontaneous feelings and impulses — is most similar to Freud's conceptualization of the _____.

3 _____ therapy uses a "hot seat" to enable group members to become aware of their feelings.

4 In marital and family therapy, the central issue is often poor _____.

Answers: 1 transactional analysis; *2* id; *3* Gestalt; *4* communication

BIOLOGICAL THERAPIES

As we discovered in Chapter 15, an important method for treating the symptoms of schizophrenia and mood disorders is drug therapy. Hundreds of thousands of severely disturbed patients, who had appeared to be doomed to spend their entire lives in institutions, have been successfully treated with antipsychotic and antidepressant drugs. Biological therapies, such as drug treatment, psychosurgery, and electroshock therapy, must be prescribed by a physician rather than a psychologist. These therapies assume that problem behaviors are caused, at least in part, by chemical imbalances or by disturbed nervous system functioning. Psychologists work with patients receiving biological therapies and are frequently involved in research programs to evaluate their effectiveness. We will begin our discussion with the most common form of biological therapy—drug treatment.

Drug therapy: Better living through chemistry?

Since the 1950s, drug companies have developed an amazing variety of chemicals to treat abnormal behaviors. In some cases, **drug therapy** corrects a chemical imbalance in the disturbed person's nervous system. In these instances, prescribing a drug is similar to administering insulin to diabetics, whose own bodies fail to manufacture enough. In other cases, the drugs are given to create effects that will relieve or suppress the symptoms of psychological disturbances even if the underlying cause is not thought to be biological.

The two major problems involved in drug therapy are maintaining the proper dosage level and controlling side effects or unwanted reactions. Like all medical treatments, effective drug therapy depends on cooperation of the patient (taking the medication as prescribed) and proper evaluation of the consequences of the treatment.

The wide range of psychiatric drugs can be classified into three major categories: antianxiety drugs, antipsychotic drugs, and mood-altering drugs. Table 16.3 lists some of the drugs included in each category.

Antianxiety drugs **Antianxiety drugs** are known as "minor tranquilizers" since they create feelings of tranquillity and calmness in addition to relief of muscle tension. These drugs have replaced sedatives (which had side effects of drowsiness and sleepiness) in the treatment of anxiety disorders. Antianxiety drugs such as Valium lower the sympathetic activity of the brain—the crisis mode of operation—so that anxiety responses are diminished or prevented. Valium is the most common drug prescribed for treating psycho-

One of the earliest biological therapies was the invention of the "tranquilizing chair" used to restrain individuals showing signs of mania.

BIOLOGICAL THERAPY: *Therapy involving physiological interventions intended to reduce symptoms associated with psychological disorders.*

DRUG THERAPY: *Use of chemicals to treat physical and psychological disorders.*

ANTIANXIETY DRUGS: *Tranquilizers used in the treatment of anxiety disorders.*

TABLE 16.3
Drug Therapy

Type of Drug	Chemical Group	Generic Name	Trade Name
Antianxiety drugs	Benzodiazepines	Chlordiazepoxide	Librium
		Diazepam	Valium
	Glycerol derivatives	Meprobamate	Miltown
			Equanil
Antipsychotic drugs	Phenothiazines	Chlorpromazine	Thorazine
		Fluphenazine	Prolixin
		Thioridazine	Mellaril
		Trifluoperazine	Stelazine
	Butyrophenones	Haloperidol	Haldol
	Thioxanthenes	Chlorprothixene	Taractan
Mood-altering drugs	Tricyclic antidepressants	Imipramine	Tofranil
		Amitriptyline	Elavil
	MAO inhibitors	Phenelzine	Nardil
		Tranylcypromine	Parnate
	Antimanic drugs	Lithium carbonate	Lithonate
			Lithane
			Eskalith

logical disorders. It was the top-selling drug of all kinds in 1970, but has since dropped to fourth place, largely as the result of efforts to control its abuse (Alper, 1986).

Question: Why are there so many warnings about the danger of drugs like Valium? Unfortunately, people can easily develop **tolerance** to antianxiety drugs, requiring increasing dosages to get the same effects. Also, people become physically dependent on these drugs, and withdrawal symptoms such as convulsions and hallucinations can occur when they stop taking the drugs. Overdosing with these drugs intentionally (to get a stronger effect) or unintentionally (by combining them with other drugs, such as alcohol) can be fatal.

TOLERANCE: *A decreased sensitivity to a drug such that larger and more frequent doses are required to produce the desired effect.*

Even though thousands of people have serious anxiety disorders that are appropriately treated with this type of medication, antianxiety drugs are seriously abused and have become popular "street drugs."

Antipsychotic drugs The drugs developed to treat psychotic disorders such as schizophrenia are often referred to as "major tranquilizers," creating the impression that they always have a strong calming or sedating effect. In fact, however, when **antipsychotic drugs** are given to severely inhibited and withdrawn patients, these drugs tend to energize the patients rather than tranquilize them. The main effect of these drugs is to diminish or terminate psychotic symptoms, such as hallucinations, delusions, and thought disorders, not to sedate the patient (Nicholi, 1988).

ANTIPSYCHOTIC DRUGS: *Chemicals administered to diminish or terminate psychotic symptoms such as hallucinations and delusions.*

Question: Do these drugs correct a chemical imbalance or just cover up symptoms? As we discussed in the previous chapter, the symptoms of schizophrenia have been related to an increase in activity of the neurotransmitter dopamine in parts of the brain. The antipsychotic drugs are thought to block the activity of dopamine receptors and therefore seem to restore a more normal chemical balance in schizophrenics (Kalat, 1988).

Studies of the effectiveness of antipsychotic drugs have consistently shown that they produce improvement in schizophrenic patients by reducing symptoms when compared to treatment with placebo medications or psychotherapy (Baldessarini, 1988; May, Tuma, and Dixon, 1981). Even patients previously destined for a lifetime in psychiatric institutions because of their distortions of reality have been improved enough to return to their homes. Not all patients are helped by the medications, however, and some may actually be harmed (Neale and Oltmanns, 1980).

Because antipsychotic medications can have serious side effects, patients often resist taking them voluntarily. These side effects include blurred vision, tachycardia (speeded heart rate), dry mouth, loss of sexual interest, stiffness of the muscles, and seizures (Tsuang, Faraone, and Day, 1988). With prolonged use, a condition called **tardive dyskinesia,** characterized by a shuffling gait and jerky, involuntary movements of the mouth, face, and diaphragm, may develop. Tardive dyskinesia has also been found in schizophrenic patients who have never received drug treatment (Crow et al., 1982; Nicoli, 1988). Although some people believe the symptoms result from organic deterioration and structural brain abnormalities, most patients on antipsychotic drugs are currently being given an additional medication (used to treat Parkinson's disease) in an attempt to prevent tardive dyskinesia.

TARDIVE DYSKINESIA: *Potential side effect of antipsychotic drugs, includes effects on voluntary muscles.*

Because of the serious side effects and the possibility of permanent damage from use of the antipsychotic drugs, many clinicians now use these drugs only during sudden flare-ups of psychotic symptoms or when the patient appears to be in danger of relapse (Herz, 1984; Carpenter and Heinrichs, 1984). In addition, many professionals are moving toward low-dose and intermittent medication strategies (Bower, 1988b; Tsuang, Faraone, and Day, 1988).

Mood-altering drugs Drug treatments are available to reduce the symptoms of both depression and bipolar disorders. Drugs used to treat major depression increase the availability of the neurotransmitters norepinephrine and serotonin and can often restore their levels to normal ranges. The two major types of antidepressant drugs are the tricyclics and MAO inhibitors. Improvement is reported in 70 percent of patients who take tricyclic antidepressants, so this type of drug is often prescribed first (Alper, 1986).

Because the adjustment of neurotransmitter levels to normal amounts takes time, it may take one to three weeks of drug therapy to relieve depression. During this time, seriously depressed patients are often hospitalized to prevent them from committing suicide.

Question: Does a depressed person have to keep taking the drugs indefinitely? When the antidepressant medication has restored the person's chemical balance, he or she may think more clearly and deal more effectively with problems in addition to feeling less depressed. By making constructive changes in their lives, some depressed persons can discontinue the antidepressant medication completely without a return of symptoms, but others need to continue this medication to prevent serious depressions.

For persons suffering from bipolar disorders, *lithium* is the drug used to treat manic episodes and prevent the occurrence of manic and depressive cycles. Lithium reduces the levels of norepinephrine in brain synapses during manic episodes and helps keep this important neurotransmitter in balance. Unfortunately, regulation of norepinephrine also means that people taking lithium will not feel euphoric even when it is appropriate. For this reason, patients sometimes "forget" to take their medication in order to elevate their moods and recapture the high-energy feelings of a manic episode (Alper, 1986). A patient taking lithium must have periodic blood tests to make sure the level of this drug is high enough to be helpful and low enough to prevent toxic reactions. Lithium can adversely affect the kidneys and thyroid gland, causing weight gain and hand tremors as noticeable symptoms of overdosage. In excessive dosages, lithium is poisonous. Thus, as with other drug therapies, it is important to monitor the proper dosage level (Baldessarini, 1990).

Electroconvulsive therapy: Promising or perilous treatment?

ELECTROCONVULSIVE THERAPY (ECT): *Passage of electrical current through the brain as a therapy technique.*

Electroconvulsive therapy (ECT) is also known as electroshock therapy (EST) or simply as "shock therapy." In an ECT treatment, 70 to 130 volts of electrical current is passed through the brain tissue between two electrodes placed on the outside of the head (Davison and Neale, 1989). This amount of electrical current applied to brain tissue for less than a second triggers a widespread firing of brain neurons that is identical to an epileptic seizure. When consciousness returns several minutes later, the patient has amnesia for the period immediately before the shock (retrograde amnesia) and is usually

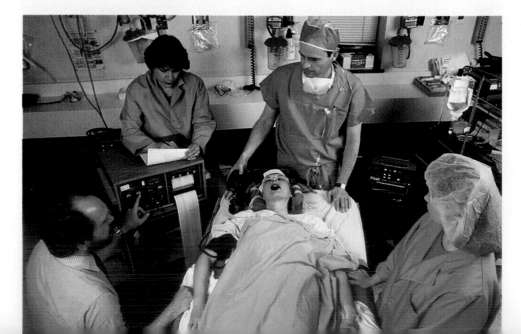

During electroconvulsive therapy (ECT), electrodes are placed on the forehead to apply electric currents to the brain and create a convulsion. ECT is used mainly to treat major depression.

somewhat confused for the next hour or so (anterograde amnesia). As treatments are continued, usually three to five times a week, the patient becomes more generally disoriented, a state that usually begins to improve soon after termination of treatments (see Chapter 7 for a discussion of the effects of ECT on memory). Most ECT patients have no memory for the shock treatments since they are usually given an anesthetic such as sodium pentothal. It is also routine to administer a muscle relaxant drug that reduces muscle contractions during the seizure to prevent injuries (Carson, Butcher, and Coleman, 1988).

Prior to the use of ECT, convulsions or comas were created by inhalation of nitrogen or carbon dioxide or by injections of chemicals such as camphor (Metrazol) or insulin. Frances Farmer received daily insulin shock therapy, a popular form of therapy during the 1940s, for 30 days.

During the early years of ECT, some patients received hundreds of treatments (Fink, 1977, 1979). In recent years, a total of less than 12 ECT treatments is most common, and sometimes the electrical current is applied only to the right hemisphere (unilateral ECT), which causes less interference with verbal memories and left hemisphere functioning.

In the 1940s and 1950s, ECT was used to treat all types of disorders, including schizophrenia. As the result of research studies that have compared changes in patients in carefully controlled experiments, ECT is now primarily administered to depressed patients who have not responded to antidepressant medication and who are suicidal (Thompson and Blaine, 1987).

Question: How does creating a convulsion relieve depression?   According to one early observer, there are at least 50 theories about how ECT can produce a beneficial effect (Gordon, 1948). The theory with the most research support is that passing an electrical current through the brain causes changes in the biochemical reactions of the synapses, making norepinephrine available to relieve the feelings of depression (Fink, 1979; Kalat, 1988).

ECT continues to be one of the most controversial biological treatments. In 1982, the voters in Berkeley, California, passed a referendum to ban the use of ECT in that city. This prohibition was subsequently overturned in the courts. Despite this opposition, many clinicians support the careful use of ECT, especially when other treatments have been found to be ineffective (Black, Winokur, and Nasrallah, 1987; Frankel, 1988).

Psychosurgery: Altering the brain

Attempts to change disturbed thinking and behavior by altering the brain have a long history. In Roman times, for example, it was believed that insanity could be relieved by a sword wound to the head. In 1936, Egaz Moniz, a Portuguese neurologist, began treating uncontrollable psychotics by cutting the nerve fibers between areas of the frontal lobes (where association areas for monitoring and planning behavior are found) and the thalamus and other midbrain structures where emotional experiences are relayed. Severing these connections decreases emotional responses and the patient accepts frustrating circumstances with a "philosophical calm." Moniz was awarded the Nobel Prize in medicine in 1949 for developing this technique, called a **frontal lobotomy,** despite the fact that he had been shot and paralyzed by one of his lobotomized patients (Valenstein, 1987).

In the years since the introduction of the lobotomy, this and other variations of **psychosurgery** have been used to treat depression, agitation, and psychotic symptoms such as hallucinations. In 1943, when hospitals were crowded with veterans discharged from military service for psychiatric problems, the Veterans Administration issued a communication that encouraged consulting and staff neurosurgeons to obtain training in lobotomy operations. They were urged to select cases for surgery "in which apprehension, anxiety, and depression are present, also cases with compulsions and obessions, with marked emotional tension," when other forms of therapy including shock therapy had failed (Valenstein, 1973, p. 390).

FRONTAL LOBOTOMY: *Alteration of the frontal lobes performed to treat psychological disorders.*

PSYCHOSURGERY: *Operative procedures on the brain designed to relieve severe mental symptoms that have not responded to other forms of treatment.*

During the 1940s, about 50,000 patients received lobotomies. One American neurosurgeon claimed that he had performed over 4,000 operations, using a gold-plated ice pick that he carried with him in a velvet-lined case. Since the procedure he performed required only a local anesthetic and a small incision at the edge of the eye socket, he often performed the surgery in the patient's home or his office (Freeman, 1959).

Question: But wouldn't there be serious side effects from damaging the brain? In some cases, lobotomy patients are calmed without dramatically affecting their behaviors. After her frontal lobotomy, Frances Farmer was able to care for herself outside the institution and to communicate well enough to write a book describing her experiences. But brain surgery is always risky and its side effects and complications may be irreversible. Patients sometimes suffer personality changes, becoming bland, colorless, and unemotional. In other cases, patients become aggressive and unable to control their impulses. Despite these problems, psychosurgery is still considered useful in some cases (Gregory, 1988).

Since the advent of drug therapy, the use of psychosurgery has dropped dramatically, and it is used only as a last resort when less radical treatments have failed. At the present time, a number of lobbying groups are actively involved in monitoring its use.

Review Questions

1 The dramatic reduction in numbers of hospitalized mental patients is attributed to the use of _____ .

2 Valium is classified as a(n) _____ drug.

3 Antipsychotic drugs are used to relieve the distortions of reality found in _____ .

4 Mood-altering drugs used to treat depression and bipolar disorders alleviate symptoms by adjusting the levels of _____ .

5 _____ is used to treat bipolar disorders, requiring the monitoring of levels of this drug in the blood.

6 ECT creates a _____ by passing an electrical current through the brain tissue.

7 A lobotomy is a _____ procedure that attempts to relieve abnormal symptoms.

Answers: 1 drug therapy; *2* antianxiety; *3* schizophrenia; *4* neurotransmitters; *5* lithium; *6* convulsion; *7* psychosurgery

ISSUES IN THERAPY

To evaluate the effectiveness of any approach to therapy, several issues need to be considered. When is it appropriate to institutionalize and treat people against their will? What qualifies therapists to decide about altering other people's behaviors? When and how should people seek therapy, and how do they know when it is helping them?

The need for therapy: Choice or coercion

It is estimated that six million Americans receive some recognized form of therapy each year. In some cases, people recognize that they could benefit from psychiatric hospitalization and commit themselves voluntarily. Others, like Frances Farmer, are involuntarily committed.

Question: What are the grounds for involuntary commitment?   It varies from state to state. Generally, people can be sent to psychiatric hospitals if they are assumed to be (1) dangerous to themselves (usually suicidal) or dangerous to others (potentially violent), (2) in need of treatment (generally applied when an individual is acting bizarrely and out of contact with reality), and (3) there must be no reasonable alternative to hospitalization that is less restrictive (Rozovsky, 1984). In emergency situations, psychologists and other professionals can authorize temporary commitment for 24 to 72 hours. During this observation period, laboratory tests can be performed to rule out medical illnesses that could be causing the symptoms, and the patient can receive psychological testing, medication, and short-term therapy (Torrey, 1988).

After the initial period of observation, patients can be legally committed to an institution if they are found to be unable to provide for their own basic needs or are presumed to be dangerous to others. In 18 states, the patient has a right to a jury trial to decide commitment, but, as you might imagine, psychotic patients are not always competent enough to understand and take advantage of their rights. In Vermont, for example, no patient has ever requested the trial option. The length of time a person can be confined after a commitment varies from 21 days in one state to 5 years in another. There are 19 states with an unspecified or indefinite commitment period, so that once the person is committed to an institution, he or she could remain there for life (Torrey, 1988). Whatever the period of commitment, most state laws specify that patients must be confined in the "least restrictive" environment.

Civil rights groups throughout the country, many of them led by ex-patients, are attempting to change laws that affect the treatment of mental patients. Recent legislation brought about by such efforts specifies that patients confined to an institution must continue to receive some form of treatment instead of receiving only custodial care. However, patients do not always wish to receive the treatments they get. In Massachusetts, for example, a patient who did not like the muscle-tightening side effects of a drug she was forced to take set herself on fire. As a result, patients' rights attorneys obtained the first court decision that guarantees a patient's right to refuse antipsychotic medication (*Mills* v. *Rogers,* 1975). Laws that protect the patient's right to refuse medication now exist in most states (Costin and Draguns, 1989).

Treatment outside mental hospitals became possible after 1963 with the passage of the Community Mental Health Centers Act. This legislation has provided federal funding for establishment of regional **community mental health (CMH) centers.** A CMH center provides outpatient services such as group and individual therapy and prevention programs, in addition to coordinating short-term inpatient care and programs for discharged patients, such as halfway houses and aftercare services. These centers are staffed by psychiatrists, psychologists, social workers, nurses, and volunteers who live in the neighborhood.

COMMUNITY MENTAL HEALTH (CMH) CENTERS: *Federally supported treatment centers providing outpatient services for psychological disorders.*

Recognition of the problems created when people are kept in large, impersonal institutions and the increased availability of community services has led in recent years to a trend toward **deinstitutionalization.** Many view this policy of discharging patients from mental hospitals to halfway houses or to the care of relatives as a positive step toward increased patients' rights (Lerman, 1981; Okin, 1987). Critics have argued, however, that thousands of ex-patients have been discharged without continuing provision for their protection (Stengel, 1987; Torrey, 1989). Many of these people have ended up living on the street with no shelter or means of support. One study of homeless adults living in beach areas near Los Angeles found that 44 percent had previously been in hospitals for psychiatric reasons (Gelberg, Linn, and Leake, 1988). In response to these problems, some communities, most notably New York City, have attempted to reinstitutionalize the mentally ill. This reinstitutionalization has also been widely criticized (Stengel, 1987).

DEINSTITUTIONALIZATION: *A practice, begun in the 1960s, and accelerated in the 1980s of releasing patients from mental hospitals.*

Question: What else can be done?   Rather than returning patients to state hospitals, most clinicians suggest an extension and improvement of community care. They recommend that general hospitals be equipped with special psychiatric units where

Although critics deplore the crowded conditions of many state hospitals, deinstitutionalization has released many former mental patients onto metropolitan streets with no facilities to care for them.

acutely ill patients could receive inpatient care. For less disturbed individuals and chronically ill patients, they recommend walk-in clinics, crisis intervention services, improved residential treatment facilities, and psychosocial and vocational rehabilitation. State hospitals would be reserved for only the most unmanageable patients.

As you can imagine, such a full range of services would be enormously expensive. Individual psychotherapy currently costs $70 to $120 an hour, and hospital costs are well over $300 a day. Specialized inpatient treatment programs for substance abuse, eating disorders, and other problems can run as high as $1,000 a day for a two- or three-week hospitalization (Meredith, 1986). Although the initial cost of providing decent, comprehensive care for the mentally ill would be high, these figures could be substantially reduced if we also invested in more *primary prevention* programs. Instead of waiting until someone loses his or her job, home, and family, we could develop more intervention programs for high-risk groups and offer short-term immediate services during crisis situations. People would also need to be educated about the pros and cons of the different therapies and how to select an appropriate therapist. These are the two topics of our next section.

Therapies and therapists: Making a choice that's best for you

As we have seen in this chapter, there are several different theoretical approaches to therapy. Many problems, such as confusion, low self-esteem, and difficulties in making decisions, can be treated equally well with all forms of psychotherapy. There are some problems, however, that respond best to specific treatments. Surveys have generally found that:

1. psychoanalysis is best for emotional-somatic symptoms and work or school adjustment problems;
2. behavior therapy works best with phobias and compulsions, emotional-somatic symptoms, sexual problems, and personal-vocational development;
3. humanistic therapy is most effective for problems of self-esteem;
4. group therapy is best for drug dependence and marital problems; and
5. biological therapies are most effective for severe depression, bipolar disorders, schizophrenia, and some anxiety disorders (Nicoli, 1988; Suinn, 1987; Zilbergeld, 1983).

TABLE 16.4
Percentages of Therapists by Type

Therapist's Orientation	Number	Percentage
Eclectic	171	41
Psychoanalytic	57	14
Humanistic	45	11
Cognitive behavioral	43	10
Behavioral	28	7
Family	11	3
Gestalt	7	2
Rational-emotive	7	2
Transactional analysis	4	1
Other	42	9
Total	415	100

Source: Smith, D. (1982). Trends in counseling and psychotherapy. *American Psychologist, 37* (3), 802–809.

In recognition of the fact that various problems respond to specific theoretical approaches, most clinicians use a combination of techniques depending on the particular individual and his or her specific problem. Such a combination of techniques is known as the **eclectic approach.** One study of 400 counseling and clinical psychologists found that 41 percent of the therapists they surveyed identified themselves with this eclectic approach (see Table 16.4). The remainder practice a particular type of therapy (Smith, 1982).

> **ECLECTIC APPROACH:** *An approach to psychotherapy where the therapist freely borrows from various theories to find the appropriate treatment for his or her client.*

Question: Are all therapists called psychiatrists or "shrinks"? "Shrink" is a slang term originally applied to psychiatrists but now often used to refer to any kind of therapist. Psychiatrists, psychoanalysts, clinical psychologists, and social workers are all therapists, but they have different educational backgrounds and are licensed to practice therapy in different ways, so these terms are not interchangeable. Each state has licensing or certification laws that limit the use of these titles.

Clinical psychologists are therapists who have an advanced degree such as a Ph.D. (Doctor of Philosophy), a Psy.D. (Doctor of Psychology), or Ed.D. (Doctor of Education). They have usually had four or more years of graduate education, including a supervised internship, and have often conducted research studies. Therapists using the humanistic, cognitive, and behavioral approaches are most often clinical psychologists.

> **CLINICAL PSYCHOLOGISTS:** *A psychologist with an advanced graduate degree who specializes in treating psychological and behavioral disturbances or who does research on such disturbances.*
> **PSYCHIATRISTS:** *A medical doctor who has additional training in the diagnosis and treatment of mental illness.*

Psychiatrists are physicians who specialize in psychiatry after graduation from medical school and completing a year of internship. The three-year residency program in psychiatry includes supervised practice in therapy techniques and training in the biological treatment of disorders. Since psychiatrists are physicians, they are the only type of therapist who can prescribe drugs for patients.

Psychoanalysts are almost always psychiatrists with additional specialized training in the techniques of psychoanalysis. (The exceptions are persons trained in analysis after completing other graduate education, such as social work.) During the specialized training period, students must themselves undergo psychoanalysis.

> **PSYCHOANALYSTS:** *A mental health professional (usually a physician) who is trained to practice psychoanalysis.*

Social workers have obtained at least a master's degree in social work (M.S.W.). During their year or two of graduate education, they are supervised in the treatment of clients in hospitals or outpatient settings. Social workers can also obtain a doctorate degree or specialize further in specific types of therapy to be certified to do private practice as licensed marriage, family, and child counselors or as licensed clinical social workers.

> **SOCIAL WORKERS:** *Therapists who have obtained at least a master's degree in social work, and who typically work with patients and their families to ease their community relations.*

 Question: When should someone see a therapist? The decision to seek therapy can be based on several considerations. When problems have increased in severity

GROUP THERAPIES

9 In the transactional analysis approach to group therapy, members examine their Parent–Adult–Child styles in communication patterns and relive childhood experiences.

10 Gestalt therapy integrates present experiences into a meaningful whole through the use of such techniques as awareness exercises and the "hot seat" or "empty chair" approach.

11 Family and marital therapy focus on improving communication patterns and solving problems within the family group.

BIOLOGICAL THERAPIES

12 Drug therapy is widely used to alleviate anxiety, reduce psychotic distortions, and alter moods.

13 Electroconvulsive therapy (ECT) applies electrical current to the brain to induce a seizure. Used as a treatment for depression, it is thought to mobilize brain neurotransmitters.

14 Psychosurgery in the form of frontal lobotomy or limbic system alterations often results in reduced emotional expression.

ISSUES IN THERAPY

15 People who are presumed to be mentally ill can be committed to mental hospitals for diagnosis and treatment, but current trends emphasize outpatient services in community mental health centers and deinstitutionalization.

16 Psychiatrists and psychoanalysts have been trained in psychoanalytic therapy techniques. Psychiatrists can prescribe drugs and administer other biological therapies. Clinical psychologists and social workers are trained to use a variety of psychotherapy techniques.

SUGGESTED READINGS

BECK, A. T. (1989). *Love is never enough.* New York: Harper & Row. A clearly written presentation of the cognitive therapy approach with extensive illustrations of its effectiveness in treatment of marital problems.

COREY, G. (1986). *Theory and practice of counseling and psychotherapy* (3rd ed.). Monterey, CA: Brooks/Cole. A practical guide to the major approaches to therapy, including therapy processes and applications.

CORSINI, R. J. (1984). *Current psychotherapies* (3rd ed.). Itasca, Ill.: Peacock. Individual and group therapies are presented with extensive case examples and research support.

DAVISON, G. C., & NEALE, J. M. (1989). *Abnormal psychology.* (5th ed.) New York: Wiley. Therapy approaches are presented for specific types of disorders. This widely used text emphasizes the similarities and differences in research methods and current therapeutic practices.

GOLDFRIED, M. R. (Ed.). (1982). *Converging themes in psychotherapy: Trends in psychodynamic, humanistic and behavioral practice.* New York: Springer. Essays on the commonalities of therapy methods, focusing on current status of the major approaches and future directions.

TORREY, E. F. (1988). *Surviving schizophrenia: A family manual.* New York: Harper & Row. Helpful for understanding the implications of short- and long-term therapy for psychotic disorders. Includes discussion of legal and ethical issues and describes resources.

ZILBERGELD, B. (1983). *The shrinking of America: Myths of psychological change.* Boston: Little, Brown. A critical look at psychotherapy and its effectiveness.

chapter seventeen
Social Interaction

ON April 15, 1989, several thousand British soccer fans were inside England's Hillsborough Stadium anxiously awaiting the start of the playoff for the national soccer championship. Outside the stadium, crowds of frustrated fans, who had been unable to gain admittance, began surging toward the closed turnstiles. Hoping to relieve this "life-threatening situation," a police official ordered a 16-foot-wide gate to be opened. This decision is now blamed for one of history's worst sports disasters. More than 200 spectators were injured and 94 people were asphyxiated or trampled to death as the crowd of fans rushed through the gate and into an enclosed and already overcrowded viewing terrace (Fisher, 1989).

For those who remember the soccer riot in Brussels four years earlier, the behavior of the English fans should come as no surprise. In May of 1985, more than 60,000 soccer fans (mostly British and Italian) rushed to fill the Heysel Stadium in Brussels in great anticipation of viewing one of the premier events in the world of soccer — the European Cup Final. About 45 minutes before the scheduled 8:15 P.M. kickoff, several British fans began to harass the opposing Italian team supporters through the wire fence that separated them. As the insults and the size of the taunting crowd increased, the fence suddenly gave way, and the British crowd charged into the Italian section, hurling rocks and bottles and setting fires. As the human tide poured across the fence, the Italian supporters panicked and made a rush for the nearest exit. Hundreds of people were pressed against a concrete side wall and wire barrier fence that faced the playing field. Thirty-eight eventually died and more than 400 were injured under the trampling feet of the crowd or by the collapsing concrete wall. "I've seen too much," moaned one bloodied Italian fan, tears streaming down his cheeks. "I've seen death" (Rosenblatt, 1985).

In spite of this mayhem, officials decided to proceed with the scheduled match after a 90-minute delay. Although West German TV stations broke off their broadcast in protest when the game began, most of the world recognized that the decision to play was based on the fear of triggering an even greater riot if the game was canceled.

The 1985 and 1989 soccer riots are not unique. A short look at the history of humankind, with its wars, murders, terrorism, infanticide, spouse abuse, and so on, shows that violence has long been a part of human existence. But history also shows that people will often rush to aid and support their fellow human beings, even when this places them at great personal risk. How do we explain these differences? Are there certain personality traits that predispose some people toward aggression and others toward helping? Or are situational factors and social forces the primary determinants of how people will behave?

Such questions are often the focus of psychologists who specialize in the field of **social psychology**. As you may remember from Chapter 1, all psychologists study behavior (which includes thoughts and feelings, as well as overt actions), but social psychologists concentrate their studies on how behavior affects, and is affected by, other people—hence the term *social* psychology.

As you may imagine, any field that attempts to study all aspects of social behavior is extremely broad. To deal with this complexity, we present two chapters. This first chapter begins with a look at the internal, thinking, and perceiving aspects of social psychology —social perception and attitude formation—and then goes on to examine the somewhat external and overt behaviors of aggression and altruism. In the second chapter, we will go even further outside the individual to look at how large social influences, such as groups and institutions, affect people's behavior.

SOCIAL PSYCHOLOGY: *The branch of psychology that studies how the thoughts, feelings, and actions of individuals are influenced by the actual, imagined, or implied presence of others.*

SOCIAL PERCEPTION

As was noted in Chapter 4, our life experiences seem to determine how we perceive or interpret the sensory world around us. Like the perception of the pygmy who spent his entire life in a dense rain forest, our perceptions of ourselves and others also reflect our unique and personal experiences in the world. The study of **social perception** helps explain how we come to know and understand the people around us, as well as ourselves. Here we will look at two of the most important areas in social perception: attribution and social cognition.

SOCIAL PERCEPTION: *Process that explains how one comes to know and understand oneself and others.*

Attribution: Perceiving the causes of behavior

In our attempt to know and understand the people around us, we often look for *reasons* for their behavior. In the case of the soccer riots in England, we seem to have a strong need to explain why the British fans rushed to their deaths in 1989 and so savagely attacked the Italian fans in 1985. Is there something unique and different about British soccer fans? Psychologists describe these attempts to understand "why" people did what they did as engaging in *attribution*. When we offer an explanation for the behavior, we "attribute" it to something (the rioters were drunk, the police were lax, and so on). **Attribution theory** describes the principles we follow in establishing such causes (Higgins and Bargh, 1987).

ATTRIBUTION THEORY: *Theory that describes the principles people follow in making judgments about the causes of events, others' behavior, and their own behavior.*

 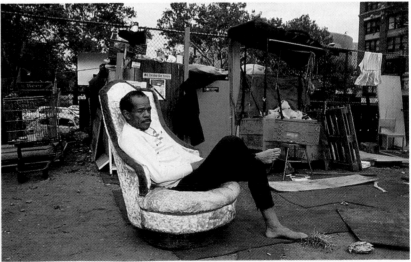

How would you explain Jimmy Swaggart's tears during his confession of sin and this man's extreme poverty? Attribution theory helps explain why your perceptions may differ from those of your parents or friends.

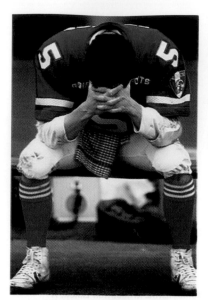

Assuming responsibility for failures (internal attributions) can help us to improve our performance, but if carried to extremes it can also lead to depression.

SOCIAL COGNITION: *Way of knowing and understanding others that involves internal, cognitive structures or patterns that are used as frameworks for organizing information.*
SCHEMATA: *An individual's basic cognitive patterns for explaining the world.*
IMPLICIT PERSONALITY THEORY: *Schema or pattern of unstated assumptions about which personality traits "go with" each other and which ones do not.*
FRAME: *Cognitive pattern that describes which behaviors are appropriate in a given social context. Frames include both role expectations and scripts for interaction.*

ILLUSORY CORRELATION: *The erroneous perception of a correlation between two characteristics that does not, in fact, exist.*

have low self-esteem tend to attribute unfavorable outcomes in their lives to their own stable personal characteristics and attribute positive outcomes to external, unstable causes such as luck. Successful coping, therefore, seems to be a careful mixture of taking credit for our successes (the self-serving bias), plus taking enough responsibility for our failures that we are motivated to change, while not blaming ourselves to the point of depression.

Social cognition: How we process social information

In coming to know other people, we rely not only on attributions but also on internal, cognitive structures or patterns that we carry with us as frameworks for organizing information about others. This way of processing social information is known as **social cognition.**

As you may remember from our discussion of the cognitive development of children in Chapter 9, Jean Piaget suggested that during the first few months of life children are actively developing **schemata,** or cognitive patterns for explaining the world around them. Just as we once developed differing "motion" schemata for eating from a spoon versus sucking from a nipple, we also develop differing *social schemata* that help to organize the vast amount of social information that bombards us each day. Schemata are invaluable for directing our attention to relevant information, for providing us a structure for organizing and evaluating information, and for creating categories necessary for long-term memory (see Chapter 7). But just as the sucking schema doesn't work when applied to eating with a spoon, our social schemata also fail us when used inappropriately. In this section we will first look at two types of social schemata (implicit personality theory and frames) and then discuss potential problems with their inappropriate use.

According to **implicit personality theory,** each of us develops a schema or pattern of unstated assumptions about which personality traits "go with" each other and which ones do not. Our schema of an "extrovert," for example, might include elements of enthusiasm, spiritedness, and self-assuredness, but not shyness, passivity, or dependence.

A second type of social schema is a cognitive pattern, or **frame,** that describes what behaviors are appropriate in a given social context. This frame provides information not only about the general behaviors expected with a particular *role* (doctor, student, husband), but that each *role* also has a specific *script* that governs interactions. When you go into a supermarket, for example, you have a particular *frame* for shopping and supermarkets that determines the *roles* that both you and the cashier will play, as well as an explicit *script* that governs all interactions. Have you ever stopped to notice how strongly these frames for roles and scripts govern your behavior? What do you think would happen if instead of responding "Fine, thank you," to the cashier's automatic question "How are you today?" you started to really tell him or her how you felt? If you went into a long story about how many tests you had to study for, how many times your car had broken down, and so on, you would not be following the generally accepted script and role and this would undoubtedly elicit a puzzled and disapproving reaction.

Question: This sounds as if schemata are useful. What are the problems you mentioned?   One of the major errors in social cognition is the tendency to "see what we want to see." If we have an implicit personality theory that "Jocks are dumb," for example, research has shown that we tend to look for information that supports this belief (M. Snyder, 1984) and will ignore contradictory information (Weber and Crocker, 1983). (This example of implicit personality theory is also known as *stereotyping* and will be discussed in the upcoming section on prejudice.)

A second potential error in social cognition is the tendency to perceive associations (correlations) between traits or behaviors that don't in fact exist (Sherman et al., 1989). One example of this **illusory correlation** effect is the common assumption that high intelligence is associated with a higher probability of psychological disorders. Despite the lack of scientific evidence, many people persist in this belief.

*Does this fit your **frame** (or social schemata) for what a "good" father does with his son?*

We not only see what we expect to see and perceive illusory correlations, we also tend to overestimate the number of people that agree with us. Research on the **false consensus bias** has shown that when people are asked to estimate the proportion of others who agree with their beliefs about drugs, abortion, toxic waste, and so on, they will significantly overestimate the degree of agreement (Nisbett and Kunda, 1985, Rodin and Salovey, 1989). Similar to the *self-serving bias* in attribution, we preserve our self-image by overestimating the "correctness" or popularity of our views.

At this point in our discussion, you may be discouraged by all the potential errors in both attribution and social cognition. Although errors do occur, it is important to remember that these are the *exceptions* in information processing, not the rule. Our judgments are generally made on the basis of ongoing interactions with others, and simply knowing about these errors may help us to overcome them.

FALSE CONSENSUS BIAS: *Tendency to believe that other people think and believe like you do more than they actually do.*

Review Questions

1 The process of making sense of a behavior by looking for explanations or causes is known as _____, and _____ _____ explains the principles that are followed in establishing such causes.

2 When judging the causes of others' behavior, we tend to overestimate personality factors and underestimate social or situational factors, a bias known as the _____ _____.

3 When judging the causes of our own behavior, we tend to take personal credit for our successes and to externalize our failures, an error known as the _____ _____.

4 Social _____ are cognitive patterns for explaining behavior.

5 The schema that assumes that certain personality traits go together is known as the _____.

6 Our _____ or schemata for appropriate behavior in certain social situations include both roles and scripts.

7 Overestimating the degree that others agree with us is known as the _____ _____.

Answers: 1 attribution, attribution theory; *2* fundamental attribution error; *3* self-serving bias; *4* schemata; *5* implicit personality theory; *6* frames; *7* false consensus bias

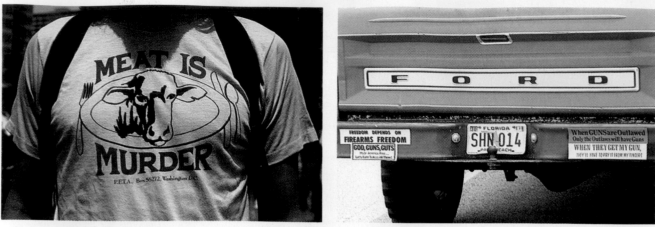

T-shirts and bumper stickers often tell others about our political and personal attitudes.

ATTITUDES

What is your attitude about the riots and violence associated with professional sports? Did you agree with the recent supreme court ruling about the legal right to abortions? How did you feel about television ads for condoms or about high school health clinics that dispense condoms free of charge? Your responses to such questions are very important to your friends and family, as well as to your college instructors, religious leaders, politicians, and salespeople. Such responses reveal your **attitudes** about these controversial topics. An attitude is a learned predisposition to respond consistently in a positive or negative way to some person, object, or situation (Petty, Ostrom, and Brock, 1981). As can be seen in Figure 17.2, each attitude has three important components: (1) the *cognitive,* which represents thoughts or beliefs; (2) the *affective,* which reflects feelings or emotional reactions; and (3) the *behavioral,* which describes tendencies or predispositions toward certain actions based on a particular attitude.

ATTITUDE: *Evaluative response to a person, object, or situation; these responses include cognitive, affective, and behavioral components.*

If we know people's attitudes, we are in a better position to meet the original goals of psychology — to describe, explain, predict, and change behavior. For example, knowing that someone supports the "Pro-Life" or "Anti-Choice" movement helps explain why he or she also bristles at the mention of abortion and votes for certain political candidates.

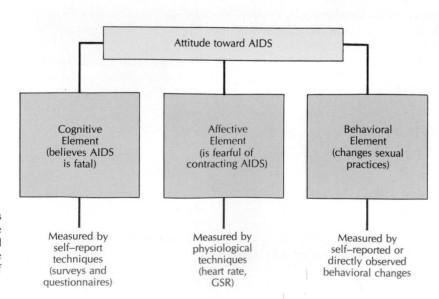

Figure 17.2 Each of our attitudes is composed of three separate elements — cognitive, affective, and behavioral. Social psychologists use differing techniques to assess each of these elements.

Question: Aren't there times when our behavior doesn't match our attitudes? Several researchers have found that people's self-reported attitudes are often poor predictors of actual behavior (Abelson, 1988; Sherman et al., 1989; Wicker, 1969). This could reflect problems in measurement of the attitude, but it could also mean that people sometimes actively suppress or distort their true attitudes, perhaps to make a good impression.

In addition, it is important to recognize that attitudes only indicate behavioral *tendencies.* Although some people may lie on self-report measures and have no intention of behaving according to their expressed attitudes, other people do provide accurate reports but their reports can be overruled by other influences. Have you ever felt bad about a racist remark made by a friend but suppressed your disapproval because you didn't want to risk losing his or her friendship? Even though your cognitive, affective, and behavioral tendencies might all be against such a negative remark, you might suppress any signs of disapproval and may even laugh at the remark because of external influences.

Attitude formation: Where do attitudes come from?

According to learning theorists, attitudes are acquired in the same manner as other types of behavior (McGuire, 1985). Just as we learn to tie our shoes, we also learn to like rock music better than classical, to prefer Pepsi over Coke, and to dislike ethnic groups different from our own. From this perspective, we learn attitudes from being exposed to similar views on the part of others (social learning), from being rewarded for expressing these attitudes (operant conditioning), and from making associations between certain people or objects and positive or negative emotions (classical conditioning).

Whereas learning theorists emphasize external factors that act on the individual to help form personal attitudes, cognitive theorists focus on the internal thoughts and reasoning of the individual. According to Daryl Bem's (1972) **self-perception theory,** people do not always know how they think or feel about an issue; as a result, they sometimes infer their attitudes from observing their own behavior. If you found yourself reading this text even when no test had been scheduled, how would you explain your behavior? You might decide that it is because you are bored and have nothing else to read, that you are a good student and want to learn the material well, or that the text is uniquely written and exciting to read. Although we would prefer that you adopt either of the last two explanations, self-perception theory is impartial and suggests that whatever reason you arrive at, your attitude will reflect this decision. Your attitudes are therefore formed by watching your own behavior and devising logical explanations for it.

SELF-PERCEPTION THEORY: *Bem's theory that people form attitudes by observing their own behavior.*

One cognitive theory that conflicts with self-perception theory is **cognitive consistency theory.** According to this perspective, people need to feel that their attitudes match or are in harmony with one another. Thus, students who are strong supporters of environmental protection issues can be expected not to wear T-shirts with "Nuke the Whales" messages on the front (unless being sarcastic) and teenagers would oppose raising the legal driving age.

COGNITIVE CONSISTENCY THEORY: *Theory that people have a strong need to feel that their attitudes match and are in harmony with one another.*

Question: What happens when a person's attitudes are not consistent? According to Leon Festinger's (1957) **cognitive dissonance theory,** we feel tension (or "dissonance") when we notice that we have two or more inconsistent (nonmatching) thoughts (or cognitions) and we are then strongly motivated to make changes in our attitudes to restore the consistency. In other words, the need for cognitive consistency leads us to experience tension or anxiety when we notice that mismatch (cognitive dissonance), and it is this tension that provides the motivation for us to change our attitudes to restore balance or consistency. Dissonance is frequently experienced (1) after making a decision (post-decision dissonance), (2) when our expectations are not fulfilled (disconfirmed expectancies), and (3) when we behave in ways that are inconsistent with our attitudes (attitude-discrepant behavior).

COGNITIVE DISSONANCE THEORY: *Festinger's theory that tension is experienced whenever one discovers that he or she has inconsistent (nonmatching) thoughts or cognitions, and that this tension drives the individual to make attitudinal changes that will restore harmony or consistency.*

increase in love was the result of his sexual abilities and his personal qualities. He now realized that it was only cognitive dissonance or self-perception at work. What do you think?

Review Questions

1   A learned predisposition to respond consistently in a positive or negative way to some person, object, or situation is known as a(n) _____.

2   The three major components of all attitudes are the _____, _____, and _____.

3   _____ theorists suggest that attitudes are formed through operant or classical conditioning.

4   The belief that people sometimes form their attitudes by observing their own behavior is known as _____ theory.

5   The need for _____ _____, or harmony between our attitudes, often leads us to change our attitudes when we experience _____ _____ from noticing the mismatch.

6   After making a decision, people will often look for evidence that confirms their choice and avoid discrepant information in an effort to avoid _____ dissonance.

7   People will often change their original attitude toward a person, object, or situation that failed to meet their expectations out of their need to avoid the dissonance associated with _____ _____.

8   When people notice that their behavior and attitudes do not match, they are motivated to change because of the dissonance associated with _____ _____.

Answers: 1 attitude;   *2* cognitive, affective, behavioral;   *3* learning;   *4* self-perception;   *5* cognitive consistency, cognitive dissonance;   *6* post-decision;   *7* disconfirmed expectancies;   *8* discrepant behavior.

Attitude change: Direct attempts at persuasion

Although the need for consistency and avoidance of dissonance can be highly effective in producing changes or adjustments in attitudes, there *are* more direct methods. What technique for attitude change would you recommend in the following situations? Joe wants to talk his parents into helping finance the purchase of an expensive car while he's still in college; Mary wants to switch colleges next year and hopes to talk her roommate into going with her; and Tom wants to convince his three-year-old that candy is not good for him. Each person wants to change an attitude of someone else, but should each use the same techniques? And what technique works best?

If you are like most people, your initial suggestions for Joe, Mary, and Tom would be based on communication techniques—"Tell them . . ." "Have someone else tell them . . ." or "Make sure they're listening when you. . . ." Such communication techniques, when designed by one source in a direct attempt to influence the attitude of another, are methods of **persuasion**. The effectiveness of persuasion depends on factors in the *source* of the communication, on the *message* itself, and on certain *audience* characteristics—in other words, on *who says what to whom.*

PERSUASION: *Direct attempts to influence the attitude of another through communication techniques.*

Characteristics of the source   If the object is to change the attitudes of others on relatively trivial matters, the source should be someone they like, identify with, and find physically attractive (Chaiken and Eagly, 1983). Beautiful models are often paid a great deal of money to endorse a certain attitude or merely to smile and stand next to a product. Despite our protests that we're *not* influenced by what some pretty girl or football player

Voters often respond favorably to this style of political campaign. Can you explain why?

has to say about dishwashers or airlines, marketing surveys and sales reports tend to contradict us.

When the attitude is not trivial but is instead a part of someone's deeply held values and convictions, the **credibility** of the source becomes the most important factor in persuasion. The two major components of credibility are trustworthiness and expertise. We seem to trust sources more when they have no apparent association with the product and have little to gain (Wood and Eagly, 1981), and we judge expertise by personal qualifications and associations with prestigious organizations. The importance of expertise has been documented in numerous studies (such as Hennigan et al., 1982).

If the communicator is knowledgeable and trustworthy, the audience is obviously more likely to be convinced. But it is also interesting to note that the *illusion* of honesty can be created simply by looking a person in the eye and by speaking confidently and fast.

Question: Don't we usually distrust "fast talkers"? Although we are often warned about the dangers of such people, it actually appears that an audience's perceptions of knowledge and trust, and thus their degree of persuasion, is positively influenced by communicators who speak at a relatively rapid rate (Apple, Streeter, and Krauss, 1979). John F. Kennedy has often been considered one of the most powerful communicators in modern times, which may in part be due to the fact that he often approached a speaking rate of over 300 words per minute (the average rate is somewhere around 140–150 words per minute). Since most people can listen and comprehend at a much faster rate than they can talk, a faster pace may attract more interest and allow less time for the audience's thoughts to drift away or to build counterarguments.

Characteristics of the message Of course, there is more to persuasion than fast-talking, likeable, or credible sources. The message itself—the content and the way it is presented—is of key importance. Although a number of researchers have emphasized the need to appeal to cognitive processes, such as logic and reason (Wood, 1982), others have emphasized the power of appeals to emotion (Abelson et al., 1982). Madison Avenue advertisers seem to agree with the latter researchers, if we are to judge by the preponderance of emotional appeals in advertising.

One common emotional appeal is that of fear induction: Politicians warn us about the threat of higher taxes and nuclear war if we don't vote for them, doctors show us graphic photos of diseased lungs in an attempt to convince us of the dangers of smoking, and product advertisements clearly depict the social rejection we face if we don't use their mouthwash, dandruff shampoo, or acne medications. For such fear tactics to work (1) the appeal must be quite strong, (2) the audience must believe the message, and (3) specific

CREDIBILITY: *Degree of trustworthiness or expertise that is associated with a particular source of persuasion.*

Fear induction is a common technique in advertisements and public service announcements.

instructions for avoiding the dangers must be presented (Bandura et al., 1982; Beck and Frankel, 1981).

Characteristics of the audience In addition to qualities of the source and the message, characteristics of the audience also influence the effectiveness of persuasion. To be fully receptive to a message and messenger, the audience must be relaxed, must have time to listen, and must be in an environment conducive to communication.

Once receptive conditions have been established, listeners must believe they are free to choose and to disagree. In fact, when people feel that they are being pushed or unduly influenced in their attitudes, they often increase their resistance to persuasion — a phenomenon termed **psychological reactance.** This "illusion of freedom" is often exploited by advertisers who offer some reward or discount to customers who try the competitor's product. Most people actually never go to the trouble to drive the other guy's car, but they do feel more attracted to the company making the offer because it seems so fair and open.

PSYCHOLOGICAL REACTANCE: *Increased resistance to persuasion that is experienced when the recipient feels that his or her freedom to choose is threatened.*

The vulnerability of the audience is also an important component in persuasibility. When people are lonely, depressed, inexperienced, poorly educated, or physically isolated, they are generally lower in self-esteem and are particularly susceptible to persuasion. Those who are willing to exploit such vulnerability can be very influential (at least for the short term) and are also potentially dangerous.

To protect yourself from this type of manipulation, it is important to recognize that during certain times of your life, such as the period following the death of a loved one or a divorce, you are particularly vulnerable and more likely to make faulty decisions. People who quickly remarry after a divorce, for example, are at much higher risk of subsequent divorce. It is also known that cults have their best recruiting success by appealing to middle-class youths who have just left home for the first time and are relatively alone (Galanter, 1989). These groups offer immediate "love" and acceptance and easy answers to questions, which many young people find comforting.

A final point about persuasion techniques involves audience participation. The more an audience becomes involved in the idea or product, the more likely they are to be convinced. If you can persuade others to sign a petition, write letters to their political representative, or do door-to-door solicitations, they are likely to become even more committed to your cause or product. (Do you recognize how this increased commitment probably results from cognitive dissonance? In their need to justify their actions and work, people convince themselves that they really approve of the cause or like the product.)

Prejudice: An attitude that hurts

PREJUDICE: *A negative attitude directed toward some people because of their membership in a specific group.*

Now that we have examined some of the most important factors in attitude formation and attitude change, we can use this information to increase our understanding of an important type of attitude that hurts everyone — **prejudice.** Prejudice is a negative atti-

Jesse Jackson often warns young black children about the limits of athletic careers and stresses the importance of higher education.

tude directed toward some people because of their membership in a specific group. The term "prejudice" is most commonly used in reference to negative **stereotypes** about members of an outgroup. But prejudice, like all attitudes, is actually composed of three separate elements: (1) the *cognitive element* (or stereotype), which is composed of negative thoughts and beliefs about the outgroup; (2) the *affective element,* which includes the feelings and emotions associated with the object of prejudice; and (3) the *behavioral element,* which consists of predispositions to act in certain ways toward members of the outgroup. Whether someone follows through on their prejudice to the point of **discrimination** is a matter of behavioral constraints. For instance, a strongly bigoted person might suppress his or her prejudicial attitude and employ a minority out of fear of legal repercussions.

For those readers who believe that great changes in prejudice have been made since the 1960s, consider the following examples. On Martin Luther King Day in 1988, CBS Sports commentator and oddsmaker Jimmy ("the Greek") Snyder suggested that "the black is a better athlete . . . because of his high thighs and big thighs that goes up into his back." He went on to explain that these differences were due to selective breeding in which "the slave owner would breed his big black to his big woman so that he could have a big black kid" ("Talking Himself Out," 1988, p. 27). In the same year, a group of "Skinheads" (members of the neo-Nazi movement) threatened to hang a black woman who was attempting to enter a public park (Leo, 1988).

At this point in our history, it is probably unnecessary to point out the long list of problems associated with being a victim of prejudice — the loss of self-esteem, unequal job opportunities, the "cycle of poverty," and so on. It may be more helpful, to look instead at the motivation behind the perpetrator of prejudice. One of the earliest attempts to study the specific personality traits associated with prejudice was done by Theodore Adorno and his associates (1950). From their initial interest in exploring the social climate and anti-Semitism (prejudice against Jews) during World War II, these researchers constructed a paper and pencil test for prejudice. The F Scale ("F" for fascism) portion of this test seemed to identify individuals with traits (rigidity, conventionality, and sadism) that predisposed them toward prejudice. People who scored high on the F Scale and possessed the corresponding traits came to be known as the **authoritarian personality type.** Examples of the questions to which an authoritarian personality readily agrees can be found in Table 17.1.

Question: What makes someone develop an authoritarian personality? Since Adorno and his colleagues were strongly influenced by Freudian personality theory, they explained authoritarianism and prejudice as an expression of unconscious needs, conflicts, and defense mechanisms. They believed that early rearing by domineering fathers and punitive mothers, who both use harsh discipline to enforce strict standards of obedience, led to insecure, dependent, hostile children. When these children grew up and

STEREOTYPE: *A set of beliefs about the characteristics of people in a group that is generalized to all group members.*

DISCRIMINATION: *Negative behaviors directed at members of an outgroup.*

AUTHORITARIAN PERSONALITY: *Personality type that includes traits of rigidity, conventionality, and sadism; these traits are said to predispose the individual toward prejudice.*

561

TABLE 17.1
The F Scale (Beliefs of an Authoritarian Personality)

America is getting so far from the true American way of life that force may be necessary to restore it.

Familiarity breeds contempt.

One of the main values of progressive education is that it gives the child great freedom in expressing those natural impulses and desires so often frowned upon by conventional middle-class society.

He is, indeed, contemptible who does not feel any undying love, gratitude, and respect for his parents.

Reports of atrocities in Europe have been greatly exaggerated for propaganda purposes.

Homosexuality is a particularly rotten form of delinquency and ought to be severely punished.

It is essential for learning or effective work that our teachers or bosses outline in detail what is to be done and exactly how to go about it.

There are some activities so flagrantly un-American that, when responsible officials won't take the proper steps, the wide-awake citizen should take the law into his own hands.

Every person should have a deep faith in some supernatural force higher than himself to which he gives allegiance and whose decisions he does not question.

Obedience and respect for authority are the most important virtues children should learn.

Nowadays when so many different kinds of people move around so much and mix together so freely, a person has to be especially careful to protect himself against infection and disease.

No sane, normal, decent person could ever think of hurting a close friend or relative.

Source: Adapted from Adorno et al. (1950). Reprinted by permission.

were in "the driver's seat," anyone who was deviant, disobedient, or a member of a minority ethnic group became a target for their unconscious anger and hatred of their parents.

As you might imagine, this theory has generated considerable controversy. Critics have argued that the items on the F Scale are slanted toward "right-wing" political conservatives even though authoritarian type personalities can be found at both ends of the political spectrum (Rokeach et al., 1960). Other critics suggest that unconscious defense mechanisms are not the primary cause of prejudice, and that children learn their prejudices directly from their parents (Brown, 1986). Still, the theory of authoritarianism has received some support (Altemeyer, 1989; Bray and Noble, 1978; McCann and Stewin, 1987). Studies on college campuses have shown a dramatic increase in authoritarianism in recent years. In the 1970s, 54 percent of college students showed authoritarian tendencies, but by 1987 over 80 percent scored in that range (Altemeyer, 1989).

Question: Since no one would want to be the victim of prejudice or to have an authoritarian personality, why does prejudice persist?   Although most parents, educators, and powers within the mass media do want to eliminate their own prejudices and to avoid inducing them in children, there still exist numerous opportunities for learning and maintaining prejudicial attitudes. Because members of racial and ethnic minorities are still absent from some occupations, members of the majority groups are seldom exposed to people who contradict the stereotypes that help perpetuate prejudices. In addition, minorities are still being portrayed in demeaning and stereotypical roles in many books, magazines, films, and television programs (Huston, Watkins, and Kunkel, 1989).

Prejudice also persists because of obvious benefits to the perpetrator. In addition to the bolstering of self-esteem that comes from feeling superior to others, there is a sense of belonging and protection that comes from being a member of an ingroup versus an outgroup. Historically, being a member of the outgroup has resulted in severe social isolation. As noted psychiatrist Thomas Szasz (1970) has observed:

Despite repeated attempts to reduce prejudice, groups such as the White Supremacists and the Ku Klux Klan still exist.

For the animal predator in the jungle, the rule of life is: Kill or be killed. For the human predator in society, the rule is stigmatize or be stigmatized. Because man's survival depends on his status in society, he must maintain himself as an acceptable member of the group. If he fails to do so, if he allows himself to be put into the role of scapegoat, he will be cast out of the social order. (p. 268)

Thus stigmatization (or prejudice) serves to reinforce the status of the majority and perpetuates injustices toward minorities. From a cognitive perspective, it is also easier to group people into specific categories (stereotyping) than to make the effort of looking for individual differences. And as we noted earlier, once schemata are formed they are highly resistant to change — we ignore contradictory information and look for confirming evidence. You might have noticed this pattern of thinking when attempting to combat prejudice by pointing out specific examples of people who don't match a stereotype. The prejudiced individual either ignores the information or creates a subcategory of "exceptions to the rule."

Question: Given all the opportunities for learning prejudice and the benefits to the perpetrator, how can prejudice ever be changed?   Research has shown that one of the best ways to combat prejudice is to *encourage cooperation versus competition* (Kohn, 1986; Rabow, 1988). Muzafer Sherif and his colleagues (1953, 1966) conducted an ingenious experiment that is often cited as an example of the role of competition in promoting prejudice. Using a group of 11- and 12-year-old boys at a typical summer camp, the researchers created strong feelings of ingroup and outgroup identification by physically separating the boys into separate housing and by assigning various projects within each group, such as building a diving board or cooking out in the woods. Once each group had developed strong feelings of group identity and allegiance, the experimenters set up a series of competitive games, including tug-of-war and touch football, and awarded desirable prizes to the winning teams. The groups began to pick fights, call each other names, and raid each other's camps — behaviors the researchers pointed to as evidence of experimentally created prejudice.

Question: Isn't this type of research unethical? Shouldn't we be trying to reduce prejudice instead of creating it?   Although this part of the experiment does seem questionable according to the research guidelines listed in Chapter 1, the second part of the experiment may offset these concerns. After using competition to create the prejudice between the two groups, the researchers then demonstrated how cooperation can be successfully used to eliminate it. The experimenters created "mini-crises" and tasks that required expertise, labor, and cooperation from both groups, and prizes were awarded to

B. TAM NOMOTO
JUDGE

One way to reduce prejudice is to portray minorities in roles that contradict popular stereotypes.

SUPERORDINATE GOAL: *Way of reducing prejudice that involves creating a goal that is "higher" than individual goals and that is of benefit to both parties.*

all. As a result, the hostilities and prejudice between groups slowly began to dissipate, and by the end of the camp the boys voted to return home in the same bus and the self-chosen seating did not reflect the earlier camp divisions. In line with our previous discussion of the fundamental attribution error, it is interesting to note that the boys attributed the change in their attitudes to changes in the outgroup's personality, not the situation (Brown, 1986).

In addition to the encouragement of cooperation versus competition, researchers have often used Sherif's study as an example of the importance of **superordinate goals** (the "mini-crises") in reducing prejudice (Johnson et al., 1984; Shofield, 1982). We may hope that international prejudice will be reduced by this principle as humankind unites to overcome our shared environmental crises. "The planet's problems could become so paramount they would force a new spirit of international partnership, one that could serve as a model for cooperation on political, economic, and military matters" (Thompson, 1988, p. 22).

A third approach to reducing prejudice is *increasing contact between groups.* According to both cognitive dissonance theory and self-perception theory, to require people to live next to one another, to share the same buses and public facilities, and to integrate their classrooms should lead to a reduction in prejudice. "I live next to blacks and I said I didn't like them (dissonance), so I guess I didn't really mean it" (it's easier to change opinions than move); "I live next to blacks, so I must like them" (self-perception theory).

Research on increased contact and prejudice reduction, however, has had mixed results (Brewer and Kramer, 1985). For contact to be successful in reducing prejudice it must involve (1) close interaction (if minority students are "tracked" into vocational educational courses and whites in the same school are primarily in college prep courses, they seldom interact with one another, and prejudice is increased); (2) interdependence (both groups must be involved in superordinate goals that require cooperation); and (3) equal status (a black janitor working for a Jewish shopkeeper obviously perpetuates stereotypes) (Worchel, Cooper, and Goethals, 1988).

As a final, biased note from your authors (who are all educators), we believe that education is also an important tool for change. If people can be educated about the costs of prejudice (for both victim and perpetrator), they may be motivated to look for solutions. And once they understand the origins and potential solutions to prejudice, they may have better tools for effecting the necessary changes.

DEVELOPING SELF-UNDERSTANDING
Social Perception and Attitude Formation

Critical thinking requires self-understanding. As we have noted in this chapter, people make numerous errors in their perception of others (e.g., selective perception and the fundamental attribution error) and in their self-perception (e.g., the self-serving bias). Fair-minded critical thinkers recognize such errors in their own way of thinking and that of others. In addition to sensitivity to errors in perception, critical thinkers are aware that their most important attitudes often developed from specific learning experiences and input from important people. They learn to carefully analyze these experiences and to critically evaluate the views of their peer group, family, and society. Critical thinkers know what their attitudes are and can talk insightfully about how and why they acquired them. Understanding one's self is the first step toward self-control and self-improvement.

To aid you in exploring your own attitudes, we offer the following exercise.

In the space next to each issue, place a number (1 to 5) that indicates your CURRENT attitude and your PAST attitude (five to ten years ago).

(1)	—	(2)	—	(3)	—	(4)	—	(5)
Strongly Support		Mildly Support		Neutral		Mildly Oppose		Strongly Oppose

	CURRENT ATTITUDE	PAST ATTITUDE
Nuclear energy	___	___
Gun control	___	___
Drinking and driving	___	___

	CURRENT ATTITUDE	PAST ATTITUDE
Smoking in public places	___	___
Divorce	___	___
Abortion	___	___
Capital punishment	___	___
Living together	___	___
Cheating on exams	___	___
Surrogate motherhood	___	___

1 Circle the top three issues you currently feel most strongly about. Briefly state your attitudes toward each of these issues. How did these attitudes develop (classical conditioning, operant conditioning, social learning, self-perception theory, cognitive dissonance, etc.)? What important experiences or significant individuals influenced these attitudes? Can you identify the three components of each of your three attitudes (cognitive, affective, and behavioral)?

2 Now compare your CURRENT attitudes to those of your PAST. Which attitudes were the most subject to change? Why? On what issues were you most resistant to change? How would you explain this?

3 How might you use the persuasion principles discussed in this chapter to change another's attitude? (Consider the characteristics of the communicator, the message, and the audience.) Can you apply the same principles to changing your own attitudes?

4 Cognitive dissonance theory asserts that "changing behavior changes attitudes." Using this theory, how would you design a program to change an undesirable attitude (in yourself and others)?

Review Questions

1 When attempting to persuade someone to change personally valued and strongly held attitudes, the _____ of the source is the most important factor.

2 Once people believe that they are no longer free to choose or to disagree with the persuader, they often increase their resistance to persuasion—a phenomenon termed _____ _____ .

3 _____ is a generally negative attitude directed toward some people because of their membership in a specific group.

4 The cognitive component of prejudice is known as _____ .

5 Those individuals who score high on the F Scale and show traits such as rigidity and conventionality are known as _____ personality types.

6 In Sherif's study with young male summer camp residents, the experimentally produced prejudice was removed by the creation of _____ goals.

Answers: 1 credibility;   2 psychological reactance;   3 prejudice;   4 stereotyping;   5 authoritarian;   6 superordinate

AGGRESSION

AGGRESSION: *Any behavior that is intended to harm someone.*

Aggression is any form of behavior directed toward harming or injuring another living being who is motivated to avoid such treatment (Baron and Byrne, 1984). The British soccer fans' verbal insults and rock and bottle throwing against the Italian fans in 1985 are clear examples of aggressive behaviors, whereas the injuries and deaths following the stampede in 1989 were unintentional. According to this definition and official crime statistics, there is ample evidence that agressive acts (rapes, homicides, spousal and child abuse) have all increased in recent years. Why do people, whether soccer fans or criminals, parents or dictators, act aggressively? In this section we will see that there are a number of internal and external explanations for aggression, as well as theories of how it can be controlled or eliminated.

Internal factors in aggression: Instinct and physiology

Because aggression has a long history and is found among all cultures, many theorists suggest humans are by nature aggressive. After personally witnessing the massive death and destruction that occurred during World War I, Sigmund Freud suggested that aggressive impulses are inborn. He argued that the drive for violence arises from the basic instinct to agress. Therefore, human aggression cannot be eliminated (Gay, 1988).

Another theory of instincts has been proposed by *ethologists,* those who study animal behavior. They believe that agression evolved over the generations because it

Drawing by John Chase

 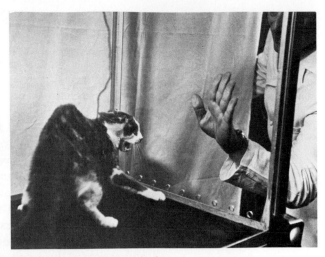

Depending on the specific area of the brain that is electrically stimulated, cats will show either unusual inhibition of aggression or extreme rage.

contributes to "survival of the fittest." Whereas Freud saw aggression as destructive and disruptive, the ethologists suggest that aggression helps to spread out animal populations, prevents overcrowding, and allows the strongest animals to win the mates and reproduce the species (Lorenz, 1981; Eibl-Eibesfeldt, 1980a).

Other psychologists who suspect a biological basis for aggression have studied the brain and nervous system in an effort to discover physiological causes of aggressive behavior. They have found that electrical stimulation or severing of various parts of an animal's brain can have a direct effect on aggression (Delgado, 1960; Kalat, 1988). Further research with brain injuries and organic disorders has identified specific aggression "centers" in the brain—in particular the hypothalamus and the limbic system (Blanchard and Blanchard, 1988). But this approach does not identify the conditions that cause the activation of these centers in the natural state.

A second line of physiological research has focused on the role of neurotransmitters and hormones in aggression. For example, many studies have linked the male gonadal hormone *testosterone* to aggressive behavior (Moyer, 1983; Freeman-Longo and Wall, 1986). As a result, there has been some experimentation with "chemical castration" for certain crimes. In the treatment of some rapists, a drug that lowers the testosterone level (depo-provera) has been used to help curb the feelings of compulsion that are sometimes reported to accompany this form of aggression.

Another important physiological factor in aggression is the use of alcohol. A considerable body of empirical evidence has demonstrated the relationship between alcohol consumption and physical aggression (Newcomb and Bentler, 1989; Siegel, 1989). A case in point: Over one-fourth of the criminals in a large survey of state prisoners admitted to heavy consumption of alcohol prior to committing their crimes (Rosewicz, 1983). The fact that alcohol is so widely available and so widely used in our culture makes it particularly important to study.

External factors in aggression: Frustration and learning

Have you ever sat down to take an important examination and found that almost everything you studied was *not* on the test? Or have you ever been in a hurry to mail a package at a crowded post office and found yourself in the *one* line where the clerk closed the window just as it was your turn? Did you feel angry about the test or tempted to shout at someone to reopen the window? The relationship between frustration and aggression was noted more than half a century ago by John Dollard and his colleagues (1939). From their research they concluded that "aggression is always a consequence of frustration" and "frustration always leads to some form of aggression."

FRUSTRATION – AGGRESSION HYPOTHESIS: *Idea that aggression is always a consequence of frustration and that frustration always leads to some form of aggression.*

Question: Does frustration *always* lead to aggression? How does this account for the differences in the amount of aggression I feel in different situations?   According to this **frustration – aggression hypothesis,** people do vary in the intensity of their response and also in the way they express it; what everyone has in common is the *motive* to aggress. You may get mad at your boss, for example, and then go home and take it out on your family — a type of *displaced aggression.* At other times you can become inwardly aggressive and self-destructive, and you may respond by quietly withdrawing, giving up, or becoming depressed. In each case, there is a buildup of tension and a desire to release that tension through aggression.

Experimental tests of the frustration – aggression hypothesis have produced conflicting results. Although frustration is undoubtedly related to aggression, it is obvious now that the case was overstated. Frustration does not *always* lead to aggression, and not all aggression is the result of frustration. For example, when someone accidentally frustrates us, or when there is a good explanation for the "blocked goal," we often do not become aggressive. Other psychologists have noted that aggression is also a common reaction to pain, heat, and general emotional arousal (as in the case of the soccer riots in England) (Berkowitz, 1983).

Besides the role of frustration, *social learning theorists* believe that we *learn* to be aggressive by observing models who are rewarded for aggression. If we see people we admire act aggressively and violently, or if we see people being rewarded for aggressive behavior, we may be more inclined to imitate them.

One of the most controversial sources of the modeling of aggression is the mass media. Despite protestations that violence in movies and on television is only "entertainment," there is considerable evidence that the media do affect aggression (Huston, Watkins, and Kunkel, 1989). Research on the media's influence has focused primarily on television programming. Results indicate that the more violent the content of a child's TV viewing, the more aggressive the child (Eron and Huesmann, 1984). A report by the National Institute of Mental Health (1982) decisively stated that children *do* imitate what they see on television and also seem to internalize the general value that violence is acceptable behavior.

Televised violence also seems to desensitize both children and adults to real life examples of aggression (Berkowitz, 1984; Geen, 1981) and to negatively affect people's perception of the world. A study by Singer and his colleagues (1984) found that both adolescents and adults who are heavy viewers of fictional crime on television are also more likely to exaggerate the frequency of violence in the world and the chances for their personal victimization. A national survey of American children between the ages of seven and eleven found that heavy TV viewers were more likely to express fears that "somebody bad might get into your house" or that "when you go outside, somebody might hurt you" (Peterson and Zill, 1981).

Can you see how the frustration-aggression hypothesis could explain sudden bursts of anger that lead to freeway shootings?

Question: How can we counteract this? With children, it is generally suggested that parents limit the amount of their TV time, monitor and control choices in programs, and encourage the children to question what they are seeing and the appropriateness of violence (Brown, 1986; Aronson, 1984). Similar principles can be applied as adults to our own viewing of violent programs.

Controlling or eliminating aggression: Can we do it?

One suggestion for general control of aggression has developed out of the Freudian belief that the biological drive toward aggression builds up a lot of pressure that must be periodically released to prevent an "explosion." Freud suggested that such aggressive impulses could be released by engaging in harmless forms of aggression, such as punching a pillow instead of your spouse, or watching others engage in violent sports matches. The Freudian approach suggests that these and other socially acceptable behaviors can provide direct or symbolic substitutes for overt aggression, thus producing **catharsis**. However, the fact that many highly contested sports events actually tend to *increase* the incidence of violence would seem to disprove this idea. Experimental studies also suggest that the "draining of the aggression reservoir" doesn't really help. Punching pillows, watching the violence of others, and even verbally expressing anger apparently do little to reduce the chances for violence (Geen, 1978; Tavris, 1989). As was discussed in Chapter 12, the expression of an emotion, anger or otherwise, tends to intensify the feeling rather than reduce it.

A second approach, which *does* seem to effectively reduce or control aggression, is to introduce incompatible responses. Because certain emotional responses, such as empathy and humor, are incompatible with aggression, Baron (1983) suggests that they can be purposely induced in the presence of anger and frustration to serve as a preventive measure. In your own experiences, you may have noticed that it is hard to keep fighting when something happens to cause you to laugh or to empathize with the other person's position.

A third approach to controlling aggression is to improve social and communication skills. Studies have found that those people who are most deficient in communication skills account for a disproportionate share of the violence in society (Toch, 1980). Unfortunately, little effort is made in our schools or families to teach basic communication skills or techniques of conflict resolution.

One final suggestion for curbing aggression is to attack it at the societal level. To reduce the incidence of child abuse, for example, efforts are needed to help reduce stress in families (Emery, 1989; McLoyd, 1989). One study of 2,143 abusive families found that the highest incidence of abuse occurred during times of economic and personal distress, as Figure 17.4 shows (Straus, Gelles, and Steinmetz, 1980). Methods must also be found to

CATHARSIS: *Freudian belief that pent-up aggressive impulses can be released through violent acts; some theorists believe it can occur vicariously, as when people watch violent sports matches.*

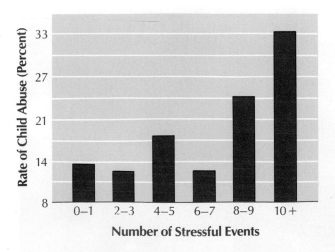

Figure 17.4 Family stress and child abuse. As the number of stressful events rises, child abuse also increases.

reduce the amount of violence in the mass media and to discourage alcohol use in potentially violent situations. In view of the fact that many of the British fans involved in the 1985 soccer riot were intoxicated at the time of the rampage, Prime Minister Margaret Thatcher suggested a voluntary ban on the sale of alcohol in stadiums. A similar ban in Scotland has greatly reduced the number of violent incidents over the past five years. Within the United States, some stadiums have attempted to reduce aggression and post-game traffic accidents by banning alcohol altogether or by stopping the sale of alcohol during the last period of play.

Review Questions

1 Any form of behavior that is directed toward harming or injuring another living being who is motivated to avoid such treatment is known as _____.

2 The drug depo-provera works to reduce _____ levels and is sometimes used to help reduce sexually compulsive behavior.

3 According to the _____ hypothesis, aggression is always a consequence of frustration and frustration always leads to some form of aggression.

4 _____ _____ theorists believe that you learn to be aggressive by observing models who are rewarded for aggression.

5 One of the clearest correlations between childhood behavior and adult aggression seems to be in the amount of _____ _____ that is watched.

6 Humor tends to _____ aggression, but harmless punching of a pillow or watching a violent sports match tends to _____ aggression.

Answers: 1 aggression; *2* testosterone; *3* frustration – aggression; *4* social learning; *5* televised violence; *6* decrease, increase

ALTRUISM

After reading about aggression, you will no doubt be relieved to discover that human beings demonstrate positive social behavior as well. People help and support one another by donating blood, giving time and money to charities, helping stranded motorists, comforting the needy, and so on. Psychologists are also interested in studying those times when people don't help. Consider the following: In 1964, on Austin Street in Queens, New

The altruistic goal of reducing or eliminating AIDS has led to several well-attended rock concerts.

On this street in Queens, New York, Kitty Genovese was stabbed to death while 38 of her neighbors failed to heed her cries for help.

York, a woman named Kitty Genovese was stabbed to death as she returned to her apartment. Thirty-eight of her neighbors heard her screams and pleas for help: "Oh my God, he stabbed me! Please help me! Please help me!" and watched as she struggled to fight off her assailant. The lights in the windows of the observers' apartments apparently scared off the attacker, who left Kitty lying in the street, wounded but still alive. But when the neighbors turned off their lights and went back to bed, the attacker returned and stabbed her again. He was once more scared off by the returning lights and attention, but the neighbors went back to bed for a second time. He then returned for his third and fatal attack.

Question: Why did the neighbors keep going back to bed, and why didn't the police come? Throughout the entire series of attacks (which lasted for over 35 minutes), not one of the 38 neighbors called either the police or an ambulance, which explains the lack of police aid. But why didn't the neighbors help? What caused their apparent indifference? More generally, under what conditions do people sometimes help and sometimes ignore others' pleas for help? These are the questions about altruism that psychologists have tried to answer.

Factors in altruism: Why we do (or don't) help

Altruism refers to actions designed to help others with no obvious benefit for oneself. One of the most controversial hypotheses concerning altruism comes from the *sociobiologists.* From their perspective altruism is an instinctual behavior that has evolved because it favors survival of one's genes. The existence of altruistic acts among lower species (e.g., worker bees living for their mother, the queen) and the fact that altruism in humans is strongest toward one's own children and other relatives have been cited as support for this position (Daly and Wilson, 1988).

The sociobiological approach is directly contradicted by learning theorists, who say that we learn altruistic behavior from our parents and our general culture. Our parents teach us that we "should" be kind and helpful to others, and our culture transmits the belief that we are responsible for helping those who are needy. We also learn to help others because we discover that the praise and attention for doing so is rewarding.

People do, however, show individual variations in their willingness to help (Clary

ALTRUISM: *Actions designed to help others with no obvious benefit to the individual.*

and Thieman, 1988). One study of in-depth interviews with 32 people who had intervened in dangerous crime situations found that these individuals were exceptionally self-assured and felt sure they could handle the potential problems (Huston et al., 1981; Kohn, 1989). They were also more likely to have specialized training in life saving, first aid, or police work.

Although many theories have been proposed concerning why people help, the question concerning the lack of help for Kitty Genovese remains. Some researchers have cited Kitty's case as evidence of "bystander apathy" and of a type of dehumanization that occurs in large cities. Soviet newspapers and textbooks often refer to this incident as evidence of the moral decay in America's "stone jungles." But is this the best explanation for the failure of neighbors to help in crimes? Although research *does* support the idea that helping is significantly less in areas of larger populations (Amato, 1983; Korte, 1980), the reasons are still being debated, and it may prove more effective to look at other explanations.

Latané and Darley (1970), for example, have suggested that whether someone helps is a result of a series of interconnected events and decisions. The potential helper must first notice what is happening, must then interpret the event as an emergency, must accept personal responsibility for helping, and then must decide how to help and actually initiate the helping behavior (see Figure 17.5).

Question: Where did the system break down for Kitty Genovese?   Since Kitty's neighbors obviously noticed what was happening and interpreted it as an emergency, the first break in the sequence was in their willingness to accept personal responsibility. But contrary to the popular portrayal of New Yorkers as uncaring and apathetic bystanders, Kitty's neighbors were *not* indifferent to her attack. Later newspaper interviews with each of the neighbors showed a great deal of anguish among the observers, but each of them "naturally" assumed that someone else had already called the police. This is an example of what has come to be known as the **diffusion of responsibility** phenomenon — the tendency when part of a group to assume that someone else will respond and take action. It is ironic that if only one of Kitty's neighbors had watched her attack, versus 38, she might still be alive today.

One of the most consistent findings in psychological experimentation is that people who are alone are much more likely to respond to an emergency (Batson et al., 1988;

DIFFUSION OF RESPONSIBILITY: *When people are in groups of two or more, there is a tendency toward less individual responsiveness due to the assumption that someone else will take action (or responsibility).*

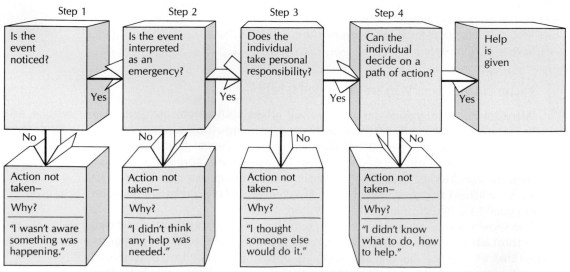

Figure 17.5 Steps that determine whether helping occurs. At each step of the way, potential helpers will not come to a person's aid if they answer no to the question in the top box. Only after they notice the situation, define it as an emergency, take personal responsibility, and decide on a course of action will they help.

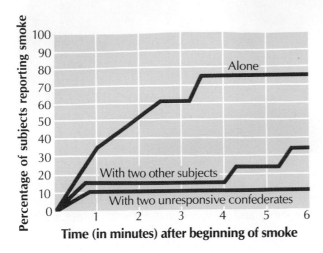

Figure 17.6 Results of Latane and Darley's smoke study. Subjects were more likely to report the smoke when they were alone than when they were with others.

Latané and Nida, 1981). This point was demonstrated in a classic social psychology study in which subjects were left in a room to complete a questionnaire. As they worked, smoke began pouring in through a small vent (Latané and Darley, 1968). When subjects were alone, they quickly jumped up and ran to report the fire to the experimenter. But when they were with two other subjects, or with two confederates who were previously told to ignore the smoke, there was virtually no reporting of the smoke (see Figure 17.6).

Question: How did the presence of others stop the subject from reporting the fire? When the subject was with two other *real* subjects, they looked at one another for cues, but since they all feared looking foolish and were waiting to see the others' reactions, they ultimately did nothing. In the condition where the subject was with two confederates who deliberately ignored the smoke, the scene became even more confusing and ambiguous and led to virtually no response.

Increasing altruism: How can we promote helping?

The most obvious way to improve the chances for altruistic behavior is to counteract ambiguous, inhibitory factors and to reward those factors that promote the chances for altruism. For example, the ambiguity of situations could be reduced by speaking up and clarifying what is going on. If you notice a situation where it seems unclear whether someone needs help, you can simply ask. On the other hand, if you are the one in need of help, you should remember the case of Kitty Genovese. Look directly at anyone who may be watching and offer specific directions, such as "Call the police."

Societal rewards for a broader range of helping behaviors could also be improved. Some researchers have suggested that states need to enact more laws that protect the helper from potential suits or recrimination and punish those who fail to respond. Certain existing police programs, such as Crime Stoppers, actively recruit public compliance in reporting crime, give monetary rewards, and assure anonymity. Such programs have apparently been highly effective in reducing crime (Rosenbaum and Lurigio, 1985).

Because people are more likely to help when they feel competent and self-assured, others have suggested that as many people as possible be trained in appropriate helping skills so they will feel less embarrassed in offering help. Such skills should also better prepare them to notice emergencies and to feel better equipped to assume responsibility. Classes in first aid and cardiopulmonary resuscitation (CPR) are two examples of such training.

Up to this point, we have attempted to explain social behavior by exploring the internal thoughts and beliefs of the individual (social perception and attitudes) and

Neighborhood Watch programs have increased altruistic behaviors and reduced robberies and other aggressive acts.

focusing on the individual and social factors in aggression and altruism. In Chapter 18 we expand this focus by looking at how the individual is affected by larger social forces — groups, social pressures to conform, comply, and obey, and environmental issues, such as pollution and crowding.

Review Questions

1 _____ refers to actions designed to help others with no obvious benefit for the respondent.

2 According to _____, altruism is an instinctual behavior that has evolved because it favors survival.

3 The major reason why Kitty Genovese's neighbors failed to respond to her cries for help was because of the _____ _____ _____ phenomenon.

4 When people are alone as compared to being in groups, they are _____ likely to help others.

5 _____ and _____ _____ _____ are two important obstacles to altruism.

Answers: 1 altruism; *2* sociobiologists; *3* diffusion of responsibility; *4* more; *5* ambiguity, diffusion of responsibility

REVIEW OF MAJOR CONCEPTS

SOCIAL PERCEPTION

1 In attempting to find answers or reasons for others' behavior (making attributions), we often seek to determine whether their actions are internally caused (from their own traits and motives) or externally caused (from the environment or situation). We also want to know if others' behavior is controllable or uncontrollable and stable or unstable.

2 Attribution is subject to several forms of error and bias. The most basic of these is the fundamental attribution error, our tendency to overestimate internal, personality influences and to underestimate external, situational influences when judging the behavior of others. When we attempt to find reasons for our own behavior, we tend to take credit for positive outcomes and attribute negative outcomes to external causes (the self-serving bias).

3 Social cognition relies on internal, cognitive schemata that organize social information. The two major social schemata are the implicit personality theory (assumptions that certain personality traits go together) and frames (schema for behavior in social interactions). Since our social schemata are often limited in detail and differ from individual to individual, we often have problems in accurate social cognition.

ATTITUDES

4 Attitudes are learned predispositions to respond consistently to some person, object, or situation. They involve not only cognitions (thoughts and beliefs), but also affective responses (feelings) and behavioral tendencies (predispositions to action).

5 Attitudes are formed through principles of learning (observation of others, operant conditioning, classical conditioning), through self-perception (we infer our attitudes by watching our own behavior), and through the need for cognitive consistency. Cognitive dissonance is the state of tension or anxiety that is felt when there is a difference between

two or more attitudes or when our attitudes do not match our behavior.

6 Attitudes can be changed through cognitive dissonance or through persuasion techniques. Persuasive communications rely on different characteristics of the audience, the message, and the source. When people are vulnerable they are more easily persuaded. A fear-inducing message and a fast-talking, credible, attractive source also increase the amount of persuasion.

7 Prejudice is an attitude that hurts everyone. The authoritarian personality type is highly correlated with increased prejudice. In spite of associated costs, prejudice persists because of numerous learning opportunities in the environment and because it increases feelings of superiority to the "outgroup" and feelings of belonging to the "ingroup." Prejudice can be reduced or eliminated by encouraging cooperation versus competition and increasing equal contact between groups.

AGGRESSION

8 Aggression is any deliberate attempt to harm or injure another living being who is motivated to avoid such treatment. In looking for biological origins for aggression, some researchers have focused on inborn, instinctual factors, whereas others have looked at physiological factors such as specific sites in the brain, testosterone levels, and alcohol.

9 External factors in aggression include frustration (blocked goals) and learning. Televised violence is one of the most important ways some children learn aggression. Attempts to control or eliminate aggression have found that catharsis doesn't seem to help, but incompatible responses such as humor and improved communication skills do seem to help.

ALTRUISM

10 Altruism involves helping without any thought of reward. Sociobiologists believe that altruism is innate and has survival value, whereas others say altruism is learned.

11 Altruism is often inhibited by the fact that many emergency situations are ambiguous and the potential respondent is unsure of what to do. Inhibition also comes from the failure to take personal responsibility for helping and assuming someone else will respond (the diffusion of responsibility phenomenon).

12 To increase the chances of altruism we should increase the rewards and decrease the costs. We can also reduce ambiguity by giving clear directions to those who may be watching. It also helps if people have training in specific helping skills.

SUGGESTED READINGS

Aronson, E. (1988). *The social animal* (5th ed.). New York: Freeman. An award-winning book that offers a witty and enjoyable overview of social psychology.

Fiske, S. T., & Taylor, S. E. (1983). *Social cognition.* Reading, MA: Addison–Wesley. A basic introduction to social cognition that is well written and should be enjoyed by those who desire more information on this topic.

Petty, R. E., & Cacioppo, J. T. (1981). *Attitudes and persuasion: Classic and contemporary approaches.* Dubuque, IA: W. C. Brown. An entertaining and informative review of the field of attitude formation and persuasion techniques with a special emphasis on practical applications.

Piliavin, J. A., Dovidio, J. F., Gaertner, S. L., & Clark, R. D. (1981). *Emergency intervention.* New York: Academic Press. A comprehensive discussion and explanation of the willingness or hesitation of people to give aid in emergency situations.

Tavris, C. (1989). *Anger: The misunderstood emotion* (2nd ed.). New York: Touchstone/Simon & Schuster. A well written and engaging overview of the research on anger and a persuasive challenge to those who advocate "letting it all hang out."

chapter eighteen
Living in Society

IT is November 18, 1978, in the northwest jungle of Guyana. A mother takes a last dazed look at the dead and dying friends around her as she puts a poison cup to her small daughter's lips, then to her own. They lie down, arm in arm, and join over 900 others in a screaming, convulsive, and finally peaceful end to their lives and to their religious community, The People's Temple. They have performed their final act of allegiance to their prophet, the Reverend Jim Jones, following him to a "promised land."

Was this an impulsive action by a distraught leader and a surprised group of religious fanatics? Apparently not. According to one report (Wooden, 1981), there were at least 42 suicide rehearsals ("white nights") that dated back to the time when the group had resided in northern California. Jones portrayed the outside world, particularly the CIA and FBI, as continually plotting to destroy their "utopian" society and convinced his followers that their mass death would be an act of "revolutionary suicide" and a historical act of great martyrdom.

The mass murder–suicide pact was precipitated in part by the visit of Congressman Leo Ryan, who was investigating charges that commune members were being mistreated and held against their will. On the afternoon of November 18, Congressman Ryan and four other people were assassinated as they attempted to board the plane that was to return them to California. After the full extent of this assassination and un-

precedented mass murder–suicide was realized, grieving relatives were joined by shocked fellow human beings throughout the world in asking why — how could such a tragedy have occurred? What kind of man was Jim Jones? What could move so many people to "willingly" abandon this life?

Some blame the leader, Jim Jones, for the disaster. They say he was demented, pointing to his childhood history of killing animals and then saying mass at their death (Iyer, 1988). Others trace events back to Jones's mother, who often predicted that her son would be a messiah, which may have led to his later fantasies of omnipotence. Certainly by all accounts Jones was a skilled manipulator of people who used a variety of techniques to recruit followers and keep them in line. He routinely broke down family ties by removing children from their parents, and he demanded that couples break up or practice celibacy — while he enjoyed sex with both women and men (Osherow, 1988; Reston, 1981).

Others lay the blame primarily with the followers for being so trusting and gullible. During Jones's rise to power, he performed questionable "cures" and "miracles" that his audience seemed all too willing to accept. One of his favorite demonstrations was to cure cancer by reaching down an affected member's throat and supposedly pulling out a mass of tissue that was then waved in front of the startled audience. The bloody piece of "cancer" was actually a chicken part that had been *palmed* (a basic trick often used by sideshow magicians and card cheats). Jones also once performed a well-publicized miracle of producing food out of thin air. He announced, "Even though there isn't enough food to feed this multitude, I am blessing the food that we have and multiplying it — just as Jesus did in biblical times" — whereupon his assistant came out of the kitchen bearing two large platters of fried chicken and was met by a loud cheer from the hungry crowd (Mills, 1979).

Why did the audience refuse to listen when critic

Chuck Beikman mentioned that trucks from the local Kentucky Fried Chicken restaurant were parked at the rear of the church (Osherow, 1988)? Was it Jim Jones or was it his followers who were most to blame for what happened in Guyana? Were his followers duped by a skillful, paranoid manipulator? Or did they follow him willingly because he offered a sense of belonging and relief from feelings of alienation and worthlessness? Or can it be, as some have suggested, that our fragmented, industrial society is most to blame (Galanter, 1989; Lifton, 1979).

The mass murder – suicide at Jonestown, Guyana, can be seen as a prime example of social processes carried to an extreme. It dramatically demonstrates the power that some individuals hold over others and the influence they can wield. Unfortunately, Jim Jones is not unique. World history is full of leaders who incite followers to behave in ways harmful to themselves and others. Although claims of divine inspiration and threats of physical force are common means of ensuring cooperation, other methods of social influence, exploited by Jones and other leaders, can be just as powerful. In this chapter we will explore several types of social influence, including conformity, compliance, and obedience. We will also look closely at group behavior. We will end our discussion with a consideration of several applications of social psychology to the problems of living in the world today.

Reprinted with special permission of King Features Syndicate, Inc.

SOCIAL INFLUENCE

The society into which we are born directly influences us from the moment of conception until the moment of death. During this lifetime, our culture transforms us from totally helpless and dependent infants into social beings capable of interacting in a highly complex society. This transformation is due in large part to pressures from the culture to believe certain things, to feel a certain way, and to act in accordance with these beliefs and feelings. Although this may sound rather manipulative, society would cease to exist without such means for assimilating new members. Thus, a society must teach its young certain behaviors and values so that they can live and work successfully within the larger culture. This transmission of the cultural ways is known as **socialization.**

Once people have been "successfully" socialized, different segments of society continue to attempt to change or modify their attitudes and behaviors. This is generally referred to as **social influence.** Influence is a common theme in social psychology. Tactics of persuasion and attitude change, discussed in Chapter 17, are attempts to influence others, as are many acts of aggression. Later in this chapter we will see how groups directly and indirectly exert social influences on their members. Here we will explore three of the most direct forms of social influence: (1) **conformity,** which is a change in behavior as a result of real or imagined group pressure; (2) **compliance,** which is altering behavior as a result of direct requests of others; and (3) **obedience,** or changing behavior as a result of direct commands from others.

Conformity: Going along with the crowd

Imagine for a moment that you have volunteered for a psychology experiment on perception. You find yourself seated around a table with six other students. You are all shown a card containing three lines labeled A, B, and C, as in Figure 18.1, and are asked to select the line that is closest in length to a fourth line, X. Each of you is asked to state your choices out loud, in order, around the table. At first, everyone agrees on the correct line, and the experiment seems pretty boring. On the third trial, however, the first subject gives what is obviously a wrong answer. You know that line B is correct but he says line A. When the second, third, fourth, and fifth subjects also say line A, you really start to wonder: "What's going on here? Are they blind? Or am I?"

What do you think you would do at this point in the experiment? Would you stick with your convictions and say line B, regardless of what the others have answered? Or would you go along with the group? In the original version of this experiment, conducted by Solomon Asch (1951), the six other subjects were actually confederates of the experimenter, and seating was arranged so that the "real" subject was always placed in the next-to-last position. The first five confederates had previously been instructed to respond

SOCIALIZATION: *The process by which people come to learn and internalize the rules and cultural ways of their society.*
SOCIAL INFLUENCE: *A change in behavior, perception, or attitude in the direction intended by another.*
CONFORMITY: *A type of social influence in which individuals change their attitudes or behavior to adhere to the expectations of others or the norms of groups to which they belong or wish to belong.*
COMPLIANCE: *A form of social influence in which individuals change their behavior in response to direct requests from others.*
OBEDIENCE: *A type of social influence in which one individual follows direct commands, usually from someone in a position of authority.*

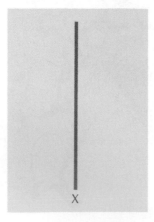
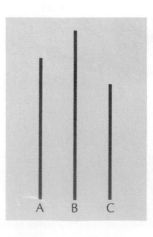

Figure 18.1 Asch's study of conformity. Subjects were shown four lines such as these and then asked which line on the right was most similar to the one on the left.

In Asch's study of conformity, the true subject (#6) was seated with six other confederate subjects who had been secretly trained ahead of time to give incorrect responses to an obvious line discrimination task.

incorrectly on the third trial and selected later trials as a way of testing the actual subject's degree of *conformity,* or going along with the crowd.

How did Asch's subjects respond? In the experimental condition where confederates gave unanimous, incorrect opinions on a prearranged set of trials, 75 percent of the subjects conformed by making one or more errors in their expressed judgments. This level of conformity is particularly shocking when it is compared to the responses of subjects in the control condition. They experienced no group pressure and chose correctly virtually 100 percent of the time.

Question: Why would so many people go along with the group on such an obviously incorrect response?   To the onlooker, conformity is often difficult to understand, and even the conformer sometimes has a hard time explaining his or her behavior. We can better understand Jones's followers, Asch's subjects, and our own forms of conformity if we look at three factors: (1) *normative* social influence, (2) *informational* social influence, and (3) the role of *reference groups.*

Normative social influence refers to the fact that people will conform to the norms of their society out of their need for approval and to be accepted by the group. A **norm** is an expected behavior that is adhered to by members of the group. Norms are society's definition of how we "should" behave. They are sometimes explicit; groups may write rules for membership and society may pass laws that determine citizenship. Most often, however, norms are more subtle and implicit; they can only be inferred by closely observing the behavior of others. Have you ever caught yourself watching the table manners of others at an important dinner party or asking what others are wearing to a social function? Such behavior reflects your desire to conform and the power of normative social influence.

The strong need for approval and group acceptance can also be seen in Asch's subjects, many of whom reported conforming out of fear of being ridiculed or excluded from the group (Asch, 1956). This type of conformity was also found in Jones's followers. Deborah Blakely, a long-time member and later defector from The People's Temple, testified: "Any disagreement with Jim Jones's dictates came to be regarded as 'trea-

NORMATIVE SOCIAL INFLUENCE: *Group pressure based on threats to reject group members who do not accept the positions of the group.*
NORM: *Unwritten rule of behavior that prescribes what is acceptable or approved in a given situation.*

Although we often recognize conformity in others, it is less noticeable in our own behavior.

581

son'... Although I felt terrible about what was happening, I was afraid to say anything because I knew that anyone with a differing opinion gained the wrath of Jones and other members" (cited in Osherow, 1984, p. 75).

INFORMATIONAL SOCIAL INFLUENCE: *Social influence produced by providing others with information.*

Informational social influence, conforming to group pressure out of the need for direction and information, is also an important factor in conformity. This is particularly the case when the situation is ambiguous and when others seem to know what they're doing. Do you remember how as a child you could trick others by getting a couple of friends together and then all start pointing and exclaiming at something in the sky? Your poor, unsuspecting victim, out of a reasonable desire to know what was going on, would then come along and look up, too, or at least ask other children, "What's happening?" In the case of Asch's subjects, their conformity seems more reasonable in the light of informational social influence since they obviously thought they were surrounded by capable people who all agreed. Similarly, Jim Jones was in sole control of information from the outside world and when he told his followers that the CIA and FBI would surely destroy them for the attack on Congressman Ryan, they had little reason to doubt him.

REFERENCE GROUPS: *Groups that we like and feel similar to and are therefore more likely to conform to.*

The third major factor in conformity is the power of **reference groups**—those people we most admire, like, and want to resemble. We are obviously more likely to conform and be influenced by some people than by others, and it is our reference groups that we most want to match. These groups also change over our life span: In early childhood our main reference group is our family; in adolescence it tends to be our peers; and in adulthood it is our marital partners or our occupational peers. By breaking down family ties and isolating the members of his congregation in a remote jungle area, Jim Jones made himself the primary referent for his followers.

In sum, conformity is a common response to normative social influence, informational social influence, and the desire for approval from our reference group. At risk of leaving you with the impression that all conformity is dangerous and destructive, it is important to point out that most people conform most of the time because it is clearly adaptive to do so. In fact, when people do *not* adhere to social norms or expectations society becomes concerned and may label them *abnormal.*

Compliance: Going along with a request

In addition to conforming to group expectations or pressures, people often *comply* (or yield) to direct requests from others. We contribute to charities, return phone calls, and sometimes buy things we don't need simply because someone asked us to do so. What makes us so willing to go along with such requests? Research has identified three major techniques that increase the odds for compliance—ingratiation, multiple requests, and guilt.

INGRATIATION: *Use of favors, flattery, and statements of shared similarities as a method of gaining increased attraction and compliance.*

Ingratiation refers to attempts to make others like us before we hit them with a request. We can increase their liking for us, and thereby obtain greater compliance, by convincing them that we are similar to them (Byrne, 1971), by doing favors for them (Isen and Levine, 1972), and by flattering them (Drachman et al., 1978). Jim Jones used ingratiation techniques when he made repeated references to his "humble beginnings"

Guilt induction is a successful form of social influence, but it can also cause resentment and anger on the part of the recipient.

and his shared feelings of powerlessness, when he offered people food and shelter, and when he repeatedly told his followers that they were "the chosen people."

Making **multiple requests** is also highly effective in eliciting compliance because the first appeal is used as a "setup" for the second or later appeals (Beaman et al., 1983; Cialdini et al., 1975). The requester may, for example, begin by asking for a small favor and then gradually increase the level of request. This is called the *foot-in-the-door* technique. The panhandler who first asks for a quarter for a cup of coffee and then works up to asking for $5 for a full meal is using this approach. In contrast, the *door-in-the-face* technique works by starting off with a large request and then backing down. "If you can't give me $5, can you at least give me a quarter?"

MULTIPLE REQUESTS: *Compliance technique in which a first request is used as a "setup" for later requests.*

> *Question:* How can such opposite techniques both work? The foot-in-the-door technique seems to result from subtle cognitive shifts in the individual being asked to comply. By agreeing to the smaller request, the person may come to see himself or herself as a helper. This shift in self-perception may then transfer over to the later, larger request. In contrast, the door-in-the-face, "hit 'em hard," technique seems to work as a result of subtle rules (or norms) for interpersonal interactions. During the socialization process, we all learn that when another person backs down or makes a concession, we are expected to make a similar response — the rule of *reciprocal concessions*. People may worry that they will appear unfriendly or hostile if they fail to comply with the smaller request after refusing the larger one (Herbert, 1988; Pendleton and Batson, 1979).

The process of **guilt induction** is another effective and popular compliance technique. We have been subjected to this tactic by friends and parents ("After all I've done for you, the least you could do is . . ."), by commercials (phone company ads that ask, "Have you phoned your grandmother today?"), and by charity organizations (photos of children with heartrending expressions asking for help). Although these techniques remind us of our social obligations, they also have a built-in cost that should be kept in mind. As you may remember from the liking and loving section in Chapter 11, we tend to like those people who make us feel good about ourselves and to avoid those who make us feel bad. Thus, we may comply with others who make us feel guilty, but afterward we might resent and avoid them.

GUILT INDUCTION: *Method of gaining compliance based on the tendency for people to comply when they feel remorse for wrong behavior.*

Obedience: Going along with a command

Pretend for a moment that it is 1968, the peak of the Vietnam War, and you are a front-line soldier in the U.S. Army. You have seen many friends killed or maimed for life, and each day you wonder whether it will be your last. You are a highly trained fighting machine, conditioned to take the rough life in the jungle and above all to trust and follow the orders of your commanding officer. On one particular day, your company has collected a group of Vietnamese villagers suspected of hiding weapons and harboring the enemy. After the men, women, and children are gathered together in a small group, your lieutenant, William Calley, yells "Shoot!" What would you do? The soldiers who were there in My Lai that day obeyed their leader's orders. One participant's report: "[Lieutenant Calley] told me to start shooting. So I started shooting. I poured about four clips into the group . . . They was begging and saying, 'No, no.' And the mothers was hugging their children, and . . . Well, we kept right on firing. They was waving their arms and begging. . . ."(Wallace, 1969).

Although almost everyone can sympathize with the plight of the soldiers who were ordered to do such a ghastly deed, many believe that they would personally defy the orders if they were in the same situation. But would they? This is the question social psychologist Stanley Milgram attempted to study in a series of experiments at Yale University. As you may remember from Chapter 1, Milgram recruited subjects to participate in a study of obedience by telling them that he was interested in testing the effects of punishment on learning. Under increasing demands and orders by the experimenter, most subjects gave dangerously high levels of shock to another research participant. Although the experi-

Military training is the most overt example of socialized obedience.

FOSTERING INDEPENDENT THINKING
Would You Have Followed Jim Jones?

After reading about the various forms of social influence and the mass suicide at Jonestown, many students find it difficult to understand why people are so easily persuaded. Experts in the field of critical thinking have suggested that some instances of destructive obedience result from a lack of education about the social forces that influence and control behavior and from a lack of practice in confronting authority figures (see Chaffee, 1988).

To encourage your own independent thinking and increase your resistance to unethical manipulation by others, we have developed the following exercise.

Part I

Rank order the following three situations by placing a 1 next to the situation you believe is the most unethical form of social influence and a 3 by the least unethical.

_____ Jane is 19 and wants very much to become a commercial artist. She has been offered a scholarship to a good art school, but her parents have repeatedly argued against this as a career. After considerable pressure, she accepts a scholarship to the same engineering school that her father attended.

_____ Bill is 21 and is having serious doubts about his decision to marry Sue. After discussing his doubts with his friends and parents, he realizes that all the plans have been made for the wedding and worries about how brokenhearted Sue would be. He decides to marry her.

_____ Mary is 20 and a senior in college. She desperately wants to get into a very important graduate school, but she is failing an important class. The instructor has made it clear that she could have an A in his course if she would sexually "cooperate" ("an A for a lay"). She agrees.

Part II

To overcome destructive obedience, John Sabini and Maury Silver (1988) have suggested that individuals should actively practice confronting authority, they should be taught about the social forces that operate on them, and they should eliminate intellectual illusions that foster nonintellectual obedience. These three suggestions can be usefully applied to the three situations you just rank ordered.

1 Mentally review the situation you ranked as most unethical and carefully rehearse how you could effectively combat a similar form of coercion. What would you say? What could you do?

2 This chapter's discussion on social influence should help to educate you about why people conform, comply, and obey, as well as how to "fight back." For example, can you see how normative social influence, reference groups, and guilt induction played a role in the three situations described above? Can you use the text material to help develop an effective rebuttal?

3 One of the most common intellectual illusions that hinders critical thinking is the belief that "only evil people do evil things" or that "evil announces itself." In Milgram's research the experimenter who ordered the subjects to continue looked and acted like a reasonable person who was simply acting out of duty to the experiment. Because he was not seen as personally corrupt and evil, the subject's normal moral "guards" were not alerted. But if we are to think critically about destructive obedience, we must avoid looking at personality and focus instead on the morality of our own and others' *acts*. In each of the three situations, can you identify the "evil" acts without looking at individual personalities?

Now that you have analyzed Jane, Bill, and Mary's situations, think of a current or past situation in your own life where you were unethically persuaded. Applying Sabini and Silver's three suggestions to your own situation can further develop your own autonomous thinking and help you to resist future manipulation.

ment was rigged and no shocks were ever administered, the subjects *believed* that the prearranged screams and groans were real and that they were causing great pain to their victim (Milgram, 1963, 1974).

What can be concluded from this experiment? One obvious conclusion is that people in positions of *authority* have a powerful ability to elicit obedience, and that this power is often underestimated. We can also conclude that the placement of *responsibility* plays an important part in the degree of obedience. Subjects in Milgram's experiment were assured early in the session that the experimenter was responsible for the well-being of the learner, which may have encouraged their high level of obedience. Finally, the *gradual* nature of many obedience situations may explain the extremes to which people may finally go. The mild level of shocks at the beginning of the session may have worked like the foot-in-the-door technique. Once a subject complied with the initial request from the experimenter, he may have felt trapped by his own behavior and the nature of the situation (Sabini and Silver, 1988). The subjects in Milgram's experiment, like the followers of Jim Jones, may have been seduced by the gradual nature of the increasing demands. Just as Milgram's subjects were asked to give higher and higher levels of shock, Jones's followers were first asked for small monetary donations, then for larger amounts of money and valuable possessions, and ultimately for their lives.

Question: Is there any way to reduce this kind of destructive obedience?   One of Milgram's strongest beliefs was that once people understand the conditions that facilitate obedience they can use this understanding to develop ways to counteract its occurrence (Milgram, 1974). Just being aware of the power of authority figures and the gradual nature of most obedience situations may be a first step toward reducing destructive obedience. Research has also found that when subjects are reminded that they will be held responsible for any harm to the victim, obedience is sharply reduced (Hamilton, 1978).

Review Questions

1 The transmission of cultural norms to the young is known as _____.
2 The three major types of social influence are _____ , _____, and _____ .
3 _____ social influence results from individuals' need for belonging and group acceptance, whereas _____ social influence involves conforming out of a need for more direction and a lack of alternatives.
4 When we point out our similarities, flatter, and do favors for others in an attempt to gain their compliance, we are using the _____ technique.
5 Asking first for a quarter and then for $5 is known as the _____ technique, whereas first asking for the $5 and backing down for a quarter is called the _____ technique.
6 Using statements like "After all I've done for you. . ." as a way to gain compliance is known as _____ .
7 The assignment of _____ is one of the best ways to decrease destructive forms of obedience.

Answers: 1 socialization;   *2* conformity, compliance, obedience;   *3* normative, informational;   *4* ingratiation;   *5* foot-in-the-door, door-in-the-face;   *6* guilt induction;   *7* responsibility.

GROUP PROCESSES

Psychologists define a **group** as "two or more persons who are interacting with one another in such a manner that each person influences and is influenced by each other person" (Shaw, 1981, p. 8). In other words, a group consists of any collection of people who have some mutually recognized relationship with one another. A couple on their first date, a family, a class in psychology, and a tennis club would all be considered groups. On the other hand, people riding together in an elevator would not be group.

GROUP: *In social psychology, two or more people who are interacting with one another and providing reciprocal influence on one another's behavior.*

Affiliation is important to most species.

Affiliation: The need to be with others

Why do people group together? There are a number of reasons. We are automatically a member of some groups, for example, our families. Other groups we voluntarily join out of some shared goal or interest. And sometimes we join with others out of the simple desire to be with others — the need for **affiliation**. If you've ever heard some really wonderful news and had to search desperately to find someone to share it with, or if you've been really frightened and wanted someone to comfort you, you understand what Aristotle meant when he called us "social animals."

AFFILIATION: *Need for friendly association with others; formation of friendships; joining of groups and cooperation.*

Question: Don't people differ in their individual need for affiliation?   Yes. Although some people seem to prefer a great deal of time alone and find isolation to be stimulating and exhilarating, others seem to like having others with them at all times and find isolation to be deeply disturbing (Suedfeld, 1982).

TABLE 18.1
Student Preferences for Being Alone or with Others in 13 Different Situations

Situations in Which	Percentage of Students Who		
	Wished To Be with Others	Wished To Be Alone	Had No Preference
Most want to be with others			
When very happy	88	2	10
When in a good mood	89	0	11
On Saturday night	85	1	14
When you are in a strange situation or doing something you've never done before	77	13	10
Most want to be alone			
When physically tired	6	85	9
When embarrassed	16	76	8
When you want to cry	8	88	4
When busy	12	70	18
After an extensive period of social contact (after being with others for a long time)	12	75	13
There is no consensus			
When depressed	42	48	10
When worried about a serious personal problem	52	44	4
When mildly ill (e.g., with a cold)	32	49	19
When feeling very guilty about something you have done	45	43	12

Source: Middlebrook, P. N. (1980). *Social psychology and modern life* (2nd ed., p. 258). Copyright © 1980 Alfred A. Knopf, Inc. Reprinted by permission.

In addition to differences between individuals, each of us also feels more affiliative in some circumstances than in others. As can be seen in Table 18.1, research finds that we most want to be with others during good times or frightening times. In a now classic experiment, Stanley Schachter (1959) first demonstrated the relation between fear and affiliation by leading subjects to believe that they would be undergoing a series of electrical shocks. He then allowed them to choose whether they wanted to wait by themselves or with others while the experiment was being set up. Half of the subjects were told that the shocks would be extremely painful but that there would be "no permanent damage" (high-fear condition). The other half of the subjects were led to expect virtually painless shocks that would feel, at worst, like a tickle (low-fear condition).

As you might imagine, those in the high-fear group were much more likely to choose to wait with others than were those in the low-fear group. Fully two-thirds of the high-level subjects chose to be with others, compared to only one-third of the low-fear subjects. As was the case with the obedience study by Stanley Milgram, no shocks were actually administered. The experiment was terminated after subjects made their choice, and the experimenter fully *debriefed* each subject by explaining the reason for the deception and fully describing the details of the experiment — what was done, why it was done, and what it meant.

Question: What is it about high stress or fear that makes us want to be with others? There are many possible explanations. People may want company because they think that others will provide important information, or perhaps they hope that the presence of others will serve as a distraction. Or, as predicted by **social comparison**

SOCIAL COMPARISON THEORY: *Festinger's view that we seek out others as a way to interpret and compare our own abilities, attitudes, and reactions.*

theory, people in this situation may be unsure of their own feelings and reactions and seek out others as a source of comparison. Leon Festinger (1954) developed this theory to explain our need to look to others as a sort of yardstick to compare our own attitudes and abilities. We want to know whether what we feel is similar to what others feel ("Is this normal?" "Am I better or worse than others in important abilities?"). The need for social comparison is particularly acute when there is no clear physical or objective standard against which to assess ourselves. This was clearly the case for subjects who believed they were waiting for a painful shock procedure. Can you also see how this theory would apply to the followers of Jim Jones, who were both physically and psychologically isolated from their families and friends? Without the opportunity for exposure to conflicting opinions, many followers looked to Jones for their social comparison data.

Group membership: How it affects the individual

Whatever the type or function of a group, membership has a variety of effects. Have you ever been with friends and found yourself doing something that you might not have done alone? Or have you ever noticed that you behave differently with your friends than with your parents or with your employer or roommates? In each situation, any variation in your behavior is largely the result of your group membership. Although we seldom recognize the power of such membership, social psychologists have noticed at least two important ways that groups affect us: (1) through the roles we play, and (2) through their ability to induce a feeling of anonymity and reduced self-monitoring (deindividuation).

ROLE: *A category of people and the set of normative expectations for people in that category.*

Roles in groups Every person in a group is expected to play one or more **roles** — a set of behavioral patterns connected with particular social positions. Some roles are very specifically spelled out and regulated (policeman), whereas others are assumed through informal learning and inference (father).

Meeting someone new may be exciting as well as awkward or uncomfortable. The discomfort is due, in part, to poorly defined social roles for "dating partners".

Roles can sometimes constrict us, tire us, or create conflicts. However, they also perform invaluable social functions. Can you imagine how difficult life would be if teachers suddenly stopped coming to class, if physicians refused to provide medical care, or if police officers no longer patrolled our streets? Have you also wondered how such "role playing" might affect the behavior and personality of the individual? This was the question that fascinated social psychologist Philip Zimbardo. In his famous study at Stanford University, 20 carefully screened, well-adjusted young college men were paid $15 a day for participating in a simulation of prison life (Haney, Banks, and Zimbardo, 1978; Zimbardo et al., 1977).

Before the study began, each subject was randomly assigned to play the role of either "prisoner" or "guard." The students assigned to be prisoners were picked up and "arrested" from their individual homes, taken to a mock police station, stripped, searched, fingerprinted, sprayed with disinfectants for delousing, and then locked in their cells in a basement at Stanford. Subjects were given little direction on how to enact their roles of prisoner or guard and the guards were told merely to "maintain law and order" without the use of physical violence. What do you think happened?

Not even Zimbardo foresaw how the experiment would turn out. Within a short time, the guards became incredibly brutal, rude, aggressive, and abusive. They insisted that all prisoners blindly obey their self-generated rules, and the slightest disobedience was punished with degrading tasks (such as cleaning the toilet with bare hands) or the loss of "privileges" (such as eating, sleeping, or washing). Although some guards were also "good guys" who did little favors for the prisoners and others were "tough but fair," they *all* became authoritarian and engaged in some abuse of power. Most prisoners initially responded to the bossing and arbitrary rules with good-humored acceptance. But as the rules increased and the abuses began, one prisoner went on a hunger strike (which was quickly punished), and a few became model prisoners who obeyed every rule. The majority became passive and depressed.

Four prisoners had to be released within the first four days because of severe

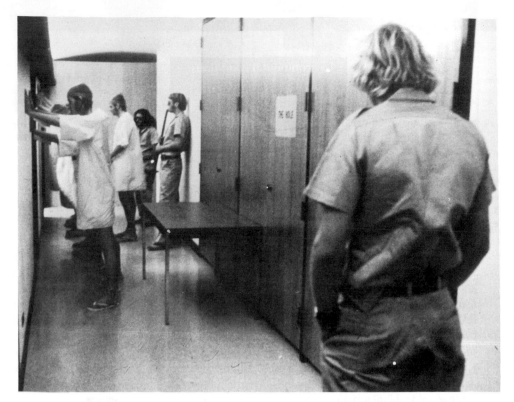

Subjects in Zimbardo's prison simulation were searched before being assigned to their cells. How do you think the sack-like uniforms affected the "prisoners" behavior?

reactions, such as uncontrollable sobbing, fits of rage, severe depression, and, in one case, a psychosomatic rash over the entire body. Although the study had originally been planned to last two weeks, it was finally stopped after only six days because of the alarming psychological changes in the student participants. The guards were seriously abusing their power, and the traumatized prisoners were becoming more and more depressed and dehumanized.

Question: How could this have happened?   According to interviews conducted after the study, the students apparently became so involved in the norms and roles associated with their assigned positions that they forgot that they were volunteers in a university experiment (Zimbardo et al., 1977). This new *social reality* was so powerful that it even trapped Zimbardo: "In the end, I called off the experiment not because of the horror I saw out there in the prison yard, but because of the horror of realizing that I could have easily traded places with the most brutal guard or have become the weakest prisoner full of hatred at being so powerless . . ." (1977, p. 9).

Although this was not a "true" experiment, in that it lacked control groups and clear measurements of the dependent variable, it does offer insights into the potential power of roles on individual behavior. If this type of personality disintegration and abuse of power could be generated in a mere six days in a "mock prison" with *volunteers,* what actually happens during life imprisonment, six-year sentences, or even overnight jail stays?

Zimbardo's study should also inspire us to question everyday roles between parents and children, teachers and students, and husbands and wives. For example, should parents have the legal right to use corporal punishment on their children? Should students have more control over course content and in faculty selection and retention? Should police take a more active role in arresting husbands who physically assault their wives?

Deindividuation   A group not only prescribes the roles each member plays but also has the power to weaken an individual's normal restraint on socially prohibited behaviors.

at how group discussions affect individual opinions (group polarization), but also at how group membership may affect access to accurate information (groupthink).

Group polarization When considering whether to trust an important decision to one individual or to a committee, most people tend to opt for a committee. They assume that any group decision will be more conservative, cautious, and "middle of the road" than an individual one. But is this true? During initial investigations of this question, it was discovered that after discussion of an issue, groups would actually support *riskier* decisions than ones they made as individuals before the discussion (Stoner, 1961). Partly because it contradicted the common belief about group caution and moderation, this *risky shift* concept sparked a great deal of research.

Subsequent research has discovered that the risky shift phenomenon is only part of the picture in group decision making. Although some groups do, in fact, make riskier decisions, others become extremely *conservative* (MacCoun and Kerr, 1988; Isenberg, 1986). Whether the final decision is risky or conservative depends primarily on the dominant preexisting tendencies of the group. That is, when individuals are polled *before* becoming a member of a group and then polled again *after* the group has made a decision, most group members will move toward the strongest initial position. This movement toward one "polar" extreme or the other is known as **group polarization.**

GROUP POLARIZATION: *Tendency for a group decision to become either more cautious or more risky than an individual decision, depending on the preexisting dominant tendencies of the group.*

Question: Why does this happen? The tendency toward group polarization generally results from a sharing of *similar* information. Since most informal, political, or business groups consist of like-minded individuals who share many similarities, during discussions each member will hear additional arguments that support and reinforce his or her original opinion. Given that jurors work as a group and also share similar information (courtroom presentations), psychologists have wondered whether their legal decisions might be affected by group polarization. Social psychological research on both *mock* and actual juries has shown that the verdict preferred by a clear majority of jurors at the onset of deliberation is, in fact, very close to the final verdict (MacCoun and Kerr, 1988; Zeisel and Diamond, 1978).

GROUPTHINK: *Condition in which a highly cohesive group with a strong desire for agreement leads to uncritical consensus and faulty decision making.*

Groupthink Although group decision making is sometimes affected by the tendency toward group polarization, it is also strongly influenced by an equally dangerous tendency toward **groupthink.** Irving Janis (1972) has defined groupthink as "a mode of thinking that people engage in when they are deeply involved in a cohesive in-group, and when the members' strivings for unanimity override their motivation to realistically appraise alter-

Group polarization and groupthink are two important explanations for the dangerous or unethical decisions that are sometimes made in groups.

native courses of action" (p. 9). That is, when groups are strongly cohesive (a family, a panel of military advisers, an athletic team) they generally share a strong desire for agreement (to see themselves as "one"). It is this desire that may lead them to overlook important criticism of certain decisions and to avoid alternative views.

After analyzing several governmental decisions, such as the U.S. invasion of Cuba (the "Bay of Pigs") in 1962, Janis concluded that many ultimately disastrous decisions were largely the result of groupthink. As outlined in Figure 18.3, the process of group-think begins with group members feeling a strong sense of cohesiveness and relative isolation from the judgments of qualified outsiders. Add a directive leader and little chance for debate, and you have the recipe for a potentially dangerous decision. During the actual discussion process, the members also come to believe they are invulnerable, tend to share rationalizations and stereotypes of the outgroup, and exert considerable pressure on anyone who dares to offer a dissenting opinion. Some members actually start to play the role of group "mindguards," working rather like bodyguards to isolate and protect the group from all differences in opinion. During the meetings that resulted in the decision to

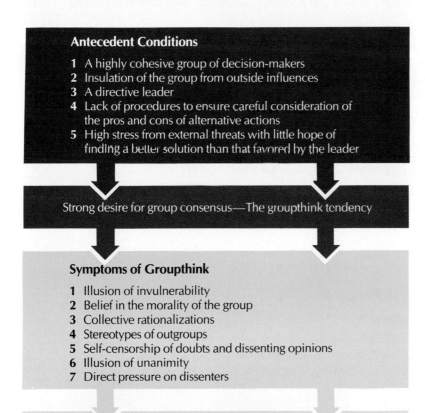

Antecedent Conditions

1 A highly cohesive group of decision-makers
2 Insulation of the group from outside influences
3 A directive leader
4 Lack of procedures to ensure careful consideration of the pros and cons of alternative actions
5 High stress from external threats with little hope of finding a better solution than that favored by the leader

Strong desire for group consensus—The groupthink tendency

Symptoms of Groupthink

1 Illusion of invulnerability
2 Belief in the morality of the group
3 Collective rationalizations
4 Stereotypes of outgroups
5 Self-censorship of doubts and dissenting opinions
6 Illusion of unanimity
7 Direct pressure on dissenters

Symptoms of Poor Decision-Making

1 An incomplete survey of alternative courses of action
2 An incomplete survey of group objectives
3 Failure to examine risks of the preferred choice
4 Failure to reappraise rejected alternatives
5 Poor search for relevant information
6 Selective bias in processing information
7 Failure to develop contingency plans

Low probability of successful outcome

Figure 18.3 An overall analysis of the antecedents, characteristics, and consequences of groupthink.

invade Cuba, for example, Robert Kennedy protected his brother, the President, and other members of the group by discouraging any direct or indirect criticism of the initial plan and even the slightest evidence of nonsupport (Janis, 1972, 1983).

Question: Does this type of thinking ever happen to groups outside of the government? One of the most immediate and personal applications of groupthink is the group decision to marry (remember that groups are composed of two or more). When dating couples begin to think about marriage, they often show several of the *antecedent conditions* for groupthink. (1) They have a strong need for cohesiveness ("we agree on almost everything"). (2) They are often insulated from others' opinions ("we do almost everything as a couple"). (3) They lack the resources or desire to methodically evaluate the correctness or advisability of their decision to marry. When discussing a pending marriage, they show many *symptoms* of groupthink: The illusion of invulnerability ("we're different, we won't ever get divorced"); collective rationalization ("two can live more cheaply than one"); and shared stereotypes of the outgroup ("couples with problems just don't know how to communicate"). It is also important to look at how couples may self-censor their own doubts and avoid any "dissenter" who tries to discourage them.

Question: Is there any way to avoid groupthink? As can be seen in Table 18.2, Janis and Mann (1977) developed several prescriptions for preventing groupthink. Some suggestions on this list obviously do not apply to a couple's decision concerning marriage, but each point has something of value that can be used in decision-making situations that you will undoubtedly encounter in your lifetime — which new member to allow into your club, which product to introduce into your business, or even where to take your family vacation.

Leadership in groups: Who makes a good leader?

LEADER: *Member of a group who has the greatest amount of power or social influence or who contributes the most toward group goals.*

In any group, there are noticeable differences in power and status among the members. Those members with the greatest amount of power or social influence, or who contribute the most toward group goals, are generally referred to as **leaders.** Do leaders

TABLE 18.2
How to Avoid Groupthink

> *1* Group members should be told about groupthink and its causes and consequences.
> *2* The leader should be impartial and should not endorse any position.
> *3* The leader should instruct everyone to critically evaluate options and should encourage objections and doubts.
> *4* One or more members should be assigned to the role of "devil's advocate."
> *5* From time to time, the group should be subdivided, with subgroups meeting separately and then coming together to air differences.
> *6* When the issue concerns relations with a rival group, time should be taken to survey all warning signals and to identify various possible actions by the rival.
> *7* After reaching a preliminary decision, a "second-chance" meeting should be called at which each member is asked to express remaining doubts.
> *8* Outside experts should attend meetings on a staggered basis and be asked to express concerns.
> *9* Each group member should air the group's deliberations to trusted associates and report their reactions.
> *10* Several independent groups should work simultaneously on the same question.

Source: Adapted from Janis (1982).

have specific personality traits that predispose them to these higher positions, or does it depend on the situation? Are different styles of leadership better in some situations than others? These are questions we will address now.

Characteristics of leaders What makes one person a leader and another a follower? Hundreds of studies have been designed to answer this question and have generally concluded that there are few, if any, specific traits that separate leaders from followers (Yukl, 1981). Those characteristics that do show a small but consistent relationship are *intelligence*— leaders tend to be more intelligent — and *motivation*— leaders tend to be more achievement oriented, dominant, and self-confident (Aron and Aron, 1989; Aronson, 1988).

Characteristics of the situation In opposition to the search for specific leadership traits is the *zeitgeist* (German for "spirit of the times") approach. According to this idea, leadership is a result of being the right person, at the right time, and in the right place (Worchel, Cooper, and Goethals, 1988). Who leads a particular group at a particular time is basically a matter of chance. Different group members emerge as leaders in those situations where they have the skills, knowledge, or qualities important to group goals or values.

Is the leadership of Lech Walesa a result of natural personality traits or was he just the right person, in the right place, at the right time?

Question: How would either of these approaches explain why Jim Jones was such a powerful leader? Jones, like all leaders, represented a combination of both personality traits and strong situational support for his leadership. Not only was he highly motivated and intelligent (particularly about social influence techniques), but he was also in the right place at the right time. Jones began his ministry with the laudable goal of eliminating racial prejudice and social injustice and first became an ordained minister in 1964. What was the national "zeitgeist" during the 1960s? As evidenced by the assassinations of President Kennedy, Martin Luther King, and Senator Robert Kennedy, and the passage of the civil rights amendment, there was obviously a strong national feeling (both pro and con) concerning the rights of the poor, black, elderly, and other socially disadvantaged groups. Jones's promise of equality and a utopian world free of prejudice, poverty, and discrimination was the "right" message at this point in history.

Leadership styles Fred Fiedler (1981) has developed an influential theory of leadership styles that specifically accounts for the interaction of leader characteristics and situational influences. His **contingency model** of leadership proposes that the effectiveness of leaders is dependent (or *contingent*) on the favorableness of the situation and on the specific style of the leader (either task-oriented or relationship-oriented).

CONTINGENCY MODEL: *Fiedler's theory that suggests the effectiveness of leaders depends on the favorableness of the situation and the specific style of the leader (either task or relationship oriented).*

Fiedler maintains that a *task-oriented leader* (one who is good at initiating and directing behavior) is more successful and effective when the situation is either highly favorable or highly unfavorable. Conversely, a *relationship-oriented leader* (one who is good at maintaining group morale, satisfaction, and motivation) is more successful when the situation is of moderate favorability. A situation is considered favorable when (1) the task is clear and well defined, (2) the leader's relations with the group are good, and (3) the leader's power is accepted and acknowledged by the group. When the reverse conditions occur, the situation is considered unfavorable.

This research has several important implications. Since Fiedler also believes that leadership styles are highly resistant to change, he suggests that managers should attempt to match the leader's style to the particular group and task. When the task is somewhat clear, the relationship-oriented leader can use his or her interpersonal skills to increase satisfaction and productivity. But when the task is either very clear or very unclear, the skills of the task-oriented leader can be used to maximize productivity (in the highly favorable situation) or to bring order from chaos (in the highly unfavorable situation).

Review Questions

1 The tendency for groups to make more daring decisions than an individual might make is known as a _____ _____.

2 _____ _____ refers to the fact that after group discussion members' preexisting and dominant tendencies or opinions will be reinforced and intensified.

3 John F. Kennedy's decision to invade Cuba can be seen as an example of _____.

4 Robert Kennedy's efforts to squelch competing ideas and criticism of his brother's plan to invade Cuba is seen as a type of _____.

5 A couple's belief that "two can live more cheaply than one" is an example of _____ _____.

6 Traits that seem to differentiate leaders from followers include _____ and _____.

7 The _____ approach suggests that leadership results from being the right person, at the right time, and in the right place.

8 According to Fiedler's contingency model, _____ leaders are most effective under highly favorable or highly unfavorable conditions, whereas _____ leaders are more effective under conditions of moderate favorability.

Answers: 1 risky shift; *2* group polarization; *3* groupthink; *4* mindguarding; *5* collective rationalization; *6* intelligence, motivation; *7* zeitgeist; *8* task-oriented, relationship-oriented

ENVIRONMENTAL PSYCHOLOGY

As you may remember, we began our study of social psychology in Chapter 17 by looking at the internal processes of the individual — social perception and attitude formation — and then discussed the more external topics of aggression and altruism. Here we have expanded our study to include the large impact that social influence and group membership has on all our lives. We now conclude with a look at the largest social factor — the environment.

Environmental psychology is an area of applied social psychology that focuses on the relationships between psychological processes and the physical environment. We will first look at rules that govern the interpersonal environment (personal space and territoriality), and then turn to some aspects that can have major psychological effects: crowding and social traps.

ENVIRONMENTAL PSYCHOLOGY: *Branch of applied social psychology that focuses on the relationship between psychological processes and the physical environment.*

Interpersonal environment: Personal space and territoriality

Suppose you are waiting in line to see a movie. How close do you stand to other people in the line? Eighteen inches? Two feet? Does it make a difference if the person next to you is a friend, a family member, or someone of the opposite sex?

Your answers to these questions demonstrate one of the most important rules or norms for social interactions: the maintenance of appropriate distances. Researchers have shown that people treat the physical space immediately around them as if it were a part of themselves — an area known as their **personal space** (Sommer, 1969). Edward T. Hall (1966, 1983), an anthropologist, has suggested that preferred interpersonal distances differ according to the situation (see Table 18.3).

PERSONAL SPACE: *Immediate physical space that surrounds each individual and is treated as if it were an extension of the self.*

Note how people tend to reserve a predictable amount of physical space between themselves and others. How would you explain this?

Question: Why do some people like to stand closer than others? There are a number of possible explanations. First, culture and socialization have a lot to do with personal space. People from Mediterranean, Moslem, and Latin American countries tend to maintain smaller interpersonal distances than North Americans and Northern Europeans (Steinhart, 1986). Children also tend to stand very close to others until they are socialized to recognize and maintain a larger personal distance (Shea, 1981). Second, certain relationships, situations, and personalities affect interpersonal distances. Friends stand closer than strangers (Ashton and Shaw, 1980), women tend to stand closer than men to whomever they are with (Harnett et al., 1970), and violent prisoners require approximately three times the personal space of nonviolent prisoners (Gilmour and Walkey, 1981).

The importance of these seemingly innocuous differences in human behavior becomes apparent when cultures, ages, or sexes are mixed. Can you see how an American and Arab might easily misinterpret each other's intentions if they were unaware of these cultural norms? An Arab, who generally prefers a smaller interpersonal distance, might try to move in closer to an American, who would most likely move back to reestablish his preferred distance. Can you see how the American might be left with the impression that Arabs are aggressive and pushy, whereas the Arab might get the impression that Americans are cold and unfriendly? If you want to test the power of this simple rule of personal space, try breaking the norm and stand about 15 inches away from a friend and then watch his or her reaction.

People seek not only to control their personal space but also to stake out and mark a certain area as their own. This behavior, generally known as **territoriality,** can be seen in

TERRITORIALITY: *Tendency to mark, maintain, or defend certain areas as one's own.*

TABLE 18.3
Appropriate Distances for Various Interpersonal Relationships and Activities

Appropriate Space	Relationship or Activity
Intimate distance (0 to 18 inches)	Lovemaking, wrestling, cuddling, fighting, and so on
Personal distance (18 inches to 4 feet)	Commonly used by friends for casual conversation
Social distance (4 to 12 feet)	Impersonal and business transactions
Public distance (more than 12 feet)	Formal contacts between an individual and the public (e.g., a speaker or actor and the audience)

Source: E. T. Hall (1966).

the form of fences around homes and in the way people will leave their coat or books to mark "their" spot in a public place.

Question: Why is this such common behavior?   Territorial marking appears to serve many functions. It distinguishes "insiders" (those who are allowed access to the area) from "outsiders," it decreases conflict (the first in line get the first tickets), and it establishes zones of privacy (a stack of books on the adjacent chair provides "protection" from unwanted intrusion).

A number of studies have also shown that territoriality is important to people's sense of control and to their vulnerability to certain types of crime. Not only do people believe that they are safer from personal assault and property loss when their property is well marked (Sommer and Becker, 1969), but crime statistics actually support their belief.

An important example of the significance of territoriality was provided by the deaths of 11 people who were trampled to death by fans at a Who concert in Cleveland in 1979. Because of a break in security, almost 7,000 fans with unreserved, general admission tickets rushed to get as close as possible to the stage. Recognizing the importance of the social control provided by the norms associated with territoriality, most concert organizers now require reserved seating.

The urban environment: Crowding and its effect on behavior

Each day the earth gains about 200,000 people. Do you realize that at this rate world population will double within the next 35 years? What will your life be like with twice as many people on our finite planet? How will colleges and the workplace deal with twice the number of students, workers, and commuters? Although some areas and groups of people will be more congested than others, everyone will experience increased competition not only for jobs and housing, but also for leisure time activities such as space on the ski slopes, camping spots at national parks, and tickets for sporting events.

Given the serious implications of our ever-increasing population, a great deal of

To study the effects of crowding on behavior, John Calhoun created a rat "utopia" where rats were allowed unlimited resources and unlimited reproduction.

Is it crowding or poverty that best explains the high level of crime, delinquency, and mental illness in certain areas?

research has been conducted concerning the effects of crowding and overpopulation. One of the earliest and most influential studies of environmental issues was done by John Calhoun (1962). To study the effects of increased population, Calhoun created a rat "utopia" with unlimited food, water, and nesting material (see the photograph). Since this study has been widely quoted in the popular press as evidence for the general problems of overpopulation, you may already be aware of the findings: The rats became aggressive, cannibalistic, hyperactive, or extremely lethargic; and some male rats responded sexually to virtually any animal in sight.

Question: How does this apply to humans? After Calhoun's study was first published, there were also several research studies that documented a strong correlation between human population density and mental illness, crime, and delinquency (Altman, 1975; Freedman, 1975). Using these data, many people concluded that the pathological behaviors found in ghetto areas in modern cities were *caused* by the overpopulation. As noted in Chapter 1, however, correlational studies can never prove causation. In this case closer examination revealed that the negative effects of crowding were confounded by the fact that socioeconomic factors are also related to crowding (Steinhart, 1986). Since it is usually the poor who live in the most crowded environments, it may be that poverty, not crowding per se, is the most important factor in the negative behaviors associated with high-density city living.

Experiments and correlational studies that *have* controlled for economic factors have found a wide variety of responses to crowding, ranging from no ill effects to serious, long-term negative reactions (Epstein, 1981; Fisher et al., 1984). Such variations led researchers to distinguish between **density,** the actual number of people in a given space, and **crowding,** the negative psychological experience of being exposed to a larger number of people than you prefer. People can obviously enjoy high-density conditions during rock concerts, football games, and parties, but they would find the same *number* of people to be highly stressful and intolerable under other conditions.

DENSITY: *Actual number of people in a given physical space.*
CROWDING: *Negative psychological experience of being overstimulated by a larger number of people than you prefer.*

The subjective experience of crowding depends on the individual's psychological appraisal, perceived control over the situation, and personality characteristics. The urban dweller who loves the exciting city night life, for example, would feel less crowded and stressed by a high-density area than would a small town resident who loves a quiet, star-lit evening. The challenge for environmental psychologists is to understand exactly what elements determine the psychological experience of crowding for each individual and to help urban and rural planners to develop strategies to maximize the pleasures and feelings of control for all.

Social traps: When individual benefits conflict with society

One major problem with any attempt to change people's behavior concerning the environment, whether it is an issue of overpopulation, noise pollution, or the nuclear arms race, is called a **social trap,** or social dilemma. These traps arise because each individual pursues his or her own immediate self-interests but does so at the expense of long-term individual benefits or the collective best interests of the group.

SOCIAL TRAP: *Dilemma created when individual short-term best interests conflict with long-term goals or group interests.*

Examples of such traps are easily found: Wilderness campers who toss their trash in the bushes ("What difference does one bag of trash make in all this space?"); automobile drivers who refuse to use mass transit systems or car pools ("What difference does my one car make?"); and citizens who ignore the fact that governments continue to stockpile nuclear weapons ("What difference does one more bomb make?"). Thanks, in part, to the "logic" of each of these positions we have highly polluted wilderness areas, dangerous smog levels and incredible traffic jams, and there are enough nuclear weapons to destroy the planet.

 Question: Are there any solutions to such traps? Research in this area has offered several suggestions:

1. *Change the payoff.* When laboratory experiments with social traps made cooperation toward mutual goals more rewarding than individualistic competition, subjects quickly recognized the difference and adjusted their behavior (Kohn, 1986; Rabow, 1988). Examples of this technique are power companies giving rebates or lower rates for use during off-peak hours, highway planners installing car pool lanes on freeways, and laws being enacted to punish those who pollute.
2. *Modeling.* In one study of water conservation, a sign was placed outside common showers asking people to turn off the water while soaping up. In other conditions either one or two students were present to actually model the behavior. The sign made some difference, but the models had a much stronger effect (Aronson and O'Leary, 1983). When social traps are composed of two opposing viewpoints, social psychologist Charles Osgood (1980) recommends another form of modeling known as the *graduated and reciprocated initiatives in tension-reduction* (GRIT) technique. With this technique, one side announces its intention to reduce tension by offering and modeling a small, conciliatory action. If the opposition responds with its own act of conciliation, the initiator responds in kind, as they would with any attempts to exploit or aggress. This strategy is apparently very effective in increasing cooperation and trust (Lindskold, Walters, and Koutsourais, 1983).
3. *Increased communication.* People who are locked into social traps must be able to communicate directly with one another (Dawes, 1987). Through improved education, people can also be encouraged to examine the long- versus short-term consequences of their behavior (Messick and Mackie, 1989).

Question: Could these techniques really work for large-scale problems? It depends. If we adopt the view that people are rational and that behavior can be described, explained, predicted, and changed, then no problem is insurmountable. As you may remember, these are the four basic goals of psychology that we discussed at the very beginning of this text.

Now that we are closing this final chapter, we sincerely hope that your brief introduction to psychology has encouraged you to see psychology as not only a science and academic discipline but also as a method for positive social influence. We encourage you to apply the information you've gained from this text and course to both personal and societal problems. We also invite you to continue your study and exploration of the subject with a career in psychology or simply as a part of your lifelong learning and personal growth.

Review Questions

1. _____ psychology is that branch of applied social psychology that deals with relationships between psychological processes and the physical environment.

2. Mediterranean cultures, children, friends, and women all tend to prefer smaller or closer _____ _____ than North American cultures, adults, strangers, and men.

3. Efforts to mark your space with books or coats, or erecting fences around homes, can be seen as evidence of _____.

4. At one time it was popular to use Calhoun's rat study as evidence for crowding being a major cause of problems in urban ghettos, but other studies found that _____ factors also played a role.

5. The term _____ refers to the actual number of people in a given space, whereas _____ is the term that describes the negative psychological experience of being exposed to more people than you prefer.

6. When people get caught between satisfying their immediate or personally rewarding best interests and sacrificing their long-term or group best interests, it is known as a _____ _____.

7. The three major steps to reducing or eliminating social traps are changing the _____, _____, and improving _____.

Answers: 1 environmental; **2** personal spaces; **3** territoriality; **4** socioeconomic; **5** density, crowding; **6** social trap; **7** payoff, modeling, communication

REVIEW OF MAJOR CONCEPTS

SOCIAL INFLUENCE

1 Through the process of socialization, children are taught important cultural values and behaviors that are essential to successful social living. These initial values are also subject to later adjustments and change through the process of social influence, which includes conformity, compliance, and obedience.

2 Conformity refers to changes in behavior in response to real or imagined pressure from others. Asch's classic study of conformity demonstrated that people will often conform and go along with group opinion even when the group is clearly wrong. People conform in order to be approved and accepted by others (normative social influence), out of a need for more information (informational social influence), and in order to match the behavior of those they admire and feel similar to (their reference group). People also conform because it is often adaptive to do so.

3 Compliance refers to giving in to the requests of others. Requestors often attempt to ingratiate themselves to us, to make multiple requests (the foot-in-the-door and door-in-the-face techniques) that "oblige" us to give in, or to make us feel guilty.

4 Obedience involves giving in to a command from others. Milgram's experiment with obedience to authority demonstrated that a large number of people will follow orders even when the physical health of another human being is threatened.

GROUP PROCESSES

5 Groups differ from mere collections of people if members share a mutually recognized relationship with one another. People join groups for a variety of reasons, one of which is the need to affiliate, or to simply be with others.

6   Schachter's classic study of affiliation demonstrated that one of the strongest factors in our desire to be with others comes from our need for social comparison. People need to compare their abilities and reactions to those of others, particularly during times of stress and fear.

7   Groups affect us through the roles we play. The importance of these roles in determining and controlling behavior was dramatically demonstrated in Philip Zimbardo's Stanford Prison Study. College students who were assigned to play the role of either a prisoner or guard in a simulated prison at Stanford University became so completely and dangerously immersed in acting out their roles that the experiment was prematurely ended.

8   Groups also affect us because they increase the chances for deindividuation among members. Deindividuation refers to the temporary suspension of self-awareness and personal restraints on behavior. The fact that people are more willing to shock others when they are in costumes, and will "bait" or encourage a potential suicide victim under the cover of darkness and distance from the victim, demonstrates the strong role of anonymity in deindividuation.

9   Groups are often trusted with decisions because we believe their response will be more conservative and "middle of the road" than the potentially extreme decision of individuals. Research shows, however, that groups are actually more extreme in their decisions. Sharing ideas with "like-minded" others often reinforces the group's preexisting and dominant tendencies.

10 Groupthink is a dangerous type of thinking that occurs when the group's desire for agreement overrules its tendency to critically evaluate information. President Kennedy's Bay of Pigs decision is often given as evidence of groupthink. Couples who are planning to marry also demonstrate many symptoms of groupthink.

11 Members of the group who hold the greatest amount of power or who contribute the most toward group goals are often seen as the leaders. Although some research shows that leaders differ from followers on the traits of intelligence and motivation, others suggest that leadership is merely being the right person, in the right place, at the right time (the zeitgeist approach).

12 According to Fiedler's contingency model of leadership effectiveness, task-oriented leaders are preferable when situations are either highly favorable or highly unfavorable. Relationship-oriented leaders, on the other hand, are preferable when the situation is moderately favorable.

ENVIRONMENTAL PSYCHOLOGY

13 Environmental psychology studies the relationship between psychological processes and the physical environment. Research concerning our interpersonal environment suggests that individuals learn to prefer certain interpersonal distances in their physical environment and that one way they protect their personal space is through territorial behaviors, such as marking the space around them with books or sweaters.

14 Environmental studies of crowding have produced conflicting results. Although research such as Calhoun's study with an overpopulation of rats has found that crowding creates a variety of negative behaviors, research with humans suggests that sheer density (the number of people in a given space) is less important than the subjective feeling of crowding.

15 When people respond to their own self-interest and short-term benefits, they often sacrifice long-term goals and the groups' best interests. This type of social trap can be avoided and eliminated by changing the payoff so that long-term benefits and group benefits are more rewarding, by modeling the individual behaviors that the group wants to establish, and by increasing communication between the individual and others in the group.

SUGGESTED READINGS

ARON, A., & ARON, E. N. (1989). *The heart of social psychology* (2nd ed.). Lexington, MA: D.C. Heath. A small paperback that provides an engaging overview of the field of social psychology.

FORSYTH, D. R. (1983). *An introduction to group dynamics.* Monterey, CA: Brooks/Cole. An up-to-date and highly readable account of the topics of conformity, leadership, and general group behavior.

JANIS, I. L. (1983). *Groupthink* (2nd ed.). Boston: Houghton Mifflin. A popular and widely read book that presents the basic theory of groupthink and how it applies to major political events.

MEHRABIAN, A. (1978). *Public places and private spaces.* New York: Basic Books. An interesting book for those seeking additional information on the environmental effects of offices, schools, dormitories, and prisons.

We are constantly bombarded by numbers: "On sale for 30 percent off," "70 percent chance of rain," "9 out of 10 doctors recommend," and so on. These numbers are meant to persuade us to buy something, to convince us of the truth of an idea, or to cajole us into thinking that one item is better than its comparison. The President uses numbers to convince us that the economy is healthy. Advertisers use numbers to convince us of the effectiveness of their products. Psychologists use numbers to demonstrate that certain behaviors are indeed results of specific causal factors. Whenever people use numbers in these ways, they are said to be using statistics. *Statistics* is a branch of applied mathematics that uses numbers to describe and analyze information on various subjects. Psychologists use statistics to support or refute various psychological theories.

Using statistics makes it possible for psychologists to quantify the information they obtain in their studies. They can then critically analyze and evaluate this information. Statistical analysis is imperative for researchers to describe, predict, or explain behavior. For instance, Albert Bandura (1973) proposed that watching violence on television causes aggressive behavior in children. In carefully controlled experiments, he gathered numerical information and analyzed it according to specific statistical methods. The statistical analysis helped him substantiate the fact that the aggression of his subjects and the aggressive acts they had previously observed on television were related, and that this relationship was not due to mere coincidence.

Although statistics is a branch of applied mathematics, you don't have to be a math whiz to use statistics. A knowledge of simple arithmetic is all you need to do most of the calculations. For more complex statistics involving more complicated mathematics, computer programs are available for virtually every type of computer. What is more important than learning the mathematical computations, however, is developing an understanding of when and why each type of statistic is used. The purpose of this appendix is to help you understand the significance of the statistics most commonly used.

GATHERING AND ORGANIZING DATA

Psychologists design their studies in ways that facilitate the gathering of information about the factors they are studying. The information they obtain is known as *data* (*data* is plural; its singular is *datum*). When the data are gathered, they are generally in the form of numbers; if they aren't, they are converted to numbers. After they are gathered, the data must be organized in such a way that statistical analysis is possible. In the following section, we will examine the methods used to gather and organize information.

Variables

When studying a behavior, psychologists normally focus on one particular factor to determine whether it has an effect on the behavior. This factor is known as a *variable,* which is in effect anything that can assume more than one value (see Chapter 1). Height, weight, sex, eye color, and scores on an IQ test or on a video game are all factors that can assume more than one value and are therefore variables. Some will vary between people, such as sex (you are either male *or* female but not both at the same time). Some may even vary within one person, such as scores on a video game (the same person might get 10,000 points on one try and only 800 on another). Opposed to a variable, anything that remains the same and does not vary is called a *constant.* If researchers use only females in their research, then sex is a constant, not a variable.

In nonexperimental studies, variables can be factors that are merely observed through naturalistic observation or case studies, or they can be factors about which people are questioned in a test or survey. In experimental studies, the two major types of variables are independent and dependent variables.

Independent variables are those that are manipulated by the experimenter. For example, suppose we were to conduct a study to determine whether the sex of the debater influences the outcome of a debate. In this study, one group of subjects watches a videotape of a debate between a male arguing the "pro" side and a female arguing the "con"; another group watches the same debate, but with the pro and con roles reversed. In such a study, the form of the presentation viewed by each group (whether "pro" is argued by a male or a female) is the independent variable because the experimenter manipulates the form of presentation seen by each group. Another example consists of a study we might conduct to determine whether a particular drug has any effect on a manual dexterity task. To effectively study this question, we would administer the drug to one group and no drug to another. The independent variable would be the amount of drug given (some or none). The independent variable is particularly important when using *inferential statistics,* which we will discuss later.

The *dependent variable* is a factor that results from, or depends on, the independent variable. It is a measure of some outcome or, most commonly, a measure of the subjects' behavior. In the debate example, each subject's choice of the winner of the debate would be the dependent variable. In the drug experiment, the dependent variable would be each subject's score on the manual dexterity task.

Frequency distributions

After conducting a study and obtaining measures of the variable(s) being studied, psychologists need to organize the data in a meaningful way. Table A.1 presents test scores from a statistics aptitude test collected from 50 college students. This information is called *raw data* because there is no order to the numbers. They are presented as they were collected and are therefore "raw." The lack of order in raw data makes them difficult to study. Thus, the first step in understanding the results of an experiment is to impose some order on the raw data. There are several ways to do this. One of the simplest is to create a *frequency distribution,* which shows the number of times a score or event occurs. Although frequency distributions are helpful in several ways, the major advantages are that they allow us to see the data in an organized manner and they make it easier to represent the data on a graph.

The simplest way to make a frequency distribution is to list all the possible test scores, then tally the number of people *(N)* who received those scores. Table A.2 presents a frequency distribution using the raw data from Table A.1. As you can see, the data are now easier to read. From looking at the frequency distribution, you can see that most of the test scores lie in the middle with only a few at

TABLE A.2
Frequency Distribution
of 50 Students
on Statistics Aptitude Test

Score	Frequency
73	2
72	3
71	0
70	1
69	0
68	5
67	1
66	2
65	3
64	2
63	5
62	5
61	2
60	2
59	5
58	1
57	3
56	1
55	0
54	1
53	0
52	2
51	1
50	3
Total	50

the very high or very low end. This was not at all evident from looking at the raw data.

This type of frequency distribution is practical when the number of possible scores is 20 or less. However, when there are more than 20 possible scores it can be even

TABLE A.1
Statistics Aptitude Test Scores
for 50 College Students

73	57	63	59	50
72	66	50	67	51
63	59	65	62	65
62	72	64	73	66
61	68	62	68	63
59	61	72	63	52
59	58	57	68	57
64	56	65	59	60
50	62	68	54	63
52	62	70	60	68

TABLE A.3
Life Change Units for 50 College Students

150	175	375	210	400
216	300	175	374	163
263	152	176	185	192
197	233	216	241	221
232	316	233	357	321
368	300	277	298	254
274	216	285	219	276
222	245	264	233	361
242	304	251	176	221
165	212	222	196	196

TABLE A.4
Group Frequency Distribution of
Life Change Unit Scores for
50 College Students

Life Change Units	
Class Interval	Frequency
400 – 424	1
375 – 399	1
350 – 374	4
325 – 349	0
300 – 324	5
275 – 299	4
250 – 274	5
225 – 249	7
200 – 224	10
175 – 199	9
150 – 174	4
Total	50

class intervals. Grouping these scores makes it much easier to make sense out of the distribution, as you can see from the relative ease in understanding Table A.4 as compared to Table A.3. Group frequency distributions are easier to represent on a graph.

When graphing data from frequency distributions, the class intervals are represented along the abscissa (the horizontal or *x* axis), whereas the frequency is represented along the ordinate (the vertical or *y* axis). Information can be graphed in the form of a bar graph, called a *histogram,* or in the form of a point or line graph, called a *polygon.* Figure A.1 shows a histogram presenting the data from Table A.4. Note that the class intervals are represented along the bottom line of the graph (the *x* axis) and the height of the bars indicates the frequency in each class interval. Now look at Figure A.2. The information presented here is exactly the same as that in Figure A.1 but is represented in the form of a polygon rather than a histogram. Can you see how both graphs illustrate the same information? Even though reading information from a graph is simple, we have found that many students have never learned to read graphs. In the next section we will explain how to read a graph.

harder to make sense out of the frequency distribution than the raw data. This can be seen in Table A.3, which presents the life change units for 50 students. Even though there are only fifty actual scores in this table, the number of possible scores ranges from a high of 400 to a low of 150. If we included zero frequencies there would be 251 entries in a frequency distribution of this data, making the frequency distribution much more difficult to understand than the raw data. If there are more than 20 possible scores, therefore, a *group* frequency distribution is normally used.

In a *group frequency distribution,* individual scores are represented as members of a group of scores or as a range of scores (see Table A.4). These groups are called

How to read a graph. Every graph has several major parts, the most important being the labels, the axes (the vertical and horizontal lines), and the points, lines, or bars. Find these parts in Figure A.1. The first things you should notice when reading a graph are the labels because they tell what data are portrayed. Usually the data consist of the descriptive statistics, or the numbers used to measure the dependent variables. For example, in Figure A.1 the horizontal axis is labeled "Life Change Units," which is the dependent variable measure; the vertical axis is labeled "Frequency," which means the number of occurrences. If a graph is not labeled, as we sometimes see in TV commercials or magazine ads, it is useless and should be ignored.

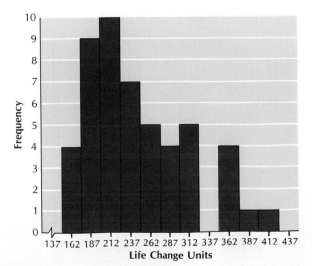

Figure A.1 A histogram illustrating the information found in Table A.4.

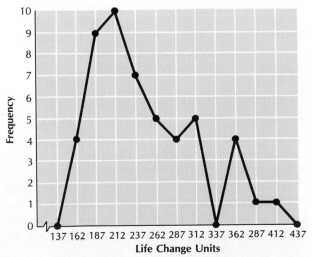

Figure A.2 A polygon illustrating the information found in Table A.4.

Even when a graph *is* labeled, the labels can be misleading. For example, if graph designers want to distort the information, they can elongate one of the axes. Thus, it is important to pay careful attention to the numbers as well as the words in graph labels.

Next, you should focus your attention on the bars, points, or lines on the graph. In the case of histograms like the one in Figure A.1, each bar represents the mean in a class interval. The width of the bar stands for the width of the class interval, whereas the height of the bar stands for the frequency in that interval. Look at the third bar from the left in Figure A.1. This bar represents the interval "200–224 life change units," which has a frequency of 10. You can see that this directly corresponds to the same class interval in Table A.4, since graphs and tables are both merely alternate ways of illustrating information.

Reading point or line graphs is the same as reading a histogram. In a point graph, each point represents two numbers, one found along the horizontal axis and the other found along the vertical axis. A polygon is identical to a point graph except that it has lines connecting the points. Figure A.2 is an example of a polygon, where each point represents a class interval and is placed at the center of the interval and at the height corresponding to the frequency of that interval. To make the graph easier to read, the points are connected by straight lines.

Displaying the data in a frequency distribution or in a graph is much more useful than merely presenting raw data and can be especially helpful when researchers are trying to find relations between certain factors. However, as mentioned previously, if psychologists want to make predictions or explanations about behavior, they need to perform mathematical computations on the data.

USES OF THE VARIOUS STATISTICS

Psychologists' selections of appropriate statistics depend on whether they are trying to describe and predict behavior or to explain it. When they use statistics to describe behavior, as in reporting the average score on the Scholastic Aptitude Test, they are using *descriptive statistics*. When they use them to explain behavior, as Bandura did in his study of children modeling aggressive behavior seen on TV, they are using *inferential statistics*.

Descriptive statistics

Descriptive statistics are the numbers used to describe the dependent variable. They can be used to describe characteristics of a *population* (an entire group, such as all people living in the United States) or a *sample* (a part of a group, such as a randomly selected group of 25 students from Cornell University). The major descriptive statistics include measures of central tendency (mean, median, and mode), measures of variation (variance and standard deviation), and correlation.

Measures of central tendency. Statistics indicating the center of the distribution are called *measures of central tendency* and include the mean, median, and mode. They are all scores that are typical of the center of the distribution. The *mean* is what most of us think of when we hear the word "average." The *median* is the middle score. The *mode* is the score that occurs most often.

Mean. What is your average golf score? What is the average yearly rainfall in your part of the country? What is the average reading test score in your city? When these questions ask for the average, they are really asking for the "mean." The arithmetic *mean* is the weighted average of all the raw scores, which is computed by totaling all the raw scores and then dividing that total by the number of scores added together. In statistical computation, the mean is represented by an "X" with a bar above it ($\overline{X}$, pronounced "X bar"), each individual raw score by an "X," and the total number of scores by an "N." For example, if we wanted to compute the $\overline{X}$ of the raw statistics test scores in Table A.1, we would sum all the X's (ΣX, with Σ meaning sum) and divide by N (number of scores). In Table A.1, the sum of all the scores is equal to 3,100 and there are 50 scores. Therefore, the mean of these scores is

$$\overline{X} = \frac{3,100}{50} = 62$$

Table A.5 illustrates how to calculate the mean for 10 IQ scores.

Median. The *median* is the middle score in the distribution once all the scores have been arranged in rank order. If N (the number of scores) is odd, then there actually is a middle score and that middle score is the median. When N

TABLE A.5
Computation of the Mean for 10 IQ Scores

IQ Scores X
143
127
116
98
85
107
106
98
104
116
$\Sigma X = 1,100$

$$\text{Mean} = \overline{X} = \frac{\Sigma X}{N} = \frac{1,100}{10} = 110$$

is even, there are two middle scores and the median is the mean of those two scores. Table A.6 shows the computation of the median for two different sets of scores, one set with 15 scores and one with 10.

Mode. Of all the measures of central tendency, the easiest to compute is the *mode,* which is merely the most frequent score. It is computed by finding the score that occurs most often. Whereas there is always only one mean and only one median for each distribution, there can be more than one mode. Table A.7 shows how to find the mode in a distribution with one mode (unimodal) and in a distribution with two modes (bimodal).

There are several advantages to each of these measures of central tendency, but in psychological research the mean is used most often. A book dealing solely with psychological statistics will provide a more thorough discussion of the relative values of these measures.

Measures of variation. When describing a distribution, it is not sufficient merely to give the central tendency; it is also necessary to give a *measure of variation,* which is a measure of the spread of the scores. By examining the spread, we can determine whether the scores are "bunched" around the middle or tend to extend away from the middle. Figure A.3 shows three different distributions, all with the same mean but with different spreads of scores. You can see from this figure that, in order to

TABLE A.6
Computation of Median for Odd and Even Numbers of IQ Scores

IQ	IQ
139	137
130	135
121	121
116	116
107	108 ← middle score
101	106 ← middle score
98	105
96 ← middle score	101
84	98
83	97
82	N = 10
75	N is even
75	
65	Median = $\frac{106 + 108}{2}$ = 107
62	

N = 15
N is odd
Median = 96

TABLE A.7
Finding the Mode for Two Different Distributions

IQ	IQ
139	139
138	138
125	125
116 ←	116 ←
116 ←	116 ←
116 ←	116 ←
107	107
100	98 ←
98	98 ←
98	98 ←

Mode = most frequent score   Mode = 116 and 98
Mode = 116

describe these different distributions accurately, there must be some measure of the variation in their spread. The most widely used measure of variation is the standard deviation, which is represented by a lowercase *s.* The standard deviation is a standard measurement of how much the scores in a distribution deviate from the mean.

Most distributions of psychological data are bell-shaped. That is, most of the scores are grouped around the mean, and the farther the scores are from the mean in either direction, the fewer the scores. Notice the bell shape of the distribution in Figure A.4. Distributions such as this are called *normal* distributions. In normal distributions, as shown in Figure A.4, approximately two-thirds of the scores fall within a range that is one standard deviation below the mean to one standard deviation above the mean. For example, the Wechsler IQ tests (see Chapter 8) have a mean of 100 and a standard deviation of 15. This means that approximately two-thirds of the people taking these tests will have scores above 85 and below 115.

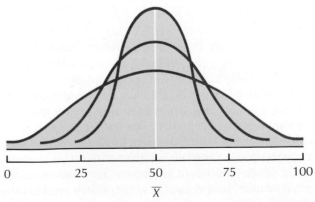

Figure A.3 Three distributions having the same mean but a different variability.

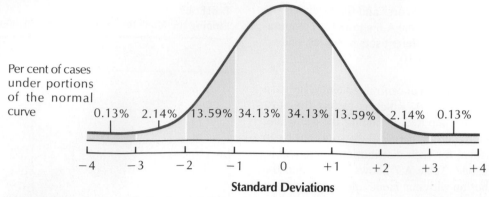

Per cent of cases under portions of the normal curve

0.13% 2.14% 13.59% 34.13% 34.13% 13.59% 2.14% 0.13%

−4   −3   −2   −1   0   +1   +2   +3   +4

Standard Deviations

Figure A.4 The normal distribution forms a bell-shaped curve. In a normal distribution, two-thirds of the scores lie between one standard deviation above and one standard deviation below the mean.

Correlation. Suppose for a moment that you are sitting in the student union with a friend. To pass the time, you and your friend decide to play a game in which you try to guess the height of the next male who enters the union. The winner, the one whose guess is closest to the person's actual height, gets a free piece of pie paid for by the loser. When it is your turn, what do you guess? If you are like most people, you will probably try to estimate the mean of all the males in the union and use that as your guess. The mean is always your best guess if you have no other information.

Now let's change the game a little and add a friend who stands outside the union and weighs the next male to enter the union. Before the male enters the union, your friend says "125 pounds." Given this new information, will you still guess the mean height? Probably not — you will probably predict *below* the mean. Why? Because there is a relationship between height and weight, with tall people usually weighing more than short people. Since 125 pounds is less than the average weight for males, you will probably guess a less-than-average height. The statistic used to measure this type of relationship between two variables is called a correlation coefficient.

Correlation coefficient. A *correlation coefficient* measures the relationship between two variables, such as height and weight or IQ and SAT scores. Given any two variables, there are three possible relationships between them: positive, negative, and zero (no relationship). A positive relationship exists when the two variables vary in the same direction (e.g., as height increases, weight normally also increases). A negative relationship occurs when the two variables vary in opposite directions (e.g., as temperatures go up, hot chocolate sales go down). There is no relationship when the two variables vary totally independently of one another (e.g., there is no relationship between peoples' height and the color of their toothbrush). Figure A.5 illustrates these three types of correlations.

The computation and the formula for a correlation coefficient (correlation coefficient is delineated by the letter "*r*") are shown in Table A.8. The correlation coefficient (*r*) always has a value between + 1 and − 1 (it is never greater than + 1 and it is never smaller than − 1). When *r* is close to + 1, it signifies a high positive relationship between the two variables (as one variable goes up, the other variable also goes up). When *r* is close to − 1, it signifies a high negative relationship between the two variables (as one variable goes up, the other variable goes down). When *r* is 0, there is no linear relationship between the two variables being measured.

Correlation coefficients can be quite helpful in making predictions. Bear in mind, however, that predictions are just that: *predictions*. They will have some error as long as the correlation coefficients on which they are based are not perfect (+ 1 or − 1). Also, correlations cannot reveal any information regarding causation. Merely because two factors are correlated, it does not mean that one factor causes the other. Consider, for example, ice cream consumption and swimming pool use. These two variables are positively correlated with one another, in that as ice cream consumption increases, so does swimming pool use. But nobody would suggest that eating ice cream *causes* swimming, or vice versa. Similarly, just because Greg Louganis eats Wheaties and can do a full twisting back double somersault off the high diving board it does not mean that you will be able to do one if you eat the same breakfast. The only way to determine the cause of behavior is to conduct an experiment and analyze the results by using inferential statistics.

Inferential statistics

Knowing the descriptive statistics associated with different distributions, such as the mean and standard deviation, can enable us to make comparisons between various distributions. By making these comparisons, we may be able to observe whether one variable is related to another or whether one variable has a causal effect on another.

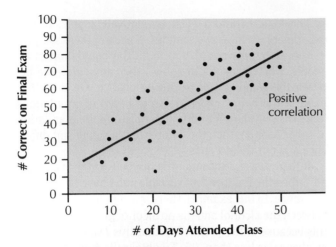

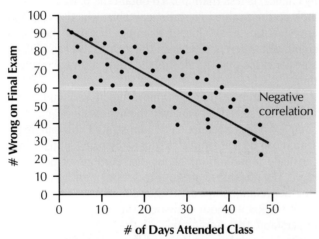

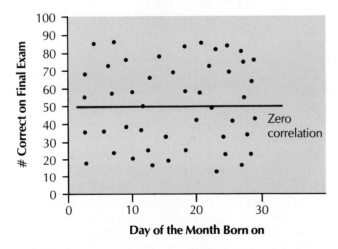

Figure A.5 Three types of correlation. Positive correlation (top): As the number of days of class attendance increases, so does the number of exam items correct. Negative correlation (middle): As the number of days of class attendance increases, the number of incorrect exam items decreases. Zero correlation (bottom): The day of the month on which one is born has no relationship to the number of exam items correct.

TABLE A.8
Computation of Correlation Coefficient between Height and Weight for 10 Male Subjects

Height (inches) X	X²	Weight (pounds) Y	Y²	XY
73	5,329	210	44,100	15,330
64	4,096	133	17,689	8,512
65	4,225	128	16,384	8,320
70	4,900	156	24,336	10,920
74	5,476	189	35,721	13,986
68	4,624	145	21,025	9,860
67	4,489	145	21,025	9,715
72	5,184	166	27,556	11,952
76	5,776	199	37,601	15,124
71	5,041	159	25,281	11,289
700	41,140	1,630	272,718	115,008

$$r = \frac{N \cdot \Sigma XY - (\Sigma X \cdot \Sigma Y)}{\sqrt{[N \cdot \Sigma X^2 - (\Sigma X)^2]} \sqrt{[N \cdot \Sigma Y^2 - (\Sigma Y)^2]}}$$

$$r = \frac{10 \cdot 115,008 - (700 \cdot 1,630)}{\sqrt{[10 \cdot 49,140 - 700^2]} \sqrt{[10 \cdot 272,718 - 1,630^2]}}$$

$$r = 0.92$$

When we design an experiment to measure causal effects between two or more variables, we use *inferential statistics* to analyze the data collected. Although there are many inferential statistics, the one we will discuss is the *t*-test, since it is the simplest.

***t*-Test.** Suppose we believe that drinking alcohol causes a person's reaction time to slow down. To test this hypothesis, we recruit 20 subjects and separate them into two groups. We ask the subjects in one group to drink a large glass of orange juice with one ounce of alcohol for every 100 pounds of body weight (e.g., a person weighing 150 pounds would get 1.5 ounces of alcohol). We ask the control group to drink an equivalent amount of orange juice with no alcohol added. Fifteen minutes after the drinks, we have each subject perform a reaction time test that consists of pushing a button as soon as a light is flashed. (The reaction time is the time between the onset of the light and the pressing of the button.) Table A.9 shows the data from this hypothetical experiment. It is clear from the data that there is definitely a difference in the reaction times of the two groups: There is an obvious difference between the means. However, it is possible that this difference is due merely to chance. To determine whether the difference is real or is due to mere chance, we can conduct a *t*-test. We have run a sample *t* test in Table A.9.

TABLE A.9
Reaction Times in Milliseconds (msec) for Subjects in
Alcohol and No Alcohol Conditions and Computation of *t*

RT (msec) Alcohol X_1	RT (msec) No Alcohol X_2
200	143
210	137
140	179
160	184
180	156
187	132
196	176
198	148
140	125
159	120
$\Sigma X_1 = 1{,}770$	$\Sigma X_2 = 1{,}500$
$N_1 = 10$	$N_1 = 10$
$\overline{X}_1 = 177$	$\overline{X}_2 = 150$
$s_1 = 24.25$	$s_2 = 21.86$

$$S_{\overline{X}_1} = \frac{s}{\sqrt{N_1 - 1}} = 8.08 \qquad S_{\overline{X}_2} = \frac{s}{\sqrt{N_1 - 1}} = 7.29$$

$$S_{\overline{X}_1 - \overline{X}_2} = \sqrt{S_{\overline{X}_1}^2 + S_{\overline{X}_2}^2} = \sqrt{8.08^2 + 7.29^2} = 10.88$$

$$t = \frac{\overline{X}_1 - \overline{X}_2}{S_{\overline{X}_1 - \overline{X}_2}} = \frac{177 - 150}{10.88} = 2.48$$

$$t = 2.48, \; p < .05$$

The logic behind a *t*-test is relatively simple. In our experiment we have two samples. If each of these samples is from the *same* population (e.g., the population of all people, whether drunk or sober), then any difference between the samples will be due to chance. On the other hand, if the two samples are from *different* populations (e.g., the population of drunk people *and* the population of sober people), then the difference is a significant difference and not due to chance.

If there is a significant difference between the two samples, then the independent variable must have caused that difference. In our example, there is a significant difference between the alcohol and the no alcohol group. We can tell this because *p* (the probability that this *t* value will occur by chance) is less than .05. To obtain the *p*, we need only look up the *t* value in a statistical table, which is found in any statistics book. In our example, because there is a significant difference between the groups, we can reasonably conclude that the alcohol did cause a slower reaction time.

As research designs grow more and more complicated, the statistics needed to analyze them grow more and more complex. This appendix has demonstrated how simple research can benefit from statistics — by using statistics we can make observations about distributions of data, observe relationships, make predictions, and determine whether relationships are real or due to mere chance. The more we know about statistics, the more likely we will understand the significance of the numbers that constantly confront us. It is urged that all students take as much mathematics as possible and at the very minimum take an elementary psychological statistics course.

Glossary

Absolute Threshold The smallest magnitude of a certain stimulus energy that can be detected.

Accommodation 1. The bulging and flattening of the lens in order to focus an image on the retina. 2. The process of adjusting existing ways of thinking (reworking schemata) to encompass new information, ideas, or objects.

Action Potential An electrochemical impulse that travels down an axon from the soma to the axon terminal buttons.

Activation–Synthesis Hypothesis The idea that dreams have no real significance, but in fact are simply unimportant by-products of random stimulation of brain cells.

Activity Theory A theory of aging that suggests that successful adjustment is fostered by a full and active commitment to life.

Adaptation Structural or functional changes that increase the organism's chances for survival.

Adaptive Theory A theory suggesting that sleep evolved as a means for conserving energy and for protecting individuals from predators.

Adolescence The psychological period of development between childhood and adulthood, which in the United States roughly corresponds to the teenage years.

Adolescent Egocentrism The belief that one is the focus of others' thoughts and attention that is common in adolescence.

Adrenogenital Syndrome A masculinization of a chromosomal female as a result of an excessive amount of androgens being produced during fetal development.

Aerial Perspective A monocular depth cue based on the fact that more distant objects appear less distinct than closer objects because of dust or haze in the air.

Afferent Incoming sensory information.

Affiliation Need for friendly association with others; formation of friendships; joining of groups and cooperation.

Ageism A discriminatory attitude (prejudice) against older adults.

Aggression Any behavior that is intended to harm someone.

Aids (Acquired Immune Deficiency Syndrome) A catastrophic illness in which a virus destroys the ability of the immune system to fight disease. Although the term "AIDS" continues to be used, the President's Commission in 1988 recommended the use of the term human immunodeficiency virus infection (HIV infection). They believe that this term more correctly defines the problem and places proper emphasis on the entire spectrum of the epidemic.

Algorithm A problem-solving strategy that always eventually leads to a solution; it often involves trying out random solutions to a problem in a systematic manner.

All-or-Nothing Principle The principle whereby an axon either fires an action potential or does not — there are no graduations; if one is fired, it is of the same intensity as any other.

Alpha Waves Brain waves that indicate drowsy relaxation.

Alternate States of Consciousness (ASC) Any state of consciousness other than normal waking consciousness.

Altruism Actions designed to help others with no obvious benefit to the individual.

Alzheimer's Disease An irreversible, progressive deterioration of the brain characterized by serious loss of memory.

Amnesia Forgetting that results from brain injury or from physical or psychological trauma.

Amplitude The height of a light or sound wave; pertaining to light, it refers to brightness; pertaining to sound, it refers to loudness.

Anal Stage Freud's psychosexual stage (from 12–18 months to 3 years) during which the anal area is the center of pleasure and toilet training is an important source of conflict.

Androgens Hormones that stimulate maturation and functioning of the male reproductive system.

Androgen-Insensitivity Syndrome A feminization of a chromosomal male as a result of a genetic defect in which androgens have no effect on the developing fetus.

Androgyny The combining of some characteristics considered to be typically male (e.g., assertive, athletic) with those that are typically female (e.g., yielding, nurturant); from the Greek *andro* meaning "male" and *gyn* meaning "female."

Animism Thinking that all things are living and capable of intentions, consciousness, and feelings.

Anorexia Nervosa An eating disorder, seen mostly in adolescent and young adult females, in which a severe loss of weight results from an obsessive fear of obesity and self-imposed starvation.

Anterograde Amnesia The inability to form new memories.

Anthropomorphism The act of attributing human characteristics to animals, gods, or inanimate objects. Also, interpreting the behavior of lower forms of animals in terms of human abilities or characteristics.

Antianxiety Drugs Tranquilizers used in the treatment of anxiety disorders.

Antipsychotic Drugs Chemicals administered to diminish or terminate psychotic symptoms such as hallucinations and delusions.

Antisocial Personality Personality disorder characterized by egocentrism, lack of conscience, impulsive behavior, and charisma.

Anxiety Disorders Type of abnormal behavior characterized by unrealistic, irrational fear.

Aphrodisiacs Substances that supposedly increase sexual desire.

Applied Research Research that utilizes the principles and discoveries of psychology for practical purposes, to solve real-world problems.

Approach–Approach Conflict Conflict in which a person must choose between two alternatives that will both lead to desirable results.

Approach–Avoidance Conflict Conflict in which a person must make a choice that will lead to both desirable and undesirable results.

Aqueous Humor The clear fluid that fills the front chamber of the eye.

Archetypes Jung's concept of images or patterns for thought, feelings, and behavior that reside in the collective unconscious.

Artificial Intelligence The creation of computer programs that enable computers to solve problems either by using algorithms or by simulating human thought processes.

Assimilation The process of responding to a new situation in the same manner that is used in a familiar situation.

Association Areas The areas in the cerebral cortex that are involved in such mental operations as thinking, memory, learning, and problem solving.

Attachment An active, intense, emotional relationship between two people that endures over time.

Attitude Evaluative response to a person, object, or situation; these responses include cognitive, affective, and behavioral components.

Attributes Characteristics such as color, shape, and size that can change from one stimulus to another.

Attribution Theory Theory that describes the principles people follow in making judgments about the causes of events, others' behavior, and their own behavior.

Auditory Canal A tubelike structure into which sound is channeled by the pinna.

Auditory Nerve The cranial nerve that carries auditory information from the hair cells to the brain.

Authoritarian Personality Personality type that includes traits of rigidity, conventionality, and sadism; these traits are said to predispose the individual toward prejudice.

Autism An abnormal condition in which an individual becomes immersed in fantasy to avoid communicating with others.

Autokinetic Effect The perceived motion of a single stationary light in the dark.

Autonomic Nervous System (ANS) A subdivision of the peripheral nervous system that maintains normal functioning of glands, heart muscles, and the smooth muscles of the blood vessels and internal organs.

Autonomy Versus Shame and Doubt Erikson's second psychosocial stage (from 12 months to 3 years), in which the child's crisis or challenge is to develop independence and self-assertion.

Aversion Therapy A classical conditioning technique used in behavior control in which the undesired behavior is paired with some kind of aversive, or intensely displeasing, stimulus.

Avoidance–Avoidance Conflict Conflict in which a person must choose between two or more alternatives that will both lead to undesirable results.

Axon A long tubelike structure attached to the neuron cell body that conveys impulses away from the cell body toward other neurons.

Axon Terminal Buttons Small structures at the ends of axons that release neurotransmitter chemicals.

Babbling An early stage of speech development in which infants emit virtually all known sounds of human speech.

Baby Biography A detailed journal or account of important changes in a child's development.

Basic Research Research conducted to study theoretical questions without trying to solve a specific problem.

Basilar Membrane The membrane in the cochlea that contains the hearing receptors.

Behavior Anything a person or animal does, feels, thinks, or experiences.

Behavior Therapy A group of techniques based on learning principles that are used to change maladaptive behaviors.

Behaviorism The school of psychology that focuses on objective or observable behaviors.

Beta Waves Brain waves associated with normal wakefulness.

Biofeedback A procedure in which people's biological functions are monitored and the results made known to them so that they can learn to control these functions.

Biological Therapy Therapy involving the application of drugs and other medical interventions intended to reduce symptoms associated with psychological disorders.

Bipolar Disorder An affective disorder characterized by manic episodes that alternate with normal feelings or with normal and depressed periods.

Bisexual An individual who engages in both heterosexual and homosexual relations.

Blaming the Victim The act of placing blame on an individual who suffers from an injustice. It involves the belief that bad things happen to people because they deserve it.

Blind Spot A part of the retina containing no receptors; the area where the optic nerve exits the eye.

Body Senses The senses that include the skin senses of pressure, warmth and cold, and pain; the vestibular sense of balance; and the kinesthetic sense of body position and movement.

Brain An extremely complex mass of nerve tissue organized into structures that control all voluntary and much involuntary behavior.

Brain Stem An area of the brain below the subcortex and in front of the cerebellum that includes the pons, the medulla, and the reticular formation.

Brainstorming A group problem-solving technique in which participants are encouraged to generate as many unique solutions to a problem as possible by building upon other's ideas and disregarding whether the solutions are practical.

Brightness Constancy The phenomenon in which objects tend to maintain their appropriate brightness even when illumination varies.

Broca's Area A brain area found in the left frontal lobe that controls the muscles used to produce speech.

Bulimia Nervosa An eating disorder in which enormous quantities of food are consumed (binges), followed by purges that are accomplished by laxatives or vomiting.

Cannon–Bard Theory Theory that the thalamus responds to emotion-arousing stimuli by sending messages simultaneously to the cerebral cortex and the autonomic system. In this view, all emotions are physiologically similar.

Cardinal Traits In Allport's theory, a pervasive, all-encompassing personality characteristic that seems to influence most areas of a person's life. Cardinal traits are relatively uncommon and are observed in only a few people.

Care Perspective An approach to moral reasoning proposed by Carol Gilligan that emphasizes interpersonal responsibility and views people in terms of their interconnectedness with others.

Carpentered Environment Hypothesis The idea that the perceptions of industrialized people are influenced by having grown up in a world of constructed objects that have numerous horizontal and vertical lines and right angles.

CAT (Computerized Axial Tomography) Scan X-ray pictures of internal organs and different parts of the brain that are clearer and more accurate than normal X rays.

Catharsis In psychoanalytic theory, the release of tensions and anxieties through the reliving of a traumatic incident.

Case Study An in-depth study of a single research subject.

Central Nervous System (CNS) The part of the nervous system that consists of the brain and the spinal cord.

Central Traits For Allport, a small number of traits that are highly characteristic of a given individual and easy to infer.

Cephalocaudal Development A general pattern of physical growth in which the greatest growth occurs first in the region of the head and later in lower regions.

Cerebellum The brain area responsible for the maintenance of smooth movement for coordinated motor activity.

Cerebral Cortex The bumpy, convoluted area on the outside surface of the brain that contains primary sensory centers, motor control centers, and areas responsible for higher mental processes.

Chromosomes Microscopic threadlike structures in the nucleus of every living cell; they carry genes, the transmitters of inheritance.

Chronic Pain Long-lasting pain that often is recurring.

Chronobiology The study of biological rhythms.

Chunking The process of grouping information into units in order to be able to store more information in short-term memory.

Ciliary Muscles Muscles attached to the lens that stretch and relax it in order to focus images on the retina.

Circadian Rhythm Biological changes that occur on a 24-hour cycle.

Clairvoyance The ability to perceive objects or events that are inaccessible to the normal senses.

Classical Conditioning Learning a response to a neutral stimulus when that neutral stimulus is paired with a stimulus that causes a reflex response.

Client-Centered Therapy A type of psychotherapy developed by Carl Rogers that emphasizes the client's natural tendency to become healthy and productive; specific techniques include empathy, unconditional positive regard, and genuineness.

Clinical Psychologists A psychologist with an advanced graduate degree who specializes in treating psychological and behavioral disturbances or who does research on such disturbances.

Closure The Gestalt principle proposing that people have a tendency to perceive a finished unit even if there are gaps in it.

Cochlea The inner ear structure that contains the receptors for hearing.

Coding The process that converts a particular sensory input into a specific sensation.

Cognition The mental activities involved in acquiring, storing, retrieving, and using knowledge; it includes such mental processes as perceiving, learning, remembering, using language, and thinking.

Cognitive Behavior Therapy A therapy that helps clients change the way they think as well as the way they behave.

Cognitive Consistency Theory Theory that people have a strong need to feel that their attitudes match and are in harmony with one another.

Cognitive Dissonance Theory Festinger's theory that tension is experienced whenever one discovers that he or she has inconsistent (nonmatching) thoughts or cognitions, and that this tension drives the individual to make attitudinal changes that will restore harmony or consistency.

Cognitive Labeling Theory Theory that the cognitive (thinking), subjective (evaluating), and physiological arousal components are all necessary to emotional experiences.

Cognitive Learning Theory The idea that learning involves more than an observable response, that often the learning that occurs involves thought processes that may not be directly observed or objectively measured.

Cognitive Map A mental image of a maze or an area that a person or animal has navigated.

Cognitive Psychology A school of psychology that focuses on reasoning and the mental processing of information.

Cognitive Therapy Therapy that focuses on faulty thought processes and beliefs to treat problem behaviors.

Cohort Effects Statistical differences between research groups as a result of their specific histories rather than because of genuine age differences.

Cohort-Sequential Research A technique of data collection in which groups of people are repeatedly tested over time while new cohorts are added to allow age comparisons.

Collective Unconscious Jung's concept of an inherited portion of the unconscious that all humans share.

Color Aftereffects Color images that are seen after staring at a particular colored pattern for a long time.

Color Constancy The tendency for the color of objects to be perceived as remaining the same even when illumination varies.

Community Mental Health (CMH) Centers Federally supported treatment centers providing outpatient services for psychological disorders.

Companionate Love A strong feeling of attraction to another person characterized by trust, caring, tolerance, and friendship. It is believed to provide an enduring basis for long-term relationships.

Compliance A form of social influence in which individuals change their behavior in response to direct requests from others.

Concept A mental structure used to categorize things that share similar characteristics.

Conception The fertilization of the female ovum or egg by the male sperm.

Concrete Operational Stage The third of Piaget's stages of cognitive development (ages 7 to 11), during which the child develops the ability to think logically but not abstractly.

Conditioned Emotional Response (CER) Any classically conditioned emotional response to a previously neutral stimulus.

Conditioned Response (CR) A learned response to a previously neutral stimulus that has been associated with stimulus through repeated pairings.

Conditioned Stimulus (CS) A previously neutral stimulus that, through conditioning, now causes a classically conditioned response.

Conditioning The type of learning involving stimulus–response connections, in which the response is conditional on the stimulus.

Cones Receptors in the retina that respond to color and fine detail.

Confederate An accomplice of the experimenter who pretends to be another subject.

Conflict A negative emotional state caused by an inability to choose between two or more incompatible goals or impulses.

Conformity A type of social influence in which individuals change their attitudes or behavior to adhere to the expectations of others or the norms of groups to which they belong or wish to belong.

Conscious In Freudian terms, thoughts or information one is currently aware of or is remembering.

Consciousness The external stimuli and internal events that we are aware of at any given moment, as opposed to mind, which is the sum of past consciousness.

Conservation The principle that a given quality, weight, or volume remains constant despite changes in shape, length, or position.

Constancy The tendency for the environment to be perceived as remaining the same even with changes in sensory input.

Contiguity The Gestalt principle stating that when two events happen at a time and place near to each other, one is perceived as causing the other.

Contingency Model Fiedler's theory that suggests the effectiveness of leaders depends on the favorableness of the situation and the specific style of the leader (either task or relationship oriented).

Continuity The Gestalt principle proposing that patterns or objects that continue in one direction, even if interrupted by another pattern, tend to be perceived as being grouped together.

Continuous Reinforcement Reinforcement in which every response is reinforced.

Control Condition A condition in an experiment in which subjects are treated identically to subjects in the experimental condition, except that the independent variable is not applied to them.

Conventional Level Kohlberg's second level of moral development, where moral judgments are based on compliance with the rules and values of society.

Convergence A binocular depth cue in which the closer the object, the more the eyes converge, or turn inward.

Convergent Thinking The type of thinking needed when there is only one correct answer or solution to a problem.

Coping Attempting to manage stress in some effective way.

Cornea The transparent bulge at the front of the eye where light enters.

Corpus Callosum A connecting bridge of nerve fibers between the left and right hemispheres of the cerebral cortex.

Correlations Relationships between variables.

Counterconditioning A procedure that replaces an anxiety response to a stimulus with a pleasure or relaxation response.

Countertransference In psychoanalysis, the analyst's experience of transferring his or her feelings and perceptions of previous relationships onto the patient.

Covert Hidden or unobservable.

Covert Sensitization Cognitive approach used in behavior control in which the individual learns to associate and aversive stimulus with the undesired behavior.

Creativity The ability to originate solutions to a problem that are also practical and useful.

Credibility Degree of trustworthiness or expertise that is associated with a particular source of persuasion.

Critical Period An optimal or sensitive time in development when the organism is most easily affected by environmental events.

Cross-Sectional Method A technique of data collection that measures individuals of various ages at one point in time and gives information about age differences.

Crowding Negative psychological experience of being overstimulated by a larger number of people than you prefer.

Crystallized Intelligence A largely cultural and educationally related intelligence that involves general knowledge, vocabulary, and the application of knowledge.

Cue A stimulus that can begin a retrieval process from long-term memory.

Cultural Bias The tendency of a test to give a lower score to a person from a culture different from the culture on which the test was standardized.

Dark Adaptation Visual adjustment that increases the sensitivity of the rods and cones and allows us to see better in dim light.

Daydreaming An alternate state of consciousness characterized by internal reverie or inwardly focused thought.

Debriefing Explaining the research process to subjects who participated.

Decay Theory The theory that memory, like all biological processes, deteriorates with the passage of time.

Defense Mechanisms In psychoanalytic theory, unconscious strategies used by the ego to attempt to avoid anxiety and resolve conflict. These mechanisms are commonly used and only cause serious problems when they are excessively used.

Deindividuation Being so caught up in a group identity that individual self-awareness and responsibility are temporarily suspended.

Deinstitutionalization A practice, begun in the 1960s and accelerated in the 1980s, of releasing patients from mental hospitals.

Delta Waves Brain waves associated with the deepest level of sleep (stages 3 and 4).

Delusions Mistaken beliefs maintained in spite of strong evidence to the contrary.

Dendrites Branching neuron structures that receive neural impulses from other neurons and convey impulses toward the cell bodies.

Density Actual number of people in a given physical space.

Dependent Variable A measurable behavior that is exhibited by a subject and is affected by the independent variable.

Depressants Psychoactive drugs that act on the central nervous system to suppress or slow down bodily processes and reduce overall responsiveness.

Depth Perception The ability to see the world in three dimensions.

Designer Drugs Drugs produced by slightly altering the molecular structure of psychoactive drugs, thereby creating a new drug that has similar effects.

Detached Retina A disconnection of the retina from the back of the eye, which causes total or partial blindness of that eye.

Developmental Psychology The branch of psychology that involves describing, explaining, predicting, and modifying age-related behaviors from conception to death. This field emphasizes maturation, early experiences, and various stages in development.

Diagnostic and Statistical Manual of Mental Disorders (DSM) A classification system, developed by a task force of the American Psychiatric Association, used to describe abnormal behaviors.

Dichromat A person having the type of color weakness in which only two types of cones are present, rather than the normal three.

Difference Threshold The smallest magnitude of difference in stimulus energy that a person can detect.

Diffusion of Responsibility When people are in groups of two or more, there is a tendency toward less individual responsiveness due to the assumption that someone else will take action (or responsibility).

Disconfirmed Expectancies The tension (dissonance) that is felt when one's expectations are not fulfilled, and the corresponding tendency to justify one's losses by rearranging original attitudes to match the outcome.

Discrepant Behavior The tension (dissonance) that is experienced when one becomes aware that one's behavior does not match one's attitudes.

Discrimination 1. The process whereby a subject learns to differentiate one stimulus from others that are similar because that stimulus is the only CS that is paired with the UCS. 2. Negative behaviors directed at members of an outgroup.

Disengagement Theory A theory of aging that suggests that successful aging involves a natural and mutual withdrawal, in which both the individual and society gradually pull away from each other as a preparation for death.

Dissociation A splitting or separating of consciousness. Under hypnosis, one part of consciousness seems to be aware and observing hypnotic suggestions, while a separate type of consciousness is responding to the suggestion.

Dissociative Disorder Stress-related disorder characterized by amnesia, fugue, or multiple personality.

Distal-Proximo Physical development in an outer to inner direction, such that peripheral development outdistances that along the central axis.

Distributed Practice A learning technique in which practice sessions are interspersed with rest periods.

Divergent Thinking The type of thinking needed when it is necessary to generate as many ideas as possible.

Dominant Genes In the process of genetic transmission, a dominant gene is one that exerts its full characteristic effect regardless of its gene partner.

Dopamine Hypothesis A theory suggesting that schizophrenic episodes occur when there is an abundance of dopamine or an oversensitivity to its effects.

Double-Blind Experiment An experiment in which neither the subject nor the experimenter knows which treatment is being given to the subject or to which group the subject has been assigned.

Double Standard The belief that different rules for sexual behavior should be applied to men and women.

Drive-Reduction Theory Theory that motivation begins with a physiological need (a lack or deficiency) that elicits a psychological energy or drive directed toward behavior that will satisfy the original need.

Drug Therapy Use of chemicals to treat physical and psychological disorders.

Dual-Coding Hypothesis The theory proposing that information is encoded into two separate but interacting systems: an imagery system for concrete items and pictures and a verbal system for abstract ideas and spoken and written words.

Dual-Coding System The process of coding information by both visual and verbal means.

Dyslexia An inability or difficulty in reading.

Eardrum (Tympanic Membrane) A membrane located between the auditory canal and the middle ear that vibrates in response to sound waves.

Eclectic Approach An approach to psychotherapy in which the therapist freely borrows from various theories to find the appropriate treatment for his or her client.

Ectomorph Sheldon's term for the tall, thin, fragile individual who is believed to be fearful, introverted, and restrained.

Efferent Outgoing motor information.

Ego In psychoanalytic theory, the rational part of the psyche that deals with reality and attempts to control the impulses of the id, while also satisfying the social approval and self-esteem needs of the superego.

Ego Integrity Versus Despair During this eighth and final stage in Erikson's theory of psychosocial development, adults review their accomplishments and feel either satisfaction or regret.

Egocentrism The inability to consider another's point of view or perspective, which Piaget considered a hallmark of the preoperational stage. In terms of mental disorders, preoccupation with one's own concerns and insensitivity to the needs of others.

Eidetic Imagery The ability to recall memories—especially visual memories—that are so clear they can be viewed like a clear picture; photographic memory.

Ejaculation The discharge of semen from the penis at orgasm.

Electra Complex The Freudian term for the sexual attachment of a girl to her father and her desire to replace her mother.

Electroconvulsive Shock (ECS) Electrical shock applied to the brain such that it causes convulsions.

Electroconvulsive Therapy (ECT) Passage of electrical current through the brain as a therapy technique.

Electrodes Small devices (normally wires) to conduct electricity to or from brain tissue.

Electroencephalograph (EEG) A machine that monitors large changes in brain activity with electrodes that are attached to a person's scalp. Recordings of these on sheets of paper are known as electroencephalograms.

Electromagnetic Spectrum The band of radiant energy generated by the sun; visible light is only a small part of this spectrum.

Electromyograph (EMG) Biofeedback device that can measure muscle tension by recording the amount of electrical activity in an area of skin to which electrodes are attached.

Embryonic Period The second stage of pregnancy (from uterine implantation to the eighth week), characterized by development of major body organs and systems.

Emotion A feeling or affective response.

Emotion-Focused Forms of Coping Coping strategies that lead to changes in one's perceptions of stressful situations.

Empathy In Rogerian terms, an insightful

awareness and ability to share another person's inner experience.

Empty Nest Syndrome A painful separation and depression that parents supposedly feel when their last child leaves home.

Endocrine System A system of glands that, by releasing bodily chemicals into the bloodstream, is responsible for distributing chemical information throughout the body to effect behavioral change or to maintain normal bodily functions.

Endomorph Sheldon's term for the soft, round, large-stomached individual who is believed to be sociable, relaxed, and affectionate.

Endorphins Morphinelike chemicals occurring naturally in the brain that can lessen pain responses.

Environmental Psychology Branch of applied social psychology that focuses on the relationship between psychological processes and the physical environment.

Envy Thoughts and feelings that arise when one's personal qualities, possessions, or achievements do not measure up to those of someone relevant to us.

Epinephrine Hormone secreted by the adrenal glands in response to messages from the hypothalamus. Secretion is associated with emotional arousal, especially fear and anger.

Episodic Memory A type of long-term memory in which memories for events are stored.

Equity Theory The theory that people are highly motivated to seek a fair share of the rewards and that they prefer a balanced relationship.

Erectile Dysfunction The inability to get or maintain an erection firm enough for intercourse.

Erogenous Zones The areas of the body that elicit sexual arousal when stimulated.

Essential Hypertension State of chronically elevated blood pressure that has no detectable medical cause.

Estrogens Hormones that stimulate maturation and functioning of the female reproductive system.

Eugenics The biosocial movement endorsing the selection of certain human traits of the species.

Evaluation The final stage in problem-solving during which hypotheses are appraised to see whether they satisfy the conditions of the goal as it was defined in the preparation stage.

Excitement Phase The first phase of the sexual response cycle, characterized by increasing levels of muscle tension and contraction and increased amounts of blood concentration in the genitals.

Experiment A carefully controlled scientific procedure conducted to determine whether certain variables manipulated by the experimenter have an effect on other variables.

Experimental Condition The condition in an experiment in which the independent variable is applied to the subjects.

Experimenter Bias The tendency of experimenters to influence the results of a research study in the expected direction.

Extinction During operant conditioning, the elimination of maladaptive behaviors by removing the rewards that were previously connected with them. During classical conditioning, the gradual unlearning of a behavior or a response that occurs when a CS is repeatedly presented without the UCS with which it had been previously associated.

Extrasensory Perception (ESP) Perceptual, or "psychic," abilities that go beyond the "known" senses, including telepathy, clairvoyance, procognition, and telekinesis.

Extrinsic Rewards External reinforcers that often work to undermine personal interest, enjoyment, and satisfaction since the person is doing it for someone else.

Facial Feedback Hypothesis Proposal that movements of the facial muscles produce emotional reactions.

Factor Analysis A mathematical procedure used to determine the basic units or factors that constitute personality or intelligence.

False Consensus Bias Tendency to believe that other people think and believe like you do more than they actually do.

Family Therapy Group therapy method that attempts to assist families to function more effectively.

Feature Detectors Specialized cells in the brain that respond only to certain sensory information.

Feedback Knowledge of the results of a particular response.

Fetal Alcohol Syndrome A combination of birth defects, including organ deformities and mental, motor, and/or growth retardation, that results from maternal alcohol abuse.

Fetal Period The third, and final, stage of prenatal development (8 weeks to birth), characterized by rapid weight gain in the fetus and the fine detailing of body organs and systems.

Figure and Ground A Gestalt law of perceptual organization stating that our perceptions consist of two aspects: the figure, which stands out and has a definite contour or shape, and the ground, which is more indistinct.

Fixed Interval A schedule of reinforcement in which a subject is reinforced for the first response after a definite period of time has elapsed.

Fixed Ratio A partial schedule of reinforcement in which a subject must make a certain number of responses before being reinforced.

Flashbulb Memories Vivid images of circumstances associated with surprising or strongly emotional events.

Fluid Intelligence A relatively culture-free type of intelligence that includes pattern recognition, spatial orientation, memory, reasoning, and abstraction.

Forgetting The unlearning of a behavior due to continued withholding of the CS as well as the UCS.

Formal Operational Stage Piaget's fourth and final stage of cognitive development (age 11 and beyond), characterized by the ability to think logically, abstractly, and hypothetically.

Fovea The point on the retina containing only cones, where light from the center of the visual field is focused; the point responsible for our clearest vision.

Frame Cognitive pattern that describes which behaviors are appropriate in a given social context. Frames include both role expectations and scripts for interaction.

Fraternal Twins Twins that develop from two eggs fertilized at the same time. From the point of heredity, they are no more alike than ordinary siblings.

Free Association In psychoanalysis, reporting whatever comes to mind, regardless of how painful, embarrassing, or irrelevant it may seem. Freud believed that the first thing to come to a patient's mind was often an important clue to what the unconscious mind wants to conceal.

Frequency The number of sound pressure waves per second; perceived as the pitch of a sound.

Freudian Slips Seemingly unintended errors in speech, memory, or behavior, thought to reveal unconscious motivational forces.

Frontal Lobes The cortical lobes located at the front of the brain whose functions include motor and speech control, the ability to plan ahead, initiative, and self-awareness.

Frontal Lobotomy Surgical alterations of the frontal lobes performed to treat psychological disorders.

Frustration An unpleasant state of tension, anxiety, and heightened sympathetic activity resulting from the blocking or thwarting of a goal.

Frustration-Aggression Hypothesis Idea that aggression is always a consequence of frustration and that frustration always leads to some form of aggression.

Functional Disorders Abnormal symptoms with psychological causes or for which no physical cause is known.

Functional Fixedness A barrier to problem solving that occurs when people are unable to recognize novel uses for an object because they are so familiar with its common usage.

Functionalism The psychological school that investigates the function of mental processes in adapting the individual to the environment.

Fundamental Attribution Error A mistake in judging the causes of others' behavior that comes from the tendency to overestimate internal, personal factors and underestimate external, situational influences.

Gain–Loss Theory The idea that increased attraction will result when we receive unexpected approval or liking from others and that attraction will decrease in the face of a loss of initial liking.

Gate-Control Theory of Pain The idea that pain sensations are processed and altered by mechanisms within the spinal cord.

Gender The stage of being male or female.

Gender Role The set of behaviors that a given culture expects of each sex.

Gender Schema Theory A theory developed by Sandra Bern that suggests that children learn gender-specific behaviors and that cognitive processes help them to interpret gender-related information.

General Adaptation Syndrome As described by Selye, a generalized physiological reaction to severe stressors consisting of three phases: the alarm reaction, the resistance phase, and the exhaustive phase.

Generalization A tendency to respond in the same way to stimuli in the environment that have similar characteristics.

Generalized Anxiety Disorder Type of long-term anxiety that is not focused on any particular object or situation.

Generativity Versus Stagnation The seventh stage in Erikson's theory of psychosocial development. To avoid stagnation, the adult must "generate" or give something back to the world beyond the concern and care for the immediate family.

Genes The basic unit for the transmission of hereditary information.

Genital Stage The stage of psychosexual development that begins in puberty and represents mature adult sexuality and personality development.

Genuineness In Rogerian terms, authenticity or congruence; the awareness of one's true inner thoughts and feelings and being able to share them honestly with others.

Germinal Period The first stage of pregnancy (conception to 2 weeks), characterized by rapid cell division.

Gestalt An organized whole or pattern of perception.

Gestalt Psychology A school of psychology that focuses on principles of perception and insists that the whole experience is qualitatively different from the total of each distinct element of the experience.

Gestalt Therapy Form of group therapy that obtains insights into one's current thoughts, feelings, and body sensations through the use of awareness exercises.

Grafenburg Spot A region in the front wall of the vagina that supposedly has a special sensitivity to erotic stimulation.

Grammar The rules of a language that specify how phonemes, morphemes, words, and phrases should be combined to express meaningful thoughts.

Grief Feelings of desolation, loneliness, and painful memories associated with loss, disaster, or misfortune.

Group In social psychology, two or more people who are interacting with one another and providing reciprocal influence on one another's behavior.

Group Polarization Tendency for a group decision to become either more cautious or more risky than an individual decision, depending on the preexisting dominant tendencies of the group.

Groupthink Condition in which a highly cohesive group with a strong desire for agreement leads to uncritical consensus and faulty decision making.

Guilt Induction Method of gaining compliance based on the tendency for people to comply when they feel remorse for wrong behavior.

Gustation The sense of taste.

Habituate To become less responsive to a stimulus as the result of repeated exposure.

Habituation The tendency of the brain to ignore environmental factors that remain constant.

Hair Cells Auditory receptors in the cochlea.

Hallucinations Sensory perceptions that occur in the absence of a real external stimulus.

Hallucinogens Drugs that produce visual, auditory, or other sensory hallucinations.

Hassles Minor daily hassles that, when they mount up, can be a major source of stress.

Health Psychology The study of the relationship between psychological behavior and physical health and illness, with an emphasis on wellness and the prevention of illness.

Heart Disease General term used to include all disorders that in some way affect the heart muscle and can ultimately result in heart failure.

Heuristics Problem-solving strategies using techniques that generally work; they involve selective searches for an appropriate solution to a problem and, although less time-consuming than algorithms, may or may not lead to a solution.

Hierarchy Ranked listing of something; used in the behavior therapy systematic desensitization process.

Hierarchy of Needs Maslow's view of motivation; that some motives (such as physiological and safety needs) have to be satisfied before advancing to higher needs (such as belonging and self-esteem).

Higher-Order Conditioning Classical conditioning in which a neutral stimulus is paired with a second stimulus that already causes a learned or conditioned response.

Homeostasis Balance or equilibrium of the internal environment, which is accomplished through constant adjustments of the nervous system.

Homophobia Irrational fears of homosexuality; the fear of the possibility of homosexuality in oneself, or self-loathing toward one's own homosexuality.

Homosexual A person who has a primary sexual preference for members of his or her own sex.

Hormones Chemicals manufactured within the body that are circulated in the bloodstream to produce bodily changes or to maintain normal bodily functions.

Hue The visual dimension seen as a particular color; determined by the length of a light wave.

Humanistic Psychology A school of psychology that emphasizes the importance of the inner, subjective self and stresses the positive side of human nature.

Humanistic Therapy Therapy approaches that assist individuals to become creative and unique persons through affective restructuring processes.

Hyperopia Farsightedness; the eye is shorter than normal and the image falls behind its ideal position on the retina.

Hypertension Excessive muscular tension and high blood pressure.

Hypnogogic State A state of consciousness at the beginning of sleep in which many people experience visual, auditory, and kinesthetic sensations.

Hypnosis An alternate state of heightened suggestibility characterized by relaxation and intense focus.

Hypothalamus A subcortical group of neuron cell bodies lying below the thalamus that ultimately controls the endocrine system and is responsible for the regulation of drives such as hunger, thirst, sex, and aggression.

Hypothesis A question or a possible explanation for a behavior being studied that can be answered or affirmed by an experiment or a series of observations.

Id In psychoanalytic theory, the reservoir of psychic energy and instincts that perpetually presses us to satisfy our basic needs.

Identical Twins Twins who share the same genetic inheritance as the result of the splitting of an already fertilized egg.

Identity Crisis According to Erikson, a period of inner conflict during which an individual examines his or her life and values and makes decisions about life roles.

Identity Versus Role Confusion Erikson's fifth stage of psychosocial development; the adolescent may become confident and purposeful through discovery of an identity, or may become confused and ill-defined.

Illusion A false impression of the environment.

Illusory Correlation The erroneous perception of a correlation between two characteristics that does not, in fact, exist.

Implicit Personality Theory Schema or pattern of unstated assumptions about which personality traits "go with" each other and which ones do not.

Imprinting The innate tendency of birds and some animals to follow and form attachment to the first moving object they see.

Incentive Theory Theory that motivation results from environmental stimuli that "pull" the organism in certain directions, as opposed to internal needs that drive the organism in certain directions.

Incubation A period of time during which active searching for a problem's solution is set aside; this is sometimes necessary for a successful solution of the problem.

Independent Variable A variable that is controlled by the experimenter and is applied to the subject to determine its effect.

Industry Versus Inferiority Erikson's fourth psychosocial stage of development (ages 6 to 11), in which the child faces the challenge of mastering the skills needed to succeed in his or her culture.

Information-Processing Approach An approach to studying mental processes that views people and computers in similar terms, as processors of information that has been gathered from the environment, then encoded for memory storage and retrieval.

Informational Social Influence Social influence produced by providing others with information.

Ingratiation Use of favors, flattery, and statements of shared similarities as a method of gaining increased attraction and compliance.

Initiative Versus Guilt The third stage in Erikson's psychosocial theory of development (ages 3 to 6), in which the child must overcome feelings of guilt and doubt and develop feelings of power and initiative.

Innate Referring to any inborn behavior that emerges during a predetermined period of an organism's life as a result of maturation only and not as a result of practice.

Insanity A legal term for those with a mental disorder that implies a lack of responsibility for their behavior and an inability to manage their affairs in a competent manner.

Insight 1. In psychoanalysis, a bringing in of awareness of motives, relationships, feelings, or impulses that had previously been poorly understood or of which the subject was totally unaware. 2. A sudden flash of understanding that occurs when one is trying to solve a problem.

Instincts Behavioral patterns that are (1) unlearned, (2) uniform in expression, and (3) universal in a species.

Intelligence The capacity to solve problems and to readily adapt to a changing environment.

Intelligence Quotient (IQ) A score on a test that is intended to measure verbal and quantitative abilities. On the Stanford–Binet Intelligence Test, the IQ is the ratio of mental age to chronological age, times 100.

Interference Task Any task that prevents maintenance rehearsal or prevents memories from being transferred to long-term memory.

Interference Theory The theory that claims we forget something because other information blocks its storage or retrieval.

Internal Locus of Control The belief that one has significant control over the events in one's life.

Interposition A monocular depth cue in which the object that partially obscures another object is seen as being closer.

Interpretation A psychoanalyst's explanation of the significance of a patient's free associations and dreams.

Intimacy Versus Isolation Erikson's sixth stage in his theory of social development; the young adult must develop a capacity for close interpersonal bonds or face isolation and loneliness.

Intrinsic Rewards Internal, personally satisfying reinforcers that motivate individuals to perform certain activities because of personal enjoyment and interest.

Insomnia A sleep disorder in which a person has repeated difficulty in falling asleep, or staying asleep, or awakens too early.

Introspection A research method popular during the late nineteenth century in which trained subjects reported their current conscious experience.

Ions Molecules that carry positive or negative electrical charges.

Iris The colored part of the eye consisting of muscles that control the size of the pupil.

James–Lange Theory Theory that emotion is the perception of one's own bodily reactions and that each emotion is physiologically distinct.

Jealousy Thoughts and feelings that arise when an actual or desired relationship is threatened.

Justice Perspective Gilligan's term for an approach to moral reasoning that emphasizes individuals' rights and views people as differentiated and standing alone.

Kinesthesis The sensory system that provides information on body posture and orientation.

Landmark Events Events that are important to us, such as high school graduation or getting married, that can be used as an aid in memory.

Language A creative form of expression in which sounds and symbols are combined according to specified rules.

Language Acquisition device (LAD) In Noam Chomsky's view, the child's inborn brain capacity to analyze language and unconsciously understand essential grammatical rules.

Latency Stage Freud's fourth psychosexual stage (age 6 to puberty), characterized by the relative lack of sexual interests.

Latent Content The true, unconscious meaning of a dream, according to Freudian dream theory.

Latent Learning Learning that occurs in the absence of a reward and remains hidden until some future time when it can be retrieved.

Lateral Hypothalamus (LH) Area of the hypothalamus responsible for stimulating eating behavior.

Leader Member of a group who has the greatest amount of power or social influence or who contributes the most toward group goals.

Learned Helplessness In Seligman's theory, a state of helplessness or resignation in which people or animals give up and quietly submit to punishment that they have previously been unable to escape.

Learned Motives Motives that are acquired through direct experience with rewards and punishments, or through the observation of others. These motives include the needs for affiliation, power, achievement, and so on.

Learning A relatively permanent change in behavior or behavioral potential as a result of practice or experience.

Lens The transparent elastic structure in the eye that focuses light on the retina by changing shape.

Lesion Techniques Any brain research technique that systematically destroys brain tissue to observe the effect of the destruction on behavior.

Levels of Processing The depth to which short-term memory contents are processed during consolidation to long-term memory.

Life Structure According to Levinson, the internal and external aspects of an individual's psychosocial development that are built up during the four eras of development and modified during periods of transition.

Light Adaptation The visual adjustment of the rods and cones that reduces sensitivity to bright light.

Light and Shadow A monocular depth cue in which brighter objects are perceived as closer, whereas darker, dimmer objects are perceived as farther away.

Limbic System An interconnected system of mainly subcortical brain structures involved with many types of emotional behavior, particularly aggression. The brain structures making up the limbic system include the hypothalamus, the fornix, the hippocampus, the amygdala, the septum, parts of the thalamus, and parts of the frontal and temporal lobes of the cerebral cortex.

Linear Development The idea that development progresses in a fairly straight line, at a steady rate, and that each new development is built on the previous stages or abilities.

Linear Perspective The principle that as parallel lines recede, they appear to come together at the horizon.

Lock and Key Theory The idea that each odor molecule will fit into only one type of smell receptor cell according to shape.

Long-Term Memory (LTM) A relatively permanent memory in which information is stored for use at a later time.

Longitudinal Method A data collection technique that measures a single individual or group of individuals over an extended period of time and gives information about age changes.

Maintenance Rehearsal The process of repeating the contents of short-term memory over and over to maintain it in STM.

Major Depression A lasting and continuous state of depression without apparent cause.

Maladaptive Functioning Approach An approach that evaluates behavior as abnormal when it interferes with an individual's functioning within his or her own life and within society.

Male Climacteric A term used to describe the physical and psychological changes associated with the male's movement into midlife.

Malleus The first of the ossicles, attached to the eardrum and the incus.

Manifest Content The surface content of a dream, containing dream symbols that distort and disguise the true meaning of the dream, according to Freudian dream theory.

Marital Therapy Marriage counselling that attempts to improve the interactions of a married couple.

Massed Practice A learning technique in which time spent learning is massed into long, unbroken intervals; cramming.

Maturation Changes in development that result from automatic, genetically determined signals.

Medical Model Perspective that assumes abnormal behaviors reflect a type of mental or physical illness.

Meditation A relaxed state of consciousness that is characterized either by detachment from the external world or by directed focus on the external world.

Medulla A structure in the brain stem responsible for automatic body functions, such as respiration.

Menopause The gradual cessation of menstruation that occurs between the ages of 45 and 55; sometimes referred to as the climacteric or change of life.

Mental Housecleaning Hypothesis A theory suggesting that the function of dreaming is to rid the brain of useless, bizarre, or redundant information.

Mental Images Mental representatives of objects and events that are not physically present; they are used during the thinking process to solve problems, express ideas, and so on.

Mesomorph Sheldon's term for the strong, athletic, and muscular individual who is said to be energetic, competitive, and aggressive.

Method of Loci A mnemonic device in which an idea is associated with a place or a part of a building.

Method of Word Association A memory method in which verbal associations are created for items to be learned.

MI (Magnetic Imaging) A research technique utilizing radio waves instead of X rays to allow researchers to see structures within the brain.

Midlife Crisis A time of psychological and emotional turmoil that supposedly occurs around the age of 35 for women and 40 for men.

Mnemonic Devices Memory strategies in which information is organized or "tagged" visually or verbally.

Modeling Learning by imitating the behaviors of others.

Monochromat A person who is truly color-blind because he or she has only rods and no cones.

Morpheme The smallest meaningful unit of language, formed from a certain combination of phonemes.

Motion Parallax A monocular depth cue that occurs when a moving observer perceives that objects at various distances move at different speeds across the retinal field.

Motivated Forgetting Theory The theory that people forget things that cause pain, threat, or embarrassment.

Motivation Goal-directed behavior.

Motor Control Area The area located at the back of the frontal lobes of the cortex that is responsible for instigating voluntary movements.

Multiple Personality Dissociative disorder characterized by the presence of two or more distinct personality systems with the same individual.

Multiple Requests Compliance technique in which a first request is used as a "setup" for later requests.

Myelin Fatty insulation that serves to greatly increase the speed at which an action potential moves down an axon.

Myelination The accumulation of myelin (a fatty tissue that coats the axons of nerve cells) in the nervous system, thereby increasing the speed of neural messages.

Myopia Nearsightedness; the eye is longer than normal and the image falls in front of the ideal position on the retina.

Narcolepsy A disease marked by sudden and irresistible onsets of sleep during normal waking hours.

Naturalistic Observation The systematic recording of behavior in the subjects's natural state or habitat.

Need Complementary The tendency to seek out and be attracted to people whose qualities we admire but personally lack.

Negative Punishment Punishment in which a rewarding stimulus is removed or taken away and the response rate decreases.

Negative Reinforcement Reinforcement in which a painful or annoying stimulus is taken away.

Neo-Freudians Contemporaries of Freud who both supported and criticized his theory.

Nerve A bundle of axons that have a similar function.

Neuron Individual nerve cells responsible for transmitting information throughout the body.

Neurosis Nonpsychotic mental disorders (usually related to anxiety) that seriously disrupt an individual's daily life but still allow moderate functioning.

Neurotransmitters Special chemicals released from axon terminal buttons that cross the synapse and bind to receptor sites on the membrane of another neuron.

Neutral Stimulus An external stimulus that does not ordinarily cause a reflex response or an emotional response.

Night Terrors Abrupt awakenings from NREM sleep accompanied by intense physiological arousal and feelings of panic.

Nightmares Anxiety-arousing dreams that generally occur near the end of the sleep cycle and during REM sleep.

Non-Rapid Eye Movement (NREM) Sleep Sleep stages 1 through 4, which are marked by an absence of rapid eye movements, relatively little dreaming, and variations in EEG activity.

Norm Unwritten rule of behavior that prescribes what is acceptable or approved in a given situation.

Normative Social Influence Group pressure based on threats to reject group members who do not accept the positions of the group.

Obedience A type of social influence in which one individual follows direct commands, usually from someone in a position of authority.

Object Permanence The understanding that objects (or people) continue to exist even when they are out of sight or disappear from view. This ability gradually develops between 6 and 18 months of age.

Observational Learning Theory The idea that we learn certain behaviors merely by watching someone else perform them.

Obsessive-Compulsive Disorder (OCD) Type of anxiety disorder characterized by persistent thoughts and repetitive, ritualistic behaviors.

Occipital Lobes The cortical lobes located at the back of the brain that are dedicated entirely to vision and visual perception.

Oedipus Complex The Freudian term for the sexual attachment of a boy to his mother and his desire to replace his father.

Olfaction The sense of smell.

Olfactory Epithelium The mucus-coated membrane lining the top of the nasal cavity and containing the receptors for smell.

Operant Conditioning Learning that occurs when a response to an environmental cue is reinforced.

Operation A set of rules for manipulating or transforming information.

Opponent-Process Theory The theory of color vision first proposed by Ewald Hering that claims that there are three color systems — blue-yellow, red-green, and black-white.

Opponent-Process Theory of Emotions Idea that an intense emotional experience elicits an opposite (opposing) emotion. With repeated experiences, the second emotion becomes stronger than the first.

Optic Nerve The cranial nerve that carries visual information from the retina to the brain.

Optimal Level of Arousal Idea that there is an ideal or optimal level of excitement that is maintained through the body's need for homeostasis in stimulus seeking.

Oral Stage Freud's psychosexual stage (from birth to 12–18 months) during which the mouth is the center of pleasure and feeding is an important source of conflict.

Organic Mental Disorders Temporary or permanent physical effects on the nervous system resulting in abnormal behavior.

Orgasm Phase The third phase of the sexual response cycle, during which pleasurable sensations peak and the body suddenly discharges its accumulated sexual tension in the process of orgasm or climax.

Orgasmic Dysfunction The inability to respond to sexual stimulation to the point of orgasm.

Ossicles Three small bones in the middle ear; the malleus, the incus, and the stapes.

Oval Window The membrane of the cochlea that is moved by the motions of the stapes.

Overgeneralize A common error in a child's language acquisition where the rules for past tense and plurals are extended to irregular forms.

Overt Observable, not concealed.

Panic Disorders Type of anxiety disorder characterized by severe attacks of exaggerated anxiety.

Papillae Small bumps on the surface of the tongue that contain the taste receptors.

Paranoia A mental disorder characterized by delusions, or mistaken beliefs, or persecution or grandeur.

Parasympathetic Nervous System The part of the autonomic nervous system that is normally dominant when a person is in a relaxed, nonstressful physical and mental state, and that restores the body to its "status quo" after sympathetic arousal.

Parietal Lobes The lobes of the cerebral cortex located at the top of the brain that contain the major projection areas for body sensation.

Parkinson's Disease A neurological disorder characterized by rigidity, tremor, and difficulty in controlling movements, believed to be caused by a dopamine deficiency.

Partial Reinforcement Reinforcement in which some, but not all, responses are reinforced.

Passive Aggressiveness A subtle form of aggression characterized by pouting, procrastination, stubbornness, or intentional inefficiency.

Peg-Word Mnemonic System A memory system in which peg words, or easy-to-visualize words in a specific order, are associated with difficult-to-remember words or numbers.

Perception The process of selecting, organizing, and interpreting sensory data into usable mental representations of the world.

Performance Anxiety A fear that one will be unable to meet the expectations for sexual "performance" of one's self or one's partner.

Peripheral Nervous System (PNS) The part of the nervous system outside the central nervous system that consists of the nerves going to and from the brain and spinal cord.

Personal Narrative A research technique based on an individual's recounting of his or her life story while the psychologist elaborates on the narrative with professional interpretations.

Personal Space Immediate physical space that surrounds each individual and is treated as if it were an extension of the self.

Personal Unconscious Jung's concept of unconscious memories created from one's own experiences.

Personality An individual's characteristic pattern of thought, emotions, and behaviors, which make him or her unique.

Personality Disorders A DSM-III category that includes antisocial personality and other maladaptive traits.

Persuasion Direct attempts to influence the attitudes of another through communication techniques.

PET (Positron Emission Tomography) Scan A type of brain scan in which radioactive glucose is injected into the bloodstream in order to see brain activity in an intact, living brain.

Phallic Stage Freud's psychosexual stage (ages 3 to 6) during which the child experiences either the Oedipus or Electra complex, which can only be resolved through identification with the same-sex parent.

Phenomenological Perspective The view that understanding another person requires knowing how he or she perceives the world. The term comes from philosophy, where the mental experiencing of the environment is called a phenomenon, and the study of how each person experiences reality is phenomenology.

Pheromones Bodily chemicals that affect others' behavior.

Phobia Mental disorder characterized by exaggerated fears of an object or situation.

Phoneme The most basic unit of speech; an individual speech sound.

Photo Receptors Receptors for vision, the rods and cones.

Phrenology Pseudoscience that measures the skull to determine personality characteristics.

Physical Attractiveness Having the physical properties (size, shape, facial characteristics, and so on) that elicit favorable evaluations from others.

Physical Dependence A condition in which bodily processes have been so modified by repeated use of a drug that continued use is required to prevent withdrawal symptoms.

Pinna The fleshy part of the outer ear that we think of as "the ear."

Pitch The highness or lowness of tones or sounds, depending on their frequency.

Placebo A substance that would normally produce no physiological effect that is used as a control technique, usually in drug research.

Plateau Phase The second phase of the sexual response cycle, characterized by maintenance and intensification of sexual tensions.

Pleasure Principle According to Freud, the id's strategy of seeking immediate and uninhibited pleasure and avoiding discomfort.

Polydrug Use The combining of several drugs, which results in unknown and potentially serious side effects.

Polygraph Instrument that measures emotional arousal through various physiological reactions, such as heart rate, blood pressure, respiration rate, and electrodermal skin response.

Pons A brain structure located at the top of the brain stem that is involved with functions such as respiration, movement, and sleep.

Population The total of all possible cases from which a sample is selected.

Positive Punishment Punishment in which an aversive or undesirable stimulus is applied or added to decrease a response.

Positive Reinforcement Reinforcement in which a stimulus is given or added that is desirable to the subject.

Post-Decision Dissonance The tension (dissonance) that is felt once a decision is made, and the corresponding need to look for confirming evidence and to avoid contradictory information.

Post-Traumatic Stress Disorder (PTSD) Type of anxiety disorder that follows an overwhelming, traumatic event.

Postconventional Level Kohlberg's highest level of moral development, which occurs when individuals develop personal standards for right and wrong.

Precognition The ability to predict the future.

Preconscious Freud's term for thoughts or information one can become aware of easily.

Preconventional Level Kohlberg's first level of moral development, characterized by moral judgments based on fear of punishment or desire for pleasure.

Prejudice A negative attitude directed toward some people because of their membership in a specific group.

Premature Ejaculation Ejaculation that takes place too quickly for the pleasure of one or both partners.

Premenstrual Syndrome (PMS) A loose cluster of symptoms that supposedly occurs in some women just prior to menstruation.

Prenatal Development Changes that occur from the point of conception to the moment of birth.

Preoperational Stage The second of Piaget's stages (ages 2 to 7), characterized by the child's ability to employ mental symbols, to engage in fantasy play, and to use words. Thinking is egocentric and animistic and the child cannot yet perform operations.

Preparation The first stage in problem solving, in which the given facts are identified, relevant facts are distinguished from irrelevant facts, and the ultimate goal is identified.

Primary Aging Gradual changes in physical and mental processes that inevitably occur with age.

Primary Motives Motives that arise from innate, biological needs, such as hunger, thirst, pain avoidance, and sleep.

Primary Reinforcers Stimuli that increase the probability of a response and whose value does not need to be learned, such as food, water, and sex.

Proactive Interference Effect that occurs when previously learned information interferes with new information.

Problem-Focused Forms of Coping Coping strategies in which one views stressful situations as problems and uses problem-solving strategies to decrease or eliminate the source of stress.

Problem Solving A series of thinking processes that are used when we want to reach a goal that is not readily attainable.

Problem-Solving Set A mental barrier to problem solving that occurs when people apply only methods that have worked in the past rather than innovative ones for solving problems.

Production The problem-solving state during which possible solutions to the problem are generated.

Programmed Instruction Personalized learning that makes use of operant conditioning techniques, whereby students read a section of text, then test themselves on the material. They continue on to the next section or review the previous one, depending on the results of the test.

Projection Areas Any area in the brain that receives incoming sensory information.

Projective Tests Techniques for assessing personality in which the individual is asked to talk about a relatively ambiguous or neutral stimulus (such as an inkblot). It is believed that inner thoughts, feelings, and conflicts will be projected onto the stimulus.

Prototype A model or best example of items belonging to a particular category.

Proximity 1. The Gestalt principle proposing that elements that are physically close together will be grouped together and perceived as a single unit. 2. Physical closeness, a factor that leads to increased attraction.

Proximodistal Development A general pattern of physical growth in which development starts at the center of the body and moves toward the extremities.

Pseudopsychologies "False psychologies"; popular systems that pretend to discover psychological information through nonscientific or deliberately fraudulent methods.

Psychiatrists A medical doctor who has additional training in the diagnosis and treatment of mental illness.

Psychiatry The specialized branch of medicine dealing with the diagnosis, treatment, and prevention of mental disorders.

Psychoactive Drugs Drugs that affect the nervous system and cause a change in perception or mood.

Psychoactive Substance Use Disorders Problematic use of drugs affecting mental functioning, such as alcohol, barbiturates, and amphetamines.

Psychoanalysis 1. Sigmund Freud's theoretical school of thought, which emphasizes the study of unconscious processes. 2. A type of psychotherapy originated by Sigmund Freud that is designed to bring relief from anxiety created by unconscious desires and motives.

Psychoanalysts A mental health professional (usually a physician) who is trained to practice psychoanalysis.

Psychoanalytic Theory Freud's theory of personality that emphasizes the influence of the unconscious mind.

Psychobiology The study of the biology of behavior.

Psychodrama A diagnostic and therapeutic technique developed by J. L. Moreno that consists of having the individual act out on stage his or her relations with others around whom conflicts center.

Psychodynamic Pertaining to processes undergoing change or development.

Psychogenic Amnesia Inability to recall the personal past as a result of psychological stress.

Psychogenic Fugue A type of amnesia in which people suddenly leave where they live and assume a new identity.

Psychokinesis The ability to move or affect objects without touching them.

Psychological Dependence A desire or craving to achieve the effects produced by a drug.

Psychological Reactance Increased resistance to persuasion that is experienced when the recipient feels that his or her freedom to choose is threatened.

Psychological Theory Erikson's theory that individuals undergo a series of eight developmental stages and that adult personality reflects successful or unsuccessful resolution of the distinct challenges or crises at each stage.

Psychology The scientific study of behavior.

Psychophysics The study of the relationships between physical stimulation and the sensations evoked by such stimulation.

Psychosexual Stages In psychoanalytic theory, a developmental period in which individual pleasures must be gratified if personality development is to proceed normally.

Psychosis Serious mental disorder characterized by loss of contact with reality and gross personality distortions. Since daily functioning is generally impossible, hospitalization is ordinarily required.

Psychosurgery Operative procedures on the brain designed to relieve severe mental symptoms that have not responded to other forms of treatment.

Psychotherapy A general term for several methods of treating psychological disorders. All psychotherapies involve the application of psychological principles and techniques in an attempt to correct problems in thinking, emotion, or behavior.

Puberty The period in life during which the sex organs mature to a point where sexual reproduction becomes possible. Puberty generally begins for girls around 8 to 12 years of age, and for boys about two years later.

Punishment Any action or event that decreases the likelihood of a response being repeated.

Pupil An opening surrounded by the iris through which light passes into the eye.

Rapid Eye Movement (REM) Sleep A stage of sleep marked by rapid eye movements, high-frequency brain waves, and dreaming.

Rational-Emotive Therapy (RET) Cognitive therapy system developed by Albert Ellis to attempt to change the troubled person's belief system.

Reality Principle According to Freud, the principle on which the conscious ego operates as it tries to meet the demands of the unconscious id and the realities of the environment.

Recall Process of using a very general stimulus cue to search the contents of long-term memory.

Receptors Body cells specialized to detect and respond to stimulus energy.

Recessive Genes During genetic transmission, a recessive gene is one whose code is masked by a dominant gene and is only expressed when paired with another recessive gene.

Recognition Process of matching a specific stimulus cue to an appropriate item in long-term memory.

Redintegration The type of remembering that occurs when something unlocks a chain of memories.

Reference Groups Groups that we like and feel similar to and are therefore more likely to conform to.

Reflexes Unlearned, involuntary responses of a part of the body to an external stimulus that do not require input from the brain.

Refractory Period The period after orgasm during which further orgasm is considered physiologically impossible. This stage is believed to be absent in the female.

Reinforcement Any action or event that increases the probability that a response will be repeated.

Reinforcement Theory The theory that attraction results from a positive emotional arousal.

We like those who make us feel good and dislike those who make us feel bad.

Relative Size A monocular cue to distance in which smaller objects appear more distant than larger objects.

Relaxation Techniques Procedures used to relieve the anxiety and bodily tension accompanying such problems as stress and chronic pain.

Relearning Learning material a second time. Relearning usually takes less time than original learning.

Reliability A measure of the consistency and stability of test scores when the test is readministered over a period of time.

Repair Theory A theory suggesting that sleep serves a restorative function by allowing organisms to recuperate from physical, emotional, and intellectual demands.

Replicate To conduct a research study again, following the same procedure.

Repression Freud's most important defense mechanism that involves unconscious blocking of unacceptable impulses to keep them from awareness.

Research Methodologies Standardized scientific procedures for conducting investigations.

Resistance A stage in psychoanalysis where the patient avoids (resists) the analyst's attempts to bring unconscious material to conscious awareness.

Resolution Phase The final stage of the sexual response cycle, characterized by continued relaxation as the body returns to its unaroused state.

Resting Potential The resting state of the axon membrane, which consists of a high concentration of sodium molecules outside the axon and a high concentration of potassium and protein molecules inside the axon.

Reticular Activating System (RAS) A network of neurons in the brain stem that filters and selects sensory input to the cerebral hemispheres.

Reticular Formation A diffuse set of cells in the medulla, pons, hypothalamus, and thalmus that serves as a filter for incoming sensory information.

Retina An area at the back of the eye containing the rods and cones.

Retinal Disparity A binocular cue to distance in which the separation of the eyes causes different images to fall on each retina.

Retrieval Process of returning long-term memory contents to short-term memory for analysis or awareness.

Retrieval Failure Theory The theory that forgetting is a problem with retrieval, not a problem with long-term storage of information.

Retroactive Interference Effect that occurs when new information interferes with previously learned information.

Retrograde Amnesia Difficulty in remembering previously learned material.

Reverberating Circuits The firing of a set of neurons over and over again during memory processing.

Reversible Figure An ambiguous figure that has more than one possible figure and ground organization.

Reward Centers Areas in the brain that, when stimulated, invoke a highly satisfying feeling.

Rods Receptors in the retina that are most sensitive in dim light; they do not respond to color.

Role A category of people and the set of normative expectations for people in that category.

Romantic Love An intense feeling of attraction to another person that is characterized by high passion, obsessive thinking, and emotional fluctuation.

Rorschach Inkblot Test A projective personality test using ambiguous "inkblots." The individual tells the examiner what he or she sees in the blots and, it is hoped, reveals hidden aspects of his or her personality.

Saliency Bias The tendency to focus attention on vivid, salient factors when explaining the causes of behavior.

Sample A selected group of subjects that is representative of a larger population.

Sample Bias The tendency for the sample of subjects in a research study to be atypical of a larger population.

Schedule of Reinforcement A schedule delineating when a response is to be reinforced.

Schemata An individual's basic cognitive patterns for explaining the world.

Schizophrenia Group of psychotic disorders involving distortions in thinking, perception, emotion, and behavior.

Sclera The white, opaque outer wall of the eye.

Secondary Aging Acceleration in the normal physical changes associated with aging as a result of abuse, neglect, disuse, or disease.

Secondary Reinforcers Stimuli that increase the probability of a response and whose reinforcing properties are learned, such as money and material possessions.

Secondary Sex Characteristics Hormonally generated sexual characteristics, secondary to the sex organs, that are not necessary for reproduction.

Secondary Traits In Allport's theory, these traits are not as important as central traits for describing personality since they influence few situations or behaviors.

Selective Attention The process whereby the brain manages to sort out and attend only to the important messages from the senses.

Self-Actualization According to humanistic theories, an innate tendency toward growth that motivates all human behavior and results in the full realization of a person's highest potential.

Self-Fulfilling Prophecy A sequence in which an individual's or other's expectations lead to behaviors that cause the expected events to occur.

Self-Hypnosis An alternate state of consciousness induced by oneself during which one is more relaxed, more alert, and more open to suggestion than in the normal state.

Self-Perception Theory Bem's theory that people form attitudes by observing their own behavior.

Self-Serving Bias Way of maintaining a positive self-image by taking credit for one's successes and emphasizing external causes for one's failures.

Semantic Memory A type of long-term memory in which facts and relations between facts are stored.

Semicircular Canals Three arching structures in the inner ear that contain the hair receptors that provide balance information from head movements.

Sensation The process of receiving, translating, and transmitting information to the brain from the external and internal environments.

Sensorimotor Stage The first of Piaget's stages (birth to age 2), in which cognitive development is acquired through exploration of the world via sensory perceptions and motor skills.

Sensory Adaptation A decrease in response of a sensory system to repeated stimulation.

Sensory Deprivation A state in which all sensory stimulation is diminished as much as possible.

Sensory Memory The type of memory that occurs within the senses while incoming messages are being transmitted to the brain.

Serial Position Effect The effect that occurs when a person remembers the material at the beginning and the end of a list better than the material in the middle.

Set Point An organism's personal homeostatic level for a particular body weight that results from factors such as early feeding experiences and heredity.

Sex-Influenced Traits Traits that are governed by genes on the sex chromosomes but are expressed in the presence of other biological factors.

Sex-Linked Traits Traits that are inherited through genes found on the sex chromosomes.

Sex-Role Stereotypes Rigid, preconceived beliefs about the characteristics of males and females.

Sexual Dysfunction Conditions in which the normal physiological processes of arousal and orgasm are impaired.

Sexual Response Cycle Masters and Johnson's description of the bodily response to sexual arousal. The four stages are excitement, plateau, orgasm, and resolution.

Sexual Scripts Socially dictated descriptions of the sequences of behavior that are considered appropriate in sexual interactions.

Shape Constancy The process in which the

perceived shape of an object remains the same, even though the retinal image of that object changes.

Shaping During behavior therapy, target behaviors are acquired by rewarding successive approximations of the desired response.

Short-Term Memory (STM) Memory containing things a person is presently thinking about and having a capacity limited to about seven items and a duration of about 30 seconds.

Shotgun Approach The technique used in behavioral change whereby there is an attempt to change all the behaviors constituting the Type A personality.

Similarity 1. The Gestalt principle proposing that things that appear similar or act in a similar fashion are perceived as being the same. 2. A sharing of common interests, values, and beliefs — an important factor in long-term attraction.

Size Constancy The process in which the perceived size of an object remains the same, even though the size of the retinal image changes.

Skin Senses The sensory system for detecting pressure, temperature, and pain.

Sleep Apnea A temporary cessation of breathing during sleep; one of the causes of snoring and a suspected cause of sudden infant death syndrome.

Social Cognition Way of knowing and understanding others that involves internal, cognitive structures or patterns that are used as frameworks for organizing information.

Social Comparison Theory Festinger's view that we seek out others as a way to interpret and compare our own abilities, attitudes, and reactions.

Social Exchange Theory The theory that interpersonal interactions are governed by the costs and benefits each gives and receives.

Social Influence A change in behavior, perception, or attitude in the direction intended by another.

Social Learning Theory A theory developed by Bandura proposing that people learn various behaviors by observing others who serve as models.

Social Perception Process that explains how one comes to know and understand oneself and others.

Social Psychology The branch of psychology that studies how the thoughts, feelings, and actions of individuals are influenced by the actual, imagined, or implied presence of others.

Social Trap Dilemma created when individual short-term best interests conflict with long-term goals or group interests.

Social Workers Therapists who have obtained at least a master's degree in social work, and who typically work with patients and their families to ease their community relations.

Socialization The process of imparting the customs, habits, folkways, and mores of a given culture to a child or a newcomer to the society.

Sodium – Potassium Pump An ongoing process whereby sodium ions are continually moved out and potassium ions are continually moved into the axon to restore and preserve the resting potential.

Soma The cell body of the neuron; it integrates incoming information from the dendrites, absorbs nutrients, and produces the majority of the protein molecules needed by the neuron.

Somatic Nervous System A subdivision of the peripheral nervous system that consists of nerves carrying afferent sensory information and efferent motor information to and from the central nervous system, and sense organs, the skeletal muscles, and the skin.

Somatotypes Sheldon's theory that body shape is associated with distinct personality patterns.

Sound Waves The mechanical movement of air molecules produced by a vibrating object.

Source Traits Cattell's term for the basic personality traits he believed were shared by most individuals.

Spinal Cord The part of the nervous system found within the spinal column that is involved in reflexes and the relay of neural information to and from the brain.

Spontaneous Recovery The reappearance of a previously extinguished response.

Standardization The process of establishing the norms of a test in order to assess which skills, knowledge, or characteristics are representative of the general population. Also, the development of standard procedures for administering and scoring a test to ensure that the conditions are the same for everyone taking the test.

Stapes The last of the ossicles, attached to the incus and to the oval window.

State-Dependent Memory Memory that is connected to a state of emotional arousal.

Statistical Standard A standard that evaluates behavior as abnormal when it deviates from average behavior in that particular culture.

Statistically Significant A relationship believed not to be caused by chance.

Statistics Data collected in a research study and the procedures used to analyze data.

Stereoscopic Three-dimensional vision that is due to overlapping views of the eyes.

Stereotype A set of beliefs about the characteristics of people in a group that is generalized to all group members.

Stimulants Drugs that act on the brain and nervous system to increase their overall activity and general responsiveness.

Stimulus An object or event that stimulates an organism to respond.

Stimulus Control A technique used in behavior control in which the individual becomes aware of the stimuli leading to the undesired behavior in order to control them by such means as avoiding them or substituting other stimuli.

Stimulus-Seeking Motives Innate, internal needs for novel cognitive, physical, and emotional stimulation.

Storm and Stress The idea that emotional turmoil and rebellion are characteristic of all adolescents.

Stress According to Selye, the nonspecific response of the body to any demand made on it.

Stressor Any stimulus that causes stress.

Stroboscopic Motion The illusion of motion in which alternating lights are seen as one moving light.

Structuralism An early psychological school that focused on the sensation and feelings of perceptual experience.

Subjective Discomfort Approach An approach that evaluates behavior as abnormal when the individual is discontented with his or her own psychological function.

Subliminal Pertaining to any stimulus presented below the threshold of conscious awareness.

Substance Abuse Use of a psychoactive drug in ways that interfere with social or occupational functioning.

Substance Dependence Abuse of a psychoactive drug that includes the physical reactions of drug tolerance or withdrawal symptoms.

Superego In psychoanalytic theory, the part of the personality that incorporates parental and societal standards for morality.

Superordinate Goal Way of reducing prejudice that involves creating a goal that is "higher" than individual goals and that is of benefit to both parties.

Superstitious Behavior Behavior that is continually repeated because it is thought to cause desired effects, though in reality the behavior and the effects are totally unrelated.

Surveys Nonexperimental research techniques that sample behaviors and attitudes of a population.

Sympathetic Nervous System The part of the autonomic nervous system that dominates when a person is under mental or physical stress, and that mobilizes the body's resources toward "fight or flight."

Synapse The junction between two neurons where neurotransmitter passes from the axon of one neuron to the dendrite or soma of another.

Synergistic Effect The interaction of two or more drugs such that the combined effects are much stronger than a simple summation of their individual doses.

Syntax The grammatical rules that specify in what order the words and phrases should be arranged in a sentence in order to convey meaning.

Systematic Desensitization Behavior therapy counterconditioning technique used to extinguish a classically conditioned anxiety response through the use of a hierarchy and relaxation.

Tardive Dyskinesia Potential side effect of antipsychotic drugs; it includes effects on voluntary muscles.

Target Behavior Approach The technique used in behavioral change where there is an attempt to change only Type A behaviors that have specifically been found to lead to heart disease, particularly those accompanied by a hostile and cynical attitude.

Telegraphic Speech The two- or three-word sentences of young children that contain only the most necessary words.

Telepathy The ability to read other people's minds.

Temperament A basic, inborn dispositional quality that appears shortly after birth and characterizes an individual's style of approaching people and situations.

Temporal Lobes the cortical lobes whose functions include auditory perception, language, memory, and some emotional control.

Teratogen An external, environmental agent that may cross the placental barrier and disrupt development, causing minor or severe birth defects.

Territoriality Tendency to mark, maintain, or defend certain areas as one's own.

Texture Gradients Monocular cue to distance based on the fact that texture changes from coarse to fine as the distance of an object increases.

Thalamus A subcortical area located below the corpus callosum that serves as the major relay area for incoming sensory information.

Thanatology The study of death and dying. The term comes from *thanatos*, the Greek name for a mythical personification of death, and was borrowed by Freud to represent the death instinct.

Thematic Apperception Test (TAT) A projective personality test requiring subjects to tell stories about pictures shown on cards. Presumably, the subjects will "project" themselves into the story, and their narrative will reflect their hidden needs.

Thinking Using knowledge that has been gathered and processed; mentally manipulating concepts and images to perform such mental activities as reasoning, solving problems, producing and understanding language, and making decisions.

Thought Stopping Behavior therapy technique for extinguishing maladaptive self-talk.

Time Out Use of negative punishment through removal of people from sources of rewards whenever they behave inappropriately.

Tip-of-the-Tongue (TOT) The feeling that a word you are trying to remember is just barely inaccessible.

Token Tangible secondary (conditioned) reinforcer that can be exchanged for primary rewards.

Token Economy System Use of secondary (conditioned) reinforcer to reward adaptive behaviors.

Tolerance A decreased sensitivity to a drug such that larger and more frequent doses are required to produce the desired effect.

Trait An enduring predisposition to respond in a particular way, often distinguishing one individual from another. People can vary in their personality traits over a wide range of values.

Transactional Analysis (TA) Group therapy approach that identifies the use of ego-state styles.

Transduction The process by which energy stimulating a receptor is converted into neural impulses.

Transference The tendency of an individual in psychoanalysis to transfer his or her feelings and perceptions of a dominant childhood figure — usually a parent — to the psychoanalyst.

Transsexual An individual who is physically one sex but psychologically the opposite and has a persistent desire to change his or her body to that of the other sex.

Transvestite An individual who gains sexual satisfaction and relief from anxiety by dressing in the clothing of the other sex.

Trephining In modern usage, any surgical procedure in which a hole is bored into the skull. In ancient times, a type of therapy that involved deliberate chipping of holes into the skull to allow evil spirits to escape.

Trichromatic Theory The theory of color vision first proposed by Thomas Young stating that there are three color systems — red, green, and blue.

Trust Versus Mistrust The first of Erikson's eight stages of psychosocial development (from birth to 12–18 months), in which the infant must determine whether the world and the people in it can be trusted.

Type A Personality Set of behavior characteristics that includes intense ambition, competition, drive, constant preoccupation with deadlines, a sense of time urgency, and a cynical, hostile outlook.

Type B Personality Set of behavior characteristics consistent with a calm, patient, relaxed attitude toward life.

Typology A system used for classification of individuals according to certain criteria.

Unconditional Positive Regard Carl Roger's term for how we should behave toward someone to increase their self-esteem; positive behavior shown toward a person with no contingencies attached.

Unconditioned Response (UCR) The reflex response evoked by a stimulus without the necessity of learning.

Unconditioned Stimulus (UCS) Any stimulus that causes a reflex or emotional response without the necessity of learning or conditioning.

Unconscious Freud's term for thoughts or information shoved far beneath our level of awareness.

Validity The ability of a test to actually measure what it is intended to measure.

Variable Interval A schedule of reinforcement in which the subject is reinforced for the first response after a specified period of time has elapsed. This period of time varies from one reinforcement to the next.

Variable Ratio A schedule of reinforcement in which the subject is reinforced, on the average, for making a specific number of responses, but the number of required responses on each trial is varied.

Variables Factors that can be varied and can assume more than one value.

Ventromedial Hypothalamus (VMH) Area of the hypothalamus responsible for signaling the organism to stop eating. If destroyed, the organism will overeat and become obese.

Vestibular Sacs Inner ear structures containing hair receptors that respond to the specific angle of the head, to provide balance information.

Vestibular Sense The sense of how the body is oriented in relation to the pull of gravity; the sense of gravity.

Vicarious Conditioning Learning by watching a model or reading about a task.

Vitreous Humor A semiliquid gel that nourishes the inside of the eye and is responsible for maintaining the eye's shape.

Wavelength The length of a sound or light wave, measured from the crest of one wave to the crest of the next.

Wernicke's Area An area of the cerebral cortex responsible for the thinking and interpreting aspect of language production.

Withdrawal Symptoms Unpleasant, painful, or agonizing physical reactions resulting from discontinued use of a drug.

Zeigarnik Effect Process of working unconsciously on a problem until it is solved.

ABBEY, A. (1982). Sex differences in attributions for friendly behavior: Do males misperceive females' friendliness? *Journal of Personality and Social Psychology, 42,* 830–838.

ABELSON, R. P. (1981). Psychological status of the script concept. *American Psychologist, 36,* 715–729.

ABELSON, R. P. (1988). Conviction. *American Psychologist, 43,* 267–275.

ABELSON, R. P., Kinder, D. R., Peters, M. D., & Fiske, S. T. (1982). Affective and semantic components in political person perception. *Journal of Personality and Social Psychology, 42,* 619–630.

ABPLANALP, J. (1983). Premenstrual syndrome: A selective review. *Women and Health,* pp. 107–123.

ABRAHAM, S. F., & BEAUMONT, P. J. V. (1982). How patients describe bulimia or binge eating. *Psychological Medicine, 12,* 625–635.

ABRAMSON, L. Y., ALLOY, L. B., & METALSKY, G. I. (1990). The cognitive diathesis–stress theories of depression: Toward an adequate evaluation of the theories' validities. In L. B. Alloy (Ed.), *Cognitive processes in depression.* New York: Guilford.

ACHTIGAL, L. (1986, January 6). Premenstrual syndrome keeps doctors guessing. *New York Times,* p. 18 (N).

ADAM, G., & FAISZT, J. (1967). Conditions for successful transfer effects. *Nature 216,* 198–200.

ADAMS, V. (1980, May). Getting at the heart of jealous love. *Psychology Today,* pp. 42–50.

ADAMS-TUCKER, C. (1982). Proximate effects of sexual abuse in childhood: A report on 28 children. *American Journal of Psychiatry, 139,* 1252–1256.

ADDIEGO, F., BELZER, E. G., COMOLI, J., MOGER, W., PERRY, J. D., & WHIPPLE, B. (1981). Female ejaculation: A case study. *Journal of Sex Research, 17,* 13–21.

ADELMAN, P. K., & ZAJONC, R. B. (1989). Facial efference and the experience of emotion. In M. R. Rosenzweig & L. W. Porter (Eds.), *Annual Review of Psychology* (pp. 249–280). Palo Alto, CA: Annual Reviews Inc.

ADELSON, J. (1979, September). Adolescence and the generation gap. *Psychology Today,* pp. 33–37.

ADER, R., & COHEN, N. (1984). Behavior and the immune system. In W. D. Gentry (Ed.),

Handbook of behavioral medicine. New York: Guilford.

ADLER, A. (1964). The individual psychology of Alfred Adler. In H. L. Ansbacher & R. R. Ansbacher (Eds.), *The individual psychology of Alfred Adler.* New York: Harper & Row (Torchbooks).

ADLER, A. (1979). *Superiority and social interest: A collection of later writings* (3rd rev. ed.). Evanston, IL: Northwestern University Press.

ADLER, T. (1989, December). Integrity test popularity prompts close scrutiny. *APA Monitor,* p. 7.

ADORNO, T. W., FRENKEL-BRUNSWICK, E., LEVINSON, D. J., & SANFORD, R. N. (1950). *The authoritarian personality.* New York: Harper & Row.

AIDS and blood donation. (1988, September). *University of California, Berkeley Wellness Letter,* p. 7.

AINSWORTH, M. D. S. (1967). *Infancy in Uganda: Infant care and the growth of love.* Baltimore: Johns Hopkins University Press.

AINSWORTH, M. D. S., BLEHAR, M., WATERS, E., & WALL, S. (1978). *Patterns of attachment: Observations in the strange situation and at home.* Hillsdale, NJ: Lawrence Erlbaum Associates.

ALAM, N., & SMIRK, F. H. (1938). Blood pressure raising reflexes in health, essential hypertension, and renal hypertension. *Clinical Science, 3,* 259–266.

ALEAMONI, L. M., & OBOLER, L. (1978). ACT versus SAT in predicting first semester GPA. *Educational and Psychological Measurement, 38,* 393–399.

ALLEN, D. M. (1988). *Unifying individual and family therapies.* San Francisco: Jossey–Bass.

ALLGEIER, A. R., & ALLGEIER, E. R. (1988). *Sexual interactions* (2nd ed.). Lexington, MA: Heath.

ALLISON, T., & CICCHETTI, D. V. (1976). Sleep in mammals: Ecological and constitutional correlates. *Science, 194,* 732–734.

ALLPORT, G. (1937). *Personality: A Psychological interpretation.* New York: Holt, Rinehart & Winston.

ALLPORT, G. W. (1966). Traits revisited. *American Psychologist, 21,* 1–10.

ALLPORT, G. W., & ODBERT, H. S. (1936). Traitnames: A psycho-lexical study. *Psychologi-*

cal Monographs: General and Applied, 47, 1–21.

ALPER, J. (1986, June). When drugs work. *Science, 86,* 45–46.

ALTEMEYER, R. (1989). *Enemies of freedom: Understanding right wing authoritarianism.* San Francisco: Jossey–Bass.

ALTMAN, I. (1975). *The environment and social behavior.* Monterey, CA: Brooks/Cole.

ALZATE, H. (1985). Vaginal eroticism: A replication study. *Archives of Sexual Behavior, 14,* 529–537.

ALZATE, H., & LONDONO, M. L. (1984). Vaginal erotic sensitivity. *Journal of Sex and Marital Therapy, 10,* 49–56.

AMABILE, T. M. (1985). Motivation and creativity: Effects of motivational orientation on creative writers. *Journal of Personality and Social Psychology, 48,* 393–399.

AMATO, P. R. (1983). Helping behavior in urban and rural environments: Field studies based on a taxonomic organization of helping episodes. *Journal of Personality and Social Psychology, 45,* 571–586.

AMERICAN PSYCHIATRIC ASSOCIATION. (1987). *Diagnostic and statistical manual of mental disorders* (3rd ed. rev.). Washington, DC: Author.

AMERICAN PSYCHOLOGICAL ASSOCIATION. (1981). *Ethical principles of psychologists.* Washington, DC: Author.

AMERICAN PSYCHOLOGICAL ASSOCIATION. (1982). *Ethical principles in the conduct of research with human participants.* Washington, DC: Author.

AMERICAN PSYCHOLOGICAL ASSOCIATION. (1984). *Behavioral research with animals.* Washington, DC: Author.

AMIR, M. (1971). *Patterns of forcible rape.* Chicago: University of Chicago Press.

AMOORE, J. E. (1977). Specific anosmia and the concept of primary odors. *Chemical Senses and Flavor, 2,* 267–281.

AMOORE, J. E., JOHNSTON, W., JR., & RUBIN, M. (1964). The stereochemical theory of odor. *Scientific American, 210*(2), 42–49.

ANAND, B. K., & BROBECK, B. R. (1951). Localization of the feeding center in the hypothalamus of the rat. *Proceedings for the Society of Experimental Biology and Medicine, 77,* 323–324.

ANASTASI, A. (1982). *Psychological testing* (5th ed.). New York: Macmillan.

ANDERSON, C. A., LEPPER, M. R., & ROSS, L. (1980). Perseverance of social theories: The role of explanation in the persistence of discredited information. *Journal of Personality and Social Psychology, 39,* 1037–1049.

ANDERSON, K. J. (1983). The interactive effects of caffeine, impulsivity, and task demands on a visual search task. *Personality and Individual Differences, 4*(2), 127–134.

ANDREASEN, N. C. (1984). *The broken brain.* New York: Harper & Row.

ANDREASEN, N. C. (1985). Positive versus negative schizophrenia: A critical evaluation. *Schizophrenia Bulletin, 11,* 380–389.

ANDREASEN, N. C. (1988). Brain imaging: Applications in psychiatry. *Science, 239,* 1381–1388.

ANGELL, M. (1985, June 13). Disease as a reflection of the psyche. *New England Journal of Medicine,* pp. 16–24.

ANNIS, L. (1978). *The child before birth.* Ithaca, NY: Cornell University Press.

ANNIS, R. C., & FROST, B. (1973). Human visual ecology and orientation anisotropies in acuity. *Science, 182,* 729–731.

APPLE, W., STREETER, L. A., & KRAUSS, R. B. (1979). Effects of pitch and speech rate on personal attributions. *Journal of Personality and Social Psychology, 37,* 715–727.

AREHART-TREICHEL, J. (1979, December 1). Down's syndrome: The father's role. *Science News,* pp. 381–382.

AREND, R., GOVE, F. L., & SROUFE, L. A. (1979). Continuity of individual adaptation from infancy to kindergarten: A predictive study of ego-resiliency and curiosity in preschoolers. *Child Development, 50,* 950–959.

ARIES, P. (1962). *Centuries of childhood: A social history of family life.* New York: Random House.

Arlin, P. K. (1975). Cognitive development in adulthood: A fifth stage? *Developmental Psychology, 11,* 602–606.

ARLIN, P. K. (1980, June). *Adolescent and adult thought: A search for structures.* Paper presented at the meeting of the Piaget Society, Philadelphia.

ARLIN, P. K. (1984). Adolescent and adult thought: A structural interpretation. In M. L. Commons, F. A. Richards, & C. Armon (Eds.), *Beyond formal operations: Late adolescent and adult cognitive development* (pp. 239–252). New York: Praeger.

ARNOLD, M. B. (1984) *Memory and the brain.* Hillsdale, NJ: Lawrence Erlbaum Associates.

AROESTY, Z. S., DALY, M., DONG, J., & ROSEN, G. D. (1986). *AIDS in the workplace.* San Francisco: San Francisco AIDS Foundation.

ARON, A., & ARON, E. N. (1989). *The heart of social psychology: A backstage view of a passionate science.* Lexington, MA: D. C. Heath.

ARONSON, E. (1984). *The social animal* (4th ed.). New York: Freeman.

ARONSON, E. (1988). *The social animal* (5th ed.). New York: Harper & Row.

ARONSON, E., & LINDER, D. (1965). Gain and loss of esteem as determinants of interpersonal attractiveness. *Journal of Experimental Social Psychology, 1,* 156–171.

ARONSON, E., & O'LEARY, M. (1983). The relative effectiveness of models and prompts on energy conservation: A field experiment in a shower room. *Journal of Energy Conservation, 12,* 219–224.

ARONSON, E., & PINES, A. (1980). *Exploring sexual jealousy.* Paper presented at the meeting of the Western Psychological Association, Honolulu, HA.

ASCH, S. E. (1951). Effects of group pressure upon the modification and distortion of judgment. In H. Guetzkow (Ed.), *Groups, leadership, and men.* Pittsburgh: Carnegie Press.

ASCH, S. E. (1956) Studies of independence and conformity: A minority of one against a unanimous majority. *Psychological Monographs, 70*(9, Whole No. 416).

ASERINSKY, E., & KLEITMAN, N. (1953). Regularly occurring periods of eye motility and concomitant phenomena during sleep. *Science, 118,* 273–274.

ASHER, J. (1987, April). Born to be shy? *Psychology Today,* pp. 56–64.

ASHTON, N. L., & SHAW, M. E. (1980). Empirical investigations of a reconceptualized personal space. *Bulletin of the Psychonomic Society, 15,* 309–312.

Ask me no questions. (1988, June 20). *Time,* p. 31.

ASTIN, A. W., GREEN, K. C., KORN, W. S., & SCHALIT, M. (1986). *The American freshman: National norms for fall 1986.* Los Angeles: University of California at Los Angeles, Higher Education Research Institute.

ASTIN, A. W., GREEN, K. C., & KORN, W. S. (1987). *The American freshman: Twenty year trends.* Los Angeles: University of California at Los Angeles, Higher Education Research Institute.

ATKINSON, R. C., & SHIFFRIN, R. M. (1968). Human memory: A proposed system and its control processes. In K. W. Spence and J. T. Spence (Eds.), *The psychology of learning and motivation* (Vol. 2). New York: Academic Press.

AVERILL, J. R. (1969). Autonomic response patterns during sadness and mirth. *Psychophysiology, 5*(4), 399–414.

AYLLON, R., & AZRIN, N. H. (1968). *The token economy.* New York: Appleton–Century–Crofts.

AYLLON, T. (1963). Intensive treatment of psychotic behavior by stimulus satiation and food reinforcement. *Behavior Research and Therapy, 1,* 33–61.

AYMAN, D., & GOLDSHINE, A. D. (1939). The breath holding test: A simple standard stimulus of blood pressure. *Archives of Internal Medicine, 63,* 899–906.

BACH, J. S. (1988). *Drug abuse: Opposing viewpoints.* St. Paul, MN: Greenhaven Press.

BACHMAN, J. G. (1971). *Youth looks at national problems: A special report from the youth in transition project.* Ann Arbor, MI: University of Michigan, Institute for Social Research.

BACHMAN, J. G., JOHNSTON, L. P., & O'MALLEY, P. M. (1981). *Monitoring the future: Questionnaire responses from the nation's high school seniors, 1980.* Ann Arbor, MI: University of Michigan, Institute of Social Research.

BACHMAN, J. G., JOHNSTON, L. P., & O'MALLEY, P. M. (1987). *Monitoring the future: Questionnaire responses from the nation's high school seniors, 1986.* Ann Arbor, MI: University of Michigan, Institute of Social Research.

BADDELEY, A. (1981). The concept of working memory: A view of its current state and probable future development. *Cognition, 10,* 17–23.

BAENNINGER, R. (1974). Some consequences of aggressive behavior: A selective review of the literature on other animals. *Aggressive Behavior, 1*(1), 17–37.

BAHRICK, H. P., BAHRICK, P. O., & WITTLINGER, R. P. (1974, December). Long-term memory: Those unforgettable high school days. *Psychology Today,* pp. 50–56.

BAILLARGEON, R. (1982, March). *Object permanence in the five-month-old infant.* Paper presented at the International Conference on Infant Studies, Austin, TX.

BAIRD, J. C. (1982). The moon illusion. II. A reference theory. *Journal of Experimental Psychology: General, 111,* 304–315.

BAIRD, J. C., & WAGNER, M. (1982). The moon illusion. I. How high is the sky? *Journal of Experimental Psychology: General, 111,* 296–303.

BALDESSARINI, R. J. (1988). Update on antipsychotic agents. *Harvard Medical School Mental Health Letter, 4*(10), 4–6.

BALDESSARINI, R. J. (1990). Update on antidepressants. *Harvard Medical School Mental Health Letter, 6*(7), 4–6.

BALDWIN, A. L. (1949). The effect of home environment on nursery school behavior. *Child Development, 20,* 49–61.

BALES, J. (1988, July). Bill reigning in polygraphs takes legislative fast track. *APA Monitor,* p. 17.

BANDURA, A. (1969). *Principles of behavior modification.* New York: Holt, Rinehart & Winston.

BANDURA, A. (1971). *Social learning theory.* New York: General Learning Press.

BANDURA, A. (1973). *Aggression: A social learning analysis.* Englewood Cliffs, NJ: Prentice–Hall.

BANDURA, A., REESE, L., & ADAMS, N. (1982). Microanalysis of action and fear arousal as a function of differential levels of perceived self-efficacy. *Journal of Personality and Social Psychology, 43*(1), 5–21.

BANDURA, A., & WALTERS, R. H. (1963). *Social*

learning and personality development. New York: Holt, Rinehart & Winston.

BARAHAL, H. S. (1958). 1000 prefrontal lobotomics: Five-to-ten-year follow-up study. *Psychiatric Quarterly, 32,* 653–678.

BARBACH, L. G. (1975). *For yourself: The fulfillment of female sexuality.* New York: Doubleday.

BARBACH, L. G. (1982). *For each other: Sharing sexual intimacy.* Garden City, NY: Anchor Press.

BARBER, T. X. (1969). *Hypnosis: A scientific approach.* New York: Van Nostrand.

BARBER, T. X. (Ed.). (1976). *Advances in sheltered states of consciousness and human potentialities* (Vol. 1.). New York: Psychological Dimensions.

BARD, C. (1934). On emotional expression after decortication with some remarks on certain theoretical views. *Psychological Review, 41,* 309–329.

BARDWICK, J. (1971). *Psychology of women: A study of biocultural conflicts.* New York: Harper & Row.

BARNES, C. A. (1980). Spatial memory and hippocampal synaptic plasticity in middle-aged and senescent rats. In D. Stein (Ed.), *The psychobiology of aging: Problems and perspectives* (pp. 253–272). Amsterdam: Elseiver.

BARNES, D. M. (1986). The biological tangle of drug addiction. *Science, 241,* 415–417.

BARNETT, P. E., & BENEDETTI, D. T. (1960, May). *A study in "vicarious conditioning."* Paper presented at the annual meeting of the Rocky Mountain Psychological Association, Glenwood Springs, CO.

BARON, R. A. (1983). The reduction of human aggression: An incompatible response strategy. In R. G. Geen & Donnerstein (Eds.), *Aggression: Theoretical and empirical reviews.* New York: Academic Press.

BARON, R. A., & BYRNE, D. (1984). *Social psychology: Understanding human interaction* (4th ed.). Boston: Allyn & Bacon.

BARRY, H. (1982). Cultural variations in alcohol abuse. In I. Al-Issa (Ed.), *Culture and psychopathology* (pp. 43–58). Baltimore: University Park Press.

BARRY, H., & PAXSON, L. M. (1971). Infancy and early childhood: Cross-cultural codes. *Ethnology, 10,* 467–508.

BARTLETT, F. C. (1958). *Thinking.* London: Allen & Unwin.

BASOW, S. A. (1986). *Gender stereotypes: Traditions and alternatives* (2nd ed.). Monterey, CA: Brooks/Cole.

BATSON, J., et al. (1989). Five studies testing two new egoistic alternatives to the empathy-altruism hypothesis. *Journal of Personality and Social Psychology, 55,* 52–77.

BAUM, A., GRUNBERG, N. E., & SINGER, J. E. (1982). The use of psychological and neuroendocrinological measurements in the study of stress. *Health Psychology, 1,* 217–236.

BAUMAN, D. J., CIALDINI, R. B., & KENRICK, D. T. (1981). Altruism as hedonism: Helping and self-gratification as equivalent responses. *Journal of Personality and Social Psychology, 40,* 1039–1046.

BAUMAN, K. E., FISHER, L. A., BRYAN, E. S., & CHENOWETH, R. L. (1985). Relationship between subjective expected utility and behavior: A longitudinal study of adolescent drinking behavior. *Journal of Studies on Alcohol, 46,* 32–38.

BAUMRIND, D. (1980). New directions in socialization research. *American Psychologist, 35,* 639–652.

BAUMRIND, D. (1983). Rejoinder to Lewis's reinterpretation of parental firm control effects: Are authoritative families really harmonious? *Psychological Bulletin, 94,* 132–142.

BAUMRIND, D. (1985). Research using intentional deception: Ethical issues revisited. *American Psychologist, 40,* 165–174.

BAUMRIND, D. (1986). Sex differences in moral reasoning: Response to Walker's (1984) conclusion that there are none. *Child Development, 57,* 511–521.

BEACH, F. A. (1977). *Human sexuality in four perspectives.* Baltimore: Johns Hopkins University Press.

BEAMAN, A. L., COLE, C. M., PRESTON, M., KLENTZ, B., & STEBLAY, N. M. (1983). Fifteen years of foot-in-the-door research: A meta-analysis. *Personality and Social Psychology Bulletin, 9,* 181–196.

BEAMAN, A. L., & KLENTZ, B. (1983). The supposed physical attractiveness bias against supporters of the women's movement: A meta-analysis. *Personality and Social Psychology Bulletin, 9(4),* 544–550.

BEATTY, J. (1987). *Biological basis of behavior.* Chicago: Dorsey.

BECK, A. T. (1976). *Cognitive therapy and the emotional disorders.* New York: International Universities Press.

BECK, A. T. (1985). Cognitive therapy of depression: New perspectives. In P. Clayton (Ed.), *Depression* (pp. 295–323). New York: Raven Press.

BECK, A. T. (1989). *Love is never enough.* New York: Harper & Row.

BECK, A. T., & YOUNG, J. E. (1978, September). College blues. *Psychology Today,* pp. 80–92.

BECK, K. H., & FRANKEL, A. (1981). A conceptualization of threat communication and protective health behavior. *Social Psychology Quarterly, 44,* 204–217.

BECKWITH, C. (1983, October). Niger's Wodaabe: "People of the taboo." *National Geographic, 164(4).*

BELL, A. P., WEINBERG, M. S., & HAMMERSMITH, S. K. (1981). *Sexual preference: Its development in men and women.* Bloomington, IN: Indiana University Press.

BELLEZZA, F. S. (1982). Updating memory using mnemonic devices. *Cognitive Psychology, 14,* 301–327.

BEM, D. J. (1972). Self-perception theory. In L. Berkowitz (Ed.), *Advances in experimental social psychology* (Vol. 6). New York: Academic Press.

BEM, D. J., & ALLEN, A. (1974). On predicting some of the people some of the time: The search for cross-situational consistencies in behavior. *Psychological Review, 81,* 506–520.

BEM, S. L. (1974). The measurement of psychological androgyny. *Journal of Consulting and Clinical Psychology, 42(2),* 155–162.

BEM, S. L. (1981). Gender schema theory: A cognitive account of sex typing. *Psychological Review, 88,* 354–364.

BEM, S. L. (1985). Androgyny and gender schema theory: A conceptual and empirical integration. *Nebraska Symposium on Motivation, 32,* 179–226.

BENNE, K. D. (1964). History of the T-Group in the laboratory setting. In L. P. Bradford, Jr., J. Gibb, & K. Benne (Eds.), *T-group theory and laboratory method.* New York: Wiley.

BENNETT, E. L., & CALVIN, M. (1964). Failure to train planarians reliably. *Neurosciences Research Program Bulletin, 2,* 3–24.

BENNETT, W., & GURIN, J. (1982). *The dieter's dilemma: Eating less and weighing more.* New York: Basic Books.

BENSON, H. (1975). *The relaxation response.* New York: Morrow.

BENSON, H. (1977). Systematic hypertension and the relaxation response. *New England Journal of Medicine, 296,* 1152–1156.

BENSON, H. (1987). *Your maximum mind.* New York: Morrow.

BENSON, H. (1988). The relaxation response: A bridge between medicine and religion. *Harvard Medical School Mental Health Letter, 4(9),* 4–6.

BENSON, H., & WALLACE, R. K. (1972). Decreased drug abuse with transcendental meditation—A study of 1,862 subjects. In C. J. Zafronetis (Ed.), *Drug abuse: Proceedings of the international conference.* New York: Lea & Febiger.

BERGER, K. S. (1986). *The developing person through childhood and adolescence,* New York: Worth.

BERGER, K. S. (1988). *The developing person through the life-span.* New York: Worth.

BERGER, P. A. (1978). Medical treatment of mental illness. *Science, 200,* 974–81.

BERGLAS, S. (1985, February). Why did this happen to me? *Psychology Today,* pp. 44–48.

BERKHOUT, J. (1979). Information transfer characteristics of moving light signals. *Human Factors, 21,* 445–455.

BERKOWITZ, L. (1983). Aversively stimulated aggression: Some parallels and differences in research with animals and humans. *American Psychologist, 38,* 1135–1144.

BERKOWITZ, L. (1984). Human aggression. In N. S. Endler & J. McV. Hunt (Eds.), *Personality and the behavioral disorders* (2nd ed., Vol. 1). New York: Wiley.

BERKOWITZ, N. (1987). Balancing the statute of limitations and the discovery rule: Some victims of incestuous abuse are denied access to Washington courts — *Tyson* versus *Tyson. University of Puget Sound Law Review, 10,* 721.

BERLYNE, D. E. (1971). *Aesthetics and psychobiology.* New York: Appleton–Century–Crofts.

BERMAN, T., & PAISEY, T. (1984). Personality in assaultive and non-assaultive juvenile male offenders. *Psychological Reports, 54*(2), 527–530.

BERMAN, W. H. (1988). The role of attachment in the post-divorce experience. *Journal of Personality and Social Psychology, 54*(3), 496–503.

BERNARD, L. L. (1924). *Instinct.* New York: Holt.

BERNARDS, N. (1988). *Teenage sexuality: Opposing viewpoints.* St. Paul, MN: Greenhaven Press.

BERNE, E. (1964). *Games people play: The psychology of human relationships.* New York: Grove Press.

BERNE, E. (1966). *Principles of group treatment.* New York: Oxford University Press.

BERNHEIM, K. F., & LEWINE, R. R. J. (1979). *Schizophrenia: Symptoms, causes, and treatments.* New York: Norton.

BERREMAN, G. (1971). *Anthropology today.* Del Mar, CA: CRM Books.

BERRY, D. S., & MCARTHUR, L. Z. (1985). Some components and consequences of a babyface. *Journal of Personality and Social Psychology, 48*(2), 312–323.

BERSCHEID, E., GRAZIANO, W., MONSON, T., & DERMER, M. (1976). Outcome dependency: Attention, attribution and attraction. *Journal of Personality and Social Psychology, 34,* 978–989.

BERSCHEID, E., & WALSTER, E. H. (1978). *Interpersonal attraction* (2nd ed.). Reading, MA: Addison–Wesley.

BERSCHEID, E., & WALSTER, E. H. (1984). *Interpersonal attraction* (3rd ed.). New York: Random House.

BEXTON, W. H., HERON, W., & SCOTT, T. H. (1954). Effects of increased variation in the sensory environment. *Canadian Journal of Psychology, 8,* 70–76.

BIDDLE, W. (1986). The detection of deception. *Discover, 1*(3), 25–33.

BIEBER, I., DAIN, H. J., DINCE, P. R., DRELLICH, M. G., GRAND H. G., GUNDLACH, R. H., KREMER, M. W., RIFKIN, A. H., WILBUR, C. G., & BIEBER, T. B. (1982). *Homosexuality: A psychoanalytic study of male homosexuals.* New York: Basic Books.

BIGLAN, A., SEVERSON, H., ARAY, D. V., FALLER, C., et al. (1987). Do smoking prevention programs really work? Attrition and the internal and external validity of an evaluation of a refusal skills training program. *Journal of Behavioral Medicine, 10*(2), 159–171.

BIRNHOLZ, J. C., & BENACERRAF, B. R. (1983). The development of human fetal learning. *Science, 222,* 516–518.

BIRRIN, J. E. (1974). Psychophysiology and speed of response. *American Psychologist, 29,* 808–815.

BISHOP, M. P., ELDER, S. T., & HEATH, R. G. (1963). Intracranial self-stimulation in man. *Science, 140,* 394–396.

BLACK, D. W., WINOKUR, G., & NASRALLAH, A. (1987). The treatment of depression: Electroconvulsive therapy versus antidepressants: A naturalistic evaluation of 1,495 patients. *Comprehensive Psychiatry, 28,* 169–182.

BLAKEMORE, C., & COOPER, G. F. (1970). Development of the brain depends on the visual environment. *Nature, 228,* 477–478.

BLANCHARD, D. R., & BLANCHARD, R. J. (1988). Ethoexperimental approaches to the biology of emotions. In M. R. Rosenzweig & L. W. Porter (Eds.), *Annual Review of Psychology* (pp. 43–68). Palo Alto, CA: Annual Review Inc.

BLASI, A. (1980). Bridging moral cognition and moral action: A critical review of the literature. *Psychological Bulletin, 88,* 1–45.

BLASS, T. (1984). Interactionism. In R. J. Corsini (Ed.), *Encyclopedia of psychology* (Vol. 2, pp. 234–235). New York: Wiley.

BLAU, Z. S. (1973). *Old age in a changing society.* New York: New Viewpoints.

BLEIER, R. (1987, October). *Sex differences research in the neurosciences.* Paper presented at the annual meeting of the American Association for the Advancement of Science, Chicago.

BLEWITT, P. (1983). Dog versus collie: Vocabulary in speech to young children. *Developmental Psychology, 19,* 602–609.

BLISS, E. L. (1980). Multiple personalities: A report of 14 cases with implications for schizophrenia and hysteria. *Archives of General Psychiatry, 37,* 1388–1397.

BLOCK, J. (1982). Assimilation, accommodation, and the dynamics of personality development. *Child Development, 53,* 281–295.

BLOCK, N. J., & DWORKIN, G. (Eds.). (1976). *The IQ controversy.* New York: Pantheon.

BLOOM, B. (1985). *Developing talent in young people.* New York: Ballantine.

BLOOM, B. L., & CALDWELL, R. A. (1981). Sex differences in adjustment during the process of marital separation. *Journal of Marriage and the Family, 43,* 693–701.

BLOOM, F. E. (1983). The endorphins: A growing family of pharmacologically pertinent peptides. *Annual Review of Pharmacology & Toxicology, 23,* 151–170.

BLOOM, F. E., LAZERSON, A., & HOFSTADTER, L. (1985). *Brain, mind, and behavior.* New York: Freeman.

BLYTH, D. A., BULCROFT, R., & SIMMONS, R. G. (1981, August). *The impact of puberty on adolescents: A longitudinal study.* Paper

presented at the annual meeting of the American Psychological Association, Los Angeles.

BOGEN, J. E., FISHER, E. D., & VOGEL., P. J. (1965). Cerebral commissurotomy. *Journal of the American Medical Association, 194*(12), 1328–1329.

BOLLES, R. C. (1970). Species-specific defense reactions and avoidance learning. *Psychological Review, 77,* 32–48.

BOLLES, R. C. (1975). *Theory of motivation* (2nd ed.). New York: Harper & Row.

BONELLO, P. H. (1982, June). The Zeigarnik effect and the recall of geometric forms. *Dissertation Abstracts International, 42* (12-A), 5060.

BONICA, J. J. (1977). Introduction to symposium on pain. *Archives of Surgery, 112,* 749.

BOOTZIN, R. R. (1980). *Abnormal psychology: Current perspectives* (3rd ed.). New York: Random House.

BORBELY, A. (1986). *Secrets of sleep.* New York: Basic Books.

BOSS, P. G. (1985). Family stress: Perception and context. In M. Sussman & S. Steinmetz (Eds.), *Handbook of marriage and the family.* New York: Plenum.

BOSSARD, M. D., REYNOLDS, C. R., & GUTKIN, T. B. (1980). A regression analysis of test bias on the Stanford–Binet Intelligence Scale for black and white children referred for psychological services. *Journal of Clinical and Child Psychology, 9,* 52–54.

BOURGUIGNON, E. (1973). Introduction: A framework for the comparative study of altered states of consciousness. In E. Bourguignon (Ed.), *Religion, altered states of consciousness and social change.* Columbus, OH: Ohio State University Press.

BOURNE, L. E. (1974). An inference model of conceptual role learning. In R. Solso (Ed.), *Theories of cognitive psychology.* Hillsdale, NJ: Lawrence Erlbaum Associates.

BOURNE, L. E., DOMINOWSKI, R. L., & LOFTUS, E. F. (1979). *Cognitive processes.* Englewood Cliffs, NJ: Prentice–Hall.

BOWEN, D. J., & PETERSON A. V. (1988, August). *Comparisons of the smoking onset process for girls and boys.* Paper presented at the meeting of the American Psychological Association, Atlanta.

BOWER, B. (1985, September 14). Social channels tune TV effects. *Science News, 128,* 166. (a)

BOWER, B. (1985, November 16). "Day after" effects of pot smoking. *Science News,* p. 310. (b)

BOWER, B. (1988). Let there be more light. *Science News, 133,* 331. (a)

BOWER, B. (1988). Low-dose advantage for schizophrenics. *Science News, 134,* 196. (b)

BOWER, B. (1988). Lungs hit harder by pot than by cigarettes. *Science News, 133,* 120. (c)

BOWER, B. (1988). Stepping out of social phobias. *Science News, 133,* 331. (d)

BOWER, B. (1989). Deceptive successes in young children. *Science News, 135,* 343. (a)

BOWER, B. (1989). The diagnostic dilemma. *Science News, 135,* 120–122. (b)

BOWER, B. (1989). Drinking while pregnant risks child's IQ. *Science News, 135,* 68. (c)

BOWER, B. (1989). PET pictures produce a palette of anxiety. *Science News, 135,* 116–117. (d)

BOWER, G. H. (1976). Experiments on story understanding and recall. *Quarterly Journal of Experimental Psychology, 28,* 211–534.

BOWER, G. H. (1981, February). Mood and memory. *American Psychologist, 36*(2), 129–148.

BOWERS, K. (1983). *Hypnosis for the seriously curious.* New York: Norton.

BOWIE, W., & MacDONALD, N. (1989). Management of sexually transmitted diseases in Canada, 1989. *Canadian Medical Association Journal, 140,* 449–501.

BOWLBY, J. (1969). *Attachment and loss,* Vol. I: *Attachment.* New York: Basic Books.

BOWLBY, J. (1970). Disruption of affectional bonds and its effects on behavior. *Journal of Contemporary Psychotherapy, 2,* 75–86.

BOWLBY, J. (1973). *Attachment and loss,* Vol. II: *Separation and anxiety.* New York: Basic Books.

BOWLBY, J. (1982). Attachment and loss: Retrospect and prospect. *American Journal of Orthopsychiatry, 52,* 664–678.

BOWLBY, J. (1988). *A secure base: Parent-child attachment and healthy human development.* New York: Basic Books.

BOYNTON, R. M. (1988). Color vision. In M. R. Rosenzweig and L. W. Porter (Eds.), *Annual review of psychology* (pp. 69–100). Palo Alto, CA: Annual Reviews.

BRACKEN, B. A. (1985). A critical review of the Kaufman Assessment Battery for Children (K-ABC). *School Psychology Review, 14*(1), 21–36.

BRADFORD, L. P., GIBB, J. R., & BENNE, K. D. (1964). *T-group theory and laboratory method: Innovation in reeducation.* New York: Wiley.

BRADLEY, M. T., & AINSWORTH, D. (1984). Alcohol and the psychophysiological detection of deception. *Psychophysiology, 21*(1), 63–71.

BRAND, D. (1988, September 5). Dying with dignity. *Time,* pp. 56–58.

BRANSFORD, J. D. (1979). *Human cognition.* Belmont, CA: Wadsworth.

BRAY, J. H. (1988). Children's development during early remarriage. In E. M. Hetherington & J. D. Arasteh (Eds.), *Impact of divorce, single-parenting, and step-parenting on children* (pp. 279–298). Hillsdale, NJ: Lawrence Erlbaum Associates.

BRAY, R. M., & NOBLE, A. M. (1978). Authoritarianism and decisions of mock juries: Evidence of jury bias and group polarization. *Journal of Personality and Social Psychology, 36,* 1424–1430.

BRECHER, E. (1969). *The sex researchers.* Boston: Little, Brown.

BRECHER, E. (1972). *Licit and illicit drugs.* Boston: Little, Brown.

BREGER, L. (1967). Function of dreams. *Journal of Abnormal Psychological Monographs, 72*(5), 1–28.

BRESLAU, N., & DAVIS, G. C. (1989). Chronic PTSD in Vietnam veterans. *Harvard Medical School Mental Health Letter, 5*(9), 3–5.

BRETT, A. S., PHILLIPS, M., & BEARY, J. F. (1986). Predictive power of the polygraph: Can the "lie detector" really detect liars? *Lancet, 1,* 544–547.

BREWER, M. B., & KRAMER, R. M. (1985). The psychology of intergroup attitudes and behavior. *Annual Review of Psychology, 36,* 219–243.

BRIGHAM, J. C. (1980). Limiting conditions of the "physical attractiveness stereotype": Attributions about divorce. *Journal of Research in Personality, 14,* 365–375.

BRIM, O. G., JR., & KAGAN, J. (1980). Constancy and change: A view of the issues. In O. G. Brim, Jr., & J. Kagan (Eds.), *Constancy and change in human development.* Cambridge, MA: Harvard University Press.

BROCA, P. (1861). Remarques sur le siege de la faculte du language articule. *Bulletin de la Societe Anatomique de Paris, 6,* 330–357.

BROD, J. (1970). Haemodynamics and emotional stress. In M. Koster, H. Musaph, & P. Visser (Eds.), *Psychosomatics in essential hypertension.* New York: Karger.

BRODT, B. B., & ZIMBARDO, P. G. (1981). Modifying shyness-related social behavior through symptom misattribution. *Journal of Personality and Social Psychology, 41*(3), 437–449.

BRODY, J. E. (1987, December 3). Jealousy: A complex emotion that can be positive as well as negative in our lives. *New York Times, 137,* pp. 16, 20.

BRODY, L. (1985). Gender differences in emotional development. *Psychology of Personality, 53,* 102–149.

BRONFENBRENNER, U., & GARBARINO, J. (1976). The socialization of moral judgment and behavior in cross-cultural perspective. In T. Lickona (Ed.), *Moral development and behavior.* New York: Holt, Rinehart & Winston.

BROOKS, A. S. (1987). Biosocial perspectives on school-age pregnancy. *Anthropology Notes, 9*(2), 1–4, 14.

BROSS, M., HARPER, D., & SICZ, G. (1980). Visual effects of auditory deprivation: Common intermodal and intramodal factors. *Science, 207,* 667–668.

BROTHERS, L. (1989). Empathy: Therapeutic and biological views. *Harvard Medical School Mental Health Letter, 6*(5), 4–6.

BROVERMAN, I. K., BROVERMAN, D. M., CLARKSON, F. E., ROSENKRANTZ, P., & VOGEL, S. R. (1970). Sex-role stereotypes and clinical judgments of mental health. *Journal of Consulting and Clinical Psychology, 34*(1), 3.

BROWN, A. L., CAMPIONE, J. C., & BARCLAY, C. R. (1978). *Training self-checking routines for estimating test readiness: Generalization from list learning to prose recall.* Unpublished manuscript. University of Illinois.

BROWN, E., DEFFENBACHER, K., & STURGILL, K. (1977). Memory for faces and the circumstances of encounter. *Journal of Applied Psychology, 62,* 311–318.

BROWN, G., BIRLEY, J., & WING, J. (1972). Influence of family life on the course of schizophrenic disorders: A replication. *British Journal of Psychiatry, 121,* 241–258.

BROWN, M. A., & MAHONEY, M. J. (1984). Sport psychology. *Annual Review of Psychology, 35,* 605–625.

BROWN, R. (1986). *Social psychology* (2nd ed.). New York: Free Press.

BROWN, R., & KULIK, J. (1977). Flashbulb memories. *Cognition, 5,* 73–99.

BROWN, R., & McNEILL, D. (1966). The "tip of the tongue" phenomenon. *Journal of Verbal Learning and Verbal Behavior, 5,* 325–337.

BROWN, T. H., CHAPMAN, P. F., KAIRISS, E. W., & KEENAN, C. L. (1988). Long-term synaptic potentiation. *Science, 242,* 724–728.

BROWNE, M. W. (1989, October 24). Problems loom in effort to control use of chemicals for illicit drugs. *New York Times,* pp. B1, B9.

BROWNELL, K. D. (1988, January). Yo-Yo dieting: Repeated attempts to lose weight can give you a hefty problem. *Psychology Today,* pp. 20–23.

BROWNELL, K. D., & VENDITTI, E. M. (1982). The etiology and treatment of obesity. In W. E. Fann, I. Karacan, A. D. Pokorny, & R. L. Williams (Eds.), *Phenomenology and treatment of psychophysiological disorders.* New York: Spectrum.

BRUNER, J. S., GOODNOW, J. J., & AUSTIN, G. A. (1956). *A study of thinking.* New York: Wiley.

BRYLAWSKI, R. (1987, November). Prenatal tests: Screening for Down's syndrome. *American Health,* pp. 18–19.

BUHRMANN, H., & ZAUGG, M. (1981). Superstitions among basketball players: An investigation of various forms of superstitious beliefs and behavior among competitive basketballers at the junior high school to university level. *Journal of Sport Behavior, 4*(4), 163–174.

BUIE, J. (1988, November). Ad campaign spotlights psychology. *APA Monitor,* p. 18. (a)

BUIE, J. (1988, November). Message catches publicity wave. *APA Monitor,* p. 20. (b)

BUIE, J. (1989, December). Age, race, gender all influence PTSD. *APA Monitor,* p. 32. (a)

BUIE, J. (1989, December), MMPI-2 earns praise as improved instrument. *APA Monitor,* p. 22. (b)

BUNNEY, W. E., JR., MURPHY, D. L., GOODWIN, F. K., & BORGE, G. F. (1972, September). The "switch process" in manic-depressive illness; A systematic study of sequential behavioral changes. *Archives of General Psychiatry, 27*(3), 295–302.

BURGER, J. M., & PETTY, R. E. (1981). The low-ball compliance technique: Task or person commitment? *Journal of Personality and Social Psychology, 40,* 492–500.

BUSH, C., BUSH, J., & JENNINGS, J. (1988). Effects of jealousy threats on relationship perceptions and emotions. *Journal of Social and Personal Relationships, 5,* 285–303.

BUSS, A. H., & PLOMIN, R. (1984). *Temperament.* Hillsdale, NJ: Lawrence Erlbaum Associates.

BUTLER, R. A. (1954, February). Curiosity in monkeys. *Scientific American, 190,* 70–75.

BUTLER, R. N., & LEWIS, M. I. (1982). *Aging and mental health* (3rd ed.). St. Louis: Mosby.

BYRNE, D. (1971). *The attraction paradigm.* New York: Academic Press.

CADORET, R. J. (1978). Psychopathology in adopted-away offspring of biologic parents with antisocial behavior. *Archives of General Psychiatry, 35,* 176–184.

CADORET, R. J. (1986). Epidemiology of antisocial personality. In W. H. Reid, D. Dorr, J. I. Walker, & J. W. Bonner III (Eds.), *Unmasking the psychopath: Antisocial personality and related syndromes.* New York: Norton.

CAIRNS, D., & PASINO, J. A. (1977). Comparison of verbal reinforcement and feedback in the operant treatment of disability due to chronic back pain. *Behavior Therapy, 8*(4), 621–630.

CAIRNS, R. B. (1972). Fighting and punishment from a developmental perspective. *Nebraska Symposium on Motivation, 20,* 59–124.

CALHOUN, J. B. (1962). Population density and social pathology. *Scientific American, 206*(3), 139–148.

CAMPOS, J. J., HIATT, S., RAMSAY, D., HENDERSON, C., & SVEJDA, M. (1978). The emergence of fear on the visual cliff. In M. Lewis & L. A. Rosenblum (Eds.), *The development of affect.* New York: Plenum.

CAMPOS, J., LAMB, M. E., GOLDSMITH, H. H., & STENBERG, C. (1983). Socio-emotional development. In J. Campos & M. M. Haith (Eds.), *Handbook of child psychology: Infancy and developmental psychobiology* (Vol. 2, pp. 783–916). New York: Wiley.

CAMPOS, J. J., LANGER, A., & KROWITZ, A. (1970). Cardiac responses on the visual cliff in prelocomotor human infants. *Science, 170,* 196–197.

CANNON, W. B. (1927). The James–Lange theory of emotions: A critical examination and an alternative theory. *American Journal of Psychology, 39,* 106–124.

CANNON, W. B., LEWIS, J. T., & BRITTON, S. W. (1927). The dispensability of the sympathetic division of the autonomic nervous system. *Boston Medical Surgery Journal, 197,* 514.

CANNON, W. B., & WASHBURN, A. (1912). An explanation of hunger. *American Journal of Physiology, 29,* 441–454.

CAPORAEL, L. R. (1981). The paralanguage of caregiving: Baby talk to the institutionalized aged. *Journal of Personality and Social Psychology, 40,* 876–884.

CARLSON, N. R. (1986). *Physiology of behavior* (3rd ed.). Boston: Allyn & Bacon.

CARPENTER, W. T., & HEINRICHS, D. W. (1984). Intermittent pharmacotherapy of schizophrenia. In J. M. Kane (Ed.), *Drug maintenance strategies in schizophrenia* (pp. 21–37). Washington, DC: American Psychiatric Press.

CARSON, R. C. (1989). Personality. In M. R. Rosenzweig & L. W. Porter (Eds.), *Annual Review of Psychology* (pp. 227–248). Palo Alto, CA: Annual Reviews Inc.

CARSON, R. C., BUTCHER, J. N., & COLEMAN, J. C. (1988). *Abnormal psychology and modern life* (8th ed.). Glenview, IL: Scott, Foresman.

CARTWRIGHT, R. D. (1977). *A primer on sleep and dreaming.* Reading, MA: Addison–Wesley.

CARTWRIGHT, R. D. (1978). Sleep and dreams, Part II. *Annual Review of psychology, 29,* 223–252.

CATTELL, R. B. (1965). *The scientific analysis of personality.* Baltimore: Penguin.

CATTELL, R. B. (1971). *Abilities: Their structure, growth, and action.* Boston, MA: Houghton Mifflin.

CATTELL, R. B. (1973, July). Personality pinned down. *Psychology Today,* pp. 41–46.

CHAFFEE, J. (1988). *Thinking critically* (2nd ed.). Boston, MA: Houghton Mifflin.

CHAGANI, H. T., & PHELPS, M. E. (1986). Maturational changes in cerebral function in infants determined by 18FDG positron emission tomography. *Science, 231,* 840–843.

CHAIKEN, S., & EAGLY, A. H. (1983). Communication modality as a determinant of persuasion: The role of communicator salience. *Journal of Personality and Social Psychology, 45,* 241–256.

CHANCE, P. (1979). *Learning and behavior.* Belmont, CA: Wadsworth.

CHANCE, P. (1986, September). The divided self. *Psychology Today,* p. 72.

CHANCE, P., & FISCHMAN, J. (1987, May). The magic of childhood. *Psychology Today,* pp. 48–58.

CHAPOUTHIER, G. (1973). Behavioral studies of the molecular basis of memory. In J. A. Deutsch (Ed.), *The physiological basis of memory* (pp. 1–25). New York: Academic Press.

CHASE, W. G., & SIMON, H. A. (1973). The mind's eye in chess. In W. Chase (Ed.), *Visual information processing.* New York: Academic Press.

CHAWALISZ, K., DIENER, E., & GALLAGHER, D. (1988). Autonomic arousal feedback and emotional experience: Evidence from the spinal cord injured. *Journal of Personality and Social Psychology, 54,* 820–828.

CHELUNE, G. J. (1984). Conversion disorders. In R. J. Corsini (Ed.), *Encyclopedia of psychology* (Vol. 1, pp. 291–292). New York: Wiley.

CHENEY, D., & FOSS, G. (1984). An examination of the social behavior of mentally retarded workers. *Education and Training of the Mentally Retarded, 19*(3), 216–221.

CHERRY, L. J. (1979). A sociocognitive approach to language development and its implications for education. In O. K. Garnica & M. L. King (Eds.), *Language, children, and society.* New York: Pergamon.

CHESNEY, M. A., EAGLESTON, J. R. (1981). Type A behavior: Assessment and intervention. In C. K. Prokop & L. A. Bradley (Eds.), *Medical Psychology: Contributions to Behavioral Medicine* (pp. 21–22). New York: Academic Press.

CHESNO, F. A., & KILMANN, P. R. (1975). Effects of stimulation on sociopathic avoidance learning. *Journal of Abnormal Psychology, 84*(2), 144–150.

CHESS, S., & THOMAS, A. (1986). *Annual progress in child psychiatry and child development.* New York: Brunner/Mazel.

CHILDERS, J. S., DURHAM, T. W., BOLEN, L. M., & TAYLOR, L. H. (1985). A predictive validity study of the Kaufman Assessment Battery for Children with the California Achievement Test. *Psychology in the Schools, 22*(1), 29–33.

CHOLLAR, S. (1989 November). Body-wise: Safe solutions for night work. *Psychology Today,* p. 26.

CHOMSKY, N. (1968). *Language and mind.* New York: Harcourt, Brace, World.

CHOMSKY, N. (1975). *Reflections of language.* New York: Pantheon.

CHOMSKY, N. (1980). *Rules and representations.* New York: Columbia University Press.

CIALDINI, R. B., CACIOPPO, J. T., BASSETT, R., & MILLER, J. A. (1978). Low-ball procedure for producing compliance: Commitment then cost. *Journal of Personality and Social Psychology, 36,* 463–476.

CIALDINI, R. B., VINCENT, J. E., LEWIS, S. K., CATALAN, J., WHEELER, D., & DARBY, B. L. (1975). Reciprocal concessions procedure for inducing compliance: The door-in-the-face technique. *Journal of Personality and Social Psychology, 31,* 206–215.

CLANTON, G. (1981). Frontiers of jealousy research: Introduction to the special issue on jealousy. *Alternative Life-styles, 4*(3), 259–273.

CLANTON, G., & SMITH, L. G. (1977). *Jealousy.* Englewood Cliffs, NJ: Prentice–Hall.

CLARK, H. H., & CLARK, E. V. (1977). *Psychology and language: An introduction to psy-*

cholinguistics. New York: Harcourt, Brace, Jovanovich.

CLARKE, A. C. (1968). *2001: A space odyssey*. New York: New American Library.

CLARKE-STEWART, K. A. (1980). The father's contribution to child development. In F. A. Pedersen (Ed.), *The father–infant relationship: Observational studies in a family context*. New York: Praeger Special Studies.

CLARKSON, M. G., & BERG, W. K. (1983). Cardiac orienting and vowel discrimination in newborns: Crucial stimulus parameters. *Child Development, 54*, 162–171.

CLARY, E. G., & THIEMAN, T. J. (1988, August). *Self perceptions of helpfulness: Different meanings for different people?* Paper presented at the annual meeting of the American Psychological Association, Atlanta.

CLAUSEN, J. A. (1981). Men's occupational careers in the middle years. In D. H. Eichorn, J. A. Clausen, N. Haan, M. P. Honzik, & P. Mussen (Eds.), *Present and past in middle life* (pp. 321–351). New York: Academic Press.

CLECKLEY, J. (1976). *The mask of sanity* (5th ed.). St. Louis: Mosby.

CLONINGER, C. R., REICH, T., SIGVARDSSON, S., VON KNORRING, A. L., & BOHMAN, M. (1986). The effects of changes in alcohol use between generations on the inheritance of alcohol abuse. In *Alcoholism: A medical disorder* (pp. 940–951). Arlington, VA: American Psychological Association.

COAN, R. W. (1984). Personality types. In R. J. Corsini, (Ed.), *Encyclopedia of Psychology* (Vol. 3, pp. 23–26). New York: Wiley.

COE, W. C. (1987, August). *Hypnosis: Where art thou?* Paper presented at the meeting of the American Psychological Association, Washington, DC.

COHEN, L. D., KIPNES, D., KUNKLE, E. G., & KUBZANSKY, P. E. (1955). Observations of a person with insensitivity to pain. *Journal of Abnormal and Social Psychology, 55*, 33–38.

COHEN, R. P., & HAMBURG, M. D. (1975). Evidence for adrenergic neurons in a memory access pathway. *Pharmacology, Biochemistry, and Behavior, 3*, 519–523.

COHEN, S. (1981). Sensory changes in the elderly. *American Journal of Nursing, 81*, 1851–1880.

COHLER, B. J. (1983). Autonomy and interdependence in the family of adulthood: A psychological perspective. *Gerontologist, 23*, 33–39.

COLE, D. L. (1982). Psychology as a liberating art. *Teaching of Psychology, 9*, 23–26.

COLE, R. A., & JAKIMIK, J. (1980). A model of speech perception. In R. A. Cole (Ed.), *Perception and production of fluent speech*. Hillsdale, NJ: Lawrence Erlbaum Associates.

COLE, S. (1980, September). Send our children to work? *Psychology Today*, p. 44.

COLEMAN, J. C., BUTCHER, J. N., & CARSON, R. C. (1984). *Abnormal psychology and modern life* (7th ed.). Glenview, IL: Scott, Foresman.

COLEMAN, R. M. (1986). *Wide awake at 3:00 A.M.: By choice or by chance?* New York: Freeman.

COLGROVE, M., BLOOMFIELD, H. H., & McWILLIAMS, P. (1976). *How to survive the loss of a love*. New York: Bantam.

COLLINS, A. M., & QUILLIAN, M. R. (1969). Retrieval time from semantic memory. *Journal of Verbal Learning and Verbal Behavior, 8*, 240–248.

COLLINS, C. C. (1970). Tactile television: Mechanical and electrical image projection. *IEEE Transactions on Man–Machine Systems, 11*(1), 65–71.

COLLINS, W. A., & RUSSELL, G. (1988). *Mother–child and father–child relationships in middle childhood and adolescence*. Minneapolis: University of Minnesota Press.

COMMONS, M. L., SINNOTT, J., RICHARDS, F. A., & ARMON, C. (Eds.) (1986). *Beyond formal operations: Comparisons and applications of adolescent and adult development models* (pp. 542–564). New York: Praeger.

CONDRY, J. C. (1977). Enemies of exploration: Self-initiated vs. other-initiated learning. *Journal of Personality and Social Psychology, 35*, 459–477.

CONGER, J. J. (1988). Hostages to fortune: Youth, values, and the public interest. *American Psychologist, 43*, 291–300.

CONNIFF, R. (1984). Living longer. In H. E. Fitzgerald & M. G. Walraven (Eds.), *Human development 84/85* (pp. 268–273). Guilford, CT: Dushkin.

COOPER, J., & McGAUGH, J. C. (1969). Leadership: Integrating principles of social psychology. In C. A. Gibb (Ed.), *Leadership*. Baltimore: Penguin.

CORCORAN, K. J. (1988). Relapse and obesity: A comment. *American Psychologist, 43*, 825–826.

COREY, G. (1986). *Theory and practice of counseling and psychotherapy* (3rd ed.). Monterey, CA: Brooks/Cole.

CORNELL J. (1984, March). Science versus the paranormal. *Psychology Today*, pp. 28–34.

CORSELLIS, J. A., BRUTON, C. J., & FREEMAN-BROWNE, D. (1973, August). The aftermath of boxing. *Psychological Medicine, 3*(3), 270–303.

CORSINI, R. J. (Ed.). (1984). *Current psychotherapies* (34th ed.). Itasca, IL.: Peacock.

CORSO, J. F. (1977). Auditory perception and communication. In J. E. Birren & K. W. Schaie (Eds.), *Handbook of the psychology of aging* (pp. 535–553). New York: Van Nostrand–Reinhold.

COSER, R. L., & COSER, L. (1979). Jonestown as a perverse utopia. *Dissent*, Spring, 158–163.

COSTA, P. T., JR., & McCRAE, R. R. (1980). Still stable after all these years: Personality as a key to some issues in adulthood and old age. In P. B. Baltes & O. G. Brim, Jr. (Eds.), *Lifespan development and behavior* (Vol. III). New York: Academic Press.

COSTA, P. T., & McCRAE, R. R. (1988). Personality in adulthood: A six-year longitudinal survey of self-reports and spouse ratings on the NEO Personality Inventory. *Journal of Personality and Social Psychology, 54*, 853–863.

COSTANTINI, E., & CRAIK, K. H. (1980). Personality and politicians: California party leaders, 1960–1976. *Journal of Personality and Social Psychology, 38*, 641–661.

COUNCIL, J. R., KIRSCH, I., & HAFNER, L. (1986). Expectancy versus absorption in the prediction of hypnotic responding. *Journal of Personality and Social Psychology, 50*(1), 182–189.

COUSINS, N. (1979). *Anatomy of an illness*. New York: Norton.

COWAN, P. A. (1978). *Piaget with feeling: Cognitive, social, and emotional dimensions*. New York: Holt, Rinehart & Winston.

COZBY, P. C. (1985). *Methods in behavioral research* (3rd ed.). Palo Alto, CA: Mayfield.

CRAIK, F. I. M., & LOCKHART, R. S. (1972). Levels of processing: A framework for memory research. *Journal of Verbal Learning and Verbal Behavior, 11*, 671–684.

CRAIK, F. I. M., & TULVING, E. (1975). Depth of processing and the retention of words in episodic memory. *Journal of Experimental Psychology: General, 104*, 268–294.

CRAIK, F. I. M., & WATKINS, M. J. (1973). The role of rehearsal in short-term memory. *Journal of Verbal Learning and Behavior, 12*, 599–607.

CRASKE, B. (1977). Perception of impossible limb positions induced by tendon vibrations. *Science, 196*, 71–73.

CRICK, F., (1982, February). Do dendritic spines twitch? *Trends in Neuroscience*, pp. 44–46.

CRICK, F., & MITCHISON, G. (1983). The function of dream sleep. *Nature, 304*, 111–114.

CRITCHLOW, B. (1985, August). *Expected utility of drinking*. Paper presented at the meeting of the American Psychological Association, Los Angeles.

CROSS, T. G. (1977). Mother's speech adjustments. In O. Ferguson & C. Snow (Eds.), *Talking to children*. Cambridge, England: Cambridge University Press.

CROSSEN, C. (1989, September 13). Bulimics take note: Personality testing is entering the '80s. *The Wall Street Journal*, pp. A4, A12.

CROW, T. J. (1985). The two syndrome concept: Origins and current status. *Schizophrenia Bulletin, 11*, 471–486.

CROW, T. J., CROSS, A. J., JOHNSTONE, E. C., OWEN, F., OWENS, D. G. C., & WADDINGTON, J. L. (1982). Abnormal involuntary movements in schizophrenia. *Journal of Clinical Psychopharmacology, 2*, 336–340.

CROWE, R. R. (1974). An adoption study of antisocial personality. *Archives of General Psychiatry, 32,* 785–791.

CUMMING, E., & HENRY, W. E. (1961). *Growing old: The process of disengagement.* New York: Basic Books.

CUNNINGHAM, J. D., & STRASSBERG, D. S. (1981). Neuroticism and disclosure reciprocity. *Journal of Counseling Psychology, 28,* 455–458.

CUNNINGHAM, W. R., & BROOKBANK, J. W. (1989). *Gerontology: The psychology, biology, and sociology of aging.* New York: Harper & Row.

CUNNINGHAM, M. R., STEINBERG, J., & GREV, R. (1980). Wanting to and having to help: Separate motivations for positive mood and guilt induced helping. *Journal of Personality and Social Psychology, 38,* 181–192.

DAILEY, R. C. (1968). *Anthropologica, 10,* 45.

DALY, M., & WILSON, M. (1988). Evolutionary social psychology and family homicide. *Science, 242,* 519–523.

DAMASIO, A. (1979). The frontal lobes. In K. M. Heilman & E. Valenstein (Eds.), *Clinical neuropsychology.* New York: Oxford University Press.

DANIELS, D., & PLOMIN, R. (1985). Origins of individual differences in infant shyness. *Developmental Psychology, 21,* 118–122.

DARLEY, J. G. (1984). Vocational interest measurement. In R. J. Corsini (Ed.) *Encyclopedia of psychology* (Vol. 3, pp. 459–462). New York: Wiley.

DARLEY, J. M., & BATSON, C. D. (1973). "From Jerusalem to Jericho": A study of situational and dispositional variables in helping behavior. *Journal of Personality and Social Psychology, 27,* 100–108.

DARWIN, C. R. (1872). *The expression of the emotions in man and animals.* London: John Murray.

DATAN, N., RODEHAEAVER, D., & HUGHES, F. (1987). Adult development and aging. In M. R. Rosenzweig & L. W. Porter (Eds.). *Annual review of psychology* (pp. 153–180). Palo Alto, CA: Annual Reviews.

DAVIDSON, B. (1984). A test of equity theory for marital adjustment. *Social Psychology Quarterly, 47,* 36–42.

DAVIDSON, R. J. (1984). Affect, cognition, and hemispheric specialization. In C. E. Izard, J. Kagan, & R. B. Zajonc (Eds.), *Emotions, cognition, and behavior.* Cambridge, MA: Cambridge University Press.

DAVIES, P. (1988). Alzheimer's Disease and related disorders: An overview. In M. K. Aronson (Ed.), *Understanding Alzheimer's Disease* (pp. 3–14). New York: Charles Scribner's Sons.

DAVIS, C. M., & YARBER, W. (Eds.). (1988). *Sexuality measures: A compendium.* Lake Mills, IA: Graphic.

DAVIS, D. (1976). On being *detectably* sane in insane places: Base rates and psychodiagnosis. *Journal of Abnormal Psychology, 85,* 416–422.

DAVIS, J. D., GALLAGHER, R. J., & LADOVE, R. F. (1967). Food intake controlled by a blood factor. *Science, 156,* 1247–1248.

DAVIS, M. H., & STEPHAN, W. G. (1980). Attributions for exam performance. *Journal of Applied Psychology, 10,* 235–248.

DAVIS, M. S. (1966). Variations in patients' compliance with doctors' orders: Analysis of congruence between survey responses and results of empirical investigations. *Journal of Medical Education, 41,* 1037–1048.

DAVIS, W. (1986). *The serpent and the rainbow.* New York: Simon & Schuster.

DAVISON, G. C., & NEALE, J. M. (1990). *Abnormal psychology* (5th ed). New York: Wiley.

DAWES, R. (1980). Social dilemmas. *Annual Review of Psychology, 31,* 169–193.

DAWES, R. M. (1987, August). *Not me or thee but we.* Paper presented at the 11th. SPUDM Conference, Cambridge, England.

DEAUX, K. (1984). From individual differences to social categories: Analysis of a decade's research on gender. *American Psychologist, 39,* 105–116.

DEAUX, K. (1985). Sex and gender. *Annual Review of Psychology, 36,* 48–81.

DEAUX, K., & WRIGHTSMAN, L. S. (1988). *Social Psychology* (5th ed.). Pacific Grove, CA: Brooks/Cole.

DE CASPER, A. J., & FIFER, W. D. (1980). Of human bonding: Newborn's prefer their mother's voices. *Science, 208,* 1174–1176.

DECI, E. L., & RYAN, R. M. (1985). *Intrinsic motivation and self-determination in human behavior.* New York: Plenum.

DE LACOSTE-UTAMSING, C., & HOLLOWAY, R. L. (1982). Sexual dimorphism in the human corpus callosum. *Science, 216,* 1431–1432.

DELGADO, J. M. R. (1960). Emotional behavior in animals and humans. *Psychiatric Research Report, 12,* 259–271.

DELONGIS, A., COYNE, J. C., DAKOF, G., FOLKMAN, S., & LAZARUS, R. S. (1982). Relationship of daily hassles, uplifts, and major life events to health status. *Health Psychology, 1,* 119–136.

DELONGIS, A., FOLKMAN, S., & LAZARUS, R. S. (1988). The impact of daily stress on health and mood: Psychological and social resources as mediators. *Journal of Personality and Social Psychology, 54,* 486–495.

DEMAREST, C. B. (1985, May 15). Relief for the patient with PMS. *Patient Care,* p. 118.

DEMBROSKI, T. M., MacDOUGALL, J. M., WILLIAMS, B., & HANEY, T. L. (1985). Components of type A, hostility, and anger in: Relationship to angiographic findings. *Psychosomatic Medicine, 47,* 219–233.

DEMENT, W. C. (1974). *Some must watch while some must sleep.* San Francisco: Freeman.

DEMENT, W. C. (1983). A life in sleep research. In M. H. Chase & E. D. Weitzman (Eds.), *Sleep disorders: basic and clinical research.* New York: Spectrum.

DEMENT, W. C., & KLEITMAN, N. (1957). Cyclic variations in EEG and their relation to eye movements, bodily motility, and dreaming. *Electroencephalography Clinical Neurophysiology, 9,* 673–690.

DEMPSTER, F. N. (1985). Proactive interference in sentence recall: Topic-similarity effects and individual differences. *Memory and Cognition, 13,* 81–89.

DENNETT, M. R. (1985). Firewalking: Reality or illusion? *The Skeptical Inquirer, 10*(1), 36–40.

DENNIS, W. (1973). *Children of the creche.* New York: Appleton–Century–Crofts.

DENNIS, W., & DENNIS, M. G. (1940). Cradles and cradling customs of the Pueblo Indians. *American Anthropologist, 42,* 107–115.

DENNY, N. W., & QUADAGNO, D. (1988). *Human sexuality.* St. Louis: Times Mirror/Mosby.

DEUTSCH, A. (1949). *The mentally ill in America.* New York: Columbia University Press.

DEUTSCH, J. A. (1983). *The physiological basis of memory.* New York: Academic Press.

DEVALOIS, R. L. (1965). Behavioral and electrophysiological studies of primate vision. In W. D. Neff (Ed.), *Contributions to sensory physiology* (Vol. 1). New York: Academic Press.

DE VRIES, H. A. (1983). Physiology of exercise and aging. In D. S. Woodruff & J. E. Birren (Eds.), *Aging: Scientific perspectives and social issues* (2nd ed., pp. 285–304). Monterey, CA: Brooks/Cole.

DEWAN, E. (1970). The programming (P) hypothesis for REM sleep. In E. Hartmann (Ed.), *Sleep and dreaming.* Boston: Little, Brown.

DEWSBURY, D. A. (1989). Comparative psychology, ethology, and animal behavior. In M. R. Rosenzweig & L. W. Porter (Eds.), *Annual Review of Psychology* (pp. 581–602). Palo Alto, CA: Annual Reviews Inc.

DIAMOND M. (1977). Human sexual development. In F. Beach (Ed.), *Human sexuality in four perspectives* (pp. 22–61). Baltimore: Johns Hopkins University Press.

DIAMOND, M. (1982). Sexual identity, monozygotic twins reared in discordant sex roles and a BBC follow-up. *Archives of Sexual Behavior, 11,* 181–186.

DIAMOND, M. (1986). *The world of sexual behavior: Sexwatching.* New York: W. H. Smith.

DIENER, E. (1980). Deindividuation: The absence of self-awareness and self-regulation in group members. In P. B. Paulus (Ed.), *The psychology of group influence.* Hillside, NJ: Lawrence Erlbaum Associates.

DIXON, B. (1986, April). Dangerous thoughts: How we think and feel can make us sick. *Science 86, 7*(3), 62–66.

DODSON, J. A., TRYBOUT, A. M., & STEINTHAL, E. (1978). Impact of deals and deal retraction on brand switching. *Journal of Marketing Research, 15*(1), 72–81.

DOLLARD, J., DOOB, L., MILLER, N., MOWRER, O. H., & SEARS, R. R. (1939). *Frustration and aggression.* New Haven, CT: Yale University Press.

DOMAN, G. (1979). *Teach your baby math.* New York: Simon & Schuster.

DONNERSTEIN, E., & BERKOWITZ, L. (1981). Victim reactions in aggressive erotic films as a factor in violence against women. *Journal of Personality and Social Psychology, 41,* 710–724.

DOREN, D. (1987). *Understanding and treating the psychopath.* New York: Wiley.

DORMAN, M. (1986, January 3). Jack La Lanne: We're just now catching up with fitness pioneer. *San Diego Tribune,* p. D-1.

DORNBUSH, R. L., & WILLIAMS, M. (1974). Memory and ECT. In M. Fink, S. Kety, J. McGaugh, & R. A. Williams (Eds.), *Psychobiology of convulsive therapy.* Washington, DC: Winston.

DOSHER, B. A. (1984). Discriminating pre-experimental (semantic) from learned (episodic) associations: A speed–accuracy study. *Cognitive Psychology, 16,* 519–555.

DOUVAN, E., & ADELSON, J. (1966). *The adolescent experience.* New York: Wiley.

DOYLE, J. (1985). *Sex and gender: The human experience.* Dubuque, IA: Brown.

DRACHMAN, D., DE CARUFEL, A., & INSKO, C. A. (1978). The extra credit effect in interpersonal attraction. *Journal of Experimental Social Psychology, 14,* 458–465.

DRISCOLL, R., DAVIS, K. E., & LIPETZ, M. E. (1972). Parental interference and romantic love: The Romeo and Juliet effect. *Journal of Personality and Social Psychology, 24,* 1–10.

DUBOIS, P. H. (1984). Q-sort technique. In R. J. Corsini (Ed.), *Encyclopedia of psychology* (Vol. 3, p. 197). New York: Wiley.

DUCK, S. (1984). A perspective on the repair of personal relationships. In S. Duck (Ed.), *Personal relationships: Repairing personal relationships.* New York: Academic Press.

DUNCAN, D., & GOLD, R. (1982). *Drugs and the whole person.* New York: Wiley.

DUNCKER, K. (1945). On problem solving. *Psychological Monographs, 58*(5, Whole No. 270).

DUSEK, J. B., & FLAHERTY, F. (1981). The development of the self-concept during the adolescent years. *Monographs of the Society for Research in Child Development, 46*(4), 191.

DYWAN, J. (1984). Hyperamnesia, hypnosis, and memory: Implications for forensic investigation. *Dissertation Abstracts International, 44*(10-B), 3190.

DYWAN, J., & BOWERS, K. A. (1983). The use of hypnosis to enhance recall. *Science, 222*(4620), 184–185.

EAGLY, A. H., & HIMMELFARB, S. (1978). Attitudes and opinions. In M. R. Rosenzweig & L. W. Porter (Eds.), *Annual review of psychology* (Vol. 29). Palo Alto, CA: Annual Reviews.

EBBINGHAUS, H. (1913). *Memory: A contribution to experimental psychology* (H. A. Ruger and C. E. Bussenius, Trans.). New York: Teacher's College. (Original work published 1885.)

EBERSOLE, P., & DE PAOLA, S. (1988). Meaning in life categories of later life couples. *Journal of Psychology, 121,* 185–191.

ECCLES (PARSONS), J., ADLER, T., & MEECE, J. L. (1984). Sex differences in achievement: A test of alternate theories. *Journal of Personality and Social Psychology, 46,* 26–43.

ECKBERG, D. L. (1979). *Intelligence and race: The origins and dimensions of the IQ controversy.* New York: Praeger.

ECKERT, E. D., BOUCHARD, T. J., BOHLEN, J., & HESTON, L. L. (1986). Homosexuality in monozygotic twins reared apart. *British Journal of Psychiatry, 148,* 421–425.

EDELMAN, M. W. (1987). *Families in peril: An agenda for social change.* New York: Allan Guttmacher Institute.

EDWARDS, G., GROSS, M. M., KELLER, J., MOSER, J., & ROOM, R. (1977). *Alcohol related disabilities.* Geneva, Switzerland: World Health Organization.

EFRAN, J. S., & SPANGLER, T. J. (1979). Why grown-ups cry: A two factor theory and evidence from *The Miracle Worker. Motivation and Emotion, 3,* 63–72.

EGAN, K. J., & KEATON, W. J. (1987). Responses to illness and health in chronic pain patients and healthy adults. *Psychosomatic Medicine, 49,* 470–481.

EGELAND, J. A., GERHARD, D. S., PAULS, D. L., SUSSEX, J. N., KIDD, K. K., ALLEN, C. R., HOSTETTER, A. M., & HOUSMAN, D. E. (1987). Bipolar affective disorders linked to DNA markers on chromosome 11. *Nature, 325,* 783–787.

EGGER, M. D., & FLYNN, J. P. (1967). Further studies on the effects on amygdaloid stimulation and ablation of hypothalamically elicited attack behavior in cats. In W. R. Adey & T. Tokizane (Eds.), *Progress in brain research,* Vol. 27: *Structure and function of the limbic system.* Amsterdam: Elsevier.

EHRHARDT, A., & MEYER-BAHLBURG, H. (1981). Effects of prenatal sex hormones on gender-related behavior. *Science, 211,* 1312–1318.

EIBL-EIBESFELDT, I. (1980). *The biology of peace and war.* New York: Viking. (a)

EIBL-EIBESFELDT, I. (1980). Strategies of social interaction. In R. Plutchik & H. Kelerman (Eds.), *Emotion: Theory, research, and experience.* New York: Academic Press. (b)

EISENBERG, N., & MILLER, P. (1989). The relation of empathy to prosocial and related behaviors. *Psychological Bulletin, 101,* 91–119.

EKMAN, P. (1972). Universals and cultural differences in facial expressions of emotion. In J. Cole (Ed.), *Nebraska symposium on motivation* (Vol. 19). Lincoln, NE: University of Nebraska Press.

EKMAN, P., & FRIESEN, W. V. (1975). *Unmasking the face.* Englewood Cliffs, NJ: Prentice–Hall.

EKMAN, P., FRIESEN, W. V., & ANCOLI, S. (1980). Facial signs and emotional experience. *Journal of Personality and Social Psychology, 39,* 1125–1134.

EKMAN, P., LEVENSON, R. W., & FRIESEN, W. V. (1983). Autonomic nervous system activity distinguishes among emotions. *Science, 221,* 1208–1210.

ELIAS, S., & ANNAS, G. (1986). Social policy considerations in noncoital reproduction. *Journal of the American Medical Society, 225,* 62–68.

EKLIND, D. (1981). *The hurried child: Growing up too fast, too soon.* Reading, MA: Addison–Wesley.

ELKIND, D. (1984). *All grown up and no place to go.* Reading, MA: Addison–Wesley.

ELKIND, D. (1987, May). Superkids and super problems. *Psychology Today,* pp. 60–61.

ELKIND, D. (1988). An essential difference. In J. Rubinstein & B. Slife (Eds.), *Taking sides: Clashing views on controversial psychological issues* (5th ed., pp. 163–173). Guilford, CT: Dushkin.

ELLINGSON, R. J. (1954). Incidence of EEG abnormality among patients with mental disorders of apparently nonorganic origin: A criminal review. *American Journal of Psychiatry, 111,* 263–275.

ELLIS, A. (1977). *How to live with and without anger.* New York: Reader's Digest Press.

ELLIS, A. (1983). *Rational-emotive therapy and cognitive behavior therapy.* New York: Springer.

ELLIS, A. (1984). Rational-emotive therapy. In R. Corsini (Ed.), *Current psychotherapies* (3rd ed.). Itasca, IL: Peacock.

ELLIS, A. (1987). The impossibility of achieving consistently good mental health. *American Psychologist, 42,* 364–375.

ELLIS, A., & HARPER, R. A. (1975). *A new guide to rational living.* Hollywood, CA: Wilshire.

ELLIS, L., & AMES, M. A. (1987). Neurohormonal functioning and sexual orientation: A theory of homosexuality–heterosexuality. *Psychological Bulletin, 101,* 223–258.

ELTON, D., BURROWS, G. D., & STANLEY, G. V. (1980). Hypnosis and chronic pain. *Australian Journal of Clinical & Experimental Hypnosis, 8,* 83–90.

EMERY, R. E. (1989). Family violence. *American Psychologist, 44,* 321–328.

ENGEL, G. (1977, November). Emotional stress and sudden death. *Psychology Today, 11*(11), 144.

ENGELMANN, S., & ENGELMANN, T. (1988). Superior minds. In J. Rubinstein & B. Slife (Eds.), *Taking sides: Clashing views on*

HOLMES, D. S. (1988). The influence of meditation versus rest on physiological considerations. In M. West (Ed.), *The psychology of meditation.* New York: Oxford University Press.

HOLMES, T. H., & RAHE, R. H. (1967). The social readjustment rating scale. *Journal of Psychosomatic Research, 11,* 213–218.

HOOLEY, J. (1988). How do family attitudes affect relapse in schizophrenia? *Harvard Medical School Mental Health Letter, 5*(4), 8.

HOPSON, J. L. (1984, November). A love affair with the brain: A conversation with Marian Diamond. *Psychology Today,* pp. 62–73.

HOPSON, J., & ROSENFELD, A. (1984, August). PMS: Puzzling monthly symptoms. *Psychology Today,* pp. 30–35.

HORN, J. C., & MEER, J. (1987, May). The vintage years. *Psychology Today,* pp. 76–90.

HORN, J. L. (1970). Organization of data on life-span development of human abilities. In L. R. Goulet & P. B. Baltes (Eds.), *Life-span development psychology: Research and theory.* New York: Academic Press.

HORN, J. L. (1978). Human ability systems. In P. B. Baltes (Ed.), *Life-span developmental psychology* (Vol. I). New York: Academic Press.

HORN, J. L. (1982). The theory of fluid and crystallized intelligence in relation to concepts of cognitive psychology and aging in adulthood. In F. I. M. Craik & S. Trehub (Eds.), *Aging and cognitive processes* (pp. 237–278). New York: Plenum.

HORN, J. L. (1984). The 16 PF questionnaire. In R. J. Corsini (Ed.), *Encyclopedia of psychology* (Vol. 3, p. 324). New York: Wiley.

HORN, J. L. & DONALDSON, G. (1976). On the myth of intellectual decline in adulthood. *American Psychologist, 31,* 701–719.

HORN, J. L., & DONALDSON, G. (1980). Cognitive development in adulthood. In O. G. Brimm, Jr., & J. Kagan (Eds.), *Constancy and change in human development.* Cambridge, MA: Harvard University Press.

HORNEY, K. (1939). *New ways in psychoanalysis.* New York: International Universities Press.

HORNEY, K. (1945). *Our inner conflicts: A constructive theory of neurosis.* New York: Norton.

HORTON, P. C., LOUY, J. W., & CAPPOLILLO, H. P. (1974). Personality disorder and transitional relatedness. *Archives of General Psychiatry, 30*(5), 618–622.

HOSTETLER, A. J. (1988, July). Why baby cries: Data may shush skeptics. *APA Monitor, p. 14.* (a).

HOSTETLER, A. J. (1988, July). Will America respond to the AIDS mailing? *APA Monitor,* p. 43. (b)

HOUSE, J. S., LANDIS, K. R. & UMBERSON, D. (1988). Social relationships and health. *Science, 241,* 540–545.

HOUSTON, J., BEE, H., & RIMM, D. (1983). *Essential of psychology.* Orlando, FL: Academic Press.

HOUTS, A. C., COOK, T. D., & SHADISH, W. R. (1986). The person–situation debate: A critical multiplist perspective. *Journal of Personality, 54,* 52–105.

HOVLAND, C. I. (1938). Experimental studies in rote-learning theory. 1. Reminiscence following learning by massed and by distributed practice. *Journal of Experimental Psychology, 22,* 201–224.

HUBEL, D. H. (1963). The visual cortex of the brain. *Scientific American, 209,* 54–62.

HUBEL, D. H. (1984). The brain. In Editors of *Scientific American, The brain.* San Francisco: Freeman.

HUBEL, D. H., & WIESEL, T. N. (1962). Receptive fields, binocular interaction and functional architecture in the cat's visual cortex. *Journal of Physiology, 160,* 106–154.

HUBEL, D. H., & WIESEL, T. N. (1965). Receptive fields and the functional architecture in two nonstriate visual areas (18 and 19) of the cat. *Journal of Neurophysiology, 28,* 229–289.

HUBEL, D. H., & WIESEL, T. N. (1968). Receptive fields and the functional architecture of the monkey striate cortex. *Journal of Physiology, 195,* 215–243.

HUESMANN, L. R. (ED.). (1978). Learned helplessness as a model of depression [Special issue]. *Journal of Abnormal Psychology, 87*(1).

HUESMANN, L. R., & ERON, L. D. (1986). *Television and the aggressive child: A cross-national comparison.* Hillsdale, NJ: Lawrence Erlbaum Associates.

HUI, Y. H. (1985). *Principles and issues in nutrition.* Belmont, CA: Wadsworth.

HULICKA, I. M. (1967). Age differences in retention as a function of interference. *Journal of Gerontology, 22,* 180–184.

HULL, C. (1952). *A behavior system.* New Haven, CT: Yale University Press.

HUNT, H. T. (1989). *The multiplicity of dreams.* New Haven, CT: Yale University Press.

HUNT, M. (1974). *Sexual behavior in the 1970's.* Chicago: Playboy Press.

HUNT, M. (1982). *The universe within.* New York: Simon & Schuster.

HUSTON, A. C., WATKINS, B. A., & KUNKEL, D. (1989). Public policy and children's television. *American Psychologist, 44,* 424–433.

HUSTON, T. L., RUGGIERO, M., CONNER, R., & GEIS, G. (1981). Bystander intervention into crime: A study based on naturally occurring episodes. *Social Psychology Quarterly, 44,* 14–23.

HUXLEY, A. (1954). *Doors of perception.* New York: Harper & Row.

HYDE, J. S. (1984). How large are gender differences in aggression? A developmental meta-analysis. *Developmental Psychology, 20,* 722–736.

HYDE, J. S. (1986). *Understanding human sexuality* (3rd ed.). New York: McGraw–Hill.

HYDE, J. S., & LINN, M. C. (1988). *The psychology of gender: Advances through meta-analysis.* Baltimore: Johns Hopkins University Press.

HYDE, T. S., & JENKINS, J. J. (1969). Differential effects of incidental tasks on the organization of recall of a list of highly associated words. *Journal of Experimental Psychology, 82,* 472–481.

HYMAN, I. A. (1978). A social science review of evidence cited in litigation on corporal punishment in the schools. *Journal of Clinical Child Psychology, 7*(3), 195–199.

HYMAN, R. (1981). Cold reading: How to convince strangers that you know all about them. In K. Frazier (Ed.), *Paranormal borderlands of science* (pp. 232–244). Buffalo, NY: Prometheus.

HYMAN, R. (1989). The psychology of deception. In M. R. Rosenzweig & L. W. Porter (Eds.), *Annual Review of Psychology* (pp. 133–154). Palo Alto CA: Annual Reviews Inc.

IANNUZZO, G. (1983). "Fire-immunity": PSI ability or psychophysiological phenomenon. *PSI Research, 2*(4), 68–74.

ILLINGWORTH, R. S. (1974). *The development of the infant and young child: Normal and abnormal.* Edinburgh, Britain: Livingstone.

IMPERATO-MCGINLEY, J., PETERSON, R. E., GAUTIER, T., & STURLA, E. (1979). Androgens and the evolution of male-gender identity among male pseudohermaphrodites with 5-α-reductase deficiency. *New England Journal of Medicine, 300,* 1233–1237.

INTRAUB, H. (1979). The role of implicit naming in pictorial encoding. *Journal of Experimental Psychology: Human Learning and Memory, 5*(2), 78–87.

ISAACS, W., THOMAS, J., & GOLDIAMOND, I. (1960). Application of operant conditioning to reinstate verbal behavior in psychotics. *Journal of Speech and Hearing Disorders, 25,* 8–12.

ISAACSON, W. (1983, July 4). Hunting for the hidden killers. *Time, 122,* 50–55.

ISEN, A. M., & LEVINE, P. F. (1972). Effect of feeling good on helping: Cookies and kindness. *Journal of Personality and Social Psychology, 21,* 384–388.

ISENBERG, D. J. (1986). Group polarization: A critical review and meta-analysis. *Journal of Personality and Social Psychology, 50,* 1141–1151.

ISMACH, J. (1988, June). What can we believe? For heterosexuals it's the doubts, not the data, that terrify. *American Health,* pp. 53–54.

IYER, P. (1988, January 18). Of weirdos and eccentrics. *Time,* p. 76.

IZARD, C. E. (1981). Differential emotions theory and the facial feedback hypothesis of emotion activation: Comments on Tourangeau and Ellsworth's "The role of facial response in the experience of emotion." *Journal of Personality and Social Psychology, 40,* 350–354.

IZARD, C. E., HUEBNER, R. R., RISSER, D., MCGINNES, G. C., & DOUGHERTY, L. M. (1980). The young infant's ability to produce discrete emotion expressions. *Development Psychology, 16,* 132–141.

IZARD, C. E. (1984). Emotion-cognition relationships and human development. In C. E. Izard, J. Kagan, & R. B. Zajonc (Eds.), *Emotion, cognitions, and behavior*. New York: Cambridge University Press.

JABLENSKY, A. (1986). Epidemiology of schizophrenia: A European perspective. *Schizophrenia Bulletin, 12*, 52–73.

JACKLIN, C. N. (1989). Female and male: Issues of gender. *American Psychologist, 44*, 127–133.

JACOBSON, A., & MCKINNEY, W. T. (1982). Affective disorders. In J. H. Greist, J. W. Jefferson, & R. L. Spitzer (Eds.), *Treatment of mental disorders*. New York: Oxford University Press.

JACOBSON, J., & WILLE, D. (1986, April). *The influence of attachment pattern on peer interaction at two and three years of age.* Paper presented at the International Conference on Infant Studies, New York, NY.

JACOBY, L. L. (1974). The role of mental contiguity in memory: Registration and retrieval effects. *Journal of Verbal Learning and Verbal Behavior, 13*: 483–496.

JAMES, S. P., WEHR, T. A., SACK, D. A., PARRY, B. L., & ROSENTHAL, N. E. (1985). Treatment of seasonal affective disorders with light in the evening. *British Journal of Psychiatry, 147*, 424–428.

JAMES, W. (1890). *The principles of psychology* (Vol. 2). New York: Holt.

JAMES, W. (1902). *The varieties of religious experience: A study in human nature.* New York: Longmans, Green.

JAMES, W. (1950). *The principles of psychology* (Vol. I). New York: Dover. (Original work published 1890).

JANCIN, B. (1989). Prenatal gender selection appears to be gaining acceptance. *Obstetrical and Gynecological News, 23*, 30.

JANIS, I. (1972). *Victims of groupthink: A psychological study of foreign-policy decisions and fiascoes.* Boston: Houghton Mifflin.

JANIS, I. (1982). Counteracting the adverse effects of concurrence-seeking in policy-planning groups. In H. Brandstatter, J. H. Davis, & G. Stocker-Kreichgauer (Eds.), *Group decision making*. New York: Academic Press.

JANIS I. (1983). *Groupthink: Psychological studies of policy decisions and fiascoes* (2nd ed.). Boston: Houghton Mifflin.

JANIS, I., & MANN, L. (1977). *Decision making: A psychological analysis of conflict, choice, and commitment.* New York: Free Press.

JANOV, A. (1970). *The primal scream.* New York: Dell.

JANOWITZ, J. F. (1967). There's no hiding place down there. *American Journal of Orthopsychiatry, 37*(2), 296.

JELLISON, J. M., & GREEN, J. (1981). A self-presentation approach to the fundamental attribution error: The norm of internality. *Journal of Personality and Social Psychology, 40*, 643–649.

JEMMOTT, J. B., & LOCKE, S. E. (1984). Psychosocial factors, immunologic meditation, and human susceptibility to infectious diseases: How much do we know? *Psychological Bulletin, 95*, 52–77.

JENKINS, J. G., & DALLENBACK, K. M. (1924). Oblivescence during sleep and waking. *American Journal of Psychology, 35*, 605–612.

JENNER, F. A., GJESSING, L. R., COX, J. R., DAVIES-JONES, H., & HULLIN, R. P. (1967). A manic-depressive psychotic with a 48 hour cycle. *British Journal of Psychiatry, 113*(501), 895–910.

JENNINGS, W. S., & KOHLBERG, L. (1983). Effects of a just community programme on the moral development of youthful offenders. *Journal of Moral Education, 12*(1), 33–50.

JENSEN, A. R. (1969). How much can we boost IQ and scholastic achievement? *Harvard Educational Review, 39*, 1–123.

JENSEN, A. R. (1984). The black–white difference on the K-ABC: Implications for future tests. *Journal of Special Education, 18*(3), 377–408.

JOAN, P. (1985). *Preventing teenage suicide.* New York: Human Sciences Press.

JOHANNSON, C. B. (1982). *Career assessment inventory.* Minneapolis: National Computer Systems.

JOHNSON, D. W., JOHNSON, R. T., & MARUYAMA, C. (1984) Goal interdependence and interpersonal attraction in heterogeneous classrooms: A meta-analysis. In N. Miller & M. B. Brewer (Eds.), *Groups in contact: The psychology of desegregation*. San Diego: Academic Press.

JOHNSON, M. K., & HASHER, L. (1987). Human learning and memory. In M. R. Rosenzweig and L. W. Porter (Eds.), *Annual review of psychology* (pp. 631–688). Palo Alto, CA: Annual Reviews.

JOHNSTON, L. D., BACHMAN, J. G., & O'MALLEY, P. M. (1986). *Monitoring the future: Questionnaire responses from the nation's high school seniors, 1985.* Ann Arbor, MI: University of Michigan, Institute of Social Research.

JOHNSTON, L. D., BACHMAN, J. G., & O'MALLEY, P. M. (1987). *Student drug use in America.* Ann Arbor, MI: Institute of Social Research.

JONES, E. (1961). *The life and work of Sigmund Freud* (L. Trilling & S. Marcus, Eds.). Garden City, NY: Anchor.

JONES, E. E., & BERGLAS, S. (1978). Control of attributions about the self through self-handicapping strategies: The appeal of alcohol and the role of underachievement. *Personality and Social Psychology Bulletin, 4*, 200–206.

JONES, E. E., & NISBETT, R. E. (1971). *The actor and the observer: Divergent perceptions of the causes of behavior.* Morristown, NJ: General Learning Press.

JONES E. R., FORREST, J. D., GOLDMAN, N., HENSHAW, S. K., LINCOLN, R., ROSOFF, J. I., WESTOFF, C. F., & WULF, D. (1985). Teen-age pregnancy in developed countries: Determinants and policy implications. *Family Planning Perspectives, 17*, 53–63.

JONES, K. L., SMITH, D. W., ULLELAND, C. N., & STREISSGUTH, A. P. (1973). Pattern of malformation in offspring of chronic alcoholic mothers. *Lancet, 1*, 1267–1271.

JONES, M. C. (1924). The elimination of children's fears. *Journal of Experimental Psychology, 7*, 382–390.

JONES, W. R., & ELLIS, N. R. (1962). Inhibitory potential in rotary pursuit acquisition. *Journal of Experimental Psychology, 63*, 534–537.

JORGENSON, D. O., & PAPCIAK, A. S. (1981). The effects of communication, resource feedback, and identifiability on behavior in a simulated commons. *Journal of Experimental Social Psychology, 17*, 373–385.

JOSEPHSON, W. L. (1987). Television violence and children's aggression: Testing the priming, social script, and disinhibition predictions. *Journal of Personality and Social Psychology, 53*, 882–890.

JOSSELSON, R. (1980). Ego development in adolescence. In J. Adelson (Ed.), *Handbook of adolescent psychology* (pp. 188–211). New York: Wiley.

JOYCE, C. (1984, February). Lie detector. *Psychology Today*, pp. 6–8.

JOYCE, C. (1988, March). Assault on the brain. *Psychology Today*, pp. 38–44.

JULIEN, R. (1985). *A primer of drug action* (4th ed.). San Francisco: Freeman.

JULIEN, R. M. (1988). *A primer of drug action* (5th ed.). Salt Lake City: Freeman.

JUNG, C. G. (1933). *Modern man in search of a soul.* New York: Harcourt, Brace, World.

JUNG, C. (1936/1969). The concept of the collective unconscious. In *Collected works* (Vol. 9, Part 1). Princeton, NJ: Princeton University Press. (Original work published 1936.)

JUTAI, J. N. (1984). Cerebral asymmetry and the psychophysiology of attention. *Journal of Psychophysiology, 1*(3), 219–225.

KAGAN, J. (1971). *Change and continuity in infancy.* New York: Wiley.

KAGAN, J. (1984). *The nature of the child.* New York: Basic Books.

KAGAN, J. (1987, May). Baby research comes of age. *Psychology Today*, pp. 46–47.

KAGAN, J., REZNICK, J. S., & SNIDMAN, N. (1988). Biological bases of childhood shyness. *Science, 240*, 167–171.

KAHN, S., ZIMMERMAN, G., CSIKSZENTMIHALYI, M., & GETZELS, J. W. (1985). Relations between identity in young adulthood and intimacy at midlife. *Journal of Personality and Social Psychology, 49*, 1316–1322.

KALAT, J. W. (1988). *Biological psychology* (3rd ed.). Belmont, CA: Wadsworth.

KALES, A., & KALES, J. (1973). Recent advances in the diagnosis and treatment of sleep disorders. In G. Usdin (Ed.), *Sleep research and clinical practice*. New York: Brunner/Mazel.

tal Methamphetamine. Oceanside, CA: McAlister Institute.

LASHLEY, K. S. (1950). In search of the engram. *Society for Experimental Biology,* Symposium No. 4, 454–482.

LATANE, B., & DARLEY, J. M. (1968). Group inhibition of bystander intervention in emergencies. *Journal of Personality and Social Psychology, 10,* 215–221.

LATANE, B., & DARLEY, J. M. (1970). *The unresponsive bystander: Why doesn't he help?* New York: Appleton–Century–Crofts.

LATANE, B., & NIDA, S. (1981). Ten years of research on group size and helping. *Psychological Bulletin, 89,* 308–324.

LAU, R. R. (1984). Dynamics of the attribution process. *Journal of Personality and Social Psychology, 46,* 1017–1028.

LA VOIE, J. C. (1976). Ego identity formation in middle adolescence. *Journal of Youth and Adolescence, 5,* 371–385.

LAZARUS, A. A. (1971). *Behavior therapy and beyond.* New York: McGraw–Hill.

LAZARUS, R. S., & FOLKMAN, S. (1984). *Stress appraisal and coping.* New York: Springer.

LEARY, W. E. (1988, January 14). Young adults show drop in cocaine use. *New York Times,* p. C1.

LEAVITT, F. (1982). *Drugs and behavior* (2nd ed.). New York: Wiley.

LEE, J. A. (1983). The role of the sympathetic nervous system in ischaemic heart disease: A review of epidemiological features and risk factors, integration with clinical and experimental evidence and hypothesis. *Activitas Nervosa Superior, 25*(2), 110–121.

LEFF, H. S., & BRADLEY, V. J. (1986). DRGs are not enough. *American Psychologist, 41*(1), 73–78.

LEIBOWITZ, (1985). Grade crossing accidents and human factors engineering. *American Scientist, 73,* 558–562.

LEIKIND, B. J., & MCCARTHY, W. J. (1985). An investigation of firewalking. *The Skeptical Inquirer, 10*(1), 23–34.

LEO, J. (1982, August 2). The new scarlet letter. *Time, 120,* 62–66.

LEO, J. (1986, July 7). How cocaine killed Leonard Bias. *Time,* p. 52.

LEO, J. (1988, January 25). A chilling wave of racism. *Time,* p. 57.

LEO, J. (1988, September 19). Drugs: A spot of tea. *Time,* p. 29.

LEON, G. R. (1977), *Anxiety neurosis: The case of Richard Benson: Case histories in deviant behavior* (2nd ed.). Boston: Holbrook Press.

LEONARD, G. R. (1974, February). Depression and suicidality. *Journal of Consulting and Clinical Psychology, 42*(1), 98–104.

LEPPER, M. R., GREENE, D., & NISBETT, R. E. (1973). Undermining children's intrinsic interest with extrinsic rewards: A test of the overjustification hypothesis. *Journal of Personality and Social Psychology, 28,* 129–137.

LERMAN, P. (1981). *Deinstitutionalization: A cross-problem-analysis* (DHHS Publication No. ADM 81–987). Washington, DC: U.S. Government Printing Office.

LERNER, M. J. (1975). The justice motive in social behavior. *Journal of Social Issues, 31*(3), 1–19.

LETTVIN, J. Y., MATURANA, H. R., MCCULLOCH, W. S., & PITTS, W. H. (1959). What the frog's eye tells the frog's brain. *Proceedings of the Institute of Radio Engineers, 47,* 1940–1951.

LEVENKRON, S. (1982). *Treating and overcoming anorexia nervosa.* New York: Scribner's.

LEVINE, M. A. (1975). *A cognitive theory of learning.* Hillsdale, NJ: Lawrence Erlbaum Associates.

LEVINSON, D. J. (1977). The mid-life transition, *Psychiatry, 40,* 99–112.

LEVINSON, D. J. (1986). A conception of adult development. *American Psychologist, 41*(1), 3–13. (a).

LEVINSON, D. J. (1986). *The seasons of a woman's life.* New York: Knopf. (b)

LEVINSON, D. J., DARROW, C. N., KLEIN, E. B., LEVINSON, M. H., & MCKEE, B. (1978). *The seasons of a man's life.* New York: Knopf.

LEVITT, E. E. (1988, April). Questions about multiple personality. *Harvard Medical School Mental Health Letter, 4*(10), 8.

LEWIN, K. (1948). *Resolving social conflicts.* New York: Harper.

LEWIS, C. C. (1981). The effects of parental firm control: A reinterpretation of findings. *Psychological Bulletin, 90,* 547–563.

LEWIS, D. (1980). *The secret language of your child.* New York: St. Martin's Press.

LEWIS, M. (1982). State as an infant–environment interaction: An analysis of mother–infant behavior as a function of sex. *Merrill-Palmer Quarterly, 18,* 95–211.

LEWIS, M., FEIRING, C., MCGUFFOG, C., & JASKIR, J. (1984). Predicting psychopathology in six-year-olds from early social relations. *Child Development, 55,* 123–136.

LEWIS, S. (1963). *Dear Shari.* New York: Stein & Day.

LI, C. (1975). *Path analysis: A primer.* Pacific Grove, CA: Boxwood Press.

LI, X., & SHEN, Z. (1985). Positive electron emission layer scanning technique and its application in psychological research. *Information on Psychological Sciences, 3,* 54–58.

LIBEN, L. S., & SIGNORELLA, M. L. (EDS.) (1987). *Children's gender schemata.* San Francisco: Jossey–Bass.

LIBERMAN, A. M. (1970). The grammars of language and speech. *Cognitive Psychology, 1,* 301–323.

LIBERMAN, R. P., CARDIN, V., MCGILL, C. W., FALLOON, I. R. H., & EVANS. C (1987). Behavioral family management of schizophrenia: Clinical outcome and costs. *Psychiatric Annals, 17,* 610–619.

LICHTENSTEIN, E., & PENNER, M. P. (1977). Long-term effects of rapid smoking treatment for dependent cigarette smokers. *Addictive Behaviors, 2,* 109–112.

LICKONA, T. (1985). *Raising good children.* New York: Bantam.

LIFTON, P. D. (1984). Personality and morality: An empirical and theoretical examination of personality development, moral reasoning, and moral behavior. *Dissertation Abstracts International, 44*(8-B), 2577.

LIFTON, R. J. (1979, January 7). Appeal of the death trip. *New York Times Magazine,* pp. 26–27.

LILLY, J. C. (1956). Mental effects of reduction of ordinary levels of physical stimuli in intact healthy persons. *Psychiatric Research Reports, 5,* 1–28.

LILLY, J. C. (1975). *Simulations of God: The science of belief.* New York: Simon & Schuster.

LINDSEY, P. H., & NORMAN, D. A. (1977). *Human information processing.* New York: Academic Press.

LINDSKOLD, S., WALTERS, P. S., & KOUTSOURAIS, H. (1983). Cooperators, competitors, and response to GRIT. *Journal of Conflict Resolution, 27,* 521–532.

LINTON, M. (1979, July). I remember it well. *Psychology Today,* pp. 81–86.

LOEHLIN, J. C., WILLERMAN, L., & HORN, J. M. (1988). Human behavior genetics. In M. R. Rosenzweig & L. W. Porter (Eds.), *Annual review of psychology* (pp. 101–133). Palo Alto, CA: Annual Reviews.

LOFTUS, E. F. (1980). *Memory.* Reading, MA: Addison–Wesley.

LOFTUS, E. F. (1982). Memory and its distortions. In A. G. Kraut (Ed.), *The G. Stanley Hall Lecture Series* (Vol. 2, pp. 123–154). Washington, DC: American Psychological Association.

LOFTUS, E. F. (1983). Whose shadow is crooked? *American Psychologist, 38,* 576–577.

LOFTUS, E. F., & LOFTUS, G. R. (1980). On the permanence of stored information in the human brain. *American Psychologist, 35*(5), 409–420.

LOGUE, A. W. (1986). *The psychology of eating and drinking.* New York: Freeman.

LONDERVILLE, S., & MAIN, M. (1981). Security of attachment, compliance, and maternal training methods in the second year of life. *Developmental Psychology, 17,* 289–299.

LONG, J. W. (1989). *The essential guide to prescription drugs.* New York: Harper & Row.

LONG, M. E. (1987). What is this thing called sleep? *National Geographic, 112,* 787–821.

LONG, P. (1986, January). Medical mesmerism. *Psychology Today,* pp. 28–29.

LONGFELLOW, C. J. (1979). Social support and mother–child interactions. *Dissertation Abstracts International, 40*(6-B), 2822.

LO PICCOLO, L. (1980). Low sexual desire. In

S. R. Leiblum & L. A. Pervin (Eds.), *Principles and practice of sex therapy* (pp. 29–64). New York: Guilford Press.

LORAYNE, H. (1985). *Harry Lorayne's page-a-minute memory book.* New York: Holt, Rinehart & Winston.

LORAYNE, H., & LUCAS, J. (1974). *The memory book.* New York: Ballantine.

LORD, L. J., GOODE, E. E., GEST, T., MCAULIFFE, K., MOORE, L. J., BLACK, R. F., & LINNON, N. (1987, November 30). Coming to grips with alcoholism. *U.S. News and World Report,* pp. 56–62.

LORENZ, K. (1937). The companion in the bird's world. *Auk, 54,* 245–273.

LORENZ, K. (1966). *On aggression.* London: Methuen.

LORENZ, K. (1974). *The eight deadly sins of civilized man.* (M. Kerr-Wilson, Trans.). New York: Harcourt Brace Jovanovich.

LORENZ, K. (1986). *Foundations of ethology.* New York: Springer-Verlag.

LOVAAS, O. I. (1977). *The autistic child: Language development through behavior modification.* New York: Irvington.

LOWRY, K. (1987, November 1). The designer babies are growing up. *Los Angeles Times Magazine,* pp. 12–32.

LOZOFF, B. (1989). Nutrition and behavior. *American Psychologist, 44,* 231–236.

LUCE, G. (1970). *Biological rhythms in psychiatry and medicine* (U.S. Public Health Service Publication No. 2088). Washington, DC: U.S. Government Printing Office.

LUCE, G. (1971). *Body time.* New York: Pantheon.

LUCE, G., & SEGAL, J. (1966). *Sleep.* New York: Lancet.

LUCHINS, A. S. (1942). Mechanization in problem solving. *Psychological Monographs, 54*(6, Whole No. 248).

LUCHINS, A. S., & LUCHINS, E. H. (1950). New experimental attempts at preventing mechanization in problem solving. *Journal of General Psychology, 42,* 279–297.

LUCINS, D. (1975). The dopamine hypothesis of schizophrenia: A critical analysis. *Neuropsychobiology, 1,* 365–378.

LUDWIG, A. M. (1966). Altered states of consciousness. *Archives of General Psychiatry, 15,* 225–233.

LUMSDEN, C. J., & WILSON, E. O. (1983). *Promethean fire: Reflections on the origin of mind.* Cambridge, MA: Harvard University Press.

LUNDEN, R. W. (1984). Horney, Karen D. In R. J. Corsini (Ed.), *Encyclopedia of psychology* (Vol. 2, pp. 139–140). New York: Wiley.

LURIA, A. R. (1968). *The mind of a mnemonist.* New York: Basic Books.

LURIA, A. R. (1973). *The working brain.* New York: Basic Books.

LURIA, A. R. (1980). *Higher cortical functions in man.* New York: Basic Books.

LURIA, Z., FRIEDMAN, S., & ROSE, M. (1986). *Human sexuality.* New York: Wiley.

LYKKEN, D. T. (1981). *A tremor in the blood: Uses and abuses of the lie detector.* New York: McGraw–Hill.

LYKKEN, D. T. (1984). Polygraphic interrogation. *Nature, 307,* 681–684.

LYNCH, G. (1984, April). A magical memory tour. *Psychology Today,* pp. 29–39.

LYNCH, G. (1988). *Identification of a memory mechanism.* Paper presented at the Cognitive Sciences Colloquium, University of California, Irvine, CA.

LYNCH, G., HALPIN, S., & BAUDRY, M. (1983). Structural and biochemical effects of high frequency stimulation in the hippocampus. In W. Seifert (Ed.), *Neurobiology of the hippocampus* (pp. 253–264). London: Academic Press.

LYNN, S. J., & RHUE, J. W. (1985, September). Daydream believers. *Psychology Today,* pp. 14–16.

LYNN, S. J., RHUE, J. W. (1988). Fantasy proneness: Hypnosis, developmental antecedents, and psychopathology. *American Psychologist, 43,* 35–44.

MACCOBY, E. E., & JACKLIN, C. N. (1974). *The psychology of sex differences.* Stanford, CA: Stanford University Press.

MacCOUN, R. J., & KERR, N. L. (1988). Asymmetric influence in mock jury deliberation: Jurors' bias for leniency. *Journal of Personality and Social Psychology, 54,* 21–33.

MACKIE, D., & COOPER, J. (1984). Attitude polarization: Effects of group membership. *Journal of Personality and Social Psychology, 46*(3), 575–583.

MacLEOD, A. D. (1983). Calenture—Missing at sea? *British Journal of Medical Psychology, 56*(4), 347–350.

MacLUSKEY, N., & NAFTOLIN, F. (1981). Sexual differentiation of the central nervous system. *Science, 211,* 1294–1303.

MADDEN, J. J., & KRASNER, N. (1984). Some changing vistas. In N. Krasner, J. S. Madden, & R. J. Walker (Eds.), *Alcohol related problems: Room for manoeuvre* (pp. 3–20). New York: Wiley.

MADDI, S. R. (1980). *Personality theories: A comparative analysis* (4th ed.). Homewood, IL: Dorsey.

MADDOX, G. L. (1970). Persistence of life style among the elderly. In E. Palmore (Ed.), *Normal aging* (pp. 329–331). Durham, NC: Duke University Press.

MADDUX, J. E., ROBERTS, M. C., SLEDDEN, E. A., & WRIGHT, L. (1986). Developmental issues in child health psychology. *American Psychologist, 1,* 25–34.

MADRAZO, I., LEON, V., TORRES, C., ET AL. (1988). Transplantation of fetal substantia nigra and adrenal medulla to the caudate nucleus in two patients with Parkinson's disease. *New England Journal of Medicine, 318,* 51.

MAGID, K., & MCKELVEY, C. A. (1987). *High risk: Children without a conscience.* New York: Bantam.

MAGNUSON, E. (1988, August 15). A house divided. *Time,* pp. 14–15.

MAJOR, R. (1979, December). The twisted roots of Jonestown. *Mother Jones,* pp. 20–22.

MALINOWSKI, B. (1929). *The sexual life of savages.* New York: Harcourt, Brace, World.

MALINOWSKI, B. (1955). *The father in primitive society.* New York: Norton.

MANDLER, G. (1980). Recognizing: The judgment of previous occurrence. *Psychological Review, 87,* 252–272.

MANGAN, G. L., & GOLDING, J. F. (1983). The effects of smoking on memory consolidation. *Journal of Psychology, 115,* 65–77.

MANGES, K., & EVENBECK, S. (1980, March). *Social power, jealousy, and dependency in the intimate dyad.* Paper presented at the meeting of the Midwestern Psychological Association, St. Louis.

MANN, L. (1981). The baiting crowd in episodes of threatened suicide. *Journal of Personality and Social Psychology, 41,* 703–709.

MARANTO, G. (1984, November). Emotions: How they affect your body. *Discover,* pp. 35–38.

MARCIA, J. E. (1980). Identity in adolescence. In J. Adelson (Ed.), *Handbook of adolescent psychology* (pp. 12–43). New York: Wiley.

MARGO, J. L. (1987). Anorexia nervosa in males: A comparison with female patients. *British Journal of Psychiatry, 151,* 80–83.

MARGOLIN, G. (1982). An interactional model for the assessment of marital relationships. *Behavioral Assessment, 5,* 175–201.

MARLATT, G. A., & GORDON, J. R. (1985). *Relapse prevention: Maintenance strategies for addictive behavior change.* New York: Guilford Press.

MARLER, P., & MUNDINGER, P. (1971). Vocal learning in birds. In H. Moltz (Ed.), *The ontogeny of vertebrate behavior.* New York: Academic Press.

MARLOWE, W. B., MANCALL, E. L., & THOMAS, J. J. (1975). Complete Kluver–Bucy syndrome in man. *Cortex, 11,* 53–59.

MARSELLA, A. J. (1980). Depressive experience and disorder across cultures. In H. Triandis & J. Draguns (Eds.), *Handbook of cross-cultural psychology,* Vol. 6: *Psychopathology.* Boston: Allyn & Bacon.

MARSHALL, G. P., & ZIMBARDO, P. G. (1979). Affective consequences of inadequately explained physiological arousal. *Journal of Personality and Social Psychology, 37,* 970–988.

MARSHALL, S. (1985, July 31). Gray panther, 80, still on the prowl. *USA Today,* p. 2.

MARTIN, G., & PEAR, J. (1983). *Behavior modification.* Englewood Cliffs, NJ: Prentice–Hall.

MARTINO, M. (1977). *Emergence: A transsexual autobiography.* New York: Crown.

MARX, J. L. (1988). Sexual responses are almost all in the brain. *Science, 241,* 903–904.

MASLACH, C. (1979). Negative emotional biasing

of unexplained arousal. *Journal of Personality and Social Psychology, 37,* 359–369.

MASLOW, A. H. (1954). *Motivation and personality.* New York: Harper & Row.

MASLOW, A. H. (1970). *Motivation and personality* (2nd ed.). New York: Harper & Row.

MASLOW, A. H. (1976). *Religions, values, and peak experiences.* New York: Penguin.

MASSEY, R. F., & GOLDMAN, M. S. (1988, August). *Manipulating expectancies as a means of altering alcohol consumption.* Paper presented at the annual meeting of the American Psychological Association, Atlanta.

MASSON, J. M. (1984). *The assault on truth: Freud's suppression of the seduction theory.* New York: Farrar, Straus, & Giroux. (a).

MASSON, J. M. (1984, February). Freud and the seduction theory. *Atlantic Monthly,* pp. 33–60. (b)

MASSON, J. M. (1988). *The shrink has no clothes.* New York: Atheneum.

MASTERS, W. H., & JOHNSON, V. E. (1966). *Human sexual response.* Boston: Little, Brown.

MASTERS, W. H., & JOHNSON, V. E. (1970). *Human sexual inadequacy.* Boston: Little, Brown.

MASTERS, W. H., & JOHNSON, V. E. (1979). *Homosexuality in perspective.* Boston: Little, Brown.

MASTERS, W. H., JOHNSON, V. E., & KOLODNY, R. C. (1986). *Sex and human loving.* Boston: Little, Brown.

MASTERS, W. H., JOHNSON, V. E., & KOLODNY, R. C. (1988). *Human Sexuality* (3rd ed.). Boston: Little, Brown.

MATHEWS, K. A. (1984). Assessment of type A, anger, and hostility in epidemiological studies of cardiovascular disease. In A. Ostfeld & E. Eaker (Eds.), *Measuring psychosocial variables in epidemiologic studies of cardiovascular disease.* Bethesda, MD: National Institute for Health.

MATLIN, M. (1983). *Cognition.* New York: Holt, Rinehart & Winston.

MAURER, D., & YOUNG, R. E. (1983). Newborn's following of natural and distorted arrangements of facial features. *Infant Behavior and Development, 6,* 127–131.

MAY, P. R. A. (1974). Psychotherapy research in schizophrenia—Another view of present reality. *Schizophrenia Bulletin,* pp. 126–132.

MAY, P. R. A., TUMA, H., & DIXON, W. J. (1981). Schizophrenia: A follow-up study of the results of five forms of treatment. *Archives of General Psychiatry, 38,* 776–784.

MAYER, J. (1952). The glucostatic theory of regulation of food intake and the problem of obesity. *Bulletin of the New England Medical Center, 14,* 43.

MAYER, J. (1955). Regulation of energy intake and the body weight: The glucostatic theory and the lipostatic hypothesis. *Annals of the New York Academy of Sciences, 63,* 15–43.

MCALLISTER, W. R., MCALLISTER, D. E., SCOLES, M. T., & HAMPTON, S. R. (1986). Persistence of fear-reducing behavior: Relevance for the conditioning theory of neurosis. *Journal of Abnormal Psychology, 95,* 365–372.

MCCANN, S. J., & STEWIN, L. L. (1987). Threat, authoritarianism, and the power of U.S. Presidents. *Journal of Psychology, 121,* 149–157.

MCCARTHY, P. (1986, July). Scent: The tie that binds. *Psychology Today,* pp. 6–10.

MCCLELLAND, D. C., CONSTANTIAN, C. A., REGALADO, D., & STONE, C. (1978). Making it to maturity. *Psychology Today,* pp. 42–53, 114.

MCCONNELL, J. V. (1962). Memory transfer through cannibalism in planarians. *Journal of Neuropsychiatry, 3,* Suppl. 1, 542–548.

MCCONNELL, J. V. (1968). The modern search for the engram. In W. C. Corning & M. Balaban (Eds.), *The mind: Biological approaches to its functions.* New York: Interscience.

MCCOURT, R. (1985, March). Walking on fire. *Science, 85,* 84.

MCCRAE, R., & COSTA, P. T., JR. (1982). Self-concept and the stability of personality: Cross-sectional comparisons of self-reports and ratings. *Journal of Personality and Social Psychology, 43,* 1282–1292.

MCDOUGALL, W. (1908). *Social psychology.* New York: Putnam's Sons.

MCGEOCH, J. A. (1942). *The psychology of human learning.* New York: Longmans, Green.

MCGILL, M. B. (1985). *The McGill Report on male intimacy.* New York: Holt, Rinehart & Winston.

MCGRADY, A., FINE, T., WOERNER, M., & YONKER, R. (1983). Maintenance of treatment effects of biofeedback-assisted relaxation on patients with essential hypertension. *American Journal of Clinical Biofeedback, 6*(1), 34–39.

MCGUIRE, W. J. (1985). Attitudes and attitude change. In G. Lindzey & E. Aronson (Eds.), *Handbook of social psychology* (Vol. II, 3rd ed.). New York: Random House.

MCINTOSH, I. D. (1984). Smoking and pregnancy: Attributable risks and public health implications. *Canadian Journal of Public Health, 75,* 141–148.

MCKELLAR, P. (1972). Imagery from the standpoint of introspection. In P. W. Sheehan (Ed.), *The function and nature of imagery.* New York: Academic Press.

MCKINLAY, J. B., & MCKINLAY, S. M. (1986, April). Depression in middle-aged women: Social circumstances versus estrogen deficiency. *Harvard Medical School Mental Health Letter, 2*(10), 4–6.

MCKOON, G., RATCLIFF, R., & DELL, G. S. (1986). A critical evaluation of the semantic-episodic distinction. *Journal of Experimental Psychology: Learning, Memory and Cognition, 12,* 295–306.

MCLOYD, V. C. (1989). Socialization and development in a changing economy. *American Psychologist, 44,* 293–302.

MCMANUS, J. A., PRYOR, J. B., REEDER, G. D. (1988, August). *Fear and loathing in the workplace: Reactions to AIDS infected coworkers.* Paper presented at the annual meeting of the American Psychological Association, Atlanta.

MCMURRAY, G. A. (1950). Experimental study of a case of insensitivity to pain. *Archives of Neurological Psychiatry, 64,* 650–667.

MCNEILL, D. (1966). Developmental psycholinguistics. In F. Smith & G. A. Miller (Eds.), *The genesis of language: A psycholinguistic approach* (pp. 15–84). Cambridge, MA: MIT Press.

MCNEILL, S. F., & KIMMEL, E. B. (1988). *Effects of extrinsic incentives on problem solving: Motivation, performance, and recall.* Paper presented at the annual meeting of the American Psychological Association, Atlanta.

MCREYNOLDS, P. (1989). Diagnosis and clinical assessment: Current status and major issues. In M. R. Rosenzweig & L. W. Porter (Eds.), *Annual Review of Psychology* (pp. 83–108). Palo Alto, CA: Annual Reviews Inc.

MEAD, M. (1964). *Continuities in cultural evolution.* New Haven, CT: Yale University Press.

MEANEY, M. J., AITKEN, D. H., VAN BERKEL, C., BHATNAGER, S., & SAPOLSKY, R. M. (1988). Effect of neonatal handling on age-related impairments associated with the hippocampus. *Science, 239,* 766–768.

MEDDIS, R., PEARSON, A. J., & LANGFORD, G. (1973). An extreme case of healthy insomnia. *Electroencephalography & Clinical Neurophysiology, 35,* 213–221.

MEDLICOT, R. W. (1948). Electronarcosis, with special reference to the treatment of paranoid schizophrenia. *Journal of Mental Science, 94,* 793–798.

MEDNICK, S. A., MOFFITT, T. E., & STACK, S. (1987). *The causes of crime: New biological approaches.* New York: Cambridge University Press.

MEDNICK, S. A., & SCHULSINGER, F. (1968). Some premorbid characteristics related to breakdown in children with schizophrenic mothers. In D. Rosenthal & S. S. Kety (Eds.), *The treatment of schizophrenia.* Elmsford, NY: Pergamon.

MEER, J. (1986, January). AIDS: The illogical connection. *Psychology Today,* p. 10. (a)

MEER, J. (1986, June). The reason of age. *Psychology Today,* pp. 60–64. (b)

MEICHENBAUM, D. (1975). A self-instructional approach to stress management: A proposal for stress inoculation training. In C. D. Spielberger & I. G. Sarason (Eds.), *Stress and anxiety* (Vol. I). New York: Halsted Press.

MELTON, G. B., & GARRISON, E. G. (1987). Fear, prejudice, and neglect: Discrimination against mentally disabled persons. *American Psychologist, 42,* 1007–1026.

NISBETT, R.
ference:
cial jud
Prentice-
NOBLE, E. P.
function
& R. Fo
research
demic Pr
NORMAN, D.
New Yor
NORMAN, W.
onomy of
factor str
ality ratir
cial Psyc
NOUWEN, A.
effectiven
low back
lation, 4,
NOVAK, M. A
recovery
year of
Developr
465.
NOVICK, B. (
overview.
(Eds.), *C*
(pp. 765
Nebraska
NOVLIN, D.,
& TORDO
the liver i
can Jour
246.
NYE, R. D. (
terey, CA
NYITI, R. M.
differenc
variation
developn
venson
child de
Francisc
OJANLATUA,
(1987). T
survivors
School H
OKIN, R. L. (
zation.
Health L
OLDS, J., &
forcemen
of septal
Journal
Psychol
OLSHAN, N. (
out drug
OLSON, J. M
tory info
nal of Pe
54, 758-
ORBACH, I. (
live. San
ORFORD, J.
York: W

MELTON, G. B., & GRAY, J. N. (1988). Ethical dilemmas in AIDS research: Individual privacy and public health. *American Psychologist, 43,* 60–64.

MELZACK, R., & PERRY, C. (1975). Self-regulation of pain: The use of alpha-feedback and hypnotic training for the control of chronic pain. *Experimental Neurology, 46,* 452–464.

MELZACK, R., & WALL, P. D. (1965). Pain mechanisms: A new theory. *Science, 150,* 971–979.

MENDLEWICZ, J., SIMON, P., SEVY, S., CHARON, F., BROCAS, H., LEGROS, S., & VASSART, G. (1987). Polymorphic DNA marker on X chromosome and manic depression. *Lancet, 1,* 1230–1232.

MENYUK, P. (1983). Language development and reading. In T. M. Gallagher & C. A. Prutting (Eds.), *Pragmatic assessment and intervention issues in language.* San Diego: College-Hill Press.

MERARI, A. (Ed.) (1985). *On terrorism and combating terrorism.* New York: University Publications of America.

MEREDITH, N. (1986, June). Testing the talking cure. *Science, 86, 7*(5), 30–37.

MERVIS, J. (1985, October). Council pledges greater support for state efforts. *APA Monitor, 16*(10), 2.

MESIROW, K. (1984, August). *Animal research survey.* Paper presented at the annual meeting of the American Psychological Association, Toronto, Ontario.

MESSER, D. J., MCCARTHY, M. E., MCQUISTON, S., MACTURK, R. H., YARROW, L. J., & VIETZE, P. M. (1986). Relation between mastery behavior in infancy and competence in early childhood. *Developmental Psychology, 22,* 366–372.

MESSICK, D. M., MACKIE, D. M. (1989). Intergroup relations. In M. R. Rosenzweig & L. W. Porter (Eds.), *Annual Review of Psychology* (pp. 45–82). Palto Alto, CA: Annual Reviews Inc.

MEYER, A. (1982, June). Do lie detectors lie? *Science, 82,* 24–26.

MEYER, A. (1984, October 8). Latest diet craze —Not for everyone. *U.S. News and World Report, 97,* 57–60.

MEYER, R. G., & SALMON, P. (1988). *Abnormal psychology* (2nd ed.). Boston: Allyn & Bacon.

MICHAEL, R. P., & KEVERNE, E. B. (1970). Primate sex pheromones of vaginal origin. *Nature, 224,* 84–85.

MICHELSON, L. (Ed.). (1985). Meta-analysis and clinical psychology [Special issue]. *Clinical Psychology Review, 5*(1).

MIKKELSEN, E. J. (1986). What is aversive treatment of autism, and when should it be used? *Harvard Medical School Mental Health Letter, 2*(10), 8.

MIKLOWITZ, D. J., STRACHAN, A. M., GOLDSTEIN, M. J., DOANE, J. A., SNYDER, K. S., HOGARTY, G. E., & FALLOON, I. R. (1986). Expressed emotion and communication de-

viance in the families of schizophrenics. *Journal of Abnormal Psychology, 95,* 60–66.

MILGRAM, S. (1963). Behavioral study of obedience. *Journal of Abnormal and Social Psychology, 67,* 371–378.

MILGRAM, S. (1974). *Obedience to authority: An experimental view.* New York: Harper & Row.

MILLER, B., & MYERS-WALL, J. (1983). Parenthood: Transitions in and out. In H. McCubbin & C. Figley (Eds.), *Stress and the family,* Vol. 3: *Coping with normative crises.* New York: Brunner/Mazel.

MILLER, C. T. (1984). Self-schemas, gender, and social comparison: A clarification of the related attributes hypothesis. *Journal of Personality and Social Psychology, 46,* 1222–1229.

MILLER, G. A. (1956). The magical number seven, plus or minus two: Some limits on our capacity for processing information. *Psychological Review, 63,* 81–97.

MILLER, J. D. (1986). *Technological literacy: Some concepts and measures.* DeKalb, IL: Northern Illinois University, Public Opinion Laboratory.

MILLER, N., MARUYAMA, G., BEABER, R. J., & VALONE, K. (1976). Speed of speech and persuasion. *Journal of Personality and Social Psychology, 34,* 615–624.

MILLER, N. E. (1978). Biofeedback and visceral learning. *Annual Review of Learning, 29,* 373–404.

MILLER, N. E., & DICARA, L. (1967). Instrumental learning of heart rate changes in curarized rats: Shaping and specificity to discriminative stimulus. *Journal of Comparative and Physiological Psychology, 63,* 12–19.

MILLER, N. M. (1982). Hypnoaversion treatment in alcoholism, nicotinism, and weight control. *Journal of the National Medical Association, 68,* 129–130.

MILLMAN, M. (1980). *Such a pretty face: Being fat in America.* New York: Norton.

MILLS, J. (1979). *Six years with God.* New York: A & W Publishers.

MILLS, J. L., BRAUBARD, B. I., HARLEY, E. E., RHOADS, G. G., & BERENDES, H. W. (1984). Maternal alcohol consumption and birth weight: How much drinking during pregnancy is safe? *Journal of the American Medical Association, 252,* 1857–1879.

MILNER, B. (1959). The memory defect in bilateral hippocampal lesions. *Psychiatric Research Reports, 11,* 43–52.

MINAMI, H., & DALLENBACH, K. M. (1946). The effect of activity on learning and retention in the cockroach. *American Journal of Psychology, 59,* 1–58.

MINDE, K. (1986). Bonding and attachment: Its relevance for the present-day clinician. *Developmental Medicine and Child Neurology, 28,* 803–806.

MISCHEL, W. (1965). Predicting the success of Peace Corps volunteers in Nigeria. *Journal*

of Personality and Social Psychology, 1, 510–517.

MISCHEL, W. (1968). *Personality and assessment.* New York: Wiley.

MISCHEL, W. (1973). Toward a cognitive social learning reconceptualization of personality. *Psychological Review, 80,* 252–283.

MISCHEL, W. (1984, April). Convergences and challenges in the search for consistency. *American Psychologist, 39*(4), 351–364.

MISCHEL, W., & PEAKE, P. K. (1982). Beyond déja vu in the search for cross-situational consistency. *Psychological Review, 89,* 730–735.

MISHKIN, M., & PRIBRAM, K. H. (1954). Visual discrimination performance following partial ablation of the temporal lobe. I. Ventral vs. lateral. *Journal of Comparative and Physiological Psychology, 47,* 14–20.

MISCHEL, W., SHODA, Y., & RODRIGUEZ, M. L. (1989). Delay of gratification in children. *Science, 244,* 933–938.

MODGLIN, T. (1986). *Suicide.* Washington, DC: National Crime Prevention Council.

MONEY, J. (1977). Determinants of human gender identity/role. In J. Money & H. Musaph (Eds.), *Handbook of sexology* (pp. 57–79). Amsterdam: Elsevier/North-Holland/Biomedical Press.

MONEY, J. (1985) *The destroying angel.* Buffalo, NY: Prometheus. (b)

MONEY, J. (1985). Sexual reformation and counter-reformation in law and medicine. *Medicine and Law, 4,* 479–488. (a)

MONEY, J. (1986). *Lovemaps: Clinical concepts of sexual/erotic health and pathology, paraphilia, and gender transposition in childhood, adolescence, and maturity.* New York: Irvington.

MONEY, J. (1988). The development of sexual orientation. *Harvard Medical School Mental Health Letter, 4,* (8), 4–6.

MONEY, J., & EHRHARDT, A. A. (1972). *Man and woman, boy and girl.* Baltimore: Johns Hopkins University Press.

MONIZ, E. (1936). *Tentatives operatories dans le traitement de certaines psychoses.* Paris: Masson.

MONK, T. H., WEITZMAN, E. D., FOOKSON, J. E., MOLINE, M. L., KRONAUER, R. E., & GANDER, P. H. (1983). Task variables determine which biological clock controls circadian-rhythms in human performance. *Nature, 304,* 543–545.

MONTAGU, A. (1971). *Touching: The human significance of the skin.* New York: Columbia University Press.

MONTAGU, A. (1976). *The nature of human aggression.* New York: Oxford University Press.

MOORE, T. E. (1982). Subliminal advertising: What you see is what you get. *Journal of Marketing, 46*(2), 38–47.

MOORE, B. N., & PARKER, R. (1989). *Critical thinking: Evaluating claims and arguments in everyday life.* Mountain View, CA: Mayfield.

MOORE-EDE, M. (
C. A. (1982).
bridge, MA: I

MORGAN, C. T., &
in hunger. II.
tion and dieta
lin upon foo
General Psyc

MORGENTHAU, T
N. F., DOHER'
uary 6). Aban

MOROKOFF, P. J
repression, se
ual experien
during erotic
sonality and
177–187.

MORRIS, C. D., I
J. J. (1977).
transfer appr
Verbal Learn
519–533.

MORRIS, N. M.,
monal influen
An experimer
cial Science,

MORRIS, R. G., B
and working
heimer-type
and Experin
279–296.

MORRIS, S. (198(
Randi. Omni,

MOSAK, H. H. (1
R. J. Corsini (l
ogy (Vols. I,

MOSCOVICI, S., &
group as a po
Personality
125–135.

MOSKOWITZ, H. (
pairment of
tive Engineer

MOSS, S., & BUTL
credibility of
Skills, 46(3),

MOYER, K. E. (19
tion: Aggress
& A. M. Roge
ture series (V
can Psycholo

MURPHY, C. (198
threshold, p
pleasantness
tology, 38, 2

MURPHY, J. M., &
ology of schiz
Klerman, M.
& L. H. Roth
cial, epidemio
234–251). N

MURRAY, D. M., Jo
& MITTELMAI
tion of cigaret
parison of fo
plied Social

PELLETIER, K. R., & PEPER, E. (1977). Developing a biofeedback model: Alpha EEG feedback as a means for pain control. International Journal of Clinical and Experimental Hypnosis, 25, 361–371.

PENDLETON, M. G., & BATSON, C. D. (1979). Self-presentation and the door-in-the-face technique for inducing compliance. Personality and Social Psychology Bulletin, 5, 77–81.

PENFIELD, W. (1975). The mystery of the mind: A critical study of consciousness and the human brain. Princeton, NJ: Princeton University Press.

PENROD, S. (1986). Social psychology (2nd ed.). Englewood Cliffs, NJ: Prentice–Hall.

PERGAMEN, K. (1976). Alcohol and crimes of violence. In R. Kissin & H. Begleiter (Eds.), The biology of alcoholism: Social aspects of alcoholism (Vol. 4, pp. 351–444). New York: Plenum

PERLS, F. S. (1969). Gestalt therapy verbatim. Layfayette, CA: Real People Press.

PERRUCCI, C., & BARG, D. (Eds.). (1974). Marriage and the family: A critical analysis and proposals for change. New York: McKay.

PERRY, J. D., & WHIPPLE, B. (1982). Multiple components of female orgasm. In B. Graber (Ed.), Circumvaginal musculature and sexual function. New York: Karger.

PERRY, N. J. (1982, November 28). Industrial time clocks—Often at odds with those inside a worker's body. New York Times, pp. F8–F9.

PERVIN, L. A. (1987, August). Current trends in personality theory. Paper presented at the annual meeting of the American Psychological Association, New York.

PERVIN, L. A. (1989). Personality: Theory and research. New York: Wiley.

PETERSEN, A. C. (1987, September). Those gangly years. Psychology Today, pp. 28–34.

PETERSEN, A. C. (1988). Adolescent development. In M. R. Rosenzweig & L. W. Porter (Eds.), Annual review of psychology (pp. 583–607). Palo Alto, CA: Annual Reviews.

PETERSEN, A. C., EBATA, A. T., GRABER, J. A. (1987). Coping with adolescence: The functions and dysfunctions of poor achievement. Paper presented at biennial meeting of the Social Research Development, Baltimore, Maryland.

PETERSON, C., & SELIGMAN, M. E. P. (1984). Causal explanations as a risk factor for depression: Theory and evidence. Psychological Review, 91, 347–374.

PETERSON, C., SCHWARTZ, S. M., & SELIGMAN, M. E. P. (1981). Self-blame and depressive symptoms. Journal of Personality and Social Psychology, 41, 253–259.

PETERSON, J. L., & ZILL, N. (1981). Television viewing in the United States and children's intellectual, social, and emotional development. Television and Children, 2(2), 21–28.

PETERSON, L. R., & PETERSON, M. J. (1959).

Short-term retention of individual verbal items. Journal of Experimental Psychology, 58, 193–198.

PETTIS, K., & HUGHES, D. (1985). Sexual victimization of children: Implications for educators. Behavioral Disorders, 10(3), 175–182.

PETTY, R. E., OSTROM, T. M., & BROCK, T. C. (Eds.). (1981). Cognitive responses in persuasion. Hillsdale, NJ: Lawrence Erlbaum Associates.

PEVSNER, J., REED, R., FEINSTEIN, G., & SNYDER, S. (1988). Molecular cloning of ordorant-binding protein: Member of a ligand carrier family. Science, 241, 336–339.

PFAFFMANN, C. (1982). Taste: A model of incentive motivation. In D. W. Pfaff (Ed.), The physiological mechanisms of motivation. New York: Springer-Verlag.

PHARES, E. J. (1984). Personality. Columbus, OH: Merrill.

PHELPS, M. E., & MAZZIOTTA, J. C. (1985). Positron emission tomography: Human brain function and biochemistry. Science, 228, 799–809.

PHILIPS, C. (1977). Modification of tension headache pain using E.M.G. biofeedback. Behavior Research and Therapy, 15, 119–129.

PHILLIPS, D., & JUDD, R. (1978). How to fall out of love. New York: Warner Books.

PIAGET, J. (1932). The moral judgment of the child. New York: Harcourt, Brace.

PIAGET, J. (1951). Play, dreams, and imitation in childhood. New York: Norton.

PIAGET, J. (1983). Piaget's theory. In P. H. Mussen (Ed.), Handbook of child psychology (Vol. 1). New York: Wiley.

PIAGET, J., & INHELDER, B. (1956). The child's conception of space. London: Routledge & Kegan Paul.

PILIAVIN, J. A., CALLERO, P. L., & EVANS, D. E. (1982). Addiction to altruism? Opponent-process theory and blood donation. Journal of Personality and Social Psychology, 43, 1200–1213.

PILIAVIN, J. A., DIVIDIO, J. F., GAERTNER, S. L., & CLARK, R. D., III. (1982). Emergency intervention. New York: Academic Press.

PILLARD, R. C., & WEINRICH, J D. (1986). Evidence of the familial nature of male homosexuality. Archives of General Psychiatry, 43, 808–812.

PINES, A., & ARONSON, E. (1983). Antecedents, correlates, and consequences of sexual jealousy. Journal of Personality, 51(12), 108–136.

PIORKOWSKE, C., & STARK, E. (1985, June). Blue-collar stress worse for boys. Psychology Today, p. 15.

PLATT, J. J. (1986). Heroin addiction (2nd ed.). Malabar, FL: Kreiger.

PLOMIN, R. (1989). Environment and genes: Determinants of behavior. American Psychologist, 44, 105–111.

PLUTCHIK, R. (1980). Emotion: A psycho-evolutionary synthesis. New York: Harper & Row.

PODOLSKY, D. M. (1988, July/August). Stress and the perception of time. American Health, p. 21.

PODOLSKY, E. (1961). Jealousy as a motive in homicide. Diseases of the Nervous System, 22, 438–441.

POLIVY, J., & HERMAN, C. P. (1985). Dieting and binging: A causal analysis. American Psychologist, 40, 193–201.

POLSTER, E., & POLSTER, M. (1973). Gestalt therapy integrated: Contours of theory and practice. New York: Brunner/Mazel.

POMEROY, W. B. (1972). Dr. Kinsey and the Institute for Sex Research. New York: Nelson.

POON, L. W. (1985). Differences in human memory with aging: Nature, causes, and clinical implications. In J. E. Birren & K. W. Schaie (Eds.), Handbook of the psychology of aging (pp. 427–462). New York: Van Nostrand–Reinhold.

POPE, J. W., & MOUNT, G. R. (1975). The control of cigarette smoking through the application of a portable electronic device designed to dispense an aversive stimulus in relation to subjects' smoking frequency. Behavioral Engineering, 2, 52–56.

POWERS, S. I., HAUSER, S. T., & KILNER, L. A. (1989). Adolescent mental health. American Psychologist, 44, 200–208.

PRATKANIS, A. R., GREENWALD, A. G., LEIPPE, M. R., & BAUMGARDNER, M. H. (1988). In search of persuasion effects. III. The sleeper effect is dead. Long live the sleeper effect. Journal of Personality and Social Psychology, 54, 203–218.

PREMACK, D. (1976). Language and intelligence in ape and man. American Scientist, 64(6), 674–683.

PRESIDENT'S COMMISSION ON MENTAL HEALTH. (1978). Report of the President's Commission on Mental Health. Washington, DC: U.S. Government Printing Office.

PRICE, L., CHARNEY, D., RUBIN, A., & HENNINGER, G. (1986). Alpha 2-adrenergic receptor function in depression. General Psychiatry, 43, 849–858.

PRIEST, R. F., & SAWYER, J. (1967). Proximity and peership: Bases of balance in interpersonal attraction. American Journal of Sociology, 72, 633–649.

PRINCE, V. (1978). Transsexuals and pseudo-transsexuals. Archives of Sexual Behavior, 7, 263–270.

PSATTA, D. (1983). EEG and clinical survey during biofeedback treatment of epileptics. Neurologie et Psychiatrie, 21(2), 63–75.

Psychedelic drugs. (1990). Harvard Medical School Mental Health Letter, 6(8), 1–4.

PULASKI, M. (1974, January). The rich rewards of make believe. Psychology Today, pp. 68–74.

PYKETT, I. L. (1982). NMR imaging in medicine. Scientific American, 246(5), 78–88.

RABKIN, J. G., & STRUENING, E. L. (1976). Life events, stress, and illness. Science, 194, 1013–1020.

RABOW, G. (1988, January). The competitive edge. *Psychology Today*, pp. 54–58.

RADKE-YARROW, M., ZAHN-WAXLER, C., & CHAPMAN, M. (1983). Children's prosocial dispositions and behavior. In *Carmichael's manual of child psychology*. New York: Wiley.

RAHE, R. H., & ARTHUR, R. J. (1978). Life changes and illness studies: Past history and future directions. *Journal of Human Stress, 4*(1), 3–15.

RAKIE, P. (1985). Limits of neurogenesis in primates. *Science, 227*(4690), 1054–1056.

RAMA, S., BALLENTINE, R., & AJAYA, S. (1976). *Yoga and psychotherapy: The evolution of consciousness*. Honesdale, PA: Himalayan International Institute.

RAMACHANDRAN, V. (1988). Perceiving shape from shading. *Scientific American, 259*(2), 76–83.

RANDI, J. (1982). *Flim-flam*. Buffalo, NY: Prometheus.

RAPOPORT, J. L. (1989). The biology of obsessions and compulsions. *Scientific American, 260*(3), 83–89.

RAPS, C. S., PETERSON, C., REINHARD, K. E., ABRAMSON, L. Y., & SELIGMAN, M. E. P. (1982). Attributional style among depressed patients. *Journal of Abnormal Psychology, 91*, 102–108.

RAPS, C. S., REINHARD, K. E., & SELIGMAN, M. E. P. (1980). Reversal of cognitive and affective deficits associated with depression and learned helplessness by mood elevation in patients. *Journal of Abnormal Psychology, 89*, 342–349.

RASKIN, M., BALI, L. R., & PEEKE, H. (1980). Muscle biofeedback and transcendental meditation: A controlled evaluation of efficacy in the treatment of chronic anxiety. *Archives of General Psychiatry, 37*(1), 93–97.

RATHUS, S. A. (1988). *Understanding child development*. New York: Holt, Rinehart & Winston.

RAWAT, A. (1982, April 19). Alcohol harms fetus, study finds. *Chicago Tribune*, Section 1, p. 13.

RAY, O. (1983). *Drugs, society, & human behavior*. St. Louis: Mosby.

RAYBURN, W. F., & ZUSPAN, F. P. (1980). Drug use during pregnancy. *Perinatal Press, 4*(134), 115–117.

READ, J. D., & BRUCE, D. (1982). Longitudinal tracking of difficult memory retrievals. *Cognitive Psychology, 14*, 280–300.

REBOK, G. W. (1987). *Life-span cognitive development*. New York: Holt, Rinehart & Winston.

REED, J. D. (1988, June 27). A disgrace to civilized society. *Time*, p. 34.

REEDG, L., & LEIDERMAN, P. H. (1983). Is imprinting an appropriate model for human infant attachment? *International Journal of Behavioral Development, 6*, 51–69.

REGIER, D. A., et al. (1988). One-month prevalence of mental disorders in the U. S. *Archives of General Psychiatry, 45*, 977–986.

REINISCH, J. M. (1988, August). *Sexual behavior in the age of AIDS*. Paper presented at the annual meeting of the American Psychological Association, Atlanta.

REISENZEIN, R. (1983). The Schachter theory of emotion: Two decades later. *Psychological Bulletin, 94*, 239–264.

REISS, T. L. (1986). *Journey into sexuality: An exploratory voyage*. Englewood Cliffs, NJ: Prentice–Hall.

REITERMAN, T. (1982). *Raven: The untold story of the Reverend Jim Jones and his people*. New York: Dutton.

RELMAN, A. S. (1982). Marijuana and health. *New England Journal of Medicine, 306*(10), 603–604.

REMINGTON, D. W., FISHER, A. G., & PARENT, E. A. (1984). *How to lower your fat thermostat*. Provo, UT: Vitality House.

REPETTI, R. L. (1984). Determinants of children's sex stereotyping: Parental sex-role traits and television viewing. *Personality and Social Psychology Bulletin, 10*(3), 457–468.

REST, J. R. (1983). Morality. In P. H. Mussen (Ed.), *Handbook of child psychology* (Vol. 3). New York: Wiley.

REST, J. R., & THOMA, S. J. (1985). Relation of moral judgment development to formal education. *Developmental Psychology, 21*(4), 709–714.

RESTON, J., JR. (1981). *Our father who art in hell*. New York: Times Books.

REUDER, M. E. (1984). Phrenology. In R. J. Corsini (Ed.), *Encyclopedia of psychology* (Vol. 3, pp. 39–40). New York: Wiley.

RHINE, J. B. (1972). Parapsychology and man. *Journal of Parapsychology, 36*(2), 101–121.

RHODES, A. J. (1961). *Virus infections and congenital malformations*. Paper delivered at the First Conference on Congenital Malformations. Philadelphia: Lippincott.

RICE, J., REICH, T., ANDREASEN, N., ENDICOTT, J., VAN EERDEGWEGH, M., FISHMAN, R., HIRSHFELD, R., & KLERMAN, G. (1987). The familial transmission of bipolar illness. *Archives of General Psychiatry, 44*, 441–450.

RICE, M. L. (1989). Children's language acquisition. *American Psychologist, 44*, 149–156.

RICH, C. L., YOUNG, D., & FOWLER, R. C. (1986). San Diego suicide study. *Archives of General Psychology, 43*, 577–582.

RICHARDS, D. D., & GOLDFARB, J. (1986). The episodic memory model of conceptual development: An integrative viewpoint. *Cognitive Development, 1*, 183–219.

RICHARDS, R., KINNEY, K. K., BENET, J., & MERZEL, A. P. C. (1988). Assessing everyday creativity: Characteristics of the lifetime creativity scales and validation with three large samples. *Journal of Personality and Social Psychology, 54*, 476–485.

RICHMOND-ABBOTT, M. (1983). *Masculine and feminine sex roles over the life cycle*. Reading, MA: Addison–Wesley.

RICHTER, C. P. (1938). Two-day cycles of alter-

nating good and bad behavior in psychotic patients. *Archives of Neurology and Psychiatry, 39*, 587–598.

RIDGEWAY, C. L. (1983). *The dynamics of small groups*. New York: St. Martin's Press.

RIESEN, A. H. (1950). Arrested vision. *Scientific American, 183*, 16–19.

RILEY, V. (1981). Psychoneuroendocrine influences on immunocompetence and neoplasia. *Science, 212*, 1100–1109.

RIMM, D. C., & MASTERS, J. C. (1979). *Behavior therapy: Techniques and empirical findings* (2nd ed.). New York: Academic Press.

RITCHEY, S., & TAPER, L. J. (1982). *Maternal and child nutrition*. New York: Harper & Row.

ROBBINS, L. N., HELZER, J. E., WEISSMAN, M. M., ORVASCHEL, H., GRUENBERG, E., BURKE, J. D., & REGIER, D. A. (1984). Lifetime prevalence of specific psychiatric disorders in three sites. *Archives of General Psychiatry, 41*, 949–958.

ROBBINS, M., & JENSON, G. (1978). Multiple orgasm in males. *Journal of Sex Research, 14*, 21–26.

ROBERTS, L. (1988). Study raises estimate of Vietnam War stress. *Science, 241*, 788.

ROBERTS, M. (1989, March). The benefits of fatherhood. *Psychology Today*, p. 76.

ROBERTS, S. B., SAVAGE, J., COWARD, W. A., CHEW, B., & LUCAS, A. (1988). Energy expenditure and intake in infants born to lean and overweight mothers. *New England Journal of Medicine, 318*, 461–466.

ROBINS, C. J. (1988). Attributions and depression: Why is the literature so inconsistent? *Journal of Personality and Social Psychology, 54*, 880–889.

ROBINS, L. N. (1966). *Deviant children grow up*. Baltimore: Williams & Wilkins.

ROBINSON, B. E., & BARRET, R. L. (1985, December). Teenage fathers. *Psychology Today*, pp. 66–70.

ROBINSON, F. P. (1970). *Effective study*. New York: Harper & Row.

ROCKSTEIN, M. J., & SUSSMAN, M. (1979). *Biology of aging*. Belmont, CA: Wadsworth.

RODGERS, J. (1984, October). Life on the cutting edge. *Psychology Today*, pp. 56–67.

RODIN, J. (1981). Current status of the internal–external hypothesis for obesity: What went wrong? *American Psychologist, 36*, 361–372.

RODIN, J. (1984, December). A sense of control: Psychology Today conversation. *Psychology Today*, pp. 38–42.

RODIN, J. (1985). Insulin levels, hunger and food intake: An example of feedback loops in body weight regulation. *Health Psychology, 4*, 1–18.

RODIN, J., & SALOVEY, P. (1989). Health Psychology. In M. R. Rosenzweig & L. W. Porter (Eds.), *Annual Review of Psychology* (pp. 533–580). Palo Alto, CA: Annual Reviews Inc.

ROEDIGER, H. L. (1980). The effectiveness of four mnemonics in ordering recall. *Journal* of Experimental Psychology: Human Learning and Memory, 6, 558–567.

ROFF, J. D., & KNIGHT, R. (1981). Family characteristics, childhood symptoms, and adult outcome in schizophrenia. *Journal of Abnormal Psychology, 90,* 510–520.

ROGERS, C. R. (1957). A note on "The nature of man." *Journal of Counseling Psychology, 4,* 199–203.

ROGERS, C. R. (1961). *On becoming a person.* Boston: Houghton Mifflin.

ROGERS, C. R. (1964). Toward a science of the person. In F. W. Wann (Ed.), *Behaviorism and phenomenology: Contrasting bases for modern psychology* (pp. 109–140). Chicago: Phoenix Books, University of Chicago Press.

ROGERS, C. R. (1970). *Carl Rogers on encounter groups.* New York: Harper & Row.

ROGERS, C. R. (1977). *Carl Rogers on personal power: Inner strength and its revolutionary impact.* New York: Delacorte Press.

ROGERS, C. R. (1980). *A way of being.* Boston: Houghton Mifflin.

ROGERS, M. F. (1985). AIDS in children: A review of the clinical, epidemiological and public health aspects. *Pediatric Infectious Disease, 4,* 230–236.

ROGOFF, B., & MORELLI, G. (1989). Perspectives on children's development from cultural psychology. *American Psychologist, 44,* 343–348.

ROKEACH, M. P., SMITH, P. W., & EVANS, R. E. (1960). Two kinds of prejudice or one? In M. Rokeach (Ed.), *The open and closed mind.* New York: Basic Books.

ROLKER-DOLINSKY, B. (1987). The premenstrual syndrome. In K. Kelley (Ed.), *Females, males and sexuality: Theories and research* (pp. 234–247). Albany, NY: State University of New York Press.

ROSCH, E. H. (1973). Natural categories. *Cognitive Psychology, 4,* 328–350.

ROSE, R. J., KOSKENVUO, M., KAPRIO, J., SARNA, S., & LANGINVAINIO, H. (1988). Shared genes, shared experiences, and similarity of personality: Data from 14,288 adult Finnish co-twins. *Journal of Personality and Social Psychology, 54,* 161–171.

ROSE, S. M. (1985). Same-sex and cross-sex friendships and the psychology of homosociality. *Sex Roles, 12,* 63–74.

ROSENBAUM, M. B., & LURIGIO, A. J. (1985, June). Crime stoppers: Paying the price. *Psychology Today,* pp. 56–61.

ROSENBERG, M. S. (1987). New directions for research on the psychological maltreatment of children. *American Psychologist, 42,* 166–171.

ROSENFELD, A., & STARK, E. (1987, May). The prime of our lives. *Psychology Today,* pp. 62–72.

ROSENFELD, D., FOLGER, R., & ADELMAN, H. F. (1980). When rewards reflect competence: A qualification of the overjustification effect. *Journal of Personality and Social Psychology, 39,* 368–376.

ROSENFELD, P., GLACALONE, R. A., & TEDESCHI, J. T. (1983). Cognitive dissonance vs. impression management. *Journal of Social Psychology, 120,* 203–211.

ROSENHAN, D. (1973). On being sane in insane places. *Science, 197,* 250–258.

ROSENHAN, D. (1988). On being sane in insane places. In J. Rubinstein & B. Slife (Eds.), *Taking sides: Clashing views on controversial psychological issues* (5th ed., pp. 220–234). Guilford, CT: Dushkin.

ROSENHAN, D. L., SALOVEY, P., & HARGIS, K. (1981). The joys of helping: Focus of attention mediates the impact of positive effect on altruism. *Journal of Personality and Social Psychology, 40,* 899–905.

ROSENTHAL, N. E., SACK, D. A., GILLIN, J. C., LEWRY, A. J., GOODWIN, F. K., DAVENPORT, Y., MUELLER, P. S., NEWSOME, D. A., & WEHR, T. A. (1984). Seasonal-affective disorder: A description of the syndrome and preliminary finding with light therapy. *Archives of General Psychiatry, 41,* 72–80.

ROSENZWEIG, M. R., BENNET, E. L., & DIAMOND, M. C. (1972). Brain changes in response to experience. *Scientific American, 226,* 22–29.

ROSEWICZ, B. (1983, January 31). Study finds grim link between liquor and crime: Figures far worse than officials expected. *Detroit Free Press,* pp. 1A, 4A.

ROSOW, I. (1963). Adjustment of the normal aged: Concept and measurement. In R. Williams, C. Tibbitts, & W. Donahue (Eds.), *Processing of aging* (Vol. 2). New York: Atherton.

ROSS, J., & LAWRENCE, K. A. (1968). Some observations on memory artifice. *Psychonomic Science, 13*(2), 107–108.

ROTH, T., & ZORICK, F. (1983). The use of hypnotics in specific disorders of initiating and maintaining sleep. In M. H. Chase & E. D. Weitzman (Eds.), *Sleep disorders: Basic and clinical research.* New York: Spectrum

ROTTER, J. B. (1966). Generalized expectancies for internal versus external control of reinforcement. *Psychological Monographs, 80*(1, Entire No. 609), 1–26.

ROTTER, J. E. (1975). Some problems and misconceptions related to the construct of internal versus external control of reinforcement. *Journal of Consulting and Clinical Psychology, 43,* 56–67.

ROZOVSKY, F. A. (1984). *Consent to treatment: A practical guide.* Boston: Little, Brown.

RUBENSTEIN, C. (1983, July). The modern art of courtly love. *Psychology Today,* pp. 40–49.

RUBIN, J., PROVENZANO, F., & LURIA, Z. (1974). The eye of the beholder: Parents' views on sex of newborns. *American Journal of Orthopsychiatry, 44,* 512–519.

RUBIN, L. (1983). *Intimate strangers: Men and women together.* New York: Harper & Row.

RUBIN, R., REINISCH, J., & HASKETT, R. (1981). Postnatal gonadal steroid effects on human behavior. *Science, 211,* 1318–1324.

RUBIN, Z. (1973). *Liking and loving: An invitation to social psychology.* New York: Holt, Rinehart & Winston.

RUBLE, D. N., BALABAN, T., & COOPER, J. (1981). Gender constancy and the effect of sex-typed televised commercials. *Child Development, 52,* 667–673.

RUBLE, D. N., FLEMING, A. S., HACKEL, L. S., & STANGOR, C. (1988). Changes in the marital relationship during the transition to first time motherhood: Effects of violated expectations concerning division of household labor. *Journal of Personality and Social Psychology, 55,* 78–87.

RUEDER, M. E. (1984). Phrenology. In R. J. Corsini (Ed.), *Encyclopedia of psychology* (Vol. 3, pp. 39–40). New York: Wiley.

RUGGIERO, V. R. (1988). *Teaching thinking across the curriculum.* New York: Harper & Row.

RUMBAUGH, D. M., et al. (1974). Lana (chimpanzee) learning language: A progress report. *Brain & Language, 1*(2), 205–212.

RUSBULT, C. E. (1983). A longitudinal test of the investment model: The development (and deterioration) of satisfaction and commitment in heterosexual involvements. *Journal of Personality and Social Psychology, 45,* 101–117.

RUSSELL, G. F., SZMUKLER, G. I., DARE, C., & EISLER, I. (1987). An evaluation of family therapy in anorexia nervosa and bulimia nervosa. *Archives of General Psychiatry, 44,* 1047–1056.

RUSSELL, M. A. H., ARMSTRONG, E., & PATEL, V. A. (1976). Temporal contiguity in electric aversion therapy for cigarette smoking. *Behavior Research and Therapy, 14,* 103–123.

RUSSELL, M. J. (1976). Human olfactory communication. *Nature, 260,* 520–522.

RYAN, W. (1971). *Blaming the victim.* New York: Vintage.

RYCKMAN, R. M. (1978). *Theories of personality.* New York: Van Nostrand.

SABINI, J., & SILVER, M. (1988). Critical thinking and obedience to authority. In J. Chaffee (Ed.), *Critical Thinking* (pp. 447–455). Palo Alto, CA: Houghton Mifflin.

SACERDOTE, P. (1978). Teaching self-hypnosis to patients with chronic pain. *Journal of Human Stress, 4,* 18–21.

SACHS, J. S. (1967). Recognition memory for syntactic and semantic aspects of connected discourse. *Perception and Psychophysics, 2,* 437–442.

SACHS, L. B., FEUERSTEIN, M., & VITALE, J. H. (1977). Hypnotic self-regulation of chronic pain. *American Journal of Clinical Hypnosis, 20*(2), 106–113.

SADKER, M., & SADKER, D. (1985, February). Sexism in the school room of the 80's. *Psychology Today,* pp. 54–57.

SALOVEY, P., & RODIN, J. (1985, September). The heart of jealousy: A report on *Psychology Today's* jealousy and envy survey. *Psychology Today,* pp. 22–26.

SALZMAN, L., & THALER, F. H. (1981). Obsessive-compulsive disorders: A review of the literature. *American Journal of Psychiatry, 138,* 286–296.

SANDERS, C. M. (1989). *Grief: The mourning after: Dealing with adult bereavement.* New York: Wiley-Interscience.

SARASON, I. G. (1982). Three lacunae of cognitive therapy. In M. R. Goldfried (Ed.), *Converging themes in psychotherapy* (pp. 353–364). New York: Springer-Verlag.

SARGENT, M. (1986). *Depressive disorders: Treatments bring new hope.* Rockville, MD: National Institute for Mental Health.

SATINOFF, E. (1974). Neural integration of thermoregulatory responses. In L. V. Di Cara (Ed.), *Limbic and autonomic nervous system research.* New York: Plenum.

SATINOFF, E., LIRAN, J., & CLAPMAN, R. (1982). Aberrations of circadian body temperature rhythms in rats with medial preoptic lesions. *American Journal of Physiology, 242,* R352–R357.

SATIR, V. (1976). *Conjoint family therapy.* Palo Alto, CA: Science and Behavior Books.

SAVAGE-RUMBAUGH, E. S. (1986). *Ape language: From conditioned response to symbol.* New York: Columbia University Press.

SAVAGE-RUMBAUGH, E. S., PATE, J. L., LAWSON, J., SMITH, S. T., & ROSENBAUM, S. (1983). Can a chimpanzee make a statement? *Journal of Experimental Psychology, 112,* 457–492.

SAVAGE-RUMBAUGH, E. S., RUMBAUGH, D. M., & BOYSEN, S. (1980). Do apes use language? *American Scientist, 68*(1), 49–61.

SAVARD, R. J. (1968). *Cultural stress and alcoholism: A study of their relationship among Navaho alcoholic men.* Unpublished doctoral dissertation, University of Minnesota. (University Microfilm No. 69–1532.)

SAVIN-WILLIAMS, R., & SMALL, S. (1986). The timing of puberty and its relationship to adolescent and parent perceptions of family interactions. *Developmental Psychology, 22,* 322–347.

SAXE, L., DOUGHERTY, D., & CROSS, T. (1985). The validity of polygraph testing. *American Psychologist, 40,* 355–366.

SCHACHTER, S. (1959). *The psychology of affiliation.* Stanford, CA: Stanford University Press.

SCHACHTER, S. (1971). *Emotion, obesity, and crime.* New York: Academic Press.

SCHACHTER, S. (1978). Pharmacological and psychological determinants of smoking. *Annals of International Medicine, 88,* 104–114.

SCHACHTER, S., & GROSS, L. P. (1968). Manipulated time and eating behavior. *Journal of Personality and Social Psychology, 10,* 98–106.

SCHACHTER, S., & LATANE, B. (1964). Crime, cognition, and the autonomic nervous system. In D. Levine (Ed.), *Nebraska symposium on motivation* (Vol. 12). Lincoln, NE: University of Nebraska Press.

SCHACHTER, S., & SINGER, J. E. (1962). Cognitive, social, and physiological determinants of emotional state. *Psychological Review, 69,* 379–399.

SCHAEFER, E. S. (1960, August). *Converging conceptual models for maternal behavior and for child behavior.* Paper presented at the Conference on Research on Parental Attitudes and Child Behavior, Washington University, St. Louis.

SCHAEFER, H. H. (1971). Accepted theories disproven. *Science News, 99,* 182.

SCHAFFER, K. (1981). *Sex roles and human behavior.* Cambridge, MA: Winthrop.

SCHAIE, K. W. (1983). The Seattle longitudinal study: A twenty-one year exploration of psychometric intelligence in adulthood. In K. W. Schaie (Ed.), *Longitudinal studies of adult psychological development.* New York: Academic Press.

SCHAIE, K. W. (1984). Midlife influences upon intellectual functioning in old age. *International Journal of Behavioral Development, 7,* 463–478.

SCHAIE, K. W. (1988). Ageism in psychological research. *American Psychologist, 43,* 179–183.

SCHAIE, K. W., & BALTES, P. B. (1977). Some faith helps to see the forest: A final comment on the Horn–Donaldson myth of the Baltes–Schaie position on adult intelligence. *American Psychologist, 32,* 1118–1120.

SCHAIE, K. W., & GEIWITZ, J. (1982). *Adult development and aging.* Boston: Little, Brown.

SCHATZBERG, A. F. (1988). New treatment for anxiety: Update on Buspirone. *Harvard Medical School Mental Health Letter, 4*(12), 8.

SCHLAADT, R. G., & SHANNON, P. T. (1982). *Drugs of choice: Current perspectives on drug use.* Englewood Cliffs, NJ: Prentice-Hall.

SCHLEIFER, S., KELLER, S., MCKEGNEY, F., & STEIN, M. (1980). *Bereavement and lymphocyte function.* Paper presented at the annual meeting of the American Psychiatric Association, Montreal.

SCHLOSSBERG, N. K. (1987, May). Taking the mystery out of change. *Psychology Today,* pp. 74–75.

SCHNEIDER, A. M., & TARSHIS, B. (1980). *An introduction to physiological psychology* (2nd ed.). New York: Random House.

SCHOFIELD, W. (1964). *Psychotherapy: The purchase of friendship.* Englewood Cliffs, NJ: Prentice-Hall.

SCHORR, L. B., & SCHORR, D. 1990. *Within our reach: Breaking the cycle of disadvantage and despair.* New York: Doubleday.

SCHRADER, W. B. (1971). The predictive validity of college board admissions tests. In W. G. Angoff (Ed.), *The college board admissions testing program: A technical report on research and development activities relating to the Scholastic Aptitude Test and achievement tests.* New York: College Entrance Examination Board.

SCHREIBER, F. R. (1973). *Sybil.* New York: Warner Books.

SCHULSINGER, F. (1972). Psychopathy: Heredity and environment. *International Journal of Mental Health, 1,* 190–206.

SCHULTZ, D. P. (1969). *A history of modern psychology.* New York: Academic Press.

SCHUMAN, H., & JOHNSON, M. P. (1976). Attitudes and behavior. *Annual Review of Sociology, 2,* 161–207.

SCHWARTZ, A. N., CAMPOS, J. J. & BAISEL, E. J. (1973). The visual cliff: Cardiac and behavioral responses on the deep and shallow sides at five and nine months of age. *Journal of Experimental Child Psychology, 15*(1), 86–89.

SCHWARTZ, B. (1982). *Diets don't work.* Houston, TX: Breakthru Publishing.

SCHWARTZ, G. E., WEINBERGER, D. A., & SINGER, J. A. (1981). Cardiovascular differentiation of happiness, sadness, anger, and fear following imagery and exercise. *Psychosomatic Medicine, 43*(4), 343–364.

SCHWARTZ, M. A. (1984). Expansionary America tightens its belt: Social scientific perspectives on obesity. *Obesity and the family: Marriage and Family Review, 7*(1,2), 49–64.

SCHWARTZ, S. H., & INBAR-SABAN, N. (1988). Value self-confrontation as a method to aid in weight loss. *Journal of Personality and Social Psychology, 54,* 396–404.

SCHWEBEL, A. I. (1982). Radio psychologists: A community psychology/psycho-educational mode. *Journal of Community Psychology, 10*(2), 180–184.

SCOTT, D. W. (1986). Anorexia nervosa: A review of possible genetic factors. *International Journal of Eating Disorders, 5,* 1–20.

SCOTT, J. (1988, February 11). Pot takes a hit in new study of health dangers. *Los Angeles (California) Times,* pp. C3, C5.

SCOTT, K. G., & CARRAN, D. T. (1987). The epidemiology and prevention of mental retardation. *American Psychologist, 42,* 801–804.

SCOVILLE, W. B., & MILNER, B., (1957). Loss of recent memory after bilateral hippocampal lesions. *Journal of Neurology, Neurosurgery, and Psychiatry, 20,* 11–21.

SEAMON, G., & GAZZANIGA, M. S. (1973). Coding strategies and cerebral laterality effects. *Cognitive Psychology, 5,* 249–256.

SEARS, D. O., FREEDMAN, J. L., & PEPLAU, L. A. (1985). *Social psychology* (5th ed.). Englewood Cliffs, NJ: Prentice-Hall.

SEECH, Z. (1987). *Logic in everyday life: Practical reasoning skills.* Belmont, CA: Wadsworth.

SEGAL, M. W. (1974). Alphabet and attraction: An unobtrusive measure of the effect of propinquity in a field setting. *Journal of Personality and Social Psychology, 30,* 654–657.

SEGALL, M. H., CAMPBELL, D. T., & HERSKOVITS, M. J. (1966). *The influence of culture on visual perception.* New York: Bobbs–Merrill.

SELIGMANN, J., & GOSNELL, M. (1986, March 3). Now the gastric bubble. *Newsweek,* p. 77.

SELIGMANN, J., & HAGAR, M. (1984, October 15). Mental state of the union. *Newsweek,* p. 113.

SELIGMAN, M. (1988, August). *Why is there so much depression today? The waxing of the individual and the waning of the commons.* Symposium conducted at the annual meeting of the American Psychological Association, Atlanta.

SELIGMAN, M. E. P. (1975). *Helplessness.* San Francisco: Freeman.

SELIGMAN, M. E. P., ABRAMSON, L. Y., SEMMEL, A., & VON BAEYER, C. (1979). Depressive attributional style. *Journal of Abnormal Psychology, 88,* 242–247.

SELYE, H. (1956). *The stress of life.* New York: McGraw–Hill.

SELYE, H. (1974). *Stress without distress.* New York: Harper & Row.

Sexual disorders—Part II. (1990). *Harvard Medical School Mental Health Letter, 6*(7), 1–4

SHANAB, M. E., & YAHYA, K. A. (1977). A behavioral study of obedience in children. *Journal of Personality and Social Psychology, 35*(7), 530–536.

SHATZ, M., & GELMAN, R. (1973). The development of communication skills: Modifications in the speech of young children as a function of the listener. *Monographs of the Society for Research in Child Development, 38*(5, Serial No. 152).

SHAVIT, H., & SHOUVAL, R. (1980). Self-esteem and cognitive consistency on self–other evaluations. *Journal of Experimental Social Psychology, 16,* 417–425.

SHAW, M. E. (1981). *Group dynamics: The psychology of small group behavior* (3rd ed.). New York: McGraw–Hill.

SHEA, J. D. (1981). Changes in interpersonal distances and categories of play behavior in the early weeks of preschool. *Developmental Psychology, 17,* 417–425.

SHEARD, M. H., & FLYNN, J. P. (1976). Facilitation of attack behavior by stimulation of the midbrain of cats. *Brain Research, 4,* 324–333.

SHEEHY, G. (1976). *Passages: Predictable crises of adult life.* New York: Dutton.

SHEIKH, A. S., & PANAGIOTOU, N. C. (1975). Use of mental imagery in psychotherapy: A critical review. *Perceptual and Motor Skills, 41,* 555–585.

SHELDON, W. H. (1954). *Atlas of men: A guide for somatotyping the adult male at all ages.* New York: Harper.

SHELDON, W. H., & STEVENS, S. S. (1942). *Varieties of human temperament: A psychology of constitutional differences.* New York: Harper.

SHELL, E. R. (1989, December). Now, which kind of preschool? *Psychology Today,* pp. 53, 56–57.

SHENGOLD, L. (1985). The effects of child abuse as seen in adults. *Psychoanalytic Quarterly, 54*(1), 20–45.

SHEPARD, R. N. (1967). Recognition memory for words, sentences and pictures. *Journal of Verbal Learning and Verbal Behavior, 6,* 156–163.

SHEPARD, R. N., & CHIPMAN, S. (1970). Second-order isomorphism of internal representation: Shapes of states. *Cognitive Psychology, 1,* 1–17.

SHEPARD, R. N., & METZLER, J. (1971). Mental rotation of three-dimensional objects. *Science, 171,* 701–703.

SHEPPARD, R. Z. (1988, April 18). A piece of the true couch. *Time,* pp. 85–86.

SHER, K. J., & LEVENSON, R. (1982). Risk for alcoholism and individual differences in the stress–response–dampening effects of alcohol. *Journal of Abnormal Psychology, 91,* 350–367.

SHERIDAN, M. (1975). Talk time for hospitalized children. *Social Work, 20,* 40–44.

SHERIF, M. (1966). *In common predicament: Social psychology of intergroup conflict and cooperation.* Boston: Houghton Mifflin.

SHERIF, M., & SHERIF, C. W. (1956). *Groups in harmony and tension.* New York: Harper & Row.

SHERMAN, J. L., KULHAVY, R. W., & BURNS, K. (1976). Cerebral laterality and verbal processes. *Journal of Experimental Psychology: Human Learning and Memory, 2,* 720–727.

SHETTEL-NEUBER, J., BRYSON, J., & YOUNG, L. E. (1978). Physical attractiveness of the "other person" and jealousy. *Personality and Social Psychology Bulletin, 4,* 612–615.

SHIONO, P. H., KLEBANOFF, M. A., & RHOADS, G. C. (1986). Smoking and drinking during pregnancy. *Journal of the American Medical Association, 225*(1), 82–84.

SHNEIDMAN, E. S. (1969). Fifty-eight years. In E. S. Shneidman (Ed.), *On the nature of suicide* (pp. 1–30). San Francisco: Jossey–Bass.

SHNEIDMAN, E. S. (1987, March). At the point of no return. *Psychology Today,* pp. 58–63.

SHODELL, M. (1984, October). The clouded mind. *Science, 84,* 68–72.

SHOFIELD, J. (1982). *Black and white in school.* New York: Praeger.

SHORE, D. (1986). *Schizophrenia: Questions and answers.* Rockville, MD: National Institute for Mental Health.

SHOTLAND, R. L. (1983). What is wrong with helping behavior research? Only the independent and dependent variables. *Academic Psychology Bulletin, 5*(2), 339–350.

SHOTLAND, R. L. (1985, June). When bystanders just stand by. *Psychology Today,* pp. 50–55.

SHURTLEFF, D., & AYRES, J. J. B. (1981). One-trial backward excitatory fear conditioning in rats: Acquisition, retention, extinction, and spontaneous recovery. *Animal Learning and Behavior, 9,* 65–74.

SIBATANI, A. (1980, December). The Japanese brain. *Science, 80,* pp. 22–27.

SIEGEL, D. J., & PIOTROWSKI, R. J. (1985). Reliability of K-ABC subtest composites. *Journal of Psychoeducational Assessment, 3*(1), 73–76.

SIEGEL, R. K. (1989). *Life in pursuit of artificial paradise.* New York: Dutton.

SIEGELMAN, M. (1987). Empirical input. In L. Diamant (Ed.), *Male and female homosexuality: Psychological approaches* (pp. 37–48). Washington, DC: Hemisphere.

SILVERMAN, L. H. (1976). Psychoanalytic theory: The reports of my death are greatly exaggerated. *American Psychologist, 31,* 621–637.

SILVERMAN, L. H. (1980). A comprehensive report of studies using the subliminal psychodynamic activation method. *Psychological Research Bulletin, Lund University, 20*(3).

SILVERMAN, L. H., & LACHMANN, F. M. (1985). The therapeutic properties of unconscious oneness fantasies: Evidence and treatment implications. *Contemporary Psychoanalysis, 21*(1), 91–115.

SILVERSTONE, J. (1969). Psychological factors in obesity. In I. Baird & A. Howard (Eds.), *Obesity: Medical and scientific aspects.* Edinburgh, Scotland: Livingstone.

SIMMONS, D. D. (1987). Self-reports of eating behavior, goals, imagery, and health status: Principal components and sex differences. *Journal of Psychology, 121,* 57–60.

SIMON, C. W., & EMMONS, W. H. (1956). Responses to material presented during various stages of sleep. *Journal of Experimental Psychology, 51,* 89–97.

SIMPSON, E. L. (1976). A holistic approach to moral development and behavior. In T. Lickona (Ed.), *Moral development and behavior: Theory, research, and social issues.* New York: Holt, Rinehart & Winston.

SINGER, B., & BENASSI, V. A. (1981). Occult beliefs. *American Scientist, 69*(1), 49–55.

SINGER, D. G., & SINGER, J. (1984). *Make believe: Games and activities to foster imagination.* Glenview, IL: Scott, Foresman.

SINGER, J. L., SINGER, D. G., & RAPACZYNSKI, W. S. (1984). Family patterns and television viewing as predictors of children's beliefs and aggression. *Journal of Communication, 34*(2), 73–89.

SINGER, M. T. (1979, January). Coming out of the cults. *Psychology Today,* pp. 72–82.

SINOWAY, C. G., RAUPP, C. D., & NEWMAN, J. (1985, August). *Binge eating and bulimia: Comparing incidence and characteristics across universities.* Poster presented at the meeting of the American Psychological Association, Los Angeles.

SKEELS, H. M. (1966). Adult status of children with contrasting early life experiences: A follow-up study. *Monographs of the Society for Research in Child Development, 31* (Serial No. 105).

SKEELS, H. M., & DYE, H. B. (1939). A study of the effects of differential stimulation on mentally retarded children. *Proceedings of the American Association for Mental Deficiency, 44,* 114–136.

SKINNER, B. F. (1948). Superstition in the pigeon. *Journal of Experimental Psychology, 38,* 168–172.

SKINNER, B. F. (1954). A critique of psychoanalytic concepts and theories. *Scientific Monthly, 79,* 300–305.

SKINNER, B. F. (1971). *Beyond freedom and dignity.* New York: Bantam.

SKINNER, B. F. (1979). *The shaping of a behaviorist.* New York: Knopf.

SKINNER, B. F. (1985) *What is wrong with daily life in the western world?* Paper presented at the annual convention of the American Psychological Association, Los Angeles.

SKODOL, A. E., & SPITZER, R. L. (1983). Depression in the elderly: Clinical criteria. In L. D. Breslau & M. R. Haug (Eds.), *Depression and aging: Causes, care and consequences.* New York: Springer-Verlag.

SLOBIN, D. I. (1979). *Psycholinguistics* (2nd ed.). Glenview, IL: Scott, Foresman.

SMITH, A. (1982). *Powers of mind.* New York: Summit.

SMITH, D. (1982). Trends in counseling and psychotherapy. *American Psychologist, 37*(3), 802–809.

SMITH, D. E. P., OLSON, M., BARGER, F., & MCCONNELL, J. V. (1981). The effects of improved auditory feedback on the verbalizations of an autistic child. *Journal of Autism and Developmental Disorders, 11*(4), 449–454.

SMITH, M. L., & GLASS, G. V. (1977). Meta-analysis of psychotherapy outcome studies. *American Psychologist, 32,* 752–760.

SMOKE, K. L. (1932). An objective study of concept formation. *Psychological Monographs, 42*(4, Whole No. 191).

SNAREY, J. R. (1985). Cross-cultural universality of social-moral development: A critical review of Kohlbergian research. *Psychological Bulletin, 97,* 202–233.

SNYDER, C. R. (1988, August). *Reality negotiation: From excuses to hope.* Symposium conducted at the annual meeting of the American Psychological Association, Atlanta.

SNYDER, C. R., STUCKY, R. J., & HIGGINS, R. L. (1983). *Excuses: Masquerades in search of grace.* New York: Wiley.

SNYDER, M. (1974). The self-monitoring of expressive behavior. *Journal of Personality and Social Psychology, 30,* 526–537.

SNYDER, M. (1984). When belief creates reality. In L. Berkowitz (Ed.), *Advances in experimental social psychology* (Vol. 18). New York: Academic Press.

SNYDER, M. (1987). *Public appearances/private realities: The psychology of self-monitoring.* New York: Freeman.

SNYDER, M., BERSCHEID, E., & MATWYCHUK, A. (1988). Orientations toward personnel selection: Differential reliance on appearance and personality. *Journal of Personality and Social Psychology, 54,* 972–979.

SNYDER, M., GANGSTAD, S., & SIMPSON, J. A. (1983). Choosing friends as activity partners: The role of self-monitoring. *Journal of Personality and Social Psychology, 45,* 1061–1072.

SNYDER, M., & SIMPSON, J. A. (1984). Self-monitoring and dating relationships. *Journal of Personality and Social Psychology, 47,* 1281–1291.

SNYDER, M., TANKE, E. D., & BERSCHEID, E. (1977). Social perception and interpersonal behavior: On the self-fulfilling nature of social stereotypes. *Journal of Personality and Social Psychology, 35,* 656–666.

SNYDER, S. H. (1980). Brain peptides as neurotransmitters. *Science, 209*(4460), 976–983.

SNYDER, S. H. (1984). Cholinergic mechanisms in affective disorders. *New England Journal of Medicine, 311*(4), 254–255.

SOKOLOV, E. N. (1977). Brain functions: Neuronal mechanisms of learning and memory. *Annual Review of Psychology, 20,* 85–112.

SOLOMON, G. F., AMKRAUT, A. A., & KASPER, P. (1974). Immunity, emotions, and stress: With special reference to the mechanisms of stress effects on the immune system. *Psychotherapy & Psychosomatics, 23,* 209–217.

SOLOMON, R. L. (1980). The opponent-process theory of acquired motivation: The costs of pleasure and the benefits of pain. *American Psychologist, 35,* 691–712.

SOLOMON, R. L. (1982). The opponent process in acquired motivation. In D. W. Pfaff (Ed.), *The physiological mechanisms of motivation.* New York: Springer-Verlag.

SOMMER, B. (1984, August). PMS in the courts: Are all women on trial? *Psychology Today,* pp. 36–38.

SOMMER, R. (1969). *Personal space.* Englewood Cliffs, NJ: Prentice–Hall.

SOMMER, R., & BECKER, F. D. (1969). Territorial defense and the good neighbor. *Journal of Personality and Social Psychology, 11,* 85–92.

SOMMERS, D., & ECK, A. (1977). Occupational mobility in the American labor force. *Monthly Labor Review, 100*(1), 3–19.

SOUCHEK, A. W. (1986). *A comparison of dynamic stereoscopic acuities in both the primary and secondary positions of gaze.* In preparation.

SPANOS, N. P. (1986). Hypnotic behavior: A social-psychological interpretation of amnesia, analgesia, and "trance logic." *Behavioral and Brain Sciences, 9,* 449–502.

SPANOS, N. P., & CHAVES, J. F. (1988). *Hypnosis: The cognitive-behavioral perspective.* New York: Prometheus.

SPANOS, N. P., GWYNN, M. L., & STAM, H. J. (1983). Instructional demands and ratings of overt and hidden pain during hypnotic analgesia. *Journal of Abnormal Psychology, 92,* 479–488.

SPANOS, N. P., WEEKES, J. R., & BERTRAND, L. D. (1985). Multiple personalities: A social psychological perspective. *Journal of Abnormal Psychology, 94,* 362–376.

SPEARMAN, C. (1972). *The abilities of man.* New York: Macmillan.

SPENCE, J., & HELMREICH, R. (1983). Achievement related motives and behavior. In J. Spence (Ed.), *Achievement and achievement motives.* San Francisco: Freeman.

SPENCE, J. T. (1984). Masculinity, femininity, and gender-related traits: A conceptual analysis and critique of current research. In B. A. Maker & W. B. Maker (Eds.), *Progress in experimental personality research: Normal personality processes* (Vol. 13). New York: Academic Press.

SPENCE, K. W. (1951). Theoretical implications of learning. In S. S. Stevens (Ed.), *Handbook of experimental psychology.* New York: Wiley.

SPERLING, D. (1985, May 30). Is ecstasy safe, or in the same league as LSD? *USA Today,* p. 3A.

SPERLING, G. (1960). The information available in brief visual presentations. *Psychological Monographs, 74,* 1–29.

SPERRY, R. W. (1968). Hemisphere deconnection and unity in conscious awareness. *American Psychologist, 23,* 723–733.

SPIEGEL, D. (1985, Winter). Trance, trauma, and testimony, *Stanford Magazine,* pp. 4–6.

SPINETTA, J. J., ELLIOTT, E. S., HENNESSEY, J. S., KNAPP, V. S., SHEPOSH, J. P., SPARTA, S. N., & SPRIGLE, R. P. (1982). The pediatric psychologist's role in catastrophic illness: Research and clinical issues. In J. M. Tuma (Ed.), *Handbook for the practice of pediatric psychology* (pp. 165–227). New York: Wiley–Interscience.

SPITZ, R. A., & WOLF, K. M. (1946). The smiling response: A contribution to the ontogenesis of social relations. *Genetic Psychology Monographs, 34,* 57–123.

SPITZER, R. L. (1988). On pseudo-science in science, logic in remission and psychiatric diagnoses. In J. Rubinstein & B. Slife (Eds.), *Taking sides: Clashing views on controversial psychological issues* (5th ed., pp. 235–248). Guilford, CT: Dushkin.

SPOCK, B. M. (1984, August). *Can our society be saved?* Invited address at the meeting of the American Psychological Association, Toronto.

SPOCK, B. (1988, May 30). A letter to the next generation. *Time,* pp. 1–2.

SPOTKOV, J., & ANDERSON, J. W. (1988). AIDS cannot be spread through casual contact. In D. L. Bender, B. Leone, L. Hall, & T. Modl (Eds.), *AIDS: Opposing viewpoints* (pp. 41–46). St. Paul, MN: Greenhaven Press.

SPRECHER, S. (1986). The relation between inequity and emotions in close relationships. *Social Psychology Quarterly, 49,* 309–321.

SPRINGER, S. P., & DEUTSCH, G. (1981). *Left brain, right brain.* San Francisco: Freeman.

SQUIRE, L. R. (1977). ECT and memory loss. *American Journal of Psychiatry, 136,* 997–1001.

SQUIRE, L. R. (1984). Memory of prose passage —ECT and memory dysfunction. In B. Lerer, R. D. Weiner, & R. H. Belmaker (Eds.), *ECT: Basic mechanisms,* (pp. 156–163). London: John Libby.

SQUIRE, L. R., & CHACE, P. W. (1975, December). Memory functions six to nine months after electroconvulsive therapy. *Archives of General Psychiatry, 32*(12), 1557–1564.

STAATS, A. W., & STAATS, C. K. (1958). Attitudes established by classical conditioning. *Journal of Experimental Psychology, 57,* 37–40.

STABENAU, J. R., & POLLIN, W. (1969). The pathogenesis of schizophrenia: 11 contributions from the NIMH study of 16 pairs of monozygotic twins discordant for schizophrenia. In D. V. Sankar (Ed.), *Schizophrenia: Current concepts and research* (pp. 336–351). Hicksville, NY: PJD Publications.

STANDING, L. (1973). Learning 10,000 pictures. *Quarterly Journal of Experimental Psychology, 25,* 207–222.

STANDING, L., CONEZIO, J., & HABER, R. N. (1970). Perception and memory for pictures: Single-trial learning of 2500 visual stimuli. *Psychonomic Science, 19,* 73–74.

STARK, E. (1984, February). Hypnosis on trial. *Psychology Today,* pp. 34–36. (a)

STARK, E. (1984, October). To sleep, perchance to dream. *Psychology Today,* p. 16, (b).

STARK, E. (1986, October). Young, innocent, and pregnant. *Psychology Today,* pp. 28–30.

STARKER, S. (1982). *Fantastic thought: All about dreams: daydreams, and hypnosis.* Englewood Cliffs, NJ: Prentice–Hall.

STEDMAN, H. J. (1975, January). We can't predict who is dangerous. *Psychology Today,* pp. 32–35.

STEELE, C. M. (1986, January). What happens when you drink too much? *Psychology Today,* pp. 48–53.

STEELE, C. M., SOUTHWICK, L. L., & CRITCHLOW, B. (1981). Dissonance and alcohol: Drinking your troubles away. *Journal of Personality and Social Psychology, 41,* 831–846.

STEELE, C. M., & SOUTHWICK, L. (1985). Alcohol and social behavior. I. The psychology of drunken excess. *Journal of Personality and Social Psychology, 48*(1), 18–34.

STEIN, A. H. (1967). Imitation of resistance to temptation. *Child Development, 38,* 159–169.

STEIN, H. (1982). *Ethics and other liabilities.* New York: St. Martin's Press.

STEIN, M. (1983). *Psychosocial perspectives on aging and the immune response.* Paper presented at Academy of Behavioral Medicine Research, Reston, VA.

STEINHART, P. (1986, March). Personal boundaries. *Audubon,* pp. 8–11.

STENGEL, R. (1985, December 9). The missing-father myth, *Time,* p. 90.

STENGEL, R. (1987, September 14). At issue: Freedom for the irrational. *Time,* p. 88.

STEPHAN, W., BERSCHEID, E., & WALSTER, E. (1971). Sexual arousal and heterosexual perception. *Journal of Personality and Social Psychology, 20*(1), 93–101.

STERN, D. N., SPIEKER, S., & MacKAIN, K. (1982). Intonation contours as signals in maternal speech to prelinguistic infants. *Development Psychology, 18,* 727–736.

STERN, M. (1980). *Sex in USSR.* New York: Times Books.

STERNBACH, R. A. (1974). *Pain patients: Traits and treatment.* New York: Academic Press.

STERNBACH, R. A. (1978). Treatment of the chronic pain patient. *Journal of Human Stress, 4*(3), 11–15.

STERNBERG, R. J. (1985). Human intelligence: The model is the message. *Science, 230*(4730), 1111–1118.

STEVENSON, J., & JONES, I. H. (1972). Behavior therapy technique for exhibitionism: A preliminary report. *Archives of General Psychiatry, 27,* 839–841.

STILE, I. L., HEGYI, T., HIATT, I. M. (1984). *Drugs used with neonates and during pregnancy* (2nd ed.). Oradell, NJ: Medical Economics Books.

STILES, W. B., SHAPIRO, D. A., & ELLIOTT, R. (1986, February). "Are all psychotherapies equivalent?" *American Psychologist, 41*(2), 165–180.

STOKES, P. E., & SIKES, C. R. (1987). Hypothalamic–pituitary–adrenal axis in affective disorders. In H. Y. Meltzer (Ed.), *Psychological pharmacology: A third generation of progress* (pp. 589–607). New York: Raven Press.

STOLER, P. (1984, October 1). Ali fights a new round. *Time,* p. 60.

STOLLER, R. J. (1969). Parental influences in male transsexualism. In R. Green & J. Money (Eds.), *Transsexualism and sex reassignment.* Baltimore: Johns Hopkins University Press.

STONE, J. (1988, August). Sex and the single gorilla. *Discover,* pp. 78–81.

STONE, J. L., & CHURCH, J. (1973). *Childhood and adolescence: A psychology of the growing person* (3rd ed.). New York: Random House.

STONE, N., FROMME, M., & KAGAN, D. (1985). *Cocaine: Seduction and solution.* New York: Pinnacle.

STONER, J. A. (1961). *A comparison of individual and group decisions involving risk.* Unpublished master's thesis, School of Industrial Management, MIT, Cambridge, MA.

STRACK, F., MARTIN, L. L., & STEPPER, S. (1988). Inhibiting and facilitating conditions of the human smile: A non-obtrusive test of the facial feedback hypothesis. *Journal of Personality and Social Psychology, 54,* 768–777.

STRATHMAN, A. J., PETTY, R. E., GLEICHER, F. H., & BOZZOLO, A. M. (1988, August). *Interpersonal judgments under scrutiny: The effects of self-monitoring.* Paper presented at the annual meeting of the American Psychological Association, Atlanta.

STRATTON, G. (1986). Some preliminary experiments on vision without inversion of the retinal image. *Psychological Review, 3,* 611–617.

STRAUS, M. A., GELLES, R. J., & STEINMETZ, S. K. (1980). *Behind closed doors: Violence in the American family.* Garden City, NY: Anchor Press.

STREISSGUTH, A. P., BARR, H. M., SAMPSON, P. D., DARBY, B. L., & MARTIN, D. C. (1989). IQ at age 4 in relation to maternal alcohol use and smoking during pregnancy. *Developmental Psychology, 25*(1), 3–11.

STREISSGUTH, A. P., MARTIN, D. C., BARR, H. M., SANDMAN, B. M., KIRCHNER, G. L., & DARBY, B. L. (1984). Intrauterine alcohol and nicotine exposure: Attention and reaction time in 4-year-old children. *Developmental Psychology, 20,* 533–542.

STRICKLAND, B. R. (1978). Internal–external expectancies and health-related behaviors. *Journal of Consulting and Clinical Psychology, 46,* 1192–1211.

STROEBE, W., & STROEBE, M. S. (1987). *Bereavement and health.* New York: Cambridge University Press.

STROMEYER, C. F. (1970, November). Eidetikers. *Psychology Today,* pp. 77–80.

STROOP, J. R. (1935). Studies of interference in serial verbal reactions. *Journal of Experimental Psychology, 18,* 643–662.

STUNKARD, A., D'A AQUILI, E., FOX, S., & FILION, R. D. L. (1972). Influence of social class on obesity and thinness in children. *Journal of the American Medical Association, 221*(6), 579–584.

SUEDFELD, P. (1975). The benefits of boredom: Sensory deprivation reconsidered. *American Scientist, 63*(1), 60–69.

SUEDFELD, P. (1980). *Restricted environmental stimulation: Research and clinical applications.* New York: Wiley–Interscience.

SUEDFELD, P. (1982). Aloneness as a healing experience. In L. A. Peplau & D. Perlman (Eds.), *Loneliness: A source-book of current theory, research, and therapy.* New York: Wiley.

SUEDFELD, P., & BAKER-BROWN, G. (1986). Restricted environmental stimulation therapy and aversion conditioning in smoking cessation: Active and placebo effects. *Behavior Research and Therapy, 24,* 421–428.

SUGARMAN, S. (1987). *Piaget's construction of the child's reality.* New York: Cambridge University Press.

SUINN, R. M. (1987). Abnormal psychology:

New challenges and basic foundations. In I. Cohen (Ed.), *G. Stanley Hall lecture series* (pp. 91–136). Washington, DC: American Psychological Association.

SUNDBERG, N. (1984). Trait psychology. In R. J. Corsini (Ed.), *Encyclopedia of psychology* (Vol. 3, pp. 436–437). New York: Wiley.

SUOMI, S., & HARLOW, H. (1972). Social rehabilitation of isolate-reared monkeys. *Developmental Psychology, 6*(3), 487–496.

SUOMI, S., & HARLOW, H. (1978). Early experience and social development in Rhesus monkeys. In M. Lamb (Ed.), *Social and personality development*. New York: Holt, Rinehart & Winston.

SUSSER, M. (1981). Prenatal nutrition, birth weight, and psychological development: An overview of experiments, quasi-experiments, and natural experiments in the past decade. *American Journal of Clinical Nutrition, 34,* 784–803.

SVENSON, O. (1981). Are we all less risky and more skillful than our fellow drivers? *Acta Psychologica, 47,* 143–148.

SWAAB, D. F., & FLIERS, E. (1985, May 31). A sexually dimorphic nucleus in the human brain. *Science, 228,* 1112–1115.

SYNDULKO, K. (1978). Electrocortical investigations of sociopathy. In R. D. Hare & D. Schalling (Eds.), *Psychopathic behavior: Approaches to research*. New York: Wiley.

SZASZ, T. S. (1960). The myth of mental illness. *American Psychologist, 15,* 113–118.

SZASZ, T. (1970). *The manufacture of madness*. New York: Harper & Row.

SZASZ, T. S. (1983). Mental illness as strategy. In P. Bean (Ed.), *Mental illness: Changes and trends*. New York: Wiley.

SZASZ, T. (1987). *Insanity: The idea and its consequences*. New York: Wiley.

Talking himself out of a job. (1988, January 25). *Time*, p. 27.

TANABE, T., INO, M., & TAKAGI, S. F. (1975). Discrimination of odors in olfactory bulb, pyriform-amygdaloid areas, and orbitofrontal cortex of the monkey. *Journal of Neurophysiology, 38,* 1284–1296.

TANNER, J. M. (1982). *Growth at adolescence* (2nd ed.). Oxford, CT: Scientific Publications.

TANNEY, F. (1988, August). *Getting the most from therapy: A consumer's guide*. Symposium presented at the annual meeting of the American Psychological Association, Atlanta.

TART, C. T. (1975). *States of consciousness*. New York: Dutton.

TAUSIG, M. (1982). Measuring life events. *Journal of Health and Social Behavior, 23,* 52–64.

TAVRIS, C. (1982, November). Anger defused. *Psychology Today, 16*(11), 25–35.

TAVRIS, C. (1986, August). *Anger: The misunderstood emotion*. Discussant at the meeting of the American Psychological Association, Washington, DC.

TAVRIS, C. (1989). *Anger: The misunderstood emotion* (2nd ed.). New York: Simon & Schuster.

TAVRIS, C., & WADE, C. (1984). *The longest war: Sex differences in perspective* (2nd ed.). San Diego: Harcourt Brace Jovanovich.

TAYLOR, D. T., BERRY, P. C., & BLOCK, C. H. (1958). Does group participation when brainstorming facilitate or inhibit creative thinking? *Administrator's Science Quarterly, 3,* 23–47.

TAYLOR, S. E. (1983). Adjustment to threatening events: A theory of cognitive adaptation. *American Psychologist, 38,* 1161–1173.

TAYLOR, S. E., COLLINS, R., SKOKAN, L., & ASPINWALL, L. (1988, August). *Illusions, reality and adjustment in coping with victimizing events*. Paper presented at the annual meeting of the American Psychological Association, Atlanta.

TEDRICK, D. (1985, May 25). Bank of sperm from "intelligent" men produces first baby. *Hartford Courant*, p. C-16.

TEGHTSOONIAN, M., & BECKWITH, J. B. (1976). Children's size judgments when size and distance vary: Is there a developmental trend to overconstancy? *Journal of Experimental Child Psychology, 22*(2), 23–39.

TEITELBAUM, P. (1955). Sensory control of hypothalamic hyperphagia. *Journal of Comparative and Physiological Psychology, 48,* 156–163.

TELLEGEN, A., LYKKEN, D. T., BOUCHARD, T. J., WILCOX, K. J., SEGAL, N. L., & RICH, S. (1988). Personality similarity in twins reared apart and together. *Journal of Personality and Social Psychology, 54,* 1031–1039.

TELLER, D. Y., PEEPLES, D. R., & SEKEL, M. (1978). Discrimination of chromatic from white light by two-month-old human infants. *Vision Research, 18*(1), 41–48.

TENNOV, D. (1979). *Love and limerence*. New York: Stein & Day.

TERMAN, L. M. (1916). *The measurement of intelligence*. Boston: Houghton Mifflin.

TERMAN, M., & LINK, M. (1989, January/February). Fighting the winter blues with bright light. *Psychology Today*, pp. 18–21.

TERRACE, H. S. (1979, November). How Nim Chimpsky changed my mind. *Psychology Today*, pp 65–76.

TESCH, S. A., & GENNELO, K. (1985, August). *Age, intimacy, and affect in young men and women*. Paper presented at the annual meeting of the American Psychological Association, Los Angeles.

THASE, M. S., FRANK, E., & KUPFER, D. J. (1985). Biological processes in major depression. In E. E. Beckham & W. R. Leber (Eds.), *Handbook of depression: Treatment, assessment, and research* (pp. 816–913). Homewood, IL: Dorsey Press.

THATCHER, R. W., WALKER, R. A., & GUIDICE, S. (1987). Human cerebral hemispheres develop at different rates and ages. *Science, 236,* 110–113.

The last word: Do lie detectors really detect lies? (1988, March). *University of California, Berkeley Wellness Letter*, p. 8.

THIEMAN, T. J., & CLARY, E. G. (1988, August). *Teaching ethically informed decision-making by experiment*. Paper presented at the annual meeting of the American Psychological Association, Atlanta.

THIGPEN, C. H., & CLECKLEY, H. (1957). *The three faces of Eve*. New York: Popular Library.

THIGPEN, C. H., & CLECKLEY, H. M. (1984). On the incidence of multiple personality disorder: A brief communication. *International Journal of Clinical and Experimental Hypnosis, 32,* 63–66.

THOMAS, A., AND CHESS, S. (1977). *Temperament and development*. New York: Brunner/Mazel.

THOMPSON, D. (1988, September 19). The environment: Cleaning up the mess. *Time*, pp. 22–24.

THOMPSON, J. K., JARVIE, G. J., LAHEY, B. B., & CURETON, K. J. (1982). Exercise and obesity: Etiology, physiology, and intervention. *Psychological Bulletin, 91,* 55–79.

THOMPSON, J. W., & BLAINE, J. D. (1987). Use of ECT in the U. S. in 1975 and 1980. *American Journal of Psychiatry, 144,* 557–562.

THOMPSON, S. C., & KELLEY, H. H. (1981). Judgments of responsibility for activities in close relationships. *Journal of Personality and Social Psychology, 41,* 469–477.

THORNDIKE, E. L. (1898). Animal intelligence. *Psychological Review Monograph, 2*(8).

THORNDIKE, E. L. (1901). The mental life of the monkeys. *Psychological Review Monograph, 3*(15).

THORNDIKE, E. L. (1931). *Human learning*. New York: Century.

THURSTONE, L. L. (1938). *Primary mental abilities*. Chicago: University of Chicago Press.

TOCH, H. (1980). *Violent men*. Cambridge, MA: Schenkman.

TOI, M., & BATSON, C. D. (1982). More evidence that empathy is a source of altruistic motivation. *Journal of Personality and Social Psychology, 43,* 281–292.

TOLMAN, E. C., & HONZIK, C. H. (1930). Introduction and removal of reward, and maze performance in rats. *University of California Publications in Psychology, 4,* 257–275.

TOMASELLO, M., & MANNLE, S. (1985). Pragmatics of sibling speech to one-year-olds. *Child Development, 56,* 911–917.

TOMKINS, S. S. (1962). *Affect, imagery, consciousness, the positive effects* (Vol. 1). New York: Springer.

TOMKINS, S. S. (1963). *Affect, imagery, consciousness, the negative effects* (Vol. 2). New York: Springer.

Toronto News, July 26, 1977.

TORREY, E. F. (1983). *Surviving schizophrenia*. New York: Harper & Row.

TORREY, E. F. (1988). *Surviving schizophrenia: A family manual*. New York: Harper & Row.

TOUFEXIS, A. (1988, February 22). Older but coming on strong. *Time*, pp. 76–79.

TREWHITT, H., PLATTNER, A., WALSH, K. T., WITKIN, G., WALLACE, J., STANGLIN, D., & CHESNOFF, R. Z. (1988, July 18). Where is the light at the end of the gulf? *U. S. News and World Report*, pp. 12–16.

TROLL, S. J., MILLER, J., & ATCHLEY, R. C. (1979). *Families in later life*. Belmont, CA: Wadsworth.

TRONICK, E. Z. (1989). Emotions and emotional communication in infants. *American Psychologist, 44*, 112–119.

TROTTER, R. J. (1987, January). The play's the thing. *Psychology Today*, pp. 27–34.

TSUANG, M. T., FARAONE, S. V., & DAY, M. (1988). Schizophrenic disorders. In A. M. Nicoli (Ed.), *New Harvard guide to psychiatry* (pp. 259–295). Cambridge, MA: Harvard University Press.

TSUSHIMA, W. T. (1984). Minnesota Multiphasic Personality Inventory. In R. J. Corsini (Ed.), *Encyclopedia of psychology* (Vol. 2, pp. 385–386). New York: Wiley.

TULVING, E. (1972). Episodic and semantic memory. In E. Tulving & W. Donaldson (Eds.), *Organization of memory*. New York: Academic Press.

TULVING, E. (1985, April). How many memory systems are there? *American Psychologist, 40*(4), 385–398.

TULVING, E. (1986). What kind of hypothesis is the distinction between episodic and semantic memory? *Journal of Experimental Psychology: Learning, Memory, and Cognition, 12*, 307–311.

TULVING, E., & THOMSON, D. M. (1973). Encoding specificity and retrieval processes in episodic memory. *Psychological Review, 80*, 352–373.

TURNBULL, C. M. (1961). Some observations regarding the experiences and behavior of the Bamputi pygmies. *American Journal of Psychology, 74*, 304–308.

ULLMANN, L. P., & KRASNER, L. (1975). *A psychological approach to abnormal behavior*. Englewood Cliffs, NJ: Prentice–Hall.

ULRICH, R. E., STACHNIK, T. J., & STAINTON, N. R. (1983). Student acceptance of generalized personality interpretations. *Psychological Reports, 13*, 831–834.

UNDERWOOD, S. L., & ALEXANDER, P. P. (1988, August). *Body image: Reformulation and assessment*. Paper presented at the annual meeting of the American Psychological Association, Atlanta.

UNGER, R. (1979). *Female and male*. New York: Harper & Row.

VAILLANT, G. E. (1977). *Adaptation to life: How the best and brightest came of age*. Boston: Little, Brown.

VALENSTEIN, E. S. (1973). *Brain control*. New York: Wiley.

VALENSTEIN, E. S. (1987). *Great and desperate cures: The rise and decline of psychosurgery and other radical treatments for mental illness*. New York: Basic Books.

VALENSTEIN, E., LIEBLICH, I., DINAR, R., COHEN, E., & BACHUS, S. (1982). Relation between eating evoked by lateral hypothalamic-stimulation and tail pinch in different rat strains. *Behavioral and Neural Biology, 34*, 271–282.

VANDENBOS, G. R., & PINO, C. D. (1980). Research in the outcome of psychotherapy. In G. R. VandenBos (Ed.), *Psychotherapy: Practice, research, policy* (pp. 23–69). Beverly Hills, CA: Sage.

VAN DYKE, C., & BYCK, R. (1982). Cocaine. *Scientific American, 10*, 128.

VAN MAANEN, J., & SCHEIN, E. H. (1977). Career development. In J. R. Hackman & J. Lloyd Suttle (Eds.), *Improving life at work*. Santa Monica, CA: Goodyear.

VAN MELIS, W. M., & STREIN, W. (1986). Materials review in comparison of the K-ABC global scales and the Stanford–Binet with young gifted children. *Topics in Early Childhood Special Education, 6*, 88–91.

VAN VOORST, B. (1988, August 29). Neither "negligent" nor "culpable." *Time*, p. 30.

VAUGHN, C., SNYDER, K., JONES, S., FREEMAN, W., & FALLOON, I. (1984). Family factors in schizophrenic relapse: A replication in California of British research in expressed emotion. *Archives of General Psychiatry, 41*, 1169–1177.

VERNON, M. D. (1969). *Human motivation*. Cambridge, England: Cambridge University Press.

VERNOY, M. W., & LURIA, S. M. (1977). Perception of, and adaptation to, a three-dimensional curvative distortion. *Perception and Psychophysics, 22*(3), 245–248.

VEROFF, J., DOUVAN, E., & KULKA, R. (1981). *The inner American: A self-portrait from 1957-1976*. New York: Basic Books.

VERVALIN, C. H. (1978). Just what is creativity? In G. A. Davis & J. A. Scott (Eds.), *Training creative thinking*. Huntington, NY: Krieger.

VESSELS, J. (1985, January). Koko's kitten. *National Geographic*, pp. 110–114.

VICTOR, M., & WOLFE, S. M. (1973). Causation and treatment of the alcohol withdrawal syndrome. In P. G. Bourne & R. Fox (Eds.), *Alcoholism: Progress in research and treatment* (pp. 137–169). New York: Academic Press.

VOKEY, J. R., & READ, J. D. (1985). Subliminal messages: Between the devil and the media. *American Psychologist, 40*, 1231–1239.

WABER, D. (1977). Sex differences in mental abilities, hemispheric lateralization and rate of physical growth at adolescence. *Developmental Psychology, 13*, 29–38.

WABER, D. (1979). Cognitive abilities and sex-related variations in the maturation of cerebral cortical functions. In M. A. Wittig & A. C. Peterson (Eds.), *Sex-related differences in cognitive functioning* (pp. 161–186). New York: Academic Press.

WADSWORTH, B. (1981, September). Misinterpretations of Piaget's theory. *Educational Digest, 47*, 56–58.

WAID, W. M., & ORNE, M. T. (1982). The physiological detection of deception. *American Scientist, 70*, 402–409.

WALD, G. (1964). The receptors for human color vision. *Science, 145*, 1007–1017.

WALDROP, M. M. (1988). Toward a unified theory of cognition. *Science, 241*, 27–29.

WALFORD, R. L. (1983). *Maximum life span*. New York: Norton.

WALKER, L. J. (1984). Sex differences in the development of moral reasoning: A critical review. *Child Development, 55*, 677–691.

WALLACE, B., & FISHER, L. E. (1983). *Consciousness and behavior*. Boston: Allyn & Bacon.

WALLACE, M. (1969, November 25). *New York Times*, p. 16.

WALLACE, R. K., DILLBECK, M., JACOBE, E., & HARRINGTON, B. (1982). The effects of transcendental meditation and TM-Sidhi program on the aging process. *International Journal of Neuroscience, 16*, 53–58.

WALLERSTEIN, J. S., & BLAKESLEE, S. (1989). *Second chances: Men, women, and children a decade after divorce*. New York: Ticknor & Fields.

WALLERSTEIN, J. S., CORBIN, S. B., & LEWIS, J. M. (1988). Children of divorce: A ten-year study. In E. M. Hetherington & J. Arasteh (Eds.), *Impact of divorce, single-parenting, and step-parenting on children* (pp. 198–214). Hillsdale, NJ: Lawrence Erlbaum Associates.

WALLERSTEIN, J. S., & KELLY, J. B. (1980). *Surviving the breakup: How children and parents cope with divorce*. New York: Basic Books.

WALLIS, C. (1985, December 9). Children having children: Teen pregnancies are corroding America's social fabric. *Time*, pp. 78–90. (a)

WALLIS, C. (1985, February 25). Gauging the fat of the land: A panel issues a warning for 34 million overweight Americans. *Time*, pp. 72–73. (b)

WALLSTON, K. A., MAIDES, S., & WALLSTON, B. S. (1976). Health-related information seeking as a function of health-related locus of control and health value. *Journal of Research in Personality, 10*, 215–222.

WALSTER, E., & WALSTER, G. W. (1978). *A new look at love*. Reading, MA: Addison–Wesley.

WARD, L. M. (1987). Remembrance of sounds past: Memory and psychophysical scaling. *Journal of Experimental Psychology: Human Perception and Performance, 13*, 216–227.

WARGA, C. (1987). Pain's gatekeeper. *Psychology Today*, pp. 50–56.

WARREN, R. M. (1970). Perceptual restoration of missing speech sounds. *Science, 167*, 392–393.

WATERMAN, A. S. (1982). Identity development from adolescence to adulthood: An extension of theory and a review of research. *Developmental Psychology, 18*, 341–358.

WATSON, J. (1913). Psychology as the behaviorist views it. *Psychological Review, 20,* 158–177.

WATSON, J. B. (1930). *Behaviorism.* Chicago: Phoenix.

WATSON, D. R., & RICHARDSON, E. (1985, April). *Children's world views: Working models and quality of attachment.* Paper presented at the biennial meeting of the Society for Research in Child Development, Toronto, Ontario.

WATSON, J. B., & RAYNER, R. (1920). Conditioned emtional reactions. *Journal of Experimental Psychology, 3,* 1–14.

WAUGH, N. C., & NORMAN, D. A. (1965). Primary memory. *Psychological Review, 72*(2), 89–104.

WEBB, W. B. (1975). *Sleep the gentle tyrant.* Englewood Cliffs, NJ: Prentice–Hall.

WEBB, W. B. (1983). Theories in modern sleep research. In A. Mayes (Ed.), *Sleep mechanisms and functions.* Wokingham, England: Van Nostrand–Reinhold.

WEBB, W., & CARTWRIGHT, R. D. (1978). Sleep and dreams. In M. Rosenzweig & L. Porter (Eds.), *Annual review of psychology* (Vol. 29, pp. 223–252). Palo Alto, CA: Annual Reviews.

WEBB, W., & FRIEL, J. (1971). Sleep stage and personality characteristics of "natural" long and short sleepers. *Science, 171,* 587–588.

WEBER, R., & CROCKER, J. (1983). Cognitive processes in the revision of stereotypic beliefs. *Journal of Personality and Social Psychology, 45,* 961–977.

WECHSLER, D. (1939). *The measurement of adult intelligence.* Baltimore: Williams & Wilkins.

WEGNER, D. (1988, August). *Unwanted thoughts: The psychology of mental control.* Invited address at the annual meeting of the American Psychological Association, Atlanta.

WEHR, T. A., JACOBSEN, F. M., SACK, D. A., ARENDT, J., TAMARKIN, L., & ROSENTHAL, N. E. (1986). Phototherapy of seasonal affective disorders. *Archives of General Psychiatry, 43,* 870–875.

WEHR, T. A., SACK, D. A., & ROSENTHAL, N. E. (1987). Seasonal affective disorder with summer depression and winter hypomania. *American Journal of Psychiatry, 144,* 1602–1603.

WEHREN, A., & DE LISI, R. (1983). The development of gender understanding: Judgments and explanations. *Child Development, 54,* 1568–1578.

WEIL, A. (1972). *The natural mind: A new way of looking at drugs and the higher consciousness.* Boston: Houghton Mifflin.

WEIL, A. (1979). *The natural mind.* Boston: Houghton Mifflin.

WEIL, A. (1980). *The marriage of the sun and moon: A quest for unity in consciousness.* Boston: Houghton Mifflin.

WEIL, A. (1985). *Health and healing: Understanding conventional and alternative medicine.* Boston: Houghton Mifflin.

WEIL, A., & ROSEN, W. (1983). *Chocolate to morphine: Understanding mind active drugs.* Boston: Houghton Mifflin.

WEIL, W. B., JR. (1984). Demographic determinants of obesity. *Obesity and the family: Marriage and Family Review, 7*(1,2), 21–32.

WEINBERGER, D., BERMAN, K., & ZEC, R. (1986). Physiologic dysfunction of dorsolateral prefrontal cortex in schizophrenia. I. Regional cerebral flow evidence. *Archives of General Psychiatry, 43,* 114–124.

WEINBERGER, D. R., WAGNER, R. J., & WYATT, R. L. (1983). Neuropathological studies of schizophrenia: A selective review. *Schizophrenia Bulletin, 9,* 198–212.

WEINER, B. (1972). *Theories of motivation.* Chicago: Rand–McNally.

WEINER, B. (1982). The emotional consequences of causal attributions. In M. S. Clark & S. T. Fiske (Eds.), *Affect and cognition.* Hillsdale, NJ: Lawrence Erlbaum Associates.

WEINER, B. (1985). An attributional theory of achievement, motivation, and emotion. *Psychological Review, 92,* 548–573.

WEINGARTNER, H., ADELFRIS, W., EICH, J. E., & MURPHY, D. L. (1976). Encoding specificity in alcohol state-dependent learning. *Journal of Experimental Psychology: Human Learning and Memory, 2,* 83–87.

WEINRAUB, M., CLEMENS, L. P., SOCKLOFF, A., ETHRIDGE, T., GRACELY, E., & MYERS, B. (1984). The development of sex role stereotypes in the third year: Relationship to gender labeling, gender identity, sex-typed toy preference and family characteristics. *Child Development, 55,* 1493–1503.

WEINSTEIN, M. S. (1969). Achievement motivation and risk preference. *Journal of Personality and Social Psychology, 13,* 153–172.

WEIR, C. (1976). Auditory frequency sensitivity in the neonate: A signal detection analysis. *Journal of Experimental Child Psychology, 21*(2), 219–225.

WEIS, C. R., ROUNDS, J. B., & ZARICHNY, K. T. (1985, August). *Longitudinal investigation of a cognitive-behavioral intervention for premenstrual distress.* Paper presented at the meeting of the American Psychological Association, Los Angeles.

WEISENBERG, M. (1980). The regulation of pain. *Annals of the New York Academy of Sciences, 340,* 102–114.

WEISS, L., KATZMAN, M., & WOLCHIK, S. (1985). *Treating bulimia: A psychoeducational approach.* New York: Pergamon.

WEISS, R. (1988). Women's skills linked to estrogen levels. *Science News, 134,* 341.

WEISS, R. (1989). Desperately seeking sexual statistics. *Science News, 136,* 28. (a)

WEISS, R. (1989). Soviet describes AIDS errors. *Science News, 135,* 382. (b)

WEISS, R. L. (1975). *Marital separation.* New York: Basic Books.

WEISS, R. L. (1979). *Going it alone: The family life and social situation of the single parent.* New York: Basic Books.

WEISSKOPF-JOELSON, E., & ELISEO, T. S. (1961). An experimental study of the effectiveness of brainstorming. *Journal of Applied Psychology, 45,* 45–49.

WEISSMAN, M. M., & MYERS, J. K. (1978). Affective disorders in a U.S. urban community. *Archives of General Psychiatry, 35,* 1304–1311.

WELLBORN, S. N. (1987, April 13). How genes shape personality. *U. S. News and World Report,* pp. 58–62.

WELLS, M. (1988, January). A schizophrenic's voices. *Psychology Today,* pp. 76–79.

WERNER, C. M., KAGEHIRO, D. K., & STRUBE, M. J. (1982). Conviction proneness and the authorization juror: Inability to disregard information or attitudinal bias? *Journal of Applied Psychology, 67,* 629–636.

WERNER, J. S., & WOOTEN, B. R. (1979). Human infant color vision and color perception. *Infant Behavior and Development, 2*(3), 241–273.

WESTON, D. R., & RICHARDSON, E. (1985, April). *Children's world views: Working models and quality of attachment.* Paper presented at the biennial meeting of the Society for Research in Child Development. Toronto, Ontario.

WEYANT, J. M. (1978). Effects of mood states, costs, and benefits on helping. *Journal of Personality and Social Psychology, 36,* 1169–1176.

WHELAN, E. (1986). *Boy or girl? The definitive work on sex selection.* New York: Simon & Schuster.

WHITE, G. L. (1980). Physical attractiveness and courtship progress. *Journal of Personality and Social Psychology, 39,* 660–669.

WHITE, G. L. (1981). Relative involvement, inadequacy, and jealousy: A test of a causal model. *Alternative Lifestyles, 4*(3), 291–309.

WHITFIELD, J. C., & EVANS, E. F. (1965). Responses of auditory and cortical neurons to stimuli of changing frequency. *Journal of Neurophysiology, 28,* 655–672.

WHITING, B. B., & EDWARDS, C. P. (1988). *Children of different worlds: The formation of social behavior.* Cambridge, MA: Harvard University Press.

WHITLEY, B. E. (1987). The effects of discredited eyewitness testimony: A meta-analysis. *Journal of Social Psychology, 127,* 209–214.

WHITTY, C. W. M., & ZANGWILL, O. L. (1977). Traumatic amnesia. In C. W. M. Whitty & O. L. Zangwill (Eds.), *Amnesia* (2nd ed.). London: Butterworths.

WHORF, B. (1956). *Language, thought, and reality.* Cambridge, MA: MIT Press.

WICKER, A. W. (1969). Attitudes versus actions: The relationship of verbal and overt behavioral responses to attitude objects. *Journal of Social Issues, 25,* 41–78.

WIERZBICKI, M. (1987). Similarity of monozygotic and dizygotic child twins in level and lability of subclinically depressed mood. *American Journal of Orthopsychiatry, 57,* 33–40.

WIGGINS, J. S. (1984). *Psychology of women: Behavior in a biosocial context.* New York: Norton.

WILBUR, R. (1986, March). A drug to fight cocaine. *Science, 86,* 42–46.

WILDER, D. A., & THOMPSON, J. E. (1988). Assimilation and contrast effects in the judgments of groups. *Journal of Personality and Social Psychology, 54,* 62–73.

WILKES, J. (1986, January). A study in hypnosis: A conversation with Ernest R. Hilgard. *Psychology Today,* pp. 23–27.

WILLIAMS, J. E., & BEST, D. L. (1982). *Measuring sex stereotypes: A thirty-nation study.* Beverly Hills, CA: Sage.

WILLIAMS, R. B. (1984). Type A behavior and coronary heart disease: Something old, something new. *Behavioral Medicine Update, 6*(3), 29–33.

WILLIAMS, T. M. (1986). *The impact of television: A natural experiment in three communities.* Orlando, FL: Academic Press.

WILSON, E. O. (1978). *On human nature.* Cambridge, MA: Harvard University Press.

WINETT, R. A. (1973). Parameters of deposit contracts in the modification of smoking. *Psychological Record, 23,* 49–60.

WINFREY, C. (1979, February). Why 900 died. *New York Times Magazine,* pp. 39–41.

WINICK, M. (1976). *Malnutrition and brain damage.* New York: Oxford University Press.

WINTERS, K. C., & NEALE, J. M. (1985). Mania and low self-esteem. *Journal of Abnormal Psychology, 94*(3), 282–290.

WISE, R. A. (1984). Neural mechanisms of the reinforcing action of cocaine. *National Institute on Drug Abuse: Research Monograph Series, 50,* 15–33.

WITTERS, W. L. (1988). *Drugs and society* (2nd ed.). Monterey, CA: Wadsworth.

WOLFF, C. (1971). *Love between women.* New York: Harper & Row.

WOLFF, P. (1969). The natural history of crying and vocalization in early infancy. In B. M. Foss (Ed.), *Determinants of infant behavior* (Vol. IV). London: Methuen.

WOLPE, J. (1958). *Psychotherapy by reciprocal inhibition.* Stanford, CA: Stanford University Press.

WOLPE, J. (1982). *The practice of behavior therapy.* New York: Pergamon.

WOLPE, J. (1987). The promotion of scientific therapy: A long voyage. In T. K. Zeig (Ed.), *The evolution of psychotherapy* (pp. 232–256). New York: Brunner/Mazel.

WOLPE, J., & RACHMAN, S. J. (1960). Psychoanalytic "evidence," a critique based on Freud's case of Little Hans. *Journal of Nervous and Mental Disease, 131,* 135–147.

WOOD, W. (1982). Retrieval of attitude-relevant information from memory: Effects on susceptibility to persuasion and on intrinsic motivation. *Journal of Personality and Social Psychology, 42,* 798–810.

WOOD, W., & EAGLY, A. H. (1981). Steps in the positive analysis of causal attributions and message comprehension. *Journal of Personality and Social Psychology, 4,* 246–259.

WOODEN, K. (1981). *The children of Jonestown.* New York: McGraw–Hill.

WORCHEL, S., COOPER, J., & GOETHALS, G. R. (1988). *Understanding social psychology* (4th ed.). Chicago: Dorsey.

Wrap-up: Alcohol and the body. University of California, Berkeley. (1986, February). *Wellness Letter, 2*(5), 1–4.

WURTMAN, J. (1987). Eating sweets when depressed or tense. *Harvard Medical School Mental Health Letter, 3,* 8.

WURTMAN, R. J., & WURTMAN, J. J. (1989). Carbohydrates and depression. *Scientific American, 260*(1), 68–75.

WYLIE, R. C. (1979). *The self-concept, Vol. 2: Theory and research on selected topics.* Lincoln, NE: University of Nebraska Press.

WYNHAUSEN, E. (1988, September). Cracked out. *MS,* pp. 69–75.

WYNNE, E. A. (1988). The great tradition in education: Transmitting moral values. In J. Rubinstein & R. Slife (Eds.), *Taking sides: Clashing views on controversial psychological issues* (pp. 145–153). Guilford, CT: Dushkin.

YOUNG, T. (1802). Color vision. *Philosophical Transactions of the Royal Society,* p. 12.

YUDOLFSKY, S., & SILVER, J. (1987). Treating performance anxiety. *Harvard Medical School Mental Health Letter, 4*(6), 8.

YUKL, G. (1981). *Leadership in organizations.* Englewood Cliffs, NJ: Prentice–Hall.

ZAIDEL, E. (1975). A technique for presenting lateralized visual input with prolonged exposure. *Vision Research, 15,* 283–289.

ZAJONC, R. B. (1985). Emotion and facial efference: A theory reclaimed. *Science, 228,* 15–21.

ZANOT, E. J., PINCUS, J. D., & LAMP, E. J. (1983). Public perceptions of subliminal advertising. *Journal of Advertising, 12*(1), 39–45.

ZEICHNER, A., & PIHL, R. O. (1979). Effects of alcohol and behavior contingencies on human aggression. *Journal of Abnormal Psychology, 88,* 153–160.

ZEIGARNIK, B. V. (1927). Untersuchungen zur Handlungsund Affektpsychologie, Herausgegeben von K. Lewin, 3. Das Behalten erledigter und unerledigter Handlungen. *Psychologisches Forschung, 9,* 1–85.

ZEISEL, H., & DIAMOND, S. S. (1978). The effect of peremptory challenges on jury and verdict: An experiment in a federal district court. *Stanford Law Review, 30,* 491–531.

ZILBERGELD, B. (1983). *The shrinking of America.* Boston: Little, Brown.

ZILBERGELD, B. (1986). Psychabuse. *Science 86, 7*(5), 48–53.

ZILBERGELD, B., & EVANS, M. (1980). The inadequacy of Masters and Johnson. *Psychology Today, 14,* 29–43.

ZILBOORG, G., & HENRY, G. W. (1941). *A history of medical psychology.* New York: Norton.

ZIMBARDO, P. G. (1970). The human choice: Individuation, reason, and order versus deindividuation, impulse, and chaos. In W. J. Arnold & D. Levine (Eds.), *Nebraska symposium on motivation.* Lincoln, NE: University of Nebraska Press.

ZIMBARDO, P. G. (1977). *Shyness: What it is, what to do about it.* Reading, MA: Addison–Wesley.

ZIMBARDO, P. G., EBBESON, E. B., & MASLACH, C. (1977). *Influencing attitudes and changing behavior.* Reading, MA: Addison–Wesley.

ZIMBARDO, P. G., & RADL, S. (1981). *The shy child.* New York: McGraw Hill.

ZIMMERMAN, D. (1985, January 10). Talking gorilla mourns dead pet. *USA Today,* p. 10.

ZIMMERMAN, M, CORYELL, W., & PFOHL, B. (1986). The validity of the dexamethasone suppression test as a marker for endogenous depression. *Archives of General Psychiatry, 43,* 347–355.

ZOLA-MORGAN, S., SQUIRE, L. R., & MISHKIN, M. (1982). The neuroanatomy of amnesia: Amygdala-hippocampus versus temporal stem. *Science, 218,* 1337–1339.

ZUCKERMAN, M. (1979). *Sensation seeking: Beyond the optimal level of arousal.* Hillsdale, NJ: Lawrence Erlbaum Associates.

ZUCKERMAN, M. (1983). Sensation seeking: The initial motive for drug abuse. In E. Gottheil, K. A. Druley, T. E. Skolada, & H. M. Waxman (Eds.), *Etiological aspects of alcohol and drug abuse* (pp. 202–220). Springfield, IL: Charles C. Thomas.

ZUCKERMAN, M. (1985, March). Can genes help helping? *Psychology Today,* p. 80.

ZUCKERMAN, M. A., BUCHSBAUM, M. S., & MURPHY, D. L. (1980). Sensation-seeking and its biological correlates. *Psychological Bulletin, 88,* 187–214.

ZUCKERMAN, M., EYSENCK, S., & EYSENCK, H. J. (1978). Sensation seeking in England and America: Cross-cultural, age, and sex comparison. *Journal of Consulting and Clinical Psychology, 46,* 139–149.

ZUCKERMAN, M., KUHLMAN, D. M., & CAMAC, C. (1988). What lies beyond E and N? Factor analyses of scales believed to measure basic dimensions of personality. *Journal of Personality and Social Psychology, 54,* 96–107.

ZUCKERMAN, M., MURTAUGH, T., & SIEGEL, V. (1974). Sensation seeking and cortical augmenting-reducing. *Psychophysiology, 11,* 535–542.

ZUGER, B. (1988). Is early effeminate behavior in boys early homosexuality? *Comprehensive Psychiatry, 29,* 509–519.

ZUGER, B. (1989). Homosexuality in families of boys with early effeminate behavior: An epidemiological study. *Archives of Sexual Behavior, 18,* 155–165.

Chapter 1 Opener: H. Wendler/The Image Bank; Page 4: from *Obedience to authority* by Stanley Milgram, Copyright © 1974 by Stanley Milgram, reprinted with permission of Harper & Row, Publishers, Inc.; Page 8: Peter Menzel/Stock, Boston; Page 9: Donna Ferrato/Black Star; Page 14: Baron Hugo Van Lawick, © National Geographic Society; Page 17: Dr. Monte Buchsbaum, University of California at Irvine, Dept. of Psychiatry and Human Behavior; Page 20: Rafael Macia/Photo Researchers, Inc.; Pages 22 and 23: Culver Pictures; Page 24: The Bettmann Archive.

Chapter 2 Opener: Petit Format/Guigoz/Steiner/Photo Researchers, Inc.; Page 36: Richard Hutchings/Photo Researchers, Inc.; Page 42: Dan Helms/Duomo; Page 43: John Dominis/*Life* Magazine, © Time Inc.; Page 46: Fred McConnaughey/Photo Researchers, Inc.; Page 49: The Warren Anatomical Museum, Harvard Medical School; Page 50:(top) British Museum (Natural History), (bottom) Courtesy of Drs. David Hubel and Torsten Wiesel; Page 54: Dan McCoy, Livingston/Rainbow; Page 57: (top) David Powers/Stock, Boston, (bottom) Courtesy James Olds, California Institute of Technology; Page 60: (left) Grant le Duc/Monkmeyer, (right) Dr. John Mazziotta et al/Neurology/Science Photo Library/Photo Researchers, Inc.; Page 61: CNRI/Science Photo Library/Photo Researchers, Inc.

Chapter 3 Opener: Arruza/Bruce Coleman, Inc.; Page 66: Rollie McKenna/Photo Researchers, Inc.; Page 69: Blair Seitz/Photo Researchers, Inc.; Page 70: George Goodwin/Monkmeyer Press; Page 77: L. Craig Jr./Bruce Coleman, Inc.; Page 82: George Hall/Woodfin Camp & Associates; Page 89: Jonathan T. Wright/ Bruce Coleman, Inc.; Page 91: Wally McNamee/Woodfin Camp & Associates; Page 92: Jeff Lowenthal/Woodfin Camp & Associates; Page 93: Christopher Brown/Stock, Boston.

Chapter 4 Opener: George Lepp/Comstock; Page 100: Michael Ventura/Bruce Coleman, Inc. Page 102: (bottom) M. C. Escher Heirs/Cordon Art Baarn-Holland, (left) Jan Halaska/Photo Researchers, Inc.; Page 103: Focus on Sports; Page 105: Courtesy American Cancer Society; Page 108: © M. C. Escher/Cordon Art-Baarn-Holland; Page 110: Baron Wolman/Woodfin Camp & Associates; Page 112: Enrico Ferorelli; Page 114: Mimi Forsyth/Monkmeyer Press; Page 116: E. R. Degginger/Bruce Coleman, Inc.; Page 124: Courtesy Dr. Alan Hein, Massachusetts Institute of Technology; Page 125: (left) B. Julesz from "Toward an axiomatic theory of preattentive vision," *Dynamic aspects of neocortical function*, Eds. G. L. Edelman, W. E. Gall, W. M. Cowan, pp. 585–612, 1984, (right) Kaiser Porcelain, Ltd., London, England.

Chapter 5 Opener: Anne Marie Rousseau/The Image Works; Page 130: Al Rubin/Stock, Boston; Page 132: (top center) Owen Franken/Stock, Boston, (bottom) Kevin Horan/Stock, Boston; Page 135: Billy E. Barnes/Stock, Boston; Page 136: Grant le Duc/Monkmeyer Press; Page 137: Edmund Apel/Photo Researchers, Inc.; Page 140: Bosch, *The Garden of Earthly Delights* (detail), Prado, Madrid. Scala/Art Resource; Page 146: (top) Bettmann Archive, (center and bottom) Bella C. Landauer Collection, The New York Historical Society. Page 148: P. Chock/Stock, Boston; Page 149: Dion Ogust/The Image Works; Page 150: Courtesy of Peter Witt, M.D.; Page 151: (left) John Feingersh/Stock, Boston; (right) Jim McHugh/Sygma; Page 152: Dr. Ronald K. Siegel; Page 153: Mike Kagan/Monkmeyer Press; Page 156: (left) The Bettmann Archive, (right) Michal Heron.

Chapter 6 Opener: Len Rue/Photo Researchers, Inc.; Page 164: Ronald H. Cohn/The Gorilla Foundation; Page 165: John Marmaras/Woodfin Camp & Associates; Page 170: Alan Carey/The Image Works; Page 171: James Balog/Black Star; Page 175: Richard Wood/The Picture Cube; Page 177: (left) Alon Reininger/Woodfin Camp & Associates, (right) Frank Siteman/The Picture Cube; Page 180: (left) Dan McCoy/Rainbow, (right) Acey Harper/Picture Group; Page 187: Pamela Price/Picture Group; Page 191: Wolfgang Köhler, *The mentality of apes*, Routledge and Kegan Paul, 1973; Page 192: Harriet Newman Brown/Monkmeyer Press; Page 193: Courtesy Albert Bandura, Stanford University.

Chapter 7 Opener: Jerry Sarapochiello/Bruce Coleman, Inc.; Page 198: UPI/Bettmann Newsphotos; Page 200: Bill Gallery/Stock, Boston; Page 202: Darlene Bordell/The Picture Cube; Page 203: Billy E. Barnes/Stock, Boston; Page 207: (top left) Owen Franken/Stock, Boston, (bottom left) Chuck Fishman/Woodfin Camp & Associates, (bottom right) Nancy Bates/The Picture Cube; Page 209: M&E Bernheim/Woodfin Camp & Associates; Page 211: Jeff Widener/AP, Wide World Photos; Page 215: Kevin Horan/Picture Group; Page 221: (top) Al Tielemans/Duomo, (bottom) Ira Wyman/Sygma; Page 222: (top and bottom) Dan McCoy/Black Star.

Chapter 8 Opener: Tom Grill/Comstock; Page 230: Courtesy Gerry Ohlinger Page 231: The Metropolitan Museum of Art, Gift of Thomas F. Ryan, 1910; Page 232: Christina Thomson/Woodfin Camp & Associates; Pages 240 and 242: Len Speier; Page 246: Mike Clemmer/Picture Group; Page 248: Courtesy Yerkes Regional Primate Center; Page 250: (top left) Bernard Gottfryd/Woodfin Camp & Associates; Page 250: (top center) Georges Merillon/Gamma Liaison, (top right) Shelly Katz/Black Star, (center left) John Barrett/Globe Photos, (center) A. Tannenbaum/Sygma, (center right) E. Adams/Sygma, (center far right) D. Kirkland/Sygma, (bottom left) Peter Turnley/Black Star, (bottom right) David Madison/Duomo; Page 252: Jim Harrison/Stock, Boston; Page 254: Dan McCoy/Rainbow; Page 257: Lowell Georgia/Photo Researchers, Inc.

Chapter 9 Opener: Michel Tcherevkoff/The Image Bank; Page 262: Jacques Chenet/Woodfin Camp & Associates; Page 264: *Nathan Hawley and Family by William Wilkie*; 1801, Collection Albany Institute of History and Art; Page 268: (bottom right) Petit Format, Nestle, Science Source/Photo Researchers, Inc., (bottom left) Lennart Nilsson from *A child is born*, Dell Publishing Co., Inc.; Page 269: Susan Leavines/Photo Researchers, Inc.; Page 270: Martha Bates/Stock, Boston; Page 276: (left) Elizabeth Crews/The Image Works, (right) David Schaefer/Monkmeyer Press; Page 277: Michal Heron/Woodfin Camp & Associates; Page 278: Gary Hutchings; Page 279: (top) Courtesy Dr. Tiffany Field, University of Miami, (bottom) Jason Lauré/Woodfin Camp & Associates; Page 281: Courtesy Dr. Carroll Izard, University of Delaware; Page 287: Lawrence Manning/Woodfin Camp & Associates; Page 288: Burt Glinn/Magnum Photos; Page 293: Nina Leen/*Life* Magazine, © Time Inc.; Page 295: Laura Dwight/Black Star; Page 296: Frank Siteman/The Picture Cube; Page 297: Anthony Jalandoni/Monkmeyer Press; Page 298: (bottom left) Nancy Sheehan/The Picture Cube, (bottom right) Richard Hutchings/Photo Researchers, Inc.

Chapter 10 Opener: F. B. Grunzweig/Photo Researchers, Inc.; Page 307: Donald Dietz/Stock, Boston; Page 308: (left and right) Wil-

Author Index